Vol. II
Part I

CONFEDERATE SOLDIERS' MONUMENT, JACKSON.

Biographical and Historical Memoirs of Mississippi

VOL. II

EMBRACING AN

AUTHENTIC AND COMPREHENSIVE ACCOUNT OF THE CHIEF EVENTS IN
THE HISTORY OF THE STATE, AND A RECORD OF THE
LIVES OF MANY OF THE MOST WORTHY AND
ILLUSTRIOUS FAMILIES AND INDIVIDUALS

Vol. II   Part I

ILLUSTRATED

A FIREBIRD PRESS BOOK

Gretna 1999

Manufactured in the United States of America
Published by Pelican Publishing Company, Inc.
1000 Burmaster Street, Gretna, Louisiana 70053

TABLE OF CONTENTS.

CHAPTER I.
Post-bellum organization 11

CHAPTER II.
Later legal and judicial history 23

CHAPTER III.
Institutions and societies 37

CHAPTER IV.
Water transportation, levees, etc. 60

CHAPTER V.
Railway transportation, etc. 77

CHAPTER VI.
Growth and development 90

CHAPTER VII.
Political history 127

CHAPTER VIII.
Cities, towns and villages 147

CHAPTER IX.
The press of Mississippi with a cursory glance at the literature of the state 242

CHAPTER X.
Physicians and their associations 252

CHAPTER XI.
Educational history 300

CHAPTER XII.
Religious history of Mississippi 348

CHAPTER XIII.
Records of families and individuals, M 384

CHAPTER XIV.
Citizens' private memoirs, N 488

CHAPTER XV.
Records of a private nature, O 524

CHAPTER XVI.
Sketches of individual life, P 547

CHAPTER XVII.
Memoirs of a few families, Q 632

CHAPTER XVIII.
Other prominent persons, R 634

CHAPTER XIX.
Selected memorials, S 717

CHAPTER XX.
Conspicuous residents of the state, T 876

CHAPTER XXI.
A few special notices, U 937

CHAPTER XXII.
A glance at individual records, V 941

CHAPTER XXIII.
Brief notices of prominent persons, W 962

CHAPTER XXIV.
Concluding individual and family notices, Y 1083

ERRATA 1091

SUPPLEMENTARY INDEX FOR VOLUME I 1093

POPULATION OF 1880–1890 1094

INDEX 1111

ILLUSTRATIONS.

	PAGE.
Confederate monument, Jackson	Frontispiece
Indian cession map	27
Charles B. Galloway	43
E. C. Walthall	59
Mrs. H. B. Theobold	75
Edmund Richardson	91
J. Z. George	123
Insane asylum, Jackson	155
Mississippi mills, View of	203
J. M. Stone	235
Siege of Vicksburg, Map of	251
William Oliver	267
Edward Mayes	315
Robert Lowry	331
W. A. Percy	363
Insane asylum, Meridian	379
D. B. Seal	411
R. Seal	427
H. S. Van Eaton	443
Jackson, Battle of	459
Tupelo, Battle of	459
J. McC. Martin	475
Charles Clark	491
John Hopkinson	507
William Starling	523
E. S. Wilson	539

Biographical and Historical Memoirs
OF
MISSISSIPPI.

CHAPTER I.

POST-BELLUM ORGANIZATION.

WHEN Mississippi came under the military law of the United States by the surrender of General Taylor's forces to General Canby, on April 9, 1865, Governor Clarke called a special session of the legislature—a legislature elected under the laws and constitution of the convention of 1861. It is not the province of this sketch to decide which idea of the status of the state at that time was the correct one; the purpose here is to show the actual changes in organization. The state, as far as actual power was concerned, was under the laws of war; this legislature, however, was the only means the people had of expressing themselves, and they forthwith passed acts providing for the appointment of commissioners to Washington to confer on the new status, and also provided for the calling of a convention to remodel the constitution to suit the new order. Even while this legislature was in session, the war department telegraphed General Canby to disperse it as unlawful, but before the new order was received the session had adjourned. The next day General Canby notified Governor Clarke that the president could not recognize any state government made since the ordinance of secession, and demand was immediately made for the turning over of all state property, archives, etc., to the officer of the army in charge. This was done at the capitol on May 22, over a month after General Taylor's surrender. However, the commissioners, Sharkey and Yerger (William), appointed by the governor, went on to Washington in an unofficial capacity and presented the situation to the president. They found that the national government and the people back of it were themselves still undecided as to the next step to pursue. There were many plans afloat; the Southern states, in the opinion of some, were simply to repeal their secession constitutions, resume their old ones with amendments forever forbidding slavery and secession—the two points secured by war; a few even thought that slavery would still be held constitutional by the Supreme court—these few, however, seemed unable to realize the laws of the war. At another extreme there were those who

A

determined not to admit a Southern state to its old footing until the negroes should be held by them as political and even social equals—these, a large number, too, seemed totally to forget that in no part of this or any other country are people all on an equal social footing. There were those, too, who held that slavery was a disease politic that required strong measures, and that now was the time to forever root out its influence by seeing to it that every state which had held it should freely and fully allow the former slave all the political rights enjoyed by any other citizens, now and forever, and that this should be the power claimed on the laws of war. This latter seemed to be the one destined to prevail, although the president held the first view presented, when he received Messrs. Sharkey and Yerger, for on May 29 he issued his amnesty proclamation, and a few days later appointed, June 13, the first of these visitors, the Hon. William L. Sharkey, provisional governor.

On July 1 Governor Sharkey issued a proclamation recognizing the exigencies of the situation and clearly pointing out what the war meant to the conquering power, and calling a convention for August 14 to prepare a constitution. This convention met and organized with one hundred delegates, seven of whom had been in the convention of 1861, and six of the seven voting against secession. It is interesting to note that, while the convention of 1861 had eighty-four democrats and twenty-five whigs, this one had seventy whigs, eighteen democrats and five conservatives. The officers of the convention were: president, J. S. Yerger, and secretary, J. L. Power. By the 24th of August amendments to the constitution were made striking out the slave article and inserting article 8, acknowledging slavery abolished forever, and making the twelfth item of the bill of rights provide for dispensing with grand jury action in certain cases. Ordinances were passed declaring all the acts pertaining to secession and rebellion null and void, and legalizing non-conflicting legislation since 1861, and providing for an election according to the constitution. On October 16 following Gen. B. G. Humphreys was elected governor, and reorganization was effected under this amended constitution of 1832, as provisional only, for the state was not admitted to representation, and the whole territory of which the state was a part was under military power.

On June 13, after Governor Humphreys' election, the famous "fourteenth amendment" was passed by congress to effect the enfranchisement of the newly-made freedmen. It became a part of the national constitution on January 31, 1867, and in February Mississippi's legislature passed resolutions refusing to ratify it. Forthwith, on March 2, congress passed "an act to provide for the more efficient government of the rebel states," and on the 23d of the same month acts were passed by congress providing for an election to be held under military authority, to decide whether or not a convention should be called for the purpose of establishing a constitution and civil government for the state, loyal to the Union." These acts are known as the "reconstruction acts," and wise or unwise, they were considered by the controlling power the legitimate fruits of war. The results of the election were announced by genrral orders No. 42, from Holly Springs, the headquarters of Major-General Ord, of the fourth military district, on December 16 of that year. The total registered vote of the state was one hundred and thirty-nine thousand three hundred and twenty-seven; votes cast, seventy-six thousand and sixteen; "for convention," sixty-nine thousand seven hundred and thirty-nine; "against convention," six thousand two hundred and seventy-seven. At this point the feelings on both sides were probably more rancorous than even during the war, and neither side could consider the other as anything less than venomous. Whether fair or unfair, it was done, and that is the only fact with which this sketch has to deal. These orders indicated by name the persons who were elected, and on January 7, 1868—exactly six years after the convention of secession—the delegates met at Jackson and continued in session until May 18, with B. B. Eggleston, of Lowndes county, as president. A new constitution was adopted on May 15, and an ordinance passed to submit it to the registered voters for ratification, and to provide for the election of state officers, as it called for. This election took place on the 22d, and some days following, under the direction of the commanding-general. The election ordinance also provided that the legislature elected should meet on the second Monday after election was decided, and, before enacting any law, should adopt the fourteenth amendment. These provisions were carried out by general orders No. 19, of May 19, 1868, issued by command of Maj.-Gen. A. C. Gillem, with headquarters at Vicksburg. Provision was also made for meeting again in case of defeat of the constitution. This constitution was chiefly characterized by franchise provisions that would have excluded all who had voted either directly or indirectly for secession. The result was that it was defeated, and the convention proceeded to amend it by striking out those sweeping particulars. Congress ordered a new election and the commanding general removed Governor Humphreys in July, replacing him with a military governor—Gen. Adelbert Ames. On December 1 (1869), over a year later, this amended constitution was ratified by the people, and James L. Alcorn was elected governor, and the lieutenant-governor chosen was R. C. Powers. On the following February 23 (1870), congress passed an act of admission to representation, on condition that state officers and legislators take prescribed oaths that would exclude from those positions men who had held any of them at any time before they took part in rebellion and because the three national amendments were ratified. Governor Alcorn was elected to the national senate, and was succeeded as governor by Lieutenant-Governor Powers in 1871.

Practically five years had elapsed since the surrender of General Taylor before Mississippi resumed her former official status in the Union, during which time she was practically under military power, although part of the time formally a civil state. Such an unfortunate condition is always one of strife and abuse, and the great mass of ignorant, newly enfranchised negroes, with exaggerated ideas of their newly found powers, made a complication of difficulties almost unparalleled in history, and a situation peculiarly humiliating to the high-spirited white citizens who had until then been the sole arbiters of the state's action. It is hardly possible that so great an accession of ignorant voters, with all the susceptibility to manipulation that ignorance implies, should not cause a weak, if not disastrous, financial and other management of the affairs of state. Intelligence in the majority of voters is an acknowledged fundamental condition of successful self-government; there can not be success without it; without it monarchy is better. It may be, however, that out of the bitter experiences of that period lessons have been learned by all concerned that will make the path for the future more plain.

Since the enfranchised population in this state embraced so large a proportion of the whole, it is probable that the situation here was aggravated above that of other states, and thus gave more force to the demand for white supremacy, which might be justly interpreted the supremacy of intelligence, which is demanded everywhere. But mass and ignorance and intelligence with less numbers when pitted against each other from natural or artificial causes, furnish one of the worst conditions in which humanity can find itself. It is a condition that stimulates the worst powers on both sides, and apparently, like a disease, must run its course. Just such a strife continued during the first five years under the new constitution and restored status of the state. The impeachment of Governor Ames, who was elected in November, 1873, was only an incident of the struggle, although the leading one, and led to his resignation and the succession to that office of John M. Stone, the present governor of the state, then president of the senate in 1876. Governor Ames, in his message, charged the successful movement with intimidation of the negro vote by an unlawful military organization and for the mere purpose of feeling their old mastery over the negro; while the legislature, charging Governor Ames and two other executive officers with corruption in office, began impeachment proceedings, which were dismissed upon assurances of his resignation.

This struggle reached its climax in the election of November, 1875, when, in what is known in political parlance as "the great revolution" occurred, which was a hotly-contested election, resulting in white supremacy or the supremacy of intelligence and property in the affairs of state. It is not the province of this sketch to determine whether the charges of intimidation are true, or if true a wrong; it is a matter of public knowledge, however, that these charges are the basis of the recently agitated national election bill. True or untrue, the charge was made, and involved the withdrawal of the large numbers of colored men who had been in prominent positions in the state and even in congress. It also resulted in the quiet and more economic administration which has since followed, and a growing prosperity that has given the state time to recuperate her wasted powers and take on the vigor of the new order. This is even more true of the condition of the colored population than the whites.

During about twenty years under the constitution of 1868-9 few amendments were made, but many causes contributed to make a demand for a new constitution whose franchise provisions would eliminate a large mass of ignorant votes, and thus remove any basis that might remain of the long-standing charge. The constitution of 1868-9 was not that of 1832 revised, but a new instrument made by a part of the population of the state, almost entirely different from that which made the constitution of 1832 or the present one. A large proportion of the convention were of the then newly enfranchised race, while the white element was largely of a class not identified with the hitherto ruling element in the state. One fact will illustrate: A prominent republican club of New York city sent to the convention copies of all the state constitutions then in existence, to aid them in forming one with, if possible, the best elements of all. Whether they succeeded is not for this sketch to determine. It is but natural from the nature of the case that this assembly should be considered by the then opposition as a burlesque on conventions, and so it was dubbed by them the "Black and Tan convention," a cognomen that will probably indefinitely attach to it. On the other hand, the convention itself, amidst all its difficulties of composition and opposition, was ablaze with that enthusiasm which the newly enfranchised freedmen felt on assuming a part in self-government for the first time, however crude the part might be. The sight could not have been otherwise than almost outrageous and ludicrous to the eyes of those who beheld their former slaves posing as their lawmakers.

The constitution made, however, was largely, if not entirely, the product of white men. While its phraseology and arrangement differed from that of 1832, and its leading features had regard to securing the new order of things, its provisions were not very dissimilar, except in a few particulars, one of the most prominent of which was an elaborate system of public schools, which, while intended for all classes, was especially directed to the education of the colored race. The system provided for state and county supervision, a system now so common and so costly, too, but one upon which its advocates believe the welfare of the state and nation both rest. The franchise was confined simply to all males of age, with the usual exceptions.

After twenty years under this constitution, and about fifteen years after the "great revolution" of 1875, there was approved, on February 5, 1890, "An act to provide for calling a convention to amend the constitution." On March 11 Governor Stone ordered an election to be held for delegates on July 29 following. The composition of the convention was to be the same as that of the house of representatives as to numbers, and fourteen delegates-at-large were to be elected. On August 12 they assembled at Jackson, and were called to order by Hon. George M. Govan, secretary of state. Hon. S. S. Calhoon, of Hinds, was chosen president, and Mr. R. E. Wilson, of the same county, was made secretary. There were one hundred and thirty-four members, of whom it is interesting to note the large proportion of lawyers and farmers; and that all were democrats, with the exception of four, two of whom were republicans, one a conservative and one a greenbacker. The convention continued in session until November 1 (1890), when the new constitution was adopted. "Our mission here," said President Calhoon in his closing address, "has been accomplished as best it could be upon adjustment of the various opinions and interests of the different sections of Mississippi. Restricted by the Federal constitution, we have tried to secure a more elective franchise without race discrimination or injustice. We knew when we assembled what the nation will yet learn—that it is hardly possible for any two of the distinct types of mankind to co-exist with divided political sovereignty. The hopelessness of the complete success of such an experiment is illustrated by all history and proved by all reasoning from natural laws. Still, it falls to our lot to repeat the effort. We will do our part in good faith, and the failure, if it shall come, will not be the fault of either race, but will result from the laws of our being, which impel each to combine to achieve or resist the domination of the other. Apprehending that harmonious political coöperation of diverse races is extremely doubtful, if not impossible, we must, nevertheless, do the best we can; and we may congratulate ourselves that it is the negro who dwells among us, as his race more readily than any other takes on the semblance of the manners, customs, religion and civilization of our own. We tax ourselves more heavily in proportion to property values than, perhaps, any other people, to educate him, and this we shall continue to do, but with faint hope of obtaining any real political homologation. In the exercise of the right of suffrage it was to be expected that there would be occasional disturbances and local conflicts between the two races. These have occurred in the past, but in fewer instances, no doubt, than would have taken place under like circumstances in any Northern state. We hope to see none in the future. Political partisanship has naturally prevented an impartial view of our situation. This we can not avoid. We can only say to our sister states that, doing the best we can, we sit patiently under the flag and await events. To that flag we are all true, because we have aided in garlanding it with that glory which hangs about its folds. To the Union we are true, because the cement of the whole is the blood of our ancestors. It is a union of strength, and should be a union of love to all its states and sections. We say to our brethren of the North, East and West, that we are willing to bear cheerfully our full share of the public burdens, to pour out our blood in equal measure for the common defense, to share in the misfortunes and rejoice in the welfare of our sister states; even willing, at their behest, to try the dangerous, and probably impracticable scheme of dividing political power with another and outnumbering race; willing to do all things except to yield up the common civilization of our common country, which civilization was constructed, has been maintained and can be continued only by the white race. There is but one sovereign by divine right. That sovereign is mind. I look in vain for any instance of African contribution to the disclosure of undiscovered truths tending to ameliorate the individual or the social condition of man. The race up to this time has shown no science, no literature, no art, no enterprise, no progress, no invention. It sometimes develops a reflected light of civilization, but never yet the life-giving heat from internal fires of intellect and energy which impel to intelligent and systematic activities. I hope better things from it in future. Withdrawn from the envelopment of white civilization, the negro race seems unable to maintain even its own imitative acquirements. It seems unfit to rule. It seems to mean, as it always has meant, stagnation, the enslavement of woman, the brutalization of man, animal savagery, universal ruin. Yet, confronted with this sad trial, it is our duty under the constitution of the United States to undertake the great task of carrying on intelligent republican government in Mississippi with his full coöperation, and with his rights and franchises, as guaranteed by the organic Federal compact, not only unimpaired, but fully protected.

"Aside from the suffrage, gentlemen," continued the speaker, "you have perfected a judiciary system, the best I know where there prevails a dual system of law and equity procedure. The limitations you have placed on legislative power in reference to local measures and other matters will soon, of themselves, largely overpay the cost of this constitutional convention, and will enforce a wiser and juster exercise of that power, and thus contribute greatly to the welfare and happiness of the masses of our people."

Further on he said: "In my judgment the material interests and moral advancement and the people of both races here depend on the predominance, in government, of that virtue of intelligence which, for the present at least, can come only from that race which in the past has shown a capacity for the successful administration of free institutions. That race alone can now safely exercise the function of ruling with moderation and justice, and accomplish the great purpose for which governments are established. Your article on corporations has emancipated the people from the thralldom of combined capital incorporated by and under the sanction of the state. You have made the creature subject to its creator. Your article on education reflects the generosity for which our state is justly famed, and if erroneous, is along the lines of noble and magnanimous endeavor. If the pockets of our impoverished people can bear the draft, you are right and they will never complain. Viewing the instrument in all its parts and as a whole, I do not hesitate to declare the opinion that there is nowhere a better constitution than the one you establish."

This instrument is practically a new constitution in provisions, arrangement and phraseology. It is simply arranged in fifteen articles and a schedule, distributed under the following subjects: 1, Distribution of powers; 2, Boundaries of the state; 3, Bill of rights; 4, Legislative department; 5, Executive; 6, Judiciary; 7, Corporations; 8, Education; 9, Militia; 10, The penitentiary and prisons; 11, Levies; 12, Franchise; 13, Apportionment; 14, General provisions; and 15, Amendments to the constitution. It is most elaborate and detailed in its provisions, and indeed seems to have adapted the best fruits of the experience of this and other states to Mississippi's present and probable future needs. The leading features have been indicated above by the address extracts, and more detailed account must here be confined to the franchise article. This feature requires an elaborate time condition of residence and registration to be complied with, and that all taxes required must be paid, a part of which is a poll tax for school purposes. Besides these provisions, another is added that, after the first day of 1892, every voter must be able to read, or sufficiently interpret when it is read to him, the state constitution.

Several ordinances were passed by the convention, among which was one providing that the system of balloting known as "the Australian system," now so generally in use, shall be used until January 1, 1896, to which time the terms of the leading state executives have been extended by a second ordinance. Others are incidental to the convention itself, in regard to penitentiary farm, the election of a land-commissioner in 1895, in regard to doubtful swamp-land claims, to issue $500,000 of bonds for levee purposes, in regard to the complete establishment of Pearl river county, and one to exempt from taxation for ten years all permanent factories hereafter located in the state before the year 1900. Such is the present constitutional condition of Mississippi after a little over a quarter of a century's existence of a new epoch in her career.

The state capital has been at Jackson so many years that it might properly be supposed to always have been so located, for he is a man older than the state itself who can remember its location elsewhere. The successive removals of the provincial and territorial capitals have been indicated. By the constitution of 1817 the first session of the legislature was to be held at Natchez and thereafter as determined by law. Very soon afterward, February 20, 1819, a grant of two sections of public land was made by the United States in any portion where the title of the Indians had been secured, and which was to be located by the state. Almost two years later (February 12, 1821), at the time the monster county of Hinds was created to include the new Choctaw cession, a commission was chosen by the state to locate their grant of two sections "within twenty miles of the true center of the state." Those commissioners were Gen. Thomas Hinds, Dr. William Lattimore and James Patton, who reported their choice, and on November 28 following, provision was made for the survey and laying out of the present capital, "the town so laid out to be called and known by the name of Jackson, in honor of Major-General Jackson." Peter A. Van Dorn succeeded James Patton, and it is interesting to note the progress of the work in reserving lots or "greens" for the capitol, court-house, college or academy, executive mansion, and the sale of lots, one incident of which was to secure the immediate building of residences by giving ten preferred lots to those purchasers who would, within a year, build a representative log or frame house, "not less than thirty feet in length." On June, 30, 1822, the plans of the commissioners were approved and the town established, whereupon the temporary state buildings were ordered and future sittings of the assembly were ordered there. We may imagine the commissioners viewing the bare landscape and pointing to this hight and that as the most commanding one above which was to rise the dome of a future stately capital, finally deciding upon one that would overlook the ferry and valley of Pearl river, and as the map lay before them, afterward choosing the names Capitol, State, President, Congress and others for the streets.

A decade passed, however, before the state was ready to grace the sites chosen with suitable architectural structures to represent the dignity and power of the state as well as furnish the government a home. On February 26, 1833, measures were taken to effect this by providing for the sale of lots and otherwise to grant $95,000 for the capitol and $10,000 for the executive mansion. As is common in such cases the completion of the buildings was delayed several years, and the cost rose to several hundred thousand dollars in the end. William Nichols was the architect chosen to complete the buildings, and was made state architect in 1836. A commissioner of public buildings was appointed in 1838 and Charles Lynch was chosen, at which date also provision was made for the reservation of a commons or park. In 1841 the office of keeper of the capitol was created and William Wing appointed to it. On January 29, 1842, the apartments of the capitol were distributed as follows: In the basement story, No. 1 was given to the governor; No. 2, the secretary of state; No. 3 to the clerk of the high court of errors and appeals; No. 4 to government stationery; No. 5 to the keeper of the capitol; No. 6 to the adjutant-general; No. 7 to the chancery court; No. 8 to the chancellor; No. 9 to the archives; No. 10 to the attorney-general; No. 11 to the clerk of chancery court; No. 12 to the state treasurer; No. 13 to the state auditor.

On the first floor, No. 1 was assigned to the senate; No. 2 to the senate committee; No. 3 to the secretary of the senate; No. 4 to the senate committee; No. 5 to the enrolling clerk of the senate; No. 6 to the high court of errors and appeals; Nos. 7 and 8 to the house committee; No. 9 to the enrolling clerk of the house; No. 10 to the chief clerk of the house, and

No. 11 to the house of representatives itself. On the second floor, No. 1 was given to the state agricultural society; No. 2 to the senate committee; No. 3 to the librarian; No. 4 to the library; No. 5 to the judges of the high court of errors and appeals, and Nos. 6 and 7 to the house committee. Of course some changes have since occurred, among which may be mentioned the removal of the library to the basement facing in the rotunda.

The capitol, now showing the effects of age and rough usage, is still a chaste and dignified piece of Greek architecture, with an Ionic face of six columns, looking down Capitol street, the main building being of a severe and somewhat earlier form, and all surmounted by a dome and extension, from which is gained a broad, picturesque view of the city, spread out in gently-rolling proportions on all sides except the east, where spreads the winding Pearl valley. Here have been enacted the varied experiences of the state for nearly three-quarters of a century, with the exception of a brief period during the war, when Columbus was the temporary capital; and in commemoration of that great tragedy of war in which was spilled much of the best blood of the state, the south part of the oblong grounds, neatly inclosed and extending along two blocks of State street, has been adorned by an elaborate and stately monument, on whose white marble one may read this legend: "To the Confederate Dead of Mississippi." This was unveiled with splendid ceremonies, on June 3, 1891, before multitudes from every part of the South, as the results of five long years of earnest effort by the ladies of Mississippi, organized on June 15, 1886, as the Confederate Monument Association of Mississippi. The piece is sixty-four feet high from the ground line, and is composed of four main parts: the die, a castled chamber thirteen feet high by fourteen feet wide, fitted to contain a life-size statue of Jefferson Davis, which is now in preparation; the plinth of four Egyptian columns, supporting an entablature, and seven feet square by nine feet high; the spire shaft, three feet eight inches square at the base, tapering thirty feet to a top two feet square, and surmounted by a statue in Italian marble, of a Confederate soldier and gun in parade rest, six feet ten inches in hight. The first public suggestion for such a monument was made by Mrs. Luther Manship, of Jackson.

Passing down Capitol street, one finds the third square on the right slightly elevated, and amidst its luxuriant foliage and lawn rises an elegant structure of Greek simplicity where the state's governors have long resided. To the north the executive mansion, first occupied by Governor Tucker in 1842, looks out upon the pleasing proportions of the public park, which occupies a square.

The governors of Mississippi have usually been among her ablest sons, and not a few among them those whom the people delight to honor. The territorial governors began with Winthrop Sargent, in the summer of 1798. His unfortunate administration has already been referred to. It closed on the 22d of November, 1801, on the arrival of the second governor, William C. C. Claiborne, after a term of about three years.

The second administration was the first really successful one, and resulted in the satisfaction of all classes. Governor Claiborne not only had to handle the affairs of the territory wisely, but kept so wisely in hand the complications due to proximity to the Indians and Louisiana that on December 2, 1803, leaving Col. Cato West, secretary of the territory, in charge, he went to New Orleans after two years of successful efforts, and became governor of that new territory in October, 1804.

On January 26, 1805, Robert Williams, of North Carolina, arrived at Washington, the capital, and succeeded Governor Claiborne. His was an administration notable for the state's prosperity and his own unpopularity. It was in this period that the famous experiences of Aaron Burr occurred, that part which occurred in this territory being due to the action of his secretary, Cowles Mead, acting as governor in his absence. It was then too that the people first elected their delegate to congress instead of the legislature. After four years he was replaced by a new appointment made by President Madison.

Governor David Holmes, a native of Virginia, was the third executive, whose long administration of over eight years began in March, 1809, and closed with the career of the territorial form of government in December, 1817. These were the eventful and trying years of the Creek wars, the British war and the evolution of statehood, and successfully did the governor guide affairs through them.

The state of Mississippi under its new constitution chose to honor Governor Holmes by election to the office he had held so long by presidential appointment; and he served during its organization for two years until 1819.

The second governor was George Poindexter, who served one term to 1821, one of the ablest men that ever graced a gubernatorial chair anywhere. His codification and revision of the state laws is a masterpiece in that line.

Governor Walter Leake served with ability during two quiet administrations (1821–5), his death occurring a few weeks before his second term closed, which period the lieutenant-governor, Gerard C. Brandon, acted as his successor. He was the first to be honored by reëlection.

The fourth governor, elected in 1825, was Mr. Leake's lieutenant-governor, Mr. Brandon, who was also the first governor and was a native of Mississippi. His four years of service as executive covered the period of agitation over the noted Planter's bank bonds, and that for a new constitution.

Gov. Abram M. Scott entered upon the duties of his office in January, 1832, but died in November, 1833, before his term was finished, Lieutenant-Governor Fountain serving the unfinished period. His administration was successful and marked chiefly by the adoption of the new constitution.

The sixth governor, serving one term during 1834–5, was Hiram G. Runnels, whose able but quiet administration was uneventful.

The administration of 1836–7 was that of Gov. Charles Lynch, the seventh governor.

Alexander G. McNutt, the eighth man who had been elected to the office of chief executive, was one of the strongest men the state has produced. His two terms covering the years 1838–42 were agitated by not only national financial trials, but the famous struggle over the Union bank bonds, whose repudiation his bold efforts secured probably more than any other one influence. It was in 1840 that Gen. Andrew Jackson was so enthusiastically received as a guest by the state.

The ninth governor, serving for 1842 to 1844, was Tilghman M. Tucker, whose administration was quiet and successful. One incident of interest was the defalcation of the state treasurer, Richard S. Graves, for about $50,000.

Gov. Albert G. Brown was another of Mississippi's stalwart statesmen, whose administration (1844–8) was chiefly marked by the state's action in the Mexican war. His wisdom is indicated among other things by his efforts to secure to the state a public-school system on an adequate scale.

The administration of the eleventh governor of Mississippi, Joseph Mathews, was uneventful and covered the years from 1848 to 1850.

Another prominent figure is the twelfth governor, Gen. John A. Quitman, who entered on his duties in 1850. His administration is complicated by his resignation, whereupon two successive presidents of the senate filled the unexpired term, namely, John I. Guion and

James Whitfield. The resignation was for the purpose of trial for complicity in the Lopez expedition against Cuba, but he was acquitted. This administration is marked by the anti-compromise convention of 1851.

Gov. Henry S. Foote succeeded as the thirteenth chief executive in 1852, and was one of the brilliant men of the state. The repudiation of the Planter's bank bonds at the polls, after the senate had unanimously declared them legal and binding, and the decision of the high court of errors and appeals that the Union bank bonds were valid, were the two prominent events of his administration.

The fourteenth governor served two terms, covering the years 1854–8, quiet but successful. This was Gov. John C. McRae.

Gov. William McWillie's administration was also a quiet one of one term, 1858–60.

In 1860 the sixteenth governor, John J. Pettus, was inaugurated, and under this vigorous executive the well-known events of the war were precipitated. He served two terms.

Gov. Charles Clarke's administration began in 1864 and ended with military control; the incidents of this period are mentioned elsewhere.

Judge William L. Sharkey was provisional governor in 1865.

Gov. Benjamin C. Humphreys entered upon the duties of his office in October, 1865, and served until removed by the military forces.

Gen. Adelbert Ames was made military governor, as has been indicated.

On March 10, 1870, Gov. James L. Alcorn was inaugurated as an elected executive, but, as has been mentioned, he was succeeded by Lieut.-Gov. R. C. Powers, on his election to the national senate.

Gov. Adelbert Ames was inaugurated in January, 1874. His administration was noted for confusion, proceedings of impeachment against him, his resignation, and "the great revolution," all of which belongs to the chapter on politics.

The president of the senate, Col. John M. Stone, succeeded to the office of chief executive by virtue of this office in 1876, and was elected in 1877, serving until 1882. Since his induction into this office the state has entered upon a career of quietness and prosperity in marked contrast to the years since 1861. The founding of the Agricultural and Mechanical college was accomplished during his term.

Gov. Robert Lowry's administration was the longest in years that the state had witnessed; it was but two terms, but their length was four years instead of two, covering the years 1882 to 1890, a period of vast recuperation and development to the state. The establishment of the Industrial institute for girls, the East Mississippi insane asylum, and the Railroad commission, as well as the unprecedented construction of railways and increase in manufactures and other industries, place this period among the most remarkable ones in the career of the state.

The present administration presents the unique and highly complimentary circumstance of the recall of a former governor to the executive chair after an interval of two terms. Gov. John M. Stone, having served six years so successfully in times of trial, entered upon his duties again in January, 1890. The adoption of the new constitution is the most prominent event so far in his administration.

The present epoch, covering the last thirty years and characterized chiefly by the new political status of the negro, presents from a governmental point of view practically three periods—the first or military period, from 1861 to 1868–9; the second period under the constitution of 1868–9, from that date to 1890, and the present period under the constitution of 1890. The first period may fall into two sections, the one under secession and that part, from

1865 to 1869, under military power. The divisions of the second period may be made on the basis of the predominance of races, the colored race previous to 1875, and the white race afterward, the former covering about eight years of the constitutional period mentioned, and the latter about fourteen years. This division is, however, less governmental than political or partisan. As a constitutional epoch its periods are necessarily based on its relations to the national constitution as well as on its internal forms. Few governments of the world present more striking evolutions in the course of a little less than two centuries, or evolutions more worthy the interest of the most profound student of governments, than does the career of the people and the boundaries known as the state of Mississippi. But more pregnant with interest and mystery than all the past is the problem that confronts her at this moment—fortunately a problem whose magnitude no one realizes more than her own citizens, and one whose solution seems so far to baffle the best minds of the civilized world. It is a question which involves so many elements—elements so elusive, too—elements totally misunderstood to those not on the field, and elements almost equally distorted by the prejudices and passions aroused in one in the midst of them. Fortunately—a tame word in this case—it has been lifted out of dense and hideous depths of ignorance and passion by over a quarter of a century of that great purifier—Time; but it has not wholly escaped either the ignorance nor the passion and prejudice yet. No one, however, who has investigated the situation at all fairly, can doubt that all concerned are manfully setting themselves to its solution. All concerned includes the civilized world; for all are interested in the capacity of republican or democratic institutions to meet every condition; but those more immediately concerned may be named, without regard to order, as the white people of this state, the colored people, the national government, and those in all lands who have especially at heart the civilization of the African race. All these have plans to offer from their own view points more or less excellent, but none wholly satisfactory to the four interested nor to themselves in all respects.

The conditions are: A population over half of which is colored and with all the ignorance and incapacity of ex-slaves as to the mass; an outnumbered white population with all the intelligence in it, refinement and culture, the product of years under a regime of aristocratic wealth; a forced political equality; the consequent struggle for mastery, because of numbers on the one hand and of intelligence on the other; both determined to stay in the state, the one because of home and property, the other because of home, inertia and climatic fitness; both bound by a certain dependence to the other, the white on the labor of the negro, apparently so necessary in this climate, and the negro on the intelligence and capital of the white people; and yet both separated by that peculiar and mysterious race instinct so beyond our grasp, and that too intensified by an irritated past.

The alternatives are: A stumbling, blundering, ignorant and inexperienced government by a colored majority; or a skilled and able government by the minority white population, with some form of suppression of the ignorant majority.

The point of issue seems to be that one race is determined to grow in self-government by blundering experiment involving the more intelligent race in the confusion, but is not strong enough to effect it; while the other race is strong enough, and is determined, by virtue of its intelligence, to govern the best for both, and let the negro grow in self-government the best he may under tutelage. It is a case in which "of two evils choose the less," and even many negroes, as well as the white race, believe the latter to be the less, and seem to be acquiescing.

Meanwhile, as said above, plans of solution are rife. Among those of every land especially interested in the civilization of the colored race, there are those that believe our colored population should be sent to Africa or to some given region like the Indians in Indian territory and colonized, but, with the exception of a few educated or aggressive colored people interested in Siberia and the evangelization of Africa, the colored people receive this coldly, many insisting that the whole world shall be free to them, and that such a course would cut them off from the civilization gained by the European races. "Besides, how long would it be before white people would be so numerous in Africa that the question would simply be revived there?" they say. The plan is held as merely speculative, even by the white people. Another class hopes and believes that, whatever happens, another generation of education and a purer religious teaching, along with the possession of property and perfected family life, will find a silent but effective solution.

The national government, when in the hands of those watchful for the infringement of the fourteenth amendment to the constitution, has proposed to resort to the measures of reconstruction, at least as far as the election of national officers is concerned, by a law that would apply equally all over the union, but, for many reasons, not the least being the fear of the precedent of introducing the army to the poles anywhere, this has not been effected. There is no doubt, too, that increasing general knowledge of the difficulties of the situation by the whole nation has also tended to discourage it. There are few, probably, who have really seen the situation but would look doubtfully upon such a measure. Besides, it would not be a solution, but only a return to the second alternative.

The colored people's solution has been described, as held by many of them. Others propose some joint division of offices between the two races on a compromise ticket, as has been secured in places where the negroes are less agricultural than in this state and more largely educated and owners of property, and where the white people, in consequence no doubt, are more inclined to concession, and the negroes prompted less by a feeling of might and right in numbers.

Finally, the white people of the state have undertaken what they hope to be an ultimate solution by an educational and tax qualification for franchise, which, while it may disqualify a few white men, will sift out large numbers of ignorant and shiftless negroes until the hitherto legal colored majority will no longer be a menace to intelligent government. This will also make a class of conservative colored voters, and constantly impress the value and responsibility of franchise upon the rest, while holding out encouragement and inducement to that education and property responsibility, the former of which, at least, is the rock of safety upon which alone successful self-government can rest.

CHAPTER II.

LATER LEGAL AND JUDICIAL HISTORY.

THE war got itself finished and done with at last, and nothing was left to the shattered state except to pull itself together as best it might and try to get over the dreadful wreck.

On the 6th of May, 1865, Governor Clarke issued a proclamation to the people, in which, among other things, he informed them that he had called the legislature to convene at Jackson on the 18th of that month. But he was not allowed to proceed. The legislature was forbidden to assemble by the Federal authorities, the governor was imprisoned in Fort Pulaski, the courts were all closed, the archives and public records of the state were seized, the administration of the laws was suspended, the civil government was totally overthrown and all of its functionaries removed from their offices. The military power reigned supreme.

What was the condition of the laws during this very critical period? This question has received judicial consideration. On the 30th of May, one John Harlan stole a gun; he was afterward indicted and convicted; he moved an arrest of judgment on the ground that at the time of the commission of the offense the constitution and laws of the state were suspended or overthrown and destroyed by the military power of the United States, and that no such sovereignty then existed or was recognized as the state of Mississippi. Of this the supreme court said: "We entertain no doubt that the laws of the state, civil and criminal, as they stood at the date of the secession ordinance, continued in force afterward, precisely as before, unaffected by that ordinance, or by the war, or by the deposition of the state magistrates in the month of May, 1865. The laws themselves were not suspended during the administration of General Canby and Provisional Governor Sharkey, but only their administration was temporarily suspended."

On the 13th of June President Johnson issued a proclamation, in which, declaring that the Rebellion had, in its revolutionary progress, deprived the people of the state of all civil government, he appointed the Hon. William L. Sharkey to be provisional governor of the state, defining some of his powers and duties.

Governor Sharkey's first act was the issuance of a proclamation, dated July 1, 1865, by which he appointed in every county the judges and clerks of probate courts, boards of police, justices of the peace and all other county officers. No provision was made for the circuit and chancery courts. Two days later he issued an order that the "act in regard to the action of replevin, and the amendments thereto passed by the legislature of Mississippi since the 9th day of January, 1861, be and the same is hereby declared to be in full force from this date." This act was one approved December 3, 1863, making provision for the speedy recovery of personal property wrongfully taken or detained, by a summary replevin before two justices of the peace. This was the only judicature created by the governor for the assertion of legal rights. All other rights of that character were left, for the time being, wholly without redress.

On July 12 was established a system of courts unknown to the constitution either of the state or of the United States. It was created by commissions, of which the material parts are as follows: "I, W. L. Sharkey, provisional governor of the state of Mississippi, do hereby appoint the said (George T. Swann) to the office of special judge, with equity jurisdiction in all contracts for cotton or other personal property in this state, with power to proceed in a summary way on petition to enforce specific performance or rescind contracts on notice to parties." The judge was empowered to issue process, to punish for contempt, and to appoint a clerk; and it was made the duty of sheriffs to execute this process and enforce its decrees. On the 25th of the month a supplementary commission was issued to the effect that "in decreeing specific performance of contracts in reference to cotton, or other property, he (Swann, or other judge) has power to make his decrees in the alternative for the cotton or other property, or for its value, if the property itself can not be had." These courts, specially organized for the sole purpose of enforcing or rescinding contracts for personal property, left all other equity jurisdiction unprovided for. They completed, with those already mentioned, the system of jurisprudence which the provisional governor thought proper to put in operation during his administration.

In the case of Scott vs. Billgerry, 40 Miss., 119, it was objected to the special courts described last above that the governor had no power to create such tribunals, and that their actions were coram non judice and void; but our supreme court decided that we were a conquered territory, and in that respect, as in others, subject to the power of the conquerer, and that the president might delegate the authority. The court, however, said: "The governor was a Federal officer, appointed to administer the Federal rule over the state, and the war-making power of that government was the source of all his authority." This tribunal, as created by the provisional governor, was not a state, but a Federal court, deriving its existence and all its powers from the Federal government.

In July also, Governor Sharkey, by proclamation, called a constitutional convention to meet in Jackson on August 14, to be composed of delegates who were loyal to the United States, for the purpose of "altering or amending the constitution," so as to enable the state to "resume its place in the Union." That body (the fourth in the state's history) met accordingly. It consisted of seventy whigs and twenty-eight democrats. J. Shall Yerger was elected president. Its membership included James T. Harrison, of Lowndes; David W. Hurst, of Amite; James S. Hamm, of Kemper; Locke E. Houston, of Monroe; George L. Potter, William Yerger and Amos B. Johnston, of Hinds; Hugh A. Barr, of Lafayette; James S. Bailey, of Tallahatchie; Thomas A. Marshall, of Warren; Will T. Martin, of Adams; Ephraim G. Peyton, of Copiah; John W. C. Watson, of Marshall; Robert A. Hill, of Tishomingo; Hampton L. Jarnagin, of Noxubee; Robert S. Hudson, of Yazoo, etc.

The convention did not frame a new constitution, but confined itself strictly to the purpose for which it was called—alteration and amendment, and the undoing of the work of the convention of 1861. The ordinance of secession, and all others intended to make it effectual, were annulled. Slavery was abolished. All legislative enactments, and all official acts of officers, not in conflict with the constitution and laws of the United States, or the constitution of the state as it was on January 1, 1861, were validated, with a few minor exceptions, as also were the proceedings of the courts, and all marriages celebrated, since the secession.

The provisions in regard to the judiciary were these:

The special courts of equity theretofore, and thereafter to be, established by the provisional governor (it seems that none were in fact afterward established) were recognized, and provision made for appeals to be taken from their judgments to the high court; but it was provided further that when the courts known to the constitution and laws of this state should be established, such special courts should be no further recognized than to allow them to conclude the cases then pending.

The twelfth section of the declaration of rights in the constitution of 1832 ran thus: "No person shall, for an indictable offense, be proceeded against criminally by information, except in cases arising in the land or naval forces, or in the militia when in actual service, or by leave of the court for misdemeanor in office." The convention added the proviso, which has continued in substance to this day, "That the legislature, in cases of petit larceny, assault, assault and battery, affray, riot, unlawful assembly, drunkenness, vagrancy, and other misdemeanors of like character, may dispense with an inquest of a grand jury, and may authorize prosecutions before justices of the peace, or such other inferior court or courts as may be established by the legislature, and the proceedings in such case shall be regulated by law." This proviso has been considered to apply to all offenses below felonies, and to empower the legislature to dispense in such cases with any trial by jury.

Section 18 of article IV was extended so as to confer on the probate courts jurisdiction in minors' business. Theretofore its jurisdiction of this class had been limited to orphans' business, and it could not, for instance, appoint a guardian of the estate or person of a child whose father was living.

The legislature was empowered to direct sessions of the high court to be held at other places than Jackson; reserving to Jackson, however, the right to at least one session per annum.

A general election was ordered for the first Monday in October for representatives in congress and all state officers and members of the legislature; also, a special election at the same time for all county, district, judicial and ministerial officers, all terms to begin on the third Monday. The legislature was directed to convene on that day.

The validity of the convention itself was in doubt, and, of course, that doubt attached to all of its measures. In the case of Thomas vs. Taylor, 42 Miss., 651, this question was raised, but the supreme court waived it so far as the point of the excess of power by the president in organizing the provisional government was concerned, "inasmuch as the congress of the United States have recognized the existing government of the state as a provisional one."

The legislature met in October, as directed. They passed quite a number of statutes, in the effort to adjust the laws of the state to conditions so embarrassing and unprecedented. The most noteworthy feature of their work was that in reference to the newly emancipated freedmen, and which, meeting the disapproval of many of the Northern people, earned for the laws of that session the unfavorable appellation of the Black Code. Generally speaking, the statutes regulated the right of the negroes to the acquisition and enjoyment of property, their power to sue and be sued and to prefer criminal charges, their marriages, their contracts and the performance of them, the apprenticing of negro children, their carrying or owning arms, and their breaches of the peace. The legislature of 1867 repealed most of the objectionable features of the acts of 1865; thereby abolishing the distinctions made in respect to the power to acquire property, the criminal laws, the apprenticing of children, etc., but left them still incompetent as jurors.

The act of November 24, 1865, established county courts, to be held once a month in each county, by the probate judge, as president, with two associates chosen by the justices of the peace for the county from their own number. The criminal jurisdiction, concurrent with the courts already invested therewith, extended to all offenses less than felonies; and it was empowered to inflict, not only the punishments already prescribed by law, but also suspension by the thumbs. The civil jurisdiction, concurrent also, embraced all civil suits at law or equity, including ejectments, where the value in controversy did not exceed $250; except that replevins were without any limit of value; and except that the jurisdiction over forcible entries and unlawful detainers was exclusive. The writ of habeas corpus could be issued and heard in all cases of crimes within their jurisdiction. Crimes were prosecuted by information; and they were authorized to employ county attorneys. Special courts of the same powers, and going under the anomalous names of "the county court of (Grenada, for instance)" were established in the towns of Jackson, Okolona, Grenada, Meridian and Corinth. Appeals from the judgments of justices' and mayors' courts were to be taken to the county courts, instead of the circuit courts; and the decisions of such courts thereon were final. Suits and prosecutions originating in the county courts might be appealed, under conditions, to the circuit courts.

An act of October 30, 1866, amended the foregoing as follows: The probate judges were made the sole judges of these courts, even for those of the towns; the county attorney was made elective; certain concurrent criminal jurisdiction in small offenses not previously cognizable by them was conferred on justices of the peace, and the terms were fixed at different intervals in different counties, ranging from one to six months.

In October, 1865, also, the election ordered by the convention took place. Judges A. H. Handy, William L. Harris and Henry T. Ellett were elected to the high court bench, and the first term of that tribunal since the war (a special one) was in January, 1866. Judge Handy was made chief justice. The circuit and other courts resumed work in November. In organizing the circuit court of De Soto county, on the 19th of February, 1866, Judge Trotter prefaced his charge to the grand jury by the remark that "It is upward of four years, I believe, since a court was organized and holden in De Soto county."

In February, 1866, occurred an interesting conflict between the courts and an officer of the Freedman's bureau. The case of one Charles Pitard, a negro apprentice, was before the county court of Madison county, apparently on a charge against him of running away from his master. The master was charged with using him badly. The matter coming to the ears of Lieut.-Col. R. S. Donaldson, acting assistant commander of the bureau, he addressed to the probate judge a letter, enclosing an order of Lieutenant-General Grant, then recently made, which gave to the military authorities the power to interfere for the protection of freedmen of all ages in cases of prosecutions for offenses and punishments where they were not treated in equal manner and degree with the whites. Besides the inclosure of this order, Colonel Donaldson undertook to instruct the judge as to what he should do in the premises. This communication was referred to Governor Humphreys, who sent it to the major-general commanding, with a letter in which he pointed out the fact that, so far as the differences in the laws of apprenticeship were concerned, the advantages were with the black children. He concluded: "Why the legislature has discriminated thus in favor of the freedman is not for the executive to inquire, but to avoid collision between the military and civil authorities, it is important for the civil officers to know, with certainty, whether these laws are to be nullified." The matter ended with a letter from Colonel Thomas, the assistant commander, to Lieutenant-Colonel Donaldson, in which these passages occur: "Nothing but the most convincing proof that the child was inhumanly treated should have caused you to take any step for his release, and then, only after the refusal of the judge of probate to release him on the presentation of the

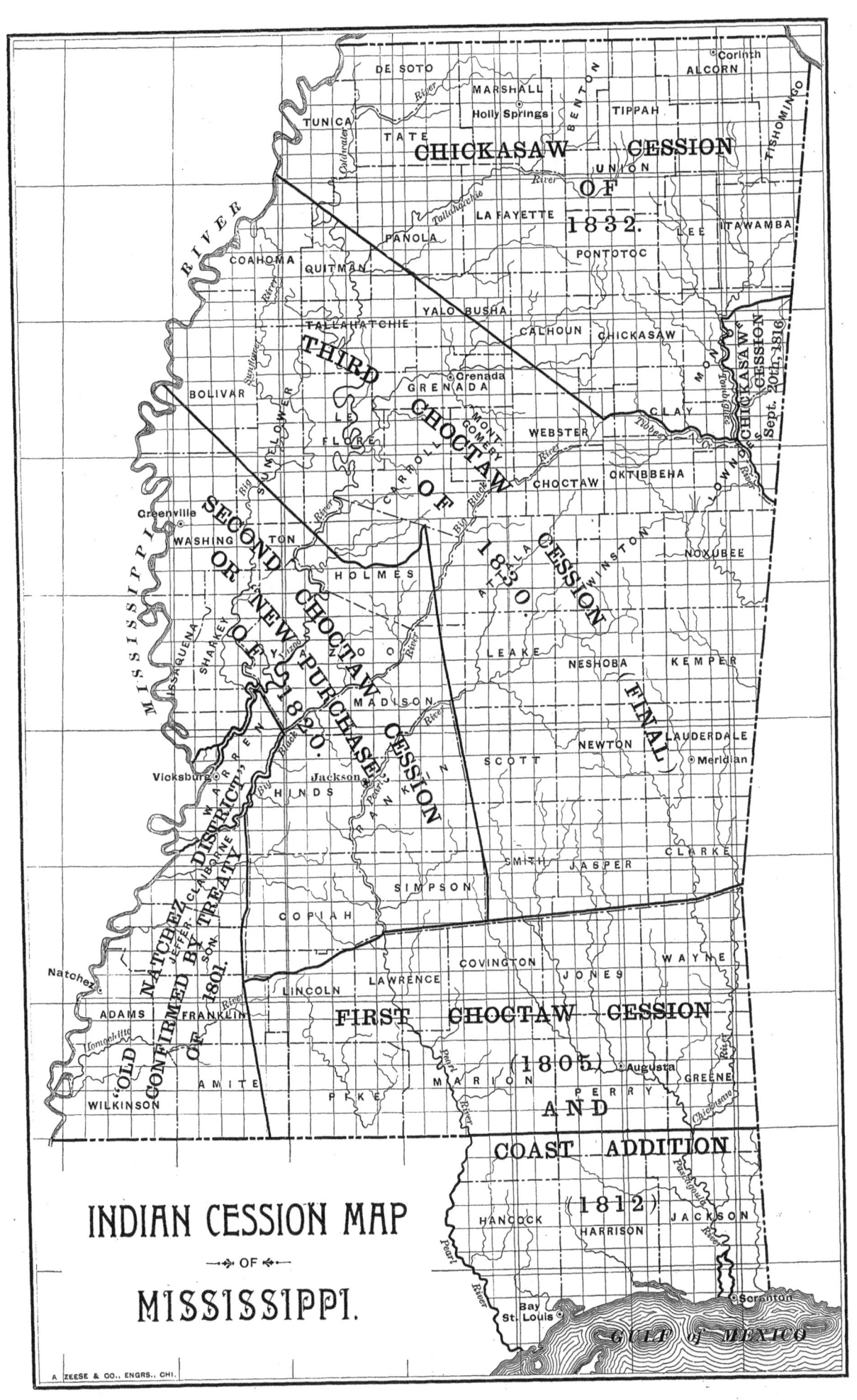

facts, as they were before you. It is the policy of the bureau to recognize the civil power of the state to the fullest extent, and infuse into the minds of the freedmen respect for the civil officers and government under which they must live at no distant day. It is not desired to nullify any state law, but to soften the application of those parts that may seem oppressive, and to interfere for the protection of freedmen only in individual cases, when local prejudices may cause the executive or judical officers of the state to deny the freedmen the rights which we are here to secure them. If you will examine the decision of Judge Campbell, attached to this paper, you will see that he is willing to give the law an interpretation that is liberal and just. It would be wrong for the bureau to assume any attitude that would injure this officer's influence. It is my opinion that the larger number of judges in the state would render the same decisions, and that only isolated cases occur where the law is interpreted oppressively. It is but treating them with due respect to make an effort to correct an evil through them, before any other method is adopted. You will see on reflection that it was not proper to write a letter of instructions to any officer of the civil government. You will therefore, in the case of Charles Pitard, write a letter to the judge of probate at Canton, Miss., saying that you withdraw your letter of instruction," etc. No fuller vindication of the impartiality of the judiciary during this trying period could be desired than is made in this "official" order of the Freedman's bureau.

The legislature met in called session on October 15, 1866, continuing, with two recesses, through February following.

An act was passed creating four high court districts, and requiring the court to be held in each district, for that district, once in each year, at the towns of Oxford, Jackson, Macon and Mississippi city. This act, however, the high court, in the case of M. & O. R. R. Co. vs. Mattan, 41 Miss., 692, decided to be unconstitutional in this: the business of the court held in a district was limited to the district, instead of embracing that of the entire state. So that the court continued, as before, to hold two terms in Jackson only.

"An act for the encouragement of agriculture," passed at this session, and approved February 18, 1867, is worthy of note. The country was in a greatly distressed condition, because of the destruction of values through the war and its ending. All of the ordinary bases of credit were destroyed or nearly so, and it became necessary to devise something to serve that purpose. The act provides that all debts for money, supplies, utensils, work-stock or other necessaries for the farm, shall constitute a prior lien on the crops not exempt, and on the animals and implements used; that advances of money, clothing or provisions, made by any owner or lessee of lands to his laborer working for a share of the crops, should constitute a lien on the share of such laborer until paid; that such liens shall be enforced by a bill in chancery, with sequestration; that mortgages might be given on crops to be produced within fifteen months; and that crops shall not be levied on or sold by any process until matured and gathered.

This statute is the origin of our present law on this important subject. It has been altered in many respects; but under various modifications it has been introduced into the codes of 1871 and 1880. The remedy has been much simplified, and is now by a summary seizure (on affidavit and warrant), much like the old distress at common law. If litigation arises, it is in the law courts, not in chancery.

In January the legislature unanimously refused to ratify the fourteenth amendment to the constitution of the United States, proposed by congress.

In March the congress passed, over the president's veto, the "Act for the more efficient government of the late insurrectionary states." It provided "that said rebel states shall be divided into military districts, and made subject to the military authority of the United States;" that "it shall be the duty of each officer assigned (to the command of such districts) to protect all persons in their rights of person and property, to suppress insurrection, disorder and violence, and to punish or cause to be punished all disturbers of the public peace and criminals; and to this end he may allow local civil tribunals to take jurisdiction of and try offenders; or when in his judgment it may be necessary for the trial of offenders, he shall have power to organize military committees or tribunals for that purpose, and all interference under color of state authority with the exercise of military authority under this act shall be null and void," etc. Mississippi was placed in the fourth district, and Gen. E. O. C. Ord made military commander. And thus, for a second time, the state was placed under a bayonet rule. In July another act of congress was passed over the president's veto, declaring that it was the true intent and meaning of the act of March that the district commanders might remove all civil and military officers claiming under authority of the states, and fill their places by appointment; and that no such commander, nor any of his appointees, should be bound by any opinion of any civil officer of the United States.

Moved by this legislation and the action inaugurated thereupon, Judges Handy, Harris and Ellett, being the entire high court bench, resigned on the 1st of October. They were just in time. Had they held on but a little longer they might have shared with Governor Humphreys the honor of ejection at the points of bayonets. General Ames, having been made military governor of the state June 15, 1868, made root-and-branch work of it. Everything was removed. For months there were no incumbents of many of the offices; not even appointees. In many of the counties even a marriage license could not be obtained so late as the spring of 1869. The clergy subjected themselves to liabilities to fines, as for violation of the law, in celebrating the nuptials of their youth. Nevertheless the marriages went on.

Two cases illustrative of the practical working of the military tribunals are those of McCardle and of Yerger.

About the 1st of November, 1867, Col. William H. McCardle, a distinguished editor, of Vicksburg, was arrested by the military authorities, under charges of, first, disturbing the public peace; second, inciting to insurrection, disorder and violence; third, libel; fourth, and impeding reconstruction. He sued out a habeas corpus before the Federal court at Jackson, but was by that court remanded to the military authorities. He then prayed an appeal to the Supreme court of the United States. The right of appeal was placed on a certain act of congress, passed February 5, 1867. The supreme court of the United States itself, shall now tell the remainder of the discreditable story: "A motion to dismiss the appeal was made here and denied. The case was then argued at the bar, and the argument having been concluded on the 9th of March, 1868, was then taken under advisement by the court. While the cause was thus held, and before the court had time to consider the decision proper to be made, the repealing act under consideration (that of March 27, 1868), was introduced into congress. It was carried through both houses, sent to the president, returned with his objections, repassed by the constitutional majority in each house, and became a law on the 27th of March, within eighteen days after the conclusion of the argument. The effect of the act was to oust the court of its jurisdiction of the particular case then before it on appeal, and it is not to be doubted that such was the effect intended. Nor will it be questioned that legislation of this character is unusual and hardly to be justified except upon some imperious public exigency" (75. U. S., 85). It was perhaps well for the supreme court which had been subjected to an indignity so great to speak of it in measured terms, but there is, and should be, no real measure for the scorn meted to a congress which, in time of profound peace, could prostitute the legislation of the United States in a conflict with the editor of a village newspaper, and that at the expense of the credit of the highest judicial tribunal of the nation.

Yerger's case arose later. On June 8, 1869, Col. E. N. Yerger slew Capt. J. G. Crane, mayor of Jackson by military appointment. A military commission was promptly organized to try him for murder. Objection was made to the competency of the mode of trial, but overruled. Pending the trial, Yerger sued out a habeas corpus in the Federal court at Jackson, under a special agreement made between his counsel and the attorney-general of the United States, in order that the important questions involved might be submitted for the consideration of the supreme court. He was remanded by the lower court to the military authorities, and took his appeal. At the December term, 1869, the case was argued specially on the point of jurisdiction, and the court held that the jurisdiction existed notwithstanding the repeal of the act of 1867, for the reason that other acts still in force gave it the power to revise the decisions of the inferior courts of the United States in such cases.

But while this important question of whether there was or was not in the United States any judicial power which could, in time of peace, revise the work of a military court in the trial of citizens was being settled, the necessity for such remedies was passing away. The constitution of 1869 had been adopted, and the state restored to its rights.

When the judges of the high court resigned in October, 1867, there was no election of their successors by the people, but by the military commandant, Thomas G. Shackleford, of Madison county, Ephraim G. Peyton, of Copiah county, and E. Jeffords, of Issaquena county, were appointed. Judge Shackleford was made chief justice. The first term under this bench was a special term in April, 1868. In 1869 Judge Jeffords was succeeded by George F. Brown.

At the October term, 1869, the important case of Thomas vs. Taylor, 42 Miss., 651, was decided. It involved the question whether the state was liable for the payment of about $5,000,000 of treasury notes, commonly called "cotton money," issued during the war, under the act of December 19, 1861. The court held that while, of course, the war and the acts leading thereto, did not abolish the state considered either as territory or as people, yet still, the government in charge of the state was not legal; it was a usurping power, revolutionary, and never recognized by the United States; that while the convention of 1865 had ratified most of its legislative acts, it had not ratified those in furtherance of the rebellion, and the issuance of the notes in question was an act of that character. The notes were void.

In the year 1867 an election was held by the military authorities, in accordance with the reconstruction act cited above, and a supplementary act of March 23, on the question whether a constitutional convention should be held, and for the choice of delegates in case it should be ordered. At this election a large number of the best and most intelligent white citizens were excluded from voting, by test oaths, penalties, etc.; while the negroes, ignorant and marshaled by unscrupulous adventurers, were allowed to vote without any pretense of a statute or constitutional provision of the state conferring that privilege on them. The qualification for suffrage was dictated by congress. Such was the foundation of the constitution of 1869.

The "Black and Tan" convention met in Jackson, January 7, 1868. It comprised a number of able, patriotic and true men, but the majority of its members were ignorant blacks and reckless white plunderers. Their work was finished on the 15th of May, 1868, and was submitted to the people for ratification as directed by the act of congress. The election resulted in its rejection. The white people of the state were deeply incensed at the whole conduct of the convention, and were especially indignant at certain clauses in the proposed constitution which disfranchised some of the best citizens. They therefore accomplished its defeat, although the election was held under military control, with troops stationed at as many as sixty different quarters in the state. The matter was brought to the attention of congress by a message of President Grant's on the 7th of April, 1869, and on the 10th a bill was approved, which authorized the president to resubmit the constitution to the electors, and, in his discretion, to submit separately any provision or provisions thereof. This was done. The election, held on the 30th of November and the 1st of December, resulted in the ratification of the constitution, except that section 5 of the article on franchise, and sections 4 to 13 inclusive of the schedule, were rejected. At this election state officers and members of congress were also voted for, by direction of the act of 10th of April.

It is to be observed that these reconstruction acts and the proceedings under them, introduced into our election system the practice of registering voters. It was incorporated into the constitution, and has been retained until now.

The most striking new features of this constitution are these: The office of lieutenant-governor is restored; imprisonment for debt is forbidden unqualifiedly; property qualifications are forbidden for any purpose; the right of secession is disclaimed forever; simple manhood qualification for suffrage, regardless of color, is established; a system of free schools is ordered to be established; the pledging of the state's credit in aid of any association, corporation or person, is forbidden, as also is the taking of stock by the state in any corporation or association; the assumption or payment of any obligation contracted in aid of the Rebellion is prohibited, as also is the making of any demand against the United States for emancipation of the slaves; the legislature is ordered to provide for the sale of delinquent tax lands, and the courts required to apply the same liberal principles in favor of such titles as in sales by execution. This extraordinary provision, generally understood as designed to enable the party in power to prosecute more successfully such white citizens as should be charged with political offenses, appears: "The legislature shall provide by law for the indictment and trial of persons charged with commission of any felony, in any county other than that in which the offense was committed, whenever, owing to prejudice, or any other cause, an impartial grand or petit jury can not be impaneled in the county in which the offense was committed." This provision, it is believed, was never put into practical operation.

Another interesting provision is section 22 of article XII: "All persons who have not been married, but are now living together cohabiting as husband and wife, shall be taken and held, for all purposes in law, as married, and their children . . . shall be legitimate." This was intended to legalize the relations of negroes, who had married while they were slaves, and were therefore incapable of making any binding contract. In the case of Dickerson vs. Brown, 49 Miss., 357, and in two others it was held that under this provision, while even those who had been previously living in unlawful relations could become husband and wife without any nuptial ceremonies, yet still their consent and acceptance of the legal relation must appear. Not even a constitution can marry two together without their consent; and the mere continuance of their intimacy after the constitution became operative was not sufficient.

The constitutional provisions in regard to the judiciary were of great importance: First, the name of the high court of errors and appeals was changed to that of the supreme court, and the terms of the judges extended to nine years; second, the circuit courts were retained, and their minimum jurisdiction raised to $150; third, chancery courts, with a distinct judiciary, were established in each county, the chancellors being assignable by law to convenient circuits, and with full jurisdiction in all matters of equity, divorce, alimony, testaments, administrations, minors' business, idiocy, lunacy and dower; chancellors and circuit judges to hold their offices four and six years, respectively; fourth, the civil jurisdiction of justices of the peace was extended to cases of $150 value of principal; fifth, the name of the board of police was changed to that of board of supervisors; sixth, the judges and chancellors alike were to be appointed by the governor, by and with the concurrence of the senate.

The effect of these provisions, and of certain statutes shortly passed in furtherance of them, was to abolish the probate courts and transfer their jurisdiction to the chancery courts; also, to abolish the county courts, and distribute their jurisdiction between the Circuit and the magistrate's courts. Existing terms were ended, and new appointments were to be made.

The legislature was required to meet annually, and the first session began January 11, 1870. That body ratified the fourteenth and fifteenth amendments to the constitution of the United States, passed elaborate statutes on the subjects of public education (a full account of which and of its results will be found in the chapter on education), of apprentices, the supreme, circuit and chancery courts, justices of the peace, besides many others of importance.

By act of June 9 it was ordered that three commissioners should be appointed to revise, digest and codify the laws, and to propose such amendments, alterations and new laws as they might deem advisable. Accordingly, J. A. P. Campbell, Amos R. Johnston and Amos Lovering, were appointed. The result of their labors revised, changed in many particulars and finally adopted by the next legislature, was the revised code of 1871, in sixty-six chapters.

Judge Johnston was a native of Tennessee. He came to Mississippi about 1830 and settled in Hinds county, living in Clinton, Raymond and Jackson at different times, as business called. Until 1839 he was an editor. In 1836 he was a member of the legislature. He was elected circuit clerk in 1839, and while in that office studied law. He served two terms, and then, in 1845, was elected probate judge. He was a member of the convention of 1851, in which he advocated acquiescence in the compromise measures, and the preservation of the Union. The fact that he was a Union man and a whig kept him out of political office, but indeed he seemed to care little for it. He was a member of the constitutional convention of 1865, and in 1875 of the state senate. He was a dignified, courteous and sympathetic gentleman; a studious, painstaking, thorough and successful lawyer. He died in 1879.

Under the direction of the new constitution, it became necessary to reorganize the judiciary. The supreme judges elected were Ephraim G. Peyton, Horatio F. Simrall and Jonathan Tarbell. They were installed about April, 1870, and their first term of court was the special May term of that year. Judge Peyton was chosen chief justice. This organization continued until May, 1876, when Judge Peyton resigned, and on the 1st Hamilton H. Chalmers was appointed, while Judge Tarbell's term expired, and on the 10th J. A. P. Campbell succeeded. Judge Simrall was then made chief justice. Judge Simrall's term expired on the 9th of May, 1879, and he was followed by James Z. George, who was made chief justice. On the 19th of February, 1881, Judge George resigned, and was succeeded by Timothy E. Cooper, Judge Chalmers becoming chief justice, under the rule of the code of 1880, to the effect that he shall be chief justice whose term is to expire first. Under this rule Judge Campbell became chief justice on the 10th of May, 1882, and Judge Cooper on the 11th of May, 1885. On the 7th of January, 1885, James M. Arnold succeeded Judge Chalmers, deceased, becoming chief justice on May 11, 1888. On the 1st of October, 1889, Thomas H. Woods was appointed, vice Judge Arnold, resigned, and became chief justice. In May, 1891,

Judge Woods was reappointed, and Judge Campbell became chief justice for the second time. Cooper and Woods associates.

Judge Ellett began his public life in Claiborne county. He was there a successful lawyer. In November, 1846, he was elected to succeed Col. Jefferson Davis in the United States congress, and served until March, 1847. Declining reëlection, he returned to the practice. He represented his county in the state senate continuously from 1854 to 1862. He was one of the commissioners who framed the code of 1857. When he resigned from the high court bench in 1867, as related, he went to Memphis, and there engaged in the practice of law until his death, which occurred in 1887. He was an enlightened, thoughtful and judicious legislator and judge, a dignified and deeply learned lawyer, a graceful and accomplished gentleman, a pure, genial and kind man.

Charles C. Shackleford was probably a Kentuckian. At all events he took a law degree at Transylvania university, and then came to Mississippi. When appointed to the high court bench he was a citizen of Madison county. He served several years as circuit judge after his retirement from that position. He did most of the work of the court while on the bench, and his opinions are very respectable.

Ephraim G. Peyton was born in Kentucky, October 29, 1802. He came to Mississippi at seventeen, and was admitted to the bar in 1825. Settling in Copiah county, he was elected district attorney in 1839. He was reëlected several times, but finally resigned in order to devote himself to a more settled practice. He was violently opposed to secession, and a lifelong antagonist to the democratic party. After the war he affiliated with the republican party, and was appointed to the supreme bench. He died in Jackson, September 5, 1876. Judge Peyton was a profound and accomplished lawyer with extraordinary assiduity in his studies. He was, too, a sincere, honest, courageous, refined, cultured and kind man. His opinions as a judge are of the finest type.

Judge Chalmers was born probably in Halifax county, Va., about the year 1833. He graduated at the University of Mississippi in 1853, and engaged in the practice of law in De Soto county. He was devoted to his profession and quickly took high rank in it. Raised to the supreme bench in 1876, he was reappointed on the expiration of his term, and died in office, January 4, 1885. Judge Chalmers was unusually gifted. Accessible, genial and even jovial, in his bearing, he still had great personal dignity. His was the fortunate talent for winning warm friends. As a lawyer, he was industrious, dexterous, faithful and successful. His speech was fluent, attractive and sometimes eloquent. He was a learned, careful, independent and conscientious judge, and his opinions are exceedingly clear and satisfactory, sometimes a little ornate. His sudden death was generally felt to be a great loss to the state, and the reputation which he left is most enviable.

Judges Simrall, Campbell, George, Cooper, Arnold and Woods are still living, and for that reason no effort will be made to enumerate their individual characteristics. Let it suffice to say that their labors have illustrated the legal literature of the state, and have placed its supreme court on a plane as high as that occupied by any state court in the Union.

The attorneys-general of the state since the war have been these: Hon. Charles E. Hooker (since, for several terms, a member of congress) was elected in the fall of 1865 and held until October, 1868. There was then a period during which the office was vacant and the state was represented by different lawyers, usually by Jasper Myers, described in the reports as "acting attorney-general." In the election of 1869 Joshua S. Morris was chosen, and held the office until the year 1874, when he was succeeded by George E. Harris, an ex-member of congress. Thomas C. Catching, afterwards and now a member of congress, followed General Harris in 1878 and pending the October term 1877. In January, 1885, Thomas S. Ford was appointed, vice Catchings, resigned; and in 1886 he was succeeded by Hon. T. Marshall Miller, the present incumbent.

The circuit judges of the period between the war and the reconstruction were James M. Smiley, James F. Trotter, Alexander M. Clayton, William Cothran, John Watts, J. A. P. Campbell, J. Shall Yerger, W. H. Killpatrick, W. D. Bradford, H. W. Foote, John E. McNair, William M. Hancock, Thomas Shackleford, James S. Hamm and B. F. Trimble. The judges for the period between the inauguration of the reconstruction and the political revolution of 1876 were James M. Smiley, W. D. Bradford, William M. Hancock, — Vance, — Gifford, — Thigpen, B. B. Boone, Jonathan Tarbell, Green C. Chandler, A. Alderson, Uriah Millsaps, Robert Leachman, Jehu A. Orr, Orlando Davis, Charles C. Shackleford, Ephraim S. Fisher, Jason Niles, W. Cunningham and George F. Brown. Those who have served since the year 1875 are James M. Smiley, James A. Green, John W. C. Watson, Samuel Powell, B. F. Trimble, William Cothran, James M. Arnold, James S. Hamm, A. G. Mayers, Sol S. Calhoon, J. B. Chrisman, Upton M. Young, Ralph North, Charles H. Campbell, Joseph W. Buchanan, Winfield S. Featherston, A. T. Roane, Samuel H. Terral, Warren Cowan, W. M. Rogers, James H. Wynn, Locke E. Houston, George Winston, J. D. Gilland and James T. Fant.

The chancellors appointed by Governor Alcorn and Governor Ames under the act of 1870 were William G. Henderson, G. S. McMillan, Wesley Drane, Thomas Christian, Theodoric C. Lyon, O. H. Whitfield, Austin Pollard, Arthur E. Reynolds, DeWitt Stearns, J. Fred Simmons, Dallas P. Coffey, J. J. Hooker, Samuel Young, Edward Hill, E. Stafford, E. W. Cabinniss, G. R. Gowen, D. N. Walker, J. W. Ellis, E. G. Peyton, Jr., W. A. Drennan, J. R. Galtney, R. Boyd, J. J. Dennis, C. A. Sullivan, William D. Frazee, C. C. Cullins, L. C. Abbott, J. N. Campbell, Peter P. Bailey, Thomas Walton, William Breck, H. R. Ware, R. B. Stone, E. H. Osgood and Hiram Cassidy, Jr. In 1876, when the democratic party came into power, the chancery districts were reduced from twenty-six to twelve, and from that time until now the chancellors have been Lafayette Haughton, A. B. Fly, Joseph C. Gray, Charles Clark, Robert W. Williamson, L. Brame, George Wood, T. B. Graham, E. G. Peyton, Jr., T. Y. Berry, Upton M. Young, Ralph North, J. Bright Morgan, W. G. Phelps, H. S. Van Eaton, Frank A. Critz, James G. Hall, Lauch McLaurin, Warren Cowan, Baxter McFarland, B. T. Kimbrough, Sylvanus Evans and W. R. Trigg. In 1888 the chancery districts were reduced to six, but increased to seven in 1890. In 1876 and 1878 the counties of Warren and Adams, respectively, were made separate circuit-court and chancery districts, the offices of judge and chancellor being held by the same person. This arrangement was terminated in 1884, those counties and Sharkey being made a district of the usual kind.

In the spring of 1866 the Hon. Robert A. Hill, of Tishomingo county, was appointed district judge of the United States for Mississippi, and the court for north Mississippi removed from Pontotoc to Oxford. In the year 1882 an eastern division of the northern district was established, the court to be held at Aberdeen, and in 1887 a western division of the southern district, the court to be at Vicksburg, and in 1888 a southern division of the southern district was established, the court to be held at Mississippi city. In 1889 the northern district was incorporated into the fifth circuit. Theretofore it had been in none, the district court exercising circuit court powers.

The literature of the legal profession, other than statutes and codes, shall now engage the attention for a period.

The first series of reports issued after the war were those of Reuben O. Reynolds—the

40th to 42d Mississippi. They embrace all of the decisions made subsequent to the war and prior to the reorganization of 1870.

The reporter, Colonel Reynolds, was born in Morgan county, Ga., and reared in Monroe county, Miss. He took an A. B. at the University of Georgia, and a B. L. at the University of Virginia. Entered upon the practice in Aberdeen, in 1856. In the army he lost an arm and rose to be lieutenant-colonel of the Eleventh Mississippi. In 1875 he was elected to the state senate, and served in that capacity for twelve years. He died in 1887. Colonel Reynolds was an accomplished, gallant and chivalric soldier, an exact, painstaking and satisfactory reporter, a most disinterested, vigilant, able, untiring and patriotic legislator, an adroit, ingenious, thorough and brave lawyer. He was a man of great versatility. Quick-tempered and impulsive, yet self-controled and generous, his varied virtues were crowned by an unobtrusive but genuine piety. Altogether it would be difficult to find his superior in the combination of graces which go to make a strong, honorable and attractive man.

His successor as reporter was Joshua S. Morris, the attorney-general. Coming into office in 1870, Judge Morris published six volumes—43d to 48th Miss.—the last terminating with the April term, 1873. The legislature of 1870 had ordered, by act approved July 18, 1870, a compilation of the criminal cases in all the volumes of Mississippi reports to date, annotated, to be called "Mississippi state cases." General Morris did this work, and the book issued in two volumes, not embraced in his regular series. General Morris was a lawyer, especially a criminal lawyer, of considerable ability. He died at Natchez in the year 1890.

He was succeeded as reporter in 1875 by Harris & Simrall, composed of George E. Harris, the attorney-general, and G. H. Simrall. They published four volumes—49th to 52d Miss.—the last ending in the midst of the October term, 1876.

Their successors were Joseph A. Brown and J. B. H. Hemingway, who published thirteen volumes, 53d to 65th Miss.; the last terminating in the October term, 1888. This series is not a work of collaboration, strictly speaking. The reporters parceled out the work, except Vol. 53. Mr. Brown alone reported 54, 57 and 59; while 61 was reported almost entirely by J. Bowmar Harris, Esq., for him. The other volumes were reported by Mr. Hemingway alone.

The next reporters are the present incumbents, Messrs. L. Brame (the ex-chancellor) and Charlton H. Alexander. The gentlemen have published two volumes, 66th and 67th Miss.

In 1872 a digest of the Mississippi reports, from Walker to 44th Miss., inclusive, by James Z. George, Esq., in which, however, the title of limitation of estates was prepared by Judge Clayton, and that of criminal law by William R. Barksdale, Esq. This digest does not include the two chancery reports of Freeman and Smedes & Marshall. These two volumes seem to have been omitted from all digests since Smede's.

In 1881 Garnett Andrews, Esq., of Yazoo city, published a digest, embracing 45th to 56th Miss., and intended as a supplement to George's digest, and in 1888 Daniel W. Heidelberg, Esq., of Shubuta, Miss., published a digest, also intended as a supplement to George's, embracing from 45th to 64th Miss.

In 1883 Marvin E. Sullivan, Esq., of Water Valley, issued the Mississippi citations, being a table of all Mississippi cases which have ever been mentioned in the opinions of the high court and the supreme court of Mississippi, from the organization of the state, including all the chancery and law reports down to Vol. 59, inclusive. Quite a useful book for briefing, but not so useful as it would have been had it included the citations of cases from other states.

On the 27th of February, 1878, by an act of that date, the legislature authorized the

Hon. J. A. P. Campbell to revise and codify all the laws of the state of a general nature, and to submit the same at their next regular meeting. This was done, and the new code was considered by the legislature, amended in some respects, and adopted on the 5th of March, to become operative (except where otherwise provided in itself) on the first of November following, and from that date it repealed all acts and parts of acts, the subjects whereof were revised, consolidated and reënacted therein, or were repugnant to its provisions.

This code is made more available by foot-notes citing the Mississippi cases in which the several statutes have been construed or applied. It is a very conservative revision. As the distinguished compiler says in the preface, "the main body of the existing statutes was preserved, and no change was made merely for the sake of change. Where alteration was not deemed important, the existing law was preserved." The most striking changes were the abolition of the estates of dower and of tenancy by courtesy, of the rule in Shelley's case, and of the use of private seals.

During the period from 1880 to 1890 there was little of general interest in this branch of state history. But on the 12th of August, 1890, pursuant to the act of February 5 previous, a constitutional convention (the sixth in the state's history) met in the city of Jackson. It elected Hon. Sol S. Calhoon president, and after a session of seventy-two days, adjourned on the 1st of November, after adopting, without submission to the people for ratification, the constitution of 1890. Some of the most noteworthy general features of this instrument are these:

Ability to read any section of the constitution, or to understand the same when read, or to give a reasonable interpretation thereof, and the payment of taxes, are made additional conditions to the right to vote. The regular sessions of the legislature are fixed at intervals of four years, with special sessions (also at four year intervals) between, and at the latter, nothing is to be considered except appropriation and revenue bills, and such other matters as may be acted on at an extraordinary session called by the governor. No appropriation-bill thereafter passed shall continue in force more than six months after the next regular meeting of the legislature. The legislature is directed to pass laws to accomplish a number of objects of general interest, such as, to regulate the acquisition and holding of lands in this state by non-resident aliens, or by corporations, etc. Quite a number of prohibitions is laid upon the legislature; e. g.: it is forbidden to pass special or local laws, for the benefit of individuals or corporations, in cases which are or can be provided for by general law, or where the relief sought can be given by any court of the state; or to pass special or local laws on any of twenty-one designated subjects (such as granting divorces, etc.), or to make donations of the public lands to individuals or incorporations. The governor is forbidden to exercise the pardoning power before conviction, and he is empowered to suspend from office any alleged defaulting state or county treasurer, or tax collector, pending the investigation of his accounts, and to make temporary appointments to fill the offices meanwhile. The governor, lieutenant-governor, auditor, treasurer, sheriffs and county treasurers, are all made ineligible as their own successors. All state executive officers are to be elected by votes of counties and representatives' districts, after the manner of the electoral college. but the electors themselves are dispensed with in this scheme. County officers, both executive and judicial, are to be selected in such manner as the legislature shall direct, but legislators are to be elected by the people; nor shall the legislature elect any other than its own officers, state librarian, United States senators, and presidential electors. The terms of all elective and county officers are fixed at four years. The leasing of convicts from the penitentiary is prohibited after January 1, 1895. Corporations shall be created only by general laws, and none granted a charter for private gain longer than ninety-nine years, and their property shall be taxed to the same extent as that of individuals. Public education is guaranteed for four months in each year, out of the public treasury. Devises of lands or money, direct or indirect, to charities or religious associations, are forbidden. The prohibitions against property qualifications, contained in the constitution of 1869, are omitted.

Not much change was made in the judiciary provisions. The supreme judges must be chosen from their respective districts as well as for them. The terms of chancellors and circuit judges are fixed at four years. If suits are brought into the circuit court, when they should have been brought into the chancery court, they shall not be dismissed, but transferred, and vice versa. The chancery court is given jurisdiction to decree possession, rents, improvements and taxes in all suits to try title and remove clouds, and in all cases in which it had jurisdiction auxiliary to courts of common law, it may exercise such jurisdiction, although the legal remedy may not have been exhausted or the legal title established by a suit at law, and it may entertain suits on the bonds of fiduciaries or public officers for property received, or wasted, or lost by neglect or failure to collect, or suits involving inquiry into mutual accounts. The jurisdiction of justices of the peace is raised to $200.

An ordinance was adopted, introducing the Australian ballot system, with Dortch's modifications, in all elections except those for congress, irrepealable before January 1, 1896.

Section 278 of this constitution provided that the governor should appoint three suitable persons as commissioners, "whose duty it shall be to draft such general laws as are contemplated in the constitution, and such other laws as shall be necessary and proper to put into operation the provisions thereof, and as may be appropriate to conform the general statutes of the state to the constitution." The governor accordingly appointed on this commission Hons. Robert H. Thompson, George C. Dillard and Robert B. Campbell, all of whom were members of the convention. These gentlemen came to the conclusion that, in order to do properly the work exacted of them, it is necessary to prepare a new code, and they are now engaged in that duty. The draft will be submitted to the legislature of 1892 for its action.

The legal and judicial history of Mississippi is now narrated to this date. But it would not be proper to end this chapter without some notice of certain gentlemen whose names have not yet been mentioned, or else mentioned so briefly as not to indicate their merit. They held no judicial offices in this state, or but humble ones, and yet they made legal and judiciary history. The names of Fulton Anderson, Roger Barton, Walter Brooke, William F. Dowd, Wiley P. Harris, James T. Harrison, Joseph Holt, Lucius Q. C. Lamar, Daniel Mayes, John T. McMurran, James Phelan, Sargeant S. Prentiss, George L. Potter, John B. Sale, Harvey W. Walter, Edward C. Walthall, John W. C. Watson, George S. Yerger and others of similar genius, constitute a galaxy which any Mississippian will regard proudly. Not all of them were gifted after the same manner. Some wielded the keen and glittering scimetar of Saladin, others the ponderous ax of Richard, but all were powerful. Nearly all are dead, yet their work remains, and with it, themselves. When the dull, cold days of winter have settled on the earth, and the glowing sunlight, the plashing and vivifying showers, the musical and strengthening breezes of summer are gone, who shall say that those beneficent and joyful agents have in truth passed away? Have they not stored themselves in a rich fruitage, in corn and wine, and more than all, the possibility of renewed life? So, the honored names above, even of those who are dead, are more than memories. They have illuminated our annals; they have enriched our jurisprudence; they have left us a noble legacy of lofty aspiration and high achievement. Let their posterity remember them lovingly and gratefully.

CHAPTER III.

INSTITUTIONS AND SOCIETIES.

A BODY of men acting as a state passes through experiences that are much like the emergence of a half-savage hunter into the highly organized life of an educated and cultured gentleman. The simple organization with a constitution, a state capitol and executives is but the hunter's eyes, arm and gun compared with the power of educated men with laboratory, library, and machinery. The state begins to develop. It provides for its sustenance in its revenue, a financial basis that grows more complex and extensive as the state develops, a history of which in any state would form a volume of marvelous interest to the thoughtful reader, but which can only be touched upon in a sketch of these limits. Almost as soon it provides for protection both from without and within by a militia organization, sometimes official and sometimes unofficial or voluntary, and this prospers or becomes weak, like a muscle, according to the varying need for its use. Protection from individuals is provided for in prisons, and as the state develops, these take on a penitentiary and reformatory character, when they fall more or less under the list of those institutions for the deformed, morally and otherwise. The deformed, as to speech, hearing, vision, or mind and often in body, are in earlier years of the state cared for by relatives and friends, but soon the people determine to share the support and aid of these under the state in schools, hospitals and asylums. At an early date the state provides itself a memory in the form of a library, which at first preserves only its necessary records made by its scribes or printers, and as the state enlarges its interests become a store of rich information, not only covering all its own affairs, but the thought and action of all states, wherein it takes continual stock of the resources of all ages. But this larger interest depends on the people individually, and so a system of public education is early begun, at first more or less primary, then slowly extending its scope to academies, high schools, normal or teachers' schools, colleges, training schools for occupations, professional schools, and universities for original investigation, the success of all which efforts is most marked when the population is homogeneous. As the state enlarges in population and becomes complex in action and interests, a more or less elaborate system of regulation is organized; easy movements through, and in and out of the state become necessary, and flat-boat, raft, sail or steam vessel regulation becomes necessary on river or ocean, or boards for the construction and care of levees to hold the streams to a fixed course, while on land the pack-horse, and stage, giving way to rapid railways, make an organization necessary to regulate the varied interests of the state in these new complications for the movement of products and people. The occupation and development of waste and unoccupied lands is another interest important enough to place in special hands; and this gives rise to the emergencies incident to an influx of population, an interest large enough to require the attention of one or more special officers. Increased population and greater intelligence usually lead to provision of officers or boards for the regulation of sanitary conditions, especially where epidemics are dangerous possibilities. In time the state advances to aggressive investigation of its own resources in various lines by bureaus or like agencies, in investigating its geological resources, in collecting information on its agricultural needs and possibilities, in studies of its wage-earners' conditions, its manufacturing powers, in periodical stocktaking oftener than the national census, and so on *ad infinitum*. So far as Mississippi has undertaken any of these lines, the most important will be indicated, some in this chapter, and others, such as the systems of public education, sanitation and the judiciary, are assigned separate chapters.

Many things are undertaken by the people associated in an unofficial or voluntary capacity, however; such as for mutual aid, social advantages, improvement, investigation, agitation, and the like. Such are the various fraternities and benefit associations, the state medical and bar associations, the press association, the various political organizations, the temperance union of women, the association of teachers, all of which are treated in separate or allied chapters, while the historical society, the Confederate veterans' association and a few others will be given brief mention here.

It is needless to say that the white race is referred to in speaking in this general line, for the intelligence and experience that is required for successful work in an organized capacity, at least any but the most crude and elementary, seems not to have been reached to an appreciable degree yet among the colored race in this state.

The militia has had a varied experience. Always provided for by law, both under the territorial governors and by every constitution, it has from the first been largely made up of volunteer companies. Many causes, both from conditions and sentiment, have contributed to make a considerable pride in excellent military companies, some of which, like the Natchez Fencibles, have had a remarkably long and well-known career. This fact in part explains the state's prompt response to calls upon it. From 1799 to 1836 the legislature passed about seventeen fragmentary acts, which were replaced by Pray's systematic act of May 5, 1837. Since then the militia has been systematically provided for in full in later constitutions.

During the period immediately succeeding the war, the militia was composed largely of colored men, but since the change of administration in 1875 they have been chiefly drawn from the white population and always in excellent training. Great care is given to this because of the liability to race conflict. Still, there is not the very general attention given to it that there was in ante-bellum days, when, under the act of 1837, there were fifty-four regiments, while there are now but three under the name Mississippi National Guard actually maintained by the state. The last report of the adjutant-general (1889) gives a roster of seventeen hundred men of infantry, artillery and cavalry, in three regiments and two battalions, who meet in annual encampment. The permanent camp-grounds are at Fort Henry near Pass Christian. The general headquarters are at Jackson, and the division headquarters at Biloxi, Joseph R. Davis, major-general commanding. The northern division, Brig.-Gen. J. S. Billups, headquarters at Columbus, with First infantry regiment, Col. R. M. Levy, centering at West Point, and the second, Col. C. L. Lincoln, at Columbus. The First cadet battalion (infantry), Maj. W. N. Hardee, headquarters at Agricultural and Mechanical college. Jackson is the rendezvous of the Third regiment, southern division, Col. George S. Green, and Biloxi of the First artillery, lieutenant-colonel commanding, E. W. Morrill. Other detached companies are the Gillsburg Rifles, Raleigh Rescues and Prairie Rifles (Okalona).

The Mississippi state penitentiary's red brick walls may be seen on an elevation in Jackson, nearly enclosing the third square north of the executive mansion. It has been nearly fifty-six years since this institution was established, the act passed being approved February 26, 1836, and directing its location within two miles of Jackson with an appropriation of $75,000 to secure its erection. By its last report it now has within its walls fifty white males, three hundred and ninety-eight black males and twenty-four black females, a total of four hundred and seventy-two prisoners on December 4, 1889. During that year one hundred and seventeen had been discharged, fifty-one had escaped, twenty-five had been pardoned, nineteen had died, three were returned for new trial, and three hundred and ninety had been let out to contractors. In charge of these, under the board of control, are these paid officers: general manager, physician, bookkeeper, chaplain, two camp sergeants, a farm sergeant, a traveling sergeant, a wall sergeant, two gate men, two night watchmen and eight wall guards. That year showed at the close a net income of $26,278.56, which shows the institution in an excellent financial condition, the board of control then consisting of J. F. Sessions, Walter McLaurin and J.C. Kyle. Measures are on foot to relocate the prison on a prison farm. The superintendent in 1887 was W. L. Doss and the general manager M. L. Jenkins. In its policy the reformatory and humane principles now so insisted upon have placed it in line with the best managed institutions elsewhere. Its career before the war was marked more by a character of punishment, before the more humane, and possibly ultra-sentimental, teachings of later days had begun. The convict-lease system has been greatly abused at times, but public sentiment has reacted against it. The labor of the convicts was used in building the Gulf-Ship Island railway to a large degree, and their use at the discretion of the governing powers in reconstruction days was a source of public dissatisfaction. This institution, like every other, suffered greatly during the war. The practice of leasing labor out through the state has found many opponents. As an illustration of the extent to which this subleasing system has been carried, take the situation in 1885, when about seven hundred convicts were subleased in as many as twelve different sections of the state in "camps," and on various kinds of labor. Many improvements were made during that year, however, some of which were a return to the policy of ante-bellum days when a cottonmill was in operation. It is probable that the new movement for the penitentiary farm will secure the abandonment of outside leasing.

The first institution anything like an asylum was the Natchez hospital, incorporated January 18, 1805, and made a state institution. Vicksburg hospital received state aid in 1846. In 1848, March 4, an act was approved establishing an asylum for the insane at Jackson. This was not completed until 1854, however, and now embraces a property worth about $500,000, and located about two miles north of Jackson. At the beginning of 1889 there were one hundred and ninety-one male and two hundred and fifty female, a total of four hundred and forty-one inmates. During the year one hundred and twenty-five more were admitted, making five hundred and sixty-six. There were fifty-one discharged recovered, eleven improved, eight unimproved, two not insane, one escaped and thirty-three died, leaving four hundred and fifty-nine at the beginning of 1890. The large proportion of women is noticeable. The total admissions since 1854, however, equalizes the sexes, there having been thirteen hundred and eighty-seven males and thirteen hundred and two females received, a total of two thousand six hundred and eighty-nine. To show the work of the institution during its career, note still farther: Of two thousand six hundred and eighty-nine received, five hundred and five males and four hundred and sixty-one females have been discharged recovered, a total of nine hundred and sixty-six; one hundred and sixty were improved, two hundred and twelve remained stationary, seventy-six eloped, thirty proved not insane; four hundred and nineteen males and three hundred and sixty-seven females, a total of seven hundred and eighty-six, died. It is interesting to note that five of the present inmates were among those admitted the first year, 1855. The disbursements for 1889 were $57,143.18, and its farm products reached $12,797.55. This institution is under the control of a board of trustees, those of 1889 being J. B. Harris, D. P. Porter, P. Fairly, James Tripp and Marcellus Green. The able superintendent is Dr. Thomas J. Mitchell.

The demands on the Jackson institution led to an act in 1882 for the founding of the East Mississippi insane asylum, which was secured by Meridian, the city donating five hundred and fifty-six acres to it. This institution was completed in 1884, and by January, 1890, had received three hundred and sixty-one males and two hundred and eighty-four females, a total of six hundred and forty-five patients, nineteen per cent. of which were epileptics. Out of one hundred and thirty-eight deaths since the beginning one-third were from epilepsy. In 1889, beginning with two hundred and fourteen, there were one hundred admitted, twenty-three were discharged recovered, fourteen improved, two unimproved, two not insane, two eloped and twenty-two died, due largely to an epidemic of dysentery and typhoid fever; and two hundred and forty-nine remained at the close of the year. The board of trustees in 1889 were Gov. Robert Lowry, W. F. Brown, S. B. Watts, George S. Covert, H. M. Street and John Stinson. Dr. C. A. Rice was the superintendent, under whom the institution was organized and so ably conducted. The present incumbent of that office is Dr. J. W. Buchanan, whose management is preserving the well-known excellence of this younger of the state's two excellent means of caring for the most unfortunate and heavily afflicted of her people.

The institution for the instruction of the blind was established in 1848, and is now in new quarters—a handsome structure at the north end of State street, Jackson, completed in 1882 at a cost of over $40,000. It is a well-known fact that the number of blind are always far less than the number of insane and less than the number of deaf. In 1883 there were fifteen male and nineteen female pupils, a total of thirty-four; in 1889 there were thirty-nine. It undertakes literary, musical instruction and certain forms of suitable manual training for both sexes, such as the manufacture of chairs, brooms, etc. The board of trustees in 1889 were C. H. Manship, H. H. Hines, J. A. Kausler, James R. Yerger and E. M. Parker. For many years Dr. W. S. Langley was superintendent, but on his death his daughter, Miss M. M. Langley, succeeded him, and Dr. P. Fairly, the present incumbent, became her successor at her death. He has a faculty of five teachers.

The Mississippi institution for the education of the deaf and dumb greets the eye of the passer-by on North State street, Jackson, as one of the most beautiful grounds in the state. An act of 1854 founded the institution, and up to 1861, when the buildings were destroyed, it grew prosperously. The state secured the admission of pupils to the Louisiana institute for a few months. Prof. A. K. Martin was superintendent at this time. It was reorganized in 1871 under Dr. J. L. Carter with about fifteen pupils, and in October, 1877, he was succeeded by Mr. Charles H. Talbot, at which time there were about forty-five pupils. In 1881, when the present superintendent, Prof. J. R. Dobyns, assumed the duties of that office, and with marked ability, there were fifty-four pupils. In 1882 several marked advances were made, among them the teaching of articulation, printing, carpentry and cabinet-work, and the establishment of a colored branch about one and a half miles in the country, where farming is taught to pupils of both races also. The total enrollment is now eighty-five and the school is in high favor with people and law-makers. The value of buildings and grounds is estimated at $75,000, and in 1888 the average cost per capita was but $141.17. The trustees in 1889 were Rev. John Hunter, D.D., D. N. Barrows, S. S. Carter, H. M. Taylor and Judge S. S. Calhoon. A force of several able instructors are employed.

The state library, in its tasteful alcoves opening into the rotunda of the capitol, is said to be "the second in value of its kind in the Union, the Massachusetts library only outranking it."* By this is meant, as a legal reference library. This condition is largely due to the efforts of a woman, Mrs. Mary Morancy, the first woman to hold a state office in Mississippi, although she was elected by proxy, during the period she held office, namely, fourteen years. The library was established by an act of February 15, 1838, with the leading state officers as trustees. The institution improved up to the war, when it suffered serious injury, and only began to be rehabilitated in 1876 under Mrs. Morancy's care. As an illustration of its progressive management the latest report, 1888-9, states that for that period two hundred volumes were added by purchase and six hundred and two by exchange, making a total of eight hundred and two volumes added in two years. Its list of its own laws, journals and reports, and the laws and reports of other states are remarkably complete. The state librarian is also keeper of the capitol. The present incumbent is Miss Rosa Lee Tucker, of Okalona.

This library may be called a part of the memory of the state. Here the state recalls her acts and the names of her servants. Let her call over the names of some of the leading lives of her public servants.

The congressmen of Mississippi have been generally her pride. In the senate, from December, 1817, to March, 1821, was Walter Leake, who resigned, to become a gubernatorial candidate, and was succeeded by David Holmes, who served by reëlection to March, 1825, when he resigned. Thomas H. Williams served from December, 1817, to March 3, 1821. Powhatan Ellis was appointed to succeed Mr. Holmes, and served by election until March 3, 1832, when he resigned, and was succeeded by John Black, appointed, who, by election, served to March, 1838. He resigned, and James F. Trotter was appointed to serve until March, 1839. Thomas B. Reed served from December, 1826, until his death, in November, 1829, when Robert H. Adams was elected to his place, but died in July, 1830. George Poindexter was then elected, and served to March 3, 1835, when Robert J. Walker was elected, and by reëlection served to March, 1845. In January, 1839, John Henderson began a full six-year term, and was succeeded, March 4, 1845, by Jesse Speight, who died May 3, 1847, and, by appointment, was replaced by Jefferson Davis. Mr. Davis resigned in the fall of 1851, but in 1857 was reëlected, and on January 12, 1861, with all this state's congressmen, withdrew. John J. McRae served by appointment from 1851 to March, 1852, and Stephen Adams served by election to March, 1857. The other senator in January, 1847, was Henry S. Foote, whose term of service extended to January, 1852, when Walker Brookes' election followed, and covered the period between the months of March, 1852 and 1853. Here Albert G. Brown's service began, that ended by his withdrawal with Mr. Davis. It was not until April 11, 1870, that the next senator took his seat—Adelbert Ames, who was succeeded by Henry R. Pease, the latter serving from February, 1874, to March 3, 1875, when the term of Blanche K. Bruce, colored, began, covering the period to March, 1881. In February, 1870, the first colored senator, Hiram R. Revels, was elected, but was succeeded in 1871 by James L. Alcorn, whose service extended to March 3, 1877. Lucius Q. C. Lamar succeeded him, and served by reëlection until March, 1885, when, by appointment, election and reëlection, Edward C. Walthall entered a service whose present term will terminate March 3, 1895. In 1881 James Z. George succeeded Mr. Bruce, the colored senator, and by election and reëlection, is holding a term at present which closes in 1893.

---
*New York World, 1891.

In the house of representatives, George Poindexter heads the list, from December, 1817, to March 3, 1819. Christopher Rankin then served until his death, at Washington, in May, 1826, when his successor's election followed. This was William Haile, who, by reëlection, served until his resignation in 1828, when Gen. Thomas Hinds succeeded him, in a term covering the time to 1831. His successor, Franklin E. Plummer, served from 1831 to 1835. A second representative was elected in 1833—Harry Cage, his term ending in 1835. Dr. David Dickson and John F. H. Claiborne were elected in 1835, but the former died in July, 1836, and his term was filled by Samuel J. Gholson, and he, with Mr. Claiborne, on their return to the twenty-fifth congress, found their seats contested by Sargent S. Prentiss and Thomas J. Word, whereupon the house decided that neither was entitled to the seats, January 31, 1838. A new election returned Messrs. Prentiss and Word, who served to 1839. Albert G. Brown and Jacob Thompson succeeded them in November, 1839, the former serving to 1841, declining reëlection, and again serving from 1848 to 1851, and the latter serving continuously to 1851. The interval between 1841 and 1848 above mentioned was covered by Dr. William M. Gwin, to 1843, declining reëlection, and Robert W. Roberts to March 3, 1847; two other representatives, William H. Hammet and Tilghman M. Tucker, in November, 1843, serving to 1845. Jefferson Davis was elected in November, 1845, but resigned in May, 1846, to take command of his regiment, and Henry T. Ellett succeeded him, serving to 1847, and declining reëlection. Patrick W. Tompkins and Winfield S. Featherston were elected in November, 1847, the former serving to 1849 and declining reëlection, and the latter to 1851, in which year the service of William McWillie, the successor of Mr. Featherston, closed. In 1851 John D. Freeman and Benjamin D. Nabors were elected, and served two years. In 1853 were elected Daniel B. Wright, Otho R. Singleton, William S. Barry and Wiley P. Harris, the last three serving to 1855, and the first to 1857; Mr. Singleton, not declining reëlection like the last two, was defeated by William A. Lake, but reëlected in 1857, and served by reëlection until the withdrawal in 1861. In 1855 ex-Gov. John A. Quitman and Henly S. Bennett were chosen, the former's service closing in 1857, and the death of the latter breaking his second term on July 17, 1858. John J. McRae was chosen to complete the unexpired term, and served by reëlection to the withdawal of January 12, 1861. Reuben Davis and Lucius Q. C. Lamar were elected in 1857, and withdrew, the former in 1861, and the latter on December 20, 1860, to become a candidate for the state secession convention from his county. When representation began again after the war, those chosen in 1870 were George C. McKee, Jason Niles, L. W. Perce, Henry W. Barry and George E. Harris, all serving to 1873, except General McKee and Mr. Barry, who continued to 1875. In 1871 the service of Albert R. Howe, John R. Lynch (colored) and Joseph L. Morphis began, and closed in 1875. In 1873 L. Q. C. Lamar was elected, and served to his election to the senate in 1877. At the great revolution in 1875, he and Mr. Lynch, the colored representative, were the only ones reëlected. Hernando D. Money, Charles E. Hooker, G. Wiley Wells and Otho R. Singleton were elected at this date, Mr. Singleton serving by reëlection to 1887, Mr. Wells to 1877, Colonel Hooker to 1883, and again to his present term, and Mr. Money to 1885. Mr. Lynch served in the forty-fourth congress, and also from 1882 to 1883, unseating James R. Chalmers. In 1877 Van H. Manning, James R. Chalmers and Henry L. Muldrow were elected. Mr. Manning served until unseated by James R. Chalmers, June 25, 1884, Mr. Chalmers until unseated by Mr. Lynch, April 29, 1882, and Mr. Muldrow by reëlection until 1885. In 1882 Ethelbert Barksdale, Henry S. Van Eaton and Elza Jeffords were elected, the first two serving to 1887, and the last to 1885. In 1884 were chosen Thomas C. Catchings, James B. Morgan, John M. Allen and Frederick G. Barry. Mr.

Allen's service closed in 1885, Mr. Barry's in 1889 and Mr. Morgan's in 1891. Mr. Catchings' service has extended to the present term, which closes in 1893. In 1886 Chapman L. Anderson and Thomas R. Stockdale's election occurred, the former's service closing in 1891, and that of the latter extending to the present term, which closes in 1893. Clark Lewis was elected in 1888, and was reëlected to his present term.

The members elected to the first Confederate congress were seven in number: J. W. Clapp, Reuben Davis, Israel Welsh, H. C. Chambers, O. R. Singleton, Ethel Barksdale and John J. McRae.

The governors of the state have already been mentioned in a preceding chapter. It is most unfortunate that the records of the state and the library branch of it should have been so despoiled during the war, that a connected list of very many lines of detail are thus rendered impossible to historical writings, and often, where apparently possible, wholly unreliable. It is only those who have attempted historical work under such circumstances that will appreciate its difficulties.

It may be of interest to note how Mississippi compares with other states as regards the salaries of her public servants, and to illustrate let one example be taken—that of the gubernatorial salary. The terms of governors in this country vary from one year, as in the case of Massachusetts, to four years, as in the case of about half the states of the Union, including Mississippi. The annual salaries also vary from $1,000, as in Rhode Island, Michigan, New Hampshire and Vermont, to the generous proportions of $10,000, as only the great and wealthy states of New York and Pennsylvania seem able to afford. Mississippi takes a stand midway and alongside of Massachusetts, Iowa, Ohio, Tennessee, Texas, Louisiana, Maryland, North Carolina and Washington, paying $4,000 per annum to her governor.

It may show her relative public spirit, too, to compare her legal holidays with those of other states, omitting Sundays and labor day, the latter a recent institution. Of fourteen such days recognized in all or parts of this country are: New year's day, January 1; anniversary of the battle of New Orleans, January 8; Washington's birthday, February 22; anniversary of Texan independence, March 2; fireman's anniversary of New Orleans, March 4; mardi-gras; anniversary of the battle of San Jacinto (Texas), April 21; Good Friday; memorial day, April 26 in Georgia; decoration day, May 30 in most Northern states; July 4; independence day; general election day; thanksgiving day and Christmas day; of which Mississippi makes legal holiday new year's day, independence day, thanksgiving and Christmas.

This state's position politically among her sister states has always been a prominent one. It has rarely been that, like Indiana or New York, the term "doubtful" could be applied to her. As a general chapter on politics elsewhere in these volumes deals with this subject, only presidential majorities will be given here, and that only since 1824. In 1821 the state joined the era of good feeling and voted for Monroe and Tompkins, but in 1824 she turned out a democratic majority of one thousand four hundred and twenty-one for her idol, in whose honor, only a short time before, she had named her capital city—Jackson. In the next campaign she increased her democratic majority to five thousand one hundred and eighty-two for him, when the ticket was Jackson and Calhoun in 1828, while in 1832, with still increasing ardor for the doughty old general who whipped Indians, the money-king Biddle, the British and most other enemies he attacked, Mississippi gave Jackson and Van Buren a democratic majority of five thousand nine hundred and nineteen. In the thirties, however, they fell upon days of financial disturbance and whig predominance, and in 1836 the democrats began to waver and the whigs to rejoice. These were the days of the great whig, Daniel

Webster, and the popular old Hoosier, Gen. William Henry Harrison, and the big democratic majority of 1832 was, in 1836, cut down to the narrow margin of two hundred and ninety-one majority for Van Buren and Johnson. The financial troubles of the great panic of 1837 caused great popular dissatisfaction all over the Union, as such times always do, and the whigs grew and waxed strong all over the broad land, and with especial strides in Mississippi under the influence of the famous "hard cider" campaign, when, in 1840, they did what has rarely been done in the entire career of the state of Mississippi—broke her democratic majority and gave the whig candidates, Harrison and Tyler, two thousand five hundred and twenty-three majority. This was destined to be but an incident, however, for the revival of financial confidence and the ominous mutterings of the fifteen or sixteen years' distant civil war led Mississippi to spring back with a bound, as if to her normal condition, with a democratic majority in 1844 almost exactly to a figure the same as that of 1832 (five thousand nine hundred and nineteen), this of 1844 being five thousand nine hundred and twenty for Polk and Dallas. These were the years of the great compromises and compromisers, and the whigs made another stupendous effort in 1848 with the great hero of the Mexican war, General Taylor, and Mississippi, whose soldiers did such noble service under their old commander of Buena Vista, as if to do him honor, dropped their democratic majority of five thousand nine hundred and twenty to only six hundred and fifteen majority for the democratic candidates, Cass and Butler. The campaigns of the fifties witnessed the increasing welding powers of the slavery agitation which swept Mississippi votes more and more into democratic lines. Of course these figures must be considered in connection with the fact of increased population—an increase in this style in round thousands by decades beginning with the year 1800: seven thousand, thirty-one thousand, seventy-five thousand, one hundred and thirty-six thousand, three hundred and seventy-five thousand, six hundred and six thousand, and seven hundred and ninety-one thousand in 1860. This shows almost doubling by decades, so the majorities must be interpreted by this fact. The first campaign of the fifties, that is in 1852, rose again to democratic majorities, state and national, Pierce and King receiving Mississippi's majority of nine thousand three hundred and twenty-eight, the largest so far ever given. In 1856 the increase is still greater, giving to Buchanan and Breckinridge a majority of eleven thousand two hundred and fifty-one. The heat of the campaign of 1860 raised the political thermometer still higher, and a majority of twelve thousand four hundred and seventy-four was given for Breckinridge and Lane, whose entire vote was only eight hundred and forty-five thousand seven hundred and sixty-three, the great mass of the democratic party of the country having gone for Stephen A. Douglas, with one million three hundred and seventy-five thousand one hundred and fifty-seven, while the republican candidate, Lincoln, went in with one million eight hundred and thirty-eight thousand one hundred and sixty-nine. The actual vote of this state was forty thousand seven hundred and ninety-seven for Breckinridge; twenty-five thousand and forty for Bell, and two thousand two hundred and eighty-three for Douglas. This was when the free population was three hundred and fifty-three thousand nine hundred and one, and the slaves four hundred and thirty-six thousand six hundred and thirty-one, this state and South Carolina being the only states having an excess of slave population over free.

This condition led to Mississippi's attempted withdrawal from the Union by unanimous vote, and the campaign of 1864 found her, with ten other states, practically defeated, and with no political status in the Union. Even the campaign of 1868 found her outside the pale when all the other of the eleven states were readmitted except herself, Texas and Virginia. Meanwhile preparations were making that provided an influx into her legal vote of the great mass of her slaves of a few years before. In 1860 the votes were drawn from a white population of three hundred and fifty-three thousand eight hundred and ninety-nine, whose slave population was nearly a hundred thousand greater—four hundred and thirty-seven thousand four hundred and four—and the voters from these were all republicans. In 1870 both were increased, but bore somewhat similar proportions—that is, three hundred and eighty-two thousand eight hundred and ninety-six white to four hundred and forty-four thousand two hundred and one colored. Of course in the campaign of 1872, although for once only, the republican majority, which means practically the colored majority, was thirty-four thousand eight hundred and eighty-seven for Grant and Wilson. The great revolution of 1876, for white supremacy, however, threw the state into the democratic ranks as of yore, with fifty-nine thousand five hundred and sixty-eight majority for Tilden and Hendricks, and she has continued democratic and under white control ever since, with immaterial variation. In the campaign of 1880 the majority for Hancock and English was thirty-five thousand and ninety-nine; the plurality for Cleveland and Hendricks, in 1884, was thirty-three thousand and one; and Cleveland and Thurman's majority, in 1888, was fifty-five thousand three hundred and seventy-five. The relative population of 1890 was five hundred and thirty-nine thousand seven hundred and three whites and seven hundred and forty-seven thousand seven hundred and twenty colored, the latter, however, representing a great mass of ignorant votes, which the new constitution makes less of a menace to intelligent government, by providing both an educational and property qualification, somewhat as Rhode Island and Delaware has long had.

The war has left many other scars and monuments in the state besides in its politics. As monuments to the fearfulness of the struggle are the all too-full cemeteries of the dead of both sides; the Confederate dead in multitudes of cemeteries throughout the state, and the Federal dead in three of the seventy-nine national cemeteries scattered throughout the Union, all but twelve of which are in the South. These three are at Vicksburg, Natchez and Corinth; that at Vicksburg containing sixteen thousand six hundred, of whom twelve thousand and thirty-two are unknown. These cemeteries are increasing somewhat in the number of their dead, especially on account of the deaths of colored men, of whom seventeen thousand eight hundred and sixty-nine out of Mississippi served in the Federal army.

One of the greatest interests of the state, however, is its financial basis and its methods in dealing with the subject. It seems strange to the present generation that the state which now receives and disburses over $1,000,000 annually for current expenses should have at one time been the property of an individual in private life, but such it was, although it scarcely amounted to more than a technicality. In 1630 it was part of a grant made by the king of Great Britain to Sir Robert Heath, and was transferred seven years later by Heath to Lord Maltravers. It afterward became the property of plain Dr. Daniel Coxe of the province of New Jersey. Now, however, a man is one of wealth if he but own a small share of this great state. Even in 1811, six years before the period of statehood began, the taxes collected for that year were $31,845.46, and economy was so well before the minds of territorial managers of the state's finances that the expenditures for that year were but little over half this amount, or $17,911.43, leaving a balance of $9,690.38. These were not the days of great state institutions, however. In 1817, the year statehood began, and but two years after the exhausting wars of the earlier half of that decade, the receipts reached a few thousand more—$45,836.66, while a balance of nearly the same proportions as above was still kept—namely, $8,269.92, after the disbursement of $37,506.74 for current expenditures. About eight years after this the receipts rose considerably above this to the sum of $77,925.00, but the expenditures rose only to $41,475. This was the year 1825, and in all these considerations of finance the remarkable increase of population, nearly or quite doubling by decades, must be taken into account. About a dozen years later, in 1838, the receipts of the treasury were the round sum of $157,198.41, and these were the days of the great panic and the bank explosions that play so large a part in Mississippi's financial history.

Let us see what state banking facilities there were in 1836. First there was that stupendous concern, the Planters' bank of Natchez, whose capital reached the, for those days, fabulous sum of $4,000,000. It was what would now be counted a syndicate of banks, however, for it had branches at Manchester, Vicksburg, Port Gibson, Woodville, Monticello, Jackson and Columbus. Its president was James C. Wilkins. Then there was another company with a like capital of $4,000,000, one of those numerous companies that arose during the years when railroad building was in the raw exuberance of an overgrown boyhood. This was the Mississippi & Alabama Railroad & Banking Company of Brandon, which also had a branch at Paulding. There were several institutions of a capitalized power of $2,000,000, and these were the Agricultural bank of Natchez, with a branch at Pontotoc; its president was Mr. A. Fisk; the Commercial bank of Natchez, president, L. R. Marshall; the Grand Gulf Railroad & Banking Company, president, Joseph Johnson, with a branch at Gallatin; the Commercial & Railroad bank of Vicksburg, president, J. M. Taylor, with its branch at Vernon, and the Commercial bank of Manchester. Those of $1,000,000 capital were the West Feliciana Railroad & Banking Company of Woodville, president, Joseph Johnson; the Commercial bank of Rodney, president, Thomas Freeland, and the Aberdeen and Pontotoc Railroad & Banking Company; one other was the Princeton & Deer Creek Railroad & Banking Company, president, Z. K. Fulton, and capital $600,000. This was in 1836, but in 1840, only four years later, there were twenty banks in the state with aggregated resources of $28,989,-090.62, while the total capital incorporated for these purposes, between 1832 and 1838 reached the princely proportions of $53,750,000. This might indicate wealth in abundance throughout this great state, but in reality it was the most rank inflation and insolvency. The only railroad that resulted from it was a few paltry miles at Natchez, and scarcely fifty miles of the Vicksburg & Brandon route. Speculation ran riot, and it is said that the wild revelry of it was stimulated by a class of speculative adventurers who afterward left the state. These banks dealt in real estate too, dealt in bonds, exchange and bills of credit, made loans and issued their own notes for circulation The crash that began in 1836 seemed to make it all the more reckless, and men seemed to lose their heads and grasp at straws in their despair, and in 1837 the hue and cry led to another great bank of a capital of $1,500,000, and this was the famous ill-fated Union bank of Mississippi, which led to the greatest stain upon the escutcheon of this state, in the eyes of the world at large, that ever soiled it. The people of the state themselves were divided on the question for many years.

A glance at the banking career of the state will explain this: Organized in territorial days the Bank of Mississippi was enlarged in 1818 with its location at Natchez, the metropolis of the state. The greatly increasing need of the growing young state for banking facilities led to the incorporation of the Planters' bank of the state of Mississippi on April 10, 1830, with $3,000,000 capital. The state was to take two-thirds of the capital stock and issue bonds on the market for it, the rest to be taken by individuals. The faith of the state was pledged to secure all losses either from principal or interest, and each and every stockholder was made individually liable to make good all losses of any character. The bonds were to be sold by the governor for specie only, and almost every section emphasized the pledging of the faith of the state to recoup all possible losses. The state was to choose seven of the thirteen members of the directory. The bonds were sold in 1830 to the amount of $500,000, and in 1833 the remaining $1,500,000 as the law directed, and the prosperity of the bank was unquestioned until the crash of 1837 throughout the union. Its bonds had "sold at a premium of thirteen and one-fourth per cent," says a writer in De Bow's Review in 1853, "so that after paying the bank two millions the state had left a net of $250,000 which was placed in the bank as a sinking fund, to which was to be added the dividends, and from which the interest was to be paid. As the dividend averaged ten per cent. for years the interest was kept up to September 1, 1839, when the state stock was transferred to the Natchez Railroad Company. At this time the balance sinking fund was about $800,000. This belonged to the state, but a large part of it was lost in the crash of 1836-9. A commission held the remainder, about $60,000 in 1854—what next? By calculation, on paying $250,000 annually it would take twenty-two years to liquidate—about 1876.". The result was, however, that in 1854 the debt of this bank was $3,518,080, as far as the state was concerned.

The new constitution of 1832, however, put the following limit on the state's financial action: "No law shall ever be passed to raise a loan of money upon the credit of the state, or to pledge the faith of the state for the payment or redemption of any loan or debt, unless such law be proposed in the senate or house of representatives, and be agreed to by a majority of the members of each house, and entered on their journals with the yeas and nays taken thereon, and be referred to the next succeeding legislature, and published for three months previous to the next regular election, in three newspapers of this state; and unless a majority of each branch of the legislature so elected, after such publication, shall agree to and pass such law, and in such case the yeas and nays shall be taken, and entered on the journals of each house; provided, that nothing in this section shall be so construed as to prevent the legislature from negotiating a further loan of one and a half million of dollars, and vesting the same in stock reserved to the state, by the charter of the Planters' bank of the state of Mississippi."

This was the condition of affairs on January 21, 1837, when the governor approved the Union Bank act "so far as the action of this legislature is recognized." This act provided that only citizen real estate owners of Mississippi could become stockholders, with privilege of transfer to other Mississippi real estate owners only after five years, with the especial stipulation that well-secured mortgages should be given even in that case. The faith of the state was pledged to secure both the capital and interest, and that she should issue seven thousand five hundred bonds of $2,000 each, eighteen hundred and seventy-five payable in twelve years, eighteen hundred and seventy-five in fifteen years, the same amount in eighteen years, and the same again in twenty years, bearing interest at five per cent. These were transferable to anyone by the governor, and special provision was made for payment of both capital and interest when due. A most elaborate security was hedged around the subscription to stock so that the certainty of its payment seemed absolute, even from that source. Of the thirteen directors, five were to be chosen by the legislature, and three commissioners were to be elected to see to the thoroughly solid condition of would-be subscribers.

All the forms of law having been carried out, in 1838 the legislature repassed it as the limitation provided, and Gov. Alexander G. McNutt, who afterward loved to be called "the great repudiator," approved it on February 5, (1838). Ten days later (15) a supplementary act was approved to clinch the bargain all the more firmly, so that, while these bonds were made as a loan to the bank the state was to take fifty thousand shares of the bank's stock and pay for it out of the proceeds of the bond sales, and the profits of it were to go to the state funds for internal improvement and educational purposes. Its most marked provision, however, was that in the sales of bonds no sale was to be made under their par value.

The bonds, to the amount of $5,000,000, were put by the bank into the hands of the following gentlemen to negotiate sale: James C. Wilkins, of Natchez; W. M. Pinckard, of Vicksburg; and E. C. Wilkinson, of Yazoo city, who succeeded in disposing of them by August 18 to Nicholas Biddle, president of the United States bank of Pennsylvania, payments being made in $1,000,000 amounts on November 1, 1838, and January 1, March 1, May 1, and July 1, 1839. About $2,000,000 of these bonds were afterward resold by Mr. Biddle, through the agency of the United States bank in Europe, and the remainder, with other state stocks, placed as security for money borrowed in England, France and Holland. "To the thinking, cool, clear-headed people, and there were many such at that day," says a recent writer, "the Union bank was foredoomed to a disastrous and ignominious failure. The entire banking system of that period was radically defective, but the theory upon which the Union bank was founded, that of 'relieving' people who were hopelessly insolvent, was a grotesque absurdity. The system of loans on mortgages of real and personal property, prescribed in the act of incorporation, for twelve months, renewable for eight years upon the payment of the interest and one-eighth of the principal, at the end of every twelve months, would have wrecked the Bank of England. The payment of the bonds as they fell due, and the interest thereon, which the bank was required to pay from the funds in its vaults, was a sheer impossibility. By the terms of the charter, the fifteen and a half millions of bonds, to be delivered to the bank, were made payable in four installments. The first installment was made payable in twelve, the second in fifteen, the third in eighteen, and the fourth in twenty years. In other words, the legislators of that period were insane enough to pledge the faith of the state for the payment of the enormous amount of fifteen and a half millions of dollars in the brief space of twenty years, together with the annually accruing interest, which amounted yearly to more than three-quarters of a million of dollars. And all this was to be the result of the profits of the Union bank in the course of two decades. Nothing can better expose the blind fatuity of the legislators of that day, or the mad, reckless temerity of the so-called financiers of the times."*

Gov. Alexander G. McNutt had somewhat of the temper of the great enemy of the United States bank, Andrew Jackson, and in his annual message of January 7, 1840, he sounded the alarm for a general onslaught on the banks of the state—Union, Planters' and all. He says: "I am induced to believe that a large portion of the property accepted as security for that stock is incumbered by judgments, mortgages and deeds of trust; that the valuations of the appraisers were generally very extravagant; that, in many instances, the titles to the property offered are yet imperfect, and that the whole management of the affairs of the bank has been disastrous to its credit, destructive to the interests of the state and ruinous to the institution. The cotton advanced upon by the bank, in some instances, has been attached and the suits decided against the institution. Many of the cotton agents and consignees are defaulters, and great loss on the cotton account is inevitable. The post notes, issued in violation of law, have greatly depreciated, and if the decisions of several of our circuit judges are affirmed by the high court of errors and appeals, actions can not be maintained on a large portion of the bills receivable of the bank. I signed and delivered to the managers last summer bonds to the amount of $5,000,000. The president of the bank was dispatched eastward to make a sale, but was unable to effect it. On the 18th of November, 1839, I received a letter from the cashier of the bank, together with two resolutions of the directors, one of which informed me that the remaining five million and a half of bonds were ready for my signature. Believing that there was no immediate prospect of sale

---

* "History of Mississippi," Lowry & McCardle.

of the bonds, and that further legislation might be required, I determined not to execute the remaining bonds." After showing the bank to have a debt due within a year of over $4,000,000, he says: "To pay the residue the bank has $5,000,000 of state bonds, and exchange, bills receivable, etc., to make the amount of $9,000,000. The state bonds can not be sold, and a sufficient sum can not be realized in time out of the other assets of the bank to pay the post notes due next April and May. It will take more than $250,000 of the available funds of the bank to pay in London the interest on the state bonds previous to the 1st of September next. It is our duty to place the institution either in liquidation, or to repeal all that portion of the charter giving to private individuals stock in the bank and privileged loans. The state debt already amounts to about $7,500,000. The interest on $7,000,000 is payable abroad, and amounts to $375,000 annually. The rights of the stockholders are yet inchoate, and until the residue of the bonds are sold they can have no peculiar claims. Influenced by no motive save that of the public good, anxious to protect the rights of all, and to advance the interests of the state, I am bound to recommend that the $5,000,000 of the state bonds last issued shall be called in and canceled, and that no more shall be hereafter issued for the Mississippi Union bank." Said he: "The existing banks can not be bolstered. Destitute as they are of credit and available means, it would be folly in us to attempt to infuse vigor and stability into their lifeless forms. They are powerless to do good, but capable of inflicting injuries irreparable." The facts afterward proved him right.

The agitation begun by the governor spread during the year, and in 1841 he struck another blow—this time at the validity of the bonds: "The situation and affairs of the Mississippi railroad company, the Planters' bank of the state and of the Mississippi Union bank will demand your calm consideration. All those institutions are insolvent, and neither of them can resume specie payment for several years or make further loans. I submit, herewith, copies of my letters to those banks, calling for specific information in relation to their condition, and the answers and statements furnished. The Union bank has $4,349 in specie on hand. Her suspended debt in suit is $2,698,869; suspended debt not sued on $1,777,337; resources, chiefly unavailable, $8,033,154; immediate liabilities $3,034,154; capital stock $5,000,000. The bank has been irretrievably ruined by making advances on cotton, issuing post notes, and loaning the principal portion of her capital to insolvent individuals and companies. The situation of the Mississippi railroad company and the Planters' bank is equally bad." Therefore he plead that, because the Union bank bonds had been practically sold below par by sale on credit, and by the bank of which Mr. Biddle was president, whose charter made the action unlawful, except for those authorized by the Keystone state or the nation, therefore they ought to be repudiated. Both senate and house disagreed with him, however, and placed themselves plainly on record in favor of paying the bonds of both banks for which the faith of the state was pledged. The campaign of 1841 was on this issue—the whigs taking a stand against repudiation, but after a hard fight they were defeated and the repudiation of the Union bonds ensued at once—and the Planters' bonds, although practically repudiated, were not formally so until eleven years later. The total debt of the two, due in 1854, aggregating over $12,000,000, was thus repudiated—technicalities which were to prove more costly than the payment would have been, although the total revenue of the state at that time would not exceed $225,000. "That the suicidal act of Mississippi has killed the credit of the slave states in Europe," says a writer in De Bow's Review in 1853, "does not admit of a doubt; and what has been the effect?" After showing that the East was getting all the credit necessary to bridge over the crash of 1837 and succeeding years, the writer continues, "The South has been forced into inaction and liquidation by the suspicion of capitalists, here and abroad, though wielding the greatest power on earth—cotton." All Southern securities were held in suspicion. On account of the trials of these years "some of the finest portions of Mississippi became partially depopulated," says a writer in 1849. "Thus in the breaking up of our miserable banking system many unhappy consequences followed, the baleful effects of which have pursued the state, kept down its natural growth and prosperity, and are yet seen and daily felt in our courts of justice and halls of legislation." The last two banks of this system to suspend were the Northern bank of Mississippi and the Commercial bank of Manchester, both of which did so in 1857. This action in regard to these bonds, ever since the governor was ordered to proclaim it on February 20, 1842, has had to be reiterated in successive constitutions; the present one says: "The credit of the state shall not be pledged or loaned in aid of any person, association or corporation; and the state shall not become a stockholder in any corporation or association, nor assume, redeem, secure or pay any indebtedness or pretended indebtedness alleged to be due by the state of Mississippi, to any person, association or corporation whatsoever, claiming the same as owners, holders or assignees of any bond or bonds, now generally known as Union bank bonds and Planters' bank bonds."

The close of the fifties saw the state in good financial condition. The total tax of 1860 was $740,276, and the disbursements of 1861 were $762,470. The two great sources of the state's wealth were cotton and slaves, and it was on these that the state expected to find a source of credit to carry on the war. The finance of the state was to be based on cotton reserves, and when it is considered that in 1859 alone Mississippi produced $45,000,000 worth of cotton, the course seemed eminently plausible. It is said that emancipation of slaves was a loss to the owners of about $600,000,000. It is natural that the war measures of the enemy should be directed to the destruction of these sources of power.* Confederate money came in use, too, and although at first at a slight premium, its depreciation was disastrous. In June, 1861, a dollar was worth ninety cents; December 1, it was eighty cents, and on the 15th, seventy-five cents; February 1, 1862, it was sixty cents; February, 1863, it fell to twenty cents; June, 1863, to eight cents; January, 1864, to two cents; November, 1864, it rose to four and one-half cents; January, 1865, it fell to two and one-half cents; April, 1865, to one and one-half cents, and after that it took $800 to $1,000 of Confederate money to equal a greenback dollar, and now it is sold as a curiosity. These circumstances will be seen by even the most uninformed observer to have been in themselves a fearful blow to this state. Then, too, the repairs of a public character during reconstruction days, together with the unskillful legislation of that time, as well as abuses, make an immense debt in 1872 a matter of no surprise. Add to this condition the $10,000,000 or thereabouts that was collected as a government cotton tax within the space of three years, and the reader is prepared for this condition in 1872. The state debt was then $2,377,342.38; the receipts in 1871 were $1,338,150.49, which, with funds, mostly of a worthless nature, in the treasury, of $828,114.16, gave a total of $2,166,264.65, from which was disbursed $1,326,161.57, leaving a nominal balance of $840,103.08; but, as the uncurrent proportion of this was $795,936.48, the current balance was but $44,166.60. The public school system was one great source of expense, too, and the increase in the state levy on the assessed valuation of land was startling. It was ten cents on a dollar in 1869, and in the successive years of 1871, 1872 and 1874 it became respectively, four times, eight and one-half times and fourteen times as great as in the first-mentioned year. The uprising of 1875–6 was a taxpayers' movement as well as a racial one.

---

*It is said that if the total cost of the Civil war was divided by the number of slaves set free it would make emancipation cost about $700 per slave.

In 1876 the state debt proper was $1,100,685.22, while the total debt, permanent and otherwise, was $3,226,847.42, distributed as follows: Due to the Chickasaw school fund, $814,743.23; interest on the same, $20,671.86; due the common-school fund, $878,572.67; interest on the same, $65,327.63; outstanding warrants, $590,368.52; certificates of indebtedness, $26,882; bonds due on January 1, of 1877, 1878, 1879 and 1896, $690,300.00; interest on the same, $32,189.50; railroad tax, $8,579.35; interest on insurance deposits, $14,476.67, and interest on bonds, $84,736. In 1882 the total debt was reduced to $2,974,832.06, and after deducting the permanent debt and cash, the debt proper was only $341,275.06. This is an excellent showing when it is recalled that from 1871 to 1875 property valuation had decreased $42,000,000, and about twenty-seven per cent. of the total area of the state had been forfeited for taxes. Taxation was reduced from nine and one-half mills in 1875 to two and one-half mills in 1883, and lands had been redeemed or purchased with the exception of seven hundred thousand acres.

In his message in 1890, Governor Lowry said: "There was cash in the treasury on the 1st day of January, 1890, $555,450.02. There can be no doubt that in the course of four years, with the present rate of taxation and the natural increase of values, the payable debt of the state can be anticipated and the bonds retired." The bonded debt of the state in 1890 was $902,437 and the floating debt $2,600,571, making a total of $3,503,008 in 1890, as against $3,324,084 in 1880, any sinking fund being deducted in both cases. As the population has increased (13.96) thirteen-and-ninety-six-hundredths per cent. during this decade, however, the per capita rate of indebtedness (less any sinking fund) has been reduced from $2.94 in 1880 to $2.72 in 1890. If the total county debt of the state be added to the totals of these two years, making a grand total (less any sinking fund in both cases) in 1880 of $4,456,847 and $4,709,807 in 1890, the per capita rate has been reduced from $3.94 in 1880, to $3.65 in 1890.

Comparing this with other states in the Union may make her standing more clearly evident. Including county indebtedness, the state having the largest total indebtedness, less any in 1890, was Virginia, with nearly thirty-three millions ($32,874,672), and that having the smallest was Vermont, with only ($153,524) a little over one hundred and fifty thousand; the per capita in these two cases however, are respectively $19.85 and forty-six cents, neither the highest nor the lowest in the Union, and, if the territories are included, Utah falls to the lowest place with a total debt of only $49,859, and the lowest per capita of only twenty-four cents. In total debt Mississippi ranks nearest to New Jersey, almost a million below Minnesota, Nebraska or Colorado, but above such states as Maine, New Hampshire, and nineteen other states and territories. In per capita rate she is likewise midway, the lowest in 1890 being Utah with twenty-four cents and the highest being the District of Columbia with $85.86, or omitting that, Arizona with $46.35, or again omitting all but states—Nevada with $28.89, Oregon with one cent, as the lowest; and Iowa with thirteen cents, coming next nearest to it, and Virginia with $18.76, as the highest among the states, is the status, excluding county indebtedness. In per capita rate the state ranks along near Ohio, New Jersey, Florida, Illinois and Michigan, if county indebtedness is included, or, if not included, with Idaho, South Dakota, Michigan and Florida.

Compared with other Southern states, however, her state per capita rate is almost the lowest, Texas being the extreme, with $1.93, and Florida only ten cents lower than Mississippi ($2.72), while Virginia, with $18.76, and Louisiana, with $14.31, are the highest two. But, including the county debt, the per capita of Mississippi is not even surpassed in lowness by Texas, and only Florida falls below her, and that only sixteen cents less.

This excellent financial condition has not prevented the state from embarking in geological stock-taking at times, or in making efforts to develop the resources by investigating them and making them known to the outside world. But these can only be, with many other subjects of interest, touched upon or altogether omitted in a sketch of these limits.

Among the many unofficial associations covering the state, a few, not elsewhere mentioned, may be noticed in this sketch.

The Confederate veterans of Mississippi was organized as a grand camp on October 15, 1889, at Aberdeen, this state, with these officers: Gen. E. C. Walthall, grand commander, Grenada; Gen. W. S. Featherston, first lieutenant grand commander, Holly Springs; Gen. S. D. Lee, second lieutenant grand commander, A. & M. college; Gen. Will T. Martin, third lieutenant grand commander, Natchez; and appointed officers of staff, Maj. E. T. Sykes, adjutant-general, Columbus; Maj. L. W. Magruder, Vicksburg, Capt. T. C. Carter, Meridian, aides-de-camp. Beginning with but three local associations, it has increased to fourteen, with a grand total membership of between fifteen hundred and two thousand veterans, these camps being located at Meridian, Aberdeen, Columbus, West Point, Vicksburg, Natchez, Lake, Hickory, Hattiesburg, Fayette, Holly Springs, Jackson, Crystal Springs and Tupelo, all organized and numbered in this order. General Walthall was succeeded in command on October 15, 1890, by Gen. W. S. Featherston, who served until his death on May 28, 1891. The present officers are Gov. John M. Stone, first lieutenant grand commander, Jackson; Gen. J. A. Smith, second lieutenant grand commander, Jackson; Capt. E. O. Sykes, third lieutenant grand commander, Aberdeen; Maj. E. T. Sykes, adjutant general, Columbus; Capts. W. H. Hardy, Meridian, and Fred J. V. Le Cand, Natchez, aides-de-camp; Gen. Joseph R. Davis, inspector-general; K. P. Lemans, quartermaster general; Dr. C. A. Rice, surgeon-general, and Rev. Louis Ball, chaplain general. The general scope of the association is indicated by the following: "Shall be strictly social, literary, historical and benevolent, and its labors shall be directed to cultivating the ties of friendship between all survivors of the armies and navies of the late Confederate states; to keep fresh the memories of our comrades who gave up their lives for the lost cause, in battle or in other fields of service, or who have died since the war; to the perpetuation of the records of their deeds of heroism, by the collection and disposition in the manner they judge best, of all materials of value for future historians; to aiding and relieving to the extent of its ability all members, their widows and orphans, in extreme cases of sickness and want, and to providing homes for them when necessary." Their headquarters are at Columbus. The Sons of Veterans also have an organization, of which R. K. Jayne is chief.

The Mississippi Historical society, whose object is "to discover, collect, preserve and perpetuate facts and events relating to the natural, aboriginal, civil, political, literary and ecclesiastical history of the territory and state of Mississippi and the territory adjoining thereto," was but recently chartered, although it has shown such vigor that its archives in the library building at the state university, its headquarters, are already of great value. Its first meeting was held at the chancellor's office, university, on May 1, 1890, the charter members being Robert Lowry, R. H. Thompson, John Hunter, A. B. Learned, W. H. Sims, T. A. McWillie, J. T. Fant, R. B. Fulton, Edward Mayes, and William R. Sims. Professor Mayes was chosen president, Professor Fulton keeper of archives, and Prof. W. R. Sims secretary and treasurer. Measures were at once taken toward gathering files of old newspapers, war relics, Indian relics, pamphlets, books, etc., in which they have been most successful. They have the earliest files in the state, except a collection owned by Mr. Stuart, of Natchez, a descendant of the first editor in the state. Its membership now embraces in the honorary list: Hon. C. C. Jones, Jr., Atlanta, Ga.; Hon. E. C. Walthall, Gen. A. P. Stewart, St. Louis, Mo.; Prof. W. H. N. Magruder, Baton Rouge, La.; Dr. John N. Waddell, Clarksville, Tenn.; Mrs. V. Jefferson Davis, Beauvoir; Hon. Charles Gayarre, New Orleans; Gen. Charles W. Darling, Utica, N. Y.; and in the active list: Hon. T. J. Wharton, E. Mayes, W. P. Harris, R. W. Jones, J. L. Alcorn, R. H. Thompson, William R. Sims, E. H. Dial, J. B. Stratton, Fred Beall, H. S. Halbert, A. G. Mayers, L. T. Fitzhugh, G. T. McGehee, C. B. Galloway, J. S. McNeilly, A. H. Stone, G. D. Shands, C. Firman Smith, S. D. Lee, R. B. Fulton, F. K. Henderson, G. R. Hill, J. G. Deupree, Jackson Reeves, Schuyler Poitevent, R. M. Leavell, J. A. Orr, W. T. Martin, T. D. Isom, H. F. Simrall, Miss Mollie Duvall, W. T. Lewis, C. B. Howry, J. W. Johnson, A. H. Whitfield and P. H. Eager. Its funds are partly derived from slight membership fees and annual dues. The society ought to be earnestly supported in aggressive efforts.

Among the extensive farmers' organizations are: The State grange, of which S. L. Wilson is master; T. L. Darden, overseer; and J. F. Dearing lecturer. The State alliance, with R. C. Patty, of Macon, president;; and C. T. Smithson, of Newport, secretary; and the Patrons' union, with headquarters at Lake, and of which J. B. Bailey is president; J. T. Hamilton vice president; J. S. Scott, secretary; and J. I. Robinson, treasurer. These are all extensive and well-organized associations, characterized by purposes of improvement in the science and art of agriculture, agitation and combination to secure legal and commercial advantages, and for social and experimental purposes. The growth of these societies has been coördinate with the general movement throughout the United States since the war. Detailed information seems unobtainable.

The State Horticultural society is the product of an agitation for the scientific prosecution of all branches of horticulture in Mississippi, and its success has been marked. Dr. H. E. McKay, of Madison station, is its president, and W. H. Cassell, of Canton, its secretary. It met at Jackson on January 25, 1883, and organized with a constitution. Its work will be noticed elsewhere.

The labor organizations are represented by the Knights of Labor, the Ancient Order of United Workmen, and various trade societies too numerous to mention.

Among religio-fraternal societies may be noticed that of the Jewish people, and the twelve branches of Catholic Knights of America, at Macomb City, Jackson, Vicksburg, Natchez, Canton, Meridian, Holly Springs, Columbus, Bay St. Louis, Greenville and Scranton, with a total membership of three hundred and seventy-two in the state.

The first lodge of the time-honored order of Free Masons* established in Mississippi was at Natchez, in October, 1801, the Grand lodge of Kentucky having chartered Harmony No. 7, on the 16th of that month. The Grand lodge of Tennessee chartered Andrew Jackson lodge No. 15, also at Natchez, August 13, 1826, and Washington lodge No. 17, at Port Gibson, April 19, 1817. The officers of these lodges, with several past masters, and other members of the craft, assembled in convention at Natchez July 27, 1818, and resolved that it was expedient and highly necessary to form a Grand lodge for the state of Mississippi. Henry Tooley was chosen grand master; Christopher Rankin, deputy grand master; Israel Loring, senior grand warden; Edward Turner, junior grand warden; Henry Postlethwaite, grand treasurer; Chilion F. Stiles, grand secretary; Christopher Miller, senior grand deacon; John Corn, junior grand deacon; Joseph Newman, grand tyler.

A committee was appointed to prepare a constitution, which was reported and adopted August 28.

---
*Contributed by J. L. Power.

Those who have filled the station of grand master are: Henry Tooley, 1818; Christopher Rankin, 1819; Edward Turner, 1820-21; Israel Loring, 1822-5; John A. Quitman, 1826-37-40-5-6; Robert Stewart 1838-9-41; George A. Wilson, 1842-3; S. W. Vanatta, 1844, died during term and succeeded by Deputy Grand Master Harvey W. Walter; Benjamin S. Tappan, 1847; Charles Scott, 1848-50; Charles A. Lacoste, 1849; William H. Stevens, 1851; James M. Howry, 1852; Joseph W. Speight, 1853; Carnot Posey, 1854; Giles M. Hillyer, 1853-4; William R. Cannon 1857; William Cothran, 1858; William P. Mellen, 1859; David Mitchell, 1860; Richard Cooper, 1861-3; William S. Patton, 1864-5; George M. Perkins, 1866; John T. Lamkin, 1867; Thomas S. Gathright, 1868-9; George R. Fearn, 1870-71; W. H. Hardy, 1872; Richard P. Bowen, 1873; A. H. Barkley, 1874-5; John Y. Murry, 1876-7; Charles T. Murphy, 1878; Frank Burkitt, 1879; William French, 1880; John F. McCormick, 1881; Frederic Speed, 1882; P. M. Savery, 1883; Robert C. Patty, 1884; J. B. Morgan, 1885; B. T. Kimbrough, 1886; E. George DeLap, 1887; M. M. Evans, 1888; William G. Paxton, 1889; John Riley, 1890; John M. Ware, 1891. Of these David Mitchell, George R. Fearn, W. H. Hardy, A. H. Barkley, John Y. Murry, Frank Burkitt, John F. McCormick, Frederic Speed, P. M. Savery, J. B. Morgan, B. T. Kimbrough, E. George DeLap, M. M. Evans, William G. Paxton, John Riley and John M. Ware are still living (in 1891).

Some of the other stations have been filled by citizens eminent in the various walks of life, and whose memory will ever be cherished by the craft. William P. Mellen served as grand secretary for eighteen years. The present grand secretary, J. L. Power, was elected in 1869, and is now (1891) serving his twenty-second year. On the completion of his twentieth year he submitted a retrospective sketch of the twenty years, giving the following interesting figures: Initiated, eight thousand seven hundred and ninety-two; passed, eight thousand four hundred and ten; raised, eight thousand one hundred and twelve; total degrees conferred in all the lodges for that period, twenty-five thousand three hundred and fourteen; affiliated, five thousand six hundred and seventy-three; reinstated, four thousand and twenty-two; dimitted, eight thousand seven hundred and two; suspended for non-payment of dues, eight thousand one hundred and thirty-nine; suspended for unmasonic conduct, three hundred and eighteen; expelled for unmasonic conduct, two hundred and thirty; died, three thousand five hundred and one. Received and accounted for in the way of dues, $186,927.87; special relief funds, $78,298; total, $265,225.87.

The Grand lodge has issued four hundred and thirteen charters. The total in force (1891) is two hundred and seventy-three. Quite a number of lodges were organized during the war period, and were known as "Army lodges." These, of course, ceased to work on the restoration of peace. Others have become consolidated, and others became extinct by the removal of members from the country to railroad towns. The numerous beneficial orders, with life insurance features, have also attracted many who might otherwise have united with the Masonic fraternity. During and immediately after the war, there was a great rush to the lodges, so that at the close of the year 1868 the total membership was twelve thousand three hundred and eight. The total membership at the close of 1890 was eight thousand three hundred and ninety, a net gain of three hundred and eighty-eight on the preceding year.

The Grand lodge meets annually, during the second week in February, and for several years it has been "on wheels." There are usually about two hundred and twenty-five lodges represented, whose delegates, with grand and past grand officers, make a total of nearly three hundred. The business is usually transacted in two days. The representatives are paid mileage and per diem from the funds of Grand lodge, which are derived from an assessment on each lodge of seventy-five cents per member, and $1 on each degree conferred—aggregating about $8,000 per annum. In addition there is a charity tax of ten cents per capita, which realizes about $800, and $500 of this is annually appropriated toward the support of the Protestant orphan asylum, at Natchez.

The principal topics that have occupied the attention of the Grand lodge of late years, are the saloon question and the establishment of a Masonic widows and orphans' home. A regulation has been adopted that no saloonkeeper can become a member of a Masonic lodge. A fund of several thousand dollars has already been collected toward establishing and endowing a home, and the interest in that behalf is steadily increasing. The Masons of Mississippi have not only the will, but the ability to thus provide for the shelter and support of the destitute widows and orphans of their brethren.

The officers of the Grand lodge for 1891 are: John M. Ware, grand master; J. L. Spinks, deputy grand master; W. A. Roane, senior grand warden; Isaac T. Hart, junior grand warden; Rev. J. A. Bowen, grand chaplain; R. B. Brannin, grand lecturer; A. P. Barry, grand treasurer; J. L. Power, grand secretary; C. N. Simpson, senior grand deacon; W. R. Woods, junior grand deacon; John Y. Murry, Jr., grand marshal; S. G. Stern, grand sword bearer; A. G. Wood, grand pursuivant; Henry Strauss, grand tyler.

The standing committees are: Law and jurisprudence, Frederic Speed, John F. McCormick, M. M. Evans; complaints and appeals, Frank Burkitt, John Y. Murry, James T. Harrison; finance and printing, William G. Paxton, E. G. DeLap, James H. Duke; state of the craft, P. M. Savery, chairman; foreign correspondence reporter, Rev. A. H. Barkley.

Pursuant to dispensation issued by the deputy general grand high priest of the General Grand chapter of the United States, dated at Baltimore March 12, 1846, the representatives of four chapters assembled in Vicksburg May 18, 1846, and organized the Grand chapter of Mississippi. Vicksburg chapter No. 3 was represented by Thomas J. Harper, Thomas Rigby and James Trowbridge; Columbus No. 4, by N. E. Goodwin; Wilson No. 5, by J. B. Day; Jackson No. 6, by A. Hutchinson, William Wing and Robert Hughes. The grand officers elected were: B. S. Tappan, grand high priest; A. Hutchinson, deputy grand high priest; Charles H. Abert, grand king; William F. Stearns, grand scribe; William Wing, grand secretary; Thomas J. Harper, grand treasurer; T. C. Thornton, grand chaplain; J. Trowbridge, grand marshal.

The first chapter organized in Mississippi was at Port Gibson, chartered September 15, 1826. A charter was issued for a chapter in Vicksburg September 17, 1841, and dispensations for chapters in Holly Springs October 30, 1841, Columbus February 7, 1842, Jackson August 28, 1843, which were chartered September 12, 1844.

The Grand chapter, like the Grand lodge, moved serenely along until its labors were interrupted by the Civil war. There were no sessions in 1862 or 1863. The convocations of 1864 and 1865 were held at Columbus, and the proceedings were printed on "Confederate" paper.

There have been one hundred and fourteen charters issued by the Grand chapter. The number in force in 1890 was forty-four, embracing a membership of eleven hundred and eighty. Its highest membership was in 1869—twenty-five hundred and sixty-five in seventy-six chapters.

The grand high priests from 1846 to 1891 are as follows: Benjamin S. Tappan, 1846–7; Walker Brooke, 1848; William H. Stevens, 1849; T. C. Tupper, 1850; Charles Scott, 1851; Charles S. Spann, 1852; A. V. Rowe, 1853; William S. Patton, 1854; William R. Cannon, 1855; William Cothran, 1856; James M. Howry, 1857; Amos R. Johnston, 1858;

M. S. Ward, 1859; Giles M. Hillyer, 1860; S. H. Johnson, 1861–4; George T. Stainback, 1865; William S. Patton, 1866; William D. Ferriss, 1867; J. O. Lusher, 1868; George D. Fee, 1869; R. B. Mayes, 1870; Charles T. Bond, 1871; H. C. Robinson, 1872; George R. Fearn, 1873–4; John Y. Murry, 1875; Harvey W. Walter, 1876–7; John S. Jones, 1878; Robert B. Brannin, 1879; Frederic Speed, 1880–81; William Richards, 1882; B. T. Kimbrough, 1883; William French, 1884; S. C. Conley, 1885; Richard P. Bowen, 1886; Charles T. Chamberlain, 1887; N. W. Bouton, 1888; A. D. Bailey, 1889; W. R. Trigg, 1890; P. M. Savery, 1891.

The Grand chapter and Grand council adopted what has been termed "the Merger," or "Mississippi plan," by which the cryptic degrees were transferred to and conferred in the chapter. This created some disturbance in the General Grand chapter and General Grand council—the course of the Mississippi companions having been ably vindicated in the General Grand bodies by Companions Harvey W. Walter, James M. Howry and Frederic Speed. After an experience of twelve years, the "Merger" was a generally admitted failure, and, by common consent, the Grand council was reorganized in February, 1889, the Grand chapter resigning all control of the degrees of royal and select master.

The officers of the Grand chapter for 1891 are: P. M. Savery, grand high priest; J. K. McLeod, deputy grand high priest; Frank Burkitt, grand king; William Starling, grand scribe; Rev. J. A. Bowen, grand chaplain; A. P. Barry, grand treasurer; J. L. Power, grand secretary; G. A. Logan, grand captain of the host; G. J. Bahin, grand principal sojourner; James T. Harrison, grand royal arch captain; Hiram Hood, grand master third vail; M. M. Evans, grand master second vail; S. R. Lamb, grand master first vail; Henry Strauss, grand sentinel. The present grand treasurer has been in office since 1869, and grand secretary since 1870.

A convention of Councils of Royal and Select Masters was held at Natchez, January 2, 1856, by the mandate of the Grand Council of the Princes of Jerusalem of the state of Mississippi. This convention drafted a constitution, which was approved by the said Grand Council of Princes of Jerusalem.

The councils represented in the convention were: Natchez No. 1, E. Craig; Vicksburg No. 7, B. Springer, William Middleton; Cayuga No. 10, William R. Lackey; Lexington No. 26, William P. Mellen, William A. McMillion.

The convention adjourned to meet at Vicksburg, January 18, 1856, adopted the constitution, and on the day following organized the Grand Council of Royal and Select Masters of the state of Mississippi by the election and installation of grand officers.

On January 26, 1856, the Grand council held an adjourned convention, when the formal ratification and confirmation of the above proceedings by the Grand Council of the Princes of Jerusalem, of the state of Mississippi, and their grant and conveyance of jurisdiction of these degrees, dated at their Grand Orient in Natchez, January 23, 1856, were presented, received and filed.

A pamphlet of thirteen pages, printed in 1855, gives the proceedings of a meeting of Royal and Select Masters, held in the Masonic hall, at the city of Jackson, January 10, 1854, when a Grand council of Royal and Select Masters was formed. The councils at Jackson, Lexington and Holly Springs were represented, and twenty-six other Royal and Select Masters were present, several of them very prominent in the craft of that day: Howry, Brooke, Cannon, Tupper, Barrows, Foute and others. The officers elected were T. C. Tupper, thrice illustrious grand master; Walker Brooke, illustrious deputy grand master; William R. Cannon, principal conductor of the work; William H. McCargo; captain of the guard; L. V. Dixon, recorder; Burton Yandel, treasurer; G. W. Johnson, sentinel.

The next assembly was held in Jackson, January 11, 1855. Seven councils were represented. A constitution was adopted. Amos R. Johnston was elected thrice illustrious grand master.

This appears to be the last of this organization, which was superseded by the Grand council formed in January, 1856, under the auspices of the Grand Council of Princes of Jerusalem.

The most puissant grand masters, from organization to 1891, are: Benjamin Springer, 1856; William P. Mellen, 1857; Jacob F. Foute, 1858; Daniel Rosser, 1859; William Cothran, 1860; Jacob F. Foute, 1861; William S. Patton, 1864-5; James M. Howry, 1866; J. O. Lusher, 1867; Giles M. Hillyer, 1868; Morris Cook, 1869; B. S. Trice, 1870-72; E. George De Lap, 1873; Harvey W. Walter, 1874-5; P. M. Savery, 1876 [merged after 1876]; William Richards, 1889; Frederic Speed, 1890-91. There were no sessions in 1861 and 1862. The highest membership was reached in 1866, nine hundred and eighty-five in forty-two councils. The total membership, December 27, 1890, was one hundred and eighty-nine in seven councils. The rite has beauties that will not fail to enlist the zealous and intelligent of the royal craft in its dissemination.

There are, at this writing, seventy-eight thousand eight hundred and eighteen Knights Templar in eight hundred and forty-three commanderies in the United States. The Grand commandery of Massachusetts and Rhode Island is the senior grand body, having been organized May 6, 1805. Mississippi ranks twelfth as to age, having been organized January 21, 1857, under letters of authority from Grand Master W. B. Hubbard, dated Columbus, Ohio, December 22, 1856. Three commanderies were represented, as follows: Mississippi No. 1, Sirs Thomas Palmer, E. P. Russell, Thomas W. Caskey; Magnolia No. 2, Sirs George P. Crump, Benjamin S. Tappan, Christopher A. Manlove; Lexington No. 3, William H. Dyson, William A. McMillion, A. V. Rowe. A constitution was adopted on the day following.

There were no grand conclaves in 1862, 1863, 1864, 1865. In January, 1866, when the Grand commandery assembled in Vicksburg, Grand Commander Tappan made appropriate and pathetic reference to the four years of pilgrimage that severely tested the faith and constancy of those who endured it; and after fitting reference to the chivalrous and knightly dead, he said: "We once more, knights and companions of our order, set our watches and pitch our tents around the hallowed temple of Zion. The civil convulsions and the armed conflicts through which we have passed have but proved the constancy of our faith in the great principles upon which that temple is founded, and that which will make it as permanent as the religion it represents, and upon which, in every great and unlooked-for emergency, like that which has so long suspended the functions of our Grand commandery, it is our privilege to look for aid."

The grand commanders, from organization, are: William H. Stevens, 1857; George P. Crump, 1858; Giles M. Hillyer, 1859; Harvey W. Walter, 1860; Benjamin S. Tappan, 1861; Edward Lea, 1866; Christopher A. Manlove, 1867; Fleet C. Mercer, 1868; John K. Fulson, 1869; Charles T. Bond, 1870; William S. Patton, 1871; E. George DeLap, 1872; E. T. Henry, 1873; P. M. Savery, 1874; Gideon W. Cox, 1875; Oliver Clifton, 1876; William A. Fairchild, 1877; William G. Paxton, 1878; Charles M. Erwin, 1879; William G. Benbrook, 1880; William French, 1881; James T. Meade, 1882; H. M. Romberger, 1883; W. P. Towler, 1884; John H. Gordon, 1885; B. A. Vaughan, 1886; N. S. Walker, 1887; Frederic Speed, 1888-9; James J. Hayes, 1890; J. E. Leigh, 1891.

The annual conclaves are held at the same place as Grand lodge, and on the Tuesday preceding.

The officers for 1891 are: J. E. Leigh, grand commander; W. A. Bodenhamer, deputy grand commander; S. W. Ferguson, grand generalissimo; J. C. French, grand captain of the guard; Rev. William Cross, grand prelate; James H. Gunning, grand senior warden; Frank Burkitt, grand junior warden; G. J. Bahin, grand treasurer; J. L. Power, grand recorder; King Dorwart, grand standard bearer; J. R. McIntosh, grand sword bearer; T. A. Teasdale, grand warder; C. W. Bolton, grand captain of the guard.

There are ten commanderies, with a membership of three hundred and twenty.

The Independent Order of Odd Fellows, on December 31, 1889, had a total lodge membership in the United States of six hundred and thirty-four thousand three hundred and thirty-five, an increase over the previous year of thirty thousand seven hundred and ninety-eight; and the relief distributed amounted to nearly $3,000,000. It is one of the great benevolent forces of the world, and, including the "Manchester Unity" in England, and membership of the order in other parts of the world, makes a grand fraternal host of nearly one and one-half million. In some of the Eastern and Western states it exceeds all other fraternal associations in numbers, but it has not been so popular or prosperous in the Southwest.

Pursuant to a charter granted by the Grand lodge of the United States to Past Grands M. Ruffner, William Dale, E. P. Pollard, S. L. Goddard, William Cannon, Joseph B. Robinson and William S. Robinson, contributing members of Mississippi lodge No. 1, and Washington lodge No. 2, both at Natchez, the Grand lodge of Mississippi was organized in that city on May 6, 1836, when Mr. Ruffner was elected grand master. The organization was conducted and the officers installed by Past Grand Sire Thomas Wildey, who founded the order in the United States on February 26, 1819. He appears to have taken a special interest in planting the order in Mississippi, and that his fostering care was appreciated by the Grand lodge is shown by the fact that he was its "permanent" grand representative for a number of years. He communicated frequently with the Grand lodge, and his recommendation always had great weight.

The Grand lodge, for several years, indulged in quarterly communications, but the quarterlies were discontinued as new lodges were established throughout the state. The order appears to have attained its greatest strength in the second term in 1860, when there were fifty-seven working lodges, a total membership of seventeen hundred and ten, two hundred and eighty-one initiations, and a total revenue of $14,127.69. There were no sessions in 1863, 1864 or 1865, so that the session in Meridian in May, 1891, was the fiftieth session and the fifty-third year of the order in Mississippi. On December 31, 1890, there were twenty-eight working lodges, with a total membership of nine hundred and ninety-four, but when the Grand lodge met in May following, the membership exceeded one thousand, so that the Grand lodge was again entitled to two representatives in the Sovereign Grand lodge. The order was greatly revived in the state in 1890, through the efforts of Grand Master Wiley N. Nash.

Its grand masters have been: M. Ruffner, William Doyle, Benjamin Walker, S. Halsey, George J. Dicks, Richard Griffith, S. B. Newman, J. R. Stockman, William H. Brown, Thomas Reed, D. N. Barrows, C. H. Stone, William Crutcher, A. M. Foute, N. G. Bryson, J. K. Connelly, W. A. Strong, A. H. Arthur, L. K. Barber, John L. Milton, H. L. Bailey, William Wyman, A. E. Love, J. P. Hawks, R. B. Mayes, C. Parish, O. T. Keeler, S. C. Cochran, George Torrey, G. K. Birchett, Ira J. Carter, Isaac T. Hart, J. S. Cain, H. S. Van Eaton, D. P. Black, R. L. Saunders, A. B. Wagner, J. H. McKenzie, Joseph Hirsh, T. J. Hanes, W. J. Bradshaw, J. L. Power, G. W. Trimble, Isaac D. Blumenthal, H.

C. Roberts, James C. Lamkin, William M. Strickland, Amos Burnett, Robert C. Patty, Wiley N. Nash. Most of these have joined the "great majority," a few have been dropped, and fifteen remain affiliated with the order. The grand master for 1891 is J. T. Thomas, of Grenada, and the grand secretary is Hon. George G. Dillard, of Macon. The session of 1892 is to be held at Holly Springs, May 3.

The saying, "Tall oaks from little acorns grow," has been forcibly illustrated in the remarkable history of the great and growing fraternity, the Knights of Honor. Organized in the city of Louisville, Ky., on June 30, 1873, with seventeen members, it had a total strength on April 1, 1891, of one hundred and thirty-eight thousand and twenty-nine; the number of subordinate lodges being two thousand five hundred and seventy, and thirty-six grand lodges. The death benefits paid during its first year amounted to $1,093.65; the death benefits paid for the year 1890 amounted to $3,848,500; the total benefits paid from organization to June 1, 1891, $34,787,034.26; the value of certificates outstanding, $256,045,000.

At the fourteenth annual session of the Grand lodge of Mississippi, August 25, 1891, the total membership in the state was six thousand and forty, a net gain of three hundred and thirty-eight on preceding year. Number of lodges, one hundred and twenty-four, six having been instituted during year. There were sixty-eight deaths during the year and the benefits paid families amounted to $135,000. Total deaths in Mississippi since organization of Grand lodge, April, 1891, seven hundred and eighty-three; total benefits for same period, $1,566,000. It is fair to presume that within the next five years the membership will reach ten thousand. It is claimed that the order is stronger in Mississippi, in proportion to white population, than in any other state in the Union. There were more applications filed at the office of the supreme reporter for the month ending July 11, 1891, than from any other state, except New York and Texas.

Hon. George G. Dillard, of Macon, is grand dictator; E. W. Smith, Hernando, grand reporter.

The order of the Knights & Ladies of Honor was organized in 1878. Its membership on June 30 of that year was nineteen hundred and twenty-five. Its membership December 31, 1890, reached sixty-seven thousand five hundred and forty-eight; benefits paid to September 1, 1891, $5,875,714.62. The benefits are from $500 to $3,000, according to division. Females are admitted on same terms as men, and it has been demonstrated that females are better risks than males. It is not necessary now, as formerly, that a person should be a Knight of Honor, or the female relative of such, in order to become a member of the Knights and Ladies of Honor; and hence the rapid growth of the order during the last few years. Mississippi had a total membership of one thousand eight hundred and eighty-one on July 1, 1891. There were twenty-eight deaths during the year ending that date, and the beneficiaries received the sum of $47,000.

The Grand lodge meets annually, in July, and the representatives and grand officers numbered at last session about seventy gentlemen and ladies. Hon. Thomas J. Wood, of Starkville, is grand protector for 1891–2; Mrs. O. A. Hastings, Port Gibson, grand secretary.

The great beneficial order, the American Legion of Honor, was organized in 1878, had a membership on January 1, 1891, of sixty-two thousand five hundred and seventy-four, and paid benefits to that date to the amount of $17,956,278.21. The benefits range from $500 to $5,000. It has twenty-seven councils in Mississippi, with a membership of about twelve hundred. It is among the most prompt of the benevolent orders in paying death losses. It has, as yet, no state organization.

The very popular benevolent order, the Knights of Pythias, is growing rapidly in Mississippi. On December 31, 1890, its total membership was three thousand one hundred and eleven; lodges, fifty-six. The endowment rank has about one thousand two hundred members, carrying an insurance of over $3,200,000. The order in the state has paid to the endowment rank $387,491.10, and received in death benefits $456,107. This order, on December 31, 1889, had a total membership in the United States of two hundred and sixty-three thousand eight hundred and forty-seven; subordinate lodges, three thousand seven hundred and twenty-four. The amount paid for relief during that year reached the magnificent sum of $789,455.53. Rev. William Cross, Greenville, grand chancellor; Joseph L. Maganos, Vicksburg, grand keeper of records and seals for 1891-2.

The Ancient Order of United Workmen is also being introduced into the state, and has strong lodges in Jackson and other places.

CHAPTER IV.

WATER TRANSPORTATION, LEVEES, ETC.

THE friction of mind against mind is one of the greatest sources of our civilization, and nothing produces this friction so much as facile means of transportation, and nothing intensifies it so much as any means of greater rapidity in such intercommunication. This feature of rapidity and the other of mere facility may each be easily marked, by the most casual student of civilizing influences, as the chief characteristics that distinguish our country and our century from other countries, and centuries now past. The amazing growth of "the great republic" and the century that has been called the "age of steam," "the age of electricity," "the railway age," "the age of iron and steel," "the age of invention," "the age of rapid transit," "the century of ocean greyhounds," and what not, springs from this one source of rapid transportation to a far greater degree than from any other direct cause. A great story of civilization lies in the simple and homely facts: A man walks about three miles an hour; a horse trots about seven miles an hour; a steamboat averages about eighteen miles an hour; and a railway train reaches near to sixty miles an hour. Civilization has moved in like manner.

But if variations in rapidity of transport make such stupendous differences in immediate results, variations in facility are equally great. The most cursory glance at the several continents will show this feature of facility of intercommunication, when climate does not interfere, to be a very practical measure of the civilization of that continent; the greater the facility of intercommunication—natural, especially—the greater the civilization. Indeed, the two continents most widely separated in degree of civilization, Europe and Africa, are also the best and worst illustrations of facility of intercommunication, although adjoining one another, and the latter even having centuries of advantage in seeds of advancement. Whatever difference of views may be held as to the bearing of race qualities on the subject, there can be no doubt that the number and depth of the water inlets into Europe, and the practical absence of them in Africa, the small continent of Europe having the longest coast line, and the vast continent of Africa having the smallest, has led to Africa being the last continent to be opened up, and that, too, by artificial means, while Europe has been advancing with an excellence and rapidity unequaled in the history of continents before the railway age.

It is Mississippi's good fortune, in this respect, that not only gave her an exceptional Indian civilization, but makes her one of the earliest to begin in that larger one of Europe. It was her ocean coast-line of magnificent harbor advantages that gave her her first settlement; her river coast-line on the longest waterway of the globe, reaching over four thousand miles from the delta to the mountains, that gave her an early and wealthy metropolis long before many of the trans-Mississippi commonwealths were deemed a possibility. Her coast-line, including the islands which are a part of the state, aggregates five hundred and twelve miles; but it must be remembered that the Mississippi allows the travel of large steamers for two thousand one hundred and sixty-one miles, while for small boats her branches in the state reach a navigation of as high as two hundred and twenty-eight miles on the Yazoo; and other branches having an easy course of over fifty miles, are the Sunflower, with two hundred seventy-one, the Tallahatchie with one hundred seventy-five, the Issaquena with one hundred sixty-one, not counting the several rivers of the sound, which are quite equal in their proportions.

It is needless to repeat here how these watercourses determined settlement in Mississippi, like such courses have in all countries before the railway age, as it is needless to show that the most advanced settlements have the best waterways. Settlements were even described by the waterway: a man lived "on the Yazoo," "over on the Big Black," "up on the Tombigbee," or "down on the Pascagoula."

It was on foot that De Soto's caravan entered this state's territory in 1540, and over a hundred years later (1690) that horses were first known to the Chickasaws. Canoes were used by those early explorers from the French posts above, and the British adventurers of the Northeast. The ocean ships of Iberville and Bienville were the first to touch her harbors on the sound, in 1699, "because of the sheltered bay or roadstead, where small vessels could come and go in safety at all times," wrote Iberville in his report.

It was not until 1736 and 1739 that bateaux or barges ascended the Mississippi river, when Bienville did so to prosecute the Chickasaw war. This was the best means then known, and these voyagers were the first. "Tuesday, the 9th, Mons. de Nouaille also set out in a separate transport," says a journal of one of his officers. "Wednesday, the 10th of June (1739), we set out at break of day, and moved with might and main to stem the terrible current of the Mississippi; a storm coming up from the northwest at about 7 A. M., we made a second landing, having gone three leagues of our route." On the 14th, when they stopped again, they were sent to barracks to rest from the fatigues of heat "and the swift currents of the river, which we had been compelled to stem." "On the 23d of September," he says, "we found ourselves engaged at the dinner hour among the three channels of the river, which are comprised within the limits of the 'Natchez' settlements. We took the middle one, fearing the currents in that on the left. We found here from three and one-half to four feet of water, and so fierce a current that half our boats were driven aground, the rest in the meantime having proceeded to encamp at the head of the channels on the right bank of the river." On the 10th of October they reached the mouth of the "Hyazous," in which one readily recognizes the Yazoo, which they could not ascend, because of the drift wood. They "continued to encounter very rapid currents, which placed several of our boats under the necessity of hauling themselves up along the shore by means of ropes." His journal illustrates the difficulties of transportation up the river at that time so well that it is here given entire, up to his arrival at the mouth of the Arkansas river:

"The 13th found us aboard at daylight, when we took the channel to the right, having on our left a small isle which lies at its head, and along which we were compelled to be towed, owing to the strength of the current. After much difficulty, we were compelled to sleep in our boats, two leagues above a channel called 'Couroit,' or 'Kourois,' so named from its being frequently visited by that nation.

"On the 14th we disembarked at daylight, to take breakfast at the foot of a small cliff. Each of the boats here provided itself with some ashwood, with which to shape some oars, which we all were more or less short of. Having, after dinner, taken up our route in the channel of a bank on the left, we found at the end that there was not sufficient water to proceed, and were compelled to retrace our course. Having then succeeded in clearing the bar, we crossed to spend the night on the opposite side of the river, having merely landed a strong guard.

"On the 15th took all aboard as soon as there was sufficient light to permit it, and having gone three and three-fourths leagues that day, slept in our boats at the lower end of the island farthest toward the north, it being one of three which we had found on our course, and where we were joined by a boat coming down from our depot to meet Mons. de Bienville.

"On the 16th, having gotten aboard at the usual hour, we proceeded. One hour afterward one of the boats sprung a considerable leak, a hidden stump having stove in the starboard bow. I immediately went to its assistance with another of our boats. We passed several hawsers beneath it to keep it afloat, and having discharged it of its load, I directed my boatswain to replace its side planks by new ones, which being done with but little delay, we reloaded it and pursued our course. We encamped in a grove at the extremity of a lengthy island, opposite that called 'Isle a la tete des morts' (the island with the heads of the dead).

"On the 17th October, all being embarked at dawn, we spent the subsequent night in our boats near the first island we had encountered that day, having made four leagues.

"On the 18th we set out with the early morn, and in the afternoon were compelled to make use of the tow-lines whilst rounding an extensive sand bank in a southerly direction, owing to the fierceness of the current. We crossed the end of the bar at sunset towards the right, and again passed the night aboard, at a distance of half a league above what is called 'the small Pointe Coupee.'

"On the 19th we set out before day, and having passed to the left of the islands, we encamped upon a large bank on our left for a short stay.

"On the 20th, being stationed on a bank over which there flew a large number of geese and ducks, we dispatched a large number from daybreak until seven in the morning, in which time we were met by a conveyance going down to New Orleans from the depot. From it we learned that our first convoy had arrived there on the 12th, the day after the arrival of the Canadians, who, including the Indians among them, were to the number of four hundred men. We also learned, from the same source, that the second convoy had lost six soldiers and one ensign.

"The 21st, after roll-call, we embarked one hour before day, and having passed to the left of the first island on our route, we slept in our boats that night one-half league beyond the island, no one having landed, owing to the fact that the landing was muddier than any previously met. We had observed, during all that day, that the waters having gone down from nine to ten feet, had caused a large diminution in the force of the current.

"The 22d we departed one hour before day, the river still falling, and encamped five in the afternoon on a bank to the right. Here we discovered the pirogue of four Arcancas Indians, who were on a hunting expedition, such being the sole occupation of all the nations in this vicinity.

"On the 23d we decamped one hour before day, and were joined soon after by a pirogue belonging to the convoy of Mons. de Bienville, from which we learned that the latter was only two leagues distant, on his way up to Arcancas, in the center channel of the three which we had discovered and was now ascending. We finally moored our vessels ashore, one-half a league further up to the left, each boat arriving separately and at intervals, owing to the violent currents which we had encountered. At ten o'clock at night we were joined by several boats belonging to the convoy of Mons. de Bienville, which soon left us to regain the latter on the opposite shore and a little above us.

"On the 24th we continued on our journey at five of the morning, and overtook Mons. de Bienville at eight o'clock. The wind being north, and the weather rainy and very threatening, both convoys set out together only after twelve. We slept two leagues further, in our boats near each other, with a separate guard on shore, of which our own was to the right.

"On the 25th, at three in the morning, the roll was beat separately, and Mons. Bienville having started, we embarked, but, half an hour afterward, taking to the channel on the left of the first island on our course, we encamped to the number of twelve boats at the first mouth of Arcancas river.

"On the 26th we were overtaken at five in the morning by one of our boats which had been unable to keep up with the rest on the preceding day, and were, consequently, unable to proceed before eight o'clock. We passed the mouth of the Arcancas river on our left. This river appeared to me to run in a north-northwest direction. The lodges of the Arcancas nation are distant seven leagues from the Mississippi. It is of considerable size, and can furnish four hundred warriors, who have ever been much attached to the French. Passing to the left of two islands, we encamped on a bank on our left, one-quarter of a league from the last of the two."

This was in 1739, when no better means was known the world over. Besides these barges or bateaux were the flatboats and keelboats, the latter the more pretentious of the two, and more or less permanent, while the flatboats were made for one trip and used for lumber at the end of the route, for they were used on the down-stream voyage. The craft used for both directions were the keelboats and barges. The keelboat, the more common one, was long, narrow and pointed at the ends, with a gangway along the gunwale for boatmen, as they poled or warped up the stream, the oars being available only when in eddies. This kind of boat only needed to have added to it a long, low, house-like structure between the gangways to be the finest boat then afloat, and bearing the more luxurious name of barge. All these vessels had immense oars for steering, the flatboats having them fixed on the sides on pivots. These were the means of transportation, not only during the days before 1798, when Mississippi was made a territory of the United States, but all the rest of that and for ten years into the present century. It must be remembered that it was only in 1753 that the first steam motor of any kind appeared in this country, and it was only ten years before Mississippi was admitted into the Union, that Robert Fulton first succeeded in applying it to boat movement as a mere experiment on the Hudson river. It is difficult for us to realize that up to 1811 no steam craft of any kind had ever floated on the thickly dotted waters before Natchez and Vicksburg, but so it was.

Two years after the success of Mr. Fulton's Hudson river exploit, his friends began to consider its adaptability to Western streams, and especially the Mississippi, between New Orleans and Natchez, the latter being the only considerable settlement below the Ohio. It was proposed to build a boat at Pittsburgh for this purpose, and Nicholas J. Roosevelt, the inventor of the boat's vertical wheel, undertook the necessary investigation of the river, which, if favorable, would determine the building of it by Chancellor Livingston, Mr. Fulton and Mr. Roosevelt, the latter to superintend the building of the boat and engine and the others to furnish the capital. "He accordingly repaired to Pittsburgh in May, 1809," says a distinguished Baltimore lawyer in an address before the historical society of his state. "The only means of conveyance to New Orleans, where his investigations were to terminate, were the keelboats, barges and flatboats," which have been described above. "None of those then in use were suited to Mr. Roosevelt's purpose, and as the accuracy of his examinations, rather than the speed of his voyage, was important, he determined to build a flatboat which should contain all necessary comforts for himself and wife, and float with the current of the Ohio and Mississippi from Pittsburgh to New Orleans. This he accordingly did, and with the exception of some three weeks passed on the shore at Louisville, and some nine or ten days in a rowboat between Natchez and New Orleans, the flatboat was the home of Mr. and Mrs. Roosevelt for the next six months. Cincinnati, Louisville and Natchez were then the only places of even the smallest note between Pittsburgh and New Orleans."

His difficulties and the remarkable incidents connected with the birth of steam power in this great valley, and for Mississippi's metropolis first, are so striking that the extract is continued: "Furnished with letters of introduction to their leading men, the travelers were most kindly received and most hospitably entertained. Mr. Roosevelt's explanations were listened to respectfully, as he stated his purpose in visiting the West, and narrated what steam had accomplished on Eastern rivers. But he was evidently regarded as a sanguine enthusiast, engaged in an impracticable undertaking. From no one individual did he receive a word of encouragement. Nor was this incredulity confined to the gentlemen he met in society; it extended to the pilots and boatmen, who, passing their lives on the Ohio and Mississippi, possessed the practical information he wanted. They heard what he had to say of the experience of Fulton and Livingston, and then pointed to the turbid and whirling waters of the great river as a conclusive answer to all his reasoning. That steam could be made to resist them they could not be made to understand. Nothing, however, shook the confidence of Mr. Roosevelt. He had made up his mind that steam was to do the work of the Western world, and his present visit was but for the purpose of ascertaining how best the work could be done upon its streams. The Ohio and Mississippi were problems that he had undertaken to study, nor did he leave them until he had mastered them in all their bearings. He gauged them; he measured their velocity at different seasons; he obtained all the statistical information within his reach, and formed a judgment with respect to the future development of the country west of the Alleghanies that has since been amply corroborated. Not only did he do this, but finding coal on the banks of the Ohio, he purchased and opened mines of the mineral; and so confident was he of the success of the project on hand, that he caused supplies of the fuel to be heaped upon the shore, in anticipation of the wants of a steamboat whose keel had yet to be laid, and whose very existence was to depend upon the impression that his report might make upon the capitalists, without whose aid the plan would, for the present at least, have to be abandoned.

"Arriving at New York in the middle of January, 1810, Mr. Roosevelt's report, bearing on its face evidence of the thoroughness of his examination, impressed Fulton and Livingston with his own convictions, and in the spring of that year he returned to Pittsburgh, to superintend the building of the first steamboat that was launched on the Western waters.

"Pittsburgh, when Mr. Roosevelt took up his residence there in 1811, had but recently commenced the career which has now entitled it to the name of the Birmingham of America. On the Allegheny side, which was liable to overflow, there were but few buildings in 1811. Close by the creek, and immediately under a lofty bluff, called Boyd's hill, was an iron foundry, known as Beelen's foundry, and in immediate proximity to this was the keel of Mr. Roosevelt's vessel laid. The depot of the Pittsburgh & Connellsville railroad now occupies the ground I am speaking of.

"The size and plan of the first steamboat had been determined on in New York, and had been furnished by Mr. Fulton. It was to be one hundred and sixteen feet in length, and twenty-foot beam. The engine was to have a thirty-four-inch cylinder, and the boiler and other parts of the machine were to be in proportion.

"The first thing to be done was to obtain the timber to build the boat, and for this purpose men were sent into the forest, there to find the necessary ribs and knees and beams, transport them to Monongahela, and raft them to the shipyard. White pine was the only material for planking that could be obtained without a delay that would be inadmissible. The sawing that was required was done in the old-fashioned and now long-forgotten saw-pits of 1811. Boat-builders, accustomed to build the barges of that day, could be obtained in Pittsburgh, but a ship-builder and the mechanics required in the machinery department, had to be shipped from New York. Under these circumstances, Mr. Roosevelt began the work. One of the first troubles that annoyed him was a rise in the Monongahela, when the waters backed into his shipyard, and set all the materials that were buoyant afloat. This occurred again and again, and on one occasion it seemed not improbable that the steamboat would be lifted from its ways and launched before its time. At length, however, all difficulties were overcome, by steady perseverance, and the boat was launched, and called, from the place of her ultimate destination, the New Orleans. It cost in the neighborhood of $38,000.

"As the New Orleans approached completion, and when it came to be known that Mrs. Roosevelt intended to accompany her husband on the voyage, the numerous friends she had made in Pittsburgh united in endeavoring to dissuade her from what they regarded as utter folly, if not absolute madness. Her husband was appealed to. The criticisms that had been freely applied to the boat by the crowds of visitors to the shipyard were now transferred to the conduct of the builder. He was told that he had no right to peril his wife's life, however reckless he might be of his own. But the wife believed in her husband, and in the latter part of September, 1811, the New Orleans, after a short experimental trip up the Monongahela, commenced her voyage.

"There were two cabins, one aft for ladies, and a larger one forward for gentlemen. In the former were four berths. It was comfortably furnished. Of this Mrs. Roosevelt took possession. Mr. Roosevelt and herself were the only passengers. There was a captain, an engineer named Baker, Andrew Jack (the pilot), six hands, two female servants, a man waiter, a cook and an immense Newfoundland dog. Thus equipped, the New Orleans began the voyage which changed the relations of the West—which may almost be said to have changed its destiny.

"The people of Pittsburgh turned out en masse, and lined the banks of the Monongahela, to witness the departure of the steamboat, and shout after shout rent the air, and handkerchiefs were waved and hats thrown up by way of God speed to the voyagers, as the anchor was raised, and, heading up stream for a short distance, a wide circuit brought the

New Orleans on her proper course, and, steam and current aiding, she disappeared behind the first headland, on the right bank of the Ohio.

"Too much excited to sleep, Mr. Roosevelt and his wife passed the greater part of the first night on deck, and watched the shore, covered then with an almost unbroken forest, as reach after reach and bend after bend were passed at a speed of from eight to ten miles an hour. The regular working of the engine, the ample supply of steam, the uniformity of the speed, inspired at last a confidence that quieted at length the nervous apprehensions of the travelers. Mr. Jack, the pilot, delighted with the facility with which the vessel was steered, and at a speed to which he was so little accustomed, ceased to express misgivings and became as sanguine as Mr. Roosevelt himself in regard to the success of the voyage. The very crew of unimaginative men were excited with the novelty of the situation; and when the following morning assembled all hands on deck to return the cheers of a village whose inhabitants had seen the boat approaching down the long reach in the river, and turned out to greet her as she sped, it probably shone upon as jolly a set as ever floated upon the Ohio.

"On the second day after leaving Pittsburgh, the New Orleans rounded to opposite Cincinnati, and cast anchor in the stream. Levees and wharfboats were things unknown in 1811*. Here, as at Pittsburgh, the whole town seemed to have assembled on the bank, and many of the acquaintances came off in small boats. 'Well, you are as good as your word; you have visited us in a steamboat,' they said; 'but we see you for the last time. Your boat may go down the river; but, as to coming up; the very idea is an absurd one.' This was one of those occasions on which seeing was not believing. The keelboatmen, whose shoulders had hardened as they pressed their poles for many a weary mile against the current, shook their heads as they crowded around the strange visitor, and bandied wit with the crew that had been selected from their own calling for the voyage. Some flatboatmen, whose ungainly arks the steamboat had passed a short distance above the town, and who now floated by with the current, seemed to have a better opinion of the new comer, and proposed a tow in case they were again overtaken. But as to the boat's returning, all agreed that that could never be.

"The stay at Cincinnati was brief, only long enough to take in a supply of wood for the voyage to Louisville, which was reached on the night of the fourth day after leaving Pittsburgh. It was midnight on the 1st of October, 1811, that the New Orleans dropped anchor opposite the town. There was a brilliant moon. It was as light as day almost, and no one on board had retired. The roar of the escaping steam, then heard for the first time at the place where now its echoes are unceasing, roused the population, and, late as it was, crowds came rushing to the banks of the river to learn the cause of the unwonted uproar. A letter now before me, written by one of those on board at the time, records the fact, that there were those who insisted that the comet of 1811 had fallen into the Ohio and produced the hubub!

"The morning after the arrival of the vessel at Louisville, Mr. Roosevelt's acquaintances and others came on board, and here the same things were said that had been said at Cincinnati. Congratulations at having descended the river were, without exception, accompanied by regrets that it was the first and last time a boat would be seen above the falls of the Ohio. Still, so far, certainly, Mr. Roosevelt's promises had been fulfilled, and there was a public dinner given to him a few days after his arrival. Here any number of complimentary toasts were drank, and the usual amount of feeling on such occasions was manifested. *Sed revocare gradum*, however, was still the burden of the song.

"Not to be outdone in hospitality, Mr. Roosevelt invited his hosts to dine on board the

---
*Levees were known in New Orleans almost a hundred years before.

New Orleans, which lay at anchor opposite the town. The company met in the forward or gentlemen's cabin, and the feast was at its hight, when suddenly there were heard unwonted rumblings, accompanied by a very perceptible motion in the vessel. The company had but one idea. The New Orleans had escaped from her anchor, and was drifting toward the falls, to the certain destruction of all on board! There was an instant and simultaneous rush to the upper deck, when the company found, that, instead of drifting toward the falls of the Ohio, the New Orleans was making good headway up the river and would soon leave Louisville in the distance down stream. As the engine warmed to its work, and the steam blew off at the safety valve, the speed increased. Mr. Roosevelt, of course, had provided this means of convincing his incredulous guests, and their surprise and delight may readily be imagined. After going up the river for a few miles, the New Orleans returned to her anchorage.

"It had been intended, on leaving Pittsburgh, to proceed as rapidly as possible to New Orleans, to place the boat on the route for which it was designed, between that city and Natchez. It was found however, on reaching Louisville, that there was not a sufficient depth of water on the falls of the Ohio to permit the vessel to pass over them in safety. Nothing was to be done, therefore, but to wait, as patiently as possible, the rise in the river. That this delay might, as far as practicable, be utilized, to the extent, at least, of convincing the incredulous Cincinnatians, the New Orleans returned to that city, where she was greeted with an enthusiasm that exceeded even what was displayed on her descent from Pittsburgh. No one doubted now. In 1832," continues the address, "I was detained for several days in Cincinnati, on my return from a visit to the South. There were numbers, then alive, who remembered the first advent of steam, and from some of these I learned what is here stated in regard to the public feeling at the time—the universal incredulity at the first visit—the unbounded confidence inspired by the second.

"Returning to Louisville, the greater interest of all on board the New Orleans centered in watching the rise in the Ohio. Rain in the upper country was what was wanted, and of this there seemed small promise. There was nothing in the aspect of the heavens that indicated it. On the contrary, there was a dull, misty sky, without a cloud, a leaden atmosphere that weighed upon the spirits, and the meaning of which would have been better understood at Naples, under the shadow of Vesuvius, than on the banks of the Ohio. The sun, when it rose, looked like a globe of red-hot iron, whose color brightened at noon, to resume the same look when it sank below the horizon. All day long one might have gazed on it with unflinching eyes. The air was still heated, and a sense of weariness was characteristic of the hours as they wore slowly by. At last, and when a nervous impatience affected every one on board, it was announced one morning that there had been a rise in the river during the night. Morning after morning the rise in the river during the night was reported, and finally, in the last week in November, it was ascertained that the depth of water in the shallowest portion of the falls exceeded by five inches the draught of the boat. It was a narrow margin, but the rise had ceased. There was no telegraph in those days to tell hourly what was the weather in the country drained by the Ohio, and Mr. Roosevelt, assuring himself, personally, of the condition of the falls, determined to take the responsibility and go over them if he could. It was an anxious time. All hands were on deck. Mrs. Roosevelt, whom her husband would willingly have left behind to join him below the falls, refused to remain on shore, and stood near the stern. The two pilots—for an extra one had been engaged for the passage through the rapids—took their places on the bow. The anchor was weighed. To get into the Indiana channel, which was the best, a wide circuit had to be made, bringing her head down stream, completing which, the New Orleans began the descent. Steerage way depended upon her speed exceeding that of the current. The faster she could be made to go the easier it would be to guide her. All the steam the boiler would bear was put upon her. The safety valve shrieked; the wheels revolved faster than they had ever done before, and the vessel, speaking figuratively, fairly flew away from the crowds collected to witness her departure from Louisville. Instinctively each one on board now grasped the nearest object, and with bated breath awaited the result. Black ledges of rock appeared only to disappear as the New Orleans flashed by them. The waters whirled and eddied, and threw their spray upon the deck, as a more rapid descent caused the vessel to pitch forward to what at times seemed inevitable destruction. Not a word was spoken. The pilots directed the men at the helm by motions of their hands. Even the great Newfoundland dog seemed affected by the apprehension of danger, and came and crouched at Mrs. Roosevelt's feet. The tension of the nervous system was too great to be long sustained. Fortunately the passage was soon made, and with feelings of profound gratitude to the Almighty, at the successful issue of the adventure, on the part of both Mr. Roosevelt and his wife, the New Orleans rounded to in safety below the falls. There was still the same leaden sky, the same dim sun during the day, the same starless night; but the great difficulty had been overcome, and it was believed that there would now be nothing but plain sailing to the port of destination. It was yet to be seen how far the expectation of those on board, in this respect, would be realized."

This birth of steam in the great valley was so great an event that even the stars and the pent-up fires of the depths of the earth were destined to celebrate it. The great comet of 1811 had now disappeared; then came the great earthquakes of that year, which, like the legendary dragons that threaten to devour, become the slave of and do obeisance to its conqueror's bravery, as the great convulsion of New Madrid seemed to do to the audacious little firecraft of Mr. Roosevelt. Says Mr. Latrobe still farther: "The first shock that was observed was felt on board the New Orleans while she lay at anchor after passing the falls. The effect was as though the vessel had been in motion and had suddenly grounded. The cable shook and trembled, and many on board for a moment experienced a nausea resembling sea-sickness. It was a little while before they could realize the presence of the dread visitor. It was wholly unexpected. The shocks succeeded each other during the night. When morning came the voyage was resumed, and while under way, the jar of the machinery, the monotonous beating of the wheels, and the steady progress of the vessel prevented the disturbance from being noticed.

"It has already been mentioned, that, in his voyage of exploration, Mr. Roosevelt had found coal on the Ohio, and that he had caused mines to be opened in anticipation. Their value was now realized, and when he reached them on his way down the river, he took on board as much coal as he could find room for.

"Some miles above the mouth of the Ohio, the diminished current indicated a rise in the Mississippi. This was found to be the case. The bottom lands on either shore were under water, and there was every sign of an unwonted flood. Canoes came and went among the boles of the trees. Sometimes the Indians attempted to approach the steamboat, and, again, fled on its approach. The Chickasaws still occupied that part of the state of Tennessee lying below the mouth of the Ohio. On one occasion a large canoe, fully manned, came out of the woods abreast of the steamboat. The Indians, outnumbering the crew of the vessel, paddled after it. There was at once a race, and for a time the contest was equal. The result, however, was what might have been anticipated. Steam had the advantage of endurance, and the Indians with wild shouts, which might have been shouts of defiance, gave up the pursuit, and turned into the forest from whence they emerged.

"While the crew was more amused than alarmed at this incident of the voyage, Mr. Roosevelt, who had not forgotten the visit to the flatboat on the preliminary exploration, was not sorry, now, when he lost sight of the canoe. That he bestowed a second thought on the matter, illustrates the nervous excitement that prevailed on board. Mrs. Roosevelt and himself were still discussing the adventure when they retired to rest. They had scarcely fallen asleep, when they were aroused by shouts on deck, and the trampling of many feet. The idea of the Indians still predominant, Mr. Roosevelt sprang from his bed, and seizing a sword —the only weapon he had—hurried from the cabin to join battle, as he thought, with the Chickasaws. It was a more alarming enemy that he encountered. The New Orleans was on fire, and flame and smoke issued from the forward cabin. The servant who attended them, had placed some green wood too close to the stove, in anticipation of the next day's wants, and, lying down beside it, had fallen sound asleep. The stove, becoming overheated, this wood had taken fire; the joiner's work close by had caught, and the entire cabin would soon have been in flames, had not the servant, half suffocated, rushed on deck and given the alarm. By dint of great exertion, the fire, which by this time was making rapid headway, was extinguished, but not until the interior woodwork had either been destroyed or grievously defaced. Few eyes were closed for the remainder of the night, nor did the accident tend to tranquillize the nerves of the travelers.

"A supply of provisions had been taken on board the New Orleans, at Louisville, amply sufficient for the voyage to Natchez, and this was occasionally supplemented by purchases at settlements along the river. These, however, were few and far between, and not at all to be relied upon. The crew, accustomed to the simple fare of boatmen on the Mississippi, were easily provided for. The commissariat of the voyage, therefore—longer than a voyage to Europe now—gave no trouble.

"Early in the afternoon of each day the steamer was rounded to and fastened to the bank, the crew going ashore to cut the wood required, after the coal was exhausted, for the next day's consumption. On some of these occasions, squatters came on board with tales of their experience upon the land, which they insisted shook and trembled under their feet. At New Madrid, a great portion of which had been engulfed, as the earth opened up in vast chasms and swallowed up houses and their inhabitants, terror-stricken people had begged to be taken on board, while others, dreading the steamboat even more than the earthquake, hid themselves as she approached. To receive the former was impossible. The would-be refugees had no homes to go to; and ample as was the supply of provision for Mr. Roosevelt and his wife, it would have been altogether insufficient for any large increase of passengers, and as to obtaining provisions on the way, the New Orleans might as well have been upon the open sea. Painful as it was, there was no choice but to turn a deaf ear to the cries of the terrified inhabitants of the doomed town.

"One of the peculiar characteristics was the silence that prevailed on board. No one seemed disposed to talk; and when there was any conversation it was carried on in whispers, almost. Tiger, who appeared, alone, to be aware of the earthquake while the vessel was in motion, prowled about, moaning and growling; and when he came and placed his head on Mrs. Roosevelt's lap, it was a sure sign of commotion of more than usual violence. Orders were given in low tones, and the usual cheerful 'Aye, aye, sir,' of the sailors, was almost inaudible. Sleeplessness was another characteristic. Sound, continuous sleep was apparently unknown. Going ashore for wood was the event of each twenty-four hours, and was looked forward to by the crew with satisfaction, notwithstanding the labor it involved. And yet the men, if not sullenly, toiled silently; and if the earth shook, as it often did, while they were at work, the uplifted axe was suspended, or placed quietly on the log, and the men stared at each other until it ceased. Nor was this depression confined to the steamer. Flat-boats and barges were passed whose crews, instead of bandying river wit, as they had done when met on the voyage from Pittsburgh to Louisville, uttered no word as the New Orleans went by. Before the travelers had been many days on the Mississippi, they fancied, as they looked at each other, that they had become haggard. Mrs. Roosevelt records ' that she lived in a constant fright, unable to sleep, or sew, or read.'

"Sometimes Indians would join the woodchoppers, and occasionally one would be able to converse in English with the men. From these it was learned that the steamer was called 'Penelore,' or 'fire canoe,' and was supposed to have some affinity with the comet that had preceded the earthquake, the sparks from the chimney of the boat being likened to the train of the celestial visitant. Again they would attribute the smoky atmosphere to the steamer, and the rumbling of the earth to the beating of the waters by the fast revolving paddles. To the native inhabitants of the boundless forest that lined the river banks, the coming of the first steamboat was an omen of evil; as it was the precursor of their own expulsion from their ancient homes, no wonder they continued, for years, to regard all steamboats with awe. As late as 1834, when the emigration of the Chickasaws to their new homes, west of the river, took place, hundreds refused to trust themselves in such conveyances, but preferred making their long and weary pilgrimage on foot.

"One of the most uncomfortable incidents of the voyage was the confusion of the pilot, who became alarmed, and declared that he was lost, so great had been the changes in the channel caused by the earthquake. Where he had expected to find deep water, roots and stumps projected above the surface. Tall trees that had been guides had disappeared. Cut-offs had been made through what was forest when he saw it last. Islands had changed their shape. Still there was no choice but to keep on. There was no place to stop at. There was no possibility of turning back.

"In the first part of the voyage when the steamboat rounded to at night she was made fast to the river bank, but when it was seen that these would occasionally topple and fall over, as the ground beneath them was shaken or gave way, it was thought safer to stop at the foot of an island, which might serve as a breakwater, taking care the trees were far enough from the boat to obviate apprehension from them. Once, however, when such a fastening had been made and a plank carried ashore, and the woodchopping had been finished at an hour earlier than usual, a new experience was had. No shock had been felt during the day, and Mrs. Roosevelt anticipated a quiet rest. In this, however, she was disappointed. All night long she was disturbed by the jar and noise produced by hard objects grating against the planking outside the boat. At times severe blows were struck that caused the vessel to tremble through its entire length. Then there would follow a continuous scratching mingled with the gurgling sound of water. Driftwood had caused sounds of the same sort before, and it was thought that driftwood was again busy in producing them. With morning came the true explanation. The island had disappeared; and it was the disintegrated fragments sweeping down the river that had struck the vessel from time to time and caused the noises that Mrs. Roosevelt had been disturbed by. At first, it was supposed that the New Orleans had been borne along by the current, but the pilot pointed to landmarks on the banks which proved that it was the island that had disappeared while the steamboat had kept its place. Where the island had been, there was now a broad reach of the river, and when the hawser was cut, for it was found impossible otherwise to free the vessel, the pilot was utterly at a loss which way to steer. Some flatboats were hailed, but they, too, were lost. Their main effort was by dint of their long oars to keep where the current was the strongest. This was evidently the best place for the New Orleans. It was not without its peculiar risks, however. In the bends, where the rushing waters struck the shore to whirl around the curve, and glance off and form a bend in the opposite direction, the deepest water was immediately under the bank, and here the trees, undermined by the current, would be seen at times to sink into the stream, often erect until the waters covered their topmost twigs, sometimes falling against each other, interlacing their great arms, as strong men might do struggling for life when drowning. Sometimes they fell outward into the water, and then woe to the vessel that happened to be near them in the bend. This danger, however, steam enabled the New Orleans to avoid. Referring to it all, it is not wonderful that the survivor still speaks of it as 'one of anxiety and terror.'

"As the New Orleans descended the river, it passed out of the region of earthquakes, and the principal inconvenience was the number of shoals, snags and sawyers. These were all safely passed, however, and the vessel came in sight of Natchez, and rounded too, opposite the landing place. Expecting to remain here for a day or two, the engineer had allowed his fires to go down, so that when the boat turned its head up stream it lost headway altogether, and was being carried down by the current, far below the intended landing. Thousands were assembled on the bluff and at the foot of it; and, for a moment, it would have seemed that the New Orleans had achieved what she had done, so far, only that she might be overcome at last. Fresh fuel, however, was added, the engine stopped that steam might accumulate; presently the safety-valve lifted—a few turns of the wheel steadied the boat—a few more gave her headway; and, overcoming even the Mississippi, she gained the shore, amid shouts of exultation and applause."

To this vivid account of Natchez' great contribution to our great valley's civilization, it may be added that Samuel Davis, who was the first to ship cotton by this boat on this trip, was standing among the spectators, when a colored drayman exclaimed: "By jolly, mass' Sam, ole Mississippi got her massa dis time!" Other steam vessels were built, the next ones being the Vesuvius and Ætna, and the great Father of waters has been dotted with them in increasing abundance ever since. It was only eight years later that the steamer Savannah did for the Atlantic what the New Orleans did for the Mississippi. The London *Times* of May 18, 1819, said: "Great experiment:—A new steam vessel of three hundred tons has been built at New York, for the express purpose of carrying passengers across the Atlantic. She is to come to Liverpool direct."

In 1820 local steamers were put on, the Mississippi being one of the first owned locally, as the most of the business was done by through steamers until nearly 1840. About the first regular packet between Vicksburg and New Orleans was the Sultana under Captain Tufts, whose son-in-law, Captain Pease, afterward ran a second Sultana, which was built by Abijah Fisk, of New Orleans. These old river captains were noted characters, many of them, one of the earliest being Capt. John W. Russell, on one of the through steamers. Capt. Abram Auter, of Vicksburg, whose life has extended into the decade just closed, was a contemporary of these old commanders, and in 1842 built and ran the Mazeppa to New Orleans, and later on ran the first steamer run above Yazoo city, even running twenty-five miles up the Yalobusha. This latter craft bore the suggestive appellation The Bully Woodsman. It was in 1843 that the floating palaces were introduced with their high style of living, by Capt. St. Clair Thomasson with his Concordia. Only a few years later he put on the Magnolia, between Vicksburg and New Orleans, and this was the passenger queen of ante-bellum days. She was sunk by a collision early in the fifties. Among other well-known captains were, C. J. Brenham, John W. Cannon, James M. White and Commodore Thomas P. Leathers, the commodore's boats almost always bearing the name Natchez.

The marvelous increase and supremacy of the shipping interests in the carrying trade from those days on, until the rise of railroads, is a matter within the memory of those now of middle age.

But Natchez distinguished herself in this line still more, late in the thirties. Not content with being the inland metropolis of the lower Mississippi, she agitated for becoming an ocean port with direct trade with Liverpool. The result was that in 1839 the legislature incorporated the Port Gibson & Grand Gulf Shipping Company and the Mississippi Importing Company. The scheme was so successful that by 1840 ships were ascending the river as high as Vicksburg, but on account of the financial disasters of those panicky times, and possibly for other reasons, the plan was not long after abandoned.

Instead of the leading river ports continuing as Natchez and Vicksburg, they have become Vicksburg and Natchez, one great reason for this, no doubt, being the construction of the old Southern, now the Alabama & Vicksburg railway.

Now, as an illustration only of river traffic, let us note the principal lines of steamboats touching at Vicksburg: The St. Louis & Vicksburg Anchor line, with several fine boats; the Vicksburg & Greenville Packet Company, owned at Vicksburg; Merchants & Planters' line to Skipwith; Vicksburg & Natchez Packet Company; Vicksburg and Davis Bend line; New Orleans & Vicksburg steamboat T. P. Leathers; New Orleans, Vicksburg & Greenville steamboat Pargoud; New Orleans & Ohio River line—a large freight line; the steamboat Headlight, up the Sunflower river; the Parisot line, up the Yazoo; the Mulhollands line, up the Yazoo, besides the steam ferry line and numerous highwater lines.

Intimately connected with the Mississippi river transportation is its levee system, which may be considered before turning attention to the coast and land transportation, especially because not a little of the railway system has been dependent on the building of levees. Only the lowland portions, of course, have any dependence on levees or dykes to protect them from overflow in times of highwater, thus rendering them cultivable and inhabitable. In the case of Mississippi, the portion of such a low level as this indicates is an immense oval-like region, formed by the river making a vast detour from Memphis to the west, and curving back on Vicksburg, and the bluffs, back of the lowlands, debouching in a similar vast curve to the east between those two cities. This vast oval is about one hundred and eighty miles long and about seventy-five miles wide, and, containing a vast area of over four million acres, about half of which is woodland, and all of which, subject to the overflows and accumulation of decayed vegetation of centuries, is of literally inexhaustible richness. To protect this from overflow was to not only make the river a better channel for transport, but practically create a country which would develop both new river and new railway transportation; but to protect a river frontage of such stupendous proportions on the greatest water-course in the world was an undertaking so vast that it had to await a late day of greatly increased population. Of course there were local lines; even in 1811 a company was incorporated for one at Warrenton. So many, however, had settled in the higher unoverflowed lands of this Mississippi-Yazoo delta, as it is called, that in 1840, before it was leveed, it produced thirty-nine thousand bales of cotton, and by 1850 a total of forty-two thousand annually. But after some meager leveeing had been done, the production increased, so that in 1860 the crop was one hundred and thirty-six thousand bales! The land, unsalable before, became at once salable.

But what were these levees? The first levee on the Mississippi was begun at New

Orleans in 1717, and not completed until 1727. The work extended, until by 1770 over fifty miles were completed. Says a recent writer in the Memphis *Commercial:* "There was a time, within the memory of men now living, when each man owning property on the great Mississippi built and kept up with his own effort the little ridges which, at that time, bore the name of levees. There were stretches of front owned by the state or government, or by non-resident land-grabbers, and these would have no protection whatever; and a levee system, above all things else, must have continuity. Its stability in all other places would be of no avail if there were gaps unfilled.

"It was then that planters took upon themselves the task of systematizing the construction of these banks of dirt, which have grown to be scientifically constructed dikes, which in time will become magnificent pikes from the bluffs almost to the sea. At first they contributed so much labor per annum, which was generally called out in one big squad, with each planter or overseer commanding his own hands. Of course, as the country opened up for some miles back, the dwellers along the river front began to feel the injustice of being compelled to keep up levees to protect men who need not do anything unless they so desired. County boards were organized, which had powers of expending the funds which were raised by taxes levied by the county police jury. The powers of these boards were enlarged as the growing importance of the interests involved and the new condition constantly being met required, until levee boards were powerful corporations, vested by the legislature with power to tax and to have the lands in the district sold for its purposes."

An act of December 2, 1858, organized a levee board, and a tax on all lands of the state was provided for levees, except on certain trust lands for school and other purposes, and about that time the government granted this land to the state for levee purposes. The delta people got in debt, too, in their efforts, and the oncoming war destroying levees, both as a war measure and by neglect, left the whole delta a wilderness as before. An act of 1865 reorganized it, but became effective in the act of February 13, 1867. Other acts followed, and by 1871 the levee district included the counties of Bolivar, Washington, Issaquena, Coahoma, Tunica, De Soto, Sunflower, Yazoo, Tallahatchie and Penola. The total acreage then in account for levee taxes was 3,484,278; the bonds issued aggregated $670,000; the state auditor became ex-officio levee commissioner; and the debt crept up, by 1876, to the round sum of $923,666,58. By 1880 the debt had fallen to $444,568.78 or nearly $500,000, and it was divided into two levee districts. By 1882 the debt had fallen to the small sum of $135,329.-06, and funds were available for clearing it all, but for a claim set up by the Mississippi & Vicksburg railway. The floods of 1882–3 caused such disaster that an additional board was organized, called the Yazoo Mississippi Delta board, and the entire system was complete by 1886. Says the writer above quoted:

"Amendments have been submitted to and passed by successive legislatures until to-day the board of Mississippi levee commissioners—embracing in its jurisdiction the great counties of Bolivar, Washington, Sharkey and Issaquena—is one of the mightiest corporations on earth. It has six members who select its secretary and treasurer, engineer and cotton-tax collector from outside its membership. This body is empowered by law to tax, not only the lands and personality in these counties, but the very products of the soil. They may issue bonds without consulting any constituency to an amount that seems fabulous, and these are held sacred and binding for all time to come—in fact, are a lien upon the taxable property in the district. No state court can enjoin this great corporation from taking private property for its use, and the just compensation is often necessarily ascertained after the appropriation by the board. The very elaborate and perfect levee laws now in force in this district are the work of that able and untiring worker in this field, the late Col. W. A. Percy, whose efforts are being more and more appreciated as the years roll by.

"For many years past this board has been constantly enlarging existing embankments, and raising them to a uniform grade, until now there is a line of levee which will hold any ordinary high water, and an extraordinary one, if it is not too prolonged nor the weather too windy.

"The work of laying out, enlarging and general supervision of a line of leeves fully two hundred miles long, is under the care of the chief engineer in this district, Maj. William Starling, one of the most accomplished engineers in the country. He looks the soldier and scholar and practical man of affairs all happily combined. His place is no sinecure at any time, but in high-water seasons it is one of the most exacting and onerous that can be imagined. People living on high hills can not imagine how one feels behind a piece of dirt which looks awfully large in summer and autumn, but is, oh, so frail when the chilly winds of March lash the waters into a seething, restless mass, seeking freedom from their artificial barriers. It is there that your chief engineer is a more important personage than governor or president. He must be apparently ubiquitous. The elements must not stand between him and any threatened point. Competent assistants are often unable to satisfy the popular demand for the chief. I have seen men after fighting for hours in mud knee deep, abandon all hope and quit, utterly broken in spirits, resume work with renewed zeal at the bare sight of the martial-looking chief, whose nerve and energy seemed to have no limit.

"A few facts in regard to the construction of levees may be of interest to your readers, many of whom have no proper idea of the subject. We shall take Skipwith as an example, as the crevasse at that point renders it a noted place. The levee, at the point which gave way, was an old one, and had been enlarged within three years past, and no fear was felt for its safety. After the break it was remembered that there was too little berme to it, and a current had washed under it until the entire structure caved in.

"It may not be understood what this berme is, and what its office in the levee may be. In all well-regulated levee building there is an unbroken strip of earth between the base of the levee and the barrow pits. This berme varies from ten to thirty feet in width, and adds greatly to the strength and length of life of the embankment. There is, of course, a very strong pressure of water against the under side of these structures, and the force is greatest at the bottom of the barrow pits on the end next to the levee, and this berme adds greatly to the power of the levee to resist the percolation of sipe water through it. Many breaks have occurred, no doubt, attributable to lack of berme in light, spongy soil. The muck ditch was at one time a very insignificant affair, which had no particular object, except the search for trees or holes in the center of the proposed embankment. Recent levee construction demands a muck ditch which will serve as a protection from sipe and crayfish.

"The Skipwith levee has under it a muck ditch six feet deep, six feet wide at bottom, and twelve feet wide on top. The board has not stopped at the size of the ditch, but on every piece of new work there is an inspector appointed to see that this muck ditch is free absolutely from all vegetable matter of any kind, and that nothing but the purest buckshot dirt finds its way into it, no matter what the character of soil through which it passes, and this is often a work of great difficulty, as on one or two sections of the new levee at Mound Landing the contractors, Messrs. Carey & Bradburn, were compelled to haul dirt nearly a quarter of a mile to get the right material.

"At this point the inspector is Judge J. L. Root, who is a levee man of great ability and experience, and whose practical knowledge of the subject makes him the terror of the con-

H. B. Theobald

tractor. The inspector sees that every shovelful of dirt that goes into the great muck ditch is thoroughly packed by boys on mules continually riding over it every few seconds. The result is a core as hard as concrete, which will add a hundredfold to the strength of the embankment.

"Levees are built now with six feet of base to every one foot of hight, and if there is variation from this rule it is on the side of wider base. The slope is gentle and will stand the greatest amount of wave-wash with the least amount of wear.

"These embankments are let to contractors by the cubic yard at prices ranging from ten cents to forty cents per yard. The cubic yard appears to be a very small lump of dirt until one begins to pull it with mules or push it with man-power up into the body of the work. There it looks and is of great bulk and weight.

"Irishmen monopolize most of the barrow work, while the negro has the call for driving the gentle and innocent mule. The negro is as good a day man as the Irishman, but the latter outdoes him in doing what is known as 'station work.' The colored man will not do any more by the job than by the day, and does not often tackle any sized stations.

"In levee building, as elsewhere, one sees a great deal of human nature among the workers. The Irishman, for example, will quit a good place if his grub varies in the smallest degree from his standard, and there is no rhyme nor reason in his manner of quitting. 'I am going to quit; give me my toime,' is often all that is heard. The writer knew a contractor to lose one hundred Irishmen at the very rush of completing his contract in time, because the baker did not have light bread ready for breakfast. A worthy Irishman explained to me the other day that his countrymen went south 'wid de geese in winter and came back wid 'em in spring.' As a rule they seem to enjoy camp life until they get a notion to move on; then all power can't stop them—go they will.

"There is a great deal of talk by outsiders about the amount of timber put in levees and railroad beds by dishonest contractors—a great deal more than the facts warrant—simply because it would not pay to do it. That it is done occasionally is shown by the following story, which is told as gospel truth: A certain contractor was not content with beating the levee board, but would not pay his laborers unless forced to do it. One of his men waited until the engineer was in easy hearing, then called out to the conductor: 'Say, now, if you don't pay me my wages, I'll set fire to your d——n dump.'

"The 'dump' is the technical term for the body of an embankment in course of construction, deriving its name from the necessary dump of scrapers or wheelbarrows of their loads of dirt. Another story has it that an engineer, in taking up some levee completed, missed his dog, and after looking around everywhere, heard him barking in the 'dump,' and before he could have a hole dug in to rescue him, the dog bounded out one hundred feet or more away. Of course there can be no such thing under the present system, and no fears need be indulged on this score in future.

"The taking charge of these great works by the national government will give a new impetus to the already rapid development of the country protected by them. They can and will be made to confine the great river in one safe, deep pathway to the sea."

But Mississippi has an ocean transportation, and a straight coast of over one hundred miles, with one of the most magnificent natural harbors in the world. So thought Bienville, in 1699, and now, after nearly two hundred years, it has four flourishing harbors—Pascagoula, Biloxi, Mississippi city and Shieldsburg. Unlike the levees, however, the states and nation have not seen fit to do much for it. Even in the year 1876 there were over seventy vessels entered and cleared for the coast-wise, and over a hundred for the foreign trade at Pascagoula alone, this being the largest shipping point at that time. Its great drawback has been its absence of direct railway connection with the center of the state, a struggle for which has been made since early in ante-bellum days, and is identical with the career of the Gulf & Ship Island railway scheme, that has lagged along in the history of the state. Thus far the lumber interests have had the bulk of the shipping, the proximity of New Orleans diverting from it many lines that might otherwise enter. The state's desire regarding it can not be better shown than by a memorial on the subject in 1872: "For the last half century the state of Mississippi has encouraged by legislation the construction of a line of railroad that would place the different parts of the state in communication with the gulf coast, and for this purpose has granted charters to companies with immunities and privileges of a most liberal character. Having on her gulf coast a deep and safe harbor, that of Ship island, with a constant depth of water twenty-four feet, with safe channels of ingress and egress, and in which was sheltered the British fleet in the war of 1812, and the Union fleet during the late war. Manifestly a wise policy dictates that this fine harbor should be made available, and the products of Mississippi's fertile soil should be transported to that point for shipment to the markets of the world. Mississippi is the largest producer of cotton of any of the Southern states, her annual crop averaging between eight and nine hundred thousand bales; and all this yield of natural wealth is carried without her borders, and pays tribute to cities beyond her limits. The mighty Mississippi flowing along her western borders, bears upon its bosom the bounteous yield from the alluvial valleys of the Yazoo and its tributaries, and the valley of the Mississippi, to the city of New Orleans. The Chicago, St. Louis & New Orleans railroad, running through the center of the state, gathers up from that portion of the state its products, and pours them into the crowded warehouses of New Orleans. The Memphis & Charleston railroad, skirting her northern line, carries to Memphis the cotton from that part of the state, and the Mobile & Ohio railroad, running along her eastern boundary, conveys to Mobile the product of that region of the state. Thus it will be seen that the state of Mississippi—rich beyond her sisters in the production of that great staple that brings so much national wealth—pays a large annual tribute to cities and communities foreign to her and her people; building them up and sustaining them in prosperity by that which should be controlled for her own benefit and the welfare of her people. Let us see what this annual revenue or tribute amounts to, that is reaped by the points hereinbefore designated. We can safely place it at $5 per bale; this includes storage, drayage, commission, labor, weighing and compressing; and by this amount let us multiply the minimum figure stated as the annual crop of Mississippi, say eight hundred thousand bales, and we have the round sum of $4,000,000 that Mississippi pays annually, a tribute to enrich cities of her sister states, when every dollar of this sum should remain with her and her people, to build up within her own territory a city that should rival those of her neighbors as a port of entry and shipment, and add to her revenues in the enhancement of the value of property subject to taxation. From the Potomac to the Rio Grande all the other sea-coast states have their port of entry and shipment, from which people derive profit and wealth and the state's increased yield of taxes. Texas has Galveston and other ports, and freights with her products vessels for all places of demand. Louisiana has New Orleans, at whose wharves are seen flying the flags of all nations. Alabama has Mobile, inviting to safe harbor and full-return cargoes the commercial marine of the world. Florida, Pensacola and San Augustine, where may be seen loading ships from all parts of the world with her cotton, sugar, timber and tropical fruit. Georgia has Savannah, and none have a better natural harbor than that of Ship island and Mississippi sound. The future is bound to make use of it."

CHAPTER V.

RAILWAY TRANSPORTATION, ETC.

As valuable as Mississippi's water transport facilities have been in furnishing communication with the outside world, she was for many years handicapped by a land transportation attended with unusual difficulties, incident to her heavy forests and numerous intercepting water courses. The difficulties attending the long route by national roads through the Chickasaw nation to the northeast settlements, and through the Choctaw country to the lower Tombigbee community have been noticed elsewhere. The long years of dependence on stage routes and horseback riding, tollroads and ferries are within the memory of many now living, and no doubt the great plantations and the comparatively meager internal commerce it fostered had much to do with it. The vast predominance of agriculture and the minimum of commerce with its consequent meager offspring of cities, the natural product of commerce, all tended to discourage it no doubt, while incidentally the public finances of the state, elsewhere noticed, was no small ingredient in the final solution. Certain it is that railway development is confined largely to the last two decades, and that, too, by far the most vigorous in the one just closed. As water development was a characteristic of ante-bellum transportation in this state, so the development of railways has been the leading feature of post-bellum intercommunication, and has been the fruitful mother of a—for this state—numerous brood of fast-growing cities, towns and villages, which will be noticed elsewhere in these volumes.

There is one marked difference between the two systems—the inflexibility and permanence of the water courses made, in their days of predominance, no uncertainty as to the location of population. Not so with the railway; in certain ways far more powerful than water courses, their projectors determine their course, and their course determines the chief seats of inhabitance.

No greater illustration of this new institution's power in this respect need be sought than in the early growth of railways in this state. We are wont to forget that the first locomotive used in this nation was only in 1820; but it was as late as 1828 that the first actual railway was in operation, so that when it is known that three years later, 1831, the Woodville people incorporated the West Feliciana railroad company to build a road from Woodville to St. Francisville, or Bayou Sara, Mississippi is seen to be near the head of the line. Vicksburg & Jackson railroad was incorporated the same year, and in 1833 the Port Gibson & Grand Gulf company. The Jackson people proposed to connect themselves with Mobile, and incorporated the Mississippi & Alabama railroad, and the same year Natchez and Jackson proposed a line joining them and extending to Canton and northward; this was the Mississippi railroad company. By this time the proposition of railway construction became epidemic in its proportions. Paper railways came thick and fast, as the sometime "leaves of Valombrosa," a total of twenty-two from 1831 to 1841: The Tombeckbee, from Columbus to the Jackson line; the Lake Washington & Deer Creek, the Benton & Manchester, the Gainsville & Narkeeta; the Yazoo, from Leflore in Carroll county; the Tallahatchie, from that river to Tillatoba; the Mississippi Springs & Clinton, and the Aberdeen & Pontotoc, all in 1836; the New Orleans & Nashville; the Hernando company, from Jefferson to the great river; the Pontotoc, Oxford & Delta; the Mississippi City company, the Grenada & Douglas, all in 1837; the Eagle & Pascagoula line, the Raymond & Bolton, the Paulding & Pontotoc, the Newton & Lauderdale, all in 1838; the Kosciusko & Canton, in 1839; the Brandon & Jackson, the Holly Springs & Tennessee, the Commerce, Hernando & East Port, and the Canton & Jackson in 1841. It will be noticed that these were the years of Mississippi's great financial distress; but they kept on; in 1846, the Southern railroad company, from Jackson toward Selma, Ala., and the Panola & Delta, and Locopolis & East Highlands, and in 1848 the Mobile & Ohio, the Hernando & Mississippi, Cold Water & Panola Hills, and the Deer Creek companies. With all this, however, we are much surprised to have a letter of 1849 sum up the state railway facilities with: "For several years we have had a railroad from Vicksburg to Jackson"! It was graded, also, to Brandon, but no tracks laid.

The meaning of this was that the financial panic of those years caused all to collapse totally, not even allowing visible progress, except Natchez, which built about thirty-five miles of her line, and then sold out and allowed it to be abandoned, and the Vicksburg & Jackson line, the solitary instance of a permanent construction. The space allowed here will not permit of an entrance into the subject of the state's aid to railways, interesting as it would be; sufficient to say that, besides money grants and loans at various times, land grants were made on the Jackson & Ship Island route, Jackson & Meridian and Mobile & Ohio, below Columbus. Neither can the connection of the railway and levee system be treated, and the mazy and numerous changes in names and combinations of railways of the state down to the present would be as uninteresting as they are inaccessible. No attempt will be made to do more than indicate the general growth to present conditions.

Moving forward about a decade from the point last noticed, it will be seen that in 1857 the Southern railroad had taken up the road east of Jackson to a junction with the new Mobile road, and was now graded to that junction, now so famous, but then scarcely named, and track laid to Brandon, with expectation of completion by January, 1860—three years. The Mobile & Ohio had grown rapidly during the decade, and was now complete to Crawfordsville station, in Lowndes county, a distance of two hundred and twenty miles from Mobile, and prospects of being through the state in three years. The New Orleans, Jackson & Great Northern, incorporated when the fifties began, and destined to become the great Illinois Central, was rapidly nearing completion from the south to Canton. The Mississippi Central was now completed sixty-two miles south of the Memphis and Charleston junction, with eighty-two miles yet to join the Great Northern at Canton. The Mississippi & Tennessee had now reached sixty miles out from Memphis toward Grenada, and with prospects of completion to that point by January, 1859—two years. But these were all. The Ship Island agitation, begun in 1837, came to an act of legislature by 1850, and resuscitation was attempted by another act in 1854, but so far in vain.

As a mere indication of the way the state had taken hold financially, by 1858, almost $20,000,000 had been invested within the state; over $10,000,000 in stock was there held, although it was quoted at fifty per cent. below par. The state itself owned $743,571.72 in stock, and held the bonds of various companies aggregating $825,396.29.

By 1859 the Great Northern had reached two hundred and six miles to Canton, and was rapidly grading toward Aberdeen. All but twenty miles of the Mississippi Central was completed, and that little gap was above Canton. The Mobile & Ohio and Mississippi & Tennessee had made large progress, but the southern tracks seemed inclined to halt at Brandon. The Memphis & Charleston had over thirty miles in the northeast corner, and the Gulf & Ship Island road had now achieved organization. This is practically the railway status of the state when the war began to paralyze the arts of peace.

In 1860 the railway mileage of the state was put at eight hundred and sixty miles. The power of the railways as connection with base of supplies, made them one of the first things to be destroyed by the army whose enemy they served. Their vast destruction is a matter of national history; suffice to say that in 1864, while there were five hundred and forty-five miles left undestroyed, only three hundred and sixty-five were in operation*. By 1870, however, the old figure of 1860 was recovered, and increased upon to nine hundred and ninety miles in the state. In 1880 the increase had reached to a total mileage of one thousand one hundred and twenty-seven. Up to this point the growth had been comparatively slow, but the decade of 1880–90 made such strides that by its close, the year 1890 saw the grand total of two thousand three hundred and sixty six miles of railway in actual operation, and more in prospect. This was considerably over a double in mileage in one decade. Note the progress in the decade: Eleven hundred and twenty-seven miles in 1880; thirteen hundred and three in 1882; eighteen hundred and forty-four in 1884; twenty-one hundred and nine in 1887, and twenty-three hundred and sixty-six in 1890, when the Georgia Pacific, the Ship Island, and the Fort Scott, Natchez & New Orleans were prospective. Compare the increase by decades in the United States: Twenty-three miles in 1830; twenty-eight hundred and eighteen in 1840—but little more than the total in this state now: ninety hundred and twenty-one miles in 1850; thirty thousand six hundred and thirty-five in 1860; fifty-two thousand nine hundred and fourteen in 1870; ninety-three thousand two hundred and ninety-six in 1880, and in 1888 a total of one hundred and fifty-six thousand and eighty-two. This showing is very favorable to Mississippi, considering the great losses of war.

This twenty-three hundred and sixty-six miles of railway is distributed among the following lines: The Illinois Central, the largest, with 636.06 miles; the Louisville, New Orleans & Texas with 584.8 miles; the Mobile & Ohio with 306 miles; the Georgia Pacific with 202.2 miles; the New Orleans & Northeastern with 153.42 miles; the Alabama & Vicksburg with 143.39 miles; the Kansas City, Memphis & Birmingham with 142.89 miles; the Natchez, Jackson & Columbus with 98.6 miles; the Louisville & Nashville with 73.83 miles; the Gulf & Chicago with 56.56 miles; the Memphis & Charleston with 33.4 miles; the Alabama Great Southern with 18.78 miles; the East Tennessee, Virginia & Georgia with 7.73 miles, and the Gulf & Ship Island with 7 miles. Thus it will be seen that the Illinois Central is much the largest, a railway that in the season of 1882–3 carried to New Orleans nearly forty-eight thousand bales of cotton more than that carried by all the rivers and bayous carrying to that port together—a total of four hundred and twenty-six thousand eight hundred and thirty-nine bales. A little more detailed sketch of each road may be of interest, at least so far as materials are accessible. The Illinois Central railroad is the great central artery of the state. To this railroad the settlement and prosperity of Illinois, Iowa, western Kentucky, western Tennessee, Mississippi and eastern Louisiana are very largely indebted. So early in the history of Illinois as 1832, Senator A. M. Jenkins suggested a road from Cairo to Peru. In 1835 William S. Waite, of Bond county, Ill., suggested the necessity of a rail-

---

*The Confederate States Almanac, 1864.

road, and in October of that year Judge Sidney Breese urged the construction of one from Cairo to Galena. Senator Stephen A. Douglas, Senator James Shields, Representatives Bissell, Harris, McClernand, Richardson, Wentworth and Young, with other prominent economists of that period, desired a central road connecting the territory of the great lakes with that of the Mississippi, and their desire was so manifestly in the interest of the state that the act of January 18, 1836—special charter—incorporating a company to build a road from Cairo to the foot of the proposed Illinois & Michigan canal, was received with favor. Let us see what the harum-scarum legislature of 1836-7 aimed at. There were $250,000 appropriated toward building the Great Western railroad from Vincennes to St. Louis; $3,500,000 to build the Central from Cairo to La Salle, and thence to Galena; $1,600,000 to construct a road from Alton to Mount Carmel and Shawneetown, to be known as the Southern Cross railroad; $1,850,000 to build the Northern Cross railroad from Quincy, on the Mississippi, to the Indiana state line; $650,000 to build a branch from the Illinois Central toward Terre Haute; $700,000 for the Peoria & Warsaw railroad; $600,000 for the branch from the Illinois Central to Lower Alton; $150,000 to build a road from Belleville to a junction with the Alton & Mount Carmel railroad; $350,000 to construct a road from Bloomington to Mackinaw, and the Freemont & Pekin branch of that proposed line, all making the modest sum of $9,650,000 at a time when the scattered citizens of Illinois had not the proper shelter from the inclement winter. Experience is a great school, but an expensive one. The next legislature repealed the act of the madmen and saved the state from irretrievable bankruptcy. In 1837 an appropriation of $3,500,000 was made under the internal improvement act of February 27, 1837; the construction of the road was entered upon in May of that year, but the credit of the state being unequal to her aspirations, she had to be content with the Northern Cross road from Menadosia to Springfield, as completed in February, 1842, at a cost of $1,000,000. Further work was abandoned. On March 6, 1843, the Great Western Railway Company was granted a preëmption right, and Darius B. Holbrook and his fellow members of the Cairo City & Canal Company of 1837, became identified with railroad history in the West. The work accomplished by the state on the Central railroad was to become the property of the new company at a stated price; but the company was bound to pay into the state treasury one-fourth of the total net income, after twelve per cent. per annum had been distributed among the stockholders. In December, 1843, this company, through Congressman Breese, petitioned congress for the right of preëmption to a portion of the public lands; but Douglas opposed the petition, and in 1844 introduced a bill providing that the lands should be preëmpted to the state. It won little attention. Similar bills introduced in January and December, 1846, by Judge Breese, failed to obtain the approval of congress, and the question of building a railroad was exactly where Holbrook & Co. found it. The Great Western Railroad Company lost their charter March 3, 1845, and for a time the contest between Chicago, represented by Douglas, and Dubuque, represented by Breese, was closed. From February, 1842, to February, 1847, the cross roads proved a losing venture, and in 1847 this $1,000,000 deal realized $21,000 in state indebtedness. The Great Western Railroad Company was revivified in 1848, and the legislature returned its charter April 13, 1849, and it may be said donated all the railroad work performed by the state in 1837, as well as right of way from Cairo to Chicago. The governor was appoined trustee *in futuro* to hold such lands as congress might donate to aid the construction of a central railroad, and altogether the Great Western Railroad Company appeared to be singularly well endowed with the friendship of the commonwealth. The return for the charter was foreshadowed by the technical defeat of Douglas' direct bills for aid to the Central railroad of 1848-9 by congressional action. On February 1, 1849, when Judge Breese introduced a general land grant bill providing for the parceling out to the several states slices of the public domain, it was purely in the interest of this road, though general in character. The senate approved the measure, but the house rejected it, thus leaving the field open to Douglas and Shields.

The senate, and, indeed, the house of representatives, saw at once the sincerity of the Little Giant and of the hero of the Mexican war, and received their direct land-grant bill of January, 1850, with favor. The promise made by the senators that the grant would not be used in the interest of speculators, as members of the Great Western railroad company, alias Holbrook & Co., were known to be, won support for this measure, and further, Alabama and Mississippi derived benefit, as the act of September 17, 1850, approved September 20, provided for the grant of lands in the states named, as well as in Illinois, as aid in the construction of a great central railroad from La Salle, Ill., to the Ohio river at Cairo (with branches to Dubuque, via Galena, and to Chicago), and thence to Mobile, Ala. Senator George W. Imes, of Iowa, urged the Dubuque clause; Thomas Childs, Jr., of New York, the Mobile clause, while Douglas and Shields watched Chicago's interests so closely that a great ovation was given to them on their return. On this occasion, each gave testimony to the work of John S. Wright in pointing out forcibly the advantages of such a grant and to the action of the congressmen from Illinois in their able support of the bill.

The action of congress did not pass unnoticed by the moneyed men of New York. No sooner was the act approved than they considered its relation to themselves, and on December 28, 1850, signed a memorial to the legislature of Illinois, showing forth their plans for constructing the Central road and its branches. This memorial was signed by Robert Schuyler, George Griswold, Governor Morris, Franklin Haven, David A. Neal, Robert Rantoul, Jr., Jona Sturges, Thomas W. Ludlow and John F. A. Sanford. The much-talked-of plan to give all control to the state and make the stock a basis for banking, as United States bonds are now in the system of national banks, opposed the plans of the Eastern men, but the people had little faith in the business qualities of this political machine, and on February 10, 1851, James L. D. Morrison's substitute for Asahel Gridley's bill, incorporating the Illinois Central railroad company, was passed. The names of the corporators were those given above as signers of the memorial, with Joseph W. Alsop, LeRoy M. Wiley and William H. Aspinwall, all of whom are gone to the dreamland of railroad builders, with the exception of Franklin Haven. On March 19, 1851, the special charter was accepted by the company, and in the shadow of former failures, work was commenced. Roswell B. Mason, of Bridgeport, Conn., was appointed chief engineer, March 22, and before May 20, he and staff were at Chicago, ready to enter upon surveying the route. In September, 1851, a mortgage for $17,000,000, on two million acres of the lands granted to secure the construction bonds, was executed. James F. Joy and Mason Brayman were employed to secure right of way in Chicago, and had their work countenanced by the ordinance of June 14, 1852, signed by Walter Smith Gurnee, mayor. John B. Calhoun, who named the original stations along the road, was accountant and financier. David A. Neal purchased eighty thousand tons of iron rails in England (at from $38.50 to $43.50 per ton, on board ship at Liverpool), and had them delivered in Chicago early in 1852, through Clark & Jessup, and on May 20 of that year the fourteen miles of track from Thirteenth street to Calumet station, now Kensington, were completed, and Michigan Central trains ran into the city on that day. Indeed, the Michigan Central railroad company made a loan to the Illinois Central to further the construction of this portion of the road. In February, 1852, charts of the road were placed before the commissioner of the land office at Washington, D. C., and in March that official approved the selection of about two million acres of the public lands. The last construction contract was entered into October 13, 1852, and one year after the Michigan Central trains steamed into Chicago over the Illinois Central tracks, sixty-one miles of the road between Bloomington and La Salle were in operation, and a temporary bridge erected over the Illinois river. In July, 1854, the road between Chicago and Urbana (one hundred and twenty-eight miles) was opened for traffic; early in November, 1854, trains were running between Freeport and Galena, and later that month passengers for the South were brought to Cairo via the Chicago & Mississippi railroad to St. Louis, the Ohio & Mississippi to Sandoval, and thence one hundred and eighteen miles on the completed southern end of the Illinois Central to Cairo, William K. Ackerman, president of the company from 1877 to 1883, being one of the through passengers. The main line, La Salle to Cairo, three hundred and one miles, was not completed until January 8, 1855; the track from Galena to Dunleith was completed June 11, 1855, and from La Salle to Dunleith, on June 12; the Chicago branch, 249.78 miles, was completed September 26, 1856, and on September 27, that year, Engineer Mason reported that the last rail on the 705.6 miles of road was placed, after a total expenditure of $35,110,-609.21, or over $18,000,000 above the estimate cost, and over the amount of the original capital stock. From September, 1856, to the beginning of the Civil war, little beyond routine work was accomplished. The Peoria & Oquaka railroad was built from Gilman to El Paso in 1857, connecting the main line with the Chicago branch. During the Civil war, the road, in all its departments, was taxed to its greatest capacity. Many of its employes entered the army, thus reducing the number of experienced railroad men; the department of war required it to carry troops and military supplies gratuitously; refugee negroes and deserters looked upon it as an eleemosynary institution, constructed solely to haul them away from danger, while war prices exercised no small influence on the company's treasury, for they balanced, if they did not overbalance, the extraordinary earnings of those terrible years of war. The views of Congressmen E. B. Washburne and others led to the observance of the charter, but congress, recognizing the services of this railroad, decided that the roadbed, and not the equipped railway, was only subject to use by the United States, and appropriated a sum equal to the value of the train service rendered.

In the fall of 1867 the Central company leased the Dubuque & Sioux City railroad and began the construction of the Dunleith-Dubuque bridge, which was completed January 1, 1869, and the transfer ferry cast aside. Later, in 1869, the Cedar Falls & Minnesota railroad (fifty-four miles in length) and the Iowa Falls & Sioux City railroad (forty-nine miles in length) were begun. They were completed in 1870, thus making the Iowa system four hundred and two miles. During the last-named year the Belleville & Southern Illinois railroad came into use as a connecting line between Cairo and St. Louis, and in 1871 the Gilman, Clinton & Springfield railroad was constructed, connecting the Chicago branch with Springfield, December 3, that year. On November 17, 1874, the trains of the Baltimore & Ohio railroad company first entered the city over the tracks of the Central, and continued to use such tracks until 1891, notwithstanding the notice of 1884 and the order of the court, requiring that company to evacuate.

The lake front act of 1869 was conceived in 1866 in the interest of local speculators, known as the Chicago Harbor & Improvement company. This improvement company did not succeed in obtaining legislative sanction for their designs. A similar measure was introduced in 1869 and passed, but was vetoed by the governor, John M. Palmer, April 14, 1869. Two days after the legislature passed the bill over the veto.

This act of 1869 turned over to the Illinois Central, the Chicago, Burlington & Quincy and the Michigan Central (which used then the same depot) the three blocks of land between Randolph and Monroe streets, they to pay therefor $800,000 to the city. With the two northern blocks the state had nothing whatever to do, they having been given to the city direct by the general government for park purposes. The block between Monroe and Madison the city held under a different title. The land had passed from the general government to the canal commissioners, and had been dedicated by them to public uses. The railroad tendered $200,000 as first installment, but the city refused acceptance, and hence litigation. On July 3, 1871, the United States proceeded to stop the company from encroaching upon the lake, and on April 15, 1873, the peculiar act of repeal, abolishing the privileges given by the legislature in the act of 1869, was passed. Litigation of course resulted and the decision of United States Circuit Judges Harlan and Blodgett, given February 23, 1888, is awaiting final approval or disapproval by the United States supreme court.

The year 1871 was an uneasy one for Illinois railroads, but more particularly for those entering Chicago, where the great fire destroyed buildings, rolling stock, grain and merchandise, as if they were so many tinder boxes. The direct loss was $300,000: but the insurance being carried by a trans-Atlantic company, who paid all policies, this loss was reduced to a nominal sum, leaving the heavy indirect losses only to be considered. The fire, after all, was only the echo of the earthquake. The granger legislature of that year enacted laws which, if left on the statute books, would have before this wiped out great enterprises in Illinois and left railroads, like some of the churches, to be operated according to one thousand different notions. The supreme court declared the foolish law unconstitutional, but mobs continued to interfere materially with the management and property of the road, causing heavy losses.

Prior to 1878 the rude primitive sleeping cars built by the company were in use. That year the contract with the Pullman palace car company was perfected. On May 26, 1880, the beginning of the town of Pullman was made, and later that year the Central company saw that the time had come to establish a thorough suburban service different in toto from that which obtained from 1856 to 1880. In 1882 two tracks for freight trains, two tracks for passenger trains, and two tracks for suburban trains were built from the Chicago yards south to the ruins of 1871, known as the Central depot, and in 1883 the South Chicago railroad, from a point near Seventieth street east to Yates avenue, and thence to South Chicago, was completed. The ordinance approving plans for a bridge over the main river, to be built by the company, was passed December 1, 1862, but not until 1879 was the bridge constructed. The St. Charles air line railroad bridge over the south branch meeting the requirements of the company up to that time. In 1880 the Kankakee & Southwestern railroad was extended to the northern division at Minonk, and the independent connection with the Chicago branch created. The erection of the six-hundred-thousand-bushel elevator at Cairo, the Randolph street viaduct, two docks, and the extension of terminal facilities must be credited to 1882, while the building of the South Chicago branch dates to 1883.

From 1866 to 1872 communication between the Northwestern and Southern states was mainly confined to the Mississippi. In the last mentioned year this company desired to establish a thorough line which, in a measure, would meet the spirit of the act of congress by bringing New Orleans, rather than Mobile, into direct communication with Chicago. A contract was made with the owners of the roads grouped under the title, the Mississippi Central railroad, the length of which system was two hundred and thirty-two miles, and the New Orleans, Jackson & Great Northern railroad, two hundred and six miles in length. Both systems were then under one management, and the owners not only agreed to an interchange of traffic with the Illinois Central, but also for the extension of the first named road one hundred and eight miles north from Jackson, Tenn., to a point opposite Cairo, Ill. The contract provided that the Illinois Central railroad company should invest one-eighth of the earnings from traffic to and from the roads named in their consolidated mortgage bonds for a decade at the rate of $100,000 per annum, but later an opportunity to purchase $200,000 of such bonds annually to the amount of $6,000,000, was given so as to enable the Southern men to build the one hundred and eight miles and improve the road generally. The gap was completed December 24, 1873, and Chicago and New Orleans, nine hundred and thirteen miles apart, were connected by iron rails. Later the Illinois Central company exchanged $5,000,000 worth of its five per cent. bonds for $5,000,000 worth of the seven per cent. bonds of the Southern roads and agreed to purchase the road under stated conditions, even in the face of a debt amounting to $18,372,834. On March 10, 1876, the Southern companies failing even to pay interest, the property was sold under foreclosure, passed into the receiver's hands, and on January 1, 1878, became an integral part of the Illinois Central under the title Chicago, St. Louis & New Orleans railroad company. On January 1, 1882, the Southern lines — five hundred and forty-eight miles of main track, thirty-one miles of branches, one hundred and six locomotives, two thousand two hundred and forty-one cars, $1,000,000 five per cent., one thousand nine hundred and fifty-one bonds, $125,000 six per cent. bonds, and $623,043.70 in cash were surrendered to the Illinois Central company.

The methodical system of James C. Clark, thoroughly inculcated in the minds of employes, also fell into the hands of the new proprietors and the bright day dreams of the railroad promoters of 1835–51 were fulfilled. During the seven years ending December 31, 1890, this great central trunk line made progress undreamed of before. The Canton, Aberdeen & Nashville railroad was begun in 1883; a controlling interest in the one hundred miles of road from Grenada to Memphis was secured; the Ohio river bridge at Cairo was constructed, and the old ferry transfer abolished; the South Chicago branch 4.76 miles in length, with double track, was built and equipped for heavy suburban and freight service; the middle division was extended to the main line near Bloomington, giving a total length of 131.26 miles. In 1886 the work of constructing the Chicago, Madison & Northern railroad was entered upon, and in August, 1888, this road was opened from Chicago to Freeport, Madison and Dodgeville, while in 1890 the right of way through Chicago was acquired. In 1887 the Chicago, Havana & Western railroad (one hundred and thirty miles in length) was purchased from the sheriff, and the Rantoul narrow gauge, connecting West Lebanon, Ind., with Leroy, Ill. (seventy-six miles in length), was acquired similarly. The gauge of the latter road was changed subsequently. In 1885 the Chicago, Burlington & Northern railroad sought right of way between East Dubuque and Portage Curve, and had thirteen miles of the Illinois Central company's right of way condemned. The supreme court decided the condemnation proceedings illegal, and the new road was purchased by the Illinois Central company, who lease it to the original builders. In 1888 the stock of the Dunleith & Dubuque bridge company was purchased by the Central company, who use it jointly with the Chicago, Burlington & Northern railroad and the Chicago, St. Paul & Kansas City railroad. The Cherokee & Dakota railroad (one hundred and fifty-three miles in length) extending from Cherokee, Iowa, to Sioux Falls, Dak., and from Cherokee to Onawa, was built, and also a road from Manchester to Cedar Rapids, Iowa. The securities of the Dubuque & Sioux City railroad company (one hundred and forty-three miles in length) and of the Iowa Falls & Sioux City railroad company (one hundred and eighty-three miles in length) were purchased, and those roads became practically the property of the company. Two grain elevators were erected, and pretentious depot buildings constructed, as at Jackson and Holly Springs, Miss., and other important points on the road.

In October, 1850, the company paid $45,000 under protest to the United States for the grant of the unused portion of the Fort Dearborn reservation. As has been stated the first depot was at Thirteenth street, and the first train to enter the city was one of the Michigan Central company's. This depot was used from May 20, 1852, to July, 1853. On June 14, 1852, the city council granted permission to lay down tracks within the limits along the margin of the lake, in accordance with the legislative act of February, 1852, authorizing a branch road from Twelfth street north to the south pier of the inner harbor, and this permission was accepted March 28, 1853. Lands for depot purposes were acquired north of Randolph street, from the United States, as shown above, or by purchase from private owners and, south of Twelfth street, by purchase. From Sixteenth street to Randolph street piles were driven in the lake bed and the track constructed thereon between 1852 and 1854. After the fire of 1871 individuals as well as the company made this piling the breastwork of a dumping ground for debris, and since that time a large area from a point northeast of Randolph street southward, has been filled in in like manner. The congressional grant to Illinois was two million five hundred and ninety-five thousand acres, and of the grant by the state to the railroad company, one hundred and seven thousand six hundred and fourteen acres were first conveyed to preëmptors. By the close of 1856 over one million acres were sold, and up to January 1, 1890, there were two million four hundred and fifty-six thousand eight hundred and twenty-nine acres sold, yielding a total of $28,742,002 or about three-fourths of the total cost of the road up to that time, $35,110,609. From 1856 to October 31, 1889, the company paid into the state treasury $11,873,337.14, being the amount of the statutory seven per cent. on the gross income, or about $350,000 per year. The road withstood the Schuyler frauds of 1853-4, the panic of 1857, the panic of 1873, the granger laws of 1871, the fire of 1871, the Iowa restrictions of 1876, the Valentine scrip of 1878, the great strike, and the latter day attacks on its Chicago right of way. Its progress in modern times is phenomenal, when its conservative policy is compared with the extension of the system and the introduction of improvements in permanent way, rolling stock and running schedules. Only on October 29, 1889, the great bridge over the Ohio was opened, giving an all-rail route between the Gulf of Mexico and Chicago. This bridge is three miles and four thousand seven hundred and twenty feet in length, and was constructed at the cost of $2,700,000. The approaches, completed in 1891, included the elevation of the tracks above flood level and entailed an extraordinary cost. By July 1, 1890, the system embraced 1,398.48 miles of Northern lines; 593.34 miles of Western lines, and 896.65 of Southern lines, or a total of 2,888.47 miles.

The presidents of the road were Robert Schuyler (deceased), March 19, 1851 to July 11, 1853; William P. Burrall (deceased), 1853-4; John N. A. Griswold, January, 1855 to December, 1855; William H. Osborn, December 1, 1855 to July 11, 1865; John M. Douglas, 1865 to March 14, 1871; John Newell, April 14, 1871 to September 11, 1874; Wilson G. Hunt, September, 1874 to January 28, 1875; John M. Douglas, January, 1875 to July 17, 1876; William K. Ackerman, October 17, 1877 to August 15, 1883, and James C. Clark, August 15, 1883 to May 18, 1887. Stuyvesant Fish elected May 18, 1887, is now president.

The names of the pioneers of this now immense system are given in former pages. The directors elected February 10, 1851, all of whom except Franklin Haven, are deceased, were men prominent in building up the country in its infancy as they were in building railroads.

In 1851 Morris Ketchum (deceased) was elected a director; in 1852, Gov. Joel A. Matteson (deceased); in 1853, William P. Burrall (deceased); in 1854, J. Newton Perkins (deceased); William H. Osborn, Frederick C. Gebhard (deceased), J. N. A. Griswold and James F. Joy; in 1855, Thomas E. Walker (deceased), and Ebenezer Lane; in 1856, Gov.

William H. Bissell (deceased), and Abram S. Hewitt; in 1857, Pierre Choteau, Jr. (deceased), and Gustavus W. Smith; in 1859, William Tracy (deceased); in 1860, Gov. Richard Yates (deceased), and Nathaniel P. Banks; in 1861, John M. Douglas; in 1862, James C. Fargo, William R. Arthur, H. H. Hunnewell, and Edwin H. Sheldon; in 1863, James Caird and Cunningham Bothwick; in 1864 Gov. Richard Oglesby, Henry Chauncey and William G. Hunt; in 1865, Ambrose E. Burnside (deceased), and R. D. Wolterbeck; in 1868, Gov. J. M. Palmer, and George Bliss; in 1871, J. Pierrepont Morgan, Louis A. Von Hoffman, John Newell, Lucius Tilton (deceased), and William H. Gebhard; in 1872, William K. Ackerman; in 1873, Gov. John L. Beveridge, and L. V. F. Randoph; in 1875, Abram R. Van Nest (deceased), Frederick Sturges, and Constantine Menelas; in 1876 Gov. Shelby M. Cullom; in 1877, A. G. Dulman, Stuyvesant Fish, Ben. F. Ayer, James C. Clarke and John Elliott (deceased); in 1879, W. Bayard Cutting; in 1882, Sydney Webster; in 1883, Gov. John M. Hamilton; in 1884, Gov. R. J. Oglesby (second term), Walter Luttgen, Robert Goelet and S. Van R. Cruger; in 1885, William W. Astor; in 1886, Oliver Harriman and Levi P. Morton; in 1888, John W. Auchincloss; in 1889, Gov. Joseph W. Fifer, J. C. Welling, Charles M. Da Costa (deceased), and George Bliss, and in 1890, J. W. Doane and Norman B. Ream.

A biography of the directors of this great corporation would bring to light many points in its history and present to the reader subjects both interesting and instructive. A sketch of each of the presidents from 1851 to 1891 would in itself make a volume worthy of study, for in it would be found an exposition of all those executive principles which lead to failure or success. Fortunately for the Illinois Central, the men who held this responsible position were, with one exception, true and capable. To the present incumbent of the office success is credited in everything, and nothing succeeds like success.

The road lines in this state are the main line, the Kosciusko branch, the Memphis division, the Canton, Aberdeen & Nashville (Kosciusko to Aberdeen), the Yazoo & Mississippi valley, and Jackson to Parsons. Its passenger earnings for this state in 1889 were $596,561.65; its freight earnings $2,674,581.84, and its taxes for nine months of that year were $106,425.

The Louisville, New Orleans & Texas railroad is the great outlet of the Yazoo delta, running parallel to the great river. It was completed January 1, 1885, and of course has a brief career, although it is the second line in the state. Its branches are: The Glendale & Eagle Nest, the Leland & Huntington, the Wilzcinski & Glen Allen, the Lamont & Rosedale and the Slaughter & Woodville. The general offices are at Memphis, and the officers are as follows: President, R. T. Wilson; general manager, James M. Edwards; secretary, C. H. Bosher; treasurer, F. H. Davis; comptroller, William Mahl; assistant general manager, A. M. Cooke; general superintendent, T. J. Nicholl; general freight and passenger agent, E. W. How; auditor, J. T. Penton, and general counsel, Yerger & Percy. Its passenger earnings for 1889 were $721,085.53; freight earnings, $1,686,746.02, and taxes paid, $64,684.12.

The Mobile & Ohio railroad was completed April 22, 1861, and although a comparatively old road the facts of its career seem unobtainable. Its branches from the main line along the eastern border of the state are the Aberdeen & Muldon, Artesia & Columbus and Artesia & Starkville. Its passenger earnings in 1889—in every case for Mississippi—were $185,317; its freight earnings, $883,069.57, and its taxes, $47,054.29.

The Georgia Pacific railroad is another late arrival, and was completed only July 8, 1889. Its branches are: Stoneville to Sharkey, and less than a mile at Columbus. Its passenger earnings for the year chosen were: $37,619.56; freight, $72,456.41, and taxes are exempt, except as to levees.

The New Orleans & Northeastern railroad was chartered March 16, 1870, Adam Thompson being the first president and G. Ingram being the first chief engineer of the company. Surveys were made, but the project lay dormant for some time. In 1881 surveys began for actual construction under John Scott, president, and W. H. Hardy, of Meridian, vice president. Construction began at the close of 1881, and the road was completed through from Meridian to New Orleans in 1883. It was opened for traffic from Meridian to Pachuta, 26.64 miles, October 25, 1882, and to New Orleans November 1, 1883. The road is 195.9 miles long, of which one hundred and fifty-one thousand five hundred and ninety-five miles are in Mississippi. The total cost was $5,612,278.24. Its earnings in 1889 were: freight, $631,774.35; passenger, $157,399.47, and taxes, $16,366.34 for 1888.

The Alabama & Vicksburg railway, from Meridian to Vicksburg, was originally built to five-foot gauge, and changed in May, 1886. Deeds for right of way, in possession of the Alabama & Vicksburg Railway Company, date back to the year 1835, and were made to the Commercial & Railroad bank of Vicksburg and to the Southern Railroad Company. The road was first built from Vicksburg to Jackson, and building of the road from Brandon to Meridian commenced in January, 1857, and was completed June 3, 1861, when the first train ran over the entire road from Vicksburg to Meridian. At this time the road was owned by the Southern Railroad Company.

M. Emanuel, president, in his annual report to the board of directors dated March 1, 1865, wrote as follows regarding the vicissitudes of the track and road bed during the war: "The first direct injury done to the road by the Federal army occurred at Newton station on April 24, 1863. Grierson's raid took it by surprise. The depot building, containing the books and papers of that office and some freight, was soon in flames. A half mile of track was torn up near the station, and ten trestles destroyed. It took nine days to repair the road. The second time the road was damaged by the enemy was in May, 1863, during the time that Grant's army occupied Jackson, previous to his march on, and investment of, Vicksburg. They then burned the Pearl river bridge and trestles, and partially destroyed the road for three miles west of Pearl river, and on their march to Vicksburg destroyed about seven miles of track between Jackson and Big Black river, including the bridge over that river and the long trestle connected with it; also Baker's Creek bridge and a number of other small ones. In July, 1863, a large army from Vicksburg, in pursuit of Gen. Joseph E. Johnston, to Jackson and thence to Brandon, again tore up the track and destroyed the bridges and trestles to such an extent, between Jackson and Brandon, and they could not run from Meridian farther west than Brandon before January 6, 1864. The last damaging blow that the road received from the enemy was in February, 1864, when General Sherman marched his army from Vicksburg to Meridian on a parallel line with the railroad, and near enough to it for the cavalry to make sudden dashes at any station on the road that he wished to destroy. The station houses at Brandon, Morton, Lake, Newton and Meridian were burned. The machine shops and other company buildings were destroyed at Lake station, forty miles west of Meridian. The enemy reached Meridian on Sunday, the 14th of February, and remained there seven days, in the meantime doing a vast amount of damage to the several roads terminating and passing there. Seven miles of track of the Southern railroad was as effectually destroyed as ingenuity and labor could do it; seven thousand feet of bridges and trestles were also destroyed, including two Chunky bridges, Tallahatta, Okatibba, and several smaller ones; also eighty-three trestles along the line of the road. The work of repair was commenced on March 29, and prosecuted with skill and energy. The repairs were completed by May 7, 1864, when the trains resumed their regular business between Meridian and Jackson." In

1867 the name of the company was changed to the Vicksburg & Meridian railroad company. The road was sold under foreclosure February 4, 1889, and a new company organized March 18, 1889, under the name of the Alabama & Vicksburg railway company. Its freight earnings in 1889 for four and a half months were $112,989.66; its passenger earnings, $76,817, and its estimated taxes about $19,000.

The Kansas City, Memphis & Birmingham Railroad Company was formed February 1, 1887, by the consolidation, in accordance with the laws of Tennessee, Mississippi and Alabama, of the Memphis & Birmingham Railroad Company, a corporation duly organized under the general laws of Alabama, with the Kansas City, Memphis & Birmingham Railroad Company, a corporation existing under the laws of Tennessee and Mississippi, and which had been formed July 26, 1886, by the consolidation, in accordance with the laws of said last two states, of the Memphis & Southeastern Railroad Company, a corporation organized under the general laws of Tennessee, with the Kansas City, Memphis & Birmingham Railroad Company, a corporation existing under an act of the legislature of Mississippi entitled "An act to incorporate the Kansas City, Memphis & Birmingham Railroad Company," approved February 18, 1886. The original corporation was chartered by an act of the legislature, approved November 23, 1859, as the Holly Springs & Mobile Railroad Company. By an act approved February 20, 1867, the name was changed to Memphis, Holly Springs, Okolona & Selma Railroad Company. By an act approved July 21, 1870, the name was again changed to the Selma, Marion & Memphis Railroad Company. In 1874 the company was reorganized as the Memphis, Holly Springs & Selma Railroad Company. In 1881 the name was again changed to Memphis, Selma & Brunswick Railroad Company. The name was again changed to the Memphis, Birmingham & Atlantic Railroad Company, and the same confirmed by an act approved January 22, 1886.

The Kansas City, Memphis & Birmingham Railroad Company of Mississippi and Tennessee, above referred to, absorbed the Memphis, Birmingham & Atlantic by purchase in September, 1886.

The main line was completed to Birmingham and opened for business on October 17, 1887; the branch to Aberdeen, Miss., January 1, 1888, and the branch to Bessemer, Ala., March 15, 1888. Its earnings for 1889 were: Freight, 51.6 per cent. of total, $719,593.15; passenger, 51.6 per cent. of total, $246,244.46, and taxes between January and September, 1889, $258.96.

The New Orleans, Mobile & Chattanooga Railroad Company, now the New Orleans, Mobile & Texas, leased by the Louisville & Nashville, was originally chartered in Alabama, in November, 1866; and on the 7th of November, 1867, an act was passed and approved by the state of Mississippi, recognizing the charter, as granted by the state of Alabama, and giving the road the same powers, privileges and franchises in the state of Mississippi. Under this charter the railroad between New Orleans and Mobile was completed, and has tended to build up numerous towns and villages on the lake coast, within the state of Mississippi. Such places as Scranton, Ocean Springs, Biloxi, Pass Christian and many other villages have been rapidly settled up and made accessible to New Orleans on the one side and to Mobile on the other, and through them both to all the world. This railroad, now known as the Louisville & Nashville railroad, runs five or six passenger trains daily through all of these towns on the Mississippi coast, is rapidly developing new industries in these towns, and large numbers of people from the North and West are making their homes there during the winter, finding a delightful and healthy climate. Much of the winter travel and sojourning which accrued to Florida is passing to this lake and gulf coast, which presents many superior advantages to anything to be found in Florida or other localities. The soil is remarkably productive when properly cared for; the roads are good, the air exhilarating and healthful. New Orleans is reached from these towns and villages in from one to three hours, according to the distance. The time made on the trains from New Orleans to Mobile is about four hours, a distance of one hundred and forty miles. The railroad company and the inhabitants on the lake shore are in accord in their desire to develop new industries along the line and to invite immigration.

Milton H. Smith, Esq., is now president of the Louisville & Nashville railroad company. Its passenger earnings in this state were, $212,504.69; freight earnings, $251,964.59; and taxes in 1887 were $9,619.07.

The Gulf & Chicago railroad is a consolidation of August 1, 1889, of this road with the Ripley, Ship Island & Kentucky and the northern division of the Gulf & Ship Island, with a lease covering the rest of the last mentioned road. Its earnings for 1889 were, freight, $17,748.90; passenger, $13,668.42; and taxes in 1888, $611.45.

The Memphis & Charleston railroad, although so small in mileage in this state, had passenger earnings in 1889 of $59,836.62; freight, $103,917.29; and taxes of $4,271.

The Alabama Great Southern railroad extends from Chattanooga, Tenn., through Alabama to Meridian, Miss., a distance of two hundred and ninety-five miles, only 18.781 of which are in Mississippi. The portion in Mississippi was built by the Northeast & Southwest Alabama railroad company, which was incorporated by the legislature of Alabama, December 12, 1853. The Alabama & Chattanooga railroad company acquired the ownership of the Northeast & Southwest Alabama railroad company December 19, 1868, and on February 11, 1870, the state of Alabama loaned its credit to the Alabama & Chattanooga railroad company for the purpose of expediting the construction of its railroad, "provided that the entire line between Meridian and Chattanooga be completed by March 1, 1871." In 1877, the Alabama Great Southern railroad company acquired the ownership of the Alabama & Chattanooga railroad. Its passenger earnings were, in 1889, $33,534; freight, $79,188.00; and taxes estimated at $2,587.62.

The Natchez, Jackson & Columbus, a narrow gauge road, was completed October 6, 1882, with 98.6 miles. Its passenger and freight earnings were respectively, $62,405, and $116,249. This is known as the "Little J."

The East Tennessee, Virginia & Georgia railway, with only 7.73 miles in this state, used the Mobile & Ohio tracks from Lauderdale to Meridian. This state's proportion of the earnings were, passenger, $10,163; and freight, $34,021; and its taxes in 1888 were $1,019.50.

The people of Mississippi have generally been friendly to these railways, but the last decade had not progressed far when it seemed wisest for the state to exercise some regulative powers over them. Accordingly, on March 11, 1884, an act was passed providing means for this in a body called the board of railroad commissioners. After its organization the apprehensions of the great railways were aroused, and all but seven, of the smaller ones chiefly, enjoined them against further proceedings, and the cases were carried up to the state courts, the "Little J" even taking it into the Federal courts, but all received decisions favorable to the commission, and the work of this body has since been carried on with the best success, securing a common regulation of all the railway transportation of the state, and with no diminution in the increase of railway building certainly.

CHAPTER VI.

GROWTH AND DEVELOPMENT.

BEFORE considering the growth of any one of the states not included in the old thirteen originals stretched along the Atlantic from New Hampshire to Georgia inclusive, one should recall that the other thirty-one are the creatures of the old thirteen in a measure, and get a clear idea of their relative periods of creation in order to fully appreciate the rapidity and magnitude of the growth of some of them. Mississippi may be called one of the old states, when we consider that in the century since "Little Rhody," the last of the thirteen*, ratified the constitution, and during which the thirty-one have been admitted, about half were created in the first half or before 1840; but Mississippi is one of the oldest states—while not the oldest of the valley sisters, like Kentucky, she follows not many years later. Vermont, the first admitted, was a mere creation of convenience; Kentucky, the second, in 1792, was the first real creation. In the next twenty-five years came at due intervals Tennessee, Ohio, Louisiana, Indiana, and, a year later than the Hoosier state, the Bayou state of Mississippi. In these words are easily seen the advancing footprints of the giant valley, and Mississippi was the sixth, not counting Vermont. Now she is almost exactly three quarters of a century old—older than the great states of Illinois, Alabama, Maine, Missouri, Arkansas, Michigan—all born in the first half of our national career. As to the later states, she is nearly thirty years older than Iowa, and a half century older than Nebraska. She has witnessed the birth of twenty-four younger sisters of Uncle Sam's numerous progeny.

In her relative progress in population, ever since her most unfavorable period began, namely, 1850, and with the disadvantage over the later trans-Mississippi states of few railways until the present decade, she has more than kept her midway place, as these figures illustrate. In 1850, when there were thirty-three states, Mississippi was fifteenth in population; in 1860, with thirty-six states, she was fourteenth; in 1870, with thirty-seven states, she was eighteenth; in 1880, with thirty-eight states, eighteenth; and in 1890, when the number sprang to forty-four, she was still on the larger side of the dividing line, and, as twenty-first in population, still counted among the larger states of the Union, there being twenty-three states with less and only twenty states with a greater population.

Before noticing the state's actual growth in figures, it may aid in realizing its greatness in size and population to compare it with some foreign countries. With an area of forty-six thousand eight hundred and ten square miles, Mississippi is about the size of Roumania; almost exactly the size of Guatemala; a little larger than Honduras; slightly

---
*1790.

smaller than Nicaragua, and some larger than Orange Free state. From these it varies comparatively little in area, while it is considerably over four times the size of Belgium; over three times the size of Switzerland; nearly four times the size of Denmark; nearly as large again as Bulgaria or Greece, and four and a half times the area of Hayti. But while Mississippi is about the size of Roumania, she has only about a fourth the population of her European sister; while almost exactly the size of Guatemala, considerably less; but as to Honduras and Nicaragua, which she approaches in area, the Bayou state is over four times their population, and Orange is so much less that it is not worth consideration. Its contrast with the other European states is more striking. Four times the area of Belgium, that country has nearly five times as many people; an area three times that of the Swiss republic, yet with less than half the inhabitance of the Alpine state; four times Denmark's area, but about three-fifths her population; nearly as large again as Bulgaria or Greece, but only about two-fifths and three-fifths their respective populations. Mississippi's counterparts in number of inhabitants approach most nearly to Ecuador, Tripoli and Wurtemberg; but in relative area and population no country so nearly reaches her size in both these features as the five-year-old republic of Guatemala. It should be remembered, however, that the comparison extends no farther, as the simple fact of the 1884 railway mileage— twenty-six miles in Guatemala to one thousand eight hundred and forty-four miles in the Bayou state—will testify; while in other respects it might not be unlike a comparison of our times of popular education with those of 1215, when, of the twenty-six English barons who signed the great Magna Charta, only three could write their names instead of making their marks. Numbers and area have most significance only when associated with the precious elements of our civilization, and Mississippi, among our United States, is twenty-eighth in area and twenty-first in population, a population but very little larger than that of the great metropolis of this valley, Chicago, a name, by a curious coincidence, that this state came near to bearing as its own, for Vega's account of De Soto's discovery of it says the name of the great river was "Chucagua," and it was so called by many early European geographers.

Mississippi's population is now one million two hundred and eighty-nine thousand six hundred souls, distributed between the races, giving the larger number, seven hundred forty-seven thousand seven hundred and twenty to the negroes, a less number, five hundred and thirty-nine thousand seven hundred and three to the whites, and a comparatively insignificant number, two thousand one hundred and seventy-seven to the Chinese, Japanese and Indians.

The white population entered, in the handful of men at Biloxi, in 1699. Some took Indian women as wives, but in 1720, says a local writer, "thirty girls from the Saltpetriere in Paris, arrived in the colony. The priests complain of the prospensity of the colonists, and especially the Canadians, for Indian wives. The dusky maidens of Mississippi, with their flashing eyes, and their voluptuous forms, and their delicate hands and feet, and their merry laugh, and their raven hair that brushed the dewdrops as they walked, modest, chaste, drooping their glances at the approach of a warrior, were preferred to the pale-faced conventional women of Paris, and the simple-minded fathers were astonished." But this all changed, and only twenty years later, 1740, says a writer in De Bow's *Review**, "The population of the French colony received a fresh accession in a large number of poor, but virtuous girls, transported from France at the royal expense, and endowed by royal bounty with a small tract of land, a cow and calf, a cock and five hens, a

---
*De Bow's Review, 1851, New Orleans.

gun and ammunition, an ax and hoe, and a supply of garden seeds. Each of these girls, with her dower, was given by Vaudreuil in marriage to some one of the soldiers, who received an honorable discharge. This importation continued annually until the year 1751, and from this source have sprung many worthy families in Louisiana, and, doubtless, in Mississippi, too." So came the first white male and female population.

The first cargo of negro slaves arrived in 1720 and a council ordinance declared a good adult negro should be rated at $176, to be paid for in three annual payments of tobacco and rice.

The census of 1721, when a considerable part of the colony was in Mississippi, gave five thousand four hundred and twenty whites and six hundred slaves. By 1785 the Natchez settlement alone contained over five thousand. Fifteen years later the present bounds of Mississippi began the present century with a population all told of seven thousand six hundred, scarcely more than the present city of Jackson contains. In 1810 it had sprung up to thirty-one thousand three hundred and six, more than quadrupled. Only two years later, 1812, it had reached forty thousand three hundred and fifty-two, of which twenty-three thousand two hundred and sixty-four were whites, owning seventeen thousand and eighty-eight slaves, and this population was all in Natchez and Washington, the two towns, and eleven counties of the Southwest, the rest being in the hands of Indians. In 1816, just before statehood, the total was forty-five thousand nine hundred and twenty-one, and four years more closed the decade with seventy-five thousand four hundred and forty-eight in 1820, more than doubling on the previous census. Of these, forty-two thousand one hundred and seventy-six were whites, four hundred and fifty-eight free blacks, and thirty-two thousand eight hundred and fourteen slaves, scattered over seventeen counties in the south and southwest, excepting Monroe county, and its largest city being Natchez, with two thousand one hundred and eighty-four inhabitants. Another decade passed with the usual doubling up of population, with most remarkable gains in slaves, so that it became a subject of great concern to public men, for heretofore the white majority had been considerable. The total population in 1830 was one hundred and thirty-six thousand six hundred and twenty-one souls.

The decade from 1830 to 1840 was marked by the opening up of Indian lands. The red race, even in 1721, had about thirty-six thousand in the state, but over a hundred years later, in this decade, the year 1834, there were resident in Mississippi twenty-three thousand four hundred Indians of the several nations. North Mississippi was an Indian wilderness, and its opening up was the signal for an influx that considerably more than doubled on the previous census, giving a grand total of three hundred and seventy-five thousand six hundred and fifty-one souls, of whom one hundred and ninety-two thousand two hundred and eleven were slaves, leaving of the whites and free blacks a minority of one hundred and eighty-three thousand four hundred and forty-one. Even the state census of 1837 gave a total of three hundred and eight thousand seven hundred and forty-four, with one hundred and sixty-four thousand three hundred and ninety-three slaves to one hundred and forty four thousand three hundred and fifty-one whites.

From 1840 to 1850 the increase was still great, but most marked in the Indian lands. A writer of 1849 says of that region: "Fifteen years ago it was an Indian wilderness, and now it has reached and passed, in its population, other portions of the state of ten times its age." The census of 1850 nearly doubles on the previous one, with six hundred and six thousand five hundred and twenty-six, of which the entire colored population was three hundred and ten thousand eight hundred and eight, including free blacks and mulattoes. These figures tell a wondrous story, and will always be kept in view by the careful student of this state's history. They are the indices of her great power and her greatest weakness, and the explanation of multitudes of her characteristic traits.

They developed in the next decade—1850-60, and the year 1860 beheld a population of seven hundred and ninety-one thousand three hundred and five, with a wealth of cotton, and four hundred and thirty-seven thousand four hundred and four, practically all slaves—a number almost equal to the entire present population of Honduras, Nicaragua, or Paraguay. No wonder the name planter took on a significance of prince!

The decade of the great tragedy seriously affected population. A powerful institution had turned over; slaves became citizens, and princely planters became poor. Soldiers were killed; the freedmen to the number of seventeen thousand eight hundred and sixty-nine became soldiers to fight their former masters, and also were thinned by death, while some left the country. Some from the invading army came in, it is true, but the population by census of 1866 showed a falling off to seven hundred and twenty-four thousand seven hundred and eighteen, there being still an excess of blacks—three hundred and eighty-one thousand two hundred and fifty-eight, and whites to the number of three hundred and forty-three thousand four hundred and sixty, showing a total loss of seventy-five thousand five hundred and eighty-five, or ten thousand four hundred and thirty-nine whites, and sixty-six thousand one hundred and forty-six blacks. After this the state advanced somewhat, so that the census of 1870 showed a population of eight hundred and twenty-seven thousand nine hundred and twenty-two, the colored part being four hundred and forty-four thousand two hundred and one, and the white three hundred and eighty-two thousand eight hundred and ninety-six, while eight hundred and twenty-five, a small showing of Mongolian and Indian races, appears, the great mass of the Indians, as mentioned elsewhere, having been removed in the thirties and forties. During this decade much of Mississippi had become a practical wilderness; the Yazoo delta, which had been partly reclaimed by levees during the previous decade, was again at the mercy of overflows, and only now began to be regained. The political troubles, and the prominence of the swamp delta region gave the state an unfortunate reputation, so that, for the first time in her history, an effort at distinctive advertising of her resources seemed necessary to attract immigration.

An act of April 6, 1874, provided for representation in the centennial exhibition, and a later act appropriated $5,000 for that purpose. A building was built of sixty-eight varieties of the state's timber, and among her exhibits were forms of cotton and woolen stuffs, corn, rice, broomcorn, syrup, tobacco, etc. On July 10, 1876, Gen. A. M. West, president of the board of managers, made an historical address on Mississippi, which gave the state an improved status. Said he: "With these vast fields of enterprise, and inspired by such important coming events, Mississippi can not be idle, but must, of necessity, join the march of enterprise and improvement, which, now, like the waves of the ocean, are moving in every direction, and pouring upon the globe a grand luminous array of the triumphs of mind over matter, as is so forcibly exemplified by this centennial exhibition; and by the rapidity with which the productions of human labor and skill are transported from farm to farm, from factory to factory, from city to city, from ocean to ocean, from county to county, exhibiting, to the amazement of the world, an activity in all the industrial pursuits of life commensurate with man's capabilities. It is a noteworthy fact that, although the late war left more than one-half the population of Mississippi homeless and penniless, and the remainder greatly impoverished, and all without credit, and frenzied by political conflicts and social disturbances, society was rapidly reorganized, domestic and social economy restored, and personal credit reëstablished. Their commercial obligations, in this and other cities, have been more promptly met the past season, than have been the obligations of the people of many of the other states. As these sudden and rapid changes affecting, as they did, society in all its varied, social, domestic and political relations, are unprecedented in the history of communities and nations, impartial judges must conclude that the resources of Mississippi are extraordinarily great, and historians must give to white and colored races credit for marvelous capacity for adaptation to circumstances, and for unparalleled recuperative powers." A considerable immigration came in up to 1880 from the northern part of the Mississippi valley, and by the close of the decade —1880—the population had arisen from eight hundred and twenty-seven thousand nine hundred and twenty-two, to the marked total of one million one hundred and thirty-one thousand five hundred and ninety-seven; both races had increased in numbers, but the colored the most, the total blacks being six hundred and fifty thousand two hundred and ninety-one, and the whites four hundred and seventy-nine thousand three hundred and ninety-eight, with the increased showing—one thousand nine hundred and eight—of third and fourth races. These figures tended still more to impress the conviction that still greater efforts should be made to stimulate immigration of Northern whites and north European people.

The decade from 1880 to 1890 witnessed strong efforts. Even Governor Alcorn had recommended efforts of this kind, and a bureau of immigration had been organized before the seventies began, and efforts were still continued during the seventies, but it remained for the reorganization of the eighties to effect the greatest results, under the commissionership of a most able manager, Maj. E. G. Wall, in the first half of the decade. These efforts were systematic and effective, aiming not only to attract agriculturists, but lumbermen, manufacturers, tradesmen, capitalists and all that make for development and internal growth, and the vigor with which it was prosecuted receives abundant testimony in the excellent statistics that work has left, as well as the diffusion of more just ideas regarding the state among people of our own and foreign countries. An exhibit was made at Louisville, too, in 1883, and with little effort to make a strong showing, premiums were taken to the amount of over $3,000. At New Orleans also, in 1884, an excellent effort was made, under the direction of Com. S. A. Jonas, and this gave especial impetus to the lumber interests and manufactures. The railways took up the refrain, and began that systematic advertising of the country along their routes that has developed the entire nation so rapidly. The result has been that while the state has witnessed more growth and development materially in this decade than in others, the population also has increased, and the census of 1890 shows an advance from one million one hundred and thirty-one thousand five hundred and ninety-seven to the total of one million two hundred and eighty-nine thousand six hundred. The race proportions are as follows: the larger part colored, seven hundred and forty-seven thousand seven hundred and twenty; and the whites numbering five hundred and thirty-nine thousand seven hundred and three; with two thousand and fifty-four Indians, one hundred and twenty-two Chinese and one Japanese. Thus it will be seen that while the per cent. of increase was only 4.6 from 1860 to 1870, and 36.7 from 1870 to 1880, the last decade has shown a good one of fourteen per cent.

To view more closely, take the figures for successive decades beginning with the year 1800: Seven thousand six hundred, thirty-one thousand three hundred and six, seventy-five thousand four hundred and forty-eight, one hundred and thirty-six thousand six hundred and twenty-one, three hundred and seventy-five thousand six hundred and fifty-one, six hundred and six thousand five hundred and twenty-six, seven hundred and ninety-one thousand three hundred and five, eight hundred and twenty-seven thousand nine hundred and twenty-two, one million one hundred and thirty-one thousand five hundred and ninety-seven, and one million two hundred and eighty-nine thousand six hundred.

But take the figures of the whites alone, beginning with 1850: Two hundred and ninety-five thousand seven hundred and eighteen, three hundred and fifty-three thousand eight hundred and ninety-nine, three hundred and eighty-two thousand eight hundred and ninety-six, four hundred and seventy-nine thousand three hundred and ninety-eight, and five hundred and thirty-nine thousand seven hundred and three. This shows a percentage of increase of 19.67, 8.19, 25.20, and 12.58, or an actual increase of fifty-eight thousand one hundred and eighty-one, twenty-eight thousand nine hundred and ninety-seven, ninety six thousand five hundred and two, and sixty thousand three hundred and five.

Compare the figures for the colored population alone during the same period, beginning with 1850: Three hundred and ten thousand eight hundred and eight, four hundred and thirty-seven thousand four hundred and four, four hundred and forty-four thousand two hundred and one, six hundred and fifty thousand two hundred and ninety-one, and seven hundred and forty-seven thousand seven hundred and twenty in 1890. This shows successive increase as follows: One hundred and twenty-six thousand five hundred and ninety-six, six thousand seven hundred and ninety-seven; two hundred and six thousand and ninety, and only ninety-seven thousand four hundred and twenty-nine in 1890. Given in percentages it is: 40.73, 1.55, 46.40, and 14.98 in 1890. So it will be seen that while the whites increased 12.58 per cent. in 1890 the blacks made a gain of 14.98 per cent.; but this is a far better showing for the white increase than the previous decade, when the per cents. were as 25.2 to 46.4 in favor of the negro.

The fact that Mississippi is 41.85 per cent. white and 57.98 per cent. colored, is the great question of all questions in her social and political life. In this she stands alongside of but two other states—South Carolina and Mississippi—but as Louisiana is so evenly balanced, being only 49.59 per cent. white to 50.32 per cent. colored, South Carolina is practically the only one to compare with her. That state is in a slightly worse condition, being 39.82 per cent. white and 60.16 per cent black. Other states hardly compare at all—Georgia is nearly fifty-three per cent. white, Alabama nearly fifty-five per cent., Florida over fifty-seven per cent., Virginia over sixty-one per cent., North Carolina nearly sixty-five per cent., Arkansas over seventy-two per cent., Tennessee over seventy-five per cent., Texas nearly seventy-eight per cent., and so on up.

It will be of interest to notice what parts of Mississippi are characterized by this excess of blacks over whites. The state has seventy-five counties in all, and thirty-seven have white and thirty-eight black excess of population, almost equally divided. Those with black excess are: Adams, Amite, Bolivar, Carroll, Chickasaw, Claiborne, Clay, Coahoma, Copiah, De Soto, Grenada, Hinds, Holmes, Issaquena, Jefferson, Kemper, Lauderdale, Leflore, Lowndes, Madison, Marshall, Monroe, Noxubee, Oktibbeha, Panola, Pike, Rankin, Sharkey, Sunflower, Tallahatchie, Tate, Tunica, Warren, Washington, Wilkinson, Yalobusha and Yazoo, the greatest excess being in Washington county in the Yazoo delta, with thirty-five thousand seven hundred and three blacks to only four thousand six hundred and sixty-nine whites. It will be noticed that these countries are chiefly either characterized by cities or lowlands, toward both of which the blacks tend to gravitate.

Since this colored element has always been the pivotal point in this state's career, we may trace it by itself. As has been said, the first cargo of black slaves came in in 1720, just one hundred years after their first arrival in this country; and one hundred years later —1820—there were thirty-two thousand eight hundred and fourteen black slaves, and four hundred and fifty-eight free blacks in this state. This last item—four hundred and fifty-eight free blacks—indicates the widespread feeling against slavery and the numerous cases of voluntary emancipation by the Christian classes. This feeling was so strong in 1823 that on the presentation and advocacy of the following police measure by Mr. Poindexter, the state's constitution maker, he was defeated because of its passage:

"Section 1. *Be it enacted by the Senate and House of Representatives of the State of Mississippi in General Assembly convened*, That if any master, overseer or employer shall knowingly permit any slave or slaves, not belonging to him or her, to be and remain in and about his or her house or kitchen, or upon his or her plantation, *above four hours at any one time*, without leave of the owner, overseer or employer of such slave or slaves, he or she so permitting shall forfeit and pay $10 for every such offense. And every master, etc., who shall, without such leave, permit or suffer *more than five* negroes, or slaves, other than those in his or her own employment, to be and remain on his or her plantation or quarter, *at any one time*, shall forfeit and pay $10 for every such negro or slave, which said several forfeitures shall be to the informer, and recoverable with costs, before any justice of the peace of the county or corporation where such offense is committed. *Provided always*, that nothing herein contained shall be construed to prohibit negroes or slaves of the *same owner*, though living at different quarters, from meeting, with their owner's or overseer's leave, upon any plantation belonging to such owner; nor to restrain the meeting of slaves on their *master's or overseer's* business, at any public place, nor on *any other lawful occasion*, by license or writing, from their master, employer or overseer.

"Sec. 2. All meetings or assemblies of slaves or free negroes or mulattoes, mixing or associating with such slaves, *above the number of five, at any place of public resort, or at any meetinghouse or houses, in the night*, or at any school or schools, for teaching them reading or writing, either in the day or night under whatsoever pretext, *shall be deemed and considered an unlawful assembly*, and any justice of the peace of the county or corporation wherein such assemblage may be, either from his own knowledge or the information of others, of such unlawful assemblage or meeting, may issue his warrant, directed to any sworn officer or officers, authorizing him or them to enter the house or houses where such unlawful assemblages or meetings may be, for the purpose of apprehending or dispersing such slaves, free negroes or mulattoes, and to inflict corporal punishment on the offender or offenders, at the discretion of such justice of the peace, not exceeding thirty-nine lashes, in the manner hereinafter directed.

"Sec. 3. The said officer or officers shall have power to summon any person or persons to aid and assist in the execution of any warrant or warrants directed to him or them, for the purpose aforesaid, who, on refusal, shall be subject to a fine, at the discretion of any such justice of the peace, not exceeding $10; *Provided*, that nothing herein contained shall be so construed as to prevent the master, employer or overseer of any slave or slaves from giving permission in writing to his, her or their slave or slaves to go to any place or places whatever, for the purpose of religious worship, *Provided*, that such worship be conducted by a regularly ordained or licensed white minister, or attended by at least two discreet and reputable white persons, appointed by some regular church or religious society."

It is well known that efforts had been made long before to prevent importation of slaves, and in 1828 Governor Brandon urged this upon the legislature: "The Southern states generally, having passed laws to prevent the importation of slaves for the purposes of traffic, has left Mississippi almost the only receptacle for the surplus black population of the middle states, where their labor is not found so productive as in the South; the vast number annually imported into our state has excited uneasiness in the minds of many of our fellow-citizens, and caused them to feel much solicitude that we should adopt the policy of our neighboring states. Slavery is an evil at best, and has invariably operated oppressively on the poorer class of every community into which it has been introduced, by destroying that mutual dependence which would otherwise exist between the rich and the poor, and excludes from the state, in proportion to the number of slaves, a free white population, through the means of which alone can we expect to take rank with our sister states. With these reflections I submit it to the wisdom of the general assembly to say whether the period has not arrived when Mississippi, in her own defense, should, as far as practicable, prevent the further introduction of slaves for sale."

It has been said, a little caustically, that "the French first introduced yellow fever and slaves, on the seacoast of Mississippi. The British afterward prosecuted the trade. And then our Northern brethren embarked in it, and by their superior energy soon monopolized the business of kidnaping Africans to sell to the Southern planter. And they received in payment indigo, tobacco, rice, sugar and cotton produced by the kidnaped slaves." Another however has spoken more truly, and truly because more fully: "They were kidnaped on their native shores by the North for money, sold to the South for money; the South bought them to make money, and kept them for money." But Mississippi aided the American Colonization society, and manumission became so frequent as to be a source of possible disorder, due no doubt to the sight of the free by the bondsmen, so that the legislature forbade it, and in 1831 free negroes and mulattoes were ordered to leave the state unless special permission was granted to remain. In 1837, when there were one hundred and sixty-four thousand three hundred and ninety-three slaves in the state, about twenty thousand more than the whites, the importation of slaves into the state was forbidden.

It was at this time that such events as the following not unfrequently occurred. Isaac Ross, of Jefferson county, died in 1836, and among numerous similar provisions in his will a few may serve to illustrate.

"First, To his granddaughter Adelaide Wade, he gave his cook, a woman named Grace, and all her children living at the time of his demise, unless the said Grace should elect of her own free will to go to Africa, in which case she and her children were to be transported there with his other slaves as hereinafter provided for. And then the said Adelaide, in lieu thereof, was to have an additional $2,000 besides her other bequests.

"Second, His aforesaid granddaughter shall take charge of and maintain comfortably during their natural lives, testator's negro man Hannibal, and his three sisters, and he gave Hannibal $100, annually, for life, and to each of his sisters $50, annually. But should they elect to go to Africa, they shall be permitted to go with and on the same footing with the other slaves; and should he so elect he shall be paid when he embarks $500, in silver, in lieu of the aforesaid legacy.

"Third, Enoch, wife and children were to be conveyed free of expense, in twelve months, to the free state they might prefer, there to be manumitted and receive $500, in coin, or to Africa if they chose, on the same footing with the others, and receive $500.

"Fourth, Excepting Tom, William, Joe, Aleck and Henrietta and Jeffers (who are to be sold as hereinafter provided), all the slaves aged twenty-one and upward, within ten days after the growing crop shall be gathered, shall be called together by the executors and the provisions of the will be fully explained. Those electing to go shall be sent to Africa under the authority of the American Colonization society. And the remainder of his estate, real, personal and mixed (excepting always the negroes whose names are mentioned above), be offered for sale at public auction, one-half the purchase money to be paid in cash and the balance in twelve months. The proceeds of sale, and any money on hand or due, after deducting enough for the aforesaid legacies, to be paid over to the American Colonization Society, provided it will consent to appropriate it as follows, to-wit: First, To pay the expense of transporting to Africa to such of my slaves as may elect to go. Second, To expend the remainder for their support and maintenance while here.

"Fifth, Should the slaves refuse to go there, they (except those that have been specially named) are to be sold, and the proceeds paid over to the American Colonization society, to be invested at six per cent., the interest to be employed for one hundred years in maintaining an institution of learning in Liberia, in Africa. If there shall be no government in Liberia, the said fund to be transferred to the state of Mississippi for a similar institution.'

This will was contested under the anti-manumission laws of the state, but failed. Judge James Green, of Adams county, emancipated one hundred and fifty negroes and provided for their colonization at Greenland, Africa. A letter from a Presbyterian minister, also a slave-owner, to General Quitman, in 1831, may illustrate another feature by a short extract:

"*Honored and Dear Sir:* I doubt not that you will excuse me for trespassing upon your attention for a few moments—especially when you learn the occasion. The church of Pine Ridge, within whose bounds you have a plantation, is now making an effort to give the gospel to every rational being under its care—the young as well as the old—the bond as well as the free.

"In order to do this effectually, it is necessary to adopt the system of plantation preaching, which is now acknowledged to possess more advantages than any other. It requires, however, a greater number of preachers, than where all can be assembled in one place.

"One minister can take charge of about nine plantations, giving them instructions, preaching and catechising every second or third Sabbath; preaching during the week when desired, celebrating marriages, visiting the sick and burying the dead.

"There are already two assistants employed in my parish, and thus far the plan has succeeded admirably.

"Nearly all the planters here feel their responsibility for their servants so deeply, that they have united to provide regular and frequent religious instruction for them by good and competent teachers. In this way the servants are made accountable for themselves, and the master is relieved from his most solemn responsibility in this respect.

"Nearly every plantation has adopted the plan, and by uniting, the expense is very trifling, about $1 per head, for all over four years of age. The services of an educated man (and none others are so well suited to the work), can not be obtained for a salary less than $500 or $600."

In 1840 there were one hundred and ninety-six thousand five hundred and seventy-seven blacks and mulattoes, of whom over two thousand were free. The danger of rapid manumission as a menace to order was felt long before this, and with the forcing of the extremists North and South, a resistance to it arose, based on the old right of non-interference, and in 1846 the prohibition of slave importation was repealed. The rest is well known; the colored population at once arose in 1850 to three hundred and ten thousand eight hundred and eight, and in 1860 to four hundred and thirty-seven thousand four hundred and four.

In 1866 there were three hundred and eighty one thousand two hundred and fifty-eight, a falling off elsewhere explained. Beginning with 1870, the figures by decades are: Four hundred and forty-four thousand two hundred and one, six hundred and fifty thousand three hundred and ninety-one, and seven hundred and forty-seven thousand seven hundred and twenty in 1890, when in all the United States there were but six million five hundred and eighty thousand seven hundred and ninety-three.

Slavery, as a labor institution, has never yet been treated fully as it deserves, and the limits of such an article as this forbid more than an indication of a few of the features connected with its change to free labor. It will have been noted by this time that no effort has been made to show up the abuses of slavery; this has been intentional, for the abuses have received plenty of public emphases in the last half century, while so very little has been said on the other side that a work in that line recently issued from a Tennessee press has been hailed with surprise. It is the conscience side of a question that always wins, and an effort has here been made to show that side.

Ex-Governor Alcorn will be admitted by all to be as fair a judge of the transition period as can be found, and his being governor in the midst of it might warrant his being called the transition governor, as Governor Pettus was called the war governor. Said he to the mixed legislature of 1871: "When it is remembered that you came together at the bidding of a

Yours truly
E. Richardson

revolution, that several of you had but just been inducted into freedom when you were called on to legislate; that very many of you, though free from birth, had had no experience in the affairs of government, and that but comparatively few of you had ever before sat in a deliberative assembly, you showed in the work of last session a moderation and wisdom highly creditable." In his treatment of comparative statistics of 1860 and 1870 in six representative counties he says: "A new feature in the census of 1870 is that of wages. An outcrop amongst us of the new order of things, this head of national stock-taking is one of peculiar interest. According to the forgoing table wages amounted, in six counties producing forty two thousand eight hundred and eighty bales of cotton, to a total of $1,355,203. This, be it understood, includes the value of board also. Now the aggregate value of farm products in those counties amounts to $6,262,144, and if this value is supposed to be the result of the wages paid for labor—be the falling off in the amount of our production what it may; be the crippling of our powers of production, for want of capital, what it may—we can congratulate ourselves on a very early restoration of these shortcomings, in presence of the fact of an income on the farming of six counties in 1869-70 to an amount approaching $5,000,000." Again he says: "I was a slave owner. Apprehensive that the restraints of reason would have been insufficient in the case of a people who had been held under lifelong restraints of force, I did not accept the facts of reconstruction without some lingering doubts," and he goes on to show hopeful proofs of growth, with all the trials of the situation: Marriage licenses among the colored people were issued in thirty-one counties from 1865 to 1870 as follows in percentages of total colored population: .23, 1.53, 1.47, 1.17, 1.49, 1.43, proving "conclusively that the colored people are striving to rise to the moral level of their new standing before the law, to the extent of a strict adherence to, at all events, the formularies of sexual propriety." "But the marriage contracts of the negroes are not mere formularies," and he shows evidence of it. "Slavery is forever dead; though flowers may not be strewn upon its tomb, as they were on the tomb of Nero, freedom can well afford to bend over it to pay its memory a tribute of justice. The peculiar institution was in truth a tender nurse! Explain this by self-interest, as you will, the fact still remains. And that nursing care withdrawn by the proclamation of freedom, I feared, in my more despondent moments, that there was something in the bad prophecies which foretold of negro annihilation." He then shows the case of children to be hopeful even in their poverty, a fact in great contrast to results in Jamaica after freedom. Colored churches in six counties numbered from 1865 for a half-decade of years: One hundred and five, one hundred and twenty-five, one hundred and sixty-five, two hundred and one, two hundred and thirty-five and two hundred and eighty-three, while in twenty-two counties the report of colored preachers employed during these years were: seventy-three, one hundred and two, one hundred and thirty-four, one hundred and seventy-seven, one hundred and ninety-four, and two hundred and sixty-two; and schools, opened in twenty counties, ran: nineteen, fifty-three, eighty-one, ninety-two, one hundred and twenty-six, one hundred and forty-eight, with teachers in eighteen counties: eighteen, forty-seven, eighty-seven, one hundred and seven, one hundred and twenty-five, one hundred and seventy. The number of colored stores ran: Seven, twenty-seven, forty-three, thirty-four, sixty, sixty; of this he says: "The upward tendency of the colored people is still put in proof in the above table, and put in proof with some force when it is remembered that they enter into competition with the whites as traders, at a starting point which found them incapable of owning capital. But the number of stores other than whisky-shops is especially significant in the fact of their increase in five years of one hundred per cent. amongst the whites, for this increase points to the breaking down of the spirit of monopoly, over which comes in, with the rush of a flood, all the previously pent-up energies of the masses of the people. The hundred customers of the new order of things demand the competition that was cut off by the system which placed the demand of that hundred customers at the disposition of an individual. And thus does the regime of freedom in Mississippi appeal to the man of small means to spring into the field of that commercial activity from which he had been excluded previously by a system that carried with it, as one of its coincident evils, a business of long credits. Because of its direct bearing on the increase of merchant stores, I ask you to glance back to the agricultural summary given above for that novelty in our industry, a system of wages. In six counties, containing at the present time a total population of seventy-six thousand eight hundred and forty, the amount of wages paid out for the crops of 1869 was $1,355,203; this would give an annual wage in the whole state to the amount of $11,000,000 or $12,000,000. Forty per cent. of this may be set down as offsetting the board which the returns of the census include. Deducting that, the balance placed in the hands of our laborers may be estimated, annually, at $6,000,000 or $7,000,000. The necessities of our present want of capital once superseded, we may look confidently for that activity of mercantile business, with the 'quick sales and light profits' incident to cash custom, which is sure to follow wherever labor throws out into trade, as the heart throws out supplies of blood into the system, a weekly wage of from $120,000 to $140,000. And as we observe business growing in all the towns of the state to dimensions that are expanding those towns into cities, so we may look for a continued increase of the number of our merchant-stores until competition shall have pressed to the limits of a moderate profit all the energies placed at its service by a system of universal liberty. The freedom of the negro, throwing thus open new fields of investment and energy, has expanded largely the freedom of the whites.''

In mechanic trades two results of the transition were remarkable. Colored shoemaker shops for the five years beginning with 1865 in seventeen counties ran: Twenty-one, twenty-eight, twenty-four, forty nine, fifty-four, sixty-three, and the blacksmiths: forty, sixty-three, seventy-four, eighty-three, ninety-eight and one hundred and thirteen. Said he regarding these figures: "They show that the shoemaker that was the servant of an individual in 1860 is now a servant of the public. The smith, who was confined in his usefulness to the demands of one great planter is, on the contrary, available now to shoe the horse and share the plow of a score of small farmers!"

As to property he says: "Tenant farming has expanded amongst the whites since 1860 about one hundred per cent. In that year it was of course unknown amongst the negroes." The product in cotton on such farms for two years is given for twenty-three counties: In 1869, whites, twenty-seven thousand and seventy-five bales, and blacks, forty thousand five hundred and sixty-one bales; in 1870, whites, twenty thousand eight hundred and ninety-three, and colored, fifty thousand nine hundred and seventy-eight. "While the industrial monopoly of the old system is seen, thus, in the act of partition amongst the masses of the people, the popularization of our production comes to us accompanied by the further gratifying fact that the negro has advanced in four short years to the condition of employing, as a farmer, active capital of his own! From twenty counties I have received full returns of the amount of cotton grown by colored people as owners of the soil. While one hundred thousand six hundred and ninety-seven bales were grown in those counties by white landowners in 1869, the number grown by colored landowners in those counties in 1869 was four thousand six hundred and forty-five. The white owner of the soil produced in those counties one hundred and two thousand four hundred and ninety-one bales in 1870; the colored owner of the soil produced in them during the same period six thousand one hundred and forty-one bales! The surprise with which these facts will come in proof before you, gentlemen, can not be greater than that with which they have come in proof before me. And my pleasure in the case is hardly less than my surprise, for one of the most serious fears for the working of reconstruction lay in the absence of a middle class constituting a link between the masses of our property-holders on the one hand, and the masses of our ballot casting labor on the other. "In seven counties selected as an illustration of the results shown by the national census, I find the following surprising evidence of negro thrift:" Sixty-nine real estate colored owners' property valued at $30,680, three thousand seven hundred and ninety-eight holding personality of $630,860, and one hundred and seventy-eight holding both realty and personality to the amount of $220,700. "Amongst forty-three thousand negroes of Washington, Madison, Holmes, Rankin, Neshoba, Jones and Lauderdale, who had been plucked penniless four short years ago from the clutches of the unwise legislation of 1865, three thousand four hundred and forty-one accumulated wealth —what the economists hold to represent the political virtue of denial—to the enormous amount of $882,240!" The language is here quoted exact, "*verbatim et literatim et punctuatim*," so it may be realized that what is now plainly evident was not so much so twenty years ago, and it may serve to illustrate the apprehensive feeling on all sides. It would be interesting to multiply studies of this kind, but enough has been given to illustrate, and that is all the limits of this article will allow.

While the negro was the pivot of this transitional movement, and so becomes the center of the problem, and, may be, attracting from its students more than its share of attention and prominence, it is a fact that the results effected by the transition on the white population are pregnant with as great, if not greater, interest to the student of economics. This phase has hardly been touched upon yet, and so intricate a situation deserves more than the mere hints that can be made in limited space.

The old regime developed planters who were princely and a very poor lower class whites; there was no great middle class, such as is now seen everywhere. The planters were, and had to be, men of large executive ability and far-seeing sagacity. Their wealth was chiefly in labor, their ownership of human labor; but they had great capital too, and the combination made, for them, remarkable resources. These gave them the opportunities and advantages, in a lavish degree, afforded by the whole earth. It enabled the women to become queenly and the men royal in all phases of life. Their hospitality is a matter of common fame. Their artistic, literary and like acquirements became their pride—and justly so. Political, military and professional careers were considered the fit courses for them to pursue. Their vast superiority over the masses of humanity nearest them gave them a sense of power that could brook little opposition, and the duel was natural; while in the minds of their inferiors a halo of hero-worship surrounded them, that is not common where a great middle class intervenes.

These conditions made a sentiment against manual labor. They made a dependence on another's labor, and the inferior, relieved of all responsibility, became childishly dependent on his master. They made a lofty pride in the one that was the parent of finest virtues as well as vices; and in the other a servility attended with like results. Every condition has its compensations.

The overturning came. The loss of wealth and labor, while not tending to create those beautiful character products that we admire as we do a statue, yet awakened new powers and energies in these old families and a self-reliance in them, especially the younger generation—which, grafted on to the old, are making the world turn to look at the new South, and placing a new term in the literature of the day—"Southern writer"—that has become its most marked feature.

But still more—a great middle class has arisen and is still rising, which loudly demands and secures recognition. Among others in this class may be found the sons and daughters of the once so-called poor whites, of which Mississippi had a less number than most Southern states. The rise of this class gives labor a new status in the sentiment of the public. But this change is only in the horizon of its progress.

Two items at this point may serve to show this state's excellent condition in regard to all classes. The number of paupers in almshouses in the United States is a little over seventy-three thousand. New York has the largest number—ten thousand two hundred and seventy-two, and New Mexico the smallest—one. Mississippi comes along among the lowest states, with only four hundred and ninety-four, of which two hundred and five are whites and two hundred and eighty-nine colored. The number of county-jail prisoners in the United States on June 1, 1890, was nineteen thousand five hundred and thirty-eight. Pennsylvania had the largest number—two thousand three hundred and eighty-six, and North Dakota the lowest, with but twenty-five; while Mississippi came below midway, with but two hundred and eighty-four—only forty-eight being white and two hundred and thirty-six colored.

From the people turn to the land development. "In one sense of the word," says Maj. A. B. Hurt, in a government report in 1884, "Mississippi is still a new state, with its immense natural advantages as yet mainly unappropriated. Its great forests of valuable woods have been comparatively little depleted; many of its numerous fine mill and manufacturing sites await the power of skill and capital; more than one-half of its area remains untouched by the husbandman, while the part already in cultivation may be made double its productive power by improved methods of agriculture." And while the opening up, by various agencies before referred to, had changed this considerably since that date, the fact in general may still be used with some allowance.

In June, 1845, there were ten million four hundred and nine thousand and thirty-four acres of unsold public land, out of a total state acreage of twenty-nine million nine hundred and fifty-eight thousand four hundred. Of this enormous amount one million and eighteen thousand one hundred and fourteen acres had been on the market five years; four hundred and fifty-one thousand three hundred and ninety had been offered for ten years; two million nine hundred and seventy-four thousand and ninety-seven acres in market for fifteen years; nine hundred and thirty-four thousand one hundred and thirty-one for twenty years; eight hundred and ninety-four thousand four hundred and twenty-four for twenty-five years; two million nine hundred and twenty-four thousand one hundred and seventy-two for thirty years; and one million two hundred and twenty-two thousand seven hundred and six for over thirty years—and all at the low rate of $1.25 an acre! Says Mr. Harper, the geologist, in 1857 of the Yazoo delta: "It is still a wilderness, the retreat of the bear, wolf and panther. The prejudice of its unfitness for cultivation has only lately been removed from the minds of the inhabitants of our own and other states, and the ax of the woodman scarcely begun its ravages."

Note what the war did. Says Governor Alcorn in 1871: "Our improved land has decreased in breadth one-ninth. This fact is very encouraging, seeing that we still retain, substantially, our conquests from the forest. The small decline of our improved land in farms, combined with the large decline in our areas of unimproved land in farms, points to the conclusion that our young 'settlements' have been given up again to the bear and panther. But, though progress is seen thus to be, for the time, arrested, we still hold, in fact, the great mass of our landed wealth of 1860. It is true the value of agricultural estate now shows a falling off on that of 1860 of nearly seventy per cent., but the basis of that wealth still unchanged in its breadth, the restoration to be effected in that case is that mainly of the establishment of order and the elevation of labor." Then came the great forfeiture of land for taxes. Between 1871 and 1875, said Governor Lowry: "About twenty-seven per cent. of the total area of this state was forfeited for taxes;" but by 1883 all except about seven hundred thousand acres had been redeemed or purchased. Between 1875 and 1885 about five million acres were restored to the tax rolls of the state; and between 1880 and 1885 the large amount of four million two hundred and three thousand one hundred and ninety acres of public land had been sold, of which five hundred and one thousand four hundred and fifty acres had been taken up under homestead laws. It should be recalled that since the congressional act of September 25, 1850, down to 1883 Mississippi had received about three million acres of swamp lands, and under the act of September 4, 1841, about five million acres for internal improvement purposes. On the first day of 1890 there remained unsold of the swamp land two hundred and twenty-seven thousand six hundred and thirty-two acres, and of the internal improvement lands only two thousand six hundred and eighty-three acres. In the two years preceding that date over twenty thousand acres of the former at a dollar an acre, and nearly ten thousand acres of the latter at fifty cents per acre show how fast available lands of all kinds have been taken up. In 1883 there was still an area of seven million acres under cultivation, less than one-fourth, but extension in this direction has been rapid since that date. The census of 1890 will show, when made public, considerable change from these figures, for the opening up of lands in the delta and elsewhere, due to railway extension, has been remarkable as a leading feature of the decade of the eighties, and especially the latter half. Said George W. Carlisle, commissioner of immigration, writing in the year 1888: "In the past two years, about one million three hundred thousand acres of land have been sold by the commissioner of lands. Most of the lands were purchased by parties from beyond the limits of the state. During the same time the register of the United States land office, at Jackson, Miss., sold in our state about one million acres of government lands. These large sales of lands prove conclusively that capitalists have confidence in our state and its prosperity. By an act of congress, approved May 16, 1888, all United States lands are withdrawn from sale by cash purchase in Mississippi; the only way by which these lands can be obtained from the government is under the homestead laws."

When this increased interest in lands began to be most marked, in 1884, Major Hurt showed the average value of land per acre was $17.79, while the averages in Illinois, Indiana and Iowa were respectively $38.65, $45.66 and $23.52, when the average acre-crop values were but a little more than half that of Mississippi's rate—$12.21 per acre. Said he: "It appears from the above, price of lands, or their market value, in Mississippi, bears no just proportion to their real intrinsic value. Lands that will average a money value product of $12.21 per acre should average a market value of at least $50 per acre, especially in such a temperate, healthy climate. Without discussing the cause of the low price of lands, it may be remarked that there is too much land for the population and capital. Land is plentiful, easy to obtain, and, therefore, cheap. If Mississippi could double or treble its population by the addition of thrifty, industrious immigrants, possessed of some capital, the price of lands would, no doubt, increase to something like their real value. This is now being accomplished, and it is stated, on the authority of the state commissioner of immigration, that lands have advanced from fifty to one hundred per cent in the past two years. It is to be regretted that the state has so little statistical data to illustrate in detail the progress made since the last census. Unfortunately, there is no statistical bureau in Mississippi.''

The foregoing will add new significance to the growth of Mississippi in wealth. This need not consider slaves after the consideration hereinbefore accorded that subject, and indicating that as the greatest source of wealth. Of the general subject it has been said that the emancipation of slaves was a loss of over $600,000,000 to their owners; and that, were the total cost of the civil war to be divided by the number of slaves set free, that freedom would cost $700 per slave.

To illustrate the general wealth development, a glance at census matter for the years 1812, 1840, 1857, 1870, 1880 and 1887 must suffice, as these dates indicate somewhat nearly the beginning, middle and close of the old labor system of slavery, and like periods in the new system.

In 1812 there were one thousand three hundred and thirty private looms at work in the state, making annually three hundred and forty-two thousand four hundred and seventy-two yards of cotton cloth, four hundred and fifty yards of linen and seven thousand eight hundred and ninety-eight yards of woolen stuffs. There was one carding machine and twenty-two mills with eight hundred and seven spindles. Ten tanneries produced $39,595 worth of leathers, while the distilleries numbered six, and the tin-shops one. The largest number of looms were in Madison and Amite counties, while the woolens were entirely in Adams, Claiborne and Wilkinson. The tanneries were in Adams, Jefferson, Claiborne, Wilkinson and Washington, while Madison reveled in over half of the entire number of distilleries. This is no small showing, and is indicative of only one line, and that the least developed line of industry—manufactures. Its agriculture, cotton, slaves and stock were its great wealth. In the absence of statistics these must be inferred for the present.

Nearly thirty years later, 1840, one hundred and thirty-nine thousand seven hundred and twenty-four whites were employed in agriculture, one thousand three hundred and three in commerce, four thousand one hundred and fifty-one in manufacture and trades, thirty-three were ocean and one hundred were river sailors, while the professions enrolled one thousand five hundred and six. In stock there were in the state one hundred and nine thousand two hundred and twenty-seven horses and mules, six hundred and twenty-three thousand one hundred and ninety-seven neat cattle, one hundred and twenty-eight thousand three hundred and sixty-seven sheep, one million one thousand two hundred and nine swine, and poultry to the value of $369,482. The granaries were full: One hundred and ninety-six thousand six hundred and twenty six bushels of wheat, eleven thousand four hundred and forty-four of rye, thirteen million one hundred and sixty-one thousand two hundred and thirty-seven of Indian corn, one thousand six hundred and fifty-four of barley, and six hundred and sixty eight thousand six hundred and twenty-four bushels of oats. Potatoes scored a total of one million six hundred and thirty thousand one hundred bushels; wax, six thousand eight hundred and thirty-five pounds; tobacco, eighty-three thousand four hundred and seventy-one pounds; rice, seven hundred and seventy-seven thousand one hundred and ninety-five pounds; wool, one hundred and seventy-five thousand one hundred and ninety-five pounds, and the great king product, cotton, rising to the immense proportions of one hundred and ninety-three million four hundred and one thousand five hundred and seventy-seven pounds—all showing wealth in these lines. The dairy made a product of value $359,585, the orchard made $14,458, and lumber $192,794, while tar, pitch and turpentine rolled out two thousand two hundred and forty-eight barrels. Trade and manufactures loomed up too. There were seven commercial companies, sixty-seven commercial houses in the foreign trade with a capital of $673,900; seven hundred and fifty-five retail dry goods stores, with a capital of $5,004,420; two hundred and eighty-eight in the lumber trade, with $132,175 capital; fifty-three cotton factories had three hundred and eighteen spindles employing eighty-one hands and capital to the sum of $6,420; $5,140 worth of hats and caps were made by thirteen persons on a capital of $8,100; one hundred and twenty eight tanneries employed one hundred and forty-nine hands and had a capital of $70,870; forty-two other leather factories produced $118,167 worth of goods on a capital of $41,945; one pottery had two hands producing wares to the amount of $1,200 on $200 capital; four drug and paint stores, with an aggregate capital of $500, sold $3,125 in profits; $10,500 worth of confectionery made in two places; machinery made to the amount of $242,225; brick and lime making was rewarded by $273,870 product on $222,745 capital; three hundred and twelve thousand and eighty-four pounds of soap were made; thirty-one thousand nine hundred and fifty-seven tallow and ninety-seven pounds of wax candles were made; wagonmaking scored $49,693, with one hundred and thirty-two men on $34,335 capital; sixteen flourmills made one thousand eight hundred and nine barrels of flour, worth $486,864, on $1,219,845 capital; $13,925 was spent in building vessels; forty-one men made furniture worth $34,450 on a capital of $28,610; fourteen distilleries produced three thousand one hundred and fifty gallons of liquor; two breweries, on a capital of $910, made one hundred and thirty-two gallons; the state boasted of one hundred and forty-four stone houses and two thousand two hundred and forty-four wooden ones, aggregating a value of $1,175,513; there were twenty-eight printing offices, one bindery, two dailies, one semi-weekly and twenty-eight weeklies, employing ninety-four men and $83,510 in capital. The total manufactured product was worth $1,797,727. There were three colleges, with two hundred and fifty students; seventy-one academies, with two thousand five hundred and fifty-three students; three hundred and eighty-two primary schools, with eight thousand two hundred and thirty-six pupils; and eight thousand three hundred and sixty whites over twenty years of age who could neither read nor write. These latter facts are given to indicate the general intelligence connected with this wealth.

Seventeen years later, 1857, figures had grown larger: There was money at interest to the amount of $6,713,658, and merchants had a trade of the comely proportions of $15,552,194. Bank stock was held to the amount of $615,100, and auctioneers had a business of $51,772. Such items as eleven thousand four hundred and eighty-six carriages valued at $1,666,079, or thirteen thousand nine hundred and forty-one watches worth $815,140, or eighteen thousand five hundred and ninety-nine clocks worth $168,939, indicate a luxurious wealth over years then past, along with $223,178 in gold and silver plate, or two thousand two hundred and thirty-three pianos worth $494,628. Counting herds of cattle only above twenty head there were two hundred and twenty thousand six hundred and sixty-four, while six thousand four hundred and forty-three horses, worth $896,044, were taxable totals in that line. Taxable slaves numbered three hundred and thirty-four thousand eight hundred and eighty-six to a total free white poll of fifty three thousand three hundred and one. The taxable land acreage was fifteen million nine hundred and thirteen thousand five hundred and twenty-two, worth $88,705,203. Now add to this a season product of cotton—taking that of 1859, two years later, for example—one million three hundred thousand bales worth $45,000,000, and the slave period closes with striking figures in wealth.

Governor Alcorn's comparison of 1860 and 1870 in six representative counties showed a decrease of melancholy proportions in everything save oats and molasses, both of which had increased. The decrease in improved farm lands was eleven per cent., in unimproved farm lands thirty-four per cent., farm values sixty-nine per cent., farm implements sixty-one per cent., stock values forty-six, cotton bales of four hundred and fifty pounds sixty-three per cent., corn sixty-five, slaughtered animals fifty-six, horses forty-nine, mules thirty-six per cent., cows twenty-seven per cent., a decrease of forty-seven per cent. in oxen, forty-three per cent. in other cattle, thirty-eight in sheep, sixty-five in swine, eighty-six per cent. in wheat, ninety-eight in rye, sixty in rice, thirty-nine in tobacco, eighty-nine in peas and beans, eighty-three per cent. loss in Irish potatoes, sixty-four in sweet potatoes, seventy-six in wool, sixty-three in butter, ninety-six in cheese, sixty-two per cent. loss in home manufactures, and eighty-two in orchard produce. And these counties represented about an eighth or ninth of the state in wealth and population.

Compare 1870 and 1880. Corn, fifteen million six hundred and thirty-seven thousand three hundred and sixteen bushels in 1870 to twenty-one thousand three hundred and forty in 1880; cotton, five hundred and sixty-four thousand nine hundred and thirty-eight bales in 1870 to nine hundred and sixty-three thousand one hundred and eleven in 1880; oats, four hundred and fourteen thousand five hundred and eighty-six bushels to one million nine hundred and fifty-nine thousand six hundred and twenty; wheat, two hundred and seventy-four thousand four hundred and seventy-nine bushels to two hundred and eighteen thousand eight hundred and ninety, a falling off; hay, eight thousand three hundred and twenty-four tons to eight thousand eight hundred and ninety-four; molasses, two hundred and nineteen thousand six hundred and seventy-four gallons in 1870 to three hundred and thirty-six thousand six hundred and twenty-five in 1880; rice, three hundred and seventy-four thousand six hundred and twenty-seven pounds to one million seven hundred and eighteen thousand nine hundred and fifty-one in 1880; Irish potatoes, two hundred and fourteen thousand one hundred and eighty-nine bushels in 1870 to three hundred and three thousand eight hundred and twenty-one; sweet potatoes, one million seven hundred and forty-three thousand four hundred and thirty-two bushels in 1870 to three million six hundred and ten thousand six hundred and sixty-three; orchard values, $71,018 to $378,145, a remarkable gain full of significance; stock, one million seven hundred and twenty-four thousand two hundred and ninety-five head to two million three hundred and ninety-eight thousand nine hundred and thirty-four in 1880, a great gain; butter, two million six hundred and thirteen thousand five hundred and twenty-one pounds in 1870 to seven million four hundred and fifty-four thousand six hundred and fifty-seven in 1880, right in line with the last; and wool, two hundred and eighty-eight thousand two hundred and eighty-five pounds to seven hundred and thirty-four thousand six hundred and forty-three pounds in 1880, and the entire assessed valuation in 1880 was $110,628,129.

At this writing the census returns for 1890 are not available. A comparison of 1880 and 1886 will show to what an advance it may be expected to reach, however. Cotton rose from over nine hundred and sixty-three thousand bales in 1880 to over one million in 1883, and only fell to eight hundred and thirty-eight thousand six hundred and ninety-two bales in 1886, valued at $37,120,000, a less variation than in most other Southern states. Corn rose from over fifteen million bushels in 1880 to twenty-five million five hundred and seven thousand in 1886. Wheat fell again from over two hundred and eighteen thousand bushels in 1880 to one hundred and seventy-three thousand bushels in 1886, but oats sprang up from over one million nine hundred and fifty-nine thousand in 1880 to three million three hundred and sixty-eight thousand bushels in 1886. Tobacco rose from over four hundred and fourteen thousand pounds to about five hundred and twenty-five thousand; Irish potatoes from over three hundred and three thousand bushels to about six hundred and thirteen thousand; sweet potatoes from over three million six hundred thousand bushels to about four million two hundred and eighty-five thousand in 1886; butter made the remarkable rise of from over seven million four hundred and fifty-four thousand pounds in 1880 to about fifteen million eight hundred and twenty-five thousand pounds in 1886; hay, also, rose from eight thousand eight hundred and ninety-four tons to fourteen thousand five hundred tons, and molasses from over three hundred and thirty-six thousand gallons in 1880 to about six hundred and fifteen thousand gallons in 1886. The acreage in farm products increased from five million two hundred and sixteen thousand nine hundred and thirty-seven acres in 1879 to five million five hundred and twelve thousand in 1886 as follows: In 1879 it was five million two hundred and sixteen thousand nine hundred and thirty-seven; in 1882 it was five million three hundred and two thousand; in 1883 it was five million three hundred thousand; in 1884 it was five million four hundred and sixty-five thousand; in 1885 it was five million four hundred and ninety-two thousand; in 1886 it was five million five hundred and twelve thousand. The value of the yield for those years varied between about $62,000,000 in 1884 and about $69,000,000 in 1883, the value, however, being less a measure of increase than the acreage, for the former often decreases in proportion to the increase of product.

These items serve merely to illustrate the state's increase in wealth, not to indicate her varied sources nor totals of wealth. These must be considered separately, farther on, as far as results are obtainable. Her wealth was once largely in but two properties, slaves and cotton; or, at an earlier date only tobacco and cotton; or, at a still later date chiefly cotton without the slaves, but now it has become divided among numerous lines. Labor and capital were once largely tied up in cotton production so in advance of all other industries as to throw them in the background, but now see the great wealth in lumber, in stockraising, in fruit culture, in manufactures, in trade, in dairy products, and numerous other lines. This is development as well as mere increase, and means a real wealth for which the past decade has been remarkable above all predecessors. Let this illustrate and prove it: The assessed valuation per capita in the state was $97.76 in 1880; in 1890 it was $122.15, an increase of 42.39 per cent., and this too when the increase in population was only 13.96 per cent. This is a better showing than for the nation as a whole, for the United States' increase was only 43.46 per cent. with 24.86 per cent. increase in population. These figures are for both personal and real property, and they mean comparative increase and development, not comparative amount of wealth, for while Mississippi has surpassed many states, even the nation at large, in rate of development, she is still below many in amount of wealth. For example, the comparison with Massachusetts' total assessed valuation in 1890 of $2,154,134,626 with that of the Bayou state, $157,518,906 is almost as twenty to one. Mississippi's assessed wealth comes more nearly reaching that of Vermont, Nebraska, West Virginia, or South Carolina, being less than the first three and greater than the last mentioned state. Those who are working to advance Mississippi's manufacturing interests find abundant encouragement in the contrast between this state and Massachusetts, the contrast of an agricultural with a manufacturing state. Mississippi's per cent. of increase, however, is almost the same to a figure as that of the wealthiest state in the nation, New York, whose assessed valuation is $3,775,325,938, namely 42.39 per cent. and 42.36 per cent. respectively, a showing slightly more favorable to this state.

But as this state probably never can be wealthy from mining, and is still only in its infancy in manufactures, it may be of interest to see to what degree it is an agricultural state. "The importance of agriculture to the people of Mississippi," said Maj. A. B.

Hurt, in his government report of 1884, "may be better appreciated when it is remembered that three hundred and thirty-nine thousand nine hundred and thirty-eight, or more than eighty-one per cent. of its entire working population, are engaged in agricultural pursuits. The distribution is as follows: All occupations, four hundred and fifteen thousand five hundred and six; agricultural laborers, two hundred and fifteen thousand four hundred and seventy-two; farmers and planters, one hundred and twenty-three thousand three hundred and eighty-two; gardeners, nurserymen and vine-growers, six hundred and twenty; stock-raisers, drovers and herders, ninety-three; turpentine farmers and laborers, two hundred and forty-eight, and others in agriculture, one hundred and twenty-three. Total, three hundred and thirty-nine thousand, nine hundred and thirty-eight."

Since this is the case, let the progress of this department of industry be traced. "Several years elapsed after the establishment of the French colony at Biloxi," writes State Geologist B. L. C. Wailes, in 1854, "before even the common vegetables of the garden were cultivated, and the sterile soil of the seashore was not calculated to invite a more extended culture, if the character and habits of the colonists, chiefly soldiers, deriving all their supplies from the mother country, had inclined them to such pursuits. It was, therefore, not until the province came under the control of the Company of the Indies that the tillage of the earth became to any extent a fixed pursuit. The first impulse was then given to planting by the large grants to European capitalists, who sent out laborers to open and improve their lands. The most efficient of these were German redemptioners; but the nature of the climate and the heavy labor of removing the dense forests, rendered the progress of improvement tedious and discouraging. It was soon found necessary to resort to Africa for suitable operatives for the prosecution of agricultural enterprise. These were introduced by the company from time to time, to a limited extent, and disposed of to the colonists at established and moderate rates, payable in annual installments in the product of the soil. These products were naturally confined, for a considerable period, to articles of necessity for home consumption, and notwithstanding some large grants were made near Natchez and on the Yazoo, ostensibly for the cultivation of tobacco and indigo; and, although some 'large plantations, with extensive improvements,' were established near the former place, it does not appear that anything beyond the spoils of the chase or the peltries procured by traffic with the Indian tribes, was exported from the country. By the massacre of the inhabitants by the Natchez, in 1729 and 1730, these establishments were broken up, and from this period the French were too much engaged in exterminating the Natchez and in hostile incursions among the Chickasaws, to reoccupy and cultivate, advantageously, their regained possessions. It was, therefore, under the occupancy of the country by the English that we trace the first germ of successful and systematic agriculture in Mississippi. The emigration which ensued, on the change of rulers, being chiefly from the Carolinas, Virginia, Jersey and New England, was from a class differing essentially in habits from their more volatile and restless predecessors, the French, who were more addicted to the chase and to trafficking with their Indian neighbors than to more laborious and settled pursuits. Many of these settlers were accustomed to agriculture, and being generally accompanied by their families, resorted at once to the tillage of the earth as a means of support. Their cultivation was necessarily rude, and their implements few and imperfect; yet their products were varied and, for the purpose of subsistence, ample. Almost every article of prime necessity which the soil could yield was produced by them to the extent of their wants," such as in 1775 Mr. Dunbar mentions—rice, tobacco, flaxseed, indigoseed, corn, buckwheat, barley, peas and other things.

The account proceeds: "Cattle and swine required little other attention than protection from the bear and wolf of the forest, and were raised abundantly, whilst the small farms, frequently confined to a few acres, exhibited a variety of production that is now (1854) rarely found together in the county. Indian corn, wheat, oats, rye, rice and potatoes, cotton flax, tobacco and indigo, were almost universally cultivated, but rarely, if at all, for exportation. In the early stages of the settlement of the colony, many of the common conveniences of life were necessarily dispensed with, or supplied with such substitutes as ingenuity or skill could devise or fabricate from the productions of the country. Not many years since, were to be seen the molds in which the head of one of the most respectable and wealthy families of the present day (1854) was wont to cast the pewter platters and spoons which constituted the only plate of himself and neighbors. The inventories of the confiscated effects of some prominent, and, as then regarded, opulent persons, yet preserved among the Spanish archives, exhibit a simplicity of attire and furniture in strong contrast with that which would now (1854) satisfy those of very contracted means or humble station. The scarcity and high price of iron, and the consequent imperfection of agricultural implements was perhaps most felt and least easily remedied. At that period cut nails were not invented, and the wrought nail cost $1 a pound. Tools and all iron implements bore a corresponding price, owing in some degree to the high freight on heavy articles up the Mississippi, the voyage from New Orleans to Natchez, made by keelboats and barges, requiring several weeks. A set of plow irons was, therefore, an acquisition of no little value. Iron entered into the composition of few of the wagons or carts, and the wheels were often made of a transverse section or disk sawed and properly fashioned from the trunk of a tree of suitable diameter. These trucks constituted, to considerable extent, the only means of transportation of heavy articles. Even as late as after the introduction of Whitney's saw-gin, a now (1854) opulent planter, a venerable and highly respected citizen, a native of Adams county, states that in a wagon of this kind he hauled his crop of cotton for two years to a neighboring gin—a framework of cane serving in lieu of plank in the construction of the body. Not many years before the same gentleman was reduced to the necessity of fabricating his only plow by framing a common mattock to a beam, that being the only implement suited to the purpose left on his plantation by the depredating Indians. This was only about sixty-five years since (i. e. before 1854), and occurred within ten miles of Natchez, and to an individual belonging to one of the most opulent and influential families in that day. Flax was raised chiefly for shoe thread and similar uses, but in some families linen cloth was made. Leather was commonly tanned throughout the country in large troughs dug out of the trunks of trees. From the earliest occupancy by the English, cotton in small quantities, sufficient for domestic purposes, was habitually cultivated. It was of the black or naked seed variety, was planted in hills and cultivated with the hoe. Fifty or sixty pounds was the ordinary quantity gathered in a day. The seeds were picked out by the hand, or separated from the lint by means of the small roller gin. It was spun and woven at home, and constituted the chief apparel of the inhabitants; the small quantity of indigo then grown, and the numerous dyestuffs the forests afforded, supplied all the coloring materials required for dyeing the cloth. Rice formed an important article of diet, supplying largely the deficiency of flour; the colonists, especially the French, accommodating themselves slowly and reluctantly to bread made from the Indian corn. It was prepared by pounding in common wooden mortars, and perhaps was not as fair as that which we now (1854) purchase, but of far richer flavor and more nutritious. In the absence of millstones, when they could not be obtained, the Indian corn was reduced to meal by pounding in the same way. Large herds of cattle were owned by the more opulent inhabitants, for which the garrison at Natchez afforded the chief market, and some were driven to New Orleans shortly previous to the change of government. The price of common stock cattle was about the same then as at this time'' (1854).

As this narrative so well shows both the early and closing years of the slave epoch, in contrast, it is continued freely: "When the country came under the dominion of Spain a market was opened in New Orleans; a trade in tobacco was established, and a fixed remunerative price was paid for it, delivered at the king's warehouses. Tobacco thus became the first marketable staple production of Mississippi. The tobacco plant, indigenous to the county, soon came into general cultivation. The larger planters packed it in the usual way in hogsheads. Much of it, however, was put up in carrets, as they were called, resembling in size and form two small sugar-loaves united at the larger ends. The stemmed tobacco was laid smoothly together in that form, coated with wrappers or the extended leaf, enveloped in a cloth, and then firmly compressed by a cord wrapped around the parcel, and was suffered to remain until the carret acquired the necessary dryness and solidity, when, together with the surrounding cloth, it was removed, and strips of lind bark were bound around it at proper distances, in such a manner as to secure it from unwrapping and losing its proportions. The rope used for this purpose was manufactured by the planter, from the inner bark of the lind, or basswood, then one of the most common trees of the forest. In those days, when the roads were indifferent, and wagons and carts few, the tobacco hogsheads were frequently geared to a horse by means of a pair of rude temporary shafts, connected with the heading, and in this manner rolled to the shipping point, or to market at Natchez; much being transported in this way from the settlements on Cole's creek, and from greater distances. To convey the tobacco to market in New Orleans, it was usual for several planters to unite and build a flatboat, with which one of the number would accompany the joint adventure, deliver the tobacco at the public warehouse, and, if it passed inspection, receive the proceeds, and return home by land, generally on foot; the payment being made on a written acknowledgment, or bon, as it was called, which entitled the holder to receive the amount from the governor or commandant at Natchez, thus obviating the labor and risk of packing the specie several hundred miles. The monopoly of the tobacco trade was retained by the king of Spain, and the price paid for all that passed inspection at his warehouses was uniform. The price was regarded as liberal, and yielded a fair return for its production, whilst the stability and certainty of a market encouraged an increased cultivation; the county began to prosper, and the planters were able to make purchases of slaves, the current price of which averaged about $350. There was no classification in the sale of tobacco. If the article passed inspection, it was taken, and the quality was generally such that for that cause it could not be rejected. Nevertheless, it sometimes happened that an unobjectionable article was left upon the planter's hands, if, from ignorance of established usage, he had omitted the customary douceur to the inspector. Whether these usages, reacting upon the producers, had any affect upon the quality or condition of the tobacco in the end, is not, perhaps, altogether clear, but it is certain that, from some cause, either from fraud in packing, the falling off in quality, or the competition of the Kentucky tobacco introduced into New Orleans, under General Wilkinson's contracts with the Spanish authorities, or by their connivance, the price was so reduced that the further cultivation of it in Mississippi, for exportation, was in a few years wholly abandoned, greatly to the injury and embarrassment of the planters, who had, for the purchase of slaves, contracted debts which they now found it difficult to discharge.''

Indigo had not been cultivated in the Natchez district as late as 1783, and until the failure of the tobacco business it was produced only for the seed, which was supplied to the various settlements below. Continuing the narrative: "The tobacco crop, being no longer profitable, indigo, which had been cultivated for some time in Louisiana, was now resorted to. This most offensive and unwholesome pursuit was, nevertheless, the most profitable one in which the planter could engage. Seed was obtained at the cost of about $50 per barrel, and some of the small farmers engaged in cultivating the indigo exclusively for the seed to supply those whose larger means enabled them to erect the necessary fixtures, and to prosecute the cultivation and manufacture on a profitable scale. Indigo ferra tinctoria, from which the indigo pigment of commerce is prepared, said to have been introduced from India, flourishes luxuriantly in the Southern states, where a variety termed the atramentum anil is said to grow spontaneously. It was cultivated in drills, and required careful handling when young and tender, the subsequent cultivation being similar to that of the cotton plant. When mature, in good land, it attained the hight of about three feet. It was then, previous to going to seed, cut with a reap-hook from day to day, tied in bundles in quantities suited to the capacity of the steeping-vats, to which it was immediately transferred." "The whole process was of the most disgusting character. Myriads of flies were generated in it, which overspread the whole country. The plant itself, when growing, was infested by swarms of grasshoppers, by which it was sometimes totally destroyed, and the fetor arising from the putrid weed thrown from the vats was intolerable. The drainings from these refuse accummulations into the adjacent streams killed the fish. Those in Second creek, previously abounding in trout and perch, it is said were destroyed in this way. It is not surprising, therefore, that the cultivation of indigo was abandoned in a few years, and gave way to that of cotton, so remarkable for its freedom from the disagreeable concomitants of tobacco and indigo culture, and comparatively so light, neat and agreeable in its handling."

Cotton is from the Italian word cotone, and so called because of its resemblance to the quince down or cotogni. Its botanical name is gossypium. It was well known to the ancients, and introduced in England so late as 1640, whence, in 1719, it was placed in South Carolina, whose first provisional congress, in 1775, "recommended to its people to raise cotton." Georgia led off, and the first cotton was shipped to Liverpool in 1784, and five years later the Sea Island variety was introduced from Jamaica. It is probable that the French introduced it into Mississippi, as it was growing in Natchez in 1722, and Bienville reports its cultivation in 1735. The Sea Island variety grew on the seaboard; the upland and Tennessee varieties were grown also; but the Mexican soon became the leader. This, it is said, was introduced from Mexico by General Wilkinson's special envoy—Walter Burling, of Natchez, who, wishing to secure some of the seed from the viceroy of Mexico, was told it was against the law, but, as Mexican dolls were not in the forbidden list, although stuffed with cotton seed, the friendly viceroy assured him he could carry all the dolls home he desired. This was in 1806. The first gin used was much like a clothes-wringer in principle and size; then a treadle was added, and so used about 1764. A few improvements were made, and bowing was used. It was on March 14, 1794, that a Yankee machine lifted the repressive difficulty of seeding off of cotton culture (Whitney's cotton-gin), and in a single decade the nation's crop was increased from about $150,000 to at least $8,000,000. In 1795 Daniel Clarke, near Fort Adams, had one of these gins made, and in 1798 cotton was shipped from the gin on Pine Ridge, near Natchez, belonging to Thomas Wilkins. David Greenleaf became probably the first ginwright, and in 1807 Eleazer Carver began their manufacture near Washington. In 1838 he made excellent improvements on the original. Cotton culture received such an impulse that the ginmakers could not supply the demand, and this state became one of the leading manufacturers of it in the United States. The stalks and seeds were burned. About 1779 square bales were made in a rough lever press. In 1801 Mr. Dunbar secured an iron screw-press from Philadelphia for $1,000, and proposed to begin the manufacture of cottonseed oil. Soon the McComb and Lewis presses were invented by Mississippians. Said Mr. Wailes in 1854: "Hoop iron has been introduced of late years, but the use, as yet, is confined to a few large planters."

Indian corn was seen by De Soto to be "of such luxuriant growth as to produce three or four ears to the stalk," and in 1854 Mr. Wailes said: "With us, as an article of food, it has become by far the most important that our soil produces. The varieties which seem best adapted to our climate are the Tuscarora, the gourd seed and the white and yellow flint." Again: "Thirty bushels are accounted a very fair crop per acre and forty a large one. The total production of corn in the state in 1849 was stated at twenty-two million four hundred and forty-six thousand bushels, equal to about thirty-seven bushels to about each individual inhabitant."

Wheat only reached a production of one hundred and thirty-eight thousand bushels in 1849. It didn't pay to raise it when the product of the Northwest could be secured so much more easily. Oats was heavily grown, so that the year 1849 produced one million five hundred thousand bushels, chiefly spring and winter or black oats. Rye and barley were pasturing crops, and only produced ten thousand of the former and two hundred and twenty-nine of the latter in 1849. Chicken corn, broom corn and "Hebron corn" were grown also before the war. Rice was generally cultivated in the southeast, especially near Mississippi city, and produced two million seven hundred thousand pounds in 1849. Sugar cane reached a crop equal to three hundred and eighty-eight hogsheads and about eighteen thousand gallons of molasses. The latter was made as far north as Chickasaw county, and many planters in the south part of the state made all their own sugar. There were sugar mills in Pike, Amite, Marion and Perry counties. The sweet potato was cultivated in five varieties, and in 1849 made the stupendous crop of four million seven hundred and forty-two thousand bushels, worth more than $2,000,000—the state taking fourth rank in this particular. The Irish potato was confined to the garden, and the crop of 1849 was only about two hundred and sixty thousand bushels. The cornfield pea was extensively grown, the crop of 1849 reaching one million bushels. It was a splendid stock feed. The Bermuda and other grasses were grown, but none compared with the magnificent Bermuda.

These were the chief agricultural products. In 1836 there were one million forty-eight thousand five hundred and thirty acres cultivated and three hundred and seventeen thousand seven hundred and eighty-three bales of cotton raised. In 1849 Mississippi was third, with four hundred and eighty-four thousand two hundred and ninety-three bales, and in 1859 she scored one million three hundred thousand bales, worth $45,000,000. In 1840 and 1850 there were produced of corn thirteen million one hundred and sixty-one thousand two hundred and thirty-seven and twenty-two million four hundred and forty-six thousand five hundred and fifty-two bushels respectively, of wheat one hundred and ninety-six thousand six hundred and twenty-six and one hundred and thirty-seven thousand nine hundred and ninety respectively, of rye and oats six hundred and eighty thousand and sixty-eight and one million five hundred and fifteen thousand eight hundred and ninety-four bushels respectively; of sweet potatoes, one million six hundred and thirty thousand and one hundred, and four million seven hundred and forty-one thousand seven hundred and ninety-five bushels respectively; of rice, seven hundred and seventy-seven thousand one hundred and ninety-five, and two million seven hundred and nineteen thousand eight hundred and fifty-six pounds respectively; of horses and mules, one hundred and nine thousand two hundred and twenty-seven, and one hundred and seventy thousand and seven, one hundred and fifteen thousand four hundred and sixty of the latter being horses; of cattle, six hundred and twenty-three thousand one hundred and ninety-seven to seven hundred and thirty-three thousand nine hundred and seventy in 1850; of sheep, one hundred and twenty-eight thousand three hundred and sixty-seven to three hundred and four thousand nine hundred and twenty-nine; and of swine, one million one thousand two hundred and nine to one million five hundred and eighty-two thousand seven hundred and thirty-four in 1850.

These are sufficient to indicate the condition of agriculture in the closing years of the old regime. This is a view from the standpoint of 1854; let a view now be taken from the view-point of 1884, after about a quarter of a century of the new regime, in the midst of its best decade:

"From the time when the first European settlement was established at the Bay of Biloxi, in 1699," wrote Major Hurt in 1884, "a variety of causes have intervened to retard that systematic, thorough, intensive cultivation of the soil, in connection with a variety of products which are required to develop to their full extent the natural advantages of an agricultural country. The system of agriculture which obtained in this state prior to the emancipation of the slave was not conducive to this end. It was an area of large estates, devoted almost exclusively to a single product, and this not with the idea to obtain the greatest results from a given area of land. Under the new order of things, after the Civil war, the farmers of Mississippi found themselves without capital with which to cultivate their lands—the only species of property, save a remnant of their stock, left to them. Millions of dollars' worth of their property had been swept away, and thus impoverished, they were compelled to invoke the yoke of debt, backed in many cases by mortgages on real estate, from which they are not yet entirely free. The system of large planting was quite extensively resumed after the war. Advance of supplies and money to make the crops were usually obtained from the local merchant, reaching the farmer after having passed through the hands of several middlemen, and compelling him to pay to them very liberal, not to say exorbitant, profits and rates of interest. The end of the year frequently found the farmer unable to meet his obligations for supplies obtained upon these terms, and in this way many fine estates were sacrificed under foreclosure of deeds of trust. Probably no other country except that of cotton production could have withstood, and even slowly prospered under, these adverse circumstances. The agriculture of Mississippi has run the course common to most states—improvident, careless farming on rich lands, exhaustion and restoration. It is now the period of restoration, and while the state has abundance of fertile land yet untouched, a great deal is being accomplished by the improvement of lands which have been heretofore impoverished by previous careless agriculture. There has been a marked improvement in the methods of culture, the treatment of the soil, and the diversification of crops in the past few years. A very encouraging advance has been made in agricultural methods, but much remains to be done to bring the state up to that high degree of agricultural prosperity which nature seems to have designed for its people to enjoy. New ideas are rapidly taking hold of the people. The obsolete agencies of the slave period have been discarded for methods better suited to the new regime. Improved implements, intensive cultivation, diversification of crops, fine stock, fruit and vegetable production, are the means which are quietly effecting a revolution in agriculture. The progress has been especially rapid in the last four years; lands have advanced in value, and there is a hopeful, cheerful, contented feeling abroad in the state."

The causes of these changes are interesting. Not the least of them were agitation for them among the farmers themselves, smaller farms, competition, and educational efforts of all kinds.

The State grange and similar societies represent the first movement mentioned. This was organized on March 15, 1872, at Rienzi, Miss., by O. H. Kelly, secretary of the National grange, and Gen. A. J. Vaughn was chosen master of the state organization. His successors have been: W. L. Hemingway, elected in 1874; Capt. P. Darden, in 1876, serving until his death in 1888; Dr. J. B. Bailey, serving from then until the election of the present incumbent in 1890—Hon. S. L. Wilson. Capt. W. L. Williams, of Alcorn county, served as secretary until 1880, since which date Mrs. Helen A. Aby of Claiborne has served. The successive annual meetings have been held as follows: Columbus, 1872; Jackson, 1873-4; Kosciusko, 1875; Jackson, 1876; Holly Springs, 1877; Okalona, 1878; Forest, 1879; Brook Haven, 1880; Durant, 1881; Jackson, 1882; Meridian, 1883; Jackson, 1884; Durant, 1885; Jackson, 1886-7; Newton, 1888; Forest, 1889; and Hickory, 1890. In March, 1872, there were but six local granges, with one hundred and twenty-three members; in December there were fifty-six, with one thousand six hundred and eighty members. The movement has enrolled from the first as high as thirty thousand members in the state, but it now has forty-six local granges, and about two thousand members. This is taken as an old and representative illustration of similar movements in the state. These movements led to the establishment of agricultural schools as means of advancement.

These schools—one for white and one for colored, with one for white girls—are treated at length in the proper place. It must suffice to say here that they are having in their respective spheres a success that proves the wisdom of their founding as powerful allies to these efforts to put all phases of agricultural life on the highest basis possible.

The change in size of farms is another vastly important feature in developing and economizing land resources. "One of the most encouraging features in the agriculture of Mississippi," said a recent writer, "is that the large plantations are being gradually subdivided into smaller holdings. As before remarked, the system prior to the close of the late war was one of large estates, and there was a strong tendency among slave-owners to enlarge annually the size of their plantations with the increase of slaves. To-day, just the contrary policy is pursued; the tendency is to contract the size of the larger plantations, intensify and improve the cultivation, and generally to obtain the highest results from a given area of land. The individual cultivation of fewer acres by improved methods is now the popular idea. The statistics of the census show that the progress in this direction is quite marked, a fact that will be gratifying to those who believe that the agricultural prosperity of the state and the value of lands will be increased by the subdivision of large plantations, and the acquisition of homesteads by an intelligent and industrious class of immigrants." From 1850, when there were thirty-three thousand nine hundred and sixty farms with an acreage of ten million four hundred and ninety thousand four hundred and nineteen, and an improved acreage of three million four hundred and forty-four thousand three hundred and fifty-eight, and with an average size of three hundred and nine acres, to 1850, when there were forty-two thousand eight hundred and forty farms of fifteen million eight hundred and thirty-nine thousand six hundred and eighty-four acres, with an improved acreage of five million sixty-five thousand seven hundred and fifty-five, and an average farm size of three hundred and seventy acres, the gain in number of farms was only twenty-six per cent.

From 1870, when there were sixty-eight thousand and twenty-three farms of thirteen million one hundred and twenty-one thousand one hundred and thirteen acres, with an improved acreage of four million two hundred and seven thousand one hundred and forty-six, and an average size of only one hundred and ninety-three acres, to 1880, when there were one hundred and one thousand seven hundred and seventy-two farms of fifteen million eight hundred and fifty-five thousand four hundred and sixty-two acres, with an improved acreage of five million two hundred and sixteen thousand nine hundred and thirty-seven, and an average size of only one hundred and fifty-six acres, the gain in number of farms was within a small fraction of fifty per cent. It will be noticed that the average size was in 1880 two hundred and fourteen acres less than in 1860, a twenty years' interval. This is striking proof of the tendency to small farms. Said Colonel Power, writing in 1889: "Large farms will soon cease to be the rule in Mississippi," and adds that in 1890, "there will be fully one hundred and twenty-five thousand farms. Lands are still very cheap, because in larger tracts than they can be profitably cultivated under the present labor system, and hence necessity forces the sale of all that can not be held or cultivated." By acres, the distribution of number of farms was as follows in 1880: eighty-four farms were below three acres; two thousand three hundred and thirty-six farms between three and ten acres; eleven thousand nine hundred and thirty-six farms between ten and twenty acres; twenty-six thousand eight hundred and thirty-six farms between twenty and fifty acres; nineteen thousand three hundred and eighteen farms between fifty and one hundred acres; thirty-five thousand four hundred and ninety-three farms between one hundred and five hundred acres; three thousand nine hundred and thirty-six farms between five hundred and one thousand acres; and only one thousand eight hundred and eighty-three farms of over one thousand acres.

In this connection it is important to note certain leading features of the labor system in agriculture, as having a most serious bearing on this greatest interest of the state. It can not be better done than by using the words of Major Hurt: "The problem of labor lies at the very foundation of all agricultural prosperity. There can be no permanent advancement in agriculture when the labor by which the soil is tilled is indolent, uncertain and difficult to control. Ever since the emancipation of the slaves, this great question has been anxiously and seriously considered by the planters of Mississippi. While it can not be said that a solution has been reached, the question is not discussed as extensively as formerly. The colored people, who form the great bulk of agricultural laborers in this state, have of late years manifested a deeper interest in their own material welfare; they have taken less interest in politics; they are no longer harassed by fears that their freedom is in peril; they realize that all the rights of citizenship are accorded them, and that as long as they live in the midst of the whites there is an interdependence of interests between the two races, to an extent that whatever promotes the welfare of their white neighbors must necessarily redound to their own advantage. They begin to understand and appreciate the full force of this mutuality of interests, and with this better understanding has come a marked improvement in their usefulness as laborers. Left to themselves, and free from the influences of designing politicians, it is but just to say that they afford perhaps the best class of laborers for the large cottonfields, especially in the Yazoo delta. Many planters, indeed, consider negro labor the only kind suited to the existing methods of cotton culture, with which long experience has made them familiar. Frequent attempts have been made to introduce labor from abroad, especially from the European countries. But little success, however, has attended these attempts, probably owing to the fact that there was no systematic and organized effort to obtain and retain this class of laborers, and the further fact that they were not introduced in sufficient numbers to overcome the objectionable competition with the colored labor already established. The difficulty was not one of climate, as has been erroneously supposed. There is no climatic bar, a fact which has been practically established. There are many instances of Swedes and others, from more northern latitudes, working successfully and without any great inconvenience throughout the hottest summer months. The main body of farm labor is, moreover, accomplished before the heated term comes fairly on, and besides there is generally a gulf breeze in Mississippi which greatly tempers the rays of the summer sun. Early corn is laid by before the hot season, while the attention which cotton requires in midsummer may be given in the cooler portions of the day. Of course there is no difficulty of this kind in the way of native white labor, as more than one-third of the cotton product of the state is the result of white labor.''

As to systems of labor, he continues: "There are three systems of cultivation as respects labor in vogue among the landowners of Mississippi, each having its advantages and defects. They are the wages system, the share system and the rental system. The wages plan, under which the laborer receives a certain stipulated sum by the month or year, is preferred by many farmers, especially those who labor for themselves, for by taking the lead and exercising close supervision they obtain better results than is possible under either of the other two systems. By this plan the farmer can control his labor, superintend the cultivation of the soil and hold in perfect discipline the forces with which to make and harvest the crops, and also to carry on the improvements necessary to keep the farm in good repair. It is not always, however, that laborers can be obtained on this plan. As a general thing, the colored people are adverse to working for wages, preferring a semi-proprietorship or partnership in the products of their labor. The share system, originating soon after the war, is quite extensively adopted throughout the state. It is, however, considered by many objectionable, as under its operation the lands are allowed to deteriorate in value, the laborer caring little for their preservation and for future results. To this system, perhaps more than anything else, may be attributed the slovenly and unremunerative methods of agriculture sometimes met with in this state. When the share system is adopted the landowner furnishes the supplies necessary to make the crop to the laborer, he has a lien to that amount, without the formality of writing, on the laborer's share of the crop, under the provisions of the existing agricultural lien law, and in like manner the laborer has a lien for his wages. In other cases the laborer gives a mortgage to the merchant on his share of the crop to secure the value of supplies advanced. The rental system has grown quite popular with many landowners. By this method the farms are rented for a specific amount of money, or pounds of cotton, the tenants making their own terms for supplies and assuming all risks. Under existing law this plan is quite safe for the landowner, for he is entitled to the crop, to the exclusion of all others, as fast as harvested, until his rent is satisfied. As to the earnings of the laborer, of course much depends on the character of the soil, season, markets and the prudence and energy exercised in cultivation. One thing, however, may be said of labor in Mississippi—the prudent and industrious laborer need not long remain simply a laborer, as the rewards of labor are nowhere more certain; land is cheap and easily secured, can be bought on long credit, and in a brief time the frugal and industrious laborer becomes himself a landed proprietor.''

Interesting as it would be to enter more in detail into these subjects, but one more feature can be noticed, namely, the restoration of land by the use of fertilizers of various sorts. Says a recent student of this subject: "The era of restoration of exhausted soils and the preservation of the fertile lands of the state, too long delayed, is now fairly inaugurated, and it is expected that there will hereafter be a large annual increase in the use of these means, promising results of the highest practical importance. More attention is being paid to the care, collection and application of barnyard manure, which costs but little time and no money, and which, by itself, supplies the ingredients necessary to insure permanent and active fertility. It is said that European agriculturists consider that anyone who even sells the manure which accumulates on his land, instead of returning it to the soil, is fast ruining his estate. The agriculturists of Mississippi have not yet reached that point of appreciation for the materials necessary to keep their soil fertile and to restore already exhausted lands, but the improvement in this respect is notable, and promises well for the future. The materials for cheap and ready fertilizing are abundant throughout the state. There are many beds of marl, calcareous and gypseous, marsh and pond muck, lignitic clays and other substances suitable for composting, and, above all, is cottonseed and its product, cottonseed meal, which have no rivals as fertilizers. The valuable purposes to which cottonseed may be now applied are such that the seed is no inconsiderable part of the profits of the crop. Many years ago cottonseed was looked on as a nuisance, and often attempts were made to get rid of it by burning in a heap, the planters seeming to entertain no suspicion of its value as an application to the land. It is said to have been a common practice with the planters of the Mississippi bottom, with whom cottonseed was a drug, to get rid of it by hauling it to the bayous, where a part was eaten by the hogs and the rest washed away. The stalks also were generally pulled up or knocked down and burned on the field." This is all changed. Fertilizer manufacturers are now in almost every city in the state, and the trade is now recognized as one of the permanent ones.

Let some of the results of the different lines of agriculture be considered. Take the great line of cotton. Says Prof. Eugene Hilgard: "There is no natural cause why Mississippi should ever cease to be what she has been for some time past, the banner state for cotton production. Texas, with its vast area, may surpass Mississippi in total product by force of numbers as it were; but it would be difficult to cut out of that state an area equal to that of Mississippi which would equal the latter state as a whole in capacity of production." The product in 1883 was one million and fifty-two thousand one hundred bales, valued at $46,292,400, and other years of the past decade have approached that figure, and it is acknowledged that the yield of this state is safer and surer than that of other states. About one-third is raised by white labor. It is noticeable, too, that the state is beginning to consume a large amount of its cotton product, as is indicated by the fact that the last two years has witnessed the consumption of over thirty thousand bales within the state.

Take the fruit-growing and vegetable lines. Truck farming on an improved scale was begun in Copiah county in 1874. Rev. J. W. McNeil and Mr. Stackhouse were pioneers at Crystal Springs. About twenty years since Mr. Cassel of Canton began advancements in horticulture, and in 1872 the McKay brothers—Dr. H. E., John and W. T. McKay—began the present extensive strawberry culture. Said a writer in a New Orleans paper in 1887:

"In the central and southern portions of Mississippi fruit and vegetable production as a business has been found so profitable as to obtain a firm footing there within the past few years. This part of the state possesses many advantages for this, and is attracting the attention of market gardeners of the North and West. The winters are mild and short, and successive crops of a large variety of vegetables can be raised during the year with outdoor culture. It is claimed that in the extreme southern portions of the state, with reasonable attention, green peas, lettuce, radishes, and a number of other vegetables, can be raised every month in the year.

"The most successful fruits in the state are the peach, apple, plum, pomegranate, pear, fig, orange, and of the smaller fruits, strawberries, raspberries, blackberries, etc.

"Of peaches there are shipped from Crystal Springs, Terry and Hazlehurst annually not less than one hundred and fifty thousand boxes, of one-third a bushel each, to New Orleans and Western markets. There are not less than two thousand acres cultivated in the peach belt, which extends about seventy-five miles along the Illinois Central. New orchards are being planted annually, and more interest has been shown during the last few years, owing to the profitableness of orchards and their not being killed as much as formerly by frosts. The most profitable varieties are the Early Rivers, May Beauty, Early Rose, Tillotson, Thurber, Crawford's and Picquet Late. The lands best adapted to peach culture are the black sandy piny woods and the deep red limy lands. Peaches which grow on this soil are noted for their beautiful red color and deliciousness, similar to those of the famous Michigan peach lands, which, before the yellows predominated, were valued at $1,000 per acre. Peach culture is one of the growing industries of the state. Some attention has also been given to the cultivation of early varieties of apples, as the Astrachan, Carolina, June and Early Harvest varieties. They generally bring remunerative prices. The Le Conte pear is being successfully introduced.

"Strawberries are also cultivated for the Northern markets, especially along the line of the Illinois Central railroad, Crystal Springs, Terry, Jackson and Durant being favorite localities. The area in strawberries at these points is two thousand one hundred and fifty acres. The most prolific varieties are the Charleston, Wilsons, Crescent Seedling and Sucker State. Strawberries have always paid well, because they get into market early. The crop this year has not been as profitable as in the past, the unseasonable spring having somewhat affected and delayed it.

"The orange grows mainly on the coast of Mississippi. Those produced there are pronounced equal to any in the market, and sell for $10 per thousand at the orchard. The severe winter of two years ago inflicted a heavy loss on the growers, killing a number of the young trees, but the industry is reviving.

"Grapes of various kinds grow throughout the state, largely on the Gulf coast, and some wine is made there, but the industry has never reached the proportions it should. The Concord, several varieties of Ives Seedlings, and some of the table grapes of France succeed well, but the native grape, the Scuppernong, is the peculiar boast. It requires no particular care and little or no pruning.

"In Winston and other more northern counties the Black Scuppernong, Flowers, Tender Pulp, Thomas, and the Sugar of the Scuppernong varieties, also, the Hartford, Ives, Concord, Delaware, Martha, Lindley, Allen's Hybrid and others are cultivated. All do well, and a dry sweet wine is made from them. One vineyard, only twenty-four acres in extent, produced one thousand two hundred gallons of wine, which sells at $2 per gallon. Other farmers in the neighborhood have lately established vineyards. There are four hundred acres in Winston county alone under cultivation in grapes, all of which are doing well and proving profitable.

"The vegetable business has assumed large proportions in Mississippi. From thirty thousand to forty thousand boxes of tomatoes are annually shipped from Crystal Springs. Melons, cucumbers, beans, peas, asparagus, egg-plant, pepper, squash, Irish potatoes and early sweet potatoes are also grown in large quantities to supply the increasing demand of Western cities. Sweet potatoes have proved to be a profitable crop, bringing $1 per bushel in the West.

"Crystal Springs makes the largest shipments of fruits and vegetables of any point in the state, the most profitable crops being strawberries, cantaloupes and tomatoes. The average yield of these is from $200 to $250 per acre. The shipments include radishes, asparagus, onions, potatoes, beets, beans, peas, strawberries, plums, peaches, tomatoes and melons.

"The Tiffany refrigerator cars, now used by the railroads, have given this early fruit and vegetable industry a great impetus. The fruit formerly sent by express paid such heavy freight charges that all the profits were eaten up, whereas now a large number of refrigerator cars are run on the Illinois Central, Mobile & Ohio, and New Orleans & Northeastern roads, carrying the fruit to the Northern markets cheaply, and getting it there in good condition.

"The Illinois Central railroad transported of fruit, from points along its line in Mississippi, two hundred and fifty-nine thousand four hundred pounds in 1884, seven hundred and thirty-six thousand seven hundred pounds in 1885, and one million two hundred and thirty-one thousand six hundred pounds in 1886. No account is given of the vegetables transported. The Louisville & Nashville railroad carried, during 1886, two hundred and fifty-one thousand eight hundred pounds of fruit and vegetables raised in the state; the New Orleans & Northeastern, five million seven hundred and ninety-eight thousand pounds; and the Vicksburg & Meridian, two million seven hundred and fifty thousand pounds.

"The total production of the state of fruits and vegetables for the past year has been $1,260,000, of which nearly two-thirds was shipped out of the state, New Orleans, Chicago and St. Louis being favorite markets. The production in 1880 was of fruit $378,145, of vegetables $61,735, so that some idea can be formed of the increase in this line and the wealth thus added to the state."

But take other lines, so well described in the article above referred to.

"It is only within the present decade that the advantages of Mississippi for stock growing and dairying have been fully recognized, and it has pushed forward and become the leading dairy state of the South. It now boasts of more creameries than any of the Gulf or Southwestern states, more breeders of blooded cattle and more high grade-cows. Difficulties have been encountered and overcome, and the great advantages far more than compensate for these.

"Mr. S. A. Jones, commissioner from Mississippi to the late World's industrial exposition, in his report to the *Times-Democrat*, calls attention to the fact that before the war almost every Mississippi farmer was a stockraiser and that thousands of blooded cattle then fed upon her prairies and luxuriated in the rich grasses of her valleys.

"It was one of the theories of Western farmers that the South could not compete with that section in grasses. The idea is to-day thoroughly exploded. It is now proved that in Mississippi, particularly in the rich lime belt in the eastern portion of the state, and even in the piny woods, grasses of all kinds, cultivated as well as native, will grow. Nowhere does Kentucky blue grass do better than here, and clover yields from six thousand to nine thousand pounds of hay per acre when planted late in October, after the other crops have been harvested, improving the land at the same time.

"Indeed, Mississippi hay has become so popular that the astonishing circumstance is seen of rich New Yorkers purchasing it in the New Orleans market for the purpose of using it in their fancy stables.

"The exhibit of grasses made by the state at the World's exposition showed its stock and dairy possibilities. It demonstrated the fact that every county was well adapted to grass-growing and stock-farming. This exhibit consisted of fifty-two bales of hay, including timothy, Japanese clover, water grass, wild millet, white clover, red clover, burr clover, crab grass, boar grass, Bermuda grass, chicken corn, red top, pea vine, Milo maize, velvet grass, all of the best quality.

"Such a display naturally gave a new impetus to the dairy industry, and in central and eastern Mississippi the amount of land planted in grass has since increased with each year.

"In consequence of the success in raising these grasses, Mississippians began improving the breed of their cattle and imported blooded stock. No state in the South has gone more extensively into the business, and every breed has been thoroughly experimented with and tested. The agricultural department, in its report on the condition of cattle in Mississippi, calculated the improvement in the standing of its stock by the importation of and crossing with better breeds, at thirty-five per cent.

The following is the view taken of the cattle industry in Mississippi by the department in its last report, published but a few months ago:

"The farmers are manifesting a determination, with a true spirit of progress, to make stockraising a success. They are improving their cattle, horses and mules by introducing fine blooded stock. A large number of counties report intense interest taken in raising horses and mules, and will, ere long, raise a sufficiency for home use. Correspondents report great improvement in building shelters for stock, and providing large quantities of hay for winter supply. They are fencing in large pastures for grazing purposes, and sowing grasses for early spring use. A very remarkable feature in the reports is, not one mentions disease of any kind among horses, mules or cattle.'

"Mississippi has the largest number of breeders of fine stock of any Southern state, the number of breeders of Jersey being two hundred and fifty, and the Jerseys registered and entitled to registration in the state being two thousand out of a total of seven thousand four hundred and twenty-five in the South.

"There is but one herd of Brittany cattle in the South—the largest in the country, and one of a very few herds owned at Starkville, Miss. One of the largest herds of Ayrshire, numbering about twenty, is also to be found in eastern Mississippi. Of Devons, there are several breeders in the state. Large importations were made of this cattle two or three years ago, but they did not do as well as other breeds and many of them died. The Agricultural and Mechanical college possesses the only herd of Herefords known to be in the state. The Holstein cattle are in great favor, and rank in point of numbers second in Mississippi; and in Holsteins and Jerseys Mississippi is far ahead of its neighbors. There are some thirty-five breeders of the former cattle, and the herds number one hundred and twenty-five, one or two being over twenty each. There are some Galloways around Starkville, almost the only ones in the South. Of Shorthorns, there are one hundred and fourteen breeders in the state, and some six hundred cattle.

"Creameries are springing up so fast in Mississippi that it is almost impossible to keep count of them. There are two at Starkville, around which there has been the greatest development in stockraising and dairy-farming—one belonging to the State Agricultural and Mechanical college, and the first creamery established in the South (and it is to be noted that this college has the only professorship of dairying in the country), one at Meridian, and others near Bolton, Macon, Aberdeen, Corinth and West Point, and a separator at Vicksburg, owned by a very eminent breeder of Jerseys—the first separator in the state. Since the success of these creameries, central and eastern Mississippi have been encouraged to embark in the dairy business, and creameries are now under way or proposed at Durant,

Holly Springs, Hernando, Crawford, Oxford, Flora, Clinton, Yazoo city, Jackson and Stanton. Macon and Aberdeen have cheese-making machinery.

"The butter made at the State Agricultural college at Starkville has gone to many of the markets of the South. It outsells creamery Elgin, and is better. From November to May, the milk of the college herd averages about one pound of butter to sixteen pounds of milk; and it has reached as high as a pound of butter to fourteen and one-half of milk—the highest average known. The herd from which this milk is taken is one-half native cattle, mixed with Jerseys and a few Holsteins.

"The dairy products of Mississippi have now reached a very respectable figure. In 1870 only two million six hundred and thirteen thousand three hundred and eleven pounds of butter were produced in the state; in 1880, seven million four hundred and fifty-four thousand six hundred and forty-three pounds; in 1885 and 1886, an average of fifteen million eight hundred and twenty-five thousand pounds, worth \$3,800,000. This is a splendid growth for six years, and the promise is even better for the future. There has been a large increase in the number of milch cows in the state, and in their average yield. The hay crop, moreover, is steadily increasing, being fourteen thousand eight hundred and seventy-five tons now against eight thousand eight hundred and ninety-four in 1880.

"In the matter of stockraising, an average of ten acres of Mississippi land is sufficient to furnish each animal with ample grazing, making the cost of pasturing a steer only \$2 per year, since nothing is paid for attendance on herds grazing at will on farms. This is less than one-quarter of the same item in Illinois.

"The advantages enumerated in favor of cattle-growing and dairying in Mississippi, as compared with the Western states, are: The cheapness of the land; the excellent pasturage to be had through the year, requiring the cattle to be fed only one or two months at most during the winter; the natural grasses and canebrakes, which afford the cattle so much extra food; the climate, which allows them to run at large without any danger; the abundance of water, etc., needed for the stock; and the nearness to excellent markets.

"Dr. W. E. Oates, of Warren county, Miss., one of the most successful raisers of Jersey cattle in the South, says:

"'After several years' experience in breeding and raising thoroughbred Jersey cattle, Southdown sheep, Berkshire and Poland China swine, I do not hesitate to say that Warren county, Miss., is equal, if not superior, in some respects, to the famous blue-grass region of Kentucky. It only needs the life-giving touch of the skilled husbandman to convert the hills and valleys into gardens of Eden. Clovers luxuriate in our soil. The Bermuda grass covers nearly all our hills and valleys, and it will pasture, acre for acre, more stock in summer than the blue-grass lands of Kentucky. Its power to resist drought is greater, and analysis places it, pound for pound, in value with blue grass. On our meadow land as much as three and a half tons per acre have been cut of very superior hay.'

"The raising of sheep, the production of wool and of mutton, has met with several very serious blows lately, growing out of economic causes, principally changes in the wool tariff. In Mississippi, however, sheep-raising still continues a profitable industry, the smaller breed of sheep being in favor, as the animals are grown principally for their wool. The pastures of the state, abandoned by the cotton planters on account of the presence of the Bermuda, may be made far more profitable as a sheep walk than when under cotton culture, with less labor, worry and risk involved in planting.

"It should be remembered that Mississippi took the first prize at the London world exhibit of thirty years ago for its wool, and that, at the World's industrial exposition, there were no less than fifty-one exhibits of wool from twenty-eight counties.

"Hogs of any breeds do well in the state, but the white breeds are not much sought after. The Berkshires and Essex are popular, on account of the readiness with which they fatten at any age. The Poland China ranks next. The Jersey reds, Yorkshires and Sussex are also among the better breeds in favor.

"The number and value of stock in the state is as follows: Horses, one hundred and thirty thousand one hundred and sixty, $9,187,566; mules, one hundred and fifty-three thousand four hundred and twelve, $12,953,958; milch cows, two hundred and eighty-three thousand and seventy-three, $4,076,251; oxen, four hundred and twenty-four thousand six hundred and sixty-two, $3,823,653; sheep, two hundred and forty-two thousand nine hundred and seventy-one, $348,664; hogs, one million one hundred and fifteen thousand one hundred and seventy-two, $3,345,516. Total, $33,735,608. As compared with $24,287,717 in 1880, this shows an increase of thirty-eight per cent., the greatest improvement being in milch cows.

"No one now disputes that Mississippi led the entire Union in the exhibits of woods at the World's industrial exposition in New Orleans. In nothing was the exposition so well represented as in the exhibits of the forest products of the Southern states, and in these Mississippi stood at the head of the list with one hundred and thirty-four varieties of wood. One specimen, a yellow poplar from Holmes county, showed a log more than twelve feet in diameter, while others were five, six and seven feet.

"There are nineteen million nine hundred thousand four hundred and ninety-two acres of forest land in Mississippi, some sixty per cent. of the entire area of the state, and nearly all of it is in wood of valuable varieties, such as pine, gum, oak and cottonwood.

"The timbers as yet most utilized in the state are pine, cypress and oak. Pine covers the southern half of the state, and constitutes about two-thirds of the lumber produced. The merits of the Southern pine need not be recapitulated here. It is one of the heaviest, strongest and most durable of woods, and is employed in all heavy edifices, in the construction of cars, for beams, etc. It is now the principal lumber used in Latin America, and large quantities are shipped there. It has also grown in favor in the North and West, and is sold extensively in the Chicago and New York markets. While rather coarser than the white pine of Michigan, it is stronger and more durable, and offers a good substitute for it. Recognizing the fact that the yellow pine forests of Mississippi must soon come into use to supply the deficiencies caused by the destruction of the woodlands in the Western states, the 'pine barons' of Illinois, Michigan and Wisconsin have bought up large areas of these lands in Mississippi, estimated at one million five hundred thousand acres; but little of which has yet been cut or utilized, but is being reserved for the time when good pine lumber becomes scarce—a time not far distant. This land, which was bought at an average of $2 per acre, has, standing on it, lumber worth $30 to $35, sawed on the place.

"The following is the estimate of the pine still standing in the state:

"Longleaf pine—standing west of Pearl river, six billion eight hundred million feet; east of Pearl river, seven billion six hundred million feet; region of mixed growth, three billion eight hundred million feet; total, eighteen billion two hundred million feet. Shortleaf pine —standing in the northwestern region, one billion six hundred million feet; standing in the northern portion of state, five billion one hundred and seventy-five million feet; total, six billion seven hundred and seventy-five million feet; grand total, twenty-four billion nine hundred and seventy-five million feet.

"Along the Gulf coast and the Illinois Central and New Orleans & Northeastern railroads are many sawmills, including two of the largest in the South, which are extensively engaged

in sawing lumber for foreign market. Mississippi supplied all the lumber used in the construction of the buildings at the World's exposition, and now supplies a large portion of the yellow pine used in Chicago in the construction of heavy buildings, while the exports from Pearl river, Pascagoula, Moss Point and other towns on the coast, go to South America, Europe, and even to Africa. A considerable portion of the lumber used in the work on the Panama canal is from Mississippi, and within the past two months there have been heavy shipments from that state to the Canary islands.

"The Yazoo valley is as abundantly wooded as the coast region, but in different varieties of timber, gum, oak, cypress and magnolia predominating. Its importance as a lumber region for the future, and the immense supply of available timber there, have only recently been recognized. As a result there have been large purchases by companies and syndicates of these woodlands, over one million two hundred thousand acres having been purchased in the last three years.

"In this valley stands the largest area of sweet gum in the world, a timber that promises to take, in time and with the proper treatment, the place of black walnut as a cabinet wood. The gum grows to a large, straight tree, ninety feet high, furnishing a considerable amount of lumber. This lumber has been found to be eminently adapted for cabinet purposes. Polished, it attains a rich and elegant satiny gloss far superior to black walnut. The wood has only one inconvenience, it warps very badly, and, unless this evil can be corrected, it will not grow in favor. This defect, however, it is claimed, can be remedied. A considerable amount of gum is now being shipped to Cincinnati and other cities engaged in the manufacture of furniture, and fine desks, armoires and tables have been made from it. It is also extensively used in house building, and lasts well.

"The rapid disappearance of black walnut, nearly all of which has been destroyed in the Northern states, renders it necessary to discover some substitute for it, and it is suggested that the sweet gum will take its place. The supply of it is practically inexhaustible, and it grows in large clumps, and is generally easy of access. During the past few years several syndicates have made extensive purchases of lands in Mississippi, well wooded, largely in gum, with the intention of bringing this lumber into general use for cabinet purposes. Experiments have been made with it, whereby its defects have been, it is said, corrected. If this can be done, it will make gum the furniture wood of the country during the next twenty years.

"One of the great advantages the timber lands of the Yazoo possess is that after the timber is cut from them, they are even more valuable than when it was standing. The soil is fertile, unlike that of most other wooded sections, and land which when timbered, was worth only $10 to $25 an acre, becomes worth $25 to $50 when cleared and suitable for crops.

"The other principal woods of the state are walnut, cypress, ash, red oak, white oak, red gum, white gum, black gum, tupelo gum, poplar, pecan and hickory. The red and other gums are used for furniture, and the Singer sewing machine company employes them almost exclusively for the woodwork of their machines. The white oak staves are sent to New Orleans and exported thence to Spain, France and other wine-producing countries, bringing at New Orleans from $75 to $140 per thousand.

"The following figures will give some idea of the improvement that has taken place in the lumbering industry of the state: Number of establishments 1886, five hundred and ninety-eight; capital, $2,698,400; hands, three thousand one hundred and twenty-five; products, $3,975,000. Number establishments 1880, three hundred and ninety-five; capital, $922,595; hands, one thousand one hundred and seventy; products, $1,920,335.

"It is in its manufactures that Mississippi is most backward. And yet it possesses all the advantages for leading in certain lines of industry. It ought to be one of the largest producers of cotton cloth in the world. It has the cotton within easy reach of the mills, and it has a fine market for the product. It ought to be the center of the lumbering industry of the country as it possesses the greatest variety of fine woods, and of furniture factories, carriage and wagon factories, etc. It formerly paid little attention to these industries, but it is now beginning to recognize the importance of greater diversification in its industries, to see that it does not benefit a state to devote itself wholly to agriculture. The towns which were formerly merely commercial and social centers are growing in population and anxious to increase their factories.

"The good will of the people of Mississippi toward manufactures, the inducements they hold out, are shown in the act of the legislature passed in 1882, exempting from taxation, for a period of ten years, the machinery used for the manufacture of cotton and woolen goods, yarns or fabrics, etc.

"As a consequence of the encouragement held out, the product of manufactures has almost doubled within the last seven years. The new industries established have been organized almost wholly with home capital.

"As is natural, this manufacturing has been confined mainly to turning the raw products of the state into more valuable forms, making the cotton into cloth, the cottonseed into oil, the timber into planks, etc.

"The cottonmills of Mississippi have been particularly prosperous, and the Mississippi mills at Wesson now turn out more goods than the whole state did in 1880. The cotton factories now give employment to two thousand and twenty-three hands, with a total annual output of $1,686,000. The products are shipped to the Northeast and West, only a small proportion remaining at home. During the past two years four new cottonmills have been erected in the state.

"Of the cottonseed oilmills that at Yazoo is the largest in the state, with an annual production of $150,000. The bulk of this product is shipped to New Orleans, whence it goes to Europe, the oil to Italy and France, to return as olive oil; the meal and cake to England for fattening cattle. Barely one-tenth of the product of the oilmills remains at home to fertilize the land and fatten stock.

"There are foundries in Jackson, Columbus, Vicksburg, Meridian, Corinth, Natchez, Canton and other points. Most of the railroads also have repair shops for the repair and rebuilding of their engines, cars, etc.

"Other industries are woolenmills, grist and flouringmills, pottery works, etc.

"The chief manufacturing interests and the amount of their products are the following: Lumber, $3,975,000; flouring and gristmills, $2,136,000; cotton goods, $1,686,000; cotton seed products, $1,120,000; woolen goods, $315,000; all other industries, $4,424,000.

"The following shows the increase in manufactures in the state in the past seven years: Number of establishments for the year 1886, two thousand three hundred and forty-two; value, $13,656,000. Number of establishments for the year 1880, one thousand four hundred and seventy-nine; value, $7,518,302. This is an improvement of seventy-nine per cent. in seven years.

"The Baltimore *Manufacturers' Record*, in reviewing the new industries established in the South, shows that the amount of capital invested in manufactures in Mississippi during the first quarter of 1887 is five times as great as during the corresponding quarter of 1886.

"Mississippi has never been regarded as much of a mineral state, and it is only within the last few years that the discoveries in Alabama have caused any examination to be made. The result has been the discovery of some minerals of undoubted and immediate value, and others whose value has not yet been definitely determined, but from which there is every reason to hope for important returns.

"The following are the most important of Mississippi minerals:

"Iron, found at Duck Hill, Enterprise and generally throughout the eastern and northern portions of the state. The ore averages from forty to seventy-five per cent. of metallic iron, sufficient to work it with great profit.

"Lignite or wood coal, underlying the entire yellow loam region in the northern portion of the state.

"Hydraulic limestone of excellent quality exists in the northeastern portion of the state. Cement made from it sets almost as rapidly as plaster of Paris, and becomes very hard. Prof. W. D. Moore, after making an examination of this limestone, said: 'I need not enlarge upon the importance to the immediate district and to the whole state of such a mineral deposit of hydraulic limestone, sufficient to supply the entire Mississippi valley with cement for generations to come, which can be worked easily, and from its vicinity to the Tennessee river, be easily transported to every part of the South and Southwest.'

"Limestone, for quicklime, building stones, grindstones and flagstones is also found in various parts of Mississippi.

"Gypsum, of a pure quality, has been found in considerable quantities throughout Mississippi, especially near Cato, in Rankin county, and near Kosciusko, Clinton, West Hinds and other places.

"The kaolin deposit in Tishomingo county is declared by Professor Harper to be the largest deposit of this mineral in the world.

"White sand fit for glass-making is found along the coast, and, indeed, a glass factory was successfully carried on at Moss Point until burned. A very superior article of glass sand is also to be obtained along the branch of the Illinois Central railroad, between Kosciusko and Aberdeen. Professor Hilgard declared that the Pearl river and its tributaries furnish 'drifts of white sand that often vie in purity with those of Ste. Genevieve in Missouri, whence the Pittsburg glassworks receive a large part of their supply.'

"Last but not least are the marls of various kinds found throughout the state. They are found in all the lower half of the state, differing somewhat in quality, but all well worth using.

"Professor Hilgard, who examined them thoroughly, said: 'My deduction from all the examinations I have given these marls is that they are far superior to the green sand marls of New Jersey in potash, for which the latter are chiefly distinguished, and also contain many other valuable elements of food life that the New Jersey marls totally lack.'

"A better manure can hardly be found. It is superior to all manure that the farmer can obtain from the farm, and is equal to guano and in some respects better, for while guano will produce a large crop the first year, its effect is not felt subsequently, while marl will exert its influence on the crop for ten years to come. In the first year its effect is but slight; it is better the second, third and fourth years. While these marls do not compare in commercial value nor in their effect upon the soil with the celebrated phosphate rocks that now make South Carolina famous and add millions of dollars a year to its wealth, yet their abundance, accessibility and diffusion make them a vast, inexhaustible source of wealth to the country where they are found, and they insure its fertility for centuries to come.

"The fisheries of the state are confined wholly to the gulf coast. Since the closing of

Bonnet Carre crevasse, which formerly allowed the water from the Mississippi to run into Mississippi sound, there has been a great improvement in the oyster beds off the gulf coast, and the oysters are now shipped not only to New Orleans, but to the North as well, where they are much relished, five canning factories being engaged in canning and preparing them.

"The fish caught off the coast are sent mainly to New Orleans and Mobile, few of them going North. The average annual catch of fish and oysters is now $225,000.

"These streams, with the railroads, give the planters four thousand and twenty-seven miles of route to market. Some of them are not to-day in complete navigable condition, but can be made so at small expense.

"The representatives of the United States statistical bureau estimate the traffic of Mississippi as follows:

"Cotton and cotton goods, $39,732,320; cottonseed oil and cake, $1,100,000; wool and woolen goods, $257,952; lumber, $3,940,000; fruit and vegetables, $250,000; fish and oysters, $235,000; cord wood, $1,500,000; total, $47,015,272. Of this $41,465,000 is exported from the state and represents its annual net earnings. Unfortunately most of this large sum goes for provisions brought from the West and manufactured goods, cottons, etc., from New England. If Mississippi raised these articles itself, as it is well able to do, it would keep all this money at home, and would soon become one of the richest states in the Union.

"In consequence of the building of railroads and the erection of factories, there has been a decided increase in population and commercial and industrial activity in the towns. Vicksburg, Natchez, Meridian, Jackson, Holly Springs, Grenada, Starkville, Columbus, Yazoo city, Water Valley, Greenville, Canton, Macon, Wesson, Brookhaven, Summit and Enterprise are all growing and prosperous places." It is greatly to be regretted that the census of 1890 is not available to make a later exhibit, especially as other sources are incomplete and therefore unavailable. Enough has been given, however, to illustrate, if not measure, Mississippi's great growth under two different systems of labor."

CHAPTER VII.

POLITICAL HISTORY.

IT is obvious to the reader that it would be impracticable to embrace within a single chapter in minute narrative and critical form a political history of the state of Mississippi, extending, as it does, through some of the most eventful periods of the general government, and covering a space of seventy-one years. It is, however, the design of the writer to state all of the important facts and interesting incidents properly belonging to such a history, accurately, uncolored by sectional prejudice or party-bias, for public information and use.

On June 12, 1797, President John Adams recommended the establishment of a government in the district at Natchez, and accordingly, by act of congress, approved April 7, 1793, all that tract of country described as bounded on the west by the Mississippi river, on the north by a line to be drawn due east from the south of the Yazoo to the Chattahoochie river, on the east by this river, and on the south by the thirty-first degree of north latitude, was constituted one district and called the Mississippi territory, and the president authorized to establish a government therein.

The territorial government, thus established, existed for fifteen years. Winthrop Sargent of Massachusetts; William Charles Cole Claiborne, of Virginia; Robert Williams, of North Carolina, and David Holmes, of Virginia, were the territorial governors. The most notable event which occurred at that time in the history of the territory and the United States, was the War of 1812. Maj. Thomas Hinds, for whom one of the most considerable counties in the state is named, and in which the capital is situated, with a battalion of Mississippi dragoons, was ordered to report to General Jackson at New Orleans. Their prowess and valor displayed upon this celebrated battlefield in history won for them the following plaudits of congratulation and praise from the General, who, possessing in an eminent degree the quality of courage and spirit of patriotism, readily discovered and generously applauded their exhibition in others. By military order he said: "The cavalry from the Mississippi territory was always ready to perform every service which the nature of the country enabled them to execute. The daring manner in which they reconnoitered the enemy on his lines excited the admiration of one army and the astonishment of the other."

Under Governor Williams' administration (extending from 1805 to 1809) of the territory this interesting episode took place. Colonel Burr and his retinue of men arrived opposite the capital site Washington, at the mouth of the Bayou Pierre run, in January, 1807, with a grotesque flotilla of nine flatboats. He soon learned that the territorial authorities would oppose his descent.

Colonel Burr in a letter to the governor " disavowed any hostile intentions toward the territory or the country; that he was en route to the Ouachita to colonize his lands and that any attempt to obstruct him would be illegal and might provoke civil war." A deputation of gentlemen, among them George Poindexter, was sent to interview Burr, with a letter from the governor. Colonel Burr, judging from all appearances, sneered at the idea of his having any hostile designs upon the country, saying that he would have gone direct to Natchez to see the governor (a point six miles distant from the capital) but for the information received at Bayou Pierre and the fear of assassination. Burr presented himself before Judge Rodney and gave his recognizance in the sum of $5,000, with sureties for his appearance at a called session of the supreme court to be held on February 2. George Poindexter was then the attorney-general for the territory. He moved the discharge of the grand jury. This was on the ground that in the depositions submitted to him by the court, he found no testimony which brought the offense charged against Colonel Burr within the jurisdiction of the courts of the Mississippi territory. He asked for the conveyance of the accused to a tribunal competent to try and punish him if guilty, and asked for the discharge of the grand jury. Judge Bruin declared against the discharge of the grand jury unless Colonel Burr was also discharged from his recognizance. The grand jury presented no bill against Colonel Burr, after a session, and were discharged. Colonel Burr then demanded a release from his recognizance, which the court refused, and he fled, forfeiting it.

At the close of the War of 1812, an exhaustive strain having been made upon the material conditions of the territory, they were appreciably stimulated with new life by increase of an enterprising population and influx of capital. The question of admitting the state into the Union was now canvassed with ardor and that pardonable sentiment of national pride which the American instinctively feels toward the government of the United States.

On March 1, 1817, President Madison approved an act to enable the people of the territory "to form for themselves a constitution and state government, and to assume such name as they deemed proper, and the state, when formed, was to be admitted into the Union upon the same footing with the original states." Qualifications of freedom, color, residence, and payment of territorial or county tax, authorized a vote in selecting delegates to form a constitution.

In accordance with this enabling act and the election held under it, the delegates, as chosen, assembled in the town of Washington in July, 1817, the convention adjourning on the 15th of August of that year. The qualifications prescribed by the constitution of 1817 for the governor were: Residence of five years in the state, the age of thirty years, possession of a freehold estate of six hundred acres of land within the state, or real estate of the value of $2,000. For the new lieutenant-governor the qualifications were the same. For a state senator: Twenty-six years of age, four years' residence in the state, to own in his own right one hundred and fifty acres of land or an interest in real estate of the value of $500 at the time of his election and for six months previous thereto. Every free white male of the age of twenty-one years or upward, a citizen of the United States, who had resided in the state one year, and the last six months in the county, city or town, and who had been enrolled in the militia, unless exempted by law from military service, and shall have paid a state or county tax, was declared to be an elector. The judicial and executive officers were made elective by the legislature. The first constitution of Mississippi was, therefore, formed and put into operation in the forty-second year of the independence of the United States of America. The earlier governors of the state under the constitution of 1817, in their consecutive order of election to office, were as follows: David Holmes, of Virginia; George Poindexter, of Virginia; Walter Leake, of Virginia; Gerard C. Brandon, a native of the territory, and Abram M. Scott, a native of South Carolina. David Holmes, the last territorial governor, was fitted by experience and ability to put into operation the machinery of the government in conformity with the provisions of the new constitution.

George Poindexter, of Virginia, is of national reputation, having been a member of both houses of the Federal congress. He is the author of Poindexter's Code of Mississippi, a work of high rank and great value in the judicial and legal annals of the state. In 1835, when Mr. Poindexter became a candidate for reëlection to the United States senate, he was defeated by Robert J. Walker, who was secretary of the treasury under President Polk.

The administration of Walter Leake was rendered conspicuous by the assembling of the constitutional convention of 1832, the convention which changed the whole structure of the organic law of the state.

The second term of Governor Brandon, covering the years 1830-31, is memorable in the state for the passage of two acts, one to establish the Planters' bank of the state of Mississippi and the other calling a convention to revise, modify or make a new constitution. Twelve years had elapsed, when the state had greatly increased in population; its agriculture had been extensively developed and the state was growing rapidly. The legislature of the state, at its annual session in 1830, determined, despite the exclusive privileges conferred upon the bank of the state of Mississippi, to incorporate an additional bank, to be known as the Planters' bank of the state of Mississippi, with a capital of $3,000,000. This act of incorporation was approved February 10, 1830. Two-thirds of the capital stock was reserved for subscription by the state, and the governor was authorized to subscribe for twenty thousand shares of the capital stock in the name and on behalf of the state, aggregating $2,000,000. The second section of the act of incorporation pledged the faith of the state to make good all losses which might accrue from a deficiency of the funds of the said bank, or by other means, in proportion to the amount of the stock which the state should have therein. The governor was empowered to have prepared and issued the bonds of the state of Mississippi for the sum of $2,000,000, to be signed by the governor and countersigned by the auditor of public accounts, and when so signed and countersigned it was made the duty of the governor to deliver the said bonds to the president and directors of the Planters' bank in payment of the subscription of the stock made for and by the state.

It was also made the duty of the president and directors of the Planters' bank to sell the bonds delivered to them by the governor for specie only. The said bonds were to be under the seal of the state, signed by the governor and countersigned by the auditor of public accounts, and made assignable by the endorsement of the president and cashier of the bank to the order of any person, or the bearer. The faith of the state was pledged for the payment of the principal and interest of these bonds upon their maturity, as well as the stock of the bank. It was also provided that if a dividend arising from the stock subscribed by the state, as specified, should be insufficient to meet the interest accruing on the bonds and the payment and extinguishment thereof when due, the bank was to supply such deficiency and charge the same to the account of the state, and for the payment thereof the faith of the state was pledged. Of the bonds of the state authorized to be delivered to the Planters' bank of Mississippi in payment of the stock subscribed for in the name of the state in that institution, $500,000 worth was sold in the year 1831 and the remaining $1,500,000 worth was disposed of in the course of the year 1833, and the money received therefor placed in the vaults of the bank. The constitution of 1817, unlike that of 1832, contained no clause prohibiting the state from pledging its face, and hence the legislature was clothed with plenary power in the premises. The bonds had been sold by the agent of the bank in strict conformity with the provisions of the law authorizing their issue, and for specie only, and the proceeds were properly paid over to the officers in charge of the institution. The bank was conducted on what are usually regarded as sound business principles and was in a highly prosperous condition until the great financial distress of 1837 came, which involved the commercial prosperity of the whole Union.

At this time the question of changing the constitution was debated, the state having outgrown the original constitution of 1817, and an organic law was demanded better calculated to meet the needs and conditions of a more prosperous and growing state. The question of the expediency and necessity of a constitutional convention was submitted by legislative act to the people, and a decided majority pronounced in favor of calling the proposed constitutional convention, which was accordingly done by legislative act passed and approved December 16, 1831. The convention convened in pursuance of the act, the 10th day of September, 1832.

The material change and distinguishing feature which characterized the constitution of 1832 was the enlargement of the liberty and power of the people through the ballot-box, by conferring authority on them to elect their own public servants, without reference to a property qualification. The most radical change, however, was that made in the judicial department of the government, making judicial functionaries, from the highest to the lowest, elective by the people. A superior court of chancery was authorized to be established and the chancellor was made elective by the people. A high court of errors and appeals was provided for, composed of three judges. Circuit and probate courts were provided for and these judges were all elected by the people, as also the district attorney.

The constitution of 1832 made Mississippi the pioneer state in embodying in her organic law the right of the people to select through the ballot box their judicial officers from those who presided over inferior tribunals to the court of last resort. At that time neither the constitution nor the laws of any state in the Union provided for a judiciary elected by the people, and in the interim, between 1832 and 1861, every state in the Union followed the example of Mississippi in this respect.

The tenure of office prescribed by the constitution of 1832 was two years, prohibiting the same individual from holding the office more than four in any six consecutive years. The powers conferred and the duties imposed on the executive were copied, in the main, from the constitution of 1817, the material difference being that the latter provided for, and prescribed, the duties of lieutenant-governor, while these duties under the constitution of 1832 were to be performed by the president of the senate when rendered necessary by reason of the death, resignation or removal from office of the governor.

Alexander G. McNutt, a native of Virginia, was the third governor of Mississippi, under the constitution of 1832, having been nominated by the democratic party, which, at that time, in 1837, had a large majority in the state over the whig party. Under his administration, the great era of the Flush Times existed, so inimitably described by Judge Baldwin in his interesting work of that name, and in his Party Leaders. The capital of the banks of the state incorporated by the legislature in less that six years after the formation of the constitution of 1832, aggregated the enormous sum of $53,750,000. To most of the railroads was given the privilege of banking; they were authorized to issue their own notes for circulation, to make loans and deals in exchange, bonds and bills of credit. The era of innumerable mushroom banks, inflated credit systems, and frenzied spirit of speculation produced an abundant harvest of distress and bankruptcy for the people of Mississippi. As this financial policy signally drew the line of division between the two prevailing parties of the state, the whigs and democrats, it will be somewhat disclosed in detail, giving rise, as it did, to a spirited and important political contest. The people at that time seemed to imagine that this species of legislature could provide substantial sources of revenue, and bring about permanent prosperity. They clamored for more banks and a still larger issue of worthless promises to pay. In obedience to this public demand for more money, the legislature early in the session of 1837 passed an act to incorporate the Union bank of Mississippi, with a capital of $15,500,000, which was approved January 21, 1837, "so far as the action of the legislature is recognized." In the original act of incorporation, in order to facilitate the said Union bank in its negotiation for this loan of $15,500,000, the faith of the state was pledged both for the security of the capital and interest, and ordered that there should be issued seven thousand five hundred bonds of $2,000 each, payable in four installments of twelve, fifteen and twenty years, and bearing interest at the rate of five per cent per annum, to be signed by the governor of the state to the order of the Mississippi Union bank, and countersigned by the state treasurer, and under the seal of the state. The bonds were made transferable by the endorsement of whomsoever or to the bearer, and the capital and interest of the bonds were payable by the bank at the time they severally fell due.

The charter of the Union bank, as originally enacted, authorized the issuance of the bonds of the state for $15,500,000, and their delivery to the bank as a loan. The bank was required to secure the payment of these bonds, and the prompt payment of the accruing interest by mortgage upon the property of the stockholders of the bank, but this did not satisfy the legislators of that day.

They passed an act to incorporate the subscribers to the Mississippi Union bank, requiring the governor to subscribe for, in behalf of the state, fifty thousand shares of the original stock of the bank, the same to be paid for out of the proceeds of the state bonds, as provided to be executed to the bank by the charter, and that the dividends and profits accruing and declared by the bank on stock subscribed for on behalf of the state, should be held by the bank subject to the control of the state legislature, for the purposes of internal improvement and promotion of education.

The president and directors of the Mississippi Union bank, or the managers, had ample power to appoint three commissioners to negotiate and sell the state bonds, provided for in the act incorporating the subscribers, in any market within the United States, or in any foreign market, under such rules and regulations as might be adopted by the president and directors, or managers, not inconsistent with the provisions of the charter of the bank providing against the sale of bonds under their par value. This supplementary act was approved by Governor McNutt on February 15, 1839, but a short time after the date of his approval of the original charter of the Union bank, after its passage by two successive legislatures, in obedience to the requirements of the constitution, during that year, bonds of the state to the amount of $5,000,000 were prepared, signed by the governor, countersigned by the treasurer of the state and delivered to the president and directors of the Union bank. The bank appointed three commissioners of integrity and purity of character to negotiate the bonds. They succeeded in disposing of the entire $5,000,000 worth of bonds to the honorable Nicholas Biddle, then the president of the United States bank of Pennsylvania. When the intelligence of the consummation of this negotiation reached the people of Mississippi they were wild with excitement, and the event was celebrated by great rejoicing and public demonstration,

In the meantime, Governor McNutt had inaugurated an unrelenting war against the Union bank, as well as all the other banks in the state. Two years previously, he had approved a law providing for the election by the legislature of three bank commissioners, who were to examine once a year into the condition of the several banks in the state and ascertain their capacity to meet their obligations, which, however, from many practical difficulties, was not productive of any good. In the governor's annual message to the legislature January, 1840, he recommended an immediate repeal of the charters of all the banks that were not able to meet promptly their obligations to their note-holders and depositors. In support of this proposition, he urged "the existing banks cannot be bolstered. Destitute as they are of credit and available means, it would be folly to attempt to infuse vigor and stability into their lifeless forms. They are powerless to do good, but capable of inflicting irreparable injuries."

In his next annual message, bearing date January 5, 1841, the governor renewed his assaults upon the Mississippi Union bank with great vigor, calling attention to the insolvent condition of the Mississippi Railway company, the Planters' bank of the state and the Mississippi Union bank, and their inability to resume specie payments or to make further loans. He favored, like his party (the democratic), the repudiation of the Union bank bonds. He argued that they were sold on a credit, instead of for cash, at their par value; that they had been purchased in the name of an institution—the United States bank of Pennsylvania—the charter of which absolutely prohibited that bank from buying or selling bonds or stocks other than issued by authority of the United States, or of the state of Pennsylvania. The legislature of that year, however, differed with the executive, and both houses, by decisive majorities, passed resolutions declaring that the honor of the state demanded that both the Union and Planters' bank bonds should be paid, both principal and interest.

The subject now had reached the proportions of a tremendous party question, and the whole state was stirred upon it with great popular excitement and partisan zeal. The democratic convention which assembled in January, 1841, nominated Tighlman M. Tucker for governor, and other officers, but made no reference in the platform adopted to the bond question. There was an ominous silence upon this point. A little later, the whigs met in convention and nominated a full ticket with Judge David O. Shattuck as governor, all in entire accord with the convention on the bond question, which had taken in its platform strong ground in favor of paying the state bonds. After one of the most exciting political campaigns in the state, the democratic party was successful in electing its whole state ticket, and a majority in both branches of the legislature. The largest taxpayers were of the opinion that the obligation on the part of the state thus created should be met honestly, basing their advocacy of payment upon the broad ground of equity and fairdealing. Leading citizens of the state at this day, survivors of that period, regard the policy of repudiation, then adopted, as a blunder of the magnitude which Talleyrand said was worse than a crime. It was a thrilling party fight. The ablest men of the time—and there were many in the state then—were engaged in it on either side of the great question. It was upon this question that the golden-mouthed orator furnished by the great state of Maine to the youthful southwestern Commonwealth, then in the zenith of his fame, extending with the confines of the Union, shed the transcendent glory of his imperial genius upon that memorable controversy in behalf of the good name and honor of Mississippi. It has been well said that he was to the whig party of Mississippi then what Charles Fox was to the whig party of England in his day. Albert Gallatin Brown, of South Carolina, was the fifth governor of the state chosen under the constitution of 1832. He was elected for two terms. During his second administration war commenced with Mexico, and with the aid of his skill, judgment and patriotism the first regiment of Mississippi, under the call made for volunteers from the Federal government, was organized and sent to that historic scene of international warfare, contributing much of the renown, prowess and valor which the American arms shed upon the flag of the United States. Governor Brown was one of the most prominent men of the state, and a strong pillar of the democratic party. He was essentially an ardent devotee to popular government and the principle of not tampering with the powers reserved to the people. He was for several terms in the national house of representatives, and from 1855 to '59 was a distinguished member of the United States senate. He and his colleague, Jefferson Davis, resigned their seats upon the receipt of the intelligence that the state had passed an ordinance of secession from the Union. His service as a member of the Confederate senate closed his public life.

John A. Quitman, of New York, after returning from Mexico with the fresh laurels won as a major-general on that foreign battlefield in behalf of his country, became the nominee of the democratic party for governor, being easily elected, and was inaugurated in January, 1850.

Under Governor Quitman's administration, the compromise measures pending in congress were the vital subject of public interest and discussion. The first legislature during the administration of Governor Quitman called a convention of delegates to meet in September, 1851, to take measures for the "redress of grievances." California, with a constitution prohibiting the introduction of slaves into her territory, had just been admitted into the Union. Public opinion in the state was to the effect that this was the denial of an inviolable right. A convention composed of delegates from several Southern states had assembled at Nashville in 1850, adopting inflammatory resolutions. Mississippi soon became precipitated into a wild scene of political excitement over the all-absorbing question. Old party ties were loosened, and new political organizations of the old ones formed.

General Quitman had been renominated for election as governor by the democratic party, and his opponents, composed in great part of the old whig party, reinforced by a considerable contingent of democrats, and calling themselves the Union party, nominated for governor Henry S. Foote, then a United States senator from Mississippi. The canvass was a warm and heady contest and much bitter feeling and excitement was engendered. Each party had its candidate for the convention and the legislature in the field in every county in the state. The election of delegates took place in August, 1851, and resulted in an overwhelming triumph of the Union party. Governor Quitman, seeing that the people had pronounced against him by very decided action, abandoned the contest. This left the party resisting the policy of the compromise measure without a leader, and all eyes were turned to Jefferson Davis, with the confident hope that he would be enabled to stand the tide that had set in with such increasing momentum and fury against the old order of political thought and organization in the state. He entered upon the herculean task of seeking to overcome a majority of nearly seven thousand which the Union party had obtained at the August election of delegates to the convention, but succeeded only in reducing it to about nine hundred votes, the majority by which Senator Foote was elected. The convention which had been called had assembled in September and declared its unalterable fealty to the Union.

Henry S. Foote, a native of Virginia, was elected governor in 1854, and was the eighth chosen under the constitution of 1832. As has been alluded to, he was a member of the United States senate when nominated for governor by the Union party. He was a doughty fighter in party warfare, and a very prominent figure in the politics of Mississippi a half century ago. During Governor Foote's administration the legislature passed an act submitting the question to the people whether or not they should repudiate the bonds of the state, the proceeds of which had been used to pay for the stock subscribed and owned by the state in the Planters' bank. The question was presented to the people at the presidential election of that year and the debt was repudiated, which had been unanimously pronounced by the senate as a legal and binding obligation, and to meet the payment of which the faith of the state had been repeatedly pledged. The high court of errors and appeals during Governor Foote's administration affirmed the validity of the issuance and sale of the bonds of Mississippi sold to raise money with which to pay for the stock owned by the state in the bank. The court was unanimous and the opinion clear and emphatic that the state was justly indebted to the holders of the bonds, and that they should be paid; but the decision of the court was of no avail, as they remain to this day unpaid.

Governor Foote removed, finally, to Tennessee, after the close of his term, which state he represented in the Confederate congress. He was appointed by General Grant superintendent of the United States mint at New Orleans, which position he held at the time of his death, in 1880.

John J. Pettus, a native of Alabama, was nominated by the democratic party in 1859 for governor, and was elected and installed in office in January, 1860. In the second year of his administration the secession convention met on the 7th day of January, 1861, in pursuance of an act of the legislature, directly representing the sovereignty of the people. Hon. William S. Barry was elected president. L. Q. C. Lamar, who has been a member of both houses of congress since the war, secretary of the interior under Cleveland's administration, and now an associate justice of the supreme court of the United States, was a member of that memorable convention. He offered a resolution that a committee of fifteen be appointed by the president to prepare and report an ordinance for the withdrawal of the state from the Federal union, with a view to the establishment of a new confederacy to be composed of the seceding states. The committee consisted of L. Q. C. Lamar, Wiley P. Harris, Samuel J. Gholson, James L. Alcorn, Henry T. Ellett, Walker Brooke, Hugh R. Miller, John A. Blair, Alexander M. Clayton, Alfred Holt, James Z. George, E. H. Sanders, Ben. King, George R. Clayton, and Orlando Davis. These were among the most leading and prominent men in the state at that period. Mr. Lamar, from the committee, reported: "An ordinance to dissolve the union between the state of Mississippi and the states united with her under the compact entitled the 'Constitution of the United States,' recommending that it do pass." Jacob S. Yerger, a member of the convention, offered an amendment by way of substitute, providing "for the final adjustment of all difficulties between the free and slave states of the United States by securing further constitutional guarantee within the present union." This substitute was lost by a vote of seventy-eight to twenty-one. James L. Alcorn offered an additional section that, "The ordinance shall not go into effect until the states of Alabama, Georgia, Florida and Louisiana shall resolve to secede from the Union and resolve their sovereignty." This was lost by a vote of seventy-four to twenty-five. ' Walker Brooke offered an amendment, submitting to the qualified electors of the state the ordinance for their ratification or rejection. This amendment was likewise voted down. Mr. Lamar then reported the following ordinance of secession, which was passed by a vote of eighty-four to fifteen: "The people of the state of Mississippi, in convention assembled, do ordain and declare, and it is hereby ordained and declared as follows, to-wit: Section 1. That all the laws and ordinances by which the said state of Mississippi became a member of the Federal union of the United States of America, be, and the same are hereby, repealed, and that all the obligations on the part of said state or people thereof, to observe the same, be withdrawn, and that the said state doth hereby assume all the rights, functions and powers which by any of said laws or ordinances were conveyed to the government of the said United States, and is absolved from all the obligations, restraints and duties incurred to the said Federal union, and shall from henceforth be a free, sovereign and independent state. Sec. 2. That so much of the first section of the seventh article of the constitution of the state as requires members of the legislature, and all officers, executive and judicial, to take an oath or affirmation to support the constitution of the United States, be, and the same is, hereby abrogated and annulled. Sec. 3. That all rights acquired and vested under the constitution of the United States, or under any act of congress passed, or treaty made, in pursuance thereof, or any law of this state, and not incompatible with this ordinance, shall remain in force, and have the same effect as if this ordinance had not been passed. Sec. 4. That the people of the state of Mississippi hereby consent to form a federal union with such of the states as may have seceded, or may secede, from the Union of the United States of America, upon the basis of the present constitution of the said United States, except such parts thereof as embrace other portions than such seceding states.

"Thus ordained and declared in convention the ninth day of January, in the year of our Lord one thousand eight hundred and sixty-one.

"In testimony of the passage of which and the determination of the members of this convention to uphold and maintain the state in the position she has assumed in said ordinance, it is signed by the president and members of this convention this the 15th day of January, A. D. 1861."

There were ninety-seven members of this convention, chosen upon the representative basis of the counties in the legislature. Every member of the convention signed the ordinance except one—Dr. J. J. Thornton, of Rankin county.

Mr. Lamar offered the following resolution in the convention: "That the commissioners appointed by his excellency the governor, in pursuance of a resolution of the legislature of the state of Mississippi providing for the appointment of commissioners, approved November 30, 1860, be furnished each with a copy of the ordinance of secession adopted by this convention, and that they be requested to submit the same to the conventions of the states to which they have been accredited and solicit the coöperation of said states with the action of South Carolina, Mississippi, Florida and Alabama." The following gentlemen were elected delegates to the Montgomery convention of the seceding states which formed the Confederate government: Wiley P. Harris, Walter Brooke, W. S. Wilson, A. M. Clayton, W. S. Barry, James T. Harrison and J. A. P. Campbell. The following were elected to the congress of the new confederacy when it should be established: Jefferson Davis and Albert G. Brown to the senate; Reuben Davis (a brother to Jefferson Davis), L. Q. C. Lamar, William Barksdale, Otho R. Singleton and John J. McRae to the house.

The governor of the state, charged with sending commissioners to several slave-holding states, asking them to coöperate with the state of Mississippi in seceding from the Federal union, appointed the following commissioners: To Tennessee, Thomas J. Wharton; to South Carolina, Charles Edward Hooker; to North Carolina, Jacob Thompson; to Louisiana, Wirt Adams; to Maryland, A. H. Handy; to Arkansas, George R. Fall; to Kentucky, W. S. Featherston: to Georgia, W. L. Harris; to Virginia, Fulton Anderson.

Governors Pettus and Charles Clark, a native of Ohio, presided over the destinies of the state during the war. In May, 1865, Governor Clarke issued the following executive order: "General Taylor informs me that all Confederate armies east of the Mississippi river are surrendered, with all government cotton, quartermaster, commissary and other stores. Federal commanders will only send such troops as may be necessary to guard public property. All officers and persons in possession of public stores will be held to a rigid accountability and all embezzlers certainly arrested. Arrangements will be made to issue supplies to the destitute. I have called the legislature to convene at Jackson on Thursday, the 18th instant. They will doubtless order a convention. The officers of the state government will immediately return with the archives to Jackson. County officers will be vigilant in the preservation of order and the protection of property. Sheriffs have power to call out the posse comitatus and the militia will keep armed and obey orders for that purpose as in times of peace. The civil laws must be enforced as they now are until repealed. If the public property be protected and the peace preserved the necessity for Federal troops in your county will be avoided. You are therefore urged to combine to arrest the marauders and plunderers. The collection of taxes should be suspended, as the laws will doubtless be changed. Masters are responsible, as heretofore, for the protection and conduct of their slaves, and they should be kept at home as heretofore. That all citizens fearlessly adhere to the fortunes of the state, aid the returned soldiers to obtain civil employment, maintain law and order, contemn all twelfth-hour vaporers and meet stern facts with fortitude and common sense.''

By order of the president Governor Clarke was imprisoned at Fort Pulaski and William L. Sharkey, an old-line whig and a prominent Union man in the secession contest, appointed by President Johnson provisional governor in 1865. Governor Sharkey issued a proclamation calling a convention, to be composed of delegates who were loyal to the United States, for the purpose of "altering or amending the constitution to enable the state to resume its place in the Union."

The convention which assembled in response to the proclamation adopted the policy suggested by it and so framed the amendment as to be in full accord with the constitution of the United States. The convention was composed of ninety-eight delegates, seventy whigs and twenty-eight democrats. The convention adopted an amendment to the constitution recognizing the abolition of slavery and providing that "Neither slavery or involuntary servitude, otherwise than in the punishment of crimes, shall hereafter exist in the state, and also declared the ordinance of secession passed by the convention of 1861 null and void."

The amendments to the constitution fully recognized the abolition of slavery and that the negroes were to be citizens of the state and that they would at least for some time reside there, and that it was not only necessary to provide such legislation for their protection and education, but also to throw all possible moral influences around them.

Benjamin G. Humphreys, a native of the state, was the first governor elected by the people after the war. He was installed in October, 1865. In his inaugural address he said:

"It has been reported from some quarters that our people are insincere and the spirit of revolt is rampant among us. But if an unflinching fidelity in war gives evidence of reliable fidelity in peace, if the unvarying professions that spring from private and public sources furnish any evidence of truth, it is sufficiently demonstrated that the people of the South, who so long and against such terrible odds maintained the mightiest conflict of modern ages, may be safely trusted when they professed more than a willingness to return to their allegiance.

"The South, having ventured all upon the arbitrament of the sword, has lost all save her honor, and now accepts the result in good faith."

At this session of the legislature Judge William L. Sharkey and James L. Alcorn were elected United States senators. They were both leading old-line whigs before the war, both gentlemen of high character, education and refinement. Judge Sharkey had been chief justice of the supreme court of the state for many years. He was eminent as a jurist of commanding and imperishable fame among Mississippians. The admirable equipoise of judgment, well-tempered views and safe conclusions which distinguished his course always in the politics of the state when called upon for advice made him the oracle of the people, without party distinction, in time of public trial, peril and calamity. General Alcorn was a leader of his party. With his enlarged views of governmental polity and attachment to American institutions and to his own state, with a trained intellect and the grasp of mind of the philosophic statesman, the state was fortunate in having his services in the executive department of the government, as well as in the national senate, where he was afterward seated during the "reconstruction era."

These gentlemen, having opposed the secession of the states, were, from the consideration of their conservatism and unquestioned abilities, selected because it was thought there would be no objection offered to their being admitted to seats in the senate, and that they would exercise a wholesome influence toward restoring the state to her former relations in the Union.

A committee had been appointed by the convention, in August, to submit to the approaching legislature such new laws and changes in existing statutes as they deemed expedient to meet the changed domestic relation, and secure obedience to law and order. It was necessary to clothe the negroes with civil rights. At the session of the legislature, Governor Humphreys, in his special message, recommended the enactment of statutes conferring upon freedmen the right to testify in all cases in court. In October, 1866, Governor Humphreys convened the legislature in extra session. In his message to the body he took the ground that the proposed amendment to the constitution of the United States would destroy the rights of the state, and referred to the antagonism existing between the president and congress.

It was at this session that the fourteenth amendment to the constitution of the United States was submitted to the legislature for its action. The joint standing committee on state and Federal relations recommended that the state refuse to ratify the amendment to the constitution of the United States, which was adopted without a dissenting vote. Judge H. F. Simrell was the chairman of this committee, who has since sat upon the supreme court bench of the state, appointed by a republican executive. Mississippi had not yet been restored to the Union. Her senators and representatives were refused seats in the national congress. The states of Mississippi and Arkansas were made a military district, with Gen. Edwin Ord in command, who issued an order in March, 1867, for an election of delegates to a convention to revise or make a new constitution of the state. This convention, on account of the many negroes of which it was in great part composed, was dubbed "the black and tan convention." The constitution of 1868 was submitted to the people for their ratification or rejection, and it was defeated. It was contended by the republican party, which was now thoroughly organized in the state, that the result was accomplished by intimidation and fraud. It was sought, when President Grant was elected, to invoke the power of the Federal government to consummate an effort which was made to save the constitution as submitted. General Grant thought, however, that it would be just and proper to recommend to congress to provide for the holding of another election, and allow the people the privilege of voting for or against the disfranchising clauses which it contained, separately, as well as for state officers, representatives in congress and in the legislature, which had been denied in the former election.

This provision, as submitted, embraced the fourteenth and fifteenth amendments to the constitution of the United States, which provided for the right of suffrage without regard to race, color or previous condition of servitude. The election was held in 1869, and the white people of the state accepted the constitution as modified and recommended by the president. This constitution has existed for sixteen years of democratic administration of the state government, and when it was changed, many leading democrats in the party of to-day, among them Gen. Edward Walthall, now in the United States senate from Mississippi, opposed it.

After the adoption of the constitution of 1868, a republican convention met and nominated B. B. Eggleston for governor and a full republican ticket. The democrats nominated B. G. Humphreys. Humphreys and Charles E. Hooker, who had been nominated as attorney-general on the democratic ticket, made a vigorous canvass of the state, as there was an estimated republican majority of twenty thousand to contend with, including the whites, then disfranchised. General McDowell, who was then in command of the military district, issued an order removing Humphreys and Hooker and other state officers, as obstructive to the reconstructive policy, and appointed Adelbert Ames as military governor of the state. The democratic canvass was made under the direction of John D. Freeman, chairman of the democratic state executive committee. Humphreys refused to obey the military order of McDowell, and continued to hold the office of governor, from which he was ejected by a military company under the order of Governor Ames. On the 15th of January, 1870, Governor Ames transmitted to the legislature copies of the fourteenth and fifteeth amendments to the constitution of the United States, which the two houses ratified, according to the prescribed terms of a resolution of congress.

James L. Alcorn was elected governor of the state in 1869, as the candidate of the republican party, and was thus the nineteenth chief magistrate of the commonwealth, and the first chosen under the constitution of 1868. It may be here remarked that the only material change in this constitution from that of 1832 was making the judiciary appointive by the governor, by and with the advice and consent of the senate. The office of lieutenant-governor was also reëstablished.

In Governor Alcorn's first inaugural address, he said: "The military government which I have the happiness to bow this day out of the state, was no more a subject of pleasure to me than it was to any other Mississippian whose blood glows with the instinct of self-government." He also said that "The ballot-box, the jury-box and the offices of the state should be thrown open to the competent and honest, without distinction of color." Previously to his accession to the gubernatorial office he had been elected United States senator, and therefore he did not remain in the office of governor long.

Ames and Alcorn were now the United States senators, and both of them, from some antagonism engendered upon the floor of the senate, decided to become candidates for governor of the state at the next election. The conservative republicans favored Alcorn, and the extreme wing of the party supported Ames. The democratic party, in convention, determined by resolution that it was "inexpedient in the approaching state election to nominate a state ticket." This left the contest to be determined between the republican candidates, and Ames was elected and installed in office in January, 1874. During his administration there was considerable race trouble and prejudice engendered through the politics of the time, the negroes then being induced to take an interest in public affairs. They, however, soon discovered that without some probationary training for this exercise of a new right, which was once suggested by President Grant, that it was a fruitless field for them, as they did their voting at the will of others, who reaped the spoils of office, and they have manifested a marked indifference to politics from that day to the present time.

In December the governor called an extra session of the legislature, which was based upon alleged disorders in Warren county. The people, who paid now a state tax of $1.40 on the dollar of assessed value of land and exorbitant levies in the counties, had insisted that the sheriff and other officers should execute new and sufficient bonds, or surrender their trusts.

Taxpayers' conventions were held all over the state. The democratic state convention assembled on August 3, 1875. It was largely attended, and gray-haired men, who had not been to the state capital for years, or participated in any political scene for a quarter of a century, were there. L. Q. C. Lamar addressed the convention, depicting with his vivid eloquence the depressed condition of the state, and the oppressive policy of taxation which had been pursued, but inspiring hope for the ultimate survival of peace, order and good government. Senator J. Z. George was elected chairman of the democratic state executive committee. The platform demanded the reduction of taxation, honest, impartial and economical government, biennial session of the legislature, an able and competent judiciary, a discontinuance of special and local legislation, protests against the arming of militia in times of peace and the encouragement of agriculture. Ex-Governor and ex-Senator A. G. Brown, then an old man, retired from the conflict of public life, at a public meeting in his county, offered the following resolution: "That, without equivocation or mental reservation, we intend to carry out the principles enunciated in the platform of the democratic party, and to this we pledge our lives, our fortunes and our sacred honor."

At this time Judge Wiley P. Harris, an eminent lawyer of the state, and democrat, addressed a club of his party, suggesting a union of the Southern people with the liberal republicans of the North, who deprecated the gross mismanagement of the Southern states under reconstruction laws, but who thought it right and wise that the constitution of the Southern states should rest on the basis of impartial suffrage.

The campaign of 1875 was organized with great spirit and skill. Clubs were formed all over the state, which was soon converted into a perfect blaze of political excitement. General George, the chairman of the democratic state executive committee, wired the attorney-general of the United States that there were no disturbances in Mississippi, and no obstruction to the execution of the laws. General Grant, though importuned to interfere, refused to do so. There were some spasmodic collisions between the leaders of the respective parties, which led to bloodshed of both whites and blacks, but there was no race conflict in the state. The public speeches delivered by the democratic orators were temperate and conservative in tone, but firm and not to be mistaken, thousands of negroes concluding at last that it was better to cast their destinies with the white leaders of public opinion, whom they had always known and could confide in. A democratic legislature was elected and an entire democratic delegation returned to congress.

Notwithstanding the charge which had been made against Governor Ames for his numerous, repeated and flagrant violations of the constitution, almost immediately after the election a democratic meeting held in one of the counties of the state passed the following resolution, showing the temper and spirit of that party, to bring about peace and harmony and satisfactory government under existing conditions, if possible:

"Resolved, That we desire that Governor Ames will persevere in the measures of retrenchment and reform heretofore recommended by him, and calculated to lighten the burdens of the people, and we hereby respectfully request our representatives, in both branches of the legislature, to give to him their confidence and support in all matters of state policy, desiring to advance the true and permanent interests of the state; and, furthermore, and as the sense of this meeting, it is right that the past be forgotten, and that the chief executive of the state, the legislature and all others of the state, act henceforth in union and harmony, and with an eye single to the public good."

The governor's message to the legislature unfortunately was not in this spirit, as he indulged to some extent in traducing the white people of the state.

In pursuance of a resolution offered to inquire into the official conduct of Adelbert Ames, a committee was appointed to make an investigation accordingly. On the 22d of February, its report was submitted, recommending the impeachment of the governor for official misconduct, on eleven separate and distinct charges. The substance of these was that he had in several specified instances refused to remove certain officials as required by law, and had in other cases made removals without cause; that he had caused a conflict between races, attended by bloodshed, at Vicksburg, in December, 1874, by directing Peter Crosby's return, in violation of law, and sustaining him in taking possession of the sheriff's office of Warren county, and that he had attempted to incite a war of races in Hinds county, in October, 1875, by causing a company of colored militia, which had taken part in the Clinton riot, to parade the streets of that town, armed and defiant. The report and the resolution of impeachment were adopted by the house February 25, by a vote of eighty-six to fourteen, all the republicans present, and two democrats voting in the negative. Twenty-three articles of impeachment were prepared and adopted. On the 13th of March, all the preliminary proceedings of the court were taken, and the trial was to begin on the 29th of March, when the following letter, addressed by the governor to his counsel, was submitted to the house: "Gentlemen: In regard to your suggestion, I beg leave to say that in consequence of the election of last November, I found myself confronted with the hostile legislature and embarrassed and baffled in my endeavors to carry out my plan for the welfare of the state and of my party. I had resolved, therefore, to resign my office as governor of the state of Mississippi. But meanwhile, proceedings of impeachment were instituted against me, and of course I could not, and would not retire from my position under the imputation of any charge affecting my honor or integrity. For the reasons indicated, I still desire to escape burdens which are compensated by no possibility of public usefulness; and if the articles of impeachment presented against me were not pending, and the proceedings were dismissed, I should feel at liberty to carry out my desire and purpose of resignation. I am very truly yours, Adelbert Ames."

The house then passed the following resolution: "That the managers on the part of this house, in the matter of the impeachment of Adelbert Ames, governor of said state, be, and they are hereby directed to dismiss the said articles against the said Adelbert Ames, governor, as aforesaid, which were heretofore exhibited by them against him at the bar of the senate."

The proceedings were accordingly dismissed in the senate by a vote of twenty-four to seven. Governor Ames immediately resigned, and Col. J. M. Stone, president pro tem. of the senate, was at once installed in the office of governor, in joint convention of the two houses.

Articles of impeachment had also been presented against the colored lieutenant-governor of the state, Alexander K. Davis, charging him, while acting as governor in the absence of Governor Ames, with receiving a bribe as consideration for granting a pardon to a man convicted of murder. He was tried and convicted, by a vote of thirty-two to four, six republicans, one of them colored, voting guilty. The four voting not guilty were all colored republicans. Sentence was passed on the 23d of March, by a vote of twenty-five to four, removing Mr. Davis from office, and disqualifying him from holding any office of profit, honor or trust in the future.

Articles of impeachment were also pending against T. W. Cardoza, a colored superintendent of public education, for converting to his own use funds of a colored normal school of the state, while treasurer of the institution; for obtaining money from the state for unnecessary books for the public schools, a portion of which was for his own benefit; and with proposing with another to divide and convert to their own use a portion of the school teachers' funds of Warren county. Mr. Cardoza asked permission to resign his office, and have the proceedings dismissed, which was accordingly done.

Two amendments to the constitution of the state were adopted. One of these abolished the office of lieutenant-governor, and the other provided for a biennial session of the legislature, beginning in January, 1878.

The republican party of the state held a convention at Jackson on the 30th of March, 1876, to appoint delegates to the national convention at Cincinnati, to nominate candidates for the presidential election, and choose a state executive committee. The following were some of the clauses of the platform adopted:

We adopt the sentiment of General Grant: "Let no guilty man escape," and we further say, Let every guilty man be brought to punishment. In view of these sentiments, we arraign the democratic leaders of Mississippi, and charge them with prosecuting impeachments for partisan purposes, and to consolidate power obtained by violence, intimidation and fraud. They charged the late governor, and the late superintendent of education, with high crimes and misdemeanors. If guilty, they should be punished; if innocent, justice and truth have been wantonly violated; whether guilty or innocent, could only be known upon a full, fair and impartial trial. This the accused parties were not only entitled to, but justice demanded it. Instead, assuming their charges to be true, democrats have compounded felonies, and have thus added another serious crime to the long catalogue of high crimes and misdemeanors on their part. We, the republicans of Mississippi, therefore arraign the democratic party of the state before an enlightened public sentiment, and charge that party with corruption in order to secure public offices for partisan purposes. The history of impeachment shows this, and nothing less.

They have usurped the power from the people, first by violence, intimidation and fraud, and thereby providing that a senator, elected as such, shall be governor, thus refusing to let the people say who shall be governor.

Themselves illegally elected, they seek to maintain power by unheard-of legislation in the interest of the democratic party, without regard to the rights or will of the people, and in disregard of both.

They have gerrymandered the state by most outrageous, unjust and partisan alteration of the congressional districts.

As important and vital as are the great principles in the foregoing, we present to the people of the state and of the whole country, as underlying and overriding all other issues, as containing all that is dear to us, as one that will invade the North and West if not arrested and crushed out, the question of the freedom of the ballot. Violence at elections is a blow at free institutions, and these, with us, are practically a mockery. This violence will destroy all other interests, social, educational, financial, business and religious.

The democratic state convention, for similar purposes, was held at Jackson on the 14th of June, and put in their answer and defense to the indictment against it, contained in the republican platform, as follows:

Resolved, That the democrats and conservatives, in convention assembled, proclaim their heartfelt gratitude for the complete victory which was won by the advocates of reform, in the election of 1875, over the incompetent, corrupt and proscriptive political organization which had held unlimited control of the state government for six years, and that they emphatically repelled the imputation that their triumph was won by any other than the legal, honest and sincere efforts which the justice of their cause, and their duty as freemen to maintain unimpaired their inalienable rights, demanded them to make.

That in proof of the sincerity of the pledges of the victorious party in that election to reduce expenditures to an honest and economical standard and elevate the scale of official qualifications, we point with pride and pleasure to the acts of its late session, to which body the thanks of the whole people are due, for its faithful discharge of duty in correcting the abuses of the public service; in diminishing the burden of taxation; in dismissing the supernumerary officials from the various branches of the public service, who consumed the earning of labor without rendering an equivalent; in dispensing the blessings of just laws without distinction of race, color or class; in holding faithless public officials to strict accountability for their misconduct; and especially does the popular branch of the legislature standing as the grand impress of the commonwealth deserve thanks for investigating the acts of the guilty officials whom it arraigned for malfeasance, corruption and usurpation of unconstitutional powers, and for driving them by the perils of the offended law into obscurity from the public trusts which they had violated.

Resolved, That in addition to the foregoing, we proclaim the following principles as the rule and guide of our political faith and conduct:

1. The doctrine of local self-government, the surest protection of personal liberty; fidelity to the constitution of the United States, and all the obligations imposed upon us as citizens of a common country.

2. Free schools, free suffrage, equal rights.

3. Equal and exact justice to all citizens of every race and clime, native and foreign born, and no discriminating legislation for the benefit of favored classes or corporations.

4. No proscription for opinion's sake; no sectional lines; no resurrection of dead issues for partisan success, and as a pretext for vindictive legislation.

5. The sacred maintenance of the public faith, and the strict performance of all obligations, state and national.

6. Retrenchment and economy in all of the departments of public service, and adherence to the time-honored Jeffersonian standard of qualification for office, "Is he honest, is he capable, is he faithful to the Constitution?"

With these declarations, we cordially invite all men to coöperate with us in establishing the permanent supremacy of the principles which they embody in the administration of public affairs.

The democrats were thoroughly organized in this canvass, but the republicans displayed little activity. At the election in November following, the whole number of votes cast for presidential electors was one hundred and sixty-four thousand seven hundred and seventy-eight. Of these, one hundred and twelve thousand one hundred and seventy-three were for the democratic, and fifty-two thousand six hundred and five for the republican ticket, making the democratic majority fifty-nine thousand five hundred and sixty-eight. The six members of congress then chosen were all democrats. The legislature of 1877 consisted of twenty-six democrats and eleven republicans in the senate, and ninety-six democrats and nineteen republicans in the house.

A committee of the United States senate was in the state for several weeks during the summer of 1876, making an investigation of the circumstances of the election of 1875. Majority and minority reports were made to the senate early in the session of 1876 and '77.

The administration of Robert Lowry, who was chief executive for two terms, covering the years 1881-9, succeeded by John M. Stone, the present governor of the state, brings the political history of Mississippi down to this day. Governor Stone had also been the immediate predecessor of Robert Lowry.

The most important question which was considered in the legislature of January, 1888, was that which contemplated calling a convention to revise the constitution of 1869. The act providing for it, after a warm discussion, was passed, but Governor Lowry vetoed it. The constitution of 1869, notwithstanding the motley composition of the convention of 1868, which adopted it, turned out to be a good one. The effort to change it was based in some degree upon the elemental self-governing idea that, as it was not altogether a genuine home product, being the handiwork of a party supposed to be hostile and alien to the state in a measure in its structure, it ought to be changed for this reason, if no other. Quite a notion, too, had taken root in the agricultural communities, nurtured by the fraternizing mood of aspiring candidates for office, that the state should return to the good old days and popular policy of the constitution of 1832, and make the judiciary elective directly by the people.

Again it was contended, with better reason than either of these, and in a straightforward spirit to deal fairly and wisely with a difficulty which was rather racial than political, that the people of the state were living under two constitutions—one of the government of the United States, and the other, of the state, and that the former was paramount and required an impartial suffrage without reference to color or race, and guaranteed the existence of a republican form of government in the states; that some positive effective method by public law must be adopted by which ignorance and incompetency should be restrained and fitted by compliance with certain constitutional requirements for the exercise of the elective franchise.

The objection chiefly urged unfavorable to the calling of the convention was that in view of the fifteenth amendment to the Federal constitution inhibitory of denial or abridgment of the right of citizens of the United States to vote, by any state on account of race or color, and that, therefore, some 15,000 ignorant whites in the state would be put in the same category with the blacks to become eligible as electors according to the design proposed in the new organic law.

However, at the next biennial legislature of 1890, another act was passed providing for a constitutional convention, which was approved by Governor Stone. It convened in August, 1890, at the capital. Sol S. Calhoun, a prominent lawyer and democrat of Hinds county, was chosen president. He made a speech in acknowledgment of the honor conferred, abounding in good sense and a full appreciation of the delicate and responsible duties devolved upon the convention. Wiley P. Harris was a member of this body, who, on account of his large experience in public affairs and his intellect, prudence and sagacious judgment, was always looked to for safe counsel by the party in emergencies. James Z. George, one of the United States senators from the state, was especially requested to leave his place of duty at Washington, congress then being in session, to become a member of this convention, as the people had great confidence in his capacity to cope satisfactorily with the more important objects had in view.

James L. Alcorn and Judge Simrall, both republicans, venerable and honored citizens of the state, were also members, chosen as delegates by both democrat and republican votes. Isaiah V. Williamson, a colored delegate from the densely black county, voted for by both races, an educated negro and property-holder, took a large and enlightened view of the situation, co-operating with the convention in its delicate and grave work of piloting the ship of state upon a narrower pathway than that in which the course of Ulysses lay between Scylla and Charybdis.

A franchise committee of fifteen was appointed, Wiley P. Harris, James Z. George, James L. Alcorn and H. F. Simrall, being among the number.

The committee brought in their report after sitting about a month and giving the subject matter confided to them profound thought and examination. As it is of importance, extracts from the report as substantially adopted in section 24 of article 12 of the constitution will be given, as follows:

Section 241. "Every male inhabitant of this state, except idiots, insane persons and Indians not taxed, who is a citizen of the United States, twenty-one years old and upwards, who has resided in this state two years and one year in the election district, or in the incorporated city or town in which he offers to vote, and who is duly registered as provided in this article, and who has never been convicted of bribery, burglary, theft, arson, obtaining money or goods under false pretenses, perjury, forgery, embezzlement or bigamy, and who has paid on or before the first day of February of the year in which he shall offer to vote, all taxes which may have been legally required of him, and which he has had an opportunity of paying according to law, for the two preceding years, and who shall produce to the officers holding the election satisfactory evidence that he has paid said taxes, is declared to be a qualified elector."

Then followed a section providing by law for the registration of all persons entitled to vote at any election and prescribing the form of oath or affirmation to be taken. The section 243 provided for the payment of a uniform poll tax of $2 to be used in the aid of common schools, the tax to be a lien only on taxable property.

Section 244 was in the following language: "On and after the first day of January A. D. 1892, every elector shall, in addition to the foregoing qualifications, be able to read any section of the constitution of this state; or he shall be able to understand the same when read to him, or give a reasonable interpretation thereof. A new registration shall be made before the next ensuing election, after January 1, A. D. 1892."

Section 244 gave rise to animated discussion, not only in the convention, but by the people and press all over the state, and there developed decided opposition to its adoption in some quarters.

It was contended that it was a contradiction in terms, and not in the frank spirit in which the convention was called and had set out upon its labors; that it would not operate impartially for the reason that the judges of the qualifications there enumerated were not provided for, this having been left to the registrars of election. It was even by an extreme expression of individual democratic opinion called a fraud.

But as a frank interchange of views and a more calm, dispassionate and analytical reflection succeeded to the impulsive impressions first taken, it was finally assented to as a fair and rational solution of the problem involved in the provision thus made from the peculiar situation of the state of Mississippi.

An amendment was offered, also proposing female suffrage. It was treated seriously and ludicrously by turns, and then dismissed rather summarily when the curious novelty of the suggestion was shorn by the robust sense of the convention of its sentimental attraction.

A scheme after the type of the Australian ballot-system was provided for, the voters receiving an official ballot containing all the names of candidates and going alone, one at a time, into compartments arranged as a voting-place, and marking, with the exercise of his own choice and discretion, the person, or persons for whom he desires to vote.

The legislature was given power to alter, annul or repeal any charter of incorporation now existing and revocable, and any that may hereafter be created whenever in its opinion it might be in the public interest to do so. This constitution finally put a quietus on the question of the Planters' and Union bank bonds which the decision of the supreme court had still left open, saying they never should be paid.

Decided restrictions were laid upon the rather liberal corporate legislation which had heretofore obtained, this action being taken responsive to the demands of the people upon this subject.

The constitution is a rather full and comprehensive one. As was facetiously remarked by a distinguished member of the convention, "They hardly left the legislature room to turn around in."

An ordinance was proposed looking to cutting up the liquor traffic, root and branch, in Mississippi, but the convention declined to go that far, the subject not having entered into the canvass for election of delegates to the convention.

The constitution was adopted November 1, 1890, the convention having been in session **nearly three months.**

Practically, since 1875, there has been but one organized party in the state, the democratic party.

This party has always been strong and controlling in the state from its early history. Prior to the Civil war, Mississippi voted at each election for the democratic candidates for the presidency and vice-presidency, the sole exception being in 1840, when it went for Harrison. After the war, when Mr. Greeley was a candidate for the presidency, the state supported him.

A few years ago a diverging effort was made to popularize a greenback theory of finance and form a party upon this basis, but it soon became apparent that the hope was as unsubstantial as a dream.

In some localities now upon the temperance question, prohibition and anti-prohibition proclivities enter as a factor in elections, but have made no impression upon the general politics of the state. A recent state prohibition convention which assembled at the capital declared in the platform adopted the positive determination of the temperance organization of the state to place no ticket in the field at any general election, or take any part in politics.

With but one political party in the state, therefore, the methods of executive committees are simply confined to declaring the manner of making nominations, supervising the agencies and providing and directing the instrumentalities in the conduct of campaign, and settling questions which grow out of this action, and disputed points of elections, such as may be properly cognizable under their management in the premises. In 1873–5, when the republican party was defeated in the state, to 1880, when a greater degree of generalship was needed, the three chairmen of the state democratic executive committee were James Z. George, John D. Freeman and Capt. Frank Johnston, a distinguished lawyer of the state.

Generally, a nomination is equivalent to an election.

The negroes, as a rule, take no interest in politics. In what are known as the black counties, in accordance with the fusion movement, which took place some years ago as between the negroes and the democrats, there is still a division made of the offices, negroes in many counties being sent to the senate and house of representatives, and elected circuit and chancery clerks and magistrates, and appointed teachers in the public schools. They serve on juries throughout the state.

There is a strong sense of the blessing derivable from the prevalence of law and order, and peace and harmony now existing between the races, and a wise and economical government in the state, which pervades every class and condition of the people. All morbid public feeling and any step taken to bring about unrest or prejudice and hurtful agitation, is reprobated by common consent. The people are willing to trust both the state and national government for protection, and the best advancement of their public interests and security, while they pursue the even tenor of their private vocations and industries.

At the juncture at which this chapter is written, the absorbing question of political interest in the state, and which has become a vital subject of controversy within the democratic party, is the subtreasury scheme, as proposed and defined in the bill of Mr. Pickler, introduced in the national house of representatives at the last session of congress, and familiar to the people of the United States since its object and purpose has been incorporated in the platform of the National Farmers' Alliance at Ocala, Fla.

This question was first presented distinctly in the politics of the state in the congressional election of the year 1890. In the seventh congressional district, now and then represented in congress by Charles E. Hooker, it was made a pregnant and controlling issue by Maj. Ethel Barksdale, who became a candidate for the nomination against Colonel Hooker, Major Barksdale then being a member of the state alliance.

It was at first thought by reason of the alacrity with which the agricultural interest, somewhat depressed in the state for several years, seized the new and facile idea of borrowing money from the government on the products enumerated in the bill, including cotton, that Major Barksdale would have, in political phraseology, a "walkover."

However, Colonel Hooker was renominated, Major Barksdale having withdraw from the canvass when the county of Madison pronounced against him in the primaries held there. In this county the question has been thoroughly ventilated by discussion pro and con in the various precincts. Many intelligent and influential farmers reside in this county.

Hooker's consistent political record, fervid oratory and great popularity, together with a masterly sounding of the issues of the campaign, turned what at one time seemed inevitable defeat into a brilliant victory.

Since that time, however, the adoption by the Ocala convention of the subtreasury scheme in its platform, the question has been freshly stimulated in Mississippi. Major Barksdale this year again entered the field as candidate for the United States senate upon this issue, against Senator J. Z. George, who had become a candidate for re-election, his colleague, Senator Edward Walthal, not entering the canvass in contemplation of retirement from the senate.

That campaign is still pending. Most of the leading men of the state are upon the hustings with the political slogan—"straightout democracy and George." General George having been always closely identified with the people through a sympathy from early struggles extending to every stratum of the social organization, and steadfastly devoted to the principles of the democratic party, believing that by it the well being of the people of Mississippi can best be subserved, it was not thought that there was any necessity for substituting another in his place, professing the same party ethics, but differing with him simply upon the expediency of the general government's adopting the economical policy proposed. John M. Allen, now in congress, the inimitable humorist and gifted politician, and a great favorite with the people, is actively engaged in the canvass in behalf of George, and Col. Charles E. Hooker is on the scene again fighting over the same battle with the same combatant of the year 1890.

Several prominent and very able alliance men of other states have taken some part in the campaign. The latest reliable intelligence of the action of the counties in choosing senators and representatives to the next legislature is, that General George's re-election is assured, the result being finally determinable by the legislature, which assembles in January, 1892.

It is obvious that the financial policy as proposed to be adopted by the national government has gained some ground in the state under the influence of the alliance organization, but still its members are democrats for the most part, and they have not tolerated any suggestion of the formation of a third party, believing that their condition can best be ameliorated within the ranks of the political party to which they have always adhered, and under a Federal policy of low taxation. The preponderating public sentiment of the state is, that while as a matter of course a logical and essential ratio should be made to exist between the expanded interstate commercial operations and increased business of the country and the volume of circulating medium, still they are not disposed, they reason, to substitute a self-evident proposition (always urged by the democracy in its advocacy of the bimetallic system of gold and silver) for the subject matter—the tariff—which has constituted the definite issue between the two great political parties of the country for an unbroken space of thirty years.

CHAPTER VIII.

CITIES, TOWNS AND VILLAGES.*

VICKSBURG is situated on the plateau overlooking the Mississippi in north latitude thirty-two degrees, twenty-one minutes, thirty-three seconds and west longitude thirteen degrees, fifteen minutes. A series of terraces mark the approach to the Hill city from the Mississippi bottom and from the bayous, giving it natural drainage in four general courses. The delta country stretching northward and the rich agricultural regions to the east and south are tributary to the city, while her railroad and steamboat facilities place her on a plane with the prosperous city of Memphis further north, bringing her within six hours' distance of the Red river country of Louisiana, Shreveport, one hundred and seventy-two miles; within seven hours' distance of the Texan cotton-fields, Marshall, two hundred and eleven miles; within twenty-four hours of Chicago, Ill., seven hundred and forty-eight miles; and Cincinnati, Ohio, seven hundred and nineteen miles; thirty hours of Washington, D. C., one thousand and fifty-four miles, and forty hours of New York city, one thousand, two hundred and eighty-two miles. The population in 1850 was two thousand six hundred and seventy-eight, in 1860, four thousand five hundred and ninety-one, in 1870, twelve thousand four hundred and forty-three, in 1880, eleven thousand and in 1890, thirteen thousand two hundred and ninety-eight.

In the matter of the sanitary condition of the city, Dr. Brisbane's report, made a few years ago, contained important points, among which are the following:

"Second to no other attraction or element of importance is the health of a town and the advantages or otherwise of its sanitary features and condition. The prospective citizen, with children to educate, is particular to estimate the educational advantages; the manufacturer and investor inquire as to taxes, encouragement offered and water or other facilities; the artisan and mechanic are specially interested in the number of factories and industries; but all alike, with one voice, demand the proof of health and sanitary guarantees of any community that invites his presence. The health of cities and growing towns, competing for attention and development, is the constant theme with their respective editors and public-spirited citizens. The sanitary condition and advantages of a community are prominent bases on which its merits and attractions are pushed and heralded with all the energy of modern booms. With any of them, in this respect particularly, Vicksburg eagerly invites comparison. The sanitary committee is one of the most important and active committees of the board of mayor and aldermen. There is a health officer, a salaried official, who acts in conjunction with the sanitary committee, and also a board of health, composed of prominent local

---

*For additional matter concerning cities, towns and villages, see Chapters VIII to XII inclusive, Vol. I.

physicians. During the summer months, sanitary inspectors are employed, and as a rule a special sanitary officer is regularly appointed by the city council. In addition, the regular police are also required to make sanitary reports, and even the fire department is not exempt when called upon to do sanitary duty. The whole is governed by a series of carefully drawn ordinances and regulations, which show to what a high degree this important part of careful municipal government has received attention. Vicksburg, like every center, has a large floating population, attracted by the construction of railroads, levees and other works of like character, and the sick and dying from this large class find an asylum in the state hospital, located at Vicksburg. The causes of death given in the records show to the discerning mind certain facts worthy of notice. For instance, there is a notable absence of the malignant forms of malaria so generally attributed to this section of country as a cause of death. There is also a comparative absence of deaths caused by typhoid fever, and likewise a very limited number of deaths under the head of contagious and infectious diseases.''

The temperature of winter seldom descends to seven degrees, and that of summer seldom exceeds seventy degrees. The change of seasons is so gradually accomplished that there is a spring and a fall distinct in character from such imaginative seasons in the North.

Vicksburg may be said to date its beginning to 1783, when the Spaniards completed Fort Nogales, garrisoned the post and armed the redoubts known as Fort Mount Virgie, Fort Gayoso and Fort St. Ignatius. For almost a century before, the site was known to Canadian and French travelers and prior to 1729 to the first colonists of the Natchez district, whose farms spread out to the Yazoo and to Walnut hills.

On March 23, 1798, the commander received orders from the governor at New Orleans to evacuate the position and return to Natchez. A few days later a company of United States troops, under Major Kersey, took possession of the works and changed the name to Fort McHenry. Its occupation was continued for a short time, when it was allowed to be used for civil purposes and became the home of Anthony Glass, Sr. Its location, ten thousand feet above the courthouse of Warren county, is to-day known as Fort Hill. The national government recognized the historic character of the place and there located the national cemetery.

The open woods, six miles east of Vicksburg, beyond the great canebrake, were selected by Newet Vick about 1811 as a homestead farm; but preferring to cultivate the land on the river front, he built a cabin for his negroes at the intersection of Washington and Belmont streets of the present city, and opened a plantation there that year. Foster Cook came before him in his interest, but can not be said to have preceded him as a settler. It was Mr. Vick who conceived the idea of planting a town on Walnut hills; but dying in 1819, his plans were not carried out until 1821, when his son-in-law, Rev. John Lane, a Methodist preacher, like the pioneer himself, had a plat of the village made. Immediately after the land was surveyed and the United States land office opened at Washington, Miss., in January, 1816, the Vicks entered the site of Vicksburg in regular form, and twenty years after the place was chosen as the seat of justice for Warren county. The first store was started at Vicksburg by Hartwell Vick, a son of Newet Vick, the proprietor of the place, in about 1820. He continued about four years, and was then succeeded by Foster Cook and partner, George Wyche, under the firm name of Cook & Wyche. They did a large business and supplied planters in many adjoining counties.

Several years ago a number of prominent citizens and capitalists of Vicksburg obtained a charter from the legislature of the state of Mississippi and organized under it the Vicksburg Wharf and Land company. This company acquired by purchase for cash all the lands south of Vicksburg, covering a river front of over a mile and a half and controlling what is known as the lower landing. This property consists of several hundred acres of land and covers as large an area as that at present occupied by the city of Vicksburg. As the growth of the city has been for years in a southerly direction, and has already reached the estate of the company, it naturally follows that in the event of Vicksburg increasing to double its present size and population—and there are strong indications of such a happening—then the property of the Wharf and Land company would become the site of a city as populous as Vicksburg now is. In 1880 Vicksburg had a population of twelve thousand, and in 1886 of eighteen thousand, thus showing a healthy and steady growth. The building of the Louisville, New Orleans & Texas railroad has given new impetus to the city, and that road is now erecting immense construction and repair shops immediately adjoining the lands of the Vicksburg Wharf and Land company, which must materially increase the demand for the company's lots. The transfer across the Mississippi river of the cars of the Cincinnati, New Orleans & Texas Pacific system is also made over the property of the company, and at this landing the various boats plying on the Mississippi and Yazoo and their tributaries connect with the Vicksburg & Meridian, Vicksburg, Shreveport & Pacific, and Louisville, New Orleans & Texas railroads.

The Vicksburg Wharf and Land company have laid out their property as an addition to the city of Vicksburg, and are at work having an electric street railroad built to it. In the meantime little or no effort is being made to dispose of the lots, the company realizing that at an early day these lots will command very liberal prices, owing to the various advantages possessed by their location both for business and residential purposes. A few lots have been sold at prices ranging from $1,500 to $2,000 each, and residences are now being erected on them. The stock of the company is not on the market. The secure position of the company, the cash value of its lands, and the stolidity with which the stockholders have held on to their shares from its earliest inception have obviated the necessity of running the capital into the millions. This amounts to $300,000 only. It is understood that this stock has never changed hands from the original holders, who have been so satisfied with the investment that they have never cared to part with it. The exceptional situation of this property, its numerous advantages for residential purposes, commanding as it does a magnificent view of the river and the surrounding country for miles, while it has in addition to the landing every railroad centering in Vicksburg immediately at its base, must make it at an early day the most sought-for and the best tract of land in and around Vicksburg. The stockolders of the company are all subtantial business men. Among them are: Thomas Rigby, ex-president of the Vicksburg and Meridian railroad; A. D. Mattingly, coal merchant; J. B. Mattingly, mill owner; Thomas M. Smedes, and Eugene Martin, all of Vicksburg; Colonel Wooldridge, Lexington, Ky.; the German Security bank of Louisville, Ky. The late Col. A. B. Pittman, of Vicksburg, was also a stockholder.

The surrender of Vicksburg, July 3, 1863, to the troops under Grant, and the defeat of Lee's army at Gettysburg on the same date, by the troops under Meade, abolished doubt in the minds of impartial observers, North and South, and pointed to the fact that, were the Federal authorities inclined to end the war, every division of the Confederacy could be garrisoned by their troops before the close of that summer. Early in the struggle the importance of Vicksburg as a strategic point was recognized by both sides. The fall of New Orleans, in 1862, gave the Federals virtual possession of the Mississippi river up to Vicksburg, down to which operations had also cleared the way from above. On the 18th of May a portion of Farragut's fleet, under Capt. S. P. Lee, appeared before the city and demanded its surrender, which was promptly refused. Every effort was made by the Confederacy to retain a strong force here. Ten thousand troops garrisoned Vicksburg at this period. On the 28th of May, General Williams, who had occupied the opposite side of the river, attempted, by means of a dug canal, to leave the city high and dry, but the uncertain stream declined to desert the city, and the scheme was a failure.

After a vain bombardment, on the 28th of June Farragut's fleet was compelled, by falling water, to descend to New Orleans. General Sherman's operations from the Yazoo quarter were equally fruitless. Grant's attack, on the 19th of May, 1863, was gallantly repulsed, but he invested the city with an overwhelming force of seventy thousand men, while the fleet co-operated from the river.

On July 3, 1863, after enduring for forty-seven days and nights the horrors of bombardment, and menaced by the pangs of hunger, Vicksburg, through General Pemberton, in command of the town, was allowed honorable terms of capitulation, and the brave struggle of the inhabitants against the inevitable was at an end. Rather less than seventeen years later, on April 12, 1880, Grant again entered Vicksburg—not this time at the head of a victorious army, but amid the plaudits of the citizens, as their invited guest, they having chivalrously forgotten the bitterness of the past and joined the whole South in welcoming the great Federal captain.

After the siege, Vicksburg struggled manfully to regain its prosperity. The reconstruction period was successfully passed through, but a disastrous fire in 1866 caused great loss of property. In 1876 the Mississippi river, most fickle and inconstant of its kind, voluntarily accomplished the task in which the Federal engineers had failed. It reached across the narrow isthmus opposite, which has ever since remained an island, while Vicksburg now stands on the borders of a lake, two miles from the main current and only reached directly by navigation during the four or five months of high water each year. Two years later, in common with other Southern cities, Vicksburg had a terrible visitation of yellow fever. Another great fire in 1883 laid a portion of the town in ruins, and as a fitting climax to this series of misfortunes, the collapse of the Mississippi bank the same year took from luckless depositors a million dollars of hard-earned money. However strange it may seem, there is a gleam of satisfaction in recalling these unhappy incidents, for they serve to set forth more eloquently than volumes of argument the strength and elasticity of the town and the unconquerable will of the people. Vicksburg has been tried in the crucible and has come out of the dread ordeal better in every way.

With the possible exception of Arlington Heights at Washington, no national cemetery in the United States can compare with that of Vicksburg, situated about two miles north of town. All that nature and art could do has been here accomplished to afford a noble resting place for over sixteen thousand Federal soldiers. Until the building of the Valley road there was a splendid wide drive from the city to the cemetery. The railroad somewhat affected the drainage and caused a slight caving in of the sides. Congress appropriated $10,000 for restoring this road in 1880 and it was made a beautiful boulevard with shade trees on each side.

The Convent and Academy of St. Francis Xavier, opened in 1860, was converted into an hospital for soldiers in 1861, and the teachers became hospital nurses there and in the principal military hospitals throughout the state. In 1863 the Federals took possession of the buildings, but they were restored to the sisters after peace was insured.

A movement was inaugurated at Vicksburg in May, 1889, to hold a reunion of Federal and Confederate veterans in May, 1890. Prominent men of the state were asked to serve upon the executive committee, such as Governor Lowry, Gen. Stephen D. Lee, Col. Charles E. Hooker, Gen. E. C. Walthall, Gen. J. Z. George, Ex-Gov. John M. Stone, Hon. T. M. Miller, Private John Allen, John R. Cameron, Gen. W. T. Martin, Gen. S. W. Ferguson, Col. Stockdale, and also distinguished ex-Federal soldiers, then citizens of the state. Their action insured success, and the Northern Decoration day of 1890 was solemnly celebrated at Vicksburg, the Blue and Gray uniting in extolling the valor of their soldiers.

The history of the part taken by the people of Warren county and Vicksburg in the Mexican and Civil wars is portrayed in the general history of the state, and there also is related much of their social, religious and commercial progress. In the brief sketch of Warren county, the character of the country, the names of its pioneers, and other facts of local interest are given, so that it is unnecessary to refer to such names and events in the sketch of the city.

The building of the county courthouse in 1858, twenty-two years after the people declared Vicksburg to be the seat of justice, and thirty-seven years after the town was surveyed, may be considered the beginning of her commercial progress. That courthouse was erected in 1858 and completed in 1861, after plans by William Weldon. It is a two-story brick (in stucco) building, which cost over $100,000. It holds the position of an ancient citadel, and like such old buildings is classic in style, the Ionic columns giving it a beauty which the colonial cupola cannot destroy. The site is terraced, and bounded by heavy stone walls. Within, the prevailing ideas of antebellum days in the South are exemplified; for the high ceilings and large rooms tell of the disposition of the people to seek light, air and space—a disposition now made subservient to economy.

The Federal building is a Florentine-Romanesque study, authorized by the last congress. The Convent and Academy of St. Francis Xavier is a great square palladium house, with a Gothic frontal or central pavilion, and is considered one of the finest educational buildings in the whole South. The Main Street public school building is a semi-Gothic house, with central tower and lantern. As a house where light and ventilation are the first objects it is a success, but from an architectural point of view the style should never show itself in the United States. There is something definite in the form of St. Aloysius' Commercial college. It is an adaptation of the Florentine school, and retains many of those features which the master, Palladio, proclaimed to be necessary. The quoin stones in the piers of the corner pavilions or projections, the pilaster strip, the Italian voussoirs and keystones are all definite, and the construction substantial.

The residences are rather in the Queen Anne style than in the classic, and in this respect Vicksburg differs materially from the sister city of Natchez.

There are eight white churches here. The Catholic church of St. Paul's has a very rich interior. There are three priests, of whom Father Petre is the chief, while among the congregation many of the best families of the city are always to be seen. The Catholic population of Vicksburg is over four thousand. The two Episcopalian churches, Holy Trinity and Christ's, are fine specimens of ecclesiastical architecture, the tall spire of the former being greatly admired. The Methodists, Presbyterians and Baptists have also convenient places of worship, while the Hebrew fraternity possesses a well-appointed synagogue. The colored people pay their devotions in six churches of different denominations. St. Paul's church is a large, gothic structure, with central tower, surmounted by a small spire, springing from within an arcade or parapet. The tower corners and buttresses are capped and each carries a pinnacle. Some years before the war a chime of ten bells was placed in the bell-tower and the interior decorated. The building suffered, of course, during the bombardment in 1863, but all damages were repaired and the decorations of the interior improved. The Baptist church presents a style of semi-gothic architecture which obtained about the middle of the first half of the century, when the sects increased in wealth and influence, as they did in numbers. A central tower with brooch, Gothic only in the formation of doors and windows, leaves it an independent architectural conception of 1879. The Church of the Holy Trinity is a Norman Gothic house, with tower, including finial or cross, two hundred and eleven feet in hight. Pilaster strip and corbel tables are extensively used, giving it a Tudor appearance. Christ church was erected in 1841-2, after the Elizabethan idea of the Gothic style. It is the same in style as those buildings erected in the United Kingdom and the British colonies in the eighteenth and in the first half of this century by the British government. The Methodist church, built in 1850, is a very independent conception of Architect Thomas Hackett. It is a combination of the Roman, Gothic and colonial—a strange combination, of course, but evidently in accord with the ideas of those who worshiped in it forty years ago. The Presbyterian building is Gothic of the Tudor school, as has all the unfinished character of that school, the buttress merging into a pilaster and vice versa. The synagogue is altogether too uncertain in its architectural features to be credited to any known style.

The Cotton exchange, organized in 1874, was incorporated in 1886. The Exchange building was purchased from the Mississippi Valley bank representatives in 1886 for $20,000. This is an Italian house with a well-proportioned Corinthian colonnade or portico, entablature, parapet, carrying statuary. The receipts of cotton are estimated at from sixty thousand to eighty-five thousand bales annually, including the greater part of the long stapled cotton produced in the tributary territory.

The first term of the United States court opened in July, 1887. The city is largely indebted for this to the Hon. T. C. Catchings, who represented the district in congress. It not only effects a great saving in the expense and inconvenience hitherto involved in the journey to Jackson, but will bring more people and more money to Vicksburg. On a hill close to the town the water-works contractors erected in 1887 a standpipe one hundred and forty feet high, twenty feet in diameter, with a capacity of three hundred and twenty-five thousand gallons. Just outside the city thirty or forty four-inch drove wells were sunk to a depth of three hundred feet. Eighty hydrants were supplied to the city, each capable of throwing a stream fifty feet high. Twelve miles of piping were laid in the streets that year, the main pipes being sixteen inches in diameter. Besides the immense boon to the general public, the improvement in sanitary arrangements, and the advantages that accrue to the manufacturers, it is estimated that the water-works effect a reduction of nearly one-half in the rates of insurance. The capacity of the pumping machinery is stated to be four million gallons.

The Hill City Electric Light company erected a plant in 1889, at a cost of $28,000, for lighting the city and private buildings, and added to the arc an incandescent system, at a cost of over $20,000 additional. The Thomson-Houston system is used, and furnishes excellent illumination for public and private purposes. Fifteen miles of wire were laid at once, and one hundred and five arc lights introduced; but one thousand incandescent lights were subsequently added and the foundations of electrical light established.

The Vicksburg Hotel company selected plans presented by Sully, Toledano & Patton, which called for a five-story commercial building, with romanesque ornament, an octagonal tower one hundred and thirty feet high, at the northeast corner, and the hight for the building proper of one hundred feet. The estimated cost of the building alone is $70,000, and of the building and site, $110,000. No commercial building in the state compares with it either in beauty or appropriateness of design, and its erection marks a new era in Vicksburg's architecture. All the requirements of light and ventilation are perfectly met. The first floor contains the main rotunda, 41x64 feet, six stores fronting on Clay street, and the bar and billiardroom in the rear, fronting on an alley twenty-five feet wide; also the office, baggageroom and laundry. On the right side of the main entrance are the elevator and grand stairway. The office or rotunda is lighted from a dome two stories high. On the second floor the entrance is into a large hall or receptionroom looking into the office below. Immediately in the rear of the dome on this floor, the dining hall, 39x82 feet, is located, as well as the ladies' ordinary, children's diningroom, kitchen and servants' rooms. The third, fourth and fifth floors are devoted entirely to the one hundred bedrooms, many of them en suite.

Many other new buildings have been erected on historical sites, and throughout the city the hum of the builders is heard. Old dwellings and stores have been remodeled within the last few years, and in all things the inactivity of the old town of a few years ago is compensated for by the activity of the people of the present city, who are determined to raise Vicksburg to that position which its location and the resources of the adjacent country fit it to occupy.

Bovina and New Town are other towns in Warren county.

Meridian, the county seat of Lauderdale county, is situated at the junction of the Vicksburg & Meridian, East Tennessee, Virginia & Georgia, Alabama, Great Southern & New Orleans and Northeastern railroads with the Mobile & Ohio railroad, one hundred and thirty-five miles north of Mobile, one hundred and forty miles east of Vicksburg and one hundred and ninety-six miles northeast of New Orleans, near the eastern border of the state. Besides the railroads above mentioned, there are three other roads certain of early completion in the next two years. These are the Warrior Coal Fields railroad, the Pensacola & Memphis railroad and the Brookhaven & Meridian railroad. Without these railroads Meridian is already, next to Atlanta, the greatest railroad center in the South. With these railroads, that are certain to be built, it will be the equal of Atlanta in railroad facilities, for these three lines, added to the present, will afford immediate connection in ten different directions.

The city of Meridian is a wonder! Of commercial expansion and business activity; of business pluck, as well as of increase of population, she is a great and growing wonder! Scarce a quarter of a century back an even one hundred people were the population of her limits. To-day about eleven thousand have their daily existence within her confines, while twice that number are interested in the rise and progress of this busy inland mart.

The past few years have witnessed wonderful progress in city-building in this magic city of the South. With no spasmodic boom, but as a result of self-confidence, the growth and development of Meridian have really been astonishing, and, if it had no prospect of further railroad facilities, her people might say to the world, without incurring the charge of vanity, nor seeming to be vainglorious: "Come to us, ye who are manufacturers and workers in every known art, and make your home with us, for we are great and growing and growing greater!" No place in the South is more favorably situated for cloth factories, furniture factories, wagon factories, implement factories and factories of every kind, than this bustling, driving, wideawake city of Meridian.

As a manufacturing center the city is now taking prominent place. Already she has recorded some fine triumphs in this direction, among which are the following: The Sash and Blind factory, the Southern Standard Press company, the Meridian Oil Mills and Manufacturing company, the Progress Machine works, the Stanford & Son's Boiler and Sheet Iron works, the Williams & Briggs Machine shops, the New Orleans & Northeastern shops, Covert's Meridian Furniture factory, the East Mississippi Cotton mills, Love & Co. and Stevenson's gristmills, Hoffer's Phœnix Iron works, the Meridian Carriage and Pump Manufacturing company, Robinson & Co.'s Terra Cotta and Brick works, the Woodward Liver Renovator company, the Meridian Phosphate company, the Meridian Planing mills, the O'Neill Marble works, the Meridian Ice factory, the Meridian Fertilizer company and the Meridian Cigar factory.

The educational interests of Meridian are extensive, and in their appointments quite as complete as may be found elsewhere, thus reflecting great credit upon this wideawake Southern city. The Meridian Female college (Baptist), the east Mississippi Female college (Methodist), the St. Aloysius Female academy (Catholic), are all notable institutions of learning, well attended and capably conducted.

The pride of Meridian is her excellent public schools. Although they were organized but five years ago, they are rapidly being recognized as among the best city schools in the state. During the last session more than fourteen hundred children matriculated. The citizens of Meridian have been aroused to the necessity of supporting these schools liberally; rapid progress is being made. The colored school has six hundred and fifty pupils enrolled, and it is prosperous. For the whites there are four large buildings, located in the different wards of the city. They have been, for four years, under the excellent superintendency of Prof. A. A. Kincannon, a native Mississippian, and one of the best known educators in the South. There is, in connection with the schools, an industrial department, where stenography, telegraphy, typewriting and architectural and mechanical drawing are taught. The main or industrial building is a magnificent structure, and was erected at a cost of $40,000.

Meridian has three strong banking institutions. The Citizens' Savings bank has a capital of $27,000. George W. Meyer is its president; J. S. Solomon, vice president; W. A. Brown, cashier. Its correspondents are the Chase National bank, New York, and the Union National bank, of New Orleans. The First National bank has a capital of $130,000, and large surplus and undivided profits. Its correspondents are the United States and National Park banks, New York, and the Union National bank, New Orleans. Charles A. Lyerly is its president, W. W. George, its vice president, C. W. Robinson, its cashier, H. L. Bardwell its assistant cashier. The Meridian National bank has a capital of $100,000, a surplus of $50,000, and undivided profits amounting to $25,000 more. Its officers are T. Wistar Brown, president; G. Q. Hall, vice president; J. H. Wright, cashier; E. B. McRaven, assistant cashier. Correspondents, Seaboard National bank, New York; State National bank, New Orleans.

Building and loan associations have had much to do with the extension of Meridian's visible limits. The eighth annual statement of the Mechanics' Aid, Building and Loan association was issued September 2, 1890. It showed that the total earnings of six series was $54,628.30; the total resources of all series were $304,973.55; the total expenses for rent, licenses, etc., were $2,601.50, remarking: "In the matter of expenses we compare favorably with the most economically conducted associations in the land; less than five per cent. of the net savings including salaries, rent, stationery, etc." This association has the following officers: George S. Covert, president; H. F. Broach, vice president; L. A. Duncan, secretary; E. E. Spinks, treasurer, Miller & Baskin, attorneys. Directors: George. S. Covert, H. F. Broach, J. C. Lloyd, A. B. Wagner, W. S. Lott, C. W. Robinson, H. M. Threefoot.

INSANE ASYLUM, JACKSON.

The second annual statement of the Savings, Building and Loan association, rendered January 6, 1891, was as follows:

"The first series of the association closes its second year, and the second series its first, with the December report. In the former the net earnings have been fully twenty per cent., and the latter something more, at an expense of less than five per cent. on profits.

"There is a growing disposition to hold the old and borrow in the latest series, which may cause a call for shares in the first series, to be retired at surrender value. This will not retard the liquidation materially beyond the five years estimated.

"Statement: Seventeen hundred shares, first series, assessed dues, $20,400; three hundred and thirty-four shares in loans, assessed interest, $3,582; shares in loans, assessed premiums, $3,362.55; fines collected, $33.40; unpaid last year, brought forward, $202.65; two hundred and fifteen shares retired during year, dues collected, $1,390; sixty-five shares loans raised during year, returned, $7,800; total enrolled, $36,770.60; uncollected, as per December, 1890, report, $591.35; net collections, 1890, $361,79.25. Gross earnings of year, $7,093.60; expenses, $478.45; net earnings, $6,615.15; resources, in loans, $40,080; investments, $8,350; unpaid balance, $910.90; total, $49,340.90. Value of shares, twenty-four months, paid, $29; surrender value, $28.65; eighteen hundred shares in force, second series, dues assessed, $21,600; two hundred and three shares in loans, interest assessed, $1,223; shares in premiums, $1,550.15; fines collected during year, $4.85; total enrolled, $24,378; uncollected, December report, 1890, $378; net collections, 1890, $24,000. Gross earnings for year, $2,778; expenses, $448.45; net earnings, $2,329.55; resources, in loans, $24,360; less advanced loans, $721.95; total, $23,638.05. Value of shares, twelve months, paid, $13.50; surrender value, $13.20.

"Shares are estimated to reach par value in a little over five years, say $120. Loans are made on the basis of running five years, monthly payments being heavier than on the $200 share plans, but premiums are not deducted, being payable in equitable installments, without interest. The third series opened with this month." The officers are: H. F. Broach, president; J. H. Wright, vice president; L. A. Duncan, secretary; Charles S. Covert, treasurer; Miller & Baskin, attorneys; directors: H. F. Broach, J. C. Lloyd, W. S. Lott, J. H. Wright, A. B. Wagner, S. B. Holt, T. B. Lamb.

The Meridian cotton exchange and board of trade was organized in 1873. Its officers are president, vice president, secretary and treasurer, and its affairs are in charge of a competent board of directors. There are the following standing committees: Inspection and classification, finance, quotations, manufactures and mechanical industries, information and statistics, membership and transportation.

The Meridian street railroad company was chartered in April, 1883.

The city fire department consists of Mechanics' steam fire company No. 1, organized in June, 1882; Clinch steam fire company No. 3, organized in June, 1886; Excelsior No. 4 hose-truck company, and Phœnix No. 2 (colored) hose-truck and hand-engine company.

Religious denominations are represented here by the following church organizations: St. Patrick's Roman Catholic, Methodist, West End Methodist, First Baptist, Calvary Baptist, Presbyterian, Cumberland Presbyterian, Protestant Episcopal, Beth Israel (Jewish), and the following colored churches: Baptist, Pilgrim's Progress Bethel, Methodist Episcopal Academy, African Methodist Episcopal, First Congregational and Mount Zion.

The list of local associations and societies is as follows: The Standard club, Young Men's Christian association, Meridian Temperance Reform club, Montefiore Social club, St. Joseph's Branch No. 105 C. K. of A., Lauderdale lodge No. 308 A. F. & A. M., King Solomon's lodge

No. 333 A. F. & A. M., Meridian lodge No. 80 I. O. O. F., Mount Barton lodge No. 13 K. of P., Mississippi lodge No. 525 K. of H., Palmetto lodge No. 320 K. & L. of H., East Mississippi council No. 1100 A. L. of H., Order of Railway Conductors, Stephenson division No. 230 B. of L. E., Knights of the Golden Rule, Brotherhood of Locomotive Firemen, Knights of Labor, Asaph lodge No. 286 I. O. B. B., Meridian lodge No. 109 I. O. F. S. of I.

The Meridian Land and Industrial company is one of the potent factors in the improvement and upbuilding of Meridian. It was organized November 1, 1888, with the following officers: J. C. Loyd, president; A. J. Weems, vice president; C. W. Robinson, secretary and treasurer. The company owns twenty hundred lots in all parts of the city and ten hundred acres of land adjacent to the city. Lots are being improved and sold on long time with a small cash payment. There is now a paid-in capital of $250,000, and since date of organization the company have sold over $160,000 worth of property, and by giving exceedingly liberal terms it has materially assisted in the upbuilding of the city.

The horoscope of Meridian appears to have been cast amid the signs of war and the rumors of war.

This city was settled by John T. Ball, and was formerly known as Ball's Log Store. It was rechristened by Mr. Ball, Meridian, and a postoffice was obtained under that name in 1854. The Mobile & Ohio railroad company, when it reached this point with the first track, in 1855, called it Sowashee station. The first railroad train arrived at this point, then the McLemore Oldfield, October, 1855. Mr. Ball erected a plain plank stationhouse, at his personal expense, aided by such individual subscription of material as could be obtained, the Mobile & Ohio railroad naming the station Sowashee, and agreeing as a special favor to grant depot privileges, provided the house according to their specifications should be furnished free, but for nearly two years afterward the place was treated as a mere flag station, and denied ordinary flag-station accommodations, while the expense of keeping up the station was borne locally. By these means the starting of a town here was prevented, the Mobile & Ohio railroad at the same time giving assistance and influence to start towns on their line on either side of and adjoining this place.

May 1, 1861, at a public barbecue at Meridian, the Meridian Invincibles were mustered into the Southern service, sixty-three strong, the Pettus guards being present. May 28, the Meridian Invincibles, eighty in number, started from Meridian northward over the Mobile & Ohio railroad at 4 P. M., three other volunteer companies starting with them. The next day the first train over the Southern, now Memphis & Vicksburg railroad, arrived at Meridian at 6:45 P. M., drawn by a handsome little engine, the Mazeppa. The train brought as passengers the volunteer company "Vicksburg Southrons," one hundred and eleven strong, and other passengers. June 3, the first train left Meridian for Vicksburg at 8:45 A. M. It is easy to imagine the flutter occasioned among the inhabitants whose places of abode lay near the line of the iron highway that placed them in direct and speedy connection with Mobile and the world beyond, through the fleet of vessels that lined the bustling wharves of the Gulf city—it is easy to imagine; but the power to depict the picture as it was, and to tell of the scenes and discussions that followed the arrival of the first train, rests only with those who were in Meridian on that day. It is not so far in the past, either, that there should not now be living those who witnessed this important event.

Hon. W. C. Smedes, the president and father of the Southern railroad, when he reached here with his track adopted the name given by Mr. Ball, and accepted by the citizens, and suggested its adoption by the Mobile & Ohio Railroad company, and from that date it has borne the name—Meridian.

It was not until the breaking out of the war that opportunities were afforded to buy property here, and during the war the uncertainty was so great as to the safety of property that nothing but inferior houses was put up, and in 1864 General Sherman reached the place and burned all of the town he could find; so that the close of the war found scarcely a vestige of what was once the town, and the people were too poor to do much in the way of improvement for a long time.

By great exertion and heavy sacrifice the owners of the property succeeded in giving the town a second start in 1866. The first manufactory established in Meridian was the foundry and machineshops of Messrs. Sellars, Murphy & Lister. They were located just above the railroad crossing north of the town. The senior partner in this firm was Mr. L. H. Sellars, now president of the Memphis & Pensacola railroad. The second was the Kewanee planingmills, located near where the Planters' compress now stands. This plant was moved from Kewanee, this county, to Meridian, by the Whiffle Brothers. Out of this beginning has grown one of the largest sash, door and blind factories in the Southwest.

In those days cotton brought fifty cents a pound, flour $14 to $16 a barrel, bacon sides twenty-five cents and hams thirty cents, whisky was twenty-five cents a drink, while the supply was unlimited. An air of prosperity pervaded the town which attracted general attention. The cessation of war seemed but to add renewed vigor to growth, and within a year the newspapers of the state had already begun to devote considerable space to the wonderful stories about Meridian. These attracted business men here from all directions. Substantial business houses had gone up, and the increase in wealth and population had exceeded anything of the kind that had ever before been known in the state. A village had within twelve months expanded into a town of one thousand five hundred.

This was before the days of the mushroom towns of the Pennsylvania oil districts and of the far West, which grew to their full stature and decayed before finishing touches could be put on the homes of the populace. It was something new for the South, especially following so closely upon the ending of a four years' war. There is little wonder that the growth of the town was considered magical. "It now numbers two thousand five hundred souls," was enthusiastically written in May, 1866, "and bids fair to become an interior commercial city. The grand advantages of the place was a phrase which found a lodgment in the heart of every Meridianite, and it was their staff of hope whenever anything happened to check the forward pace of their town. In 1870 it had a population of two thousand seven hundred and nine, and had as many handsome two and three-story brick stores and blocks as many of the large cities of the state of ten times its age, and its growth and improvement have been rapid and steady since. In 1880 the population was four thousand and eight; in 1890, ten thousand eight hundred and eighty-nine.

During the first half of the period from 1865 to 1875, Meridian was substantially dead, many of her most enterprising citizens having lost their all during the closing years of the war, which rendered them unable to contribute anything toward the development of the town. In the latter half of this decade Meridian passed successfully the point of doubt and uncertainty. Railroads projected were constructed, and Meridian's rivals reluctantly conceded its preeminence. In 1870 the Memphis *Avalanche* said: "Meridian is the most rapidly growing town in the state of Mississippi, and its future still brighter. Sherman burned it up in 1864, but it now has a population greater than that of any town in the state except Vicksburg. The Mobile & Ohio and the Vicksburg & Selma railroads cross there, and the most important road she has projected will be completed this year. This is the direct line to Chattanooga, up the Wills valley, and it is the air line from New Orleans to New York, passing by Meridian,

Chattanooga, Knoxville, Lynchburg and Washington. A bill has been introduced in the legislature at Jackson, Miss., to extend the Chattanooga & Meridian road to New Orleans; and a like bill has already passed the legislature of Louisiana. The same Boston capitalists that now have the construction of the road from Chattanooga to Meridian propose to make it directly to New Orleans, on an air line, and they want no help. This means that they know it will pay its stockholders, as it is the shortest line that will ever be built between New Orleans and New York. This is the future of Meridian; and another road will be built there; we allude to that from Grenada. Such a line can not long remain unoccupied; and its extension to Pensacola will soon follow, thus placing Memphis as near the Gulf as she now is to Louisville."

A letter to the *Clarion* from Baldwyn dated March, 1870, has the following allusion to this thriving young city: "The growth of Meridian is truly wonderful. The latest and most noticeable improvement is a large and handsome brick hotel, which will be ready for guests this summer. It presents a truly metropolitan appearance. It is being erected by a stock company and will be an ornament in its line. With the location of the courthouse, the establishment of gas works, and the converging here of so many railroads, Meridian may yet be the Chicago of the South. She should not be ambitious, however, to attain to the distinction which the latter enjoys in the way of morals." From this time on Meridian's progress was great. The period from 1875 to 1880 witnessed still greater progress in Meridian's commercial and financial growth than even the last decade had done. Notwithstanding the draft upon her resources caused by the Civil war, her advance was rapid and substantial, and some of the city's fine buildings were erected during that period, and some of its large manufactories and other enterprises were started about this time. The impetus that Meridian has acquired during the past ten years is certainly accelerating. Since the census of 1880 the population has increased nearly seven thousand, and, with extended railroad facilities, the future outlook for Meridian is tinted with a roseate hue, with every prospect that another year will see her population fully doubled, and the busy hum of machinery heard upon every side. Never in the history of Meridian was there such a need of houses as exists at present, and there are a great number in process of erection.

Other towns of this county are Marion, which was the county seat until 1866, when the courthouse was removed to Marion Station, where it remained until the establishment of the seat of justice at Meridian in 1870; Lockhart, Lauderdale Station (near old Lauderdale Springs, a popular resort in the ante-bellum days), Toomsuba, and Daleville.

Summit is distant one hundred and eight miles from New Orleans and seventy-five miles from Jackson, the state capital. It stands on one of the highest points in the state, four hundred and twenty feet above tide-water. The business portion of Summit is almost entirely of brick, several fire experiences having taught the advisability of such construction. About thirty stores are here in full operation, the principal of these being on a very extensive scale. The cotton trade of the town is a weighty item, the average receipts being from thirteen thousand to fifteen thousand bales each season, as large in comparison to the size of the place as that of any town on the Illinois Central road. A compress will doubtless be built ere long. The shipment of country produce is becoming more and more important. Chickens and eggs are being sent in quantities to New Orleans.

Summit's location, in the heart of the pine belt, offers advantages in timber well worth notice. There is within four miles, just the other side of McComb city, one of the most complete sawmill, planing, drying establishments in the state. J. White is the proprietor. The business gives employment to about one hundred and fifty men. Three miles north of Summit Messrs. Johnson & Whitney have another complete mill, while still more are projected.

To the advancement of this place the admirable religious and educational institutions of the city have largely contributed. The churches, five in number, are in every respect commodious, thoroughly fitted places of worship. The colored race have also three good churches. This is the seat of Lea Female college, and has first-class public schools for whites and blacks.

Natchez was visited by La Salle and party in 1682, but did not receive its first white settlers until 1698, when Pere Davion, who shortly after located where Fort Adams now is, and Pere St. Cosme, who remained among the Indians at that point and remained until the year 1707 arrived. The latter was killed by the Chittimaches near Donaldsonville, La., while en route to that Indian town. On February 11, 1700, Lemoyne d'Iberville and Lemoyne Bienville, accompanied by Henri de Tonti, who visited them at Biloxi, arrived at Natchez and were welcomed by Pere St. Cosme. The proposition to establish a post there was well received and the name La Ville de Rosalie aux Natchez was bestowed upon the site. The cabin of the chief and the temple of the sun were soon given neighbors in the shape of stately log huts and the foundations of a city were made. In 1716 a fort was constructed at that point, and in 1718 the plantation of M. de la Houssaye, on St. Catherine's creek, was opened, and a house for the owner erected in the village. The farms of Pellerin and Bellecourt were opened close by in 1819, and in 1820 the great plantation of Hubert was cleared on that creek, the gristmill, the forge, the armory and the machine-shop were erected and equipped, and the Montplaisir tobacco farm, within a half-myriameter, or about three miles of the village, established. No sooner was this settlement made than British intrigue introduced trouble, and the disagreements between the colonists and Indians, leading up to the massacre of 1729, were commenced. The history of this terrible affair is given in the second chapter of the general history of the state. Enough here to state that the French colony at Natchez was exterminated, and, in turn, the Natchez themselves were blotted off the face of the earth by the French colonial troops and Choctaws in 1732. In 1745 there were eight white males (soldiers), two negro families, and fifteen negro slaves at Natchez. In 1751 there were fifty soldiers in garrison there. In 1772 the British ventured in, and their leader, Col. Anthony Hutchins, located lands on St. Catherine's creek. Five years later the British purchased the Natchez district from the Choctaws for a few presents, although they had parceled it out to favorites in 1772, Hutchins being given a large tract, including the White Apple village and twenty-five thousand acres to Amos Ogden. In 1772 Richard and Samuel Swayze of New Jersey purchased nineteen thousand acres from Captain Ogden at twenty cents per acre, and in the fall settled where is now Kingston, in Adams county. Samuel was a Congregational preacher, and as his own and other families who came with them to settle here were members of this society, he had little trouble in organizing the first protestant religious association in the Natchez country, or even in the whole South. In 1780 fears of Indian attack drove those settlers to Natchez post, where Samuel took up lands on the east bank of St. Catherine's bayou. They selected lands on the Homochitto. Four years later (1776) the new town of Natchez boasted of twenty houses, log and frame, located under the bluff. The merchants were James Willing, an American; Captain Bloomart, a British pensioner; Thomas Barber and Hanchett & Newman. The planters in the neighborhood had almost reached that stage of prosperity which the French planters were enjoying when the massacre of 1729 wiped them out. The new British colonists of Natchez were not to be exempt, their unreasonable exhibition of tory proclivities, their professed preference for British rule and the opportunities to aid the British soldiery attracted the attention of the fathers of the republic, and James Willing, who resided among and knew them, was commissioned to win them over to the Revolution or crush their power to help the enemy. How well he succeeded is part of the national history as it is of that of the state. In 1779-80 the Spanish troops drove the British from west Florida and placed Colonel Grand Pre in charge of a small garrison at Natchez. In April, 1782, colonists made a demonstration against the Spanish, and by the use of a forged letter urged the Spanish officer to surrender Fort Panmure (named so by the British in 1764), then the name of the post. The Britishers took possession and sent the garrison under guard to Loftus hights. Arrived at that point a Spanish force was observed ascending the river. The captors released the captives and fled. The commander of the Spaniards was Major Mulligan, and he, without delay, went in pursuit, came up with the fugitives, killed fourteen, and captured many. The colonists fled in mortal fear, among the first to go being the Hutchins, Dwights, and Lymans, leaders of the opposition; but the Spaniards exercised the greatest moderation and there was little or no loss inflicted upon the miserable sectionalists.

On March 29, 1798, the Spanish garrison evacuated Natchez, and Captain Guion installed a garrison of United States troops.

The population of Natchez in 1785 was one thousand five hundred and fifty, and in 1788, two thousand six hundred and seventy-nine; in 1812, one thousand and twenty-one whites, four hundred and fifty-nine slaves, and thirty-one others, numbering one thousand five hundred and eleven; in 1820, one thousand four hundred and forty-eight whites, and seven hundred and thirty-six negroes; in 1837, three thousand seven hundred and thirty-one; in 1870, nine thousand and fifty-seven; in 1880, seven thousand and fifty-eight; and in 1890, ten thousand one hundred and forty-nine.

An act to incorporate the city of Natchez was passed by the territorial legislature March 10, 1803. The first meeting of the common council was held April 9, 1803, with Samuel Brooks, mayor; Lewis Kerr, recorder; and Samuel Neil, an alderman. Samuel Brooks was mayor a long time; but as the record books were destroyed nothing is certain regarding his immediate successors. The mayors and presidents of the council from 1815 to the present time are named as follows: Edward Turner, 1815; William McComas, 1818; Robert W. Wood, 1855; John Hunter, 1859-63; William Dix, 1866; John W. Weldon, 1869; Robert H. Wood, 1871-4; Henry C. Griffin, 1874-83; I. Lowenberg, 1883-7; William H. Mallery, 1887-9, and W. G. Benbrook, 1889-91.

The first postmaster appointed for Natchez by the United States was Abijah Hunt, commissioned July 1, 1800. This was the first postoffice established in Mississippi by the United States, that at the Chickasaw agency, in charge of James McIntosh, being the second, January 1, 1802, and that at Greenville, established September 10, 1803, with John Shaw master, the third.

Natchez in 1812 was no unimportant place. There was nothing to interfere with the prosperity, save the threatened invasion and subjection of the United States by the British. Marchalk's almanac of that year paints the town in words and figures thus:

"Four tailor shops, three blacksmiths, four saddlers, six carpenters, five cabinetmakers, one coach and sign painter, three hatters, two tinners, four boot and shoemakers, one trunkmaker, one bookbinder, one wagonmaker, one chairmaker, one nail factory, three barbers, four brickyards, one butcher, four bakers, one brushmaker, three gold and silversmiths, one confectioner and distiller, four bricklayers, one horsemill (corn), one plasterer, twelve watercarts, eight physicians, seven lawyers, three English schools, one incorporated mechanics' society, one Free Mason lodge, four magistrates, three printing offices, with weekly papers, two porterhouses, six public inns, five warehouses, one readingroom and coffeehouse, twenty-four drygoods stores, four groceries, two wholesale stores, seventeen catalenes, one commission store, one bank of Mississippi, capital $500,000, managed by thirteen directors, with Stephen Minor president. Under the 'Hill' were two blacksmith shops, one tavern and thirteen catalenes."

Among the giants of the old Natchez bar were: Wm. B. Griffith; Robert Walker, United States senator from Mississippi, and secretary of the treasury under Polk; Felix and Eli Houston; John A. Quitman, governor of state and member to congress, and a distinguished general in the Mexican war; Thomas B. Reed; George Winchester; John T. McMurrain; S. S. Boyd; William Vannerson, who died in 1871, and is spoken of as the Nestor of the Mississippi bar; Alexander Montgomery; G. M. Davis; Grafton Baker; Aylett Baker; Ralph North, ex-circuit judge, and Gen. Wm. T. Martin. Among these might be mentioned Hon. S. S. Prentiss, though he practiced here but a short time.

Church societies of nearly all denominations are represented in Natchez. The Catholic church dates its foundation here to 1698, when Father John B. Buisson de St. Cosme, Father Davion, and other priests established missions among the Natchez. In 1885 St. Mary's cathedral was dedicated. The erection of this magnificent church edifice was begun in 1841 and completed in 1885 at a total cost of $78,241. St. Mary's cathedral is a handsome Gothic structure of brick, the most graceful building in the state. It has a beautiful and well proportioned spire, one hundred and ninety-six feet high, surmounted with a cross. In this steeple there was placed in 1881, the result of a provision in the will of P. H. McGraw, a fine clock with four large dials, one of which is illuminated. The Protestant churches date to a period early in the eighteenth century; indeed, the Methodists had missionaries or itinerants here in 1799. A Presbyterian church was organized at Pine Ridge February 25, 1807, by Rev. J. Smylie. This church is still in existence, and is the oldest Presbyterian church in Adams county.

The organization of the Presbyterian church at Natchez was practically effected in 1817 by the enrollment of eight persons as members. The Rev. Daniel Smith, a clergyman from New England, who had been laboring as a domestic missionary in the community for more than a year, was invited to minister to it as a stated supply; and John Henderson, Joseph Forman, Richard Pearce and William B. Noyes were ordained as its bench of ruling elders. To this body Samuel S. Spencer was added in 1818. Steps had been taken as early as 1810 for the erection of a Presbyterian house of worship, and in 1812 the corner-stone of the building was laid. It was a brick structure, located on the spot where the present church stands. It was dedicated in February, 1815. The engagement with the Rev. Mr. Smith having terminated in 1819, the Rev. William Weir, a native of Ireland, was elected pastor, and on the 31st of March, 1820, was installed by the Mississippi presbytery. This gentleman, therefore, was the first regular pastor of this church. He is remembered by some few aged citizens, and is spoken of as a man of learning, of great purity of character, and eminently zealous in his work. His period of labor, however, was a short one, his death having occurred on the 25th of November, 1822. The square marble tomb which marks the spot of his sepulture may still be found in a neglected lot which belongs to the church in the city cemetery.

The second pastor of the church was the Rev. George Potts, who first visited Natchez as a licentiate of the presbytery of Philadelphia. Having been subsequently ordained by the presbytery, he was installed pastor by the presbytery of Mississippi in December, 1823. The number of communicants at this time was forty-nine. The first donations reported to have been made by this congregation were in the year 1825, and consisted of $20 to the missionary fund, and $30 to the educational society. In the beginning of 1825 Samuel Postlethwaite was ordained as a ruling elder—a man distinguished for his urbanity as a gentleman and for his integrity as a Christian, and a fine type of that band of merchants who, in the earlier times of Natchez, made their class noble. In 1828, the church edifice originally erected being found inconvenient, the trustees resolved to erect a new one, which work was in the course of the next two years successfully effected. This second building was the original of the one now occupied, a large and handsome brick edifice, and was dedicated on the first Sabbath of January, 1830. The pastorate of Mr. Potts terminated in November, 1835, having continued thirteen years. His removal from Natchez was occasioned by his acceptance of a call from the Duane Street church, New York. He left a communion list of one hundred and thirty-five persons. During his incumbency another addition had been made to the ruling eldership in the person of Dr. Andrew Macrery.

The successor of Mr. Potts was the Rev. Samuel G. Winchester, a native of Baltimore, and previously pastor of a church in Philadelphia. His installation took place on December 24, 1837. The bench of elders having been reduced by deaths and removals to two members—the venerable John Henderson and Dr. Macrery—the congregation elected to that office Thomas Henderson, William Pearce and Franklin Beaumont, who were ordained February 25, 1838. In the year following the church building was repaired, and its means of accommodation enlarged by the introduction of the galleries which are at present standing. About the same time the very neat and commodious parsonage belonging to the church was purchased for the use of the pastor. Mr. Winchester's labors were brought to a close unexpectedly by his death, in August, 1841, while he was absent at the North, whither he had gone as commissioner of the general assembly, which met that year in Philadelphia. He was succeeded by Rev. Joseph B. Stratton, whose pastorate has been a successful one.

The Baptist church was organized in Natchez in January, 1837. Rev. Ashley Vaughn was the first pastor. This society never erected a church and soon after the society became extinct.

The Wall Street Baptist church was organized in 1850, by Rev. T. J. Freeman. A tasty and commodious brick church was erected at once at a cost of about $15,000 and was dedicated April 6, 1851.

The introduction of Methodism into Natchez occurred in 1798, and Tobias Gibson, of South Carolina, was the first minister. Their large and handsome church, corner Jefferson and Union streets, is supplemented by Wesley chapel for the benefit of the factory operatives and citizens of the north part of the city, and also a commodious brick structure on Pine street, occupied by the colored Methodists.

The conception of the English Protestant Episcopal church of Natchez dates back to 1821, and on May 10, 1822, Rev. James Pilmore was installed as the first rector. A church was erected in 1823; alterations and improvements were instituted later, and now they have an elegant house of worship which cost some $35,000.

The Temple B'Nai Israel is a brick house presenting some architectural features and good interior decoration. The one Methodist and two Baptist churches of the negro societies are commonplace structures.

Of benevolent institutions there are the following: St. Mary's Orphan home, for girls, and D'Evereaux hall, an orphan asylum for boys, both of them being conducted under the auspices of the Catholic church. A Protestant orphan home, for boys and girls, is also well sustained.

D'Evereux Hall, the Catholic home for orphan boys, is possessed of a fine property, including many acres of valuable land, thirty-four of which are cultivated by the boys, producing a handsome income. In the midst of this, and surrounded by lawn, grove and flower garden, stands D'Evereux Hall, a substantial brick structure of two floors, handsome in design and well adapted to the purpose for which it is employed. This institution is under the immediate management of the Christian Brotherhood, and is presided over by Brother Gontran, whose fine executive ability, experience, economic management, energy and devotion to the undertaking, have rendered the establishment partially independent of outside support. This institution was chartered January 25, 1858, by Rt. Rev. Bishop Elder, then bishop of Natchez, and a number of Catholic gentlemen. From limited operations in a small wooden building, the institution has been enlarged until it has called into requisition a fine and valuable estate. From fifty to sixty orphans form the average charge of the establishment, whose maintenance costs some $4,500 per year. Its income is derived from the following sources: One half proceeds annual orphans' fair, $1,400; proceeds market garden, $1,800; from guardians and friends of orphans, $600; Christmas collections in church, $250; a total of $4,050 per annum. This is the reliable income of the establishment, the difference between this and the expenditure being met by various means. The Hall is a perfect model of domestic economy. The garden, of between thirty-four and thirty-five acres, is worked by the boys, one hour per day being all of this description of labor required from each individual.

St. Mary's orphan asylum has been in existence a great number of years and is under the excellent management of the Sisters of Charity, an order whose glorious services amid the horrors of the battlefield and among the sickening scenes of the dreadful epidemic are indelibly inscribed upon the heart of hearts of the people of the South. This establishment maintains at present sixty-six orphan girls at a yearly cost of about $4,500. The income of the asylum is derived in part from the following: From proceeds annual Catholic fair, $2,000; from bequest late Dr. O'Riley, of Canton, Miss., $250; from Christmas and other collections, $608; total, $2,858.

The needles of the girls assist somewhat toward their maintenance. The receipts from this source, however, consequent on the extensive and increasing employment of the sewing-machine, lessen every year. The asylum occupies a substantial and commodious brick building on the corner of Rankin and Jefferson streets, with vegetable and flower gardens attached, the former of which, worked by the orphans, supplies the table with excellent vegetables the year round. The children are comfortably clothed, receive a good English education, and in all the domestic duties are thoroughly qualified, and so excellently trained they are eagerly sought for for adoption and service, and many a girl whose career has started in the chilling shadows of the most distressing auspices has, thanks to the beneficence of St. Mary's, been ushered into a womanhood surrounded with all the comforts and refinement of independence. The house is presided over by Sister Tatiana, who is assisted by a community of sisters and a board of trustees composed of Catholic gentlemen. After looking over the books of both these Catholic orphan asylums it is found that fully one-third of the children for whom they provide are either of Protestant or non-Catholic parentage.

The Protestant orphan asylum dates back to March 12, 1816, when a few ladies of

Natchez met together and organized an association for providing a home for the friendless children of the state, the result of which was the establishment of the Protestant orphan asylum, an institution which, through all these years, a period marked with the calamities of plague, bankruptcy, devastations by storm and ravage of war, has offered a roof for the roofless, meat for the hungry and friendship for the friendless. The history of this establishment is a relation of everything pleasant to remember of the former and present generation of amiable Protestant ladies of Natchez, a recital of which, I regret, is not within the province of the present undertaking. The asylum occupies a substantial and roomy building on Union street, in the northern outskirts of the city and in the midst of a delightful grove. At present there are some forty inmates, principally female, though the asylum admits children of both sexes, the support of which cost last year $2,559.95. The receipts from various sources, principally from voluntary subscription of the citizens of Natchez, and a donation by the grand lodge of Masons amounted to $3,055.35, leaving a balance in the treasury of $445. For some time past the citizens of Natchez have experienced a burden in the chief support of this institution, and one too, unfairly imposed upon them, when it is considered that the city furnishes but one-tenth of the children here provided for, while nine-tenths are waifs from all quarters of the state. Considering it the duty of the state at large to contribute to the support of the establishment the lady managers a short time ago called in the advice of a committee composed of members of all the Protestant churches and Hebrews, the latter of whom, though they have derived no benefit from the asylum, have both by their purse and influence done much in assisting it. They called in the aid of this committee, as I have stated, to advise as to the most effective means to arouse the Protestants of the state to a sense of their duty in the premises. The result of this was the issuing of an appeal to the churches, Masonic and other bodies, Protestant, Christian and Hebrew, for contributions. The response exceeded expectation.

Harmony lodge No. 33 (now Harmony lodge No. 1), A. F. & A. M. was chartered by the grand lodge of Kentucky in 1801. On August 25, 1818, it was rechartered by the grand lodge of Mississippi as Harmony No. 1. The first officers were: Seth Lewis, W. M.; James Farrell, S. W.; William Brooks, J. W.; David Lattermer, treasurer; John Girault, secretary; St. James Beauvis, S. D.; Israel E. Trask, J. D.. Joseph Newman, S.; William Mitchell, Tyler. This lodge is now in a flourishing condition, with E. G. De Lap, W. M.

Jackson lodge No. 15 (now Andrew Jackson lodge No. 2), was chartered under the grand lodge of Tennessee, October 8, 1816. This lodge was rechartered by the grand lodge of Mississippi in 1818. It now has a large membership, and J. Peeples is W. M.

The grand lodge of Mississippi, A. F. & A. M., was organized at Natchez July 27, 1818, when Henry Tooley was elected M. W. grand master.

Lock lodge, A. F. & A. M., No. 52, of Natchez, was chartered by the grand lodge of Mississippi February 9, 1842, with John M. Duffield, W. M. The charter of this lodge was surrendered November 29, 1849, the members joining other lodges in Natchez.

Natchez R. A. chapter No. 1 is in flourishing existence here, with Dr. J. C. French high priest.

Rosalie commandery No. 5, K. T. of Natchez, is at present presided over by W. G. Benbrook, E. C. The other officers of the commandery are: J. C. French, M. D., general; J. Peebles, C. G.; E. G. De Lap, prelate; C. T. Chamberlin, S. W.; F. S. Shaw, J. W.; Geo. W. Kuntz, treasurer; John R. Bledsoe, recorder; E. J. Guice, standard-bearer; W. B. Irwin, sword-bearer; C. H. Keirn, warder; C. M. Sawyer, captain-general.

The cornerstone of the old Masonic temple was laid June 25, 1827. It was quite an imposing stone edifice, and was used till 1889, when it was torn down and its site utilized for the erection of a new Masonic temple and operahouse now in course of erection. It will be a most imposing structure, five stories in hight, built with brick and stone trimmings. The ground plan is 119x60 feet, with a sixteen-foot L architectural design, modern and stately; interior decorations artistic. The building would be a pride to any city.

Mississippi lodge No. 1, Odd Fellows, was established in Natchez in 1836. Marion Ruffner was the first noble grand.

The grand lodge of Odd Fellows was established here in 1838, and Marion Ruffner was the first grand master. Thomas Reed, of Natchez, is now the oldest surviving grand master.

Natchez lodge No. 3, Knights of Pythias, was organized October 7, 1873, with Allison H. Foster past commander.

Knights of Honor lodge No. 1145, was organized a few years ago and won to its banner a large membership.

The Catholic Knights is a new and widespread order, similar in its plan to the Knights of Honor. Though not a secret order, it is well established here, in St. Martin's branch No. 88, and includes in its membership many of the influential and prominent Catholic citizens.

Ezra lodge No. 134, I. O. B. B., includes in its membership the majority of the Hebrews of Natchez.

St. Joseph's Total Abstinence and Benevolent society and many literary and benevolent associations are doing effective work.

In the thirties, Natchez, Vicksburg and Woodville began railroad building. The first two towns reached out to connect with Jackson, the state capital—the town of Woodville desiring to reach the Mississippi at Bayou Sara. The financial crisis of 1836-40 put a damper upon railroad interests and checked operations in that line almost entirely. After building only thirty-five miles of their road the Natchez company sold out to parties who, in turn, abandoned the project and disposed of the locomotives, iron, etc. Unfortunate mistake was this, and one that cost the town a large portion of the traffic that had hitherto been her own, but which now went to Vicksburg and Jackson. Again, the New Orleans, Jackson & Great Northern (now the Illinois Central) might have been induced by proper efforts to run their line through Natchez, and much valuable business territory might have thus been saved to her merchants. Yet a third time Natchez slept upon her opportunity and permitted the Louisville, New Orleans & Texas road to pass to the east of her when it was in her power to secure the important connections offered by this great railway.

But, these mistakes aside, Natchez is to-day one of the most promising cities of the South. Always conservative, her merchants are doing business with their own capital and upon a solid financial basis. The railroad to Jackson has been constructed by her own means and its final completion to Columbus is one of the certainties of the near future. Another improvement in this road will be the broadening of the gauge to the standard width. At last awakened to the importance of railroads and finally realizing their great value, the business men of the town are working with energy and perseverance to secure the New Orleans, Natchez & Fort Scott railroad, which will doubtless prove one of the most important railways ever built upon American soil. From present indications the running of this line through Natchez seems a matter of fact.

The Natchez, Jackson & Columbus railroad, or the Little J, as it is called, has done a world of good to the town of Natchez, and its value is appreciated. General Martin, the brainy and energetic president of this line, is indefatigable in his efforts to secure the extension and broadening of his road and its equipment as a first-class highway. A recent visit to New York in the interest of the road was highly satisfactory and the General was able to say to the directory upon his return that the future of the road would be all that could be wished. The management of the Little J road has been exceptionally good. The officers of the company are capable, courteous officials, and take pleasure in consulting the public weal while faithfully performing the duties of their several departments. Major Williams, the general superintendent (a New Orleans gentleman), is an official whose fitness for the important office he holds is a matter of record, while his urbanity is known to all business men, rendering him a general favorite both in railroad and business circles. In 1882–3 the growth of the business interests of the city was so great that it became necessary to connect the wharves, the railroad depots and the mills by rail; so the Bluff City railway was organized for the purpose. Right of way was obtained from the city, the track was laid and an incline was constructed from the general level of the town to the water's edge. This railway has proved a valuable institution and more than justifies the expenditure necessary to its construction. The street railway was built in 1885–6 to connect the business part of the city with the ferryboat that plies between the city and Vidalia, La. The city is supplied with an excellent quality of gas from the city gas works, located in the northern part of the town. As the demand for extra supply is created it is promptly met by the company.

The cotton exchange was commenced early in 1886, and on the 20th of May, 1886, a charter was obtained from the legislature. The organization started out under the most auspicious conditions and has been steadily maintained, while daily growing in popular favor. The objects and purposes of the exchange, as set forth in the charter, are the same as those of similar institutions in the cities throughout the country. Cotton has met with a ready sale here at remunerative prices, which have been satisfactory to all parties concerned. There is a large and efficient corps of buyers in the town, who will compare favorably in all respects with those of any town in the South. A large portion of the cotton bought in Natchez has been bought for export. The river or bend cotton is not surpassed by any section on the Mississippi, and has always been in excellent demand at good prices. The sales of staple cotton have also been large at prices equal to the best markets in the South. As a cotton market Natchez has taken a prominent stand, and it is confidently predicted by those competent to judge that she will handle about fifty thousand bales per annum.

A new cotton compress was erected in 1886 at a cost of about $75,000. With improved machinery and in the hands of live, go-ahead business men, this important adjunct to the business of the town has proved a valuable factor in the increase of trade. Perhaps no single institution of the city speaks more unerringly of her future.

No city of its size in the Southwest has built as many manufacturing establishments as Natchez. The first of these was the Natchez cottonmills, a factory occupying a space of fifty feet front by a depth running the entire square, three stories high and fitted with the most improved machinery for the manufacture of cotton in the various grades of yarn, batting, cloth, etc. This mill employs over three hundred looms, ten thousand spindles and three hundred people, whose wages aggregate about $4,000 monthly. Between three and four thousand bales of cotton are consumed annually in producing the sheetings, shirtings, drills and brown cottons that the factory turns out.

Another important institution of the kind is the Rosalie mills, the products of which are similar to the other, and the capacity of which is almost as great. Both of these mills are being operated profitably, and find markets for all the goods they can manufacture.

Two cotton-seed oilmills, the Carpenter-Dickens company (Lee oilworks) and the Adams manufacturing company, are engaged in the manufacture of cotton-seed oil, cake, meal, cotton batting and fertilizers. These companies employ a number of operatives and are important institutions of the town. They were under the control of the Oil Trust company, as are most of the similar institutions in the South. An iron and brass foundry meets an important demand in this direction and employs skilled workmen. The work executed at these foundries is said to be very superior, while the charges are very reasonable. The ice factory, public cottongins and lumbermills are all large industrial concerns.

The press of the city has played an important part in the whole drama of progress. *The Daily Democrat* and *The Banner* have always inculcated the opinions and ideas of progressists.

In the northern portion of the city is the National cemetery, under the sod of which are interred the remains of the Federal dead who fell in the conflicts in which they were engaged on the soil of Mississippi and Louisiana, as well as those who died in the service at the various hospitals and upon the tented fields. The number of graves in this beautiful cemetery is very large. From a central mound, all carpeted with greensward, a tall flagstaff rises heavenward. This spot, sacred to the memory of the Union soldiers, is one of the loveliest in the state, which abounds in attractive locations. The National cemetery is justly a favorite resort for equestrians and drivers in equipages.

The City cemetery is likewise a most attractive spot of this unusually attractive city on the bluff. Massive structures of marble and granite commemorate the virtues of many of the honored dead of the town, while the graves of others are traced by less pretentious tombs and slabs — all combining to indicate in one solemnly beautiful segregation, within the city of the living, this sacred and honored city of the dead.

The churches, public buildings and residences of Natchez point out the spirit of the Renaissance, which took possession of her people long before it dawned on the inhabitants of the North Atlantic states. The Doric and Ionic orders, with entablatures in Greek and Roman form, prevail here. The Gothic cathedral speaks of thirteenth century glories and the colonial style is not wanting in the architectural panorama. The streets of Natchez are well drained and kept clean. The residences in the city and throughout its suburbs are many of them palatial. The drives about the town are among the most delightful to be found in the county. Fragrant blossoms greet the senses at every turn, while in many gardens is seen a wealth of floral productions that is simply intoxicating. Natchez is especially noted for its picturesque landscapes, its luxurious homes and its delightful climate. Here the Northerner may find health and comfort in the winter months, and almost perfect freedom from the severity and harsh frigidity of his ice-clad home. The grand old hill, selected first by the Roman missioners and secondly by the French officer, Bienville, commands a view of the Mississippi. While wanting in the primitive grandeur of 1698, it has raised up a beautiful civilization which breathes harmony around and renders it what Maryland was in early years. It is a typical Southern city, where much of the old manners and social forms still obtain and one where the educated citizen of the Republic finds much to admire and little to condemn.

Washington, in Adams county, was important in the earlier history of Mississippi. "The town of Washington, six miles east of Natchez, in a rich, elevated and picturesque country, was then the seat of government," wrote Colonel Claiborne. "The land office, the surveyor-general's office, the office of the commissioner of claims, and the courts of the United States, were all there. In the immediate vicinity was Fort Dearborn, and a permanent cantonment of United States troops. The high officials of the territory made it their residence, and many gentlemen of fortune, attracted by its advantages, went there to reside. There were three large hotels, and the academical department of Jefferson college, established during the administration of Governor Claiborne, was in successful operation. The society was highly cultivated and refined. The conflicting land titles had drawn there a large crowd of lawyers, generally young men of fine attainments and brilliant talents. The medical profession was equally well represented, at the head of which was Dr. Daniel Rawlings, a native of Calvert county, Md., a man of high moral character and exalted patriotism, eminent in his profession and who, as a vigorous writer and acute reasoner, had no superior and few equals. The emigration from Maryland, chiefly from Calvert, Prince George and Montgomery counties, consisted, for the most part, of educated and wealthy planters, the Covingtons, Chews, Calvits, Wilkinsons, Graysons, Freelands, Wailes, Bowies and Magruders; and the Winstons, Dangerfields and others from Virginia, who for a long time gave tone to the society of the territorial capital. It was a gay and fashionable place, compactly built for a mile or more from east to west, every hill in the neighborhood occupied by some gentleman's chateau. The presence of the military had its influence on society; punctilio and ceremony, parades and public entertainments were the features of the place. It was, of course, the haunt of politicians and office hunters; the center of political intrigue; the point to which all persons in the pursuit of land or occupation first came. It was famous for its wine parties and its dinners, not unfrequently enlivened by one or more duels directly afterward. Such was this now deserted and forlorn looking little village during the territorial organization. In its forums there was more oratory, in the salons more wit and beauty than we have ever witnessed since, all now moldering, neglected and forgotten in the desolate graveyard of the ancient capital of Mississippi."

Greenville is the courthouse town of the county, as well as the capital of the levee district. Its population is six thousand six hundred and fifty-five. In 1880 it was twenty-five hundred. Old Greenville was burned during the war by the Federal naval authorities. A postoffice was established there September 10, 1803, with John Shaw as postmaster. The present town was laid off in 1865, though it was not incorporated until 1870. K. R. Wilson, a young man of New Jersey birth, who had come to Mississippi in 1858, and had served in company D of the Twenty-eighth Mississippi cavalry, returned from the war, and in May built a crude warehouse at Greenville, which was used for shipping and receiving purposes. This was on Blantonia plantation, and was the first thing in the way of a business house at Greenville. L. L. Alexander and M. Weiss built the first store, and were the first merchants. Following them were B. Cohn, Selig & Co., A. B. Finlay & Co., Cox & Everman. B. Hanway was an early merchant.

Such, in brief, is the early commercial history of this bright and attractive Mississippi city. In front of it the Father of Waters flows majestically, acting as the great regulator of freight rates by rail, and is of incalculable benefit to all classes doing business in this market. Of railways there are three; the Lake Washington and Bolivar loop lines of the Louisville, New Orleans & Texas railway, and the main line of the Georgia Pacific railway, and others will be built in the near future. That the Illinois Central will construct a line to Greenville during the next eighteen months is now an open secret; in fact, in order to protect its valuable carrying trade from and to the great delta region, that company sees and appreciates the necessity for paralleling the Georgia Pacific. Surveys have already been made and the favored route will doubtless be the one directly through that section, via Grenada. It will thus be noticed how complete and comprehensive Greenville's transportation facilities are, and that it must always retain a commanding position as a distributing center. That Greenville, therefore, reasonably may aspire to become a city of the magnitude of Memphis is by no means extravagant, particularly as, in connection with all the natural advantages, its citizens are imbued with such enterprise, push and progress that they do their utmost to advance its interests upon all occasions. The streets are wide, beautifully graded, well guttered and kept clean; consequently it is a healthy city, and free from all local diseases liable to become epidemic. The business streets present a fine and imposing appearance, the buildings being principally constructed of brick, having iron and plate-glass fronts, while some of their occupants transact fully $750,000 worth of business per annum. Good sidewalks have also been laid in every portion, and a good street car line furnishes excellent transit facilities between the business and residence quarters. At night the city is illuminated by means of electricity, the streets presenting a thoroughly metropolitan appearance. A system of waterworks is being constructed, calculated to supply a city of twenty-five thousand inhabitants, about the size Greenville fully, and with reason, expects to attain in less than a decade. A fine telephone exchange is also another modern feature enjoyed by this modern ideal community. Large and costly business houses, residences and cottages are being constructed in all portions of the city, and improvements of a substantial character are being made in every direction, plainly indicating the prosperity and enterprise of the inhabitants who are widely known for their hospitality, kindness, culture and refinement. Very creditable educational facilities also existing have a tendency to draw to Greenville a very superior citizenship. The city is provided with a good opera-house and a large number of churches, while the different leading civic societies are well represented. Real estate is steadily advancing in value, and heavy deals are being made almost every day, often involving large sums. Some very fine additions to the original site have been laid out, and the city seems to be visibly growing and becoming more of a cosmopolitan metropolis every day. It boasts of four banks, with a combined capital of $600,000, and a line of deposits averaging $750,000. There are also two large and first-class compresses and two cottonseed-oil mills, representing a total investment of $495,000.

The cornerstone of the new Washington county courthouse was laid recently. N. Goldstein was master of ceremonies, and delivered an address in opening the proceedings. Rev. Stevenson Archer invoked God's blessing. Mayor J. H. Winn delivered an address of welcome. Judge W. R. Trigg spoke as the orator of the occasion, in place of Capt. W. W. Stone, who could not possibly be present. Rev. William Cross directed the Masonic ceremonies. The following is the record of the contents of the stone: Holy Bible, laws of Free Masonry and constitution of the grand lodge, proceedings of the grand commandery of 1891, names and officers of the grand lodge, names of acting officers of the grand lodge, order of procession, program of ceremonies, names of Washington county's officials, names of Greenville's municipal officials, copies of the Greenville *Times* and *Democrat*, copies of daily and weekly *Clarion-Ledger*, history of Greenville, United States coins. The inscriptions upon the stone are as follows: Dedicated to justice, October 20, 1891, A. L. 5891. John M. Ware, grand master. Laid by William Cross, D. D. G.

As yet, Greenville depends for its commerce almost wholly upon the cotton, of which staple it receives some one hundred thousand bales per annum, and the receipts are rapidly and very largely increasing each season, as new railroads are built and new plantations opened. An active cotton exchange aids very materially in making of this so important a cotton market and a Liverpool rate of sixty-five cents per hundred pounds has been secured.

There is naturally a limit to the growth of any town or city wholly supported by its surrounding agricultural country, and knowing this, the people of Greenville believe in fostering and encouraging industrial enterprises, and local capitalists will cheerfully and liberally coöperate with the outside men of means and practical knowledge of manufacturing, and invite their attention to their city. Its present industries comprise two large cotton compresses, costing $165,000, two oilmills, costing $325,000, one of which is the largest and finest plant in the South, its cost having been $250,000. The electric light plant represents an investment of $65,000. There are two large saw and one planingmill, a sash, door and blind factory, an ice factory, one foundry, two cistern or tank factories, and a steam bottling works. One large brick works, conducted by a strong stock company, produces millions of first-class bricks for local use as well as export. Besides these, there are a number of smaller establishments of various kinds, every one being prosperous and busy, all of which shows plainly that manufacturing pays well in Greenville, if practically prosecuted. By means of Greenville's splendid railway system, every important market and consuming center in the Union is made readily accessible by routes and at rates as low as are enjoyed by any other Southern city. The attention of practical manufacturers is therefore specially directed to Greenville as being in all respects a most favorable location for industries. A large cotton and woolen mill could not be located elsewhere to better advantage, this being King Cotton's capital realm, the product of which is eagerly sought and well paid for in every cotton manufacturing center in the United States and Europe.

The press is creditably represented in Greenville by three first-class weekly newpapers, one of which runs its presses by an electric motor, having been the first and for some time the only office thus equipped in the state, or, as far as is known, in the South. The *Democrat* now in its thirteenth volume, is an eight-page paper, all home print, well edited, and the advertising columns are an index to the character of its constituents. Enterprise and prosperity are plainly visible on every page.

The *Times* was established as the *Washington County Times* in 1868, is ably edited and well supported by all classes throughout the city and country. In politics it is democratic. John W. Ward, its former publisher, sold the paper to J. S. McNeily, who gave it its present title.

The *Spirit* is a successful candidate for public favor, and was established February 18, 1889, by John W. Ward. It is a four-page folio, and its circulation is growing rapidly.

All these journals may be taken with profit by anyone intending to locate in the Delta, as they are full of information concerning that desirable country.

The *Greenville Republican*, H. T. Florey, proprietor, was published by John W. Ward during the administration of Governor Alcorn.

In 1880, James E. Negus and Henry T. Iries opened a private bankinghouse. After some time Mr. Iries withdrew and Mr. Negus continued the business some time under the name of the Merchants' bank. In 1887 it was merged into the First national bank. This institution has a capital of $100,000, and a surplus of $30,000. James E. Negus is its president, and Thomas Mount, cashier.

The Bank of Greenville was organized in 1869 by W. A. Pollock, and in 1887 was incorporated under the state laws. This, the first bank in the Delta, was a private bank operated by Mr. Pollock at first. At the time of incorporation the concern was capitalized at $250,000, with Mr. Pollock as president and A. S. Olin as cashier. This bank is the pioneer in this part of Mississippi.

September 15, 1888, the Merchants and Planters' bank was organized by James Robertshaw with a capital of $100,000. J. S. Walker was president, W. E. Hunt vice president and J. Robertshaw cashier. The present officers are J. S. Walker, president; W. E. Hunt, vice president; S. C. Lane, cashier, and George Wheatley, assistant cashier.

The Citizens' bank of Greenville was organized December 1, 1888, with $50,000 capital. Its president was A. P. Keesecker and J. S. McDonald was cashier. Its present officers are J. A. Deaton, president; W. S. Hamilton, cashier. The capital is now $85,000.

In 1868 the Greenville Compress company was established with a capital of $100,000; W. A. Pollock, president; T. J. Irwine, secretary and treasurer.

The Planters' Compress company was incorporated in 1887 with $50,000 capital; James E. Negus, president; Joseph Uhl, secretary and treasurer.

The Greenville oil works is a branch of the great oil interest. The investment in its plant and realty is $150,000. Jos. Allison, of Memphis, is president, and King Dowarth, secretary and treasurer.

The Planters' cottonseed crushing association has a home capital of $100,000. C. H. Smith is president, George Alexander superintendent.

Nearly all religious denominations are represented in Greenville, among them the Presbyterian, Baptist, Methodist Episcopal, Protestant Episcopal, Catholic and Jewish. They all have substantial frame edifices and most of them have good membership and are in a prosperous condition.

The Young Men's Christian association has its own building, a fine brick structure, erected in 1890, which with the lot and fixtures cost $12,000. It is well supported and is doing much good. It was organized in 1878, after the yellow fever epidemic, and incorporated a few years later.

The Greenville cemetery association was incorporated in 1887.

Greenville lodge No. 94, I. O. O. F.; Mississippi Valley lodge Knights of Honor No. 723, C. P. Huntington council No. 973 Legion of Honor, the Benevolent Protective order of Elks No. 50 and Hebrew union are among the societies that have good membership here.

Delta Commandery No. 16, Hillyer Royal Arch Chapter, No. 113 and Greenville lodge No. 206, represent the Masonic order at Greenville, and are all in a flourishing condition and have a good membership.

The Knights of Pythias have two strong lodges at Greenville—Stonewall Jackson lodge No. 7, and W. A. Percy lodge No. 57. There are a number of social clubs in Greenville, having elegantly furnished rooms, equal to many found in large cities. The citizens are generally speaking, social in their habits, and take special delight in entertaining strangers. The Greenville Rifles is a splendid militia company, handsomely uniformed, well accoutered and perfect in the manual of arms.

Greenville's leading industries and notable features may be thus summarized: two oil mills, two cotton compresses, a land and improvement company, an ice factory, an electric power and light company, the Greenville street railway company, the Greenville brick and improvement company, the Delta land and improvement company, thirteen miles of electric wire, and about seven miles of street railway.

Leland is situated east from Greenville about ten miles, on the banks of Deer creek, and has a population of six hundred. The main line of the Louisville, New Orleans & Texas railway passes through Leland, which is also the diverging point for the Greenville, Arkansas City, Lake Washington and Bolivar Loop branches of that road, while the Georgia

Pacific railway crosses the main line one-half mile from the town. Leland is surrounded by a well-settled and rich cotton and corn growing section. Within the past few years some twenty thousand acres have been put into cultivation near Leland. Leland is substantially built of brick and presents a fine appearance. The merchants carry large stocks and are doing a prosperous business, while not less than ten thousand bales of cotton are handled. The annual business of the town will aggregate fully $1,000,000. The Louisville, New Orleans & Texas railway company has erected there one of the finest hotel buildings in the state, having accommodations for over one hundred guests, which station at Clarksdale, conceded to be one of the finest, was opened by Mr. Blake in 1887.

A large sawmill, a large stove factory and two gins are in operation at Leland, and not less than thirty-two business houses, representing every line of trade. There are two handsome, well equipped schoolhouses, affording excellent educational facilities for both races. Three good church buildings have been erected, while several secret societies are represented by flourishing lodges and well appointed halls.

The streets are wide, graded, and good sidewalks have been put down and improvements of a substantial character are visible on every hand.

Leland is the end of two divisions of the Louisville, New Orleans & Texas railway, and that company has large workshops and lumber yards there, employing a large force of men. Capt. J. A. V. Feltus, the father of Leland, founded the town in 1884, having ever fostered its interests to the extent of his by no means limited ability.

Jackson City was established November 28, 1821, and named in honor of Andrew Jackson, the hero of New Orleans. A road from Vicksburg to that point was completed about the same time, and this faint gleam of civilization was first shed on that section of the Pearl river wilderness. It was the same road over which Jackson was carried in triumph in 1840 to a capital of a state whose people aided him a quarter of a century before in opposing British occupation. Jackson lies on the western bank of the Pearl river, a beautiful stream flowing into the gulf of Mexico, navigable for small boats above and below the city for eight months in the year, and furnishing at all times a never failing and abundant supply of the purest water. Being situated about the geographical center of the state it was naturally made the capital city. It is also one of the county sites of Hinds county, one of the most fertile and productive counties in the state, being second only to the best delta lands in cotton production. The advantages of Jackson are not factitious; they are natural, real and permanent, and are unaided by any adventitious circumstances, auguring it a prominence and prosperity which can not be forced down. Jackson has never been boomed as some towns are; it has never been pushed forward by any aggregated or concerted efforts of its citizens; such things, so far, are unknown to it. Its growth and development are but the nominal results of the natural course of events, and it may be truthfully said that in spite of itself nature has made it what it is; a prosperous and growing city of over six thousand inhabitants, with a brilliant and promising future of illimitable possibilities. The advantages of the place cannot be overestimated; and in considering what it is to-day it must be remembered that Jackson is a city which was practically destroyed by and rebuilt since the war. The Jackson of to-day is to all intents and purposes a city dating from the surrender, and it has attained its present importance in spite of certain obstacles, now removed, which would have forever prostrated any less favored locality. No town in the state suffered by the war as Jackson did. It was subjected to the ravages of a friendly as well as hostile army. And during the tedious years of reconstruction which followed, the city, more than any in the state, felt the depressing blight of unsettled political affairs. All this is now happily a thing of the past. A new era has been entered upon; nature has again asserted itself, and Jackson is marching to the front steadily and surely.

The population in 1870, was four thousand two hundred and thirty-four; in 1880, five thousand two hundred and four; and in 1890, six thousand and forty-one. The editor of the *Clarion-Ledger*, speaking of her progress under date May 11, 1891, says: "It is usually admitted that no town of its size in Mississippi equals it in its industrial life or the general hospitality of its citizens. Far and wide it is noted for its push, and the late census shows a marked progress in every branch of industry, as well as a large increase in population. In 1880 the census gave the population of the town at five thousand, while she to-day boasts of nine thousand." Under date October 21, 1891, the same paper says: "The census of 1890 may be a true and correct estimate of the population of Jackson, but the *Clarion-Ledger* does not believe it, and the people do not believe it. And, another thing, Jackson has a populous suburb that is, in point of fact, a part and parcel of the city. Mercerville and West End are as much a portion of Jackson as if they were located within the sacred precincts of the corporation line. Several of the leading and most substantial business men of the city have handsome residences and valuable lots in that suburb, and by right should be included not only in the census of Jackson, but on the city assessment rolls, and pay their quota of the expenses. The board of trade could not turn its attention to a more important matter than the annexation of that part of Jackson known as West End or Mercerville. The corporation line should be extended one mile on the other side of the depot. At present it is not a quarter beyond the railroad, and thus some of the most valuable properties of the city escape city taxes and at the same time enjoy the many privileges and conveniences of city life. It is only a matter of time when the annexation will be made, and why not now? The board of trade should move in the matter. Let it be one of the subjects for discussion at the next meeting, and a committee appointed to properly lay the subject before the legislature in January next. Jackson has now a population of ten thousand or more, and is increasing at the rate of five hundred per annum. The fact of the business is, Jackson is a prosperous and growing city in point of size, business and numbers."

The acts relating to the incorporation of Jackson are those of December 25, 1833, February 14, 1839, and February 22, 1840. On March 5, 1846, the act authorizing a bridge over Pearl river was approved; in 1846 acts relating to schools; in 1846, also, one providing for the forfeiture of vote in the case of the non-payment of street tax, and in 1848 one extending the limits and one regulating bridge affairs. The city records, prior to 1854, could not be found, but from unofficial documents it is learned that John P. Oldham was mayor for nine years prior to that date and that Joseph Spengler served as a member of the old council.

The mayors of the city since 1854 are named as follows: Richard Fletcher*, 1854; William H. Taylor, 1855-7; James H. Boyd*, 1858; W. A. Purdon,* 1859; R. C. Kerr, 1860-1; C. H. Manship, 1862-3; D. N. Barrows, 1864 to May, 1868, (removed by military authorities); Thomas H. Norton, from May 8, 1868, to July 9, 1868, (removed by military authorities); James Biddle, from July 9, to July 31, 1868, (removed by military authorities); James P. Sessions*, from July 31, 1868, to January 12, 1869, (removed by military authorities); Rhesa Hatcher*, from January 12, 1869, to April 2, 1869, (removed by military authorities); Joseph G. Crane*, from April 2, 1869, to June 8, 1869, (killed); F. A. Field, from June 16, to July 16, 1869, (removed by military authorities); A. W. Kelly, from July

---

*Deceased.

16 to November 5, 1869, (removed by military authorities); E. W. Cabaniss*, from November 9, 1869, to June 22, 1870, when Governor Alcorn appointed Oliver Clifton. The latter resigned October 17, 1871, and ten days later Rhesa Hatcher* was appointed and served until January 3, 1872, when the days of appointments passed away and Marion Smith was elected mayor; John McGill was elected January 5, 1874, and served until January, 1888, when the present mayor, William Henry, was elected.

The aldermen in 1854 were C. R. Dickson*, C. A. Moore*, Stephen P. Bailey*, R. M. Hobson*, W. D. Bibb* and J. W. Shaw*. Bailey* was reëlected in 1855–6 and 7; E. M. Avery*, 1855–6; W. H. Donnell*, 1855–7 and 1862; Rhesa Hatcher*, 1855–6 and 1870–1; W. W. Langley*, 1855–6; James T. Rucks*, 1855–6 and 1858; O. Barrett*, 1857; L. V. Dixon*, 1857; Thomas Green*, 1857–67; Hiram Hilzheim*, 1857 and 1871; Jo. Bell*, 1858–60–2; C. H. Manship, 1858–9–60; D. N. Barrows, 1858–9–62–3; W. M. Estelle*, 1858–9–60; T. W. Caskey, 1858; L. Julienne*, 1859–60; C. A. Moore*, 1859–60; H. Spengler, 1859 and 1876–84; J. H. Bowman, 1860; M. W. Boyd*, 1861; W. M. Patton*, 1861; C. S. Knapp*, 1861; J. O. Stevens, 1861–6; M. C. Russell*, 1861; John H. Echols*, 1861; G. H. Sutherland*, 1862–3; J. H. Boyd*, 1862–7; R. M. Hobson*, 1862–3, R. O. Edwards*, 1863; W. W. Hardy, 1863; J. W. K. Lucy*, 1864, (killéd by Deputy United States Marshal Winders); A. Virden, 1864–9; Samuel French, 1864; M. McLaughlin*, 1864–73; Ned Farish, 1864; James Tapley*, 1865–9; John Nelson*, 1865–7 and 72; Angelo Miazza*, 1867–70 and 1872–3; Marcus Hilzheim*, 1867–9; Rufus Arnold, 1867–9 (appointed by military authorities to fill vacancy, October 8, 1867); Thomas Green*, and John Nelson*, (resigned October 4, 1867); John Burns*, 1869–70; E. Bloom, 1869; Charles Williams, 1869–70; Thomas Palmer, 1869–70; James Lynch*, 1869–71. The five last named were appointed May 15, 1869, by the military authorities *vice* Virden, Tapley, McLaughlin, Arnold and Hilzheim, removed, and served until March 28, 1870, when Samuel Lemly*, Henry Musgrove*, E. A. Peyton*, James Lynch* (colored) and G. Richards* were appointed by Governor Alcorn. Musgrove, Peyton and Lynch served in the council in 1871, with R. Hatcher and M. McLaughlin, the latter being appointed *vice* Lemly. On July 6, 1871, the six last named councilmen were removed, when A. N. Kimball*, James Peachey, E. D. Fisher (later postmaster), James R. Yerger and T. Anderson were appointed. In 1872 George H. Clint succeeded McLaughlin and I. Strauss succeeded Clint in June, 1872. John McGill (who took J. J. Rorhbacher's place in February, 1873), P. O. Leary, Jacob Kausler (who took A. Miazza's place in June, 1872) and Harris Barksdale*, all were members of the aldermanic board. In 1874 C. B. Smith (killed by accident), Thomas Anderson (colored), Charles Williams, D. Ward, W. Q. Lowd and M. Stamps (colored) were members. Messrs. Anderson, Lowd, Ward and Williams were reëlected in 1876 and H. Spengler and L. Kavanaugh* elected. In 1878 Spengler, Williams, Lowd and Anderson, with J. S. Hamilton and J. W. Harrington*, were aldermen. In 1880 S. E. Virden replaced Hamilton, and J. W. Clingan took the place of Harrington, the other members being reëlected. The elections of 1882 resulted in the choice of H. Spengler, J. S. Hamilton, F. B. Hull, W. Q. Lowd, W. H. Taylor and Ben Jones. The two last named were reëlected in 1884, with E. Watkins, W. H. Gibbs, J. Braun and H. K. Hardy. In 1886 W. S. Lemly took the place of Gibbs and the other members were reëlected. E. Watkins, W. S. Lemly and W. H. Taylor, with L. F. Chiles, H. M. Taylor and George Lemon, were elected in 1888, and in 1890 Messrs. Chiles, Lemon and H. M. Taylor, with B. W. Griffith, E. Von Seutter, L. Manship and James Ewing, formed the board of aldermen.

---
*Deceased.

So early as February 20, 1819, congress donated one thousand two hundred and eighty acres to the state, to be selected by the legislature, and made the site of the state capital. Two years after, the legislature named Thomas Hinds, James Patton and William Lattimore commissioners to locate such capital town within twenty miles of the geographical center of Mississippi. For some reason, William Lattimore did not take part in the final action of the commissioners, for on November 28, 1821, the first and last named, with Peter A. Van Dorn, were directed expressly by the legislature to locate the capital land grant on the east half of sections three and ten, and the west half of sections two and eleven, in town five north, and range one, east of the Choctaw meridian, to name the land so selected Jackson, and to have a temporary building for legislative sessions erected thereon before December, 1822. The sale of lots in the new town was authorized June 30, 1822, and the terms of sale placed at ten per cent. cash, and the balance in three years. The particulars are given in page ninety-nine, Hutchinson's Mississippi code. On February 26, 1833, the act for the erection of the capitol and executive mansion was approved and $105,000 appropriated. Three years later, William Nichols was appointed state architect (office abolished in 1842), and Richard Davidson, Perry Cohea, and Henry K. Moss commissioners of public buildings. In February, 1836, the act to establish a penitentiary was approved; in 1848, that establishing the institute for the blind; in 1853 the state lunatic asylum was authorized, and in 1854 the institute for the deaf and dumb. Work on the statehouse was commenced in 1833, the contract for woodwork being entered into by E. S. Farish.

Of the pioneers of the city very few remain. David Shelton settled here in 1836; Herbert Spengler came about 1837, and in October, 1838, laid the foundation of the businesses, which he has built up within the last fifty-five years; William J. Brown, who was a printer here in 1836; Charles H. Manship, a settler of 1836, and Alexander Virden, who also came in 1836, George Langley, Edward Virden, Thomas Helm, Jacob Kausler, and John Clinghen are still residents of the city. In 1844, D. N. Barrows established an insurance office; in 1850, Isadore Strauss came; in 1850 or 1851, E. Von Seutter; in 1853, E. D. Patton; in 1855, H. M. Taylor, and in 1858, L. Fraggiacoma. They are to-day among the most enterprising men of the commercial circle. Many children of the pioneers of the county and state reside at Jackson, and are found in all branches of trade and in the professions. Many of the old settlers, men and women who were here before the war, and passed through the trials of the city's occupation by opposing armies, are now witnessing the extraordinary progress of a new city under a new idea of civilization. Some landmarks of the original town have survived time, as well as the large public buildings completed within the decade ending in 1860, and a few of the principal residences of antebellum days, but the hand of the modernizer is more manifest and architectural styles and conveniences undreamed of even twenty years ago exist on every side. The last decade, which did so much for civilization in the Northern states, has not overlooked the Southern country, and in the advance Jackson city has been foremost.

The old frame house known as the Eagle hotel, forty rooms, stood where the Brown residence now is. The brick hotel of one hundred rooms erected on this site in 1854, and known as the Bowman house, was burned during the war. George Langley, now a resident of the city, was a prime mover in urging the erection of a large hotel, and suggested the purchase and donation of the ground.

Jackson is the railroad center of the state, and one of the most important in the South. The great Illinois Central railroad, from Chicago to New Orleans, divides the state north and south, and at Jackson intersects the Vicksburg & Meridian, running east and west from Vicksburg on the Mississippi and forming a link in the chain of roads connecting the Atlantic and Pacific oceans. Jackson is the present terminus of the Yazoo & Mississippi Valley railroad, a line operated by the Illinois Central and extending northwest from Jackson through the world-renowned Yazoo and Mississippi delta, the most fertile and productive body of land in the world, to a point on the Mississippi river opposite Helena, Ark., where it connects with the Great Western and Northwestern systems of railroads. The Natchez, Jackson & Columbus railroad, with its present termini at Jackson and Natchez on the Mississippi river, runs southwest from Jackson, and will be completed beyond Jackson northeast, to the coal fields of Alabama. The Gulf & Chicago railroad, now rapidly approaching completion, will give Jackson as direct and quick connection with the Gulf of Mexico as it has now with New Orleans. A branch of the Queen & Crescent railroad from a point near the Pearl river bridge to Pearl street, in the rear of State street, was completed October 22, 1891. Jackson has now within its corporate limits between seven thousand and nine thousand inhabitants, including a large and rapidly increasing suburban population. The streets are all named and houses numbered, and a free postal delivery system is in operation. At least five hundred buildings have been completed in the last five years, and more are constantly going up. It has one of the largest cotton compresses in the world, being the same which was awarded the first premium at the World's exposition in New Orleans. It has gas and street railways, two prosperous banks, an ice factory with a daily capacity of fifteen tons, three steam foundries and small factories of agricultural implements running to their full capacity; two large brick factories, two fertilizer factories, one furniture factory, one broom factory, ten churches, six newspapers (five weeklies and one daily), and three large hotels. Being the capital of the state, nearly all the important state institutions and buildings are located here. The State library in the capital building is the third largest state law library in the Union. The miscellaneous library, being also large and well selected, is free to the public. At Jackson are held the state supreme, chancery, and circuit courts; also the circuit and district courts of the United States. At Jackson also assemble the legislature and all the important conventions. In 1887 the Illinois Central company built at Jackson a passenger depot unsurpassed by any in the South, and early in 1891 designed a grander building for this important railroad center.

The Jackson Land and Improvement company, organized in 1886–7, is a joint stock company, gotten up exclusively on home capital, and has for its object the advancement and general improvement of the material interests of the city. It is composed of gentlemen of standing and respectability. Its charter gives it full power to conduct and operate all branches of business which will tend to increase the comfort and business prosperity of the city. This company now owns the most desirable suburban property to be found near Jackson, lying just in the path of its present growth. This land is divided into lots and offered as cheap homes for persons desiring to locate permanently here. One of the main objects of the company, by means of co-operation, is to make known to the outside world the many substantial attractions of their city; to correspond with outside capitalists seeking investments, and to show to them the many reasons why Jackson is the most desirable and eligible place in the state or the South for the establishment of any and all kinds of industries which manufacture wood or cotton or wool. Few places can show such inducements in these lines as this offers, with its rivers and railroads and cheap and accessible adjacent forests abounding in the finest lumber of multiplied varieties, in addition to being in the very center of the largest cotton-producing state.

The educational advantages of Jackson, for both sexes and all colors, are excellent.

There is also a first-class commercial college here, a convent school and classical schools. The churches are well administered and exert a most beneficent influence upon the people of the city.

The secret and benevolent societies are thoroughly organized, while social and literary associations attain a rare excellence. The newspapers of the city, past and present, are referred to in other pages.

The Capital State bank is the oldest bank in Jackson. It was founded by Col. Thos. E. Helm, in 1872-3, the reorganization taking place in January, 1888, with the following officers: R. W. Millsaps, president; Thos. E. Helm, vice president; B. W. Griffith, cashier, and E. M. Parker, assistant cashier. The directors are: R. W. Millsaps, Thos. E. Helm, C. A. Alexander, E. Virden and I. Strauss, of Jackson, Walter Heilman, of Clinton, and W. H. Tribette, of Terry, all of whom are gentlemen of the highest financial, commercial and social standing in this state. The bank operates with a capital of $100,000, and has a surplus and undivided profits amounting to $15,733.00 additional.

The First National bank was established May 1st, 1885. Its capital is $100,000, to which has been added a surplus of $30,000. The officers are: Samuel S. Carter, president; Charles A. Lyerly, vice president; O. J. White, cashier, and A. C. Jones, assistant cashier. These are also directors, together with R. L. Saunders, Byron Lemly, S. S. Calhoon, P. W. Peeples and C. W. Robinson. These names will be recognized as being borne by the most substantial men of central Mississippi.

The Jackson bank was organized December 19, 1889, with a cash capital of $100,000; the officers are: P. W. Peeples, president; R. L. Saunders, vice president; A. M. Nelson, cashier; J. W. Cooper, assistant cashier, and directors P. W. Peeples, John McDonnell, G. Y. Freeman, W. W. Stone, W. J. Davis, R. Griffith, E. H. Anderson, R. L. Saunders, J. B. Ross, Wirt Adams and A. M. Nelson.

State Building and Loan association was organized April 22, 1890, but incorporated February 21st of that year, with an authorized capital stock of $3,000,000. The following well-known citizens of Mississippi form the directory: J. M. Lambert, Natchez, Geo. M. Govan, McComb City; R. K. Jayne, Jackson; D. D. Boyd, Jackson; T. M. Miller, Vicksburg; A. H. Jayne, Jackson; A. B. Watts, Meridian; John H. Odeneal, Jackson; J. M. Lambert, president; Geo. M. Govan, vice president, R. K. Jayne, secretary and D. D. Boyd, trustee; T. M. Miller and A. H. Jayne, general attorneys; John H. Odeneal and A. B. Watts, inspectors.

One of the most valuable improvements is the water system, completed in 1889. The water works are owned by the Light, Heat & Water company, of which R. L. Saunders is president, P. W. Peeples vice president and M. Green secretary and treasurer, who are also directors, together with C. W. Robinson, S. S. Carter, R. W. Millsaps, S. S. Calhoon and B. Lemly, all business men and capitalists of the city. The capital stock is $100,000. The system employed is gravity pressure for domestic and direct pressure for fire service. A steel stand pipe one hundred and twenty feet in hight, twenty-four feet in diameter, with a capacity of two hundred and eighty thousand gallons, has been constructed upon a hill about one and one-half miles from the city limits, the elevation being seventy-three feet above the ground where the capitol stands. The water is obtained from Pearl river, some three miles above the city, and also the same distance along mains. The pumping plant consists of two duplex double-acting Deane steam pumps, one compound and one high pressure, each having a daily capacity of one million gallons. The boilers are of steel, fifty-four inches in diameter. The pumps are set in a circular well, twenty-one feet deep, the lift from low water being eleven feet. The pumphouse is built of brick, and of sufficient size to admit of the doubling of the capacity at any time. The plant is entirely above the high water mark and five hundred feet above low water. In addition to the direct suction, an independent suction admits water being taken from a well excavated near the pumphouse for filtering purposes. The stand pipe is one and one-quarter miles from the pumps and one hundred and twenty feet above them; an electrical call, by which the engineer can turn the water off from the stand pipe and apply direct pressure in case of fire, is a part of the apparatus. The mains range from twelve to four inches in diameter, and eight miles are laid within and three without the city limits for supplying the various state institutions, which require twenty-one hydrants in addition to the number required by the city. These works have been constructed in the most thorough and systematic manner by Moffitt, Hodgkins & Clarke of Watertown, N. Y., while all the material and machinery used are of the very best, latest and most highly improved patterns. The gas works preceded the water works, and even the electric light was introduced before the boon of a good water supply was given.

The Mississippi Compress & Warehouse company owns and operates one of the largest and finest cotton compresses in the entire South, its plant representing an outlay of fully $60,000. The press is a ninety-inch Morse, the same which was on exhibition at the exposition in New Orleans, where it carried off all the honors. The press, warehouses, platforms, sheds, etc., cover an area of five acres, having storage capacity of ten thousand bales, located upon the tracks of the different railways entering Jackson, having a frontage on the Illinois Central railroad of three hundred feet, and on the Vickburg & Meridian railroad of two hundred feet. Every facility and all late improvements have been added and exist for the rapid and effective work required in this business, and the press has a record of loading one hundred compressed bales into one car.

The Capital City Oil works were built in the summer of 1889, and commenced operation in the fall of the same year. The following citizens are the officers: John A. Lewis, president; E. T. George, secretary and treasurer; John W. Todd, general agent. Since the date of the establishment of this concern its volume of business has grown to an immense degree and to-day it takes front rank with all similar industries. It is located in West Jackson on a plat of ground covering about five acres. There are three distinct buildings: The mill, which is built of brick, 270x40 feet; the seedhouse, 400x50 feet; and the office building, a handsome two-story brick house. The engineroom is 50x60 feet, and the boilerroom, 40x50 feet. Two switches of the Illinois Central and one of the Little J run through the yards, thus furnishing excellent shipping facilities. The mill is fitted throughout with most improved machinery, and contains eight (Buckeye) presses, with a capacity of crushing seventy-five tons of seed per day. The company have their own dynamo, and during the busy season, when they are compelled to run both night and day, furnish lighting material. The oil manufactured is sent to the North, where it goes through a process of refining.

A number of manufacturing industries, such as the Enoch's Lumber and Manufacturing company, the sawmills, planingmills, foundries, etc., are in operation, each one worked to its full capacity.

The mercantile houses are large, prosperous concerns, always telling of business principles in their conduct, and in the manners of merchants and employes.

The cotton market of the city is, of course, an interesting point, as it is in all such Southern cities.

The board of trade was chartered April 18, 1888, the following named being among its first officers: Dr. P. W. Peeples, president; Maj. R. W. Millsaps, first vice president; E. Virden, second vice president; A. Virden, Jr., secretary; and Dr. S. S. Carter, treasurer. The board of directors is made up as follows: R. W. Millsaps, J. A. Shingleur, R. L. Saunders, Dr. B. Lemly, Isadore Strauss, John McDonnell and J. H. Odeneal.

The Edwards house, the Lawrence and the Spengler are the principal hotels of the city. The first named is one of great old houses of the state, speaking of days before its institutions were overturned by war. A modern brick addition and interior decoration bring it into harmony with the present. The Lawrence house, established in 1858, is undoubtedly the leading commercial hotel of central Mississippi. The owner established himself at Jackson in 1858, served with the Confederate troops during the war, and resuming the business raised the business of hotel keeping to a profession. The addition to the house was completed in 1890. The Spengler house, opposite the capitol, occupies one of the finest business sites in the city. Removed from the railroad depot, it is on the borders of the principal business and residence districts. The improvements completed in January, 1891, including the important brick addition, render it a modern house. The owners are among the pioneers of Jackson, and connected closely with the building of the city. The large hotel at Cooper's well, three and one-half miles from Raymond, is the property of the Spenglers. Mrs. T. B. J. Hadley, a daughter of the Indian fighter, David Smith, after whom Smith county was named, and the wife of Auditor Hadley, of Wilkinson county, kept the leading boardinghouse at Jackson in 1837. She was a great admirer of the Indian laws providing for the protection of married women's property, and was instrumental in urging the adoption of such a law by Mississippi.

The capitol, governor's residence, city hall, deaf and dumb institute, Federal building, state school for the blind, insane asylum and state penitentiary are the public buildings of the city. The four first named buildings show adherence to definite architectural forms, the Federal building is an adaptation of the Palladian, and the penitentiary building a mixture of the Tudor and Colonial, with the finer parts of each style ignored. The church buildings are Gothic, the Illinois Central depot Queen Anne, and the modern residences partake, in a measure, of the last-mentioned style, or are decidedly French of the suburban type.

Throughout the city brick or wooden sidewalks and macadamized streets prevail, street cars traverse the principal streets, gas or electricity lights up the thoroughfares, and the water system extends through every ward. In the residence portion the parkways, while not as wide as they should be, are well kept, but to large grounds surrounding each residence credit must be given for being faultless in the arrangement of shrubbery and lawn. It is a garden city, boasting of all the light and air of the country and all the advantages of a modern city.

At the meeting of the board of trade October 20, 1891, several topics of practical interest to the city were considered. Dr. Peeples, as chairman of a committee, reported some progress in the matter of securing the arrival of morning trains on the Little J and Yazoo branch roads. He called attention to what was manifestly a discrimination against Jackson in the matter of rates on cotton from Flora to Jackson and from same point to Yazoo City. Flora is nearer Jackson than Yazoo City, and yet the freight is seventy-five cents to Jackson, and only forty cents to Yazoo City. A member suggested that perhaps the Illinois Central owned or had an interest in the Yazoo City Compress. The committee was continued to press the matter of morning trains, and to interview the railroad commission, if necessary, for removal of the discrimination stated. General Henry reported that $500 in cash had been subscribed for the repair of the turnpike, and that contracts would be let on Saturday next.

The matter of incessant switching at and near the railroad junction, the delays to vehicles and persons desiring to cross the numerous tracks, the danger to life, and the accidents occurring, was a subject of earnest and protracted conversation. Mr. Montgomery said the railroad people were anxious to provide a remedy, but it could only be done by removal of freight depots out of town, which would result in great inconvenience to the business community. The opening of more streets from East to West Jackson, above and below the city, it was suggested, would solve the problem. Mr. Odeneal thought a bridge over the Capitol street crossing would be a great relief, that it was now very dangerous for school children to cross the track, and that wagons were provokingly delayed in coming to and going from town. Colonel Power suggested that the school population of West Jackson seemed to require a public school building in that part of the city, and that the children over there should not be subjected to the dangers mentioned by Mr. Odeneal. General Henry remarked that the necessity for a West End school was becoming very apparent. The removal of the penitentiary was the special topic of discussion. Colonel Hooker, Captain Stone, Colonel Hamilton, Dr. Peeples and Major Millsaps all spoke earnestly in that behalf, and finally it was ordered that the president of the board should, at his convenience, appoint a committee of nine to prepare a memorial to the legislature urging the early removal of the prison, which was a continual menace to the health, and an obstacle to the growth of the city. Dr. P. W. Peeples, chairman; W. W. Stone, J. L. Power, B. W. Griffith, Oliver Clifton, R. L. Saunders, John McDonnell, M. Green, L. F. Chiles, R. W. Millsaps, were appointed a committee to wait upon the legislature to urge the removal of the penitentiary from the city limits.

The following brief city directory of Jackson's municipal, fraternal, judicial, religious and other interests was compiled in October, 1891:

William Henry, mayor; W. R. Harper, police justice; J. B. Harris, city attorney; John T. Buck, city clerk and collector; Isadore Strauss, treasurer; A. G. Lewis, chief of police; Henry Taylor, white sexton; Alex. Wilson, colored sexton.

Aldermen—North ward, B. W. Griffith, Luther Manship; South ward, H. M. Taylor, L. F. Chiles; West ward, George Lemon, James Ewing. Regular meetings of the board on Wednesday after first Tuesday each month.

Fraternal societies—Pearl Masonic lodge No. 23, first Saturday night each month; Jackson Royal Arch chapter No. 6, fourth Monday night each month; Mississippi commandery No. 1, Knights Templar, second Monday night each month; Capitol lodge No. 11, I. O. O. F., every Thursday night; Central lodge No. 764, K. of H., first and third Tuesday nights in each month; Jackson lodge No. 163, K. and L. of H., every third Monday; Pearl lodge No. 23, Knights of Pythias, second and fourth Tuesday nights in each month; Manassah lodge No. 202, I. O. O. B., second and fourth Sundays, 10 A. M., in lodge room, Temple basement; Capitol lodge No. 11, A. O. of U. W., first and third Monday nights in each month; United Brotherhood of Carpenters and Joiners of America meets every Friday night, at 7:30, in Richardson building, West Jackson; Capitol Light guards, regular meetings first Thursdays, regular drill every Monday night.

The firemen—Jackson Fire department, L. B. Moseley president, Oliver Clifton chief; Jackson No. 1, first Monday night in each month; West Jackson No. 1, second Tuesday night in each month; Gem No. 2, second Tuesday night in each month; Pearl Hook and Ladder No. 1, first Thursday night in each month; Hope No. 3, second Tuesday night in each month.

Supreme court—J. A. P. Campbell, chief justice, Third district; Thomas H. Woods, associate justice, Second district; T. E. Cooper, associate justice, Fourth district; Oliver

Clifton, clerk. Semi-annual terms commence on third Monday of October and first Monday of April.

United States court—Circuit and chancery courts, first Monday in May and November, Henry C. Niles, judge; R. H. Winter, clerk; F. H. Collins, marshal.

Circuit court, Hinds county—First district, Jackson, first Monday in January and June (eighteen days); Second district, Raymond, fourth Monday in January and June (twelve days). J. B. Chrisman, judge; W. H. Potter, clerk; R. J. Harding, sheriff.

Chancery court, Hinds county—First district, Jackson, first Monday in March and October (twelve days); Second district, Raymond, third Monday in February and September (twelve days). H. C. Conn, chancellor; W. W. Downing, clerk.

Hinds county supervisors—Meetings on first Monday in each month, alternately at Raymond and Jackson. In Raymond, January, March, May, July, September and November; Jackson, February, April, June, August, October and December. W. W. Downing, clerk, office in Raymond; Ramsey Wharton, deputy, office in Jackson.

The churches—West Jackson Methodist, B. F. Lewis, pastor; preaching 11 A. M. and 8 P. M.; Sunday school 9:30 A. M.; J. T. H. Laird, superintendent; prayer-meeting Thursday, 8 P. M. Baptist church, H. F. Sproles, pastor; preaching 11 A. M. and 7:30 P. M.; Sunday-school 9:30 A. M.; B. W. Griffith, superintendent; prayer meeting Wednesday, 7:30 P. M. Presbyterian church, John Hunter, pastor; preaching 11 A. M. and 7:30 P. M.; Sunday-school 9 A. M.; W. S. Lemly, superintendent; prayer-meeting Wednesday night, 7:39; West Jackson Sunday school 9 A. M., Dr. B. H. Cully, superintendent. Methodist church, Rev. W. C. Black, D. D., pastor; preaching every Sabbath at 11 A. M. and 7:30 P. M.; prayer-meeting Wednesday night at 7:30; Sabbath-school 9:30 A. M., W. L. Nugent, superintendent. St. Peter's Catholic church, Rev. Louis A. Dutto, pastor; services every Sunday; early mass 7:00 A. M.; high mass, 10 A. M.; vespers 4 P. M. Episcopal (St. Andrew's) church, Sunday service 11 A. M. and 7 P. M.; Sunday school 9:30 A. M., M. Green, superintendent. Christian church, M. F. Harmon, pastor; preaching every Sunday, 10:45 A. M. and 7:15 P. M.; Sunday school 9:30 A. M. Beth Israel congregation, no pastor at present; services every Friday night at 7:30, conducted by laymen.

The monument erected at Jackson to perpetuate the memory of those who gave their lives to the Southern cause during the Civil war was unveiled June 4, 1891, with appropriate ceremonies in the presence of twenty thousand people. It stands in the southern portion of the capitol enclosure, on grounds donated by the legislature for the purpose, in full view of the principal street of the city.

The hight of the monument from the ground line to the soldier on top is sixty feet and four inches. It stands upon a solid concrete foundation twenty-four feet square and two feet and eight inches thick. The base of the monument at Jackson, Miss., is almost a duplicate in miniature of the temple at Pandrethan. The three platform stone bases are built of white limestone from the quarries at Bowling Green, Ky. Each is eight inches thick and the lower is twenty-four feet long by twenty feet wide. On the outside of these bases there is a granolithic stone pavement four feet wide, extending entirely around the monument. The die resting on these stone bases represents the wall of an old castle, and is thirteen feet high by fourteen feet wide. The walls above the receding buttresses or plinths are equally divided and cut up into seventy-four blocks. It was originally intended to have each of these blocks represent one of the seventy-four counties of the state (the number in the state at that time) with the name of the county chiseled thereon and number of soldiers it furnished the Confederacy. This, however, for the present has been abandoned and the blocks are perfectly plain. On the north and south sides of the die there is an inscription on raised marble, extending two-thirds across the monument, containing these words: "To the Confederate Dead of Mississippi." On the west and east sides are the doorways, about seven feet high and two feet and eight inches in width. They are ornamented by beautiful and heavily molded doorjams, extending to the sides and tops of the openings and resting upon ornamental scroll buttresses. Curving to the outside and securely fastened to the doorjams are heavy vault doors of malleable galvanized iron. The pattern of this is scroll and flower work. There are no bars. Each of the doors is provided with locks, so that the vaulted chamber containing Jefferson Davis' statue and the inscriptions, can be secured from intrusion. Each of these doorways is further ornamented and protected by an arched portico, projecting five feet from the face of the die and about ten feet high. Each of these arched canopies of the portico is supported by two highly polished red beech granite columns. Crowning the arch of these appears the monogram, C. S. A. (Confederate States of America), raised in heavy bold letters and gilded. They form the approach to the vault, immediately in the center of the monument. The vault is octagonal in shape and has a red and white marble floor, seven feet two inches in diameter. In the center is the corner, or more appropriately speaking the centerstone, which was laid with imposing Masonic ceremonies three years ago. This stone is of Italian marble, beautifully polished, and projects six inches above the floor. Resting upon this as a pedestal, is to stand the life-sized statue of Jefferson Davis, president of the Confederacy. This piece of work was executed by one of the finest artists in Italy, and represents Mr. Davis standing with left hand extended in the attitude of delivering a speech. In his right hand he has a roll of manuscript and at his feet lays a pile of books. The sides of this chamber are wainscoted with Italian marble six feet in hight. Including the doors there are eight sides to the chamber, the doors forming two sides. On the six marble slabs there are engraved the following inscriptions in beautifully gilded letters.

Officers of the Confederate Monument association of Mississippi, A. D., 1890: Miss Sallie B. Morgan, president; Mrs. Belmont Phelps Manship, vice-president; Mrs. Elenor H. Stone, treasurer; Miss Sophie D. Langley, secretary; Mrs. Virginia P. McKay, corresponding secretary.

"All lost! but by the grave
 Where martyred heroes rest,
He wins the most who honor saves—
 Success is not the test."

"It recks not where their bodies lie,
 By bloody hillside, plain, or river;
Their names are bright on fame's proud sky;
 Their deeds of valor live forever."

The noble women of Mississippi, moved by grateful hearts and loving zeal, organized June 15, A. D. 1886, the Confederate Monument association; their efforts and appropriation of the state of Mississippi, were crowned with success in the erection of a monument to the Confederate dead of Mississippi, in the year 1891.

The men to whom this monument is dedicated were the martyrs of their creed; their justification is in the holy keeping of the God of history.

God and our consciences alone
 Give us measures of right and wrong.
The race may fall unto the swift
 And the battle to the strong;
But the truth will shine in history
 And blossom into song.

From the top of the marble slabs springs a balled arch canopy to the highth of nine feet six inches, making an octagonal arch chamber. Among the battlements of the die arise the bases of the plinth of the spire, of which the plinth proper is the most attractive, being seven feet square and nine feet high. Four Egyptian columns on the corners support the marble entablatures, on which are cut in bold relief on the west side the eagle and coat of arms of Mississippi; on the north side a piece of artillery with Confederate flags; on the east side crossed cavalry sabers and belts; on the south side crossed Enfield rifles within a shield on which is inscribed: "Mississippi Volunteers." Above the plinth starts the spire, which is three feet and eight inches square at the bottom, tapering gradually to two feet square on the top, the shaft proper being thirty feet high. The top of the shaft is surmounted with a statue of a Confederate soldier, his feet and the butt of his gun being in the position of parade rest, his head depressed and his left arm resting on the muzzle of his gun in an easy and graceful position. The statue is six feet and ten inches high and was sculptured at the monument by J. T. Whitehead, from a rough block of Italian marble. Excepting the material mentioned, the monument is built of calcareous limestone from Bedford, Ind.

The first public suggestion for the monument was made by Mrs. Luther Manship, of Jackson. So that the scheme may be said to have originated and culminated at the capital. In the spring of 1886 there appeared in the *Clarion* an article announcing a concert to be given by Mr. and Mrs. Luther Manship to raise a nucleus fund for this purpose. In the next issue a delicate and beautiful appeal to patriotism and Confederate memories from the pen of the young and gifted Charles Hooker attracted the attention of the ladies of the commonwealth to the holy cause. The united press came to their aid with everything beautiful in poesy, song and prose. Friday, May 28, 1886, the concert was announced, the following being the program:

PART FIRST.

Piano Accompaniment.....Miss Florence Bowmar, Mrs. A. L. Julienne, and Prof. Doe.
Selection..Gem Band.
Sound of Harps..Chorus.
Our National Banner..Recitation.
       Willie Nugent.
Address..Col. C. E. Hooker.
Conquered Banner, by Father Ryan......................................Luther Manship.
The Spell..Solo Lurine.
      Miss Bessie Clark.
After the Battle...Recitation.
      Mrs. Luther Manship.
Erin on the Rhine..Solo.
       Mr. Oram.
Ernani...Solo.
      Mrs. Bella McLeod Smith.

PART SECOND.

Come Rise with the Lark..Quartette.
   Messrs. Julienne, Zehnder and Ligon.
Bird From O'er the Sea...Solo.
      Miss Ayda Terrell.
Selected...Prof. Borneman.
Miss Hulda's Offer...Miss Annie Manship.
See the Pale Moon..Duet.
      Misses Wolfe.
The Dutch Volunteer..Luther Manship.
Tantum Ergo..Duo.
    Mrs. Smith and Prof. Borneman.
Suwanee River..Chorus.
  Misses Langley, Wolfe, Manship, Fletcher, Clarke, Mrs. Julienne, and Messrs.
    Julienne, Ligon, Oram, Skellenger, Zehnder, Schulze and Manship.

A small fund was the result, and thus the monument was inaugurated. The 16th of June following, responding to a call of Miss Sophie Langley, nine ladies met in the senate chamber and organized the Confederate Monument association. They were Mrs. Luther Manship, Miss Sophie Langley, Mrs. A. L. Brunson, Mrs. V. P. McKay, Miss Mary Andrews, Miss Jennie Fontaine, Miss Rebecca Smith, Miss Mary Lou Langley, Miss Mary Belle Morgan, Miss Sallie B. Morgan. The last named lady was called to the chair, and an organization was effected, pledging themselves to work for the cause. Mrs. C. E. Hooker, though not present, was elected president, afterward declining for satisfactory reasons. Mrs. A. L. Brunson was vice president; Mrs. Manship, corresponding secretary; Miss Sophie Langley, assistant corresponding secretary. Miss Fontaine, then a girl scarcely fourteen, was made local secretary, and held the place with assiduity and energy until her removal from Jackson, after most of the work was accomplished. Miss Anderson was treasurer of the association, which she held also until her parents moved from Jackson.

Moving on without a president, the association gained strength and membership, reorganizing in the fall of 1886 under a charter prepared by Capt. D. P. Porter. February 24, 1887, Mrs. Manship resigned the office of corresponding secretary and was elected president, and at the same meeting Mrs. W. W. Stone was elected treasurer of the monument fund, which position she holds still, being reëlected from term to term. At the meeting March 3, 1887, a letter of encouragement was received from Gen. Stephen D. Lee, containing a handsome contribution, the first donation to the monument. Mrs. Hooker, Mrs. Stone and Mrs. John Dunning were appointed a committee to draft a constitution and by-laws for the government of the association. They met November 10, 1887, and adopted the constitution and by-laws as reported, and the following officers were elected: Mrs. Manship, president; Mrs. A. L. Brunson, vice president; Miss Jennie Fontaine, secretary; Mrs. V. P. McKay, corresponding secretary; Miss Sophie Langley, assistant corresponding secretary; Mrs. W. W. Stone, treasurer monumental fund, and Miss Mary Anderson, treasurer of association. Capt. D. P. Porter and Capt. W. W. Stone were made honorary members. In the annual election of 1888 the same officers were mostly elected, Miss Kate Power becoming local treasurer, and Mrs. C. C. Campbell being chosen vice president.

The ladies struggled on in so many ways that it is impossible to go into detail. A bill to aid them was passed by the senate in 1888. It was drafted by Judge Thrasher, of Claiborne, and introduced and warmly advocated by Senator Binford; Senators Wilson, Yerger and others made speeches in its favor. The house defeated it by a small majority, Messrs. Sharp, Magruder, Watkins and Jones warmly supporting it. Finding legislative aid failing, the ladies signed a contract for a modest, but enduring monument, to be built by Mr. J. T. Whitehead, an ex-Confederate soldier. The cornerstone was laid with well-remembered Masonic ceremonies, May 25, 1888. It was not to be costly, because hope from other than little sources had failed. Mrs. C. C. Campbell, aided by Mr. Luther Manship, got up a kirmess, to which call the people of Jackson nobly responded. One thousand dollars was the result, the largest sum from any one source donated. The towns of Greenville, Greenwood and Yazoo City each gave the proceeds of an entertainment given for the purpose. Mrs. C. E. Hooker and Mrs. J. H. Dunning made an afghan that brought a considerable sum. A bazar and restaurant at the fair, and a table conducted by Mrs. Dunning and Mrs. Brougher and Miss Rebecca Smith, on the occasion of the laying of the cornerstone, added greatly to the fund. Again Judge Thrasher drafted the bill for the ladies, asking $10,000 to complete the monument. The senate listened to the advocacy of Gen. J. H. Jones and others patiently, and with but five against the bill they sent it to the house. Those senators who opposed it did not do so for want of feeling. The house received the bill most kindly and passed it, despite some violent opposition not engendered by any bad feeling. Various were the reasons for this opposition, but none of them were for the want of a proper Confederate feeling or an appreciation of the cause. Many donations came in small sums from the citizens and soldiers and the Confederate organizations. The contract called for an artistic and endurable work, and it has been faithfully filled.*

Mississippi presented to the Washington monument a white marble rock, with the inscription "The State of Mississippi to the Father of his Country;" the grand Masonic lodge of Mississippi, a gray marble rock, with emblems and words inscribed; Oakland college, a coarse-grained sandstone, and the grand lodge of Odd Fellows, a gray stone with three links in bas-relief.

Raymond was established as the seat of justice of Hinds county January 17, 1829, in accordance with the report of locating commissioners appointed February 4, 1828. The population in 1890 according to the census was five hundred; but on May 11, 1891, the *Clarion-Ledger* claimed for it one thousand more, or a total of fifteen hundred. Each year, as it is numbered with the past, shows a large increase of population. It has good schools, good society, good water; and the ministers look after the spiritual affairs of the people. The business men, as a class, are spirited, enterprising and progressive, well disciplined in the best way of trade, carry unusually large stocks, classify and handle them by metropolitan methods, are sagacious and public-spirited merchants, and a more generous or wholesouled class was never gathered in one city of its size. They have an elegant $60,000 courthouse and a $40,000 jail and many fine buildings, evidences of thrift and prosperity. It would seem as though the citizens of Raymond had adopted the word Excelsior for their motto. The famous Cooper's wells are but a few miles from the city. During the summer an immense number reside in Raymond on account of the proximity of these wells.

The history of the old settlers of Hinds county contains many references to Raymond, Mount Salus, or Clinton, and other towns of historic interest; while in the first chapter of volume I the physical characteristics of these neighborhoods are noted. Courts for this county are held at Jackson also.

Bolton, twenty miles east of Jackson, on the Queen & Crescent railroad, as described by the *Clarion-Ledger* of May 11, 1891, is located in that portion of Hinds county which is attracting the attention of citizens. Its elements of wealth surpass Persia of old. Bolton has always been a favored little town, and by the enterprise and liberality of its citizens it is growing rapidly in wealth, culture and education. It is surrounded by a fertile country, with its fields of snowy cotton and orchards, and settled by an industrious population. Bolton is a live center, and all the influences which characterize refined life are found here. It became the nucleus of a city in 1847. Naught could be seen then but a few cleared fields, around which basked the June sun; the dense forest, as up into the clear blue sky wreathed lazily, or swayed fantastically in the evening breeze, the pale blue smoke from the wooden chimneys of the few log huts that then comprised the embryo village, clothed in all her natural grandeur. The Indian hunted lazily through the forest, while the dark-eyed damsel made love to the brave, as the wild flowers kissed the morning dew, or as the luminary of the universe cast its scintillant rays o'er forest and departing day. But behold the change. The iron horse carries the products of the plantations and the orchard to the markets in the

---

*Largely from the *Clarion-Ledger*.

great world beyond. Fine buildings are filled with varied stocks which attract the eye. Church and school buildings send forth morality and education, which sow the crop of genius in future great men. Large moneyed interests and young industries are here, working forward steadily to place the town where ambition points, and good hotels afford entertainment to the traveler. Terry is fifteen miles south of Jackson, on the Illinois Central railroad. It is in the midst of a great fruit country, and boasts of a few industries. Other towns in this county are Clinton, Edwards, Utica, Learned, Adams, Oakley, Byram, and a few more.

Columbus, the county town of Lowndes county, has a population of four thousand five hundred and fifty-two. The Columbus of Mississippi is one of at least thirty towns in differents parts of the Union to which the bold navigator who landed in the West Indies less than four hundred years ago has given his name. If unable to claim originality of nomenclature this Columbus can proudly take a pedestal by itself in respect of its many unique advantages. It is a dignified, substantial and cultured city, more conspicuous even in respect of its educational, sanitary and social claims than by reason of its other attributes. It is one of the largest and most progressive in its way of Mississippi towns. It is characterized by wide rectangular streets, solid brick buildings devoted to business, and an almost unequaled wealth of costly and luxurious homes. Even beyond these are its schools and churches, the former headed by the famed Columbus Industrial institute and college, a state institution which, in many respects, stands peerless in the South. The city lies on the east bank of the Tombigbee river, two miles above its confluence with the Luxapalila and on the Mobile & Ohio and the Richmond & Danville railroads. Columbus has an area of about one and one-half miles north and south, by one mile east and west. Situated upon a level plateau, it has an admirable drainage on either side. It lies upon a range of hills which bluff up to the Tombigbee river on the west to a hight of over one hundred feet, sloping gradually eastward to Luxapalila plateau, about sixty feet above low water mark. Columbus has thirty-five miles of excellent macadamized gravel roads, shaded for the most part by innumerable live oak trees on either side. Gas has been used to light both residences and streets. The works cost upwards of $25,000. An electric light company has been just organized. The telephone system is one of the most complete in the state. The Columbus Street Railroad company was organized under an amended charter, originally granted in 1882. Its capital of $20,000 was subscribed for in less than an hour. The city has about one hundred business houses, and an estimate of the business transacted places it at $2,750,000. There are six real estate agents, four merchandise brokers, three hotels and some good local newspapers. Of the latter, the *Dispatch* weekly and (tri-weekly) is owned and edited by Mrs. S. C. Maer. It has stamped itself as one of the brightest and most intelligently conducted papers in the state. The *Index* is another well-conducted weekly and tri-weekly paper, ably edited by Miss Lucile Banks. The *Sunday Morning Telegram* was started at Columbus in 1887, by Martyn & Johnson. There is a large and prosperous oilmill, admirably managed; an extensive sawmill, five gristmills, a flouring mill, a foundry, a carriage and wagon factory and a broom manufactory; while among the most valued institutions of the town must be placed the Columbus Ice company, which is well situated on ground belonging to the company and on the same square with the Gilmer hotel. The daily capacity of the factory is about five tons of clear, merchantable ice, and with ample room in the large building to increase the output if it should be necessary. The company is incorporated by state charter; its president and manager, Mr. L. M. Tucker, is the largest stockholder. The local cotton trade is large, and an important adjunct to it is the compress. The oldest financial institution here is the Columbus Banking and Insurance company, which has a capital paid up of $300,000. This is a splendid and substantial bank, with very perfect premises and vaults. The First National bank, dating back to April, 1882, was the first national bank organized in the state. It has a paid up capital of $75,000 and a large cash surplus, and has returned its stockholders ten per cent. every year. Its deposits average between $250,000 and $300,000, and it has one of the most costly steel vaults in the South. There are two fire companies, with a hook and ladder company, and a superb steam fire engine, with an ample water supply, to protect the city from the ravages of fire. Columbus has private academies of great merit, such as Professor Belcher's high school for boys, one of the best in Mississippi. The city schools are three in number, two white and one colored. The schools have a handsome balance on hand. In efficiency and completeness the schools are unsurpassed. The term is nine months in the year. The county schools number seventy-six, of which twenty-nine are for the white and forty-seven for the colored children. There are nine thousand four hundred and twelve educable children and a total enrollment of four thousand five hundred and two; number of teachers, seventy-nine. As in the city schools, everything is in an eminently satisfactory condition. Columbus is equally well endowed with churches. Seven of all denominations are open to the whites, most of them being ornate internally and externally. The colored people have five good churches. The crowning feature of the city's educational attractions, however, is the Industrial institute and college for the education of white girls of Mississippi.

The institute was established by authority of an act approved March 12, 1884. In December of the same year Hon. James T. Harrison, Hon. J. J. Thornton and R. W. Jones, the president of the college, were appointed a building committee, with instructions to enlarge and improve the unfinished brick dormitory which was upon the grounds when donated to the state by the city of Columbus. The committee entered vigorously upon the work, and succeeded in bringing the buildings to that state of approximation to completeness which enabled the opening of the college under the most favorable auspices on October 22, 1886. The building is one of the handsomest to be seen anywhere. It is massive and beautiful in design and finish, being of presssed brick and stone, and surrounded by handsome grounds, with greensward, marked with graveled walks leading to every entrance to the building and all parts of the spacious grounds, with just enough of well-cared-for trees to lend picturesqueness to the scene. The dormitory is a massive brick structure three stories and a mansard high, one hundred and seventy-five feet front and running back one hundred and seventy feet—large, well arranged, well lighted and ventilated diningroom, with all modern improvements and conveniences for the three hundred pupils, besides matron, housekeepers and teachers lodging there. Connected with this building by a covered passage is the chapel building, three stories in hight, containing assemblyroom, president's office, secretary's office, eight recitation rooms, chemical and physical laboratories and several storage rooms. A building in the rear of the chapel, connected by passageway and containing twenty-five rooms, is devoted to music, painting and the industrial arts.

None but Mississippi girls are admitted, although applications are received daily from Texas, Arkansas, Louisiana, Alabama and other states. The charter defines the design of the college to be to confer a thorough general education; to give the best normal training, together with teaching and practice in the kindergarden and to train pupils in the various industrial arts, by which to enable them to more readily earn a living and make woman a significant factor in the modern problem of material progress. The course of study is divided into four departments: collegiate, normal, industrial and the department of music and fine arts. There is a marked advance upon the usual course of study in girl's colleges, especially in elements of a solid education and in the mathematical and scientific studies. Tuition is made free to Mississippi girls in the collegiate, normal and industrial departments. Students are paid for work, many of them being dependent upon it to continue in the course of instruction. There is no disposition to disparage those who work. The dignity of labor is respected, and the daughters of the rich, of those of moderate means, and of the poor, are together in one harmonious body. There earnestness and excellent deportment impresses every visitor. They have formed among themselves two organizations: a Young Woman's Christian association and a literary society. The institute has thus far cost the state $90,-000, and, it is claimed, has recompensed it a thousand fold. A. H. Beals, president, took charge of the institute June 14, 1890. John A. Nelson is the proctor.

The town of Columbus was incorporated in 1822, and William L. Moore was the first mayor. The first house erected on the present site of Columbus was a small split log hut, built by Thomas Thomas in 1817. There was nothing like a settlement till about the middle of June, 1819, when Thomas Sampson (who was afterward probate judge), William Vizerspirous Roach and William Poor came to the place, and a short time afterward the citizens of the neighborhood had a meeting, and at the suggestion of Silas McBee, Esq., the town was called Columbus. About this time came Thomas Townsend, Green Bailey, Dr. B. C. Barry, Silas Brown, Hancock Chisholm, William Conover, William Fernandes, John H. Leech and several others. In September, 1830, the treaty of Dancing Rabbit creek was held by the United States and the Choctaws, whereby they were required to remove during the falls of 1831-3. In 1832 the government made a treaty with the Chickasaws at Pontotoc creek, and both nations were removed by 1833. This threw open an immense body of the finest lands in the South for settlement, and the county rapidly filled with a wealthy and enterprising population. The Columbus *Whig* and Columbus *Democrat* were two of the first newspapers of the town. The former was edited by W. A. Short and William P. Donnell, and the latter by Worthington & Thompson. The first death in Columbus was that of Mrs. Keziah Cocke, wife of William Cocke and stepmother of Hon. Stephen Cocke. In 1837 occurred the hanging of the gamblers at Vicksburg and Natchez. This caused a stampede of large numbers of those who congregated in Columbus. They were all well dressed and fine looking men. They turned every room they could get into a gambling resort, and in every part of the public streets could be heard the rattling dice and poker chips. The mayor (Squire Donald) was determined to get rid of them, and notified them that they must leave, at which they were very defiant, and proceeded to arm themselves, buying up all the ammunition and arms that they could get and fortifying themselves in up-stair rooms. The mayor gave them one week to leave and ordered two companies of volunteers to report to him with ammunition and arms on the following Monday. The gamblers held out until Friday, when nine of them applied to Dr. T. H. Mayo, then stage manager, for seats, paid for them and left at dark. The next morning several more applied, and in the next few hours all the vehicles that could be had were carrying the gamblers out of town, and by Monday all had disappeared.

Tombigbee Cottonmills company was organized in 1887, with H. Johnston president, W. C. Richards vice president and W. Johnston secretary and treasurer. The building, which is a four-story brick 50x200, with two wings, was completed in 1888 at a cost of about $44,000. It is well equipped with modern machinery at a cost of about $75,000. The mill is in operation the year round and employs about one hundred men and women. They manufacture shirting, sheeting, osnaburgs and B drilling.

Columbus lodge No. 5, A. F. & A. M., was organized February 24, 1821. The first officers were: Thomas Sampson, W. M.; William Cocke, S. W.; B. C. Barry, J. W.; William W. Bell, treasurer; R. D. Haden, secretary; Titus Howard, S. D.; Edward Kewen, J. D.; Samuel Cowell, secretary and treasurer. The lodge did not get its charter until January 8, 1822, when it was granted to the following charter members: Gideon Lincecum, W. M.; R. D. Haden, S. W.; John H. Morris, J. W.; Ovid P. Brown, Silas Brown, B. C. Barry, Thomas Sampson, John Pitchlyn, Thomas Townsend, David Folsom, William Cooke, William W. Bell, Littlebury Hawkins, John Bell, D. Lawrence. The present officers are: T. B. Franklin, W. M.; J. H. Stevens, S. W.; W. H. Coburn, J. W.; C. L. Lincoln, treasurer; C. S. Franklin, secretary; E. S. Donald, S. D.; A. J. Owings, J. D.; Charles Calhoun, tyler. The lodge meets on the first Friday night of each month. The membership is ninety five. For the year 1890 it conferred about two hundred and fifty degrees in the different ranks of its order.

Covenant lodge No. 20, I. O. O. F., was organized October 1, 1846, with William Cady as noble grand. McKendree lodge No. 32, I. O. O. F., was organized October 7, 1847. From these two lodges emerged Union lodge No. 35, I. O. O. F. They consolidated in 1868 and the new lodge received its charter August 5, 1868. The first officers were: W. C. Hearn, N. G.; G. T. Stainback, V. G.; J. P. Krecker, secretary; H. Hale, treasurer. The present officers are: J. D. Hutchinson, N. G.; H. M. Lanier, V. G.; J. H. Stevens, secretary; C. L. Lincoln, treasurer. The lodge meets Monday night each week. The membership is fifty-five. This organization owns its hall and three-story building with store and offices, all of which are rented. The property is valued at $15,000. The lodge has also a fine cemetery consisting of thirty acres, known as Friendship cemetery, a portion of which was purchased in 1848. The first person buried therein was Mrs. Elizabeth St. Clair.

Joachim lodge I. O. O. B. No. 181, was instituted October, 1871, belonging to districts Nos. 7 and 6. In November, 1872, district No. 7 was made independent, with headquarters at Memphis, Tenn. At the same time an endowment law was enacted which gave $1,000 to the widows of deceased brothers. The first officers were: S. Lichenstadter, president; J. Bluhm, vice president; Charles Schuster, secretary; L. Fleishman, financial secretary; J. Hirshman, treasurer. The present officers are: S. Wolff, president; Mr. Loeb, vice president; S. Schwab, secretary; L. Fleishman, treasurer. The lodge meets first and third Sundays of each month. Its membership is twenty-one.

Columbus lodge No. 26, K. of H., was organized on March 20, 1877, with thirteen charter members. Its officers were composed of W. B. Bryan, past dictator; J. W. Worrell, dictator; George Whitfield, vice dictator; C. H. Worrell, assistant dictator; A. J. McDowell, reporter; S. Lichenstadter, financial reporter; R. R. Spiers, guide. The time of meeting is on first and third Thursday nights in each month. The membership is fifty-eight.

Tombigbee lodge No. 12, K. of P., was instituted July 10, 1889. Its first officers were W. L. Kemp, C. C.; W. A. J. Jones, V. C.; H. A. Osborne, prelate; C. S. W. Price, M. of Ex.; George F. Shattuck, M. of F.; S. Schwab, K. of R. & S.; R. R. Spiers, M. at A. Its present officers are W. A. J. Jones, P. C.; D. P. Davis, C. C.; A. A. Wofford, V. C.; W. L. Jobe, prelate; S. Schwab, K. of R. & S.; Mr. Loeb, M. of F.; George F. Shattuck, M. of Ex.; R. R. Spiers, M. at A. The lodge meets on the first and third Tuesdays in each month. The membership is forty-four.

The last election for mayor and council in Columbus occurred December 1, 1890. There was no opposition to the democratic ticket. Captain Moore has been elected mayor three times, and his administration of affairs has given great satisfaction. E. T. Sykes, J. M. McGown, D. M. Richards, W. W. Westmoreland, J. M. Street and C. S. Franklin constitute the board of councilmen. Among the several villages of this county are Crawford, Arteria and Caledonia.

Aberdeen, the seat of justice of Monroe county, and one of the oldest towns in the northern part of the state, is situated on the west bank of the Tombigbee river, and has a population of about three thousand four hundred and forty-five. It is beautifully located and has a good trade, although it is not as extensive as formerly, as only branch lines are built to Aberdeen. The Mobile & Ohio, Kansas City, Memphis & Birmingham and the Illinois Central lines all have branches terminating at Aberdeen. The United States courthouse and post-office building cost in the neighborhood of $100,000, and is a beautiful and imposing structure. The town has a cotton campus, an ice factory, a spoke factory and other manufactures, and two flourishing banks; The First National, organized May 1, 1887, with a capital of $75,000, formerly the private bank of Jinkins Bros., and the bank of Aberdeen, organized October 10, 1888, with a capital stock of $50,000. The city has one of the finest and most complete public school buildings in the state, and several elegant church buildings.

Aberdeen possesses many advantages as a manufacturing and distributing center, and will in the course of time develop into an important city. The present conspicuous advantages of Aberdeen will be greatly improved with the completion of prospective railroads, which, besides giving increased transportation facilities, will also place it in direct communication with the great coal and iron districts of Alabama, located within a reasonable distance, and giving access to the great forests of valuable timber which form one of the most valuable, while least appreciated, of the resources of the Southern states.

Prof. Lawrence C. Johnson, of the United States Geological survey, recently expressed himself as follows, concerning Aberdeen and its surroundings:

"At the head of navigation, this is the natural and nearest outlet to a large territory of both Mississippi and Alabama. It should control the coal and iron regions of at least Lamar and Marion counties, Ala., and have an equal chance at the grand coal fields of Walker. With your population and position you already possess two kinds of capital necessary to enter the lists in the great iron industries of what we may term the New South. Your position, geologically considered, is advantageous. Situated at the eastern edge of what the books call the Eutaw formation of the cretaceous group, you have behind you all the wealth of the calcareous soils of the prairie. Beyond the Tombigbee you have thin soils, it is true, in the sharp hills of what we call the Tuscaloosa formation; but these hills are clothed with the finest timber, and when that is removed it becomes the land of the mulberry, grape, peach, and all the fruits of our climate. In this formation let it be understood that you have no gold, no silver, no lead, nor any coal; do not waste your time upon them; but you have an abundance of iron ores, carbonates and limonites of various grades. In Lamar county, from ten to fifteen miles of the Mississippi line, there are many deposits of limonite ore. The old Hale & Murdock mines are well known. This is not an accidental, sporadic case of the occurrence of ore, but belongs to a system — belongs to the lower division of the Tuscaloosa formation, which we have traced from Autauga county, Ala., to Tishomingo county, Miss. It may not be discovered as a continuous iron belt, because erosion has played a big part here, and has cut many gaps in it; and another later formation, called the Orange sand, has in many places covered up, and now conceals the older strata. The Tuscaloosa formation has another in its upper division; not as rich, perhaps, as the lower, and is still more interfered with by erosions and by Orange sand deposits, but of much importance to Aberdeen, because it lies up and down the headwaters of your river and approaches quite near to your city. This might well be called the Greenwood springs belt, for it appears in Monroe county in greatest force in that vicinity. It is two or three miles in breadth, extending to the high hills east of Buttahatchie river, opposite the mouth of Sipsey, and southeastward from that point; on the west of the Buttahatchie it tends northward, up Sipsey. This belt exhibits two classes of ore: one superficial, found only on the tops of the ridge, as well as seen in two of the cuts of the Kansas City, Memphis & Birmingham railroad, east and west of Wise's gap; the other ore springs from a different source, and is found in the foot hills near Greenwood springs. This last is a limonite that is formed from a change of the carbonate; a carbonate I did not actually see, but know its presence, not only from the resultant ziodic chambered ore seen there, but from the abundance of springs charged with bicarbonate of iron. Of these the chief is Greenwood."

Aberdeen commandery, U. D., was organized in 1891. Frank P. Jinkins is eminent commander. Wildy lodge No. 21, I. O. O. F., is an old lodge, of which W. S. Lindamood is noble grand.

Eureka lodge No. 719, Knights of Honor, organized about 1875, with Dr. William G. Sykes as dictator, is in a prosperous condition. It has about one hundred members, and J. M. Acker is the dictator. Castle Gray lodge No. 198, Knights of the Golden Rule, organized December 21, 1881, by Deputy Supreme Commander J. R. Hodges, has about one hundred members. Apollo lodge No. 14, Knights of Pythias, established in 1878, with William Howard as chancellor commander, now has a membership of about forty-five, and Kirby Lann is its chancellor commander.

Aberdeen lodge No. 32, A. F. & A. M., was organized in 1837, with J. H. Lawson as worshipful master, and the following members: David Hall, Nathaniel W. Walton, T. B. Pollard, John Franks, James G. Williams, Daniel Burnett, Thomas J. Ford, George Weightman, Parker Alexander, A. R. Hunter, A. J. Holliday, John Abbott and Alex Baker. Dr. William G. Sykes is now worshipful master. In 1884 the lodge erected a magnificent three-story brick temple at a cost of about $38,000. This beautiful structure, which also contains the operahouse, has a seating capacity of six hundred.

Amory lodge No. 165, A. F. & A. M., at Amory, organized with Hon. Wright Cunningham as worshipful master. W. A. Griffith is now worshipful master. This lodge was formed by the consolidation of lodges Nos. 165 and 178.

Euphemia Royal Arch chapter No. 13, at Aberdeen, was organized in 1847, with R. H. Dalton as high priest. Frank P. Jinkins is the present high priest.

Aberdeen council, R. & S. M., No. 28, was organized in 1860, with B. B. Barker, J. N. Walton and W. S. Vestal as first officials. Present officers are R. B. Brannin, C. N. Simpson and S. H. Berg.

Other towns in this county are Amory, Smithville, Quincy, Gattman, Strongs, Reynolds, Prairie and Muldon.

Water Valley is situated on the Illinois Central railroad, about ninety miles southeast of Memphis, midway between Jackson, Tenn., and Canton, Miss. Water Valley has risen from a heap of ashes since the war and grown to a population of two thousand, eight hundred and twenty-eight and in wealth to several millions. The Indians still roamed the forest in the neighborhood in 1840, while some rude habitations indicated the thrift with which a live population were beginning to enter upon the work of reducing to civilization an unbroken wilderness. The first house in or near the town was built about this time by a Mr. Ragland, and is now occupied by Dr. Askew. It was a stage stand along a public highway between Oxford and Coffeeville. About 1847 Capt. P. D. Woods built near the same spot a rude storehouse and kept a stock of goods which would not now compare with the most unpretentious house in the city. The goods were brought by chance wagons from Memphis and other points. Capt. William Carr had already built a log house which now stands near the center of the business portion of town, east of the railroad. Mr. Rasha Robinson settled about a half-mile north. The town was incorporated in 1848 and B. H. Collins was the first mayor. About 1850 there had sprung up two or three business houses near the present site of the town. In 1856 the Mississippi Central railroad was complete to this point, and the little town of a half-dozen business houses began to assume the airs of a railway station. In 1861 there were perhaps a dozen places of business. A company was raised in the town and surrounding country which for gallantry and courage stand prominent in the history of the lost cause. The Federal army pushed its way to the city in the winter of 1862–3 and burned the little wooden village, and its people returned to find the rewards of their industry a heap of ashes. In 1865 there were left from the ravages of war two or three business houses. Oxford and Holly Springs suffered also, and at the latter place the car shops of the railroad were burned. Inducements were offered to the railway company to rebuild its shops in Water Valley, which was determined upon in 1867. Now began an era of prosperity, and handsome buildings sprang up like magic. With the meager facilities merchants were scarcely able to handle the immense business which crowded upon them, but it seemed well nigh impossible to overtax the resources and tact of those who guided the destinies of the young city. Buildings sprang into existence every day and the population increased faster than industry could furnish shelter; yet the spirit of improvement never flagged, and in 1874 the population had grown from two hundred to twenty-five hundred. Already the city had overshadowed her plucky little neighbor. Coffeeville had wrung from her a division of the courts, and was fast absorbing the trade that formerly went to that place and Oxford. Other causes tended to cause a cessation of growth for some years; but her plucky business men faced the storm of depression and maintained a brave front, and now have finally overcome all difficulties and are on a solid financial basis.

Within the past three years many handsome buildings have gone up. Real estate has nearly doubled in value. The population is increasing.

Water Valley bank was chartered in 1888. The company is successor to Bryant & Shackelford, who began business in 1882. Mr. G. D. Able, formerly of Oxford, is the cashier, and Mr. John Wagner bookkeeper, the latter the son of Mr. D. R. Wagner. Both of them are native Mississippians. The bank does a daily business of about $15,000.

The cotton factory enterprise was begun by a joint stock company about 1870. The building was nearly completed by the company when it failed, and it stood idle for some years, when Mr. D. R. Wagner determined that an enterprise so important to the city should be enlivened by the hum of machinery. He, with his associates, purchased the property and imported the machinery at once. The value of this property to the city may easily be estimated when it is known that seven hundred and fifty thousand pounds of cotton are consumed yearly, and the gross earnings amount to nearly $40,000, a large part of which is paid to operatives, and the surplus of profit on the capital invested, goes into investment here. The Water Valley Manufacturing company, which began operations in 1866, was later merged into the concern controlling the mills.

Around Water Valley, imbedded under the soil, is the best of clays for the manufacture of earthenware. The factory commenced operations a little more than two years ago, and has demonstrated the fact that a profitable enterprise is open for development here.

The planingmill and sash, door and blind factory is doing a good business.

Water Valley lodge No. 132, A. F. & A. M., was chartered in 1847. Valley City lodge

No. 402 was organized July 5, 1888. St. Cyr commandery No. 6, K. T., was organized January 25, 1867. Water Valley lodge No. 82, I. O. O. F., was chartered January 23, 1867; Grand Encampment No. 22, March 1, 1887. Knights of Honor lodge No. 1062, is a prosperous organization. Lochinvar lodge No. 55, K. of P., was organized May 14, 1890.

The Water Valley *Courier* was established April 5, 1867, by E. A. Goodland, editor and proprietor. It was afterward sold to W. B. Yowell, who changed its name to the *Southern Eagle*. About one year later it was sold to F. W. Merrin, who called it *The Vallonian*, and afterward restored to it its original name. In 1882 he moved the plant to Plant City, Fla., where the paper is published as the *South Florida Courier* by S. W. Merrin & Son.

The Mississippi *Central* was founded in 1869 by Capt. R. M. Brown and A. V. Rowe. In 1875 it was purchased by S. B. Brown. In 1881 it was published by Johnson Ater, with E. A. Garland as editor. In 1885 it was changed to the *Free Churchman*, and edited by M. B. Fly. In 1887, as the *People's Friend*, it was published by G. Aycock. In 1888 it was purchased by McFarland & Lee, and published as the *North Mississippi Herald*.

The *Progress* was founded in 1882 by S. B. Brown as editor and publisher, with his son, T. D. Brown, as assistant editor.

The Cumberland Presbyterian church of Water Valley was organized October 14, 1843. Rev. Angus Johnson was first pastor, with James M. Morrison and Robert Nickle as elders. The organization was originally known as the Otuckaloffe church, but its name was soon after changed to Water Valley church. W. V. Johnson had charge in 1843–59; E. C. Davidson, 1860–78; J. W. Roseborough, 1878–80; S. I. Reid, 1881–2; H. M. Sydenstricker, 1883–5; J. D. Lester, the present pastor, came in 1886. The church now has a membership of one hundred and ninety-three, and the house of worship was completed in 1868 at a cost of $8,000. Mr. Lester, the present pastor, is a native of Union county, Tenn., and was ordained in 1883 at Memphis, Tenn. He is stated clerk of the synod of Memphis, and clerk of the North Mississippi presbytery. The elders of the church and the dates of their ordination are: J. C. Mury, 1859; A. G. Buford, 1861; W. E. Benson, 1883; R. R. Pate, 1883, and Baron Leland, 1883. Elder T. J. Price, ordained in 1887, died in 1890.

Methodist Episcopal church of Water Valley was organized in 1858, by Rev. Robert Martin, with a membership of twenty. Services were held in the Masonic building. In 1859 the church erected a house of worship, completed in 1861, which was replaced by the present building in 1870, at a cost of $6,000. Rev. Mr. Martin was succeeded by Revs. M. D. Fly, W. S. Harrison, J. M. Boone, J. W. Honnol, J. W. Price, J. S. Oakley, J. M. Wyatt, and the present pastor, Rev. T. W. Dye. The church has a membership of three hundred and fifty, and its Sunday-school numbers three hundred. The church received its largest accession of membership during the labors of Rev. Harrison, a most noble man, now of Starksville, Miss.

Missionary Baptist church of Water Valley was organized August 19, 1859, with a membership of five, all of whom are now deceased except Mr. and Mrs. Shaw, of Natchez, Miss. The present membership is about one hundred and fifty. Rev. E. L. Wesson is pastor. There are other religious organizations represented here.

Coffeeville is one of the goahead cities on the Illinois Central, and has a population of eight hundred. It is one of the county seats of Yalobusha, located in the southwestern portion of the county, and is surrounded by a rich country and was incorporated in 1836. It has no boom, but each year shows a large increase of population. It has good schools, good society, and many churches. The business men, as a class, are spirited, enterprising, progressive, sagacious and public-spirited merchants, and a more generous or wholesouled class was never gathered in one city of its size. The new and elegant courthouse and many fine stores and buildings are evidences of thrift and prosperity.

The Coffeeville high school has quite recently moved into new buildings. The number of pupils enrolled has greatly increased during the current year. By the introduction of all the many branches taught in the higher schools, the advantage to be derived from attending this school has been greatly increased. An endeavor is being made to make the school so thorough that it will not be necessary for students to go from home to receive an education. The school has been brought to such a standard that it has few rivals in Mississippi. The Wynn and Preston institute, with a large two-story building, was founded in 1890.

Coffeeville was a very popular and flourishing city in the antebellum days, and had among its citizens some of the highest men of the South.

The first paper published at Coffeeville was the *Yalobusha Pioneer*. The pioneer editor was E. Percy Howe. Beginning about 1850, the *Southern Appeal* was published for some years. Coffeeville Masonic lodge No. 83 was founded in 1818.

The first merchants of Coffeeville were D. M. Rayburn, Bridges & Shaw, and James Jones. The first white child born in Yalobusha county was James D. Haile, now bookkeeper for Herron & Co., of Coffeeville. S. McCreles built the first house in Coffeeville some time in 1830, and gave the place its name.

The Methodist church was probably the first religious body formed here. It now has a neat building and a membership of about eighty-five.

The Cumberland Presbyterian church was organized by Rev. W. S. Burney, of Oxford, Miss., in 1845. Rev. Mr. Burney was succeeded by Dr. J. C. Provine, now of Nashville, Tenn., and he by Dr. R. S. Thomas, the present pastor, for over forty years in charge of the church. When he came in 1848 the church had only eight members. The present membership is sixty-five. The first building was erected in old Coffeeville in 1850, the present brick structure in 1877.

The Baptists have a building here. Their pastor is Rev. Mr. Farris.

The Coffeeville academy was founded by Dr. Thomas in 1850, and flourished until the war. The Coffeeville institute, founded in 1867, flourished about ten years.

Other towns and villages in this county are Torrance, Oakland, Garner and Tillatoba. Coffeeville, Water Valley and Torrance are on the Illinois Central railroad; the other places mentioned, on the Mississippi & Tennessee railroad. Pine Valley is an old and well-known business point. Tabernacle lodge No. 340 was organized there with thirty members. Tabernacle Methodist Episcopal Church South was organized in 1840. It now occupies its third house of worship, a large structure, with a Masonic hall in connection.

Corinth, the seat of justice of Alcorn county, is the most prominent city in northern Mississippi, and has a population of twenty-five hundred. It is situated on the Memphis & Charleston and Mobile & Ohio railroads, ninety-three miles from Memphis. During the Civil war it was occupied successively by the Federal and Confederate forces, it having been regarded as a point of much strategic importance. The Confederate army fell back on Corinth after the battle of Pittsburg landing. Upon its evacuation by Beauregard, Corinth was invested by Halleck. General Rosecrans made his headquarters at Corinth while in command of the district. General Van Dorn attacked Corinth later and made determined battle, directing his troops in person, but was driven back and pursued by Generals Hurlbut and Ord, but escaped beyond the Hatchie river.

Corinth has grown steadily and substantially since the war. It has ten churches, is amply supplied with good public schools and other institutions of learning, and has numerous commercial, manufacturing and financial institutions.

Jacinto, the former seat of justice, is a small place but the center of considerable local trade. Other towns are Danville, Rienzi, Wenasoga and Glendale. Rienzi has a population of three hundred and seventy-five. Its first plat was near its present site, where at the outbreak of the war quite a village had grown up which had considerable prestige until the division of Tishomingo county. In 1875 Rienzi was visited by a destructive storm by which it was destroyed and a number of its citizens were killed. The Methodists, Baptists and Cumberland Presbyterians all have good houses of worship; they now meet in the Methodist church and in Mason's hall.

Grenada, the capital of Grenada county, is a bustling, thriving little city of twenty-three hundred inhabitants, beautifully located on a level plateau at the head of navigation of the Yalobusha river, and on the main line of the Illinois Central railway, and is the terminus of the Mississippi & Tennessee railroad, a branch of the Illinois Central from Memphis to Grenada. Grenada has four churches: Methodist, Baptist, Presbyterian and Episcopal. Each has a good congregation and a flourishing Sunday-school.

The Grenada Collegiate institute, costing $40,000, for the education of young ladies, and under the supervision of the North Mississippi conference, is located here and has about two hundred students. There is a high school for boys, and several smaller schools, besides two free schools (one white and one colored), with large attendance, presided over by competent teachers. Two public-school buildings, one for each race, have been erected, costing $15,000.

In the management of the corporate affairs the strictest business rules are observed, and everything is done upon a cash basis. There are in successful operation a cotton compress, a cottonseed oilmill, a steamgin and gristmill, a collar factory, a tannery, a creamery, ice factory and cold storage warehouse and other smaller enterprises. Other enterprises could be opened with profit, and the people of Grenada will advance means to worthy and competent persons coming here to engage in creditable enterprises. There is a bank here with a paid-up capital of $60,000, and deposits of over $100,000, and a building and loan association which has proven a benefit to the community. The assessed value of the property in the city is over $650,000. All branches of the mercantile business are represented. Grenada is one of the largest receivers of cotton on the Illinois Central railway, the average receipts being about fifteen thousand bales. The various secret orders are represented, and flourishing lodges of Masons, Odd Fellows, Knights of Pythias, and Knights of Honor are here.

The city proper is just one mile square, and is laid off into beautiful lots and wide streets. The stores are handsome, and the residences comfortable and convenient. Many of the houses are of the latest styles of architecture.

The cotton trade is extensive and growing, two thousand bales being handled each year. The town has the additional advantages of a cotton compress, which was erected in 1885. The business portion of Grenada lies about half a mile from the railroad. It comprises between forty and fifty stores. Every branch of business is well represented, some of the houses doing a very heavy trade. There are three good hotels and two lively newspapers. In banking facilities the city is well to the front. The Merchants' bank has a paid up capital of $40,000, and a large support from the district. A handsome new building has been erected for it on the public square. Grenada is not as yet rich in manufactories, but there are a successful oilmill and gristmill and gin.

The trade which supports this active town is drawn from a circuit of seventy to eighty miles, and extends over five counties. There is a fair jobbing trade, and in some branches, notably hardware, dry goods and drugs, Grenada merchants launch out far beyond the limits of their territory. Excellent freestone water is supplied by wells and pumps, and there is good natural drainage. The system of sidewalks is complete and commendable. The most prominent building is the courthouse, an ornate structure of brick, erected in 1884 at a cost of $25,000. There is also a large public hall, with a capacity of eight hundred.

Grenada has had some rough experiences. The town is older than the railroad. In 1847 it was devastated by a cyclone. In 1855 it was partially burnt. Early in 1884 the sudden failure of a bank sadly demoralized the business of the town. On the 16th of August, in the same year, a disastrous fire laid one side of Grenada in ruins, doing damage to the extent of more than $250,000. To crown all these misfortunes the remaining bank closed its doors before the end of the year. The stores were rebuilt more substantially than ever; money was forthcoming; a sound financial system replaced the erratic methods of the broken institutions, and Grenada is to-day in every way, stronger, healthier and more prosperous than at any period of its existence. All the buildings on the public square are now of brick, with metal roofs. Property is increasing in value, and many new enterprises are in contemplation.

Grenada lies in the mineral district of which Duck hill is the most prominent exponent. It is notable, also, that Grenada capitalists are largely interested in Duck hill's mineral land company.

The town is located on the land which John Donly, a mailcarrier for the Choctaw Indians, obtained by the Dancing Rabbit treaty. On this land, which lies on the left bank of Yalobusha river near the center of what is now Grenada county, sprang up the thriving village of Pittsburg, and on an adjoining tract of land and only a short distance away grew up the village of Tullahoma. They were rivals for some years, neither surrendering its name to the other, and they finally compromised on the name of Grenada, under which it was incorporated in 1836.

In 1882 Grenada Female college was transferred to the north Mississippi conference, and has since been known as Grenada Collegiate institute, with Rev. Thomas J. Newell, a graduate from Emory and Henry college, Virginia, as president. There are five instructors besides the president, and the school has a dormitory for about eighty boarding pupils, and a chapel with a seating capacity of about three hundred. The Methodist is probably the oldest church society in Grenada county, it having had an organization in Grenada as early as 1836. It erected a building about 1837, and in 1852 built its present house of worship. The Presbyterians organized about 1837 and built a house soon after. The Baptists came next, and built about 1845, but their house was destroyed in 1846 by a tornado. They at once built another structure and occupied it till 1891; they have just completed a handsome brick building. The old Baptist church is now owned by the Cumberland Presbyterians, who organized a society in 1891.

In 1851 the Baptists founded Yalobusha female institute at Grenada, and began the erection of a large four-story brick building, which was completed about 1857 at a cost of $47,000. Some time afterward the name was changed to Mercer institute, owing to a liberal endowment by a Mrs. Mercer. During the war the building was used as a hospital for the Confederate soldiers, and sometime after the war the institution fell into the hands of private individuals, and later into the possession of a Mr. Radsdale, who expended about $10,000 in improving the building, etc.

Grenada lodge No. 31, A. F. & A. M., was incorporated in 1838.

The Graysport lodge No. 289, A. F. & A. M., was organized a few years after the war, and was in existence some ten years, when it surrendered its charter.

Grenada lodge No. 6, I. O. O. F., was chartered about 1840, with Mr. Tyler as noble grand; has a membership of about fifty, and owns a fine brick hall, and is in a flourishing condition. L. P. Doty is noble grand. Grenada lodge, K. of H., No. 983, was organized in 1878 with A. V. B. Thomas as dictator. The membership is about sixty. J. Ash is the dictator.

Grenada lodge No. 158, K. & L. of H., was organized in 1879. The membership is about forty-five.

Ivanhoe lodge No. 8, K. of P., was organized in March, 1876, and has about fifty members. W. P. Ferguson is chancellor commander.

Calumet encampment, I. O. O. F., No. 16, first organized about 1853, and surrendered its charter about 1880. It was chartered in 1890, and has about fifteen members. Julius Ash is chief patriarch.

Protection lodge No. 2, A. O. U. W., chartered about 1877, in 1878 paid out about $40,000 as a result of the yellow fever. It has about twelve members, and Rias Carl is master workman.

The *Grenada Bulletin* was doubtless the first newspaper published in what is now Grenada county, having been issued as early as 1836, by William McClellan. Other papers that were published from time to time were the *South Rural Gentleman*, by Jerry Davis, followed by the *Whig*, the *Grenada Republican*, the *Locomotive*, the *Grenada Gazette*, afterward the *New Era*, and the Grenada *New South*. The Grenada *Sentinel* succeeded the *Locomotive* in 1855, and is now the only paper in the county. Volume XXXVI is the current volume. J. W. Buchanan is the editor and proprietor. Other towns in this county are Elliott, Graysport and Hardy.

Holly Springs, the beautiful and attractive seat of justice of Marshall county, dates back as far as the year 1836. Long before the war it was a prosperous town. Unfortunately, in the course of events Holly Springs suffered terribly. It was almost entirely destroyed during the war, and has never yet thoroughly recovered its status. Holly Springs is famous historically as the scene of Van Dorn's raid on the Federal stores. Many interesting incidents of the raid are told by the old residents. The old courthouse was burnt by Grant and most of the rest of the city by Van Dorn. Soon after the war the present courthouse was erected. It is a large two-story brick building, surrounded by an unusually well-kept grass lawn, at whose edge shade trees in great and rare variety give an additionally charming effect. Holly Springs is the market town of a varied and productive district. Cotton is the chief item of trade. A prominent druggist of Holly Springs has a very complete creamery near at hand, with fifteen Jersey cows and fifteen graded. He ships milk and cream to Memphis, besides supplying a portion of the home demand. Holly Springs also boasts of the only Holstein registry in the state. This is under the direction of Capt. Buchanan, and is doing excellent service. Trotting horses are being raised to quite an extent. There are some superb Kentucky stallions here. The farmers are devoting much attention to the breeding of horses and mules. Holly Springs is an important station on the Illinois Central railroad. The railroad company have established here an excellent hotel. The Memphis & Birmingham branch of the Kansas City, Fort Scott & Gulf road also runs through here. This road connects the West with the Alabama mineral district. The public schools of Holly Springs are of a high grade of excellence, and this is the site of the State Normal Colored school, the Maury Institute for girls, the Franklin Female college and the Bethlehem academy.

Holly Springs has a population of two thousand two hundred and thirty-two. It is built on the west side of the ridge that divides the state on a north and south line, and Memphis is only fifty miles away. The soil round about, very much like the famous Mississippi swamp lands, is fertile in the extreme, and the surface of the county is beautiful. From the beginning there it was patent that the town would become one of importance, and it soon left other towns in the territory far behind in the race for commercial and municipal supremacy. The stream of immigration was then flowing southward and it bore to Holly Springs many well known planters, eminent lawyers and talented and scholarly physicians, who at once identified themselves with its interests, and were instrumental in placing it upon a solid foundation conducive to future growth and prosperity. With the early history of Holly Springs such names as Roger Barton, Hon. Joe Chalmers, Gen. Alexander Bradford and John W. Watson are inseparably connected. From an early day the average population of the county was refined and educated, and down to the present time no community has stood higher than that of Holly Springs. Its business men as a class have been noted for the most rigid commercial integrity. Its banks have been strong and reliable. Its professional men have stood high at the bar of the county and state and upon the roll of those who elevate their lives to the alleviation of the suffering of their fellow men. Its churches have been strong numerically and of farreaching spiritual influence, its preachers, some of them, among the most noted divines of the South. Its educational institutions, including its excellent public schools, have been thorough, efficient and popular, some of the men and women having oversight of them distinguished in literature and art. Holly Springs is a pushing, enterprising, advancing city, full of enterprise and ambition, and in the highest degree typical of the progressive spirit of the new South.

Byhalia, Redbank, Victoria and Potts' Camp on the Kansas City, Memphis & Birmingham railroad, and Waterford and Hudsonville on the Illinois Central railroad, are small railroad towns of growing importance. The following villages and trading points in the county have no railroad facilities: Early Grove, Mount Pleasant, Bainesville, Oak Grove, Cornersville, Bethlehem, Chulahoma Watson and Wall Hill.

The city of Canton is situated almost in the center of Madison county, upon the main line of the Illinois Central railroad, at an altitude of three hundred and twenty feet above the Gulf. The site is a very desirable one, and Canton does not without good cause claim to be the prettiest city in the state.

The streets are wide, and well graded and guttered, aggregating some twenty miles. The principal business center is the public square, around whose four sides the merchants have erected their establishments, many of which are large, ornamental and costly brick structures, while the immense stocks carried indicate that a very large and flourishing trade is enjoyed in every line. In the residence portion are found many large and ornate homes, indicative of wealth and a cultivated taste, while an air of solidity is everywhere observable that is both refreshing and confidence-inspiring to the stranger. One of the pleasing features of Canton is the large numbers of noble trees by which its streets and private grounds are shaded.

The county courthouse occupies the center of the public square, and is a beautiful and imposing brick, stone and iron structure, which was erected in 1852, but is in a splendid state of preservation. It stands in the center of a four-acre plat, surrounded by stately trees, and the ground is covered with a thick carpet of grass. Both the brick and stone of which this building was constructed are products of Madison county.

The Illinois Central railroad runs through the corporation in the western portion, and Canton is conceded to be one of the greatest cotton and live stock shipping stations between Durant and New Orleans. Near the depot are seen a large cotton seed oilmill, several large cotton warehouses, icehouses, etc., which give the place an air of activity. The local manufacturing establishments are the oilmill, two steam gristmills and gins, two carriage and wagon shops, a planingmill and a number of minor shops, including a fruit and vegetable box factory. A large cotton factory was in operation some time ago.

Canton, being situated on an altitude of three hundred and twenty feet above the Gulf, on a rolling, well-drained site, which guarantees immunity against epidemics and infectious diseases generally, besides having a rich, well settled tributary country, which insures cheap living for employes, is certainly well adapted for the location of large factories, from these material and important standpoints. Being also located on a great trunk line railroad, its transportation facilities for reaching all the important markets and consuming centers of the country are most excellent, while the near future will doubtless witness the building of one or more competing lines, notably one from Canton to Vicksburg, to connect with the Mississippi river and the railroad systems centering at that point. Several miles of this road have already been graded, and there is no doubt of its ultimate completion.

Socially, Canton is a delightful place, and its people are widely known for culture, intelligence and their many accomplishments. This is made apparent by the city's educational facilities, both public and private, which are of the very highest order, placing the benefits of a thorough and practical education within the reach of all. Six church buildings, representing the leading denominations, are found, while the colored portion of the population worship in not less than five separate edifices. The civic societies, as Masons, Odd Fellows, Knights of Pythias, and others, are represented by strong and flourishing lodges. A large and well arranged hall serves for the reception of dramatic companies, who frequently contribute to the social pleasure of the citizens. The city government is vested in a mayor and six aldermen, city clerk, treasurer, marshal and taxcollector. These offices are held by citizens of probity and integrity, who manage the city's affairs wisely and well.

Real estate values have an upward tendency, although nothing resembling a boom has ever occurred to inflate them, the increase and advance being rather of a steady and substantial kind, which, after all, is the safest and best in the end. There are two substantial and amply capitalized bankinghouses in Canton, which, as yet, are all that its commerce demands. Some little jobbing business is transacted in a few lines, but the retail trade forms the principal industries among the merchants, who, as a general thing, are strong, solvent, and rated high in commercial circles.

The press is well represented by one daily and two weekly publications, which evince more than the ordinary editorial ability of journals published in towns of this size. Outside of Vicksburg, Natchez and Meridian, this city is the only one in the state that supports a daily paper, which speaks well for the enterprise and liberality of its citizens. The *Picket*, daily and weekly, is a progressive, live journal, ably conducted by a gentleman widely and favorably known among, as well as outside, of the profession, Capt. Emmett L. Ross. This journal, as well as the *Citizen*, may be taken with profit to themselves by Northern people who contemplate immigrating to Mississippi, as they always contain many items of interest concerning the city, county and state.

Canton's population does not exceed twenty-five hundred souls, resident therein, but it is a nucleus around which will gradually gather new and fresh elements, which will eventually result in the upbuilding of a large, prosperous and wealthy commercial and industrial city, a distinction to which its geographical position, rich tributary country, excellent transportation facilities and the enterprise of its citizens clearly entitle it to aspire.

The Canton cotton warehouse was built during 1888 by a company organized for that purpose. Over $6,200 have been invested in a fine brick and iron building, 62x120 feet, fitted up with sliding doors, and all the features which go to make up a standard warehouse according to insurance rules. Its capacity is fifteen hundred bales. Platforms and office buildings have also been erected, and a large business has been developed.

A new bridge across Pearl river was built a few years ago at a cost of $4,000 by the county and private subscriptions combined. This serves to largely increase Canton's trade territory from the counties lying east, whose people have heretofore gone to other markets.

Madison and Flora are prosperous railroad towns in Madison county of large and increasing business.

Bay St. Louis, the seat of justice of Hancock county, is located in the southeastern part of the county, on the Louisville & Nashville railway, and on the shore of Mississippi sound. It has a population of twenty-two hundred, and is a prosperous and pleasant little city, popular among health and pleasure seekers of the South.

Pearlington, on Pearl river, was intended by its founders to become a place of much commercial importance, and they dedicated a large area of land for the purpose of building up a city. That was in the old territorial days, and Pearlington for a time had a small boom. Its population is now eight hundred and fifty.

Gainesville, farther up the Pearl river, has a population of two hundred and twenty-seven.

The town of Macon, the seat of justice of Noxubee county, was laid out by Charles W. Allen in April, 1834. It was called Macon in honor of Nathaniel Macon, one of the first settlers of the place. It is located on the line of the Mobile & Ohio railroad, and has a population of twenty-two hundred. Early in the forties a two-story brick courthouse was built there. Just before the war the present courthouse was built, at an expense of $60,000. The town has five churches where white people worship: Methodist, Presbyterian, Baptist, Episcopal and Catholic; and two for colored people: Methodist Episcopal and Baptist.

Stockman lodge No. 19, I. O. O. F., is one of the oldest lodges in the state. Its charter and records were destroyed by fire in 1878, and the lodge was granted a new charter July 22, 1879.

Macon lodge No. 40, A. F. & A. M., was instituted February 7, 1840. The first officers were: F. C. Ellis, master; R. D. Barker, S. W.; Samuel Moore, J. W. The present officers are: C. C. Sessions, master; J. L. Ford, S. W.; W. S. Farmer, J. W.; W. T. Hodges, treasurer; W. P. Minor, secretary; J. W. Halbrook, Sr. D. and P. M.; F. W. Bransby, J. D.; Jacob Faser, S. and T. This lodge has a total membership of sixty-eight, owns its hall and has money at interest. It meets on the second Friday night of each month.

Macon chapter No. 11, R. A. M., was organized in 1849, with F. G. Ferguson as high priest. Its membership is now thirty-nine, and it meets on the third Friday night of each month.

Mauldin lodge No. 2937, K. of H., was instituted April 6, 1883, with twenty-six charter members. The first officers were: George D. Dillard, P. D.; Jacob Holberg, D.; J. S. Scott, V. D.; J. J. Callaway, A. D.; R. R. Jeffries, reporter; W. G. Sellick, F. R.; J. W.

Patty, Jr., treasurer; W. M. Jones, guide; Thomas Foote, sentinel; trustees, A. Klaus, W. B. Barker, R. K. Wooten. The present officers are: J. W. Patty, D.; M. L. Wells, V. D.; A. Klaus, A. D.; J. S. Scott, reporter; W. M. Jones, F. R.; Jacob Holberg, treasurer; T. J. O'Neill, guide; T. T. Patty, guard; Lewis Luclis, sentinel; trustees: C. M. Carter, J. L. Griggs, G. D. Dillard. The lodge meets on the second and fourth Tuesday nights of each month. The membership is twenty-eight.

Noxubee lodge No. 63, K. of P., was instituted June 19, 1890, with twenty-six charter members. The first officers were: H. F. Van Kohn, P. C. C.; T. J. O'Neill, C. C.; W. S. Farmer, V. C.; J. L. Patty, prelate; W. T. Hodges, M. E.; L. M. Scales, M. F. and K. R. S.; J. W. Holt, M. A.; G. A. Freeman, I. G.; L. Ludi, O. G. The present officers are: T. J. O'Neill, P. C. C.; C. C.; F. W. Bransby, V. C. C.; S. J. Feibeman, K. R. S. and M. F.; George A. Freeman, prelate; W. L. Hodges, M. E.; J. W. Holt, M. A.; Luther Freeman, I. G.; L. Ludi, O. G. The membership is forty-four. The lodge meets on the first and third Tuesday nights of each month.

Besides Macon the towns in Noxubee county are Brookville, Shuqualak, Summerville and Cooksville.

Mississippi City, the seat of justice of Harrison county, is located on the Louisville & Nashville railroad near the Mississippi sound, and has a population of three hundred. This city; Biloxi, population two thousand; Pass Christian, population one thousand; Handsboro, population six hundred and ten, and Beauvoir are dotted along the coast, with ample hotel accommodations at Mississippi City, Pass Christian, Biloxi and Handsboro, which are frequented the year round by visitors from north, east and west as well as by thousands of Mississippians. Beauvoir is noted as having been long, and until his death, the residence of Hon. Jefferson Davis. Handsboro is the seat of Gulf Coast college. Stonewall, Long Beach and De Lisle are flourishing towns in this county.

Public schools are maintained throughout the county for a term of four and five months during each year, and in Pass Christian and Biloxi for eight months. The Catholic churches of Pass Christian and Biloxi are in the lead in Mississippi, next is the Episcopalian, next the Methodist, next the Presbyterian, and then the Baptist.

The leading industries are the planting of oysters, canning of the oysters and vegetables, milling and truck farming.

Starkville, the county town of Oktibbeha county, is located at the intersection of the Mobile & Ohio, Illinois Central and Georgia Pacific railway lines, and has a population of two thousand. It is the largest town and principal shipping point of the county.

There are in this town live congregations of the following named religious denominations, all of whom own good houses of worship: Methodist, Baptist, Presbyterian, Associate Reformed Presbyterian, Cumberland Presbyterian and Episcopalian. There are three colored churches, two Methodist and one Baptist, all with substantial buildings and large congregations.

The Starkville Female institute, a chartered institution opened in 1889 by Rev. T. G. Sellers, D. D., provides a complete collegiate course for young ladies. The average attendance for the past seventeen years has been nearly two hundred pupils. This school takes first rank among the seminaries of the South. Starkville high school, founded in 1880 by its present principal, Mr. W. E. Saunders, prepares its students for practical business lives or to enter college. This school has an average attendance of one hundred and fifty. There are also several private schools, besides two colored schools. The Agricultural college of Mississippi was opened in 1880; it is pleasantly situated just outside the city limits, and has an average attendance of three hundred and fifty students. This college is ably managed by its president, S. D. Lee, and a large faculty of the best men that can be secured in the country. It has enjoyed unusual prosperity, is popular with the people of the state, and takes first rank with the agricultural colleges in the country. $325,000 have been expended in the equipment and support of this college. The curriculum embraces technical training of students in agriculture, and to carry out this work a large farm has been equipped as a model farm, on which the breeding and feeding of stock, the growing of all crops adapted to the climate, fruits, vegetables, nursery stock, etc., is pursued in a skilled manner. Among other things the college carries on a creamery, from which butter and cream are shipped daily through the year to towns in this and other states. The influence of the college is felt in the surrounding country, and is shown by the attention being paid to stockgrowing and the improvement of the lands, which is carried to a greater extent than will be found in any other portion of the state.

Three papers are published in Starkville, *The Southern Live-Stock Journal*, devoted specially to the live-stock interests of the South, a well edited paper, and having a wide circulation. It is the leading stock and agricultural journal of the Southern states. The *East Mississippi Times* and *Oktibbeha Citizen*, political and general newspapers, both have a good circulation in the eastern portion of the state.

Abert lodge No. 89, A. F. &. A. M. (formerly Oktibbeha lodge), was organized under a dispensation granted in 1847 and was chartered 1848. O. L. Nash, past master; William R. Cannon, W. M.; Simeon Muldrow, S. W.; S. W. Easley, J. W.; Moses F. Westbrook, treasurer; William G. Lampkin, secretary; John T. Freeman, S. D.; Alex Walker, J. D.; Charles Dibrell, S. and tyler. Other lodges A. F. &. A. M. in this county are Big Creek lodge No. 204, Double Springs lodge No. 251, and Whitfield lodge No. 365, the last at Sturgis. Ridgeley lodge No. 23, I. O. O. F., was organized December 23, 1846, with A. J. Maxwell as N. G. E. L. Tarry is the present N. G. Starkville lodge No. 783, K. of H., was organized October 29, 1877, with W. E. Saunders as dictator. T. M. Cummings is the present dictator. Starkville council No. 900, A. L. of H., was established April 1, 1882, with C. E. Gay as commander. The original membership was twenty-seven; the present membership is fifty-seven. Oktibbeha lodge No. 38, K. of P., was established November 23, 1883, with Simon Field as C. C., and a membership of twenty-five. The members now number twenty-six, and T. J. James is C. C.

Whitfield, Salem and Montgomery are other towns in Oktibbeha county.

Hazlehurst, the seat of justice of Copiah county, is favorably located a little east of the center of the county and has a population of one thousand five hundred and fifteen. It is a station on the Illinois Central railway, has much business activity and commands a good trade.

There is perhaps no point on the line of the Illinois Central railroad of more interest to the agricultural and farming communities than Wesson, Miss. (population two thousand), the point at which the celebrated Mississippi mills are located. This cotton and woolen manufactory employs a large number of hands, furnishing not only work for many men and women, but it necessarily creates a local demand for all kinds of farm produce which is felt in all that section of country. We quote from an address of Gen. A. M. West, of Holly Springs, delivered before the international exhibition at Philadelphia, Penn., July 10, 1878, the following concerning the great enterprise at Wesson: "In 1847 Col. J. M. Wesson, of Geor-

MISSISSIPPI MILLS, WESSON, MISSISSIPPI.

Manufacturers of Cotton and Woolen Goods.

gia, organized a company for manufacturing cotton and woolen goods, cornmeal and flour, and located in the same year in Mississippi, and commenced operations in 1848. This enterprise was eminently successful. It commenced with a capital of $50,000, and within a few years increased the same to $300,000. It was destroyed by the Federal army in 1864. Colonel Wesson, encouraged by previous success, located, after the war, in a vast pine forest in Copiah county, and named the place Wesson, and entered at once upon the erection of suitable factory buildings, which he soon furnished with machinery and put into operation. These mills were destroyed by fire and were then rebuilt by Mr. E. Richardson." The further history of this great industrial enterprise is given elsewhere in this volume. Quite a large town is growing up around the mills. There is a demand for all the goods they can make, and they are unable to keep up with orders for styles. Large sales are made in the Western states, in New York, and what is better they have a large local and home patronage; thus demonstrating that cotton can be more economically manufactured in the immediate vicinity of its production than elsewhere.

The town of Wesson has never had a saloon, deeds for the lots containing a clause which prohibits forever the sale of intoxicating liquors on them. There are three white churches, Methodist, Baptist and Presbyterian, all handsome structures, and one colored church, though the population is made up almost exclusively of white people, there being not more than a score of negroes living within the corporate limits.

The town is well supplied with water for protection from fire through the public spirit of the mill company in placing fire plugs at convenient points, the supply coming through the company's pumps at a creek and reservoir a mile distant. There are lodges of Masons, Odd Fellows, Knights of Honor and other like organizations. The banking business of the place is transacted through the Mississippi mills. The town raised $10,000 bonus and the site to secure the location of the state female college which, however, went to Columbus, notwithstanding Wesson was the home of one thousand four hundred young ladies, drawn thither from various counties by the prospect of employment in the mills. There is a large and successful free school in session the entire year, besides several private schools.

Wesson was visited on April 22, 1883, by a cyclone, the most destructive ever known in the state. Its track was one-fourth of a mile wide and thirty miles long, sweeping away in its course two towns, Beauregard and Georgetown—Wesson, however, suffering severely. The storm cloud came from the southwest, at about three o'clock in the afternoon, and with a frightful roar carried away houses, trees, fences, human beings, and all manner of debris in indescribable confusion. There were one hundred and ninety persons wounded and seventy-six killed, while hundreds were left homeless and destitute. An associate society of Red Cross for Copiah county was formed at Wesson, and over five hundred and fifty destitute people received aid in this vicinity, exclusive of aid given by agents of the society along the track of the storm. The society received and disbursed $7,943, exclusive of large supplies of food and clothing.

Other towns in this county are Crystal Springs and Beauregard. Crystal Springs has a population of one thousand one hundred and twenty-five, and is a flourishing station on the Illinois Central railroad. It is a well built and handsome place, widely known for its extensive garden truck and fruit-growing interests. Beauregard, on the same railway line, has a population of six hundred and three. It was almost totally destroyed by a cyclone in 1883 and has been only partially rebuilt.

Hazlehurst lodge No. 25, A. F. & A. M., consolidated in 1870 with Gallatin lodge No. 25, has twenty-six members, and D. B. Low is worshipful master. Quitman lodge, A. F. & M

A. M., is located at Rockport postoffice, near Pearl river, and has twenty-nine members, its worshipful master being M. D. L. Crawford. Charles Scott lodge No. 136, A. F. & A. M., is located east of Crystal Springs. J. M. Wesson lodge No. 317, of Wesson, has sixty-seven members, and Miles Cannon is worshipful master.

Copiah lodge No. 1422, Knights of Honor, was organized in 1879. Its first dictator was Judge T. E. Cooper. It now has about sixty-six members and Hon. Geo. L. Dodds is dictator. Excelsior lodge No. 365, Knights and Ladies of Honor, of which Capt. J. L. Ard is protector, has about thirty-five members. There is a Knights of Pythias lodge in the county known as Copiah lodge No. 60. Signal Assembly No. 5739 Knights of Labor, has a goodly membership, and there is a lodge of A. L. of H. The following lodges are located at Crystal Springs: Knights of Pythias No. 21, established about 1880, which has about fifty-one members. Knights of Honor No. 1420, established about 1879, and has about one hundred and five members. At Wesson are Harmony lodge Knights of Honor No. 1851, a Knights and Ladies of Honor lodge, an I. O. O. F. lodge, and a Good Templars lodge.

West Point, the seat of justice of Clay county, on the Illinois Central & Mobile & Ohio railroads, has a population of twenty-two hundred, and is a trading point of growing importance. West Point has a fine brick public school building. Its churches are as follows: Missionary Baptist, Christian, Methodist, Cumberland Presbyterian, Old School Presbyterian and the Protestant Episcopal. The Baptists were the first to organize here. Secret societies are represented thus: Cannon lodge No. 159, A. F. & A. M., of which Moses Jordan was the first worshipful master, and J. H. Shipman is the present one, and which has surrendered its charter twice, and been twice revived; Star lodge No. 84, I. O. O. F., established January 1869, with W. J. Howell as noble grand, and of which Tol. Hobbler is present noble grand; West Point lodge No. 527, Knights of Honor, organized March, 1877, with nine members, J. H. Shipman first dictator, and now having one hundred and sixty-one members. West Point lodge No. 224, Knights and Ladies of Honor, which was organized January, 1880, with thirty-four members, I. W. Foster first protector, and now has sixty-one members; Fred Daggett being protector. Prairie lodge No. 42, Knights of Pythias, which was organized in June, 1885, with W. E. Motford as chancellor commander, and Security lodge No. 254, Knights of the Golden Rule.

Tibbee, Palo Alto and Siloam are several small towns in this county.

The village of Abbott is situated near the geographical center of Clay county, eleven miles northwest from West Point, the county seat, and eight miles from Muldon on the Mobile & Ohio railroad, which is the nearest railroad point. That a railway will be built here at an early day seems probable. There has been a line surveyed from Muldon station, and an excellent route, affording easy grades and but few bridges, has been located. It is believed that the Mobile & Ohio railroad company will recognize the necessity of building this important branch soon. When it is borne in mind that at least two-thirds of the twenty thousand bales of cotton annually shipped from West Point come from the country around and naturally tributary to Abbott, some idea of the importance of a feeder into this district becomes apparent.

At present the population of Abbott scarcely reaches two hundred. There are three mercantile houses doing an annual business of $35,000, a saddlery and harness shop, a wagon shop and blacksmith shop, gristmill and gin. There is also a double daily mail.

Abbott was named in honor of Capt. F. M. Abbott, its founder, a native of the state of Pennsylvania, who located here immediately subsequent to the war, has since that time devoted himself to making a home worthy of the name, and to proving by living witnesses that not only can a Northern man live, be respected and prosper here, but also that improved modes of farming and diversified agriculture can be carried on as successfully, and even carried to a higher point of perfection, than in any of the Northern or Eastern states.

Winona, the county seat of Montgomery county, is situated on the Illinois Central railroad, at its intersection with the Richmond & Danville road, two hundred and seventy-one miles from New Orleans and two hundred and seventy-nine from Cairo. It has a population of twenty-one hundred people, contains between twenty and thirty substantial stores, and does a trade of over half a million dollars a year. Winona has a good bank with ample capital, which moves the extensive cotton business of the town, which amounts to over two thousand bales yearly, the bulk of which goes East.

Winona is said to be the name given by an Indian chief to his first-born female child. The building of what is now the Illinois Central railroad caused a small town to spring into existence within two miles of Middleton, then the educational center of Mississippi. The new town was christened Winona, and it soon distanced its older neighbor. Middleton is now a place of the past; its famous schools have been scattered over the state, but Winona lives and grows. Winona has two banks. Its railroad facilities make it a very desirable location for mills and factories of any kind, and such enterprises would receive great encouragement and support in the town. At present there are here two carriage and wagon factories and a gristmill. A compress has been talked of, and will soon be built if it has not been already. Among the other institutions of Winona is the rifle corps, of which it is justly proud, an exceedingly well-drilled body. The town also has a brass band and a capacious public hall.

Winona is in no respect lacking in educational facilities. There are three very well organized public schools, largely attended. Two private academies of a high order are also located here. Winona is in the mineral district in which Duck Hill is the most conspicuous point, and must profit by the general development of the district, some of its capitalists being interested in Duck Hill's mineral land company.

Winona has the following named churches: Methodist Episcopal, Presbyterian, Baptist and Christian, all strong of membership and having good houses of worship; and Methodist, Baptist and Presbyterian colored congregations all have adequate buildings. Here are two Masonic lodges, one of white men, the other of blacks. The business buildings in Winona are mostly of brick, and with few exceptions they are large and in every way creditable to their owners and to the town. The Winona *Times* is published by Walter N. Hurt. It is in its ninth volume, in size a five column quarto. The Winona *Democrat* was published for a time under that name and was afterward known as the *Advocate*.

Duck Hill is the name given to a pleasant little town in Montgomery county, and situated on the Illinois Central railroad between Winona and Grenada, at a distance of two hundred and eighty-two miles from New Orleans, ninety-nine miles from Jackson, and two hundred and sixty-eight miles from Cairo, Ill. Duck Hill lies in one of the most beautiful valleys in the state, which extends for miles up to the road. Near the town towers the real hill called after the Indian chieftain Duck, while on either side, for miles up the valley, and running back for miles on ridges—on either side lie the hills lately discovered to be rich in ores. Almost within a stone's throw of the town in its rear there appears to be a solid mountain of iron. Professor Johnson, the well-known United States geologist, has distinctly located these ores. A strong company of local and outside capitalists has been formed under a state charter to purchase and to operate these mineral lands.

Other towns in Montgomery county are Lodi, Mayfield, Sawyers and Kilmichael.

Tupelo, the seat of justice of Lee county, is a town of one thousand five hundred and twenty-five inhabitants, at the junction of the Kansas City, Memphis & Birmingham and Mobile & Ohio railroads, two of the greatest trunk line railways on the continent. During the past three years over one hundred new residences, about fifteen elegant brick storehouses, four factories, and a number of other substantial improvements were made. The trade has been largely increased, and prosperity is evidenced on every hand. The citizens are wideawake, enterprising and progressive. They intend that Tupelo shall, with her superior advantages, be the leading cotton and manufacturing town in northeast Mississippi. With a $15,000 public schoolbuilding, a splendidly equipped operahouse, three excellent hotels, five factories, two solid firms of cotton buyers, a number of the wealthiest merchants in the state, an immense cotton compress and cotton warehouse, a fine dairy farm, and one of the richest agricultural sections on the globe to support the town, there seems no reason to doubt that their expectations will be realized. The cash cotton buyers, representing eastern mills, Liverpool and Manchester, England, located in Tupelo, have the means to purchase all the cotton produced in the state of Mississippi, and are determined to handle large quantities of the fleecy staple in this section of the state if the highest cash prices will buy. The leading merchants, Messrs. Clark, Hood & Co., J. J. Rogers, Greener Bros. & Co., F. Elliott, and others, purchase all the cotton brought to Tupelo by wagons, and sell it to the exclusive cotton buyers representing the Eastern mills.

Besides its commercial advantages, Tupelo is one of the healthiest places of its size in the state. Within her limits are twenty-seven sparkling and free-flowing artesian wells, providing pure water. Tupelo has one splendid banking institution—B. C. Clark, president; John Clark, vice president; H. A. Kincannon, cashier, T. M. Clark, assistant cashier. Its capital stock is $80,000, and deposits about $100,000.

Tupelo has to-day one thousand five hundred and twenty-five people, seven churches, thirty business firms, two splendid hotels, one $15,000 schoolbuilding, two jewelers, one furniture factory, one spoke factory, one livery stable, one fine operahouse, one photograph gallery, one tin shop, five superior physicians, one extensive dairy, twelve lawyers, two meat markets, four painters, six brickyards, one cotton compress, two first-class railroads, two newspapers, one bank, six boardinghouses, one colored school, one ice factory, one chair factory, one broom factory, two barber shops, three blacksmith shops, one excellent bakery, one small graveyard, three firms of exclusive cotton buyers, thirty-seven artesian wells, twenty-five brick masons, one bakery and lunchhouse, a number of contractors and builders, fifty mechanics, one large cotton warehouse.

An institution that will add much to Tupelo's prosperity is the handsome two-story brick public schoolbuilding now in course of erection in Freeman's grove at West End. This building will be a monument to the progressive spirit of its enterprising citizens for years to come. The old schoolhouse was incapable of accommodating the pupils of the town.

Tupelo lodge No. 318, A. F. & A. M., was organized in 1869 with twenty members. Royal Arch chapter No. 7 has forty-three members, the Royal Arch commandery fifty-one members, the local organization of Knights of the Golden Rule has fifteen members.

Tupelo Methodist Church South was organized in 1868, with about twenty members, with Rev. Mr. Plummer as pastor. A frame house, 40x60 feet, was built in 1872, on Church street. The church has about one hundred members. Rev. A. G. Augustus is pastor. The Presbyterian church of Tupelo has a membership of eighty-five, and a fine brick house of worship. It is in charge of Rev. G. H. Steen, pastor, formerly of Okolona, Miss. The Cumberland Presbyterian church has a membership of sixty and a good frame house. The pastor is Rev. T. H. Padgett, from Bowling Green, Ky., who began his ministerial career in Mississippi, and subsequently continued it for a time in Missouri.

The Baptist church of Tupelo, Miss., was organized August 19, 1850, at a place called Hickory Grove, then Pontotoc county, in a loghouse about three miles west of its present site, by Elders E. Smith, C. C. Malon and Elijah Moore, with eleven members. Elder E. Smith was the first pastor chosen, and served the church until 1853. J. O. R. Word first church clerk. At the December meeting 1850, B. Jenkins, Burrell Jackson and Robert Fears were chosen deacons. In 1851 the Hickory Grove Baptist church was admitted into the Chickasaw association. The membership of the church increased gradually under the pastorate of Elder E. Smith until 1853, when he was succeeded by Elder A. L. Stovall. In 1853 the congregation built a nice frame meetinghouse a short distance from the old loghouse in which they organized. The church increased her membership rapidly under the ministrations of Elder Stovall, and in connection with a few other churches organized the Judson association in October, 1853. The membership of Hickory Grove continued to increase, and in eight years from her organization numbered one hundred and sixty-three members, eighty-seven having been received by baptism.

December, 1859, Elder A. L. Stovall resigned the pastoral care of the church, after having served them faithfully and acceptably for six years, and Elder William Young succeeded him as pastor, and continued in charge until the breaking out of the Civil war, in 1861. At night, on April 4, 1860, the Hickory Grove church house was fired by an incendiary, and burned down. In August, following, the church decided in conference to build a new house of worship, and selected Tupelo for its location, since which time it has been known as the Tupelo Baptist church. Elder A. L. Stovall was again called to the pastorate of the church in October, 1861, and continued to serve them as pastor continuously, except the year 1866, up to the time of his death, which occurred July 4, 1872. From the year 1872 to April, 1891, the following pastors have supplied the Tupelo Baptist church: G. W. Potter, J. T. Freeman, J. T. Christian, of Kentucky; then J. T. Freeman, L. R. Burress, J. L. Tumage, J. R. Sumner and S. G. Cooper, the present pastor.

Saltillo, Lee county, is a place of two hundred and fifty, and a station on the Mobile & Ohio railroad. It was settled by James Kyle, but little business was done there until after the completion of the railroad. After the county was organized the first grand jury met here previous to meeting at Tupelo.

The town has five church organizations. The Presbyterian church was organized about 1850, the Methodist church in 1868, the Baptist church in the early seventies. These three denominations had a union church erected about 1875. The Christian church owns a building valued at $1,000, erected in 1876. The Catholic church has an adequate building.

Saltillo was incorporated about ten years ago. James Heidleberg was its first mayor. The present incumbent of the office is J. D. Barton. The town has seven stores and a gin and a sawmill. There is here a good public school, of three departments, with an average attendance of ninety. Saltillo lodge No. 294, A. F. & A. M., was organized in 1868, and has a membership of fifteen.

The growing village of Nettleton was named in honor of George H. Nettleton, the Kansas City railroad magnate, and is situated in Lee and Monroe counties, about half in each county, on the Kansas City, Memphis & Birmingham railroad. It was laid out in the fall of 1887. Dr. M. M. Davis & Co. built the first storehouse. Soon after another was built by

Mullens, Frances & Co. The town now has two churches and two more are being built. The Nettleton Hardwood Manufacturing company, organized in 1890 with a capital of $50,-000, has an extensive sawmill with a capacity of forty thousand feet per day, which gives employment to eighty hands. Providence college, situated near by, was charterd in the spring of 1886. It was a frame building, built by subscription, 40x100 feet in size, with a capacity for seating five hundred students. The average attendance is about three hundred, and five teachers are employed. Nettleton Missionary Baptist church, known as the Town Creek church, was organized about 1855, with Rev. William Hood as pastor, with only five or six members. In 1858 a frame church was built. At that time there were about forty members. In 1880 the church declined, and had preaching only occasionally, till 1888, when it reorganized, with Rev. W. F. Davis as pastor, with about seventeen members. At the end of 1888 it had fifty members. Rev. D. J. Austin is the pastor at this time, and the church has about fifty-three members. Nettleton Christian church was organized in 1888, with Rev. Patterson as pastor and twenty-five members, increased now to thirty. The house of worship, a 40x60 frame structure, was built in 1889, at a cost of $1,500. It has a seating capacity of about three hundred and fifty. Rev. Armont is pastor. Two other organizations hold meetings in the same house, the Methodist Episcopal Church South and the Cumberland Presbyterian church. Rev. M. E. Tumbin is pastor of the Methodist Episcopal Church South, and Rev. Blanton of the Presbyterian church.

Baldwyn is situated in Lee and Prentiss counties, about equally divided between the two, but the postoffice is in Lee county, on the Mobile & Ohio railroad. It was named in honor of Mr. Baldwyn, who was one of the principal projectors of the Mobile & Ohio railroad. Its first storehouse was built in 1860 by Col. Robert Lowry. E. Oliver, Zebedee Williams, I. R. Wallis all built before the war. Since the war the population has grown to five hundred. The town has four churches, a gristmill, sawmill and cottongin all combined, and a gristmill and cottongin combined.

Masonic lodge No. 108, of Baldwyn, was organized in 1849 at old Carrollville, with only seven members. It was moved to Baldwyn in 1860, and now has thirty-six members.

Cumberland Presbyterian church, at Baldwyn, was first organized at old Carrollville in an early day, and moved to Baldwyn in 1860, when a frame house, 35x60, was built. At that time all Christian denominations of the community worshiped in it. The first pastor was Rev. William Wear. The church now has about thirty members, and a good Sunday-school, with Rev. J. E. McShan now as pastor.

The Missionary Baptist church at Baldwyn was organized about 1862, with Rev. L. R. Burress as pastor. The congregation built a frame house in 1870, 50x90 feet, with a seating capacity of about four hundred, well finished and elegantly appointed. Since its foundation various ministers have been employed by the church, but at present has its first pastor, Rev. L. R. Burress. The membership is about forty-five, and there is a good Sunday-school, with J. W. Burress as superintendent.

The Methodist Episcopal church at Baldwyn was established about 1851 at old Carrollville, and moved to Baldwyn just after the war. A frame house was built about 1869 with a seating capacity of four hundred. That house was torn down and a new one built about 1876. The church now has about fifty members, with Rev. K. M. Harrison as pastor. It has a successful Sunday-school.

The Christian church of Baldwyn was organized about 1869. An early, if not the first, pastor was Rev. R. B. Trimble. The church was erected in 1873 and cost about $3,000. The membership is seventy-five. Rev. H. M. Armor is pastor.

The Presbyterian church of Baldwyn was organized November 23, 1872. The constituent members were A. Cox, Mrs. N. T. Cox, Mrs. M. A. Stevenson, A. G. Wescott, John Stevenson and W. M. Cox. The present membership is about fifty. The pastor is Rev. J. H. Gaillard, who is concerned in the organization of the church.

Shannon, Lee county, was laid out in 1858, by G. F. Simonton, and named in honor of Col. E. G. Shannon, and is favorably situated on the line of the Mobile & Ohio railroad. The first building was erected for a store, by John M. Simonton, and goods were sold from it by Simonton & Buchanan, general merchants. Soon afterward other stores were built, and Shannon became quite a trading point. The population is four hundred and fifty.

The Methodist Episcopal Church South, at Shannon, was organized about 1869, with Rev. E. B. Plummer as pastor. The members numbered seventeen—seven males and ten females. The house of worship was erected about 1872, at a cost of about $1,000. The present pastor is Rev. C. P. Barnes. The members number seventy-five.

The Baptist church at Shannon was organized about 1867, with about seventy members, with Rev. William Thomas as pastor. A frame church was built about 1873, and dedicated by Rev. J. R. Graves. It has a seating capacity of five hundred. The church numbers about sixty-five members, and is under the pastoral care of Rev. T. H. Padgett, of Tupelo.

The Cumberland Presbyterian church at Shannon was organized at an early day, at a place near by, and soon after moved to Shannon and erected a frame building with a seating capacity of five hundred.

Palmetto Lodge No. 152, A. F. & A. M., organized at Palmetto Church, west of Verona, before the war, and transferred to Shannon about 1868 or 1869. It has a membership of twenty-five.

Shannon Graded institute was chartered in the spring of 1890, has a frame building 40x80 feet, two stories high, employs five teachers, and has an attendance of from one hundred to one hundred and twenty-five students. The house is situated on a beautiful hill, is well ventilated and is the best seated and equipped school building in the county. It was built by subscription through the efforts of Prof. W. T. Foster, the principal. This gentleman is a native of Tennessee, and has been a successful educator for thirteen years.

Five miles southwest of Baldwyn is Bethany, a small trading point. Here was organized the Associate Reformed church of Bethany, on Saturday, June 5, 1852, agreeable to an order of the Associate Reformed presbytery of Alabama, by Revs. H. H. Robison and J. L. Young, assisted by ruling elders Maj. Robert McBryde, Alexander Foster and Hugh Wiseman. The following persons became members of the church by certificate: Thomas Bryson and wife, Mrs. Martha Bryson, Miss Jane Bryson, Miss Elizabeth A. Bryson, Miss Mary Bryson, Miss Eliza Bryson, Miss Emily Bryson, Hampton Bryson, Samuel Bryson and wife, Mrs. Jane Bryson, David Lemmon and wife, Mrs. Martha Jane Lemmon, Mrs. Margaret O'Shields, and Mrs. Margaret I. Young, from Providence church, Laurens district, S. C.; James Turner and wife, Mrs. Nancy C. Turner, John Watt and wife, Mrs. Sarah Watt, and Mrs. Martha E. McGee, from Generostee church, Anderson district, S. C.; John K. Crockett and wife, Mrs. Rachel Crockett, from Ebenezer church, Tippah county, Miss. Besides these white persons, four colored members were at the same time received, viz.: Lunnon, Patience and Joseph, servants of Rev. J. L. Young, from Providence church, Laurens district, S. C., and Nelly, servant of John Watt, from Generostee church, Anderson district, S. C. There was at that time a total membership of twenty-five persons, twenty-one being whites and four colored. Thomas Bryson, Samuel Bryson and John K. Crockett were elected ruling elders. Thomas

Bryson had been ordained a ruling elder at Providence, S. C. Samuel Bryson and John K. Crockett were ordained on June 5, 1852.

During the war, Tupelo and other points in Lee county witnessed many exciting scenes. Early in 1862 the war drew nearer and nearer to them. The battle of Shiloh was fought April 6 and 7, 1862. Corinth became a military camp, commissaries scoured the country, gathering up all the beeves and forage they could obtain. Hospitals were established at Guntown, and citizens brought sick soldiers to their homes and nursed them. This state of excitement continued till the last of May, when General Beauregard evacuated Corinth, and moved the Southern army to Tupelo. The retreat then became a visible reality to the people. Many of the blacks fled to the Federal lines. General Chalmers had a picket line at the church and along the Pontotoc road, and no one was permitted to pass without permission of the military authorities. And, to add to the troubles of the time, in January, 1863, the smallpox was brought into the neighborhood, and several good citizens died, among whom was Dr. Washington Agnew. The year 1863 may be termed the year of raids. As soon as the spring opened, raids from Corinth became common. There was a cavalry fight at Birmingham, on April 24, 1863. The next week another raid passed down the railroad, burning the Guntown steammill, May 4, 1863. From that time on, raids were reported every few weeks in some part of the country. In consequence of them, the citizens were compelled to hide their stock and valuables, to prevent them from falling into the hands of a foe as ruthless as the Vandals of the middle ages. June 10, 1864, a battle was fought immediately around Bethany, which has been variously designated as the battle of Guntown, the battle of Tishomingo creek, the battle of Brice's crossroads and Sturgis' defeat. In the official medical history of the war the losses on both sides in this engagement are given as follows: Federals killed, two hundred and twenty-three; wounded, three hundred and ninety-four; missing, one thousand six hundred and twenty-three. Confederates killed, one hundred and thirty-one; wounded, four hundred and seventy-five.

Guntown, in Lee county, on the Mobile & Ohio railroad, has a population of three hundred. Shortly after the Revolutionary war an heir to a baronetcy in England, possessing the warlike name of Gunn, proved himself a tory of the most notorious stripe. Rather than live in commune with the creatures of a republic, he joined the Chickasaw Indians and became a chief. He married a fair daughter of the tribe, and by the marriage a lovely child was born, and Okalallah became the pride of the Chickasaw nation and was noted for her beauty, comeliness and modesty. Hence the name of Guntown.

In the early fifties a village was started on nearly the highest point between Cairo and Mobile, and in 1855 D. N. Cayce arrived, bought a plantation, opened a store and made things hum. There were two stores on his arrival, and Guntown grew until about half a dozen establishments were doing business, when the war clarion sounded. D. N. Cayce was a Tennesseean, who located at Fulton, Miss., in 1842, and moved therefrom merely to invest, and maintained his home at Fulton, where he died about three years ago, deeply regretted. He had been a power in the land, owning several plantations and several stores, but always eschewed official ambition.

His son, J. M. Cayce, was born in Lawrence county, Tenn., and studied at the celebrated Emory and Henry college, Virginia. When his father purchased the Guntown properties he was made overseer, and with this region he has been prominently identified ever since.

The town of Fayette, the seat of justice of Jefferson county since 1825, was incorporated in 1842. Its first mayor was J. B. Carpenter, its first clerk G. A. Guilminot, its first council

M. C. Dixon, R. H. Truly, Thomas Devenport. Its present mayor is W. F. Faulk, its present clerk Henry Key, its present council George D. Forman, James McClurg, Jr., S. Hirsch.

The town contains three churches, viz.: Methodist Episcopal, Presbyterian and Christian. Its schools are the Fayette female academy, the boys' high school and the public or free school. There are within its borders the following brick buildings: The courthouse and jail, three churches, the female academy and five business houses. The courthouse was erected in 1881 at a cost of $15,000. The jail cost $10,000.

The Fayette academy was chartered in 1827 through the efforts of Gov. Cowles Mead. The Rev. Mr. Sanford and wife were the first principals. In 1858 the charter was amended and collegiate power given, its name being changed to the Fayette Female college. This institution has a large two-story brick building, nicely located on a rise of ground in the eastern part of the city.

The first Baptist church in Jefferson county was established by Rev. Richard Curtis, Jr., near the south fork of Coles creek in 1798. It was called Salem. He (Rev. Curtis) was at one time with one of the members of his church, named Stephen De Alvo, a converted Spaniard, banished from the territory by Gov. Gayoso De Lemos. The Fayette Methodist Episcopal church was organized about 1825 by Rev. John C. Johnson. The present pastor is Rev. Ralph Bradley. The number of members is eighty-five. The denomination had an organization in the county as early as 1802, meeting at the old Spring Hill church, four miles south of Fayette. The organization was effected by Rev. Tobias Gibson, and is still kept up. The society at Fayette has a large and commodious house of worship, a brick building erected in 1829. The first Presbyterian church in the county was organized in 1804 by Rev. Joseph Bullen, of Vermont, who was sent as a missionary to the Chickasaw Indians in the year 1800. The Fayette Presbyterian church was organized December 9, 1854; its first pastor, Henry McDonald; first clerk, J. H. Darden. The original membership was thirty-three. The present pastor, W. B. Bingham; the present clerk, P. K. Whitney; the present membership, fifty-eight. A good Sunday-school is kept up. The house of worship is a good brick structure. There is regular preaching twice each month. The Christian church of Fayette was organized March 29, 1851, by Rev. J. T. Johnston, of Kentucky, and has a brick house of worship. Among the original members were David Darden, John P. Darden, James Stowers and John D. Burch. The present pastor is Rev. Philip Vawter.

The physicians of Jefferson county, in the order of their advent, have been Drs. J. H. Duncan, Key, Thomas H. Young, Farrar, B. F. Fox, James Brown, William C. Walker, Thomas Walton, Penquite, E. J. H. White, A. K. McNair and R. C. Love.

Jefferson lodge, I. O. O. F., No. 14, was chartered in 1821. Among the charter members were Thomas Reed, J. C. Fletcher and others. The present noble grand is James McClure, Jr. J. A. Donald is secretary. The membership is twenty-five, and the lodge is in a good financial condition.

Thomas Hines lodge No. 58, F. & A. M., was chartered April 12, 1843. John H. Duncan was first worshipful master, the first senior warden was Philip O. Hughes, the first junior warden Isaac Dunbar. The charter members were Philip O. Hughes, J. H. Duncan, Isaac Dunbar, S. B. McLeod, Charles West, Thomas M. Nash and Chesley S. Coffey.

The officers of this lodge in 1890 were: Charles Cooper, W. M.; G. D. McNair, S. W.; C. E. Robertson, J. W.; J. J. Robertson, S. D.; James McClure, Jr., J. D.; James McClure, treasurer; Henry Key, secretary; T. J. Key, S. & T. The membership was forty-one. The organization is strong financially, owning a hall and lot and having money in the treasury.

Fayette lodge No. 1389, Knights of Honor, was chartered in October, 1879. The charter members were: Ben Eiseman, Henry Key, William Thompson, C. M. Eiseman, W. L. Stephen, O. H. McGinty, F. Krauss, C. Cooper, S. Heildron, I. B. Stewart, E. M. Keyes, W. L. Guice, R. H. Truly, G. W. Rembert, M. Eisman, N. Eilbott.

Fayette lodge No. 404, Knights and Ladies of Honor, was chartered April 9, 1889. The official members were: W. D. Torrey, protector; T. L. Darden, past protector; William Gohazen, vice protector; Mrs. M. I. Key, secretary; L. R. Harrison, treasurer; C. W. Whitney, guide.

The old childhood home of Jefferson Davis was at old Greenville, the old county seat of Jefferson county, where he lived with an elder brother. Aaron Burr was arrested on the banks of Coles creek, in this county. Buena Vista plantation, owned by General Taylor at the time of his election to the presidency, is located on the Mississippi river, eight miles below Rodney. General Jackson was married at the residence of and by Thomas Green, near old Fort Gayoso. General Gayoso first resided in this county.

The Rodney *Gazette*, published at Rodney by Thomas Palmer, Thomas J. Johnson editor, politically whig, was established in 1830. The Fayette *Watch Tower* was established at Fayette in 1839 by William B. Tebo, editor and proprietor. The Fayette *Times* was published in 1858 by J. H. King. The Jefferson *Journal* was started in 1862 by Andrew Marschalk, Jr. The Fayette *Chronicle* was established by W. A. Marschalk in 1865. In 1870 he sold the paper to B. B. Paddock and F. H. Cully, and Mr. Paddock became its editor. In 1872 he sold it to R. H. Truly.

Flora McDonald, celebrated in romance as the savior of Charles Edward after the battle of Culloden, resided at Fayette for a time.

Harriston, located at the junction of the Louisville, New Orleans & Texas, the Natchez, Jackson & Columbus railroads, northeast of Fayette, contains six general stores, one drug store, two hotels, one newspaper, three saloons, two livery stables, three lodges and one church building, a frame structure now in course of erection, to cost $2,000. The secret societies mentioned are the Knights of Pythias, the American Legion of Honor and the Order of Railroad Sectionmen. The postoffice was established in January, 1885; Mrs. M. L. Jones was first postmistress. The office is now in charge of Mrs. E. B. Hammond. Griffin & Patton are the publishers of a bright and newsy local paper, which was established in the fall of 1890. The town was incorporated in 1886 with James M. Love as mayor and John Gillis and C. H. Gates as members of the town board.

July 4, 1864, a fleet under General Ellett, landing at Rodney, sent a detachment of troops through this county in search of cotton. They met four companies of Confederate cavalry at the crossroads near Dr. Coleman's place, now known as Clifton. A brief but sharp engagement took place and the Federals were driven to their boats, with slight loss. The Confederates lost four killed and several wounded. Major Morman led the Confederates.

Harriston, near Fayette, is a thriving village. Greenville, once the seat of justice, is now a cotton field, but there are those who can still point to the locality of the county buildings, the gallows and other landmarks.

Lying almost in the center of Claiborne county, occupying an advantageous and beautiful location in the midst of a fine cotton, corn, fruit, vegetables and grass-growing section, is found the pretty little city of Port Gibson, one of the state's oldest municipalities, as the county also is one of the oldest, having been organized in the beginning of the present century, or in 1802, on January 27. Port Gibson, the beautiful county seat of Claiborne county, was first founded and laid out by Samuel Gibson, Esq.; who was a native of South Carolina, born August 1, 1748. Mr. Gibson came to Mississippi in 1772, at the age of twenty-four, and first settled in what is now known as Jefferson county. The records in the national land office at Washington, D. C., show that in October, 1777, he obtained from the British authorities, then in power here, a grant of land on Boyd's (now Cole's) creek. He also acquired two tracts of land on St. Catharine's creek, in Adams county, one tract bearing date of 1784, the other 1788. He obtained from the Spanish government then established at Natchez, which had supplanted the British, a grant of eight hundred and fifty acres on the waters of Bayou Pierre. This tract covered the site of Port Gibson, since the first settlement of which, therefore, over ninety-nine years have passed. Mr. Gibson was the second man to penetrate so far from the river into the untrodden forest and wilderness. All around him, and for an unknown distance to the east, stretched a trackless forest, inhabited only by savages and wild animals.

The pioneer who preceded Mr. Gibson to this neighborhood was Jacob Cobun (in all probability his father-in-law), who the year before, January 11, 1787, had located a Spanish grant of eight hundred acres near here, which land was subsequently held by Elizabeth and Ann Cobun, sisters of Mrs. Samuel Gibson, and lay three or four miles south of Port Gibson, on Red Lick road.

When Mr. Gibson settled on the beautiful plateau of country now the site of Port Gibson, it was an almost impenetrable forest, with a huge undergrowth of cane. Port Gibson was in its early days known as Gibson's Landing, but in 1803 an act was passed by the legislature, declaring the name should be changed to Port Gibson. At the same time the above act was passed by the legislature Messrs. Thomas White, Daniel Burnet, G. W. Humphreys and John McCaleb were appointed commissioners to buy two acres of land from Samuel Gibson, and to contract for the erection thereon of a courthouse, jail, stock, pillory and whipping-post. Accordingly two acres of land were purchased, the site of the present courthouse and jail, and Joseph Davenport undertook the erection of the public buildings. They were completed that winter, and in February, 1804, the justices held their first meeting in the new courthouse.

The first license to keep a public house (tavern) in Port Gibson was granted in July, 1803, to Moses Armstrong and Robert Ashley. Immediately after, Gibson's Landing, or Port Gibson, was chosen by the legislature as the county seat, people began to purchase lots from Mr. Gibson and to build.

The first sale was made July 10, 1803, to Frederick Myers, and the price paid was $115. It was lot No. 3, in square No. 8, and soon there was a brisk demand for lots, and by November, 1804, the village contained thirty houses, with a total population of about one hundred souls. In the early history of Port Gibson the pseudonym Gibson's Landing clung to it, but in the course of twelve to fifteen years the former name prevailed.

The first fire company in Port Gibson, so far as known, was a chartered organization incorporated by an act of the legislature passed January 26, 1821. The charter members were as follows: Amos Whiting, James Burbridge, Harvey Bradford, James Hughes, Orran Faulk, Tobias Gibson, Horace Carpenter, Cornelius Haring, John H. Esty, Benjamin Shields, George Lake, Alfred Faulk, A. G. Cage, W. R. McAlpine, Thomas Cotton, John L. Buck, Fieldner Offutt, James Maxwell, Joseph Briggs, David D. Downing.

The Bank of Port Gibson was incorporated in May, 1836. A company was organized under the name of the Grand Gulf & Port Gibson Exporting company, in 1829.

Previous to the war Port Gibson was noted far and wide for the wealth and culture of its inhabitants, as it was the home of a large number of Mississippi's most wealthy cotton planters. It still retains the reputation of being the home of a cultivated, refined and hospitable population, and is indeed one of the most charming little cities in the state, being a seat of learning of no mean importance, and containing a very superior citizenship, among which the social graces and amenities are assiduously cultivated.

The advent, a few years ago, of the Louisville, New Orleans & Texas railroad had the effect of placing Port Gibson in direct communication with the outside world, and served to stimulate its commercial and industrial activity to a gratifying extent, and since then its growth has been marked, steady and substantial. Its population in 1890 was one thousand six hundred, and new accessions are being received. The municipality embraces something more than one-half mile square, the streets being regularly laid out and well improved, while good sidewalks prevail. A profusion of ornamental trees shade the streets, giving the place a charming, home-like appearance, while the many beautiful residences indicate the wealth and cultivated tastes of the inhabitants. In the business portion are seen many large, substantial mercantile houses, some being modern structures of elegant architectural design; their heavy stocks showing plainly that a large and lucrative business is transacted. Investigation only confirms this, and the merchants, as a class, are regarded as far above the average in point of solvency and reliability. The corporation is also out of debt, and its warrants are worth their face value. The town handles, annually, from twelve thousand to fifteen thousand bales of cotton, and the receipts are increasing each season. The citizens have displayed the most commendable zeal and activity in the efforts to locate industrial enterprises, and have now two very important ones in operation, namely, a cottonmill and a cottonseed oilmill, which are successfully conducted and add largely to the commercial and economical prosperity of the place.

Trade is principally confined to Claiborne county, and the cotton receipts reach fifteen thousand bales per annum. Some thirty-seven business houses, of different kinds, constitute the commercial world at present, and no line is, we learn, overdone; hence the merchants are prosperous and rate high in commercial circles.

As an educational center Port Gibson occupies a commanding position among Misissippi towns, and its female college and male academy are educational institutions which attract pupils from all parts of the state, as well as other states. There are also two public schools which afford ample educational facilities for the youth of both races, the scholastic term extending over a period of six months. In the important matter of educating its youth, Claiborne county is by no means remiss, as is shown by its seventy-nine public schools, and the $10,000 annually paid for their support by the taxpayers.

That a Christian and moral people comprise the population is well attested by the fact that there are five white and three negro churches, the former Methodist, Episcopalian, Presbyterian, Catholic and Christian, the latter being Methodist, Baptist and Christian. The principal civic societies are also represented and have flourishing, well attended lodges and well equipped halls. A very good and well arranged hall serves to accommodate dramatic troupes who visit the place during the theatrical season.

The location is a healthy one, the town site being rolling and allowing of perfect natural drainage. Water of excellent quality is obtained from wells and cisterns, and is abundant and pure at all seasons. As a consequence of these advantages, there is no danger of the outbreak of dangerous fevers and epidemics, and such ordinary diseases as prevail are easily controlled by the resident physicians. The city government is a safe and conservative one, and is vested in a mayor and five aldermen.

The First Methodist Episcopal church in Claiborne county, Miss., was organized in 1828; Hebron Methodist Episcopal in February, 1830; the Presbyterian church was organized in 1827.

The Masonic order was organized in Port Gibson, 1818, and was known as Washington lodge No. 17. Its charter was surrendered and a new charter was granted to Washington lodge No. 3, under which name the lodge still exists. Grand Gulf lodge No. 41 was chartered February 6, 1840, under a dispensation granted January 10, 1839. Franklin lodge No. 5, I. O. O. F., was organized at Port Gibson January 12, 1848.

The first academy in the neighborhood of Port Gibson was the Madison academy. It was situated about three miles from Port Gibson, on land belonging to William Lindsay. The tract was afterward owned by Dr. Dorsey and now is the property of Mrs. Clara Purnell. On the 5th of December, 1809, the territorial legislature passed an act of incorporation whereby "the school on the north fork of Bayou Pierre, in the neighborhood of Port Gibson, now under the direction of Henry C. Cox, is erected into an academy, hereafter to bear the name of Madison academy." By the same act the following trustees were appointed: Samuel Gibson, Thomas White, Stephen Bullock, Peter Lyon, Thomas Barnes, Ralph Regan, Allen Barnes, Waterman Crane, Daniel Burnet, Samuel Cobun, Edan Brashear, Andrew Mundell and Hezekiah Harman. The act provided that students of all denominations should enter the institution on an equality and be admitted to the same advantages. The trustees were authorized to raise by lottery, for the benefit of the academy, a sum not exceeding $2,000. In 1810 Mr. Lindsay gave the academy twenty-four acres of land, including the buildings in which the institution was established. It would seem, however, that it did not prosper, owing probably to the fact that its situation between the two forks of Bayou Pierre rendered it difficult of access during the frequent occurrence of high water. It is likely that there were a few boarders, but its chief patronage must have been from day scholars. At any rate, whatever the reason may have been, the legislature in 1814 authorized the trustees to remove the academy to a "more eligible site, not to be more than three miles from Port Gibson." There are no means of learning to what place— whether to Port Gibson or elsewhere—the school was removed, nor what its after-fortunes and fate were.

St. James' church, Port Gibson, dates its history from the 9th of April, 1826, when the Rev. Albert A. Muller visited Port Gibson and organized a parish of the Protestant Episcopal church, under the name of St. John's church. On the 17th of May in the same year eleven clerical and lay delegates, representing this newly-organized parish and three others, met in convention in Trinity church, Natchez, for the purpose of organizing a diocese of the Protestant Episcopal church in the state of Mississippi. St. John's church was represented by the Rev. John Wurts Cloud, rector-elect, and the Hon. Joshua G. Clarke, chancellor of the state, and Mr. I. W. Foote, lay delegates.

In 1848 a reorganization of the parish was effected under the Rev. F. W. Boyd, and its present name of St. James' church was adopted. Under a succession of rectors services were held in the courthouse and in hired rooms. In 1860 a further and final reorganization was effected and the sum of $5,000 was promptly subscribed toward the purchase of land and the erection of a church edifice. A lot was selected and partly paid for, but during the Civil war which ensued, although the organization was kept alive, the results of the previous efforts to secure a place of worship were engulfed in the general disaster. The amount subscribed was not realized and the purchased lot was lost. After the war a ladies' aid association was organized and incorporated. Its energy was soon rewarded by success in raising $2,500, with which a plat of ground on the corner of Church and Jackson streets was purchased. It contained a dwellinghouse (a small portion of which, said to have been originally built of logs and more recently clapboarded, is, as is claimed, the oldest building in Port Gibson,) which being removed so as to front on Jackson street, was converted into a rectory, leaving ample space for the erection of a church upon the corner. In the meantime the congregation worshiped in the brick building (now used by a colored congregation) on Church street, in the northern part of the town. At this time (1869 to 1876) the rector of the church was the Rev. James S. Johnston, now bishop of western Texas.

In 1881, under the energetic administration of the Rev. Nowell Logan (now rector of Holy Trinity church, Vicksburg), the work of raising funds for the building of a church was renewed, and with success. On the 30th of October, 1884, the cornerstone of a handsome brick church, designed by W. P. Wentworth, architect, Boston, was laid by the grand lodge of F. & A. M. of Mississippi. The building was completed early the following year, and presents a very attractive appearance, both without and within, being one of the most prominent of the few striking architectural features of the town. The total cost was $5,600. Of its stained-glass windows, the triple lancet over the altar is a memorial of the late Rev. Charles B. Dana, D. D., who was rector of the parish (1861–1866) throughout the gloomy period of the Civil war. One of the side windows is a memorial of Mr. Charles A. Pearson, a devout layman of the parish who died in 1878. A fund has been raised by the Sunday-school guild toward the purchase of a peal of bells, which will be placed as soon as sufficient tower room can be erected.

The parish received its charter in 1882 and the Ladies' Aid association deeded the property, church and rectory to the incorporated parish. But the association has continued its existence and still renders efficient service in the parochial work. The parish made material progress during the rectorate of the Rev. Mr. Logan (1881 to 1888). It now reports seventy communicants. Its present vestry is composed of Dr. W. Myles and Capt. N. S. Walker, wardens, and Capt. W. W. Moore, Capt. A. K. Jones, chancery clerk, John A. Shreve and Senator Stephen Thrasher vestrymen. The present rector, the Rev. Arthur Howard Noll, entered upon his duties in October, 1889. He is a New Jerseyman by birth, and was called to the bar of that state in 1876. He was engaged in railways in Mexico 1882–5, and then prepared for the ministry. He entered upon his missionary work a deacon in 1887 in western Texas. He was ordained a priest in Eagle Pass, Tex., in 1888, by the Rt. Rev. James S. Johnston, bishop of western Texas, wholly unconscious that in a year's time he was to become the successor of that prelate in his first parish.

Ministers of the Methodist church preached occasionally at Port Gibson before 1820, but no regular organization was made until 1827, when Rev. Thomas Griffin gathered some persons into the church. Port Gibson at that period was considered quite an irreligious community, and Mr. Griffin met great opposition. Among the early members were the Humphreys and Jeffries families, Joshua Kelley and his wife, Mrs. Isabella Kelley, Thomas Loury and Mrs. Susan Loury, James S. Mason and J. L. Foote. Of these, Mrs. Kelley, Mrs. Loury and Mr. Foote still survive. In the early history of the church it was favored with the ministrations of those eminent men, Dr. William Winans, Dr. Bill Drake, Rev. John G. Jones and Rev. Elias Porter. For a time the congregation, as all others, worshiped in the courthouse. A church was erected in 1830, which was in a few years destroyed by fire. Another was then built on the same spot. This was removed, and the present imposing brick structure was completed on the old site in 1859, costing $20,000. The church now numbers one hundred and fifty. Rev. E. H. Moureger is the present pastor (1890).

Besides Port Gibson, the towns of Claiborne county are Grand Gulf, Rocky Springs, St. Elmo, Hermanville, Carlisle, Tillman and Martin, all, except Rocky Springs and Grand Gulf, on the Louisville, New Orleans & Texas railroad. The history of Grand Gulf is interesting in its way. It was once a bustling little river city and handled forty thousand bales of cotton every year. Its first and a subsequent location caved into the river; it was three times visited with destructive fires, the last time burned by Federal troops; a cut off of the Mississippi placed it two miles from the river, and its only railway, extending from Grand Gulf to Port Gibson, was not only abandoned, but taken up, and Grand Gulf is little more than a memory.

The city of Brookhaven is located on the Illinois Central railroad one hundred and twenty-nine miles north of New Orleans, fifty-five miles south of Jackson, the state capital, and seven hundred and eighty-six miles south of Chicago. It is five hundred feet above tidewater and is the highest point on the Illinois Central railroad between New Orleans and Holly Springs, Miss. It is the county seat of Lincoln county, where all county business is transacted. The corporate limits embrace a square mile, of which the railroad depot is the center. The first settlement of the place was in the fall of 1856 and spring of 1857. John Storm, who closed a useful and well-spent life a few years ago, after having raised a large family who are now among Brookhaven's most active and respected citizens, and Mr. Jesse Warren, who also raised a large family and was long circuit clerk of the county, were among the first settlers. Messrs. Warren and Storm were also the first regular merchants of the town; what few shops existed before they opened business in the spring of 1857 having been of a very inferior and unpretentious order.

For a year or two the railroad extended no farther from New Orleans than Summit, which was its northern terminus and the distributing point for freights for all of the surrounding towns and counties. Finally, however, the road was completed to this point, and in May, 1857, the first train reached Brookhaven. It was a freight, and Mr. A. O. Cox, ex-sheriff of the county, who was the first station agent of the railroad, stated that the tariff on the cargo for delivery at this place was $1,350.

For eight or ten months Brookhaven continued as the northern terminus of the railroad, and during this time its growth was very rapid and its business large. The first year it was a railroad town, the shipment of cotton amounted to eighteen thousand bales. But the railroad was soon completed to Beauregard, Hazlehurst and other points farther north, thus dividing the business, and from that time its growth was more gradual and business settled down to the permanent basis which it has since maintained. The population has increased steadily and is now fifteen hundred.

The business of Brookhaven is of a stable and promising character. The record will show that there have been fewer failures among her business men than in any other town of like size in the state. It is the market and trading point of a majority of the people of the county, as well as a very large proportion from Franklin, Jefferson and Lawrence counties. The building of the Meridian and Northeastern and the Mississippi Valley railroads has no perceptible effect toward drawing away trade, nor is it feared that it will, as this will only take off a few from the outskirts of Brookhaven's trade territory and will be more than offset by the constant development that is going on. The twenty-seven sawmills of the county, with their hundreds of employes and dependents, and the sturdy agricultural population will sustain and continually increase its commercial importance.

The city is under the direction of a board of mayor and aldermen and a marshal (who is also ex-officio taxcollecter), elected every two years.

Brookhaven has ever been noted for the beauty of her women and the gallantry of her men, and in point of intelligence, culture and animation her society circles will compare favorably with those of any other community. With schools the city is peculiarly favored. First and foremost among these is the now famous Whitworth Female college. In addition to this a male academy of high grade is conducted, and several competent and experienced teachers; each conducts a mixed school for small boys and girls. The public schools of the city are also run four months of each year.

The Presbyterians, Catholics, Methodists, Baptists and Episcopalians all have commodious and comfortable churches, and all except the latter have regular religious services and Sunday-schools.

Though owning no synagogue the Jewish citizens also maintain a religious organization and hold worship at stated periods. The colored population likewise display a creditable interest in religious matters, and support one Baptist and two Methodist churches with very comfortable houses of worship.

Secret societies are represented by lodges of I. O. O. F., Masons, Knights of Honor and Knights and Ladies of Honor, which meet in a large and commodious hall built and owned by the Masonic fraternity. Heuck's hall, capable of seating six hundred persons and equipped with a well arranged stage and fine scenery, furnishes accommodation to various excellent traveling combinations during the winter months, and amusement to lovers of the drama.

Other towns in this county are Bogue Chitto, Montgomery and Caseyville.

Bogue Chitto, about ten miles south of Brookhaven on the Illinois Central railroad, is situated on the Bogue Chitto river. It is one of the oldest towns along the road, having been in existence ever since the railroad was built. Owing to various causes, the growth of this town has been very slow. Its buildings being entirely wooden structures, it has been twice destroyed by fire and until within the past few years has had a hard struggle for existence. The population of Bogue Chitto is two hundred and twenty-five, nearly double what it was a few years past, and is increasing rapidly and steadily. Its volume of business has swelled until it is ten times greater. There are five dry goods and grocery stores. Messrs. B. E. Brister & Co. own two large saw and planingmills, besides doing a flourishing mercantile business. J. M. Tyler also owns a fine watermill and gin about a half-mile from town. The lumber manufacturing interests of Bogue Chitto are equal to those of any and superior to those of a great many places of much greater pretensions. There are seven mills for manufacturing rough and dressed lumber in the vicinity of the place. The annual shipment of lumber is about $40,000 to $50,000. Messrs. Wesson & Money own one of the finest bodies of pine timber in the country, with a narrow gauge railroad and locomotive running through it to a distance of eight miles east, and there is a probability that the road will be extended to Pearl river. The Natchez, Bogue Chitto & Ship Island railroad will possibly become a fixed fact in the near future, though it may take a different name, and in view of that fact the value of property in and around Bogue Chitto is increasing. The corporate limits of the town include about a mile square. There are some very sightly residences and very fine sites for many more. The school facilities are fine. There are two churches, one white (Methodist) and one colored (Baptist); one Masonic and town hall.

Woodville (population one thousand) the seat of justice for Wilkinson county, is one of the oldest towns in the state, and prior to its incorporation (which dates back to about 1808) was one of the earliest settlements in the then Natchez district. Peopled by one of th proudest races on earth, its population comprised men whose sense of honor was the most exalted, and whose chivalry, exhibited whenever occasion presented, led them to deeds of valor and heroism.

It would be difficult to point out a location for a town that would combine more advantages than that of Woodville. Situated upon an elevation four hundred and fifty feet above the river level at Bayou Sara, the breezes of the gulf are here distinctly felt and enjoyed. The topography of Woodville and its immediate environments is one that is admirably adapted to thorough drainage and perfect sanitation. The watershed of the town is fourfold, and drainage occurs at the four cardinal points of the compass. The inevitable consequence of all this is that Woodville is one of the most healthful spots in the country, and enjoys unusual immunity from the ills that flesh is heir to.

Woodville is supported wholly by the trade afforded by its surrounding agricultural country, whose inhabitants raise principally cotton, corn, oats, hay and live stock for the market, the county being specially adapted to the successful cultivation and growing of either. Wilkinson county contains twenty-five townships, and has a population of about seventeen thousand five hundred and sixty-four, the principal portion of which is engaged in agricultural pursuits. Were its arable lands wholly occupied it could, with ease, sustain a population of from sixty thousand to seventy-five thousand souls. It will thus be seen that excellent opportunities exist for the acquirement of land and homes by immigrants from other states and countries. Quite a number of large, well supplied stores provide the agricultural population with all needful supplies, and during the busy cotton season this town wears an aspect of thrift and bustle that would be creditable to much larger business places. The enterprise and promptness of her business men are proverbial.

Perhaps no town in the state takes greater pride in her secret organizations than Woodville. The Masons have a lodge, a Royal Arch chapter and council, all of which have large membership and are in first-rate financial condition. The Odd Fellows have a lodge and encampment in like excellent standing. This latter order is in a flourishing state financially. The Knights of Honor have a large membership and a flourishing lodge, the order being justly popular here. The American Legion of Honor is also represented in a lodge numbering about forty-five members.

The Protestant Episcopal church (St. Paul's) is one of the oldest churches in the town, and has its pulpit regularly supplied. This church has a fine organ and a choice choir. The Catholic congregation of Woodville has an attractive, commodious house of worship, where services are held every fourth Sunday in each month. The Methodists have a large congregation and a handsome church edifice, where they worship every Sunday. The Baptist church is likewise a very handsome building. This denomination is also a large one. They have services on the first and third Sundays in each month. The Presbyterian congregation worship in a large and comfortable church in the town, and number among their worshipers a goodly list of the old residents of the town and county. The Hebrew population of Woodville numbers about twenty families, who hold their regular weekly services in the Jewish temple, Beth Israel, which was built in 1878. The congregation wasorganized a few years prior to the construction of the temple. Rabbi Henry Cohen, formerly of Kingston, Jamaica, and London, England, is the spiritual head of the congregation. Besides filling the pulpit at the synagogue here, his labors extend to Bayou Sara, where he has a large Sabbath-school, and to other neighboring localities. There is also a Jewish cemetery here, which was dedicated about twenty years ago.

There is a large public school for whites in Woodville, in a most satisfactory and flourishing condition. There is also a public school for colored people in the town. This is perhaps one of the best colored schools in the South. The late Judge Edward McGehee donated, during his life, a handsome sum of money toward the education of the youth of Woodville, which was one of the many generous benefactions bestowed by this big-hearted philanthropist. The donation is represented in a fine building and ample grounds, in the corporate limits of Woodville, and is under the management of the conference of the Methodist Episcopal church. Though controlled by the Methodist church the school is in no wise sectarian. The public schools throughout the county are sufficiently numerous to meet the requirements of the school population, and here, as elsewhere in the South, there are ample educational advantages for all.

Woodville has only one direct connection by rail with Bayou Sarah, via the West Feliciana railroad, over which trains leave Woodville at 7 A. M., on Mondays, Wednesdays, Fridays and Saturdays; returning, arrive here at 4:30 the same day. A mail is carried over this route.

There is also a regular hack line (conducted by Mr. G. M. Petty), which connects Woodville with the Mississippi Valley railroad. The hack leaves Woodville every morning at 7:30 o'clock, making close connection with the south-bound train at Centerville, Miss. The hack lays over and connects also with the north-bound train, and, returning, arrives here at 4:30 P. M. This gives Woodville a daily mail from New Orleans, as well as from the North.

The Woodville *Republican* is the name of the local paper, whose editor and proprietor, Mr. J. S. Lewis, devotes himself assiduously to its publication. The *Republican* is a handsome county paper and deserves to be well supported.

The patriotic ladies of Wilkinson county organized themselves into a Confederate monumental association, and through their noble efforts, ably seconded by the veterans of the lost cause in the town and county, erected a beautiful monument in a square lot opposite the south side of the courthouse, "In memory of the Confederate soldiers of Wilkinson county—1861 to 1865." The foregoing inscription appears upon one side of the shaft, near the base, and just above the word "Confederate." Upon another side appears the Confederate battle-flag, and just beneath a private soldier wearing the gray, his musket held at rest. On a third surface is the coat of arms of the Confederate states, and upon the front a Confederate cavalryman, mounted and equipped for battle. Above this figure a second battle-flag is unfurled. The shaft is sixteen feet high and surmounts a mound covered with an evergreen sward. It is a very handsome monument, and the entire work reflects credit upon the dutiful daughters of patriotic old Wilkinson. A suitable iron railing to inclose the monument square completes the work.

Fort Adams was settled by Wilkinson's army in 1798, when the soldiers were in cantonment until about 1807. Fort Adams was named in 1800, in honor of the president. Pinckneyville, the original seat of justice, was founded in the first settlement of the territory. It was platted in 1805 by Thomas Dawson, and its plat was recorded in 1806 by James Johnson, clerk.

Jackson academy, incorporated in 1814, was located in what is now John A. Redhead's yard, where the site is still to be seen. The school flourished for a number of years, and afterward the place was known as a stand for physicians. The Wilkinson lodge No. 10, I. O. O. F., was started in 1846. Asylum lodge No. 63 was chartered about the same time.

The Baptist church in Woodville was incorporated in 1824; the Presbyterian church at

Cold Spring in 1825; St. Paul's Episcopal church in 1825; Consolation church below old Mount Pleasant, in this county, in 1831; Bethel church, at the old camping grounds near Thompson creek, the present site of Bethel church, was first built of logs by Edward McGehee, William James and friends, and was dedicated by Rev. Lewis Hobbs in 1813. Some years after this building was replaced by a frame church, that later by a brick building, which stands as a monument to the honor of Judge Edward McGehee. The Methodists had a church at Pinckneyville some years before this, and another at Loftus Heights. The next oldest church was at Midway, first known as Grave's church, founded by the Bowman family and established about 1815 or 1817 by Mark Moore, afterward moved to Centerville, where there is a flourishing organization with a membership of one hundred. The Presbyterian church of Centerville has a neat frame building and a membership of fifty. The Baptist church at same place numbers about thirty-five members.

In the western part of Wilkinson county, Miss., is a stream running almost due north and south. It runs through an alluvial country and in many places has high banks. With almost every overflow, like the Mississippi river, it changes its current and causes large caving of the banks. For many years these caving banks have brought to light remains, such as bones, tusks and teeth, of some extinct animal, said to be the mastodon. In one instance a tusk was found measuring five feet, from the point, in length, and six inches in diameter at the largest part. Unfortunately this specimen was neglected and gradually crumbled away from the action of the air. If varnished with common copal varnish these specimens may be preserved indefinitely, otherwise they soon crumble and perish. There are in the county many valuable specimens, such as jaw teeth, front teeth, points of tusks and larger bones, which have been treated with varnish and are well preserved. One specimen consists of the jawbone with the teeth all in good state of preservation. The negroes gather up these remains after an overflow, and for a consideration bring them to the curious in such matters. The supply seems to be inexhaustible.

Oxford, the seat of justice of Lafayette county, is a flourishing town of two thousand population on the line of the Illinois Central railroad. The city was almost totally destroyed by the Federal army during the war.

The legal bar of Oxford has always ranked high, and in the biographical department of this work will be found sketches of the leading lawyers of the past as well as the present day.

The Bank of Oxford was organized February 1, 1872, with a paid-up capital of $33,333.33, and an authorized capital of $100,000. W. L. Archibald was the first president, and W. A. West its first cashier.

A. T. Owens is the present president, and Ben Price cashier. It is one of the sound and prosperous banking institutions of the state. Another bank at Oxford is the Merchants & Farmers, which was established in September, 1889, with a capital of $50,000. Charles Roberts was its first and he is its present president, and W. A West is cashier.

Other towns in Lafayette county are Taylor, Springdale and Abbeville.

Scranton, the seat of justice of Jackson county, is a growingly important town of one thousand one hundred and fifty inhabitants, on the Southern border of the county and state on the shore of the Mississippi sound, and on the Louisville & Nashville railroad.

Other towns in this county are East Pascagoula, West Pascagoula and Ocean Springs. The two Pascagoulas depend on Scranton for mail facilities. Ocean Springs, which is noted chiefly for the extensive pecan culture of Col. W. R. Stuart, has a population of five hundred.

Pascagoula lodge No. 202, A. F. & A. M., is situated at Moss Point, and has seventy-five members. It was organized at East Pascagoula in 1855. Its charter members were Thomas L. Sumrall, W. M.; A. E. Lewis, S. W.; W. G. Elder, J. W.; J. E. Sarozin, secretary; Cheri Sarozin, treasurer; W. Griffin, S. D.; Lyman Randall, J. D.; Bernard Gillsley, tyler. The lodge was cordially supported, and grew and prospered till 1862, when the environments of war became too great for it, and in common with nearly all other interests it was compelled to succumb. Nothing is found of its work till it was reorganized in 1866 by H. B. Griffin, senior warden, holding over from 1862, H. L. Houze, a past master of Wilson lodge No. 72, acting as W. M.; J. M. McInnis, J. W.; A. H. Delmas, secretary; H. Krebs, treasurer; W. G. Elder, J. D.; J. B. Delmas, tyler. After its reorganization the lodge took on its old-time vigor and prosperity, and speedily took high rank among the Masonic institutions of the state. About this time it was removed to Moss Point, where a suitable building awaited it. It soon numbered among its members nearly all the leading citizens of the vicinity, and has for many years impressed itself upon the morals of the community, as well as contributed largely to all charitable enterprises. Its charities reach away up into the thousands. In each of the yellow-fever epidemics of 1874 and 1878, this lodge dispensed hundreds of dollars indiscriminately to initiated and profane alike. In the Masonic councils of the jurisdiction of Mississippi, Pascagoula lodge No. 202 has not been without her honors. In 1881 one of her past masters, J. W. Morris, was appointed senior grand deacon, and another, M. M. Evans, district deputy grand master, in 1880 and 1881. The same individual was appointed deputy grand master by the lamented Grand Master Patty, in 1884, and was elected junior grand warden in 1886, senior grand warden in 1887, and grand master in 1888; was appointed on the committee of complaints and offenses in 1889 and 1890, and on the committee of law and jurisprudence in 1891. J. K. McLeod, another past master, was appointed on the committee on complaints and offenses in 1886 and 1887. The lodge at this writing is occupying its accustomed position among the lodges in the state, and will doubtless continue to write itself in the history of Free Masonry in Mississippi. Its worshipful masters were: Thomas L. Samrall, two years; A. E. Lewis, five years; W. G. Elder, one year; H. B. Griffin, one year; H. L. Houze, seven years; S. A. McInnis, three years; M. M. Evans, three years; J. K. McLeod, six years; J. W. Morris, one year; T. A. Coulson, two years; W. Watkins, one year; J. H. Rolls, one year; J. W. Stewart, present incumbent.

H. L. Houze R. A. chapter No. 108, situated at Moss Point, was organized January 17, 1876, with the following charter members: H. L. Houze, H. P.; D. M. Dunlap, king; Nelson Wood, scribe; W. H. Rolls, C. of host; J. W. Griffin, P. S.; W. C. Morrow, R. A. C.; George Wood, M of third V.; D. A. Yates, M. of second V.; C. W. Calhoun, M. of first V.; H. C. Horens, treasurer. This chapter was named in honor of its first high priest, a patriarch in Masonry. One who had devoted much of his life to its service, and who has always loved Masonry for its pure and elevating influence, his life has been an exemplification of Masonic tenets and principles. It was therefore but a just tribute to call the chapter which he did so much to establish and maintain after his name. H. L. Houze chapter No. 108 has contributed its share toward charitable enterprises, always joining with Pascagoula lodge for that purpose. Among the leading members of the grand chapter, she has her representative in the person of J. K. McLeod, one of the past high priests, who was installed grand principal sojourner in 1887, grand captain of host in 1888, grand scribe in 1889, grand king in 1890 and deputy grand high priest in 1891.

Pride of Moss Point lodge No. 1913, grand united order of Odd Fellows in America, composed exclusively of colored persons, was organized in 1879, with the following as charter members: D. Anderson, C. S. Colland, A. Haskins, B. J. Mayo and W. W. McInyon.

It now has thirty members, and is devoted to the care of the sick and destitute of its members. It expends considerable in this direction.

Scranton lodge No. 45, I. O. O. F., was instituted April 5, 1886. Its charter members were W. F. A. Parker, J. H. Rolls, R. P. Blalack, S. J. Armstrong, J. S. Blalack, W. K. Mead and J. W. Mead. It has at present writing eighty members, and is a thrifty and prosperous lodge, embodying most of the prominent citizens of Scranton and vicinity among its members. It annually dispenses large amounts in charity, and is a useful, moral agent. Its members are liberal in its financial views, having built a very imposing edifice for the occupancy of the lodge, with several rooms and halls for rent for offices and other purposes. This building cost upward of $5,000 and is a beauty in architecture. Scranton lodge No. 45, stands in the front rank of Odd Fellows' lodges in the state, and will doubtless impress itself upon the history of that order.

Gulf lodge No. 2884, Knights of Honor, situated at Moss Point, Miss., was organized June 8, 1881, with the following charter members: W. D. Bragg, W. E. Bingham, A. Blumer, S. J. Bingham, George N. Cook, Burton Goode, W. Fred Herrin, John W. Morris, E. C. Woods and D. A. Yates. It numbers at present seventy-five members, including most of the leading persons of the community. It has always been a useful adjunct to the moral and financial forces of the county, having in its brief existence contributed largely not only to the healthy, moral sentiment of the town and vicinity, but has dispensed to the widows and orphans of its deceased members amounts aggregating $18,000.

Escatawpa lodge No. 3115, Knights of Honor, was organized in 1884 with sixteen charter members. It now has thirty-two. It has paid out $6,000 in benefits.

Gulf lodge U. D., A. F. & A. M., is in process of organization at Scranton, Miss. Its charter members are S. T. Hariland, M. C. Pankey, W. M. Denny, R. D. Smith, J. A. Miller, M. C. Allman, W. A. Chapel, C. P. Bowman and C. H. Alley. They are all wellknown gentlemen and will doubtless conduct this new lodge successfully.

Greenwood, the county seat of Leflore county, is located on the left bank of the Yazoo river about three miles below where that river is formed by the confluence of the Yalobusha and Tallahatchie rivers and has a population of one thousand souls. Here also the Yazoo & Mississippi Valley railroad has an incline for the ready transfer of freights from steamboats, a number of which ply daily carrying on a lucrative business up and down the river from this point. The growth of the town in the past six years has been almost phenomenal, it having grown in that time from a village of about five hundred inhabitants. Beside a large local trade there are several large wholesale establishments located at Greenwood and a number of cotton buyers and it is a lively business point. It has three churches, Methodist, Presbyterian and Episcopal, for the whites, and a large Methodist church for the colored population, besides two public schoolhouses one for each race, also an elegant operahouse and ample lodgerooms for the various secret and benevolent orders. A number of manufacturing companies have been incorporated and facilities will be supplied to handle the immense amount of cotton shipped from this and adjacent points. Here too a packery of beef could find the material necessary for carrying on that business, since a large number of cattle are raised in this and adjoining counties.

South of Greenwood, on the line of the Yazoo & Mississippi Valley railroad, is the thriving village of Rising Sun, at which place the railroad taps the Yazoo river, and there is probably the best dirt road in the country leading from there to the hill country on the east.

Ten miles south from Greenwood on the same railroad where it taps the river is the town of Sidon, second in size and importance in the county which has kept proportionate pace in improvements with the county seat, and where a number of roads coming in from the hill country make a desirable trading point where are ample church and school facilities and a live whole-souled people.

Going north from Greenwood ten miles is found the third town of size and importance in the county, Shell Mound, on the right bank of the Tallahatchie river, which is the entrepot of supplies for a large territory embracing the farms on the McNutt lake and Quiver river, where is raised the finest staple of cotton in the world. McNutt, situated on a lake of the same name, was once the county seat of old Sunflower county, and while the march of improvement has turned aside from this once thriving inland town, it still boasts of its school and church and is noted for the hospitality of its people.

Emmaville is a pretty village on the right bank of the Tallahatchie. Railway facilities which are promised will cause Red Cross, Shannondale and Minter city, three beautiful little villages on the Tallahatchie river, to develop into towns of some size.

Sheppardtown, ten miles south from Sidon, on the right bank of the Yazoo river, is another thriving village having the rich land of Bear creek from which to draw its trade and still farther down the Yazoo at stated intervals can be found large storehouses where clever merchants do a good business. Between Sidon and Rising Sun, on the right bank of the river, is Roebuck landing, one of the best trading points in the county, where an immense business is done. Going west from there around Roebuck lake, a cutoff of the Yazoo, are to be found several stores, and at Itta Bena, where the line of the Georgia Pacific railroad crosses that lake, quite a village has been built. Fort Loring, where the same railroad crosses the Yazoo river three miles west from Greenwood, has attained importance.

Besides Greenwood, this county has the following towns and villages: Itta Bena, Sidon, Shell Mound, Minter city, Sunnyside, Old McNutt, Rising Sun and Red Cross.

Friar's Point, the seat of justice of Coahoma county, is located on the Mississippi river and on the Louisville, New Orleans & Texas railroad, and has a population of seven hundred and seventy-six. Coahoma county was established February 9, 1836, and its courthouse and public offices have been located at various times at Delta, Port Royal, again at Delta and at Friar's Point, where good county buildings have been erected. Since the construction of the railroads, of which several lines intersect the county, Friar's Point has greatly improved, and is now, with a good hotel, several manufacturing establishments and the bank of Friar's Point, Friar's Point Improvement company, and the Friar's Point Building & Loan association, and many large mercantile houses, one of the busiest towns of its size in any state.

Clarksdale is a new town, having been built up since the advent of the railroad in 1884, but is now the metropolis of the county, with eight hundred. It is a railroad junction of importance, and its site is well chosen, beautiful and advantageous, on high ground above overflow at the head of navigation of Sunflower river. Clarksdale, Coahoma county, has grown up since 1884. Until then its site was occupied by only the store of John Clark, the owner of a plantation including the site. The advent of the Louisville, New Orleans & Texas railway, about that time, caused the beginning of the growth of a town which now has a population of eight hundred and is incorporated. Clarksdale lies in the very heart of the great delta region, one hundred and seventy-seven miles from Memphis and three hundred and eighty-three miles from New Orleans. The amount of cotton handled reaches fifteen thousand bales per season, with good prospects for from eighteen thousand to twenty thousand bales during the present one, based upon the increased acreage and unusually fine crop prospects. Clarksdale has recently been made an interior town by the New York cotton exchange, something unusual for a place of its population. One among the largest and most complete cotton-seed oilmills in the South is located there, and a cotton compress has been built. There are also a large sawmill, public gin and gristmill in Clarksdale, and a substantial banking house, the Clarksdale Bank & Trust company, the successors of the Central City bank, organized in 1888. The civic societies, Masons, Odd Fellows, Knights of Pythias, Knights of Honor and others, have flourishing lodges and strong memberships.

About fifty-five years ago the wife of a Choctaw chief gave her name to Attala county, and the settlement known then as Redbud was rechristened after the illustrious Polish hero. Kosciusko, in its early days, must have been a wild place. It was the haunt of robbers and desperadoes of all kinds, but it has undergone a very radical change, so that at present Mississippi knows no more orderly, peaceable or proportionately solid constituency. The county seat of Attala is a cotton town of one thousand six hundred and fifty inhabitants. Kosciusko enjoys the trade of three adjoining counties—Leake, Winston and Neshoba. It also draws a little from Choctaw and Montgomery counties. The country around is almost entirely in the hands of white small farmers, and a large proportion of the colored people own their own lands.

About twelve years ago Kosciusko became a railroad town, and is now one of the most prominent stations on the Canton, Aberdeen & Nashville branch of the Illinois Central railroad. The coming of the railroad naturally helped to develop the place.

The Yockanowkaney river, one and a half miles from the town, affords a wonderful natural water power, which would be invaluable for mill purposes. Kosciusko would, in fact, be a first-rate location for a mill or factory. Already two wagon factories are in full operation here and are supplying all the home demand. All except the wheel timber is of local growth. Other industries here are a barrel factory, a furniture factory, two sawmills, a gristmill and gin and an extensive flouringmill.

Kosciusko is a well-governed, orderly, breezy little city. It boasts of a cozy little opera house, has good public schools, open ten months in the year, and its churches are eight in number, of which three belong to the colored people. The denominations represented are Presbyterian, Methodist, Cumberland Presbyterian and Baptist. Rev. Dr. J. H. Alexander has been pastor of the Presbyterian church since 1855. The town was named Pekin in 1833, was later called Paris, and since about 1830 has been known as Kosciusko.

Trinity lodge No. 88, A. F. & A. M., Royal Arch chapter No. 20, the local lodge K. & L. of H., and Farmers' Alliance No. 105 are flourishing societies at Kosciusko.

Other towns in this county are Ethel, named in honor of a daughter of Capt. S. B. McConnies; Sallis, named in honor of Dr. James Sallis, and McCool, named in honor of Hon. James F. McCool. The Methodists and Presbyterians have good houses of worship at Sallis.

Quitman, the seat of justice of Clarke county, was named in honor of Gen. John A. Quitman. The land upon which the town is built was owned and laid off into town lots by Gen. John Watts, afterward for many years judge of the circuit court. The population is four hundred and ten.

Enterprise, Miss., lies in the northwestern portion of Clarke county, and has both the Mississippi & Ohio and New Orleans & Northeastern railways to carry its products to all the great markets of the country. It also lies at the junction of Chunkey and Tibbee creeks, which here form the important Chickasawhay river, which in times gone by was navigable to the gulf, and from this place alone was wont to transport sixty-five thousand bales of cotton annually.

This place was founded by John J. McRae, afterward governor of the state. Its population, one thousand one hundred and thirty, and its annual cotton shipment amounts to four thousand bales. It has a number of substantial business houses, a cottonmill, gristmill and gin and the Wanita woolenmills a short distance from the corporation limits. There is also a line of street railway which connects the two depots, furnishing transit between the east and west ends, as the river divides the town. Schools, churches, and civil societies are found here, and as a place of residence it is highly spoken of. An excellent agricultural country surrounds the town, and its trade is largely drawn from adjoining counties, whose people find a good market.

Take the agricultural and timber resources of the county alone and they will, when fully developed, serve to support a place of ten thousand inhabitants, but when to these be added inexhaustible deposits of the richest iron ores, it will rightly be conjectured that Enterprise has a magnificent future before it, and that a second Birmingham will soon be found here.

From the explorations already made, it has been determined that heavy deposits of liminite ores exist in this vicinity, covering an area of country four miles wide by ten long, the trend being from northwest to southeast, and the dip of the strata being about thirty feet to the mile. From the analyses given farther along, it will be observed that being exceedingly rich in quartz, clay and lime, it will require little if any other additional flux; but if it should, there exist in close proximity, great ledges of the finest limestone, which will yield an abundance of flux for centuries. The ore stratum is solid and well defined, and runs in an average depth of twelve and one-half feet, although it often reaches a depth of twenty feet and more. Another peculiarity of this ore is that it is easily mined, and it is loose as a gravel bed almost, and can in many places be mined with a steam shovel. That it is exceedingly rich in iron and is easily reduced, the analyses show and furnace tests will confirm this. It now only remains for some one to erect a blast furnace between the two lines of railway, northeast of the city, right in the heart of the ore beds, where excellent water is abundant, and where charcoal can be made in the great forests surrounding. There is a most excellent site in the locality mentioned that ought, and doubtless will be, utilized for that purpose. But in the event that charcoal should not be found desirable for reduction purposes, it is but a short distance to the Warrior coal fields and great coke arms at and near Birmingham, with a line of road directly to them, or to the Patton mines reached via the Mississippi & Ohio and Grand Pacific railways, either of which could lay the coke down here at rates that would render the smelting at this point profitable. The Alabama Land & Development company has more than one hundred thousand acres of land in Clarke county.

The following analysis of the iron ore found at Enterprise will prove conclusively that the deposits of iron in this section, while inexhaustible, are also of remarkable richness and very easy of reduction, besides containing the requisite flux without the addition of limestone. Of a specimen of iron ore received from Mr. L. B. Brown for Dr. Moore, Enterprise: Carbonate of protoxide of iron, 37.5; peroxide of iron, 17.14; sulphuric acid, 1.52; phosphoric acid, 1.4; carbonate of lime, 5.5; quartz, sand, clay and organic matter, 36.; metallic iron in ore, 30.12; phosphorous in phosphoric acid, .62; sulphur in sulphuric acid, .61. Extract from a letter from Joseph Albrecht, analytical chemist, New Orleans, accompanying the above analysis: "The ore contains no manganese and no other deleterious matters except those stated in the analysis; it must be roasted before it can be melted, but it is of easy reduction, wants no addition (in my opinion), as the quartz, clay and lime will form the necessary flux or slag required." Report of analysis by Charles Mohr & Son, analytical chemists, Mobile: "The material sent to us has been submitted to chemical analysis with the following results: Volatile matter (moisture and combined water and organic matter), 24.3; oxide of iron, 45.4; other metallic oxides, principally alumina, 7.8; silica (sand), 22.5. The 45.4 per cent. ferric oxide represents 35.58 per cent. metallic iron."

Pontotoc, the seat of justice of Pontotoc county, was long the second town in North Mississippi in population and importance. The location of the land offices for the Chickasaw Indians, it early became a favorite field for commerce and speculation, and was the scene of busines transactions involving goodly amounts for the time. Among its early men of prominence were: William Y. Gholson, Charles Fontaine, Thomas J. Word, Judge R. Miller, William and James Davis and others equally well known. In point of intelligence the men and women of Pontotoc have always ranked above the average, and many of them amassed good fortunes and lived lives of leisure, devoted to the pursuit of art, literature and science. The United States court was held here for some years. The town was incorporated in 1837, and now has a population of about one thousand. It is located on the Gulf & Chicago railroad, being the terminus of the Pontotoc & Middleton branch of that system, and is the only place in the county except Cherry Creek (population one hundred and seventy-five) that has railroad facilities. Its business men are enterprising and progressive, and it is the center of a good country trade.

Ripley, the seat of justice of Tippah county, has a population of seven hundred and fifty, which ranks high for refinement, intelligence and enterprise, and is an important station of the Gulf & Chicago railroad. It is the center of a growing trade, and has attracted the attention of manufacturers. Its merchants, lawyers, physicians, and business men generally, are noted for their integrity and their ability. Other towns in Tippah county are, Dumas, Falkner, Brooklyn, Ruckenville, Guyton, Tiplersville, Cotton Plant, Blue Mountain, Lowrey, Silver Springs and Brigaba.

Iuka, the seat of justice of Tishomingo county, has over one thousand inhabitants and is situated on the Memphis & Charleston railroad. One hundred and fifteen miles east of Memphis, six miles from Alabama line, seven miles from the Tennessee river, upon one of the most elevated sections of Mississippi; readily accessible by the Memphis & Charleston railroad and its connections. The country around is hilly, and has been termed "The Switzerland of Mississippi." The corporation is one mile square. Every house is surrounded by ample grounds of orchard, park and garden. There are five churches, all with active, earnest membership, and a flourishing normal school. Cordial, hospitable, wide-awake, and energetic, the inhabitants of Iuka are pleasant people with whom to cast one's lot. Its people are educated and refined, and its business is flourishing and growing. Other towns in the county are Bay Springs, Cartersville, Eastport and Burnsville.

The site of Yazoo City, the justice seat of Yazoo county, was an Indian reservation, entered by Greenwood Le Fleur in 1827, under the provisions of the treaty of Washington, concluded January 20, 1825, with the Choctaw Indians. Yazoo City was first called Hannon's Bluff and afterward incorporated as Manchester, and subsequently as Yazoo City, the name having been changed about 1845. This town, the gem city of the world-famous Yazoo, Miss., delta country, is situated upon the eastern bank of the Yazoo river. The site is a well-chosen and wonderfully advantageous one, gently sloping back to the bluffs in the rear. A better or prettier site for a city could not have been selected. At its wharves are always seen steamboats loading and unloading, while along the levee run the tracks of the Illinois Central railroad, its depot, freight and warehouses presenting an equally busy scene. Along its principal business street are large, substantial brick business houses, fronted with iron, stone and plate glass, presenting a metropolitan appearance, giving the stranger an agreeable impression of its commercial importance. The streets are broad, beautifully graded, macadamized with gravel and well guttered.

Its population is five thousand two hundred and forty-seven, and its growth is steady, it having more than doubled since the close of the war. During the past few years improvements have been more rapid and of a much superior nature. Owing to its splendid navigation and railroad system it should, and doubtless will, become Mississippi's greatest industrial city. Its present industries consist of one large sawmill, a cotton seedmill, containing all the latest improved machinery, a large, first-class compress, a mill and gin, one ice factory and four substantial brick cotton warehouses. There are also brickyards, making an excellent quality of brick, used locally and shipped to other points. Two creameries are in operation, turning out large quantities of fine butter. Two amply capitalized banking houses furnish satisfactory facilities.

Two steamboat lines run regular packets from Yazoo City. The river navigation extends north over two hundred miles, and to the Mississippi river south, connecting with the Big and Little Sunflower rivers, and Lake George, etc. Some twelve hundred and fifty miles of navigable rivers, penetrating the South's greatest cotton and corn regions, are made accessible and tributary to Yazoo City, which, by reason of its comprehensive railroad and river navigation system, should naturally develop into a great jobbing center, as well as an industrial city.

In the matter of public schools, Yazoo City is well supplied, there being not less than three, with a large enrollment of pupils. There are also private schools, notably, the convent or Catholic school. There are also five white churches in the city, some of whose edifices of worship are noble and imposing specimens of architectural beauty. The principal civic societies are also represented by flourishing lodges, while a public library and social club are attractive and pleasing features. There is an operahouse with a seating capacity of seven hundred.

The city limits extend one mile north and south, and a mile and a half east and west. The sidewalks are usually of brick. Another attractive feature is the great number of ornamental trees by which the streets are shaded, as well as the evergreen shrubbery and semitropical exotics adorning the grounds of the different residences. The city has an efficient and well-equipped fire department, having two engines and one hook and ladder company.

The county courthouse, a beautiful and imposing structure, was erected at a cost of $80,000. A substantial city jail has also been built at an outlay of $12,500. A fine iron bridge has been built across the Yazoo river, in order to facilitate trade from the west, at a cost of $30,000.

Socially, as well as in a business sense, the people of Yazoo City are a very superior class, being noted for enterprise and progressive tendencies. They have full faith in the future of their charming little city, and are ever ready to further its interests by all means within their power. The city government is vested in a mayor and board of aldermen, numbering eight, a clerk, treasurer, assessor and collector, attorney and city marshal. It is a popular administration, and is made up of men who guard the interests of the public with conservative care.

The local capitalists are not averse to engaging in new enterprises, and will meet outside men of means half way in the matter of sites for manufacturing establishments or taking stock in the same. But Yazoo City has something better to offer the manufacturer and capitalist than a mere subsidy of money or land, and that is location, which, after all, is what insures the success of every industrial enterprise. By its railroad system not less than thirty counties in Mississippi and six different states and territories are reached, while its fine navigable river makes tributary the most fertile and productive portion of the lower Mississippi valley, with all the tributary streams of the Father of Waters. The raw material can be floated to its factory doors, almost without cost, while the same highway, aided by the railroad, serves to distribute the product to every great consuming center in the country. The First National bank was organized in September, 1886, with a capital paid up of $50,000, to which has since been added a large surplus. It is located in a new building at the corner of Main and Bridge streets, specially arranged for the business, the interior being arranged in modern style, while fire and burglar-proof vault and safes effectually guard the treasure. A general banking, exchange, deposit and collection business is transacted by this bank, and any one requiring the services of a reliable correspondent in this section will do well to engage its services. The officers of the First National are: L. Lippman, president; Charles Mann, vice president; and R. L. Bennett, cashier, under whose careful and conservative management its affairs have thriven and the business widely extended. The directory is made up of L. Lippman, Charles Mann, L. B. Warren, J. H. D. Haverkamp, John Lear, E. A. Jackson and E. Drenning, who are all well known as leading capitalists, merchants and professional men of Yazoo City. The bank's correspondents are the Mercantile National, New York; Union National, New Orleans; Kentucky National, Louisville; and the Prairie State National, Chicago. The establishment of this bank was the outgrowth of Yazoo City's urgent demand for increased banking facilities.

The Bank of Yazoo City, the pioneer banking house of Yazoo City, was established in the year 1876, with a paid-up capital of $100,000, to which has since been added a large surplus. This bank has the handsomest and most attractive building on Main street. The interior is fitted up in elegant style, such as prevails in metropolitan banking houses, and is equipped with fireproof vaults, steel safes and time lock. The building was erected at a cost of $10,000. This institution does a general banking business in all its branches, and is regarded as one of the safest banks in the state. Its correspondents are the National Park bank, New York, and the Louisiana National bank, of New Orleans. The officers are R. C. Shepherd, president; Charles Roberts, vice president, and S. R. Berry, cashier, men of extensive experience as bank managers, who are well known and stand high in financial circles. The directors are R. C. Shepherd, J. H. D. Haverkamp, J. J. Fouche, J. N. Gilruth, J. F. Powell, William Hamel, W. C. Craig and Louis Wise, all of whom will be recognized as being among Yazoo City's leading capitalists, largest and most successful business men and manufacturers.

Walthall is the seat of justice of Webster county. It is located near the center of the county and has a population of two hundred and fifty. It was named in honor of Senator Walthall. This is a good interior trading point, which, though remote from railroads, has attained to some local commercial importance.

Among the secret orders represented in Webster, as elsewhere, the Masonic order is prominent. Among the A. F. & A. M. lodges organized here are the following: Adelphi lodge No. 174 of Walthall, which was chartered January 17, 1853, and for many years held its meetings at Bellefontaine; Eldorado lodge No. 184, at Cumberland; New Hope lodge, which for some years met at New Hope church, now meets at Maben, Oktibbeha county, and Greensboro lodge No. 49, which was chartered early in the forties, and is the oldest lodge in the county.

Eupora, on the Richmond & Danville railroad, is a point of growing importance.

Waynesboro, the seat of justice of Wayne county, is situated northwest of the center of the county, on the Mobile & Ohio railroad, and has a population of three hundred. The first county seat of this county was Winchester, five miles south of Waynesboro, and on the Mobile & Ohio railroad. About 1822 the courthouse at Winchester was destroyed by fire. It was rebuilt and is now standing. The old jail also yet stands at Winchester, built in the forties, with walls three feet thick of heavy hewed pine, by John McDonald, at a cost to the county of $400 or $500. The county seat was located at Waynesboro in 1870. Schools were introduced in this county by itinerant teachers. One of them, Samuel M. Dickson, taught a classical school three miles and a half south of Winchester, on the Mobile road. Patterson taught on the Ridge next; Jacob Collins taught also on the Ridge east of Winchester; General Falconer and John A. Edwards alternated at the Ridge about 1828.

Among early churches in Wayne county were: Zion (Baptist), on the Ridge, of which William Powell and Nathan Clay, Jr., were early pastors; Salem (Baptist), in the present town of Waynesboro, though it stood at first on the Winchester road, William Morris, noted for his arbitrary rulings, acting as pastor in the twenties. Rev. Mr. Chambers was another early Baptist preacher here. The Methodists preached in the old Winchester courthouse in early days. Rev. William A. Cotton was a noted early circuit rider, and is said to have been something of a fighter when occasion demanded.

Magnolia, on the Illinois Central railroad, is the seat of justice of Pike county. It had its start upon the completion of the railroad to that point in 1856. The county seat was located here in 1875. Among Magnolia's early business men were: L. R. Jones, carpenter, who built the first business house in the town; Robert L. Carter, W. H. Joyner, W. H. B. Crosswell, Joseph Evans and Abraham Hiller, merchants; L. Gournly, first postmaster, and E. M. Bee, the first depot agent, who served nineteen years. The population is seven hundred and fifty.

Holmesville was the first incorporated village of the county. It was incorporated in 1817. Osyka was the next, and for two years was the terminus of the Illinois Central railroad.

Meadville, the seat of justice of Franklin county, is located near the center of the county, and has a population of two hundred and fifty. The Franklin *Journal* was the first newspaper published in this county. It was issued in the summer of 1866 by one Crawford, who was a deaf mute. After several changes in ownership it became known as the Franklin *Banner*, and was published under that name by a son of Judge McGee for three years, until the death of the publisher. The Franklin *Herald* was established at Hamburg in 1886. In 1890 P. C. Thompson bought the material and took it to Knoxville, and there published the *Southern Progress* until the latter part of that year, when it was removed to Garden City, where it is still issued, with C. F. Thompson as editor, and P. C. Thompson as manager. Hamburg, on the Louisville, New Orleans & Texas railroad, in Franklin county, has a population of one hundred and fifty. Roxie, south of Hamburg, on the same line, dates its history from 1885, and has a population of two hundred and twenty-five. Knoxville, on the railroad still farther south, has a population of one hundred and fifty. The county seat was at first located at Franklin, which was two and a half miles west of the site of Meadville. Early churches of this county are mentioned elsewhere.

Indianola, the seat of justice of Sunflower county, is a thrifty and prosperous little town on the Georgia Pacific railroad, in close proximity to some plantations and farms, and has grown steadily since the date of its location. Its population at this time is three hundred and seventy-five. It was incorporated in 1886, and its first mayor was I. C. W. McLeod. The first seat of justice of this county was at McNutt, later it was removed to Johnsonville, on Sunflower river, and thence, a few years after, to Indianola.

De Kalb, the seat of justice of Kemper county, is located as nearly as may be in the geographical center of the county, and has a population of three hundred and four. It has no railway facilities, but is the trading point for a considerable area round about and is prosperous in all its interests.

The Free-Will Baptist church was founded in Kemper county in 1882 by Rev. C. F. Johnson, a sketch of whose life appears in this work. The doctrine of the church indicates salvation free to all and obedience and faith in Christ, also free communion at the Lord's Supper with all orthodox Christians, and baptism by immersion exclusively. The government is congregational. The church consists of about thirty members.

The courthouse in Kemper county, with the county records and public documents, was burned in 1881.

Other towns in this county are Oak Grove, Scooba, Wahalak, Moscow and Kellis Store.

Neshoba county is remote from railroads and has never felt the influence of railway facilities upon its development. Hence its towns, though enjoying a good local trade and peopled by a sturdy, enterprising and intelligent class, have none of them attained to any considerable size. Philadelphia, the seat of justice, has a population of about one hundred. Other villages within the borders of the county are Dowdville, Laurel Hill, Dixon, New Hope, Java, North Bend and Milldale.

Booneville, the seat of justice of Prentiss county, is a thriving station on the Mobile & Ohio railroad, and has a population of eight hundred. It is the center of a good trade, and has good schools, ample church accommodations and an intelligent, well-educated, progressive class of citizens. Other towns in this county are Marietta, Carrollsville, Elma, Baldwyn (See Tupelo, Lee county, etc.), old Cairo and Beulah.

Monticello, Lawrence county's seat of justice, was incorporated in 1818. Monticello academy was established in 1836 with John E. McNair as its first principal. Mr. McNair was afterward a circuit judge of great popularity. One of the first papers was the *Southern Journal*, edited by John R. Chambers. Among local papers well known in this part of the state may be mentioned the Monticello *Advocate*, by S. W. Dale, and the *Sunny South*, by C. N. Jones. The *Lawrence County Press*, by Joseph Dale, son of S. W. Dale, is an able journal, and the only paper now published in the county. The first church in the county was established at Monticello. It was of the Methodist denomination. The Baptists organized a few years afterward. Silver Creek Baptist church was organized in 1815, and has a membership of two hundred. Bethany church (Baptist), on White Sand, was organized in 1819, under the labors of Elder John P. Martin, one of the leading pioneer ministers of the state, who was succeeded by Norvel Robertson for more than forty years. A branch of the Planters' bank was established at Monticello soon after 1830. Monticello at one time did a large and extensive business, and had an able bar, comprising some of the best talent in the South. The superior court was held at this place for some years, and the vice chancery court until 1854. It was here that the lamented S. S. Prentis[s] received his license to practice law. Monticello was selected as the site of the state cap[i]tal at a session of the legislature convened at Columbia—just before Jackson was made th[e] capital of the state—when Mr. Runnels was in the senate and Mr. Cooper in the house [of] representatives. They were both prominent citizens of Monticello and leaders in selectin[g] Monticello as the state capital, and by their efforts it was located here. After they ha[d] secured the vote in favor of Monticello, they returned to their home to bear the news [of] their success to their constituents, and in their absence a motion was made to reconsider th[e] vote, and Jackson was then given the honor thus unfairly wrested from Monticello.

Following is Monticello's church and society directory: Churches: Baptist—Thir[d] Sunday and Saturday in every month at 11 o'clock A. M.; Sunday-school every Sun[-]day at 3 P. M.; Rev. R. W. Hall, pastor. Presbyterian—First Sunday in every month [at] 11 o'clock A. M. and 7:30 P. M.; Sunday-school every Sunday at 10 A. M.; Rev. George [C.] Woodbridge, pastor. Methodist—Fourth Sunday in each month at 11 A. M. and 7:30 P. M[.] Rev. R. Havers, pastor. A. F. & A. M. lodge—Third Saturday in every month at 1 o'clock A. M.; Z. P. Jones, W. M. Monticello Farmers' Alliance—First Saturday in ever[y] month at 3 o'clock P. M.; Will C. Cannon, president.

Sardis, one of the two seats of justice of Panola county, was incorporated in 1857, an[d] Dr. S. F. Dunlap was its first mayor. The town was named by Mr. W. H. Alexander, wh[o] was the first postmaster and is now proprietor of the town of Mastodon in the western pa[rt] of the county. The church houses in Sardis are Methodist (South), Presbyterian, Baptis[t,] Episcopal and Catholic. Other denominations have organizations but no house of worshi[p.] Sardis has a population of one thousand, and is an enterprising station on the Illino[is] Central railroad.

Batesville, farther south on the same line, is the seat of justice of the second judici[al] district of Panola county. It has a population of six hundred and twenty-five.

Belen and Marks are the towns of Quitman county. Belen, the seat of justice, has [a] population of about one hundred and twenty-five. There are in this county good publi[c] schools and quite a number of churches of different denominations.

Brandon, the county town of Rankin county, is a station on the Alabama & Vicksbur[g] railroad and has a population of six hundred. It was named after Gov. Gerard C. Brando[n] and was early known as the seat of the famous Brandon bank, of which Col. William H. Shelto[n] was president. Situated on the highest point between Vicksburg and Jackson, this place [is] exceptionally healthy. For years it was the terminus of the Vicksburg & Meridian railroa[d] and the trading point for several adjacent counties. For more than twenty-five years th[e] Brandon Female college has been in charge of Miss Johnston, one of the most celebrate[d] teachers in Mississippi, who has perhaps done more to enrich the culture and intelligence [of] the town and its vicinity than any one else. Other towns in this county are Steen's Creek[,] Cato, Fannin, Pelahatchee and Armistead.

Paulding, the county seat of Jasper county, has a population of two hundred and thirt[y.] It is situated a little east of the center of the county and has no railway communication. [It] has a good country trade, however, and is the center of a considerable business.

It was in Jasper county that Dr. J. N. Waddell, who afterward became chancellor [of] the University of Mississippi and later of the Southwestern university at Clarksville, Tenn.[,] began his career as a teacher. The *Clarion Ledger* was first edited here under the name [of] the *Eastern Clarion*.

Garlandsville, Heidelburg. Lake Como and Vosburg are other towns in this county.

Louisville, the county seat of Winston county, has a population of three hundred and seventy-five, and is a thriving and progressive inland town with no railroad connection. It contains several good store buildings, some sightly church edifices and a creditable courthouse. The land on which the county buildings are located was donated to Winston county by Jane Dodson.

The first newspaper issued in Winston county was the *Times-Tablet* and *Mississippi Gazette*, published in 1844, at Louisville. The next paper was the *Chronicle*, established prior to the war, and after the war came the *Bulletin*, and later the *Banner*, followed by the *Index* and the *Signal*. The last mentioned paper was started by W. J. Newsom, present editor and proprietor.

Louisville lodge No. 75, A. F. & A. M., was organized under a dispensation granted in 1845, and was chartered January 10, 1846. Other lodges in the county are Webster lodge No. 205, Winstonville lodge No. 277, and Perkinsville lodge No. 331.

In Winston the Masonic society, Odd Fellows, Grange, Alliance, etc., are represented. There are several normal and low-grade schools throughout the county. At Louisville, Plattsburg and Betheden there are churches of the Methodist, Baptist, old style Presbyterians, Cumberland Presbyterians, Catholic, Lutheran and Campbellite or Christian denominations.

The county seat of Scott county, in 1836, was established at Hillsboro, which was well located and has grown to a prosperous little town of about one hundred and seventy five. Thirty years later it was removed to Forest, on the Vicksburg & Meridian railroad, a good trading point, which has six hundred and three inhabitants, with good schools, a number of churches, several stores and manufactories, and other claims to growth and prosperity. Other towns in this county are Lake, Raworth and Morton.

Charleston, the county seat of Tallahatchie county, is a flourishing trading point of four hundred and seventy-five population, situated east of the center of the county, in the forks of the Tillataba. Sharkey and Graball are small trading points. Harrison station on the Illinois Central railroad has a population of three hundred.

Churches abound all over Tallahatchie county, the prevailing denominations being Baptist, Presbyterian and Methodist. The educational advantages afforded are equal to those in other counties, except in those having cities and large towns. The common-school system is well sustained. There are in this county thirty-two free white schools and thirty-eight colored. The white educable children number one thousand four hundred and forty-one—seven hundred and thirteen males and seven hundred and twenty-eight females; two thousand one hundred and six colored; of these, one thousand and ninety-two males and one thousand and fourteen females. There are two high schools in the county, each with a commodious and handsome building, one at Spring Hill (the Cascilla Male and Female high school, established in 1889), and the other at Cascilla (the Tallahatchie high school, established in 1889). The school at Charleston is also of high grade and prospering.

George Washington lodge No. 157, A. F. & A. M., at Charleston, is the oldest lodge in the county. It was chartered in 1851 and James W. Rhew was its first worshipful master. Glasgow lodge No. 354, at Harrison Station, has a good membership. Cascilla lodge No. 411 was established in 1890, with Thomas Denman as worshipful master. Tallahatchie lodge once flourished. Sycamore and Hood lodges have a healthy existence. A. Mason Leigh lodge No. 3233, K. of H., at Charleston, was organized in 1886. Charleston lodge No.

108, I. O. O. F., was established March 4, 1880. T. W. White was its first noble grand. Rebecca degree No. 3 was established in 1891. Sam Lawrence lodge No. 110, I. O. O. F., at Cascilla, was established in April, 1890, with H. M. Moore as noble grand. Rebecca degree No. 2 was chartered in 1891.

Westville, the seat of justice of Simpson county, was named in honor of Col. Cato West. It is located a little south and west of the center of the county and has a population of two hundred. As a business point it draws a good trade from the surrounding country, and it is peopled with an educated and intelligent population and well provided with churches and schools. Jaynesville and Harrisville are other towns in this county.

Raleigh, the county seat of Smith county, received its name in honor of the dashing but ill-fated Sir Walter Raleigh. It is located a little west of the center of the county, and has a population of two hundred. Its churches and schools are adequate to its needs, and its people are refined, educated and intelligent. It has a good variety and number of business places, and its merchants and professional men take high rank for integrity and talent. The first seat of justice was four miles distant from Raleigh, and was called Fairfield. In this county Parkville grew up on the west side of Strong river more than forty years ago, and Trenton, on the east side, had its beginning a few years later. Other towns and trading points are Sylvarena, Pineville, Taylorsville and Bunker Hill.

Carrollton, on the Richmond & Danville railroad, is the seat of justice of Carroll county, and has a population of four hundred and seventy-five. It has a good local trade, and its future is as promising as that of any town of its size in that part of the state. A Baptist church was organized ten miles from Carrollton, in 1833, with nine members, and was moved to Carrollton in 1839 and named Carrollton church, afterward growing rapidly. Its first pastor was Rev. Joseph Morris. About 1839 Rev. S. S. Lattimore, one of the first and most prominent preachers in the state, served one year as pastor. In all, the church has had nineteen pastors, some of them very talented men. The Presbyterian church was established here about 1836, and the church house was built about 1837. The Methodist Episcopal and the Protestant Episcopal churches were established before the war. Carrollton lodge No. 36, A. F. & A. M., was organized about 1837, Judge Blanks, V. M. Butler and O. L. Kimbrough being among the early members. This lodge had at one time about seventy-five members, and has now about twenty-eight. Its present master is G. S. Fox. Benjamin Roach has been secretary since 1856.

Vaiden, on the Illinois Central railroad, is a flourishing town of nine hundred population. Black Hawk and Shongaloo are other towns in Carroll county.

When the Mississippi Central railroad was built the people of Carrollton projected two large enterprises: The factory and the Carrollton Female college. They erected a massive structure for manufacturing, covering an acre of ground. The Carrollton Female college building they made ample and commodious. It has been under the management of some fine educators, among whom, worthy of especial mention, are Rev. Mr. Colmery and Captain Belcher. Under its present management, that of Rev. Z. T. Leavell, its success has been remarkable. The faculty is not excelled by any institution for young ladies in the state, for thoroughness and conscientious work. The friends of the college are now very sanguine as to its future.

Senatobia, the seat of justice of Tate county, is located on the Illinois Central railroad a little south of the center of the county, and has a population of one thousand one hundred

and twenty-five. This town is one of the most enterprising of the smaller important towns of the state, is handsomely located and well sustained in its every interest, business, professional, religious, educational and social. It is a cotton-shipping point of prominence and has a large general trade. Other towns in this county are Coldwater Depot, Arkabutla, Independence, Looxahoma, Tyro and Strayhorn.

Houston, the seat of justice of Chickasaw county, is an attractive town of six hundred and fifty population, located near Chico creek, west of the center of the county. It was incorporated in May, 1837.

Okolona, the metropolis of Chickasaw county, on the Mobile & Ohio railroad, has a population of nineteen hundred and fifty, and is a good business point. The town is forty odd years old, and the post office was formerly Rose Hill, about one mile west of where the town now is. It has Presbyterian, Baptist, Methodist and Catholic churches. There is a fine brick public school building erected in 1890, at a cost of about $18,000.

Prof. H. B. Abernethy, founder of the Mississippi Normal college, Houston, is a native of Mississippi, born near Troy, Pontotoc county, in 1854. His father, J. T., and his mother, Emmaline (Porter) Abernethy, were natives of Alabama and South Carolina, respectively. They reared a family of eight children, of whom Professor Abernethy is the eldest. The father, who was a farmer, and was for a number of years bailiff of the county, died in 1875; the mother is yet living. No educational advantages, other than those afforded by public schools, were given our subject up to the time he was grown; such school he attended not less than four months in the year. At eighteen years of age he began teaching, and followed that occupation four years, and during the vacations in which there were no schools he conducted a farm. He married, in 1876, Miss Sallie L. Gossett, a native of Pontotoc county, a graduate of the Baptist Female college, and at the time of her marriage a teacher. Four years later they attended the National Normal university at Lebanon, Ohio, where they remained two years, graduating in 1882, Mr. Abernethy with the degree of B. S., Mrs. A. with the degree of A. B. Immediately upon their return they opened a school at Troy. At its start, in 1882, that now noted school, the Mississippi Normal college, the first of its class in Mississippi, was located at Troy, Pontotoc county. It was opened with four teachers: Prof. H. B. Abernethy, the founder, was principal; Mrs. S. G. Abernethy, assistant; J. U. Abernethy, in charge of the preparatory class; Miss Dora Abernethy, teacher of music. The school was the private enterprise of Professor Abernethy. The buildings used were Professor Abernethy's one building, 30x60, two stories high, with six recitation rooms and a large hall. There was a separate boardinghouse, with a capacity for forty boarders. This was for ladies only; gentlemen boarded at private houses. The first year the school had one hundred and seventeen pupils, principally local, only about twenty-five being boarders. The succeeding five years, during which the school was located at Troy, were marked by steady growth, until the last year three hundred and twenty pupils were enrolled, twelve teachers were employed, and the institution had primary, preparatory, teachers,' commercial, scientific, classical, music (instrumental and vocal) and art departments. Mr. and Mrs. Abernethy have a son named Jene, born in 1878.

Okalona, the seat of the second judicial district, where the circuit and chancery courts are held, is a town of about two thousand inhabitants on the Mobile & Ohio railroad near the eastern border of Chickasaw county. It is surrounded by a fertile prairie and has considerable commercial importance and the best of educational and religious advantages.

Palo Alto, Buena Vista and Sparta are flourishing interior villages having good local trade.

The founders of the Buena Vista Normal college, appreciating the great need of an institution where a liberal education could be obtained at a minimum cost, organized that institution in 1885, and the state legislature chartered it in 1886. The great advantages offered by this institution have been recognized from the beginning. Its magic growth rests on the fact that it offers superior advantages and facilities for obtaining an education at less cost than any school of equal merit in the South. Neither money nor labor has been spared in maintaining the elevated position of the Buena Vista Normal college. Young men and young women who want an education, and are willing to study and work for it, can find here all the advantages and aids wanted. The charges for board and tuition have been placed at the smallest figures that can be afforded. Board, $7 to $10; tuition, $2 to $4; music and use of piano, $4; art, $2 to $4 per month. Prof. W. S. Burkes, the president of this institution, is an active, energetic, industrious and thoroughly equipped educator. The college is under the supervision of the following board of directors: Dr. J. T. Murdock, J. T. Parker, M. D., Capt. J. L. Pulliam, Dr. U. S. Williams, Maj. L. C. Sugg, G. T. Stillman, A. J. Aycock, A. A. Thompson, J. Y. Ball, J. C. Williams.

Prairie lodge No. 87, A. F. & A. M., was chartered in 1848, with Isaac Mullen as worshipful master. Okolona chapter No. 27 is a flourishing institution, with W. J. Lacy as high priest. Ivanhoe commandry No. 10 was chartered about 1872, with P. M. Lavery as commander. W. A. Bodembimer is the present commander. Okolona lodge No. 37, I. O. O. F., and Eva Clara lodge No. 5, Knights of Pythias, have large lists of members. Chickasaw lodge No. 720, Knights of Honor, was chartered in 1877, with J. S. Dugger as dictator. Victor lodge No. 199, Knights of the Golden Rule, was established in 1888. Atlanta lodge No. 362, A. F. & A. M., at Atlanta, is a popular institution of that place.

Tunica, the seat of justice of Tunica county, is a town of four hundred and fifty inhabitants, on the Louisville, New Orleans & Texas railroad, which is a shipping point for much cotton and has a large general trade. Its churches and schools are adequate to its needs, and its inhabitants are intelligent and well educated as a class. It has numerous stores and other business enterprises. Other towns in the county are Austin, Hollywood, Evansville and Robinsonville.

Chester, the seat of justice of Choctaw county, has a population of two hundred. It is an interior trading point which is gaining in importance. French Camp has two hundred and seventy-five inhabitants and a good local trade.

One of the best schools in the state is at French Camps, Choctaw county, under the management of the Central Mississippi presbytery, and is in two divisions: first, the Central Mississippi institute for females, established in 1886, Rev. A. H. Macklin being president of the faculty; second, the French Camps academy for males, established in 1887, of which J. A. Macklin is president. Each has commodious buildings and boardinghouses, and a beautiful campus, about $15,000 having been expended on these improvements. These institutions have a high course of study, including the languages, arts and sciences, fitting students in some branches to enter the state university.

Among the societies of Choctaw county may be mentioned: Snowsville lodge No. 119, A. F. & A. M., which met for some time at Bankston, then at different places, and afterward for a time at Chester, now meets at Ackerman; Bankston lodge No. 296, A. F. & A. M., which was organized and for some years met at Bankston, and at Chester since 1889; La Grange lodge No. 263, A. F. & A. M., at La Grange; Ackerman lodge No. 1290, K. & L. of H., which was established in 1888 with E. R. Seward as protector; French Camp lodge No. 1312, K. & L. of H., at French Camp, and lodge of K. of H., which was recently organized at Ackerman.

Hartford, the original seat of justice of Calhoun county, is now extinct. It was originally an old Indian settlement. In its prime it had several stores and other business and small manufacturing interests. Hartford lodge, A. F. & A. M., No. 155, was organized there in 1850, and in 1853 was removed to Pittsborough, where it became known as Pittsborough lodge No. 155. Early in the settlement there a Methodist church was organized and a house of worship was erected, and a large membership secured. The religious and all other interests here later clustered around Pittsborough.

Pittsborough was first settled in 1850. The Methodist Episcopal church was organized there in 1852, and the house of worship was erected in 1853. The Baptists erected their church in 1860. Thomas Odom put up the first building in the place for a grocery; Mr. Johnson the first hotel. Judge D. N. Bessy was the oldest settler. The town now has a population of three hundred and twenty-five.

Benela, originally an old Indian settlement, was settled by whites about 1840 by James McCright, and Richard Griffin came soon after. Capt. T. T. Enochs was the first merchant there. Benela lodge No. 140, A. F. & A. M., was organized in 1840; had at one time six hundred members, and is the oldest lodge in the county. The Methodist Episcopal church was organized soon after 1850 and has a large two-story building, which was built in 1886 at a cost of $1,000. Bentley was settled in 1844 by the Bentley family. The postoffice was established in 1878, and the first store was opened in 1879 by Patterson & St. Clair. Bethlehem Methodist Episcopal Church South was organized by the first settlers, and had at one time about eighty members. A good building was erected in 1880. There is here a good graded school conducted in a fine two-story building. Slate Spring was settled about 1857. The first house was built by Joseph Fox. This is the seat of one of the best graded schools in the county, with three hundred pupils, under the principalship of Prof. J. J. Higgins. Bethany church was organized in 1857 and has a membership of one hundred and fifty. The Methodist Episcopal church was organized in 1887. Slate Spring has a population of two hundred and fifty.

The first store at Sabougla was built by Stevens & Holden. The postoffice was established in 1878. The Cumberland Presbyterian church is the oldest organization in the place and was organized in 1884. It was a fine church building that cost $1,500. The Baptists have a church of small membership.

Big Creek was settled by Henry and James Bounds and D. A. Covington. J. J. Ramsey built the first store in 1846 and was succeeded as merchant here by J. R. M. Du Barry. The present village site was settled by the Boland family, and M. M. Boland began merchandising there in 1871. Chapel Hill lodge No. 227 was organized in 1857. The Methodist Episcopal Church South erected its house of worship in 1856 and has a membership of one hundred and fifty. Cole's Creek was settled by Samuel F. Provine in 1838. R. N. Provine established the first store in 1868. The postoffice was established in 1870. Shiloh Baptist church was organized in 1870, but a Baptist organization had existed here since 1840. There is a membership of one hundred. The school known as Cole's Creek academy was founded by R. N. Provine.

At Banner, William Redwine started a cooper shop, the first enterprise on the ground Brower & McCord were the first merchants. Banner lodge, A. F. & A. M., No. 329 was organized in 1870.

The Methodist Episcopal church was organized in 1858, and has a membership of fifty. The Banner academy was founded in 1886 by C. P. Gilmore. A. M. Arnold is its oldest settler now living in the place. Spring Creek Missionary Baptist church was organized by some of the first settlers, and has a membership of one hundred and fifty. Turkey Creek Missionary Baptist church was organized in 1840, and has a membership of one hundred and twenty-five. Sarepta was settled early. Theodosia lodge, A. F. & A. M., No. 182, once flourished here, but is now extinct. The Baptist church here has a membership of forty. The Methodists organized soon after 1830. Mr. A. McDonald is the oldest merhant and settler now living in the place.

The seat of justice of Union county is New Albany, which is located at the intersection of the Gulf & Chicago and Kansas City, Memphis & Birmingham railways, and has a population of eleven hundred and twenty-five. It is the center of a growing local trade, and a shipping point of importance. Its schools and churches are numerous, and its business and professional men and citizens generally are of a class unusually intelligent, well educated and refined. Wallerville, Ellistown, Blue Springs, Keownville, Baker, Ingomar, Rocky Ford and Myrtle are the other towns and trading points in Union county.

Poplarville, the seat of justice of the newly created Pearl River county, is located near the center of the county on the New Orleans & Northeastern railway, and has a population of about two hundred. Derby and Hillsdale are railway trading and shipping villages.

Rosedale, the seat of justice of Bolivar county, was incorporated in 1882. Ten years after it became the county seat, which in 1872 was removed from Beulah, six miles southwest, this point affording many advantages over the latter. Outside of the new additions recently laid out, the corporation contains fifty-two acres, the site being particularly well chosen and thoroughly protected from the encroachments of the river by the splendid levees of the lower levee district.

The river does not flow directly up to the city, but about three-fourths of a mile distant, a great advantage in itself, while Rosedale is at the same time the only river point touched by the Louisville, New Orleans & Texas railway (Bolivar loop) between Friar's Point and Greenville, a fortunate circumstance, as it is thus made a competitive point between river and rail transportation lines, and insures favorable rates to eastern and European markets.

Until the completion of the Bolivar loop line from Greenville, in December, 1888, Rosedale did not show any signs of ever becoming anything beyond a river town of one or two hundred inhabitants, and made little if any progress after the excitement attendant upon the county seat removal had died out; so that whatever of improvements one sees at present dates from that time. These improvements are many, and of a very creditable and substantial character indeed, and new buildings, public and private, representing an outlay of over $75,000, have been erected since the railroad entered the corporation limits, among them the new county courthouse, a beautiful and imposing structure of pressed brick, trimmed with white stone, which occupies the square in the center of the city. This is one of the handsomest courthouses in the state, and was erected at a cost of more than $30,000. In its rear has been built a handsome brick jail, which cost $16,000. The building occupied by the Bank of Rosedale also attracts much attention. The business of Rosedale is represented by four general stores, one drug store, one hotel, a number of liquor stores, restaurants, livery stable, two blacksmiths, a public ginnery, an ice house, one butcher, barbers, two newspapers and one bank, which has a paid-up capital of $100,000. There are also eleven attorneys, one insurance agent, three physicians and two real estate agents.

Carthage, the county town of Leake county, is located near the geographical center of the county and has a population of four hundred and twenty-five. It is an enterprising and progressive town and its citizens are ambitious and pushing. The former name, Leakeville, was superseded by the present name of Carthage, July 31, 1834. Other towns in this county are Ofahoma, Thomastown, Edinburgh, St. Anne, Good Hope, Lena, Grove and Madden, all small places, but each the center of a good local trade.

Augusta, the seat of justice of Perry county, is situated on the Pascagoula river north of the center of the county, and is a good local trading point. The population is one hundred and twenty-five.

Hattiesburgh, with a population of six hundred and fifty, is the only important town in Perry county. Perry lodge, Enon lodge and Hattiesburg lodge and chapter (at Hattiesburgh) are the Masonic bodies of Perry county. Crescent lodge No. 47, Knights of Pythias, at Hattiesburgh, is the only Pythian lodge. There was one lodge of Grangers of quite a membership which formerly existed; there are several lodges of the Farmers' Alliance, and there was formerly a lodge of the K. of L. The only pretentious schools in Perry county are at Hattiesburgh, Augusta and Central. The Baptist, Methodist, Presbyterian and Catholic denominations are all represented, the Baptist and Methodists having the larger memberships, the Presbyterian churches numbering two and the Catholic one.

Rolling Fork, the county seat of Sharkey county, is located west of the center of the county, and is a junction station on the Louisville, New Orleans & Texas railway. It has four hundred inhabitants and does a good local and shipping trade. Other towns in the county are Egremont, Smedes, Anguilla, Nitta Yuma and McKinneyville.

The Methodists were the first to hold religious services within the present limits of Sharkey county. In 1840 Rev. John Fullerton preached in a log schoolhouse on the Rolling Fork plantation, built by Thomas Y. Chaney for his private use as a schoolhouse. Here, in 1840, Mr. Fullerton founded the first Methodist society in the county, known as Union church. This society afterward held services in the Masonic hall till 1888, when it erected a frame building of its own on Race street, Rolling Fork, the first church house in the county.

Soon after the war, under the influence of Colonel Ball, the Baptists organized a society at Rolling Fork, and they held services in Masonic hall.

In 1886 J. C. Burruss organized a society of Universalists at Vickland church, which now has a membership of twenty-five.

In 1874 Bishop W. H. Green organized an Episcopal church at Rolling Fork, where services are still held.

Decatur, the seat of justice of Newton county, was named in honor of Commodore Stephen Decatur, and has about two hundred inhabitants. Hickory, on the Alabama & Vicksburg railroad, has a population of two hundred and ninety-four; Newton, on the same line, has a population of five hundred. Lawrence is a smaller railroad station. A good local trade is done at all these points.

In Newton county Masonic lodges are established at Newton, Decatur, Conehatta, New Ireland, Pinckney, Chunkey and Hickory; Masonic Royal Arch chapters at Newton and Decatur; one lodge of K. of P. at Newton, one of K. of H. at Newton.

There are three academies or high schools for white boys and girls at Newton, Conehatta and Hickory. The county supports eighty free schools, four months each year, forty-six white and thirty-four colored. The churches of this county are as follows: Baptist, regular white churches, twenty-four; colored, twelve; primitive white, five; members white regular Baptists, one thousand six hundred; colored, one thousand two hundred; white primitive, one hundred and fifty; total, three thousand nine hundred and fifty. Methodist white churches, ten; colored, six; white members, about eight hundred; colored members, about six hundred. Presbyterian white churches, four; members, two hundred and fifty. The first Baptist church was instituted in 1836. The first Baptist members conducting the churches and living in the county at that time were Revs. James Merchant and Cuder Price. The great civilizer and missionary of east Mississippi, Rev. N. L. Clarke, of the Regular Baptist church, now in his four-score years, lives at Newton, edits the *Mississippi Baptist*, supplies his churches and travels to the neighboring country when called to preach the Word.

Liberty, the seat of justice of Amite county, has a population of four hundred and twenty-six. It is a handsome village and has always supported and encouraged schools. Its college hall was burned by Federal soldiers during their occupancy of the town in 1863. The buildings that were spared were later acquired by Prof. C. F. Manales, a native Amite countian and an educator of successful experience.

Other towns in the county are Gloster and Gillisburg. The educational institutions at East Fork and Ebenegon are liberally patronized.

Hernando, the seat of justice of De Soto county, on the Illinois Central railroad, has a population of six hundred and twenty. It is a busy town full of men of vigorous enterprise, and was incorporated in 1839. E. W. Caldwell was its first mayor. Joseph Payne its first marshal. It has five churches for whites and two for colored people. The Methodist Episcopal South, Baptist, Episcopal, Presbyterians and Cumberland Presbyterians have houses of worship. There is a good school for white and another for colored pupils. The town has twenty business houses and an ax-handle factory.

Ashland, the seat of justice of Benton county, was named in honor of the home of Henry Clay. It has a population of two hundred and twenty-seven, and does a good local trade. Other towns in this county are Lamar, Michigan City and Hickory Flat.

Rosedale, the seat of justice of Bolivar county, is a prosperous and attractive town of three hundred and fifty inhabitants. It has fine public buildings, and its financial and mercantile concerns are substantial and adequate to the demands of its trade. Benoit, Bolivar, Shaw, Huntington, Shelby, Cleveland, Alligator, Duncan, Australia, Concordia and Beulah are all business points of local importance.

Williamsburgh, the seat of justice of Covington county, had a population of one hundred and twenty-four in 1890. It is located about in the geographical center of the county, and though it has no railway facilities as yet, has a good local trade. Its bar is able, and its business men are enterprising and successful. Mount Carmel and Jaynesville are trading points in this county.

Leakesville, the seat of justice of Greene county, has but a small population and no railway advantages, but its school, church and other interests are well promoted and its prospects are improving. It was named in honor of Hon. Walter Leake, formerly governor of the state. State Line, in the southeast corner of the county, on the Mobile & Ohio railroad, is a local trading point.

Mayersville, the seat of justice of Issquena, was named in honor of David Mayer, an extensive cotton planter, formerly of that county, now of Vicksburg, is located on the Mississippi river and is a shipping point of importance, with good educational and religious institutions and a progressive class of business men and citizens.

Lexington, the seat of justice of Holmes county, is a town of ten hundred population, on the Illinois Central railroad, which has long been noted for the refinement and intelligence of its people and commands a fair trade.

Holmes county has churches of the Methodist, Baptist, Presbyterian, Episcopalian and Catholic denominations, all strong and owning houses of worship. There are colored Methodist and Baptist churches, two of them with buildings. The Masonic order, the Knights of Pythias and the Knights of Honor are all represented in this county.

Durant is a junction town with a population a little larger than that of Lexington, in which business of all kinds is flourishing. Tchula Junction is also a town of some importance in its relations to the surrounding country.

Fulton, the seat of justice of Itawamba county, is located about the center of the county north and south, and a little west of the center east and west, and is the only town in the county, though there are stores at different points in all directions. The population was two hundred and seventy-nine in 1890. It has no railway facilities, but is in the center of a substantial country trade, and has good educational and religious institutions.

Ellisville, the seat of justice of Jones county, is situated as nearly as may be in the geographical center of the county, and has a good trade with the township round about. Other small towns in the county are Laurel, Sandersville, Estabutchee and Tuscaloma. All of the points above mentioned are stations on the New Orleans & Northeastern railroad.

Carthage, the seat of justice of Leake county, is situated in the geographical center of that county and has a population of four hundred and twenty-five. It is a prosperous town, the center of the local trade of near portions of the Pearl river valley, peopled with enterprising, progressive business men and farmers and their families and possessed of ample church and school facilities. Its progress has been measurably restricted by its remoteness from railways, and a line from Macon to Jackson, which is the natural order of development, will be constructed almost inevitably, would do much to advance the interests of this pretty inland county town. Other towns and trading points in this county are Ofahoma, Edinburgh, Thomastown, Good Hope, St Anne, Madden, Grove and Lena.

Columbia, the county seat of Marion county, was long the only town within its borders. Richburgh, Purvis and Piotona, on the Northeastern railroad have developed within the past few years and are advancing with much rapidity. Purvis has three hundred and twenty-five population, Columbia about two hundred. The latter has no railway facilities, but is pleasantly situated on the west shore of the Pearl river a little north of the center of the eastern half of the county. Its business and professional men take high rank and it is well supplied with churches and schools.

CHAPTER IX.

THE PRESS OF MISSISSIPPI, WITH A CURSORY GLANCE AT THE LITERATURE OF THE STATE.

THE press of Mississippi, in a most remarkable manner, has kept in advance of the actual wants and necessities of the people, and the enterprise, progress and stability of the state. The publishers, printers and editors, from the very year of the introduction of the first wooden hand printing press to the present day, with all its rapid, complicated and ponderous hand and steam printing machinery, and telegraph and railroad facilities, have been men of a very high order of intellect, genius and perseverance, men of remarkable sprightliness, patriotism, determination and courage, men who have adorned in all the walks of life the communities in which their lots have been cast, men who have contributed most wonderfully to the onward march of the state and its rapid advancement in all that constitutes true greatness and nobility.

At the early period (we may say, indeed, from 1800 to 1860) the village and town printer, or editor, as he was usually termed, was a man of all work in and about the newspaper printing office. That is to say, he was, almost invariably, printer, publisher, reporter, business manager and editor, all combined. The cities were the only exceptions to this rule. In the cities, the editors were usually resident lawyers, temporarily called to lead a campaign, or prospective or actual candidates for official positions; but it is true that the best equipped and most successful editors of the early times were from the ranks of the men who came into the state from other sections of the Union, and worked their way from the printing office proper to the editorial room and into the editorial harness. We assert it as a truth, and, in our judgment, the statement must be admitted as a truth by all who passed through any number of the years of the early times, that there was a something about the old-time newspaper printing office which suddenly transformed the intelligent, observing, industrious and conscientious youth connected therewith, however slight may have been his previous opportunities, into the accomplished, self-reliant and successful editor, the most useful and valued citizen, the highly popular and most substantial public servant.

The first printing press introduced into what is now known as the state of Mississippi, was brought here by Mr. Andrew Marschalk, between the years 1790 and 1800. Mr. Marschalk was a Marylander by birth, and as an ensign, came down the Mississippi river with the first detachment of United States troops that appeared after the withdrawal of the Spanish authorities. The detachment to which he belonged was on duty for some years, we believe, on the river at and between the first rude forts constructed by our government at the points now known as Vicksburg and Natchez. The press was quite diminutive, and was made of mahogany, and came originally from London, England. Its first work in this country was turned out at Walnut Hill, or Fort Nogales (now the city of Vicksburg), and was a song, printed at the full capacity of the press, which was 4x6 inches. Soon after this, say in 1800, Mr. Marsckalk himself built a press, a larger press, no doubt using a part of the London press in its construction—one capable of printing a foolscap sheet, 11x14 inches, and upon this large, Mississippi manufactured press was printed at Natchez the territorial laws soon after the organization of Mississippi territory. At no distant day Mr. Marschalk sold this press to one B. M. Stokes, who at once commenced the publication at Natchez, on a foolscap sheet, of the first newspaper published and printed in what is now known as the state of Mississippi, and it was called the Mississippi *Gazette*.

The Mississippi *Gazette* proved quite a success supplying "a want long felt," and the field enlarging, and there being a demand for a larger sheet, and the facilities having increased, Robert Green reached Natchez, from Baltimore, Md., with a printing press, and another paper was soon established, but its life was short. Then, as now, the business could be overdone, and newspaper enterprises, however deserving, could not in every case be crowned with success. With the declining fortunes of Mr. Green's journal, Mr. Marschalk again entered the field, and with largely increased facilities, and issued at Natchez, the Mississippi *Herald*, in the year 1802 or 1803—say about five years after the organization of the territory, and fourteen years before the admission of Mississippi as a state into the Federal Union. And soon after the appearance of the *Herald*, came the *Halcyon*, the *Messenger*, and other papers, all manifesting industry and talent; in almost every instance, however, they proved unsuccessful ventures, but they supplied the famishing people with what they craved, viz.: Political reading as well as the news not only about their homes but from the old states from which they had come.

In 1810, or thereabouts, John A. Winn, a man of education and business energy, established the *Chronicle* at Natchez, and a year or two later appeared a paper, also at Natchez, under the management of Peter Isler, who, years afterward, established a paper at Jackson. Then came the *Ariel*, then the *Natchez*, and others followed, not only in Natchez, but in the towns in the adjacent counties. The Woodville *Republican*, if we are not mistaken, was established about 1812. A paper is still published carrying that name.

From 1810 to 1820, as from the first, very nearly all the printers, as well as very nearly all the printing material in the territory, remained at Natchez, which was then, as for many subsequent years, the overshadowing and ruling locality—the center of intelligence, wealth, political power and influence—and then and there commenced the fierce political battles for which Mississippi has ever been noted.

The *Natchez*, a journal under the management of James H. Cook, soon after its establishment became a power in the state, bringing to its political views many of the most prominent, influential and wealthy men of what was then known as the Natchez country, which embraced perhaps a half dozen of the counties which now constitute the extreme southwestern corner of the state. In time it became the champion of what was known as the John Quincy Adams party—the forerunner of what was subsequently known as the whig party—and, consequently, the opponent of Gen. Andrew Jackson. There were then but few, very few, native Mississippians, the population consisting almost exclusively of enterprising and ardent young men, immigrants from the states north and east; some of them mere adventurers, and men of desperate fortunes, but for the most part true men, and men of unblemished character and great intelligence and brilliancy. The two political parties were well arrayed against each other as early as 1822, and very soon the *Statesman* appeared as the exponent and defender of the Jackson party, established by Mr. Marschalk (the same who brought into the country the first printing press), with distinguished and able gentlemen presiding over the editorial columns. The political fight was very warm and decided from the beginning, and all intelligent citizens at once became politicians. As years rolled along Col. I. F. H. Claiborne (afterward a member of congress) became its editor, and again Robert J. Walker (afterward United States senator, secretary of the treasury, etc.).

During this interesting period (1820 to 1830) the newspaper press commenced pushing its way with surprising rapidity into the interior of the state, north and east, keeping pace with, if not leading, the tide of immigration as it appeared in those early times. The delightful climate, the virgin soil of unequaled virtue for cotton and other agricultural productions, the multiplicity of navigable streams (for the small flat boats of the early times) and the very superior class of men who were pushing forward and making settlements in every part of the state, combined to bring Mississippi to the front in a most enviable light, and soon the state commenced filling up with wonderful rapidity for those early times, and with highly intelligent, wealthy and substantial men from all the old states, east to the Atlantic and north to the lakes, and especially from Virginia, the Carolinas, Tennessee, Kentucky, etc., who, with their slaves, at once commenced opening up the wilderness, removing impediments, organizing new counties, building courthouses and establishing newspapers of the most sprightly character. The newspapers were, without exception, political journals, all specially charged with politics, personal, state and Federal, outspoken and defiant for Jackson or Adams, for Clay or Van Buren, whig or democratic. There was no Northern or Southern party then, no talk of anti-slavery or secession. It is true, at a great distance there was a cloud, about the size of a man's hand, which threatened nullification, but the idea found no lodgment among the then Union-loving people of Mississippi.

At an early day the *Mississippi Free Trader* was established at Natchez, by Besancon and others, with Colonel Claiborne and Forbes as editors, and at once assumed the position as the leading Jackson or democratic paper of the state, and continued to hold that proud position for many years. And with the *Free Trader* came very soon the Natchez *Courier*, as the exponent of the gallant old Henry Clay or whig party. And very soon other bright, influential and forcible journals followed, always political, with eminent men as editors among whom were Black, Mellen, Van Winkle, Baldwin, Risk, Duffield, Prewitt, Hillyer, etc, Like the *Free Trader* the *Courier* remained a power in the state until about 1860.

The press assumed its proper position at Vicksburg during this period. Here the first press was planted (the wooden one brought from England by Mr. Marschalk), and here was received and operated many years afterward the first power press introduced into the state. The *Republican*, the *Advocate*, the *Mississippian*, the *Sentinel*, the *Register*, the *Sun*, and others, led the Jackson or democratic hosts, with such editors as Fall, Hagan, Green, Jenkins, Jones, Roy, Wood, McCallum and others; while the grand old party led by Henry Clay was represented at different times by papers of very superior ability and nerve and of wonderful resources and vitality. The *Whig* continued from its establishment (by Marmaduke Shannon), one of the leading journals of the state, if not of the Southwest, until the entire establishment was destroyed by fire in 1863. Shannon and Henderson were its founders, and Shannon continued as its publisher to its last isssue. It was for a considerable period, between 1840 and 1860, the only daily paper in the state, and its influence was always very great. It had as its editors, at different times, some of the brighest editorial lights of the Southwest, some of whom we may name: Griffin, Tyler, McCardle, Hammet, A. H. Arthur, R. Arthur, Carnes, Brooks, Partridge, etc.

Between 1830 and 1840 came the *Vicksburg Mississippian*, with Gen. H. S. Foote (afterward governor and United States senator), and his brother-in-law, F. H. Catlett, as editors and publishers. They were both Virginians, and both lawyers, having little, if any, previous knowledge of the publishing business. In a year or two they moved their paper to Clinton, Hinds county, and from there it soon found its way to Jackson, which had become the state capital, and soon it became one of the leading democratic papers of the state, which position it continued to hold until 1862. The *Southern Intelligencer*, the *True Issue*, the *Constitutionalist*, the *Southern*, and sundry other creditable journals appeared at Vicksburg during the same period, with McCreery, Hurst, Miller, Buck, McCardle and others as editors, but their existence was temporary.

Jackson, now the state capital, sprang into existence and importance long after the settlements made at Natchez and Vicksburg. Indeed, for years after the first printing presses were operated at the points named, the country where Jackson now stands in all its beauty, prosperity and importance, was a howling wilderness and the property of the red man, and the red man was its occupant. The Anglo-Saxon put in his appearance there between 1820 and 1830, and true to his character and customs, he brought with him the great civilizer and christianizer, the political newspaper. Many were the journalistic ventures, which came with its early history, and which continued until about the time of the Civil war. The *Mississippian* as the organ of the democratic party, with Foote, the Howards, Price, Fall, Barksdale and perhaps others, as editors, was ever a vigorous and popular journal and ever enjoyed the patronage of the democratic party. It ever gave a hearty support to McNutt, Brown, Jefferson Davis, McRae and the other leaders of the party, and ever enjoyed a large patronage, which must have been highly remunerative.

The Southern, the *Flag of the Union* and two or three other journals, under the editorial management of A. R. Johnston, Thomas Palmer, Dr. Pickett, H. V. Barr, Colonel Purdom and others, ever commanded the admiration and generous support of the old whig party, giving their support to Prentiss, Guion, Tompkins, Bingaman and a host of other leaders in opposition to General Jackson. While the *Reformer*, under the control of the Smythes, with the brilliant John Marshall as editor, stood very high in the affections of both of the political parties of its day.

The first power printing press in Jackson was brought in by Price & Fall, about 1848; and another was introduced in January, 1852, by Thomas Palmer, for the purpose of executing public work (The *Flag of the Union*, Mr. Palmer's paper at that time), having been elected state printer by the union-whig legislature of that year.

The *Eastern Clarion* was established at Paulding, Jasper county, between 1830 and 1840, with John I. McRae (afterward governor and member of congress) as editor. Soon, however, it passed into the hands of Simeon R. Adams, who made it a power, not only in east Mississippi, but throughout the state, drawing not only a tremendous circulation, for that period, but an influence which was coextensive with the state, and freely acknowledged at all hands. Under the leadership and superior tactics of the *Clarion* east Mississippi became the political power of the state, and for some years had but to assert its wants and they were cheerfully accorded. Upon the death of Mr. Adams, about the year 1859 or 1860, the *Clarion* was bought by Col. J. J. Shannon, who removed it to Meridian about 1862, and in 1865 or 1866 it was removed to Jackson, where it is now, as a part of the *Clarion-Ledger*, under the control of Messrs. I. L. Power and R. H. Henry. Mr. Shannon continues his editorial labors in east Mississippi.

Port Gibson was settled at a very early period, and was a growing and thriving town when Mississippi territory was admitted into the union as a state, in 1817, and when by far the larger portion of the territory was inhabited by the red man. The printing press was put in motion there before the state was organized, and first-class papers have been issued there from the first, conducted by Marschalk, Mason, Morris, etc.

The first paper at Macon, Noxubee county, on the Alabama border, was established in 1836 and was called the *Mississippi Star*. It was established by A. G. Horn, afterward of the *Meridian Mercury*, a gentleman of very superior literary attainments and wonderful perseverance. He died but a few years ago.

The three decades which we are now endeavoring to trace (1830 to 1860) were prolific of political papers. They appeared as if by magic, in every village, town and city in every part of the state from the great river to the Alabama line, and from the Tennessee border to the gulf. The mania for banking, the excitement as to railroads, the building of new towns (real as well as visionary towns), the purchase of the land from the Chickasaws and Choctaws, the creation of new counties, the demand throughout the world for more cotton, the rapidly increasing population through emigration from the old states as well as from Europe, the opening of the delta of the Mississippi with its virgin lands of truly wonderful productiveness, with the extraordinary political contests of 1840, 1850, 1851 and 1860, no doubt combined to cause the extraordinary increase in the number of public journals, and to build up and strengthen those already long established. During the bank period, especially, from 1836 to 1840, the wildest schemes for villages and towns and cities were planned, and every one had its newspaper, while the whole state resounded with the woodsman's ax and the plowman's merry song. No other people on the continent, perhaps, were ever so prosperous as were the people of Mississippi from 1845 to 1860, and it was a substantial and solid prosperity; and the press was in its glory.

Holly Springs, Columbus, Aberdeen, Coffeeville, Canton, Hernando, Oxford, Yazoo City, Carrollton and Lexington, in the northern part of the state, and Liberty, Woodville, Monticello, Fayette and various others, then mere villages, in the southern counties, came to the front, and in each was planted one or more printing presses, and from them were issued creditable journals, brimful of political matter, state and Federal. There was no use for neutral or independent papers in those stirring times, for the public appetite craved politics, politics only, in good column articles, at the hand of the newspaper.

Among the towns hewn out of the high hills and dense pine forests at this period (between 1830 and 1840), was Raymond, for the county seat of Hinds county. The geographical center of the county was found, and there a courthouse was to be built, and Raymond was the name taken, and Raymond at once assumed an air of importance, and a very considerable town arose from the thick forest, as if by magic, and to the prospective city at once removed a number of the ablest young lawyers of the state. Among them were H. S. Foote, Anderson Hutchison, A. R. Johnston, T. J. Wharton, E. W. F. Sloan, John Shelton, William M. Rives, etc., and for a decade or more the sessions of the court in Raymond had a bar from abroad, consisting of S. S. Prentiss, Powhattan Ellis, Governor McNutt, P. W. Tompkins, W. A. Lake, John I. Guion, Judge Sharkey, and other men of like repute. Before a house was fully completed a printing press was brought in, and the *Public Echo*, by S. T. King, a 10x12-inch sheet, was issued, which was succeeded, in 1836, by the Raymond *Times*, by King & Dabney; which gave place, in 1841, to the *Southwestern Farmer*, by King, North, Jenkins & Phillips; which gave place, in 1844, to the Raymond *Gazette*, by George W. Harper and S. T. King. In 1852 King retired, and Harper continued as publisher and editor until 1884—making an uninterrupted editorship of forty years by George W. Harper —when he turned the establishment over to his son, Samuel D. Harper, who had been engaged in the office since 1870, by whom it is still edited and published—perhaps the oldest continuously published paper in the state. During its publication the office was once destroyed by fire (1859), and once by General Grant's invading army (1863). Within the same time Raymond had the *Comet*, the *Snag Boat*, the *Fencible*, and the *Young Christian*, all of which were short lived.

Brandon, Rankin county, came to the surface as a progressive town about the year 1830. Andrew Harper established a creditable newspaper there, which in 1852, became the property of A. J. Frantz, who continues its publication to this day, having breasted triumphantly all the storms which have howled so fiercely and so unmercifully around him. A number of other papers have appeared in Brandon since the establishment of the *Republican*, some before the Civil war, and some since the war, but they have fallen by the wayside.

During the war period, 1860 to 1865, the fortunes of the newspaper press in Mississippi were most trying and overwhelming. The first great difficulty that presented itself was the want of practical printers—men to set the type, work the press, and manage the office. Printers, of all classes of American citizens, are eminent when the country needs friends and protection, when patriotism calls, when honor is at stake. It is not strange, then, that when the drums beat for volunteers in 1861, that very nearly every able-bodied printer was anxious to enroll; that the printers, almost to a man, shouldered muskets and fell into line, announcing their readiness and anxiety to march instantly for the hottest of the fight. Very nearly every printing office in the state was at once without a working force, while many were left utterly prostrate—editors, printers, pressmen, devils, and all, having taken up arms in defense of their beloved Southland. And very soon a greater difficulty presented itself. Females and children could in time acquire some knowledge of type-setting and the routine work of the small printing office—but paper, paper on which to print—was soon the great overshadowing want. It could not be obtained. It was not in the Confederacy in anything like a sufficient supply—it could not be manufactured here, for the material was wanting and the machinery was not within reach. It could not be brought from abroad, for the North would not supply it, nor would the Northern gunboats allow it to be brought from foreign countries. Frequently were papers seen in 1863 and 1864 printed on coarse brown wrapping paper, on common wall paper, on sheets torn from large blank books, etc. The invading armies, too, contributed largely to the suppression of the newspapers. The printing offices, as the invading armies came upon them, were pretty generally destroyed, some by fire and some by ordinary means of destruction. We do not now remember that, when the war closed, April, 1865, there was a legitimate newspaper in the state in regular publication. The invaders had swept the field, had blotted out the newspaper press, and in a manner before unheard of in the annals of civilized warfare. For instance, an Iowa regiment was quartered for a day or two (in 1863) in Raymond. Some of its men proceeded at once to the village printing office, which they found utterly unprotected. They used the material for their own purposes, and then dumped it into an adjacent well, forty feet deep! Other printing offices, as they encountered them on their onward march, were treated even more harshly.

With the brushing away in 1866 of the terrible and fearful effects of the war, no people in the state went to work more energetically and efficiently than the journalists, editors, publishers and printers, and no industry was guided by more skillful hands, more earnest desire, or was more successful. The old papers, for the most part (at least in name), were permitted to slumber, and new papers came bristling forth from almost every town and city of the state, north, south, east and west. New type, new and improved printing machinery, and new editors (for the most part), had the field, and patriotically and well did they improve the opportunity afforded. Jackson, Vicksburg, Natchez, Meridian, and the other cities of the state, especially, at once came up abreast with the cities of the surrounding states, issuing sheets which, in their contents, compared most favorably with any in the land, and for a time all were highly successful as literary, political and pecuniary ventures. At Jackson, there was the *Mississippian*, by Yerger; the *Clarion*, by Shannon; the *Standard*, by Power, Hamilton and Jones, with A. R. Johnson as editor, and others. At Vicksburg, there was the *Herald*, by Swords and Partridge; the *Times*, by McCardle, Manlove and H. Shannon. At Natchez, there was the *Democrat*, by Botto; the *Courier*, by Hillyer, and others; at Meridian, the *Mercury*, *Tropic*, etc. And in every other part of the state the press was up with, if not far ahead of, all other enterprises, and gallantly battling for the rights of the people, for the rights of the state, and for its favorites for the public offices.

In June, 1866, some of the editors and publishers met for the purpose of organizing a press association. The meeting was held at the capitol in Jackson, and J. M. Partridge, of the Vicksburg *Herald*, presided. The following was the membership roll at this first meeting:

Jackson *Clarion and Standard*—J. J. Shannon, Jones S. Hamilton, B. F. Jones, J. L. Power. Jackson *Mississippian*—E. W. Yerger; *Christian Watchman*, A. N. Kimball, H. M. Aikin. Brandon *Republican*—A. J. Frantz. Meridian *Tropic*—Jere Gibson. Vicksburg *Herald*—J. M. Partridge, J. M. Swords. Vicksburg *Journal*—T. B. Manlove. Handsboro *Democrat*—P. K. Mayers. Lexington *Advertiser*—J. D. Houston. Canton *Mail*—Singleton Garrett. Brookhaven *Journal*—S. W. Dale. Panola *Star*—M. S. Ward. Natchez *Democrat*—J. F. Mead. *Mississippi Conservative*—J. L. McCullum, F. T. Cooper.

Journalism had assumed its proper business proportions and its proper attitude when the 1870 decade was ushered in. Almost every county in the state had its newspaper journal or journals, and its well-known editor or editors, and the Mississippi was marching on in the faithful discharge of its duty. There was the Jackson *Clarion*, with Power & Barksdale; the Natchez *Democrat*, with Thomas Grafton; the Goodman *Star*, with McCullum & Walpole; the Brookhaven *Citizen*, with Cassidy; the *Hazlehurst Copiahan*, with Vance; the Port Gibson *Reveille*, with J. S Mason; the Handsboro *Democrat*, with Mayers; the Winona *Democrat*, with Boothe; the Oxford *Falcon*, with Thompson; the Vicksburg *Herald*, with Spears & Jewel; the Crystal Springs *Herald*, with Stackhouse; the Canton *Herald*, with Garrette; the Water Valley *Central*, with Brown; the Charleston *News*, with Hall; the Brandon *Republican*, with Frantz; the Raymond *Gazette*, with George W. Harper; the Holly Springs *Reporter*, with Falconer; the Panola *Star*, with Randolph; the Senatobia *Times*, with Shands; the Summit *Times*, with Cooper; the Iuka *Gazette*, with Davis; the Scooba *Spectator*, with Woods, etc. It is true that at this period the Federal government was holding Mississippi by the throat, but the newspapers, with but here and there an exception, were outspoken, bold and defiant. Indeed, as shown by the press, there was fire in the air, and they were but awaiting a favorable opportunity to restore the proud state of Mississippi to the custodianship of the Anglo-Saxon people within its borders.

The Press association organized in 1866, was revived in 1874, and on its rolls were, entered not only the business and practical men of the press, but the editors, publishers and reporters. In 1875 it was in its prime, and its ranks contained the following heroic list: Jackson *Clarion*, E. Barksdale, J. L. Powers; Jackson *Sunburst*, S. R. Jones; Jackson *Vindicator*, E. G. Wall, D. Denneit, E. Elliott; Jackson *Banner*, Rev. C. B. Galloway; Vicksburg *Herald*, W. H. McCardle; Brandon *Republican*, A. J. Frantz; Yazoo *Herald*, J. L.

McCullum; Summit *Sentinel*, H. S. Bonney, N. P. Bonney; *Mississippi Democrat*, J. D. Burke; Crystal Springs *Monitor*, J. S. Harris, C. N. Harris; Raymond *Gazette*, George W. Harper, Samuel D. Harper; *Southern Homestead*, J. J. Shannon; Enterprise *Courier*, W. J. Adams; Forest *Register*, S. Davis; *Calhoun Democrat*, I. T. Blount; Columbus *Index*, G. C. Tucker; West Point *Citizen*, D. L. Love; Winona *Advance*, H. D. Money, B. F. Jones; Canton *Mail*, E. L. Ross; Holly Springs *Reporter*, W. J. L. Holland; Holly Springs *South*, H. C. Myers; Oxford *Falcon*, I. M. Howry; *Rural Gentleman*, J. M. Davis; Durant *Advertiser*, J. S. Hoskins; *Central Star*, R. Walpole: Newton *Ledger*, R. H. Henry; Hernando *Press*, Ira D. Oglesby; Handsboro *Democrat*, P. K. Mayers; Tallahatchie *News*, L. G. Polk; Yazoo *Democrat*, Frank Campbell; Aberdeen *Examiner*, H. R. Dixon; *Carthagenian*, L. W. Garrett; Panola *Star*, J. A. Pope; Winona *Pioneer*, C. M. Erwin; Water Valley *Courier*, F. M. Merrin; Senatobia *Times*, G. D. Shands.

In 1875 occurred the grand overthrow of carpetbag and negro rule in the state, which had prevailed for five or six years, and the reëstablishment of white supremacy, and it may be justly said that the battle was fought, on the part of the white race, by the journals and journalists enumerated above. Great credit was awarded them at the time and the recollection of their efforts in behalf of the white people and their rights under the Federal constitution are not yet forgotten.

The press of Mississippi to-day is infinitely stronger and more commanding in its influence than ever before, and its number is greater. The papers are, in the main, larger, better printed, better edited and better arranged than ever before, and it is reasonable to conclude that they are better supported, that is to say, have a better paying and more commanding patronage than at any former period. Besides, the association and other causes, have brought about a better understanding among the business managers and editors, and to-day a better feeling exists among the newspaper journals and journalists, than ever before. And hence it is, that the newspaper press now commands a respect from the educated and patriotic people, and has a pecuniary support, in and out of the state, never before enjoyed. A half century ago there were two magnificent newspaper journals at Washington city, whose political utterances controlled the newspapers of the country, and in turn the newspapers outside of Washington formed the political sentiments of the two grand parties of the country of those years. One was the *National Intelligencer*, the national organ of the old whig party; the other, the *Globe*, the organ of the old democratic party. The two old parties received their orders through the two magnificent papers named, and there were none to object—none to rebel. Now, however, Washington city and its newspapers do not inspire the people of distant states—have really no influence whatever in molding public opinion or controlling public sentiment—certainly not in Mississippi. The public men and newspapers of the state now mold and control public sentiment here; and hence it is that more care is observed in the conduct of the state press, and that more patronage is bestowed. It is safe to say that the seventy-four counties of the state have to-day more than one hundred daily, weekly and monthly journals, and that all are well conducted and apparently prosperous. It is true, that now, Claiborne, Marschalk, McCardle, Price, Adams, Prewitt, Mason, Johnston, Hillyer, Botto, Grafton, Jenkins, Cooper, Barksdale, Watson and a host of others, who were magnificent editors in past years, are gone from the press—gone, as to the most of them, to that land whence no traveler returns, yet the press of the state to-day stands out in all its grandeur, purity and strength, challenging the admiration of all intelligent and patriotic men of every race and nationality.

Mississippi, a rural state, without other publishing houses than those controlled by the county newspaper press, has offered few temptations and little encouragement to bookmakers, and yet if time was afforded—and considerable time would be needed—to assemble the facts the commonwealth would make quite a presentable showing.

In the matter of history, Col. J. H. F. Claiborne, of Natchez, in his story of the settlement and progress of the commonwealth, has left to chroniclers an amount of data that is invaluable.

Hon. Jefferson Davis, of Beauvoir, has given the world in his memoirs,—completed by his wife—a work that is destined to hold a lasting place in literature.

Gen. Reuben Davis, of Aberdeen, in his recollection of Mississippians written in his old age, has given the world a book of generally conceded power and merit.

Ex-Governor Lowry and Col. William H. McCardle, of Jackson, have just issued from the *Clarion-Ledger* press, of that city, a history of Mississippi that in addition to being exhaustive in its reach and scope is a work exhibiting literary excellence, and is soon to be followed by a school history from the same pens and press.

Miss Duval, of Sardis, has published a school history of Mississippi that possesses great merit and has been adopted as a text book in several counties.

Chancellor Edward Mayes, of the state university, has just completed—to be published under the auspices of the United States Bureau of Education—a history of education and educational institutions in the territory and state of Mississippi that will take rank as among the ablest books of the kind ever given to the American press.

Capt. John R. Lynch, of West Point, published, a few years ago, a book on the bar and bench of Mississippi that had an extensive sale and possessed great merit. He also published in book form a history of the thrilling events that occurred in Kemper county during the days of military reconstruction, that has been regarded as an important addition to the literature of that stormy period.

In general history, the rector of St. James (Protestant Episcopal) church of Port Gibson, Rev. Arthur Howard Noll, has written a small work of original research, bearing the title, A Short History of Mexico. Mr. Noll is also a magazine writer.

Several books of poems have been published by ladies of West Point since the war, chiefly meeting local demand.

Col. Holt, of Natchez, deceased, was the author of several works of fiction of rare excellence.

Prof. E. W. Hilgard, while a member of the faculty of the state university, wrote and published a work upon the geology of Mississippi that has ever since been regarded as an authority upon the subject. He was followed in the same line by Prof. Harper, with a valuable publication.

Miss Ellen Martin, of Vicksburg, has written a novel of considerable power, and has written much in other lines.

Miss Poitevant, of Pearlington, Miss., Johnnie Hunt, of Vicksburg, and many others whose names I can not hastily recall, have published charming collections of poems, and from the earliest days of Mississippi her local journals and those of Mobile, New Orleans and Memphis, have contained poems from the pens of Mississippi's sons and daughters that would be regarded as gems wherever published or read, and you can seldom open an issue of New Orleans Sunday paper, without finding in some poem or other writing of merit over a Mississippi name and date.

Magazine writing has largely engaged the attention of our people, and as we have no such publications within our bounds, the little waifs have generally found auditors among strangers,

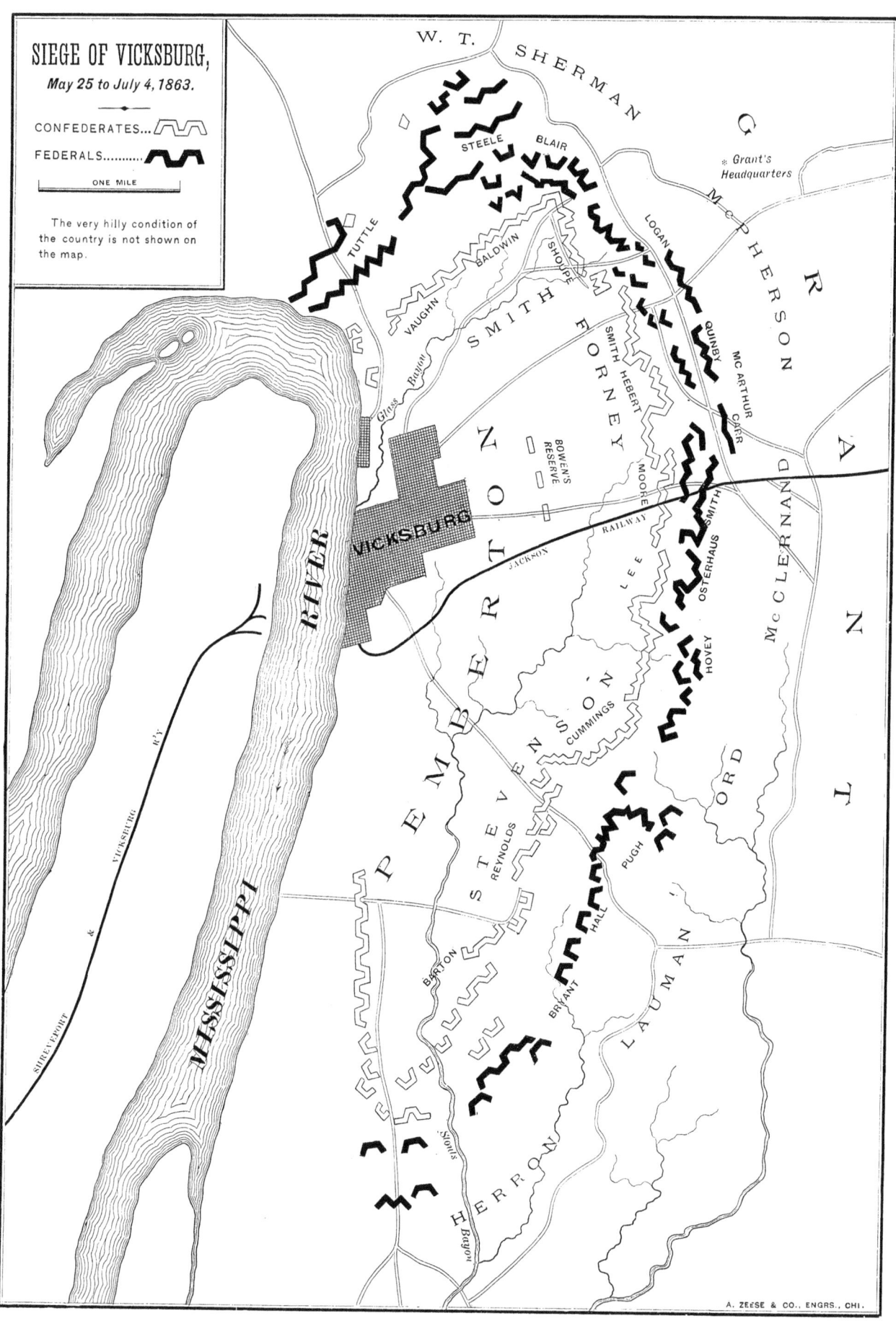

and the authors have been content to accept pecuniary compensation in lieu of local fame and neighborhood praise.

It is the vicinity of the factory and machine shop that prompts mechanical research and encourages inventing or at least patenting. It is the vicinage of publishing houses and magazine offices that encourages literary production and stimulates ambition to appear as authors or bookmakers. A few years ago, Maj. R. M. Bradford, of Aberdeen, wrote a most charming and beautiful fairy tale. Had a publishing house been convenient, he would probably have sought an audience, but being very poor and forced to work hard for a livelihood, he delayed sending forward his production, and it is probably now moldering among other hoarded papers.

Prof. G. M. Lovejoy, of Aberdeen, has recently written an epic poem that will make a book of several hundred pages, and probably create a decided sensation when given to the world. Men and women in various parts of this state are taking out a livelihood by receipts from prominent publications for stories, essays and poems. In dialect stories and poems—Negro dialect—many of our people have obtained entry to leading journals and magazines, and many a "prose poem" has come from pens, the world ought to know—in the way of newspaper communications—that were of very high and rare literary excellence.

In the lecture field and in the matter of contributions to medical journals and associations, we have heard and read many wonderful Mississippi productions. Among the authors at this writing the following names occur: Dr. Hill, of Macon; Dr. Ward, of Winona; Drs. J. M. Greene, E. P. Sale, John T. Lowe and W. G. Evans, Jr., of Aberdeen; A. H. Whitfield and Edward Mayes, of Oxford; F. G. Barry, of West Point; E. H. Bristow, of Aberdeen; Major Magruder, of Vicksburg; Robert McIntosh, of Meridian; E. L. Russell, of Tupelo; Gen. S. D. Lee, of Starkville.

Among the writers who have published books in Mississippi upon practical or progressive themes, one may recall Dr. D. L. Phares, of Woodville, whose work upon the grasses and herbage plants of the gulf states is exhaustive upon those subjects and regarded in all quarters as standard authority. Dr. Phares has also published a work of great merit upon the diseases of domestic animals.

In the progressive line Mr. A. B. Hurst, of Winona, under commission from the agricultural department, a few years ago compiled and published a very valuable book in regard to the resources and productions of Mississippi.

In the field of statistics we have had many able writers, while finance and tariff have supplied texts that have given Mississippians great audiences through the magazines and metropolitan press. Among these writers in olden times was Robert J. Walker, whose pen won him the Federal treasury portfolio.

Lacking other fields, the tendency of Mississippi writers has been toward the newspaper press, and to-day one finds them mainly filling the Memphis "sanctuaries," and upon leading journals in all large American cities, while in our state there are many obscure country journals whose columns in each succeeding issue contain as able editorials as the American press can anywhere exhibit. These people if invited into a broader field would win fame and fortune, but literature is timid as a general rule, and its true devotees are wofully lacking in all of the aggressive attributes of the pioneer. They do not know their own power, as a general rule, and where knowing it doubt their ability to obtain acknowledgment from others.

CHAPTER X.

PHYSICIANS AND THEIR ASSOCIATIONS.

THE repeated references to the old physicians of Mississippi, made in other chapters of this work, leaves little to be written here. In all the principal American settlements of the state the physician was then found, but the sparse population and comparative freedom from dangerous diseases, afforded him but little opportunity to exhibit those high qualities of mind and body which are manifested daily by his brother of modern times. There is scarcely a necessity for him to think; for he felt that

"God takes the good, too good on earth to stay,
And leaves the bad, too bad to take away."

In 1828 some exception was taken to their views. Dr. Reuben Davis disagreed with their method of treatment pursued by Drs. Gray and Holland during the pneumonia epidemic of that year. Their patients dying daily, even Dr. Davis confessed to a man named Harall that he killed one of his negro boys by the same treatment that Gray and Holland observed. Davis' bold confession and his advocacy of whisky and Peruvian bark, attached the people to him, and he was very successful. In 1838 he moved to Aberdeen from Athens. The rebellion against old methods has been carried on from that time down to 1870, when the whole system appears to have been revolutionized, and new ideas of cause, effect and remedy installed. Dr. Wirt Johnston, in his address to the medical association, in April, 1883, reviewed the profession in Mississippi as it stands to-day. He pointed to the progress made by the professon, and credited the association of physicians with that progress. He said:

"The association together of the members of a learned and liberal profession is not purposeless. The advancement of medical knowledge, the elevation of the character and standing of the profession and the enlargement of its sphere of usefulness to the public, and, incidentally, the enjoyment of social pleasures, are among the definite and practical objects in view. I dare say there is not one among us who does not return to his home after these annual meetings with a consciousness that something has been learned, with a more elevated opinion of his profession, and with freshly-aroused interest in the work before him. It is true that by individual effort one may acquire distinction and wealth, but it is to be expected that well-directed organized work alone will result in general and permanent good to the whole profession. I am proud to-day to be able to congratulate you upon the success and standing of this association. It is strong in numbers and intelligence, and upon its roll of members are the names of many of the most learned and eminent of the medical profession in the state. It can be said to be on a sure and permanent foundation, and it is safe to predict for it a future of great usefulness. Its scientific papers will compare favorably with those of kindred organizations, and have received favorable comment from the medical press of the country. This, while gratifying, should only serve to stimulate us to greater improvement.

"Scientific contributions, original in character, while being those most desired, receive the largest share of attention, and are calculated to reflect the greatest amount of credit upon their authors. But to originate, it is evident that the most patient research and investigation and careful observation are necessary. There are, however, broad, uncultivated fields before us into which all earnest workers would be welcomed and which give promise of a rich harvest. The profession to-day seeks eagerly for every original contribution and is ready to honor the author of every new discovery. We constantly encounter diseases whose etiology and pathology are imperfectly understood and whose treatment is not based upon sound principles. The list is long, and some time would be required to even enumerate them.

"There is one cause of disease especially, however, whose influence is so widespread and whose manifestations in their protean forms are so often encountered that it deserves and should receive a large share of our attention. To ascertain what malaria is would immortalize any one. To ascertain the exact pathology of and proper treatment for hæmaturic and other forms of hemorrhagic malarial fever, and malarial continued fever, would surely bring distinction. I venture to suggest to the association, as a means of encouraging original investigation and research among our members, that prize essays be invited. A commendable spirit of competition might thus be aroused, which would, no doubt, result in the production of papers that would add to the reputation of their authors and reflect credit upon the association. The essays should be original in character and upon some practical subject. At each annual meeting a sum of money could be appropriated out of the treasury for the procurement of a suitable prize, a subject selected and a committee appointed to decide between the competitors and award the prize. The prize essay and such of the others as may be deemed worthy and of sufficient interest could be read before the association. A number of interesting and valuable contributions to the literature of the profession might by this means be obtained.

"For the elevation of the character and standing of the medical profession and to enlarge its sphere of usefulness, this association, while it has already done much, is capable of doing more. Through it the physicians of the state are brought together annually for interchange of views, to place upon record such information of value as they may have acquired, and for the discussion of matters of interest to the profession with a view to the advancement of its interests. By it also the public are made aware that the physicians of the state are not behind in the march of progress, but are active in their efforts to advance science and are desirous, as citizens, of discharging the duty to the state for which they are peculiarly fitted by virtue of their calling.

"It was through your efforts that a law was enacted by the last legislature to regulate the practice of medicine in this state. A law which, if it should continue in operation, and is wisely administered, is sure, in the course of time, to elevate the character of the profession. It will not only accomplish this, but will also result in even more good to the people of the state, as by it they will be protected in life from the ignorance of the incompetent, and in purse from the cupidity of quacks. Section seventeen of the law is liberal in its spirit, and was so construed by the attorney-general, and under its provisions some obtained license, it is true, who fall short of the standard erected by this association for the admission of its members and who are not physicians in accordance with a strictly technical defi[nition] of the term. This section became inoperative after June 30, 1882, at which time the [pros]pective operation of the law commenced. Now only two kinds of licenses are provide[d,] one of which serves a temporary purpose only, as it becomes void at the time of th[e] meeting of the censors succeeding its issuance, and which, under the rules of the bo[ard of] health, can only be issued to graduates; the other can only be procured after passing [sat]isfactory examination before the censors. It seems to me that the standard thus erect[ed is] high enough, and that the only point in the law as it now stands upon which there cou[ld be] any difference of opinion among the members of the regular profession, is the require[ment] that those holding diplomas from medical colleges of good standing shall also under[go] examination. It was doubtless thought by the authors of the law that it would be p[olitic] in urging its passage to give to the legislature the assurance that regular graduates [were] willing to be subjected to the same test as to competency as it was asked should be ap[plied] to those who hold no diplomas.

"As it may be of some interest to those present to learn something of the number and [char]acter of the licentiates, as well as the result of the examinations by the censors, the fo[llow]ing statement is made: Number of licenses issued under the provisions of section seve[n] of the law, 1,785; number issued after examination by the censors, 55; making a tot[al of] 1,840 licentiates. This, it is fair to presume, approximates closely to the number of p[rac]tioners of medicine in this state. Taking the last census of the state it shows that the[re is] one licentiate to about every 615 of population. There are, as shown by the applica[tions,] 1,180 graduates, 149 non-graduates, and 511 who fail to state whether or not they are [grad]uates, and whom it is fair to suppose are not graduates, or they would have so stated in [their] applications. The licentiates belong to the different schools of practice as follows: Re[gular] and allopathic 158; eclectic, 84; homeopathic, 11; botanic, 7; botanic and eclectic, 4; [homeo]pathic and mineral, 5; eclectic and allopathic, 8; mineral, 11; allopathic and botan[ic,] eclectic or reformed, 1; hydropathic, 1; eclectic, allopathic and homeopathic, 1; dosim[etric,] 1; physio-medical, 1; idiopathic 1; herb doctor 1; root doctor, 1; and 119 who either sta[te no] school or use obscure expressions. The censors have examined 60 applicants, of whic[h 55] received a favorable endorsement and 5 were refused license.

"In another particular, gentlemen, you are not only up with the times, but occupy a [posi]tion in the front of the army of progress. It was with you that the idea of a state boa[rd of] health originated, and through your efforts that it came into existence. At first, it is [true] it was created without power and pecuniary means, but by your assistance it is now cl[othed] with ample power, has abundant resources at its command, and is in a position to re[nder] efficient service to the state.

"Preventive medicine, yet in its infancy, has made wonderful progress in late years [and] has already been of incalculable benefit to mankind, but it is reasonable to assume [that] future investigations, conducted with the same precision that has characterized them i[n the] past, will elucidate much that is now obscure in the etiology of disease, and as a consequ[ence] lead on to accurate methods of prevention. Let me suggest that this subject present[s an] inviting field for investigation and is worthy of the attention of every one who is desiro[us of] contributing to science or who has the good of mankind at heart. That the public ar[e not] fully informed of the great protection that proper sanitation offers to their health and [life] is but too evident. It is a subject which does not receive the share of attention it dese[rves,] and upon us especially it devolves to inform the people of its importance."

In the early years of the state Dr. Samuel Brown, Dr. William M. Gwin, Dr. Ste[phen]

Duncan, who was also president of the Bank of Mississippi, and other physicians, directed the profession along the Mississippi front. Dr. Robert Dalton, who came from North Carolina to Aberdeen, Dr. John Clopton, Dr. Hatch, Dr. John M. Tindall, the Sykes brothers, all of Aberdeen; Dr. Green, of Pontotoc, Dr. Higgason and Dr. Reuben Davis, of Athens; Drs. Gray and Holland and a few younger men controlled the profession in the eastern counties. Sixty years ago their rulings on medical and sanitary subjects were laws to be observed. To-day physicians wonder how any one escaped from their hands alive. Changed conditions of life did necessarily suggest changes in practice, so that the youngest physician in the state to-day knows a thousand methods and remedies which were hidden from the pioneers of the profession here.

The roll of members of the Mississippi State Medical association in 1891 is as follows:*

William Aills, Steen's Creek, Rankin; W. N. Ames, Starkville, Oktibbeha; W. H. Anderson, Pickens, Holmes; J. A. Alexander, Bolton, Hinds; M. J. Alexander, Austin, Tunica.

John Brownrigg, Columbus, Lowndes; J. L. Baskin, Itta Bena, Leflore; J. W. Bennett, Brookhaven, Lincoln; T. G. Birchett, Vicksburg, Warren; O. C. Brothers, West Point, Clay; J. H. Blanks, Nashville, Tenn.; H. P. Brisbane, Vicksburg, Warren; W. H. Barr, Starkville, Oktibbeha; T. T. Beall, Vicksburg, Warren; G. P. Blundell, Yazoo City, Yazoo; J. M. Buchanan, Meridian, Lauderdale; J. C. Brooks, Bolivar, Bolivar; F. A. Brizzell, Arcola, Washington; R. L. Buck, Jackson, Hinds; A. J. Borroum, Corinth, Alcorn; J. B. Bailey, Conehatta, Newton; J. T. B. Berry, Brandon, Rankin; G. M. Barrier, Alsatia, La.; W. D. Bragg, Moss Point, Jackson; H. D. Butler, Wilzinski, Washington; T. E. Butler, Glen Allen, Washington; E. R. Bragg, Moss Point, Jackson; A. S. Baugh, Polkville, Smith; J. D. Barfield, Mayfield, Montgomery; J. P. Bailey, Bailey's, Lauderdale; E. S. Beadles, Water Valley, Yalobusha; Patton R. Brown, Liddell, Montgomery; William Ball, Greenville, Washington; C. W. Bufkin, Vosburg, Jasper; W. T. Bolton, Perkinston, Harrison; W. C. Brooke, Meridian, Lauderdale; Mimms Blewett, Meridian, Lauderdale; J. A. Barber, Meridian, Lauderdale; R. M. Bishop, Corinth, Alcorn; M. Britt, Como, Panola.

J. A. Crisler, Livingston, Madison; C. P. Conerly, Summit, Pike; N. G. Carter, Ripley, Tippah; N. L. Clarke, A. S., Meridian, Lauderdale; Matthew Clay, Vicksburg, Warren; J. T. Chandler, V. P., Oxford, Lafayette; A. P. Champlin, Bay St. Louis, Harrison; B. B. Carson, Durant, Holmes; G. M. D. Chester, Free Run, Yazoo; B. L. Culley, Jackson, Hinds; B. D. Cooper, Mansfield, La.; Henry Christmas, Tchula, Holmes; J. M. Catchings, Georgetown, Copiah; A. L. Cannon, Indianola, Sunflower; P. M. Catchings, Georgetown, Copiah; S. K. Coleman, Canton, Madison; L. M. Clark, Newton, Newton; J. G. Cherry, Lumberton, Pearl river; H. L. Crook, Pelahatchie, Rankin; H. C. Cook, Augusta, Perry.

J. D. Dabney, Tchula, Holmes; Chesley Daniel, Holly Springs, Marshall; M. G. Davis, Greenwood, Leflore; R. L. Dunn, Yazoo City, Yazoo; B. F. Duke, Lake Como Jasper; G. T. Darden, Blanton, Sharkey; B. A. Duncan, West Point, Clay; J. C. Denson, Ludlow, Scott; S. R. Dunn, V. P., Greenville, Washington; J. W. Dulaney, Rosedale, Bolivar; D. M. Diggs, Black Hawk, Carroll; S. T. Dunning, Utica, Hinds; J. L. Dodge, Bolivar, Bolivar; S. R. Deans, Abbott, Clay; John E. Davis, Ben Lomand, Issaquena.

---

*Throughout the list the letter P. denotes service as president; V. P., vice president; R. S., recording secretary; C. S., corresponding secretary; A. S., assistant secretary; T., treasurer; O., orator; *, removed from the state.

C. C. Ewing, Aberdeen, Monroe; W. A. Evans, Jr., Aberdeen, Monroe; J. W. Elliott, Lake City, Yazoo; L. C. Elliott, Yazoo City, Yazoo; J. D. Egger, Caledonia, Lowndes.

J. M. Farrish, Satartia, Yazoo; J. S. Featherston, Brooksville, Noxubee; T. W. Fullilove, Vaiden, Carroll; F. B. Forbes, Othello, Tunica; T. B. Ford, Columbia, Marion; F. L. Fulgham, Jackson, Hinds; T. W. Foster, Zeiglerville, Yazoo; Frank Ferrell, Ashland, Benton.

Harris A. Gant, Water Valley, Yalobusha; W. P. Gatlin, McComb City, Pike; W. R. Greenlee, Harriston, Jefferson; S. C. Gholson, Holly Springs, Marshall; W. F. Gresham, Durant, Holmes; N. C. Gulledge, Durant, Holmes; T. H. Gordon, Oakland, Grenada; N. L. Guice, P. Natchez, Adams; F. H. Gulledge, Jackson, Hinds; H. S. Gully, Meridian, Lauderdale; J. M. Greene, V. P., P., Aberdeen, Monroe; J. B. Gresham, V. P., P., West Point, Clay; D. M. Gardner, Oxford, Lafayette; R. W. Gulledge, Durant, Holmes; F. L. Gipson, Pelahatchie, Rankin; D. W. Goodman, Matherville, Wayne; J. W. Gilbert, Verona, Lee; Walton S. Greene, Aberdeen, Monroe; J. C. Gathings, Prairie Station, Monroe.

S. H. Howard, Tchula, Holmes; A. C. Halbert, Cobb Switch, Lowndes; J. D. Harrell, De Soto, Clarke; C. R. Henderson, Deasonville, Yazoo; A. B. Holder, Memphis, Tenn.; C. M. Henderson, Sardis, Panola; J. J. Harralson, Conehatta, Newton; George W. Howard, Vicksburg, Warren; W. F. Hyer, T., V. P., P., Meridian, Lauderdale; J. C. Hall, Anguilla, Sharkey; William Preston Hughes, Port Gibson, Claiborne; George K. Harrington, Jackson, Hinds; H. H. Harralson, Forest, Scott; O. A. Harrison, Meridian, Lauderdale; J. E. Halbert, V. P., Mound Landing, Washington; W. W. Hamilton, Brooksville, Noxubee; R. E. Howard, Durant, Holmes; C. S. Hudson, Yazoo City, Yazoo; T. R. Henderson, Greenwood, Leflore; T. A. Heath, Hays' Landing, Issaquena; J. P. Hamer, Kilmichael, Montgomery; J. M. Hicks, Goodman, Holmes; J. F. Hunter, T., Jackson, Hinds; G. S. Hunter, A. S., Bolton, Hinds; W. W. Hall, Meridian, Lauderdale; W. R. Harper, Rolling Fork, Sharkey; D. S. Humphreys, Leota Landing, Washington; A. G. Hall, Natchez, Adams; R. M. Hand, Shubuta, Clarke; H. B. Hunter, Decatur, Newton.

Thomas D. Isom, Oxford, Lafayette; T. G. Ivy, West Point, Clay; B. W. Inman Woodville, Wilkinson; Henry Izard, Meridian, Lauderdale; George Izard, Meridian, Lauderdale.

Wirt Johnston, R. S., P., Jackson, Hinds; R. B. Johnson, Kirkwood, Madison; Charles H. Jones, Greenville, Washington; C. W. Jordan, West Point, Clay; R. E. Jones, Crystal Springs, Copiah; W. T. Johnson, Black Hawk, Carroll; J. W. Jordan, Black Hawk, Carroll; E. P. Jones, Hermanville, Claiborne; L. H. Jones, Phœnix, Yazoo; L. C. Jones, Madison Station, Madison; J. O. Jones, Beulah, Bolivar; W. W. Johnson, Melvin, Choctaw.

R. S. Knox, Enterprise, Clarke; Carroll Kendrick, Corinth, Alcorn; B. F. Kittrell, V. P., O., P., Black Hawk, Carroll; D. A. Kinchloe, Star Place, Panola; A. C. Kuykendall, Grenada, Grenada; W. G. Kiger, Brunswick, Warren; J. G. Knox, Toomsuba, Lauderdale; W. T. Kendall, Meridian, Lauderdale; W. S. Kent, Sharon, Madison.

W. B. Loyd, Myles, Copiah; T. P. Lockwood, Crystal Springs, Copiah; John H. Lucas, Greenwood, Leflore; W. C. Lawrence, Crawfordsville, Lowndes; Robert Lowry, Canton, Madison; M. J. Lowry, Meridian, Lauderdale; John Long, Coffadeliah, Neshoba; J. H. Love, Newport, Attala; George W. Luster, Cayuga, Hinds; Buford Larkins, Oakdale, Lawrence.

M. V. B. Miller, Meridian, Lauderdale; C. M. Murry, Ripley, Tippah; S. A. Morris, Belzonia, Washington; H. C. McLaurin, Brandywine, Claiborne; W. H. Miller, Okolona,

Chickasaw; J. H. Murfee, Okolona, Chickasaw; D. McCallum, V. P., Westville, Simpson; P. J. Maxwell, Columbus, Lowndes; Thomas H. Mays, Columbus, Lowndes; L. M. Mays, Graysport, Grenada; P. J. McCormick, Yazoo City, Yazoo; T. J. Mitchell, Jackson, Hinds; J. P. Moore, V. P., Yazoo City, Yazoo; T. H. Marselis, Nunnery, Amite; George H. McNeil, Newton, Newton; A. G. McLaurin, Trenton, Smith; J. F. Moore, Enterprise, Clarke; W. Myles, Port Gibson, Claiborne; William McSwine, Grenada, Grenada; R. C. Myles, New York; H. A. Minor, Macon, Noxubee; E. L. McGehee, Woodville, Wilkinson; L. W. Mabry, Goodman, Holmes; Aurelius Martin, Hardy, Grenada; Daniel M. McGehee, Shell Mound, Leflore; D. D. Montgomery, Greenville, Washington; J. Y. Murry, Ripley, Tippah; Joseph L. Murrell, Benoit, Bolivar; W. H. McFarland, Vaiden, Carroll; J. S. McCain, Lexington, Holmes; J. L. McLean, Winona, Montgomery; A. McCallum, Edwards, Hinds; A. K. McNair, Fayette, Jefferson; James L. Minor, Memphis, Tenn.; M. D. Morgan, Jackson, Hinds; G. M. Mott, Ellisville, Jones; A. L. Morris, Lena, Leake; J. H. Maddox, Concordia, Bolivar; R. D. Miller, Clinton, Hinds; Anthony Miller, Rosedale, Bolivar; J. W. Malpus, Meridian, Lauderdale; F. McCormack, Vosburg, Jasper; W. J. McNair, Quitman, Clarke; J. L. Myers, Meridian, Lauderdale; W. O. McNeill, Eucutta, Wayne.

R. Anderson New, Rodney, Jefferson; E. A. Neely, Memphis, Tenn.; N. Y. Nelson, Myles, Copiah; J. O. Newman, Vicksburg, Warren; J. E. Noble, Fannin, Rankin; F. B. Nimocks, Lawrence, Newton.

J. L. Owen, Benoit, Bolivar; J. F. O'Leary, Shreveport, La.; T. T. Orendoff, Rolling Fork, Sharkey; C. E. Oatis, Hazlehurst, Copiah.

A. B. Pitts, Hazlehurst, Copiah; K. P. Perkin, Batesville, Panola; J. H. Plunkett, Flora, Madison; W. O. Porter, Meridian, Lauderdale; W. M. Paine, Aberdeen, Monroe; Joseph B. Perkins, Choctaw Agency, Oktibbeha; J. R. Prince, Summerville, Noxubee; Isaac P. Partin, Meridian, Lauderdale; E. B. Poole, Clinton, Hinds; George C. Phillips, Lexington, Holmes; G. L. Pope, Stoneville, Washington; B. J. Pate, Sidon, Leflore; C. S. Priestley, Canton, Madison; D. L. Phares, Madison Station, Madison; J. B. Pease, Concordia, Coahoma; W. W. Payne, Meridian, Lauderdale; R. E. Patrick, Lynwood, Rankin.

R. A. Quin, T., Vicksburg, Warren; D. H. Quin, McComb City, Pike; O. B. Quin, McComb City, Pike.

P. W. Rowland, Coffeeville, Yalobusha; S. D. Robertson, Dover, Yazoo; W. D. Redus, Port Gibson, Claiborne; S. M. Rainey, Osborne, Oktibbeha; C. A. Rice, Meridian, Lauderdale; J. H. Rhodes, Learned, Hinds; J. C. Roberts, Centerville, Wilkinson; W. B. Rogers, Memphis, Tenn.; R. W. Rowland, Flora, Madison; S. D. Robbins, Vicksburg, Warren; E. A. Rowan, Wesson, Copiah; L. S. Rogers, West, Holmes.

B. A. Sheppard, Lexington, Holmes; H. Shannon, V. P., Nashville, Tenn.; J. S. Sizer, Fort Stevens, Yazoo; R. G. Southall, Jr., Arcola, Washington; Z. Y. Scott, Crystal Springs, Copiah; S. O. Smith, Ellisville, Jones; A. H. Smith, V. P., Meridian, Lauderdale; J. Mell Smith, Coffeeville, Yalobusha; John W. Spellman, Columbus, Lowndes; S. D. G. Scruggs, Grenada, Grenada; A. B. Smith, Hatton, Yalobusha; Nolan Stewart, Fort Apache, Ariz.; A. P. Sims, Morton, Scott; L. Sexton, Wesson, Copiah, Newton C. Steele, Chattanooga, Tenn.; H. L. Sutherland, Bolivar, Bolivar; W. J. Sykes, P., Aberdeen, Monroe; Robert Smith, Kosciusko, Attala; A. J. Sanderson, Vaiden, Carroll; E. P. Sale, V. P., P., Memphis, Tenn.; W. B. Sanford, Corinth, Alcorn; O. J. Sherman*, Harrison, Tallahatchie; J. D. Staples, Huntsville, Montgomery; J. M. Shivers, Sidon, Leflore; J. M. Shamburger, Toomsuba, Lauderdale; W. J. Stevenson, Lauderdale, Lauderdale; J. D. Smythe, Greenville,

Washington; E. F. Shuler, Greenville, Washington; J. A. Shackleford, Greenville, Washington; G. A. Spivey*, Texas; C. C. Stockard, Columbus, Lowndes; A. G. Sinclair, Memphis, Tenn.; Owen Stone, Stoneville, Washington; John Seay, Glenora, Washington; O. H. Spence, Utica, Hinds; W. S. Sims, Meridian, Lauderdale.

J. M. Taylor, V. P., P.; Corinth, Alcorn; R. S. Toombs, P., P. P.; Greenville, Washington; T. R. Trotter, Duck Hill, Montgomery; G. W. Trimble, O. P.; Grenada, Grenada; J. E. Talbert, Memphis, Tenn.; W. E. Todd, R. S., S.; Jackson, Hinds; W. A. Taylor, Booneville, Prentiss; M. J. Thompson, Meridian, Lauderdale; J. F. Taylor, Anguilla, Sharkey; George A. Teunisson, Monticello, Lawrence; B. F. Travis, Heidelburg, Jasper; J. C. Terrell, Leland, Washington; M. H. Turner, Brownsville, Hinds; E. S. Turner, Ashland, Benton; R. L. Turner, Ellisville, Jones; J. R. Tackett, Pickens, Holmes.

B. A. Vaughan, V. P., C. S., P., Columbus, Lowndes; G. W. Vassar, Carrollton, Carroll.

J. D. Walker, Kings, Rankin; W. E. Whitehead, Greenwood, Leflore; R. G. Wharton, V. P., Port Gibson, Claiborne; John Wright, Sardis, Panola; T. L. Wilburn, Winona, Montgomery; S. L. Wynne, Looxahoma, Lea Williamson, Como, Panola; B. F. Ward, O., P., Winona, Montgomery; A. A. Wheat, Harrison, Tallahatchie; William H. White, V. P., Brandon, Rankin; C. Weathersby, Clarksdale, Coahoma; T. W. Wright, Pickens, Holmes; J. D. Weeks, Ackerman, Choctaw; Edwin Wright, Sardis, Panola; J. L. Walker, Nicholson, Hancock; J. H. Watson, Thornton, Holmes; F. L. Walton, Quitman, Clarke; W. H. Whittle, De Soto, Clarke.

H. Yandell, Yazoo City, Yazoo; J. W. Young, Grenada, Grenada.

The honorary members of the Mississippi State Medical association are: Hon. E. Barksdale, Jackson; Hon. F. G. Barry, West Point; T. J. Crofford, M. D., Memphis; W. Y. Cadberry, Yazoo City; Frank Johnston, Esq., Jackson; J. C. Longstreet, Grenada; Ex-Gov. Robert Lowry, Jackson; A. H. Smith, M. D., Meridian; W. D. Powell, M. D., Torrance; Gen. J. S. Sharp, Crawford; L. M. Southworth, Carrollton; D. Sutton, M. D., Lexington; John Tackett, M. D., Richland.

Throughout the state are many local associations; all organized on the principles of the state society. The Columbus and Lowndes association of 1872, the Marshall county of 1872, the Lee county, of 1878; the Copiah county, of 1878, and the Grenada Medical association, of 1876, are represented in the state society.

The Mississippi State Medical association was organized in 1866-7, and the first annual meeting held in 1868. An old roll of membership credits P. T. Baley of Jackson, L. P. Blackburn of Natchez, M. S. Craft of Jackson, A. H. Cabaniss of Jackson, S. C. Farrar of Jackson, W. Y. Gadberry of Yazoo City, J. F. Harrington of Jackson, W. B. Harvey of Canton, W. B. Williamson of Edwards, with joining the association in 1866; D. W. Booth, William H. Baird, James R. Barnett, E. G. Banks, T. G. Birchett, W. M. Compton, John S. Featherston, C. B. Galloway, A. J. Curtiss, W. D. Bragg, J. H. Gibbs, J. M. Hunt, E. T. Henry, S. V. D. Hill, J. R. Hicks, J. D. Harrell, Thomas D. Isom, J. R. Kirkland, John D. Kline, Edward Lea, James M. Lewis, A. A. Lyon, W. L. Lipscomb, John D. McConnell, W. E. Monette, C. J. Mitchell, Frank Nailer, J. Nailer, D. B. Nailer, N. Pettit, B. B. Palmer, Robert A. Quinn, D. H. Quinn, George E. Redwood, J. L. Reilly, H. Shannon, J. W. M. Shattuck, James Steinriede, A. H. Smith, J. C. Spinks, L. Shackleford, J. S. Sizer, C. Y. Thompson, J. M. Taylor, Z. T. Woodruff, P. F. Whitehead, B. H. Whitfield, M. F. Wakefield and E. M. Alexander became members between April, 1869, and December, 1871.

It appears that no permanent organization was effected until 1868, but as the minute books for 1866, 1867, 1868, 1869, 1870 and 1871 can not be found, nothing can be stated with certainty respecting meetings or officers.

The fifth annual meeting was held at Holly Springs in April, 1872, Dr. W. M. Compton, the outgoing president, presiding with Dr. J. W. M. Shattuck, secretary. The election of officers took place April 4, when Dr. C. B. Galloway of Canton was chosen president; D. W. Booth, W. M. Lea, J. D. Burche and L. Shackleford, vice presidents; J. W. M. Shattuck, recording secretary; P. F. Whitehead, corresponding secretary, and W. G. Sykes, treasurer. The delegates to the American Medical association then appointed were J. R. Hicks, W. Y. Gadberry, W. L. Lipscomb, Thomas D. Isom, Lee Shackleford, W. M. Compton, J. M. Taylor and S. C. Gholson. A motion by Dr. Capers to refuse affiliation with the national association, owing to "legislation partisan in its course" being on their record books, was not entertained. The motion of Dr. Gadberry, to publish the proceedings of the fifth meeting of the association with names of members, constitution, laws and papers on special subjects, was adopted and the work therein outlined carried out in the Excelsior book and job office at Columbus, Miss., under the supervision of Drs. A. A. Lyon, J. W. M. Shattuck, and C. B. Galloway.

The roll of members of 1872 presents the following names:

*E. M. Alexander, Ripley; *William H. Baird, Vicksburg; *P. T. Baley, Jackson; *W. T. Balfour, Vicksburg; E. G. Banks, Clinton; *J. R. Barnett, Vicksburg; T. G. Birchett, Vicksburg; *D. W. Booth, Vicksburg; W. D. Bragg, Garlandsville; J. D. Burche, Yazoo City; J. F. Butler, Holly Springs; *A. B. Cabaniss (1873), Jackson; A. H. Cage, Canton; *L. G. Capers, Vicksburg; J. L. Carter, Jackson; *William M. Compton, Jackson; *M. S. Craft, Jackson; A. J. Curtiss, Meridian; F. W. Dancy, Holly Springs; J. R. Dougherty, Holly Springs; Chesley Daniel, Holly Springs; J. S. Davis, Iuka; K. C. Devine (moved in 1872), Madison county; W. J. Dulaney, Madison county; R. L. Dunn, Yazoo county; J. C. Fant, Macon; J. S. Featherston, Macon; Frank Ferrell, Salem; *C. B. Galloway, Canton; *W. A. Galloway, Canton; W. Y. Gadberry (first president), Yazoo City; S. C. Gholson, Holly Springs; J. H. Gibbs, Meridian; J. W. Gray, Hudsonville; J. D. Harrell, De Soto; J. F. Harrington, Jackson; W. B. Harvey, Canton; *E. T. Henry, Vicksburg; *J. R. Hicks, Vicksburg; *S. V. D. Hill, Macon; J. M. Hunt, Vicksburg; W. F. Hyer, Chulahoma; Thomas D. Isom, Oxford; *Robert Kells, Jackson; H. B. Kidd, Yazoo county; V. O. King, Black Hawk; J. R. Kirkland, Meridian; B. F. Kittrell, Black Hawk; John D. Kline, Meridian; Edward Lea, Holly Springs; W. M. Lea, Holly Springs; R. O'Leary, Vicksburg; C. J. Mitchell, Vicksburg; *W. E. Monette, Vicksburg; Frank Nailer, Vicksburg; J. Nailer, Vicksburg; R. A. Quinn, Vicksburg; *H. Shannon, Vicksburg; *P. F. Whitehead, Vicksburg; *Z. T. Woodruff, Vicksburg; James M. Lewis, Kosciusko; W. L. Lipscomb, Columbus; A. A. Lyon, Columbus; J. W. M. Shuttuck, Columbus; B. A. Vaughan, Columbus; *J. D. McConnell, Brownsville; J. P. Moore, Jackson; D. D. Nailer, Warren county; B. B. Palmer, Lake; *D. R. Pettit, Warren county; George E. Redwood, Meridian; L. Shackleford, Meridian; A. H. Smith, Meridian; J. L. Riley, Lake; J. S. Sizer, Yazoo county; H. Yandell, Yazoo county; B. H. Whitfield, Clinton; M. F. Wakefield, Starkville; J. C. Spinks, Fort Stephens; James Steinride, Benton; W. G. Sykes, Aberdeen; J. M. Taylor, Corinth; C. Y. Thompson, Macon.

The president's address is not given in the first printed report. Special papers by C. B. Galloway on Chloroform in obstetrics, by J. M. Taylor on Chronic constipation, by J. W. M. Shattuck on Hypodermic medication, by James M. Lewis on Treatment of pneu-

---
*Deceased or removed from the state.

monia, by B. A. Vaughan on Clinical thermometry and critical days, by E. H. Anderson on Malarial hæmaturia, by A. A. Lyon on Conservative surgery and by J. M. Taylor a Report of cases in practice.

A synopsis of proceedings of the Columbus and Lowndes County Medical society for the year ending March 26, 1872, was printed to prove what a local society may accomplish in the study and discussion of medical and surgical subjects.

The sixth annual meeting of the association was held at Vicksburg in April, 1873. There were enrolled the following named members: D. W. Adams, W. L. Ainsworth, William Aills, W. H. Armistead, M. T. Anderson, J. W. Bennett, R. B. Banks, J. D. Beck, J. M. Boyle, R. L. Boyle, W. G. Davis, F. M. Fitzhugh, George W. Howard, C. R. Henderson, A. C. Hulbert, Wirt Johnson, Dudley W. Jones, George L. Latimer, P. T. McCormick, N. W. McKie, R. D. McLaurin, W. H. McDougal, L. M. Mays, W. J. N. E. Smith, James C. Newman, R. Anderson New, William E. Oates, J. F. O'Leary, Thomas A. Phillips, L. Richardson, James M. Smith, H. C. Stackhouse, R. R. Stockard, H. L. Sutherland, George Sumrall, R. S. Toombs, A. M. Waddill, L. White, R. G. Wharton, W. B. Williamson.

The expenditure of the association for the year ending March 31, 1873, was $125, all of which was paid for stationery, printing reports and postage. The election of officers resulted in the choice of J. M. Taylor, president; M. S. Craft, B. A. Vaughan, P. F. Whitehead and J. W. Bennett, vice presidents; J. W. M. Shattuck, permanent recording secretary; W. A. Galloway, correspondent; W. J. Hyer, treasurer, and J. R. Hicks and Wirt Johnson, orators. The death of Dr. John R. Coffman, of Grenada, was reported January 16, 1873.

The delegates to the American association were J. F. O'Leary, I. F. Harrington, P. J. McCormick, B. A. Vaughan, E. G. Banks, R. G. Wharton, J. W. M. Shattuck, A. A. Lyon, W. Y. Godberry, M. S. Craft, and S. V. D. Hill. The constitution and by-laws were revised during this meeting and measures suggested for improving the condition of the profession. C. B. Galloway delivered the president's address; A. A. Lyon, the annual oration; J. P. Moore, a paper on Malarial hæmaturia; S. V. D. Hill, one on Cerebro-spinal meningitis; J. W. M. Shattuck, one on the Sequelæ of malarial diseases; J. R. Barnett, one on Scarlatina and its sequelæ; A. A. Lyon, one on Conservative surgery; J. D. McConnell, one on Dysmenorrhœa; D. W. Booth, one on the Progress of materia medica and therapeutics during the years 1871-2; P. F. Whitehead, one on the Epidemic of 1871 at Jackson, Vicksburg and Natchez; M. S. Craft, one on the Epidemic at Jackson; William M. Compton, one on Medical experts; J. M. Hunt, one on Removal of ovarian tumor; P. F. Whitehead, one on Tetanus treated with calabar bean; A. A. Lyon, one on Loss by sloughing with reproduction of the glans penis; J. R. Barnett, one on Entra abdominal orchitis; J. R. Hicks, one on fracture of the femur treated by simplification of Smith's anterior splint; D. W. Booth, one on Operation for strangulated femoral hernia, and J. M. Taylor, one on Skin grafting. In 1874 Dr. P. F. Whitehead was elected president.

The eighth annual meeting was held at Vicksburg in April, 1875. Dr. P. F. Whitehead presided, with Dr. R. A. New, recording secretary. Dr. Richard O'Leary, then mayor of the city, delivered the address of welcome. Papers by R. R. Stockard and J. H. Murfee were read. One by P. J. McCormick, on the Use of chloroform in obstetrics, was ably discussed by several members. Dr. Whitfield's papers on Double hearing and monstrous dentition; Dr. W. A. Galloway's, on Syphilis; Dr. R. G. Wharton's, on the use of Electricity as a therapeutic agent; Dr. E. G. Bank's, on Meningitis; Dr. R. J. Turnbull's Report on cases; Dr. J. R. Hicks', on Endemics and epidemics of 1874; Dr. W. L. Lipscomb's address; Dr. B. H. Whitefield, on the Eye, and Dr. R. A. Quinn's, on Traumatic tetanus and strangulated inguinal hernia, were ordered to be published. The election of officers resulted in the choice of M. S. Craft, president; B. A. Vaughan, E. W. Hughes, W. H. Armistead and John Brownrigg, vice presidents; R. A. New was reëlected recording secretary; John W. King, correspondent; J. A. Campbell, treasurer; E. G. Banks and R. A. Quinn, orators.

The ninth annual meeting was held at Jackson, in May and June, 1876. P. J. McCormick was elected president, R. G. Wharton, A. G. Smythe, W. W. Hall and D. C. McCallum, vice presidents; C. A. Rice, corresponding secretary; Wirt Johnson, recorder; Robert Kells, treasurer; B. F. Kittrell and M. S. Craft, orators. There were one hundred and seventy-five members on the roll at the close of the year. The address by Dr. M. S. Craft, a paper on Electro-therapeutics, by R. G. Wharton; one on Ramollissement, by W. M. Compton; one on Cerebro-spinal meningitis, by John Brownrigg; one on Hemiplegia, by B. F. Kittrell; one on the Antiseptic treatment of wounds, by J. M. Taylor; one on A Case of necrosis of inferior-maxillary bone, with festulous opening on lip and plastic operation, by J. M. Taylor; one on Capillary bronchitis in children, by R. Fowler; one on Chloroform and ether, by E. G. Banks; one on Indigenous remedies of Mississippi, by B. H. Whitfield; and one on Diseases of north Mississippi, by E. W. Hughes, were read before the association in Centennial year, each being an excellent review of the subject under notice.

The tenth annual meeting was held at Grenada in April, 1877. B. A. Vaughan was chosen president; E. W. Hughes, T. R. Trotter, T. P. Lockwood and J. T. Parker, vice-presidents; Wert Johnston, recording secretary; C. A. Rice, corresponding secretary; Robert Kells, treasurer; and D. W. Booth and J. E. Halbert, orators. The papers read comprised The Mission of medicine, by B. F. Kittrell; The State board of health, by W. M. Compton; Puerperal fever, by S. V. D. Hill; Veratrum in puerperal convulsions, by P. F. Whitehead; Scarlatina anginosa heated with sulpho-carbolate of sodium, by H. C. McLaurin; Four cases of laceration of the perineum, by S. V. D. Hill; Resuscitation from death by chloroform, by C. A. Rice; Ergot in the treatment of pneumonia, by J. E. Halbert; Method of treating epidemic dysentery by the use of iodine, by J. C. Hall; Operation in a case of vesico-vaginal fistula, by C. A. Rice; The Surgical history of Mississippi, by W. W. Hall; and Surgical cases, by M. S. Craft. The historical paper by Dr. Hall covers a large number of surgical cases throughout the state. The subject is treated so exhaustively that it would make a volume in itself, at once practical and instructive.

The eleventh annual meeting was opened at Jackson April 3, 1878. B. L. Kittrell was elected president, R. G. Wharton, H. Hanslow, G. W. Vasser and E. P. Sale, vice presidents; Wirt Johnston, recorder; M. S. Crafts, correspondent; Robert Kells, treasurer; E. G. Banks and John Brownrigg, orators. The members in 1878 are named in the history of the board of health. Dr. Vaughan's address was a masterly review of medical methods; Dr. Halbert's oration was historical and descriptive, but, like other annual orators, he indulged in lashing the ancient physicians for their supposed ignorance, when in fact they were as learned in the diseases and remedies of the ancients as the physicians of the present are in the diseases of the moderns. The ancient physicians were learned, honorable men, who always acknowledged the ideas they received from the tribal doctors of an earlier civilization. Dr. Wirt Johnston treated the Manufacture and uses of salicylic acid, Dr. P. F. Whitehead, the Treatment of diphtheria; Dr. Hill, A Case of poisoning with arsenious acid; Dr. J. R. Barnett, A Case of suppuration of antrum highmorianum; Dr. William Powell, Syphilis in the negro as differing from syphilis in the white race; Dr. H. J. Ray, A Case of hydrophobia; D. L. Phares, Posture in treatment of colic; Dr. J. W. Holman, Croupous pneumonia; Dr. Thomas Bryan, Malaria, what it is, how produced and how prevented; Dr. R. G. Wharton, Chronic catarrh; Dr. H. Hanslow, A Case of poisoning by hydrate chloral and camphor, and report on the wound of plantar arch; Dr. J. E. Halbert, Chloral hydrate in obstetrics; Dr. B. F. Kittrell, Treatment of cholera; E. W. Hughes, Epidemic of cerebro-spinal meningitis round Grenada in 1862; Dr. J. T. Parker, Early management of the infant; A. H. Cage, Typhlitis, and Dr. W. W. Hall, Continuation of surgical history of Mississippi.

Each paper is a testimonial to the earnestness of its author and a valuable addition to medical and surgical literature, as well as to sanitary science.

Dr. W. T. Balfour, who located at Jackson, Miss., in 1837, and shortly after moved to Vicksburg, to fight the yellow-fever epidemic, died there December 12, 1877; Dr. LeGrand G. Capers died December 2, 1877; Dr. H. B. Kidd, who located at Yazoo City in 1845, died there August 11, 1877; Dr. L. L. Gadberry died at Yazoo City, December 12, 1877; Dr. Henry C. Stackhouse, born at Crystal Springs, Miss., died at Utica in 1877, and Dr. C. B. Galloway, of Canton, died there in 1877.

The twelfth annual meeting was held at Aberdeen, April 1, 2 and 3, 1879. The first two days were devoted to memorial services for the members of the association and other physicians who died while on duty during the epidemic of 1878. On the 3d, members to fill vacancies on the state board of health were nominated as follows: First district, Dr. E. P. Sale; second district, Dr. John Wright; third district, Dr. S. V. D. Hill; third district, Dr. B. F. Kittrell; fourth district, George E. Redwood; fifth district, Dr. J. W. Bennett; sixth district, Dr. C. A. Rice.

The officers chosen were: E. P. Sale, M. D., Aberdeen, president; W. F. Hyer, M. D., Hudsonville, first vice president; W. C. Jarnagin, M. D., Macon, second vice president; William Powell, M. D., Torrance, third vice president; J. S. Cain, M. D., Okolona, fourth vice president; Wirt Johnston, M. D., Jackson, recording secretary; M. S. Craft, M. D., Jackson, corresponding secretary; George K. Harrington, M. D., Jackson, treasurer; B. F. Ward, M. D., Winona, orator; and W. H. Baird, M. D., Indian Bayou, alternate orator.

The papers read before the association in 1879 were: Address, by Dr. B. F. Kittrell; The Spas of Mississippi, by Dr. D. L. Phares; Helenium tenifolium, by Dr. D. L. Phares, Bayou Sara vs. Yellow fever, by Dr. D. L. Phares; Surgical diseases of the rectum, by Dr. M. S. Craft; Malarial fevers, by Dr. N. L. Guice; Intentional anæsthesia, by Dr. J. M. Taylor; Ligation of the femoral artery, by Dr. E. P. Sale; Use of the obstetric forceps, by Dr. S. V. D. Hill; Climo-therapy of phthisis pulmonalis, by Dr. John Brownrigg; New remedies, by Dr. B. A. Vaughan; Report of a case of meningitis, by Dr. A. G. Smythe; Diagnosis and treatment of yellow fever, by Dr. W. F. Hyer; Wound of the knee joint, by Dr. S. V. D. Hill.

The members of the association who fell in the epidemic of 1878 were: W. H. Armistead, Lee Shackleford, D. W. Booth, P. F. Whitehead, A. H. Cage, W. M. Lea, G. C. McCallum, E. W. Hughes, D. A. Kinchloe, W. B. Williamson, W. M. Compton, N. W. McKie, W. W. Hall, P. F. Fitzgerald, W. J. Nesmith, J. R. Hicks, W. E. Monette, R. S. Ringgold, Z. T. Woodruff, and H. W. Johnson.

The physicians who were not members, but who died while attending the sick, were: Dr. V. F. P. Alexander, Greenville; Dr. M. Blackburn, Vicksburg; Dr. Barber, Vicksburg; Dr. Birdsong, Vicksburg; Dr. George Dickson, Crystal Springs; Dr. J. S. Roach, Vicksburg; Dr. Sappington, Vicksburg; Dr. W. B. Wilkerson, Vicksburg; Dr. Gilliland, Vicksburg; Dr. Hayes, Vicksburg; Dr. Happolat, Vicksburg; Dr. Glass, Vicksburg; Dr. E. W. Hughes, Grenada; Dr. Lindley, Grenada; Dr. W. B. May, Grenada; Dr. G. W. Woolfolk, Grenada; Dr. Gillespie, Grenada; Dr. Hawkins, Grenada; Dr. J. L. Milton, Grenada; Dr. Lewis, Holly Springs; Dr. Leach, Holly Springs; Dr. Thomas Manning, Holly Springs; Dr. W. O. McKinney, Holly Springs; Dr. Frank Fennell, Holly Springs; Dr. J. M. Fennell, Holly Springs; Dr. Fenton, Holly Springs; Dr. M. J. McKie, Canton; Dr. J. S. McCall, Greenville; Dr. William Montgomery, Greenville; Dr. James Newman, Vicksburg; Dr. J. P. Norris, Vicksburg; Dr. Potts, Vicksburg; Dr. M. C. Blackman, Vicksburg; Dr. A. S. Gardner, Greenville; Dr. Stafford, Greenville; Dr. J. J. Tate, Lake; Dr. Powell, Hernando; Dr. W. D. Sprott, Port Gibson; Dr. J. C. Strowbridge, Port Gibson; Dr. Thomas Young, Port Gibson; Dr. Blickfeldt, Port Gibson; Dr. Barber.

Dr. William Henry Armistead, son of John and Julia E. (Gaines) Armistead, was born in Randolph county, N. C., on the 5th of August, 1820. At the age of fifteen his father removed to Alabama. Of his early education but little is known. He graduated at the University of Louisville, Ky., in the spring of 1848; commenced the practice of medicine in the county of Choctaw, Miss., where he continued until May, 1854, when he removed to Shongalo, Carroll county, Miss., and married Miss Mary E. Wilson. After a time he removed to Vaiden. While Dr. Armistead was all his life engaged in practice, he was, from time to time, a representative from the counties of Choctaw and Carroll, in the state legislature. He was a member of his county medical society; also a member of the state and American Medical associations, and served as a delegate to the latter in Louisville in 1875. In the latter years of his life Dr. Armistead suffered much from rheumatism, declining rapidly, and finally fell a prey to paralysis, and died at his residence in Vaiden, on the 30th day of November, 1878, aged fifty-eight years and three months, leaving a wife and several children to mourn his irreparable loss. Honored and respected by all who knew him.

Dr. David W. Booth was born in the city of Vicksburg, Miss., of American parents, who were of English and Irish origin, on the 17th of July, 1840. Received his elementary education at Hampden Sydney college, Virginia, and his medical training at the University of Louisiana, where he graduated in the spring of 1861. During the late war he served as assistant regimental and brigade surgeon, also as medical inspector. At the close of the war he settled in his native city. In 1865 he was elected physician to the city hospital, of which he continued in charge until 1869. In 1875 he leased the same and established the Hill City infirmary, of which he was in charge at the time of his death. He fell a victim to the terrific plague of yellow fever, at his home in Vicksburg, on the 27th of August, 1878, aged thirty-eight years, leaving a wife and four children to mourn his untimely death. Thus has fallen, in the prime of life and eminent usefulness, one of our fellows, who was an ornament to the profession, and who bid fair to attain to an elevated position in the ranks of the medical men of the state. Of his private life and social relations we know but little, but presume they were pleasant and honorable. Said to have appeared to be cold, stiff and formal to strangers, but warm, genial and generous to a fault with friends and acquaintances. *Pax ad rejus memoria.*

Dr. Peter Flanagan Whitehead, a descendant of English and Irish ancestry, was born at Winchester, Ky., on the 9th of June, 1838. Was educated at the academy of his native town. Studied medicine at Jefferson Medical college, and graduated in 1859. Remained in Philadelphia hospital one year, after which he located at Independence, Mo. At the commencement of the late war he entered the Confederate army, in which he served three years as regimental surgeon, and one year as chief surgeon of General Loring's division. After the war he settled in the city of Vicksburg, where he soon obtained a respectable and lucrative practice.

In 1874 he was chosen president of this association, and represented it in the American Medical association in 1875. He was also a member of the state board of health. He was an occasional contributor to the current medical literature of the day, and nearly every recent volume of our transactions contained one or more papers from his pen, of bold, pointed and practical articles. On the approach of the late epidemic of yellow fever, he remained at his post, and fell a victim to that terrible scourge on the 5th day of September, 1878, in the prime of a life of honorable usefulness, mourned by his family and lamented by his friends.

Dr. Willis M. Lea, of Marshall county, Miss., was born at Leesburg, in North Carolina, on the 5th day of November, 1802. He took the degree of A. B. at the university of his native state, in 1821, and the degree of M. D. at the University of Pennsylvania in the year 1826. Located and practiced in his native town ten years, after which he removed and settled near Holly Springs, in Marshall county, Miss., where he engaged in practice and planting until he was disabled by a fall from a horse, which misfortune was followed by paralysis. His early training and close application placed him above a large number of those by whom he was surrounded. He was for many years president of his county medical society; was a member of the state convention which passed the ordinance of secession. He died of paralysis in Marshall county, Miss., on the 8th day of December, mourned by his family, and respected and venerated by a large circle of friends and acquaintances.

Dr. John R. Hicks was born on the 18th of November, 1839, in the city of Vicksburg. Of his early education the committee knew nothing. Received his professional training in the medical department of the University of Louisiana, graduating in 1861. Was valedictorian of his class. Entered and served in the army of Virginia until the latter part of 1862. Was transferred to the department of Mississippi, serving as surgeon to the close of the war. Married Miss Ida Yerger in 1865. Located in his native town. Had charge of the city hospital for a time. Died in Alabama, where he was resuscitating his health, on the 7th of October, 1878. Particulars not known.

Dr. Z. Taylor Woodruff was born in Tuscaloosa, Ala., on the 22d of June, 1849. Removed to Vicksburg when a youth. Studied medicine with hospital advantages; took his course at the University of Louisiana, graduating in 1872. Practiced one year at St. Louis, Mo., and for a time in Hale county, Ala.; but finally settled in Vicksburg, where he was made health officer, and continued to fill that office up to a short time before his death. His health being seriously impaired, he went to Turk, Ala., where he had friends, at which place he died just fifteen days after leaving Vicksburg, and on the 17th of July, 1878. *Ita est vita.*

Dr. G. C. McCallum, son of Judge A. McCallum, was born near Claiborne, Jasper county, Miss., on the 9th day of August, 1845. Received his primary education at the neighboring schools of the county. He graduated in the medical department of the University of Louisiana, in March, 1867. In January, 1870, married Miss M. J., daughter of the late S. R. Adams, of Paulding. He was located at Lake Station, Miss., where he died of yellow fever on the 7th of September, 1878. His whole family, except a son of six years, having died of the same scourge.

Dr. Edward W. Hughes descended from Irish ancestors, and was born on the 15th of March, 1819, in Charleston, Va. Received his education, first at the academy of his native town and last at the Classical and Mathematical high school, in Washington City. He graduated at the University of Louisville, Ky., in March, 1847, and settled in Grenada, Miss.

Was a member of his county society, also its president. Was vice-president of this association, and but for his extreme retiring modesty, would have been its president. Was a member of the International congress in 1876, and a member of the state board of health. Author of many valuable papers. Had a large and interesting family. He fell with his armor on in the cause of humanity, August 31, 1878, battling against disease, suffering and death, in the terrible scourge which visited the doomed little city of his home. He died as he had lived, a faithful physician, a man of honor, and Christian gentleman.

Dr. W. E. Monette was born in Warren county, Miss., the 7th of January, 1834. Obtained his early education at Oakland college. Graduated at the University of Pennsylvania in 1857. Attended a course at the University of Louisiana, and practiced for a time in that state. Served as a brigade surgeon in the Confederate army. Had resided in his native county since the war. Was a member of this association. Fell a prey to the epidemic of 1878. It is to be regretted that the day of his death, place and circumstances of his last illness are unknown to the committee.

Dr. David Anderson Kinchloe, of Scotch-Irish parentage, was born in Barren county, Ky., October 18, 1823. Was educated at Farmington academy, Missouri. Studied medicine and graduated on the 4th of March, 1846, in the medical college of Ohio. Located at Belmont, Panola county, Miss., but on the declaration of war with Mexico he entered the volunteer service as surgeon under contract. Was afterward commissioned and assigned to duty in the Second regiment of Mississippi volunteers. Was afterward placed in charge of the hospital at Buena Vista, where he remained until the close of the war. He served as captain, and afterward as surgeon in various commands, and finally as chief surgeon in the staff of Major-General Withers, in the Confederate army, and was surrendered with the army of Tennessee at Greensboro, N. C. After the war he located at Sardis, Miss., and was in practice when able until he was prostrated by disease. He contracted chronic bronchitis in Mexico, from which he suffered in his last illness. But the final cause of his death was chronic enlargement of the liver, inflammation of the stomach and alimentary canal. Dr. K. was a fair contributor to the medical literature of his time. He died at Sardis on the 9th day of September, 1878, aged fifty-five years.

Dr. William Boswell Williamson was born on the 23d of November, 1812, at Sussex courthouse, Va. Graduated at the University of Pennsylvania in 1835. Was surgeon of volunteers in the revolution of Texas in 1836. He afterward settled and remained several years in Hinds county, Miss. He removed to New Orleans, but returned and settled at Edwards. He was secretary of the first state medical society formed in Mississippi. Was a member of the Medico-Physico society of New Orleans. He was a member of the Hinds County Medical association. He was superintendent of the state lunatic asylum in 1857 and 1858. He was a surgeon in the Confederate states army during the Civil war. He died with yellow fever at his home in Edwards, on the 27th day of September, 1878.

Dr. William McCorkle Compton, of American parentage and Irish ancestors, was born in Madisonville, Hopkins county, Ky., on the 4th of March, 1833. His early education was obtained in Alabama. His professional course was commenced at Louisville, Ky., and completed at Jefferson Medical college, where he took the degree of M. D. in 1854. He commenced practice in Marshall county, Miss. During the war of the states he served as a private and as surgeon in the Confederate army. He was a member of the state legislature in 1861, and a delegate to the constitutional convention in 1865 and 1868. He removed to the city of Jackson to take charge of the state lunatic asylum, and was superintendent eight years. While he was a general practitioner he devoted much time and study to special subjects—insanity, public health and kindred subjects. Was author of a number of papers upon various topics in relation to medicine of high character and peculiar merit. After the expiration of his time of service as superintendent he removed to Holly Springs, where he was preparing to erect a private asylum or hospital for the treatment of the insane. He was not engaged in practice at the time of his death. He was member of the state and American Medical associations and had been president of the former. He was a member of the state board of health for the state at large, and was probably a member of the International Medical congress at Philadelphia in 1876. He was probably one of the most prominent general practitioners in the Southern states. In the prospect of a brilliant success in his new enterprise he fell a victim to the terrible scourge of yellow fever. He died at his home near Holly Springs on the 23d of October, 1878, leaving seven motherless children to mourn his untimely death. Dr. Compton was the last physician who died in the epidemic in this state.

Dr. Nathan W. McKie, son of Dr. M. J. McKie, was born in Canton, Madison county, Miss., on the 5th day of July, 1849. His elementary education was obtained at Canton and Sharon, in his native county, and was a superior scholar of the grammar-school class. Had charge of the postoffice in Vicksburg in 1866. Commenced the study of medicine quite early under his father. Took his first course at New Orleans, in 1868, and graduated at the Washington university, of Baltimore, Md., in 1870, dividing first honors with two others in a class of forty or fifty. Immediately after his return commenced to practice at Sharon with his father, even rivaling him in the estimation of the people. Married Miss Molly McCool in 1871. Removed to Canton in 1877, and after a time he in a measure secured the confidence and practice of the lamented Cage during the temporary absence of the latter. At the breaking out of the yellow fever at Canton, when all was confusion and dismay, he, like a true hero, remained at his post surrounded by disease, suffering and death, doing his utmost to relieve suffering humanity until stricken himself, and fell a victim to the relentless plague on the 19th of August, 1878. Thus has passed from the stage of life, in the full vigor of manhood, with the prospect of a long life and a brilliant future in the practice of the profession of his choice. He left a wife and three small children to buffet the cold charities of a hard world.

The late lamented Dr. William Wood Hall was (probably) born at or near Grenada, Miss., on the 17th of August, 1839. His early education was chiefly obtained by his personal exertion, and it may be said truly that he was a self-made man. He began the study of medicine under the direction of the late Dr. E. W. Hughes, and took his course at the University of Nashville, where he graduated in 1861. Practiced one year in the swamp region; entered the Confederate army, a lieutenant, then a captain, promoted to be regimental surgeon of Taylor's regiment, serving with credit to the close of the war. Went to Coffeeville, but removed to Grenada in 1866, and settled permanently and did a fair and successful practice; was at one time vice president of this association; was and had been engaged by appointment of the same for two or three years in collecting material and writing the surgical history of the state, which labor bid fair to be an honor to the author and an ornament to the professional literature of the state and county. Dr. Hall had received the appointment to fill the chair of gynecology in the new medical college at Memphis, Tenn. Dr. Hall died as he had lived, sacrificing his life to his profession and humanity. Thus has fallen at the premature age of thirty-nine years, at the very threshold of a new field where his energy of character and persevering labor were almost sure to have been crowned with success. He fell a prey to the fell destroyer on the 29th of August, 1878, like a hero with his face to the foe with no hope of success. *Sic transit.*

Eng^d by H.B. Hall's Sons, New York.

Dr. Peter Fletcher Fitzgerald was born in Smithville, Brunswick county, N. C., on the 2d of November, 1836; was raised at Grenada, Miss.; received a liberal academic education; took his first course at the University of Nashville, and graduated at the University of Louisiana in 1858; located twelve miles south of Grenada, in the county of Carroll, and commenced practice; married Miss Eliza A. Purnell; entered the war of the states as a private, was promoted to assistant surgeon and served to the end of the war; returned and married a sister of her former wife, she having died some years before. At the time the epidemic made its appearance in Grenada, Dr. Fitzgerald tendered his services to the board of health, which were not accepted for the reason that he would be likely to fall a prey to the disease, but urged that he await and hold himself in readiness to meet it provided it should, as it did, spread to the country. He met it as a hero should meet a foe, face to face, and although not strong physically, he continued to respond to all calls, until, worn out and exhausted, he fell a prey to the relentless plague of yellow fever, on the 13th of October, 1878. He was a man of modest and unpretending demeanor, animated by a generous sympathy and possessed an unblemished character.

Dr. Lee Shackleford was born in Perry county, Ala., December 15, 1833, and died May 19, 1878, being in the forty-fifth year of his age. He graduated in medicine in the University of Louisiana, New Orleans, in 1858, and subsequently attended a course of lectures at the Jefferson Medical college, Philadelphia. He commenced the practice of his profession at or near Meridian, Miss., 1860, but the war breaking out soon after he volunteered as a private in the Thirty-seventh Mississippi regiment, then under the command of Col. Ro. McLain, but was detailed as a surgeon of the same. He was soon promoted, upon examination, to the full work of surgeon, in which capacity he served on various duties, with great fidelity and ability till the close of the war. He then resumed practice in Meridian, and prosecuted it with distinguished ability and success till stricken down by disease.

Dr. A. H. Cage, of Canton, Miss., was forty-seven years old and graduated in medicine at the University of Louisiana, in March, 1846. He was an educated, polished, Christian gentleman and physician far above mediocrity. Always courteous and hospitable to his brother physicians, kind and sympathetic in the sick room, the rich and the poor were alike the recipients of his faithful care. His health of late years had been much impaired, and for this reason he thought that to remain in Canton during the epidemic would be certain death to him, and frequently so expressed himself, but when urged to leave by both citizens and physicians, his reply was that death to him was preferable to disgrace, and that the profession should not suffer dishonor at his hands.

The thirteenth annual meeting was held at Vicksburg in April, 1880. The address of Dr. Shannon in welcoming the association was the beginning of one of the most interesting and instructive conventions of the association ever held. He said: "As chairman of the committee of arrangements, and in behalf of the physicians of Vicksburg, it becomes my duty and pleasure to welcome you to our city. We welcome you as citizens of a great and populous state, as patriots and Christian gentlemen, as well as members of a learned and honorable profession. Since Vicksburg was last honored by the presence of this association, our fair city, as well as many portions of our beloved state, has been desolated by an epidemic which will ever stand as a memorable epoch in history. I need not remind you, that when so many fell victims to the scourge, that some of the brightest and most useful members of this association went down at the post of duty. The places of such men as Hughes, Hall, Whitehead, Booth and others whom I could name, are not easily filled in society or in the ranks of the profession. Difficult as the task may seem, we have an abiding faith that the younger members of the profession, full of hope, of energy and of professional pride, will strive to emulate the example and worth of the illustrious dead, and push forward the car of progressive medicine. We are hopeful for the future prosperity of our city. Though we have some days of darkness and discouragement, the light is breaking and a brighter day is dawning. And when the association again assembles in this place in the near future, we hope to show you our restored harbor, a quickened commerce, successful factories and a city of largely increased wealth and population. We have recently been honored with a visit from that distinguished civil engineer, Capt. James B. Eads, whose fame is only coextensive with the splendor of his scientific achievements. Under his wise leadership, aided by a generous appropriation by the general government, we hope to show you in successful operation the most wonderful feat of engineering skill ever devised—the subduing and absolute controlling of the turbid and turbulent waters of the mighty Mississippi. This fact demonstrated as it must and will be, to the satisfaction of the commercial world, who can foretell its measureless influence in the development and enriching of this great and fertile valley?

Our historic city has withstood the rude shock of war, for months beleaguered by sword and famine. She has been wasted by a pestilence appalling and almost without parallel. She has been left high and dry by the great Father of Waters in his tireless march to the sea. Yet, by the energy and enterprise of her chivalrous people, she is destined to achieve a greater glory, and in the very heart of this marvelous cotton belt, sit enthroned like a crowned and sceptered queen amid her thousand hills. In addition to many other attractions, we may be able to show you the completion of the several railroad lines now contemplated, leading to this city and emptying here their untold treasures of wealth. Especially as we hope you may see here the completed transcontinental railroad, that indissoluble iron band that shall link together the great oceans, one on the east and the other on the west, along the thirty-second parallel of latitude. Then, in the days of her increased prosperity, Vicksburg will open her heart and welcome the men whose heroic deeds at the bedside of the sick and dying, in hovel as well as mansion, are too often unknown and unappreciated, save by Him who ruleth above and with whom dwelleth all wisdom. In conclusion, gentlemen, we congratulate you upon the large number of intelligent and experienced medical men present, and express the hope that this reunion of the Mississippi State Medical association may be harmonious and profitable not only to those present but to the profession and people at large.''

The following gentlemen were admitted to membership at this session: Drs. R. E. Howard, W. G. Stone, C. S. Hudson, W. E. Satterfield, George C. Phillips, O. B. Quin, John H. Lucas, T. J. Crofford, A. P. Harris, E. Fox, Daniel M. McGehee, R. T. Edwards, W. G. Kiger, G. W. Baskett, T. R. Henderson, J. A. Hull, W. P. Younge, F. M. Halbert, T. T. Beall, T. J. Murray, J. B. Pease, W. R. Blailock, S. D. Robbins, E. L. McGehee, O. S. Iglehart, J. R. Hill, Thomas A. Catchings, S. R. Dunn, F. W. Forbes, T. B. Ford, T. J. Lee, C. Hoover, R. E. Jones and W. F. Toombs.

The memorial to the senate and house of representatives, and the draft of a bill to incorporate the Mississippi State Medical association with power, to regulate the practice of medicine in the state of Mississippi, were presented. Dr. Taylor, in reviewing the history of this attempt to regulate medical practice, said: "It will be observed that in drafting this bill the two-fold object aimed at was kept in view, and the provisions intended solely for the charter of the association were restricted to the three first sections, whilst all the balance of the bill was devoted to the subject of regulating the practice of medicine. This was done that the charter might not fail on account of any objections to the balance of the bill, as it would be easy to strike off all after the third section. The bill was introduced in the senate, read and referred to the judiciary committee, from which it was never reported. The failure of the bill was not at all unexpected, and should not at all discourage its advocates. A measure of such vast importance should not be adopted until after it has been carefully and thoroughly considered, and, as far as possible, perfected. The bill, as presented, was not supposed to be free from imperfections and objections; but its principles and objects were thought to be sufficiently clearly indicated to serve as a basis for a more perfect bill to be presented and urged at the next session of the legislature. But it was thought a formal presentation of the subject before the legislature, even in an immature form, would bring it before the profession and the public more prominently and more forcibly than could be done by any other course. It is a subject which needs only to be fairly presented to commend itself to all intelligent minds. The better it is understood the more highly its importance will be appreciated. The enactment of similar laws in other states will cause hundreds of peripatetic charlatans to migrate into our state, where they can pursue their nefarious calling with impunity, inflicting upon the uninformed and credulous untold injury in purse and in health. A similar law in Illinois, passed in 1877, had the effect, in one year, to drive fourteen hundred of these gentry from that state, and to send four hundred and fifty non-graduated practitioners to medical schools to qualify themselves for practice.

The officers elected in 1880 were: W. F. Hyer, M. D., Hudsonville, president; D. L. Phares, M. D., Woodville, first vice president; H. Shannon, M. D., Vicksburg, second vice president; R. S. Toombs, M. D., Greenville, third vice president; W. D. Carter, M. D., Ripley, fourth vice president; Wirt Johnston, M. D., Jackson, recording secretary; M. S. Craft, M. D., Jackson, corresponding secretary; George K. Harrington, M. D., Jackson, treasurer; S. D. Robbins, M. D., Vicksburg, orator; S. R. Dunn, M. D., Greenville, alternate orator.

The papers read before the association in 1880 are of interest even to-day. The subjects treated were: The duties we owe to our women, by E. P. Sale; Medicine in the cotton states, by B. F. Ward; Recent advances in surgery, by S. V. D. Hill; Recent advances in obstetrics, by N. L. Guise; New remedies, by B. A. Vaughan; Ascyrum crux-andreae, for pertussis, by D. L. Phares; Malarial hematuria, by J. M. Greene; Hemorrhagic malarial fever, by B. F. Kittrell; Treatment of wounds by C. A. Rice; Operation for strangulated inguinal hernia, by John Brownrigg; a Case of amputation of both legs—thymol being used as a dressing in one and salicylic acid in the other, by Wirt Johnston; a Case of amputation of the leg in which secondary hemorrhage occurred, by Wirt Johnston; a Case of traumatic tetanus that resulted in recovery, by Wirt Johnston; Notes on some cases of interest, by W. A. Taylor; Removal of urethral calculi by perineal section, by J. E. Hulbert; a Case in practice, by John S. Featherston; a Case of lithotomy, by J. W. Bennett; an Unusual case of congenital malformation of the anus, by J. C. Hall; a Simple uterine and vaginal irrigator, by John S. Featherston; a Case of artesia, vaginæ, complicated with pregnancy, by E. P. Sale, and the History of yellow fever at Concordia in 1879, by John B. Pease.

The deaths of Drs. Turner, Sykes, Dulaney, Lowe, McLaurin and Davis were recorded in 1879–80, and the following tributes placed on record:

The tribute to David B. Turner, M. D., was written by T. L. Wilburn, M. D., of Winona, in 1880. "After hearing the report on necrology, and comparing its smallness to the long list of those faithful martyrs who perished at the post of duty during that memor able year 1878, we are forcibly struck with the gentleness with which a benign Providence has seen fit to deal with us since the last meeting of our association. But while we have abundant reasons for gratulations and rejoicing, the black angel, death, has not been entirely stayed in his work of destruction, but has seen fit to appear again in our ranks and select, as his victim, one of our most worthy, esteemed and useful members. I refer to Dr. David B. Turner, who, in the prime of his manhood and usefulness, when the hand upon the dial-plate of time denoted the sun had just crossed the meridian, and life to him was offering its sweetest charms, was called to rest from his labors, it was my good fortune to meet him frequently when I first espoused the cause of the healing art—a time in our history when we feel so sensibly the need of wise counsel and encouragement, which he always gave in such a manner as to impress me so forcibly with his strict integrity of character as a man and physician—I deem it nothing more than a simple act of justice to pay some human tribute to his memory.

"He graduated in the medical department of the University of Louisiana in 1859; moved to Winona and commenced the practice of medicine there in 1861, where he remained, doing a lucrative practice until his death in September, 1879. His wife died soon after he moved to Winona, and he afterward married Miss Laura Moore, daughter of Col. O. J. Moore, who now, with five children, mourn their irreparable loss. In his death we can truly say a good man has fallen—one who ever enjoyed the confidence and love of his patrons and friends, and commanded the respect and esteem of his professional brethren. He was of the highest order of professional honor and medical attainments; if not seemingly as impressive as some, it was due to that modesty and unobtrusiveness which ever characterized his nature.

"Kind and attentive to his patients, generous to a fault, he faithfully performed his mission: Going about doing good. In August, 1878, when it was announced the fair city of Grenada was visited by a scourge unparalleled in her history for the immensity of its proportions, we watched with eagerness the daily mortuary reports, bearing the sad tidings of departed loved ones, until at last it was flashed across the wires, "Drs. Hall and Hughes are no more." Dr. Turner remarked upon receiving the sad intelligence, "Two men have gone whose places in society and in our ranks will be hard to fill." Soon his own town was visited by the same destroying angel, and, her citizens thrown into sudden consternation, were fleeing hither and thither, seeking refuge from the grim monster, until the business little town of Winona, almost depopulated, assumed the aspect of some of Sherman's sentinels in his famous march to the sea. He remained faithful at the post of duty, contending with the insiduous foe, alleviating pain, and smoothing the path of the doomed to the grave."

"The tribute to Lucian Melville Sykes, M. D., was written by E. P. Sale, M. D., of Aberdeen, in 1880. Dr. Sykes, third son of the late Dr. William A. and Rebecca Barret Sykes, was born in Decatur, Ala., May 4, 1838. Whilst quite young his father moved near, and afterward to Aberdeen, Miss., where the subject of this sketch was brought up. Having been prepared by excellent high-school teaching for a collegiate education, he entered, in 1854, the University of Mississippi at Oxford, where he graduated in 1857, with credit to himself and alma mater. After graduation Dr. Sykes chose medicine for his profession, and with this in view he entered the medical department, University of New York, in 1858, where he attended one course of lectures. His inherited delicate constitution refused to tolerate heavy drafts made on it in following his professional studies, consequently he was compelled to abandon them and engage in an occupation not so taxing to his health. He decided on farming, and having received as his patrimony, a plantation in Boliver county, Miss., he moved on it and remained until the commencement of the late war. He enlisted amongst the first volunteers from his county, and was in the Confederate army until its surrender. After the war he collected the debris of a once handsome fortune and determined to complete his medical education, which he did by again entering the medical department, University of New York, where he graduated in March, 1866. He selected for his field of labor a point in the prairie district, northeast Mississippi, near what is now the railroad depot, Muldon, on the Mobile & Ohio railroad. Having well fitted himself for the practice of his profession, Dr. Sykes brought to bear in its pursuit great energy and skill, until he soon attained, for a young practitioner, quite an enviable reputation. About the period of the acme of his professional success, his health for the second time gave way, and for about a year he had almost abandoned his profession; but upon it's restoration he recommenced an active practice in which he continued up to the period of his death, which occurred suddenly from lightning stroke July 16, 1879. In April, 1868, he married Miss Lou A. Walker, daughter of the late John A. Walker, a prominent citizen and planter of Monroe county, Miss. To them were born three children—two girls and a boy, the latter, his namesake."

"The tribute to William J. Dulaney, M. D., was written in 1880, by Wirt Johnston, M. D., of Jackson. Dr. Dulaney was born in Orange county, Va., in 1813. His family was an old and highly respected one, and he was a most worthy descendant of a worthy line of ancestors. He evinced a partiality early in life for the study of medicine, and graduated in his chosen profession at the University of Virginia in the year 1833. Of a strong and independent character, anxious to work out his own fortunes unaided, he came to the state of Mississippi in 1835, and located at Society Ridge in Hinds county, where he resided until about the year 1846. He then removed to Madison county where he resided at the time of his death, which sad event occurred on February 14, 1880. Dr. Dulaney was sincerely devoted to his profession, and of a kind and sympathetic nature; he was ever ready to respond to the calls of the afflicted. He did a large and arduous practice, extending over a number of years, and the last days of his life were devoted to a patient afflicted with a fatal disease. He was a close student, a strong and original thinker, and a successful practitioner of medicine. As a professional man he not only won in early life, but he retained to the end the confidence of his neighbors and friends. As a citizen, as a father and husband, and, indeed, in a word, in all the relations of life, he was an admirable and exemplary character. He was just and fair in all of his dealings with his fellowmen, and was evidently actuated in all things by strong conscientious convictions."

"Dr. Hugh C. McLaurin, son of Daniel McLaurin, a Scotch emigrant, was born in Marlborough district, in the state of South Carolina, on the 30th day of September, 1813. His father moved to Wayne county, in this (Miss.) state. Living there only two years, he removed first to Covington, then to Simpson county, in 1822, continuing there the remainder of his life. In 1835 Dr. McLaurin went to South Hanover college, in Indiana; after a time, he went to the celebrated school of Hudson, in South Carolina; he read medicine in the office of Dr. Robertson, of Fayetteville, N. C., in 1839, and attended his first course of lectures, the following winter, in the medical department of the University of Pennsylvania; returned to Simpson county, and commenced the practice of medicine; graduated in the same school in 1844; married Miss Harriet E. Lowe, of Madison county, December 16, 1845; continued to practice in Simpson county, until he removed to Hinds county, in December, 1860. He removed to Brandon in 1865, where he established a respectable and successful practice, and maintained it up to the time of his death, which occurred suddenly, from a paroxysm of apoplexy, of only about thirty-six hours' duration, on the 13th day of July, 1880, aged sixty-six years ten months and thirteen days."

"James Shelton Davis, third son and fourth child of James R. Davis and Elenora Tinsely Davis, was born in Madison county, Ala., March 24, 1819, and died at Iuka, Miss., November 29, 1879. When quite young, he removed, with his parents, to Limestone county, where he received a common English education, and a slight acquaintance with the Latin language. In 1837, he removed to Athens, Ala., where he did business in the mercantile house of J. H. & R. Hine. In 1839 he entered the office of Dr. John C. Spotswood, with whom he read medicine. He married, July 21, 1838, Nancy E., daughter of Samuel Tanner, of that place. In 1839 he attended a course of medical lectures at Louisville, Ky., and engaged in the practice on his return home, the following spring. In 1845 he removed to Marshall county, Miss., where he practiced till 1852, when he moved to Salem, Tippah county, Miss. In 1860, he was elected to the Secession convention at Jackson, and served in that body, voting for the ordinance of secession, the proudest act of his life. He was connected with the war that followed. After the convention, he moved to Iuka, and soon after commenced editing the Iuka Springs *Gazette*. He graduated in medicine at the Jefferson Medical college, Philadelphia, in 1854. At the commencement of the University of Louisville, Ky., in 1871, the *ad eundum gradum* was conferred upon him. In 1872 he was one of the democratic electors for president and vice president, for the state of Mississippi, on the O'Connor ticket."

The fourteenth annual meeting was held at Winona, in April, 1881. Papers were read in the following order: Surgery of Mississippi, by M. S. Craft; Cases, by Dr. Brownrigg, R. A. Cunningham, R. R. Blailock, J. H. Banks, W. D. Carter, S. V. D. Hill, F. E. Daniel, J. M. Green, B. F. Kittrell, L. M. Mays, A. P. Harris and M. S. Craft. Dr. W. Y. Gadbury explained the new appliance for fracture of lower extremities. Dr. Hyer delivered the address. A paper on the Abortive treatment of pneumonia was read by Dr. W. Y. Gadbury; one on New remedies by B. A. Vaughan; one on Diphtheria by Dr. J. B. Gresham; one on Recent advances in general pathology by Dr. B. F. Ward; one on the Diseases of gastroenteric mucous membrane in infancy and childhood by Dr. B. F. Ward; and one on the Rights, duties and responsibilities of physicians before the courts by J. S. Morris. Two members were expelled from the association on April 6.

The officers elected in April, 1881, were B. F. Ward, M. D., president, Winona; J. P. Moore, M. D., first vice president, Yazoo City; T. W. Fullilove, M. D., second vice president, Vaiden; John Tackett, M. D., third vice president, Richland; W. W. Hart, M. D., fourth vice president, Lodi. Wirt Johnston, M. D., recording secretary, Jackson; M. S. Craft, M. D., corresponding secretary, Jackson; G. K. Harrington, M. D., treasurer, Jackson; F. E. Daniel, M. D., orator, Jackson; T. R. Henderson, M. D., alternate orator, Greenwood.

The members of the executive committee appointed were: J. M. Taylor, M. D., Robert Kells, M. D., E. G. Banks, M. D., R. G. Wharton, M. D., B. A. Vaughan, M. D., A. G. Smythe, M. D., D. C. McCallum, M. D., B. F. Kittrell, M. D., S. V. D. Hill, M. D., W. F. Hyer, M. D., B. F. Ward, M. D., N. L. Guice, M. D., George E. Redwood, M. D. Of the judicial committee: W. Y. Gadbury, M. D., Wirt Johnston, M. D., secretary, George K. Harrington, M. D., treasurer, S. V. D. Hill, M. D., B. F. Ward, M. D., B. F. Kittrell, M. D., J. M. Taylor, M. D. Of the committee on publication: M. S. Craft, M. D., Robert Kells, M. D., P. T. Baley, M. D., T. J. Mitchell, M. D.. Of the committee on necrology: A. G. Smythe, M. D., W. W. Hart, M. D., Robert Smith, M. D. And of the committee of arrangements: J. T. Chandler, M. D., T. D. Isom, M. D., and Paul A. Burt, M. D.

The only death recorded was that of Dr. W. P. Finley. He was born in Madison county, Miss., on December 25, 1836, and died at Fannin, Rankin county, Miss., May 15, 1881, of pneumonia with asthma, being forty-four years of age. He graduated in the medical department of the University of Louisiana, in 1859. Soon after this he began practice in Kosciusko, and thence moved to Greensborough, Choctaw county, Miss. The war coming on, he was made regimental surgeon in the army of northern Virginia, in which capacity he served his country with success and credit. He was married during the war to Miss K. C. Carlton, of North Carolina.

Dr. James Wilson Holman died of meningitis, at Winona, Miss., April 21, 1881. He was born in Perry county, Ala., October 5, 1829. At an early age his parents moved to Mississippi. His father, by great industry, frugality and integrity, amassed a large fortune. The deceased might, if it had suited him, have lived the life of an idler, as so many of our young men have done who were similarly situated, but Dr. Holman was made of a different kind of material, and as soon as he reached man's estate he determined to pursue the profession of medicine, believing that no calling could be more honorable than that of alleviating human suffering. He graduated at Louisville, Ky., in the year 1851, and immediately located at Middleton, Miss. Soon after this he married Martha W., daughter of E. W. Bennett. After the war between the sections, when the town of Winona rose upon the ashes of Middleton, he located there, and from that day until the hour of his death his name was inseparably interwoven with the history of the busy and prosperous little city of Winona.

The rules and regulations adopted by the board of health in March, 1882, for the government of boards of censors, in their examination for license to practice medicine under the provisions of "an act to regulate the practice of medicine in the state of Mississippi," approved February 28, 1882, were stringent, though few in number.

The fifteenth annual meeting was held in April, 1882, when the following-named officers were chosen for the year ending April, 1892: Wirt Johnston, M. D., Jackson, president; J. M. Greene, M. D., Aberdeen, J. E. Halbert, M. D., Leota Landing, J. T. Chandler, M. D., Oxford, E. L. McGehee, M. D., Woodville, vice presidents; T. W. Fullilove, M. D., Vaiden, recording secretary; M. S. Craft, M. D., Jackson, corresponding secretary; Robert Kells, M. D. Jackson, treasurer; G. W. Trimble, M. D., Grenada, orator; J. B. Sanford, M. D., Corinth, alternate orator.

Dr. J. Y. Murry, chairman of the committee on the nomination of delegates to the American Medical association, and other state medical associations, reported the following as delegates to the American Medical association: Drs. B. F. Ward, B. F. Kittrell, E. L. McGehee, J. P. Moore, W. D. Carter, T. J. Mitchell, J. H. Blanks, C. E. Oates, W. F. Hyer, William Powell, C. A. Rice, R. M. Young, T. D. Isom, J. E. Halbert; J. M. Greene, T. R. Trotter, H. A. Gant. To Tri-State Medical association: T. J. Chandler, W. R. Blailock, Frank Ferrall, W. B. Sanford, S. N. Walker, R. E. Howard, J. M. Hicks, T. J. Crofford, F. W. Dancy, R. S. Toombs, O. J. Sherman. Alabama association: J. M. Taylor, B. A. Vaughan, R. E. Jones, P. J. McCormick, L. W. Mabry, W. E. Todd, F. P. Bibby.

The papers read before the meeting included: on Alcohol, by Dr. B. F. Ward; New remedies, by Dr. B. F. Kittrell; Senecio lobatus, by Dr. D. L. Phares; Retained placenta, by Dr. T. R. Trotter; Scarlet fever, by Dr. F. W. Dancy; Traumatic tetanus, by Dr. H. A. Grant; Abortive treatment of puerperal convulsions, by Dr. T. H. Gordon; Infantile convulsions, by Dr. J. P. Moore; Puerperal eclampsia, successfully treated with veratrum viride, with cases, by Dr. N. L. Guice; Case of perforation of the illium by worms, by Dr. T. J. Crofford; Three cases of embryotomy, by Dr. J. D. Talbert; Spinal curvature, by Dr. Chesley Daniel; Surgical cases, by Dr. W. R. Blailock, and Report on the surgery of Mississippi, by Dr. M. S. Craft. Cases were reported by Dr. T. J. Crofford, of Coffeeville, Dr. R. C. Cunningham, of Verona, Dr. George C. Phillips, of Lexington, Dr. J. M. Taylor, of Corinth, Dr. D. C. Montgomery, of Greenville, Dr. R. E. Jones, of Crystal Springs, Dr. E. L. McGehee, of Woodville, Dr. J. E. Halbert, of Leota Landing, Dr. J. M. Green, of Aberdeen, Dr. S. V. D. Hill, of Macon, Dr. R. F. Edwards, of Edwards, Dr. F. W. Dancy, of Holly Springs, Dr. W. R. Blailock, of Carthage, Dr. W. B. Sanford, of Corinth, Dr. C. R. Henderson, of Deasonville, Dr. R. M. Young, of Corinth, Dr. J. H. Blanks, of Meridian, Dr. M. S. Craft, of Jackson.

The sixteenth annual meeting was held at Meridian in April, 1883. Col. W. H. Hardy, welcoming the physicians, said:

"We understand the objects of this association to be to combine and direct the moral and intellectual forces of the profession, to incite its members to reach out and up for higher planes of professional excellency; and to guard the profession and the public from quacks and charlatans. It is, therefore, with unfeigned pleasure that we hail you as true philanthropists, real benefactors, and we deeply regret that our facilities for entertaining you are not what we would wish them to be, for our little city is an unpretentious child of the new South, scarcely sixteen years old. We have no ancient classic halls, whose towers look down upon the buried ages; no monuments of marble or brass perpetually proclaiming the renowned achievements of warriors and statesmen; no splendid parks, studded with trees and fragrant with flowers; no towering mountains reflecting the golden beauty and glory of a Southern sunset to ravish your visions. We have only our youthful blushes, our generous hearts, our humble but hospitable homes, and to all these, in the name of all our people, I bid you a most cordial and thrice hearty welcome."

The officers elected were: J. M. Greene, M. D., Aberdeen, president; S. N. Walker, M. D., Baldwyn, D. McCallum, M. D., Westville, vice presidents; W. E. Todd, M. D., Clinton, recording secretary; J. F. Hunter, M. D., Jackson, assistant secretary; Robert Kells, M. D., Jackson, treasurer; M. S. Craft, M. D., Jackson, corresponding secretary.

An election to make nominations to fill the vacancies on the state board of health, resulted as follows: S. V. D. Hill, M. D., first district; J. P. Moore, M. D., fourth district; J. W. Bennett, M. D., Robert Kells, M. D., fifth district; R. S. Toombs, M. D., sixth district.

The subjects discussed were the objects of the association, treated in the president's address, by Dr. Wirt Johnston; Intemperance as a disease, by Dr. G. W. Trimble; Recent advances in surgery, by Dr. S. V. D. Hill; Malarial hematuria, by Dr. J. E. Halbert; Hypodermic use of sulphate of quinine, by Dr. N. L. Guice; Vaccination, by Dr. B. A. Vaughan; a Splint for Barton's fracture of the radius, by Dr. John Brownrigg; Appliances for the treatment of fracture of the femur, by Dr. John Brownrigg; External urethrotomy, by Dr. John Brownrigg; Rupture of uterus, by Dr. W. E. Todd; Typhoid pneumonia, by Dr. W. E. Todd; Whooping cough, by Dr. E. L. McGehee; Trismus nascentium, by Dr. T. J. Hancock; Abortive treatment of pneumonia, by Dr. T. J. Hancock; Puerperal convulsions, by Dr. L. W. Mabry; A case of chronic hydrocephalus, by Dr. B. F. Kittrell; Mumps (Metastasis), by Dr. D. L. Phares; A surgical case, by Dr. R. S. Toombs; Case of chronic synovitis, by Dr. J. W. Bennett; and Surgical cases, by Dr. M. S. Craft.

The death of Dr. A. I. Ellis, at Sardis, occurred April 11, 1883. He was sixty-one years of age.

The seventeenth annual meeting was held at West Point, April 2, 3 and 4, 1884. No less than forty-three papers were read, together with the address of President Greene. As recorded they are named in order: President's address, Dr. J. M. Greene; The Germ theory, Dr. W. D. Carter; Diphtheria, Dr. W. E. Todd; Endometritis, Dr. J. T. Hancock; Areolar hyperplasia of the uterus, Dr. E. P. Sale; Third stage of labor, Dr. Samuel Walker; Chronic inflammation of the bladder, Dr. S. V. D. Hill; Small pox, Dr. W. D. Wall; A case of twin labor, Dr. B. F. Kittrell; Vaginismus, Dr. B. F. Ward; Epidemico-zootic plagues, Splenic fever, Dr. D. L. Phares; Abdominal palpation in obstetric practice, Dr. C. C. Stockard; Empyema, Dr. B. F. Ward; The disposal of wastes, Its relation to public health, B. A. Vaughan. Surgery of Mississippi, cases reported: Gun shot wound, Dr. John S. Featherston; Removal of a breach pin of a gun from the brain, followed by recovery, Dr. T. B. Elkin; Excision of tumor, Dr. B. F. Duke; Tracheotomy, Dr. B. F. Duke; Imperforate anus, with operation, Dr. C. M. Jordan; Excision of left mammary gland, for hand cancer, Dr. W. N. Ames; Wound of the carotid artery, Dr. W. N. Ames; Double amputation—death, Dr. Luther Sexton; Twelve gallons of pus removed from peritoneal cavity at seven tappings—recovery, Dr. Luther Sexton; New operation for hydrocele, by laying open and obliterating the sac, Dr. Luther Sexton; Abscess of liver, incision into abscess and recovery, Dr. W. T. Balfour; Railroad injury, Dr. W. T. Balfour; Strangulated hernia—operation and recovery, Dr. W. H. White; Fracture of a skull into frontal sinus, Dr. B. A. Duncan; Severe wound of abdomen, involving stomach and liver, Dr. B. A. Duncan; Fatty tumor of abdomen successfully removed, Dr. B. A. Duncan; Two cases of gunshot fracture of femur, Dr. C. A. Rice; Double Hey's operation, Dr. W. H. Barr; Polypus of the rectum, Dr. C. Kendrick; Traumatic gangrene, amputation—death; Retention of urine from stricture, relieved by aspiration, Dr. C. C. Stockard; Epithelionia, with operation, Dr. John Brownrigg; Stone in the bladder, with operation, Dr. J. M. Greene; Strangulated hernia, Dr. S. V. D. Hill; Pott's fracture, Dr. S. V. D. Hill; Osteo sarcoma, Dr. S. V. D. Hill; Death from syphilis, Dr. M. S. Craft; Epithelionia of the cervix uteri, Dr. M. S. Craft; Two cases of benign stricture of rectum relieved by operation, Dr. M. S. Craft, and Second case of stricture, Dr. M. S. Craft.

The officers elected in 1884 were: D. L. Phares, M. D., A. and M. College, Starkville, president; J. B. Gresham, West Point, and W. A. Taylor, Booneville, vice presidents; W. E. Tood, M. D., Clinton, recording secretary; N. L. Clarke, M. D., Hickory, assistant secretary; M. S. Craft, M. D., Jackson, corresponding secretary; John F. Hunter, M. D., Jackson, treasurer. The members of the judicial council were N. L. Guice, M. D., Fayette, W. D. Carter, M. D., Ripley, William Powell, M. D., Torrance, each for one year; S. V. D. Hill, M. D., Macon, J. P. Moore, M. D., Yazoo City, B. F. Kittrell, M. D., Black Hawk, each for two years; J. M. Taylor, M. D., Corinth, R. S. Toombs, M. D., Greenville, B. F. Ward, M. D., Winona, each for three years. The officers of judicial council were W. D. Carter, M. D., president, and B. F. Kittrell, M. D., secretary. The delegates to American association were Drs. M. S. Craft, B. A. Duncan, N. L. Guice, J. M. Greene, S. V. D. Hill, Wirt Johnston, T. J. Mitchell, C. A. Rice, W. A. Taylor, R. S. Toombs, W. B. Sanford, B. F. Ward, S. N. Walker, F. R. Van Eaton and S. R. Dunn.

The eighteenth annual meeting was held at Greenville in April, 1885. The following were nominated to fill the vacancies on the state board of health:

E. P. Sale, M. D., first district; John Wright, M. D., second district; S. V. D. Hill, M. D., third district; J. H. Blanks, M. D., fourth district; R. T. Edwards, M. D., and N. L. Guice, M. D., sixth district.

The committee on delegates to American Medical association reported the following names for the year 1885: Drs. J. B. Pease, M. S. Craft, E. P. Sale, J. M. Taylor, W. A. Taylor, W. Y. Gadbury, J. S. Walker, J. C. Denson, William H. White, T. T. Beall, T. W. Fullilove, Aurelius Martin, J. C. Brooks, R. S. Toombs, J. E. Halbert. Any member who desired to attend the American association as a delegate would, by notifying the secretary, be furnished with proper credentials.

The papers and reports on medical topics read before the meeting included those entitled: Two cases of abscess of the liver, treated by incision and free drainage, by Dr. J. H. Shackleford; Removal of nails, by Dr. E. L. McGehee; Veratrum and gelsemium compared, by Dr. J. Brownrigg; The euphorbiaceæ or spurgeworts, by Dr. D. L. Phares; Tracheotomy for membranous croup, by Dr. Luther Sexton; Case of traumatic tetanus—recovery, by Dr. B. F. Ward; Some of the recent improvements in the treatment of fractures, by Dr. J. Brownrigg; Report of a case, by Dr. W. H. White; Alcohol, its effects on the system in health and in disease, by Dr. J. C. Robert; The sanitary examination of water, by Joseph Waldauer, Ph. G. The cases reported by Dr. Wirt Johnston were: Abscess of the liver, Empyema (pyothorax), Aspiration of the bladder, Two cases of hydrocephalus, Amputation of the arm, Wound of the brachial artery, Fracture of arm near elbow-joint, and Morphia administered hypodermically. A paper entitled Vaginismus, by Dr. E. P. Sale; Diagnosis and treatment of lacerations of the cervix uteri, by Dr. J. H. Blanks, were also read.

The officers of the association for the year 1885-6 were J. B. Gresham, M. D., of West Point, president; J. B. Pease, M. D., of Concordia, and S. R. Dunn, M. D., of Greenville, vice presidents; W. E. Todd, M. D., of Clinton, recording secretary; G. K. Harrington, M. D., of Jackson, assistant secretary; M. S. Craft, M. D., of Jackson, corresponding secretary; John F. Hunter, M. D. of Jackson, treasurer.

The members of the judicial council were N. L. Guice, M. D., Fayette; W. D. Carter, M. D., Ripley; William Powell, M. D., Torrance (each for one year); E. P. Sale, M. D., Aberdeen; W. F. Hyer, M. D., Holly Springs; B. F. Kittrell, M. D., Black Hawk (each for two years); J. M. Taylor, M. D., Corinth; R. S. Toombs, M. D., Greenville; B. F. Ward, M. D., Winona (each for three years).

The officers of judicial council were J. M. Taylor, M. D., president; B. F. Kittrell, M. D., secretary.

The nineteenth annual meeting was held at Jackson April 21 and 22, 1886. The officers of the association elected were R. S. Toombs, M. D., of Greenville, president; W. B. Sanford, M. D., of Corinth, and G. W. Trimble, of Grenada, vice presidents; W. E. Todd, M. D., of Clinton, recording secretary; P. W. Rowland, M. D., of Coffeeville, assistant secretary; M. S. Craft, M. D., of Jackson, corresponding secretary; John F. Hunter, M. D., of Jackson, treasurer.

The members of judicial council were N. L. Guice, M. D., Fayette; W. D. Carter, M. D., Ripley; William Powell, M. D., Torrance; W. F. Hyer, M. D., Holly Springs; E. P. Sale, M. D., Aberdeen; B. F. Kittrell, M. D., Black Hawk; N. L. Guice, M. D., Fayette; W. D. Carter, M. D., Ripley; S. V. D. Hill, M. D., Macon.

Drs. Guice and Carter were appointed by the president at the meeting at West Point in 1884 for a term of three years, and were elected at the meeting in Jackson in 1886 for a term of three years.

Governor Lowry, in welcoming the delegates, said: "It is safe to assume that the learned profession to which you belong has made greater progress in the last quarter of a century than that of any other; indeed, the advancement has been more marked in the last thirty than the preceding fifty years. I may add, in this connection, that the state medical association and state boards of health have given to the people a security and confidence for the protection of life and health never before felt in the American Union. But a few years ago this commonwealth was subjected to epidemics, occurring in neighboring states, and entirely powerless to invoke the necessary sanitary and quarantine preventives. I remember, in this hall, to have witnessed a meeting, composed not only of eminent physicians, but of representative business men of the great Mississippi valley, when there was a free interchange of opinions touching the public health, which culminated in the co-operation of the sanitary council of the Mississippi valley with the several state boards of health, which rendered the latter more effective. From that day a better understanding has prevailed between neighboring states, and when occasion required those of your number charged with the duty have in a great measure prevented the spread of contagious and infectious diseases. The friendly intercourse between boards of health of the several states, and each with that of the general government, insures the most prompt information; so that in any emergency active steps are assured to prevent the spread of epidemics."

Addresses on medical topics were delivered in the order of the following record: Address of president, Dr. J. B. Gresham; Antiseptic treatment of pulmonary diseases by means of pneumatic differentiation, by Dr. J. H. Blanks; A case of puerperal nephritis, by Dr. N. L. Guice; Traumatic tetanus in a child of five years, by Dr. George C. Phillips; External urethrotomy, by Dr. J. A. Shackleford; Ulcerative tonsilitis, by Dr. B. F. Duke; Cocaine, by Dr. B. F. Kittrell; Report of a case of glaucoma, by Dr. R. B. Carson; The use of antiseptics in obstetrics, by Dr. E. P. Sale; Malarial flux, by Dr. E. L. McGehee; Dysentery, by Dr. W. H. White; A Case of opium poisoning, by Dr. T. T. Beall; Lacerated cervix operations, by Dr. T. T. Beall; Five cases of cataract extractions, by Dr. A. G. Sinclair; Some of the complications of typhoid fever, by Dr. Henry Izard; The treatment of malarial hæmaturia, by Dr. J. C. Hall; Surgery of Mississippi, report by Dr. M. S. Craft, chairman of cases for 1886; by Dr. C. W. Jordan, West Point, Tracheotomy for the removal of a cockleburr; by Dr. J. G. Knox, Toomsuba, A case of herniotomy; by Dr. C. C. Stockard, Columbus, Amputation for recurring hemorrhage sarcoma; by Dr. W. W. Hamilton, Brooksville, Elephantiasis; by Dr. J. Brownrigg, Columbus, Dislocation of the thumb, Occlusion of the vagina; by Dr. L. W. Magruder, Congenital absence of os uteri; by Dr. B. F. Duke, Fistula in ano; by Dr. E. L. McGehee, A punctured wound through the abdominal and uterine walls; by Dr. J. C. Robert, A Case of laceration of bladder, with probable wound of intestines; by Dr. John M. Whitson, Pistol-shot wound in the chest, Excision of a tumor of the face, Extraction of a calculus from the urethra of a two-year-old baby; by Dr. Luther Sexton, Don't mix surgery and obstetrics, Fluid extract marigold, Extensive burns, Needle in the foot for eighteen months; by Dr. T. R. Lockwood, Pirigoff's operation; by Dr. W. B. Sanford, Two operations for lacerated perineum; by Dr. J. W. Bennett, Tracheotomy; by Dr. W. B. Sanford, Two operations for strangulated inguina hernia; by —— ——, Aneurism of the femoral artery, Gangrene and death; by Dr. J. W. Dulaney, Wounds of abdomen from kick of a horse; and by Dr. M. S. Craft, Reports of tumors.

The twentieth annual session was held at Jackson April 20, 21 and 22, 1887. The address of welcome was delivered by Charles E. Hooker. The papers on professional topics read before the association are named as follows: Erysipelas, by Dr. W. A. Galloway; Uterine surgery, by Dr. J. A. Shackleford; A case of embolism, by Dr. B. F. Kittrell; A case of ovariotomy, Presenting some features of interest, by Dr. W. F. Hyer; Case of malarial cachexia of two years' duration, Purgative action of minute doses of strychnine, by Dr. N. L. Guice; A few suggestions of the treatment of diseases of the eye and ear, by Dr. J. L. Minor; Chloral hydrate as a remedy in two forms of acute malarial diseases, by Dr. T. T. Beall; Hereditary progressive muscular atrophy, by Dr. J. W. Bennett; Modified phimosis operation, by Dr. T. T. Beall; Iritis, by Dr. A. G. Sinclair; Abscess of the liver treated by aspiration and incision, by Dr. J. E. Halbert; A case of fracture of the skull, by Dr. B. F. Duke; Two cases of chronic suppurative inflammation of the middle ear (atorrhea) successfully treated by boracic acid, by Dr. T. T. Beall; Suppurative hepatitis, by Dr. G. L. Pope; Report of three cases of fluid in plueral cavity, and One case of extirpation testicles for sarcocelle, Dr. O. B. Quinn; Wound of the head, with considerable loss of brain, by Dr. W. G. Lawrence; An unusual sequence to reduction of dislocation of hip joint, by Dr. T. T. Beall; Fatal issue from intra-uterine injection, by Dr. T. T. Beall; Epidemic dysentery, by Dr. W. E. Herring; Modern treatment of phthisis pulmonalis, by Dr. S. V. D. Hill; Report of two cases of urethral stricture, with operation and results, by Dr. R. B. Carson; Phlegmasia dolens, by Dr. Sexton; Serious result of a trivial wound, by Dr. W. H. White; Treatment of pneumonia, by Dr. H. H. Haralson; Abcess of the anterior mediastenum, by Dr. A. L. Morris; Heart disease, by Dr. E. L. McGehee; Malarial flux, by Dr. E. L. McGehee.

The first true effort made since 1878 by the committee on necrology was that of this year. Doctors Sexton and Blanks reported that the following names were found on the roll though the parties had been dead for years (too long, many of them, to obtain any correct data for report): J. L. Cloud, Water Valley; E. Fox, Forrest; C. C. Lee, Graysport; W. D. McMartin, Black Hawk; A. G. Smythe, Baldwyn; J. O. Saunders, Carrollton; L. White, Utica. Dr. C. E. Hoover died of some heart trouble in 1886. He graduated in the medical department of the University of Louisiana, and practiced medicine at Summit and McComb up to the time of his death. He had been a consistent member of the association for years, and loved his profession next to his family and his God. He was district surgeon of the Illinois Central railroad, and had acted as sanitary inspector of the state board of health during the epidemic of small pox in Pike county in 1884. Dr. T. A. Phillips died at Fort Smith, Ark., in 1886, of Bright's disease of the kidneys. He practiced at Canton for a decade. Dr. W. L. Ainsworth, of Copiah county, though he had been dead for several years, his name still appeared on the roll. The doctor was a graduate of the medical department of the University of Louisiana, and practiced at Hazlehurst for four or five years after graduating. Finding that he was physically unable for the task of an active practice, he reluctantly gave up his profession and accepted the office of county treasurer of Copiah county, which office he filled at the time of his death.

The officers of the association elected in April, 1887, were: N. L. Guice, M. D., Natchez, president; L. Sexton, M. D., Wesson, and M. J. Thompson, Meridian, vice presidents; W. E. Todd, M. D., Clinton, recording secretary; W. M. Paine, M. D., Aberdeen, assistant recording secretary; M. S. Craft, M. D., Jackson, corresponding secretary; John F. Hunter, M. D., Jackson, treasurer.

The members of judicial council chosen were: J. E. Halbert, M. D., Mount Landing; B. F. Ward, M. D., Winona; Luther Sexton, M. D., Wesson; W. F. Hyer, M. D., Holly Springs; E. P. Sale, M. D., Aberdeen; B. F. Kittrell, M. D., Black Hawk; N. L. Guice, M. D., Fayette; W. D. Carter, M. D., Ripley; S. V. D. Hill, M. D., Macon. Drs. Guice and Carter were appointed by the president at the meeting at West Point, in 1884, for a term of three years, and were elected at the meeting in Jackson, in 1886, for a term of three years.

The twenty-first annual meeting was held at Jackson, April 18 and 19, 1888, when the following named officers were elected: Luther Sexton, M. D., Wesson, president; R. E. Howard, M. D., Durant, first vice president; E. F. Shuler, M D., Greenville, second vice president; W. E. Todd, M. D. Jackson, recording secretary; George S. Hunter, M. D., Bolton, assistant recording secretary; John F. Hunter, M. D., Jackson, treasurer; W. A. Galloway, M. D., Jackson, corresponding secretary.

The members of judicial council were: J. E. Halbert, M. D., Mount Landing, B. F. Ward, M. D., Winona, and Luther Sexton, M. D., Wesson, each to serve until 1890; W. F. Hyer, M. D., Holly Springs, B. F. Kittrell, M. D., Black Hawk, and E. L. McGehee, M. D., Woodville, each to serve until 1891; N. L. Guice, M. D., Natchez, W. D. Carter, M. D., Ripley, and S. V. D. Hill, M. D., Macon, each to serve until 1889.

The address of welcome was delivered by E. Barksdale, who referred to the death of Dr. M. S. Craft in the following words: "Your reunion is saddened by the recent death of one of the most beloved and distinguished of the resident physicians of this city, Dr. M. S. Craft, whom you have been accustomed to meet around your council board, and in professional and social life. He has crossed the river and rests in the shade of the trees beyond. His duties have been transferred to a higher sphere of existence. A strong pillar of your profession has fallen. The able physician who fought many a successful battle for the relief of suffering humanity, has succumbed to the last enemy. He fell in the zenith of his fame, and his usefulness, as the 'great oak uplifted by the storms, fell with its garlands of ivy around it.' If the beautiful legend be true that the spirits of the dead revisit the scenes they loved in life, we may cherish the hope that our departed friend is not absent from us in spirit to-day "

The following papers were read on medical subjects: Intestinal obstruction, J. A. Shackelford, M. D., Greenville; Diseases common to manufacturing towns, and sanitary recommendations for same, Luther Sexton, M. D., Wesson; Typho-malarial fever, P. W. Rowland, M. D., Coffeeville; Brass pin in Wharton's duct, W. E. Herring, M. D., Terry; Abdominal pregnancy, Laparotomy, John S. Featherston, M. D., Brookville; Post-mortems, A. B. Holder, M. D., Crow Agency; A Case of moist gangrene, B. F. Duke, M. D., Lake Como; Quinine, B. A. Vaughan, M. D.; Malarial cachexia, B. F. Travis, M. D., Heidelberg.

Of the physicians who died during the year, the committee on necrology succeeded in obtaining facts from which the following sketches were written:

Mijaman Sidney Craft was born in Jackson, Miss., August 6, 1827, and was educated in the town schools. Early in life he manifested a desire to learn the healing art, and when he was nineteen years of age he began his professional studies under the supervision of the late Dr. William R. Gist, as preceptor, and continued them for three years. He then attended two courses of lectures at the University of Louisville, where he graduated, and afterward two courses at the Jefferson Medical college, where he enjoyed special privileges and facilities through the kindness of the elder Pancoast, then in the zenith of his fame. He began the practice of medicine in Jackson, Miss., in 1853, and had firmly established himself when the Civil war began. He was appointed surgeon in the provisional army of the Confederate states, May 18, 1861, and was assigned to duty with the Twelfth Mississippi regiment, which formed part of that famous brigade, commanded at different times by Featherston, Posey and Harris. He was at Corinth when he received his commission, having already joined his fortunes with the Confederacy. He served until February 6, 1865, with the Army of Northern Virginia, when, on account of ill-health, he was relieved from duty with that army and directed to report to Medical Director Scott, at Meridian, Miss., for hospital duty. The estimate which the soldiers put upon him is well expressed by one of them who has not seen him since the war. Writing for a contemporary newspaper since Dr. Craft's death, he says: "We, of the line, had a blind confidence in the ability of Dr. Craft, and our anxiety was, that if wounded he should pronounce on the case. That confidence was second only to that so implicitly placed in Generals Lee, Jackson and A. P. Hill."

After the war Dr. Craft resumed the practice of his profession in the city of Jackson, where he soon secured an enviable patronage and reputation. He was often urged by friends to seek a larger field for the exercise of his brilliant talents, but he was too much endeared to the people among whom he had been reared to entertain the thought of going among others. He was one of the promoters and organizers of the Mississippi State Medical association, and its third president, serving in that office during the years 1875-6. For many years he had made a collection of the cases of surgery in Mississippi reported by the members, filling out short or deficient reports, pruning voluminous ones, and making this feature of the transactions of the association an honor to the medical profession. He contributed many valuable papers himself. In December, 1878, following the terrible epidemic of that year, the lower house of congress created a select committee to inquire into the origin, introduction and prevention of epidemic diseases in the United States, with power to employ experts and scientists, not to exceed seven in number, and to act in connection with a like committee created by the senate. Dr. Craft was selected as one of the experts, and in conjunction with his associates and members of the committee visited many of the points where the fever had been epidemic, and assisted in procuring and furnishing the evidence on which the report of the committee was based. While Dr. Craft's tastes ran in the line of surgery, he having performed, first and last, nearly all the capital operations, his knowledge of the practice of medicine and therapeutics was profound. His abilities were not appreciated at home alone, for many of his patients came to him from a distance, and wherever he went he received the most distinguished attention. He was happily married in 1871 to Miss Julia Barr, and was the father of four children, of whom the first born died in infancy. The others, with his devoted wife, survive him. He died in Jackson, Miss., April 8, 1888, of locomotor ataxia, after a lingering illness of more than twelve months.

Robert Kells was born near Hudson, N. Y., in the year of 1818, and died in Jackson, Miss., April, 1888. He came to Mississippi in 1840 and located at Edwards, Hinds county, where he engaged in the practice of medicine and planting. He married Miss Mary Phillips, January 13, 1846, with whom he lived until her death, June 15, 1871. Dr. Kells always took an active interest in the State Medical association and State Board of health. He was superintendent of the state lunatic asylum for seven years, including the war period. After retiring from this position he engaged in the practice of medicine at Jackson, where he enjoyed the confidence of a large clientage until old age, and his large property interest caused him to give up active practice. He still retained his interest in the State Medical association and a position on the State Board of health until his death.

J. W. Ellis was born in West Point, Miss., in 1851, and graduated when twenty-one years old, with the honors of his class, at Jefferson Medical college, Philadelphia. He practiced his profession in the Delta up to 1879, when he located in Canton, Miss., where he soon made many warm friends, and built up a lucrative practice. He was married to Miss Adah Lowry in 1875, who with two sweet little girls survives him, and to whom he has left an honorable name as a priceless legacy.

W. W. Hart, son of Henry and Judith P. Hart, was born in Robinson county, Tenn., April, 1828. After receiving a liberal education he studied medicine in Clarksville, Tenn., and graduated in the University of Louisville in 1849. He then moved to Mississippi and settled in Carrollton, where he remained actively engaged in the practice of his profession until the breaking out of the Civil war. He volunteered and went out with the first company that left Carrollton; was soon after appointed surgeon, in which capacity he served with distinction until the close of the war. After hostilities ceased he returned home and located near Lodi, in Montgomery county, and commenced again the practice of his profession, and remained in active practice until his death, May 27, 1887. He was married three times. Miss Laura A. Peeples, June 4, 1850; Mrs. Mary Laggins, January 11, 1871, and Mrs. A. F. Adair, May 2, 1872. His last wife survives him. He was a good citizen, a kind and indulgent father and husband, an eminent physician and surgeon. He represented his county one term in the state legislature.

The twenty-second annual meeting was held at Jackson April 17, 18, and 19, 1889. The address of welcome was delivered by T. M. Miller, who, after paying a high tribute to the profession, said: "I would speak to you from a politico-legal point of view. You all have your hobbies, so bear with mine. One doctor rides full tilt on quinine; another phosphates, another mustard, and so on. My hobby, now, or rather what seems to me to be the crying evil of our state and time, is the light esteem in which human life is held in our midst. To you I appeal to help in righting this wrong thing; in bringing about a higher standard in elevating public opinion; in cultivating a popular sentiment against it. You are drawn from the upper classes of society—from the cultivated and refined—yet you not only have access to these, but to all. Your hold on the affections of your patients, your influence in the families where you practice, is unbounded. To whom do they turn for help, counsel, and sympathy but to the family doctor? The radius of that influence extends to the haunt of infamy, where the step of the minister is never suffered; to the den of ignorance, where the schoolmaster has never penetrated; to the retreat of lawlessness, where the officer of the law is baffled. You leave the deathbed of the outlaw, your soul harrowed by his remorse, or shocked by his effrontery, to visit the desolated home of his victim. Who can draw such a moral; who can tell such a tale; who can speak with such dreadful force as you?"

The officers elected in 1889 were: Dr. J. E. Halbert, Mound Landing, president; Dr. W. A. Evans, Jr., Aberdeen, first vice president; Dr. W. H. White, Brandon, second vice president; Dr. W. E. Todd, Jackson, recording secretary; Dr. B. D. Cooper, Jackson, assistant recording secretary; Dr. J. F. Hunter, Jackson, treasurer; and Dr. J. M. Buchanan, Meridan, corresponding secretary.

The members of judicial council chosen were: J. E. Halbert, M. D., Mound Landing; B. F. Ward, M. D., Winona; Luther Sexton, M. D., Wesson; W. F. Hyer, M. D., Meridian; B. F. Kittrell, M. D., Black Hawk; E. L. McGehee, M. D., Woodville; J. W. Bennett, M. D., Brookhaven; J. Y. Murry, M. D., Ripley; J. C. Hall; M. D., Anguilla.

The papers read in 1889 are recorded by title and reader as follows: President's address, by Dr. Luther Sexton; Medical legislation, by Dr. B. F. Kittrell; Report of surgical cases, by Dr. J. M. Greene; Some cases in practice, by Dr. John S. Featherston; Pelvic reflexes, by Dr. W. F. Hyer; Treatment of dysentery, by Dr. D. L. Phares; New method of performing hysterectomy, by Dr. T. J. Crofford; Reflex phenomena incident to perineal rupture, by Dr. M. J. Thompson; Therapeutic progress, by Dr. H. H. Haralson; Placenta previa, by Dr. T. W. Fullilove; Penetrating wounds of the cornea, by Dr. W. S. Sims; When is the induction of premature labor justifiable? by Dr. E. L. McGehee; Heroic conservatism, by Dr. E. L. McGehee; Amputation on account of diseased joint, by Dr. C. Kendrick; Management of insane asylums, by Dr. T. J. Mitchell; Antagonism of therapeutic agents, by Dr. B. A. Vaughan; Medicine and law in Mississippi, by Dr. A. J. Jagoe; Mammary tumors, by Dr. W. B. Rogers; Pelvic cellulitis, by Dr. F. B. Nimocks; Scarlet fever, by Dr. P. W. Rowland; and Fever with special reference to its thermogenesis, by Dr. Gus Evans.

The twenty-third annual meeting was held at Jackson, April 16, 17, 18, 1890. Capt. Frank Johnston delivered the address of welcome. He reviewed the history of the profession from a serio-comic point of view, and in his comparison of law and medicine, spoke as follows: "Gentlemen, your profession, like my own, has been the subject of witticisms since the beginning of the world. Some of us might say, though not witty ourselves, we 'are the cause of wit in others.' But the world can not get along without us, laugh and jest as it may. When a man wants a doctor he is like the chap in Texas and the pistol, who said he did not need a pistol often in Texas, but when he did he wanted it bad." The conclusion of his address was an eloquent tribute to physicians.

The papers read before the meeting were the president's annual address, Dr. J. E. Halbert; Three cases of orthopœdic surgery, Dr. S. K. Coleman; Ligation of femoral artery for popliteal aneurism, Dr. W. M. Paine; Two cases of abdominal tumors, Dr. William Aills; Obstruction of the bowels, Report of two cases, Dr. F. B. Nimocks; Chloroform and alleged double rape in dentist's office, Dr. D. L. Phares; Diseases of the eye in renal disorders, Dr. A. G. Sinclair; Craniotomy, Dr. P. J. McCormick; A few points in the treatment of endometritis, Dr. T. J. Crofford; Some cases in gynecological surgery, Dr. T. T. Beall; A rare case of delivery, Dr. B. A. Vaughan; Pelvic abscess, Dr. J. M. Thompson; Pistol ball through left lung—recovery, Dr. B. A. Duncan; Exsection of scaphoid, etc., Dr. M. J. Lowry; Operation for the extraction of hard cataract, and a report of twenty-six cases, Dr. W. S. Sims; Some observations during a visit to Cooper's well, Dr. E. L. McGehee: Malaria, Dr. Gus Evans; A case, Dr. T. P. Lockwood.

The officers for 1890–91 are: G. W. Trimble, M. D., Grenada, president; J. Y. Murry, M. D., Ripley, first vice president; P. W. Rowland, M. D., Flora, second vice president; W. E. Todd, M. D., Jackson, recording secretary; B. L. Cully, M. D., Jackson, assistant recording secretary; S. K. Coleman, M. D., Canton, corresponding secretary; J. F. Hunter, M. D., Jackson, treasurer.

The members of the judicial council chosen were: W. F. Hyer, M. D., Meridian; B. F. Kittrell, M. D., Black Hawk; E. L. McGehee, M. D., Woodville; each to serve until 1891; J. W. Bennett, M. D., Brookhaven; J. Y. Murry, M. D., Ripley; J. C. Hall, M. D., Anguilla—each to serve until 1892; J. E. Halbert, M. D., Mound Landing; B. F. Ward, M. D., Winona; Luther Sexton, M. D., Wesson—each to serve until 1893.

The deceased members* are named as follows: W. L. Ainsworth, Hazlehurst; William T. Balfour, Vicksburg; P. T. Baley, Jackson; M. S. Craft, Jackson; *F. W. Dancy, Holly Springs; *R. T. Edwards, Vicksburg; *T. B. Elkin, Aberdeen; J. W. Ellis, Canton; E. Fox, Forest; *W. A. Galloway, Jackson; *S. V. D. Hill, Macon; W. W. Hart, Lodi; C. Hoover, McComb City; R. E. Hutchins, Greenville; W. E. Herring, Terry; Robert Kells, Jackson; L. C. Lee, Graysport; *T. J. Lee, Philadelphia; *James McWillie, Jackson; J. A. Mead, Pearlington; C. J. Mitchell, Vicksburg; Thomas L. Neal, Ben Lomond; *William Powell, Grenada; T. A. Phillips, Canton; George C. Redwood, Meridian; L. Richardson, Bolivar Landing; *Sid B. Smith, Grenada; James M. Smith, Eggs Point; J. O. Sanders, Carrollton; J. D. Staple, Huntsville; L. White, Utica; A. S. Thompson, Buena Vista.

*Died during the year.

Dr. Sid B. Smith was born in Tuscaloosa county, Ala., and died of consumption at Lane Park, Fla., May 13, 1889, aged forty-four years. Dr. Smith enlisted in the Confederate army at the early age of fifteen years, and commanded a company of sharpshooters two last years of the war. He was wounded six times during that memorable struggle. After the war he studied medicine and graduated at Mobile Medical college. He went to Grenada at the hight of the yellow-fever epidemic in 1878, and was for seven years a partner of Dr. G. W. Trimble, of that city.

Dr. James McWillie was born in Madison county, Miss., December 21, 1847, and died at his home in Jackson, Miss., March 1, 1890. He was a brave and fearless soldier of the Confederacy, and after the war studied medicine. He graduated with honors in Baltimore in 1870. In 1871 he was appointed assistant superintendent of the state lunatic asylum and retained that position until a few months before his death when he resigned in consequence of bad health. He made an efficient officer and was devoted to his profession. Truth, honor and unswerving fidelity to his sense of duty were fixed principles of his life. In 1875 he married Miss Nannie Compton, who, with five children, survive him.

Dr. W. A. Galloway was born in Kosciusko, Miss., February 9, 1851, and died in Jackson, Miss., March 1, 1890, in the thirty-ninth year of his age. He prosecuted the study of his profession in the medical colleges of Louisville, but graduated in New Orleans, having attended his last course of lectures in the medical department of the University of Louisiana. After graduating he was associated with his father in the practice of medicine in Canton, Miss. In 1879 he married Mrs. Bettie Williams, of Jackson, Miss., who survives him. He moved to Jackson in 1883, where he resided at the time of his death. Dr. Galloway was a man of brilliant gifts, and his distinguished ability was recognized by the profession all over the state. He died in the prime of life and in the possession of a large and appreciative patronage.

Dr. William Powell was born in Nottoway county, Va., January 20, 1819. He graduated in medicine in Louisville, Ky., in 1838, and afterward graduated in Cincinnati, Ohio, where he was an intimate friend of Professor Drake. He began the practice of his profession in Yalobusha county, Miss., in 1839. His distinguished abilities soon won for him a large and lucrative practice. He was at the organization of the State Medical association and was afterward often urged to accept its presidency, but always declined, perferring the labors of a more subordinate position. Modesty was one of his chief characteristics. In the death of Dr. Powell this association has lost one of its most valued friends and honored members. He retired from active work in 1889 and died of prostatitis, February 15, 1890.

Dr. T. B. Elkin was born January 21, 1837. He was educated in the common schools of the neighborhood. He attended his first course of medical lectures in Jefferson Medical college in the winter of 1857–8 and attended the University of the city of New York during the following summer. He graduated at Jefferson Medical college in March, 1860, and attended lectures in New Orleans during the winter of 1860. He was appointed assistant surgeon of Forty-third Mississippi regiment and afterward promoted to surgeon. After the war he again attended lectures in New Orleans. One of his colleagues has said of him: "As a practitioner of medicine he was studious, earnest, well informed, evenly balanced, careful, conscientious and able. As a man he was honest, noble, honorable and true; as husband, father and brother, he was one of the most loving, kind, considerate men I have known." He died on the 9th of March, 1890.

Dr. Thomas Jefferson Lee was born in Farmersville, Ala., August 26, 1840, and died at Philadelphia, Miss., February 14, 1888, aged forty-four years, five months and nineteen days. As a physician Dr. Lee was skillful, popular and unusually successful; as a physician he was beloved and honored. Being a leading man in his community, his death is sorely felt. He leaves a wife and several children to mourn his loss, and to them we tender our sympathies.

Dr. Joshua C. Fant was born in South Carolina in 1832, and moved with his parents to Noxubee county, Miss., when quite a small boy. He graduated in medicine in Charleston, S. C., in 1857, and located in Macon, Miss., where he lived until removed by death, October 25, 1889, fifty-seven years of age. Dr. Fant was a true and faithful Christian, a useful and honored citizen, and a popular and successful physician.

The deaths of Dr. Edwards, of Vicksburg, and Dr. Sherman, of Harrison, were reported in 1890.

Samuel Van Dyke Hill was born in Nashville, Tenn., January 25, 1835, and died in St. Louis, Mo., whither he had gone for medical treatment, October 14, 1889. Dr. Kittrell states: "In his eighth year his father removed the family from Tennessee to Chickasaw county, Miss., and in this state Dr. Hill resided continuously for forty-six years, except during his absence in the Confederate army. He was educated in the schools in his vicinity, and at the Columbus high school. He attended courses of medical lectures at the University of Louisville, and the University of New York, graduating from the latter institution in March, 1857. Until the breaking out of the war he practiced his profession at Palo Alto, Miss. In January, 1861, he was appointed assistant surgeon in the Confederate army, and was appointed to be surgeon in January, 1863; from October, 1862, to the end of the war, he was in charge of Quintard general hospital. October 10, 1861, he married Miss Jennie Calvert, of Chickasaw county, Miss., who, with true wifely devotion, accompanied him to Virginia, and remained near him during the war. At the close of the war, in October, 1865, he established himself at Macon, Miss, where he remained actively engaged in practice until the inroads of fatal disease compelled him to desist from his labors. He was a member of the State Medical association from its organization after the war until his death, and was elected and served as its president in 1871. He was a member of the American Medical association, having been several times elected a delegate from the State Medical association. He was elected a delegate to represent the state association in the International Medical congress that convened at Washington. He was appointed a member of the state board of health at its organization in 1877, and was continuously reappointed at the expiration of each term of his service. He was twice elected president of the board, and was filling that position at the time of his death.

The twenty-fourth annual meeting was held at Meridian in April, 1891; Col. J. R. McIntosh delivered the address of welcome, and the following-named papers were read: Some remarks on fevers, Dr. J. M. Greene; Vessical hemorrhage, Dr. H. A. Gant; Recent advancement in therapeutics, or new remedies, Dr. Chesley Daniel; Infant feeding, Dr. N. L. Clarke; The nose, its diseases and their treatment, Dr. B. M. Bishop; Two cases of external urethrotomy, Dr. J. A. Shackleford; The value of albuminuria in diagnosing diseases of the kidney, Dr. J. M. Buchanan; Noise, Dr. B. F. Duke; Glandular disease of strumous character, Dr. R. C. Gulledge; Knife wound penetrating abdominal cavity, Dr. Henry Izard; Laparotomy for gunshot wound of abdomen, Dr. Henry Izard; Phimosis, a report of cases, Dr. E. S. Beadles.

The officers elected for 1891-2 were: J. Y. Murry, M. D., Ripley, president; W. E. Todd, M. D., Jackson, first vice president; N. L. Clarke, M. D., Meridian, second vice president; H. H. Harralson, M. D., Forest, recording secretary; G. S. Hunter, M. D., Bolton, assistant recording secretary; B. F. Duke, M. D., Como, corresponding secretary, and J. F. Hunter, M. D., Jackson, treasurer.

The judicial council chosen comprises J. W. Bennett, M. D., Brookhaven; R. S. Toombs, M. D., Grenada; J. C. Hall, M. D., Anguilla; J. E. Halbert, M. D., Mound Landing; B. F. Ward, M. D., Winona; Luther Sexton, M. D., Wesson; W. F. Hyer, M. D., Meridian; B. F. Kittrell, M. D., Black Hawk; E. L. McGehee, Woodville.

Dr. John Ames Mead was born in Portland, Me., July 16, 1842, and died in New Orleans, La., January 30, 1891. In his infancy his parents moved to Massachusetts, where he attended the public schools and Woburn high school. He afterward attended Amherst college, but left in 1862 to enlist in the Thirty-ninth regiment Massachusetts volunteers. He was taken a prisoner in 1863, and remained such one year. After his release he returned home and finished his collegiate course. He studied medicine in Harvard Medical school, of Boston, from which he graduated in 1869. He came south in October, 1869, and settled in Pearlington, Miss., where he practiced his profession up to death. In 1880 he married Miss Amelia S. Mead, of New Orleans, La., who with two children — a daughter, age nine years, and a son, age six years — mourn his loss.

Dr. James D. Staples was born near Huntsville, Miss., November 13, 1850, and died of pneumonia at Huntsville, Miss. He graduated at the University of Nashville, in the class of 1871. He died in the prime of life and in possession of a large and appreciative patronage. As a physician he was studious, earnest, well informed, evenly balanced, careful, conscientious and able, not given to criticism of his professional brethren, "not a man, who for the poor renown of being smart, would leave a sting within a brother's heart."

Dr. F. W. Dancy died November 7, 1890. He was born near Roanoke river, in Warren county, N. C., in the year 1810. Having prepared for college in the classical schools of Huntsville, Ala., and vicinity, he entered the University of Nashville, Tenn., from which he graduated in 1831, beginning soon after the study of medicine under Dr. I. W. Bibb, of Athens, Ala. He matriculated in the medical department of the University of Pennsylvania in 1832, becoming a private pupil of Prof. W. E. Horner. At the opening of his second course his health was so impaired that, by the advice of Drs. Jackson and Physick, he returned to Alabama. At the end of a year, with recovered health, he entered the medical department of Transylvania university, in Lexington, Ky., from which he graduated in 1835. He first settled in Greensboro, Ala., where he remained eight years, removing to Holly Springs, Miss., in 1844. He was a member of the Marshall County Medical society, of which he was president, of the State Medical association, sanitary commissioner for the state at large, member of the board of health of the state of Mississippi, organized on the 7th of April, 1877, and a permanent member of the American Medical association. He was married in his twenty-seventh year to Miss Rebecca Elizabeth Mason, of Jackson, Tenn., who died in 1866. The result of this union was eleven children, nine of whom are yet living. In 1876, ten years after the death of his first wife, he married Mrs. Kate McCorkle Nelms, who survives him.

The profession of medicine in Mississippi is fast rising to the same position in national estimation which the old bar attained. Throughout the state physicians are found who for two decades have reflected honor on the state and county. The association has exerted a most beneficial influence during the twenty years of its active life, and the time is at hand when the medical and surgical practice of the state must claim the same attention from physicians throughout the country that the Mississippi law reports claim from lawyers.

The system of homeopathic medicine was introduced into the state about the year 1849 by the late Dr. Davis, of Natchez, and Dr. Harper, of Vicksburg, both allopaths who embraced the homeopathic practice and carried it on with remarkable success until their death within the last half decade. In 1851 Dr. J. W. Hough introduced the practice at Jackson and is to-day the oldest and most successful homeopathic physician in the state. Dr. Hardenstein resided at Jackson for some years, until his removal to Vicksburg after the war, and died there about seven years ago, leaving a large practice and reputation to his son, Dr. Otto Hardenstein. Dr. Gilman, a contemporary of Dr. Harper, died about fifteen years ago. Dr. Gilbert, who died in September, 1891, at Jackson, practiced there for several years.

Dr. Pierce, who settled at Jackson in 1891, is a younger member of the school, being a graduate of the Hahnemann college of Chicago. Dr. French, of Natchez, settled there a short time before the death of the pioneer, Dr. Davis, and Dr. Chase have practiced there for over a quarter of a century.

The names of homeopathic physicians registered are: F. A. M. Davis, the first old school, now homeopathic, B. D. Chase and J. D. Smith, of Adams county; J. W. Hough, Hinds county; J. Galdechens, Hinds county; H. J. Coleman, Jefferson; E. T. Harding, Pike; A. O. Hardenstein, Warren; T. J. Harper, Warren; G. O. Furry, Warren.

The registry of Mississippi physicians dates back only to 1882. Of the total number, one thousand eight hundred and sixteen whose names and records are entered in the books of Secretary Johnston of the board of health, all presented evidence of their right to practice medicine in Mississippi in 1882, with the exception of one who registered in 1884 and fifteen in 1890. In the record the allopathic school is represented by seventeen-eighteenths of the whole number. The eclectic school claims seventy-six members exclusive of those who are both allopathic and eclectic physicians; the homeopathic school claims ten members, and sundry other schools twenty-six members. The number of physicians in each county, according to the record of 1882, is shown by the following table:

Adams, fifteen; Alcorn, twenty-four; Amite, twenty; Attala, thirty-eight, two in 1890; Benton, twenty-two; Bolivar, seventeen; Calhoun, thirty-one, one in 1884; Carroll, twenty-four, one in 1890; Chickasaw, thirty-five; Choctaw, twenty-one, one in 1890; Claiborne, twenty-seven; Clay, twenty-seven; Clarke, twenty; Coahoma, twenty-one; Copiah, fifty-four; Covington, nine; De Soto, thirty-six; Franklin, seventeen; Greene, four; Grenada, eleven; Hancock, seven; Harrison, eleven; Hinds, fifty-eight; Holmes, forty; Issaquena, eight; Itawamba, twenty-four; Jackson, sixteen; Jasper, eighteen; Jefferson, eighteen, one in 1890; Jones, eleven; Kemper, twenty-five; Lafayette, thirty-seven; Lauderdale, thirty-six; Lawrence, twenty-two; Leake, thirty-two; Lee, fifty-four; Lincoln, twenty-five; Lowndes, forty-four; Le Flore, nineteen, two in 1890; Madison, thirty-five; Marion, three; Marshall, forty-one; Monroe, forty; Montgomery, twenty-five, three in 1890; Neshoba, eighteen; Newton, twenty-three; Noxubee, thirty, two in 1890; Oktibbeha, twenty-seven; Panola, fifty; Perry, four; Pike, thirty-five; Ponotoc thirty-four; Prentiss, twenty-four; Quitman, three; Rankin, twenty-six; Scott, twenty; Sharkey, thirteen, one in 1890; Simpson, nine; Smith, eighteen; Sunflower, eight; Tallahatchie, twenty; Tate, thirty-three; Tippah, thirty; Tishomingo, twenty-one; Tunica, seven; Union, twenty-five; Warren, thirty-six, one in 1890; Washington, thirty-seven; two in 1890; Wayne, ten; Webster, twenty-three; Wilkinson, thirteen; Winston, twenty-five; Yalobusha, thirty; Yazoo, forty-two.

The Botanic school enrolls seven members; the mineral school, thirteen; the dosimetric, one; the Esculapian, one; the hydropathic, one, and the idopathic one. Joe Barnes' name appears as herb doctor of Lowndes county and Ned McDuff's as root doctor of Leake county. Among the systems of practice or schcols written in the record the following are given:

"Don't recognize any," "scientific," "ordinary standard or allopathic," "allopathic and eclectic," "the legitimate profession," "old school," "clinical medicine and gynecology," "common school or regular," "botanic and eclectic," "truth and common sense," "old regular school," "the regular advanced science," "mineral, mineral or allopathic," "old blue school," "whatever is indicated," "medical reform," "homeopathic," some combine eclectic with allopathic practice.

The state board of health was created by an act approved February 1, 1877. Under authority vested in the governor by section number one of this act, he commissioned Drs. W. M. Compton,* F. W. Dancy,* and D. L. Phares members from the state at large; J. M. Taylor,* and A. G. Smythe,* from the first congressional district; T. D. Isom and John Wright,* from the second; E. W. Hughes* and S. V. D. Hill,* from the third; C. B. Galloway and P. J. McCormick,* from the fourth; Robert Kells* and C. A. Rice,* from the fifth; and R. G. Wharton and P. F. Whitehead,* from the sixth district. The meeting to organize was held at Jackson, April 7, 1877, Dr. Whitehead presiding, with Dr. Rice, secretary. The members present were those whose names are marked thus * in the foregoing list. Drs. Compton, Taylor, McCormick, Kells and Rice were chosen members of an executive committee for six years; Drs. Phares, Isom, Hughes, Wharton, and Whitehead, for four years; Drs. Dancy, Smythe, Wright, Hill, and Galloway, for two years. Dr. Kells was subsequently elected president and Dr. Wirt Johnston, secretary.

Reporters or writers on special subjects pertaining to sanitation were appointed in the following order: Epidemic and endemic and contagious diseases, Dr. J. M. Taylor; Diseases of the swamp district, Dr. P. J. McCormick; Diseases of the prairie region,† Dr. S. V. D. Hill; Diseases of the sea coast and the sea coast as a sanitary resort,† Dr. D. L. Phares; Vaccination and compulsory vaccination,† Dr. E. W. Hughes; The influence of syphilis on public health, Dr. P. F. Whitehead; The effects of food and clothing on public health,† Dr. F. W. Dancy; Drainage, Dr. John Wright; Indigenous remedies of Mississippi, Dr. D. L. Phares; Cleanliness, its general and special influence,† Dr. A. G. Smythe; The influence of alcohol,† Dr. W. M. Compton; The architecture of prisons, asylums and hospitals,† Dr. C. A. Rice; The proper organization and objects of city, county, state and national boards of health, including the registration of births, marriages and deaths,† Dr. J. M. Taylor. The subjects marked † were ably treated before the close of the year, and papers on the prevailing diseases of the sixth congressional district by Dr. R. G. Wharton, and of the first congressional district by Dr. A. G. Smythe were read. The sanitary commissioners appointed in the order of congressional districts, were: Drs. Smythe, Isom, Hill, Galloway, Rice and Wharton. A resolution of thanks to the state librarian for permitting the meeting to be held in the senate chamber closed the first meeting of this board.

An epidemic known as phlegmonous erysipelas appeared in that part of Tishomingo county, now Prentiss county, in February, 1845, and before the close of May carried off a number of women and girls, but no adult males. One third of the sufferers succumbed to the disease and the recovery of the others was slow. This statement is taken from Dr. Smythe's paper read before the state board of health in 1877. In 1877, Secretary Johnston communicated with sanitary associations throughout the country, and mailed one hundred and sixty-four circular letters to physicians throughout Mississippi. Before the close of the year many responses came in and the march of old and the introduction of new diseases are accounted for. The death of Dr. C. B. Galloway at Canton, June 3, 1877, was made part of the record of the board. The papers presented brought forth clearly the preventable side of disease and showed that by proper attention to personal cleanliness and the least attention to the laws of sanitation in the house, village and city, the great majority of diseases could then be banished from the state.

The meeting of April, 1878, was presided over by Dr. Kells, with Dr. Wirt Johnston secretary. The latter was then member of the board from the state at large, vice W. M. Compton, deceased. In December C. A. Rice presided as president pro tem. His address tells of the action of the board during the prevalence of the yellow fever, and makes special mention of Dr. Johnston and the late Dr. Crafts. Resolutions on the death of Drs. Hughes, Whitehead, Cage and Compton were adopted; measures were proposed for guarding the state against disease, and copies of rules and regulations were sent to the county and municipal boards, organized under the amendment of 1878.

In November, 1878, the American Public Health association met at Richmond, Va., and there Mississippi was to be represented by Drs. R. G. Wharton, J. M. Taylor, P. J. McCormick, S. D. Robbins, F. W. Dancy, George E. Redwood and Wirt Johnston, but Drs. Johnston and Robbins, with Mr. Marshall, were the only delegates present to present the report from this state.

The following roll embraces the membership of the Mississippi Medical association in 1878. The letters and marks after each are explained thus: P., last president of association; V. P., vice-president; R. S., recording secretary; C. S., corresponding secretary; T., treasurer; O., orator; * removed from the state; †deceased. The star before a name denotes the president of a county or city board of health in 1878-9.

D. W. Adams, Floreyville; W. G. Allen, Skipwith's Landing; E. M. Alexander, Ripley; *William Aills, Steen's Creek; *W. N. Ames, Starkville; William H. Armistead, V. P., Vaiden; W. L. Ainsworth, Hazlehurst; M. T. Anderson, Brownsville; T. M. Anderson, Pickens; Theodore Artaud, Jackson; W. H. Baird, Vaiden; *P. T. Baley, T., Jackson; W. T. Balfour †, Vicksburg; E. G. Banks, V. P., O., Clinton; R. B. Banks, Jackson; J. R. Barnett, C. S., Vicksburg; *J. D. Beck, Corinth; J. W. Bennett, Brookhaven; T. G. Birchett, Vicksburg; John Brownrigg, V. P., Columbus; W. Y. Gadberry, first president, Yazoo city; †L. L. Gadberry, Yazoo city; *Harris A. Gant, Water Valley; S. C. Gholson, Holly Springs; J. H. Gibbs, Meridian; *John Gordin, Corinth; *J. W. Gray, or H. W. Gray, Holly Springs; W. F. Gresham, West Station; T. H. Gordon, Grenada; *N. L. Guice, Fayette; F. H. Gulledge, Durant; A. C. Halbert, Artesia; J. D. Harrell, DeSoto; W. B. Harvey, Canton; C. R. Henderson, Deasonville; E. T. Henry, P., Vicksburg; J. R. Hicks, O., Vicksburg; S. V. D. Hill, P., Macon; George W. Howard, Vicksburg; E. W. Hughes, V. P., Grenada; J. M. Hunt, Vicksburg; *W. F. Hyer, T., Chulahoma; J. C. Hall, McKinneyville; William Preston Hughes, Fort Gibson; George K. Harrington, Jackson; A. E. Hardin, Abbeville; W. W. Hall, V. P., Grenada; John L. Hebron, Bovina; J. W. Holman, Winona; J. E. Halbert, Leota Landing; W. W. Hart, Lodi; J. J. Houston, Tillatoba; H. Hanslow, V. P., Hazlehurst; Thomas D. Isom, V., P., Oxford; Henry Izard, Garlansville; D. W. Jones, Hazlehurst; Wirt Johnston, R. S., Jackson; R. B. Johnson, Madison county; H. W. Johnston, Clinton; Robt. Kells, T., Jackson; Carroll Kendrick, Corinth; H. B. Kidd, Yazoo City; D. A. Kinchloe, Sardis; J. R. Kirkland, Meridian; William T. Balfour, Jr., Vicksburg; J. M. Bogle, Raymond; *R. L. Bogle, Raymond; D. W. Booth, V. P., O., Vicksburg; W. D. Bragg, Garlandville; O. C. Brothers, Artesia; J. D. Burch, V. P., Yazoo City; Samuel T. Birdsong, Conway; T. C. Bryan, Pope; W. F. Barksdale, Hardy's Station; A. M. Brown, Coffeeville; Charles Baskerville, Horn Lake; A. H. Cage, Canton; *J. S. Cain, Okolona; LeGrand G. Capers,† Vicksburg; J. A. Campbell, T., Shaqualak; Matt. Clay, Brooksville; William M. Compton, P., Holly Springs; *E. A. Cox, Baldwyn; M. S. Craft, C. S., V. P., P., Jackson; N. G. Carter,

Ripley; *R. C. Cunningham, Verona; *F. W. Dancy, Holly Springs; Chesley Daniel, Holly Springs; J. S. Davis, Iuka; *M. G. Davis, Greenwood; J. R. Dougherty, Holly Springs; *W. J. Dulaney, Jackson; R. L. Dunn, Yazoo City; F. G. Ervin, Columbus; A. I. Ellis, Sardis; J. T. Evans, Oakland; C. C. Ewing, Aberdeen; R. D. Farish, Mayersville; J. C. Fant, Macon; *J. S. Featherston, Macon; *Frank Ferrell, Ashland; F. M. Fitzhugh, Warren county; W. P. Finley, Fannin; Dr. Fielder, ——; P. F. Fitzgerald, Grenada; *T. W. Fullilove, Vaiden; C. B. Galloway, P†, Canton; W. A. Galloway, C. S. Beauregard; *B. F. Kittrell, V. P., O., P., Black Hawk; John D. Kline, Meridian; John W. King, C. S., Vicksburg; D. A. Kinchloe, Jr., Sardis; W. M. Lea, V. P., Holly Springs; *James M. Lewis, Kosciusko; W. L. Lipscomb, O., Columbus; T. P. Lockwood, V. P., Crystal Springs; L. C. Lee, Graysport; C. J. Mitchell, Vicksburg; W. H. Miller, Okolona; J. H. Murfree, Okolona; D. McCallum, V. P., Westville; P. J. Maxwell, Columbus; Thomas H. Mays, V. P., Columbus; L. M. Mays, Graysport; J. D. McConnell, R. S., Brownsville; P. J. McCormick, V. P., P., Yazoo City; W. H. McDougal, Rienzi; N. W. McKie, Sharon; R. D. McLaurin, Sidon; T. J. Mitchell, Jackson; W. E. Monette, Warren county; *J. P. Moore, Yazoo City; G. C. McCallum, Lake; W. Myles, Utica; H. C. McLaurin, Brandon; William McSwine, Grenada; James McWillie, Jackson; J. M. McFarland, Water Valley; C. J. F. Meriwether, Charleston; J. L. McLean, Winona; R. C. Myles, Burtonton; Frank Nailer, Vicksburg; J. Nailer, Vicksburg; D. B. Nailer, Warren county; W. J. Nesmith, Vicksburg; R. Anderson New, P., R. S., Port Gibson; James C. Newman, Vicksburg; William E. Oates, Vicksburg; R. O'Leary, Vicksburg; J. F. O'Leary, Vicksburg; T. T. Orendorf, McKinneyville; S. L. Paine, V. P., Corinth; T. A. Phillips, Canton; J. T. Parker, V. P., Buena Vista; William Powell, Torrance; D. R. Pettit, Warren county; K. P. Perkins, Eureka; A. J. Pulliam, Grenada; D. L. Phares, Woodville; R. A. Quinn, T., Vicksburg; D. H. Quinn, Summit; *H. J. Ray, Grenada; *George E. Redwood, Meridian; W. D. Redus, Port Gibson; L. Richardson, Bolivar Landing; C. A. Rice, C. S., Brandon; J. L. Riley, Lake; R. S. Ringgold, Grenada; R. W. Roland, Oakland; H. Shannon, Vicksburg; Lee Shackleford, V. P., Meridian; J. S. Sizer, Fort Stephens; A. H. Smith, V. P., Meridian; James M. Smith, Egg's Point; A. G. Smythe, V. P., Baldwyn; John W. Spillman, Columbus; J. C. Spinks, Shubuta; A. P. Sims, Morton; Newton C. Steele, Kossuth; R. R. Stockard, Greenville; Joseph Steinride, Benton; H. L. Sutherland, Glencoe; W. J. Sykes, T., Aberdeen; Robert Smith, Kosciusko; B. A. Shepherd, Goodman; A. J. Sanderson, Vaiden; *E. P. Sale, V. P., Aberdeen; J. Mell Smith, Coffeeville; J. O. Sanders, Carrollton; J. M. Taylor, P., Corinth; C. Y. Thompson, Macon; R. S. Toombs, Greenville; R. J. Turnbull, Duncansby Landing; G. W. Trimble, Grenada; J. Tackett, Richland; David B. Turner, Winona; *T. R. Trotter, V. P., Duck Hill; J. D. Talbert, Cold Water; W. E. Todd, Clinton; F. R. VanEaton, Dowd's Landing; *B. A. Vaughan, V. P., C. S., P., Columbus; *G. W. Vassar, V. P., Carrollton; A. M. Waddill, Rolling Fork; M. F. Wakefield, Starkville; *R. G. Wharton, V. P., Port Gibson; L. White, Utica; P. F. Whitehead, C. S., P., Vicksburg; B. H. Whitfield, Clinton; John Wright, Sardis; *T. W. Wright, Pickens; W. B. Williamson, C. S., Edwards; Z. T. Woodruff, Vicksburg; *J. S. Walker, Greenville; A. M. West, Holly Springs; T. L. Wilburn, Winona; S. L. Wynne, Looxahoma; Lea Williamson, Como; *B. F. Ward, Winona; N. M. Woods, Oakland; *H. Yandell, Benton; J. W. Young, Carrollton.

The presidents of county municipal boards in 1878-9, who were not then members of the state medical association, are named as follows: T. J. Jackson, Liberty; T. S. Sharpe, Natchez; J. A. Cooper, Friar's Point; G. W. Purnell, Hazlehurst; W. E. Jones, Quitman; J. W. George, Chester; Alex. Fairly, Williamsburg; J. E. McEachin, West Point; J. P. H.

Westbrook, Hernando; Geo. N. Smith, Pass Christian; Edward Latham, Bay St. Louis; W. W. Durden, Lexington: B. D. McGown, Mayersville; W. G. Bailey, Claiborne; E. F. Griffin, Scranton; L. M. McLendon, Sucarnochee; J. T. Chandler, Lafayette; B. Noah Ward, Leake Co.; B. T. Semmes, Canton; T. B. Ford, Columbia; C. P. Parton, Decatur; M. N. Phillips, Batesville; D. T. Price, Booneville; M. R. Fontaine, Pontotoc; J. W. Ellis, Deer Creek; William Giles, Westville; A. H. Bays, Walthall; W. D. Carter, Ripley; J. R. Slaton, Senatobia; A. S. Kirk, Louisville; L. W. Magruder, Woodville; W. J. Nelson, Austin; C. A. Pegues, Abbeville; J. H. Hays, Byhalia; S. P. Lester, Batesville; S. F. Sorsby, Byram; Frank McIntosh, Beauregard; O. B. Cooke, Cumberland; C. R. Norman, Cato; F. L. Fulgham, Crystal Springs; A. A. Powell, Coffeeville; W. R. Blailock, Carthage; John B. Pease, Concordia; R. B. Carson, Durant; A. L. Kline, Enterprise; J. W. Lack, Hillsboro; D. H. Bryant, Liberty; M. H. Allen, Lodi; J. L. Gresham, Lake; J. A. Fox, Louisville; D. P. Rawles, Morton; D. U. Ford, McComb City; D. C. McCampbell, Mt. Pleasant; A. Le Blance, Magnolia; H. A. Minor, Macon; J. W. Cutrev, Osyka; W. R. Manniece, Pontotoc: J. W. Bynum, Rienzi; T. W. Coleman, Rodney; W. D. Heflin, Sardis; J. R. Sample, Summit; L. W. Tuttle, Satartia; B. F. Archer, Taylor's Depot; O. S. Iglehart, Vicksburg; J. Pitts, Waynesboro; R. W. Rea, Wesson.

The report of Dr. T. B. Ford on small-pox in Marion county, in the spring of 1878; that on the epidemic in Grenada was presented by Dr. H. J. Ray; in Canton, by Dr. A. T. Semmes: that on the epidemic at Lake, Scott county, by Dr. F. E. Daniel, of Jackson, Miss.; that on Holly Springs, by Dr. F. W. Dancy; that on Greenville, by Dr. R. S. Toombs; that on Water Valley, by Dr. H. A. Gant; that on Hernando, by Dr. J. M. Jones; that on Harrison county, by Charles Pelaez; that on Pass Christian, by Dr. George N. Smith; that on Tillatoba and vicinity, by Dr. T. H. Gordon; that on Yazoo City, by P. J. McCormick; that on the epidemic at Y. F. Griffin's house, near Summit, by Dr. W. W. Moore; that on Winona, by Dr. B. F. Ward; that on Meridian, by Dr. P. H. Griffin; that at Valley Home, by Dr. J. M. Calhoun. The several reports form a history well worthy of study. Each one goes from the beginning to the end of disease in 1878, deals with the causes and effects and points out where care and cleanliness could have averted the troubles of that year. The history of quarantine regulations in the counties and towns of the state was contributed by Dr. T. S. Sharpe, of Adams; J. T. Chandler, of Lafayette; G. W. Vasser, of Carroll; C. Y. Thompson, of Noxubee; Frank Ferrell, of Benton; T. J. Jackson, of Amite; Alex. Fairly, of Covington; H. H. Holbert, of Scott; B. N. Warde, of Leake; K. P. Clark, of Lincoln; W. F. Stansbury, of Holmes; A. T. Semmes, of Madison; R. C. Cunningham, of Lee; C. P. Partin, of Newton; J. S. Cain, of Chickasaw; George M. Powell, of Yazoo; W. N. Ames, of Oktibbeha; George E. Redwood, of Lauderdale; W. L. Carter, of Tippah; H. J. Ray, of Grenada; J. A. Cooper, of Coahoma; T. B. Ford, of Marion; A. L. Kirk, of Winston; R. G. Wharton, of Claiborne; M. G. Davis, of Le Flore; James D. Beck, of Alcorn; A. H. Bays, of Sumner; Marshall R. Smith, of Issaquena; W. E. Jones, of Black; W. J. Bailey, of Jasper; J. F. Pitts, of Pontotoc; and J. S. Walker, of Washington.

Reports on the quarantine of 1878 were also made, by H. A. Minor, of Macon; N. L. Guice, of Fayette; B. A. Vaughan, of Columbus; J. M. Lewis, of Kosciusko; M. D. Vance, of Oxford; F. L. Fulgham, of Crystal Springs; H. S. Van Eaton, of Woodville; John B. Peace, of Concordia; H. Wood, Jr., of Scooba; J. A. Hartin, of Banner; J. D. Talbert, of Cold Water; R. B. Carson, of Durant; I. B. Luck, of Mount Pleasant; R. Thompson, of Hillsboro; N. Vernor, of Cornersville; Howell Whitsill, of Wahalak; W. D. Heflin, of Sardis; J. E. McEachin, of West Point; R. H. Parham, of Michigan City; Mayor George W. Rice, of Harrison; L. W. Tuttle, of Satartia; J. A. Fox, of Louisville; J. P. Alvis, of Waterford; W. E. Jones, of Quitman; Wyatt Wooten, of Forest; D. T. Price, of Booneville; A. T. Whitfield, of Artesia; J. W. Bennet, of Brookhaven; A. C. Webster of Toccopola; C. R. Norman, of Cato; Frank McIntosh, of Beauregard; D. N. Lawrence, of Crawford; W. L. Lee, of Ellisville; H. D. Thrower, of Mayhew; D. P. Rawles, of Morton; W. F. Cross, of Lexington; M. G. Davis, of Greenwood; S. A. Cooper, of Friar's Point; Mayor S. Hearle, of New Albany; P. T. Raeford, of Byhalia; G. W. Vasser, of Carrollton; T. W. Wright, of Pickens; Thomas Bryan, of Pope; J. S. Smith, of Chester; Mayor J. W. Woods, of Love's station; W. J. Nelson, of Austin; W. A. McAnulty and William F. Wallace, of Kossuth; Mayor C. C. Shipp, of Springdale; J. L. Plunkett, of Carthage; Mayor Josiah Hester, of Martinsville; M. W. Howard, of Fulton; Henry Yandell, of Benton; C. M. Williamson, of Raymond; John H. Morgan, of Ashland; Thomas G. Brewer, of Lamar; J. R. Slaton, of Senatobia; C. Baskerville, of Horn Lake; H. C. McLaurin, of Brandon; P. H. Hamilton, of Shuqualak; T. R. Trotter, of Duck Hill; Mayor W. J. Taylor, of Charleston; J. D. Dabney, of Tchula; W. R. Minniece, of Pontotoc; V. W. Fullilove, of Vaiden; E. P. Sale, of Aberdeen; H. W. Gray, of Pleasant Hill; G. W. Tribble, of Guntown; J. T. Parker, of Buena Vista; W. T. Holland, of Marion; G. H. Gray, of Raleigh; S. P. Lester, and W. O. Harris, of Batesville; F. W. Coleman, of Rodney; A. W. Hunter, of Tupelo; J. S. Rosborough, of Como; W. D. Carter, of Ripley; A. Le Blanc, of Magnolia; J. T. Alvis, of Taylor; L. M. Sykes, of Muldon; Benjamin F. Kittrell, of Black Hawk; Mayor Thomas H. Hull, of Grand Gulf; W. E. Thomas, of Leakesville; G. S. Matlock, of Hickory Flats; Mayor H. L. Dicken, of Newport; Mayor L. A. Powers, of West Station; J. G. Sallis, of Sallis; B. F. Archer, of Taylor's Depot; J. B. Greaves, of Edwards; D. H. Wallace, of Goodman; C. A. Pegues, of Abbeville; J. R. S. Pitts, of Waynesboro; Mayor J. B. Shaw, of Pittsboro; H. C. Mayer, of Meadville; A. A. Powell, of Coffeeville, and G. S. Henderson, of Birmingham.

The measures taken, according to the reports, were effective in checking the march of disease and were so far useful. Had they been taken before the disease appeared there would be little or nothing to fear and regulations opposed to commerce and personal liberty would not have to be enforced so radically as it became necessary to enforce them.

The transactions of the board for 1879 were insignificant when compared with those of 1878. The members and people rested after a year of alarms, fatigues and losses. Dr. F. W. Dancy was reappointed by the governor a member of the board and was present at the annual meeting, April 5, 1879. B. F. Kittrell was commissioned a member, vice E. W. Hughes, deceased. George E. Redwood, vice A. H. Cage, deceased, and C. A. Rice, vice P. F. Whitehead, deceased. E. P. Sale, John Wright, S. D. V. Hill, and J. W. Bennett were appointed or reappointed members. In August, 1879, the following points were established as quarantine stations: Osyka, Michigan City, Fort Adams, and a point between Commerce and the Tennessee line on the Mississippi river. The quarantine officers appointed were Dr. W. C. Warren at Osyka, Dr. J. M. Taylor at Corinth, Dr. C. A. Rice at Polk's Landing, near Commerce, Dr. E. L. McGehee at Fort Adams and Dr. Geo. E. Redwood at Michigan City. Prior to November 8th, all the stations were vacated, including the station at Horn Lake, established at the close of August. The fever at Concordia, Oak Grove and Harrison Station was stamped out immediately, the national board of health appropriating money toward that end.

The annual meeting of 1880 was held at Jackson in April, 1880. Dr. S. V. D. Hill was elected president, and Dr. Johnston reëlected secretary. The law approved March 4, 1880, abolished county boards of health and provided for the appointment of a county health officer, by the governor, on the nomination of the state board.

The chief health officers of counties appointed under the act of March 4, 1880, and holding office in 1880-1, were: Adams, Dr. T. S. Sharpe, Natchez; Alcorn, Dr. W. B. Sanford, Corinth; Amite, Dr. C. H. Bates; Attala, Dr. J. M. Lewis, Kosciusko; Benton, Dr. T. L. Jackson, Michigan City; Bolivar, Dr. J. W. Dulaney, Rosedale; Calhoun, Dr. W. L. Dottery, Bentley; Carroll, Dr. G. W. Vassar, Carrollton; Chickasaw, Dr. J. S. Cain, Okolona; Claiborne, Dr. W. D. Redus, Port Gibson; Clarke, Dr. A. V. Wolverton, Enterprise: Coahoma, Dr. J. A. Cooper, Friar's Point; Copiah, Dr. G. W. Purnell, Hazlehurst; Covington, Dr. Alex Fairley, Mt. Olive; Clay, Dr. J. E. McEachen, West Point; De Soto, Dr. J. H. P. Westbrook, Hernando; Greene, Dr. B. F. Hamrick, State Line; Grenada, Dr. G. W. Trimble, Grenada; Holmes, Dr. G. C. Phillips, Lexington; Jefferson, Dr. N. L. Guice, Fayette; Jones, Dr. John M. Baylis, Ellisville; Kemper, Dr. L. M. McLendon; Lafayette, Dr. J. T. Chandler, Oxford; Lauderdale, Dr. A. H. Smith, Meridian; Lawrence, Dr. James A. Rowan, Silver Creek; Leake, Dr. W. R. Blailock, Carthage; Lee, Dr. R. C. Cunningham, Verona; Lincoln, Dr. E. J. Bowen, Brookhaven; Lowndes, Dr. B. A. Vaughan, Columbus; Le Flore, Dr. M. G. Davis, Greenwood; Madison, Dr. A. T. Semmes, Canton; Marshall, Dr. A. M. West, Holly Springs; Monroe, Dr. J. M. Greene, Aberdeen; Montgomery, Dr. B. F. Ward, Winona; Neshoba, Dr. T. J. Lee, Philadelphia; Newton, Dr. C. P. Partin, Decatur; Noxubee, Dr. H. A. Minor, Macon; Oktibbeha, Dr. W. N. Ames, Starkville; Panola, Dr. A. I. Ellis, Sardis; Pike, Dr. B. U. Ford, McComb City; Prentiss, Dr. W. A. Taylor, Booneville; Rankin, Dr. P. Fairley, Brandon; Scott, Dr. J. L. Gresham, Forest; Sharkey, Dr. J. C. Hall, McKinneyville; Simpson, Dr. William Giles, Westville; Smith, Dr. A. G. McLaurin, Raleigh; Sumner, Dr. A. H. Bays, Walthall; Sunflower, Dr. W. H. Baird, Indian Bayou; Tallahatchie, Dr. James Calhoun, Garner's Station; Tippah, Dr. W. D. Carter, Ripley; Tishomingo, Dr. Carroll, Kendrick, Corinth; Tunica, Dr. J. M. Phillips, Austin; Warren, Dr. W. T. Balfour, Vicksburg; Washington, Dr. R. S. Toombs, Greenville; Wilkinson, Dr. L. W. Magruder, Woodville; Yalobusha, Dr. H. A. Gant, Water Valley; Yazoo, Dr. R. L. Dunn, Yazoo City; J. R. Slaton, of Tate; A. A. Wheat, of Tallahatchie, and G. K. Harrington, of Hinds county, resigned; R. D. Farish, of Issaquena, declined to accept the office, and Dr. H. C. McLaurin, of Rankin county, died. The reports of health officers and of quarantine affairs at Pascagoula occupy a large space in the annual reports for 1880 and 1881.

In March, 1882, the board adopted rules for the guidance of censors or examiners of physicians seeking a license to practice in this state. Dr. Johnson resigned the office of secretary on March 17, so that the tenure of the office should be fixed, and was immediately elected to fill that position for a term of six years. Dr. F. W. Dancy was elected president. During the year five hundred and seventy cases of small pox were reported, but inspectors were only sent to De Soto, Panola, Coahoma, Bolivar, Pike, Tallahatchie, Le Flore, Holmes and Warren counties. In September the question of guarding against the introduction of yellow fever, then prevailing at Pensacola, Matamoras, Brownsville and Havana, was discussed; quarantine regulations were ordered to be enforced in Jackson county and at Osyka. The reports on the small pox epidemic of 1882, given in the report of the state board for 1882-3, are valuable contributions to the history of this disease in Mississippi. The number of licenses issued under section 17 of the act of March 17, was seventeen hundred and eighty-five, exclusive of twenty-six temporary licenses and eighty-four after examination by the censors. Dr. J. M. Taylor was elected president in May, 1883.

The annual meeting of 1884 resulted in the choice of Dr. B. F. Kittrell for president. Correspondence on the subject of the small-pox epidemic claimed attention first and reports of health officers next. Small-pox was reported in nineteen counties during the year 1884, as follows: Adams, Amite, Claiborne, Clarke, Copiah, Hancock, Hinds, Holmes, Jefferson, Lee, Marshall, Pike, Prentiss, Sharkey, Sunflower, Warren, Washington, Wilkinson and Yalobusha, continuing in Warren county from 1883. A case in a county warranted mention, but the state may be considered as free from disease. In 1885 Dr. Kittrell was reëlected president. Owing to reports from New Orleans, La., on June 10, the necessity for establishing quarantine stations on the New Orleans & Northeastern railroad and the Louisville, New Orleans & Texas railroad appeared urgent, and preparations were at once made to quarantine against New Orleans. Fortunately nothing more than preparation for defense was necessary, and the year became noted as one in which the state reveled in good health. The issue of a circular by the board, drawing the attention of the people to the possibility of a cholera invasion and pointing out the means to prevent or restrict it, was not the least of the good deeds of this body.

In April, 1886, Dr. E. P. Sale was elected president and chief health officers nominated for thirty-eight counties. The epidemic of yellow fever at Biloxi and one case of small-pox at Natchez were the only blots on the very healthful condition of the state. The record of 1887 was equally good. In March, 1888, Dr. J. M. Taylor was elected president pro tem. and Dr. Wirt Johnston reëlected secretary for six years. On November 12, 1889, the death of Dr. Hill was announced and Dr. Taylor was elected president to fill the vacancy occasioned by such death.

The report of the secretary presented in 1889, is substantially as follows: "It gives me pleasure to report that during the years 1888 and 1889, the state has been comparatively exempt from contagious and infectious diseases. Cases of scarlet fever, diphtheria, measles, mumps and whooping-cough were reported in a few localities, and a case of small-pox in Lowndes county, but nothing occurred to excite general alarm except the limited outbreak of yellow fever in Jackson in 1888.

"On account of the prevalence of yellow fever in Florida in 1888, it was deemed prudent by the executive committee to declare quarantine against the infected places in that state, and this was accordingly done on August 13th, and steps were at once taken to establish stations as follows: On the Mobile & Ohio railroad, near state line, Dr. G. L. Izard, quarantine officer; Louisville & Nashville railroad, near Murray Station, Dr. W. A. Cox, quarantine officer; Alabama Great Southern railroad, near Kewanee Station, Dr. J. M. Buchanan, quarantine officer; East Tennessee, Virginia & Georgia railroad, near Bell Station, Dr. E. F. Crowther, quarantine officer; Georgia Pacific railroad, near Steens Station, Dr. A. C. Halbert, quarantine officer; Kansas City, Memphis & Birmingham railroad, near Gattman Station, Dr. W. A. Evans, Jr., quarantine officer; Memphis & Charleston railroad, near Iuka, Dr. H. G. McEachin, quarantine officer. The quarantine property of the board, which was stored at Osyka and Nicholson Station, was used for the partial equipment of these stations, and Adjutant General Henry, of the State National guard, kindly permitted us to use a sufficient number of tents and cots, belonging to that department, to complete their equipment. This property was shipped from Pass Christian for the purpose and afterward returned to that point by us."

In December, 1889, Dr. Taylor, then president of the board, issued his address on the work of his associates since organization. He states: "Scarcely had the members of the board returned from the first annual meeting to their several homes, when, like a besom of destruction, the great scourge of 1878 swept over the state, as if intended by an outraged Providence to teach a lesson which no amount of argument or reason could teach. In this epidemic, three members of the board, 'the noblest Romans of them all,' fell at their posts of duty, and many hundreds of good citizens, and millions of dollars, were lost to the state. Since that time the board has subserved the purpose of a convenient scapegoat, if nothing else. A small appropriation has been made, not to pay for valuable services, but to defray actual expenses, and a pittance for lost time. The result of this epidemic visitation was a literal demonstration of the truth of a statement made by our worthy secretary in his first report: 'When epidemics come to blight the prosperity of their towns, to carry off their most useful citizens, to rob them of their loved ones, and to bring mourning into their households, communities are struck with awe. They turn to the medical profession for protection. Thus aroused to the realization of the insecurity of the population against pestilence, and the powerlessness of the board of health to afford any protection, it is true the legislature did make a very liberal appropriation for the prevention and control of epidemic diseases, for which it is entitled to the gratitude of all benevolent citizens. But it is also true that the management of epidemics is only a part, and that not the most important part, of the duties devolving on a state board of health.'

"While epidemics appall and paralyze the whole country by their violence and suddenness of attack, they come only occasionally, and in many instances it is possible to evade them by flight or other precautions, but it is a fact well known to all sanitarians, that there are many agencies constantly and silently at work everywhere, causing sickness and death at all seasons, and in all ranks of society, which might and should be prevented. Many of these causes are enumerated in the law, and the board of health is authorized and instructed to abate them, but, notwithstanding the total of sickness and deaths, and consequently loss to the state from these causes is far greater than those from all epidemics combined, no appropriations have ever been made for the former, while, as before said, ample provisions have been made for the latter.

"It is very gratifying to know that, from the first organization of the board to the present time, it has uniformly had the sympathy and moral support of the governor, and the uniform and substantial support of the press is no less creditable to the newspapers of the state than it is gratifying to the board. The columns of the papers have ever been open for any communication in behalf of state medicine and public health. I am free to say that, without this support, the board could never have succeeded. The newspapers of the state, like the board of health, have done much gratuitous service, for which they are entitled to the gratitude of all right-minded people. Now, after an active service of thirteen years, the state board of health can refer with pride to its record for the manner in which it has discharged its duties with the means at its command. Its action has been characterized throughout by the strictest economy compatible with efficiency. We claim that no department of the state government can show a cleaner record than ours.

"As this is probably the last official paper which I shall ever have the honor to write, I desire to renew the unqualified testimony of the entire board of health to the beneficent results of the law to regulate the practice of medicine in the state. The law is not perfect, by any means, but it is such an improvement on the old regime that we are loth to have any radical changes made in it. Pecuniarily, it is self-sustaining, and every year it is becoming more and more efficient. But not until the licentiates under section seventeen of the law have disappeared, will the full force of the law be realized. Unavoidably, many totally incompetent and unworthy persons were licensed under that section. This was clearly foreseen, and carefully considered in the formulation of the law, but it was deemed best, for obvious reasons, not to produce any violent and sudden perturbation in the status of the medical profession of the state. This class of practitioners will constantly decrease, and finally cease, in a few years, by natural limitation. In the meantime, both the people and the profession will adapt themselves to the new order, the change being so gradually and quietly effected that it will scarcely be appreciated, except in the improved character of the practice which it will secure. The process of elimination might have been greatly expedited by incorporating in the law a clause for the revocation of license for incompetency and immorality. But the same conservative and cautious policy which characterizes all the medical legislation in the state, prevented the urging of such a measure.

"Some legislation should be enacted to facilitate the co-operation of our board with other state boards of health. Interstate co-operation should be encouraged, as the most effectual way to prevent such senseless and ruinous panics as we had last year throughout the Southern states. With the proper interstate regulations, there could be no necessity nor excuse for local or shotgun quarantines. And any incorporated town should be held responsible for all damages caused by unnecessary interference with commerce and travel. I can not discuss these subjects further now, nor have I any definite or matured propositions to make. But their importance demands, and should receive, the most careful consideration of the legislative department of the state government. It is very unjust to require delegates appointed to represent our board of health in conventions and conferences with other boards of health, not only to give their time and services, but to pay their own expenses, as has been the practice heretofore. Some conditional appropriation, at least, should be made for this purpose.

"I feel it to be my duty, as a medical censor of the state, to protest against the enactment of special laws for the exclusive benefit of pretenders claiming to have specific remedies or methods for the treatment of cancers, consumption and other diseases, many of them incurable, obtained from Indians or other equally absurd source. Often, too, the parties so favored are totally illiterate and make no claim to any knowledge of the first principles of medicine. Such legislation not only ignores all medical science but licenses unfeeling harpies to filch the last cent from the poor drowning wretch who will ever grasp at a straw. It is no less cruel to the poor deluded sufferer than unjust to the qualified practitioner, and should receive the prompt veto of the governor."

The following report on the yellow fever at Jackson was presented in 1889.

"On September 20, 1888, at about noon, two of the local physicians, Drs. Harrington and Morgan, reported that they had patients sick with a suspicious fever. The former declared his belief that his patient had yellow fever, and the suspicions of the latter were so strong as to almost amount to a conviction that his two patients also had the disease. It was at once arranged for me to visit the patients. Before doing so, however, fully appreciating the great responsibility involved in a final decision as to the character of the disease, and after consultation with Dr. J. F. Hunter, a member of the executive committee, it was decided to telegraph Drs. Robbins and Iglehart, of Vicksburg, and invite them to come out on the evening train to see the cases with the local physicians. Then, in company with Drs. Harrington and Galloway, I visited Mr. Calhoun, the patient of the former. In company with Drs. Morgan, Galloway and Harrington, the two patients of Dr. Morgan were then visited, viz.: Mr. Lorance and Mr. Lee. After a careful examination of the cases, a consultation was held by the physicians named, and it was agreed to pronounce the cases as suspicious, and to await the arrival of the physicians from Vicksburg before positively deciding the character of the disease. We were all of the opinion that the disease was yellow fever, but appreciating the gravity of the situation preferred to see the cases again before announcing a final decision. At the conclusion of this consultation the cases were announced as suspicious. Upon the arrival of Dr. Iglehart, president of the Vicksburg board of health, and Dr. Purnell, of the hospital of that city, at six o'clock p. m., the following local physicians, in company with them, visited the cases, viz.: Drs. Harrington, Morgan, Galloway, Todd, health officer of the county, Hunter, a member of the state board of health, and myself. At the consultation held, all of these gentlemen agreed that the disease was yellow fever, and it was at once reported as such. Under the laws of the state, the state board of health assumed control of the sanitary management of the town, and the following was issued:

"To the citizens of Jackson: Under the laws of the state of Mississippi, the state board of health assumes control of the sanitary affairs of the city. All persons who have not been exposed to the disease are advised to leave the city at once. Certificates should be obtained at the office of the state board of health. WIRT JOHNSTON, secretary state board of health.

"The first object in the way of preventing the spread of the disease was depopulation, and this had already commenced upon the first announcement of the fever, and was being rapidly accomplished without much assistance from us. Many of the citizens sought refuge in the surrounding country, and arrangements were made with the Illinois Central railroad, through Captain Mann, superintendent, to run special trains to convey the people to northern points. A census taken at the time showed that the following population remained: Whites, three hundred and ninety-eight; colored one thousand five hundred ninety-three; total, one thousand nine hundred and ninety-one. Whites protected by an attack of the disease, one hundred and twenty-six; colored protected, two hundred and ninety-nine; total protected, four hundred and twenty-five. Only a few of the citizens had been exposed to the disease, and those who had not been and applied for it before leaving, were provided with a certificate to that effect. It would have been perfectly safe to have admitted the citizens who had not been exposed into any place. In the sanitary management it was our purpose to protect not only the citizens of Jackson, but of the entire state.

"Arrangements were made as speedily as possible for the establishment of a refugee camp for the safety of those who had not been able to leave the town. This camp was not, however, used to any great extent, on account of the fortunate termination of the fever.

"The town covers a considerable area, and the residences for the most part have large grounds and are widely separated. The exodus of citizens almost depopulated the infected district, and created long distances between inhabited dwellings.

"Guards were stationed at the infected houses, with instructions to permit no one to have access except physicians and nurses; and an effort was made to keep under observation every one who had been exposed to the disease. The houses were designated by yellow flags.

"As soon as the depopulation of the town had been accomplished, as far as practicable a night and day force of guards were stationed on all avenues of escape, with instructions to permit no one to pass either in or out without written permission.

"Three of the four railroads entering the town were compelled to stop running their trains on account of the quarantine restrictions along their lines. Only one road, the Illinois Central, continued to run its trains, and on this road a mile and a half north of the town, we established a quarantine station, where trains stopped, under the supervision of a quarantine officer, and freight and express matter was discharged; which was subsequently brought into the town by a locomotive located there. No person was permitted to get on board or off the cars at this station, and no freight or other article from the town was permitted to be taken on board. All cars on sidetracks were detained. No mails left the town, not that we thought they would be dangerous after fumigation, but because other localities refused to receive them.

"As soon as practicable, disinfection was resorted to as follows: Infected bedding was burned, linen and cotton fabrics were boiled in a one to five hundred bichloride of mercury solution; the floors and walls of infected houses were scrubbed with the bichloride solution, and the rooms with their contents were subjected to sulphurous fumigation. Of the thirteen cases reported five died. All the persons attacked were employed around the Illinois Central depot. The last cases were reported September 22, but quarantine was continued until October 12."

The officers for 1890-2 are: J. M. Greene, M. D., president, Aberdeen; Wirt Johnston, M. D., secretary, Jackson; members for the state at large, W. F. Hyer, M. D., Meridian; B. F. Ward, M. D., Winona; Wirt Johnston, M. D., Jackson; members for the first district, J. M. Taylor, M. D., Corinth; J. M. Greene, M. D., Aberdeen; for the second district, H. A. Gant, M. D., Water Valley; Chesley Daniel, M. D., Holly Springs; for the third district, T. R. Trotter, M. D., Winona; B. F. Kittrell, M. D., Black Hawk; for the fourth district, M. J. Lowry, M. D., Meridian; R. E. Howard, M. D., Durant; for the fifth district, J. F. Hunter, M. D., Jackson; L. Sexton, M. D., Wesson; and for the sixth district, R. S. Toombs, M. D., Greenville; E. L. McGehee, M. D., Woodville. The executive committee comprises Wirt Johnston, M. D., J. F. Hunter, M. D., L. Sexton, M. D.

The transactions of the board for the two past years are not yet compiled. The reports made by the chief health officers of counties since 1884 form an important part of the transactions of the board. A report from each of forty-four counties is appended. All would be given for this year were it possible to obtain them; but all which could be obtained find a place as a supplement to the history of the board of health, and as a record of the recognition by the people of the value of sanitary science and knowledge of health conditions.

What was written a year ago on the health of Mississippi, applies more strongly to-day. In every particular the sanitary conditions of the state have been improved and the people show the result of such improved conditions in feature and movement. There are general exceptions, of course. Malarial districts are found here as in every other state east of the Mississippi, and people are found inhabiting them. Careless men and women exist here, also, who fail to recognize the fact that disease is the companion of uncleanliness. The board of health has tried every argument with such persons, but not always with success. A general communal effort in this direction, such as that resorted to to clear a county of horse-thieves, is necessary now; for a neighbor who noes not observe cleanliness and the laws of sanitation robs village and city life of a treasure much more valuable than horses and should have no place in a community.

The records of the Board of Health and State Medical association points out the variety of ailments, ordinary and extraordinary, which come under the notice of Mississippi physicians. The great majority of such ailments are common throughout the United States, and of the minority it may be said, that they are more virulent in some of the Northern states than in the South. Like la grippe, they are not native. They have been brought hither, and under certain conditions grow into epidemics. Such conditions are explained in other pages and the efforts to abolish them told.

The principal disease of Mississippi is malarial fever, which is widespread during the summer and fall seasons, seldom or never proves fatal in the hill region, but often becomes pernicious in the alluvial or bottom lands, and fatal when it takes a hemorrhagic character.

In 1856 two cases of pernicious malarial fever were brought under the observation of Dr. E. W. Hughes for the first time in his life, while in later years a few cases of malarial hemorrhagic fever were reported near Sidon on the Yazoo.

During the winters of 1848, 1850, 1855 and 1858 typhoid fever prevailed in Carroll, Grenada, Tallahatchie, Yalobusha and adjoining counties. Before the habits of the monster were understood many patients died under a too active treatment, but for the last quarter of a century there have not been twenty-five cases of true typhoid brought under the notice of physicians in northern Mississippi. In 1866 a disease which has been called continued fever appeared. The symptoms resembled those of cerebro-spinal meningitis.

The first extensive inroad of cholera into north Mississippi was made at Duck Hill, Montgomery county, in 1866, when one, Hazlehurst, was stricken by the disease. Of the total number of inhabitants—sixty—twenty-two were attacked; and of that number thirteen died. The stagnant ponds and lakes in the neighborhood aided in bringing on the village this terrible scourge.

Scarlatina has been known here since 1846. In 1854 every form of this disease was presented at Grenada. In 1853, 1854, 1857 and 1858 the winter brought with it this scourge.

Dysentery, sporadic, is common from April to September, but easily mastered. In 1849 and 1852 dysentery, epidemic, took possession of Carroll and Grenada counties. So severe was it in 1852, that two Caucasians and ten negroes were carried off, within the first fifteen days of July, on the plantation of Henry Purnell, and all cases might have proved fatal had not the whites and negroes removed to camps on July 16 of that year.

The epidemic of erysipelas of 1844 was the most serious ever known in northern Mississippi. Since that time cases are occasionally presented, but never in epidemic form.

Diphtheria was common in the upper Yalobusha and Tallahatchie country before the war, particularly in 1859 and 1860. In one case tracheotomy was resorted to with success by a Dr. B. B. Drane. In the summer of 1858 it appeared in Tippah county.

Small-pox was introduced by Memphis, Tenn., negroes in 1872, into Grenada. Of ten Caucasians attacked all recovered; but twenty-five of the fifty negro sufferers died.

Whooping-cough, measles and mumps present themselves annually as in all other sections of the country. Pneumonia, phthisis, rheumatism and other diseases common throughout the world are presented here occasionally, but generally wanting in virulence. In November, 1862, however, rheumatism took possession of the negroes working on the forts at Grenada, and before April, 1863, one hundred of them died of this disease.

The epidemic of 1871 at Jackson, Vicksburg and Natchez assumed a type so peculiar in characteristics that for a long time physicians were slow to pronounce it yellow fever. On July 22, 1871, an Englishman residing at Vicksburg was attacked; but the fever did not reach its highest point until November 1, that year. The disease at Natchez was called yellow fever by all the physicians there except Dr. Bonduvant, who inclined to the belief that it was typho-malarial fever. Dr. P. F. Whitehead, writing on the subject in 1872, inclines to the opinion that the disease at Natchez was of local origin, beginning under the hill and extending to the city. Dr. M. S. Craft places the date of the first case at Jackson, September 7, 1871, and pronounced the epidemic yellow fever. Of thirty cases within the United States garrison at Jackson, twenty-four were fatal. Dr. Craft's paper, given in the reports of the medical society for 1873, is a brief but extraordinarily complete description of the dreaded disease as diagnosed by him at Jackson in 1871.

The first mention of yellow fever in Mississippi is made under date August 22, 1701, when

Antoine Lemoyne Sauvolle died at Fort Maurepas, near Biloxi. The disease was carried from St. Domingo by one or more of the ships touching at that point, and was not then, nor is it now, indigenous. Over a century and a half passed away before any serious invasion was made. In 1853 many persons were carried off; again, in 1871 it was introduced, but not until 1878 was the character of the dreadful scourge realized.

In dealing with the botany of Mississippi, in the first chapter, the names and character of the medicinal plants of the state were not given, as such a list appeared to belong to this chapter, pointing out the fact that where disease is there also is the remedy. There are at least eighty-six species of medicinal plants in the state, which may be distributed under the following heads as arranged by Dr. B. H. Whitehead: Tonics—Dogwood, American columbine, poplar, magnolia, sweet bay, umbrella tree, wild cherry, willow, boneset-thoroughwort, dogfennel, wild camomile, swamp dogwood, button bush, century plant. Sedatives—Yellow jasmine. Narcotics—Thorn apple, jamestown weed, lobelia, American water hemlock, cherry laurel, swamp laurel, locust, mountain ivy. Aromatic Stimulants—Indian turnip, sweet flag, cedar, hoarhound, peppermint, spearmint, horsemint, spicewood, laurus benzoin, wild ginger, Canada snakeroot. Astringents—Persimmon, white oak, black oak, Spanish oak, live oak, dewberry, blackberry, sumac, dock, water lily, wax myrtle, chinquapin, common thick shell hickorynut, pecan, shellbark, witch hazel. Spastics—Poison oak. Emetics—Milkweed, bloodroot, pocoon, pokeroot, pokeberry, latherwood. Cathartics—American senna, wild senna, palma christi, may apple, elder, black walnut, wild potato vine, castor oil plant. Diaphoretics—Sassafras, butterfly weed, pleurisy root, holly, hercules club. Diuretics—Burdock, dandelion, purslane, dwarf stinging nettle, hydrangea seven barks. Blennorhetics—Long-leaf pine, short-leaf pine, pitch pine, trailing arbutus, ground laurel, mayflower, sweet gum. Emmenagogues—Spanish needles. Alteratives—Southern prickly ash, China briar, sarsaparilla. Demulcents—Red elm, slippery elm, mullien, pansy violets. Anthelmintics—Pink root, worm seed, jerusalem oak, China berry tree. Other indigenous remedies are the sneezewood, an erbine, and the mulberry.

The remedies named are here to meet the natural troubles of the body. Many of them were known to the Indian medicine men and were the only remedies resorted to prior to the settlement of the country by the Caucasians. When new diseases were introduced by violation of natural laws, stronger remedies were called for, and as civilization advanced calls for still more radical remedies increased, until now there is scarcely a place for the medicinal plants of Mississippi in the pharmacopœa.

Chapter XI.

EDUCATIONAL HISTORY.

FROM the period of the first Protestant-English settlements in what is now the state of Mississippi, in the latter half of the last century, the majority of those settlements sustained small neighborhood schools. These schools were of the very simplest character. Usually they were kept in log houses, with rough plank benches for the only furniture. They were supported wholly by private contributions, or by the tuition fees paid. The course of study rarely embraced more than the rudiments: reading, writing by copy, and arithmetic so far as the double rule of three. However, where conditions were favorable, as along the Mississippi river, in the rich-land counties, would be found a gathering of families comparatively wealthy and often highly cultivated, whose schools would be of a better type, and include the classics and English grammar. Noteworthy among these were the Swayzes, of Adams county; the Lymans, of Claiborne; the Vicks and Cooks, of Warren.

The first known public school of any reputation in the territory was a female school established at Natchez, in the year of 1801, by the Rev. David Ker. He was assisted by his wife and daughters, who were highly finished scholars and very elegant ladies. He was of Irish birth, was an ex-professor of the University of North Carolina, and 1802 was appointed judge of the superior court. He left descendants of his name, who are yet about Natchez.

Jefferson college, located at Washington, Adams county, was incorporated on the 13th of May, 1802. The institution still exists. It had no endowment at the first, the plan being that it should be supported by voluntary contributions. A site was donated by John and James Foster and Randall Gibson. On the 3d of March, 1803, congress granted to it a township of land and some lots in the city of Natchez. These grants, however, did not yield any available funds for a number of years. The city lots were adversely held, and litigation ensued, while the township lands were not yet subject to entry. Toward the close of the year 1810, an arrangement was effected whereby the buildings and subscriptions of the Washington academy, which was at work under the Rev. James Smiley, were transferred to the college, and thereby the institution was enabled to make a beginning. It was opened, on the 1st of January, 1811, on the footing of an humble academy, under the charge of Dr. Edwin Reese; Mr. Samuel Graham, assistant. In the year 1812 about $5,000 was derived from a grant of escheats made by the legislature. In 1816 the sum of $6,000, payable in four annual installments, was appropriated by the territorial legislature, and a Mr. James McAllister employed as principal. In August, 1817, the suit with the city of Natchez over one of the lots granted by congress, was compromised by the payment to the college of $5,000; and thereupon the east wing of the college edifice was erected. In 1818 the township lands began to yield something, and about $8,000 was obtained from that source.

This sum, with about $13,000 more, borrowed from the state and from bank, was applied to the completion of the buildings. Shortly afterward the values of lands declined, and the policy of the Federal government, in making land-grants on extraordinarily liberal terms, practically excluded competition, so that the college was disappointed in its expectations of further revenue from that source. A period of great financial difficulty ensued, from which it was not rescued for years, and in which executions were sometimes levied on its property, which was preserved only by the generous intervention of its trustees, who paid the debts, in some instances, from their private means. In June, 1821, Mr. McAllister retired. The academy was kept up, on a reduced scale, until 1826, when the instructor then in charge died, and the institution was closed for a period. This emergency led to a final compromise of the remaining litigation with the city of Natchez by which it was agreed to sell the property in controversy and divide the proceeds. Still, but little benefit was derived from this expedient. Sales were slow, and at low prices. However, an agreement was made with Mr. E. B. Williston, as president, and Maj. John Holbrook, as superintendent, on a five years' lease, for the reopening of the college, on the West Point plan, at their own expense. It was so reopened December 1, 1829, and with great success. In 1832, however, Mr. Williston resigned, because of failing health, and Major Holbrook died. Capt. Alden Patridge, formerly superintendent at West Point, succeeded as president. He remained but a few months. The military system was then abandoned, and the trustees determined to employ teachers at fixed salaries. One of those teachers, Mr. Charles L. Dubuisson, was made president in June, 1835. The school, however, did not flourish. It so declined that in March, 1838, there were only twenty-five students, of whom only five were in the college proper. The collegiate department was therefore suspended for one year, and a thorough reorganization effected. Work was resumed in 1840, with an extensive course of study and a faculty of five professors, Rev. A. Stephens, president. The attendance of students was largely increased. At this time the estate of the college amounted to $251,671. This included the site and buildings, library and apparatus, bank stock, and purchase-debts of the lots in Natchez and of the township lands, the latter having been at last located and sold. Most of these funds were, however, soon lost by unfortunate investments. In 1845 the college was under the charge of Professors Jacob Ammen, John Rowland and Orrick Metcalfe, and was flourishing. In October, 1850, it passed into the hands of President Ashbel Green, son of Dr. Green, president of Princeton college. In April, 1853, the Rev. Charles Reighly became president, and he was followed, in July, 1856, by the Rev. E. J. Cornish. On his death, which occurred in 1859, Prof. J. J. Critchlow was appointed president pro tempore, and remained in charge until the summer of 1861. At this time, owing to the stress of finances caused by the war, salaries were suspended, and Professor Critchlow and the Rev. W. K. Douglass, as associates, were employed under a special arrangement. They conducted the school until the summer of 1863, when it was suspended. The buildings were later occupied by the Federal troops as barracks, and were not restored to the trustees until November, 1865. For seven years thereafter the college was presided over by Mr. Jesse Andrews. In the summer of 1872 Prof. J. S. Raymond, the present president, was elected, and authorized to employ an assistant. Tuition was made free, and so remained until the summer of 1875. The session of 1879–80 was a very prosperous one, and the employment of two additional assistants was authorized. Since that time the history of the college has been one of success. President Raymond is at present assisted by Prof. Matthew C. Harper and Prof. Jackson Reeves, both graduates of the state university. The effective endowment is about $40,000. This institution occupies the interesting attitude that its charter was the first granted in Mississippi for any purpose; that it is the oldest existent school in the entire South perhaps, outside of North Carolina and Virginia; that it has still never granted a baccalaureate degree; that its students have included J. F. H. Claiborne, B. L. C. Wailes, A. G. Brown and Jefferson Davis; and that the great naturalist, J. J. Audubon, was once its drawing master.

The story of Jefferson college has carried us far beyond the period of its origin. It will be necessary now to return to the date, about 1802. The limits fixed for this publication forbid a full history of all the excellent schools of which information more or less satisfactory is attainable. Many quite deserving of distinct chapters will have to be dispatched with brief mention. It is to be remembered, too, that many other fine schools are not only extinct, but also lost to memory.

The Franklin Society academies.—By an act passed January 8, 1807, Cato West and twenty-one others were incorporated as The Franklin society, for the purpose of establishing an academy at the town of Greenville, or its vicinity, in Jefferson county. The academy was successfully established, in two distinct branches, one for each sex. The Rev. and Hon. David Ker was in charge of the female academy for a period about 1810.

Madison academy.—By an act passed December 5th, 1809, Samuel Gibson and twelve others were incorporated under this name, and empowered to establish the academy in the county of Claiborne, on the north fork of the Bayou Pierre, near the town of Port Gibson, under the presidency of Henry C. Cox. By an amendatory act, passed December 1, 1814, the removal of the academy to any site within three miles of Port Gibson was authorized; it was removed to that town.

Washington academy, at Washington, Adams county; established about 1808, by Rev. James Smiley. In 1810, it was absorbed by Jefferson college, as related.

Rickhow's academy was established for boys, at Natchez, in 1811, by the Rev. Jacob Rickhow, from New Jersey. It continued for several years. Mr. Rickhow was one of the pioneer Presbyterian ministers, and is a historical character in his church.

Green academy was located in what was then Madison county, Mississippi territory, but what is now the vicinity of Huntsville, Alabama. It was incorporated in 1812, and received a donation from the territory of $500, in 1816.

Washington academy was located in what was then Washington county, Mississippi territory, but is now Washington county, Ala., at Fort St. Stephens. It was incorporated in 1814, and received a donation from the territory of $500, in 1816.

The Jackson academy, in Wilkinson county, was a mixed boardingschool. Mr. William Connell was principal: Mr. Booth, steward. Board and washing were restricted to $60 per annum. It was incorporated December 27, 1814; Daniel Williams, Sr., and eight others, incorporators and trustees.

The Pine Grove grammar school, in Amite county, was established in 1814; perhaps earlier. Rev. James Smiley was principal; Mr. H. Wiley, assistant. It was a boarding-school, with a steward. Tuition, board and washing, $100 per annum. This was merged in the Amite academy, at Liberty, Amite county, which was incorporated December 8, 1815; James Smiley and ten others, incorporators. A $1,500 house was erected by subscription. The school prospered for a time, but wasted away, and in 1829 the house was occupied by a sixteenth section free school.

The Pinckneyville academy, at Pinckneyville, Wilkinson county, was incorporated December 23, 1815: Gerard C. Brandon and eight others, incorporators and trustees. It was still at work in 1825-6; Mr. William Smart, principal.

The Wilkinson academy, two and one-half miles east of Woodville, was incorporated December 23, 1815; Abram M. Scott (afterward governor) and eight others, incorporators and trustees. In the year 1825-6, Mr. Charles H. Talbot, late of Tennessee, was principal; in 1826, Mr. S. Hill; in 1831, Mr. J. A. Shaw; in 1832, Samuel McLelland; in 1833, Mr. Z. S. Lyons; and in 1834, a Mr. Black. Shortly after this, it seems to have become extinct.

Richard Pearce and Israel Spencer, elders in the Presbyterian church, conducted a high school in Natchez from 1815 to 1820.

The Shieldsboro college, located at Shieldsboro, in Hancock county, was incorporated in 1818.

The first aid extended by either Federal or state government to the cause of common-school education, came in the establishment of the sixteenth section funds. On April 7, 1798, the Mississippi territory was organized. In offering the public lands, acquired from the Indians, for sale, the government pursued the usual policy of reserving in each township the section numbered sixteen (or some other in lieu thereof, whenever that section had been otherwise lawfully disposed of), for the support of schools within the township.*

The act of congress of January 9, 1815, inaugurated a policy of leasing the lands on short terms. The state statute of February 5, 1818, passed pursuant to the injunction of the constitution of 1817, adopted the same plan. At first the lands were managed by the county courts, but the act of January 9, 1824, authorized the election, by the resident heads of families, of trustees, who were empowered to rent, collect and disburse the rents, erect school-houses, employ teachers, etc.

The act of February 27, 1833, authorized the sale, on a credit of one to four years, of ninety-nine year leases; the purchase money to be secured by lien on the lands. The proceeds, when collected, to be invested in the Planters' bank stock. The amendment of February 27, 1836, allowed the proceeds to be lent to private borrowers, at ten per cent., with security or to be invested in stock of solvent banks. Various alterations of detail were made by statute; but the foregoing system was substantially adhered to for many years.

The act of 1842 required the distribution of the proceeds among all the schools of the township, in proportion to the resident scholars attending

There was much mismanagement. The money invested in Planters' bank stock was lost; that invested in other banks met the same fate; many of the purchase notes were permitted to become barred by the statute of limitations; many that were collected were so collected after protracted and costly litigation; much of the money lent out proved to be lent on worthless endorsements, etc. It is a disgusting story.

Even where there was a fund preserved it was practically useless, except in rare instances. It was a troublesome business, and the trustees were generally indifferent. Where they were not, they were embarrassed to the point of paralysis by uncertainty as to the laws. By the year 1845, no less than fifty-three statutes, local and other, had been passed in reference to these lands. Those statutes were scattered through numerous volumes of session laws. None knew where to turn for certain knowledge. The statues were generally ill drawn, hardly ever requiring the officers to give bonds for the discharge of their duties.

The landssharks were about, of course. Plots to lease cheap, plots to engross the desirable parts of a section, and defy competition as to the residue, etc., abounded. Timber thieves were not wanting either.

---

*A somewhat different policy was adopted in the Chickasaw cession, embracing about the northern one-fifth of the state; whence came the Chickasaw school fund, of which later.

Governor Brown, in his message of January 6, 1846, called the attention of the legislature to the manner in which this interest had been most shamefully neglected, and urged the establishment of a system of schools under a general head responsible to the state.

Nothing was done. Notwithstanding the governor's message the matter went as before. In a few counties there was a semblance of attention; in the most, none; and after the Civil war, in the days of reconstruction, the greater part of what was left was either squandered or stolen.

Meanwhile, the lands are out of hand for ninety-nine years, with a few exceptions where they have not been in request. They will begin to revert about 1933; but what will then be their value agriculturally, after a century of skinning, it needs no prophet to foresee. As the county superintendent of Sharkey county put it, "boards of supervisors are, from time to time, donating, as it were, to individuals valuable sections of land belonging to the people, upon the virtual condition that, after enriching the happy individual and his offspring, it shall be turned over, worn out and worthless, to the remote posterity."

To sum up, there are fifty-seven counties that should be largely endowed from this source. Of that number, nineteen have no trace of the fund left; three have an income for the whole county of less than $100; twelve others have incomes of $300 or less; seven others, incomes between $300 and $500; two others, incomes of about $800; three others, between $1,000 and $2,000; and one, an income of about $3,000. Eleven others report lands of more or less value still on hand (mainly of little account); and the remaining counties make no report.

The Beach Hill academy and Methodist meeting-house (sic) was incorporated on February 6th, 1818; Isaac Dunbar and four others being incorporators and trustees.

The Elizabeth Female academy, located at Washington, Adams county, was the first high school exclusively for girls in the state; and was the first school established by any Protestant denomination in all the extreme South. In the year 1818 Mrs. Elizabeth Roach donated the land and buildings, on condition that the donees, the Mississippi conference of the Methodist Episcopal church, should maintain there a high school for the education of girls. It was incorporated in 1819. It maintained until the day of extinction a very high character for thoroughness of tuitional work. In all but name it was a college. The first president was Mr. C. Stiles, from Claiborne county; Mrs. Jane B. Sanderson, governess. Mr. Stiles died in 1822, and was succeeded by the Rev. John C. Burruss, a most accomplished gentleman. Under him, Mrs. Caroline M. Thayer, a near relative of Dr. Warren, the hero of Bunker Hill, was governess. From 1828 to 1832 the Rev. Benjamin M. Drake was president. In 1833 he was followed by the Rev. J. P. Thomas, and Mrs. Thayer was succeeded by Mrs. Susan Brewer. In 1836, the Rev. Bradford Frazee became president; and in 1839, the Rev. R. D. Smith, Miss Lucy A. Stillman being governess. There is extant an old report which shows the number of boarders (but not of the day scholars) for the first eleven years. They were as follows: for 1819, twenty-eight; for 1820, twenty-eight; for 1821, seventeen; for 1822, thirteen; for 1823, eighteen; for 1824, twenty-five; for 1825, ten; for 1826, thirty; for 1827, forty; for 1828, forty-five; for 1829, sixty-three. The course of study embraced penmanship, English, French, Latin, geography, ancient and modern history, belles lettres, arithmetic with the elements of mathematical sciences, astronomy with the use of the globes, chemistry, natural, moral and mental philosophy, constitution and government of the United States, the Bible and evidences of Christianity. About 1844, after a career of about twenty-five years of great usefulness, the academy was abandoned, other schools more favorably located having drawn its patronage away.

The Natchez academy was incorporated February 12, 1819; Dr. John Hosmer and thirteen others being incorporators and trustees. Dr. Hosmer was the principal. He and his wife had come from Lexington, Ky., in the December previous, for the express purpose of opening a female academy, "as good as any in the United States." The institution seems to have perished soon. Its charter and property were used later, as will be shown under the date 1829.

Pearl River academy, in Lawrence county, was incorporated February 12, 1819; William Cooper, Sr., and four others being incorporators and trustees.

The Wilkinson Female academy, of Wilkinson county, was incorporated February 19, 1819; John Joor and five others being incorporators and trustees.

The Columbian academy, of Marion county, was incorporated February 10, 1820; Benjamin Lee and seven others being incorporators and trustees.

The first effort made by the state in aid of general education was in the establishment of the literary fund. This was done by the act of 26th of November, 1821. All escheats, confiscations, forfeitures, and derelict; all fines, penalties and forfeitures not otherwise appropriated; all goods of persons dying intestate and without heirs, were appointed to this fund. It was directed to be invested in bank stock or lent on security. Its object was, first, to aid in the education of poor children; secondly, to endow and encourage schools. Such portion of the fund as should be left unused in the education of poor children was to be divided among schools to be kept in the different counties, for such purposes as the legislature should deem best for the promotion of literature; but no distribution of this kind could be made until the surplus should amount to $50,000.

The Planters' bank, in the stock of which nearly all, if not quite all, of the fund was invested, failed, and was put into liquidation in 1844. Its stockholders realized nothing from their stock. The fund proper was wiped out of existence at one sweep. It would hardly have been worth while to dwell on the Literary fund, so barren was it of visible fruit, except that the establishment and cherishing of it for a period of eighteen years discloses an anxiety in the minds of the people of the state to further the cause of education, and except for the further fact that it was one of the progressive steps by which, through failure and disaster, the present stage was reached.

The Franklin academy, located at Columbus in Lowndes county, was established in 1821, by authority of the legislature. It was, by twenty-four years, the earliest free school of note and permanency in the state. It was and is a sixteenth section school. At the time of its foundation the county of Lowndes formed a part of Monroe, and was separated from the residue of the state in white occupancy, by the intervening lands of the Choctaw Indians. The school section was divided into lots and leased for ninety-nine years. At first they paid an annual rental of about $8,000; but in the financial troubles of 1837-40, a system was inaugurated of forfeiting the leases, and releasing at lower rates, the result of which was that the income dwindled to about $2,400 per annum from that source. It has, however, been supplemented by taxation so as to maintain the school on an efficient basis. From the beginning, there were distinct male and female departments. Until the year 1839, there was a full collegiate course free, but at that time, owing to complaint that the resources of the institution were taxed for the support of a high curriculum to the partial exclusion of the children of the poor, a reorganization was made by which the higher courses, especially of Latin and Greek, were left off. In 1842, there was a further modification, by which the course was divided into five classes, all except the first being required to pay tuition fees ranging from $4 to $12 per session of four months. Under this management less attention was paid to the higher branches, and other schools were established for them. Later, the Odd Fellows school was destroyed by fire, which led to the gradual re-establishment of the former high grade at the academy; and that high grade has been maintained ever since that time. In 1876, a branch for colored children was established. A very handsome additional building has been recently erected, and the school is kept open for nine months of the year. So early as 1837 the attendance of pupils had reached about two hundred; but prior to the reorganization of 1839, it had fallen away to about one hundred. That measure immediately brought the number up to about four hundred. The numbers since have varied. The annual attendance is now about one thousand, of which about six hundred and fifty are white. A full account cannot now be given of the various principals. In 1836, Prof. Robert B. Witter was in charge of the male department, with two assistants, while Mrs. M. A. Innes and an assistant were in charge of the female department. In September, 1837, a Mr. Swift was in charge, and he was followed, in June, 1838, by the Rev. H. Ried. In July, 1839, Mr. James T. Hoskins was elected principal of the male branch and given two assistants, while Miss C. Mathieson was placed in charge of the female, also with two teachers. In 1841 the male department was under Mr. J. J. W. Payne, with one assistant; and the female, under Mr. McLean and wife. Passing over the long list of other teachers, it remains to note that the academy is now under the presidency of Prof. Pope Barrow, a graduate of Randolph-Macon college, and that he has a corps of eleven assistants in the white branch alone. This school has been always a progressive one. As far back as 1841, is to be found a communication in the *Argus* making a protest against "the new experiment now being tried in Columbus of teaching our children to spell before they learn their alphabet."

The Sligo academy, of Wilkinson county was incorporated November 20, 1821; John B. Posey and seven others being incorporators and trustees.

Brevost's academy was established at Natchez in 1822. Mr. Brevost employed the celebrated naturalist, John J. Audubon, to teach drawing.

The Lancastrian academy was in operation in Natchez in 1825.

Mr. A. Kinsey conducted an academy for young ladies in the same city at the same time.

Cicero Jefferson and Alva Farnsworth kept a classical school on Main street, in Natchez, in 1825, and it had an evening-school feature.

The Flower Hill academy was incorporated in 1825, but the statute does not name the location of the school

Fox academy, a boarding school for girls, was opened near Woodville, in March, 1826, by the Rev. James A. Fox, an Episcopalian clergyman. His wife assisted. The school continued a number of years.

Burroughs seminary was opened at Woodville in 1826, by three sisters: Hannah, Cornelia A., and Caroline M. Burroughs. It was a boarding school for girls. Music and dancing were taught. A popular and useful school for, at the least, ten years.

The Port Gibson academy was incorporated in 1826, under the name of Clinton academy. The name was changed by an amendatory act in 1829. Who first had it in charge is not known. In 1835 the principals of the female branch were E. A. and S. Royce. In 1838 it was under the presidency of a Mr. Smith, who was "an experienced teacher and a graduate of Brown university." He was assisted by his wife and two others. The senior course embraced mineralogy, geology, trigonometry, mensuration, astronomy (including astronomical calculations), political economy, mental and moral philosophy, logic, elocution, analogy, sacred history, Latin, Greek, French and German. There were art and music departments on a considerable scale. In 1840 Mr. Smith was succeeded by Prof. George P. Strong, just from Mississippi college. The school seems to have failed about the year 1844.

The Mississippi college. The foundation of this institution was laid in 1826 by the incorporation of the Hampstead academy, located at Mt. Salus (now Clinton). It is noteworthy as being the first school of a successful character established in the territory acquired by the treaty at Doak's Stand, by which the Choctaws ceded the country lying, roughly speaking, between the south boundary of Hinds and the north boundary of Holmes, the east boundary of Rankin and the Mississippi river. The school was, at first, a village school, the fruit of private enterprise. It began work in January, 1827. In February its name was changed to the Mississippi academy, and the state granted to it for five years from February, 1825, the rents of the seminary lands. At this time Mr. G. F. Hopkins was principal, and there were over thirty pupils. Males and females had separate rooms. The classics, higher mathematics, with their practical applications, chemistry, astronomy, rhetoric, etc., were taught. In 1829, Daniel Comfort was president; there were about ninety pupils; and the state lent the institution $5,000 for the purpose of erecting buildings. In 1830 the name was changed to the Mississippi college; two handsome buildings were completed, one for boys and one for girls. In June, 1832, there was a grand commencement, and two young ladies, Miss Lucinda F. Bagley, of Covington, La., and Miss Caroline H. Couluer, of Vicksburg, graduated, and received degrees. The president delivered a baccalaureate. The first degrees conferred in this state, therefore, were conferred on women. In 1834 the college was organized into two distinct departments, one for each sex; each with a distinct faculty, but under a common president. In 1835 and 1836, the male branch was under I. N. Shepherd and E. W. F. Sloane. It was thriving. The teachers claimed their course of study to be of the best. They delivered public lectures on natural philosophy and chemistry every Friday evening. The female branch was under Mrs. Thayer (late of Elizabeth Female academy), and a Miss Parker. Until October, 1836, however, there was no president. Prof. E. N. Elliott, of the Indiana university, was then engaged, and there was a complete change of faculties. President Elliott took personal charge of the male department with two professors.

The female department was placed under Profs. Henry and George P. Strong and Mrs. Sarah K. P. Failes, as associate principals, with three assistants. At this time the institution became involved financially. Unable to meet its engagements to the professors of the male department, they resigned in November, 1837. Toward the end of 1839, Professor Strong gave up the female branch, and both departments were then placed under Prof. H. Dwight, then lately from the University of Louisiana, who was assisted by his wife and a Miss Potter. After an unsuccessful attempt, in 1841, to negotiate for the adoption of the college by the Methodists for their Centenary college (then in the process of establishment), it was placed, in 1842, under the fostering care of the Clinton presbytery. A strong faculty was then organized: Rev. Alexander Campbell, former president of Sharon academy, was president; assisted, in the male branch, by Rev. Robert McLain, Rev. C. Parish, Dr. E. Pickett and U. W. Moffit; in the female branch, by Miss H. E. Gillespie. For some years the college did well. In July, 1845, Mr. M. A. Foute, of Jackson, received the degree of bachelor of arts, and is therefore the first male graduate of this institution. At this time the Rev. A. Newton, an educator of high standing and great experience, was in charge of the female department with two assistants. In 1846 the Rev. P. Cotton was president. He was followed, in 1848, by the Rev. C. Parish. Again financial troubles arose and the college began to decline. Whereupon, in July, 1850, the presbytery surrendered their control over it. In the following November the property was transferred to the Mississippi Baptist state convention, and in the same fall, the first session under that management was opened. The female feature was dropped. It did not at first aspire to be considered a college. Mr. I. N. Urner was made principal. Eighty-four students were enrolled, and the session closed with three teachers. In 1851 a movement was inaugurated to secure an endowment of $100,000 by subscriptions. In 1853 college classes were organized, and in 1854 Mr. C. C. Granberry graduated, the first under the Baptist management. In 1858 the subscription to the endowment had reached $102,800, and a special subscription was started for the building of a chapel, to be used also as a church. This building was completed in 1860 at a cost of about $30,000. In that year, also, Mr. Urner was formally made president. When the war broke out some of the students and three of the professors formed the company called the Mississippi College Rifles and joined the Confederate army. A small school was continued at a heavy expense. The war was very disastrous. Not only was the endowment fund practically annihilated, but, also, the owners of the scholarships which were purchased by such parts of it as had been paid up, called for their rights of free tuition, so that receipts from that quarter were very largely prevented. However, they struggled along. In September, 1867, Dr. Walter Hillman, a graduate of Brown university, was elected president. He began with one assistant and eleven pupils. The total enrollment for the year was twenty-nine. Year by year there was improvement. In 1872 Dr. Hillman resigned and was succeeded by the present incumbent, Dr. W. S. Webb, a graduate of Madison university. In that year, also, another endowment subscription was started. It soon grew to about $40,000, but the financial crash of 1873 rendered it almost worthless. In 1891 a third effort was made to this end, and at last success has crowned the so persistent labor, the sum of $60,000 having been secured. The convention furnishes, from year to year, a contribution to the running expenses. This institution, after all of its interesting vicissitudes, seems to be at last on an assured basis. There are in the faculty the president, five professors, a principal and an assistant for the preparatory department. There is a high collegiate curriculum, and about two hundred and fifty pupils attend annually, while the troublesome scholarships of the date prior to the war have been all, or nearly all, surrendered.

Fayette academy—Incorporated in 1827 and organized with distinct male and female departments at Fayette, in Jefferson county. Its earliest management is now unknown, but in 1831 the male department was under the charge of Messrs. J. J. Sanford and Charles Clarke, gentlemen of collegiate training, the female department being managed by Mr. Sanford and his wife. In 1837 a Mr. Scheling and his wife assumed charge of the academy, and they were followed, in November, 1838, by Mr. Thomas Brown, Jr., of Carlisle, Penn., his wife (a French lady) and her sister. In December, 1840, the Browns left and the academy passed into the hands of Miss Ann Jenkins. She was followed, in 1842, by Rev. Mr. Morris, son and daughter. They, in turn, in 1850, by Rev. William M. Curtiss, a Methodist clergyman, then of New Orleans, whose extensive personal influence brought the academy to a measure of success it had not before known. Mr. Curtiss resigned in 1855. In 1857 the charter was amended so as to authorize the transfer of the academy to the Mississippi presbytery. This being done, Rev. Mr. Tenney was made principal. Under this arrangement the school prospered. There was an average attendance of about eighty boarding pupils, with the usual complement of day scholars. After the Civil war a Mr. Hay conducted the school, but it languished and he resigned. The building became dilapidated, the property passed into the hands of the county and was used for free school purposes. In 1883 it was retransferred to the presbytery, and this body, in 1884, appointed Miss Kate Wharton principal. This lady, in the following year, purchased the property and it has prospered with her. There are about sixty scholars; property worth about $20,000. This is the oldest existing female school in the state.

The Westville academy, of Simpson county, was incorporated in 1827.

The Spring Ridge academy, of Madison county, was established in the summer of 1828 under the charge of Rev. M. Marshall. In 1830 he associated with himself the Rev. A. Newton. Apparently the first high school north of Clinton, it was incorporated in 1833.

The Natchez academy seems to have been revived in the spring of 1829. The old charter and the same building were used. It was opened in September; Rev. Isaac S. Demund, principal. Latin, Greek, French, the higher mathematics, and the usual English branches were taught. Edward Turner and John A. Quitman were members of the board of trustees. In 1832, the academy was under N. Shotwell and S. H. B. Black, as coprincipals; in 1833, under Mr. Black alone. It seems to have become extinct about the year 1840.

Zion Hill academy, in the northern portion of Amite county, was flourishing in 1829, and before. Messrs. Borden and Taylor, Northerners, founded it, and were credited with great industry and ability. In 1839, the school was still at work, under Mr. L. E. Davess.

Mr. and Mrs. Lawrence kept a high school in Natchez in 1829.

Nathaniel Hunt kept another in the same city, at the same time.

Baldwin's seminary, a boarding school for girls, was flourishing in the same city in 1829; M. W. Baldwin was principal, assisted by the Misses Rogers and Dunlap; Mrs. Richard Walsh music teacher.

Mrs Cornell's academy, another boarding school for girls, was also kept in Natchez in 1829, by Mrs. M. F. R. L. Cornell. This lady in 1832 had associated with herself as coprincipal Mr. John H. Black, A. M. There were teachers of modern languages and of music, and a scientific apparatus.

Elvah academy was established in 1829, at Brighton, on Second creek, in Adams county. It was a flourishing and noted school for a number of years. In 1841, a Mr. John S. Mosby was principal. He was much praised. In 1848, a Mr. Cykaski was instructor in French, music, fencing and gymnastics. In June, 1850, the Rev. Joseph Brown, of Memphis, Tenn., was engaged to take charge of the mathematics and the classics, and in November of that year Mr. Mosby added a department of natural sciences.

The Pearl River academy, at Brandon, in Rankin county, was incorporated in 1829. In the year 1834, the male branch was in successful operation, and efforts were making to establish a female branch. A lottery was on foot for that purpose. In 1837 and 1838 the male department was under a Mr. Boynton, who gave great satisfaction. In 1836, 1837, and until July, 1838, the female department was under Miss Cynthia A. Lovell, of Vermont (afterward Mrs. Miller). She then died, greatly regretted, and the school passed into the hands of a second Miss Lovell. In 1846, the male department was under Mr. H. H. Horner.

The Benton academy, at Benton in Yazoo county, was incorporated in 1829. This school is remarkable as being the first to be incorporated north of what is now the Vicksburg and Meridian railroad.

Levin and Bynum's academy, with male and female departments, was opened in Woodville, May 10th 1830, by Lewis C. Levin, afterward a member of congress from Pennsylvania. In April, 1831, he associated Mr. Alfred Bynum, afterward editor of the Woodville *Republican*. Levin retired in August, and the school seems to have suspended for a period. It was revived in 1833, and was conducted through two years, perhaps longer.

The Brandon academy was flourishing in 1830, near Fort Adams in Wilkinson county. It was a noted and useful school. Mr. John J. Michie was principal; followed in July, 1832, by the Rev. Samuel R. Bertron. This was a sixteenth section school, named in honor of

Governor Brandon; a boardingschool. In the years 1834 and 1835, James O. H. VanVacter was principal; in 1836, the Rev. Dr. John Gibson.

The Hampden academy, of Raymond, Hinds county, was incorporated in 1830.

The Union academy, of Jefferson county, was incorporated in 1830.

The Marion academy, of Wilkinson county, was also incorporated in that year.

Oakland college, located in Claiborne county, was established in 1830, mainly through the efforts of the Rev. Dr. Jeremiah Chamberlain. It was under the care of the Mississippi presbytery. Dr. Chamberlain was the first president. It opened May 14th as a mere grammar school, with three pupils; but at the end of the session there were sixty-five, two of whom were sophomores and five freshmen. Mr. John Chamberlain gave instruction in mathematics and English. In 1831 a charter was obtained, as the institution of learning, under the care of the Mississippi presbytery. The first commencement was held in 1833, and Mr. James M. Smiley, afterward vice chancellor of the state, received an A. B., being the first man to take a degree at any institution in this state. The principal object of Oakland college was to educate young men for the ministry. Dr. John Ker, son of the Rev. David Ker, secretly denoted the sum of $25,000 for the endowment of a theological professorship; and in 1837 the Rev. Zebulon Butler was made temporary professor. In a short time the Rev. S. Beach Jones, of New Jersey, was elected to that chair. This professorship was continued only until 1841, but during that time many young men entered, by its aid, not only the Presbyterian ministry, but also that of other denominations. In 1839 the college was transferred to the synod of Mississippi, under which management it remained until the year 1871. At this time the college was very prosperous. It owned two hundred and fifty acres of land; there were three professors' houses, fifteen cottages, a main building of three stories in the course of erection, an apparatus which had cost $1,500, a library of one thousand volumes, two societies' libraries of three thousand volumes more, and an endowment subscription of $100,000. Improvements were made from time to time, until it became one of the handsomest and most equipped institutions of its period in the South. In September, 1851, Dr. Chamberlain was killed. The Rev. R. L. Stanton, D. D., succeeded him. The faculty at this time was composed of five members; one thousand youths had attended the different sessions, and of them one hundred and twenty had graduated. The Rev. James Purviance followed Dr. Stanton as president; and he, in turn, was followed in 1860 by the Rev. William L. Breckinridge, of Kentucky. The Civil war soon terminated his service. After the cessation of hostilities the institution resumed it labors. The Rev. Joseph Calvin, D. D., was made president, but he soon died, and on that event the doors of the college were virtually closed. In 1871, because of the destruction of its resources through the calamities of war, the property of the college was sold to the state, which used it for the establishment of the Alcorn university for colored youths. The funds remaining after the payment of debts were transferred by the synod to the presbytery of Mississippi for the establishment of an institution of learning; and thereupon, in 1877, the presbytery established the Chamberlain-Hunt academy, at Port Gibson. Incorporated in 1877, it was named after Dr. Chamberlain and David Hunt, one of the most generous founders of Oakland college. The first session was that of 1879. The buildings are mainly of brick, and are large and well arranged. The library has about two thousand volumes. The endowment is about $40,000. In the academic department are taught Latin, Greek, French, English, English literature, natural sciences, bookkeeping, history, and mathematics as far as, and including trigonometry and surveying. Prof. W. C. Guthrie, A. B., of Washington and Lee, is principal, and has been from the beginning. There are four other teachers, and an annual attendance of about one hundred and twenty pupils.

Mount Carmel academy was situated at Mount Carmel, in Covington county. Founded by John Ryan, Esq., at a date not exactly known, but prior to 1830, it is remarkable as the first school of the class established in southeast Mississippi. On Mr. Ryan's death, about 1832, there was a suspension of several years; but in 1835 it was revived, and three buildings, designed for the male and female departments and music hall, were erected by subscription. About this time it was conducted by Rev. W. H. Taylor, a graduate of Brown university, recommended by Doctor Wayland. On the 13th of May, 1837, it was incorporated, Samuel Hemphill and eleven others being incorporators and trustees. For two years there were seventy to eighty students. After that, a suspension for a few months caused by want of suitable teachers. In 1840, Mr. Robert C. Cohean, an able teacher and accomplished scholar, was engaged, and he conducted several prosperous sessions. About 1842, the Rev. Azariah R. Graves, a Presbyterian minister, took charge. Mr. Graves did not long maintain this school. Having determined that another locality in the same county offered better advantages, about the year 1845 Mount Carmel was finally abandoned in favor of Zion seminary, also in Covington county. In this connection, Mr. Graves deserves more than a passing notice. His was one of those admirable souls filled with a deep and fruitful sympathy for the poor and the ignorant. He was a missionary in a remote extremity of the presbytery, where schools were almost unknown. The earliest history of him now obtainable is that, in the early winter of 1837-8, he was employed, under strong recommendations from Rev. Dr. Chamberlain, president of Oakland college, and other distinguished gentlemen, a man of unblemished character, a ripe scholar and a skillful teacher, to conduct the Monticello academy. He remained at Monticello only one year, leaving in the autumn of 1838, under the highest commendations both as teacher and minister, for a better field in the neighborhood of Gallatin, in Copiah county. At Zion, seminary buildings were erected; teachers were brought from the North, who in several instances, being ministers, combined the work of an evangelist with that of a teacher; instruction was offered upon such easy terms that all who wished could avail themselves of it; and the expenses of the institution were provided for by donations solicited by Mr. Graves from benevolent patrons in all parts of the presbytery. This process was kept up for a series of years, and the good effects of it were seen in the elevation of a generation of youth, and in the general diffusion through the community of a conviction of the value of mental and religious culture. It had been Mr. Graves' hope that the school he had begun would become ultimately self-sustaining, or so well endowed as to become permanent, but this hope was frustrated by the calamities attending and following the war. The institution was suspended and finally was abandoned, and Mr. Graves himself did not long survive its extinction. From the outset, he had placed Zion seminary under the care and supervision of the presbytery.

Mrs. Dunlap's academy was at work in Woodville, in the year 1831.

The Meridian Springs academy, of Hinds county, was incorporated in 1831.

W. H. Bruner and wife were conducting an academy in Vicksburg, in and before the year 1832, probably the Vicksburg institute, incorporated in 1831. Prior to 1837, they removed to Natchez.

Mrs. Callan's female academy was opened in Vicksburg, March, 1832.

Leigh's classical school, in Vicksburg, was established by Junius E. Leigh, in March, 1832.

The Mount Hope seminary, one and one-half miles east of Woodville, a boarding-school for girls, was opened in January, 1832, by the Misses A. and L. Calder. It was moved into Woodville, nearly opposite Baptist church, in 1836, and was called the Wilkinson Female seminary. A solid and lasting school, it was still at work in 1849.

Marshall's classical school for both sexes was opened in Wilkinson county, in 1832, by the Rev. Mr. M. Marshall, formerly of Spring Ridge academy, Madison county.

Mrs. Stark's boarding school for girls was at work in Woodville in 1832; probably continued into, or through 1835.

The Gallatin male and female academies at Gallatin in Copiah county. The female academy was incorporated in 1833; the male academy in 1836. In 1839, the female academy, taught in the Masonic hall, was prospering under the government of a Mrs. Speer, late from Natchez; the male academy, with a building of its own, under a Mr. Monfort.

The Oak Ridge academy, in Warren county, was opened, for girls exclusively, in 1833.

Mr. and Miss Goddard opened a sixteenth section school of high grade, for both sexes, in Warren county, in 1833.

Bristol and Featherston were conducting a classical school in Vicksburg, in 1833.

The Pearl River academy, of Madison county, was incorporated in 1833. A good school, of a long career. It was at work in 1846, under the charge of J. W. Dana.

The Yazoo academy, of Benton, in Yazoo county, was incorporated in 1833. It had a long and chequered career. In 1842 the female department was under charge of Mrs. A. Goodrich and Miss Healy, Mr. Alfred Goodrich professor of music; the male department was under Mr. John Fulton, late of Kentucky. In the fall Mr. Fulton was succeeded by a Mr. Campbell; and a Mr. Keeparis appears as classical teacher and assistant in physical sciences. When the county seat was removed to Yazoo City, about 1850, the old courthouse was donated for school uses. In 1864 the schoolhouse and boardinghouse were destroyed by the Federal army; rebuilt since, by private enterprise, but on a reduced scale. Merged in the Benton high school, chartered in 1883 through efforts of Prof. J. G. Wooten, then principal. Present principal, C. D. Thompson; annual attendance about ninety; and confers degrees.

The Judson institute was remarkable for two reasons: it was the first appearance of the Baptists in the educational work, and of the manual labor plan. The movement was inaugurated by the Baptists of Hinds county, and perhaps of other counties, in March, 1835. In May, 1837, upward of $135,000 had been subscribed, and between $6,000 and $7,000 had been collected. A tract of land containing more than six hundred acres had been purchased a farm was going on, and the institution was ready for the reception of students. Provision was made for the education of pious young men for the ministry. The institute had been incorporated in the year previous, and the location was at Spring Ridge, near Palestine church, five miles south of Raymond, in Hinds county. It was not a convention school, but belonged to an independent society styled the Mississippi Baptist Education society. S. S. Lattimore was its first financial agent, and L. B. Holloway the first teacher and president. In November, 1838, Mr. Holloway had been succeeded by Rev. W. H. Taylor, a graduate of Brown university, who had taught successfully at Mt. Carmel. The farm, it seems, had been purchased in part on credit. 1839 efforts were making to sell residence lots to persons desirous of living at the institute to educate their children; the proceeds to be devoted to paying for the farm, and in part to the erection of suitable buildings. In 1839, the location in Hinds county was abandoned, and the institution moved to Middleton, in Carroll county, Mr. Taylor continuing a classical school at the old site, under the name of Taylor's institute. The move to Middleton did not produce the good results hoped for. There seems to have been an indifference to the institution which was fatal. The great financial disasters of 1837-40 apparently prevented the collection of any great part of the subscriptions which had been made. An attempt of the convention of 1842 to adopt the institution was defective, for want of an amendment of the charter. The Judson does not seem to have ever rallied, but fell into other hands and was lost to the denomination, and, indeed, lost to everybody.

The Grand Gulf academy was opened in April, 1835, under the charge of Calvin Miller, a former student of the Miami university and the United States Military academy. In 1837 Mr. Miller moved to Clinton, to practice law; and the academy passed into other hands.

The Tuscahoma academy was opened at Tuscahoma, in Tallahatchie county, in 1835. The Rev. Francis Rutherford and wife were placed in charge. A spacious two-story brick building was erected, and a high grade of study was established. Incorporated in 1838.

The Holly Springs Female institute was organized in 1836—the same year in which the Chickasaw cession was organized into counties. Trustees were appointed at a meeting of the citizens held for the purpose, and a Miss Mosely was employed to teach the first session. In 1837, a Mr. Baker and his wife were principals. In the same year Holly Springs was incorporated. The sum of $10,500 was appropriated by the corporate authorities for the development of the academy. In 1838, Mr. Thomas Johnson was made principal; a more desirable lot was purchased, containing four acres; the cornerstone of a handsome brick structure, two stories high, and 60x64 feet, was laid, and pianos were purchased. There were about eighty pupils. The music department was under the care of Mr. and Mrs. Kenno, and was well conducted. There was a collegiate department, with a high curriculum. In May, 1839, Mr. Johnson was succeeded by the Rev. C. Parish, late a professor in the Holly Springs university. He was assisted by Miss Ruth Beach, Rufus Beach, Esq., and his daughter Eliza were the music teachers, and Mrs E. Langley in the ornamental branches. In this year the institute was incorporated. In January, 1842, Mr. Parish resigned. He was followed by the Rev. C. A. Foster, an Episcopalian clergyman, under a lease for five and a half years. He was assisted by the Rev. A. P. Merrill and wife, and Miss Martha W. Frazer; J. F. Goneke and daughter music teachers. A fine cabinet of minerals, a good philosophical apparatus, and a library, were provided, and part of the grounds was laid off as a botanical garden. The attendance of pupils for 1842 was about one hundred, for 1843 about one hundred and twenty, for 1844 about one hundred and fifty. In 1843 Prof. Goneke and daughter were succeeded by a Mr. Morse, late of Jackson, and a Miss Covington. The school made quite an enviable reputation. The examinations were held in public, and the pupils were questioned on the higher branches, such as geometry, geology and mental philosophy, and were required to converse in public in the French tongue. In 1845 Professor Foster resigned and was succeeded by the Rev. James Weatherby, late of the Oxford Female academy. The Rev. G. W. Sill became president in the fall of 1848, and under him the institute came to its best career. The buildings were all completed, and the halls were crowded with bright girls from all the country round about. In 1856 the Rev. N. Chevalier became president, and he was succeeded in 1858 by J. H. Hackleton. This gentleman remained in charge until the Civil war swept the institution out of existence. It was burned by an incendiary.

The University of Holly Springs gives the first appearance in the state of a title so pretentious. It was first agitated in the summer of 1836 (being the same year in which the Chickasaw cession was organized into counties) by the Rev. Robert Hardin, a Presbyterian minister who had come down from Maury county, Tenn., on a prospecting expedition. There was a town meeting, there were addresses, committees were appointed, and a board of trustees organized; but there the matter stopped for a while, on Dr. Hardin's final determination to remain in Maury county. However, a classical school was established and placed under the care of Mr. F. A. Brown. The question of the university was revived in June,

1837, by Dr. W. P. King. The trustees were increased; a subscription, aggregating $22,650, was raised. A two-story brick building was erected in 1837, and the academical department of the school opened with considerable advertisement, under the charge of Rev. C. Parish and Mr. Brown. The collegiate department was opened in 1838; Rev. Joseph Travis, president pro tem.; Rev. C. Parish, professor of ancient languages; J. B. Clausel, professor of mathematics and natural philosophy; Charles R. Lemanski, professor of modern languages; William H. Blake, principal of preparatory department. In 1839 the university was incorporated. Being pressed for money and patronage, it was shortly afterward transferred to the Methodist church, the faculty remaining unchanged. This experiment proved also a failure; and the church soon gave it up. The Holly Springs *Gazette* of November 4, 1842, says of it: "With the buildings sufficient for a college, it seems to have been neglected, if not wholly abandoned." In 1843, an effort was made to reanimate the university. The services of Elisha Bass, Jr., and Frederic Sanborn were secured. Still no success followed. It is a significant fact that editorials in the *Gazette*, of date December 1, 1843, and December 13, 1844, on the schools of Holly Springs, make not the least mention of the university.

Richland academy, located at Shongalo, a village now deserted, but formerly in Carroll county, about one mile west of Vaiden, was incorporated in 1836. A two-story building, 26x46 feet, with three apartments, sufficiently large for the accommodation of one hundred pupils, was erected in 1837–8. The first session began April 22, 1839, under Mr. and Mrs. Emmons (formerly of the Raymond Female academy); with Mr. A. P. Hill, A. B., from the South Carolina college, as assistant in the male department, with fifty pupils.

The Carrollton academy was also incorporated in 1836. In January, 1840, the male department was placed in the hands of Mr. James M. McLean, who gave general satisfaction, and was still in charge in July, 1841.

The Paulding academy, at Paulding, in Jasper county, was incorporated in 1836. It took rank quickly as a first-rate school. In 1845 and 1846 it was under John E. Seaman, as principal.

The Madisonville academy, and the Canton Female academy, both in Madison county, were incorporated in 1836.

The Monticello academy, located at Monticello, once capital of the state, and in Lawrence county, was founded by A. M. Keegan and others by voluntary donations. Incorporated February 4, 1836, Arthur Fox, president of the trustees. Distinct male and female department; in 1838 Rev. A. R. Graves was in charge of the former, Miss Sophia Royce, of the latter; in 1839, Prof. J. M. Ellis was in charge; in 1840, Francis P. Montfort, late from Gallatin, was preceptor of the former; Mrs. S. J. Sawkins, preceptress of the latter. Property, a handsome two-story building, lot ninety-nine feet square; valued at $4,000.

The Oakland Female seminary, located at Oakland, in Claiborne county, near Oakland college, was opened in January, 1836, by J. Black.

The Port Gibson seminary was established in Port Gibson in the fall of 1836, by Mann Butler, a gentleman who brought to his work an experience of several years, acquired in some of the best institutions of Kentucky. Still open in the winter of 1840–1.

The Raymond academy probably was the successor of the Hampden academy of 1830. Perhaps no school in Mississippi more thoroughly exemplified the evil of an unceasing change of teachers. It was bad everywhere, but here was at its very worst. The female department was capable af accommodating one hundred pupils, and in 1836 was under Mr. and Mrs. Emmons; in 1838, under Miss L. Parker; in 1839, under the Rev. Bradford Frazee, some time president of Elizabeth academy; in 1840, under Mrs. Jane Clark, from

Edward Mayes.

Carlisle, Penn., and later Columbia, Tenn. Exactly when Mrs. Clark left is not now known, but in 1845-6 the principal was E. Ames. After this, the school seems to have failed, as there were in 1847 a number of private schools, and no mention made of the academy. The male department was, if possible, even worse. In 1836 it was under Mr. C. Ramsay; in 1837, under James C. Campbell, A. M., of New York; in 1838, under Mr. Heywood Foote; in 1839, under Mr. F. D. Cowles; in 1840, under W. Richard Ellis, A. B., and Jean Joseph Giers, associates, of Kentucky; in 1841, under Albert W. Ely, A. B., in January, and S. E. Goddard, in June. There is no further history, except a notice in the Raymond *Times* of October 10, 1845, that the building was tumbled to pieces, discreditable to our town and neighborhood.

The Woodville Female academy was opened in August, 1836, at the house formerly occupied by Mrs. Stark (see date 1832) by a Miss Chapman, late from Tuscaloosa, Ala. In June, 1838, Miss Chapman was succeeded by Mr. and Mrs. Halsey, who retained control of it until 1846, when Miss Clarissa M. Chapman (afterward Mrs. Dunbar) succeeded them and conducted the academy successfully for a number of years.

The Natchez Female academy, kept by Rev. W. H. Bruner and wife, who had formerly taught in Vicksburg (see date of 1832), was probably open before 1837. At all events, it was at work in November, 1837, and continued until the summer of 1839.

The Liberty academy, located at Liberty, in Amite county, was probably a continuation of the old Amite academy. In April, 1837, it was under the management of Mr. George W. Rudd. He was followed in February, 1839, by Mr. John R. Caulfield. At this time the old charter was revived by the legislature. In November, 1841, Mr. J. R. Knox, a graduate of Miami university, was principal, and he was followed in February, 1844, by J. H. Black, A. M.

The Mississippi Female college, located at Columbus, was the first exclusively female school to assume the name of college. Exactly when the institution was established is doubtful, but it is certain that it was at work in 1837. The Rev. Abram Maer was president; a man described as of extensive literary research, of long tried worth and established reputation, and possessing that rare faculty of governing with ease and communicating knowledge with facility, which constitute at once the ornament and usefulness of an instructor. The building was tasteful and elegant in its structure, and commodious in the number and arrangement of its apartments, situated on the most elevated point in the town. Thomas G. Blewett was president of the trustees. The curriculum embraced, besides the common branches, belle lettres, French, Latin, geometry, algebra, natural philosophy, chemistry, botany, mental philosophy, evidences of Christianity, music, drawing and painting. The college was incorporated in 1840. In 1838 there were about ninety pupils. In July, 1844, Mr. Maer had left, and the college was probably suspended.

The Louisville academy, located at Louisville, in Winston county, was incorporated May 9, 1837; founded by contributions, aggregating $5,152. The building was a two-story frame structure. James Martin was president of the trustees. The first teachers were: John W. Morrison, in the male department, and James Martin, in the female department. In 1842 the male department was under George G. Snedicor, who was followed in July, 1843, by the Rev. J. I. Jones and Mr. D. W. Seiders. In 1843 the female department was under Mr. and Mrs. Godden.

The college and academy at Sharon, in Madison county, at first a university school of the Methodist, Baptist, Old School and Cumberland Presbyterian churches, was incorporated in 1837. The town was created for and by the school. The female academy was opened in April, and was in the hands of Misses J. H. and H. W. Copes, of Maryland. Early in 1838 the preparatory department of the male school was opened, with about forty pupils; and in the October following the college proper got under way. Five professors were elected to the faculty, four of them clergymen; one from each of the patronizing denominations. The idea was to distribute the chairs after that plan, so as to prevent the exclusive sectarian influence. The Rev. Alexander Campbell was president of both schools. In the college Rev. Richard Beard, William L. Williford and John F. Little were of the faculty. In the academy Rev. H. W. Smith was principal, assisted by his wife and Miss Stratton; Mr. C. Brachus, music teacher. There were two distinct lots, with buildings, for the two schools, and a subscription of about $20,000 for endowment. The pupils in the college, including preparatory, for 1839, were one hundred. In 1841 President Campbell resigned, accepting the presidency of Mississippi college, and the schools seem to have been placed under Professor Beard. In the early part of 1843 the female academy was transferred to the Mississippi conference of the Methodist Episcopal church. It was reorganized under the name of the Sharon female college. The male school seems to have become extinct, probably because of the vicinity of Mississippi college, then fostered by the Presbyterians, and of Centenary college, then fostered by the Methodists. Rev. E. S. Robinson was made president of the female college, assisted by his wife, Mr. C. W. F. Muller and others. There were over eighty students that year. In 1845 President Robinson was succeeded by the Rev. Pleasant J. Eckles. Under him the reputation of the college greatly increased. He was followed, in 1854, by the Rev. J. W. Shelton. He was soon succeeded by the Rev. Mr. Guard, who had charge until 1861, when the Rev. William L. C. Hunnicutt, now president of Centenary college, became president. Dr. Hunnicutt soon enlisted as a chaplain in the Confederate army, and was followed by the Rev. Samuel D. Aikin. In 1867 Dr. Aikin removed to Texas, and Dr. Hunnicutt again became president. He was followed, in 1869, by the Rev. Josiah M. Pugh, formerly of Madison college, who retired in the following year, when Dr. Hunnicutt still again took charge; and again, in the next year, 1871, Dr. Pugh succeeded Dr. Hunnicutt. In July, 1872, Dr. Pugh accepted the presidency of Marvin college, in Texas, and was followed by the Rev. Mr. Moss, from Alabama, but the college had run its course. The class of 1872 was the last to graduate, and the doors were soon closed. This failure was the result of several causes, mainly the shifting of population, the impoverishment of the surrounding country, and an unfortunate fire in 1868, which destroyed the main building.

The Cayuga academy, at Cayuga, in Hinds county, was opened in February, 1837. A new, spacious and comfortable building was provided. Mr. R. A. Carloss and wife were principals.

The Lane academy, named for the Rev. John Lane, a Methodist minister of prominence who was devoted to educational interests, and located at Vicksburg, was incorporated in May, 1837. A. B. Reading, Esq., gave a building lot, valued at $10,000, for the site. Revenue was drawn from the sixteenth section funds. In 1838, the academy was at work, under the Rev. A. W. Chapman, a Methodist minister, with two assistants. In December, 1839, Mr. Chapman retired, to devote himself to the female academy recently established, and this school passed under the control of Mr. Richard Griffith, of Ohio, a graduate of the Ohio university, and of Mr. Robert D. Howe. In October, 1844, Mr. Griffith had retired, and Mr. Howe was assisted by Mr. J. G. Parham, Jr.

The Greensboro academy, at Greensboro, in Choctaw county, was incorporated May 11, 1837; Erasmus L. Acee, and forty others being incorporators and trustees. There was a fine building. In 1842 Mr. and Mrs. Melton were in charge; but differences among us had " about ruined our schools."

The Pinckney academy, at Pinckney, Newton county, was incorporated May 13, 1837; Michael Thomas and six other being incorporators and trustees.

The Marion academy, in Lauderdale county, was incorporated in 1837.

The Hernando academy, at Hernando, in De Soto county, was incorporated May 11, 1837, being the first incorporated in the Chickasaw cession. Rev. McMahon (sic) and eight others were incorporators and trustees. The first principal of the female department of whom any trace is now discoverable was Mrs. Dockery, in 1839. She was followed in December by Mrs. Caroline C. Jones. In 1845, Mrs. M. W. Simmons was in charge, and the Rev. A. P. Henderson, a graduate of Glasgow college, opened a male school in the male academy. In 1847 a better building, containing three rooms, was erected. In 1850, by authority of the legislature, the academy was transferred to the Methodist Church South; new buildings were erected. Col. Warner M. Yates, an eminent teacher, was called to preside over it, which he did with great success for several years. He was succeeded by Mrs. M. A. Moseley, who for several years prior to 1861 maintained a school highly approved and numerously attended. Meanwhile debts accumulated, and the trustees were finally forced to sell the property, which passed into private hands, but is still used for school purposes.

The Preston academy was established in Yalobusha county as early as 1837. In that year and in 1838 it was under Thomas J. Jenkins, as rector. The village itself was planted exclusively for the encouragement of education, like Sharon. In 1842, and before, Mr. R. G. Wilder, was rector, and the trustees boasted of the character of Preston as one of the oldest and most respectable seats of learning in north Mississippi. Mr. A. W. Kilpatrick took charge in April, 1843.

The Colbert Male and Female academy, of Lowndes county, was incorporated February 15, 1838; Timothy L. Rogers and six others being incorporators and trustees. It was opened January, 1838, under the Rev. Jacob Lindly, assisted by Mrs. Maria M. Gay, both originally from Pennsylvania. In June, Mr. Lindly, who took charge only to start the school, withdrew in favor of Mrs. Gay, with Miss Lindly as assistant. An accomplished music teacher was engaged. In July, 1841, Miss Charlotte Paine, from the Oxford Female academy, took charge; but her health failed, and, in January, 1842, she was followed by the Rev. W. W. Burch and wife.

The Aberdeen Female academy, located at Aberdeen, in Monroe county, was opened February 1, 1838, under the charge of James A. McLean and wife, assisted by Miss Norris; musical department under Mrs. Brown. It was incorporated in 1845.

The Liberty Female seminary, at Liberty, in Amite county, was opened in the spring of 1838, by the Misses Ring, who proposed to teach the whole system of female education generally adopted in female schools. They were followed, in 1843, by Misses S. T. and S. A. Russell.

The Vicksburg Female seminary, under Rev. Samuel W. Speer, with four assistants, in 1838 justly ranked among the best institutions in the state. It became extinct in 1840, or about that time.

The Union Female academy is the earliest of the Attala county schools traceable. It was twelve miles above Kosciusko, and in 1838 was under the charge of Mrs. M. P. Caffrey.

The Oxford Female academy, located at Oxford, Lafayette county, was incorporated in 1838. The first principal was Miss Charlotte Paine, whose first session closed in December, 1839, with a roster of thirty-four scholars. She was succeeded by the Rev. James A. Weatherby, with three assistants. In 1842 there were eighty-four pupils, drawn from three states. The building was a two-story brick structure. In 1844 S. Leak Slack, of Philadelphia, took charge. He was assisted by his wife, Miss Ann C. Smith and Miss E. D. Ware. After a short time he was followed by a Mr. Collins, from Vermont. In 1854 the school was transferred to the Cumberland Presbyterian church and reincorporated under the name of the Union Female college. Under this name and management the school is still a working institution of high order. Its presidents have been successively: Rev. Dr. Stanford G. Burney, afterward professor of English in the university, and now principal of the department of theology at Cumberland university; Rev. Dr. C. H. Bell, now of St. Louis, Mo.; Prof. Robert J. Guthrie; Rev. J. S. Howard; Prof. W. I. Davis; and Prof. H. N. Robertson, the present incumbent. This college, although the Fayette academy was established many years before it, still enjoys the distinction of being the oldest female school in the state of unbroken history (leaving out of view the interruption of the war). Its first class under the charter of 1854, graduated in 1856. It has graduated two hundred and thirty-one. The average attendance is about one hundred and fifty. Young boys are admitted as day scholars. The premises are ten acres in extent, and the main building is a large and commodious three-story brick. The old structure is still in use as a music hall.

Franklin Female academy, located at Franklin, Holmes county, was opened in the summer of 1838, under Mrs. Rose and Miss Merriwether. In July, 1842, it was taken in charge by Col. G. D. Mitchell, from Grenada academy.

The Emery academy, located at Emery, Holmes county, was established in January, 1839, under the auspices of the Mississippi conference of the Methodist church, Rev. Bradford Frazee and wife were the principals; incorporated that same year; Hon. David O. Shattuck and thirteen others being incorporators and trustees.

The Richland Male and Female academy, located at Richland, Holmes county, was opened before 1839; but in January of that year, its capacity was enlarged, by the addition of a new building, to one hundred and thirty pupils. It was under Mr. Hollis Holman and his sister, Mary B. Holman. In 1842 Rev. D. L. Russell, assisted by his wife, took charge; Mr. P. Kenna and wife having the musical department. This institution seems, in 1848, to have been superseded by the Eureka Masonic college, incorporated that year, and located at the same place. Lemuel Doty was president of the trustees; Rev. D. L. Russell was president and professor of moral and mental science; Mr. Z. Mott Lawrence, professor of languages; Mr. W. L. Wright, professor of natural sciences, and principal of the primary department.

The Winston Female seminary, in Winston county, was opened in January, 1839, under Mr. Eugene Ferris and Susan B. Micou. No day scholars admitted.

The Vicksburg Female academy was established at a meeting of citizens on July 24, 1839. Rev. John Lane and eighteen others were elected trustees. Rev. A. W. Chapman, who had been acting as agent on subscription and building, was continued. The academy was opened on the fourth Monday of October, 1839, Mr. and Mrs. Chapman principals. The buildings were large and convenient, with accommodation for fifty boarders; incorporated in 1840. It derived some revenue from the sixteenth section. The Misses Grandier were assistants. In September, 1840, Miss A. M. Foster was engaged in addition. In 1841 there was a library of six hundred volumes. Striby was professor of music. In 1844 Miss Sarah Boyer was assistant in the literary department; P. Schmidt, music; Mons. Vallett, French, etc. In 1846 Professor Nash was in charge of the music.

The Woodville Male academy was established in January, 1839, by Mr. Halsey, then principal, also, of the Woodville Female academy. He was assisted by Rev. Mr. Mudge, formerly a member of Wesleyan university, and who, in 1837, had opened a classical and scientific school, which was merged in this. Mr. Mudge left in 1841, and was followed by

Mr. Ulysses Chapman, a graduate of Wesleyan university. In 1845, Mr. Halsey, having relinquished the female academy, took personal charge, but in 1846 he was succeeded by a Mr. Soule, and he, in turn, and in the same year, by John S. McLean. In June, 1847, Mr. McLean was followed by Mr. George H. Wiley, who, however, soon moved to Jackson, La., and accepted a position in Centenary college.

The Woodville Classical school was incorporated February 14, 1839. It was promptly opened in the basement of the Presbyterian church, S. A. Phelps, A. B., principal. In September, at the beginning of the third term, Mr. M. B. Green, A. M., was engaged as a coprincipal, and the school divided into two departments. How long this school continued to exist is not now known. It was at work in the session of 1842–3.

The Wahalak Female academy, in Kemper county; the Farmington academy, in Tishomingo county; the Plymouth academy, in Lowndes county; the Wyatt Male and Female academy, in Lafayette county, and the Chulahoma academy, in Marshall county, were also incorporated in 1839.

The Sylvestria academy, male, was opened at Sylvestria, in Marshall county, in 1839, by Z. D. Cottrell, late principal of the Oxford Female academy. It was converted into a female academy about 1841.

The Centenary college originated at a convention of the members of the Mississippi conference of the Methodist Episcopal church held at Jackson on the 7th of August, 1839. It was there determined to commemorate the centennial year of Methodism by raising a charitable fund, of which seven-tenths should be devoted to the establishment of a college to be located as near the center of the conference as practicable. The Rev. C. K. Marshall was appointed canvassing agent by the December conference, and a committee on location was appointed. In a few months subscriptions, in the shape of the purchase of scholarships, to the amount of $76,000 had been raised, in addition to some donations of lands. Much of this subscription was, however, never paid. In 1841 the college was located at Brandon Springs, in Rankin county. An extensive and valuable property, originally designed for a watering place, was purchased at $30,000, on favorable terms as to payments, and was considered a great bargain. The first session opened in 1841. Dr. Thomas C. Thornton was president and professor of moral science and sacred literature; Dr. James B. C. Thornton, M. D., was professor of natural sciences; N. W. Magruder was professor of ancient languages, and James B. Dodd was professor of mathematics. There was a preparatory department, of which the Rev. E. S. Robertson, A. M., was principal, and Mr. Robert D. Howe, assistant. The college opened well, the attendance of pupils being sixty in the first month. In 1842 a school of medicine was established, and placed under the charge of Dr. James Thornton, and a law school projected. In the fall of that year the college opened with one hundred and seventy-five students in attendance. In 1843 a charter was granted to the college. In 1844 a great deal of discontent arose in regard to the management of the college, both as to tuition and finances. This spirit became so intense as to cause the resignation of Dr. Thornton. The Rev. David O. Shattuck, of Carroll county, was then elected president pro tem., and the institution was reorganized so far as to establish an exclusively English and classical school, and to place the preparatory classes under the direct charge of the respective professors. This allayed the discontent, and the session of 1844–5 opened well; but the trustees still determined that the location at Brandon Springs was a mistake. The surrounding country was poor and the population was sparse. The result of it all was that in 1845 the institution was moved to Jackson, La., where it now is.

The Rocky Spring academy, located at Rocky Spring, in Claiborne county, was opened on the 1st of January, 1839, under the direction of Mr. Holmes, a graduate of Miami university.

The Summerville academy, a female school of high grade, was established at Summerville, in Noxubee county, in 1839; Mrs. Vaughn, principal.

The Middleton Female academy seems to have been an appendage of the Judson institute after its removal to Middleton. In 1840 Dr. E. J. White was principal, assisted by his wife and a Miss Bustead. In 1843 Mr. B. Holt, of Vicksburg, became its president. There was a chemical and philosophical apparatus, and in 1846 Colonel Holt added a superior astronomical apparatus. Shortly after this, however, the school became extinct.

The People's academy was also located at Middleton. In fact, this now almost forgotten village, about two miles west of the present Winona, was, at this time, quite an educational center. It was a prominent candidate for the location of the university. This was the Presbyterian school. In 1841 it was under the charge of the Rev. Elijah Graves, assisted by his wife and daughter. In 1842, the female department was under a Mrs. Thompson; Mrs. Graves, music teacher. In 1843 Mr. Reuben Nason leased this academy, and seems to have converted it into a male school exclusively. He was still in charge in 1845-6. A sectarian controversy, it is said, destroyed the usefulness of both these schools.

The Almucha academy, in (probably) Lauderdale county; the Thickwoods academy, of Amite county; the Rienzi academy, of Tishomingo county, and the Constantine Male and Female academy, of Noxubee county, were incorporated in 1840.

The Grenada Male and Female academy, located at Grenada, in Yalobusha county (now in Grenada county), was incorporated February 15, 1839. It was preceded by certain classical schools, still traceable; by a Mrs. S. M. Orrel, in 1835; succeeded by Prof. G. D. Mitchell, from Tennessee, in 1836. Rev. Joseph E. Douglass, of the Methodist church, taught in 1837; followed, in 1839, by R. J. Mendum, from La Grange college, Ala. In 1838 a Mr. William Duncan had opened a female seminary of some pretensions. The academy seems not to have been organized until 1841; then with distinct establishments for the different sexes — even distinct boards of trustees. The earlier schools were displaced by it. Professor Mitchell, assisted by Mr. Edward Hughes, Jr., took charge of the male branch. Professor Mitchell retired in 1842, leaving Mr. Hughes in charge. In 1844 Mr. G. B. Clark became principal; followed, in the same year, by Mr. John P. Povall; and in 1845 by Mr. A. L. Lewis, a graduate of the University of Georgia, under whom the school was removed to the building theretofore occupied by the female department. Mr. Lewis was followed, after one year, by Mr. John M. Sample, a graduate of the North Carolina university; and after him, the institution seems to have become extinct. The female department, in 1841, was put under the charge of Mr. Edward Hughes, Sr., and his wife, and the property formerly occupied by the Douglass school purchased for it. In 1842 Mrs. H. B. J. Eager, wife of the Baptist minister, took charge, but shortly afterward gave it up, when the academy was displaced apparently by a school conducted by the Rev. Joseph A. Ranney, assisted by Miss Catherine Sawyer, a lady of a high order of qualifications. In December, 1845, there was an effort to shake the trustees of the academy out of their Rip Van Winkle nap, and a Miss Harriet Washburn (afterward Mrs. Stratton) was employed to conduct it. The advertisement was prefaced by the editorial query, "Who knows when it will rain again?" and that was the last appearance.

The Coffeeville Male and Female academy, at Coffeeville, in Yalobusha county, was incorporated in 1839; placed under Mr. Hughes, Sr., and his wife. They were followed in 1841 by Miss E. Lyman (afterward Mrs. Smith) in the female school. There is only the most meager general information about these schools. They seem to have been well kept. The building was destroyed by fire about 1850.

The Macon academy, located at Macon, in Noxubee county, was incorporated in 1839. Mr. and Mrs. Melvin were the first teachers; afterward Mr. James Wallace and wife were placed in charge. There were eighty-five students at the first term. The building was a two-story framed structure. By the same statute were also incorporated the Mt. Pleasant academy, which had been at work since March, 1838, under Rev. Mr. Archibald, and the Shuqualak academy, in the same county.

The De Kalb academy, located at De Kalb, in Kemper county, was incorporated in 1839. There was a good two-story school building.

The North Mississippi college, located at College Hill, Lafayette county, was incorporated in 1840. A quarter section of land was donated for a site, and buildings regarded as of temporary character erected. Opened for reception of students in January, 1840. Rev. S. Hurd was president, Rev. D. L. Russell, vice president, and J. B. Clausel, professor of mathematics; P. A. Yancey, tutor. Full collegiate courses were offered in Latin, Greek, mathematics, chemistry, astronomy, engineering, mental and moral philosophy, etc. A bureau of correspondence was projected for the introduction into the state of desirable teachers for other institutions. This school continued to flourish for several years. It made some reputation and drew students from adjoining counties. The University of Mississippi was opened in 1848, only six miles away, and overshadowed it, however; the Civil war destroyed it. Its property is still used as the site of a public school. At one time it was under the charge of Professor Jeffreys, a man of considerable scholarship.

Rose Hill seminary was opened in Natchez in 1841, by Miss E. Marcilly. French was the language of the family, and the students were required to use it both in their recitations and in their recreations. The school seems to have been a favorite with the Natchez people. The course of instruction, besides the lower studies, embraced algebra, astronomy, natural philosophy, chemistry, history, chronology, mythology, logic, ethics, French, Italian, Spanish, music, dancing, drawing, plain and ornamental needlework. The school was still flourishing in the year 1851.

The Natchez institute (Brown's), a seminary for young ladies, was established near Natchez, in 1841, by Thomas Brown, Jr., formerly president of Fayette academy. General Quitman, ex-Governor Brandon, Hon. Edward Turner and other distinguished Mississippians were referred to as its patrons. After a period it was suspended by the removal of Mr. Brown from Natchez, but in March, 1847, he returned for the purpose of reopening the institute. The Natchez *Free Trader*, noticing this fact, says that his former teaching was successful.

Ford's seminary for girls was opened in Natchez in November, 1841. The usual higher English branches were taught, also the Latin, French and Italian languages, music, drawing, painting and perspective.

Montrose academy, at Montrose, in Jasper county, was founded in 1841, by Rev. John N. Waddel, its proprietor. James Denison and Henry Sturgis were assistants. Property, eighty acres of wild land and a $1,000 building. No apparatus; a small library. From such meager outfit Mr. Waddel built up a school whose reputation survives to this day. No degrees were conferred. Students were thoroughly prepared for the junior class in college. They came from the adjoining counties, and the annual examinations drew visitors from so far as Jackson. The largest patronage was about seventy-five per annum. Mr. Waddel was elected professor of ancient and modern languages at the university in 1848, and the academy was then abandoned.

The Carrollville Literary institution, of Tishomingo county, was established in January, 1841, with Rev. M. B. Feemster the first principal.

The Jackson Female seminary was opened in January, 1841, by Miss Silphina M. Roscoe, from Nashville, Tenn. It was developed into quite a considerable school. In 1842 the services of Prof. A. S. Villeplait (a native of Paris, and late professor of modern languages at the university at Nashville) and his wife were secured. In 1845 this academy was suspended, and Miss Roscoe took charge of the Woodville Female academy.

The Oakland Male and Female academy, of Yalobusha county, was incorporated in 1841, but did not commence work until January, 1843. At this time the Rev. Marcus C. Henderson was principal of the female department, and James Moore president of the trustees. This institution, with varying fortunes has continued up to this day.

The Wahalak Male academy, of Kemper county; the Commerce academy, of Tunica county, and the Williamsburg Male and Female academy, of Covington county, were also incorporated in 1841.

The Whitesville academy, of Wilkinson county, was established in 1841. It was a sixteenth section school, of high grade, fund about $3,200 at ten per cent interest. D. L. Phares was first president of the trustees. It was ably managed for about ten years by Messrs. Morell, W. McPhaul and others, only one teacher being employed at a time. In 1847 there were forty-two pupils. The free pupils were taught an average of thirty-three weeks each; the pay pupils much more. Became extinct about 1850.

The Newton Female institute, also at Whitesville, and also drawing aid from the sixteenth section fund (township one, range one west), was organized at his own expense, in 1842, by Dr. D. L. Phares. Supplied with a fine apparatus, a library of over two thousand volumes and all other appliances. There was a full collegiate curriculum. A celebrated school of great merit and influence. Dr. Phares, at various times, was assisted by his wife, Miss Irene Merrill, Misses M. E. and Sarah Swan, Mrs. Lavinia D. Wright (of New York city), Miss Laura Stebbins, Dr. and Mrs. Slosson, Miss Mary J. Putnam (a relative of old Israel's) the Misses and Hattie Dailey, Miss Fay, Miss Rachel Harris, Miss M. L. Phares, Prof. Alexander Ellett (a man of gigantic mind, versed in many sciences, and several modern languages), L. Berg and C. Brackenhoff. The number of pupils in attendance rose to about seventy-five per annum. Quite a large number of the pupils became teachers. After the war, the property having been much depredated upon, and the health of Mrs. Phares failing, the institute ceased to be in 1865.

The University of Mississippi owes its origin to the acts of congress of March 3, 1815, and February 20, 1819, by which thirty-six sections of public land were conveyed to the state in trust for the support of a seminary of learning. The lands were located in 1823; for a few years the policy was adopted of renting them on short leases; but this was abandoned in 1833, and the lands sold at public auction, bringing in notes running one, two and three years with ten per cent. interest, the sum of $277,332.52. Of this, the sum of $129,300, including interest, was invested in stock of the Planters' bank, and thereby lost when that institution broke, about 1840. About $90,000 was collected and used by the state—about its ordinary expenses. The remainder was never collected. No steps were taken to establish the seminary until 1840, when a committee was appointed to visit seven designated towns and make report to the next legislature as to the best site. In January, 1841, on the reception of the report, the location was made at Oxford by a majority of one vote over Mississippi City. The citizens of Lafayette county had already donated conditionally a beautiful section of land adjacent to the town for the site. Still the university was not incorporated until the

24th of February, 1844. The first meeting of trustees was on the 15th of January, 1845, but nothing substantial could be accomplished for want of funds. In January, 1846, however, the legislature appropriated $50,000, and with that money the buildings were immediately undertaken. This work progressed during 1846, 1847, and a part of 1848. In January, 1848, an income was provided by the act of the 25th of February which made an appropriation slightly variable, but which amounted to about $11,000 per annum. In July the first faculty was organized. George Frederick Holmes, an Englishman by birth, and then a professor at William and Mary college, Virginia, was made president, and assigned to give instruction in mental and moral philosophy, logic, belles lettres, political economy, and international law. Albert Taylor Bledsoe, a native of Kentucky and a graduate of West Point, was elected a professor of mathematics and astronomy; John Millington, M. D., an Englishman and a professor in William and Mary college, was elected to the chair of natural philosophy and chemistry, and John N. Waddel, D. D., was elected professor of ancient and modern languages. On the 6th of November the first session began. Thomas E. Bugg, of Chickasaw county, was the first student enrolled. The total attendance was eighty. At the close of the first term President Holmes returned to Virginia, and Professor Bledsoe acted *ad interim*. In July, 1849, Rev. Augustus B. Longstreet, D. D., was chosen president, and the foundation of the library was laid by a donation of books from the Hon. Jacob Thompson. In March, 1850, the legislature directed an agricultural and geological survey of the state to be made under the direction of the university, and to that end established the chair of agricultural and geological sciences, with an assistant, and added $3,000 per annum to the college revenues. This work was prosecuted until the year 1874, when it was completed. The first graduating class was that of 1851, with fifteen members, and in this year a chair of modern languages was established. In 1854 the law school was established, and William F. Stearns, Esq., of Holly Springs, was elected professor, continuing in office until the war. The first class embraced seven members. In 1856 the legislature appropriated the sum of $100,000 to the aid of the university, payable in five annual installments. An additional dormitory, a new steward's hall, the observatory, and the magnetic laboratory were then erected, and large additions were made to the apparatus and collections, including the Markoe collection of minerals and the Budd cabinet of shells. The faculty was increased by the election of four tutors. In July President Longstreet resigned and was succeeded by Prof. Frederick A. P. Barnard, LL.D., who had in 1854 followed Bledsoe as professor of mathematics and astronomy.

In 1858, chairs of English and mathematics were established. In 1859 the title of president was changed for that of chancellor. In 1860 the law school had so enlarged that a second professorship was established and Hon. James F. Trotter elected. When the Civil war broke out many of the students formed a military company called the University grays, and joined the Confederate army as a company in the Eleventh Mississippi regiment. The exercises of the institution were suspended. In July 1865 measures were taken to reopen. Dr. Waddel was elected chancellor; Dr. John J. Wheat, professor of Greek; Dr. Alexandre J. Quinche, professor of Latin; Gen. Claudius W. Sears, professor of mathematics, and Gen. Francis A. Shoup (in October) professor of physics, astronomy and civil engineering, and Dr. Stanford G. Burney, professor of English. Dr. Eugene W. Hilgard, state geologist, was requested to discharge, provisionally, the duties of professor of chemistry, geology and mineralogy. College opened in October, and the attendance for the year was one hundred and ninety-three. In June, 1866, Hon. Lucius Q. C. Lamar was elected professor of ethics and metaphysics, while Dr. Hilgard was also made a professor. It was determined to reëstablish the law school, and Hon. H. F. Simrall was elected professor, Mr. Lamar being requested to discharge the duties provisionally. In 1867 Judge Simrall having failed to accept, Professor Lamar was transferred to the chair of law. The ethics and metaphysics were assigned to Professor Shoup, who was relieved of a portion of the work heretofore done by him by the election of Dr. Landon C. Garland as professor of experimental philosophy and astronomy. In 1870 there was a reorganization of the university, a result of the reconstruction acts of congress. None of the professors were removed. Mr. Lamar, however, resigned. He was followed by Hon. Henry Craft, Jordan M. Phipps, assistant. There was a general remodeling of the scheme of work in the literary department, and arrangements were made for thirteen professorships, of which, however, only eleven were actually filled. By the revised code of 1871 the charter was altered in some respects, the most material of which was the substitution of a general annual appropriation of $50,000 for all previous arrangements. This year, also, Mr. Craft resigned, and Thomas Walton, Esq., was elected professor of law. Also two-fifths of the income from the agricultural land-scrip fund, amounting to about $7,600 per annum, was assigned to the university, and a department of agriculture established, Professor Hilgard being made professor of agricultural chemistry and the special geology and agriculture of the state. Dr. M. W. Phillips was made adjunct professor of agriculture and superintendent of the farm. This enterprise was never very successful. The means for the establishment were never provided by the state. In 1875 the appropriation for the support of the university was reduced to $35,000, and in 1876 to $21,000, whereupon the agricultural department was abandoned. In July, 1874, Dr. Waddel resigned the chancellorship, and was succeeded by Gen. A. P. Stewart. In 1877 Edward Mayes, Esq., was elected law professor. In 1877, also, Dr. Cowles M. Vaiden, a member of the board of trustees, began to send large numbers of poor but deserving boys to the university; the plan being to lend them the money needed, on their personal notes. At one time there were one hundred of those beneficiaries, but when he died the practice ceased. In 1879 Col. Felix Labauve, of De Soto county, died and left by his will a residuary legacy in trust, that the net income should be devoted to the education of poor orphan boys of that county at the university. This fund now amounts to about $20,000, paying about $1,500 per annum, and on it five beneficiaries attend the university each year. In 1882, the doors of the institution were opened to females, and from that time there has been an attendance of girls every year. They have done exceedingly well. Girls have graduated in five classes, and in two instances made the highest records of the class: Miss Sallie Vick Hill, of Macon, in 1885, and Miss Mattie J. Smythe, of Leake county, in 1888. The largest attendance for one year was twenty three. No modified curriculum is provided for them, but they take exactly the courses prescribed for all students. There are now (1890–1) four female candidates for the post-graduate degree of master of arts. In July, 1886, the chancellor resigned. Professor Mayes was chosen chairman of the faculty, and the chancellorship abolished; but in 1889 the office was restored and Professor Mayes made chancellor. At the same time the scheme of education was revised, and the work of the institution divided into schools, of which nineteen, each being independent of the others, were established: Latin, Greek, French, German, English, belles lettres, mathematics, physics, astronomy, history, political economy, mental and moral philosophy, logic, botany, zoology, mineralogy, geology, theoretical chemistry and practical chemistry. The courses in several of the schools were made more extensive, especially in mathematics, French and German. The school of belles lettres was entirely a new introduction. In 1890 four fellowships were established, designed to encourage graduates to pursue higher work, and thus to qualify themselves for life as scientists or professors. One such fellowship had been previously established. The five are now in chemistry, natural history, physics and astronomy, mathematics and English. Elocution was at this time added as a twentieth school, and is, as it has been for several years, under the charge of Miss Sallie McGehee Isom. Since its establishment four thousand three hundred and thirty-three students have attended the university, of which four hundred and six have been law students. Of these, six hundred and sixty-seven have taken baccalaureate degrees, two hundred and sixty-five the degree of bachelor of laws, and twenty-three that of master of arts. The average attendance in the literary department has been two hundred and three, while that in the law school has been twenty-two.

The Vicksburg Female institute was established under the Rev. A. B. Lawrence, some time editor of the New Orleans *Observer*, and his wife, in February, 1842. In 1844 it was conducted in that extensive building formerly known as the Vicksburg hotel, and William H. Vick was president of the trustees.

The Friendship Male academy of Panola county was established in 1842, under the charge of Joseph Y. Boyd, a graduate of Miami university, incorporated in 1844, Mr. Boyd being still principal.

The Kosciusko Male and Female academy, in Attala county, was at work in 1842, Mr. and Mrs. Charles W. Emmons principals. They were followed, in 1843, by a Mrs. McCary.

The Raleigh academy, of Smith county, was incorporated in 1843.

The Port Gibson Female college, in Claiborne county, was founded in September, 1843. Mr. John Harvie was in charge, assisted by his wife and four other teachers. The grounds and buildings were worth about $15,000, and there was an extensive apparatus. In 1854 it was incorporated as the Port Gibson Collegiate academy. In 1859 the Rev. Benjamin Jones was president, and again in 1871. In 1869 it was taken into the connection of the Methodist Church South. The Rev. John A. B. Jones was president from 1875 to 1881. He was followed by the Rev. Thomas C. Bradford from 1882 to 1887. In 1888 the Rev. Edwin H. Mounger was made president, and is so still. The turmoil of the late Civil war did not interrupt the work of this college, and consequently it can claim the longest uninterrupted career of any female school in the state. The attendance has ranged from sixty to one hundred and twenty-five, and to date it has graduated sixty-four young ladies.

St. Thomas' hall, located at Holly Springs, in Marshall county, in January, 1844, by the Rev. Dr. Francis L. Hawkes, former rector of St. Thomas church, New York city, with an able and learned corps of teachers, it achieved a high reputation, and attracted a large number of pupils. One of the best schools ever in the state. The necessary grounds and buildings were donated by the citizens of the county. The first faculty were Dr. Hawkes, president and professor of English literature; John Q. Bradford, A. M., professor of Latin and Greek; Claudius W. Sears, of the United States Military academy, afterward brigadier-general of the Confederate States of America, and for over twenty-four years professor of mathematics in the University of Mississippi, professor of mathematics; Thomas K. Wharton, professor of French and drawing. In January, 1845, the institution suffered a serious and for a time apparently irremediable loss in the departure of Dr. Hawkes for New Orleans, where he was made president of the University of Louisiana. However, a rally was made, and the hall was reopened in October, under the auspices of the Protestant Episcopal church, probably the first appearance of that body in the educational work of the state. The Rev. David C. Page, rector of Christ church, was principal. On the 4th of July, 1846, there was a grand celebration, one feature of which was a parade of the student military company, Ed. C. Walthall, ensign. In 1847 Prof. Henry Whitehorne was teacher of ancient languages, a Mr. Wright being professor of mathematics. In 1857 Professor Whitehorne was elected to the chair of Greek in the university. In 1849 the institution was reorganized as a military school; the Rev. J. H. Ingraham, LL. D., president and professor of English; C. W. Sears, commandant and professor of mathematics; William A. Clark, A. M., professor of Latin and Greek. At this period the average annual attendance was about seventy-five. This excellent school continued until the Civil war. During that calamitous period the buildings were destroyed, and the institution has not been revived.

The Wesleyan Female college, located in Jackson, was in operation in 1843. Mrs. Louisa C. W. Judd was principal. It had considerable success. The faculty for the year 1845-6 was as follows: Mrs. Judd, Col. Guilford D. Mitchell, Misses A. and M. Mitchell, M. L. Julienne, professor of French; Mr. Stribey, of music. In the year following Colonel Mitchell established an independent school, and Mrs. Judd reorganized her faculty thus: C. M. Murch, music; Julienne, modern languages; Mrs. J. H. Kimberly, ornamental work; Miss Hannah Merrill, primary. In 1847 the school seems to have been suspended, and the premises occupied for school purposes by the Rev. Amos Cleaver, an Episcopalian clergyman who had opened a high grade female school in the year 1846. About 1850 a company bought the property, and Mr. A. R. Green opened a fine female academy there, which was maintained until the outbreak of the war.

The Oakland institute, a school for girls, was established at Jackson in 1844, by Mr. and Mrs. Oakley. It had a prosperous career of near twenty years, continuing until the Civil war.

The Lexington Male and Female academy, at Lexington, in Holmes county, was incorporated in 1844. The male department was under Mr. G. Zelotes Adams, a graduate of Washington college, Connecticut, who had already taught seven years South.

The Houston academy, located at Houston, Chickasaw county, was incorporated in 1844. A lot was procured and a schoolbuilding erected. The building was destroyed by fire; and the lot, being deemed ineligible, was abandoned. A more desirable one was obtained, upon which was built a two-story structure at a cost of $5,000. By authority of an act of the legislature passed in 1884, the county authorities conveyed the property to the town of Houston; which, in turn, leased it for twenty-five years to Prof. H. B. Abernathy, for the uses of the Mississippi Normal college (q.v.).

The Decatur academy, located at Decatur, in Newton county, was incorporated in 1844.

Mount Sylvan academy, for boys, located at Mount Sylvan, in Lafayette county, was established in 1845, under the Rev. S. G. Burney, D. D., and the Rev. Robert Morris, D. D. Col. James Brown was its chief benefactor, by his donations of more than $1,200; Hon. Jacob Thompson made valuable donations of books and public documents, and many others were generous. In 1846, the pupils numbered fifty-five. This school continued for a number of years one of the best. Quite a number of youths there received the education which afterward enabled them to assume prominent positions in church and state. Doctor Burney, later, held for a number of years the chair of English in the university, and is now at the head of the theological school of Cumberland university.

The Chulahoma Female institute, located at Chulahoma, in Marshall county, was in operation in 1845, under the management of Mr. and Mrs. Howze, Mr. D. Brewer professor of music. Long a prosperous and useful school.

The Seneca institute, for girls, located at Brandon, Rankin county, was opened in 1845, under Mr. Robert Anderson, a graduate of South Carolina college. Philip L. Bode, professor of music. A good school.

The Natchez institute was opened in 1845. It originated with Alvarez Fisk, who donated to the city property valued at $13,000, on condition that it would establish a school for the gratuitous education of the youth within its limits. The condition was agreed to, and an annual tax ordered of $6,000, which was increased $542.60 by private subscriptions and by the literary fund. Although Franklin academy was established in 1845, yet inasmuch as it was supported by the sixteenth section fund, the Natchez institute may fairly claim the credit of being the first free school established on individual and municipal liberality. It was successful from the beginning. The principal, Mr. Joshua Pearl, A. M., of Yale college, was a ripe scholar and a laborious and experienced teacher. Much of the permanent success achieved must be attributed to his skillful initiative. He was assisted by two male and five female teachers. The attendance of the first term was: Males, two hundred and twelve; females, one hundred and ninety-six. The total of the second year was six hundred; the third year opened with five hundred in attendance. A board of visitors visited the school regularly, examined the teachers, and established by-laws. Many of the children had been nuisances in the streets, but were made orderly, studious and ambitious. Latin, Greek and the higher mathematics were taught from the first. We may not follow this fine school through its long but not very eventful career. It is happy in having but little history. It is still in existence and flourishing.

The Vicksburg institute, similar to that at Natchez, and yet in existence, was founded in the same year.

The Salem High school, on Leaf river, in Greene county, was established in 1845 by a class of citizens known as North Carolina Scotch Presbyterians. Prominent among them was the Rev. James H. Thomson. No endowment. The school was supported by annual contributions from the trustees and by the tuition fees. A log house, 30x50 feet, was built, and later three others were added, with a small framed building for a musicroom. Incorporated in 1850. The first session began in October, 1846; David Moore, A. M., a graduate of Lafayette college, principal; Mrs. S. D. Pierce, female department; Mary Stewart, music; R. S. Shannon, primary. In 1852 W. E. Hall succeeded Mr. Moore. He was followed by Lewis Tice, M. D., of Union college, New York, and he by E. W. Larkin, A. M. The assistants at various periods were Angus R. Fairley, John R. Fairley, E. F. Griffin, Miss Godfrey, Miss Black, Miss Shannon, Miss Mary E. Connelly and Mrs. Mary Hall. The apparatus was good, and the library contained about five hundred volumes. The average attendance was about one hundred, of whom about two-thirds were from a distance. About one-fourth took courses which may be considered as of collegiate grade. Suspended in 1862, and never revived.

The college in Jackson was organized by Dr. Thomas C. Thornton immediately after his resignation from Centenary college. It was opened on January 1, 1845. Doctor Thornton was president and professor of history, political economy, intellectual and moral philosophy; Rev. Norman W. Camp, A. M., professor of ancient languages and rhetoric; J. M. Pugh, A. M., professor of mathematics and civil engineering; James B. C. Thornton, M. D., professor of natural history, experimental philosophy and chemistry and medicine; Louis Julienne, teacher of French; Daniel Mayes, Esq., professor of law. The college was kept in the old Eagle hotel, on the site now occupied by the residence of Joseph Brown, Esq. The plan was to make it a college of higher grade than the state had yet seen, and to get it taken under the patronage of the state and of the city. It was incorporated in 1846, but the effort to procure subsidies for it failed. After two years it was abandoned, having graduated four students.

The common schools. In 1846 was passed the first statute in Mississippi contemplating the establishment of a uniform system of free schools, supported by license fees and taxation. Through a faulty construction of the statute, however, as well as a narrow interpretation of it, the enterprise did not get well under way. While efforts were made to put the system into operation, and with some success in a few localities, yet as a whole the undertaking proved a failure. Numerous local acts were passed inaugurating various schemes. There was neither unity of plan nor perseverance in effort. The schools of Hinds county flourished, and presented some semblance of the present system; but in all other parts of the state the movement was more or less crippled, and in many completely paralyzed, by the want of a uniform and vigorous policy.

Milton academy, about three miles west of (present) Vaiden, in Carroll county, was established in 1846 by the Rev. W. H. Harris, who conducted it very successfully until his death in 1855. He was followed by the Rev. S. S. Brown. In 1859 Mr. Brown sold to Prof. J. Smith Colmery, who converted it into a female school, under the name of the Milton Female seminary, and as such conducted it until 1875, when it was abandoned. Some of Mississippi's best men were educated at Milton academy.

Morey's school, established in Carroll county, about three miles north of Carrollton, is interesting as a forerunner, by some forty years, of a style of school now quite common in the state under the name of Normal schools. He advertised it the Practical school, on a time and money-saving plan!

The Planters' academy, in the southern part of Attala county, was at work in 1846, and gained some reputation.

The Pleasant Grove Female academy, in Marshall county, was in operation in 1846, under Miss Mary C. McCollum.

The Central academy, in Marshall county, about eight miles southwest of Holly Springs, was flourishing in 1846 and 1847. The female school was under Mrs. M. A. Holliday, and the male school under Mr. Elden.

The Pontotoc Male academy was incorporated in 1846.

The Black Hawk Male and Female seminary, located at Black Hawk, in Carroll county, was organized and incorporated in 1846, Mr. D. A. Bland and Miss A. Nixon in charge. The male and female schools were situated in different parts of the village. The buildings were comfortable. In January, 1847, Mr. Tripp and Miss Kingsbury were in charge; Prof. George Wear, music; Mrs. Wear, art. In 1848 Miss Kingsbury was in charge, with a lady assistant. From 1849 to 1853, inclusive, the Rev. Benjamin Holt, a Methodist minister, was principal, assisted by Miss Harriet Magruder. In 1850 the institution was enlarged, and the female department incorporated under the name of the Eudocia Female college. In 1853 Mr. Holt was succeeded by Mr. James Gillespie, and he, in turn, by Dr. W. S. Young, from Vicksburg, who remained until June, 1856. Meanwhile the male department was, in 1850 and 1851, taught by Dr. William Bennett, from North Carolina. He was succeeded by the Rev. S. S. Brown, from Ohio, who remained until the summer of 1855. Mr. Gillespie, and, after him, Mr. Robert R. L. Harris taught for a few months; and then came, in June, 1856, Mr. William H. Johnson. At this time it was determined to reduce the scale of the school. Mr. Johnson purchased the property, and consolidated the two branches. He conducted the consolidated school until the outbreak of the Civil war. He joined the Confederate army, and the school was taught, during most of the war period, by a Mr. Akin. On the termination of hostilities Mr. Johnson resumed the control, and remained until the summer of 1867. Mr. C. T. Adams, from Virginia, took charge in the fall of 1868, but leaving before the year was out, he was followed by the Rev. Charles B. Galloway, A. B. of the University of Mississippi, and now a bishop of the Methodist Episcopal Church South, assisted by Miss Patty Cross and Miss McCrosky. About September, 1869, a Mr. Combs took charge; followed in 1872 by Rev. Thomas A. S. Adams, afterward president of the Centenary college. At this time it was brought into the connectional relations of the Methodist Church South, and so remained until the end. In 1875 it was reincorporated under the name of the Yazoo District High school. In 1875-6 a Mr. Carter was in charge; and in 1876-7 Miss Alice Kittrell. Then came Edward W. Tarrant until 1883; at which time it passed into the hands of Mr. John P. Marshall. After him came, in quick succession, Mr. William H. Johnson, again, in 1885; Miss Sallie Morgan and a Mr. Shivers, in 1886; Mr. B. P. Patterson, in 1887; and in 1888 Mr. Leland B. Abell, LL.B. of the University of Mississippi, under whom it remained until destroyed by fire 1890. The curriculum was high; and the last two or three years of its existence was under the name of the Winona District High school.

The Franklin Female college, located at Holly Springs, in Marshall county, was founded in 1846, by the Rev. S. G. Starks, an eminent Methodist minister. For a number of years it was under the patronage of the denomination. Its faculty was the best, and its attendance amounted to three hundred pupils, coming from Louisiana and south Mississippi. There was a valuable apparatus, and a well selected library. Mr. Starks was succeeded in 1857 by the Rev. David J. Allen, and he, in 1859, by the Rev. J. E. Douglass. In 1862, when the wounded from the battle of Corinth were brought to Holly Springs, the school was suspended and the buildings used for hospitals. After the war closed, they were used by the United States soldiery for barracks. In 1869 they were thoroughly refitted, and leased by Capt. William Clark, a finished scholar and eminent teacher, associated with the Rev. H. H. Paine, a Presbyterian minister. In 1870, Mr. Paine retired. In 1878, Mr. Clark fell a victim to the great epidemic of yellow fever, and was succeeded by his widow, Mrs. Mary B. Clark, daughter of the celebrated lawyer, Roger Barton. Under her, the college maintained its high reputation. She died in 1888, and was followed by her sister, Mrs. F. A. Tyler, and daughter, Mrs. R. H. Tunstall, ladies well qualified for the position. Since the war, the pupils have ranged from seventy-five to one hundred and fifty, from one half to three-fourths in the collegiate course. The first class to graduate was that of 1850, and its alumnae embrace many of the most accomplished ladies of the state. Of late years, the patronage is mainly from Mississippi, although pupils still come occasionally from Louisiana, Arkansas, Tennessee, Alabama, and Texas. Incorporated in 1873.

Wildmarth hall, at Natchez, was established by Mrs. A. F. W. Speer, in the fall of 1846. A select school, limited at first to twenty-five pupils, and enlarging gradually, and always full. Patronized largely by Louisianians. The Rev. S. W. Speer taught for his wife the classes in mental and moral philosophy, sciences and astronomy; Mons. F. Prou, professor of modern languages; T. Crouch, professor of music; Misses Maria H. Weldin, C. B. Armington, and Eliza A. Dodson, assistants, composing the faculty for 1848-9. In 1852, the institution seems to have been enlarged. It was incorporated as Wildmarth Female college, Rev. Mr. Speer being principal.

The Brandon college was established by Dr. Thomas C. Thornton, and Professor Pugh in 1847, after the failure of the college in Jackson. They took the old academy, with the two commodious buildings erected in 1838, and reorganized it into a college, obtaining a charter in 1849. In 1851, it was abandoned under the circumstances explained in the notice of Madison college. Eight students had graduated; among them Miss Veturia J. Finley, probably the first young lady in this state to complete the entire collegiate course prescribed for young men. When Dr. Thornton left the school was taken in charge by W. H. Potter, of Mystic, Conn., who conducted it until 1855 as an academy. Afterward it changed hands frequently. In 1865, it was taken in hand by Miss Frank A. Johnson, who has held it until now. In February, 1867, it was incorporated under the name of the Brandon Female college, and for a period was the only institution of high grade in the state under the management of ladies alone. Under Miss Johnson it has been a successful and most useful school. The attendance has ranged from sixty-five to eighty-five per annum. It is now one of the separate district schools, having been adopted as such by the town.

The Crystal Springs academy, in Copiah county, was opened in 1847: John P. Mapes, principal; Livingston Mims in the male department; Mrs. Asenath Evans in the female department; Prof. E. A. Haug music.

The Marshall Female institute, located in Marshall county near the Tennessee line, was established in 1848, under the auspices of the Methodist church. The Rev. Joseph E. Douglass was president, assisted by his wife, Prof. John J. Steger and Miss Anna Boley. This was a very celebrated, useful and prosperous school for many years. From 1852 to 1856 the matriculations averaged about two hundred. The course of study was high. In 1856 the building was burned by an incendiary, and President Douglass entered the itinerancy, being succeeded by Dr. Speer; but he returned the following year, the house having been rebuilt. In 1859 Professor Watkins was made president. In 1863 Mrs. Douglass became principal, and in 1868 Miss Margaret Johnson. Various influences have caused it to decline from its former proud position. It was made a district high school of the church under a Professor Johnson from Virginia. In 1874 it was destroyed by fire.

The Columbus Female institute was incorporated and established in 1848. There were four collegiate classes in addition to the usual preparatory ones, with a full curriculum of ancient and modern languages, mathematics, sciences, philosophy, art and music. A frame building was erected at a cost of $3,330; about $9,000 was realized from the sale of perpetual scholarships, and devoted to the further improvement of the property. In 1860 the building was destroyed by fire. The sum of $32,465 was then raised in cash, bonds and subscriptions, for the purpose of rebuilding. A large brick dormitory was commenced, which, however, was not completed (until the state did so later). Only the interior of the first story was finished for the present. In 1862 the school was suspended for about six months, as the building was used as a hospital. There were on resumption in 1863 one hundred and thirty-seven pupils. In 1872 a scheme was agitated to make the institution a female department of the university, but it came to nothing. In 1875 another plan to make it a part of the Franklin academy, thus bringing it into the public school system, but neither did that result in anything. Finally, in 1884, it was donated to the state, and formed the basis for the present establishment of the industrial institute and college.

The following academies not elsewhere mentioned, for they are now getting too numerous to describe in detail, were incorporated about this period:

1848—Enterprise academy, Clarke county; Raymond Female institution, Hinds county; Pleasant Hill Male and Female academy, Jasper county; Canton Male academy, Madison county; the Female institute, Noxubee county.

1850.—Pearl River Female academy, Madison county; Polkville Male and Female academy, Smith county: Almucha academy (the second), Lauderdale county; Kemper college Kemper county.

Very Truly
Robert Lowry

1852.—Collegiate High School of Odd Fellows, Columbus; Coldwater Baptist Female seminary (Chulahoma), Marshall county; Mary Washington Female college (Baptist), Pontotoc; Mississippi Female college, Hernando; Greenwood Female institute, Jasper county; Maple Spring Male academy, Tippah county; Masonic and Odd Fellows' high school (Bankston), Choctaw county; Pleasant Ridge Male and Female academy, Tippah county; Middleton Female seminary, Carroll county; Southern Scientific institute, Claiborne county; Simpson Male and Female seminary, Simpson county; Yalobusha Baptist Female institute, Yalobusha county; Choctaw Collegiate institute (Baptist), Choctaw county; College of St. Andrew (Episcopalian), Jackson, Hinds county; Canton Female institute, Madison county; Presbyterian Female Collegiate institute, Pontotoc; Crawfordville Male and Female institute, Lowndes county.

1854.—Good Hope academy, Leake county; Westminster academy, Tippah county; Hill City Collegiate institute, Vicksburg; Central Mississippi Female college, Lexington; Monroe Female institute, Aberdeen; Octograde seminary, Yalobusha county; Union seminary, De Soto county.

The Chickasaw school fund originated in the sale by the state of the lands donated by congress for common-school purposes to the inhabitants of that portion of the state which was ceded by the Chickasaw Indians. This sale was made in 1848. The state appropriated the money to general uses and acknowledged itself debtor therefor. The amount of the fund is now about $816,617, on which is paid semi-annually to the counties entitled interest at six per cent. per annum.

The Liberty Female institute, at Liberty, in Amite county, was opened in July, 1849; Rev. A. B. Lawrence and his wife, formerly of Vicksburg, principals. They were assisted by able teachers.

Chalmers institute, located at Holly Springs, was founded in 1850 by the Rev. Samuel McKinney. It was possessed of the property of the old university of Holly Springs, and was regarded as the successor of that institution. In 1873 it was incorporated. Meanwhile it had been in operation since its foundation as a male school. In 1854 it was under charge of Messrs. Hackleton, Hoole, Pike and Hume, and they established a military feature. From 1855 to 1861 it was presided over by Rev. S. I. Reid, A. Enloe, Henry Paine, William M. Walkup and Rev. W. C. Young (now of Center college, Kentucky). During the war its work was interrupted. Exercises were resumed in 1865. In 1869 the military feature was revived. In 1879 the school was suspended. The following gentlemen had been connected with it since the war: Rev. S. I. Reid, William M. Walkup, Col. George M. Edgar, W. A. Anderson, A. S. Marye, John Creighton and William M. Rogers.

The Mississippi Female college, located at Hernando, De Soto county, was established, under the name of the De Soto Female seminary, in 1850, by subscriptions of the citizens of the county. It was incorporated under the general laws of the state. A brick building was erected in 1850-51, at a cost of $6,500. The Rev. William Cary Crane, an Episcopalian clergyman, was elected president in the fall of 1850, and the school opened successfully in the spring following. In 1852 a charter was granted by the legislature, under the name above. In 1856 President Crane was succeeded by Prof. James C. Dockery, former professor of French at the University of Alabama. In the spring of 1858 he was followed, pro tem. by Dr. H. M. Jeter, and early in 1859 Rev. Champ C. Connor was made president. The college had been successful, and enlargements were about to be made; but in the winter of 1859-60, a fire destroyed the buildings. In 1861 a handsome new brick building was completed, but the Civil war interrupted. In 1865 Mrs. Mary Pope kept a successful school in the building, followed in 1866 by Mrs. Emma Holcombe, who, in turn, was succeeded in 1869 by Mrs. M. P. Southworth, of Memphis, as a lessee, until 1874. The property was then sold for debts growing out of the rebuilding, and passed into private hands. Since that time it has been constantly used for school purposes.

Madison college was established at Sharon, in Madison county, in 1851, by Dr. Thomas C. Thornton and Professor Pugh, in response to an invitation extended by the citizens of that village. It was conducted at first in a frame building formerly used for a hotel; but soon a good brick house was built at an outlay of $5,000. The faculty was shortly after the opening enlarged, and was composed of Dr. Thornton, president and professor of moral and intellectual science and sacred literature; Rev. J. M. Pugh, vice president and professor of mathematics, natural philosophy and astronomy; H. W. Pierce, professor of English literature; Rev. W. L. C. Hunnicutt, professor of ancient languages; J. C. Pitchford, principal of the preparatory department; Wm. H. Hartwell, professor of music. During the most prosperous period, from 1852 to 1859, the annual attendance of pupils was about one hundred and fifty, of whom about two-thirds were usually in the college proper. In March, 1860, President Thornton died. He was succeeded by Professor Pugh, but in December he resigned to take the presidency of Centenary college, and was followed by Professor Pierce. After the interruption of the late Civil war, the college was reopned in 1866, Rev. Harvey W. Johnson president. In 1867 President Johnson left to take charge of Whitworth college, and was followed, in 1868, by Dr. Hunnicutt. At this time Rev. Charles B. Galloway was a professor there. In 1870 Dr. Hunnicutt was succeeded by Dr. Pugh again. In 1872 the institution suspended finally, for want of endowment and patronage.

The Yalobusha Baptist Female institute was founded in 1851, by the Yalobusha Baptist association. For its accommodation the existing edifice was erected at a cost of $30,000. The Rev. Dr. W. S. Webb, now president of Mississippi college, was its president. He conducted it successfully for six years, when he was followed by Mr. George Granberry. It continued to prosper until the outbreak of the war, when it met the common fate of suspension. After the war ceased the property was sold for debt and was purchased by Geo. W. Ragsdale, who refitted it and leased it to Mrs. Holcombe in 1867. She opened then the Emma Mercer institute. After several years she failed and was followed by Prof. R. A. Irwin. He did well, having about eighty pupils. In 1875 the property was again sold for the debts of its owner, and it was purchased by a joint-stock company of citizens, who changed its name to the Grenada female college. Rev. D. D. Moore was made president. In 1879 he was followed by Dr. N. T. Scruggs, and he, in 1881, by Rev. Dr. T. C. Weir. In 1882 the property was purchased at a low price by the North Mississippi conference of the Methodist Episcopal Church South, and the Rev. Thomas J. Newell made president. He has filled that place ever since. A charter was obtained in 1884 as the Grenada Collegiate institute. The faculty embraces eight teachers in addition to the president. The annual attendance is about one hundred and seventy-five. The alumni number to date is twenty-two.

The Hernando Male seminary was incorporated under the general laws of the state about the year 1852. Stock to the amount of $6,000 or $7,000 was subscribed, and a suitable building of six or seven rooms, including two large study halls, erected. A good school was maintained until 1861, patronized by the surrounding counties. In 1866 the building was burned, but the school was continued under Rev. S. I. Reid, and in 1867 the house was rebuilt. The Rev. J. W. Tipsey then took charge, under a lease. He was followed in 1869 by R. N. J. Wilson. The school was finally displaced by the free-schools, under the system of 1870.

The Coffeeville academy was established in 1852, chartered under the general laws of the state. Miss Margaret Stein conducted it until 1854, when she was succeeded by the Rev. R. S. Thomas, of the Cumberland Presbyterian church, with Misses Ingles and Patton assistants. In 1856 Mr. Thomas retired, and the ladies conducted the school until 1857, when Prof. Eli G. Burney, A. B. of the university, took it. He was followed by Miss Bettie Martin, who kept it until the war broke it up entirely.

Enon high school, located in the central-western portion of Perry county, was incorporated in 1852. It was in operation about ten years, with a yearly attendance of about one hundred, and did great good for that portion of the state.

The Kosciusko Masonic Female college, at Kosciusko, Attala county, was incorporated in 1852. Mrs. Tilton, from New York, was principal; succeeded by Prof. Hatfield. Assistants were employed as needed. Attendance about seventy-five, mostly local. No endowment, but occasionally aided by the Masons. During the war, and later, it was presided over by the Rev. J. H. Alexander, assisted by Mrs. West and Mrs. Thompson, daughters of Rev. John N. Waddel. Situated on a desirable lot, and with three good houses (one of brick), in 1870 the Masonic fraternity sold it to the public school officials for $4,000, and it became, and now is, one of the separate district schools.

Newton college, located in Wilkinson county, was about one-fourth of a mile from Newton institute. It was established in 1852, for youngmen; incorporated in 1854. Dr. Phares was president until 1859, and then Prof. Alexander Ellett, who continued until the school ceased to exist, which was in 1861. William Baxter, F. H. Rislay, J. H. McKay, H. Kirk Baxter, and others, served as professors. A number of gentlemen were educated at this college, some becoming distinguished in the learned professions.

The Central Female institute, located at Clinton, in Hinds county, was founded in 1853, under the patronage of the Baptist church. Its first president was Prof. William Duncan. He was soon followed by the Rev. Walter Hillman, who has remained in charge until the present time. The attendance of pupils has averaged about one hundred and twenty per annum, and it is now completing its thirty-seventh year of uninterrupted work; the late Civil war causing no suspension. President Hillman has six assistants in his faculty. There are two large dormitories, a variety of smaller buildings detached, and a very handsome main building completed within the year. The equipment of apparatus and specimens for illustration of the sciences is exceptionally fine.

The Summerville institute, located at Summerville, in Noxubee county, was established in 1853, as a private enterprise, by Thomas S. Gathright, from Alabama. With two or three assistants each year, Professor Gathright maintained an unusually fine school for many years. The yearly attendance was about eighty, the expenses about $200. About 1877 Professor Gathright moved to Texas, and the school was abandoned. Many of the best men in the state received education there.

The St. Stanislaus Commercial college, located at Bay St. Louis, in Hancock county, was established in 1855, by the Brothers of the Sacred Heart, of the Catholic church. Pleasantly located on the shore of Mississippi sound, and the buildings spacious. The special object of the institution is to prepare young men for a mercantile life. At first the attendance was small, but soon it grew large, and students came from the surrounding states. During the late war, efforts were made to continue the work, but a suspension was forced by the drift of events. Labor was resumed when peace came. There was no endowment. The members of the society contributed the means needed to erect buildings, etc. At first, there were three professors for the commercial department, but it soon became necessary to appoint two others. Incorporated in 1870. The course of study is divided into four grades. The highest includes geometry, with applications to drawing and mensuration, trigonometry, surveying, navigation, astronomy, conic sections, calculus, physics, chemistry and commercial law. There are nine professors. The attendance has averaged about one hundred and fifty per annum.

The Warren Female institute, located at Oxford, Lafayette county, was founded about 1855, by Mrs. Harper, wife of the professor of agriculture and geology in the university. She was followed by Miss Sallie Giles; and she by Miss Hull, now Mrs. Smither, of Oxford; and she, by Miss Lewis, in whose hands it was well attended, and tided over the critical period of the Civil war. During all this time it made but little pretension beyond that of a good grammar school, but about 1870, a Mrs. Hays took charge, elevated the course and did much toward its improvement. She was succeeded by the Misses Miller. In 1880 Mrs. C. A. Lancaster, the present owner and principal, from Virginia, took the school. She still further elevated the grade, gave it the present name, and it was incorporated in 1882. An excellent school; buildings, a two-story framed structure, with accommodations for twenty-five lodgers.

The Odd Fellows' Female college, located at Carrollton, in Carroll county, was opened under the auspices of the Odd Fellows in 1857. The first principal was J. Smith Colmery. Provided with a fine lot of about three acres and a commodious framed building of three stories. The school was at once successful. In 1859 there were one hundred and thirty pupils. After varying fortunes of prosperity, decadence and suspension, and several changes of ownership, it is now flourishing in the hands of the Rev. Z. T. Leavell, a Baptist minister.

The Vernal Springs Male and Female academy, located in the south central part of Greene county, was founded and incorporated in 1860; J. B. Smith, principal; Kate Smith, assistant. Its career, though brief, was prosperous. Average attendance, about fifty; about one-fifth boarders. There was a small patronage from Alabama and Texas.

The Woodville Female academy, located at Woodville, Wilkinson county, was founded in 1860, by the liberality of Hon. Edward McGehee, who donated the land and erected the buildings at his own cost. The building was not completed when the war broke out, but a small school was taught in it, Professor Holcombe, principal. In October, 1865, the academy proper was opened. It was a Methodist church school, and the Rev. W. T. J. Sullivan was principal, with eight lady assistants. The academy was quite prosperous at first, drawing patronage from Louisiana as well as from Mississippi; but in the fall of 1867 an epidemic of yellow fever caused a back-set from which it never entirely recovered. Dr. Sullivan retired in 1870. Since then the school has led a rather precarious existence. Its name has recently been changed to Edward McGehee college, and under the presidency of the Rev. H. Walter Featherston a larger future is promising. The buildings cost about $10,000; and the property is now worth about that amount.

The following additional academies, many of them of great merit, were incorporated at this time:

1856. Oak Bowery academy, unknown; Byhalia Male academy, Marshall county; Okolona Male academy, Chickasaw county; Canaan Male and Female academy, Tippah county; Mississippi Masonic Female college, Claiborne county; Calhoun institute (Macon), Noxubee county; Eastport Female institute, Tishomingo county; Okolona Female institute, Chickasaw county; Amite Female seminary, Amite county.

1858. Semple Broadus college (Baptist), De Soto county.

1860. Brandon State Military institution, Rankin county; Aberdeen Masonic Male high school, Monroe county; Amite County Female academy (Liberty), Amite county; Willard Male and Female academies, De Soto county; Masonic Female seminary (Mount Pleasant), Marshall county; Yazoo Educational association, Yazoo county.

Whitworth female college, located at Brookhaven, in Lincoln county, was founded in 1859, by Rev. M. J. Whitworth, a Methodist preacher. It was incorporated in 1860, and opened in the spring of that year, under Rev. J. P. Lee as president. A frame building was erected, at a cost of about $15,000. In June, 1861, President Lee because of the war, resigned, and the school was suspended until April, 1862. It was then reopened, with Rev. E. L. Crosby president. In the following July, however, Mr. Crosby died, and the buildings were then used for a hospital until the close of the war. In January, 1865, the Rev. George F. Thompson was elected, and conducted the school with moderate success until 1867. In April, of this year, Rev. Harvey W. Johnson, then president of Madison college, was elected, and under him the college had extraordinary success. He repaired the property, paid off a debt of $2,800 and built the chapel and music hall, at a cost of $8,500. In 1878 a handsome brick dormitory, valued at $15,000, was erected, and in 1883 a commodious brick main building, worth about $20,000. This valuable property, erected from the earnings of the school, with some generous assistance from others, was by President Johnson donated to the conference. In August, 1886, Dr. Johnson died, and Prof. Lewis T. Fitzhugh, principal of the high school of the university, was elected to succeed him. Under this gentleman the school has greatly prospered. The annual attendance is about two hundred and fifty pupils. There is a conservatory of music, organized on a large scale, with about two hundred pupils. The faculty in the college embraces seven teachers, besides the president. That in the conservatory embraces six others. There is also an art department. The alumni are three hundred and fifty-five in number.

The suspension of hostilities at the close of the late Civil war was immediately followed by a resumption of labor in the field of education.

Cooper Normal college, located at Daleville, in Lauderdale county, was established in 1865, under the name of the Spring Hill Male and Female academy, by the Rev. J. L. Cooper. It was a private enterprise. The property was worth about $5,000; there was no endowment. The library contained about two thousand volumes. Mr. Cooper was assisted by three able teachers. In 1873 the institution was chartered as the Cooper institute. There were then seven assistants, three thousand volumes in the library and about one hundred and sixty pupils, coming from four states. The museum contained about three thousand specimens, and there was a fine illustrative apparatus. A three-months' commercial course had been organized. In 1885 the institute passed into the hands of Prof. Thomas T. McBeath, and in 1886 was incorporated anew, as the Cooper Normal college. There are five assistants. There are five courses of study: The literary, the scientific, the classic, the languages and literature, the commercial and technical. The last includes bookkeeping and business forms, shorthand, typewriting, telegraphy and engineering. There is also a department of pedagogics; also one of music and fine arts; average attendance about one hundred and seventy-five per annum; that for the year 1888-9 was two hundred and fifty; total graduates, about two hundred and fifty; property, one hundred and ninety-two acres of land, three large two-story frame buildings and six cottages; library, about forty-five hundred volumes.

The Meridian Female college was established in 1865, and ran a successful career of many years, and the Newton female academy, of Crystal Springs, was founded at the same time and incorporated.

In 1866 were incorporated the following academies: St. Joseph's School for Females at Natchez (Catholic); Pass Christian college, in Harrison county; East Mississippi Female college, at Aberdeen, and the Franklin Masonic high school, at Meadville.

The University of Columbus, located at Columbus, was established in 1867, by Profs. Thaddeus C. Belsher and George B. McClelland, under the name of the Columbus Male high school. An effort was made to raise the standard of scholarship above that of the schools of the country then in existence. In 1873 a charter was obtained under the present name. This was the most prosperous period of the school. In 1875 there were one hundred and twenty-two students, from four different states, five professors, a collegiate department and a commercial course. Since that time there has been a shrinkage in patronage. There is now only one teacher. The library contains two thousand volumes, and the building is the old Methodist church, a handsome brick structure;

The State Teachers' association was organized at Jackson in January, 1867. An earlier organization had been effected in the year 1838, which continued during four years. The association of 1867 was, therefore, the second. Its second meeting was in July, 1867, also at Jackson. Forty-two teachers were present. There was discussion of the educational funds, of a system of common schools, on music in education, on the education of the negro. This organization, however, dissolved in the anxieties and troubles of the reconstruction. The meeting appointed for 1868 was never held. On Wednesday, August 8, 1877, a third organization was effected at a meeting held in Jackson for that purpose, thirty-four teachers being present, of whom four were colored. This association has continued until the present time, meeting in Jackson every year during the Christmas holidays, and discussing all subjects of interest to the profession. Besides the state association, three minor associations, known respectively as the East Mississippi, the Northwestern and the South Central Teachers' associations, have been formed.

The Stonewall institute, at Arkabutla, in De Soto county, was at work in 1867 under Prof. R. L. McElree, with two assistants.

The Oak Hill academy, in De Soto county, was flourishing at the same time, under Prof. S. S. Robinson, as also were the Horn Lake academy, under E. R. Gill; the Sylvarena institute, in Smith county, under Prof. Lewis T. Fitzhugh, incorporated; the Hebron academy, in Rankin county, under R. A. Whitfield; the Union high school, at Pleasant Hill, under D. W. Bristol; the Anna Lee institute, under W. D. Howze; the Charleston seminary, in Tallahatchie county, under W. J. Blanks, and the Fair Lawn institute, at Jackson, under the Misses Moseley, incorporated in 1871, and a most useful school for many years, besides the schools and colleges described in the chapter in Volume I of this work, and in addition, of course, to many others, the names of which have not reached the writer. In this year were incorporated, also, the Ripley institute, of Tippah county; the Live Oak academy, of Jackson county; the Bluff Spring academy, of Tippah county; the Russell institute, at Hickory, in Newton county; the Zion Hill high school, of Jefferson county; the Verona Male academy (under Prof. Richard M. Leavell, now of the state university), and the Shubuta Female institute, of Clarke county.

The Peabody public school, located at Summit, in Pike county, was established in 1868 by the joint agreement of Dr. B. Sears, general agent of the Peabody fund, and the town. The former agreed to contribute $1,000 per annum from the fund, and the latter $2,000 per annum from taxation. Rev. Charles H. Otken was elected principal; Mrs. Josephine Newton, assistant. Pupils registered the first year, one hundred and forty-two; in the second, two hundred and twenty-nine pupils and three assistants. In 1870 a charter was obtained for the Peabody Educational association, which erected a good building, with capacity for five hundred pupils, at a cost of $7,000. A high school feature was adopted. Students of the third session, three hundred and forty-seven, of which forty-seven were in the high school; six teachers. A full collegiate curriculum was offered. The school was adopted as a part of the general free-school system of the state, and drew some revenue from that fund. Enrollment for 1871-2 (fourth session), three hundred and thirty-eight, of which sixty-two were high school. A large immigration was drawn to the town by the school. Factions arose, however, and led in 1875 to the abolition of tuition fees in the high school, and a still further reduction of income. The allowance from the Peabody fund was thereupon reduced to $500. The high school was then abolished in June, 1876, and from that date the school has been conducted as an ordinary grammar school. In June, 1877, the principal's salary having been reduced from $1,200 to $800, Dr Otken resigned and established Lea Female college.

The Starkville Female institute, in Oktibbeha county, was founded in 1869 by Mr. W. B. Montgomery and the Rev. T. G. Sellers. Dr. Sellers, a Baptist minister of high culture, has remained at the head of the institute from that time until now. Incorporated in 1873. Average attendance about one hundred and eighty; number of graduates, eighty-eight; value of property, about $10,000; library, about ten hundred volumes; eight assistant teachers.

The Blue Mountain Female college, at Blue Mountain, in Tippah county, was founded in 1869, by Gen. M. P. Lowrey, a prominent member of the Baptist church. It was opened in 1873; General Lowrey, principal, with two assistants. Fifty students were enrolled. From that time the school, being a favorite of the Baptists, and generously patronized by them, has steadily grown. In 1877 it was incorporated. In 1885 General Lowrey died, and was succeeded by his son, the Rev. W. T. Lowrey. The annual enrollment is now about two hundred and twenty-five, two-thirds of whom are boarders. The faculty number seventeen, prominent among whom is Rev. W. E. Berry, A. M., who became at the opening of the fourth session one of the proprietors, and professor of Latin and Greek, and has done much toward the success of the school. The school property has been enlarged and improved until it is valued at $25,000. The alumni number seventy-five. Instruction is given in music, art, and various industries; and there is a library of about six hundred volumes.

The Bethlehem academy, at Holly Springs, a Catholic institution, was established as a female school in 1869, by the Sisters of Charity, from Nazareth, Ky., and has been a prosperous and useful school until now.

The Tougaloo university, for colored youths, was founded in Madison county, on the co-educational plan, in 1869, by the American Missionary association. Designed to be an agricultural and mechanical school, five hundred acres of land, with buildings, were purchased and improved at an outlay of $25,000. In May, 1871, it was incorporated, and a normal department was organized. In January, 1872, this normal department was taken under the patronage of the state, the annual sum of $4,000 being appropriated for the support of it. This appropriation has been continued ever since that date (reduced in amount, however), except that none was made for the years 1878 and 1879. In 1873 a theological school was added. There is a music department, a library and readingroom, and a quarterly journal is published. The graduates have been thirty-seven, of whom eleven were women. The institution has received valuable aid from the Slater fund. Its property is valued at $60,000. The present faculty consists of the Rev. Frank G. Woodworth, president, and eleven teachers.

The common schools: At the teachers' meeting of January, 1867, resolutions were adopted, looking toward the establishment of a common school system, and of normal schools for the education of colored teachers, but the reconstruction measures interfered and stopped all action of a public character. The constitution of 1869 made it the duty of the legislature to establish a uniform system of free public schools, to be supported by taxation, or otherwise, for all children between the ages of five and twenty-one years. This injunction was obeyed by the act of July 4, 1870. Schools were ordered to be maintained for four months in each year, a state board of education was provided for, and a state superintendent of public education and a county superintendent in each county. At first there was much opposition to the system; more in some localities than in others. It was regarded as a system of taxation without representation, imposed by adventurers and plunderers, rather for the purpose of riveting their fetters on the people of the state than for any humanitarian object. However, that opposition gradually died away. The system, with some minor alterations and adjustments of details, has been not only preserved, but even enlarged, since the democratic party regained control of the state affairs. The new constitution of 1890 devotes to the common schools all the poll taxes collected in the respective counties, and such additional sum from the general funds in the state treasury as shall be necessary in order to maintain the schools for at least four months. Any county or separate school district is authorized to levy such further local taxes as may be desired for the purpose of continuing the schools beyond the four months. It is estimated that the amount needed to carry on the four months' term will be $800,000 per annum, to which must be added the further local levies for the prolonged terms. The expenditures for common schools for the year 1888-9 aggregated $1,117,110.82. The children enrolled were: whites, one hundred and forty-eight thousand four hundred and thirty-five; colored, one hundred and seventy-three thousand five hundred and fifty-two. The teachers employed were: whites, four thousand and eighteen; colored, three thousand and ninety-seven.

The separate district schools constitute a most important feature of the common-school system. The act of 1870 provided that any incorporated city of five thousand inhabitants might constitute itself a separate district for school purposes, with the privilege of raising and extending its school work, and with the power to collect special taxes to that end. Subsequent statutes have admitted smaller cities to this privilege, until now any town of one thousand or more inhabitants may exercise it. Under this plan numerous such schools have been established at intervals, and that work is still going on. Aberdeen, Bay St. Louis, Biloxi, Brookhaven, Canton, Coffeeville, Corinth, Crystal Springs, Greenville, Grenada, Hazlehurst, Holly Springs, Jackson, Kosciusko, Macon, Meridian, Oxford, Okolona, Port Gibson, Sardis, Starkville, Tupelo, Water Valley, Wesson, West Point, Winona and Yazoo City have established fine schools, in many instances at an outlay for buildings and equipment of from $25,000 to $50,000. So, also, the existing schools, already mentioned, at Brandon, Columbus, Natchez, Summit and Vicksburg have been brought into this system, and form parts of it, although themselves founded long before that system was inaugurated. The general plan of this class of schools is, the division into annual grades (from six to thirteen in number), and the extension of the free term from four months, as in the ordinary school, to terms ranging from seven to ten months. Several of them are provided with large corps of teachers, and are ready to prepare boys for the sophomore classes of college, and to carry young ladies to a very respectable graduation.

The Toccopola academy, in Pontotoc county, was founded in 1870 by W. B. Gilmer; incorporated in 1873 as the Toccopola college. A music department was established, and seven teachers were employed. Patronized from five states, about one-fourth of the students being boarders. Highest attendance, two hundred and three. This was a most useful school for many years. Noteworthy as being the only academy that ever sent a youth to the university prepared for the junior class, and it sent two. Now under J. W. Furr, B. S., of the university.

The Cato high school, of Rankin county, was established in 1870. William Buchanan was principal. He was followed in 1873 by P. B. Bridges, and he, in 1876, by H. M. Long. This also was long a useful school.

The Shaw university, at Holly Springs, now called Rust university by the act of 1890, was established in 1870 by the Mississippi conference of the Methodist Episcopal church, for the education of colored youths, and was incorporated in the same year. It has been in operation, more or less successfully, ever since that time. It has a commercial and a medical school; also a preparatory academy located at Meridian. Rev. C. E. Libby is president, and the faculty is composed of nine members. There are fifteen alumni. Females are admitted.

The State Normal school, at Holly Springs, also for colored youths, was established by the state in 1870. For two years the normal department of Shaw university was leased; afterward distinct quarters were provided. Professor Gorman was first principal; in the second year Miss M. E. Hunter. She was followed in 1875 by W. B. Highgate, and he, in 1886, by the present principal, J. H. Henderson. The average attendance has been, of males, eighty-three; of females, forty-three. The appropriations made by the state aggregate $96,950. The grounds embrace about five acres, and, with the building of brick, cost $10,000. There is a good chemical and physical laboratory, and a library of about three thousand volumes. Incorporated in 1890.

The Alcorn Agricultural and Mechanical college, at Oakland, in Claiborne county, was also established by the state for the education of colored youths, in 1871. The property of old Oakland college was purchased for it at a cost of $42,500. Designed for higher education, it opened February 7, 1872, under the presidency of ex-Senator Hiram R. Revels, who had two assistants. An agricultural department was added in 1872. In 1873-4 the faculty had increased to nine members, and a superintendent of mechanic arts was added. In 1882 J. H. Burrus, of Tennessee, was made president, and yet holds that office. In 1884 females were admitted, and more or less of them have attended on each subsequent session. The attendance for the last ten years has averaged one hundred and eighty-four. The graduates number forty-six. The appropriations by the state have been as follows: For the years 1871 to 1874, $175,000; from 1875 to 1891, $95,640; total, $270,640. To this must be added the interest from the agricultural land-scrip fund, being the congressional donation, which is $5,678.75 per annum; total, $116,991.25.

In 1871 the Masonic Male and Female institute was flourishing at Pleasant Hill, in De Soto county, under Prof. S. B. Pankey, and in 1872 under D. W. Bristol. In the same year the following academies were incorporated: The Coffeeville Female seminary of Yalobusha county; the St. Joseph academy, of Hancock county; the Baptist Female seminary, at West Point, Clay county; the Guntown Male and Female institute, of Lee county; the Belmont academy, of Carroll county.

The Kosciusko Male and Female institute, at Kosciusko, in Attala county, was founded in 1871 by the Methodist church at that place. It had no endowment, but at the first a little aid from the Peabody fund; property worth about $2,500; attendance for 1872, one hundred and seventy. In 1874 the institute was taken into the connection of the North Mississippi conference and the Rev. W. P. Barton made principal. In 1879 Mr. Barton was succeeded by the Rev. T. A. S. Adams, who had three assistants. Incorporated in 1878. In 1884 Dr. Adams resigned, and shortly afterward the institute became extinct.

The East Mississippi Female college, located in Meridian, Lauderdale county, was established in 1871 under the auspices of the Mississippi conference of the Methodist Episcopal Church South. Incorporated in 1872. Prof. S. P. Rice, of Florence, Ala., was first president. In 1873 he was followed by the Rev. John W. Adkisson, of Shelbyville, Mo., who remained in charge until 1883. Under his administration the college so prospered that the faculty was increased from three assistants to six. Accepting the presidency of Central college, in Texas, he was followed by the Rev. A. D. McVoy, and he, in turn, was succeeded in 1888 by the Rev. R. M. Saunders, former president of Norfolk college, Virginia. The alumni are one hundred and twenty in number; attendance about one hundred and fifty, from five states. The course of study embraces the following schools: English language and literature, including Anglo-Saxon; ancient languages, modern languages, mathematics, history, physical sciences, mental and moral science, music and fine arts, industrial arts. There is a good library; also a fine collection of minerals; also a good scientific apparatus. The buildings are of brick and are commodious. The faculty includes eleven members.

The Slate Springs Male and Female college, located at Slate Springs, in Calhoun county, was established in 1872 by Mr. Fuller Fox, with two assistants. Incorporated in 1873. Buildings with accommodation for three hundred students were erected and a music department added.

The Paine high school, at Booneville, in Prentiss county, was established in 1872 by the Iuka, Verona, Columbus and Macon district conferences of the Methodist Episcopal Church South. Citizens of Booneville subscribed $10,000 toward the necessary funds. The building was completed in 1874 and the school opened in September, with Prof. C. M. Verdell as principal. Meanwhile the financial crash of 1873 caused the loss of much of the subscription. In 1876 the property was sold for a debt due the builders and was purchased by the town. Judge J. P. Povall was then chosen principal and the school became a mixed school for two years. In 1878 George W. Turner and W. R. Davenport became joint principals. In 1881 John W. Johnson, A. B., of the university, became principal, and under him the institution was chartered as the Johnson institute. In 1886 Prof. H. L. Atkinson was elected principal, and one year afterward Prof. J. C. Benedict, of Ohio.

In 1872 the Coldwater Male and Female institute was in successful operation in De Soto county, under the supervision of Maj. E. Porter, and the Masonic institute at Senatobia, under Mr. Samuel F. Massey.

In 1873 the Mississippi Military institute was in operation under E. H. Murphy, superintendent, at West Point, Miss. It was incorporated in 1875, and was removed to Aberdeen. It registered one hundred and nine students in the session of 1875–6. Shortly afterward it seems to have been removed to Pass Christian, Miss., where it was maintained for a few years. From this place Colonel Murfee went to Arkansas to accept a chair in the university, and the school became extinct.

In 1873, also, the Brandon Male high school, under Gen. J. A. Smith, as also was the Jackson high school, under George W. McLaurin, was in successful operation, and the following academies were incorporated: The Corinth Female college, of Alcorn county; the Langston school, at Holly Springs, the Colfax institute, at Spring Valley, Choctaw county; the Baldwin Female college, of Prentiss county; the Educational society of South Mississippi and East Louisiana, and the Summit commercial college, both of Summit, in Pike county; and the Mississippi Female institute, for colored girls, now located at Clinton, Miss.

In 1874 the Sardis Female college, of Panola county, and the Abbeville Female college, of Lafayette county, were incorporated; and the Mississippi Female college, under Miss Josephine Freeman, her sister, and a Miss Morgan, was in good condition at Jackson, being taught at St. Andrew's church.

In 1875 the Stonewall-Jackson institute was organized at Harperville, in Scott county. In 1881 it was incorporated under the name of Harperville college. In 1884 the Hunt and Huddleston College Faculty association was incorporated, with power to maintain a principal college and establish preparatory and high schools as auxiliaries. Harperville college has about one hundred and twenty-five students annually, drawn from four states; about three-fifths collegiate. It is a mixed school, and offers three degrees, viz.: B. A., B. S., and M. E. L. There is a good apparatus, and a library of about seven hundred and fifty volumes.

In 1875, also, were incorporated the West Point Female institute, of Clay county; the Brookhaven Male Academical association, of Lincoln county; and the Southern Christian institute, near Edwards, in Hinds county. The last is a school for colored people of both sexes, with an industrial and a normal feature, established at a cost of about $10,000 by the Christian church, with a special view to the preparation of young colored men for its ministry It was opened in 1882. Randall Faurot was the first president. He died in October, 1882, and was followed by Jephtha Hobbs. The attendance grew to about three hundred, but the free school was discontinued in 1887, and the attendance was thereby much reduced.

The Lea Female college, at Summit, in Pike county, was established in 1877, by Rev. Charles H. Otken, and was incorporated that same year. The attendance has averaged about sixty-five per annum, of which about one-half were of collegiate grade, and about one-third were boarders from a distance. The faculty has five members. Music and accounts are taught.

The Corinth Female college (now existing), of Alcorn county, was founded in 1877, by Mary C. Conally, with two assistants. It was incorporated in 1878. In 1887 Miss N. Lena Elgin became president. The attendance is a little over one hundred per annum, of which about forty per cent. are of collegiate grade, and about one-eighth boarders. There is a framed two-story building; property worth about $4,000. This school works in conjunction with the free-school system of Corinth, as part of it.

In 1877 the Calhoun institute was established at Macon, and the following schools, all for females, were incorporated: The Elisha Calloway Female institute at Macon, in Noxubee county; the Edgworth Hall Female college at Aberdeen, in Monroe county; the Sardis Female college in Panola county, and the North Mississippi college at Verona, in Lee county.

Zealy's seminary, by Dr. J. T. Zealy, was at work in Jackson in 1878, with a full corps of teachers. It was incorporated that year, and so were the following: The Iuka Presbyterian Male high school of Tishomingo county; the Beth Eden collegiate institute, of Winston county; the Batesville high school, of Panola county; the Grange Agricultural school, of Coahoma county; the name of the last being changed to the Clarksdale high school, by the act of 1890.

The Agricultural and Mechanical college, located at Starkville, in Oktibbeha county, was incorporated February 28, 1878. It was the outcome of an act of congress passed July 2, 1862, whereby was donated to each state, which should provide colleges for the benefit of agriculture and the mechanic arts, an amount of public land equal to 30,000 acres for each representative and senator in congress. The half of that fund, amounting to $113,575, was secured to this institution by its charter; on which sum is realized an annual interest income of $4,928.75. In addition to that income the state has made the following appropriations for the support of the college: In 1880, $85,000; in 1882, $120,000; in 1884, $65,000; in 1886, $50,000; in 1888, $35,320, in 1890, $58,760. The college was opened, after the purchase of the necessary farm and the erection of the proper buildings, in the fall of 1880. The average attendance has been three hundred and fifteen students per annum. Only Mississippi boys are received, since they exhaust the capacity of the institution. The military methods are followed. The literary schools are divided into a preparatory department and a college. In the college are taught drawing, bookkeeping, English history, rhetoric, mathematics, natural philosophy, natural history, chemistry, political economy, constitution of the United States, moral science, astronomy, civil engineering, literature, physiology, veterinary science, in addition to the schools of agriculture, horticulture, biology, dairy husbandry and military science, which the undergraduates are required to attend. The academic building is of brick, 127x70 feet, and three stories high; the dormitory, brick also, and three stories high, is 275x140 feet, with capacity for two hundred and fifty students. There are, besides, a chemical laboratory, a mess hall, residences for the professors, and a large outfit of barns, stables, etc. The property is valued at $188,617. From its foundation the college has been under the presidency of Gen. Stephen D. Lee, whose able management has extended its reputation far beyond the limits of the state. The faculty is usually composed of about eighteen professors and assistants. There is a readingroom and a library of about three thousand volumes. Connected with the college is an agricultural experiment station, established under the act of congress of March 2, 1887, and supported by annual payments from the United States. This station is a department of the college, but has its distinct functions, and its separate working force and equipment. At the same time the farming department of the college proper is much relieved by it, both of work and expense, and it furnishes a continual and valuable object lesson to the students. The station has published one annual report and ten bulletins, which are sent free of charge to all farmers of the state who apply for them. Already the influence of the Agricultural and Mechanical has been sensibly felt in the agriculture of Mississippi, and if no short-sighted policy cripples it, great things may be expected in the near future.

In 1879 and prior thereto St. Margaret's hall, a boarding and day school for girls, was successfully conducted in Jackson by Mrs. S. B. Ware. In 1888 Mrs. Lucy S. Smith was principal.

The Holly Springs normal institute was founded in 1879 by Maj. T. C. Anderson, using the property of the old university of Holly Springs. It was incorporated. There were four assistants. The attendance of pupils ranged from one hundred and fifty to three hundred, and a few of them took collegiate grade.

The Poplar Springs normal college in Union county was founded in 1880 by Jasper N. Davis. Incorporated in 1886, the first class graduated in that year. There are teachers', business, scientific and classical courses. J. M. Langston and D. H. Davis are co-principals, with three assistants. The attendance of pupils is about two hundred. The school property is worth about $3,000. The library is valued at $1,000 additional, and there is a scientific apparatus.

In 1880 were incorporated the Waverly institute, of Byhalia, in Marshall county, the Dido Male and Female academy, the Prewitt Center Ridge academy, the West Point seminary, and the Carrollton Female college. The last is now prospering under the presidency of the Rev. Z. T. Leavell, a Baptist minister.

The Okolona Male academy was flourishing in 1880, with G. W. Turner and W. R. Harper as principals, while the Okolona Female college was prospering under the presidency of Prof. J. G. Deupree, now of Mississippi college. In the same year Anselm H. Jayne established the Jackson high school, and the Rev. L. M. Stone founded the Shuqualak Female college. Invested in the last institution is about $10,000. There is a music department, also one of art.

The Sallis Male and Female academy was founded in 1881; P. W. Corr, principal. Incorporated in 1886.

The Riverview seminary, Mr. and Mrs. Snead, principals, was founded in Vicksburg in 1881. It still continues to thrive.

The Iuka normal institute, of Tishomingo county, was organized in 1882 by Profs. H. A. Dean and John Neuhardt. Two well-known schools, the Iuka Male academy and the Iuka Female institute, had been previously conducted in that place. Their buildings were leased for a term of years by the normal institute. This school opened with a faculty of six. It has been very prosperous. The attendance has averaged about two hundred and eighty. There are eight departments: Primary, preparatory, training, commercial, scientific, classic, music and fine arts. In 1885 it was incorporated, and Professor Dean became sole proprietor. The property is valued at $7,000, and there is besides a good scientific apparatus and a library of seven hundred volumes.

The Mississippi normal college was founded at Troy, in Pontotoc county, in 1882, by H. B. Abernethy. Incorporated in 1884. In 1888 it was removed to Houston in Chickasaw county. Average attendance about two hundred and forty. It is of the same type as the preceding school. Telegraphy, typewriting and phonography are taught. The faculty comprises eleven members. There is some apparatus, and a library of three hundred volumes. The school property, formerly occupied by the Houston Male and Female academies, is owned by the town, and is leased to Professor Abernethy for twenty-five years.

The Ashland academy, of Benton county, was established in 1882 by a joint stock company. Rev. Enoch Wines was the first principal, with two assistants. Incorporated in 1888. Graded into primary, intermediate and collegiate. Music is taught. The attendance has ranged from forty to one hundred. Prof. W. P. Gunn is now principal, with two assistants.

The Maury institute, an excellent female school at Holly Springs, was established in 1882, by Miss E. D. Watson, incorporated in 1884, and continues to flourish.

In 1882, also, the following institutions were incorporated: the Palo Alto academy, of Clay county; the Guntown Male and Female academy, of Lee county; the Blue Mountain academy, of Tippah county; the Camp Ground academy, of Jonesboro, in Tippah county; the Louisville Male and Female seminary, of Winston county; the Fannin high school, of Rankin county, and the Rose Hill institute, of Jasper county.

Kavanaugh college, at Holmesville, in Pike county, was founded, in 1884, by the Rev. Walter Featherstun, and shortly afterward was taken under the patronage of the Methodist Episcopal Church South. It was designed to accomplish a missionary work by carrying education to a large class of youth of the poorer country who were unable to seek it away from home. A mixed school; and music and art were taught. The faculty comprised four members. The attendance ranged from one hundred to one hundred and fifty. The property was valued at about $1,500. In 1889 the institution was sold to the Baptists, Mr. Featherstun taking charge of Edward McGehee college.

The Union Church high school, of Jefferson county, was founded in 1884 by the Rev. C. W. Grafton, a Presbyterian minister, and an A. B. of the State university. A most prosperous and useful school, now having about one hundred and fifty scholars. There are primary, academic and collegiate departments. Music is taught. Boys and girls admitted. The faculty are five in number.

The Montrose high school, of Jasper county, was founded in 1884 by W. B. Massey, with one assistant. There are now three. The attendance has ranged from seventy-seven to one hundred and sixteen. The three departments of primary, preparatory and collegiate exist. Incorporated in 1887. Patronized by the Brandon district of the Methodist Episcopal Church South.

The Pittsboro Male and Female college was founded, in 1884, by private subscriptions; W. Wyatt principal, with three assistants. Incorporated in 1886, and presided over then by Prof. George L. Gordon. This gentleman called the school the Calhoun Graded Normal college, and published a catalogue under that name. Rev. William Rivers, B. A., of the University of Mississippi, was president in 1889. Attendance about one hundred and seventy-five. Music is taught. Property valued at $2,000.

The Industrial institute and college, for white girls of Mississippi, was chartered in 1884. Miss Sallie E. Reneau, of Grenada, first agitated in this state the question of state aid for the higher education of girls. Her labors began in 1856, and were prosecuted at intervals until 1874, but without any substantial success. In 1879 Mrs. Annie C. Peyton, of Hazlehurst, took up the cause. She had many zealous and influential colaborers, and after several discouraging failures success crowned their efforts in 1884. The legislature appropriated $40,000 for the years 1884-5. To win the location of it the city of Columbus donated $50,000 of city bonds and the property of the old Columbus Female institute. The Industrial institute and college was opened in October, 1885, under the presidency of Richard W. Jones, ex-professor of chemistry of the university. Its entire success was at once assured, and its career of prosperity has been unbroken. The Industrial institute and college is designed to fit women for particular spheres and lines of work, and to open up to her new avenues to employment and to wider and more varied modes of usefulness. Its organization contemplates collegiate education, normal training and industrial preparation. Under the last head are taught music, oil painting, free-hand drawing, designing, wood carving, modeling, crayon portraiture, hammering in thin metals, decoration of porcelain ware, needle work (fancy and plain), dressmaking, phonography, typewriting, bookkeeping, telegraphy, practical printing and housekeeping. The Normal school and the college are fully developed and of high grade. The attendance of pupils is on scholarships awarded by the county superintendents of education in the several counties. Of these there are four hundred and six, one half with the privilege of board in the dormitories, and one-half without such privilege. The latter class of students get board out in the town. The scholarships are distributed among the counties of the state as follows: Of those with privilege of board in dormitory, the counties of Bolivar, Claiborne, Coahoma, Covington, Greene, Grenada, Issaquena, Le Flore, Perry, Quitman, Sharkey, Sunflower, Tunica, Washington, Wayne and Wilkinson, have one each; Adams, Amite, Benton, Choctaw, Clay, Hancock, Holmes, Jasper, Jefferson, Lawrence, Madison, Marion, Montgomery, Neshoba, Noxubee, Oktibbeha, Simpson, Tallahatchie, Warren and Winston, two each; Alcorn, Clarke, De Soto, Franklin, Harrison, Jackson, Kemper, Leake, Lincoln, Rankin, Scott, Smith, Tate, Union, Webster and Yalobusha, three each; Carroll, Chickasaw, Hinds, Itawamba, Jones, Lafayette, Lowndes, Marshall, Newton, Pike, Pontotoc, Prentiss, Tippah, Tishomingo and Yazoo, four each; Attala, Lauderdale and Lee, five each; Calhoun, Copiah, Monroe and Panola, six each. Of scholarships without privilege of board in the dormitory each county has a similar number.

Further appropriations have been made as follows: In 1886, $59,875.50; in 1888, $45,177.50; in 1890, $50,000. Large additions have been made to the buildings. The dormitory is a massive brick structure, three stories and a mansard high, one hundred and seventy-five feet front, and running back one hundred and fifty feet. It has a large and well arranged, well lighted and ventilated diningroom, capacious kitchen for instruction in cookery, washingroom, room for soapmaking, boilerroom, ironingroom, bathroom, waterclosets, seventy-six well-built and ventilated rooms for sleeping, and a parlor. Connected with this building by a covered passage is the new chapel building, which is three stories high, well and strongly built, which has a large assembly room, president's office, secretary's office, eight recitation rooms, chemical and physical laboratories and storage rooms, all arranged with full regard to convenience, health and efficient work.

In 1878 President Jones resigned to accept the presidency of Emory and Henry college, and Charles H. Cocke, of Columbus, was elected to succeed him. In March, 1890, President Cocke resigned, and the duties of his office were temporarily discharged to Miss M. J. S. Callaway, mistress of mathematics. In June, 1890, Prof. Arthur H. Beals, of Paducah, Ky., was elected president for one year. In June, 1891, he was not a candidate for re-election. The office has not, at this time, been filled. The faculty comprises twenty members besides the president.

The Cool Springs academy, of Cool Springs, in Union county, was incorporated in 1884.

The Buena Vista Normal college, of Chickasaw county, was chartered in 1885. It was very prosperous for a time under J. S. and L. T. Dickey, of Kentucky. In 1887-8 the attendance of pupils was three hundred and two, and the faculty numbered nine. Music and art were taught. It was patronized from seven states, and from thirty-nine counties in Mississippi. In 1889, however, it had retrograded, and the faculty was reduced to four. Profs. W. S. Burks, of Texas, and W. M. Morrison, of Virginia, then leased the property, and organized a new faculty. In 1891 Rev. E. A. Smith and Prof. R. L. McDonnold took charge. The standard has been raised under every new administration, and this school has few equals in the state.

The Phœnix high school, of Yazoo county, was established in 1885, with R. W. Jones as principal, and one assistant. M. I. Bass became principal in 1888. There are two buildings of moderate cost, also an endowment income of about $125 per annum, and a rental of $300 from school lands. The attendance is about one hundred.

The Pass Christian institute for girls, under the auspices of the Protestant Episcopal church, was incorporated in 1885. Its president was and is the Rev. H. C. Mayer. Attendance about sixty, drawn from four states. Music, phonography, typewriting, telegraphy and dressmaking are taught, in addition to the usual studies. There are seven teachers and four lecturers, in addition to the president; among the latter, Bishop Thompson. This school is beautifully located on the Mississippi sound. It has a library of about four hundred volumes.

The Liberty Male and Female college, of Amite county, was incorporated in 1886; founded by J. R. Edmunds, with two assistants. The attendance is about one hundred. There are seven departments—the model, normal, business, music, art, preparatory and collegiate. The present faculty are J. H. Patterorn, principal, and four assistants. Property valued at $15,000.

In 1886 were also incorporated the following schools: The Durant academy, of Holmes county; the Gibson high school, at Rienzi, Alcorn county; the Knoxville White Male and Female academy, at Knoxville, Franklin county.

In 1887 the Scooba high school, of Kemper county, was established; F. E. Porter, principal, with two assistants. The attendance of the first year was fifty-five. Music is taught. There is a good building with four rooms. Incorporated in 1888. At the same time the Fairview White Male and Female institute was flourishing at Binnsville, in Kemper county, and was incorporated in 1888. The same year witnessed, also, these incorporations: The Mount Carmel normal college, of Covington county; the Jefferson High School association, of Carroll county; the Tombigbee normal institute at Fulton, Itawamba county; the Philadelphia high school of Neshoba county; the Deasonville high school, of Yazoo county; the Providence Male and Female college, at Nettleton, Lee county; the Newton Male and Female college, of Newton county; and the Centre high school of De Soto county.

The Houlka high school, of Chickasaw county, was established in this year; Rev. E. A. Smith, principal, until June, 1891. Incorporated in 1890, its growth has been slow, but steady; and it has more advanced students, and a higher moral tone, than many institutions of far greater pretentions.

Banner college, located at Banner, in Calhoun county, was established in 1887, and incorporated in 1888. Cortez P. Gilmer, M. A., of University of Mississippi, was president, with four assistants. There was a collegiate course, and one of commerce. Music was taught also. Attendance about one hundred and seventy-five.

The Mississippi normal high school, of Troy, in Pontotoc county, orginated in 1888, from the removal of the Mississippi normal college to Houston. A school was continued at Troy, under the name above given, and under the management of B. M. Bell.

The Lexington normal school was established at Lexington, in Holmes county, by Prof. Dickey; was formerly of the Buena Vista normal college in 1888–9. It has been a flourishing school.

The Meridian normal college, located at Poplar Springs, in Lauderdale county, two miles from Meridian, was established in 1888 by W. E. Johnson and Rev. R. F. Johnson, with seven members of the faculty. The first session enrolled one hundred pupils. There is a philosophical apparatus, and a library of about one thousand volumes.

The St. Aloysius Commercial college was established October 16, 1879, by the Brothers of the Sacred Heart, of Vicksburg, Miss. The present building is a large three-story brick structure at Grove and First North streets, and the corner-stone was laid in the month of June, 1878, by Rev. Father McManus, and was completed at a cost of about $18,000. It comprises eight classrooms, and various other room accommodations for two hundred and fifty pupils, and the school, at the present time, has all the pupils it can accommodate. They have primary, scientific and commercial courses, and also teach modern languages. This admirably conducted educational institution is under the charge of Brother Charles, who was one of the original brothers who assisted in arranging the course. The establishment was chartered in 1882, and is acknowledged to be one of the finest institutions in the state, if not in the South. It is devoted to the education of boys and young men, and many of the graduates have reflected great credit upon its management.

Millsaps college, established by the two conferences of the Methodist Episcopal Church South in Mississippi, was incorporated in 1890. The munificence of Maj. R. W. Millsaps, of Jackson, who contributed $50,000 to the institution, on condition that the church should bestow a similar sum, and the zeal and influence of Bishop C. B. Galloway, who canvassed the state and procured subscriptions wherewith to meet the offer of Major Millsaps, have equipped this infant college with more than $100,000 of endowment. Efforts are still making by those gentlemen, on the same terms, to add $50,000 more. The people of the city of

Jackson, by subscription, have donated property and money to the extent of about $40,000, for site and buildings, to induce the location of the college in their midst, and this has been done. It is expected to have the new institution at active work by the fall of 1892.

In addition to the institutions already mentioned, the following were incorporated in 1890: The Castalian Springs graded institute, the Goodman high school, the Ebenezer high school, and the Pickens high school, all of Holmes county; Harper's Baptist college, near Gloster, in Amite county; the Hickory White Male and Female institute, of Hickory, in Newton county; the Pleasant Hill high school, of Jasper county; the Hebron high school, of Lawrence county; the Cedar Bluff high school, of Clay county; the Bellefountaine Male and Female high school, of Webster county; the Shannon graded institute, and the Saltillo high school, of Lee county; the Louisville normal school, and the Winston normal high school, at Plattsville, both of Winston county; the Waynesboro normal institute and college, of Wayne county, and old Myrtle normal college.

Also at this time (1890) the following schools not yet mentioned were flourishing. Of these, some are schools of many years' standing, but the exact dates of the foundation of them are not obtainable. The Lumberton high school, of Marion county; the McBride school, of Jefferson county; the Cascilla Male and Female high school, of Tallahatchie county; the Capital Commercial college, of Wyatt and Sharp, at Jackson; the Rural Hill high school, of Winston county; the Decatur college, of Newton county; the French Camps academy, conducted for now many years by the Rev. James A. Mecklin, with great success, in Choctaw county, and the Central Mississippi institute for girls, also at French Camps, conducted by J. A. Sanderson.

It only remains to say that it is not claimed that this chapter and the corresponding chapter in Volume I exhaust the subject of education in Mississippi. Scores of schools of great merit have probably been left without mention. The labor of a lifetime even would have been insufficient for the accumulation of material for an exhaustive history, for the reasons: first, that all record and memory of many are lost, and secondly, that the schools change so constantly that a chapter complete to-day would be incomplete to-morrow.

It is claimed that these two chapters come far nearer to a complete history than any ever before given.

CHAPTER XII.

RELIGIOUS HISTORY OF MISSISSIPPI.

THE record of the Protestant Episcopal church in Mississippi, of which we are asked to write an historical sketch, goes back to the Spanish domination, when what is now the state of Mississippi formed part of the Natchez district of the province of west Florida.

The Rev. Adam Cloud, a Virginian by birth, settled on St. Catherine's creek, in Adams county, in 1792. Though all public worship not under control of the Roman *curia* was still interdicted by the Spanish government, he baptized the children and buried the dead of the Protestant families in his neighborhood, preaching also an occasional sermon and ministering as best he could to their spiritual needs. At the end of three years, however, he was arrested, put in irons and sent to New Orleans, to be tried for preaching, baptizing and marrying people contrary to the laws of the existing government. After long delay Governor Carondelet submitted to him two alternatives. Either to be sent to Spain to be tried by an ecclesiastical court, under the specified allegations, or to leave forever the Spanish dominions. Too familiar with the history of the Spanish inquisition to risk himself before one of its courts on a charge of heretical preaching, he chose the latter alternative, and spent the next twenty years of his life in South Carolina and Georgia. In 1816 he returned to Mississippi and settled in Jefferson county. In 1820 he organized the parish of Christ church, at Church Hill, in that county, of which he remained rector for many years.

Mr. Cloud was followed by the Rev. James A. Fox, the Rev. James Pilmore and other devoted missionaries, and congregations were established and churches erected wherever an opening was afforded.

On the 17th of May, 1826, the first convention of the Protestant Episcopal church in the state of Mississippi met in Trinity church, Natchez. There were present of the clergy the Rev. Albert A. Muller, rector of that parish; the Rev. James Pilmore, rector of Christ church, Church Hill; the Rev. James A. Fox, of St. Paul's, Woodville, and the Rev. John W. Cloud, of St. John's, Port Gibson. The Rev. Adam Cloud, residing then in Jefferson county, was not present.

The lay delegates to this primary convention were John I. Griffith, Joseph Dunbar, Levin R. Marshall, Robert Moore, A. P. Merrill, M. D., and Col. Henry W. Huntingdon, of Natchez; Gen. John Ioor, Judge Randolph and Judge Prosser, from Woodville; Hon. Joshua G. Clarke, chancellor of the state, and J. W. Foote, from Port Gibson, and Col. James G. Wood and Dr. S. G. Cloud, from Christ church, Jefferson county. As no other congregations are mentioned in the journal of this convention, or in that of the one succeeding, it is proper to conclude that the only then existing parishes were those of Natchez, Church Hill, Woodville and Port Gibson.

We have seen, however, that the Rev. Adam Cloud had been actively at work in this frontier territory since 1820, and that the work had also been prosecuted by other devoted missionaries of the church for some years prior to this movement for a diocesan organization. In the proceedings of this convention we read that the Rev. Mr. Pilmore arrived in Mississippi in 1822, and finding several families in Natchez and the vicinity attached to the communion of the Episcopal church, organized a congregation. Steps were at once taken for the erection of a church, which was commenced in May, 1822, upon a large and expensive scale and completed in 1825. The number of communicants reported for this parish, then as now, numerically the strongest in the diocese, was thirty-five.

The Rev. James A. Fox, the minister of St. Paul's, Woodville, reports to the convention that he began his ministerial duties in this state in August, 1823, at the village of Pinckneyville, in Wilkinson county, and soon after visited Woodville, in the same county, and held divine service. At Woodville he found a considerable number of families attached to the church, and by the spring of 1825 a very neat frame building had been erected, which stands to-day, unaltered as to its identity, a monument to the honesty and thoroughness of the workmen of sixty years ago. In May, 1825, the Rev. Mr. Fox, who, after Mr. Cloud, seems to have been the pioneer in the work of the diocese, visited Port Gibson, in Claiborne county, where a parish was organized under the name of St. John's (changed many years after to St. James; for what reason does not appear), which was represented in the primary convention of the diocese. He visited also Jefferson county "for the purpose of inquiring into the state of a society of the Episcopalians formerly established in the neighborhood of Greenville." He found their number much diminished by deaths and removals; yet Christ church of Church Hill, in Jefferson county, was represented in the first convention and still remains in union with the council.

In striking contrast to the methods adopted in the latter days, and elsewhere, these four feeble parishes, the strongest of them numbering thirty-five communicants, proceeded to organize the diocese of Mississippi, and to elect "two clerical and two lay delegates, who may represent this diocese (sic) in the general convention of the Protestant Episcopal church in the United States of America, to be held in Philadelphia in November next." The gentlemen elected, says the journal, were "the Rev. Albert A. Muller and the Rev. James A. Fox, of the clergy, and Levin Covington and J. W. Foote, Esqs., of the laity." They also adopted a constitution and canons for the government of the church in the "diocese of Mississippi," and set forth a declaration of conformity to the constitution and canons of the Protestant Episcopal church in the United States of America. Having done this the convention adjourned to meet again in Trinity church, Natchez, on the 2d of May, 1827.

The president of this first convention of the diocese was the Rev. Albert A. Muller, and the secretary the Rev. James Pilmore. In his closing address to the convention the president said: "But a few years have passed away since in this place the lawless savages of the forest held their feasts of revelry and meditated their hostile plans of revenge and murder, and now a Christian people stand in their places devising suitable means for the advancement of that gospel which has brought 'peace on earth and good will toward men.' May we not then in regard to this opening of our church, adopt the forcible and appropriate language of the Psalmist, 'Thou, O God, hast brought a vine out of Egypt; Thou hast cast out the heathen and planted it. And may we not hope that its fruit may cover the hills, and its limbs be like the goodly cedar, whose boughs shall extend to the sea, and its branches unto the river.'"

The brief space allotted to this sketch will not suffer us to follow very closely the growth of the vine planted in a faith so sublime and a hope so heroic. We pass on to the year 1832, when the dioceses of Alabama and Mississippi, and the clergy and churches in the state of Louisiana, were authorized to associate and join in the election of a bishop. A convention was accordingly held in Christ church, New Orleans, on the 4th and 5th days of March, 1835, which resulted in the election of the Rev. Francis L. Hawks, D.D., rector of St. Thomas' church, New York, as bishop of the southwestern diocese. Dr. Hawks, however, declined his election and the project fell through.

In 1838 we find the Rt.-Rev. Leonidas Polk, missionary bishop of Arkansas, exercising Episcopal jurisdiction in the diocese of Mississippi by authority of the general convention, an arrangement which continued in force until the spring of 1841, when Bishop Polk, having been elected to the episcopate of Louisiana, the Rt.-Rev. James H. Otey, bishop of Tennessee, was by the convention of that year chosen provisional bishop of Mississippi. Bishop Otey sustained this relation to the diocese until the election of Bishop Green, although in the meantime more than one attempt was made by the brave and struggling diocese to elect a bishop of her own. In his address to the convention of 1844, Bishop Otey strongly urged the election of a diocesan for Mississippi. He tells the convention that "eight years ago there was not more than one regular settler and officiating minister in the diocese." In the journal of 1844 we find seventeen names on the clergy list and the number of parishes increased to twenty. In accordance with this urgent desire and recommendation of the provisional bishop, the convention proceeded to an election, and the Rev. Francis L. Hawks, D.D., rector of Holly Springs, Miss., was chosen. The general convention, however, failed to confirm the election of Dr. Hawks, and Bishop Otey resumed charge of the diocese.

The twenty-third annual convention met in Natchez May 17, 1849. Bishop Otey having again resigned the office of provisional bishop, requesting to be relieved for reasons of increasing infirmity as well as accumulated labor, the convention proceeded, on Saturday, May 19, to the election of a bishop, which resulted in the unanimous choice of the Rev. William Mercer Green, D. D., of the diocese of North Carolina, who also was by agreement to become rector of Trinity church, Natchez. The Rev. Dr. Green accepted his election, and was consecrated on Sunday the 24th of February, 1850, being the festival of St. Matthias. The Rt.-Rev. James H. Otey, late provisional bishop, was the consecrator. He was assisted by Bishops Polk, Cobb and Freeman, all of whom had at some time performed Episcopal offices in the diocese. The journal of the first convention over which Bishop Green presided shows a clergy list of seventeen names and a roll of twenty-four parishes.

"The Rt.-Rev. William Mercer Green, D. D., LL.D., the first bishop of Mississippi, was sixty and six years in the ministry of Christ and His church. He was thirty-seven years in the episcopate, and in spite of the burden and weight of age, and the remonstrance of friends and sudden illness falling oft upon him, and perils of travel and inclement seasons, and of exposure, he pressed on with a resolute and heroic courage, fondly hoping to die in the very act of duty. He was born May 2, 1798. He died the 13th of February, 1887, in the midst of his kindred and friends, and in the shadow of the great university he helped to found. He was buried in the capitol of his own diocese, by his successor in office, his clergy and his people, the triumphant song of the church filling all that quiet grove in which we laid him. *
Let us look for a moment at the period of his episcopate. He was consecrated in February, 1850. Then followed eleven years, which we may call day, in which a man ought

to work. Then came the war four years. Following these, ten years during which the whole state lay prostrate and bleeding at every pore. When these ten years were ended and the night, the long night, was fairly over, our bishop was now in the seventy-eighth year of his age. He was never a strong man, and seventy-eight years are a heavy load to bear. But to his honor be it remembered ever that, even at his age, he held the diocese together during a crisis that threatened the very life of many of our Southern churches; and who does not know that there are conditions when merely to maintain life and organization a force is needed that, under favorable auspices, would manifest itself in a decided and rapid onward movement. It is interesting to note that during the war his aged and venerable form was familiar to both armies, that he was enabled to do what perhaps no other man in the state could have done. He visited both within and without the lines of the contending forces. He held up his Episcopal banneret, and he held it full high advanced, and the stars and the stripes and the stars and the bars willingly made way for it. Again and again he passed through the lines of the besieging and the besieged upon a mission against which there is no law.

"Our bishop was a gentle man and his had been in the main a gentle and a calm life, and yet he had, like others, his periods of storm. He had known sorrow and become acquainted with grief. Of these trials he rarely spoke. Now and then upon a long and tiresome journey, meditating as men will at such times, he would lift the veil and suffer you to glance for a moment at the tracks of blood that he had left behind him, and upon the dark arena which had been the scene of his fiercest battles. But these times were rare. For the most part he took into his council and innermost cabinet only the Almighty Comforter and Lord of Life, who has the balm of Gilead for our wounds, a lethe and a grave for our painful memories, and an immortal crown for our reward."*

So writes one who, better able than any other for the task, delivered before the council of 1887 the most beautiful and touching memorial it was ever our fortune to hear. "His life had been in the main a gentle and a calm life," he tells us, and yet into this life had fallen the bloody rain of a cruel and fratricidal war, followed by the fiery trials of a period ten times more cruel, "which tried men's souls" as war itself has never tried them! But founded upon a rock, the church of which he was the chief pastor in this diocese came out purified and exalted, with not so much as even the smell of burning upon her garments.

During the period of the war between the states, the diocese of Mississippi, following the tradition of the Catholic church in all ages, united with her sister dioceses of the South in a convention which formed that branch of the Holy Catholic church, known for four brief years as the Protestant Episcopal church in the Confederate States of America. Upon the cessation of hostilities and the return of the state to the Federal Union, the diocese of Mississippi in common with the other Southern dioceses, resumed her connection with the general convention of the church in the United States.

During Bishop Green's administration the church continued steadily to advance as she became known, though hindered as we have seen by events of unusual character and far-reaching consequence. The Bishop, never a strong man physically, had to contend with difficulties in the discharge of his episcopal functions which are now hardly credible. Nights and days of anxious waiting upon the river bank for the arrival of an uncertain steamer, long journeys by land over well nigh impassable roads and across creeks and rivers swollen often by sudden freshet, and frequent exposure to inclement weather made the annual visitation of his diocese a serious task for one who when he entered upon it had already passed the meridian of life.

*Memorial address, Rt.-Rev. W. E. Adams, D. C. L., 1887.

At length in the thirty-sixth year of his episcopate he asked that an assistant be given him, and at the meeting of the fifty-fifth annual* council an effort was made to afford the Bishop the needed assistance. On the 19th of April, 1882, the council met in Christ church, Vicksburg, and on the third day of its session proceeded to the election of an assistant bishop, voting by orders and parishes. The Rt.-Rev. W. F. Adams, D. C. L., now bishop of Easton, was the first choice of the clergy, but this choice failed of confirmation by the laity. The Rev. Dr. Alex. I. Drysdale was then nominated by the clergy, but this nomination was also rejected by the laity. A third attempt resulted in the election of the Rt.-Rev. J. H. D. Wingfield, missionary bishop of northern California. Bishop Wingfield, however, being unable to sever his connection with his important jurisdiction, declined the election.

A special council was then called by the Bishop, which met in St. Andrew's church, Jackson, November 28, 1882, and unanimously elected the Rev. Hugh Miller Thompson, S. T. D., to be assistant bishop of the diocese of Mississippi. Dr. Thompson accepted his election and was consecrated on St. Matthias' day, February 24, 1883, in Trinity church, New Orleans, Bishop Green being the corsecrator and the bishops of Alabama, Louisiana, Georgia, Arkansas and Michigan assisting.

Bishop Thompson is too well known to make necessary, and this not the place for, any distinctly personal sketch of that distinguished prelate and scholar. Suffice it to say now that his accession to the episcopate was like the infusion of new blood into the diocese, and yet nothing about him was more admirable than his filial regard for the aged bishop, and his absolute subordination to his every wish. On May 8, 1884, however, the Bishop transferred the administration of the diocese to his coadjutor, and retired to Sewanee, where as chancellor of the University of the South, he continued to reside, making brief annual visitations to his diocese, until he was called to his reward. Upon the death of Bishop Green, February 13, 1887, Bishop Thompson became bishop of the diocese.

It remains now to give some brief account of the diocese as it is to-day.

We have seen that in the primary convention of 1826 only four parishes were represented, viz., those of Natchez, Woodville, Church Hill and Port Gibson. Of these places Natchez is the only one which even now can properly be called a city, and nothing is more remarkable as an illustration of the changed aspect of many things since the war than the decadence of prosperous parishes drawing their support from the neighborhood settlements of wealthy planters, now planters no more, and the coming into prominence of railroad towns and cities as the centers of educational and religious effort.

The parish of Natchez, the oldest and most important in the diocese, attained its greatest growth under the Rev. Alex. Marks, for thirteen years rector of the parish, a member of the standing committee of the diocese, dean of the convocation of Natchez and deputy to the general convention. He entered into rest on August 28, 1886. The parish numbers now some three hundred and fifty families and four hundred and eleven communicants, owning also besides the church a large and commodious rectory and a parish building used for school and other purposes. The Rev. F. A. De Rosset, who succeeded Mr. Marks, is the present rector.

One of the first parishes of any note, added to the courageous and faithful four comprising the primary convention, was the parish of Christ church, Vicksburg, which appears first upon the journal of the convention of 1839. The Rev. Dr. George Weller, then rector, reports the number of communicants as twenty-seven, and says "at present we worship in a

*Changed from convention to council in 1869.

large room over a storehouse, but active exertions are making for the erection of a handsome church, the corner-stone of which was laid by Bishop Polk, during his visitation of that year, on February 19, 1839. The parish now and for twenty-five years, under the care of the venerable rector, the Rev. Henry Sansom, D. D., numbers nearly two hundred communicants and four hundred and fifty souls. Its church, chapel and rectory are complete and commodious, and the parish is a power for good in the city of Vicksburg.

The increasing membership of Christ church which kept pace with the growth of the city led to the formation of the parish of the church of the Holy Trinity, Vicksburg, which was organized September 29, 1869, and soon became one of the leading parishes of the diocese. To the untiring energy of its first rector, the Rev. W. W. Lord, is due the massive and imposing edifice in which the congregation now worships. This, by far the most beautiful church building in the diocese, was completed in 1874, at a cost of about $70,000. Dr. Lord was succeeded by the Rt.-Rev. W. F. Adams, D. D., now bishop of Easton, under whom the parish grew and flourished. The present rector is the Rev. Nowell Logan, who succeeded Bishop Adams in 1888.

St. Andrew' church, Jackson, was organized in 1838, and admitted into union with the council in 1843. This parish, including within its limits the state capital, is one of the most important in the diocese. St. Paul's, Columbus; St. Mark's, Raymond, and St. Paul's, Grenada, were admitted into union with the convention in 1840, and Christ church, Holly Springs, in 1842. Other important points now occupied by parishes of later date are Aberdeen, Biloxi, Greenville, Meridian, Oxford, Yazoo City, etc.

Our space does not permit us to give more than a very general view of the statistics and present condition of the diocese.

The diocese of Mississippi is co-terminous with the state, and therefore covers some forty thousand three hundred and forty square miles. The number of families reported in the journal of 1891 as attached to the church is one thousand eight hundred and seventy-eight embracing some seven thousand souls. The communicants reported are three thousand and sixty-six, and confirmed persons, three thousand four hundred and forty-six; but as these figures cover only the reports from parishes, and some of these very defective, they do not fairly represent the strength of the church in the state. The proper total of communicants, could it be ascertained, would be found not far from four thousand.

The number of clergy reported in 1891 is thirty-two, parishes and missions seventy-seven, church edifices fifty-six, rectories and parish buildings twenty-five. The contributions for all purposes during the last year as reported were $45,028.94, and the total value of church property reported by the parishes, $328,155. To this should be added the property of the diocese, including the bishop's residence on Battle Hill, near Jackson. Here on the very site of the old residence of Bishop Green, destroyed by the Federal troops, during the war, is situated the Episcopal residence where Bishop Thompson dispenses a hospitality as refined and generous as it is scriptural. The residence and ground occupy about twenty acres, forming a gentle eminence called Battle Hill, upon the side of which looking toward Jackson is to be built a stone chapel in memory of Bishop Green; most of the material being now on the spot.

The present officers of the dioceses are the Rt.-Rev. Hugh Miller Thompson, S. T. D., LL. D., bishop, whose residence, as we have seen, is at Battle Hill, Jackson; the Rev. Henry Sansom, D. D., president of the standing committee; the Rev. Nowell Logan, secretary and registrator; Mr. A. M. Leigh, treasurer; Hon. William G. Yerger, of Greenville, chancellor; the Rev. William Cross, secretary, and Dr. G. W. Howard, treasurer of the missionary committee, and Messrs. R. L. Saunders, Q. O. Eckford and Frederic Speed, trustees of the Episcopal fund and church property.

In bringing to a close this brief and imperfect sketch, we can not do better than to quote the language of one of our bishops. Bishop Thompson in his latest charge to the clergy and laity of the diocese, summing up the progress of the diocese in the first septennate of his administration, says:

"It seems fitting, in this seventh anniversary of presiding in this council, to make you an address and charge, as it were, instead of the usual council sermon. One need not believe in the doctrine of mystic numbers to be impressed with the passage of a period of seven years of his life in a new office and responsibility, and to desire to review somewhat and take account of his work in them. Seven years and a month ago the fifty-sixth annual council met in Grace church, Canton, and I presided, for the first time, in the diocese of Mississippi. * * * * Seven years ago, including the bishop and assistant, and the Rt.-Rev. Dr. Adams, there were in the diocese twenty-seven clergy. Of these six were non-residents, leaving twenty-one as our actual working force. There are now twenty six priests, seven deacons and the bishop. Thirty-four in all, of whom but two are not engaged actively in the work. There have been ten churches built during these years where none existed before, three of them brick. Nine churches have been restored, enlarged, completed or cleared of debt. Two have been built to take the place of others burned; each a great improvement upon its predecessor. Seven rectories have been built or purchased. One parish building, creditable to any parish in the church, has been erected at Natchez, and a very neat and sufficient one at Biloxi. A residence for the bishop has been built in this city, and above all a church school for girls, by the devoted faithfulness of one clergyman, has been established, worked to a high prosperity, and housed in perhaps the most elegant and perfect school building in the state.

"Seven years ago there was no missionary board and no missionary fund. A canon creating such a board was passed in the council of 1883. No funds came to be administered till 1884. At that date we began our present system of pledges, and since then we have dispensed, in support of missionaries, in educating candidates, in helping in church building— the purposes for which the board exists—something over $10,000. During the same period the obligations of the diocese to its episcopate have been, in contrast to a long previous experience, promptly met, at least, at every year's close, and all in the face of my first year's experience, the loss by a treasurer's failure of all our diocesan funds. Certainly there has been a bracing up of our diocesan administration, a confidence and feeling of strength on which we may congratulate ourselves, and take courage for the future.

"Thus have we endeavored to follow the growth of the 'vine planted in the wilderness' so many years ago. It will be seen that the church has kept pace steadily with the state, sharing the fortunes of the commonwealth in the evil days as in the good. But the hand of man can not really come near to do her evil, for she is of God. Her boughs are 'like the goodly cedar whose branches shall extend to the sea and her boughs to the river'; and she must increase and prosper, until in His good time shall come to pass the saying that is written, 'the earth shall be full of the knowledge of the Lord, as the waters cover the sea.'"

The Presbyterian church in Mississippi began its existence as an organized body in Mississippi in the first decade of the present century. Prior to this date, during the long predominance of the French and Spanish authorities in the region known as west Florida, in which Mississippi was included, no toleration was extended to the professors of Protestant

Christianity. After the requisition of this region by the United States, and the erection by congress of a part of it, first into the territory of Mississippi, in 1798, and subsequently, in 1817, into the state of Mississippi, all such obstructions were removed, and representatives of the different Protestant denominations poured rapidly into the country. The first settlements were made in the southwestern section of the territory, in the counties bordering on, or contiguous to, the Mississippi river, in what was called the Natchez district. The northern part of the territory was claimed and occupied by the Choctaw and Chickasaw Indians. Many of the emigrants came from the Carolinas, and were of Scotch and Scotch-Irish descent, strongly tenacious of their Presbyterian traditions and usages. Others of a kindred type came from the Western states, and some from New England.

The first stage in the history of the church may be said to extend from 1800 to 1815, and may be called the pioneer period. The effort to organize the Presbyterian material in Mississippi began in 1801, when this frontier region was visited by three clergymen—the Rev. William Montgomery, the Rev. James Hall and the Rev. James Bowman—under a commission from the synod of Carolina. They made their way on horseback, through the wilderness, to Mississippi. These ministers spent part of a year in the territory, exploring the country, preaching in the different settlements, and gathering the Presbyterian population into congregations. They were followed in 1803 by the Rev. Joseph Bullen, a native of Massachusetts, and for many years a pastor in Vermont, who had been sent out by the New York Missionary society to establish a mission among the Indians in the northern part of the territory. After spending four years in this work, Mr. Bullen removed with his family into the southern settlements, where he had purchased a tract of land, about twenty miles northeast of the town of Natchez. Here, besides cultivating his farm, he occasionally taught a school, and statedly held religious services among the neighboring communities. In 1804 he constituted, in regular form, the first Presbyterian church in Mississippi, at Uniontown, in Jefferson county, under the name of the Bethel church. From this date till 1812 the work of organizing congregations into regular churches was carried on by Mr. Bullen and other ministers who had come into the territory, until the number had reached eight. Four ministers were in the field supplying these flocks with the means of grace—the Rev. Joseph Bullen, the Rev. James Smylie, the Rev. Jacob Rickhow and the Rev. William Montgomery.

The second stage in the progress of the church may be noted in 1815, when the above-named ministers and churches were constituted by an act of the synod of Kentucky into a new and independent presbytery, to be known as the Mississippi presbytery. The first meeting of this presbytery was held at the Salem church on Pine ridge, in Adams county, on the 6th of March, 1816. The territory assigned to the Mississippi presbytery was originally of immense extent, and in some directions without limit. It embraced a large part of Alabama, the whole of Mississippi and Louisiana, and portions of Arkansas and Texas. In 1817 that part of the Mississippi territory which now constitutes the state of Mississippi, was by act of congress admitted into the Union as a sovereign state. From this fact it will be seen that the population of Mississippi had been largely increased. The interior of the state had been penetrated by immigrants, and the section previously occupied by Indians had been, after their removal, rapidly peopled by settlers. Presbyterian communities and churches were multiplied in proportion to this increase of population. As the result of these changes within the twenty years succeeding the creation of the Mississippi presbytery the vast field originally included in that body was subdivided by the carving of new presbyteries out of its territory until 1835. Instead of being the sole ecclesiastical judiciary of the Presbyterian order in the Southwest it found itself reduced to the position of one of a numerous sisterhood of presbyteries. The period now under consideration was one of great activity in the Presbyterian church. The obligation to carry the gospel to parts beyond was fully recognized, and the work of propagating religion was prosecuted in every available direction. Besides the care of organized churches missions were maintained among the Indians, plans for the religious instruction of the slave population were adopted in all the presbyteries, and special attention was given to the founding of schools of learning. The records of the Missionary society of the Mississippi presbytery abound in traces on the part of its agents of a zeal and a hardihood in enduring labor and trial that were truly apostolic. The work of these men was that of quarrying stones from a mass of shapeless rock for the rearing of a future temple. One of them, the Rev. John H. Vancourt, in his report, made in 1823, gives this notice of his visit to Jackson, now the seat of government of the state Mississippi: "On the 29th of May I arrived at Jackson. This town now contains about a dozen families. There are likewise several settled in the country around within a few miles of the town. There are in the town three members of the Presbyterian church and several Presbyterian families. There is no regular preaching here of any kind. The pious mourn over the loss of religious privileges and ardently desire to have some one to break unto them the bread of life. I preached three times to this people." It is, perhaps, not claiming too much to say that at this early date the Presbyterian church was the forerunner of all others in the work of popular education in Mississippi. As an evidence of its zeal and of its actual achievement in this department it may be mentioned that in 1829 the presbytery of Mississippi resolved to establish within its bounds an institution of learning of the highest order then existing in the country. This project was consummated in 1830 by the inauguration of Oakland college in a rural district in Claiborne county, about four miles distant from the town of Rodney, on the Mississippi river. The Rev. Jeremiah Chamberlain, D. D., was installed as its first president, under whose administration the institution rapidly attained a respectable maturity. After preserving its useful mission for more than forty years, Oakland college was constrained through loss of funds consequent upon the Civil war, to close its doors. Its property was purchased by the state of Mississippi for the purpose of founding the Alcorn university for colored young man. The funds of Oakland college, after the payment of its debts, were devoted to the establishing of the Chamberlain-Hunt academy at Port Gibson, an institution of a high order, which has ever since continued to maintain a vigorous existence. During its whole history Oakland college was sustained entirely by the contributions of private individuals, mostly Presbyterians, in Mississippi.

The church reached the third stage of its history in 1835, when by act of the general assembly of the Presbyterian church in the United States of America, the present synod of Mississippi was formed. Under this act it attained organic completeness, presenting in a gradation of courts the development of the Presbyterian idea of church order. The synod of Mississippi was composed of all the presbyteries lying within the bounds of the state of Mississippi (except two on the northern border, which from contiguity were attached to the synod of Memphis), together with those belonging to the state of Louisiana. The synod of Mississippi has ever since constituted a bond of union among the churches of the state, exercising within constitutional limits the power of review and control over all the presbyteries. Under this arrangement, from 1835 to 1861, the church continued to expand and prosper. Its ministry and eldership included in them men of marked ability, and its policy was distinguished by zeal and activity in every department of evangelical work. The doctrinal complexion of the churches was strictly in harmony with the standards of Presbyterianism, as formulated by the Westminster assembly of divines, and has continued to be so until the present time. This conservatism was evinced when, in 1837, the rupture which divided the Presbyterian church in the United States of America into the old school and new school parties occurred. The synod of Mississippi on that occasion, with the exception of a single presbytery, decided to adhere to the old school party. In this connection it remained, being annually represented in the general assembly of that body, through commissions from its presbyteries, till the secession of the Southern states, and the opening of the Civil war threw such obstacles in the way of fellowship with the Northern section as required the churches within the bounds of the Confederacy to dissolve their connection with it and organize themselves as a distinct corporation, under a general assembly of their own.

This change of relation marks the fourth and final stage of the Presbyterian church in Mississippi. The Presbyterian Church South was regularly constituted under the title of the Presbyterian Church in the Confederate States of America, by the convening of a general assembly, composed of commissioners from the presbyteries of the seceding states, at Augusta, Ga., on the 4th of December, 1861. Representatives from most of the presbyteries belonging to Mississippi were present at this meeting. The reasons which justified the act of severance were published to "all the churches of Jesus Christ throughout the earth" in an able address prepared by the Rev. Dr. Thornwell, of South Carolina. The separation thus created between the Presbyterian Church North and South, survived the reunion of the states at the close of the war, and has been maintained till the present day. It is maintained, however, solely as an organic arrangement and in consistency with the most cordial fraternal relations between the two bodies. After the extinction of the Confederacy the title of the Southern church was changed to that of the Presbyterian Church in the United States. Of this body the churches of Mississippi have, since 1861, formed a constituent part.

The disastrous effects of the Civil war in the state of Mississippi was as apparent in the department of religious life and work as they were in all others. For the first fifteen years after that great convulsion the Presbyterian church, in common with all other denominations, was enfeebled by the exhaustion and embarrassed by the confusion which prevailed throughout the country. Its resources were enormously reduced by the extinction of slavery and the general depreciation of property. Agriculture was impeded by the introduction of a new and experimental system of labor. The survival of debts, where assets and incomes had disappeared, involved the leading landholders largely in bankruptcy. The unsettled state of society and the absence of means of livelihood arrested immigration, and in fact, led to a considerable drifting of population away from the state. As the result, the strong churches at the commercial centers became weak; and the rural churches, which were dependant for their support upon planting neighborhoods, unable to maintain an organization by their own efforts, sank into the position of missionary stations or became extinct. Happily this season of depression has passed away. Within the last decade a marked revival in the enterprise and prosperity of Mississippi has been witnessed. The state has become interlaced by a system of railways, new marts for traffic have sprung up in every direction, some of them rapidly reaching imposing dimensions, the relations of capital to labor have been adjusted to new conditions, manufactories have been introduced, new industries have been inaugurated, and a new commonwealth is rising out of the wreck of the old. The stimulus of this healthful reaction has been felt by the churches, and the Presbyterian church has kept pace with the others in the attempt to meet the moral and religious wants created by the new era. It may be said to have guided itself, at the close of the century, with the missionary armor which it wore and wielded so effectively at the beginning of it. It is aiming to raise its fallen sanctuaries, and to plant new ones in infant settlements, to increase the ranks of its ministry, and by a wide system of evangelistic work, supplemental to that of the local pastorate, to convey the influence of Christian doctrine and ordinance into every destitute portion of the state.

The territory of the state is divided, ecclesiastically, into 1. The presbyteries of Chickasaw and north Mississippi, in connection with the synod of Memphis. 2. The presbytery of Tombeckbee. 3. The presbytery of central Mississippi. 4. The presbytery of Mississippi. 5. Parts of the presbyteries of Louisiana and New Orleans, including the southern counties of the state, to the Gulf of Mexico. These presbyteries report as having under their care some two hundred churches, and about eighty-five ministers, with several licentiates, and a number of candidates for the ministry. In addition to these, there are in Mississippi, at least, six colored churches and four or more colored ministers of the Presbyterian order, besides two licentiates and five candidates.

It is an interesting fact that at the last meeting of the synod of Mississippi, in November, 1890, in compliance with the petition from the parties, all the colored ministers and elders within the bounds of the synod were erected into a separate presbytery. The number of communicants in the Presbyterian church in Mississippi may be stated, proximately, as ten thousand.

The church has, from the beginning, thrown its influence into the scale of every philanthropic movement and every scheme of social reform which has been projected in the state. It has been the vigilant guardian of the sanctity of the Sabbath. It has been the patron of literary and benevolent institutions. It has advocated the purity of public morals. As early as 1829 we find on the records of the Mississippi presbytery a resolution in which the ministers pledge themselves to abstain from the use of ardent spirits, and earnestly and affectionately call upon the churches under their care to co-operate with them in the effort to suppress the enormous evil of intemperance. The attitude of the church at the present time on this subject is stated in certain resolutions of the last synod, to the effect that "while we heartily sympathize with every legitimate and judicious effort to check the prevalence of intemperance, and urge upon our ministers and church sessions renewed diligence and faithfulness in dealing with the subject, we hold that the political aspects of the temperance question do not fall within the province of our body as a church court, and that we are, therefore, not at liberty to recommend any particular course of legislation respecting the matter to the civil government"

It only remains to say that the Presbyterian church in Mississippi has always been recognized as a potent and a wholesome leavening element in the body politic. Its members have been prominent factors in every community in which they have been found. Its ministry has uniformly received the respect to which it has entitled itself by the culture, the integrity and the disinterested devotion to its work which have characterized its members. With a few exceptions, these men have consented to live and to die under a yoke of privation and of penury which would have been considered an insuperable objection to an entrance upon any other walk of life. The heroic fathers who led the van in the moral conquest of this primitive wilderness have passed away, and some of them are sleeping in unmarked if not forgotten graves; but their work abides, and a new generation, apparently emulous of their zeal and their prowess has entered into their labors.

The Cumberland Presbyterian church in Mississippi, although fourth in point of membership among the other Protestant denominations of the state, is not widely known over the state, especially in the southern part, the reason being that its organized membership is confined exclusively to the northern half of the state. Because of this fact it is but justice to this denomination to allow a brief statement in this sketch, defining its position in the general family of Presbyterianism.

The denomination grew out of what at first appeared to be an unavoidable doctrinal schism in the Presbyterian church in Kentucky. Its first presbytery, from which the church took its name, was organized by Samuel McAdow, Samuel King and Finis Ewing, regularly ordained ministers in the Presbyterian church. This was the Cumberland presbytery, and embraced parts of Tennessee and Kentucky. It was organized in 1810. Soon after the organization, a brief authoritative statement was given to the world, setting forth the reasons for the organization of another Presbyterian church. We can do no better than to give that statement here:

"The founders of the Cumberland Presbyterian church, in their licensure and ordination by the Presbyterian church, were permitted to 'except the idea of fatality,' as they believed it to be embraced in the doctrines of unconditional election and reprobation, and an atonement limited to a definitely elected number, as taught in the Westminster Confession of Faith. Subsequently, having for this been cut off from the parent church, in fixing a standard of doctrines for the Cumberland Presbyterian church, which they organized, they adopted the Westminster Confession of Faith (which is the Presbyterian confession), modified in the following particulars:

First. That there are no eternal reprobates.

Second. That Jesus died, not for a part only, but for all men, and in the same sense.

Third. That all infants dying in infancy are saved.

Fourth. That the Holy Spirit operates on all the world, all for whom Christ died, in such a manner as to render all men responsible, and therefore, inexcusable." *

The first work done in Mississippi by Cumberland Presbyterians was by Rev. Robert Bell, who was sent as a missionary to the Chickasaw Indians in 1820. This was in the northeast part of the state. Soon after Bell's settlement among the Indians he was joined by Rev. John C. Smith. Bell continued in this mission for several years, until the agitation of the removal of the Indians, and the final removal resulted in the abandonment of the mission. In the meantime, many white settlers penetrated into this Indian territory. To these early pioneers Mr. Bell and his co-laborers preached, but it was rather incidental, as their time and strength were consumed in maintaining schools among the Indians. But from this incidental seed-sowing sprang the first white Cumberland Presbyterian churches in Mississippi.

It should be noted that much of the immigration into this Indian country was from the sections where Cumberland Presbyterians had established churches. By and by demands began to increase for Cumberland Presbyterian preaching. This was not true of south Mississippi, which had been settling up long prior to this, even before 1810, when the church first assumed an independent existence. Very few Cumberland Presbyterians went to that portion of the state. Most of the settlers in this part of the state were from the Atlantic states, where Cumberland Presbyterians never attempted to penetrate, so numerous were the calls in the West. This fact accounts largely for the absence of the church in lower Mississippi. The first congregations were not organized much before the beginning of the removal of the Indians (1833). It was stated in the church paper in 1836 that all the congregations in the state had been organized in the preceding five years. The first presbytery, known as

* For a fuller statement see "Our Position, or Cumberland Presbyterians in Relation to the Presbyterian Family," by Rev. W. J. Darby, D. D., Cumberland Publishing House, Nashville, Tenn.

the Mississippi, held its first meeting at Gallatin, in Copiah county. Its original members were Thomas J. Bryan, Robert Molloy, Samuel W. Sparks and Isaac Shook. This first meeting was in April, 1832.

During the early period the struggling congregations suffered much because of the secularization of many of the ministry. For several years after the opening of the Indian country the spirit of speculation ran high and wild. This period was regarded as a golden opportunity to amass fortunes. This wild spirit seized the ministry. The sentiment was largely prevalent that Mississippians would not listen with any respect to a preacher who let this golden opportunity for independence slip, and then expected the people to support him. The advice to the preacher was: "Get you a plantation and hands to cultivate it; get them paid for; and then you can go preach as much as you please." Unfortunately for the Cumberland Presbyterian church in Mississippi, and other churches as well, too many of the ministry acted on this advice. One instance will suffice to illustrate this secularized condition of the ministry. I quote from McDonnold's history: "In the diary of the Rev. Isaac Shook is an account of a visit to a Mississippi town in 1834. There were seven hundred inhabitants, and among them five Protestant ministers all secularized. One was a merchant, one a schoolteacher, one a lawyer, and two slavedrivers, as Shook calls them. They were seizing the golden opportunity to secure independence. Shook began a series of meetings. By and by the schoolteacher began to attend. There was a revival. Then the merchant, who also sold whisky, came of nights and grew wonderfully zealous, but he still sold whisky. The others would drop in occasionally, but took no special interest. The meeting closed. One of these preachers was afterward silenced; all of them utterly lost the confidence of the people. The town became noted for its contempt of Christianity."

During this early period much was lost to the church because of the scarcity of consecrated preachers. An illustration of this we find in the history of the evangelistic labors of Mr. Shook. In May, 1832, finding himself, as if by accident, in the then little town of Columbus, he was prevailed upon to hold a series of services. The interest spread. He held meetings in the surrounding country. Within two months there were three hundred conversions. Of these, Shook received only twenty into the Cumberland Presbyterian church. The reason of this, as given by Mr. Shook, was that he did not encourage them to join the Cumberland Presbyterian church, because he saw no means of supplying them with the word. He says these twenty would go nowhere else.

Besides those already mentioned, who figure in the early establishment of the church in Mississippi, many others should be mentioned. The evangelistic labors of H. H. Hill were greatly blessed. This was in 1832. Especial mention should be made of Rev. R. L. Ross, who was a convert of these meetings. Many are the congregations that were established by him. About the last work of his devoted life was the establishment of the church in Meridian. In 1834 Rev. W. S. Burney began his work in the state by holding camp meetings. He was assisted by A. P. Bradley. Great success attended them. To these names should be added those of Jefferson Brown, Joseph Harrison, Cyrus Wilson, Elane Waddell, Jabez Hickman and F. M. Fincher. Later on came Wayman Adair, Joe Bell, James W. Dickey and F. E. Harris, besides others equally as worthy of mention. While the Cumberland Presbyterian church in Mississippi has never established male schools of a high grade, being convenient to Bethel college and the Cumberland university, Tennessee, denominational schools, yet she has not been indifferent to the matter of education. Very early (1838) we find one of her leading ministers, the Rev. Richard Beard, afterward professor of theology in the Cumberland university, in charge of Sharon academy, in Madison county. His influence and labors were of great help to the church in the state.

In this connection especial mention should be made of the Rev. Stanford G. Burney. Through the special efforts of Rev. W. S. Burney and Elder James G. Trigg, of Oxford, Mr. Burney was induced to come to Mississippi from Tennessee, and take charge of what was known as Mount Sylvan academy, in Lafayette county, and which had been established the year previous by the Rev. Robert Morris, of Masonic fame. This was in 1846 or 1847. In the meantime Mr. Burney was active as a preacher. When the church estalished Union Female college, Oxford, Mr. Burney became its first president. This was in 1854. This school is still maintained by the Mississippi synod of the Cumberland Presbyterian church. As a teacher Mr. Burney did much good for the denomination. For years he was pastor at Oxford, succeeding the Rev. W. S. Burney, who organized the congregation. Perhaps no preacher throughout north Mississippi had greater reputation and influence than S. G. Burney. He is now professor of theology in Cumberland university.

But this sketch would not be complete without a notice of the educational efforts of the Rev. Leonard Cooper. Soon after the war he established at Daleville a school of high order—Cooper institute. Mr. Cooper continued this school for many years, educating many young men for the ministry of the church. Not only so, Mr. Cooper took rank as one of the leading educators of the state. All things considered, perhaps Mr. Cooper contributed as much, and probably more, to the educational interests of the state, and of the denomination in the state, as any other one Cumberland Presbyterian.

Space forbids a further notice of those among the laity, as well as among the ministry, living as well as dead, who have given of their thought and substance in the establishment of the Cumberland Presbyterian church in Mississippi. As pickets they have stood faithfully on the border line of the denomination. In serving their church, they have served the state none the less. To the social, material, educational and religious interests of the state Cumberland Presbyterians have contributed faithfully and liberally. Cumberland Presbyterians are Presbyterian, though not Calvinistic (they reverence John Calvin as much as any man, living or dead, should be reverenced), and that means they are a liberty-loving and a liberty-guarding people, whether in the church or in the state. With them the liberty of conscience and head is a priceless jewel and they have but little respect and less patience for the man or institution who would interfere with either.

The Cumberland Presbyterian church in Mississippi, while not large, is making a steady advance. Like other churches and institutions of the state, it suffered much by the war and the reconstruction period. Also by the shifting of the white population from the rural districts to the towns and cities. But the denomination is fast adjusting itself to this new condition of things. Its ministry is all the time improving, comparing favorably with that of any other denomination in the state.

The outlook is encouraging. The membership is becoming more and more active to the matter of state evangelization. Infant congregations are all the while being planted under the supervision of a state superintendent of missions and Sunday-school work, but unfortunately the calls for such work are more numerous than can be supplied. Yet there is one encouraging feature in the failure to answer all the calls, namely, that the denomination as such is appreciated and demanded in the state. There are at present, 1891, in round numbers, seven thousand communicants. This does not include baptized children, but the actual membership in communion. There are one hundred and fifty congregations. There are fifty-one regularly ordained ministers, and twenty-four licentiates and candidates, making a total of seventy-five. There are now five presbyteries: Bell, Oxford, Mississippi, New Hope and the Yazoo. These are all embraced in one synod, the synod of Mississippi, and they include the northern half of the state, there being no congregations, or few at least, south of Winston and Attala counties. There are congregations at Corinth, Tupelo, Oxford, West Point, Columbus, Starkville, Meridian, Coffeeville, Grenada, Batesville, Kosciusko, Louisville, Water Valley, besides other smaller towns. Of course the country districts come in for a large share.

The entrance of the Methodist church into Mississippi was the commencement of Protestant Christianity in the same country. On March 30, 1798, the Spanish government ceased to exist in the western part of the Mississippi territory, then known as the Natchez country, and was immediately succeeded by that of the United States. For more than thirty years before this a Protestant population had been gradually accumulating in the Natchez district. This country, not very accurately defined, was claimed as belonging to the English colony of Georgia, and after the Revolutionary war it was claimed as belonging to the United States. This afforded reasonable belief to border settlers that Protestant Christianity would soon be protected. But the first Protestant families coming into this country had to endure much hardship and persecution from the Spanish Catholics. At this time Bishop Francis Asbury was general superintendent of the Methodist Episcopal church in the United States. So soon as he had learned that the Spanish government in the Natchez district had been superseded by that of the United States he determined to send missionaries into it, and the Rev. Tobias Gibson, of South Carolina, volunteered for that service; and accordingly, at the next meeting of the South Carolina conference, Mr. Gibson was appointed to that new, important and hazardous ministry. Mr. Gibson was then twenty-eight years old and in the eighth year of his ministry. At that time the white settlements in Mississippi were confined to a very narrow strip of country extending along the Mississippi river from Fort Adams to Walnut Hills, now Vicksburg. All the rest of Mississippi, all Alabama, with the exception of some settlements close around Mobile, and a considerable part of Georgia was an unbroken wilderness, inhabited solely by Indians. As a journey through this trackless wilderness would be extremely hazardous, Mr. Gibson took the more circuitous route by way of Nashville, Tenn., and the Mississippi river. So, after traveling six hundred miles on horseback, he reached the Cumberland settlement, then in the state of Georgia, at or near where Nashville now stands. Here he sold his horse and procured a canoe, into which he packed his traveling equipage, with a supply of provisions, descended the Cumberland, then the Ohio and then the Mississippi, and landed at Natchez about the last of March, 1799.

Mr. Gibson's ministry was the only Methodist, and with very little exception the only Protestant ministry within five hundred miles of Mississippi for several years. It was very successful. In the first year he gathered into the church sixty members. The second year the church was increased to eighty, and in 1801 to a hundred. This Natchez country was now included in the South Carolina conference. This Natchez country took its name from a large and powerful tribe of Indians who once inhabited this region, but the name in time came to be confined to the then little town of Natchez and Fort Rosalie. The South Carolina conference, of which Mississippi was a territorial portion, formed Natchez into a circuit, as its geographical country pastorates are called. They generally consist of four or five local country churches under one pastorate. This Natchez circuit included nearly or quite all of the Mississippi territory. Mr. Gibson was reappointed to Natchez in 1801 and again in 1802. In 1802 he traveled on horseback to a conference held in Harrison county, Ky., to procure ministerial help. At this time this Natchez circuit was placed in the Western conference, so called, which then included the states of Tennessee, Kentucky, Ohio, Illinois and part of Virginia. Mr. Gibson was for several years the only Methodist preacher within five hundred miles of his field of labor. Although Methodist preachers were increasing every

The Goodspeed Pub.Co.Chicago.

W R Perry

year, the demand for their services in the West increased in a greater ratio. At this session of the Western conference, held in Kentucky, Moses Floyd, a young preacher from Georgia, volunteered to go to Natchez and was accepted by the bishop. At this conference Natchez circuit was placed in the Cumberland district, with John Page as presiding elder. Mr. Gibson's health having seriously failed, the Natchez church was placed in charge of Mr. Floyd. Mr. Gibson's health continued to fail and he died in April, 1804.

In 1805 Natchez circuit had two preachers, Launer Blackman and T. C. N. Barnes. It throws light on these times to state that during the first five years of his ministry Mr. Blackman traveled in five states—Maryland, Delaware, Virginia, Kentucky and Mississippi. In order to reach Natchez he traveled fourteen days in the savage wilderness, and eleven of the fourteen nights he slept on the ground, with his saddlebags for his pillow and the sky for his covering. He was an orator of high order and of social qualities that endeared him to all classes.

At the session of the Western conference held in Scott county, Ky., Natchez circuit was divided into four circuits, Wilkinson on the south, Claiborne on the north and Opelousas, in Louisiana, being added. These four constituted a district called the Mississippi district, and Mr. Blackman, though only twenty-four years of age, was appointed presiding elder. He was the first presiding elder ever in Mississippi. He was a man of extraordinary labors, visiting many places and organizing churches.

In 1806 Natchez had two preachers, Mr. Barnes and Thomas Larley. In 1807 C. W. Cloud was appointed to Natchez circuit. This year the first church edifice was built in Natchez.

Drifting down those brief sketches, necessarily in great haste, we come to 1810. Here we meet with Miles Harper, a most extraordinary man. He came from Tennessee, was junior preacher on Natchez circuit. Though not a man of extensive learning he had rare gifts as a public speaker. His voice was strong, musical and captivating. The power of his preaching was immense. His converts were many. But he was not a student, and like many preachers who cease to study, he to a considerable extent outlived his usefulness. In 1829 he retired from the itinerancy and died a local preacher in 1843.

Perhaps the most remarkable man of the Natchez preachers in those times in some respects was John Johnson. He was from Virginia. He was entirely illiterate until about twenty years old. Working daily on a farm, he engaged the services of an old negro man to teach him to read. Spending his evenings in this way he soon mastered the spelling book and could read the Bible. He was licensed to preach and soon became a power in the pulpit, and was received a member of the Western conference, preached two years in Ohio and then came to Mississippi, and for many years was one of the most powerful and effective preachers of his time.

Another of the most noted and most useful preachers of the Southwest in those early times was William Winans. He was a very complete self-made man; never went to school; born in 1788; worked in an iron foundry; was admitted into the Western conference in 1808; traveled two years in the Northwest and was sent to Mississippi in 1810 and was soon appointed presiding elder. He was a very constant reader and with great natural endowments soon acquired a high position. He was a member of every general conference from 1824 until his death in 1857. He was uniformly regarded one of the best debators in the general conference.

To notice the preachers who distinguished themselves in those early times would lengthen these brief notes too much. Natchez district, which included this whole region of country,
W

continued a portion of the Western conference, which included nearly the entire Mississippi valley until 1813, when the Mississippi conference was organized. This improved things greatly. Now we have a conference at home. The first session of the Mississippi annual conference was held at the residence of the Rev. Newet Vick, about five miles southwest of where Fayette now is, in Jefferson county, Miss., on November 1, 1813. Present: Samuel Sellers, president; members, Miles Harper, Richard Nolley, Lewis Hobbs, John S. Ford, John Phipps, John Shrock, William Winans, Thomas Griffin, John I. E. Bird; William Winans, secretary. The bishop ordering the conference could not get there on account of Indian troubles, but appointed a president pro tem.

At the next session, in 1814, Simon Gentry, Jonathan Kemp, Peter James and Josiah Dougherty were received on trial. This second session has been for some time confounded with the first, but Rev. J. G. Jones, in his history of Methodism in Mississippi, holds as above, which is, no doubt, correct.

The conference now embraced what is Mississippi, Alabama and Louisiana, with other adjacent, but not well-defined territory. For a few years the operations of the church were considerably interrupted by hostile armies or troops. The Creek Indian war, and the British invasion caused much disturbance, but still the church increased.

The first conference attended by bishops was in 1816. Bishop Robert R. Roberts traveled some four hundred miles on horseback, mostly through a wilderness country to get to it. It was held in the country near Natchez. Ten preachers were assigned to as many pastoral charges. Five of these were in Mississippi, two in Alabama and three in Louisiana. These were all circuits, each one including several separate congregations. The first station was Natchez, in 1826.

This much of detail has been necessary in order to give the reader some idea in outline of Methodism in this country in its formative state. Henceforth the necessary brevity of these notes require that we proceed much faster and deal less in particulars. After the Indian and British troubles were settled the church increased much more rapidly, and a few years separate annual conferences were set apart in Louisiana and Alabama respectively, and the Mississippi conferences were confined to the state of Mississippi and included that part of Louisiana lying east of the Mississippi river, except the cities of New Orleans and Baton Rouge.

These notes are understood to refer to Episcopal Methodism, but after about 1830 the Protestant or non-Episcopal Methodists became organized, and for many years had quite a number of circuits in several parts of the state, but in 1871 they disbanded, that is, those in Mississippi, and united in a body with the Episcopal Methodists.

These notes must not omit to mention what this writer regards as the most extraordinary preacher of modern times the world-renowned John Newland Moffit. In 1836 he visited Natchez, where he spent a considerable portion of the year, but the points of that brief ministry will long remain. And also Charles K. Marshall, who for half a century was always recognized as a master of pulpit eloquence, standing a head and shoulders above other men. He died at his home in Vicksburg in 1891.

For twenty years and more after about 1830 the wilderness part of the state opened up largely and rapidly to agriculture, commerce, education and religion. And the Mississippi conference increased greatly both in its ministry, laity and educational institutes. There was before the war scarcely a township (fourteen miles square) of land in the state not occupied by the Methodist ministry.

In 1858 the Mississippi conference had eight colleges, viz.: Centenary college, with a president and seven professors, one hundred and seventy-five students, with buildings, apparatus and endowment worth $150,000, and library of seven thousand five hundred volumes; Sharon Female college, ninety students and buildings worth $10,000; Feliciana Female institute, buildings, $4,000; Walls' Female institute, fifty pupils; Port Gibson collegiate academy, eighty pupils, building $10,000; Southern Female college, eighty-five pupils, property $8,000; Mount Hermon Female institute, seventy pupils, property $5,000; Madison college, one hundred scholars, building $8,000. The first Sunday-school in the United States south of Philadelphia, was permanently organized in the Methodist church at Natchez in 1827.

In 1855 the Mississippi conference established a book and tract society at Vicksburg for the more ready sale and distribution of religious literature. Its capital was raised by voluntary subscription. This, together with its business, increased until in the time of the war it amounted to some $6,000 or $7,000. But on the fall of Vicksburg it fell into the hands of the army and was destroyed.

It has always been a leading policy of Methodism in the South to preach the gospel to the colored people, no more nor no less in Mississippi than in other Southern states. Before the war where the negroes were somewhat numerous, separate churches were built for their accommodation, or otherwise ample galleries were built in almost all the churches for their use. The number of colored members was sometimes nearly or quite equal to that of the whites, but generally the number of colored members was probably half that of the whites. Large plantations were generally supplied with a missionary, or sometimes two adjoining places.

On the division of the church at the general conference at New York, in 1844, of course Mississippi allied itself with the other conferences in the South in a separate organization under the name of the Methodist Episcopal Church South. This, however, made no change of any sort in the annual conferences, and the church continued to prosper until its labors were measurably interrupted by the tramp of hostile armies in 1862 and thereafter.

The war produced a state of things in the church in Mississippi, and in other parts of the South, quite anomalous and rarely, if ever, encountered by any church before. The entrance of the United States army into Kentucky, Tennessee, Georgia, etc., in its march southward had the natural and necessary effect of dividing the Methodist Episcopal Church South into two churches, with an impassable wall of fire between them. This separation, as things turned out, was but temporary, continuing only four or five years, when they came together again. But for the time it was complete. When this army line came to be established, seven of the annual conferences, or the greater part of each, were found to lie north of the army line, viz.: Tennessee, Louisville, Western Virginia, Indian Mission, Arkansas and Missouri, with all the rest of the conferences south of the main army line. Of course, the Mississippi conference fell in the Southern group. So that for the space of four years or more, in common with its neighbors, its public operations were very much restricted and confused. Its annual and quarterly conferences were much frustrated and neglected. Local disturbance created general disturbance. The church or denomination of which the Mississippi conference formed a part suffered disruption for a time, not only from the near presence and hostilities of the contending armies but from legal consequences. Wars disturb the possession as well as titles to property. Conquest gives ownership to property, and it requires treaties of peace and diplomacy to settle these things afterward. As this war turned out much of this church property was restored after the war, though much in a damaged condition. Churches, colleges, schoolhouses and private residences had been long used as hospitals, army quarters, etc., and many of them damaged or totally destroyed.

But on the close of the war, in 1865, the church in Mississippi, as elsewhere, rallied rapidly, so that in 1870 it was found necessary to divide the Mississippi conference into two conferences. This was done by the general conference of that year, which sat in Memphis, Tenn., by an east and west line, dividing Yazoo and Holmes counties and following other county lines; the southern portion retaining the name of Mississippi conference, and the northern taking that of Northern Mississippi. But these lines do not follow state lines strictly, for the Mississippi conference still includes those parishes of Louisiana which lie east of the Mississippi river except the cities of New Orleans and Baton Rouge.

Educational interests have been reasonably well attended to by the Methodists of this state from the first. Besides primary schools, which have generally been plentiful, the Elizabeth Female academy, of Washington, in Adams county, was established in 1824, and was kept in successful operation about three-quarters of a century, and was one of the best and most useful colleges for girls in the United States.

Centenary college was established in the centenary of Methodism and named in commemoration of it. It was first located near Brandon, Miss., in 1839, and was afterward, in 1845, removed to Jackson, La., near the line dividing those states, but still in the Mississippi conference, and has since borne the title of Centenary College of Louisiana, though mainly patronized by Mississippi.

At Brandon, Dr. Thomas C. Thornton, Judge D. O. Shattuck, Prof. W. H. N. Magruder, and other distinguished educators, were connected with it.

At Jackson, La., money was largely expended in erecting handsome buildings, which still adorn its campus. The late Judge Edward McGehee and others gave largely for these buildings and endowment, etc. Among its presidents were Dr. R. H. Rivers, W. H. Watkins, John C. Miller, before the war, and Dr. C. G. Andrwes, D. M. Rush and Dr. T. A. S. Adams since the war. The present president is Dr. W. L. C. Hunnicutt.

The present faculty consists of ten professors and teachers, and the number of students last session was one hundred and thirty-eight; of these twenty-two are licensed preachers and fifteen others sons of preachers, all of whom receive tuition free of cost. The college has an endowment of over $60,000, which fund is increasing.

The two literary societies, the four libraries and the Y. M. C. A. are very valuable adjuncts to the college. All its professors and teachers are members of the Methodist Episcopal Church South, and Christianity is emphasized in all its teachings. The trustees, at their last meeting, invited persons who are able to endow scholarships and professorships in the college.

Millsaps college, of Mississippi, is in its embryo state, but is destined in the very near future to become one of the best colleges in the Southwest. Maj. R. W. Millsaps, a wealthy gentleman of Jackson, Miss., a few years ago proposed to give $50,000 to found a first-class college for boys in Mississippi, on condition that the proposition should be accepted by the two annual conferences of the state, and that a like amount be raised by private subscription for the same purpose. In 1889 the two conferences respectively accepted the proposition of Mr. Millsaps and encouraged the raising of the requisite $50,000 to be added. Bishop Galloway, who also resides at Jackson, and several other ministers, took hold of this enterprise, and in some months the other $50,000 was on hand. It was understood that the proposed college should be in Mississippi, without designating any particular location.

And also, besides the $100,000, as above, other funds were raised for permanent endowment. Several towns and other handsome sites were ready to take the college, and this competition had the effect of raising an endowment fund of over $100,000, and which is still being increased. A short time ago, in this present year, it was decided by the trustees to locate the college at Jackson, the capital of the state. A very handsome piece of ground has been selected for this purpose, north of the city. The buildings are commenced and ample facilities will soon be afforded for the best collegiate training.

The college is in the hands of a very competent board of trustees. Several architects have for some time been at work on the proposed buildings, and before the close of 1892 they, with their enclosures, are expected to present a handsome appearance.

Since the war it is probable that no state, North or South, is much, if any, ahead of Mississippi in furnishing educational facilities to the negro population. The restricted limits of these notes will not admit of enlargement on this subject. The public records must be looked to for such information. But colored schools are sure all over the state at about every crossroad and in every city, town and village. Several of the colored churches in the state are Methodist and furnish their full share of teachers and pupils for the various schools.

The public schools, primary and of high grade, all over the state, are numerous. These are patronized by the Methodists in common with other denominations. The limits of this chapter will not admit of particular mention of them. Besides these, the state has five Methodist female colleges of high character and respectable patronage, viz.: Whitworth Female college, at Brookhaven; Port Gibson Female college, at Port Gibson; East Mississippi Female college, at Meridian; Grenada Female college, at Grenada, and Edward McGehee College for Girls, at Woodville.

The strength of Methodism in the state may be gathered in a general way from the following figures: The Mississippi conference has one hundred and fifty-five traveling preachers, and the North Mississippi conference one hundred and sixty-six. Total, three hundred and twenty-one. Of local preachers, the Mississippi conference has one hundred and sixty and the North Mississippi one hundred and fifty-five, making three hundred and eleven. Whole number of preachers, six hundred and thirty-two. The North Mississippi conference has forty thousand nine hundred and ninety-one members, and the Mississippi thirty-six thousand two hundred and twelve. In all, seventy-seven thousand two hundred and two. There are in the state, that is, in the two conferences, which includes a fraction of east Louisiana, not easily separated, four hundred and thirty-two churches in the Mississippi and five hundred in the North Mississippi conference. Total, nine hundred and thirty-two.

The value of these church buildings is $905,858. Of Sunday-schools exclusively under Methodist control, there are eight hundred and forty-eight, nearly equally divided between the two conferences, with thirty-six thousand nine hundred and sixty-three scholars, besides officers and teachers, which would increase the number of persons engaged in Sunday-school work to something over forty thousand. These statistics refer to the reports of 1890.

Besides these, there are a considerable number of mixed Sunday-schools. In many sparsely-settled regions where the Methodists are not strong enough to have a Sunday-school of their own, or where other churches are not strong enough, they unite in mixed schools. Including the Methodists in these schools, it will swell the Methodist Sunday-school of these two conferences to over fifty thousand strong.

Mississippi has furnished two bishops for the church. Bishop Robert Paine was born in North Carolina in 1799, but spent most of his life, especially the latter part of it, in Mississippi. He was ordained a minister in early life, preached mostly in north Mississippi and west Tennessee, and was a number of years president of La Grange college, in Tennessee. He was elected and ordained bishop in 1846, which active service he continued during life. He died at his home in Aberdeen, Miss., in 1882.

Bishop Charles B. Galloway is a native Mississippian, the youngest man ever ordained bishop in the Methodist church. He graduated in the University of Mississippi in 1868, and immediately on his return home from school was licensed to preach, and at the same time was recommended for the traveling connection, and was received into the Mississippi conference at the earliest period allowable by the law of the church and soon took a leading position for a man of his age. He was several years editor of the New Orleans *Christian Advocate*, and was elected and ordained bishop in 1886, which office he now holds.

The history of the Christian church in Mississippi is less important than in most of the Southern states, as their membership is smaller, the progress of the church being greatly impeded by the late war. Since that time the great mass of emigration has gone West, made up mostly from the central states, where the Christian church is very strong, and it furnished a great many emigrants, and consequently is very strong in the West as well as in central states. The first organization of this church in the state was at Battle Springs, about the year 1836. This congregation was organized by Gen. William Clark, who preached for them once a month for many years after. This church was about eight miles from Jackson, but no organization has existed there for many years. An organization was effected at Utica, about thirty-three miles from Jackson, on the Jackson and Natchez road, about the same time as the one at Battle Springs. Jefferson H. Johnson was the organizer of this church. About the year 1838 President Tolbert Fanning, of Tennessee, and James A. Butler, two prominent ministers of the church, organized a congregation at Columbus, in the northeastern part of the state, while William E. Mathes, an able minister, organized several small congregations in Wilkinson county. Gen. William Clark, who was state treasurer, and Joseph E. Mathes, state auditor, organized a congregation in Jackson in 1841. The first regular pastor laboring for the Jackson congregation was T. W. Caskey, a talented man, who served from 1854 to 1860, when he went into the army as a chaplain, where he served in that capacity very acceptably till the close of the war. Since then the church has been ministered to by Elisha Pinkerton, Elder Snow, of Virginia, George A. Smythe, for several years, and lately by Joseph Sharp, Robert Mayes, T. A. White, and by the present pastor, M. F. Harmon. The congregation in Jackson previous to the war was one of the wealthiest and most influential churches in the state. The church house, which was a brick, and a good one for its day, was greatly damaged by soldiers during the war and was in 1884 condemned and torn down. A small, neat chapel stands in the rear of where the old church stood, and a fine modern style building is soon to be erected on the old site.

There are in the state now thirty-two church houses reported, and valued at $34,000. There are about sixty organizations in the state, thirty of them having no meetinghouse, and there are about forty little unorganized bands. The total white membership is between five thousand and six thousand. There are about thirty-two preachers who give part or all their time to the ministry, and about fifteen who give but little or none of their time. There are twenty-seven colored congregations in the state, with about two thousand membership; twenty-one church houses valued at $8,630, and thirty-two preachers. This church teaches strict adherence to the New Testament as the "all sufficient rule of faith and practice," are opposed to all human creeds, believe in the co-operation of all their congregations in sending the gospel to all parts of the earth. They believe in every Christian reading, studying and interpreting the Bible for himself. They have an educated ministry and believe in a consistent Christian life. They hold, in common with all the so-called evangelical churches, the fundamental principles of Christianity, rejecting from their faith and practice only those things which are not commanded in the New Testament, or are not of divine precedent. They believe in the union of all Christians upon the Bible, and the Bible alone. They call themselves Christians or Disciples, as the followers of Christ were called in the beginning. This people believe in missions, both home and foreign. Besides collections taken from the congregations at regular times for foreign missions they have a regular state board of missions that keeps an evangelist in the state all the time. This state work was begun with the labors of F. W. Caskey from 1841 to 1854, and William E. Hooker and Robert Ursey labored in the same capacity from 1854 to 1860. B. F. Manire, a talented Christian minister, evangelized throughout the state for several years independent of any board.

The Mississippi Christian Missionary convention, which is operating now in doing state missionary work, was organized in 1884, with Dr. D. B. Hill, of Palo Alto, president, who served till 1887. From that time to the present (June, 1891) Dr. D. L. Phares, of Madison Station, has been president. This board holds annual conventions, the last week in August, for the purpose of reviewing the work of the past, and planning for the future. Their work is altogether advisory. Joseph Sharp was the first evangelist under the new board, serving from 1885 to 1890, A. C. Smither serving from January, 1890, to August of same year. January, 1891, John A. Stephens accepted the position of evangelist, and is filling it acceptably yet.

Newton college, located near Woodville, was opened March 7, 1843, to both sexes. It closed in 1860. A great many young men were educated here, several for the ministry, who have made useful men. A number made distinguished doctors, lawyers and educators. A great many grand women were educated here.

Southern Christian institute is a mission school with plantation, organized in 1877, for the colored people, with an organized stock basis of $10,000. The present site of the institute was selected in 1882, near Edwards, in Hinds county, twenty-six miles west of Jackson, on the Virginia & Mississippi railroad. The plantation consists of eight hundred acres of number one cotton land. The school at present is under the control of J. B. Lehman and wife, thorough educators.

In 1875 S. R. Jones edited a paper known as the *Unitist*, in the interest of the church. It continued for a year or more and suspended. An attempt or two has since been made to publish a church paper, but owing to the weak condition of the churches, and perhaps more properly to bad, inefficient management in the projectors, none of these attempts have amounted to much, except the last, which promises to prove a valuable church organ—the *Messenger*, an eight-page, three-column paper, published monthly in Jackson, by M. F. Harmon.

It would be unjust to the man, as well as the church in Mississippi, to fail to make special mention of B. F. Manire, a consecrated minister, who has spent a great portion of his life in evangelizing throughout the state, and adding more souls to the church than any other man of his church. The Christian church stands in the front ranks in every reform movement that is calculated to benefit humanity.

The early history of the Baptist denomination in the territory of Mississippi is rendered obscure in consequence of there having been so little attention paid to church records and other written documents. The fact that so many of the early settlers were illiterate, and many in aftertimes looked with indifference, not to say contempt, on the early Baptists and their labors in this country, is the main reason why they were almost forgotten. Yet by diligent search and comparing many documents, a tolerably accurate history of these early pioneers can be written. From this obscure beginning they have grown to be a great and prosperous people.

T. M. Bond, the only historian of this early period, relates that in the spring of 1780, there was a number of emigrants who left South Carolina for the country of the Natchez. On arriving at the Holston river, in Tennessee, they provided themselves with boats, three in number, and undertook the perilous task of passing down the waters of Tennessee, Ohio and Mississippi, to their place of destination. Among these emigrants were some ten or a dozen members of the Baptist church. One of the members was Richard Curtis, a licensed minister, with a large family. We have also learned the following names, as heads of families, viz.: John Courtney, John Jones, Daniel Ogden, William Ogden, —— Perkins. The emigrants, in descending the streams, had to pass through the country owned by the Cherokee and other Indian tribes, having to pass shoals and narrows, and bends that very much exposed them to the hostility of the Indians, who availed themselves of one of these places, and fired on the foremost boat, in which was Elder Curtis and his family. The wife of William Curtis shielded her husband with a thick poplar stool, which caught one or more bullets, while he was plying the oar. Another female sized the steering oar, that her husband might use his rifle, and with dauntless heroism guided the vessel, until disabled by a wound.

The second boat passed unharmed. The third boat was considerably behind, in consequence of having the small-pox on board, and the Indians captured it and massacred all on board, except one woman, who was taken captive. She remained two or three years among the Indians, when, by treaty, she was restored to her friends. She stated that the Indians took the small-pox, and great numbers of them died. The other two boats after a long and perilous voyage, landed at Cole's creek, a few miles above Natchez, and formed a settlement. After they had reared their cabins in the forest, they immediately instituted the worship of God in these far western wilds, by holding meetings in their private houses, which were blest of the Lord to the comforting of the followers of the Savior. This was the first Protestant community formed in all the wide region of the Southwest, below the Cumberland settlements in middle Tennessee. At that period the Natchez county nominally belonged to Great Britain, but after the treaty of 1783 passed, for a time, into the hands of Spain.

In this community was soon organized a Baptist church called Salem. It was constituted without a presbytery, or even the presence of a single ordained minister. They simply agreed to meet together statedly, and worship God according to His word, and to exercise gospel discipline over one another, and called Elder Curtis to preach to them, whose labors were eventually greatly blessed. This course was a matter of necessity with them, and the Lord greatly owned and blessed his labors in the conversion of many sinners. As it was probable that they would never see an ordained Baptist minister the converts were baptised by Curtis.

We know but little of the church and its affairs until 1793 or 1794. About that time a Spanish Catholic, by the name of Stephen de Alvo, renounced the Romish religion and joined the Baptists. This, together with the denunciation of the Catholics by a man by the name of Harigail, greatly incensed the Catholics, so that they determined to make an example of some of the leaders. William Hamberlin, Richard Curtis and Stephen de Alvo were selected as the chief offenders. A letter was written by Gayoso, the Spanish commandant, to Curtis, expostulating with him upon his course. To this Curtis replied bluntly, and an order for his arrest was issued and he was brought before Gayoso April 6, 1795. After threatening to send Curtis, Hamberlin and de Alvo to the mines in Mexico, they were discharged, with an injunction not to offend again. An edict was also issued that if nine persons were found worshiping together, except according to the form of the Catholic church, they should suffer imprisonment. But the church continued to meet privately for worship, and Mr. Curtis officiated publicly in a marriage ceremony in 1795. This was considered a violation of the law, and an attempt was made to arrest him, but he made good his escape in company with Hamberlin and de Alvo, and they made their journey across the country to South Carolina, where they arrived in the fall of 1795. At the end of two years and a half Curtis returned, having been ordained during his stay in South Carolina. The country now passed into the hands of the United States, the Baptists had rest and prospered greatly.

In 1800 a church was constituted in Wilkinson county, four miles from Woodville, by a part of the Ogden family and others. About the same time one was constituted on Second creek, and possibly was called New Hope. In 1805 the New Providence church, Amite county, was constituted, and Ebenezer in 1806. These five churches met, by their delegates, in September, 1806, and organized the first association and called it the Mississippi. It has had a long and honored career and still exists.

The denomination grew rapidly. In 1812 there were seventeen churches in the state with a membership of seven hundred and sixty-four. In 1836 there were one hundred and seven churches, ninety-two pastors, and four thousand eight hundred and sixty-five members. In 1860 there were five hundred and ninety-six churches, three hundred and five pastors, forty-one thousand four hundred and eighty-two members.

In 1820 the Pearl River and Union associations were organized. In 1835 there were six associations, and in 1859 there were twenty-one associations.

A Baptist state convention was organized in 1822. The sixth annual session was held October 21, 1828. After that period the convention declined and soon afterward became extinct. The present state convention was organized at Palestine church, Hinds county, in 1837. Rev. L. B. Holloway preached the introductory sermon from the words: "Thy Kingdom Come." Rev. Ashley Vaughn was president. Prominent in the counsels of this meeting were Benjamin Whitfield, W. J. Denson, S. S. Lattimore, Ashley Vaughn, L. B. Holloway, Charles Felder, Lee Compere, R. G. Green, Norvel Robertson and T. S. N. King.

The call for this convention was made by the Mississippi association, at its session October, 1836. The following resolutions were passed by that body:

Resolved, that this association deem it important that the Baptists in this state should unite in convention by delegates at a proper time and place, to take into consideration the adoption of some systematic plan by which the efforts of the denomination may be united, her resources drawn out, the gospel preached to the destitute, religious information disseminated, and such other objects as may be important to the advancement of the Redeemer's kingdom promoted.

Resolved, that we unite in recommending a meeting consisting of delegates from churches, missionary societies, and also of individuals in good standing in the regular Baptist denomination, to be held in Washington, on Friday before the fourth Lord's day in December next, to consider the propriety of forming a state convention of our denomination.

The Bethel association joined in with the call from the Mississippi, and accordingly the meeting was held at Washington preliminary to the organization of the state convention. An address was drawn up by Ashley Vaughn, S. S. Lattimore and T. S. N. King. "The proceedings of these two associations," declared the address, "were in perfect accordance with the feelings and wishes of a large number of the churches and individuals belonging to the various associations in the state."

An extended editorial in the *Luminary* for November, 1836, disclaims for the convention all right to usurp any authority whatever over churches, or associations, or individuals, and makes the following points in favor of the state convention:

What, then, are the advantages which it is supposed will accrue to the cause of Christ from the formation of a state convention?

1. The gospel will be more extensively and habitually preached to the destitute in the bounds of the state.

2. Feeble and destitute churches will be sought out and visited, and encouraged to "strengthen the things that remain that are ready to die."

3. A more general interest will be taken in relation to the extension of the Redeemer's kingdom in foreign lands.

4. The strength and energies of the denomination in the state will be more entirely and harmoniously concentrated.

5. Religious information, generally, will be more widely disseminated, and the cause of education—particularly the religious education of youth—encouraged.

6. Christian intercourse, and Christian fellowship, and Christian union, will be greatly promoted.

The meeting was accordingly held at Washington. The constitution that was adopted is strikingly like the one the convention now has. The second article sets forth that the objects of this convention shall be to organize and digest an operative system of measures in relation to missionary exertions throughout the state of Mississippi; to promote religious education; support missionary service among the destitute, both at home and abroad; and to adopt from time to time such measures as shall be considered by the convention calculated to promote the general interest of the Redeemer's kingdom, particularly within the bounds of the state.

At this preliminary meeting at Washington, and at the first annual meeting at Palestine, the convention put itself squarely upon missionary and educational grounds. So far back as 1811, the Mississippi association had taken steps to supply the destitution in her own borders, and the convention organized upon the basis of missionary work.

At a very early period Mississippi Baptists began to move in educational matters. Their first efforts were far from successful, but they never faltered till ultimate success was reached. Dr. William Carey Crane wrote of these early efforts: "Prior to the adoption of the college at Clinton by the convention, sad failures were made. The Judson institute was located on Society ridge, Hinds county, in 1836, under the charge of Elder L. B. Holloway, but the location (so says a circular of 1841) was found so unhealthy that, after having expended a considerable amount of money, our denomination saw the necessity of removing it, and accordingly removed it to Palestine, in an opposite extreme of the same county, to which, after two years' experience, it was found that there existed not only the same objection, but another, if possible, worse—the surrounding country was too poor to support a school. It was then determined to locate and found the school at Middleton, and accordingly, under the presidency of Elder S. S. Latimore, and A. S. Bayley and R. Nason, professors, the institution lived a fitful life till about 1842, it declined, and the convention, in 1844, appointed a committee to ascertain what connection it had with it, inasmuch as the legislature, which had chartered it, had never passed any act recognizing a conventional connection with it. Since that time it has never been spoken of in the convention. An abortive effort was made to purchase the Mississippi Springs property, in Hinds county, in 1847."

But at this time Mississippi college became the property of the Baptists. It was one of the oldest schools of the state. It was chartered in 1826 as Hemstead academy, and was the first school in the state that ever conferred a diploma. In 1830 its name was changed to Mississippi college; in 1842 it was transferred to the Presbyterians, and in 1850 passed into the hands of the Baptists. This was the long-hoped-for opportunity. An agent was put in the field, and by 1860 a cash endowment of $100,000 was raised, with $30,000 more pledged and $20,000 worth of buildings erected. Unfortunately, the whole endowment was lost by the war and the college suspended.

At this period female colleges were in successful operation at Grenada, Chulahoma, Clinton, Lexington, Hernando and Castillian Springs.

The history of Baptist newspapers in the state, preceding the war, is suggestive of wise reflection. Dr. Crane, writing in 1858, says: "The *Southwestern Luminary* was conducted by Elder A. Vaughn through the year 1837, and in February, 1838, was merged into the Mobile *Monitor and Southwestern Luminary*, under the care of Elder G. F. Heard. The *Mississippi Baptist* was commenced in January, 1846, by Elder W. H. Taylor, who was associated with Elder W. C. Crane from July, 1847, to July, 1848, in its editorial care. It was then placed under a committee, consisting of W. C. Crane, W. H. Taylor and L. J. Caldwell. In January, 1849, it was placed under the editorial management of the lamented Elder J. B. Hiteler, and was discontinued in April of that year. A committee, consisting of Elders I. T. Tichenor, G. W. Allen, L. J. Caldwell and G. H. Martin, edited it for a short time. In January, 1857, it was revived at Grenada, under the editorial care of Elder J. T. Freeman, and removed to Jackson. It is now spreading itself like the green bay tree, and commanding the warmest regard and cordial support of the denomination throughout the state." But, like every other institution of the state, the *Mississippi Baptist* was wrecked by the war.

From 1861 to 1865 the whole country was desolated by the ravages of war. The *Mississippi Baptist* suspended publication, our institutions of learning were closed, some of them never to open again; missionary work ceased, except among the soldiers, wealth gone, the churches disrupted, the Baptist denomination had scarcely more than a name to live. Worse than all of this, the war had fired the fiercest passions of the human breast, and the terrible days of reconstruction blighted and demoralized the moral and religious sentiment of the entire country. It took brave and stout hearts for leaders in those days; but the Lord did not fail for men to stand before Him. Gen. M. P. Lowry, Col. L. Ball, and a host of others, laid aside the sword and musket, declined every political preferment, and gave themselves to the moral uplifting of the state. It was an arduous work, but the results have been entirely satisfactory.

One of the first things done was to reopen Mississippi college. Not only was the endowment swept away, but a great debt in the shape of scholarships threatened the existence of the college. Dr. Walter Hillman became president, and through his management the debt was removed and the success of the institution was assured. For nearly twenty years Rev. W. S. Webb, D. D., has been the efficient president. The college now has an endowment of about $50,000, and the outlook is encouraging. The catalogue of 1890-91 shows eight instructors and two hundred and fifty students.

A number of flourishing female colleges have also been established. Central Female institute, now Hillman college, Dr. Walter Hillman, president; Blue Mountain Female college, Dr. W. T. Lowrey, president; Starkville Female institute, Dr. T. G. Sellers, president; Shuqualak Female college, Rev. L. M. Stone, president; Lea Female college, Dr. C. H. Otkin, president, and Carrollton Female college, Rev. Z. T. Leavell, president, all have an honored history. Besides these, numerous high schools have been planted in various localities, and it is likely that many more will be founded.

Following the war, as we have intimated already, there was a great missionary work to be done. The Baptists were scattered and discouraged, while the destitution was appalling. For a time every man worked on the wall over and against his own house, and did that which was right in his own eyes. After a time organized work was begun in associations, and the Domestic Mission board was able to do something.

In 1873 the convention met at Aberdeen, Miss. A committee consisting of T. J. Walne, C. Smith, W. H. Hardy, J. A. Hackett and E. Smith reported a plan of work as follows:

1. That this convention appoint a board on state missions, to be known as the "State Mission Board of the Mississippi Baptist State Convention."

2. This board shall be located at Hazlehurst, Copiah county, Miss., and shall be composed of fifteen members, who shall elect from their own number a president, two vice presidents, a recording secretary and a treasurer.

3. This board, when duly organized, shall have charge of the domestic mission work within the bounds of this convention, and shall be empowered and instructed to employ a corresponding secretary; to secure the closest and heartiest co-operation possible with all the churches and associations within our bounds in domestic mission work; to raise funds, employ missionaries, and supply, so far as possible, the destitution throughout the state.

Thus was the State Mission board organized, which under God did such a great and mighty work. Oxford at length became its local habitation, and Rev. T. J. Walne became corresponding secretary. He served faithfully and successfully for eleven years, when he was succeeded by Rev. L. Ball. This board strengthened the places that were ready to die, preached the gospel in many waste places, and was a powerful agency in putting the Baptists of the state in the front rank of missionary work.

In 1885 the convention again met at Aberdeen. It was felt that the work of the state must be put upon still broader basis. Accordingly the old State Mission board, which had done so grandly, was abolished, and the convention board was organized and took its place. It was declared that this board should take collections for state missions, home missions, foreign missions, Mississippi college, ministerial education and sustentation. Rev. J. B. Gambrell, who had been foremost in presenting and urging this plan, was elected corresponding secretary. He served two years, and resigned on account of other pressing duties. Rev. J. T. Christian, the present incumbent, was then elected. The work of this board has been successful from the start. It has now sixty missionaries in the field, and its financial report for the year just closed aggregated over $70,000 for missions and educational purposes.

A Baptist newspaper was established in Jackson in 1867 called the *Christian Watchman*. It lived only a few months. It was, however, not until 1877 that a successful enterprise of this kind was established. Rev. M. T. Martin began the publication, and Rev. J. B. Gambrell became editor of the *Baptist Record*. This paper continues to be a great power for good. The general association had an organ called the *Southern Baptist*, which was merged into the *Baptist Record*. It now has a paper edited by Rev. N. L. Clarke, called the *Mississippi Baptist*. The progress of the denomination has been great. The statistics in 1891 are as follows: White and colored, ninety-seven associations, one thousand five hundred and eighteen ministers, two thousand five hundred and eighty-seven churches, and one hundred and ninety-one thousand four hundred and twenty-four members.

The history of the American continent for the most part, up to the present century, is practically a history of the Roman Catholic church. We have but to recall the names of Columbus, De Soto, Joliet, La Salle, Marquette and multitudes of others to remind ourselves of the fact. This is partly because state and church were united, and what the church of Rome did was credited to the state from which the instrument of the deed came, or what France, Spain, Italy and other Roman Catholic countries did were all done in the name of the church. Thus so intimately intertwined are the deeds of both on this continent in early days, that history of that period is history of both church and state.

This is true of the territory covered by the state of Mississippi previous to 1798, when it came under the government of the United States, where church and state were and have ever been separate. Since that time the Catholic church has not prospered in Mississippi as has other churches, and, since it is smaller, is so intimately connected with early history in general as to receive considerable mention, but especially because the facts of its career here have been so inaccessible, this sketch must be limited to scarcely more than a general description.

It is well known that De Soto had his priests along with him in 1539-42, when he crossed the present limits of the state, but it was over a hundred years later that we hear much about missionary effort among the Indians of this region by Roman Catholic missionaries. In 1682 Ricollet, Father Zenobius Membre, of La Salle's company, was probably the first to celebrate mass among the Natchez Indians. This was on March 29, 1682, as is learned from Father Membre's account of it. In 1699, when Bienville settled at Biloxi, his chaplain was De Bordenac. In 1701 Father Joliet de Montigny visited the Natchez and Tunicas, but as he made no converts, he returned north to Quebec again. "Father Davion and Montigny arrived at Biloxi in a pirogue," says a local writer. "Father Davion had originally settled at Natchez for a year, but making no converts he went to the Tunicas, and erected a cross on the highest bluffs, where he said mass every morning. It was called Roche a Davion until 1764, when it became known as Loftus Heights, and afterward and ever since as Fort Adams. To this remote cliff, conciliating the various tribes as he traveled, the devoted priest had come bearing upon his shoulders the sacred symbols, with no hope of earthly reward, sustained only by the sublime faith that triumphs even over the terrors of death. Father Montigny had come from the posts on the Illinois to inquire for him, and to take his place if he had perished; and hearing from the Indians of the colony at Biloxi, they journeyed thither, down the Mississippi, down the Mauchac, along Lakes Maurepas and Ponchartrain, through the Rigolets and along the Mississippi sound, under the burning sun and profuse dust of July, camping on the desert shores at night amid myriads of mosquitoes, with no refreshment but a calabash of tepid water and a little dried meat or parched corn! Ten days only they allowed themselves to commune with their countrymen, and then these devoted men set out, as they came, the one to resume his labors among the Tunicas, the other to establish a mission on the Yazoo, or river of death."

By 1722, when the colony had five thousand four hundred and twenty whites and six hundred negroes, about as much in four states as is now in the single city of Jackson, it was organized into three ecclesiastical divisions: From the mouth of the Mississippi to the mouth of the Illinois was the first, and placed in charge of the Capuchin monks; between the Illinois and Wabash was given to the Jesuit fathers; and at Biloxi, Mobile and Toulouse fort were placed the Carmelites. Thus Mississippi's present territory was under the Capuchins and Carmelites in its first organization. It was but a couple of years later that laws were passed, as a feature of the union of church and state, compelling owners to bring up their slaves in the faith of the Catholics, or, if the owners were not good Catholics themselves, their slaves should be owned by the government; amalgamation of races was forbidden also; Jews were expelled and no other religion was to be tolerated. These laws were called the Black code. Father Philibert, a Capuchin, was curé at Natchez about this time, and certainly in 1727.

For the next half century the church grew among the Indians, as well as among the

Caucasian and Negro inhabitants, and was the only church within the present boundaries of Mississippi. Under the Spanish control of Don Gayoso, and others, later in the eighteenth century, and when Natchez was the metropolis, it bore a prominent part in public life. "The Catholic religion was the only one tolerated in the country," said an old citizen of Natchez, resident there at that date. "The priests exercised much influence, and were very generally loved. They had great power and used it very mildly. Irish priests were usually selected for Natchez, because there were so many English-speaking people. I well remember Father Brady—the best shot, the best rider, and the best judge of horses in the district. And Father Malone, with a wink and a joke, and a blessing and an alms for every one—welcome at every wedding, every frolic and every dinner—most exemplary in the discharge of every duty, but with a slight weakness for his national beverage on St. Patrick's day, when his patriotism would prove stronger than his head. However, in these days, and for years after, the clergy of all denominations took their morning nips and their midday toddy and were always considered the best judges of Maderia. Attempts were made by several Protestant ministers to preach but were not encouraged. The only sermon I remember to have heard during the Spanish rule was preached by an Episcopalian named Cloud. [Rev. Adam Cloud. See sketch of the Episcopal church in these volumes—Ed.] Governor Gayoso was present and walked home with my father after the service. He expressed himself in their conversation as being individually in favor of religious toleration, 'but', he added, 'you know I have a master.' The next day Cloud was notified that he must not preach again; but, he, persisting in doing so, was shortly arrested and sent out of the country."

It was the friction of the intense Protestant and Catholic feeling against each other in those days that added to the discord of the transfer of the territory to American hands. The first governor-sergeant, native of a Puritan region, unused to the customs of Catholic countries, such as attending mass in the morning and attending picnics, and having similar pleasures in the afternoon, even contemplated seizing the Catholic church building and using it for a courthouse, and was only prevented from doing so by motives of expediency. One reason for the decrease of the church after 1798 was the removal of many Catholics in sympathy with the Spanish power beyond the boundaries of Mississippi territory.

During the present century, however, they have not decreased, but while reaching far below the numbers of the great denominations of the state, it has made substantial progress and extended all over the state. In the year 1876, they had within one of as many organizations as the Episcopal church, and was next in size to the Baptist, Methodist, Presbyterian and Episcopalian churches. At that date there were thirty-two organizations scattered over the state, chiefly in the cities and along the gulf coast. There were nine chapels erected, and in various parishes there was a total of twenty-six priests, four of whom were not employed in parish work. They also had several flourishing institutions, one of which was a literary one for young men; for the young ladies there were five female academies; and the primary work for children was cared for in eleven parochial free schools. In their care for orphans they had provided two schools, one for each sex. The extra Catholic population at this time, including all members of Catholic families, was estimated at twelve thousand.

It is very difficult to compare churches bearing the organizing principles of this one with those of a different method of government and arrangement. The membership of the Catholic church includes all who are born into it as well as those who enter by conversion. Even their communicant list includes all above an age that varies between nine and eleven years, while such denominations as the Baptist church seldom have members below the age of maturity. Therefore, when it is stated that the Catholic church in Mississippi had eleven thousand three hundred and forty-eight communicants in 1890, the membership of mature age would be considerably less. This (eleven thousand three hundred and forty-eight) was the number in 1890. The great mass of these are chiefly in five different counties, and the larger number in the respective counties is indicated by the order in which they are mentioned: Harrison county, with one thousand nine hundred and fifteen; Hancock, with one thousand six hundred and eighty-two; Warren, with one thousand four hundred and twenty-six; Jackson county, with one thousand one hundred and forty; Adams, with one thousand and fifty. All other counties contain less than five hundred each, the smallest number being seven in Coahoma county, and the largest, four hundred and fifty in Madison county. The total number of organizations in the state is sixty-seven, the largest number, ten, being in Harrison county, and the second largest in Hancock county. There are nearly as many church edifices as organizations, the number being sixty, the largest numbers of these in any one county being in those last mentioned, and they are capable of seating in all about thirteen thousand four hundred and forty-eight persons. The value of the property of the church in this state is $321,525, the most expensive proportions being in Natchez, Vicksburg, Meridian and the coast counties. There are but three counties in which property is not owned, where there is a Catholic population, and there are thirty-seven counties that have such population, namely: Adams, Alcorn, Bolivar, Chickasaw, Claiborne, Clarke, Clay, Coahoma, Copiah, Covington, Hancock, Harrison, Hinds, Holmes, Jackson, Jasper, Jefferson, Lauderdale, Leake, Lee, Leflore, Lincoln, Lowndes, Madison, Marshall, Monroe, Neshoba, Noxubee, Panola, Perry, Pike, Warren, Washington, Wilkinson, Winston, Yalobusha and Yazoo.

The church in Mississippi is in the province of New Orleans, and the diocese of Natchez, which is coincident in its boundaries with the boundaries of the state. The bishop of the diocese is located at Natchez, whose beautiful cathedral is one of the prominent historical and architectural features of the city.

As the city of Natchez has always been the headquarters for Catholicity in the state, it may suggest some further features, for two years before the site was chosen for a city a permanent mission had been established there. The priests located at this time were as follows: Father St. Cosme among the Natchez, Father Montigny among the Tensas, and Father Davion among the Tunicas. In 1702 Father Foucault was among the Yazoos, and was the first martyr of the region, being killed by his treacherous Koroas guides. Father Charlevoix visited the place in 1721, and found that for several years no priest had been there to replace the dead. In 1729 Father Du Poisson was the first victim of the great massacre, and these martyrs are remembered by three arrows in the coat of arms of the bishop of Natchez. From 1763 to 1783 under British rule, no mention of priest or church can be found.* In 1779 the new Spanish Governor Grandpré, re-established the services, and on April 11, 1788, the square included in Franklin, Rankin, State and Wall streets was bought for a parochial residence, and a two-story frame church in the center of Natchez was erected, and three Irish priests arrived before 1790: Revs. William Savage, Gregory White and Constantine McKenna, the superior being Rev. Savage. Very soon, March 29, 1798, the clergy retired with the Spanish government, and on the theory of union of church and state, the property fell to the United States government. Natchez was under the Havana see in 1793, and later on of New Orleans and Baltimore. After the governmental change the first priest to return was Rev. F. Lennon, and in 1802 Father Boudin. In 1819, after several years of misfortune, a Kentucky priest arrived, and from 1820 to 1824 Rev. Maenhut was priest.

---
*Sketch of Catholic Church in Natchez, pamphlet of 1886.

Other priests followed, but on December 28, 1832, the church building was destroyed by fire, and in 1838 Father Van de Velde was sent to make preliminaries for the establishment of an episcopal see, and the next year Father Brogard became pastor and remained until after his consecration in Baltimore. March 14, 1841, Bishop J. J. Chanche, the first Natchez bishop arrived, and the diocese, covering the state, began with two priests only and not a church in the state. His first services were at Mechanics' hall, and on February 24, 1842, there was laid the corner-stone of the noble cathedral of St. Mary's. Among his earliest missionaries to the central parts of the state were Rev. Father Francois, A. Desgaultiers, L. Muller, S. H. Montgomery and G. S. Bohme. In 1849 several came, and among them was the Very Rev. M. F. Grignon. Bishop Chanche died July 22, 1853, after a service of years marked with great growth. His successor was Bishop Van de Velde, December 18, 1853, but the prevailing epidemic caused his death only two years later on November 13, 1855. He it was who began the college, besides increasing the mission. Bishop William H. Elder was his successor—a name very dear to the people of his church, and to the sufferers whom he relieved during the bloody scenes of war. On account of his refusal to comply with a military order in 1863 that public prayer should be offered for the president, and for the rebellious intents he construed it to indicate, he was removed to Vidalia, but on petitions was released August 12 of that year. On January 30, 1880, he was appointed to the archiepiscopal see of Cincinnati, and was succeeded here by Bishop F. Janssens on May 7, 1881. The cherished work of this bishop has been that of education, and it is largely to his efforts that the schools before mentioned are in existence. After his promotion to the archbishopric of New Orleans, he was succeeded by the present incumbent—the Rt.-Rev. Thomas Heslin, D. D., who is too well and favorably known to need comment.

While the larger religious bodies are the Methodists, Baptists, Presbyterians, Cumberland Presbyterians, Protestant Episcopalians, Christians (commonly called Campbellites, after their great leader), and Roman Catholic, there are numerous other smaller churches and miscellaneous religious and reformatory bodies that deserve mention. In the northern part of the state is a considerable body of the Associate Reformed Presbyterians, and also numbers of the Primitive Baptists, whose strict tenets have won them the sobriquet of Hard Shell among the uninitiated. To the south are some Seventh Day Adventists, and scattered here and there in the state some English Lutherans. Here and there are a few Congregationalists also, but their work is chiefly among the colored people and of an excellent character. One mission of the Latter Day Saints exists. Jewish synagogues also may be found in the leading cities.

Among other religious societies are the Young Men's Christian association, the Young Women's Christian association, the Woman's Christian Temperance union, the King's Daughters and the Young People's Society of Christian Endeavor, their relative size being estimated in this order. The temperance movement has been distinctive enough to warrant a separate sketch of that. The largest of the others, the Young Men's Christian association, was not very vigorous until the year 1887, when the first state convention was held at Columbus, on March 25-29. Annual conventions have been held since at Greenville, Meridian, West Point and Natchez, and several associations have been organized through the state, a few of which have women's auxiliaries.

The state has five hundred and thirty-nine thousand seven hundred and three white people, and the above refers chiefly to religious activity among them; but the state has seven hundred and forty-seven thousand seven hundred and twenty colored people, and two thousand one hundred and seventy-seven Indians and Chinese, and the religious life among them, while

EAST MISSISSIPPI INSANE ASYLUM, MERIDIAN.

crude and not unmixed with superstition in the mass, has made rapid strides in improvement in the last decade. Previous to the war the slaves were attached to the churches of their masters, and at service usually had seats in a gallery to the rear. Many masters secured preachers to minister to their slaves, and many an old "uncle," with his old "missus" to read and interpret the Bible, held services on the plantation in the "quarters." As the Methodist, Baptist and Presbyterian churches were the largest, the great mass of the colored people, who were thus interested, were organized separately in those denominations after the war, and those now embrace by far the greater part of the church membership among them. In the larger educational centers, where an educated ministry are used, the service is not far below that of many white churches among the laboring classes of Northern states, but in the country, where the old "uncle" still holds forth, the scenes are often as ludicrous as they are sad, and the interpretations of the Scriptures take on the wonders of the Arabian Nights' Entertainment, yet withal their rapid progress gives large hopes for the future, as they are the subject of the interest and efforts of every religious body in the United States, as well as of the white churches of their own state.

The Woman's Christian Temperance union. In 1881 Miss Frances E. Willard, president of the National Woman's Christian Temperance union, left the first Woman's Christian Temperance union footprint made on Mississippi soil. Miss Willard was then on that grand pilgrimage—the most heroic ever attempted—to every town in the United States numbering ten thousand inhabitants. Constrained by an overmastering pity for human blight and weakness to preach a gospel men did not wish to hear; to meet limp fingers, hearts frostbitten by indifference, custom, prejudice, conservatism outraged by a woman's public speaking—all braved for the sublime faith in everybody's noble soul, if it could only be gotten at, that—

"She who most believes in man,
Makes him what she believes"—

thus it was that the Woman's Christian Temperance union introduced itself to Mississippi, "coming up," as Miss Willard said in a personal letter, "forlorn enough, all alone, from New Orleans; taking tea with Mrs. Judge Sharkey in Jackson, to whom I had a letter; speaking to a small audience, convened, I think, by a Good Templar, and leaving on the night train for Georgia. Nothing came of that, to human vision."

In 1882 Miss Willard, accompanied by her private secretary, Miss Anna Gordon, invested the month of January in Mississippi. It rained the whole month, with that lavish prodigality for which the South is famed; and "surely," as Miss Gordon remarked, "their work ought to grow and the seed to sprout, for it was literally sown under water." Quoting from the above mentioned letter, Miss Willard says: "I came by invitation of Judge J. W. C. Watson, of Holly Springs, one of the ex-Confederate senate, a graduate of the University of Virginia, and one of La Fayette's attendant guards when he visited the Old Dominion. This good and earnest Presbyterian elder and temperance man had kindly welcomed me, I think, on that pioneer trip in 1881, and visited Lake Bluff, near Chicago, the following summer, inviting us to make this visit, he paying traveling expenses and providing entertainment. He was circuit judge and made my engagements in his own district, at Holly Springs, Grenada, Oxford, Water Valley, etc., and taking Anna and me to the capital, where I spoke before the legislature, Rev. Dr. C. K. Marshall presiding, and making me altogether at home by his noble, brotherly words. He was a good friend always. I have been entertained in his Vicksburg home, and earnestly lament his loss to every good cause. Colonel Inge, of Corinth, was speaker of the house that winter, and through him and his wife we were invited to Corinth. I have been in Natchez, Meridian, Fayette and several other Mississippi towns, but most of all enjoyed the convention at Crystal Springs, where you were present. On that trip we had a meeting at Jackson, making three in all, and this time in a church. That showed decided gains, and I verily believe it was Presbyterian at that."

It was in the good old Methodist church, that has always helped those women; but Rev. Dr. Hunter, the well beloved pastor of the Presbyterian church at Jackson for more than thirty years, was in the pulpit, and Mr. Charlton Alexander, a Presbyterian elder, introduced Miss Willard. Rev. Drs. W. C. Black and C. K. Marshall, of the Methodist church, were also in the pulpit. Miss Willard spoke to an overwhelming, enthusiastic and representative audience of Jackson.

On January 19, 1882, Miss Willard made an address in Oxford. Sixteen ladies gave their names to form a W. C. T. U., and the number was soon increased to thirty-six. Mrs. A. P. Stewart was elected president, and was virtually state president (this being then the only union in Mississippi) till November 20, 1883. At that date Miss Willard and Miss Gordon came to Corinth, wishing to organize a state W. C. T. U. Colonel Inge, Rev. Dr. Steel, Rev. J. A. Bowen and others took the matter in hand and advertised it as freely as possible. In the afternoon and evening of that day Miss Willard made two addresses. That night the state W. C. T. U. was formally organized, with Mrs. F. E. Steele, of Corinth, president. The following are the minutes of that convention: The next morning Miss Willard made another address, and the Corinth local union was formed, with Mrs. Dr. T. Wilson as president. Mrs. Steele explains that this first state organization had its officers all from Corinth because but one lady from outside that town was present. Mrs. Steele also states: "It seemed almost impossible to arouse the women. We sent out an organizer and partly formed several unions, but they soon fell through for lack of help and information. In the summer of 1884, I heard of Mrs. M. E. Ervin, of Columbus, and appointed her to represent Mississippi in the national W. C. T. U. convention at St. Louis.

At the instance of Miss Frances E. Willard, of Chicago, president of the Women's National Christian Temperance union, a large meeting was held at the Methodist Episcopal Church South, in Corinth, November 20, 1883, for the purpose of organizing a State Woman's Christian Temperance union. The object of the meeting was explained by Miss Willard, prayer offered by Rev. Amos Kendall, Colonel Inge was elected chairman and Rev. Eugene Johnson secretary of the meeting. Committees were appointed as follows: On credentials—Rev. I. D. Steele, Miss Anna Gordon and Mrs. S. E. McCord. On plans and constitution—Dr. N. C. Steele, Elder M. Kendrick, Rev. R. Young, Mrs. N. S. Moore, Mrs. W. G. Kimmons, Mrs. T. D. Duncan and Miss Anna Gordon. On nomination of officers— Col. J. D. Bills, Col. C. W. McCord, J. M. Martin, Mrs. J. E. Gift, Mrs. W. M. Inge, Mrs. T. B. Hale and Mrs. Kirk Hall. After some routine business and short addresses the convention adjourned till the following morning at nine o'clock. A mass meeting was held at night in the Cumberland Presbyterian church, at which time and place Miss Willard delivered an able and heartily appreciated address to a crowded house of listeners.

"Officers for the state union: President, Mrs. N. C. Steele, Corinth, First congressional district; vice president, Mrs. W. M. Inge, Corinth, First congressional district; vice president, Miss Lizzie Watson, Holly Springs, Second congressional district; vice president, Mrs. Dr. Slack, Friar's Point, Third congressional district; vice president, Mrs. Octavia Wofford, Okolona, Fourth congressional district; vice president, Mrs. Mary Hoskins, Lexington, Fifth congressional district; vice president, Mrs. Neilson, Natchez, Sixth congressional district; vice president, Mrs. C. B. Galloway, Jackson, Seventh congressional district; recording secretary,

Miss Mamie Caldwell, Corinth; treasurer, Mrs. Kirk Hall, Corinth; corresponding secretary, Mrs. S. E. McCord, Corinth; superintendent of temperance literature, juvenile work and publications, Mrs. N. Steele, Corinth."

Mrs. Ervin says: "When I received Mrs. Steele's letter in October I had never heard of the state organization. I replied that I was the Lord's and He could send me wherever he willed in His service. I had ever regarded this glorious work as a vine of His own planting. It had been dear to me since the 'Crusade days' when a 'shut-in' invalid. I had crept to the closet many times a day to pray with those who were going into the saloons to pray. Although I had less than a week's notice, 'I will direct thy work in truth' was a proven promise, and I went."

A state convention had been called to meet at Winona, Miss., two days after the national convention. Owing to the illness of her private secretary Miss Willard failed to meet her appointment but sent Mrs. C. B. Buell, national corresponding secretary, and Mrs. Sallie F. Chapin, superintendent of Southern work. A local union had been formed at Columbus and Mrs. M. E. Ervin elected to represent it at Winona. Lifted skyward on the afflatus of the great St. Louis meeting, these three sisters entered Winona. Doors were all open for delegates. Speakers were ready, but where was the convention? Rev. L. E. Hall, of Shubuta, and Mrs. Ervin represented the whole state! Even the president, Mrs. Steele, was absent, detained by sickness in her home. There was a rousing time anyhow, for Mrs. Chapin's tragic eloquence and Mrs. Buell's sledge-hammer logic brought out crowded houses and applied power at their end of the lever raised Mississippi up into range of vision. Mrs. M. L. Wells, of Tennessee, gave six weeks of pioneer service this year to Mississippi, organizing many unions that still hold up a brave standard. Governor St. John also visited the eastern portion of the state in 1884; he was heartily welcomed and the prohibition banners he set up then have never been furled, nor will be till they have signaled the destruction of the liquor traffic from the dome of the state capitol.

In September, 1885, the state held its first delegated convention at Meridian. Nineteen local unions had paid state dues that year and seventeen were represented in convention. On account of failing health Mrs. Steele had resigned the state presidency immediately after the annual meeting at Winona; by her appointment Mrs. M. E. Ervin acting as president.

At Meridian the following state officers were elected: Mrs. M. E. Ervin, president; Mesdames S. F. Clark of Shannon, A. E. Harper, Fayette, vice presidents; Mrs. M. M. Snell, corresponding secretary; Miss Jimmie Petty, Meridian, recording secretary; Mrs. F. E. Steele, Corinth, treasurer.

Annual conventions have been held since at Jackson, Columbus, Natchez, Crystal Springs, Oxford, Brookhaven. Mrs. Ervin resigned at Natchez and Mrs. Lavinia S. Mount was elected president. Mrs. Chattie Beall of West Point and Mrs. M. J. Quinche of Oxford have served the state as vice presidents; Mrs. Helen R. Garner of Columbus, Mrs. E. C. Hurlbutt of Meridian and Mrs. Vic Gambrell of Brookhaven, as corresponding secretaries. Mrs. Chattie Beall, Mrs. M. L. Hood, of Tupelo, and Miss Zelle McLaurin, of Meridian, as treasurers. Mrs. L. S. Mount, Miss Madge Montgomery, of Stockville, as recording secretaries.

The W. C. T. U. has brought here Mrs. Caroline Buell, Mrs. S. F. Chapin, Mrs. Lydia Hoffman, Mrs. J. K. Barney, Mrs. Mary T. Lathrop, Mrs. Mary Reade Goodale, Mrs. M. L. Wells, Miss Anna Gordon; and Mother Wallace gave a month's work in the state. It is due to this brave old friend of women to say that nobody ever came at our call who so universally won the people's heart, and great was the lamentation in Mississippi when the news of her recent violent illness was made public. Men, rather more than women, paid her homage, as might have been expected in a state which in a constitutional convention has brought the question of woman's enfranchisement, with an educational qualification, into open discussion and serious consideration; introduced by Hon. John Tewell and supported by such men as Gen. S. D. Lee, Judge J. B. Chrisman and Judge Woods, of the supreme bench.

The greater part of the public men of Mississippi favor woman's ballot, limited by an educational test. Every community has its advocates. That it is an open question in the state is perhaps due to the noble handling of the subject by Mrs. Zerelda Wallace in her progress through the chief towns, as well as to a universal habit of justice to women in the state's administration, as evinced by the perfect equality of men and women before the law respecting property.

The chief legal measures which the W. C. T. U. has influenced have been the removing of the liquor licenses from the public education fund; the raising of the age of consent from ten years to protection for a woman of any age; the making a woman eligible to the state office of librarian. Mrs. H. B. Kells was perhaps the first person to advocate the latter through the press, claiming that the person who discharged the duties of the office should be voted for as though an elector. Mrs. Mary Morancy, of Jackson, had filled the place for fourteen years, and by her superior qualification had made that of Mississippi the second state library in the nation.

The measure which has most universally received the support of the W. C. T. U. is scientific temperance instruction for the public schools. This department was adopted in 1885, and Mrs. H. B. Kells appointed superintendent. A bill was introduced into the legislature of 1886, which received sufficient support to be appended to an amendment of the educational laws, but it was lost in engrossment. The legislature of 1888 passed another bill by a unanimous vote in the senate and an overwhelming majority in the house. This bill was vetoed by Governor Lowry, on the ground that the teachers were not educated sufficiently to teach physiology with reference to the effects of alcohol and narcotics on the human system, and because the books would cost too much. In 1890 another bill was lost by a majority of two, owing to the fact that many members of the house were at home in the custody of la grippe. The subject, however, has been introduced into the highest grade of the public schools, and is taught probably in every county in the state, through the personal efforts of the superintendent with county superintendents of public instruction and teachers' institutes and with presidents of private schools and colleges and the state university.

No history of the Mississippi W. C. T. U. would be complete without mention of Mrs. Mollie McGee Snell, of Columbus, who has been identified with the temperance movement since its infancy in Mississippi. Her bold, incisive pen and fearless advocacy on the platform have done much to create sentiment, and hers is one of the best known names in the cause in the Southwest. When Mr. Jefferson Davis opposed constitutional prohibition just as Texas was about to vote on it, it was Mrs. Snell who most ably and successfully answered his arguments.

Nor would W. C. T. U. annals be complete without notice of W. H. Patton, of Shubuta, and Henry Ware, of Pass Christian. It was the former who sent Rev. L. E. Hall to Winona in representation of the prohibitionists of Mississippi in the convention which failed to convene at Winona. There has been no hour in which his brotherly hand has not grasped ours, in which it has failed to hold sympathy, cash, aid in every line, for the W. C. T. U. He has stood by us when no other man cared to face the music of public criticism. Friends have deserted, enemies have been converted, foes have been routed and have overwhelmed us, but through all the din of battle, persistent as fate, W. H. Patton has come out of the cloud of defeat, the tumult of triumph, serene and in steady step with the women who never know when they are defeated.

Henry Ware is one of the clearest thinkers in the South on prohibition questions. He is impervious to questions of expediency; he believes God leads in this cause, and that those who have enlisted under the god of battles must follow without questioning or attempts to change the plans of battle to suit the weak-kneed or non-combatants. He has furnished more money for prohibition than any man, perhaps more than any other hundred men, in the state. He says he believes in God and the good women, and he acts as if he did. Many a time the waves would have seemed too deep for the W. C. T. U. had it not been for the timely outstretching of his strong, full hand and his hearty "Sister, be of good cheer!" He is the best loved Roman of them all, and it will be a sad day in Mississippi when his venerable, obstinate, clear-thinking head no longer crowns the W. C. T. U. conventions.

One other work the W. C. T. U. has made successful. They own and publish, print and edit the strongest W. C. T. U. paper in the land. Now, in its fourth year, it is the organ of the Southern W. C. T. U., established at Waynesville, N. C. Mississippi is the strongest of the Southern state W. C. T. U. organizations, and has nearly doubled its number of unions since May 1. It believes in prohibition and no compromises. It has many warm friends and cordial enemies, whose persecutions have but taught it to bear burdens like good soldiers. Using a strong figure for small trials, certainly the blood of the martyr has proved its seed as much as of the church: "In Christ it beareth all things, believeth all things, hopeth all things." It loves Frances Willard, and believes her called of God to this work, and is raising up an army of young women to follow her, led to-day by Miss Belle Kearney, of Madison county, who is state organizer for the Y's.; a brilliant young woman, native born, who has already won her laurels, and of whom the world may expect to hear more.

The chrysanthemum is the chosen flower of the Mississippi union. The state motto is its inspiration:

"Give to the wind the fears,
Hope and be undismayed.
God hears thy sighs, He counts thy tears;
He shall lift up thy head."

CHAPTER XIII.

RECORDS OF FAMILIES AND INDIVIDUALS, M.

DURING the year 1816, and on the 24th of June, John Mackey, one of the oldest citizens of Coahoma county, Miss., was born in South Carolina, being the second of ten children born to Thomas and Martha (Bowdon) Mackey, they being also natives of South Carolina. The former moved from his native state to Alabama, and at the end of thirteen years went to Tennessee, and fifteen years later came to Marshall, Miss., where he remained a worthy citizen and planter until his death, in 1864. His parents were Charles and Lydia (Isom) Mackey, the former being a Revolutionary soldier under Francis Marion, with whom he served throughout his entire campaign. He and his wife were each eighty-seven years of age at the time of their deaths. He was one of the leaders in the capture of a band of tories by Marion, at the time the latter painted the mouths of cannons on the logs of the breastworks. John Mackey's great-great-grandfather was an Irishman by birth, and was considered a rebel by the English government and was compelled to flee the country. He was smuggled to America on board a sailing vessel. The maternal grandfather, Travis Bowdon, was a native of South Carolina. John Mackey was reared principally in Alabama, and was educated by his mother, who was a highly cultivated lady. At the age of twenty-five years he came to Mississippi and located where he now lives and engaged in planting. He has been honest and industrious, and is now the owner of six hundred acres of land, of which two hundred and sixty-seven are under cultivation. He is one of the oldest and most prominent citizens of the county, is well posted on the general topics of the day, and is an entertaining and intelligent conversationalist. Although he had never held an official position, he has always been a stanch democrat, and for some time he has been chairman of the democratic executive committee. He was first married in 1838 to Mrs. Julia C. Moore, a native of Virginia, who was a Miss Adams prior to her first marriage. To this union one child was born: Henry N., who died in infancy. Mrs. Mackey died in 1839, and in 1847 Mr. Mackey took for his second wife, Miss Dorothea R. Cammack, native of Kentucky, and a daughter of Lomax and Dorothea (Robinson) Cammack, natives of Virginia and Kentucky respectively. This wife died in 1877, leaving five children, only one of whom is now living, John B. Mr. Mackey married a third time in 1882, but his wife lived only nine months after their union.

Among the very foremost of the professional men and also of the sturdy and independent class of planters of the state is James H. Maddox, M. D., physician and surgeon, and dealer in general merchandise, drugs, staple and fancy family groceries, Perthshire, Boliver county, Miss. He was born in Mercer county, Ky., on the 2d of July, 1849, the eldest of three children born to James and Ellen (Duncan) Maddox, both of whom were born on blue grass soil. The former was an extensive planter in his native state, but dropped his farming implements for service in the Mexican war, at the end of which he returned to planting, and in 1854 came to Mississippi, where he died in 1873, at the age of sixty-one years. He inherited Welsh blood of his parents, who were Virginians by birth, in which state their ancestors settled during the colonial history of this country. Dr. James H. Maddox came to Mississippi at the age of five years, but at the end of five years he was put to school in Louisville, Ky., the greater part of ten years being spent in educational institutions of that city, during which time he became an exceptionally well-informed young man. His learning was not confined merely to books, but he was well posted on general topics, and possessed an original and thoughtful mind, being, in fact, admirably qualified for a successful and useful career. He returned to Mississippi, and for the past twenty years has been a resident of Bolivar county. In 1870, at the age of twenty-one years, he commenced for himself without any capital whatsoever, but by applying himself diligently to business has made for himself not only the reputation of being a good physician, but a fortune of at least $50,000. He is extensively engaged in planting and is the owner of nine hundred and fifty acres of fine land, eight hundred acres being under cultivation, on which he is erecting a residence which, when completed, will cost at least $6,000, and will be a handsome and modern structure. His plantation is one of the most fertile in this section, and everything about it shows that a man of enlightened and progressive views and energy is at the helm. In 1876 he was united in marriage to Miss Laura A. Blanchard, a daughter of John and Mary (Whitson) Blanchard, and by her is the father of two bright and interesting children: Mary E. and John C. His present wife, whom he married in 1890, was formerly Miss Laura Love. Dr. Maddox is a worthy member of the A. F. & A. M. In personal appearance he is quite distinguished and possesses a fine physique. His hair and eyes are black. He is kind, generous and hospitable, and in him are found the characteristics of the true gentleman.

Hon. James S. Madison, who is classed among the most prominent and successful of Mississippians, is the son of L. W. and Frances Delilah Tucker, the father a native of Laurens district, S. C., born in 1818, and the mother of Marengo county, Ala., in 1829. The parents removed to Lowndes county, Miss., in December, 1850, and after remaining there five years removed to Noxubee county, that state, where they now reside. James S. Madison, one of a family of ten children, was born in Marengo county, Ala., in March, 1834, and was married in Noxubee county in 1876 to Miss Nettie Carpenter, of the same county. Their union has been blessed by the birth of six children, five of whom survive: Edmund C., James J., John L., Josie Inez, Winnie Lee and an infant daughter. Mr. Madison has been engaged in planting all his life, and from his extensive and very productive plantation he raises from one hundred and fifty to two hundred and fifty bales of cotton annually. Mr. Madison was a member of the state troops under Colonel Patton, and in 1876, on the restoration of white rule, he was elected justice of the peace of his district. In 1885 he was elected to represent his county in the lower house of the legislature, and succeeded himself in 1887 and 1889. On the organization of the house in January, 1890, he was chosen its speaker by acclamation, a compliment never before paid in the selection of a presiding officer. Among the members, when the vote was taken, were six republicans, all colored. On the expiration of the session of 1890, Speaker Madison was the recipient of many valuable presents; one of these, a silver water pitcher, was much prized because of its peculiar significance, in that it was presented by the six colored members as a token of their appreciation of his firm and impartial ruling during the session. Speaker Madison also received from the pages a gold-headed cane as a testimonial of their respect. On accepting it he expressed the hope that at some future day they (the pages) might rise to the distinction of representing their people, that some might attain to speaker, but expressed a fear that none of them would ever become as big a man as their present speaker. (Mr. Madison weighs three hundred and twenty pounds.) In 1888 Mr. Madison was the author of the bill for the relief of certain soldiers, sailors and servants of the late war between the states, resident in Mississippi, which feature has since been engrafted upon the constitution of the state. He was also the author of the bill requiring chancery clerks to keep ledger accounts against each office, each official and each line of road in the state; a bill making it a misdemeanor for failure to pay poll-tax, which bill the late constitution virtually repeats; the Madison assessment bill, a bill to equalize assessments which threw the counties into five different grades and the lands in each county in seven different classes, with a cash value upon each class. On the adjournment of the legislature Speaker Madison was by acclamation recommended to the people as a delegate to the constitutional convention, state at large, but circumstances intervened preventing his standing for the position. Mr. Madison is president of the Noxubee County Farmers' Alliance, which office he has held for two years, and he is a member of the Masonic fraternity. His brother, Hon. John E. Madison, third child of the above mentioned union, was educated at Washington and Lee university, Virginia, and took a degree at law at the Mississippi State university, at Oxford. He was a prominent lawyer at Macon, and was the youngest member of the legislature of 1880. He was at one time editor of the *Mississippi Sun*, and later of the Noxubee *Democrat*, and a practitioner at the Macon bar at the time of his death, which occurred in April, 1890.

Hon. Eugene C. Magee was born in Ireland. In 1830 he was practicing law at Vicksburg. In 1835 he represented Warren and Washington counties in the state senate.

Laurin R. Magee has resided in Covington county, Miss., since his birth, in 1825, and is one of a family of the following children: Mary A., Sarah, Caroline, Amanda, Turpen D., Laurin R., Jehu G., Emanuel I., Robert P., Warren G., Jane and Martha. The parents, Robert and Margaret (Graves) Magee, were natives of Chesterfield district, S. C. The father was born in 1791, and grew up to be a soldier in the War of 1812. His father, Philip Magee, was a native of either Virginia or South Carolina. Laurin R. passed his youth in his native county, and served in the war with Mexico under General Quitman. He was in the siege of Vera Cruz, and was a faithful and gallant soldier. At the close of this war he returned to his home, and before the gold fever had abated determined to go to California. In the spring of 1850 he made the journey, and after his arrival there he engaged in mining. Afterward he was engaged in packing supplies to the mines, and remained there until 1856, when he came back home. He was then married to Miss Euphemia Milloy, and engaged in agriculture, which occupation he has since followed. In 1863 he enlisted in the Fourth Mississippi cavalry under Col. T. R. Stockdale, and served until the close of the war. Once more he returned from the battlefield to the pursuits of civilization, which have not been interrupted by the bugle call since 1865. Mr. Magee owns a plantation of one thousand acres of good land, and is one of the most successful planters in the county. He was president of the board of supervisors for the years 1886, 1887, 1888 and 1889. He belongs to the Presbyterian church and occupies a high social standing in the community. He and his wife have reared a family of nine children: Martha I., wife of A. I. Walker; Belle, wife of W. N. Williamson; Sallie, wife of R. A. Campbell; Virginia, Mary, Leroy, Eddie, Wade H. and Estella.

Dr. John W. Magee, a prominent physician and planter of Lincoln county, who lives seventeen miles northwest of Brookhaven, was a native of that part of Copiah county which was set off in the formation of Lincoln county. He was born in 1851, and is a son of Chester and Rachel (Hartley) Magee. His father was a native of Tennessee, his mother of Mississippi. They were married in Copiah county at the residence of Jesse Thompson, the father of Mrs. Magee, who had been previously married to a Mr. Hartley, and by whom she had four children: Jessie, Harvey T., Susan N. and Catherine. She has borne Mr. Magee six children—four sons and two daughters: Mary M., the wife of B. F. Anding, a planter living in Lincoln county, and who has nine children—four sons and five daughters—of whom seven are living; James M., who married Anna Macillas, who is a schoolmaster, living in Texas and who has had five children—two sons and three daughters—of whom one is deceased; Thomas C., who died at Corinth, during the war, and was brought home for burial; Evan, who died at home during the war, leaving a wife, formerly Miss Margaret Anding, and one child; Eliza J., who married J. L. Anding, and died leaving five children, of five sons and two daughters born to them. Dr. Magee was the youngest of six children. Both his father and mother died in the same week in 1866. At that time the subject of our sketch was fourteen years old, and he found a home with an uncle, J. H. Thompson, and three years later he took up the battle of life for himself as a schoolteacher. Later he attended the Summerville institute at Noxubee, county, Miss. After teaching for a time, he entered the employ of Thompson, Lamkin & Co., of Beauregard, Miss., as a clerk in a mercantile establishment. After serving there faithfully for a year, he engaged in planting, but after making one crop, he took up the study of medicine, in due time entering the University of Louisiana, from which he graduated after the usual course. In 1874 he began practicing medicine in Copiah county, Miss., where he has continued with much success until the present time, being in great demand throughout Copiah and Lincoln counties. In 1882 Dr. Magee was married to Miss Anna E. McRee, daughter of David and Epsey (Leech) McRee, who was born in Mississippi in 1853. (See sketch of Samuel P. McRee.) Mrs. Magee was educated at Whitworth Female college, at Brookhaven. She has borne her husband four children, three of whom are now living: David, Lamar, Johnnie, all of whom are living at home, Ida Belle having died in infancy. The family have occupied their present residence since December, 1882. The Doctor and his wife are members of the Methodist Episcopal Church South. Politically, he is a democrat, but he is not, in the ordinary sense, a very active politician, never having sought or accepted offices of any kind, but, at the same time, his interest in the public weal is deep and abiding, and he has ever been a strong and willing supporter of churches, schools, and all laudable public enterprises. He is very prominent as a physician, and, socially, he is regarded very highly by all who know him.

M. G. Maggard is an Alabamian by birth, in which state he first saw the light of day in 1849. After attaining manhood on a farm he removed to Lauderdale county, Miss., in 1860, where he turned his attention to planting, with which calling he was thoroughly familiar. He is now one of the thriftiest and most practical of the planters of the county, and owns one hundred and sixty acres of its choice land. He is one of those progressive planters who makes his land strictly self-sustaining, and to this end raises a diversity of crops, corn and cotton, however, predominating. He began life for himself at the close of the war in very straitened circumstances, but at the present time is entirely free from indebtedness of any kind and is the owner of a fertile and well-kept plantation. During the twenty-two years that he has devoted to agriculture he has never purchased a bushel of corn, which is more than the majority of the planters from his section can say. In the tilling of his land he employs home composts and commercial fertilizers, and being strictly self made, his example is worthy of imitation by others. He is of an honest, frank and generous disposition, is energetic and capable, and moves in the best society. He is a Methodist in his religious views and leads an exemplary life. In 1869 he was married to Miss Mollie Coker, of Lauderdale county, by whom he has six children: John, Effie, Pernecia, Maggie, Zula and Cynthia. Three children are married. The father of M. G. Maggard, David Maggard, was a Virginian, born about 1818, and after reaching manhood was married to Miss Pernecia Gary, of Alabama.

J. H. Magruder, D. D. S., is a skilled and experienced dentist of Jackson, Miss., who, by his superior workmanship and his accommodating and agreeable manners, has built up an extensive practice. He was born in Yazoo City, Miss., in January, 1858, being the second in a family of eleven children born to Dr. A. F. and Julia (Abbey) Magruder, both of whom were Mississippians. The paternal grandfather, John H. Magruder, came to this state from Maryland, and at a very early day settled at Washington, Miss., near Natchez, but later he removed to Madison county, where he spent the remainder of his days. A sketch of the maternal grandfather, Rev. R. Abbey, of Yazoo City, appears in this work. Dr. A. F. Magruder, after finishing his literary education, began the study of medicine at Louisville, Ky., graduating as a medical doctor in 1855. After practicing in Louisiana and Madison county, Miss., he went to Yazoo City in 1870, where he was residing at the time of his death, in 1884. He was a fine general practitioner, but was especially skilled in surgery, and had a large practice. He was of a modest and retiring disposition, was a public-spirited citizen and his death, which occurred on the 14th of December, at the age of fifty-three years and eight months, was a great loss to his family and the community in which he labored. He was a trustee and a member of the Methodist Episcopal Church South. His widow, who survives him, also belongs to that church. Their son, J. H. Magruder, is a steward in the First Methodist church, Jackson. Their marriage was celebrated on the 2d of May, 1855. J. H. Magruder was educated at Yazoo City and in and near Nashville, Tenn. He began the study of dentistry in 1877, and graduated from this department of the Vanderbilt university, of Nashville, in the session of 1881-2. He first began practicing in St. Joseph, La., then at Hazelhurst, Miss., and finally settled in the city of Jackson, in January, 1889, and although he has been here a comparatively short time, he is already well known and has built up a splendid reputation and a fine practice. He is progressive and enterprising and gives every promise of becoming eminent in his profession. He is first vice president of the Mississippi State Dental association and keeps fully abreast of the progress made in his profession. He is a member of the A. F. & A. M. lodge of Jackson. He was first married in October, 1883, to Miss Emma Wailes, daughter of Col. E. Floyd Wailes and niece of B. L. C. Wailes, a native of Louisiana, who died at Yazoo City on the 2d of January, 1885. In 1888 Dr. Magruder was again married to Miss Agnes Harris, of Hazlehurst, a daughter of Capt. L. B. Harris, a prominent lawyer of that place. She is a worthy member of the Methodist Episcopal Church South and has borne her husband two children: Julia Ella and Freeland B.

Dr. Thomas B. Magruder (deceased) was born September 25, 1800, at the ancient family mansion, near Upper Marlboro, Prince George's county, Md., and had he lived one month longer would have reached the age of eighty-five years. After graduating in his profession, Dr. Magruder determined to venture out to the then sparsely populated Southern states, and in 1822, rode on horseback from his native county to this region through the wild, unsettled intervening country, and at the end of a journey of two months, reached Port Gibson, which city and vicinity continued to be his home until his death. He entered at once upon a successful professional career, and he it was who established the first drug store in the town. A year or two after his arrival in this country he was united in marriage to Miss Elizabeth Harrington, by whom he became the father of three sons: Calvit, Hon. W. T. (see sketch), and the late gallant Captain Joseph M., who fell in defense of the lost cause and the land of his nativity. Mrs. Magruder died on the 5th of July, 1844, at the age of forty-six years, after having lived a useful and truly Christian life. In her day it was the custom of the Choctaw Indians, who then inhabited Claiborne county in great numbers, to camp at Gruders, as they pronounced the name, and they were always kindly treated by the mistress of Cabinwood. At her death large numbers of them attended her funeral and expressed the deepest sorrow for the loss of the friend whose kindness and consideration for them never wavered or knew diminution. She was noted for her many acts of charity, and her truly Christian character is well worthy of emulation. In 1845 the Doctor wedded his second wife, Mrs. Sarah Olivia (Dunbar) West, daughter of Isaac Dunbar, of Adams county. Four sons and five daughters blessed this union, one son and two daughters of whom are dead. Those yet living are: Isaac D., Robert W., Mrs. Alice McDougal, Herbert S., Mrs. Anna T. Wade and Rosa. Dr. Magruder was an active participant in public affairs for sixty odd years, and scarcely a public meeting was held in which he did not figure conspicuously, and always in a useful way. He possessed an excellent memory, and the reminiscences of his career would fill a volume. There was not one of the olden time homes in the county which he had not visited in his professional capacity, nor a square mile which he had not traveled over. Very often in his early life he was called upon to act as arbiter in personal difficulties, and although of quick temper and great personal courage, he always advocated peaceable adjustment as the best way. He was for many years the only survivor of those who were participants in the Ross-Gibbs duel in 1826, being present in the capacity of surgeon and attended upon each of the participants when the affair was over. In 1839 the Doctor was elected to the lower house of the state legislature as a whig, of which party he was an earnest advocate and leader, and in 1842 was re-elected to the position. In the following year he was his party's candidate for the state senate against Gen. Parmenas Briscoe, but was defeated by one vote. In 1860 he was brought out by his adherents and admirers as a candidate for the state convention, which passed the ordinance of secession, and as he was a Union man in sentiment he was not a strong supporter of the measure, but advocated a convention of all the Southern states to secure united co-operation before adopting the measure. As the secession measure had found great favor with the masses, and owing to the great ability and popularity of his competitor, Hon. Henry T. Elliott, he was defeated. After the war was over he became an active, prominent and trusted democrat, and as a testimonial of his worth he was elected to the state legislature in 1881, at the age of four-score years. He was very active and earnest in his desire to do himself and his friends justice, and notwithstanding his advanced age he made an able and intelligent legislator, and during his entire term of service he was never absent from his seat. Although he was reared in the Episcopal faith he became connected with the Methodist church after coming to Mississippi, but upon the establishment of an Episcopal church he at once transferred to it his membership, and with it remained connected until his death, its impressive and solemn burial service being read at his funeral and over his grave. He was also buried with Masonic honors, for of that order he had been a member from 1825, holding membership in Washington lodge No. 3. A volume could be profitably filled in writing of the life and adventures of this venerable and worthy man, but panegyric is not praise, nor is adulation a biographical ornament. He possessed very social and refined tastes and his hospitality was often enjoyed by his numerous friends. Although he had his ups and downs in business life he always maintained the strictest integrity, and always managed to surround his family with many comforts, and give his children good educational advantages. During his last illness his physician, Dr. Redus, gave him constant attention, and his devoted children, grandchildren and sons-in-law were ever at his bedside anticipating every want with tenderness and affection. He told his physician it was useless to minister to so feeble a frame, in which there was nothing to rally, nothing recuperative, and he expressed willingness and desire to leave his earthly life behind him and be at rest. He died Sunday evening, August 22, 1885, and was buried Monday afternoon from St. James' Episcopal church, Rev. Nowell Logan officiating. An immense concourse of relatives and friends paid their last respects to the dead and followed his remains to the city of the dead, where they now repose in peace. Of him it may be said: "Mark the perfect man, and behold the upright, for the end of that man is peace." R. W. Magruder, his son, was educated in the public schools of Port Gibson, and completed his literary education in the Port Gibson academy. At the age of eighteen years he began earning his own living, and in 1875 began the study of law under J. D. Vertner, of Port Gibson, being admitted to the bar in November, 1877. He successfully followed the practice of his profession until after the death of his father-in-law, Mr. Sims, at which time he took upon himself the management of the latter's entire estate, in which capacity he has displayed much executive ability. He was married to Miss Carrie J. Sims, who was born July 7, 1860, and died December 10, 1880, having borne one child, John M. Mrs. Magruder was highly accomplished, and owing to the many Christian qualities which she displayed she won the affection and respect of all who knew her. Mr. Magruder is a democrat in politics, and is a successful and thoroughly practical business man. He possesses many of his father's amiable qualities, being hospitable, generous and kindhearted.

Hon. William T. Magruder (deceased), was one of the county's most illustrious citizens, and from the time of attaining his majority until his death he occupied himself incessantly with plans for the political and industrial advancement of his section. He was born in Port Gibson, Miss., January 16, 1825, and in that city was reared, his education, which thoroughly fitted him for a life of usefulness, being received in his native city and in Oakland college. After attaining his senior year in this institution he left college to take up the study of law, but later abandoned this to become a disciple of Æsculapius. Failing eyesight, however, compelled him to give up a professional life, and as he had been brought up to a knowledge of planting he began ardently to devote himself to this calling, being at that time in his nineteenth year. Being a young man of strong character and tireless energy he soon began to gather about him considerable means and, though assuming a debt of $5,000, soon purchased for $18,000 the plantation known as Askamala; his sole property which was free from incumbrance being two or three slaves and the same number of mules given him by his father. By careful management and industry he afterward became very wealthy and purchased two large tracts of land in addition to his home place, one being the Oak Grove plantation, making him the owner of nearly three thousand acres of some of the best land in the county, one thousand and three hundred acres being under cultivation. Mr. Magruder was deeply interested in the proper management and cultivation of his broad acres, and as he at all times endeavored to keep out of the beaten path and to adopt new and improved methods his operations were attended with remarkably satisfactory results. He possessed a brilliant intellect and his views, in nearly every instance, were intelligent, broad and comprehensive, and being devoted to the interests of the planters, their affection and respect for him was unbounded. His fidelity to his section and party was rewarded, and in 1884 he was elected by his numerous friends to represent Claiborne county in the state legislature, a position he filled with eminent ability for two terms. While a member of this body he was the founder of the Industrial Reform bill, and on the 25th of January, 1886, made an able and eloquent speech in its defense, solving the industrial features of the race problem. This speech was delivered in the hall of the house of representatives, was a model of logic, eloquence and strength, and thoroughly exhausted every detail of the subject and wielded a widespread influence among the members. Mr. Magruder was considered one of the deepest thinkers of the county, and was the inventor of several agricultural implements, one being a cotton planter, which he had patented in 1887, and which has met with universal satisfaction wherever used throughout the South. He always interested himself in the political affairs of the state and was an earnest patron of education. At the time of his death, on the 8th of December, 1889, he was a member of the house of representatives. His death, which was mourned by all who knew him, was caused by an apoplectic stroke. He was married to Maria, daughter of Benjamin Hughes (see sketch of William Hughes), her birth occurring in this county in 1833, and her death on the 25th of April, 1871. She was educated in Port Gibson Female college, and throughout the greater portion of her life she was an active and earnest worker in the Presbyterian church. She and her husband contributed some of the brick which was made on his place, for the erection of the Presbyterian church of Port Gibson, of which Mrs. Magruder was an active member, and to which she was always a liberal contributor. She was a devoted mother, an earnest Christian and a faithful friend, beloved by all who knew her. She bore her husband thirteen children, eight of whom are living: Joseph, who married Miss Priscilla Daniell, resides on the old Windsor plantation. Robert H. was educated in the university of Oxford, and resides on the home place. Benjamin H. also attended at that institution for two years, after which he entered college at Danville, Ky., graduating in 1882. Since that time he has taught school four years, being in the Chamberlain & Hunt academy for two years, at Okolona, Miss., one year, and one year at Pecos, Tex. He is now bookkeeper and assistant cashier in the Port Gibson bank. Lizzie is the wife of George Disharoon. She was educated in the female college of Port Gibson, and she and her husband reside on the home place with his parents. Thomas was educated in the schools of Port Gibson, and is now filling a trusted position with the Delta Bank, Loan & Trust company of Vicksburg; Mary and Nannie were given the advantages of the Port Gibson schools and the schools of Holly Springs, Miss.; James also attended the schools of Port Gibson, and Henry, who died at the age of twenty-three years, attended school at Port Gibson and the military institute of Kentucky, being a bright and promising young man. The brother of Hon. William T. Magruder, Joseph Magruder, attained his majority in this county, and was married to a Miss McCray, by whom he had one daughter, Mrs. W. B. Lean, now of New Orleans. Joseph was captain of a company in the Confederate army, and while making a charge at Canton in 1863, was killed. Mr. William T. Magruder reared his family to honorable manhood and womanhood, and they are now classed among the leading citizens of Claiborne county.

M. Mahorner is a planter and stockdealer at Macon, Miss., but is a native of Baltimore, Md., where he was born in September, 1837, to M. and Sarah A. Mahorner, the former of whom was born in Virginia and the latter in Baltimore. The father was a captain on the high seas until 1839, at which time, having married in Baltimore, he immigrated to Mississippi, and engaged in planting in Noxubee county. He was very successful, became wealthy, and his broad acres were carefully tilled and cultivated by his numerous slaves. In 1869 he moved back to Maryland, and there died in 1872, his wife dying at the same place two years earlier. They reared a large family of children only two of whom survive: M. Mahorner, of Macon, Miss., and R. Mahorner who is in the comptroller's office at Austin, Tex. Five sons were in the Confederate army during the war, and Bernard and Harris, who were wounded in the battle of Gettysburg, died from the effects of the same. Lewis was captured at Fort Morgan and died in prison at Elmira, N. Y. Matthias and Rienzi both went through the service. Mathias Mahorner, the subject of this sketch, resided in Baltimore from the time he was sixteen until he was twenty-two years of age, during which he served an apprenticeship in the machine shop of Poole & Hunt, and was afterward employed in a commission house. In 1860 he came to Mobile, Ala., where he was employed as bookkeeper until the war broke out, but upon the opening of the war in 1861, he dropped his pen and enlisted in the Third Alabama regiment. In 1863 he was transferred to the First Maryland cavalry, in which he served until the close of the war, taking part in many cavalry engagements. Since the close of the war he has been a planter of Noxubee county, Miss., and in addition to this calling he has given considerable attention to the raising of fine stock, his herds of Jersey cattle and Southdown sheep being especially fine. He also raises an excellent grade of horses and hogs, and keeps a fine lot of fancy poultry. He is the owner of three thousand acres of fine land nine miles southeast of Macon, of which about one thousand one hundred acres are under cultivation, and eight hundred acres devoted to pasturage. All kinds of native grasses grow in abundance on this tract and Bermuda, Lespedeza, red clover and Johnson grass are also grown for the benefit of his stock. The greater part of Mr. Mahorner's attention is given to stockraising, at which he has been remarkably successful. He was married in 1871 to Miss Mary A. Teague, of Sumter county, Ala., by whom he has one son, Mathias, Jr., who is attending college at Spring Hill, Ala., near Mobile. Mr. Mahorner is a member the Farmers' Alliance, is a wideawake and enterprising gentleman, and is well fitted for the calling in which he is engaged.

Maj. Lewis C. Majet, planter, Grenada, is a native of the Old North state, born in 1836, and is the second of four children—two sons and two daughters—born to the union of Nicholas and Sarah (Walters) Majet, natives also of North Carolina, born in 1787 and 1801 respectively. The parents made their home in their native state until 1836, and then removed to Yalobusha county, Miss. (now Grenada county), and settled ten miles east of Grenada, where they improved a good farm of about eight hundred acres. They were among the pioneers, and there they passed the remainder of their days, the father dying in 1859 and the mother in 1872. He was an old line whig, was very active in politics and all matters of public interest. He was a great hunter, horse-racer and general sportsman, but after removing to Mississippi, abandoned all those amusements but hunting, and became a prosperous planter and a representative citizen. His father was a descendant of one of the old French Huguenot families of North Carolina. The maternal grandfather, Lewis Walters, died in North Carolina. He was at one time sheriff of Northampton county. His father was of English descent and was a soldier in the Revolution. Maj. Lewis C. Majet is the only one living of the four children born to his parents. They were named as follows: Cuthbert, who served in the Confederate army and was wounded at Port Hudson. He has never been heard from since Christmas, 1865, when he stopped at a house in Mississippi, enroute from his home in Arkansas to Mobile, Ala. It is supposed he was murdered for his money; Elizabeth was the wife of Capt. N. B. Ingram (deceased), and died of yellow fever in 1878; and Caroline was the wife of Dr. S. C. Glover, and died about 1880. Major Majet received the rudiments of an education at home and later attended Grenada and Oxford and finished his education in the military institute at Frankfort, Ky., just before the war broke out. He then joined company E, Fifteenth Mississippi infantry as a private, but was afterward made sergeant-major, and with the exception of about six months on detached service in an artillery, he served in that command until the close of war, fighting at Fishing Creek, Vicksburg, Port Hudson, Baton Rouge and was in the Georgia and Atlanta campaigns. He was then sent back to Corinth, Miss., and served for some time in the commissary department. He was then sent back to join General Johnston, whom he reached just prior to the surrender. Returning to Mississippi, he followed farming, and in 1867 was married to Miss Louise Ingram, who was born in the house in which she is now residing in Grenada county, and who is the daughter of Capt. N. B. and Margaret Ingram. Captain Ingram was married twice, his first wife being the mother of Mrs. Majet. He and first wife were born in South Carolina, but came to what is now Grenada county about 1837, and settled a number of miles east of Grenada, where he improved a good farm. He subsequently removed to Grenada and followed merchandising until his death in 1874. To Mr. and Mrs. Majet have been born eight children, two sons and three daughters now living. When first married Mr. Majet lived about twelve years in Le Flore county, then in the neighborhood where his boyhood days were spent and recently in Grenada. He is one of the leading planters of the county, owning about three thousand acres with twenty-five hundred acres in the bottoms of Le Flore county, mostly the result of his own efforts but partly the result of inheritance. He is sparing no pains to educate his children and make his home pleasant.

Dr. Thomas J. Malone's residence in Mississippi dates from the year 1835, when he moved from Madison county, Tenn., and settled within the present limits of Marshall county, eight miles south of what is now Holly Springs. He was born in Sussex county, Va., December 31, 1806, and was the son of Thomas and Rebecca (Green) Malone, natives, also, of that county and state. The father was a prosperous planter, removed to Alabama in 1825, and there continued his former calling until his death, in about 1837. He was a leading Methodist in Virginia, and his home was the gathering place of all the early preachers. The Malone family is of Irish-English extraction. Dr. Thomas J. Malone received his education in the common schools of Virginia, where he remained until, in his eighteenth year, he removed with his parents to Alabama. He was engaged in teaching school for about three years, and in 1833 was married to Miss Julia Owen, a native, also, of the Old Dominion. The following year he and wife settled in Madison county, Tenn., remained there one year, and in 1835, as above stated, came to Mississippi, settling in Marshall county. He located among the Indians, purchased four hundred and eighty acres in 1836, and remained in that place two years. He then purchased his present plantation, sixteen hundred acres, south of the present site of Waterford, and has cleared most of this tract. He became at once active in politics, and in 1845 was elected by the democratic party to the state legislature. He was re-elected in 1849, but declined renomination in 1852. For ten years after that he followed planting, and greatly improved and beautified his place. Mrs. Malone died in 1853, and the Doctor was married the second time, in about 1857, to Mrs. Lucy Alderson, widow of Maj. James Alderson, and soon moved to Holly Springs, where he has since resided. He had the misfortune to lose his second wife in 1887. Both ladies were members of the Methodist church. Dr. Malone has been a member of the same church since boyhood, a worker and officer for years, and a liberal supporter of the same. He is also a strong supporter and liberal contributor to all educational matters, and has been a trustee of Rust university since its establishment. He was a director in the bank for years. The Doctor studied medicine for individual benefit, has never practiced, but is universally called Doctor. He accumulated a large fortune prior to the war by planting and speculating in land, and this was mainly swept away during the struggle. He was a plain and pronounced Union man before secession, treated his negroes well and was thought much of by them. He has many old servants around him now, to some of whom he has given property. Although he lost much during the war, he soon recovered his fallen fortune after cessation of hostilities, and for years has been a donator and contributor to all worthy or laudable enterprises. He has given much to his relatives, and often gives a tract of land or bonds to an old servant. He is one of the oldest persons in the county, has resided here since its earliest white settlement, and is loved and respected by every one. Although a leading and prominent politician when elected to the legislature, he was no officeseeker, being naturally modest and retiring, and his entrance into the office was accidental. He is a fluent speaker, a shrewd reasoner, and a man of keen perception and intelligence. Although of a yielding temperament, yet he is firmly rooted to practical demonstrated facts. He is now studying Methodist history, is active for his age, and transacts all his business. He owns property adjoining town, and also about five thousand acres throughout the county. His social relations have been of the pleasantest, and he was never sued but once. He bought railroad bonds before the war, and after that eventful period was for a long time the only bond man in the county. He is strictly honest and upright, and has been known for years as an advocate and promoter of Marshall county's interests.

S. H. Mangum, a native of Mississippi, born in 1837, is a well-known planter of this section, and his plantation which comprises one thousand and forty acres, with about two hundred acres admirably tilled, yields a fine crop of corn and cotton annually. His ideas in regard to agriculture are shrewd, practical and progressive, and a secret, no doubt, of his success is that his work is very congenial to his tastes. He takes great pride in keeping his plantation in admirable order, and everything about the place indicates his care and attention. He has erected a fine sawmill on his place, and the attention which he devotes to this industry and time he bestows on his plantation and in the raising and care of his stock, keeps him fully occupied. He is every respect a trustworthy gentleman, and the respect which is bestowed upon him by all who know him speaks volumes in his praise. He has taken much interest in the politics of the county and has been a member of the A. F. & A. M. since 1856, at which time he became a member of Cato lodge No. 230. He was also a charter member of the grange, which he joined in 1875. On the 15th of December, 1867, he was married to Miss Minnie J. Martin, who was born in Mississippi in 1844, and their union has resulted in the birth of the following children: W. P., Nancy C., J. S., R. L., Emma and Augusta, all of whom are living. During the war he was a member of company D, Forty-sixth Mississippi infantry and served throughout the entire war. His parents, Solomon and Zilla (Chapman) Mangum, were born in Georgia and Kentucky respectively, the former's birth occurring in 1787. Their union was consummated in 1818 and resulted in the birth of nine children: G. W., Nancy C., Caroline, Eliza, William, Mary, Alfred, W. P. and S. H., of whom four are deceased. Solomon Mangum came to Mississippi in 1812 and located in Rankin county, where he died December 29, 1852, his widow surviving him until February 21, 1879, when she, too, passed away.

Theophilus J. Manley, chancery clerk of Tallahatchie county, was born in the old town of Belmont, Fayette county, Tenn., in 1854. His parents were Capt. T. J. and Mary R. Manley, cousins, the former a native of Virginia, the latter of Fayette county, Tenn., born about 1822 and 1829 respectively. They were married in Fayette county, Tenn., and removed from there to Pine Bluff, Ark., and during the war to Tunica county, Miss., and thence to Cold Water, where they remained until 1865 when they removed to Charleston, removing thence four years later to a plantation, where the father was engaged in farming until 1871, when his death occurred. Captain Manley was a planter during most of his life.

He organized, drilled and was made captain of a company for the United States service in the Mexican war, which, however, was never formally accepted by the government. He was a prominent Royal Arch Mason and took the highest degree in the I. O. O. F., his connection with the last mentioned order extending through many years. He has long been a devoted member of the Methodist Episcopal church, is highly honorable, strictly moral and temperate, and is everywhere recognized as a high-minded man. The mother of our subject is living at Charleston. She had four children: Clarence W., architect and builder of Charleston; Ida A., wife of W. B. Marshall, a lawyer of Charleston; T. J. and Mary, who died when two years old. Theophilus J. Manley received a limited common-school education, and in 1871 started out in life for himself as an employe in a printing office at Charleston, and after five years' experience purchased the Tallahatchie News, a paper upon which he had been working, and which he published about one year. At the end of this time he sold out and engaged in clerking in a store in 1879, when he bought the Charleston News, which he published till 1884, when he again relinquished newspaper work and was connected with a mercantile establishment till his election in 1887 to the office he now holds. He has been clerk and treasurer of the board of aldermen in his town for eight years. He is a prominent member of the I. O. O. F., and a charter member of the Charleston lodge No. 108, of which he has twice been noble grand. He is a prominent member of the Methodist Episcopal church, earnestly and actively interested in Sunday-school work. During his journalistic career he took a prominent part in the meetings of the Press association, which called him to various parts of the country, which, in connection with his prominence with the Odd Fellows and in church and Sunday-school work has given him a wide acquaintance in Mississippi, and made him very popular among the best classes of citizens.

Saunders J. Manor, Yazoo City, Miss., a thoroughly reliable planter of Yazoo county, was born in Rutherford county, Tenn., March 31, 1825, and is the eldest of a family of seven children. His parents, Levi and Levina (Jarrett) Manor, were natives of North Carolina and Virginia, respectively. The father removed to Mississippi in 1834, and was prominently identified with the early political history of the community in which he resided; he was a candidate for sheriff of Yazoo county at the time of his death which was in 1839. His widow lived until 1884. The paternal grandparents of our subject were Aaron and Rhoda Manor. The maternal grandparents were Thomas and Susan Jarrett, Virginians by birth. Saunders J. Manor grew to maturity in the county where he was born; he acquired a plain, practical education in the private schools of that day, fitting himself for all the duties which have fallen to his lot. He is a planter by occupation, owning one hundred and eighty acres of land; he has placed sixty acres under cultivation which yield a generous harvest. He was married in 1848 to Miss Margaret J. Swain, a native of South Carolina. They have had born to them a family of twelve children: William T. (deceased), Levi D., Elizabeth A. (deceased), Rhoda O., Evelyn H., Mary S., Margaret S., Drucilla, Roxanna L., Ada W., Sam R. and Giles M. Mr. Saunders is a member of the Farmers' Alliance, and in his political convictions sympathizes with the Democratic party. He has contributed liberally to all public enterprises which have had for their object the upbuilding of the community and the uplifting of the moral and religious element of society. He is a man plain of manner and speech, and a citizen who has the respect of the entire community.

Clifton H. Marshall, a planter of Monroe county, whose postoffice address is Nettleton, Lee county, Miss., was born in 1849, a son of William L. and Eliza P. Marshall. His father was born near Rome, Ga., in 1825, and came to Monroe county in 1844, locating on a farm near that on which he and his son Clifton now live. He was married in 1847 to Eliza Conniway by whom he had five children: Clifton H., Leonora M. (deceased), Oscar P., Richard L. and Comander. Mr. Marshall is the son of Neighew Marshall, who was born in Georgia and came to Monroe county in 1845, was a planter for the remainder of his life. Richard Conniway, father of Mrs. William L. Marshall, was one of the first settlers west of the Tombigbee river, who began life by buying land of the Indians, later becoming a wealthly planter and slaveholder. Although he received but a common-school education, Clifton H. Marshall is one of the most intelligent men of the county; a diligent reader of the newspapers, and well posted not only upon current events but upon historical subjects generally. In 1871 he married Fannie E. Johnson of Monroe county, and they had five children: Hattie, Daisy, Clarice L., William A. and Dellie V. In 1889 he was elected justice of the peace, and is yet serving efficiently in that office. He and his wife are members of the Methodist Episcopal church. He is an extensive and successful planter, genial and very popular.

In Madison county, Ala., January 1, 1812, Judge John P. Marshall first saw the light of day. His father, Thomas M. Marshall, was born in South Carolina, and there married Mary Malone, a daughter of William Malone, of South Carolina; his father, Col. James M. Marshall, was a native of the same state, and was a soldier in the war of the Revolution where he distinguished himself in gallant service to his country. The Marshalls are of English descent. Thomas M. Marshall was a planter in South Carolina, and removed to Alabama, settling near Huntsville, Madison county; there he lived until his death which was in 1844; his wife died in 1831; John P. is one of a family of seven sons and four daughters, and he and two brothers are the only surviving members; Hon. Benjamin T. is a planter in the county of Carroll, and Samuel G. also resides in Mississippi. John P. passed his youth in Madison county, Ala., and acquired the best education his limited circumstances afforded. At the age of twenty-one years he came to Mississippi and settled in Hinds county; two years later he went to Choctaw county, where he resided about one year. In 1835 he was married to Martha B. Long, a native of Mississippi, and a daughter of the Rev. Stephen Long, of the Methodist Episcopal church. In 1837 he removed to Carroll county and bought land on Palucia creek. This was in a wild, uncultivated state, but he had willing hands and a determination to succeed, and this is as good capital as a pioneer needs. He built a cabin, cleared some of the land, and made a comfortable home. In 1849 he removed to the place where he has since resided; here he had the same obstacles to overcome, but he cleared away the forest, and now has three hundred acres of as fine farming land as can be found in the county of Carroll. In his political opinions Mr. Marshall was formerly a whig, and was opposed to the late war. In 1839 he was elected ranger, and in 1842 he made the first assessment of lands ever made in this county, which is said to be a marvel of accuracy. In 1843 he was elected justice of the peace, and a greater part of the past twenty-six years he has held that office. In 1865 he was appointed probate judge by Judge Sharkey, and soon after he was appointed chancery clerk. He was next elected to that office, and continued to hold it for a period of eighteen years, winning the reputation of being the best clerk in the state. In 1852 Mrs. Marshall died leaving three sons and three daughters, only three of whom are living: Mrs. M. A. Wood, Mrs. T. H. Oury, and William B. Marshall, a planter of this county. The Judge was married a second time, December 23, 1852, to Mrs. Martha W. Baskett, a widow, a daughter of Russell Beall, member of a prominent family of Mississippi; she died December 7, 1883; there were no children of this marriage. Judge Marshall was married October 16, 1884, to Mrs. Florence Ory, a Virginian by birth. He has reared a number of orphan children, and now has two grandchildren with him. He and his wife are members of the Methodist Episcopal church. He belongs to the Masonic lodge, being a member of both the chapter and commandry. He is the oldest living member of the Carrollton lodge. Judge Marshall is a man who gives character to a community; he is a philanthropist; he has a keen sense of right and wrong, and as a public servant gave entire satisfaction. The most elegant hospitality is always dispensed in his home, and as a citizen he stands with few peers and no superiors.

Levin R. Marshall (deceased), one of the wealthy bankers and business men of Natchez, formerly, was born in Alexandria, Va., on the 10th of October, 1800; was the son of Henry Marshall, who was a native of Maryland, but who spent his latter years in Virginia. The elder Marshall was of English parentage and he was of the same family as the distinguished Chief Justice Marshall. Levin R. received a good practical education and when about seventeen years of age went to Mississippi, located in Woodville, where he was soon made cashier of the United States bank at that place. While there, and in 1826, he married Miss Maria Chotard, daughter of the celebrated John Marie Chotard (see sketch.) She was born in Mississippi territory in 1807 and died in Natchez in 1834. She was the mother of four children, all deceased but Hon. George M. Marshall, of Natchez. Mr. Marshall afterward married Mrs. Sarah E. (Elliott) Ross, widow of Isaac Ross and daughter of Dr. Elliott. The latter came to Port Gibson at an early day and spent the balance of his days as a successful physician and a prominent citizen. His wife's maiden name was D'Evereux. She was a native of the Emerald isle and a sister of John D'Evereux, who was an officer in the English army and who, after the Irish troubles, was under Robert Emmett and served in a very satisfactory way to Ireland. For this he was banished from the country and after a short time in Baltimore, Md., he went to South America, where he was made a general under General Bolivar, serving in the Bolivian army. After this he was pardoned by the English government and allowed to return home, and there spent the closing scenes of his life in peace and quiet. He made frequent visits to his relatives and numerous friends at Natchez, but made his permanent home in his native county. By his second marriage Mr. Marshall became the father of eight children, only two of whom survive: Josephine E., wife of J. R. Ogden of New York, and Stephen Duncan Marshall, who was born in Natchez, educated principally in New York, and who married Miss Catharine Maria Calhoun in 1872. She was a native of Natchez and a daughter of the late Dr. Gustavus Calhoun, a Pennsylvanian by birth but a pioneer of Natchez, where he died. Mrs. Calhoun is still living at Natchez and is quite aged. Mr. and Mrs. Stephen Marshall are prominent members of the Episcopal church. As a financier and general business man Levin R. Marshall was probably not excelled in the Southwest. He began for himself with no capital, but by his untiring industry and excellent business ability he became a leader in financial circles in the palmiest days of Natchez. He began his career at Woodville and, as before stated, he became cashier of the United States bank. In 1831 he removed to Natchez and became cashier of the United States bank there. He was afterward instrumental in establishing the Commercial bank at Natchez, of which he served as president for a number of years. He also followed merchandising quite extensively and was at one time connected with the commission house of J. B. Byrne & Co., of New Orleans, also the commission house of Marshall, Reynolds & Co., at Natchez. He became the owner of extensive sugar and cotton plantations, and soon after removing to Natchez he erected a magnificent suburban residence one mile south of the city, it being known as Richmond. He passed his time alternately between that place and Westchester county, N. Y., and his death occurred in the last named place on the 24th of July, 1870, after a long and useful life. He was one of the class of men singled out by nature to show what a man can do when he sets his mind on accomplishing a certain object. He was a self-made man, and what he accomplished in the way of this world's goods and personal achievement was wholly due to his own good fighting qualities. He was all that goes to make up a true, noble and generous man. His widow still occupies the old Richmond house and is eighty-eight years of age. She is an accomplished and much esteemed lady and has been a prominent member of the Presbyterian church for many years.

Hon. George M. Marshall, representative of Adams county, and a prominent planter of the same, was born in Woodville, Miss., in 1830, and is the son of Levin R. Marshall and the grandson of Henry Marshall, who was a native of Maryland, but who spent the closing scenes of his life in the Old Dominion. Levin R. Marshall was born in Fauquier county, Va., in 1800, received a fair scholastic education, and when a young man left the parental roof to seek his fortune in the Southwest. He located first in Natchez, and then at Woodville, Miss., became cashier of a branch of the United States bank, and in 1826, while holding that position, he met and married his first wife, whose maiden name was Maria Chotard. She was a daughter of the celebrated John Marie Chotard, whose sketch appears in another part of this work. In 1831 Mr. Marshall removed to Natchez, became cashier of the branch of the United States bank there, and afterward was instrumental in establishing the Commercial bank, of which he was the first president. He had previously engaged in mercantile pursuits, and was at one time prominently connected with the well known commission house of J. B. Byrne & Co., of New Orleans, and with the firm of Marshall, Reynolds & Co., commission merchants of Natchez. Mrs. Marshall died in 1834. To this union were born four children, Hon. George M. Marshall being the third in order of birth and the only one now living. Mr. Marshall took for his second wife Mrs. Sarah E. Ross (nee Elliott), a native of Maryland. She is still living. Mr. Marshall started in life in moderate circumstances, and his vast estate was the result of his own efforts altogether. He owned extensive sugar and cotton plantations and at the time of his death, which occurred in Westchester county, N. Y., on July 24, 1870, he left one of the most valuable estates in Mississippi, besides a large estate in New York. For many years he was a leader in the financial circles of Mississippi, and much of the early enterprise and success of Natchez was due to his great ability as a financier and general business capacity. He was a man of firmness and great decision of character and his high sense of honor, his integrity and liberality of heart, won for him many warm friends, who honor and respect his memory. Hon. George M. Marshall received his earlier education in Jefferson college and finished at Princeton college, N. J., where he received the degree of A. M. In 1852 he married Miss Charlotte Hunt, a native of Jefferson county, Miss., born in 1831 and the daughter of David and Ann (Ferguson) Hunt, the father born in New Jersey in 1779, and the mother in Mississippi in 1797. David Hunt came to Mississippi when a boy with an uncle, Abijah Hunt, who was a native of New Jersey. At an early day the latter went to Ohio, thence to Mississippi territory, and there became one of the most extensive merchants and planters of the territory, owning large establishments and public gins at Natchez, Washington, Greenville, Port Hudson and Big Black. By his intelligence, enterprise and wealth he exerted a great social and political influence, and was a decided partisan of what was then known as the Federal party. He took an active part against George Poindexter, and as a result Hunt was challenged to fight a duel. This took place in Louisiana a short distance above Concordia, opposite Natchez, and Mr. Hunt received a wound in the abdomen which proved fatal in a few hours. His death occurred on June 8, 1811. David Hunt married, settled in Jefferson county, and became a very wealthy planter.

There he received his final summons in 1861. His widow followed him to the grave in 1874. Both were prominent Presbyterians. Mr. Hunt was intelligent, generous and warm-hearted in all his social relations and to everything pertaining to his town and county he was a public-spirited citizen. He was one of the founders of Oakland college, now Alcorn university. To Mr. and Mrs. Marshall were born seven children, three of whom survive: Ann Hunt, wife of Henry B. Gaither, of Natchez; Sarah E., wife of Theodoret Bartow, of Long island, N. Y., and George M., Jr. The two daughters were educated at Natchez and New Orleans, and the son received his education at Natchez and Baltimore, Md. Mr. Marshall resided near Natchez with his father until 1855, when he erected his fine residence, having already embarked in the planting industry in 1853. In the spring of 1862 he joined the Natchez southrons as a private and served in Chalmers's brigade, participating in the battle of Shiloh, but after a few months' service he was discharged on account of disability. Prior to the war he had served about five years as a member of the board of supervisors of Adams county, and about three years of that time he was president. In 1888 he was elected to represent his county in the state legislature and was reëlected in 1890. During the sessions of 1888 and 1890 he was chairman of the committee on contingent expenses, and served as a member of the committee on appropriation and education. He has always been an active worker for his party, and for the advancement of the town and county, and has frequently been a delegate to state and other conventions. He was one of the two who were appointed by Governor Stone as delegates from his state senatorial district to attend the Southern state immigration convention held at Asheville, N. C., in December, 1890, but Mr. Marshall did not attend. He is a member of the Bluff City lodge No. 1145, Knights of Honor, and of Natchez lodge No. 3, Knights of Pythias. He and wife are quite prominent Episcopalians and he is one of the vestry of Trinity church, Natchez.

Judge Thomas Alexander Marshall is a Kentuckian by birth, born March 29, 1812, at Augusta, in which town he was reared and educated, graduating from Augusta college when eighteen years of age. His parents, Martin and Martha Battaile (Taliaferro) Marshall, were Virginians, and his grandfather, William Marshall, was a Baptist minister of considerable renown, who settled at Shelbyville, Ky., at a very early day. After finishing his literary education, Judge Thomas A. Marshall entered the clerk's office of Mason county, Ky., where he remained three years, and then began the study of law under Judge Key and his father, at Augusta, and was there admitted to the bar in 1835, his first law suit being tried before Jesse Grant, Esq., the father of the distinguished General Grant. In 1836 Mr. Marshall came to Mississippi on horseback, and had the distinction of being one of the few men of his class who did not carry arms. The February following his arrival he was admitted by the high court of errors and appeals, at Jackson, to practice his profession throughout the state of Mississippi, and as Vicksburg, at that time, was an inviting field for lawyers, he determined to make that city the field of his future operations. He entered the office of Harrison & Holt, who were the ablest and most extensive lawyers of the place, but afterward formed a partnership with William C. Smeder, who was a noted attorney of Mississippi, their partnership being a very strong and able one. He devoted his life to his large law practice, but did not seek political preferment, his remarkable modesty, independence of character and contempt for the arts of the demagogue being distasteful to him. However he was elected to the state legislature on the Union ticket in 1851 by his numerous friends, and served throughout 1852. He was also elected to the secession convention of 1861 as a Union man—an unsought honor, but conferred upon him by the people of Warren county as the best exponent of their opposition to disunion. He was one of the thirteen members who voted against secession, but when the war became inevitable his age and delicate health unfitted him for military service. After the capture of Vicksburg he was invited there by General Grant, who urged him to use his efforts to end the strife. Although Mr. Marshall, like all his family, was devoted to the Union, he submitted to the decision of his own people, and cast his lot with them. After the close of the war he returned to Vicksburg, and was a member of the reconstruction convention of 1865, being almost unanimously elected. He took the position that Mississippi had never been legally out of the Union, and was, therefore, entitled to all the rights of states, and this view, advanced by him and other Southerners, and practically conceded by Chief Justice Chase, as much as the magnanimity of the conqueror, saved the South from the usual consequences of armed resistance to national authority. In 1844 Mr. Marshall married Miss Letitia, daughter of Maj. Anderson Miller, who was of a Kentucky family of Virginia descent, and was one of the pioneers of steamboat navigation of the Western rivers, and also in the cotton-seed oil manufacture, being at the time of his daughter's marriage United States marshal of Mississippi. After a long and successful career at the bar, Mr. Marshall's health gave way, and since 1873 he has been retired from the active duties of life. He has been an invalid for years, and his peaceful old age is cheered by the affection of his family and friends, who highly respect and honor him. Martin Marshall, his son, was born in 1846, and until 1862 was educated by private tutors. He then entered the military institute of Virginia at Jackson, and in 1864 joined a cadet corps of Confederate troops, and was badly wounded at New Market in May, 1864. In 1865, at the close of the war, he began the study of law with his father, and in 1867-8 he attended the law university of Virginia, and began practicing in 1870, which calling has received his attention ever since. He has followed in his illustrious father's footsteps, and is one of the foremost attorneys of the state. In 1878 he was elected a member of the house of representatives, being on the judiciary committee, and in 1884 he was elected to the state senate. In 1871 he was married to Miss Ella Bush, of Hinds county, a daughter of John Bush, a pioneer of that county, and six children have blessed their union.

George Marshall is a Kentuckian by birth, born at Augusta, March 5, 1829, the seventh child born to Martin Marshall and Matilda B. (Taliaferro) Marshall, natives of Virginia, the former of whom was a distinguished lawyer and practiced his profession in Kentucky. He represented the county in which he lived in the state legislature of Kentucky for one term, and in that state passed from life in 1853, his wife's death having occurred in 1846. Her people were farmers. George Marshall came to Mississippi in 1850, and for a number of years lived with his brother in Vicksburg (the Hon. T. A. Marshall). He attended the common schools until fitted for college, after which he entered Augusta college, of Kentucky, where such eminent men as Tomlinson, Bascom, Trimbell, McCowan and Robbins were professors. After graduating from this institution he came to Vicksburg, where he read law with his brother, but never practiced. In 1855 he began planting, and followed this calling up to the breaking out of the war. Prior to this he had been a stanch Union man, but after the state of Mississippi had seceded he took up arms in defense of the Confederate cause, and in 1861 went to the front with Cowan's battery, with which he remained one year. He then became a volunteer on General Green's staff, soon after which he was appointed adjutant of the Ninth Mississippi cavalry, and took part in the battles of Vicksburg, Champion hill, Atlanta, Jonesboro and Franklin. In the latter part of the war he had charge of the courier department, so far as orders were concerned, from Sugsville to Demopolis, Ala. Upon being paroled by General Canby he returned to Mississippi and went into the real estate business in Vicksburg, where he remained two years. He then moved to his plantation on Big Black river, where he has remained ever since, living the quiet life of a planter. Mr. Marshall came into possession of his plantation in 1855. It contains seven hundred acres, nearly all of which is fine bottom land in Hinds county. He has five hundred acres under cultivation, and although cotton is his principal crop he also raises some corn. Mr. Marshall was married in 1853 to Miss Harris, daughter of Dr. Hartwell Harris, of Virginia, the latter being a very early settler of Mississippi and becoming the owner of a large amount of real estate. To Mr. and Mrs. Marshall four children have been born: Leila, Thomas A., Elizabeth C. and T. D. Leila and Thomas A. are deceased. Elizabeth became the wife of Hon. Marye Dabney, a prominent attorney of Vicksburg, of which city T. D. Marshall is a rising attorney, the latter having graduated from Oxford university with second honors. Mr. Marshall is very fond of field sports, and takes an eight or nine mile chase with his hounds almost daily, his vigor and energy being remarkable for one of his years. His residence, which is situated in a handsome grove of oak trees, is situated about one-half mile from Smith's Station.

E. J. Martin, president and general manager of the Progress Manufacturing company, of Meridian, Miss., was born in Clarke county of this state in September, 1851, the only child born to Norman and Eleanor (Chapman) Martin, the former a native of Georgia, and the latter of Alabama. They were married in Mississippi, whither they had removed at an early day, she being his second wife. He was first married to Miss Anna Morrison, by whom he became the father of four sons and three daughters. He was a planter and stockraiser by occupation; was a plain, practical and successful planter, and prior to the Civil war was the owner of a large amount of land, and between seventy-five and one hundred slaves. He never aspired to any official position, but quietly pursued the even tenor of his way, and was highly respected by all who knew him. He was a member of the Methodist Episcopal church, and died in Clarke county, Miss., in 1883, his widow (the mother of the subject of this sketch), who was a member of the Baptist church, breathing her last in Lauderdale county, in 1886. Only four of Mr. Martin's children are now living. E. J. Martin began making his own way as a planter after attaining his majority, and is still following this calling in connection with his manufacturing interests. He has been associated with the Progress Manufacturing company since its organization, the plant at that time being worth about $16,000. It has since so increased in value that it is now worth at least $40,000. Mr. Martin has been the president of the concern since 1888, and their cotton and hay presses, their engines and boilers are of admirable workmanship, and readily demonstrate the fact that none but skilled mechanics are employed in the establishment. They also do a general foundry and machineshop business and give employment to about fifty hands throughout the year. The annual business done amounts to about $100,000, is founded on a substantial basis, and bids fair to double its capacity in a short time. Mr. Martin has been a member of the city council two terms, is a conservative democrat, and has never participated in the political affairs of the county to any great extent. He was married in 1873 to Miss Jennie McLemone, of Lauderdale county, and by her is the father of four sons and two daughters: Louella, Percy, Edwin, Leon, Mary and Robert. Mr. Martin and his wife are members of the Baptist church, and socially he is a member of the A. F. & A. M. and the K. of P. fraternities. He is the owner of one hundred acres of land near Meridian, also considerable land in Clarke county, and is the owner of other valuable property. He has been liberal in contributing of his means to schools and churches, etc., and is a public-spirited and useful citizen. He is now devoting his time and energies to the successful management of the Progress Manufacturing company.

One of the brightest lights and ornaments in Mississippi journalism and one of the state's most widely and favorably known citizens is Edward L. Martin, editor of the *Mississippian*, a leading democratic journal published at Jackson, Miss. Mr. Martin is a native of Copiah county, Miss., where he first saw the light of day in 1861. Studious, ambitious and energetic, his youth was spent in the schoolroom and in work whereby he might acquire sufficient means to complete his education. He left the state university in 1879 with a splendid record for deportment and scholarship and after a few years spent in the railway service embarked in journalism, becoming joint owner with his brother, John H., of the *New Mississippian* of Jackson. He assumed the business management and by his personal popularity and untiring energy soon trebled its circulation and patronage. Though modestly conceding to his brother the control of the paper's editorial policy, his frequent valuable contributions to its columns and earnest sympathy with the cause of reform attracted general attention and favorable comment. He connected himself with the Independent Order of Good Templars and the Farmers' Alliance movement. As delegate from Mississippi he attended the international meeting of the former organization at Saratoga, N. Y., and enjoyed the distinction of being the youngest and tallest of six hundred members present from all quarters of the globe. He three times represented Mississippi in the national alliance and was chairman of the committee that framed that order's first platform of demands for national legislation. He has held the positions of respondent to the address of welcome, essayist and annual orator in the Mississippi press association, and was chosen to represent that body in the national editorial convention which met at San Antonio in 1888, at Boston in 1890 and St. Paul in 1891. He attended both the latter and was each time honored with appointment as member of the standing committee on legislation. His address at the St. Paul meeting on the subject of the country weekly, before one thousand journalists from every state of the Union, won for him at a single bound a national reputation, being universally pronounced the most humorous and eloquent delivered on that occasion. Mr. Martin is the constant recipient of invitations to make alliance, temperance and political speeches and has made the annual literary address before no less than a dozen male and female colleges of the state. His hight, commanding bearing, clear articulation, easy grace of manner, choice language and ringing musical voice have won for him the justly deserved sobriquet of the silver-tongued editor of Mississippi. Mr. Martin jocularly declares that he has never been a candidate for anything but matrimony, but nevertheless he has held the positions of secretary of the legislature and the late constitutional convention, and is conceded to be the best public reader in Mississippi. No public convention ever assembles at Jackson without enlisting his services as secretary or reading clerk. As he is just entering his thirtieth year, the horizon of his life is bright with the rainbow of hope and promise. Mr. Martin has been recently chosen president, at a handsome salary, of the Gulf Coast Building and Loan association, with an authorized capital of $5,000,000.

Mississippi has had no son who at the early age of twenty-five achieved more signal success and widespread reputation as a litterateur and journalist than the subject of this sketch. Born in Pike county, Miss., in 1862, he developed a youthful precocity and love of learning that made him famous in that section of country before he reached the age of seven. In Shaksperean dialogue and recitation he was completely at home and participated in many public theatricals, in which he won lasting renown. His tastes and talents carried him, at the age of fifteen, into the newspaper business, and he went to the top at the first bound. In Westville, Brookhaven, Crystal Springs, Utica and other places he conducted papers of his own with unvarying success. At the age of twenty-two, with his brother E. L. Martin, he purchased the *New Mississippian*, of Jackson, Miss., and assumed editorial control. His facile pen, at one time mirthful and humorous, at another bitterly sarcastic, again tender, pathetic and kind, and always brilliant and eloquent, moving the hearts and minds of men as with a magician's wand, soon attracted the attention of the state. His versatile genius burst upon them suddenly and with dazzling splendor, as though the sun, too impatient to ascend by regular gradations the heavenly horizon, should, without premonition, burst upon a startled and unexpectant world in all its meridian brilliancy and glory. Prison reform, prohibition, governmental reform, etc., found in him a bold, brilliant and uncompromising champion. With one acclaim prohibitionists and others interested in the movements seeking to elevate humanity proclaimed him leader. He stumped the state for temperance and rendered invaluable assistance in reclaiming more than half its territory from the curse of the licensed saloon. As a speaker he united the wit and humor of Mark Twain, the strength of Edmund Burke and the flowery and impassioned eloquence of Prentiss. His addresses bore the polish of the cut diamond and shone resplendent with all the bright hues that mark its luster. The State Press association had showered their honors upon his head and heaped them with profuse hand at his feet. In him were centered at once their hopes and pride. The tragic occurrence on May 1, 1888, in which he and his assailant, General Adams, both instantly lost their lives, spread a pall of gloom over the city and state. He was at that time a candidate for congress, with excellent promise of success. The funeral cortege to his old home at Brookhaven, fifty-five miles south on the Illinois Central railroad, was besieged with large crowds at every intermediate station. Floral tributes were presented by the ladies and temperance bands until the car could hold no more. Loving hands tenderly laid him away in the city of the dead, and above his breast was inscribed in silver the words: "John H. Martin—1888—Pure and noble. He died as bravely as he lived."

John Martin, a prominent planter of Lincoln county, whose postoffice address is Bogue Chitto, lives ten miles south of Brookhaven. He is the son of James and Mary (Gill) Martin, who were born and married in North Carolina, where the subject of our sketch was born in 1813. Their other children—John, Thomas, James and Daniel—are deceased. Melinda is the wife of Warrick Brister, a prominent farmer of Lincoln county, and is the mother of eight children. The mother of our subject died in 1825. Mr. Martin married for his second wife, Alice Gill, and to them were born four children, of whom two—Albert J. and Hamilton —are now living. Mr. Martin was a very prominent planter in his native state. He came to Mississippi with his family in 1809 and located in Lawrence county on the farm on which he lived the life of a planter until his death. John Martin began active life for himself when still quite young. While having no educational advantages, he managed to get a large amount of general information, being observing of everything about him, and an apt student of human nature, which, with his other good qualities, caused him to become a highly respected and highly influential citizen of Lawrence county. He was married in 1846, to Mrs. Elphany (Obier) Weathersby, who at that time had five children by her former marriage with Ludwick L. Weathersby. The names of the children are as follows: Lewis, Missouri, Virginia, William J. and Solomon C. This lady was a native of South Carolina, and a daughter of John and Elizabeth (Adams) Obier, to whom were born four children: James, William, Mary and Elphany, now Mrs. Martin. To Mr. and Mrs. Martin one child has been born—a son—John O., who married Miss Julia Gardner, and after her death he married Miss Dora Huffman, who died after having borne him one child. He then married Miss Maggie C. Smith, who has borne him a family of five children: Smith, Nellie, Pollie, Virginia and John A. This son with his family lives with Mr. and Mrs. Martin, and he assists his father in the management of the plantation. In 1863 Mr. Martin was drafted to serve in the Mississippi state militia and went into service in Captain Grag's company of Colonel Quin's regiment. He served a very brief time, and then came home on a furlough and did not return. Mr. Martin may truly be called an Andrew Jackson democrat, for he cast his first presidential vote for Old Hickory, and has voted the democratic ticket ever since. He is a supporter of churches, schools and everything that has a tendency to promote the general welfare. He is a member of the Methodist Episcopal church and a Master Mason. He came upon his present plantation in 1866 and was obliged to clear the land and erect buildings for himself and his family. His home is one of the most comfortable in the county, and the hospitality of the family is such that it is truly a home to all who seek admission.

Hon. John H. Martin was born in Albemarle county, Va., in 1790. He was a soldier under General Jackson during the Indian wars and was made a major in recognition of distinguished services. He commanded the Tennessee troops at the battle of New Orleans. After the war he practiced law with success at Glasgow, Ky., until 1826, when he removed to Nashville, Tenn., and associated himself with Hon. John Bell and Judge Henry A Crabb. Later he was a partner of George S. Yerger, and that firm prepared Martin & Yerger's Tennessee reports. Later he was for a short time circuit judge by appointment. He removed to Vicksburg in 1836 and died of yellow fever in 1841.

Hon. Jonathan McCaleb Martin is a personage of such importance and prestige in his county and district, as well as in the state, that a brief review of his career will be of more than passing interest to the readers of this volume. Although his early manhood was devoted to the cause of secession and was full of thrilling incidents his subsequent career has been devoted to peaceful pursuits and his success has been a steady and constant growth, for he is possessed of excellent judgment, strong common sense and indomitable energy, and in his life and character have evinced great symmetry, completeness and moral standing of a high order. He was born in Claiborne county, Miss., June 2, 1846, being the sixth in a family of ten children, six sons and four daughters, of whom only four are living. The names of his brothers and sisters are as follows: Caroline M., a literary lady of note residing in New York city; George H., a resident of Wichita Falls, Tex., and Fletcher C., who is a graduate of the University of Texas, and is now practicising law in Seymour of that state. Those deceased are: Jones E., who was a student of high rank in Williams college, after leaving which he began devoting his attention to agriculture. He entered the Confederate service as captain in a company of infantry and during his career as a soldier showed remarkable courage and bravery. He was killed at the terrible battle of Sharpsburg, having, just prior to his death, been promoted to the rank of lieutenant-colonel in the Forty-eighth Mississippi infantry volunteers. William M., another brother, entered the Confederate service in the Claiborne guards, in which he was soon promoted to first lieutenant, but resigned this position to return home and raise a cavalry company in connection with Captain McGruder, in which he assumed the role of first lieutenant. In an engagement which took place soon after, Captain McGruder was killed and Lieutenant Martin was promoted to the captaincy of his company. Captain Martin was shot three times and was killed at Harrisburg, Miss., in 1864. He was a young man of brilliant prospects, was a graduate of Yale college, and was expecting to make law his profession. Charles Henry, who died in early manhood, possessed a fine analytical mind and gave every promise of making name and fame for himself, but ere these expectations could be realized his sun had set forever. Sarah H. was a graduate of the famous Female college of New Haven, Conn., of which Mrs. Edwards was president, and died in 1866. Mary E. died of yellow fever in 1878, she having also been a graduate of the Female college of New Haven. Melinda A. died at the age of nine years. The father of these children, William Heyward Martin, was born in Maryland in 1800, and was a graduate of the famous Princeton college of New Jersey, afterward becoming an eminent lawyer in his native state. He first read law under William Bullit, and after graduating in his calling moved to Louisville, Ky., where he formed a partnership with Humphrey Marshall, a man of renown, stability and wide reputation.

After making his home in Louisville for one year he came to Port Gibson, Miss., where he opened a law office, and soon won the reputation of being one of the most talented lawyers of Claiborne county, if not of the state. After a time, at the solicitation of his wife, he gave up his chosen profession and engaged in looking up his large landed interests, which were wrecked by the war. He died in 1878 of that terrible scourge, yellow fever. He often told of witnessing the passage of the British ships up Chesapeake bay and also saw the bombardment of Fort William Henry. His wife, whose maiden name was Mary M. McCaleb, was born in Mississippi in 1814 and died in 1865. Her mother was a native of South Carolina and her grandfather was a soldier in the Revolutionary war. The paternal grandfather of the subject of this sketch, Dr. Ennels Martin of Maryland, was surgeon's mate of Dr. Shippen's staff. Hon. J. McC. Martin's early education was received under a governess and private tutor, also the country schools, from which he entered the Seidlitz school at Port Gibson, Miss. His education was interfered with by the bursting of the war cloud which was hanging over the country, and he left the halls of erudition at the early age of fifteen years to shoulder his musket, don his suit of gray, and defend his country. Prior to his enlistment, however, he had taken part in the battle of Port Gibson, and only three days after entering the service he had his horse shot from under him, this being at the battle of Harris' Landing. He became a member of the Fourth Mississippi cavalry in 1863, and was assigned to Mississippi River department, but was afterward transferred to the famous Gen. Bedford Forrest's command and took part in the engagements at Flenker's Field, where Col. Frank P. Powers was his commander; Harrisburg, Miss., where his brother was killed within a short distance of him; Johnsonville, Tenn., where the Confederates destroyed the arsenal and sunk several steam and gun boats, and where Captain Martin came very near being killed by a bursting shell. He also took part in the engagement at Oxford, Miss., the fight taking place on the campus of the college grounds. In this engagement Captain Martin was promoted to fifth sergeant for gallant conduct, by Capt. Charles E. Buck. He next took part in the engagement at Selma, Ala., and surrendered at Gainesville of that state, soon after returning home. He at once engaged in hauling cotton and superintending wagoning, for as he had not a dollar in his pocket he concluded that there was no time to waste in vain regrets, but with his characteristic energy, immediately put his shoulder to the wheel in order to retrieve his fallen fortune. He had to commence at the very bottom of the ladder, but he wisely saved the money he earned and with it determined to finish his education. He entered the famous University of Virginia, at Charlottsville, in 1866, and after taking a general course for two years he returned home and began teaching school in Copiah county, the money he thus earned being sent to his brother, with which to cultivate the home farm. He afterward followed agricultural pursuits for a short time, then decided to take up the study of law, and with this end in view went to New Orleans, but finding that he must engage in some business in order to carry on his course of study, he applied for, and obtained the chair of English and mathematics in Prytonnia high school of that city. In 1874 he engaged with the White league in the famous battle of the Levee, and narrowly escaped being shot as a ball passed through his hat close to his head. He was admitted to the Louisiana bar in 1875, but shortly after left New Orleans, having received a telegram from his sister calling him home on important business, and here he drifted into politics. In 1875 he was the prime organizer of the revolt against the republicans and pushed his venture to a successful issue. Three years later he was elected to the house of representatives and was re-elected in 1879 and 1881, and was also chosen to the state senate from Claiborne and Copiah counties. His measures which were successfully handled and perfected were the following: The Emigration law of 1880, The State census of 1880, The Compromise of Mobile and Ohio railroad, of money borrowed from the Chickasaw school fund in 1857, The Act creating the Mississippi institute and college for the white girls in 1884," which bill he drafted, and secured its passage after a bitter fight. He had been a trustee of the college ever since its erection, and at the present time about four hundred names are enrolled. He commenced the practice of law in 1876, and is considered by all the leading members of the bar as one of the best counselors of the state, and his work as a skillful, shrewd and farseeing attorney has won for him a national reputation. By his earnest endeavors he has amassed a fortune of $60,000, and by dint of perseverance, ability, industry, frugality and honest toil, has arisen to an exalted position in the state. During the first four years of his career as a professional man, he was a partner of the late chancellor of Mississippi, L. McLaurin, now of Dallas, Tex., but since that time has been associated with several gentlemen who have formed the basis of their legal education under the admirable tutelage of Hon. J. McC. Martin. One young gentleman, S. R. Bertron, a graduate of Yale college, is now prominently connected with the Equitable Loan and Trust Company, of Boston, Mass. Hon. J. McC. Martin also educated his brother Fletcher C. in the University of Texas, the latter being now a successful legal practitioner. Mr. Martin is trustee of the Industrial institute and college of Columbus, Miss.; is a member of the I. O. O. F. at Port Gibson, Miss., and is also a member of the Knights & Ladies of Honor and the American Legion of Honor. He is a gentleman who firmly believes in insurance and is now carrying over $30,000 in the heavy stock companies of the East.

He was married to Miss Amanda M. Myles, a native of Mississippi, and a daughter of Dr. William and Amanda (Wood, nee McCall) Myles. Mrs. Martin is an accomplished and intelligent lady and received her education in the Columbian Female institute, at Columbia, Tenn. Mr. Martin is a member of the Methodist Episcopal Church South, of Port Gibson, and his wife of the Episcopal church of that place. He is an openhanded and generous gentleman, whose benevolence is well known by all who are acquainted with him. He is ever awake to the demands and interests of his country and state and at all times uses his influence for the advancement of morality, intellectual vigor, the rise and growth of the country and the general welfare of the race. Although his legal learning is profound he is yet a close student, and in his handsome and well appointed library many pleasant and profitable hours are spent. His law library contains twelve hundred volumes, valued at $4,000, and his library of general works is remarkably well selected, contains eight hundred volumes, worth about $2,000. He possesses strong and resolute will, great firmness, practical sagacity, a keen insight into the motives and methods of men, and in all respects is admirably fitted for the profession he has followed. His home in Port Gibson is one of the most beautiful and attractive private residences of which the city can boast; an air of refinement and taste pervades all its surroundings, and the generous and truehearted, yet unostentatious hospitality displayed there by himself and his accomplished wife is the delight of the many friends who gather beneath their rooftree.

Norman Martin is the sixth son of Norman Martin, Sr., who was of Scotch descent, born in South Carolina in January, 1798. His son, Norman, was born in Lauderdale county, Miss., in 1842, was brought up to a farm life and was educated in the common country schools. In 1860 he began work on his own account, but in 1861 responded to the call of the Confederacy for troops, and being at that time a resident of Louisiana he joined the Nineteenth Louisiana regiment, under command of Colonel Hodge, afterward successively commanded by Hollingsworth, Winding, Turner and others. Although his regiment participated in the battle of Shiloh, he was sick at the time and did not take part in that battle but was afterward at Chickamauga and Missionary ridge. He was at Atlanta with Johnston, was at Resaca, New Hope church, was at Atlanta again on the 28th of July, after which he went with Hood on his Tennessee campaign, participating in the battle of Nashville. Upon Hood's army being routed he made his escape from Tennessee and arriving in Mississippi went to Spanish Fort, Alabama and after the close of hostilities came home and once more engaged in agricultural pursuits at his old home in Clarke county. He was given onehundred and sixty acres of land by his father, which by good management he has increased to between eight hundred and one thousand acres of average land. From the cultivated portion of this land he raises about twenty-five bales of cotton each year, the average being about one-half bale of cotton to the acre. The average yield of corn is about twenty bushels to the acre, but oats, potatoes and sugarcane are also raised to a considerable extent. He uses home compost and commercial fertilizers and considers it a paying investment. He was married in 1866 to Miss Martin Anderson, of Lauderdale county, Miss., by whom he has five children: George W., Lucy C., Joseph L., Thomas F. and Sarah Hayes. He was elected a member of the board of supervisors in 1876 and was twice re-elected, doing much to improve the county during his term of service. His well known efficiency has again brought him before the public for the position this year (1891) and he no doubt will again be elected. He is a member of the Farmers' Alliance, and he and his wife are members of the Baptist church of many years standing. Mr. Martin is liberal and charitable, is a warm patron of education, is thrifty and industrious and occupies a high social position.

Judge Thomas N. Martin (deceased), a prominent and distinguished attorney at law, was born in North Carolina in 1807, being the third son born to William Martin. The eldest son, James was a pioneer minister of the Baptist church, and it is said of him that though illiterate he did untold good for the cause of Christianity. The second son, Osborn, was an itinerant Methodist minister. As Thomas came of humble parentage he only received about three months' schooling in his boyhood, his time being spent in tilling the soil. When about twenty-one years of age he secured a position in an iron foundry on Broad river, North Carolina, being in the employ of a Mr. Black, who afterward became a congressman. The political preferment of Mr. Black served as a spur to the ambition of Mr. Martin and he set about securing a better education than he had. About the time he had attained his majority he had married a Miss Parthenia Howser, the daughter of a well-to-do planter of Dutch parentage, after which he remained in the employ of Mr. Black until about 1835 or '36, when he removed to Mississippi and settled in what is known as the Dark corner of Chickasaw county. He chose for his home a sterile piece of land because he discovered that a spring of clear water flowed through it, and here he opened a school and cleared him a little farm. The story of his early struggles against privation, the hardships he endured and the dangers he encountered are but the repetition of the story of other worthy and ambitious pioneers. At about the time the county of Chickasaw was organized he was appointed one of the commissioners to lay out a road from Houston to Grenada, also served as a member of the board of police and was afterward made a justice of the peace. His next advancement upon the ladder of success was when he was elected clerk of the probate court, although at that time he was still a resident of an obscure portion of the county, being elected to this office about the year 1840. He removed to Houston in 1841 and served in the capacity of clerk for about twelve years. In 1852 or '53 he became assistant clerk of the house of representatives, in which capacity he was faithful, efficient and upright. In 1846 his genius found an outlet as editor of the Houston *Patriot*, of which he continued to be the successful editor and proprietor for five or six years. Under his able management the paper became a decided success and became largely patronized. In 1865 Judge Martin was elected a member of the state senate, and during his term as senator he became noted as a conservative, thorough and ardent democrat. He was instrumental in securing the passage of a number of important bills, but the one which won him his greatest distinction and in which he took greater pride than in any other act of his senatorial career was an act providing for the recovery of the Chickasaw school funds from the several railroads to which it had been loaned. In November, 1869, Mr. Martin was elected to congress, his opponent being a Mr. Railsback, receiving a very flattering majority, but was not permitted to take his seat in congress. This closed his political career. His ambition aspired to greater honors and his advancing years made the latter part of his political career odious to him. Mr. Martin was admitted to the bar without special preparation, save that which was gained from his service as a public officer. He at once took rank with the leading members of the local bar, which at that time was very able. Realizing his defective early education, he formed a partnership with J. M. Thompson, now of Birmingham, Ala., and together they built up a very successful and lucrative practice. This partnership lasted up to 1858, at which time Mr. Martin associated himself with his son-in-law, William S Bates, of Pontotoc, under the firm name of Martin & Bates, which partnership lasted up to the time of Mr. Martin's death, May 19, 1886. By the time the war opened Judge Martin had acquired a large property, consisting principally of real estate. When the war opened he began merchandising, but had the misfortune to lose a considerable amount of his property in the general collapse that followed. He had, however, prior to his death, been able to partially retrieve his fortune, and was the owner of fifteen hundred acres of good land in Chickasaw and adjoining counties. To himself and wife the following children were born: Mary Jane, widow of William Scott, of Houston; Sallie A., widow of Judge S. A. Dulavey, of Houston; Susan, wife of Judge William S. Bates; William O., who grew to be a young man of excellent principles and fine intellect, joined the army of Virginia in 1862 as a private in the Eleventh Mississippi infantry and was killed at the battle of Malvern hill; Virginia, wife of Capt. J. W. Howell, of Greenwood, Miss.; Martha O., widow of Mr. Roberts, and Laura S., widow of Clay Prewit, of Houston. Judge Martin was from boyhood a member of the church and was for the last twenty years of his life an elder in the Presbyterian church. His widow, who survives him, is also a member of that church. He was a leading member of the local lodge of the A. F. & A. M., of Houston, represented his lodge in the grand lodge of the state and was at one time assistant lecturer of the state. He was an advocate of temperance and identified himself with temperance organizations. He was a man who possessed very superior mental qualifications, and weight and power accompanied all his words and writings and inspired respect. His leading characteristics were extreme frankness, honesty of purpose, indomitable will and energy. Full of generosity and charity he rarely suspected others of sordid or improper motives, and his criticisms, when provoked, were tempered with mildness and forbearance. In the domestic circle he was devoted to his family and in social life he was highly esteemed for his kindly and courtly manners. He was keenly alive to the sufferings and misfortunes of others, and no one ever appealed to him in vain for consolation or succor.

William B. Martin, M. D., of Indianola, Miss. Among the pioneer families of Mississippi that settled in Copiah county, was that of the Rev. Dr. Martin, who took up his abode there about 1816. He was a pioneer minister of the Baptist faith, but in addition to attending to the spiritual wants of his fellowmen he was engaged in planting also, and reared his family on his plantation in that county. Hon. W. W. Martin, his son and father of Dr. William B., was born in one of the Carolinas about the year 1814, but from his infancy until the time of his death he was a resident of Mississippi. Miss Mary A. Miller, a native of Copiah county and a daughter of Squire Miller, a prominent and wealthy planter of that county, became his wife, after which they settled on a plantation and in time became wealthy. He interested himself in the political affairs of his day, showed excellent qualities of leadership, was a thoroughly independent thinker and for the sound judgment and practical ability which he at all times manifested he was elected to represent Copiah county in the general assembly of the state one or more terms. He was called from life in 1858, his widow surviving him until 1890. Dr. William B. Martin was the youngest of their five sons and two daughters that grew to mature years, and his youth, like that of his father, was spent in Copiah county, on a plantation. Besides receiving his primary education at home he finished his education in Mississippi college, nearly completing the regular course of that institution. His first work in the way of earning his own living was as a school teacher in Holmes county, being principal of the Wesson high school for one year, where he earned the reputation of being an able instructor and a fine disciplinarian. While in that town he studied medicine under Drs. Rea and Sexton, two local physicians of the place, and took his first course of lectures in Tulane Medical college of New Orleans in the winter of 1884-5. After completing his first course he returned to Wesson, and during the summer of 1885 was there engaged in the practice of his profession, after which he returned to his former alma mater and finished his medical course, graduating in the spring of 1886. Soon after this he came to Indianola and here has been actively engaged in practicing ever since. He has done much to alleviate the ills of suffering humanity in this section, and has shown that as a physician he is possessed of more than ordinary skill and talent. He brings the magnetism of his presence to bear upon his patients, and his cheerful countenance, his cordial ways and encouraging words, aid largely in carrying out the work which his medicines inaugurate. In 1888 he formed a partnership with Dr. Cannon and the following year this firm opened a drug establishment and are now carrying a fine line of drugs and medicines that would do credit to a much larger town. They have a fine trade and practice and are the leading physicians of Sunflower county. Dr. Martin was married here in November, 1887, to Miss Georgia Smith, a native of the county, being reared here by an uncle, G. K. Smith, now a resident of Oxford, Miss. Mrs. Martin is the daughter of William and Nannie (Gillespie) Smith, both of whom died when she was a child. The Smiths were among the prominent early families of this section. Mrs. Martin, as well as the Doctor, is a member of the Baptist church. The latter is a member of the state board of medical examiners and also belongs to the state board of health. He is one of the leading inhabitants of Indianola and is public-spirited and enterprising.

The individual members of the firm of Martin Bros., merchants, Hardy Station, Miss., are Dr. A. Martin, J. A. Martin and W. F. Martin, who are classed among the prominent business men of the county. They are the sons of James A. Martin and the grandsons of Aurelius Martin, after whom Dr. A. Martin was named. Grandfather Martin was a native of

South Carolina and came to Mississippi with his family in the forties, settling in Yalobusha county, where he resided for a number of years. He afterward moved to a place near Coffeeville, then the county seat of that county, and there his death occurred. He was the father of six children, three sons and three daughters, all of whom lived to be grown and settled in the vicinity of the home place. Only one, Savanah, is now living. She first married Jesse Hardy and after his death was united in marriage to J. E. Laycook. She now resides on the old home place and in the same house built by her father. The children deceased were: Joseph, John, James A., Elizabeth and Rebecca. Joseph and John died when young, on the home place, and just after completing their education. Elizabeth was the wife of Thomas Atkinson, and after his death was married to J. W. Harris, now of Hardy Station. Rebecca married Col. Richard Stokes, and both are now deceased, she dying in 1881 at the age of forty-seven years. Their sons are prominent merchants of Hardy Station. James A. Martin was born in Edgefield district, S. C., on the 11th of October, 1831, and there received his education. He was married to Miss Marthy Hill, daughter of Joel Hill, of South Carolina, who afterward moved to Mississippi and became one of the foremost planters. She was educated at Grenada and afterward taught school in the academy for a number of years. She was a member of the Baptist church and was a good and noble woman. She died when her youngest child was eight months, leaving three children, who now compose the above mentioned firm. The father was married the second time to Miss Frances Griffis, daughter of Jesse Griffis (see sketch of John W. Griffis) and by her became the father of three children: Jannie, a graduate at the school at Columbus, Miss., and who is now completing a musical course at Iuka, of this state. Blanche is attending school at Columbus, and John E. is a bright little fellow of eleven years. In 1862 Mr. Martin settled in Hardy Station, commenced merchandising and continued this until his death, on the 9th of December, 1889. He had won the reputation of a good, law-abiding citizen, a kind neighbor, a generous friend, an honest merchant and a successful farmer. His house was so emphatically the home of hospitality that strangers as well as friends naturally gravitated to it for its generous kindness. Mr. Martin was intelligent, genial, and warmhearted in all his social relations and was a kind, loving and devoted husband and father. He took a very active part in politics and was one of the foremost democrats of the county. He was a member of the Baptist church in early life. He was a member of the A. F. & A. M., Grenada lodge No. 31, and was buried by the beautiful ritual of the Masonic order. Dr. A. Martin, the senior member of the firm of Martin Bros., is a graduate of the University Medical college at Louisville, Ky., and commenced his practice at Hardy Station in partnership with Dr. Barksdale, of that place. He has not married. He is a member of the I. O. O. F., Ivanhoe lodge No. 8, at Grenada. James A. Martin was educated in the vicinity of Hardy Station and was married to Miss May Smith of that place, she being a daughter of Joseph and L. A. Smith. James A. is a member of the grand lodge of Odd Fellows, No. 6, is a Knight Templar in the Masonic fraternity and is a member of the Knights and Ladies of Honor. He first engaged in merchandising at Hardy Station about five years before the death of his father, and after the above firm was established they succeeded the latter in the mercantile business. William F. Martin, the junior member of the firm, was educated at Oxford, Miss., and is now depot and express agent, also postmaster at Hardy Station. The brothers, like their father, are all stanch democrats and take a lively interest in politics. They are the owners of large tracts of lands in Yalobusha and Tallahatchie counties and with several hundred acres under cultivation. They handle about three hundred and fifty bales of cotton every year and are live, energetic business men.

T. Staige Marye, resident of Greenwood, Miss., has for many years been prominently identified with the history of Le Flore county, and is justly entitled to the space allotted him in this record of the leading citizens of the state of Mississippi. He was born at Port Gibson, Claiborne county, Miss., August 12, 1849. James T. Marye, his father, was born in Virginia, about the year 1814, and came to Mississippi when a young man, and settled at Port Gibson. There he married Mary P. Hoopes, a native of the city of Philadelphia, and a daughter of Passmore Hoopes, one of the pioneers of Claiborne county and a leading merchant of Port Gibson for a number of years. He died there about the year 1868, his wife following him three years later, in 1871. Our subject is one of a family of two sons and two daughters who grew to maturity. He spent his youth in Port Gibson, and received his education there. When he started out in life for himself he came to what is now Le Flore county, and engaged in planting on Roebuck lake. In a few years he went to California, but Our Italy failed to chain him to the Pacific coast, and at the end of a year he returned. He then entered the mercantile trade at Greenwood, and did business there for a number of years; he finally removed his store to his plantation, and has carried on a neighborhood and plantation store. He was one of the prime movers in the establishment of the oilmill at Greenwood, in 1890. On the organization of this company he was elected treasurer, secretary and manager. The mill was in running operation in February, 1890, and is doing a fine business; two forces of men are worked, so the mill runs day and night; about sixty tons of seed are used every twenty-four hours. This is a very important institution to Greenwood and the surrounding country. The pay roll amounts to $400 per week, and the industry is one of the most profitable. In addition to his commercial interests Mr. Marye takes an active part in local politics. He is a strong adherent to democratic principles, and zealously supports all the men and measures of that body. He is one of the county board of supervisors, and has occupied this position for the past ten years. He is president of the present board. He has served as the mayor of Greenwood, carrying out an economical and satisfactory policy. He is vice president of the Delta bank, being elected to this office on the organization of that institution; he is a member of the Yazoo and Mississippi River Delta Levee board, and has belonged to this body since its inception in 1884. Mr. Marye was married in Le Flore county, Miss., in 1870, to Miss Mary Emma Harper, a native of Le Flore county, and a daughter of J. P. Harper. Mrs. Marye was reared in Le Flore county, but received her education in Carroll county. She is the mother of one son, W. S. Marye. Our subject is one of the heaviest landowners in Le Flore county; he has two thousand acres, thirteen hundred of which are under excellent cultivation. About eight hundred bales of cotton are produced annually. This places Mr. Marye among the largest planters of the state, and he is known to be among the most public-spirited and enterprising of her citizens.

Presly Mason, of Meridian, Lauderdale county, Miss., was born in 1840 in Richmond county, N. C., and, coming to Lauderdale county, Miss., in 1870, settled in the southeastern part. Isaac Mason, his father, was born in Richmond county, N. C., about 1815, and was married about 1837, to Miss Hicks, of North Carolina. He was a soldier in the Confederate states army. Presly Mason also went to the war, enlisting in company D, Capt. A. T. Cole commanding, twenty-third North Carolina regiment, Colonel Hoke's command; was in the battles of Williamsburg, Seven Pines and South mountain, and in the campaign to Maryland; captured at Antietam, and imprisoned at Fort Delaware for one month; exchanged and paroled, he went back with his old regiment; was at Gettysburg, was here slightly wounded and again captured, and imprisoned at Point Lookout, Md.; remained there eighteen months, during which time he suffered much from cold and hunger, from the effects of which he has never fully recovered. He held some non-commissioned positions during his war service; was appointed orderly sergeant by his captain as a token of merit. After the general surrender of the Confederate forces he engaged in agriculture in North Carolina, and, as indicated above, removed to Mississippi. He owns three hundred acres of land and has been engaged in sawmilling and ginning. Among the branches of his agriculture may be mentioned stockraising, truckfarming, etc. He aims at extensive and intensive farming and has much faith in truckfarming. Mr. Mason was married in 1867 to Miss S. J. Covington, of North Carolina, and has had ten children: John C., Maggie J., Francis I., Corrie M., James D., Sudie M., Sadie F., Ruby, Presly Edwin and Bessie. Eight of these survive. Miss Sue Covington, a sister of Mrs. Mason, resides with the family. Mr. Mason acquired his education in the common schools. His son, Francis I., is a student of the Agricultural and Mechanical college, at Starkville, while his daughter, Miss Maggie J., is a student at the East Mississippi Female college, at Meridian, Miss. Mr. Mason is a friend to education, and the principal founder of the Pleasant Hill high school, an institution of worth and merit, located near his home. Mrs. Mason is a lady of literary turn of mind and presides with dignity over her interesting family. Mr. Mason has affiliated with the Masonic order, is a member of the Alliance, a stanch democrat, and is a Missionary Baptist. He is of a benevolent disposition, and bestows charity with a liberal hand. December 10, 1884, his oldest son, John C., was killed by a boiler explosion on the premises. He was a young man of promise and his death threw a gloom over the family which can never be wholly dispelled. How true it seems, in this instance, that death loves a shining mark. Little Bessie, a tender flower, was transplanted to unfold its loveliness in a fairer world. Mr. Mason is deservedly popular with his people, being a man of prudent, conservative ideas as regards the financial and political condition of the country. He has been solicited to represent them in the legislature, though he prefers the quiet walks of life.

George M. Massingale, general merchant and planter, of Quitman, Clarke county, Miss., was born near Goldsboro, N. C., in 1830, a son of George W. and Polly (Cotton) Massingale. His father was a native of North Carolina, and was reared on his father's farm, at an early day starting in life as a farmer, an occupation which he followed all his life. He was married in North Carolina, and reared a family of ten children: Young B., Robert B., Allie C., Epsie, Mary A., George M., Curtis B., Julia A., Julian A., Julius M. The family emigrated to Alabama in 1831, and from there to this state in 1846, living a short time in Jasper county and locating permanently in Clarke county. He was a successful planter and became a well-to-do citizen. He was a public spirited man, an active member of the Baptist church, and died in this county in 1863. The mother, a native of North Carolina, and a member of the Baptist church, died in Jasper county in 1857. Mr. and Mrs. Massingale were among the early pioneers of this section of the state, and had their share in the troubles and vicissitudes of that period. Four of the brothers of our subject served the Confederate cause during the late war, in which he also did gallant service. Young B., Robert B., Julian A. and Julius M. are all of them now residents of Mississippi except Julius M., who lives in Arkansas. The boyhood and youth of our subject were passed at Quitman, and he was reared to a thorough knowledge of farm and plantation work. At the age of twenty-one he engaged as a clerk in a store of that town, and in September, 1859, he was married to Martha M. McGowan, a daughter of Elbert McGown, a native of Alabama, who became a well known planter of this county. Mrs. Massingale was born in Pickens county, Ala., in 1839. After his marriage Mr. Massingale accepted a position as a bookkeeper at Shubuta, where he remained till he entered the Confederate service in 1862 in company E, of the Thirty-seventh Mississippi volunteers, in which he was lieutenant, and later became captain. He participated in the battles at Iuka and at Vicksburg, where he was wounded in the left leg by a rifle ball so severely as to disable him for a year and prevent his going into action again. He surrendered in 1865. On returning to Clarke county he was elected probate clerk, a position he held for three years, when he engaged in his present occupations of farming and merchandising. He does a large mercantile trade, and is the owner of about five thousand acres of land in Clarke county, where he is heavily interested in planting. Mr. and Mrs. Massingale have eight children: Howard, who is in the mercantile business at Quitman, and has a family of wife and three children; Estelle, who died at college; Maud, who married James A. Terral, and is dead; Sallie, wife of Mr. C. B. Weir, an attorney at Heflin, Ala.; George M., at home; Samuel C., at the State University of Mississippi; Nannie and Earl, at home. He and his family are members of the Methodist Episcopal church, in which he holds the office of steward. He represented his county in the state legislature in 1875 to 1877, and has been president of the county board of supervisors of Clarke county for two years, besides serving his fellow-townsmen in the city council. He is a self-made man in the best sense of that often-abused term, and what he owns he became the possessor of by right of laborious acquisition. He is a democrat in politics, and takes a deep and abiding interest not only in state and county affairs but also in small local matters that promise to benefit the population among whom they have arisen.

Edwin Mathis, of Energy, Clarke county, Miss., is a son of Frederick Mathis. The latter was born in South Carolina and lived successively in South Carolina, Georgia, Alabama, Mississippi and Texas, and died in the latter state in 1862. He married Miss Sarah Waites, of Georgia. Edwin Mathis was born in Henry county, Ga., in October, 1825, and came to Mississippi in 1844 and settled in Lauderdale county. He received an ordinary education in the schools of the period and locality. At the age of twenty-one years he began farming for himself. He was married in 1851 to Miss Caroline Bontwell, of Choctaw county, Ala., and has eleven children: Sarah Levisa, George W., John C., James Buchanan, Amelia, William Breckinridge, Mary Ellen, Louvenia Caroline, Edwin Jones, Mattie Ann, and Ann Eliza. He purchased land in 1847 and by additional purchases now owns a great deal of average Clarke county land. His usual crop of cotton is fifteen bales, and his average yield of corn is twenty or twenty-five bushels per acre. He also produces oats, sugarcane and potatoes. He uses commercial fertilizer and home compost. A part of his land is covered with fine, longleaf pine timber and hard woods. In 1863 he enlisted in the Eighth Mississippi regiment, Col. Wilkinson commanding, and was in the battle of Missionary ridge, falling back to Dalton and taking part in the defense of Atlanta. He was wounded at the battle of Kenesaw mountain, and went into Marietta hospital. After remaining there for a short time he went to Atlanta, La Grange and Columbus, successively, and was in the battle of Jonesboro. He returned to his command at Atlanta and was present at the evacuation of that place. He then went with Hood to Tennessee and took part in the battle of Franklin, as a member of Claiborne's division, of Lowrey's brigade in Lashly's company of Tyson's regiment. There Captain Lashly was killed and Mr. Mathis was wounded and went into the hospital at Columbia. He rejoined his command at Corinth and came home on a furlough, and then became sick and had not recovered at the time of Lee's surrender. Mr. Mathis re-engaged in farming with much energy and stands to-day as the most successful representative of agriculture in all his section of the country. He was once elected justice of the peace of his district. In 1874 he was chosen a member of the board of supervisors of his county, and served two years. Mr. Mathis is a Mason; is a member of the Methodist church of forty-three years' standing; Mrs. Mathis is also a Methodist. Their children are highly respected and most of them are members of the Methodist church. All of his children survive except William Breckinridge, who mysteriously disappeared years ago in Texas, whither he had gone to try his fortune. The supposition is that he perished at the hands of an assassin. E. J. Mathis is a practitioner of medicine in Louisiana. He graduated from Mobile medical college in 1890. Prior to this he graduated from the Bowling Green, Ky., business college, and is one of the leading men, financially, in his county, having a standing second to none.

An old and highly respected citizen of Covington county, Miss., Neill Mathison, was born in Twiggs county, Ga., in 1818, and is a son of James Mathison, a native of South Carolina. His father came to Mississippi when he was an infant seven months old, and lived in Jackson county during the first three years of his residence here. He then went to Perry county and lived there four years. He finally settled in Covington county, where our subject grew to manhood. During his youth he became initiated into the mysteries of agriculture, and for a short time during the winter season attended the common schools; his advantages in this direction, however, were extremely limited, as the public-school system of that day had not reached a point when it could be called a system. In 1860 Mr. Mathison was married to Miss Damie, a daughter of Wesley Gray. Her father was a substantial planter, owning a considerable amount of property before the war. Mr. and Mr. Mathison are the parents of nine children, six of whom grew to maturity. The eldest son, Louis, was a promising young man, possessed of an excellent education; he died at the age of twenty-five years, when he was sheriff of the county. Mr. Mathison has been prominently connected with much of the history of Covington county, and is a representative man. For two terms he was a member of the state legislature, serving with much credit to himself and the entire satisfaction of his constituency. He is a member of the Masonic order, belonging both to the Blue lodge and chapter. He is an active member of the Presbyterian church. He is living quietly on his plantation a few miles southeast from Mount Carmel, where he is enjoying the fruits of his earlier days of toil and industry.

Ex-Governor Joseph Matthews, who was well known throughout the length and breadth of Mississippi, first made his entrance in this state as a government surveyor. He made a permanent settlement near Salem, engaged in planting, and this was his principal occupation through life. He became very prominent as a politician, and was frequently a member of both branches of the state legislature. In 1850 he was elected governor of Mississippi, and served in that honorable position one term. He was one of the first stump speakers in the state, was original and peculiar, and wielded a great influence both socially and politically. He was a man of rigid economical habits and lived quite plainly. His death occurred in 1863 or 1864 during the war. He reared several children, all of whom became honorable and useful citizens.

R. F. Matthews, M. D., although born in Huntsville, Ala., has been a resident of Lowndes county, Miss., since about 1844, at which time he removed thither with his mother, who was widowed. His parents, Thomas and Kittie (Hughes) Matthews, were born in the Old Dominion, but were among the early settlers of the state of Alabama. The father was a planter, but while in the meridian of life was cut down by death. His widow died in 1862, having borne a family of five children, two of whom are living: Dr. R. F., and Samuel, of Louisiana. Dr. R. F. Matthews spent a considerable portion of the early part of his life in the state of his birth, and was given a public school education, afterward attending school in Tuscaloosa. He was quite a youth when he entered upon the study of medicine, and after becoming sufficiently fitted he entered the medical college at Transylvania, Ky. (which was merged with the Louisville school in 1845), and after graduating immediately came to Columbus, Miss., of which place he has since been a resident and an active practitioner. He was post surgeon at Macon, Miss., during the war, and was also a member of the board of surgeons at Columbus. Dr. Matthews is undoubtedly a skilled physician, and during his many years of practice in this county his success has been phenomenal. Being of a cheerful and happy disposition, his very presence in the sickroom does much toward inspiring his patients with hope and confidence, and therefore greatly augments their recovery. He is a member of the Masonic fraternity, and he and his worthy and amiable wife are members of the Presbyterian church. In 1846 he was married to Miss Amanda Barry, a sister of Col. W. S. Barry, a member of congress from this district. They have one child living: Mary S., wife of T. B. Bradford.

Capt. S. A. Matthews, one of Pike county's oldest settlers, was born in Brook county, Va., June 27th, 1822, and while an infant his parents removed to Jefferson county, Ohio, locating at Smithfield, where his father engaged in mercantile pursuits. His father, William Matthews, was a Virginian by birth, and married Mary Pennel, a native of Lancaster county, Penn. The father of Mrs. William Matthews, William Pennel, was one of the early pioneers in Brook county, Va., and was a companion of the celebrated Poe brothers. He was a valiant warrior, participating in the Indian wars of that period, and serving in the War of 1812 under Gen. William Henry Harrison. He had also when a mere lad served in the Revolutionary war as a light horseman. Mr. and Mrs. Matthews had five children born to them, three boys and two girls, of whom two only survive, viz.: William Matthews, named after his father, and Capt. S. A. Matthews. The Captain is the oldest child of this worthy couple and spent his early boyhood days in Jefferson county, Ohio, in the primitive days of that section of the state. At about the age of fourteen he entered the Grove academy at Steubenville, Ohio, and remained there for two years. He then entered upon a course of study at Franklin college, New Athens, where he had for a room mate an intimate associate Gen. G. W. McCook. Hon. John A. Bingham, who was afterward elected to the United States senate from Ohio, and was appointed special judge advocate in the trial of the assassins of President Lincoln, was also a student at this college and a friend of Captain Matthews. A third associate student was Hon. William Lawrence, who was elected to represent his state in the United States congress. In 1840 Captain Matthews began the study of law at Steubenville, Ohio, under the tutelage of General Stokely, who was then a member of congress from that district. He remained in General Stokely's office until the winter of 1842, when he took a trip through the South with a view to locating in some advantageous portion of the country, and, after visiting New Orleans and various places, settled permanently at Holmesville, Miss. Here the position of teacher in the public schools was tendered him, which he accepted, in the meantime continuing his law studies. In April, 1843, though yet under age, he was admitted to the bar, after passing an examination and being granted a lisense by Hon. Van Tramp Crawford, district judge of Pike county. Captain Matthews at once began to practice law in the village of Homesville, which he continued until 1849, when he was elected to the lower branch of the legislature, and sat during the regular session of 1850 and the extra session of 1851, acting as a member of the committee of military affairs. While he was representative he cast one ballot for Jefferson Davis as United States senator. He was very active in his efforts to secure the charter for the construction of the Illinois Central railroad through the state, this road at that time being known as the New Orleans & Jackson railroad. This bill, after having passed both houses, was vetoed by General Quitman, who was then governor of the state of Mississippi, but after a hard struggle the bill was passed over his head. During all this time Captain Matthews' efforts to push this bill through were indefatigable, and it was largely due to him that the charter was secured when it was. In 1851 he helped to establish and became a stockholder in *The Southron*, a weekly paper published at Holmesville, and the first democratic paper of the county. For the ensuing year he was engaged as managing editor of the paper and resigned this to accept the position of probate clerk, to which he had been elected in 1852. Afterwards he was elected circuit clerk and took charge of both offices till the year 1860, when he devoted his attention to his profession till the war cloud burst which had been hovering so long over the horizon. On April 15, 1861, he was mustered into the service of the state as captain of the Quitman guards, which he himself had organized. This company was mustered into the Confederate service May 27, 1861, and was known as company E, of the Sixteenth regiment, Mississippi volunteers. This regiment was attached to the Army of Northern Virginia, under the command of General Ewell. Captain Matthews served with this company in all of its engagements until January 1, 1864, when he was transferred to the department of trans-Mississippi, under Gen. E. Kirby Smith, and was placed on special duty on account of disabilities incurred in the hard service he had seen. He surrendered at Shreveport, La., July, 1865. Upon his return to his old home in Pike county he resumed the practice of law, and in 1868 he removed with his family to Magnolia, and from there he moved again to Summit, in 1871, where he formed a law partnership with H. Q. Bridges. In 1875 he was elected justice of the peace, serving until 1887. In 1888 he gave up his law practice, being appointed county superintendent of education, which position he held for two years. In July, 1887, he was also appointed notary public, which position he still holds. June 9th, 1849, he married Carrie J. Ellzey, a native of Pike county, Miss., and a daughter of William Ellzey, a prominent planter here. They have four offspring: Ida B., now Mrs. C. H. Hosmer, of Summit; George D., messenger of the Southern Express Company, and resides at New Orleans; Mamie E., who is married to H. C. Dunn and resides at Macomb City; and Eugene W., the eldest child, who was accidentally killed at Indian Bay, Ark., in 1879. Captain Matthews has been a member of the Masonic order since 1854; is a prominent member of the I. O. O. F. and is serving his second term as D. D. G. M. of the tenth district of Mississippi.

John B. Mattingly is a coal merchant and president of the Home Insurance company and of the Hill City Electric Light company. He was born in the city in which he is now residing in 1844, being the eldest child born to Austin D. and Mary (Bobb) Mattingly, who were born in Kentucky and Mississippi respectively. The maternal grandfather, John Bobb, was born in Philadelphia, Penn., and came to Mississippi at an early day, settling at Natchez, where he engaged in contracting and building. After remaining in that city for a short time he came to Vicksburg, and here followed the same calling, erecting the marine hospital, besides many other of the handsome structures of the city. He was the owner of a good brickyard, being the first manufacturer in his line in the city, and this, as well as his building operations, brought him in a substantial income. He in later years retired to a small plantation near the city, upon which he died, in 1863. Austin D. Mattingly was reared and educated in the state of his birth, but in 1823 came to Mississippi, and for some time was engaged in teaching at Washington, near the city of Natchez. He soon removed to Vicksburg, and first engaged in the manufacture of shingles, then in lumber, and afterward established a sawmill, which for a time was one of the largest in the state. In 1855 he began planting in the upper part of the county, and as his plantation was large his business was correspondingly extensive until the opening of the war. During the Rebellion he served with General Cheatham's division as assistant commissary, and after the war he returned to Vicksburg and began work with Victor Wilson in the coal business, and soon became a partner and a short time after sole proprietor. He then built up the business known as Mattingly, Floweree & Co., afterward Mattingly, Son & Co. He was deeply interested in the prosperity of Vicksburg, and was usually one of the organizers of its numerous enterprises. He died July 6, 1889, and his wife in 1854. John B. Mattingly was educated in Bardstown, Ky., but left school in May, 1861, to enlist in the Confederate army, becoming a member of Wirt Adams' company and a participant in the battle of Shiloh. He was also in the engagements around Corinth, and was fighting Sherman during the latter's raids in and around Vicksburg. He was in the Georgia campaign; was with Hood in Tennessee; then came back to Mississippi, and was near Tupelo at the close of the war, but was paroled at Jackson. He was captured at Mechanicsville, but made his escape by jumping from a steamboat near Friar's Point and working his way, with great difficulty and many dangers, through the swamps back to the Confederate lines. After the war he began planting in the southern part of Warren county, continuing until 1878, when he moved to Vicksburg and engaged in business with his father, purchasing the interest of Mr. Floweree, the firm then becoming Mattingly, Son & Co. He is now in business with his son Walter, and the firm, which is doing a coal and milling business, is known as Mattingly & Son. Mr. Mattingly was one of the organizers of the Home Insurance company, of Vicksburg, in 1886, of which he was elected president; is president of the Hill City Electric Light company, which was organized in 1887 with a paid up capital of $25,000, and is one of the finest plants in the state; and has been otherwise interested in the welfare of the city, there being few industries which have not received his support. He made a faithful soldier, is a stirring and enterprising business man, and is a worthy and honorable citizen. He is prepossessing in personal appearance, and is courteous and agreeable in manners. In 1865 he was married to Miss Catherine Hullum, a native of this county and a daughter of B. S. Hullum, one of the early settlers and planters of this county. To Mr. and Mrs. Mattingly a family of seven children have been born, but only three are living at the present time: Walter, who graduated from the Montgomery Bell college, of Nashville, and is now the electrician of the electric light company of Vicksburg; Mary, who is the wife of D. N. Road, of Yazoo county, and Irene. Mr. Mattingly and his wife are members of the Methodist Episcopal church, and he is a member of the K. of P., the K. of H. and the A. F. & A. M.

Hon. H. P. Maxwell was born on the farm on which he now lives, eight miles northwest of Ashland, the county seat of Benton county, the eldest son in a family of two sons and three daughters, born to Harrison P. and Charlotte (Mooman) Maxwell, natives of Kentucky and Virginia respectively, but who were married in Tennessee. The father immigrated to Mississippi at an early day and bought land of the Indians— a fact which entitled him to rank among the pioneers of this county. He was a brickmason by trade, but after locating in Mississippi he engaged in planting, which was his lifelong occupation. Prior to the war he was very successful, becoming owner of fourteen hundred acres of land and one hundred slaves. He was well and favorably known throughout the country, not alone as one of its earliest settlers, but as one of its most prominent citizens. He was a liberal contributor to schools, churches, and to all public institutions, and he and his wife were members of the Old School Presbyterian church. At the time of the war he was too old for military service, but for some time acted as agent for the Confederacy, buying up small arms through the country. He died in 1876, and his wife in 1884, at their old homestead where they lived all their married life, and upon which our subject was born and has lived until the present time. At the age of twenty-two H. P. Maxwell began life for himself as a farmer and planter. He was married in 1870 to Miss A. E. Treadwell, daughter of F. L. Treadwell, who bore him four sons: Harrison P. (deceased), Louis, Mooman T. (deceased), and Robert C. He was a member of the county board of supervisors for one term, and in 1886 his fellow-citizens still more strongly expressed their confidence in him by electing him to represent them in the state legislature. He is well and favorably known throughout this section of the state; is industrious, enterprising, honorable and a highminded gentleman; a most successful planter and a man of uncommon integrity. He and his wife are members of the Cumberland Presbyterian church, toward the support of which he is very liberal, as he has been for the support of other churches, as well as schools and other benevolent institutions. He is the owner of seven hundred and forty acres of land, four hundred of which are under cultivation. He is a member of the Knights of Honor, and he and his family rank high in social circles.

P. J. Maxwell, M. D., is a physician and surgeon whose reputation for skill and ability has become widespread. The first work he did as a practitioner of the healing art was as a surgeon in the Confederate army during the turbulent times of the Rebellion. He was born in Charleston, S. C., January 3, 1834, a son of William R. and Anna M. (Johnston) Maxwell, natives of South Carolina, and of English origin. His great-grandfather was born near Stirling in Scotland, and immigrated to America in the reign of George III., or about 1756. The lands he settled on, known as Jashey island, at the mouth of the Port Royal river, South Carolina, are now in possession of Hon. William Aiken. His grandfather, James Maxwell, was a graduate of the Edinburgh college, and finished his education in that institution of learning in 1776. He became a wealthy planter of South Carolina, and died at Charleston, S. C., when in the prime of life, leaving two children, William R. and Sarah Pringle, both of whom are now deceased. William R. Maxwell was a rice planter on the Santee river, in Georgetown district, S. C., and in 1871 removed to Columbus, Miss., and died there some three years later. His wife died in 1866, having borne him five children who grew to maturity, three of whom are now living: Mrs. Wilson, William J. and Dr. P. J. The latter was reared in the Palmetto state, and received his education in Charleston. He began the study of medicine when quite young with Dr. W. M. Michel, and graduated from the Medical College of the State of South Carolina, at Charleston, in 1854. After attending the University of Philadelphia, Penn., for some time, he entered the Bellevue hospital of New York city, in which institution he acquired a practical knowledge of his profession. In October, 1858, he crossed the Atlantic to Europe and studied in the Hotel Dieu of Paris, France, remaining abroad eighteen months to perfect himself in his studies. He returned to his native land in time to witness the bursting of the war cloud that had so long hovered over the country. He immediately enlisted as a surgeon of the Charleston light dragoons, and served on the coast of South Carolina with that company. He was afterward transferred to the twenty-fourth South Carolina regiment under command of Col. E. Capers, attached to Gist's brigade, Hardee's corps, of Bragg's army, following Joseph E. Johnston through his Georgia campaign, at the close of which he found himself in charge of a hospital in Columbus, Miss. At the battle of Jonesboro, Ga., late in the evening, a number of wounded were lying on the platform at the station, and the doctor was busily attending to them, when he came across a Federal soldier, an Irishman, who was bleeding to death. He set to work at once to stop the flow of blood by tying up the artery, and while so doing was tapped on the shoulder by a Federal cavalryman, who said, "You are my prisoner;" whereupon the Irishman remarked with an oath, "Leave the doctor alone, he is trying to save my life." The cavalryman, leaving his horse quite near, went into the station office, and the doctor, taking advantage of his absence, mounted his horse and made his escape. Notwithstanding bullets whistled thick, fast and furious in close proximity around him, he succeeded in reaching the Confederate lines and rejoining his regiment, much to their joy and surprise, as they had made sure of his having been captured. He returned to his old home at the close of the war to see what property the war might have left him, and soon returned to Columbus, in which place he settled permanently in 1866. He has built up a very large practice among the leading citizens of this section, and is considered by all to be an exceptionally skillful and successful medical practitioner and surgeon. He is a member of the American Medical association, the State Medical association and the Lowndes County Medical society. He has attained to the chapter in the A. F. & A. M., and for ten years has been treasurer in the Episcopal church. He has been and is a stockholder in nearly all the public institutions of Columbus. He owns many cottages and cabins in Columbus, besides other valuable property, all of which he has earned since coming to this city. He has been president of the Building & Loan association, in which he is a stockholder. He was married in 1865 to Miss F. N., daughter of John C. Ramsey, by whom he has one child, John Ramsey.

One of the best examples of what may be accomplished by perseverance and industry is to be seen in the career of W. L. Maxwell, druggist and grocer, who is now one of the prominent business men of Camden. He was born in Madison county, Miss., in 1838, and of the ten children born to his parents, Willis and Catherine (Cooper) Maxwell, he was third in order of birth. The parents were natives of Georgia and North Carolina respectively. They came to Madison county at quite an early day and both are still living, the father at the age of eighty-four and the mother at eighty years of age. Seven of their children are living in this county and are useful and law-abiding citizens. W. L. Maxwell entered the Confederate service in 1861, company G, Eighteenth Mississippi infantry, as a private, and was promoted to the rank of lieutenant, which position he held one year. He then resigned and joined Word's battery, light artillery, Poague's battalion, Third army corps, Army of Northern Virginia, and served one year in the battery. He was appointed to the medical department as hospital steward for the chief surgeon. At Appomattox he lost all his medicine, it being captured by the enemy, and after surrendering he returned to Camden, where he established a drug store. This business he has continued to follow and has added a general line of dry goods, etc. He takes an active part in politics, but has never aspired to any political position. He started in business on a borrowed capital of $1,000, but he is now out of debt, has a stock of goods valued at $3,500 and is the owner of three hundred acres of land with one hundred and fifty acres under cultivation. His marriage, which occurred in 1868 to Miss Fanny Thornhill, has been blessed by the birth of seven children: Willis A., in the dry goods business in Camden; Gus C., who conducts the drug store; Lillie, Kitty, Annie, Magruder and John (twins). Mrs. Maxwell is a worthy member of the Methodist church and an active worker in the same.

Albert Quitman May, Chancery clerk, Westville, Miss., was born on a farm within nine miles of Westville, Miss., on the 17th of June, 1857, and his father, William May, who comes of an old Kentucky family, is also a native of that state, born in Pike county. The father removed to Simpson county, Miss., when a boy and was there married to Miss Nancy Ross, the mother of our subject. After this he gave his attention exclusively to planting and is now a resident of this county. Prior to the war he was probate judge of Simpson county and held other offices of trust. He was an old school democrat and favored secession, but since the war he has steadfastly refused to accept any political honors. He is an active member of the Baptist church. Albert Q. May received his early education in the schools of his locality and at Westville, but later attended Mississippi college at Clinton. The two years following after leaving school he was engaged as clerk and bookkeeper in a general mercantile establishment at Harrisville, Simpson county, and while there he was elected sheriff (1881) being the youngest official for that position in the state. He declined to become a candidate for a second term and in the spring of 1884 he was appointed by Judge Mayers to fill the unexpired term of W. L. Drummond and was elected to that position by a special election ordered by the board of supervisors in May of that year. Mr. May was elected by an overwhelming majority, his popularity as a public official being evinced in that manner. In 1887 he was elected by an immense majority over a strong candidate and in the campaign of 1889 he came out as a candidate for state treasurer only two months before the election and made a very limited canvass. Under the circumstances he developed a greater strength than his friends had dared to anticipate, receiving a very complimentary ballot. Mr. May is a very popular young man and wields an enviable influence. He is at present a member of the democratic state executive committee. The strength developed by Mr. May and the esteem in which he is held by his large circle of friends, cause him to be looked upon as a most promising subject for future honors.

One of the leading residents of Biloxi, Miss., J. W. Maybin, M. D., is descended from a long line of English ancestors, many of whom have been prominent in the politics of the country. He was born in Natchez, Miss., October 12, 1837, and is a son of Lawrence and Caroline Maybin, natives of Tennessee and Mississippi respectively. His grandfather Alexander was a native of North Carolina and a member of the colonial congress from that state. He was a lawyer by profession and became one of the most eminent members of the bar. Lawrence Maybin, grandson, was a planter by occupation. He was one of the first settlers in Natchez and was elected a member to the legislature from Adams county, but from ill health did not serve. He was a man of wealth, owning a large amount of real estate, personal property and slaves. Dr. Maybin is the only child of his parents. He was reared on the plantation in Yazoo county and received his education at Centenary college, Miss., and at the University of North Carolina. At the age of nineteen years he began the study of medicine and was graduated from Jefferson Medical college, Philadelphia, in the class of 1856. He returned to Mississippi and located in Yazoo county, where he was at the breaking out of the Civil war. In 1863 he served as a surgeon in the Eightieth Tennessee regiment and served until the end of the war. At the surrender of Atlanta he was in the hospital at Marietta, Ga., and remained there until the cessation of hostilities. When he returned to Yazoo county it was a discouraging prospect, indeed, and required all the bravery of heart and determination he could summon to take up again the pursuits of civilization. He resumed his professional work and superintended his planting until 1876, when he removed to Canton, Miss. He practiced there until 1880, going thence to Jackson, Miss. He resided there until 1882, when he came to Biloxi. Here he has established himself among the leading practitioners of the county and has won a large and intelligent patronage. He was first married to Miss Mary Brien, one son being born of the union, William H. Maybin. Dr. Maybin was married a second time in 1876, being united to Miss Lee, a daughter of Dr. L. C. Lee, of Grenada, Miss., a cousin to Gen. Robert E. Lee. Two children were born to the Doctor and his wife: Warren (aged fourteen years) and Willie (aged four years). William H. Maybin is a promising young lawyer of Biloxi, Miss. He was graduated from the University of Oxford, Miss., in 1886, and later from the law department of the Tulane university.

He was married, May 23, 1888, to Miss Bulah Alvis. Dr. Maybin is a member of the Masonic fraternity and of the I. O. O. F. He also belongs to the Episcopal church.

Dr. Maybin is a brilliant orator and a forcible speaker, as will be seen by the following extracts from Mississippi newspapers. The following extract is taken from the *American Citizen*: "On Friday evening, the 12th instant, a large and intelligent audience assembled at the courthouse to listen to the speeches of Hon. Robert Powell and Dr. J. W. Maybin, who had been elected by the Democratic club to entertain our citizens on that evening. The meeting was opened by the president of the club, Mr. J. M. Anderson, Sr., who briefly introduced Mayor Powell. The latter gentlemen made a few remarks in his own happy way. He appealed to his hearers to stand by the good old democratic party and its nominees, and fired a hot shot at all independent candidates. He was glad to see the ladies present, was glad to see the interest they manifested in the political welfare of our country. He said he must necessarily be brief, because he knew the audience was impatient to hear the gallant orator who would follow him. He then introduced Dr. Maybin. The fame of this gentleman as a political speaker was known to many of his auditors, but none there were prepared for the brilliant effort that crowned the occasion. Commencing in a calm, silvery voice, the gifted orator carried his audience spellbound, as it were, to the very acme of delight. Long, loud, and deafening applause followed the words of wisdom and patriotism that fell from his lips. Time and again the noble speaker was compelled to pause in his impassioned utterances before the tumult of cheers that followed his lofty eloquence. After a time, which seemed only too short to his charmed hearers, the Doctor closed his address with a beautiful, poetic, and touching tribute to the fair daughters of the sunny Southland. As he retired from the rostrum, cries of 'Go on!' 'Go on!' proceeded from every side. Never have we seen an audience so completely charmed by the power of words. Later in the evening the speaker was serenaded at his residence. We but echo the universal wish of our citizens when we say we hope to hear Dr. Maybin again at an early day." The Canton *Mail*, in speaking of the same occason, alludes to Dr. Maybin as follows: "Dr. Maybin was then loudly called for, and, when the noise had subsided, began one of the most entertaining addresses it was ever our privilege to listen to. His language was chaste, and his utterances soul-stirring and eloquent. He fairly brought down the house in wild and enthusiastic applause, so great at times that it was almost impossible for him to proceed. Dr. Maybin proved himself on this occasion to be one of the best campaign orators in the democratic party. His address occupied about forty minutes' time, but his audience would have cheerfully listened to him for another forty minutes." The following extract we take from the Chicago *Tribune*: "The Canton (Miss.) *Mail* contains a full account of a democratic meeting, in that town recently, at which Dr. J. W. Maybin made a speech, the spirit of which can be understood by the following extracts: 'In 1875 we awoke as from a death-like sleep, arose in our manhood, wrenched from our benumbed limbs the great political hand-cuffs that bound our manhood; our tongues became as the pen of ready writers, and by the help of Almighty God and the double-barreled gun and Colt's repeaters, we drove them back from our own sunny South to their own cold, heartless and selfish Northland. Last but not least of our democratic sisterhood comes Ohio, the great state of Ohio, from whence comes the fraudulent president, Rutherford B. Hayes. Though Ohio has been on the wrong side of politics for many weary years, she is right to-day and appreciates as we do the outrage and wrong of placing a man in the presidential chair by corrupt and fraudulent means. She spurns the insult heaped on her and the American people. Yes, from the cold and frozen regions of Maine to the flowery groves of Florida, along the orange groves of Louisiana and the gulf coast to the Rocky mountains, to the golden shores of California, has the fraud been rebuked in thunder tones. * * * These are the blows dealt by a solid South upon the cooler metal of the North that will arouse and weld its people into a unity of action and purpose as solid as that which inspired us during the bloody years of the Rebellion. Go on, gentlemen. 'Providence moves in a mysterious way his wonders to perform.'"

The following letter was received by Dr. Maybin from Governor Lowry:

DEAR DOCTOR:—I have carefully read your speech, which you had the kindness to send me, and if I am any judge, the matter is most excellent. Your description of our wrongs and sufferings could not fail to find a hearty response in the hearts of our people. The description of the moral and intellectual worth of the Southern people is certainly not overdrawn. The distinction drawn between the carpet-bagger and the good citizens of the North was most apt and a truth that our people should under no circumstances forget. We need and want good people, representing all the various industries, to settle among us and become identified with us. The appeal to your hearers to preserve their political integrity could not be surpassed; indeed, this was the only safety for our prosperity; the defeat of the democratic party would have entailed untold suffering on the people of the South, and at the same time revived and placed firmly in power the wreckers to whom we are indebted for all the wrongs and oppressions which you describe. I was equally impressed with the soundness of your views on agriculture; the correction mentioned must be adopted or poverty will be the result. On the whole your speech came up to the full measure of a good one, and I am only sorry that you could not have made it all over the state. With assurances of high regard, I am very truly your friend,

ROBERT LOWRY.

Doctor Maybin took an active part in politics from his early manhood, and during the reconstruction of his native state, being an ardent and zealous democrat, and being a states-rights man of the strictest construction, took the stump in Mississippi in 1875-6 in defense of her people and denounced the carpet-bagger and scalawag at every available opportunity until home rule was accomplished. Doctor Maybin never asked for or held office, feeling that the private station was the post of honor.

Judge Alonzo Gustavus Mayers' professional career embraces an eventful and interesting period of forty years. He was born in Winchester, Wayne county, Miss., March 6, 1821, a son of James Mayers, who was a native of Richmond, Va. He removed to Wayne county, Miss., early in life, where he married Miss Jane Cole and became a man of considerable local prominence, filling with ability nearly every office in the county. He died in 1834. Judge Mayers left home at the early age of fourteen years to make his own way in the world, at which time he had a very limited education and no means, but with the energy and determination that has since marked his career he began at once to seek his fortune and secured a position in a store at Quitman, and later at Garlandsville, in the meantime availing himself of every opportunity for self-improvement. He began reading law with Judge Watts, at Garlandsville, and was admitted to the bar at Winchester before he was twenty-one years of age. Some time afterward he formed a partnership with his former preceptor with whom, however, he was associated only a short time. In 1844 he located at Raleigh, where he practiced until 1847, when he removed to Paulding and was associated with Judge Mounger until the death of the latter in 1851. During this time, in 1845, he was a candidate for district attorney in a strong democratic district and though a whig was defeated by only two votes. In 1852 he removed to Brandon (where he has since resided), and in 1860 formed a partnership with Ex-Governor Lowry, whose tutor he was and with whom he remained professionally associated for sixteen years. In 1876 Governor Stone appointed Mr. Mayers judge for the Eighth judicial district, to which he was reappointed by Governor Lowry in 1882 and in 1888. Notwithstanding his advanced age Judge Mayers is possessed of an excellent constitution and elasticity of step that might well be envied by many men a quarter of a century his junior. His mind is as clear, active and bright as in his early manhood, and his sound judgment and sagacity admirably fitted him for the responsible position of judge. He was presiding judge in the famous trial of Col. Jones S. Hamilton, charged with the murder of Roderick D. Gambrill, at the February (1888) term of the circuit court of Rankin county, which occupied forty-six days and created more excitement than perhaps any criminal case in the history of the state. Judge Myers was married in 1848 to Miss Elizabeth C. King, of Rankin county. Mrs. Mayers died in 1852, leaving two children who died that year, and in 1856 the judge married Miss Nancy L. McLaurin, of Covington county, Miss., by whom he has four children: Mary, wife of Olin Green of Meridan; Daniel, a merchant of Brandon; Henry, an insurance agent of Union City, Tenn., and Miss Nannie. Judge Mayers is a conservative democrat, a prohibitionist and a member of the Methodist Episcopal Church South.

Edward Mayes, a prominent lawyer of Oxford, and chancellor and professor of law in the university of the state of Mississippi, was born in Hinds county, Miss., December 15, 1846. He is the youngest of a family of four children born to Daniel and Elizabeth (Rigg) Mayes. The father was a native of Virginia, but grew to manhood in Kentucky. After serving on the circuit bench and in the law professorship of Transylvania university, he removed to Jackson, Miss., and engaged in the practice of law; this was in 1839. Edward Mayes was prepared for college at Jackson by the private schools, and in 1860 he became a student at Bethany college, Virginia, now West Virginia. He was driven home by the breaking out of the Civil war, and was employed as a clerk until the destruction of Jackson by the Federal troops in May, 1863. He was then engaged in teaching in Carrollton for three or four months. In April, 1864, he volunteered as a private in company H, Fourth Mississippi cavalry, Confederate States Army, and served until the termination of the war. In October, 1865, he entered the freshman class of the University of Mississippi, and was graduated with the degree of A. B., taking the four years' course in three years. In 1869 he received the degree of B. L. from the same institution. In 1869-70 he taught in the university. May 5, 1869, he was united in marriage to Miss Frances Eliza Lamar, daughter of Prof. L. Q. C. Lamar, of the law department of the university, now Justice Lamar, of the United States supreme court, and granddaughter of Dr. A. B. Longstreet, second president of the university. In 1871 Mr. Mayes began the practice of law at Coffeeville, Miss., but in May, 1872, he removed to Oxford, where he has since resided. In 1877 he was elected to the law professorship in the university, and has occupied that chair from that date until the present. Upon the reorganization of the faculty in August, 1886, he was elected chairman of the faculty by that body. In June, 1889, the office of chancellor having been reëstablished, he was elected to fill it. Mr. and Mrs. Mayes are the parents of seven children: Mary L.; Lucius L., who died at the age of four months; Elizabeth L.; Edward W., who died at the age of six years; Lucius L., Francis L. and Basil R. The family are members of the Methodist Episcopal church, and are quite active in church work. Mr. Mayes was a member of the general conference held at St. Louis in 1890, and is lay delegate to the ecumenical conference of 1891. He is a member of the Knights of Honor, and was a member of the constitutional convention of 1890, serving as chairman of the committee on bill of rights and general provisions.

George F. Maynard, attorney, Friar's Point, Miss. Mr. Maynard's parents, Decatur B. and Mary E. (Saunders) Maynard, were natives of Virginia and Alabama respectively, and descendants of old and very prominent families of those states. His paternal grandfather was a native of Virginia, received his final summons in that state, and was a prosperous merchant and a very wealthy man. The Maynard family is of Norman French descent and was among the early settlers of the Old Dominion. Decatur B. Maynard came to Mississippi with an elder brother (Magnus L.) and settled in Coffeeville. There Magnus married Miss Frances Saunders and later Decatur was wedded to her sister, Miss Mary E. Saunders, both daughters of George N. Saunders. This last named gentleman was a planter and purchased a tract of land near Friar's Point. This is still known as the Old Saunders place. He made extensive improvements and there received his final summons in 1875. He was a veteran of the war of 1812, was at the battle of New Orleans, and was a brave and patriotic soldier. He was also with General Jackson in the Indian war. He was a substantial and prosperous citizen. The Saunders family is of Irish descent. His wife was a relative of Pres. William H. Harrison. One of his sons, Capt. B. F. Saunders, was a soldier in the Mexican war, and later filled the position of sheriff of Coahoma county. The captain lost his right arm in an accident while hunting, but raised a company at the outbreak of the Civil war, served as captain through the stirring scenes of the war and was noted for his bravery. He was an active citizen and a man highly esteemed for his many good qualities. He died at Asheville, N. C., in 1868. Decatur Maynard removed to Washington county (now Coahoma), Miss., soon after his marriage and later came to Friar's Point, where he was a land speculator and merchant, being one of the early merchants of that place. He could not enter the army on account of physical disability and after the war he did not take advantage of the bankrupt law but paid to Northern creditors $60,000 all of which he made after peace was declared. He had been ruined by the war and the freedom of the slaves. He was a tender and loving husband and father, and after his wife's death in 1873 he never recovered from the shock, but died of grief, it is said, the following year. He left a large estate but slightly encumbered, and this his daughter cleared from all claims. Both Mr. and Mrs. Maynard were members of the Methodist Episcopal Church South, and he was a most pious and devout Christian. He was of small stature and had quite a fair complexion. George F. Maynard, whose birth occurred in Friar's Point in 1853, was the sixth of eleven children born to his parents. He was reared at Friar's Point, graduated at Emory and Henry college, Virginia, in 1875, and then taught school in order to obtain the means to take him through his law course. Three years later, or in 1878, he graduated in law at Mississippi university, Oxford, and in 1879 he began practicing at Friar's Point in partnership with E. M. Yerger. In 1880 he took a short course at the University of Virginia, and nine years later he formed his present partnership, Fitzgerald & Maynard. The firm own about three thousand five hundred acres of wild land. Mr. Maynard is president of the Friar's Point oilmill, is secretary and treasurer of the Friar's Point Building and Loan association, and has assisted in organizing all the enterprises of the place. He is one of the rising lawyers of the state. He owns a plantation of six hundred acres with three hundred and fifty acres under cultivation at Burk station.

Col. Samuel Mills Meek was born in Tuscaloosa, Ala., on Nov. 11, 1835, and graduated at the university of his native state in 1850. After leaving college he engaged in teaching for two years in the county of Oktibbeha, Miss., and afterward for one year filled the position of assistant to Prof. Thomas B. Bailey, now of the Agricultural and Mechanical college, of this state, in the Odd Fellows' Collegiate high school at Columbus, which he made his home, and where he now resides. Having adopted the law as his profession, Colonel Meek was admitted to the bar at Columbus in 1854. About this time, being an ardent, zealous democrat, he was chosen by his party elector for the county of Lowndes, and in conjunction with Capt. Thomas I. Sharp, who was his colleague, made a vigorous canvass against knownothingism. The ability he displayed at once gave him prominence, and his party attested its appreciation of his worth by nominating him, in 1858, for the position of district attorney of the sixth judicial district. In the race he was opposed by three or four popular and formidable competitors, but was elected by an overwhelming majority.

In 1856 he married Miss Mary L. Cannon, daughter of the late Col. William R. Cannon, who represented for several terms Chickasaw and Oktibbeha, then a senatorial district, in the state senate. When the war between the states came on, with true patriotic ardor Colonel Meek enlisted in the service of his section as a private soldier, though by virtue of his office he was exempt from military duty. He was at an early day promoted to a lieutenancy of infantry. Whilst holding this position he was, in 1862, re-elected district attorney. He preferred, however, to remain in the army, and was shortly afterward made lieutenant-colonel of a Mississippi regiment which was for a long while attached to Price's command, and which followed the fortunes of the army of the West from Bowling Green to Vicksburg.

When the war closed he again pursued the practice of his profession, in all the branches of which he gained a high and enviable reputation. As a criminal lawyer he has been engaged in the prosecution and defense of more capital felonies than perhaps any man of his age in the state or county. In civil practice also he has been eminently successful. During the memorable campaign of 1872 Colonel Meek was a democratic elector, during which he espoused warmly and vigorously maintained the cause headed by Horace Greeley. During this campaign he made a thorough canvass of his district, delivering eighty-two speeches in behalf of the cause of reform and local self-government. Although a wheelhorse in the ranks of democracy, ever willing and ready to respond to any call, he has yet never sought a political office. In the summer of 1880, yielding to the urgent solicitations of friends, he allowed his name to be used as a candidate for congress in the First district. He was defeated in the convention after about four hundred ballots, and gave way gracefully, and to his credit it must be said never gave sign that he cherished any ill will toward any of his opponents and never displayed any of the acerbities of a foiled politician. Indeed, it can with truth be said that Colonel Meek possesses many noble attributes. Free as he is from petty jealousies that so often dwarf the character of public men, he rejoices in the success of others when that success is attained through merit. In the arena of politics, as in that of law, he has never asked or claimed anything but an open field and a fair fight. Generous to a fault, his rivalry never exceeds the emulation of a noble mind; and after a contest is declared at an end he seeks to forget whatever of acrimony may have been engendered and to cherish only a desire to soothe the hurt feelings and wounded pride of his antagonists.

In person Col. Meek is of majestic statue, standing, like Saul, a head and shoulders above his fellows. His countenance is of the cast that wins you on approach. Kindness, benignity and amiability shine forth in its every lineament and proclaims the friend of man. In his intercourse with others he brings much of the *bonhomie* so indicative of an open, candid and truly genial nature. Col. Meek is remarkable for his success in criminal cases. His reputation in this branch of his profession has extended beyond the limits of the state. No one, it is said, is more happy in selecting jurors than he, and he displays much tact in the management of delicate cases which oftentimes involve the life of his clients. In the style characteristic of him in the speeches he delivers, one would say he modeled after Burke, giving to the class of declamation the varnish and coloring of Curran and Phillips. In manner he has evidently carefully studied the examples of those three great men who have passed away from the stage of action; and he prefers their stately periods and lofty address to the buffoonery of modern foemen. As an advocate in the criminal branch of the law, to which he has devoted so much time and labor, and in which he has won so many bright and enduring laurels, he has probably not an equal, certainly not a superior in the Southwest. His native powers of mind, magnetic, and remarkably quick in their movements, seize the strong points of cases in which he is interested, or trials in which he is engaged, as they spring up in discussion at the time, and grasping with remarkable celerity and masculine force their weight and bearing where they may prove favorable or prejudicial to his clients, presents them with a strength, a vigor and a cogency, at the same time a clearness, which carries conviction to bench, jury and audience. In many respects he resembles the late Col. John T. Brady, of New York. In the case of the latter it has been said that no emergency ever arose to which he was not equal, and the more closely he was pressed the greater the resources he displayed and the readier, happier and stronger he appeared. The same can be said of Colonel Meek, and as with Mr. Brady, it can with truth be remarked of him the faculty of readiness in debate has contributed much to the brilliant success he has achieved.

In the management especially of difficult uncertain cases, Colonel Meek is justly regarded as one of the safest and most reliable lawyers in the South. His conception takes in at a glance all the difficulties likely to arise when an issue is joined, and enables him like a skillful general to be strong at every weak point. He rarely, if ever, no matter what the circumstances may be makes blunders, and to this fact is largely due the reputation he enjoys. Colonel Meek belongs to a long line of distinguished ancestry. His grndfather on his father's side was a soldier in the American Revolution, and lost a leg at the battle of Cowpens. His father was a distinguished physician, for twenty years president of the medical board of the state of Alabama, and also a Methodist minister. His mother was a Miss McDowell, a native of Charleton, S. C., but a relative of the celebrated Virginia family of that name, Governor McDowell being her second cousin. His immediate family have all been distinguished. Five brothers graduated at the University of Alabama, with high honors, one of them, Judge A. B. Meek, eminent as a poet, orator and statesman, is very well known throughout the country. His younger brother, B. F. Meek, LL. D., is now professor in the University of Alabama. His other brothers died before they were old enough to gain anything more than a collegiate reputation. Colonel Meek is now in the prime and vigor of manhood and we trust will live long to battle for the interest of his native section.

Colonel Meek has in his possession some rare relics, among which is a tomahawk said to have been owned by Pocahontas, who saved the life of John Smith in the seventeenth century. This was handed down by the Col. William S. Bollinger family, and Smithsonian institute of Washington, D. C., has offered a handsome price for it. This is without doubt genuine. Another relic is a pair of large fieldglasses which was presented by Louis Napoleon to the great cavalry leader Gen. N. B. Forrest, who used them during the Civil war. They were presented to Col. S. M. Meek by Gen. Forrest at his death.

Thomas M. Meeks and J. T. Meeks comprise the firm of T. M. Meeks & Sons, prominent planters, merchants and sawmill men of Alcorn county, Miss. T. M. Meeks owes his nativity to Bedford county, Tenn.; born June 30, 1829, and lived there until five years of age, when he came with his parents to Mississippi and remained there until nineteen years of age receiving his education. He then returned to Tennessee, remaining there five years. While there he was married, in 1852, to Miss Sophia A. Moore, daughter of Henry and Bethenia (Hill) Moore, both natives of the Old North state. Mr. Moore was a farmer, and followed that occupation in Tennessee until his death. The mother also died in that state.

Faithfully yours
R. Seal.

Both were members of the Christian church. To Mr. and Mrs. Thomas Meeks were born four children: William L., deceased; James W., deceased; Robert G., deceased, and J. T. Meeks. The latter married Miss Dona McPeters, a native of Mississippi, and the daughter of Robert and Hattie F. (Gains) McPeters; Mrs. McPeters being a direct descendant of old General Gains, who distinguished himself in the War of 1812 at New Orleans under General Jackson; Mrs. McPeter's father was a distinguished Methodist preacher in north Mississippi and Alabama. Robert McPeters was a native of Alabama. He was reared and educated there, and was a successful planter in that state until 1852. He then moved to Mississippi and opened a large plantation, which he ran successfully until his death, which occurred in 1861, and now lies buried in the Shiloh cemetery, in Alcorn county. His widow was remarried to W. R. Richardson, in 1870, a native of South Carolina. To J. T. Meeks and wife were born three children; Hubert E., Lula M., and T. DeWitt. J. T. Meeks was educated at Henderson, Tenn., under the management of Rev. George Savage, now principal of the Southern Baptist university, of Jackson, Tenn.

Miss Dona Meeks was educated at the Female college at Corinth, Miss. In 1864 our subject, Thomas M. Meeks, enlisted in the Confederate army under Colonel Lowry, company B, Mississippi infantry from Mississippi. He went to Bowling Green, Ky.; then being discharged returned to Mississippi; then enlisted in the Seventh Mississippi Partisan rangers under Col. W. C. Falkner, and was in the battle of Iuka and Burnt Mills. He was in the retreat from Burnt Mills to Tupelo. He joined Van Dorn at Ripley and went to Pocahontas, Tenn., thence to Corinth, Miss., and was in the battle at that place. He returned from there to Holly Springs on his retreat. He was in the battle at Davis' Ferry; returning from there he went to Hernando; from there he went to Grenada, Miss., then to Houston, from there to Oxford, then to Varona and from there to the state of Alabama. Then he returned to Mississippi. He was in the battle of Collierville, Tenn., and at Wyatt. He was also in the battle of Leaf river, and was in several skirmishes in north Mississippi and Alabama. He was discharged in 1865. Mr. Meeks is a democrat in politics, and socially he is a member of the Masonic order. He has been a member of the Missionary Baptist church ever since 1859, and his wife is also a member of that church. He has been postmaster at Theo since 1879. He and J. T. Meeks (his son) now own three thousand six hundred acres of land, a sawmill and store, and have been successful in each occupation. He is one of the prominent men of Alcorn county, and is the son of Littleton and Millie (Morris) Meeks, natives of Franklin county, Ga, the father a prominent planter of his county, who at an early date moved from his native state to middle Tennessee, thence to Mississippi, and settled in Tippah county. He followed farming there for several years and then went to Arkansas, where his wife died. He afterward returned to Mississippi and died there in March, 1848. Both he and wife were members of the Primitive Baptist church.

He had been married three times, his first union being to Miss Susie Womick. They had three children: John W., Melissie and Minerva, all deceased. The mother of these children died about 1824, and Mr. Meeks' second union was to Miss Millie Morris, who bore him five children: Mary, Thomas M. (subject), Frances, Sarah, Nacy and James, all deceased but the subject of this sketch. The mother died in July, 1844, and is buried in Arkansas. Mr. Meeks' third marriage was to Mrs. Conner. His death occurred in 1848, and his wife followed him to the grave soon afterward. His parents were Nacy and Frances (Holt) Meeks, natives of Georgia, it is supposed. Nacy Meeks was a farmer and a Primitive Baptist minister. He was the father of ten children, of whom Littleton was second in order of birth: John, Littleton, Martin, James, Nacy, Josephus, Martha, Jane, Mary and Nancy, all

AA

of whom emigrated to Texas at an early date except three: Littleton and James and Martin, who died in the state of Mississippi.

Jefferson county, Miss., has many estimable citizens, but she has none more highly respected, or for conscientious discharge of duty in every relation of life, more worthy of respect and esteem than is Abram J. Melton. He has been intimately connected, not only with the farming and stockraising interests, but also with mercantile life, and as each of these branches of business has received his attention from early boyhood, he has gained for himself a reputation which may be a source of pardonable pride. His birth occurred in Selma, Ala., January 17, 1839, and as he was thrown upon his own resources at an early day, his opportunities for obtaining an education were somewhat limited. At the early age of thirteen years he entered a general mercantile store at Selma, where he remained as a clerk for about six years, thus obtaining a thorough knowledge of mercantile life. When the mutterings of war first resounded throughout the land he cast aside all personal considerations, gave up his position and with the enthusiasm of youth and full of patriotic devotion to the land of his birth, espoused the cause of the Confederacy, enlisting as a private soldier in company F Fourth regiment of Alabama infantry, but was soon promoted to the rank of lieutenant. Later he was transferred to the Third Alabama cavalry with the rank of captain, and at a still later period was promoted to the rank of quartermaster. He was a participant in many of the leading engagements of the war and on four different occasions was severely wounded, first at Manassas, second at Shiloh, third at Perryville and fourth at Murfreesboro. He remained in the service until the 26th of April, 1865, when he returned to his home. On the 12th of February, 1863, he had married Miss Chestina Farley, a daughter of G. P. and Charlotte P. Farley, of this state and county, and upon the close of hostilities he settled here and engaged in planting, but with the expectation of bettering his financial condition he went to the state of Louisiana, but while there unfortunately lost a large amount of property and money by the overflow of the Mississippi river. Nothing daunted, he returned to Jefferson county, Miss., and with the courage, perseverance and indomitable pluck and energy which have ever characterized his endeavors he set about retrieving his losses, and on land which he rented he once more started anew. This state of affairs did not last long, however, for being a man of exceptionally shrewd views and very pushing, it was not in the nature of things that he should long remain a renter, and he soon gathered about him considerable means. In time his well established reputation as an able financier brought him safe returns and he is now the possessor of six thousand acres of valuable land, well improved and well tilled, for all is under his watchful eye. A fine steam cottongin and gristmill add much to the appearance of prosperity which surrounds his property, while on his broad acres a fine herd of five hundred head of cattle, as well as a large number of horses and mules, are pastured annually. Mr. Melton does not confine himself merely to the raising of cotton, but also raises hay and his own corn. He has at all times endeavored to keep out of the beaten path, and the new, improved and valuable farm machinery that is used on his plantation fully testifies to his progressive, enterprising and intelligent views. He ships large quantities of tomatoes and small fruits to different cities in the spring of the year, also. He has an excellent blacksmith and repair shop on his place, and in his mercantile house, which he established in 1885, he carries the best assortment of general merchandise to be found in the county. He gives employment to about two hundred Africans the year round, and will soon require the help of many more in a large oilmill which he expects to erect in the year 1891. Here he will use about nine hundred tons of cottonseed during the year. He has already purchased this year, for shipment, about seven hundred tons of seed, and twelve hundred bales of cotton. His handsome and commodious residence is beautifully located on a rising piece of ground near the center of his plantation, and in this typical Southern mansion he and his accomplished and amiable wife delight to welcome their friends. In disposition Mr. Melton is genial and liberal, distributing his wealth with an unstinted hand wherever it is essential to the pleasure or welfare of himself and family or those around him, and as a result commands the respect and liking of all with whom he comes in contact. He and his wife have no children of their own, but they have reared and educated two orphan children, a boy and girl, both of whom are now grown. For the past fourteen years Mr. Melton has served as a member of the board of supervisors, and in this capacity has had abundant opportunity to display his practical and intelligent views. The term self-made man may be appropriately applied to Mr. Melton, for since a young lad he has earned his own living and the magnificent property of which he is now the owner has been earned by his own efforts. For the admirable way he has conquered the many difficulties that have strewn his pathway he deserves great credit, and where many others would have fainted and fallen by the wayside, he has kept sturdily on, and is now reaping his reward in the shape of a handsome competency and the admiration and respect of his numerous friends.

E. W. Melvin, farmer and merchant, Camden, Miss., is a descendant of Irish ancestors on his father's side, his grandparents being natives of the Emerald isle, from which they emigrated to the United States in about 1790. His father, Robert E. Melvin, was born in Washington county, Penn., but was married in Kentucky to Miss Nancy Waller, a native of Shelby county, Ky. In 1845 they removed to Pike county, Mo., thence to Hinds county in 1851, and settled in Jackson, where he acted as deputy clerk for a number of years. During that time he studied law under Judge Clifton, and practiced his profession until the opening of the conflict between the North and South. In 1875 he entered the ministry of the Baptist church, which he continued until his death, in August, 1890. The mother died in 1864. Four of the five children born to this union grew to maturity, and one besides our subject is now living: Mary E., wife of J. A. Fleming, of Madison county. E. W. Melvin was born in Pike county, Mo., in 1849, but until eleven years of age was reared in Hinds county, of this state. He then went to live with an uncle, with whom he remained six years, but on account of the uncle not living up to his promise of sending him to school, he ran away and came to Madison county. He began attending school when in his nineteenth year, and spent six years in getting an education. He attended the Cooper institute, in Lauderdale county, for one year, and by close application to his books received a good education. He subsequently came to Camden, taught school from 1875 to 1878, and in 1880 began merchandising where he is now located. He started with a stock of general merchandise valued at about $2,000, and has increased this from time to time, until at present he carries a stock of goods valued at about $8,000, and does an annual business of about $40,000. About 1887 he bought two hundred acres of land, engaged in farming, and has since added six hundred acres, making eight hundred altogether. He also owns several small tracts in the county, amounting to about eight hundred acres more. On his farm here he has a large watermill and gin, which he operates successfully. He is actively engaged in raising Poland China hogs, and has at the head of his herd a fine thoroughbred animal imported from New York. Mr. Melvin was married in 1875 to Miss Elizabeth A. McMurtray, daughter of J. A. and Telitha (Cobb) McMurtray, natives of the Palmetto state. To this union have been born six sons: Marion E., Walter G., James H., Robert A., George M. and John W. Socially Mr. Melvin is a member of the Knights of Honor. He and Mrs. Melvin are members of the Presbyterian church at Camden, of which he is elder, and he has been superintendent of the Sunday-school for the past ten years.

Hon. T. L. Mendenhall was born August 19, 1830, in Anson county, N. C. When fifteen years of age his father, Dr. William Mendenhall, died, in consequence of which he received only an academic education. In 1849 he emigrated to Westville, Simpson county, Miss., where he now lives. In 1855 he was elected clerk of the circuit and probate courts of said county, and performed the duties of these offices twelve years, having been reëlected five times. During his service as clerk, he devoted his spare time to reading law, and after he declined to become a candidate for reëlection, in 1867, he obtained license to practice law, which profession he has followed ever since. In 1873 he was elected democratic state senator from the counties of Simpson, Smith, Covington, Jones and Wayne, for the term of four years, and consequently was a member of that body during the notable impeachment trials of Governor Ames, Lieut.-Gov. A. K. Davis and G. W. Cardoza. In 1890 he was elected a delegate to the state constitutional convention from Simpson county and represented his county in that capacity.

Mrs. Roena V. Mendrop was born in Southampton county, Va., a daughter of Newet Drew, who was born in the Old Dominion in 1804. He was a farmer and distiller, and was the owner of an immense amount of land and an extensive distillery. He was married to Miss Lucy Wesbrook. His father was a planter by occupation, and soldier during the Revolutionary war. Mrs. Mendrop received only a common school education, and at the age of eight years she left her native state with her mother's family, and with them located first near Memphis, Tenn. In January, 1851, she came to Vicksburg and settled on a plantation belonging to Judge Noland, on the Big Black river, but at the end of two years purchased the Morgan place, and in 1864 became the owner of her present plantation, which consists of three hundred and twenty acres, two hundred of which are under cultivation. She was married January 3, 1856, to C. A. Betts, of Virginia, and by him became the mother of four children: James T., Carlous E., Lucy A., and Mary A. Mr. Betts was a planter by occupation, and while just in the prime of life was cut down by the hand of death in December, 1865. On the 15th of May, 1869, his widow married E. W. Mendrop, a Prussian by birth, who served in the Confederate army in Barnes' cavalry company, Stark's regiment, enlisting in 1861, and continuing in the service until 1865. During this time he was a participant in the battles of Shiloh, Murfreesboro, Corinth, Forts Henry and Donelson, Missionary ridge, the engagements before Atlanta, Port Gibson, and other important engagements. To Mr. Mendrop and his wife the following children have been born: Susie, Herman, Roena, George, Grace, Ernest and Elden; Herman is deceased. Mr. Mendrop, who died in 1884, was an honorable and useful citizen, and his death was regretted by a large circle of friends and acquaintances. Mrs. Mendrop is a member of the Baptist church and is justly proud of the large family she has reared.

Dunbar Surget Merrill, planter and stockbreeder, Natchez, Miss. Major Merill, the great-grandfather of Dunbar S. Merrill, held the rank of major in the Revolutionary war and was one of those who assisted in removing the British prisoners to Canada, which many others refused to do. His son, Dr. Ayres P. Merrill, was a native of Pittsfield, Mass., and a man of education and learning. He came to Natchez when a young man and was married there to a Miss Jane Moore, a native of Adams county, Miss. The Doctor was cashier of the Agricultural bank a number of years, but afterward removed to Memphis, Tenn., where he resided for some time. During the last years of his life he was an invalid and died in St. Cloud hotel, New York city, in 1874. He was a surgeon in the Seminole war. His son, Hon. Ayres P. Merrill, was born in Natchez, Miss., where he was ably tutored, and he was a graduate of Harvard college in the class of 1849. After this he studied law in New

Orleans, with the late distinguished Hon. S. S. Prentiss, and practiced his profession in that city until about 1854, when he returned to Natchez. He was there married to Miss Jane Surget, who was a native of Adams county, Miss., and who died in 1864. She was the daughter of Frank Surget, a wealthy planter of Adams county, and a granddaughter of Peter Surget (see sketch of James Surget). Her mother was a Miss Dunbar, daughter of Sir William Dunbar. After his marriage Mr. Merrill settled at Elmscourt, a place in the suburbs of Natchez, and engaged in planting until after the war, when he removed to New York city. He was there engaged in the firm of Goodman & Merrill, Southern commission merchants, and continued with the same until the death of Mr. Goodman, when business was suspended. He continued to reside in New York and during General Grant's first term in the presidential chair he served about three years as minister to Belgium. He was then compelled to resign on account of paralysis. He died at his home near Natchez in 1883. He was the owner of considerable real estate there, valuable business interests, and was the owner of residence property in New York city, and a summer residence at Newport. To his marriage were born seven children: Catherine B.; Ann M., wife of H. Albert de Bary, of Antwerp, Belgium; Dunbar Surget, Ayres P., Jennie, Frank and Surget. The third child in order of birth, Dunbar Surget Merrill, was born on Elmscourt plantation, near Natchez, in 1859, and was educated at Brussels and Paris. Since the return of the family to Natchez he has followed planting and is an energetic young man. He was married in 1887 to Miss Charlotte Stanton, who was born at Brandon hall, Adams county, Miss., and who is a daughter of Aaron Stanton and the great-granddaughter of ex-Governor Gerard Brandon (see sketch of Aaron Stanton). Since his marriage Mr. Merrill has lived on his present farm, Hedges plantation, consisting of eighteen hundred and fifty acres, which he has greatly improved since becoming the owner. He is engaged in breeding a fine grade of Ayershire, Devon and Jersey cattle. To Mr. and Mrs. Merrill have been born two interesting children.

Ayres P. Merrill, a prosperous planter of Adams county, Mississippi, is residing at his beautiful country seat, Elmscourt, which is situated about one and one half miles from Natchez. He was born in 1862 to Ayres P. and Jane (Surget) Merrill, both of whom were born in Adams county, the father receiving his literary education in Harvard college, after which he studied law and practiced for a short time. He afterward turned his attention to planting but was also in business in New York city as a commission merchant. During President Grant's administration he was sent as a minister to Belgium but died in his native land in 1882. His father, who also bore the name of Ayres P. Merrill, was a physician and a native of Massachusetts. In an early day he became a resident of Natchez and for some time was a surgeon in the Mexican war. He was connected with the commercial bank and other business enterprises and died at the St. Cloud hotel in New York in 1873. His wife was a Miss Moore. Mrs. Jane (Surget) Merrill was a daughter of Frank Surget, an early pioneer and the richest and most successful planter of this section, who passed from life here on his home plantation. Mrs. Merrill died in 1865. Ayres P. Merrill, the immediate subject of this biography, is one of a family of ten children, seven of whom are living: Catharine, Anna M., wife of H. Albert de Bary, of Belgium, Dunbar S., Jennie S., Ayres P., Frank S. and Eustis. Ayres P. Merrill was educated in Burlington, N. J., and at Brussels, Belgium. In 1883 he was married to Miss Pauline, daughter of Dr. Walter, a native of New York, and Jane Stewart, a native of Natchez, Miss., the former of whom came to Natchez, Miss., in youth and was married here, this place afterward being the home of Mr. and Mrs. Stewart until their death, which occurred during the war. Mrs. Stewart was a daughter of Hon. Aylett Buckner, a Virginian who went with his parents to Kentucky, coming in 1832 to

Natchez, where he practiced law until just prior to the war, when he retired from active life. He was United States attorney for the closing up of the Mississippi state bonds of the Planters' bank, was a faithful official, and was noted as a talented and brilliant attorney. His wife was Charlotte Buckner, who was born in Adams county and died here about 1886. Mrs. Merrill was born in Natchez but was given a thorough education in the city of New Orleans. She and Mr. Merrill are members in good standing of the Episcopal church, are prominent people of this section, and move in the highest social circles in Natchez. Elmscourt, their home, is one of the old-time houses of Adams county and is still kept in good condition and style. It has one hundred and forty-two acres of park, woodland, garden and cultivated fields, and the house, which is a stately and imposing mansion, is situated on rising ground and is completely embowered by a magnificent park of magnolias and liveoaks. Flowering plants and shrubs border the driveway to the house, and taken all in all it is an ideal home.

Dr. J. F. Merritt was born in Fayette county, Ala., and when but a child was brought to Tippah county, where he grew to manhood and received a common school education. At the breaking out of the Civil war he entered company C, of the First Mississippi cavalry, and served until the battle of Selma, Ala., in 1864. Here his command was captured, but Dr. Merritt succeeded in making his escape and returned to his home in Mississippi and engaged in teaching school and studying medicine. In 1869 he entered the Medical University of Kentucky at Louisville, and after leaving this institution he located at Connorsville, Marshall county, Miss., where he remained until 1873. Since that time he has resided at Blue Mountain and has devoted his time to the practice of his profession, his name becoming a very familiar one in many homes. He has shown himself eminently worthy the trust and confidence reposed in him by all classes, and has unquestionably shown himself to be a physician of decided merit. At the time of his locating in Blue Mountain there was but one family in the place, Gen. M. T. Lowrey's, but it is now a thriving little town and Dr. Merritt is its leading physician. He is a member of the Tri-State Medical association, which comprises Mississippi, Tennessee and Arkansas, and is eminently capable of successfully practicing his calling, for he makes a point of keeping thoroughly posted in his profession, and also relies upon his own sound judgment in the treatment of his cases. He is a member of the Masonic fraternity, and has been a member of the Baptist church since 1860. He has been remarkably temperate all his life and is a liberal patron of all worthy enterprises, aiding them by every possible means. He was married in 1858 to Miss Sarah J. Robinson, of Tippah county, by whom he has four daughters and two sons.

Oren Metcalfe has been a resident of the state of Mississippi since the year 1833, and during the long term of years that he has resided here he has been earnest and able in his advocacy of what he thinks best calculated to promote the best interests of his country. Being a man of indomitable will power he has been the means of pushing many enterprises that have come up before him to a successful issue, and as his leading characteristics are extreme frankness, honesty of purpose and energy, his influence is widespread. He was born in Connecticut in 1810, the youngest of twelve children born to Thomas and Sybil (Chapin) Metcalfe, the former a native of New Hampshire and the latter of Connecticut. The paternal grandfather came from England and settled in New Hampshire, but his son Thomas afterward moved to Connecticut, where he met and married Miss Chapin. In this state he resided for many years, but in 1819 he again made a change of residence, this time taking up his abode at Chardon, Ohio; but here he passed from life three years later, having been one of the honorable, successful and worthy tillers of the soil of the different states in which he resided. His widow, who lived to be ninety-three years of age, passed from life in Ohio, having been an affectionate mother and a true Christian. After leaving the common schools, where he received his education, Oren Metcalfe began clerking in a store, a calling he followed for some years, but in 1830 made a trip to Natchez to visit his brother Asa B., who was a practicing physician, but soon after returned to Ohio, where he remained three years longer. He then took up his permanent abode in the state of Mississippi and for some time thereafter was engaged in merchandising. In 1838 Miss Zuleika, a daughter of Joseph B. and Amora (Cox) Lyons, became his wife, and after a married life of thirty-three years he was called upon to mourn her death, the date of her demise being May, 1871. To them a family of twelve children were born, three sons and two daughters of whom are living: Zuleika (wife of George D. Lawrence, who is a resident of Vicksburg, Miss., and is the present superintendent of the southern department of the Louisville, New Orleans & Texas railroad), Anna (wife of James S. Fleming, merchant, a resident of Natchez), Richard Inge (a clerk in a bank), James B. (a lawyer at Seattle, Wash., he being the first attorney-general of that territory and now the head of a well-known legal firm of that city known as Metcalfe, Turner & Burleigh), and William, who is a lawyer of Oregon. The members of the family that are deceased are as follows: Joseph A., Thomas W., who was killed during the war; Julius O., Charles, John Inge, Medora and Belle. Mr. Metcalfe followed the occupation of merchant until 1850, being also engaged in planting; but in 1851 he was elected to the office of county sheriff, and as the duties of his trial term was discharged in a manner highly satisfactory to all, and very much to his credit, he was reëlected to the position at each succeeding election until he had filled the office for twelve years, at the end of which time he was appointed for one year longer by Governor Sharkey. At the end of this term he once more embarked in mercantile life, and for five years followed an active business life, during which time his efforts to accumulate some worldly goods were highly successful and reflected great credit upon his ability as a financier, his sound judgment and practical views. At the end of this time he engaged in his present business, that of general life and fire insurance, and now represents the Queen insurance company of England, the Providence of Washington, R. I., the Security of New Haven, Conn., and the Home of Georgia. In May, 1850, Mr. Metcalfe was appointed trustee of Jefferson college, and four years later was elected treasurer of that institution, which office he has since continuously held, being the oldest trustee and officer. He is an elder in the Presbyterian church of this place, a position he has filled for some thirty-five years, and for his many Christian qualities, his kindness, charity and love for his fellowmen, his friends are numerous and his enemies extremely few.

P. S. Miazza, proprietor of the Commercial hotel of Greenville, Miss., was born in Jackson in 1866, the fifth of six children born to Angelo and Elizabeth (Quinn) Miazza, the former a native of Italy and the latter of Illinois. P. S. Miazza attended school until he was eleven years only, at which age he began working in a printing office at Jackson, later entering a telegraph office, where he remained two years. He then went to Wesson, Miss., where he secured employment in the Mississippi mills. In January, 1881, he became an office boy in a hotel belonging to L. Fragiacomo in Jackson, and during this time his evenings were spent in attending night school, where he finished a commercial course in about a year and a half. He was soon advanced to the position of clerk in the hotel and for several years thereafter was manager of Mr. Fragiacomo's hotel. After remaining with him until July, 1890, he came to Greenville and purchased the Scobely house, near the Louisiana, New Orleans & Texas railroad depot, and changed the name of this establishment to the Commercial House. He had it thoroughly renovated, repaired and refitted up from garret to basement and now has seventeen well appointed sleepingrooms, a pleasant parlor, samplerooms, etc., and a commodious diningroom. Mr. Miazza is an experienced hotel man, is anxious to please his patrons, spares no expense in keeping his table supplied with the delicacies of the season, and being a jovial and agreeable companion, his house is a popular resort, especially for the traveling public. Although young he is exceptionally intelligent, for he was early compelled to rely upon his own resources, and is self-educated. He possesses rare business qualifications, his hotel is rapidly growing in popularity, and a bright future is before him. He was married on the 31st of December, 1889, to Miss Emma Spengler, a daughter of H. Spengler, Sr., of Jackson, and to their union one child has been born, whom they have named Emma. Both Mr. Miazza and his wife are worthy members of the Catholic church.

Daniel A. Mickle, planter, Duck Hill, Miss., is another of the many prominent citizens of Montgomery county, Miss., who owes his nativity to the Palmetto state, his birth occurring in Barnwell district on the 17th of December, 1820. His father, John M. Mickle, was born in the same state and district in 1787, and his grandfather was a native of the Emerald isle, but an early settler of South Carolina and a soldier in the Revolution. John M. Mickle was married in Barnwell district to Miss Elizabeth Touchstone, daughter of Stephen Touchstone, who was of German parentage. Mr. Mickle moved to Alabama about 1832, located on a farm and there reared his family. He was a soldier in the War of 1812 and held a lieutenant's commission. About 1850 he moved to Mississippi and spent his last days with his son, his death occurring in 1871. His widow died about 1874. Daniel A. Mickle, who was one of the children born to the above mentioned union, remained with his parents until eighteen years of age and in 1838 came to Carroll county, now forming a part of Montgomery county, and bought land near his present residence. He followed farming until 1864, when he enlisted in the Confederate army, and his regiment was located at Grenada for home protection. Returning to his home after cessation of hostilities he remained there until 1870, when he moved to his present property, consisting of about seven hundred acres, with one hundred acres under cultivation. Mr. Mickle was married in this county in 1846 to Miss Jane Margaret Sally, daughter of Capt. John H. Sally, and a native of South Carolina, although reared in Mississippi. Mr. and Mrs. Mickle have no children of their own, but have reared a number of orphan children. Mrs. Mickle holds membership in the Missionary Baptist church. Mr. Mickle is one of the successful and substantial citizens of Montgomery county, and boasts of always having raised his own corn and fattened his own meat. He is a social, honorable gentleman, and is highly esteemed by his friends and neighbors.

Edward E. Middleton, a planter of Yazoo county, was born in Franklin county, Miss., in 1833, and is the elder of two sons of Martin and Lucretia (Epps) Middleton. His parents were born in South Carolina, where they grew up and were married. They removed to Mississippi in the pioneer days of the state, and endured all the privations and trials incident to the settling of a comparatively new country. His mother came to Mississippi from South Carolina when she was only five years old, in 1819, and his father came in 1812, when he was seven years old. The father died in 1835, in Franklin county, Miss., but the mother still survives. Edward E. passed his boyhood and youth in Hinds county, Miss., and at the age of twenty-three years started out in the world to seek his fortune. He had been trained to agriculture, so he began planting for himself. He settled in Yazoo county in 1852, but at the end of two years he removed to Holmes county. In 1862 he entered the service, enlisting in company D, First Mississippi light artillery. He passed through the hardships of warfare, and was a brave and faithful soldier until the declaration of peace. In 1856 he was married to Miss N. C. Barksdale, a daughter of Joseph and Annie (Carter) Barksdale, who were among the early and influential settlers of Mississippi. Mr. and Mrs. Middleton are the parents of twelve children, ten of whom are living: Louisa M., wife of R. S. Evans; Edward and Joseph, farmers; Lily, William, Fannie, Eva, Annie, Rufus and Pearl. Mrs. Middleton is a member of the Methodist Episcopal church. Mr. Middleton belongs to the Masonic order in Benton, of which he has been W. M. four years. He gives his attention to planting, and owns three hundred and seventy-eight acres of good land; one hundred and fifty acres are under cultivation, and yield abundant harvests. He has traveled frequently through the southern portion of Mississippi, and has been a witness to the wonderful changes which have been wrought by the hand of industry since the place was laid desolate by the ravages of war.

Rufus M. Middleton was born in Franklin county, Miss., January 9, 1835, and is the son of Martin C. and Lucretia (Epps) Middleton, natives of South Carolina. There were two children, and Rufus M. was but six weeks old when the father died. Two years afterward the mother was married to the Rev. Preston Cooper, a member of the Methodist Episcopal conference of Mississippi. The family removed to Hinds county, Miss., in the fall of 1837, and settled on a farm. About the year 1840 Mr. Cooper discovered the mineral wells known as Cooper's wells, which are considered of excellent quality. Mr. Middleton's two sons grew to maturity, and are still living; the mother also survives, and resides at Hazlehurst. Rufus M. Middleton grew to manhood in Hinds county, and spent his school days at Raymond. In 1853 he came to this county, and engaged in farming. In 1859 he purchased the plantation on which he has since lived; he cultivates half of the four hundred acres of which the farm consists at the present time; his first purchase was of two hundred and eighty acres of land which was little improved; this he had in a good state of cultivation at the breaking out of the Civil war, but at the close of the conflict there was little left to tell of what had been; the improvements were all swept away, and the livestock and crops were stolen. In 1862 he entered the Confederate service as a member of company B, Wither's light artillery. He was at Port Hudson, Harrisburg and Blakely, and in numerous smaller engagements. At Port Hudson he was taken prisoner, was paroled, and again, at Blakely he was captured. When the war was ended he returned to his home, and set bravely to work to retrieve his broken fortune. Of late years he has given special attention to improving the breeds of farm stock of all kinds. Politically he affiliates with the democratic party, and is actively interested in all the movements of that body. He has served as magistrate, and is a member of the school commission. He belongs to P. B. Tutt lodge No. 17, A. F. & A. M., also to the W. D. Farris chapter, R. A. M., and to the Knights of Honor. He has been secretary of the Blue lodge for twenty years. Mr. Middleton was united in marriage in Yazoo county in 1855, to Johanna A. Mays, a daughter of John and Mary B. (Churchwell) Mays. Mrs. Middleton's parents were of English ancestry, and removed from Virginia to Mississippi. Mr. and Mrs. Middleton had born to them eight children: Mary L., wife of F. B. Thompson, of Madison county; Laura H., wife of James P. Rose, of Benton; Henry P., who married Miss Birdie Carmouche; Rufus M., Jr., of Madison county; John D., of Louisiana; Frank E., Maud G. and Allen F. Mr. Middleton has been a witness to the advance of Yazoo county since the war, and, as all true Southerners are, is an ardent admirer of the courage and will with which the men of the South applied themselves to the rebuilding of their shattered fortunes.

E. S. Middleton was born at Crosswicks, N. J., January 13, 1831, the eldest of three children born to Aaron and Martha S. S. (Cottongood) Middleton, the latter inheriting Dutch blood of her ancestors. The great-great-grandfather of E. S. Middleton came from England and settled in New Jersey, and nearly all the male members of the family down to the present day have been farmers and tanners. Aaron Middleton was a blacksmith by trade, but farmed the most of his life. He was a well-informed man, having received an academic education in his youth, was progressive and enterprising in his views and of kindly and charitable disposition. E. S. Middleton attended the old fieldschools up to the age of sixteen years, then went to the city of brotherly love, where he began learning the carpenter's trade, afterward working at the same for five years in Philadelphia, five months in Georgia, six months in St. Louis, after which he came to Mississippi, and settled in Hinds county, working on the insane asylum of Jackson in the fall of 1853. He afterward took charge of a sawmill for A. G. Grant for about six months, and after quitting his employ began contracting as a carpenter, which calling he continued to follow until the breaking out of the war. He then joined the Confederate army, but only remained in the service for a short time, his services being principally required as a shipbuilder. He spent four months in Savannah, where he helped to repair and refit an ironclad which had been made in Scotland to run the blockade. When the war closed he returned to Hinds county, Miss., where he has since been engaged in farming. He made considerable money prior to the opening of the war, but lost it all, and had, like many others, to commence the battle of life anew after hostilities had ceased. In payment of a debt he took some cotton, which he sold for $8,000. He now owns two thousand acres of land, about seven hundred and fifty of which are under cultivation, and on which he raises two hundred and twenty-five bales of cotton and one thousand five hundred bushels of corn annually. He has a fine steam cottongin and gristmill, the former of which turns out about six hundred bales each year. He keeps constantly on hand about eighty head of cattle, which he fattens for beef, and ships some occasionally to New Orleans. He also raises quite a large number of cattle each year. In 1881 he was elected a member of the board of supervisors of Hinds county, and during the four years that he served he filled the position of president of the board two years. During this time a large portion of the county debt was paid off. The board was very economical and made a new issue of bonds to cover a debt of $100,000, all of which bonds the president of the board was compelled to sign. He also served in the capacity of magistrate during Alcorn's administration as governor. He was married in 1862 to Miss Mary Baskins, of Madison county, Miss., and by her has three sons and two daughters: E. S., Jr., who attended the high school of Philadelphia, Penn., for four years, and afterward graduated from the law department of the University of Mississippi, standing very high in his class; Elwood Kirby, who attended Clinton college three years; Caleb S., who spent two years in the Agricultural and Mechanical college and studied medicine in Philadelphia, Penn.; Jesse Stewart and Anna, both of whom are graduates of Hamilton college, of Lexington, Ky. Mr. Middleton is and has every reason to be proud of his family, for they all promise to become upright, useful and intelligent citizens. Mr. Middleton is of a kindly and charitable disposition and is liberal in the use of his means in aiding the poor and needy and in encouraging worthy enterprises.

Dr. J. D. Miles is a prominent and skillful dentist of Vicksburg, but was born in Natchez, March 15, 1829, being the third child born to David and Eleanor (Brownjohn) Miles, the former of whom was born in Wales. He came to the United States and settled in Natchez, Mississippi, in 1816, and there followed his calling, that of a civil engineer, and laid out many of the streets of that city, at the same time being engaged in street contracting. He died in 1830. The mother was born in London, England, a daughter of John Brownjohn, and in 1816 came with her people to the United States, settling in Natchez, where her father and mother died. After the death of her husband Mrs. Miles married a Dr. R. Chambers and removed to Illinois, where she resided until 1850, when they returned and settled in

Vicksburg. Dr. R. Chambers was a popular and successful dentist and followed his profession in Vicksburg until his demise. The mother died in March, 1886, at the age of seventy-nine years, having been an earnest member of the Episcopal church. To her union with Dr. Chambers six children were born, only Mrs. J. F. Baum being now alive, her home being in Vicksburg. Dr. J. D. Miles resided in Illinois until he was sixteen years of age and there received the principal part of his education. He began the practice of dentistry in 1851 in Natchez. The following year he was married to Miss Hattie Paine, a daughter of Thomas Paine, an old settler of Natchez, and in 1855 came to Vicksburg, where he has been in the constant practice of his profession ever since. He has devoted the greater part of his life to his profession and is a skilled operator, his patronage being large and lucrative. In 1875 he with six other dentists organized the Mississippi State Dental association in his office in Vicksburg, was its first president and has since been its president on two different occasions. He has for five years served as a member of the Mississippi state board of dental examiners, and has in numerous other ways shown a deep interest in his profession. To Dr. Miles and his wife six children have been born: John Joseph, a broker at Seattle, Wash.; Mary M., wife of George A. Myer of Washington, D. C.; Charlotte, who died in infancy; Benjamin C., who is in the transfer business at Vicksburg; Freddie Baum, who died of yellow fever in 1878, and Eliza J., wife of S. Q. Kline of Vicksburg. The family are members of the Episcopal church and move in the highest social circles of Vicksburg.

Rev. E. D. Miller, principal of the State normal school at Holly Springs, and an educator of prominence, is a native of the Buckeye state, his birth occurring in 1827, and was the eighth in order of birth, and a twin, of ten children born to Godlove and Susanna (Sims) Miller, both natives of Virginia. The parents were married in the Old Dominion, but moved to Ohio in 1818, and there the father followed mechanical pursuits and farming until his death in 1837. The mother died in 1877. She was a member of the Baptist church. The paternal grandfather was a native of Germany, and came to America in colonial times, settling in Virginia, where he reared four children. He was a Baptist minister, and was well known as a ripe scholar and a great linguist, few individuals at that time being his equal in scholarship. The maternal grandfather, George Sims, was a native Virginian and of English descent. He was also a Baptist preacher, and left a large family. Rev. E. D. Miller received a thorough theological education at Georgetown, Ky., and graduated there in 1854. He subsequently went South, settling in Decatur, Ala. After one year he went to Elizabethtown, Ky., was in charge of a church there for one year, and then, in 1857, came to Mississippi, settling in Marshall county. He lived on a plantation, and in connection with his ministerial duties carried on farming there for some time. In 1870 he came to Holly Springs, and four years later became actively connected with educational matters. In 1878 he was appointed county superintendent of schools, and served in that capacity with credit to himself and satisfaction to the people for twelve years. During that time he made many changes in the schools of the county, advocated and employed the best systems of instruction, and thus elevated the tone and credit of the schools. In 1884 he was appointed one of the trustees of the State normal school, and in 1889 was appointed superintendent of that institution. He is a student of psychology, as it relates to the child and its power of learning, also the theory and practice of teaching, and is also studying history and theology. He has a good, useful library and a pleasant home. He was married first, in 1857, to Miss Margaret E. Ford, a native of Virginia, who died in 1878. The second union occurred in 1881, Mrs. Mary V. Mayer, *nee* Mallory, a native of Alabama, becoming his wife.

Judge Hugh R. Miller was born in South Carolina in 1815. He came to Pontotoc,

Miss., about 1840, and immediately made his influence felt at the bar of his county. By his genius and close application to the duties of his profession he climbed to the topmost round of the ladder in his legal practice of this section. Way back in the forties he was elected to represent his county in the legislature. He was elected circuit judge, and was noted for the fairness of his decision. Refusing reëlection, he resumed the practice of his profession, in which he continued until the opening of hostilities between the North and South. He organized a company in Pontotoc and went directly to Virginia, participating in the battle of Manassas junction, where he distinguished himself so largely that, at the solicitation of his commanding officers, he returned home and raised the Forty-third regiment of Mississippi volunteers, which he commanded with great credit until his brilliant military career was cut short by his death at the battle of Vicksburg.

Rev. Irvin Miller, merchant, Walnut Grove, Miss., was born in the Blue Grass state, Marion county, near Lebanon, on the 11th of November, 1836, and is of Scotch descent, his paternal grandfather being a native of that country. His father, James Irvin Miller, was born in Pennsylvania, and there grew to manhood. He went from there to Kentucky, and was married in that state to Miss Adaline Evans, daughter of Edward Evans, a native of the Old Dominion and a pioneer settler of Kentucky, in which state Mrs. Miller was born and reared. Soon after his marriage Mr. Miller settled in Marion county, followed farming, and there reared his family. He was an active member of the Presbyterian church, and an elder in the same for a number of years. He died in 1846, and his wife followed him to the grave in 1879. Rev. Irvin Miller was educated in his native county at Lebanon Male seminary, under the supervision of Prof. W. T. Knott, and after completing his studies, or in 1855, he came to Mississippi, locating in Hillsboro, Scott county, where he engaged in clerking. He there practically learned the mercantile business. In 1859 he began merchandising at Damascus, and sold goods up to 1863, when in January of that year he enlisted, first, in the Fourth Mississippi cavalry, which was afterward reorganized and known as the Second Mississippi. Mr. Miller served until the close of the war, and participated in a number of important engagements. He was wounded at Spring Hill, Tenn., by concussion of shell and disabled from further active duty. After sufficiently recovering he served on detached and post duty until cessation of hostilities. Returning then to Damascus, Miss., he resumed merchandising, and continued this occupation successfully until 1868, when he removed to Walnut Grove, located where he now resides, and has been in active business since. He was the second man to locate and engage in business at this place; the surrounding country was a wilderness, and there were only a few farms scattered here and there. He erected a large store building, a good residence, and has been an active business man here since. In connection he has also been engaged in farming for a number of years, and is the owner of several farms in Leake county. Mr. Miller was married on the 4th of December, 1856, to Miss Melissa Brewer, daughter of Wiche Brewer, one of the early settlers of Scott county. Mrs. Miller was born in Alabama and reared in Scott county, Miss. The fruits of this union were six children, viz.: John E., married, and depot agent at Hattiesburg, Miss.; Ada M., widow of Prof. W. W. Graham, who was a native of Leake county, and a teacher in the Lone Star state (Mrs. Graham has one child, Miller, a boy of two years); Jennie, wife of Dr. W. A. Kelly, who is a physician of Walnut Grove; Gussie, wife of Luther Sparling, a farmer of Leake county; Irvin K., a lad of twelve, and Edith Love, nine years old. Mr. Miller joined the Methodist Episcopal Church South, in 1848, and was licensed to preach in 1865, and has been an active minister of the same ever since. He is a local preacher, and has regular appointments. He is an eloquent and gifted speaker on nearly all subjects, and has the faculty of holding the attention of his audience. He has never aspired to political honors, but was elected to represent Leake county in the last constitutional convention. He is a member of the Masonic fraternity, and of White Plains lodge No. 192, joining the same in 1859, and is master of his lodge. He is also a member of the Knights of Honor. He has served as postmaster at Walnut Grove for the past twenty-three years, and at Damascus eleven years prior to his removal to Walnut Grove. Mr. Miller is a typical Southern gentleman, hospitable and chivalrous, and no man stands higher in the estimation of the people than he.

Prof. John C. Miller, of Clay county, Miss., was a well-known and successful educator up to 1886, but since that time has devoted his attention to farming, milling and stockraising. He was born in Spartanburg, S. C., in 1836, to Alexander and Sylvia (Whetstone) Miller, both of whom were born in the Palmetto state, the former's birth occurring in 1800. He was a farmer and mechanic, and about 1844 moved to Mississippi, and settled in that part of Chickasaw county that is now Clay county. He died at the home of his son John C. in 1875. To his marriage, which occurred in 1825, the following children were born: William H., a resident of Clay county; James M., who was killed in the battle of Chickamauga during the war; Nancy M., wife of William Linn, both deceased; John C.; Mary J., wife of S. McKenney, deceased, of Clay county; Thomas W., a resident of this county; and two children deceased. John C. Miller was educated in the state university of Mississippi at Oxford, and was graduated from that institution in 1858. He immediately began teaching in Long Branch academy near Palo Alto, and up to 1886 followed this calling, with the exception of the time that he was in the army, teaching nine years at one place. He also carried on planting in connection with these duties, but since the above mentioned date has given up pedagoguing. In April, 1861, he joined company A, Seventeenth Mississippi regiment, and served until after the first battle of Manassas, in which he participated. After this he was taken ill and honorably discharged. Upon recovering he again enlisted in the service, but this time became a member of company F, Ninth Mississippi cavalry, and before the close of the war took part in many engagements, and was appointed quartermaster sergeant. He was paroled at Gainesville, Ala., in 1865, and returned to his home in Mississippi. He has since filled the offices of justice of the peace, a member of the school board in Chickasaw county, and in 1872 was elected to the office of county supervisor, a position he filled with ability for two years in Chickasaw county. He has been very successful as a planter, and is now the owner of one thousand five hundred and twenty acres of land, and has five hundred acres in cultivation. There has never been a mortgage on any of his property, and he has always been abundantly able to live up to his obligations, and to meet all demands upon his purse. He is a member of the Methodist church, of Pikeville lodge No. 85, of the A. F. & A. M., at Buena Vista, the Golden Rule, the Farmers' Alliance and the Patrons of Husbandry (grange). In all these he held important and prominent positions. He was married in 1866 to Miss Jennie Brownlee, a daughter of A. M. and Florinda Brownlee, and to them a family of twelve children have been born: Cheves, wife of Dr. J. S. Evans; Dora L., deceased; Zalla, successful schoolteacher; Florinda, James M., Walter V. (deceased), John C., Jr., Evans, Goldie L., Una E., Albert P. and Percy De W., all of whom any parent might be proud.

John H. Miller, planter, Waterford, Miss. There are a number of men prominently identified with the agricultural affairs of Marshall county, but none among them is more deserving of mention than John H. Miller, who, in the management of his farm, displays excellent judgment and thoroughness, qualities which can not fail of success. He is a native

Virginian, and comes of old Virginia stock, his parents, John and Mahala (White) Miller, being natives also of the Old Dominion. The paternal grandfather was a native of Scotland. The parents were reared in their native state, were there married, and there reared a family of eleven children, six of whom are now living, and all in Virginia, with the exception of John H. The parents both died in Virginia, the mother in 1875 and the father in 1885. John H. Miller, the eldest son of the above-mentioned family, was married in his native state in 1846 to Miss Mary Susan Harris, of Buckingham county, Va., and daughter of Col. John M. Harris. In 1848 he moved to Mississippi, located in Marshall county, and has been a resident and honored and respected citizen since. His marriage was blessed by the birth of eight children—six sons and two daughters—five sons and one daughter now living. Mr. Miller is the owner of nine hundred acres of land, five hundred acres under cultivation, and is engaged in raising cotton principally. He is a practical agriculturist, and keeps thoroughly apace with the times. His sons are all farmers, but in connection also deal largely in mules. His sons, Eugene and J. C., have a large livery business in Greenwood, Miss., and are successful business men. Mr. Miller and wife are members of the Christian church, Mr. Miller having joined nearly fifty years ago. He is now in his seventy-fourth year, but is still hale and hearty. He has been a resident of Marshall county for forty-two years, and his reputation in that and adjoining counties is that of a first-class citizen, and an honest, upright man. He is universally respected, and no man stands higher in the estimation of the people. He was appointed by Governor Lowry as one of the commissioners to represent the state at the State fair of Georgia, held at Atlanta. The Miller family is one among the oldest of Marshall county, and the members have ever been honorable and esteemed citizens.

Among the substantial and reliable men of Greenwood, Miss., is Eugene L. Miller, a native of Marshall county, Miss., born December 17, 1851. John H. Miller, his father, was born in the state of Virginia, where he grew to man's estate. He was there united in marriage to Mary S. Harris, also a Virginian by birth. He removed to Mississippi about the year 1849, and was one of the pioneer settlers of Marshall county. He opened a plantation near Holly Springs, where he now resides, and is one of the prominent planters of the county. Eugene L. Miller is one of a family of five sons and one daughter, all of whom have grown to maturity, and three of whom are heads of families. Our subject spent his youth on his father's plantation, receiving a common English education in the county in which he was born. After reaching his majority he engaged in planting in Marshall county; also trading and dealing in livestock. He removed to Greenwood in January, 1889, and in that city erected a large barn and embarked in the livery business. He buys large numbers of horses and mules, and is one of the most successful livestock dealers in Le Flore county. He has won for himself an enviable position in the business circles of Greenwood. He was married in Virginia, in October, 1874, to Miss Mary Ann Lipscomb, daughter of George Lipscomb, Esq., and a native of Virginia. Mr. and Mrs. Miller have one son, Robert Miller, a lad of thirteen years. Mr. Miller is a member of the Masonic fraternity, and also belongs to the Knights of Pythias and the Knights of Honor. He is a man of genial disposition, enterprising and public-spirited, and possessed of those sterling traits of character that go to make the best citizenship.

A livery stable is a most essential institution, both for pleasure and convenience, and to be able to command at any moment a horse and rig for a drive in the country, or for business or other purposes, is a great privilege, indeed. Foremost among the prominent business men of Booneville stands the name of J. T. Miller, who is a native of this state, born in Marshall county on the 25th of July, 1841. His father, Kedar Miller, was born in Tennessee in 1815, and the latter's first marriage was to Miss Ann Campbell, daughter of John K. Campbell. She died, leaving three children: John, Thomas and Mary. Mr. Miller was then married to Miss Parthenia Dalton, daughter of Terry and Nancy (Low) Dalton, and five children are the fruits of this union: Kedar, James T. (subject of this sketch), Anna L., William L. and Emma. The mother of these children was a member of the Methodist church, and died in Prentiss county in 1852. Subsequently Mr. Miller took for his third wife Priscilla Forbes, who bore him five children: Parthenia, Jessie, Benjamin, Sallie, and Katie (who is in the millinery business at Booneville). Mr. Miller died about 1876. He was a member of the Methodist church, and was active in his support of all public affairs of a laudable nature. He was a Mason, and in his political views was a democrat. Kedar Miller was the son of James and Pollie Miller, both of whom died when their grandson, James T., was small. It was the latter's lot to grow up with a farm experience, but at the age of twenty-five years he started out to fight life's battles for himself. Miss Sallie Perkins, who became his wife, and who was the daughter of E. M. and Elizabeth Perkins, was a native of Tennessee. This felicitous union resulted in the birth of six children: Ebby Terry, William Albert, Elizabeth, Katie, Lucian and Esma, all now living. Mr. Miller followed farming until about 1870, when he moved to Booneville and engaged in the draying business. Later he embarked in the livery business, and has won the reputation of being one of the thorough, wideawake business men of the place. He is what is called a self-made man, and what he has acquired in the way of this world's goods is the result of hard work and close attention to business. He is a member of the Methodist church, and in politics is strongly democratic. He espoused the cause of the Confederacy, and in 1861 enlisted in a company of the Twenty-sixth Mississippi, under Captain Davenport. He was in the battles of Collinsville and Town creek, and was wounded in the ankle at the former place, being disabled from duty for a month. He then enlisted in the Seventh Mississippi cavalry, company A, Capt. Tom Ford, Colonel Falconer, and was in regular service for two years, participating in the battles of Harrisburg and Tupelo. He was discharged in 1865. Aside from his livery business, Mr. Miller is the owner of two hundred and eight acres of land on Wolf creek, and has about one hundred acres of this under cultivation. He also owns property in Booneville.

William D. Miller's parents, Calvin and Catherine B. (Comfort) Miller, were natives respectively of North Carolina and New Jersey, and his father left his native state to locate in Hinds county, Miss., in 1836. He was reared in North Carolina, but was educated at Miami, Ohio, and later entered the West Point Military college, where he was not able to finish his course on account of ill health. After leaving the school he was offered an appointment in the navy, which he did not accept, but instead accepted a professorship in Washington, D. C., which he held up to the time of his removal to Mississippi. Soon after being admitted to the bar of the supreme court he practiced law in Jackson, Miss., until 1839, when he removed to Panola county, where he had a very successful practice for nearly forty-two years. As a lawyer he was well read and profound, and his argumentative powers were clear, vigorous and incisive. He never saw but one side to a case, and that was his own. He possessed to an eminent degree the two most requisite characteristics of a successful lawyer—patience and perseverance. He had an aversion to politics, and could never, though often solicited to do so, run for any political office. He was a Mason of high rank, and was instrumental in establishing many lodges of that order in the state. He was a gifted and polished gentleman, and a strict member of the Episcopal church. It is said of him that he never swore an oath in his life, and never permitted any one to tell a vulgar joke or story in his presence. His death occurred in 1881, and his widow followed him to the grave seven years later. The paternal grandfather, John Miller, was one of North Carolina's most prominent men, and lived on a farm that was first settled by Daniel Boone. He was a member of the state senate of North Carolina. The maternal grandfather, Daniel Comfort, was a native of New Jersey, and came to Clinton, Miss., at an early day. He accepted the presidency of the school at that place, and retained his position in the college until his death in 1859. He was an educator of rare ability, and many prominent men of Mississippi, among whom are several ex-governors, received their education under him. He was a minister in the Presbyterian church. William D. Miller was born in Hinds county, Miss., on the 17th of November, 1840, and was the second in order of birth of three children born to his parents. His boyhood days were pased in Panola county, and his literary education was obtained at La Grange, Tenn., and Frankfort, Ky. He subsequently attended law school at Oxford, Miss., but was kept from graduating by the breaking out of the war. Soon after leaving school he entered the Confederate army, attached himself to company F, Twenty-eighth Mississippi cavalry, commanded by Col. P. B. Stork, and participated in the battles of Franklin, Atlanta, siege of Vicksburg and surrender at Oakland, Miss. When the war ended he returned to Panola county, began the practice of law and has continued this up to the present time. He is an able attorney, and as custodian of the people's interests he has ever been vigilant and watchful. His practice has been very gratifying and satisfactory in every way. From 1878 to 1879 Mr. Miller was a member of the legislature, and his career as a public man has been characterized by honesty and perseverance. He has inherited many of his father's good qualities, and his aim in life is to do credit to his father's memory. He is the owner of nine hundred acres of land, a handsome residence in Sardis, and a well-equipped office. In 1871 he married Miss Annie Gillion, a native of Mississippi, and a daughter of John Gillion, who was born in Georgia. This union resulted in the birth of two children: Katie Heard and Caloin. The daughter was educated at Stanton, Va., and the son is now in school at Oxford. Mr. Miller and family are members of the Episcopal church.

Maj. R. W. Millsaps, president of the Capital State bank, of Jackson, Miss., is a native of Copiah county, Miss., where he was born on the 30th of May, 1833, being the second in a family of eight children born to Reuben and Lavinia (Clowers) Millsaps, both of whom were Georgians by birth. The paternal grandfather, William Millsaps, who was also a Georgian, came to Mississippi with his family in 1830, and was a resident of Copiah county when that country was a wilderness, inhabited by wild animals and Indians, having first made a temporary residence in Jasper county. He became a planter, reared a large family of children, and died in 1834. His family, which was of Irish lineage, settled in South Carolina during colonial times. The maternal grandfather, William Clowers, was born in Georgia and came to Mississippi about 1830, settling in Copiah county, where he became a prominent citizen. Reuben Millsaps was reared in Copiah county, and by his own efforts secured a good education, becoming the first schoolteacher of that county. He afterward married, and became a planter, but throughout life was deeply interested in the cause of education, and gave his children good advantages. He was called from life in 1854, his wife having died the year previous, both being earnest members of the Methodist Episcopal church. Maj. R. W. Millsaps was educated in Hanover college, which he attended two years, afterward entering Asbury university (now De Pauw university), from which he graduated in 1854. After returning to Mississippi he taught school, in order to obtain means to enter the law department of Harvard university, from which he was honorably graduated in 1858, locating soon after at Pine Bluff, Ark., where he practiced until the opening of the late war. He then joined company A, Ninth Arkansas infantry, and on the day on which it was organized he was

elected lieutenant, and was soon after chosen adjutant, and was afterward made lieutenant-colonel. The regiment was sent to Kentucky and Tennessee, during which time he participated in the battle of Shiloh, where he was wounded. After remaining in the hospital at Jackson for some time, he rejoined his command at Corinth in 1862, and was in the movements about Vicksburg in 1863, being a participant in the battle of Champion's Hill. He then joined Bragg's army in Georgia, after which he was transferred to the inspector's department, and was inspector-general of Loring's division, with the rank of major. He was in all the fighting about Atlanta, was then with Bragg on his Tennessee campaign, was a participant in the battle of Franklin, and was wounded in the engagement at Nashville. Following this, he went to North Carolina with Johnston, and was in the last battle of the war at Bentonville. While on his way back to join the trans-Mississippi department, and had reached Jackson, Miss., the news came of Lee's surrender. Immediately succeeding this, he turned his attention to cotton dealing in several counties until 1866, when he began merchandising at Brookhaven, where he continued in business for about sixteen years, having branch establishments at Hazlehurst and Union Church. In 1880 he closed out all his interests in Mississippi, and went to St. Louis, Mo., where he started a wholesale grocery and cotton commission business, under the firm name of Millsaps, Magee & Co. In 1884 he closed out this business, and for one year thereafter traveled with his family in Europe. After returning to America, he established the Merchants and Planters' bank at Hazlehurst, of which he had charge until 1887, when he moved to Jackson, and the next year, with a few others, bought out the Capital State bank, and was elected its president. He is also a stockholder and director of the Delta Trust and Banking company, of Vicksburg; the First National bank, of Greenville; the Bank of Greenville; the Merchants and Planters' bank, of Greenville; the Bank of Rosedale, at Rosedale, and the Clarksville Bank and Trust company, of Clarksville. He owns large planting interests in Washington and Sunflower counties, some of his land being the finest in the state. He is president of the Jackson Compress company, treasurer of the Jackson Fertilizer company, and a director of the Jackson Light, Heat and Water company. Major Millsaps was married in 1869 to Mrs. Mary F. Younkin, a daughter of Horace Bean, a wealthy banker, of New Orleans, and as their union has not resulted in the birth of any children, they have an adopted daughter, named Josie. The Major and his wife are members of the Methodist Episcopal Church South, in which he is a very active worker. It has long been a cherished scheme of Major Millsaps to found a college in Mississippi, for the general and economical education of the youth of the state, the germ of this idea being originated in the fact that his own early opportunities for obtaining an education were very meager, notwithstanding the fact that he was very desirous of obtaining a good education. A short time since he offered $50,000, should a like sum be raised, to make a fund of $100,000, to found a college at some point in the state. Although various towns were anxious to secure the honor of the site, Jackson finally won, and the ground for the same was donated by Major Millsaps, who also made further cash contributions, amounting to nearly $75,000 in all. The college will soon be an established fact, to the pride and satisfaction of all loyal Mississippians and to the honor and credit of Major Millsaps. Although the Major has been compelled to make his own way in the world from earliest youth, he has been successful, for he has been devoted to his business, and is now one of the wealthiest and most prominent men of the state. He is of unpretending disposition, but his numerous admirable qualities are well known and highly appreciated.

Judge Uriah Millsaps, a retired lawyer and a prominent citizen of Hazlehurst, a son of Thomas and Elizabeth (Holliday) Millsaps, was born in Copiah county in 1828. His father was born in Pendleton district, S. C., January 1, 1799, and his mother was born in Georgia about 1804. They came to Mississippi with their parents, and were married in Copiah county, about 1824, beginning life in the woods, near the waters of Bayou Pierre. There Mr. Millsaps cleared and improved a plantation, and there he lived until his death in 1882, his wife having died in 1841. Mr. Millsaps married Mrs. Hanna Griffith, of Covington county, the second time. He was one of twelve children, who came with their parents to Copiah county. The educational advantages were limited, but he was an energetic and successful business man, who had the respect of the community at large. His father was William Millsaps, of South Carolina, who lived in that state until about 1810, when he came to Perry county, Miss., moving his family and all his earthly psssessions through the then wilderness. He located in Copiah county, about 1823, and both he and his wife died about ten years later, while on a visit to a son in Perry county. He was a successful planter and amassed a considerable property. Some of his sons became well known in the state. His father, Thomas Millsaps, was a native of Ireland. Ayres Holliday, Judge Millsaps' grandfather on his mother's side, was a Georgian, who removed to Washington parish, La., at an early date, and thence to Copiah county, afterward returning to Louisiana, where he died. Thomas Holliday, one of his sons, was for many years sheriff of Copiah county. Our subject was the second of three sons and three daughters born to his parents: William died when young; Martha, who is also dead, became the wife of John S. Beesley; Mary, married Thomas E. Millsaps; Sarah is the widow of the Rev. William Wadsworth, a Methodist minister; Hon. Thomas J. Millsaps, the youngest brother of the Judge, was born in Copiah county in 1834. He passed his early life on a farm, receiving his primary education at the country schools, afterward attending Hanover college, in Indiana, and later attending the Centenary college, in Louisiana. He afterward read law until the beginning of the war. In 1862 he joined the Thirty-sixth Mississippi infantry as a private. He was in the battles of Corinth, Iuka and Vicksburg, being captured at the last-named place, and held as a prisoner for some time. Rejoining the army just before it reached Atlanta, he came back with Hood's command to Franklin and Nashville and on the retreat south was taken sick and was in the hospital at Macon, Ga., at the time of the surrender. After his recovery he walked home to Copiah county. Soon after his arrival he engaged in planting, which he has continued till the present time. In 1870 he was married to Mississippi, the daughter of Hon. John Fatheree, and a native of Holmes county, which he once represented in the legislature with much honor. After his removal to Copiah county he became one of the leading planters, and one of the most prominent citizens. He was a widely known and brilliant member of the Masonic fraternity. When he died he was universally respected. Mrs. Millsaps, his daughter, was born in Copiah county. In 1887 Mr. Millsaps was elected to represent Copiah county in the state legislature. He was reëlected in 1889, and served as chairman of the committee on commerce and manufactures. He was a member of the executive committee of the state alliance, and was in every way a useful citizen, honored for what he has accomplished. Our subject, Judge Uriah Millsaps, was educated at Hanover college, Indiana, and at Danville, Ky., where he graduated. He afterward studied law with Judge Daniel Mayes, of Jackson, and was admitted to the bar in 1854. He hung out his professional shingle at Gallatin, and was a successful legal practitioner there for some time until after the war, when he removed to Hazlehurst, where he has since lived. In 1856 he married Sarah Lewis, the daughter of Bryant Lewis, who was born in Copiah county, being one of nine children, two of whom are still living. Her father was a native of South Carolina and removed to Copiah county, where he became a prominent citizen, and there ended his days. In 1862 Judge Millsaps joined the Confederate cavalry as a private, but later he recruited the company in which he was first lieutenant, and afterward captain, which was attached to the army of the West, and which he commanded until the close of the war. After peace was established he resumed the practice of his profession. In 1869 he was appointed judge of the fifth judicial district, and served with much honor until 1876, when he again returned to his legal practice, in which he has since been practically succeeded by his son, H. T. Millsaps. He is the owner of considerable real estate, the management of which requires much of his attention, and which brings him a comfortable income. He is a Royal Arch Mason, and he and his wife are members of the Methodist church. Judge Millsaps is practically a self-made man, and he is a good and well-known citizen, and a member of one of the best families in the state. Major Millsaps, of Jackson, the founder of Millsaps college, is a son of one of his father's brothers.

Dr. William D. Mims, physician, Wall Hill, Miss., the great-grandfather of David Mims, who married Miss Martha Dinguid, the 5th day of October, 1773. To them was born a son, Dinguid Mims, who was married to Miss Martha Massie the 1st day of November, 1804, of which marriage David Henry Mims, the father of Dr. Mims, was born on February 9, 1806. Dr. Mims' parents, David H. and Eliza A. (Cochran) Mims, were natives of Virginia and Georgia, respectively, and both came to Mississippi when single, settling in Marshall county early in the thirties. They were married in that county, and there the father followed planting for the most part, but was also engaged in merchandising for some time in the thirties. Both died in Marshall county, the father in 1872, at the age of sixty-six years, and the mother in 1877, at the age of fifty-nine years. Both were consistent members of the Methodist Church South. They were the parents of ten children—five sons and five daughters—eight of whom are yet living. Dr. William D. Mims was born in Marshall county, Miss., on the 24th of November, 1840, and when twenty-one years of age enlisted in the Confederate army, company B, Seventeenth Mississippi infantry, under Col. W. S. Featherston, and was in the army of Virginia, participating in nearly all the hard fighting in that state. He was in the first Manassas, Leesburg, Richmond, Sharpsburg, Petersburg, Wilderness and various others. He was wounded and captured at Gettysburg, was in the hospital at David's island, N. Y., for nearly four months, and was then paroled and sent to Richmond. He rejoined his old command the following March and was captured again on the 6th day of April, 1865, near Petersburg, a few days before the surrender. He was taken to Point Lookout, Md., and was on the road back to Petersburg when General Lee surrendered. He was kept a prisoner until July, 1865, and after being released he returned to his old home in Marshall county, Miss. He engaged in farming for about five years and then took up the study of medicine in 1871, graduating at the University of Louisiana, now Tulane university, in 1873. He began practicing the same year at Red Banks, Miss., and removed to Wall Hill in the fall of the same year. There he has practiced his profession ever since, and has been very successful. He has availed himself of all new ideas and has put them in practice. He is in partnership with Dr. J. W. Sharp, under the firm name of Sharp & Mims. Aside from his profession the Doctor is now the owner of eight hundred acres of land, four hundred of which are under cultivation, and his principal crop is cotton, averaging one fourth of a bale to the acre. His farm is run by tenants. The Doctor also owns a nice residence in Wall Hill, where he makes his home. He was married in 1866 to Miss Martha E. Horn, of Byhalia, and two children were born to this union, both now deceased. Mrs. Mims died in 1870, near Byhalia. The Doctor's second marriage occurred in 1881, to Miss Emma Knight, daughter of R. K. and Violet (Aughey) Knight, the father a native of Tennessee and the mother of New York. Mr. and Mrs. Knight were married near Memphis, Tenn., and had a family of seven children—three sons and four daughters—Mrs. Mims being the eldest of the family. The parents are still living and Mr. Knight is engaged as an educator. The Doctor and Mrs. Mims are both members of the Methodist Church South, and the Doctor has been a member of the Masonic fraternity for twenty years, Albert Pike lodge. Dr. Mims being a native of Marshall county, the people have had every opportunity to judge of his character and qualification, and he is not only one of the prominent physicians of the county, but one of its most esteemed citizens.

Gov. Don Stephen Minor (deceased) was a Pennsylvanian by birth, and comes of a well-known and prominent family. He was given excellent educational advantages of a high order, and being a young man of enterprise and energy he, at an early day, pushed westward, visiting while enroute Pittsburgh, Vincennes and St. Louis, at the latter place making the acquaintance of Colonel Howard, an Irishman in the Spanish service. By this gentleman he was sent with dispatches to the governor-general at New Orleans, and upon holding audience with that gentleman created a very favorable impression, as he invariably did on all whom he endeavored to please. He was soon commissioned a captain in the Royal army, and was assigned to duty at Natchez, Miss., where he remained until the final evacuation of that post by the Spanish, in 1798. He was then appointed governor to succeed Gayoso, and was also one of the commissioners for Spain in the location of the boundary line in that year. He was always held in high esteem, and had the unbounded confidence of the Spanish authorities, and it may with truth be said that he wielded more influence than any other foreigner in their service. He was a man of commanding and dignified presence, well calculated to maintain the honor of his position, possessed a brilliant, shrewd and practical mind, and with these admirable qualities was blended a social temperament, rare conversational powers and a winning manner, that inspired ease and confidence in his presence. His financial abilities were of a high order, and he rapidly accumulated property, but was very liberal and charitable with his means. He purchased the home of Governor Gayoso (Concord) upon the removal of the latter from Natchez, and in this home he lived in princely style, dispensing a splendid hospitality until his death in 1815. No mansion in Mississippi has so many historic memories clustering about it as the old Gayoso-Minor house, which is still standing in the suburbs of the city. Governor Minor was married twice, his second union being to Miss Catharine Lintot, who was born in Connecticut in 1770, and bore her husband five children: Fannie, wife of Maj. Henry Chotard (see sketch); Catherine, wife of J. C. Williams; Stephen, William J., and one that died in infancy.

Dr. H. A. Minor. The citizens of Noxubee, as well as the surrounding counties, are familiar with the name that heads this sketch, for the greater part of his life has been devoted to healing the sick and afflicted throughout this section, and a portion of his reward has been received in this world, for he has the respect, confidence and love of his fellowmen, and the consciousness that he has driven sorrow and despair from many homes by his skill and talent as a physician. He was born in Mooreville, Limestone county, Ala., February 25, 1835, a son of Dr. William T. and Fannie (Washington) Minor, natives of Virginia, who emigrated to northern Alabama in about 1818, where the father practiced medicine throughout the remainder of his days. He was a graduate of Jefferson Medical college, of Philadelphia, Penn., about 1817, and as a professional man his life was a success. He died in 1854, and his widow in 1879. Their union resulted in the birth of nine children, three sons and four daughters, of whom are living: Dr. Lucian of Alabama; Dr. H. A.; W.

P.; Mary A. (Mosely) of Decatur, Ala.; Louisa (Lisle), of northern Alabama; Minnie (Waldon) and Sallie (Ferris), also of that state. Dr. H. A. Minor was reared and received his literary education in the state of his birth, but completed his knowledge of books in the high school near Nashville, Tenn., and in the college at La Grange, Ala. After deciding to make the practice of medicine his calling through life, he entered the University of Virginia, from which he was graduated as an M. D. in 1857, and immediately entered upon the practice of his profession in Decatur, Ala. In the spring of 1859 he moved to Macon, Miss., where he continued to follow his calling until the opening of the war, in 1861, at which time he abandoned the calling of Æsculapius to become a votary of Mars, and enlisted in company F, Eleventh Mississippi infantry, which was the first company from this place that was sent to Virginia. He was wounded at the first battle of Manassas by a gunshot in the leg, and in September, 1861, he was commissioned assistant surgeon in P——— A———, Confederate States, and was assigned to the Nineteenth Mississippi regiment, in which capacity he served until February, 1862, when he was made surgeon of the Ninth Alabama regiment, in which he served until the surrender at Appomattox. He then returned to Macon and resumed his practice, since which time he has continued a zealous and laborious physician. January 1, 1866, he formed a partnership with Dr. S. V. D. Hill, an eminent physician of the state, and their partnership lasted harmoniously for nineteen years. The Doctor has been health officer of Noxubee county for about twenty years, and a trustee of the A. M. college for five years. He is a member of the state Medical society, the Tri-state Medical society and the county association. Socially he is a member of the A. F. & A. M. and the I. O. O. F. He was married in November, 1865, to Mrs. Kimble, a daughter of Dr. H. Dent, of Macon, by whom he has five children living: Anna D., wife of A. T. Dent; H. Dent, an attorney, of Long Island, N. Y.; Fannie; Henry M., in business in Birmingham, Ala., and Launcelot, at home. The mother of these children died in 1883, after which the Doctor married Mrs. Baechtel. He has been a member of the Methodist Episcopal church for the past twenty-five years, and has risen to prominence in his profession as well as a citizen. The Doctor is a grandnephew of Col. William Washington, and his first wife was a niece of Gen. James Longstreet, and grandniece of Judge Longstreet, of Oxford. The Doctor is also a nephew of Prof. John B. Minor, of the University of Virginia, who has been connected with that institution for over fifty years.

Capt. Matthew K. Mister, postmaster at Grenada and proprietor of New Era plantation at Blaine Station, Miss., was born in Baltimore, Md., in 1845. The father, Matthew K. Mister, was born in Maryland, in 1810, and was married in that state, in 1835, to Miss Julia A. Lake, also a native of Maryland, born in 1812. In 1840 they moved to Grenada, Miss., but only resided there until 1845, when they returned to Baltimore. After making their home there until 1850, they again came to Grenada, and here the father, in connection with merchandising, engaged quite extensively in planting until 1873. He was a member of the Mississippi legislature from Yalobusha county in 1870, when Grenada county was formed. In reconstruction times he was appointed judge of the county court of Yalobusha county; also alderman of Grenada, by the general in command at Vicksburg, but was removed by General Ames. He was a stanch Union man during the war, but was not an extremist. In his religious views he was a Methodist all his life, and a liberal supporter of that church. His death occurred in 1880. The mother, who was also a member of the same church, died in 1873. The paternal grandfather of our subject, Lowder Mister, was probably born in Maryland. Capt. Matthew K. Mister was the third of nine children—six sons and three daughter—five of whom are living: James F., an attorney, now living in Kansas City, Mo., was attending college when the war broke out. He joined Wise's legion of Virginia, University grays, and remained in service for twelve months. He then returned home and joined General Forrest's cavalry, serving with him until the close of the war. He was captured near Holly Springs and imprisoned at Alton, Ill., and other places until exchanged in 1863 in Virginia. He then rejoined his command and served until the close of war. He was reporter of the Missouri supreme court. Prof. Wilbur F., of Plano, Tex., and a teacher by profession, was educated in the University of Mississippi, Princeton, N. J., and Columbia, S. C., graduating from the last-named institution. He is now a teacher and minister of Texas. He was in company G, Fifteenth Mississippi regiment, at Vicksburg and vicinity a short time, and was afterward chaplain in General Forrest's cavalry until the close of war. Edward C., a traveling salesman of Baltimore, was educated at Grenada, and Eugene, a merchant of Texas, was also educated at Grenada. At twelve years of age Matthew K. Mister left school and clerked in his father's store until the breaking out of hostilities. He then joined the Fifteenth Tennessee as first lieutenant and was assigned staff duty in the first brigade and first division of General Forrest's cavalry, acting assistant adjutant-general until the surrender. He was in many severe engagements in Tennessee and Mississippi and was paroled at Meridian, Miss., by General Canby. After the war Captain Mister engaged in merchandise in partnership with his father until 1873. Since that time he has been engaged in planting, and is the owner of two thousand seven hundred and sixty acres, with about one thousand six hundred under cultivation, producing three hundred bales of cotton and hay and corn to supply the plantation. He is a director in the Grenada creamery, Cold Storage company, and of the Alliance Warehouse company. In 1882 he was made postmaster, served in that capacity until 1885, and was appointed to the same position in May, 1890. He is a member of the I. O. O. F., Grenada lodge No. 6, and is county lecturer of the Farmers' Alliance. He is also a Knight of Honor, Grenada lodge No. 983. The Captain was married in 1878 to Miss Jennie Topp, a native of Nashville, Tenn., and a member of the Episcopal church. Her parents, Dixon C. and Mary Topp, were natives of Tennessee also, and were there reared and married. Mr. Topp, who was a planter and commission merchant, died at Holly Springs in 1890. Captain Mister is a self-made man, and owes his success to his own industry and good management. He is a republican in principle and is prominent in politics, being the choice of his party as a candidate for congress in 1890.

Eli S. Mitchell, real estate agent, is one of the first settlers of Corinth, and is a man of thought and action, as is clearly shown by the achievements of his long and useful life. He was born in east Tennessee on the 1st of December, 1819, and was the son of H. B. and Mary (Houston) Mitchell, and grandson of Adam Mitchell, a native of North Carolina and a farmer by occupation. The father and mother were both natives of Tennessee and the father was a merchant and farmer, and followed these all his life. The mother was a second cousin of Sam Houston, of Texas. Eli S. Mitchell, the eldest of eight children (Nancy A., Adam, Houston, L. B., Martha, Catherine and Mary, two besides our subject now living, L. B. and Nancy), came with his parents to Alabama when an infant, but subsequently moved back with them to Tennessee. He made his home in McNairy county, Tenn., and Alcorn county, Miss., until 1840, when he went to Indian territory, following merchandising there for thirty years. From there he went to Fort Smith, Ark., and then back to Alcorn county, Miss., where he has followed the real estate business ever since. He always considered Alcorn county his home, and in 1854 he and his brother, Houston, together with a Mr. Hamp Mask, bought the ground where Corinth now stands, laid it off in lots, and began selling these. Mr. Mitchell came to Corinth in 1877 to take charge of the business, sell lots, etc. There he has resided ever since. He is a gentleman of extensive general information, is thoroughly versed in his business, and all business entrusted to him receives his prompt attention. He was married in 1850, in Alcorn county, to Miss Martha A. Phillips, a native of Tennessee, born in 1830, and the daughter of Joe and Mary (McQueen) Phillips; the father a native of Virginia and the mother of Tennessee. Mrs. Mitchell was one of eleven children: Avarilla, Mary, Louisa, Martha A., Susan, Virginia, John, Hill C., Joseph J., Thomas J. and Malcom. Mr. Mitchell was suttler for a Choctaw regiment for the Confederate army from 1861 to 1865. He is a democrat in politics, but has never aspired to any public office. Mrs. Mitchell is a member of the Presbyterian church, and he is a believer in the same and contributes liberally to religious and educational enterprises.

Hon. James C. Mitchell was born near the Peaks of Otter, in Virginia, to which fact he sometimes laughingly attributed his lofty stature and his soaring ambition. He removed to east Tennessee at an early age, and turning his attention to the law rapidly rose to eminence. He was a whig in politics and a warm admirer of General Harrison. He was, while in congress, a warm personal friend of Gen. Sam Houston. At the expiration of his term in congress, in 1828, he was elected to the circuit bench of Tennessee. He was the author of Mitchell's Justice. He came in 1837 to Hinds county, Miss., then advanced in years, and died there in 1843.

Dr. T. J. Mitchell, superintendent of the state insane asylum, at Jackson, Miss., was born in Livingston county, Ala., in 1830, the eighth of nine children born to Cullen and Mary T. (Sykes) Mitchell, who were born in North Carolina and Virginia, respectively, the former being one of the early pioneers of Alabama, in which state he successfully followed the calling of a planter until his death in 1832, his wife dying in 1849, both members of the Methodist Episcopal church. The paternal grandfather was of Scotch-Irish ancestry, and a pioneer of the Old North state. James Sykes, the mother's father, a planter of Virginia, was of English descent, and served in the continental army during the Revolutionary war. Dr. T. J. Mitchell was educated at Tuscaloosa university, Alabama, but left while in his junior year, in 1848, to begin the study of medicine, graduating from the University of Pennsylvania as an M. D. in 1852. He at once began practicing at Jackson, but in order to perfect himself in his profession he abandoned his practice to pursue his medical studies and researches in Europe, where he remained during 1856-7. In 1862 he entered the Confederate army, as surgeon of the Thirty-ninth Mississippi regiment, but as his health at this time was rather poor, he only served irregularly. After the war he practiced in Jackson until 1878, when he was appointed by Governor Stone to his present position at the insane asylum, which he has held by reappointment ever since. Under his management the institution has attained a high degree of perfection, and as his reputation for wonderful cures has gone abroad the attendance at the asylum is large. The Doctor is especially skilled and well posted in that branch of his profession which treats of abberation of the mind, and there could be found no more fitting person for the position than he, for aside from possessing the above mentioned qualification, he is kind-hearted, considerate, and possesses sound judgment. He was married in 1858 to Miss Annie McWillie, a daughter of ex-Governor McWillie, a sketch of whom appears in this volume. To their union five children were born: Kate, wife of Carroll Johnston, of New Orleans; Ida, wife of J. W. Robinson, a merchant of Jackson; Henrietta, Thomas J., and Cullen Calhoun. The mother of these children, who was a worthy member of the Episcopal church, was called from life in 1878, having been an earnest Christian and an exemplary wife and mother. The Doctor is also a member of the Episcopal church. He is the owner of some three thousand acres of land in Copiah and Attala counties, which is considered very valuable land.

Hon. Alexander Montgomery was born and reared in Natchez in the old territorial days. He received an exceptional literary education, and then addressed himself to the study of law. He is regarded as having been one of the most profound lawyers ever produced by this state. In 1831 he was appointed judge of the supreme court, but his official career as such was terminated the following year by the elective judiciary introduced under the new constitution. On retiring from the bench he resumed the practice of his profession in Natchez, where he was for a time a partner of the distinguished Samuel S. Boyd, and was an active practitioner to a very advanced age. He died at the home of a relative in Warren county.

Hon. A. A. Montgomery, farmer, Osborn, Miss. Mr. Montgomery's parents, Samuel A. and Elizabeth (McClary) Montgomery, where natives of the Palmetto state, the father born in Fairfield district in 1824, and the mother near Charleston about 1830. The paternal grandfather, Charles Montgomery, who was also a native of South Carolina, was of Scotch-Irish origin. The latter left his native state, removed to Oktibbeha county, Miss., and settled on the present site of Osborn, where he purchased a large tract of land. The maternal grandfather, David McClary, moved from South Carolina to Alabama, and thence to Columbus, Miss., when Mrs. Montgomery was but a child. He was a prosperous planter. Samuel A. Montgomery reached the age of nineteen years on his father's farm in South Carolina, and then came with the latter to Oktibbeha county, Miss. Two years later his father gave him a small farm, and he started out for himself as an agriculturist. In 1847 or 1848 he married Miss Elizabeth McClurg, who bore him three interesting children: Sanuella (deceased), Alvin A. and Samuel A. (who is now a successful physician of Osborn). Samuel A. Montgomery, Sr., became the owner of about four hundred acres of land in Oktibbeha county, and there his death occurred in 1854. His widow survived until 1878. Both were members of the Old School Presbyterian church, and he was an elder in the same. Alvin A. Montgomery was born in Oktibbeha county, Miss., in 1851, and comes of a prominent and highly respected family. Until seventeen years of age his time was divided between assisting his father on the farm and in attending the common country schools. He then engaged as clerk, and continued this three years, first, one year at West Point, then a year at Mayhew, and finally a year near Osborn. He then began farming where he now lives, cultivating about one hundred and thirty acres; has about seventy-five acres in native grass and the remainder in timber. His principal crops are corn and cotton. He is also interested in stockraising, horses and cattle principally, and is a prosperous young planter of the county. He was married in December, 1890, to Miss Lulu Muldrow, a native of Lowndes county, Miss., born in 1866, and the daughter of Robert and Annie (Oliver) Muldrow, natives, respectively, of South Carolina and Georgia. Mr. Montgomery was elected to the state senate in November, 1887. For a number of years he was judge of elections in the county. He is a member of the Farmers' Alliance, and he and Mrs. Montgomery are members of the Presbyterian church, in which he holds the office of elder. His brother, Dr. Samuel A. Montgomery, was born in Oktibbeha county, Miss., and was also reared on a farm, receiving the foundation of his education in the common schools, which he attended until about fifteen years of age. He then entered Salem college, Garnettsville, Ky., remained there two years, and subsequently took a literary course in Erskine college, South Carolina, for the same length of time. After this he took a full course in medicine at a medical college in Nashville, Tenn., and graduated in 1872. After practicing his profession for three years at Osborn, Miss., he removed to Starkville, where he resided seven years. On the 15th of December, 1874, he wedded Miss Margaret Watt, a native of Oktibbeha county, born in 1852, and the daughter of Dr. William and Virginia (Childs) Watt, the former from South Carolina and the latter from Mississippi. After leaving Starkville, Dr. Montgomery engaged as agent with Illinois Central railroad, and in this capacity he still serves. In connection he is also engaged in farming, owns two hundred acres of land and has one hundred acres under cultivation. He raises cotton and corn, and is also engaged in stockraising. He is a member of the Knights of Honor, at Starkville, and he and wife are members of the Presbyterian church, of which Dr. Montgomery is deacon. He is the father of four children: Eva May, Bessie Lou, Grace and Ruth.

Dr. D. C. Montgomery, the second in order of birth of nine children born to W. P. and Catherine (Cameron) Montgomery, owes his nativity to Franklin county, Miss., where his birth occurred in 1835, and is of Scotch-Irish descent. His parents were natives of South Carolina and descendants of representative families in that state. The father grew to manhood in North Carolina, and after marriage came to Mississippi, settling in Adams county about 1820. Some time after this he came to the present site of Greenville, and, with his brother A. B. and others, entered a tract of five thousand acres. He made many and vast improvements until his death, in 1886. The mother had died in 1852. Both were members of the Presbyterian church. Mr. Montgomery opened about twelve hundred acres of land and became an extensive planter. Of their large family of children only three are now living. Dr. Montgomery was educated in Centenary college, Louisiana, and graduated in medicine from the University of Pennsylvania, in 1855. One year later he located in Bolivar county, and at the breaking out of hostilities during the late unpleasantness, he enlisted in the Confederate service as a private in the Bolivar troops. He was in the battles of Shiloh and Corinth. In 1862 he was appointed surgeon of the First Mississippi cavalry, and was taken ill while in Hood's retreat from Nashville. Later he was captured and detained until July 23, 1865, when he returned to his practice in Bolivar county. In 1869 he came to Greenville, and here he has since been located, being justly regarded as one of the thoroughly reliable and efficient physicians of Greenville. He was married first in 1866, to Miss Fannie Semmes Harris, daughter of Judge William L. Harris, of Columbus. She died in 1881. One child, Harris, who died at the age of three years, was the fruit of this union. Dr. Montgomery's second marriage occurred in 1883, to Mrs. M. N. Sims, nee Finley, daughter of Dr. John L. Finley, of Greenville. To this union one child, Cameron, has been born. Mrs. Montgomery had two children by a former marriage. The Doctor is a member of the state medical association, and is a vigorous supporter of all enterprises of local interest. The family are members of the Methodist Episcopal church.

William Eugene Montgomery was the son of William Pinckney Montgomery and Catherine Cameron, and was born in Franklin county, Miss. W. P. Montgomery was born in South Carolina, and was the son of William Montgomery and Agnes Barclay, who moved from South Carolina and settled in Adams county, Miss., about the time the state was admitted into the Union. Catherine Cameron was the daughter of Daniel Cameron and Mary McMillan and came from North Carolina about the same time, settling in Franklin county, Miss. They were all of Scotch parentage. In 1857 W. E. Montgomery married Mary Adelia Clark, the daughter of Charles Clark, who was the governor of the state of Mississippi at the close of the war between the states. W. E. Montgomery was appointed first lieutenant in the First Mississippi battalion of cavalry, then to the rank of captain and then to that of major, and commanded the First Mississippi battalion until the surrender. At the date of the surrender he was operating with a portion of his battalion in the swamps of Mississippi, along the Mississippi river, and owing to the floods from the Mississippi river at the time of the surrender, he did not receive orders to surrender from Col. William S. Yerger, with whose regiment he had been consolidated, until long after the surrender of the state. The order to surrender from Colonel Yerger was delivered to Major Montgomery under a flag of truce by a Green Boat captain, to whom he surrendered his command near the mouth of White river and were probably the last Confederate troops surrendered in Mississippi. Major Montgomery has two brothers residing in Washington county, Miss., Dr. Daniel Cameron Montgomery, who was brigadier-surgeon in General Armstrong's cavalry brigade, and Captain John Malcom Montgomery, of Col. Richard A. Pruson's regiment in same brigade. Both served until the close of the war. W. E. Montgomery resides at Natchez, Miss.

Col. F. A. Montgomery, attorney at law, of Rosedale, Miss., was born in Adams county, of this state in 1830, the only child that lived beyond infancy born to Thomas Jefferson and Martha (West) Montgomery, who were also natives of this state, the former being a planter by occupation and dying when the subject of this sketch was three years of age. The Montgomery family originated in the famous old Waxhaw settlement of South Carolina, and like the majority of the settlers they were of Scotch ancestry, but previously residents of the north of Ireland. They became wealthy settlers of South Carolina, for those early days, but were robbed and impoverished by the British tories during Revolutionary times. Alexander Montgomery, the first of the name known in this country and the grandfather of the immediate subject of this sketch, was born in South Carolina, and first removed from his native state to Tennessee, thence to Mississippi, at which time he was wholly without means. He received limited educational advantages, but he possessed a vigorous and inquisitive mind and always desired to know the why and wherefore of everything, great or small. He rapidly acquired property and position, became a leader of the republican party, was year after year placed at the head of the legislative ticket, filled the prominent and responsible position of speaker of the house, and had he lived two years longer would have undoubtedly been elected governor of the state of Mississippi. He first married a daughter of Maj. Richard King, and secondly a Miss Swayze, both members of highly respected and very prominent families that came to Natchez when the country was under Spanish rule. By these wives he became the father of a large family, and a number of his sons became prominent in Mississippi history and left many descendants who now reside in the state. He himself came of a very influential family, and was related both by blood and marriage to some of the most noted and prominent people of the South. It is to such men as Mr. Montgomery that the gratitude of the present generation is due, for he was not only a believer in law and order, but he was a patron of all good works and his efforts in behalf of suffering humanity were unceasing. The maternal grandfather, Cato West, was born in Halifax county, Va., was of an influential family and sprung from an ancient earldom of England. He was a man of talent, education and fortune, and, with his father-in-law, Col. Thomas Green, emigrated to Georgia, thence to Natchez, where he settled and became an ardent republican, leading the opposition to Governor Sargent. He became secretary of the territory under Claiborne, and after the latter went to New Orleans, he conducted the executive office. He was frequently elected to the legislature, and on several occasions presided over the senate. He possessed an original and brilliant mind, was a forcible writer and speaker, and during early times was a leader of the territory. He was a resident of Pickering (now Jefferson) county, and was a very extensive and prominent planter there for many years. Col. F. A. Montgomery, whose name heads this sketch, was educated chiefly at Oakland college in Jefferson county, but also spent one year at Allegheny college, in Meadville, Penn., after which he returned to his home. In 1848 he was married to Miss Charlotte Clark, of Ohio, whose father came to this state in early life, here spending the rest of his days. Her brother Charles, who was a lawyer, came to this state also at an early day, and being exceptionally talented soon rose to eminence. His qualities of leadership were signally displayed in the arena of politics, and he was regarded as one of the most able, active, indefatigable leaders of his party in the state, his numerous friends showing their appreciation of his ability by electing him to the legislature. He went out as a captain of a company in the Second regiment of Mississippi volunteers for the Mexican war; was soon elected colonel, in which capacity he served until the war ended. When the Civil war came he was first a brigadier-general of state troops, afterward becoming major-general, and as soon as the Confederacy was formed he was appointed, by Jefferson Davis, a brigadier-general in the Confederate army and commanded a division at the battle of Shiloh, where he was wounded in the shoulder. He also commanded a division at Baton Rouge, at which place was so severely wounded in the hip that he was unfitted for further duty. At this time he was taken prisoner and conveyed to New Orleans, where he was exchanged and returned home. He was at once elected governor (in 1862) of Mississippi, at the end of which term he was re-elected. After the war closed he was taken a prisoner to Fort Pulaski, and upon being released returned to his home in Bolivar county and resumed the practice of law, receiving the appointment, in 1876, of chancellor of his district, and died in 1877, while serving in office. He was for many years a conspicuous leader in the affairs of the state and was well known for his sagacity, skill and sound and practical views on all subjects. After the celebration of Mr. Montgomery's nuptials, he continued planting, first in Jefferson county, but since 1855 has been a resident of Bolivar county. In 1858 he opened up a plantation on the Mississippi river, which he called Beulah, and where the present village of that name now stands he cut the first cane and made many improvements in the way of buildings, etc., which were destroyed by the Federal soldiers during the war, with the exception of one negro cabin. The first election in the county after his arrival was held in 1855, and at that time he was elected president of the board of supervisors, a position he held until the opening of the war, when he cast aside personal considerations to enlist in the Confederate army in defense of home and friends, and was chosen captain of a cavalry company, which he organized, called the Bolivar troops, it being the first company to be organized in the county. He was in many bloody combats along the Mississippi river, the most noted of which was Belmont, and upon the reorganization of his regiment he was elected lieutenant-colonel, an office he held until the war closed. He often commanded his regiment and was in the campaigns of Hood and Johnston, and while with them was captured at Selma, Ala., and was taken to Columbus, Ga. Here he was sick for some time and after being paroled returned to Mississippi and entered upon the practice of law. He was elected to represent the county in the state legislature in 1879, serving by re-election for three terms when he declined further re-election and once more began giving his time exclusively to his practice, and for years has been one of the leading lawyers of the county. He is one of three oldest men who came as pioneers to this county, and it can with truth be said that there is not a man of greater personal popularity or who possesses intelligence of higher or more practical or useful order than does he. As a citizen he has been of material benefit to the section in which he has resided, and as an officer he was cool in judgement, fruitful in resources, skillful in planning, excellent in execution and no braver or more courageous soldier ever faced the enemy.

Colonel Montgomery about seven years ago united with other old comrades in forming an association, which has met annually since in some part of the state, and with the pledge, as long as any are left, to continue to meet. This association is composed of surviving members of the four regiments, comprising a cavalry brigade commanded by Gen. Frank C. Armstrong, a splendid man and gallant soldier, who now lives in Washington, D. C., and whose name is a household word among them. From its organization till the present time Colonel Montgomery has each year been honored by being elected the president of the association, and its gallant commanders were honored by being permitted to name it the Armstrong Brigade association. The brigade was composed of the First (of which Colonel Montgomery was lieutenant-colonel), Second, Twenty-eighth and Ballentine's Mississippi cavalry regiments. General Armstrong's letter, which follows, explains itself, and is here inserted as a well deserved tribute to this gallant soldier, who, though not a Mississippian, commanded Mississippi troops, and is closely allied to the family of the late Col. W. A. Perry, of Gainesville, Washington county. It is signed Frank C. Armstrong, and dated Washington, D. C., May 30, 1891:

COL. A. F. MONTGOMERY, PRESIDENT OF ARMSTRONG'S BRIGADE ASSOCIATION:

My Dear Colonel:—I am in receipt of a notice of the annual reunion of the "Armstrong Brigade," which I had the honor to command. It is with more than usual regret that I am compelled to write that my engagements will not permit me to be with you on the 3d of June. Each year I have promised myself the great pleasure of meeting in reunion my dear old comrades of the great war time, but I am again disappointed. My heart and sympathy are, and always will be, with the Confederate soldiers, and though the banner under which we marched and fought together has gone down, the sentiments of honor and courage inculcated outlasted the war, and will always be the heritage of those who survive it. The lesson of faith, self-reliance and soldierly manhood were never stronger than among those who shared the blanket, drank from the same canteen, and divided the last rations. I should have particularly liked to have been present and added my share of respect, honor and love to those heroic Mississippians who gave their lives under the battle flag of our states and our cause. I will do it, in spirit, in memory. I will never forget the fortitude, courage and unfaltering valor of the First, Second, Twenty-eighth, and Ballentine's Mississippi cavalry, during all my service with them, and particularly in the last days of the Confederacy, when all was dark, and delay the only hope. Every regiment, company and man seemed to vie with each other as to who could stand the most in the front of overwhelming odds, and the manly, soldierly manner in which they all did their duty to the end. I hope the association will be made a permanent one, and the yearly reunions many. Again regretting that I can not be with you and my old comrades, I am, faithfully your friend.

Colonel Montgomery is descended from families historic in the early days of Mississippi, and has been an honor not only to the state, but also to his illustrious name. His residence was the first to be erected in the town of Rosedale, and besides the ground on which his residence is located he owns several acres in the town. To himself and wife twelve children were born: Louisana, who died in 1868, at the age of nineteen years; Jefferson, who is married and a successful lawyer of Rosedale; Tillie, principal of the schools of Rosedale; Martha, wife of E. H. Moore, a sketch of whom appears in this work; Harriet, wife of Dr. John W. Dulaney, of Rosedale (see sketch); Frank, who is married and the leading lawyer of Tunica county; Lottie, Fadjie; Joseph, a lawyer of Quitman county, and Anna. Two children died unnamed. The family are members of the Methodist Episcopal church and Mr. Montgomery may be said to be the father of the church of that denomination at Rosedale. He has contributed to it large amounts of money and has in all ways aided its advancement and the handsome structure is a monument to his Christian spirit and liberality. He was the first city attorney of Rosedale, a position he filled one year, and socially is a member of the A. F. & A. M., Bolivar lodge No. 210. The Colonel is stately and commanding in appearance, being tall and slender, in complexion is a blonde, and is known throughout this section as a charitable, kind and hospitable gentleman.

Lafayette Montgomery is the efficient passenger agent for the Illinois Central railroad at Jackson, but in 1855 was born in Madison county, the third in a family of eight children born to Andrew J. and Susan L. (Dixon) Montgomery, who were also born in this state, the father's people being among the earliest settlers of southwest Mississippi, and the mother's, who were of English descent, of Jefferson county. Andrew Montgomery was a planter, in which occupation he become quite successful. He died in Madison county in 1868, his widow still surviving him. Lafayette F. Montgomery was educated in the public schools, which he attended until 1868. In 1870 he become an employe on the Illinois Central railroad, in the employ of which company he has been continuously ever since. In 1878 he remained faithfully and fearlessly at his post, notwithstanding the fact that yellow fever was raging, and for this act of bravery and disinterestedness he was promoted to an easier and more lucrative position soon after. He first filled the position of telegraph operator, then became chief clerk of the freight office, was then made assistant ticket agent, then ticket agent and is now agent of the passenger depot at Jackson, which position is a responsible one. In 1884 he was married to Miss Clara Atkinson, a native of this county and a daughter of Hon. Thomas Atkinson, a sketch of whom appears in this volume. Mrs. Montgomery was called from life in 1885, leaving one child, which also soon died. Mr. Montgomery is a gentleman in every sense of the word and is a pleasing and entertaining conversationalist. He is a member of the Knights of Honor and the Knights of Pythias.

Capt. W. A. Montgomery, of Edwards, Hinds county, Miss., is one of the successful and talented attorneys of the state and has made his way to the front in the practice of his profession, for he possesses in a more than ordinary degree the natural attributes essential to a successful career at the bar and in public. He was born in Winston county, October 18, 1844, a son of C. W. and Olivia F. (Moore) Montgomery, the former of whom was also born in Mississippi, although his ancestors were natives of the state of South Carolina, coming thither about 1820 and settling near Starkville. The mother's father, Gen. William Moore, was a Tennesseean, and won his title while serving in the War of 1812 and Indian war, and was a representative to the Tennessee legislature for many years Capt. W. A. Montgomery was called from school at Murfreesboro, Tenn., by his father, who desired that his son should be near him during the pending struggle between the North and South, and soon after returning to the state of his birth he enlisted in the Hinds county light guards for three years or during the war. This enlistment was, however, against his father's wishes, and the latter was instrumental in securing his release. He was later made a member of the Raymond fencibles, of the Twelfth Mississippi regiment, and remained with this regiment until the spring of 1862, when he was discharged, on account of ill health; went into the service again in the fall of the same year, with the First Mississippi regiment of state militia. In May, 1863, he rejoined the regular army as a scout, reported to General Pemberton for duty, and the first work given him was the burning of the Dillon bridge over Fourteen-mile creek, which he performed successfully, and with seventeen men and a hastily constructed breastwork impeded Grant's whole army for almost an entire day. He took part in the battle of Champion's hill, and during the progress of that noted battle made himself so conspicuous for gallantry that Gen. Wirt Adams had him detailed as a regular scout, after which he took part in the engagements at Clinton, Jackson, Livingston, second battle of Champion's hill, Coleman's plantation, Mechanicsburg, Concord church and Grand Gulf, during which time he so won the respect and admiration of his superior officers that he was commissioned captain March 4, 1864, and was authorized to raise a company of mounted men for service on the Mississippi front. During his career as a scout he captured many prisoners, and kept the Union army in constant dread of Montgomery scouts. The Captain served his state most conspicuously during the oppressive carpet-bag reign of

Governor Ames, when he was among the number who incited the populace by his leadership to such determined opposition to the governor that he was compelled to disband his colored troops, stationed at different points throughout the state, and a great eyesore to the whites. He commanded the five hundred men who marched to Jackson and brought Governor Ames to a full knowledge of their determination, and to submission. Captain Montgomery was elected to the state senate from Hinds and Rankin counties, to fill the unexpired term of A. R. Johnson, in 1868, and ably and faithfully did he discharge every duty of this responsible position. He has interested himself in all enterprises looking to the advancement of his county and state, and is exceptionally well known, respected and liked throughout Hinds county. He was first married to Miss Mella Dupree, a daughter of Capt. James Dupree, of Brownsville, Miss., with whom he lived happily until 1882, when he was called upon to mourn her death. To their union five children were born: Patrick H., Charles W., Ollie, Hugh R. and W. A., Jr. In 1884 he was married to Miss Bettie C. Henry, of Mississippi, by whom he has one child, William A. The Captain is a Royal Arch Mason, and also belongs to the I. O. O. F., the K. of P., the K. of H. and the American Legion of Honor. The Captain has always been a man of indomitable pluck and energy, and in addition to his brilliant career as a soldier he ranks among the highest civilians, and has been a valuable acquisition to the county of Hinds. He is a strict member of the Baptist church, and joins heartily in all the moral reforms advocated by that sect.

B. S. Moore, planter, Kosciusko, Miss. On his present homestead of one hundred and sixty acres of good tillable soil, one hundred acres of which are under cultivation, Mr. Moore is actively engaged in stockraising in connection with his farming. His parents were natives of Alabama, and in that state their nuptials were celebrated. They moved to Mississippi in January, 1855, located in Scott county, and there the father died in 1875, after following the life of a successful agriculturist. He was a member of the Methodist church, a member of the Grange, but took very little interest in politics. His widow is still living and makes her home at Walnut Grove, Leake county, Miss. The paternal grandfather was a native of Tennessee but was a resident of Scott county, Miss., at the time of his death. The maternal grandfather, Benjamin Sims, was a native of Georgia, and was a Baptist minister. He died in Mississippi. B. S. Moore, the only child born to his parents, owes his nativity to Mississippi, his birth occurring in Scott county in 1855, shortly after his parents moved to that county. He grew to manhood there, received his education and in December 1876 he was united in marriage to Miss Bailey, a native also of Scott county, Miss. Since that time Mr. Moore has been engaged in planting, and although his farm is not as large as some it is one of the best improved in the county. He raises a superior grade of stock, principally Jersey cattle, and is enterprising and progressive. He has ever taken an active part in politics and at the present time is a candidate for circuit clerk. He is a worthy member of the Methodist church, contributes liberally to the same, and gives his hearty support to all worthy movements. He is a Royal Arch Mason, having joined Morton lodge No. 254 in 1879 and he obtained a dimit from that lodge and joined Bethel lodge No. 107, in 1886. He is senior deacon of the same. He is also a charter member of Springdale lodge, Alliance, held the office of vice president for two terms, and is now the incumbent of that position.

C. C. Moore, merchant and planter, was born in 1842, in Chickasaw county, where he still resides, three miles from Houlka, on a plantation of which he is now the owner. His father, Lewis Moore, was born in Georgia in 1803, a son of John and Willie (Rice) Moore, both of whom were native Georgians and at an early day removed to Alabama. John Moore became a wealthy planter, and he and his wife reared a family of seven children, of whom Lewis was the eldest. The latter was reared in Alabama, and his early advantages for acquiring an education were rather limited, although he was an intelligent and well informed man. His marriage to Miss Rice took place about 1828, at which time she was in her fifteenth year, a daughter of Hopkins Rice, a very successful planter of Greene county, Miss., originally from North Carolina. Mr. Moore became a resident of Chickasaw county, Miss., in 1840, settling on the plantation of which the subject of this sketch is now the owner, at which time he purchased three sections of land, and some years later a section of prairie land at Egypt, Miss. Lewis Moore and wife reared ten out of the eleven children born to them, all of whom married with the exception of one who was killed while serving in the Confederate army. They are: Elizabeth J. (wife of B. F. Fitzpatrick, of Mobile, Ala.); John P. (a banker, real estate agent, planter and merchant, of Helena, Ark.), Mary A. (the deceased wife of Dr. J. B. Rockett), William T. (a merchant and planter of La Grange, Ark.), J. H. (who commanded company H, Eleventh Mississippi infantry, and was killed at the battle of Gettysburg on the 5th of July, 1863), L. C. (is a planter of Chickasaw county), C. C., J. B. (a planter and magistrate of Pickens county, Ala.), Cora F. (widow of S. C. Pippin, of Helena, Ark.), and Dora A. (wife of Mr. Bass, a merchant of Helena, Ark.). The parents have been members of the Baptist church for many years, in which church Mr. Moore held the position of deacon. He died on the 16th of February, 1866, his wife's death having occurred on the 5th of February. The boyhood days of C. C. Moore were spent on a plantation near Houlka, Miss., but at the age of fourteen years he was sent to Marietta, Ga., where he attended a military school for some time, and attended an educational institution at La Grange, Ala., until the opening of the war. In 1861 he organized a company of infantry (company D), of which he was elected first lieutenant, and became a part of the Fourth Confederate regiment, so called because it was made up of companies from Alabama, Mississippi and Tennessee. He was a participant in the battles of Fort Pillow, New Madrid, Island No. 10, being captured in the last named engagement and conveyed to Camp Chase, at Columbus, Ohio, thence to Johnson's island in Lake Erie, three miles from Sandusky, where he was kept nine months and was then exchanged. He then returned to Vicksburg, but soon went to Jackson, where he joined General Tillman's command, and was in the battle of Baker's creek. He was next at Vicksburg, from whence he retreated across the state to Montgomery, Ala., where his regiment was recruited, and acted as military conductor on the railroad between Montgomery, Ala., and West Point, Ga., in which capacity he served until the close of the war. Upon his return home he engaged in planting, on his own account, on the old homestead, on which he has ever since been actively engaged in planting. He is the owner of two sections of land, and is actively engaged in cultivating about five hundred acres. He makes cotton his principal crop, raising a sufficient amount of other products to make his plantation self-supporting. He is a progressive planter, believes in building up and enriching the soil, and is at present experimenting with the commercial fertilizer. He gives some attention to stockraising. At the beginning of 1878 he engaged in merchandising at Houston, purchasing the stock of goods belonging to A. L. Hill & Son. At first the firm name was Jamison, Moore & Co., but in January, 1889, Mr. Moore sold his interest in the business and started for himself with a new stock of goods. He has been a successful business manager, has proved himself an able financier, and now commands a large patronage. He was married on the 19th of March, 1866, to Miss Mollie L. Jamison, who was born in Pontotoc county, Miss., July 23, 1851, a daughter of Andrew J. and Amarilla (Stone) Jamison, a sketch of whom appears in this work. Mr. and Mrs. Moore have four living children: Andrew J. (the eldest, is a clerk and bookkeeper in his father's store at Houston; he was married December 31, 1890, to Miss Nettie Evans, daughter of Dr. J. L. Evans, of Houston), L. Evans (is attending school at Starkville), Inez and C. C., Jr. (are at home). Zelia A. and Paul Bertram died in childhood. Mr. Moore is a member of the Masonic fraternity, and is a charter member of the Knights of the Golden Rule, of Houston. He and his wife are members of the Methodist church at Houston, in which he is a steward. His sound and practical views on all subjects, his capability and his honorable business methods admirably fit him for any position within the gift of the county, but he does not aspire to political life, the turmoil and strife of politics being very distasteful to him.

Edward H. Moore, lawyer, Rosedale, Miss. Judge William H. and Margaret C. (Harris) Moore, natives respectively of North Carolina and the Old Dominion, were the parents of fifteen children, of whom the subject of this sketch was second in order of birth. The father is now residing in Alabama and is an able lawyer. The paternal grandfather, Edward Moore, was born in North Carolina, and followed the occupation of a planter. He was the brother of Gabriel Moore, governor of Alabama. The maternal grandfather, B. D. Harris, was of old Virginia stock. He emigrated to Tennessee at an early day. Edward H. Moore was born in Alabama in 1849, and although reared in that state he received the principal part of his education at Lexington, Ky. He then began reading law in his native state with Judge Lewis, and in 1873 came to Bolivar county, Miss., where he was admitted to the bar the same year. He has been practicing in this county since and is one of the leading lawyers. He is courteous and pleasant and a gentleman highly esteemed for his many estimable qualities. In connection with his practice he also carries on agricultural pursuits, and is the owner of twelve hundred acres, with five hundred acres under cultivation, most of which he has cleared himself. The soil is rich and tillable, and everything about the place indicates the owner to be a man of good judgment and advanced ideas. In 1890 he improved, remodeled and rebuilt his residence, and has a pleasant cottage home. He has been rather active in local politics, and in 1889 was elected a member of the board of supervisors, of which he was made president. He was married in 1873 to Miss Mattie Montgomery, daughter of Colonel Montgomery (see sketch), and one child has blessed this union, Lottie Clarke. The family are members of the Methodist Episcopal church, Mr. Moore having joined that denomination in boyhood. He is an earnest advocate and gives his hearty support to all measures to improve Rosedale or benefit Bolivar county.

James Moore, senior member of the firm of James Moore & Co., Oakland, was born near that place October 7, 1839, a son of James and Harriet Gaston (Davidson) Moore, born near Wadesboro, N. C., July 5, 1800, and about 1808, respectively. They were married at Wadesboro, and from there moved to Dyer county, Tenn., whence they came to Yalobusha county and settled on a small improvement near where Oakland now is, where Mrs. Moore died in 1844. Mr. Moore took for a second wife Martha A. Henderson, a daughter of a Methodist minister well known throughout this part of the country. In 1850 Mr. Moore moved to Tallahatchie county and located in the valley north of Charleston, where he died in 1857, at Eolia, where he had established a postoffice and store. He was a man of good attainments and had inherited considerable property. His business qualifications were first class, and he left a considerable estate. He and his wife are prominent in the Methodist church. Mr. Moore had nine children by his first wife and three sons and two daughters by his second wife. Of his family by his first marriage Green D. died in 1888; Caroline H. became the wife of James H. Rayburn and they are both deceased; Alexander H., Sidney and Anne died young; Harriet A. married T. M. Harton, a planter of this county; James

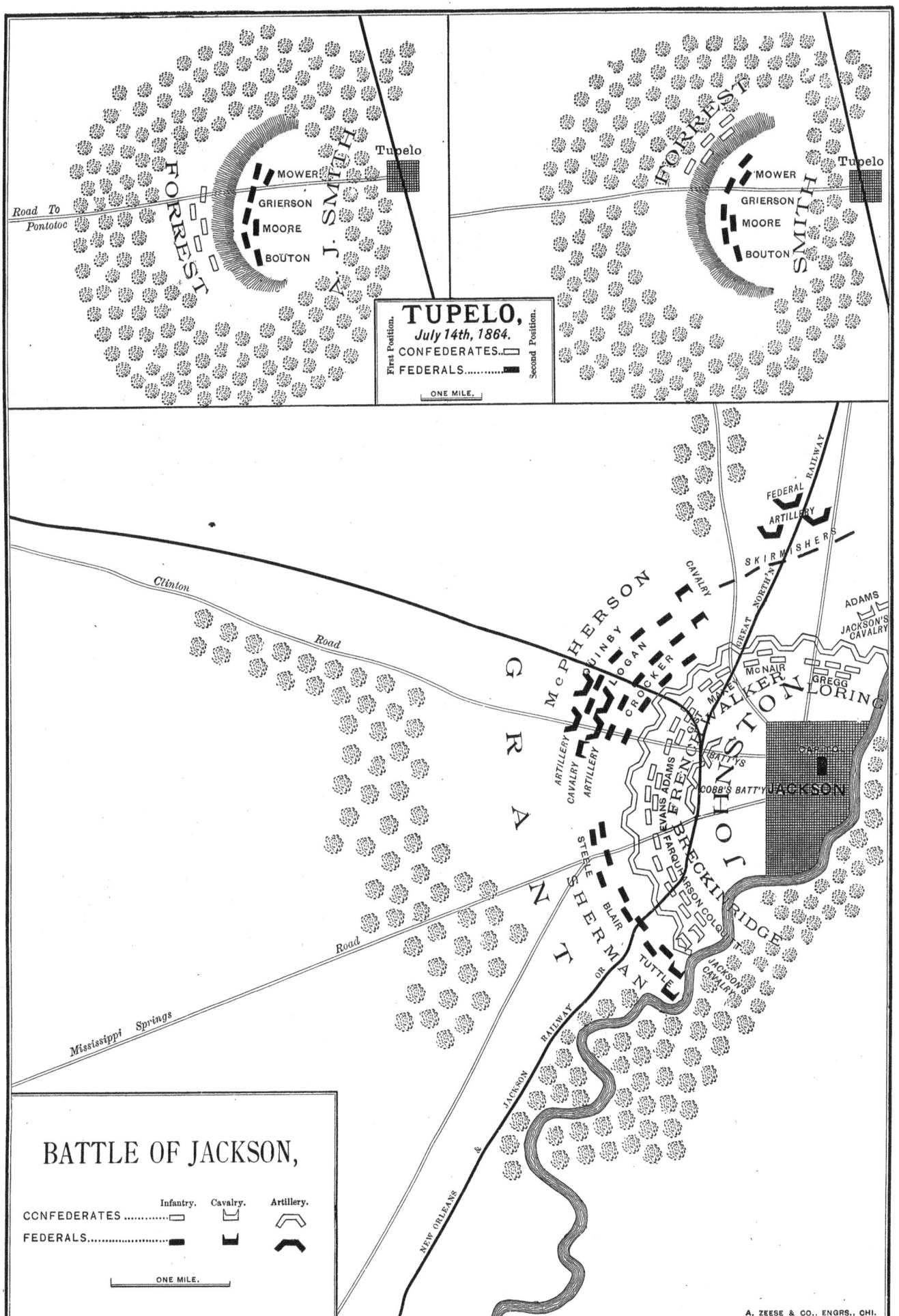

The location of the subordinate commands, as shown in the map of the battle of Jackson above, must not be considered as definitely established. From the best information obtainable, however, the troops were posted as here shown.

and John M. are living, and Lawrence died when quite young. Of the children by the second wife Marcus H., Edward M. and Adelaide died young. Henry Moore, of the firm of James Moore & Co., is a young business man well known throughout this section. Lawrence Moore, grandfather of the subject of this sketch, was born and lived out his days in North Carolina. He served his country as a soldier during the Revolutionary war, and represented his district a number of times in both branches of the North Carolina legislature. He was active and prominent in all public matters and one of the most successful planters in his part of the state. He reared a large family of sons and daughters, some of whom have become prominent in Alabama, Louisiana and other Southern states. Many of his descendants are living in different parts of the South, all of them honored and respected wherever their lots may be cast. Mr. Moore's great-grandfather, James Moore, was also a North Carolinian planter, and died in that state. He was a man of exceptional talent, a fine classical scholar and an able lawyer and physician. He was colonel of a regiment during the Revolutionary war, and was a member of the colonial assembly of North Carolina. Mr. Moore's maternal grandfather, Green Davidson, was also a native of North Carolina, where he lived for many years, but removed to Tennessee, whence in 1836 he came to Yalobusha county, where he became a well known planter and died in 1861. He was of English descent and in every sense a prominent citizen. Our subject was reared on his father's plantation and acquired an intimate knowledge of the details of planting. He received a good English education and became a fair Latin and Greek scholar. At the age of seventeen he became a clerk in a drygoods store at Memphis, Tenn. In this position he labored for three years. In 1859 he married Emily J., daughter of Benjamin and Sarah A. Carson, who are natives of South Carolina and Mississippi, respectively, and both of whom came to Tallahatchie county about 1836, where the parents of both Mr. and Mrs. Carson died. Here Mr. and Mrs. Carson married and lived the balance of their lives. Mr. Carson died in 1848 and his wife in 1856. Mr. Carson's father, William Carson, was one of the first settlers of Tallahatchie county, and became one of its best known planters. Mrs. Carson's father, William Lott, was an early settler where Charleston now stands. Mrs. Moore was born in Tallahatchie county and is the mother of three sons and one daughter: James B., who died in infancy; Green Harris was educated at the home school and at Oxford, and was married in February, 1891, to Zana Herron; Benjamin C. received a good common school education, and, as does his brother, Green D., finds employment at the store of James Moore & Co.; the daughter was an infant, unnamed. Soon after his marriage Mr. Moore engaged in merchandising in Charleston, which he continued up to the time of the war. He was a member of the First Mississippi cavalry regiment, furnished a substitute and was honorably discharged from service in 1862, afterward doing service in the state militia and in McLendon's battery, to which organization he belonged until the end of the Civil war. He had been an old line whig and had strenuously opposed secession. After the war he was a planter in Tallahatchie and lived there until 1878, when he took charge of the store of his brother, Green D. Moore, at Oakland, which he managed until 1881. In the year last mentioned he turned his attention to planting, which he gave his undivided attention to until 1886, when the firm of James Moore & Co. was organized, to succeed Green D. Moore & Sons, who had succeeded Moore & Davidson, the successors of Buntin & Moore, who had become proprietors of a business which had been established by Green D. Moore a short distance from the present town of Oakland. James Moore & Co. are one of the best known mercantile firms in northern Mississippi. They own about five thousand acres of land in different tracts, and handle about twelve hundred bales of cotton annually. Mr. Moore owns about eighteen hundred acres individually and produces about two hundred bales of cotton annually. Mr. Moore's success in life has been great, although it was interrupted by the war. Since the war period he has accumulated this fine property and placed himself at the head of this magnificent business through his own untiring effort, by the exercise of his well-known enterprise, unimpeachable honor and integrity. He has for many years been connected with the Masonic fraternity, and is worshipful master of Oakland lodge, A. F. & A. M., No. 82. He stands high, not only in this order, but also in the Knights of Honor, being a member of Scott lodge, Knights of Honor, of Oakland. Mr. and Mrs. Moore are prominent members of the Methodist church. The former is a cousin of Senator Isom G. Harris and of Hon. J. D. Adkins, of Tennessee.

James Bright Morgan, of Hernando, was born in Lincoln county, Tenn., March 14, 1835; was brought by his parents to De Soto county, Miss., in 1840, where he has since resided; received an academic education; studied law at Hernando, under John K. Connelly, and was admitted to the bar in 1857; when not engaged in the public service, has practiced his profession; was elected judge of probate before the war; resigned, and was mustered into the Confederate states service as a private; was elected captain, and in the organization of the Twenty-ninth Mississippi infantry was elected major; was promoted lieutenant-colonel and colonel; at the close of the war was again elected judge; was a member of the state senate of Mississippi in 1876, 1877 and 1878, and was chairman of the committee on the judiciary; was appointed, in October, 1878, by the governor, chancellor of the Third chancery district, and served for four years; was elected to the XLIXth and Lth congresses, and was reëlected to the LIst congress as a democrat, receiving thirteen thousand nine hundred and seventy-eight votes, against five thousand eight hundred and seventeen votes for James Reynolds Chalmers, republican, and one hundred and seven votes for James Witherspoon, independent candidate.

Hon. John M. Moore, mayor of Oakland, proprietor of the Craig hotel, planter and liveryman, was born near Oakland in 1841. He is the son of James Moore, a sketch of whom appears in these pages. He received a good common-school education in the schools of Oakland and vicinity. At eighteen he became a salesman in a store, an occupation which he followed until 1862. In that year he served sixty days as a private. Later he was engaged for some years in planting and after that was for considerable time a merchant at Harrison. From 1873 to 1882 he traveled for the firm of Bishop Brothers, of Cincinnati, Ohio, and during this time, in 1877, he was elected to represent Yalobusha county in the legislature and served two years to the entire satisfaction of his constituents. During the past ten years he has been repeatedly elected mayor of Oakland. He was chairman of the county democratic central committee for some years and held this position during the perilous times of the notorious A. T. Wimberley, a period of greenbackism, and took an active part in allaying the disturbances which were then rife in that part of the country. He is a member of the Oakland lodge of the I. O. O. F. and is prominent in that order. He has held every official position in his lodge and has been district deputy grand master and several times a representative to the grand lodge. He is also a member of the Oakland lodge of the Knights of Honor and has identified himself with the Farmers' Alliance. In 1862 he was married to Mrs. P. D. Shaw, a daughter of Sampson Bridgers. She died in 1887, and in 1889 Mr. Moore married Mrs. M. J. Craig, a daughter of Dr. Preston W. and Amanda Caroline Davis, who were natives, respectively, of Kentucky and Tennessee. The marriage occurred at Oakland, Miss. Dr. Davis was for many years engaged in the practice of his profession with marked success at Nashville, Tenn., where he died in 1878, aged about eighty-one years. He received his medical education at the Transylvania college, at Lexington, Ky., and died a devout member of the Christian church. His widow survived him and made her home with her daughter, Mrs. Moore. Mr. and Mrs. Moore are prominent Methodists. They own together about one thousand acres of land and their planting operations are very extensive. The Craig hotel is very popular among traveling people, and Mr. Moore is widely known as one of the most genial and accommodating landlords in this part of the state. He stands high as a citizen, and as a public official has acquitted himself with much ability and credit. Mrs. M. J. Craig, whom Mr. Moore married, was the widow of Capt. Blunt Craig, a large planter of Yalobusha and Tallahatchie counties, who responded to the first call for volunteers to serve in the late war, raised two companies during the war, was elected captain by acclamation and made a brave and noble officer, returning bearing the laurels of honor and respect, beloved by friends and comrades and dying at his home in Oakland in 1869. James Craig, his father, a soldier of the War of 1812 under General Jackson, and a wealthy planter of Limestone county, Ala., moved to this state among the first settlers. While the Indians still claimed their hunting grounds and race tracks he purchased much of his land from them. He was an extensive and successful planter. Owning a large number of slaves he made generally from five hundred to one thousand bales of cotton each year. He lived in a beautiful country home near Oakland, surrounded with such comforts and luxuries as enabled him to act the part of a bountiful host and most pleasing entertainer, his home being known far and near for its almost lordly hospitality.

James F. Moore was born in Lauderdale county, Miss., in September, 1850, and is a son of James and Caroline (Price) Moore, natives of North Carolina and Alabama respectively. The father went from his native state to Alabama at the age of twenty-three years, and was married there at the age of twenty-eight years. For ten years he was engaged in agricultural pursuits, his work being that of overseer. In 1845 he removed with his family to Lauderdale county, Miss., and bought land, which he immediately began to place under cultivation. His efforts in this direction were rewarded with more than ordinary success. When the war arose, he had accumulated a considerable amount of property, and owned fifteen slaves. He enlisted in the state militia, and was first lieutenant of his company. While the war was in progress he was employed by the Confederate government to tan hides, as he had a large tannery on his farm; much of the leather he had manufactured into boots and shoes, the tanyard, ginhouse, and thirty bales of cotton were burned by Sherman's army in 1864. After the war he passed through the trials experienced by the whole Southern population in regaining a foothold in the business world. Mrs. Moore died in June, 1878, on the home plantation. She was a consistent member of the Baptist church. Mr. Moore is living in the seventy-eighth year of his age, and is strong and active, and in full possession of his mental faculties. He has been a deacon in the Baptist church for thirty years. They reared a family of ten children: William H. died in 1872; Thomas J. died in the army in 1861; Sallie, the wife of A. J. Cansler is deceased; Susan, wife of M. G. Terry, is not living; James F. is the next in order of birth; Martha died at the age of twenty-one years; Elizabeth died in infancy; Cornelius D. is unmarried; Margaret is the wife of C. W. Jones; Georgia is the wife of John T. Ethridge. James remained at home until he was twenty-one years of age, and then took charge of his father's farm on his own account. He was married at the age of thirty years to Mary E. Miller, a daughter of Daniel and Mary (Pippin) Miller. Her mother was a native of Alabama, and her father was born in Pennsylvania. They had five children born to them: Daniel I., Caroline, Thomas M., Virginia, Jane E. Mr. Moore owns one hundred and ten acres of land, three miles from Meridian, and devotes his time to truck gardening and fruit culture. He also owns residence property in Meridian. He is public weigher of Meridian, his duties being to weigh and reweigh cotton. He is the land inspector of the British American Loan company, and is considered one of the most progressive and energetic young business men in the county. He is well known throughout the surrounding country, and the family name is honored and respected wherever it is heard. Mr. Moore was employed as a clerk by A. Threefoot & Son one year, but he prefers outdoor work, and so stays on his farm in the summer, and spends the winter season in Meridian. He and his wife are members of the Baptist church, and he belongs to the Knights of Honor. His brother Cornelius and he are associated in business, and both are members of the Farmers' Alliance.

James S. Moore is a prosperous farmer and stockman of Tate county, Miss., but was born in Marshall county of this state on the 24th of December, 1840, a son of Robert J. and Elva (Clementine) Moore, both natives of South Carolina. Here they were reared and married, but in 1834 removed to Marshall county, Miss., which was before the Indians had been removed from the state. They continued to reside in Marshall county until 1850, then came to Tate county, Mr. Moore purchasing an unimproved tract of government land. He also speculated in land to some extent, and at his death, which occurred in 1859, he was in good circumstances. His wife survived him until February, 1890, when she passed away at the age of seventy-five years. They reared a family of eight children, six of whom are still living: Jane C., widow of William Embry; Mary, wife of William T. Meeks of this county; James S., Eliza P., living with her brother John; Margaret A., wife of W. J. Veazey, Jr., of this county, and John A., a planter on the old homestead. James S. Moore spent his school days in this county, and in the spring of 1862 he entered the Confederate service. He became a member of company B, Forty-second Mississippi infantry, which was commanded by Capt. L. G. Woollard, Hill's army corps, army of northern Virginia, and was in all the battles from the seven days' fight near Richmond until the surrender. He was wounded at Falling Water, and in the battle of Wilderness. He served until the 2d of April, 1865, when he was captured, and on the 2d of July he was paroled from Point Lookout, Md., after which he returned home. From that time until 1870 he farmed on the old homestead, then purchased the plantation on which he is now residing, having rented it two years previous to making the purchase. This place amounted to three hundred and twenty acres, to which he has added from time to time until he now has sixteen hundred and thirty acres in three bodies, of which some eight hundred acres are under cultivation. He had to practice the closest economy and the most untiring industry upon first starting out for himself, and in this he was aided largely by his faithful and estimable wife, who assisted him in ginning cotton and in other outdoor work. Their efforts have been rewarded, and they now have a comfortable fortune and a pleasant and commodious home, which they enjoy to the utmost. Although their prudence has gathered around them an excellent amount of worldly goods, they have been the friends of the poor and needy, and have always been interested in the upbuilding of schools, churches and all worthy enterprises, and have given liberally in their support. In 1870 he was married to Miss Laura E., daughter of William J. and E. J. Veazey, who were among the early settlers of this county. To Mr. and Mrs. Moore five children are living of seven born: Laura E., James V., Robert S., Mary A. and Jessie L. Mr. and Mrs. Moore are members of the Methodist Episcopal Church South, in which he is a steward. He has always taken an active interest in politics, and has affiliated with the democrat party for many years.

James W. Moore, who is not only a successful planter of the county, but a business man of considerable experience, was originally from the Palmetto state, his birth occurring in Lawrence county. His father, George M. Moore, was also a native of South Carolina, and was married in that state to Miss Elsie M. Crook, who owed her nativity to that state also. After the birth of their son, James W., they removed to Chattooga county, Ga., and resided there six or seven years, the father engaged in farming. From there he removed to Marshall county, Miss., settled near Red Banks, purchased land, and became one of the prosperous planters of the county. He died in 1873, at his home near Red Bank, in the sixty-third year of his life. Mrs. Moore is still living, and although seventy-four years of age, is still hale and hearty. Of the six children born to this union, of whom our subject was the eldest, only three sisters and James W. are now living: Mary, the widow of James Hardy; Sallie, wife of P. L. Gray, of Memphis, and Eliza. James W. Moore began life for himself by enlisting in the Confederate army, Seventeenth Mississippi infantry, under Colonel Featherstone, in the spring of 1862. He was in the army of Virginia, and was in the battles of Gettysburg, Fredericksburg, Chickamauga, Knoxville, and others. He served through it all without being wounded or captured, and surrendered with General Lee at Appomattox. He then returned to his home and resumed farming. He was married in 1869 to Miss Jane McFadyen, who bore him five children: George P., Thomas A., Mary P., Edna C. and Elsie C. Mr. Moore owns two thousand acres of land, eight hundred acres under cultivation, and is one of the prominent men of the county. He is also engaged in merchandising at Red Banks, under the firm name of Moore & Crook, and is doing well. The Moore family was among the first settlers of the county, and was highly respected. Mr. Moore was deputy sheriff for eight years, and at the present time is deputy United States marshal and has held the position two years.

Among the prominent business enterprises of a town and county that of merchandising takes a leading part. Mr. John R. Moore, who is a merchant of Booneville, has been a resident of Prentiss county, Miss., since 1847, and is thoroughly identified with the business interests of the same. He was originally from Bedford county, Tenn., born June 23, 1834, and his parents, Thomas and Nancy (Allen) Moore were natives of Wake county, N. C., and Warren county, Tenn., respectively. The father was born on March 17, 1804, and was the son of Randolph Moore, a native of Virginia and a soldier in the Revolutionary war. The latter came to Bedford county, Tenn., in 1830, bringing his family in a wagon, and there his death occurred three years later. He was the father of the following children: Elizabeth, Stansill, Nathan, John, James, Thomas, Zilpha, Rebecca, Celia and Piety, all of whom lived to be grown except Elizabeth, and all to a ripe old age except the father of our subject, the latter dying at the age of fifty-five years. Celia lived to be over eighty years of age, and died in Lincoln county, Tenn. The paternal grandmother of our subject, Elizabeth (Stansill) Moore, died in Bedford county, Tenn., in 1843 or 1844. Thomas Moore, father of subject, was reared in Bedford county, Tenn., and in 1847 came to Mississippi. His death occurred in 1859. In 1833, while a resident of Bedford county, Tenn., he married Miss Allen, and after coming to Mississippi he was engaged in agricultural pursuits until his death. He opened up a small farm three miles west of Rienzi. He and his wife, who was born in 1812, were members of the Methodist church. Her father, John Allen, was a native of Mecklenburg county, N. C., and an early settler of Tennessee. Mr. Allen's wife, Nancy (Carr) Allen, was born in the same county in North Carolina. Her father, Joseph Carr, was a native of Ireland, and was a soldier in the Revolutionary war. He and wife were residing at Mecklenburg Courthouse at the time of the signing of the declaration of independence. Mrs. Moore, mother of the subject of this sketch, was one of the following children: William, Joseph, Mary, Margaret, Nancy, John, James, Newton and Abigail. Of these James and Newton are still living—Newton at Shelbyville, Tenn., James in this county. To Thomas and Nancy (Allen) Moore were born seven children, three of whom are yet living: John R., Newton and George, all residents of Prentiss county. Those deceased were Violet, Margaret, Milton M. and Thomas. Milton was killed at Peach Tree creek, on July 22, 1863; Thomas died in Texas in 1873; Violet was the wife of George Anderson, and died in this county, leaving seven children, and Margaret, who was the wife of M. B. Armor, died at Rienzi, Miss., in 1881. John R. Moore, the eldest child living, was reared within six miles of his present place of residence, and since 1867 has been engaged in business in the county. He secured an ordinary education in the common schools of the county, and followed farming until the breaking out of the war. He enlisted in company A, Thirty-second Mississippi infantry as a private, and served as orderly sergeant, then first lieutenant, and held that position until the surrender. He was in the battles of Chickamauga, Springhill and Franklin. He surrendered at Greensboro, N. C., after which he returned to Prentiss county. Miss Sarah Anderson, who became his wife in 1856, was born in Bedford county, Tenn., in 1839, and died in 1868, leaving four children: Virginia Ann, now the wife of Thomas L. Bettersworth, who is the editor of the *Prentiss Plaindealer*, Booneville, Miss.; S. Thomas, William P. and John R., Jr. S. Thomas is in a bank at Union city, Tenn.; William P. is engaged in photography at Aberdeen, and John R., Jr., is in a railroad office at Artesia, Miss. Mr. Moore was married a second time in 1872, to Miss Sallie Marshall, a native of Virginia, and the daughter of Dr. R. T. Marshall, also of the Old Diminion. She was the eldest of six children, two besides herself now living: Robert and Hamilton. To Mr. Moore's second union were born two children: Elizabeth M. and Mary H. Mr. Moore was elected a member of the board of police of Tishomingo county in 1865, and was also appointed a member of the board of supervisors of Prentiss county, holding that position until relieved by Governor Ames. He was appointed to the latter position by Governor Alcorn upon the organization of Prentiss county. In politics he is strictly democratic. He is a member of the A. F. & A. M., Booneville lodge No. 305; was the first one to join that lodge, and was secretary for several years. He is a member of the mercantile firm of John R. Moore & Co., which firm does an annual business of about $18,000.

John R. Moore, planter, Holly Springs, Miss. The subject of this sketch needs no introduction to the people of Marshall county, for he is well and favorably known all over the same. His birth occurred in this county in April, 1840, and he is the eighth in order of birth of twelve children born to Austin E. and Elizabeth (Reeves) Moore, the father a native of North Carolina and the mother of South Carolina. The Moores are of Irish and the Reeves of Scotch descent. The parents were married in Tennessee, and there resided until 1837, when they moved to the wilds of Marshall county, Miss. They were among the earliest settlers, and the father bought his land from the government. His estate was near Holly Springs, and he followed farming on the same the remainder of his days, his death occurring there in 1874, at the age of seventy years. The mother died in 1878. Both were consistent members of the Methodist church. Of the large family of children born to this union there are only six now living, John R. being the only son surviving. The daughters are: Mary, wife of W. T. Cooper; Zenobia; Nannie, wife of James McAlexander; Elizabeth, wife of F. E. Waller; and Donia, wife of Dr. G. E. Kelsey. John R. Moore and two brothers enlisted in the Confederate army, and one of the brothers was killed at the battle of Chickamauga. The other died in the evacuation of Atlanta, John R. alone surviving the bloody struggle. He was wounded by a minie-ball in the right side at Hernando, Miss., and was so disabled from his wound that he was unfit for active service from that time on. He remained in the army until the close and surrendered at Memphis. Returning home he resumed his former occupation, farming, and was married in 1882 to Miss Sophia H. Lord, daughter of William and Ellen D. (Smith) Lord. The result of this union was one son, Warren, who died when nearly two years old. Mr. Moore is the owner of one thousand one hundred acres of land, has four hundred acres under cultivation, and has a nice frame residence situated four miles from Holly Springs. He is a practical farmer, is advanced and progressive in his ideas, and is one of the county's thoroughgoing citizens. Mrs. Moore is a member of the Methodist church. Both she and her husband obtained their education in the common schools of the county. They are held in high estimation by all who know them.

Joseph F. Moore, M. D., of Estabutchie, Miss., was born in Fairfield district, S. C. December 16, 1829. His parents were William F. and Lydia A. (Stanton) Moore, both also natives of Fairfield district, S. C., where they were reared and married and lived until they moved to Sumter county, Ala., where the father died in 1881 and the mother in 1883. Of their six children Doctor Moore was the eldest except one. He moved to Alabama with his parents when quite young, and was educated at Oxford, Ala., and Marion, Miss. Early in the spring of 1853 he began to read medicine under the direction of W. C. Silliman and John Gambrell, of what was then Payneville, Ala. In the winter of 1853–4 he attended medical lectures at the Tulane university of New Orleans, La. After availing himself of this course of lectures, he went to Enterprise, Miss., and entered the office of Dr. J. L. George. Under his instructions he read and practiced medicine until the winter of 1854–5, when he took his second course of lectures at the University of Louisiana, graduating with the degree of M. D. March 15, 1855. Returning to Enterprise, he began the practice of medicine, entering upon a partnership with his old preceptor, Dr. J. L. George, which continued until the beginning of the war, in 1861. In the years 1856 and 1857–8 he attended two courses of lectures as a post-graduate in the Tulane university of Louisiana. Dr. Moore then gave up his practice and accepted a position as surgeon in the Eighth Mississippi regiment, and received his commission as such from Gov. John J. Pettus, August 7, 1861. When the regiment was transferred to the service of the Confederate States, he was commissioned by Secretary Judah T. Benjamin as surgeon of the Confederate States army, October 11, 1861, after an examination by the army medical board, and as such served during the remainder of the war, acting as chief inspector of recruits for the state of Mississippi, with headquarters at Enterprise, also having charge of the hospitals there at the same time. During this period he served as surgeon at Pensacola, Fla., for one year, and was in charge of the hospitals at that place. During the last year of the war he was surgeon of General Lowering's division of General Johnston's army in northern Georgia. He was paroled at Meridian, Miss., May 13, 1865, and immediately returned to Enterprise, Miss., and resumed the practice of his profession. In 1882 he was one of five commissioners, and being the only physician of the board he was given charge of the erection of the insane asylum at Meridian, Miss., Col. H. M. Street directing its financial department, everything connected with its style of construction left practically to his dictation. Early in 1889 he removed to Estabutchie, Miss., where he has since lived. Under his supervision the Estabutchie Lumber Manufacturing company was chartered and organized in 1889, and he still retains an interest in it. Dr. Moore was married at Shubuta, Miss., in 1859, to Matilda D., daughter of Gen. A. Carr, of Shubuta, Miss., who died in 1880, having borne him five children:

Pinkie, Terrie L., Joseph F., Bessie F. and James A. In 1884 the doctor married for his second wife Kate Virginia, daughter of William Griffin, of Moss Point, Miss. They have no children. The doctor is a member of the State Medical association and of Lauderdale Medical association, and he also is a Mason. He is a man of more than ordinary enterprise, and during his whole life has been prominently connected with many of the most important interests of the communities in which he has lived. At Estabutchie he ranks among the leading business men, and there are few who have done more than he in the assistance of the public welfare.

Lod Moore was born in Alabama in July, 1821. Robert Moore, his father, was born in Kentucky in 1790, and moved to Tennessee with his parents in 1805, and his wife, Ladocia Hamilton, was born in Tennessee in 1800. His parents were married in Tennessee in 1816, and had nine children, of whom our subject is the third in order of birth. His father removed from Tennessee to Greene county, Ala., in 1819, and located where Greensboro now stands, and was there engaged in a mercantile business, with Mr. Peck as a partner, and was one of the early settlers in that part of the country. In 1824 he moved to Marengo county, of the same state. He followed planting for a livelihood, and in 1831 located in the rich portion of Sumter county, Ala. In 1834 he moved to Kemper county, Miss., where he died in 1836. After the death of his father our subject returned to Alabama with his mother, and grew to manhood there. His mother married, for her second husband, Robert Allison, of North Carolina, then resident in Alabama, by whom she had one child. His father served under General Jackson in the War of 1812, and took part in that useless battle—New Orleans. In 1842 Lod Moore married Elizabeth Thompson, a daughter of Daniel and Sarah Thompson, of Georgia. Lod Moore is a prominent planter, who has a family of twelve children. His daughters Sarah, Fannie, Margaret, Ellen, Donna and Kate were educated at Whitworth college, Mississippi. Mr. Moore and his family, as were his parents before him, are members of the Methodist Episcopal church. Mr. Moore is connected with the Masonic fraternity. He is the owner of two thousand acres of land, about one-fourth of which is improved and under cultivation, and of three store buildings in Forest, where he is interested in the mercantile establishment of the local Farmers' Alliance. In 1863 Mr. Moore enlisted in the state militia, under Capt. J. C. Harper, and served until the close of the war, when he returned home, and engaged energetically in planting and business operations. Although obliged to work against many disadvantages and discouragements, he has met with satisfactory success, and ranks among the well-to-do planters and business men of this county.

The subject of this sketch, Dr. L. R. Moore, was born in Sumter county, Ala., in 1833. He was one of a family of thirteen children who sprang from the union of his parents and lived to smooth the declining years of the old couple. His father was Alfred Moore and his mother Catherine (Hamilton) Moore, who were natives of Tennessee and Kentucky respectively. Alfred Moore was born in 1792, and was a veteran of the War of 1812. He was a planter by occupation, at which he proved himself very successful. Dr. Moore came to Scott county, Miss., when he was thirteen years of age and has continued to live here the most of the time ever since. In 1862 he obeyed the patriotic impulses of his heart and enlisted in the army, but his will being stronger than his body, he was placed in hospital service instead of active duty in the field. This opened up an opportunity for him to study medicine, which he at once embraced, and after the war continued his studies by attending a series of lectures at the University of Louisiana, New Orleans. He located in Morton in the year 1866, where he has ever since plied his profession with untiring zeal. The Doctor first took unto himself a wife in the person of Miss Virginia Simms, who presented him with two children, all of whom died during the war. Later he again married, this time to a Miss Patti Pettus. Dr. Moore is a member of the Masonic fraternity. He is also an active member of the Methodist Episcopal Church South, of which he is an acknowledged leader, having been steward in the church for twenty-two years.

Col. O. J. Moore, one among the pioneer settlers of Montgomery county, was originally from the Old Dominion, born in Mecklenburg county in April, 1812, and his father, Capt. Warren Moore, was also a native of that state. The elder Moore was a man of fair education and commanded a company in the War of 1812. He contracted disease in the army and died from the effects. He married Miss Elizabeth Worthington, a native also of Mecklenburg county, Va., and a descendant of an old and prominent family of that state. Our subject's paternal grandfather was an Englishman. Colonel Moore was one of four sons and one daughter born to the above mentioned union who grew to mature years, and he is the only one now living. After the age of nine years he was reared by his guardian and received a fair business education at a private school. After arriving at mature years Mr. Moore moved to Greenville county, Va., where he bought an interest in a tannery and followed this business for about four years. He was married in Virginia in 1834 to Miss Rebecca N. Gee, daughter of Benjamin Gee, of a prominent Virginia family. After his marriage Colonel Moore located in Brunswick county, Va., and engaged in farming, which he carried on for about ten years. In 1844 he moved to Mississippi and located in what is now Montgomery county, about one mile from the present town of Winona. In 1848 he bought the place where he now resides, which was then but partially improved, and he now has a fine plantation. On the building of the Illinois Central railroad, in 1860, Colonel Moore laid out the town of Winona, which was incorporated about four or five years later and now is the county seat of Montgomery county, and a town of about two thousand inhabitants. The Colonel has been an active planter all his life and is one of the successful ones of this county. He has always espoused the principles of the democratic party and has held several local positions of honor and trust. He was a member of the old Virginia cavalry, commanded a company, and was afterward made colonel of a regiment. After coming to Mississippi he was made colonel of the Mississippi militia, which was organized during the war for home protection. He served on the old board of police jury, was a member of the town board and was treasurer of same for a number of terms. Colonel Moore's residence, which once stood isolated and alone, is now surrounded on every side, the town gradually growing up around it. He is a prominent member of the Methodist church and has been an officer in the same since 1834, serving as recorder and steward for a number of years. He was a delegate to the Memphis general conference in 1870 and also to the Louisville conference, in 1874, and is still active and foremost in church matters. He is a Knight Templar in the Masonic fraternity, which organization he joined in 1856, and he has represented his lodge in the grand lodge of Mississippi. Mr. and Mrs. Moore have reared five children: Benjamin died in the fall of 1860, just after reaching his twenty-first year; Dr. E. D. graduated in medicine and practiced his profession for a few years; his death occurred in 1889 in Norfolk, Va.; L. N. is a prominent merchant of Winona, Ella A. is the wife of J. T. Lay, of Winona, and Laura J. is the widow of Dr. D. B. Turner. The last named daughter resides with her parents. She is the mother of four children, one of her daughters being the wife of A. A. Green, of Jackson, Miss. One of her sons is a student of medicine at New Orleans and another son is attending the Memphis Commercial college. The youngest child, a miss of fourteen, is at home.

Capt. R. J. Moore, farmer, Hazel Dell, Miss. In the early settlement of Mississippi, and among the families who were closely identified with its material affairs and associated with its progress and development, were the Moores. The respected representative of this family is found in the subject of this sketch, who was born in Itawamba county, Miss., on the 16th of March, 1837, and who was the fourth in order of birth of seven children born to Stephen R. and Lucy (McDougal) Moore, both natives of the Old North state. The paternal grandfather was of Irish descent, and lived to be ninety years of age. He removed to Alabama at an early date, thence to Mississippi in 1838, and settled in Tishomingo county, where he died in 1860. The maternal grandparents also moved from North Carolina to Alabama at an early date. The parents of Captain Moore were reared in Alabama, and were married in Lauderdale county of that state. There they resided for several years, and then in 1836 moved to Itawamba county, Miss., bought land, and were among the first settlers. The father was a plain, practical farmer and never aspired to any official positions. He removed from Itawamba to Tishomingo county in 1844, and resided there until the breaking out of the war. He was then taken from his home by the Union troops, placed in prison at Alton, Ill., and there his death occurred in 1863, four months after being imprisoned. His wife had died in 1845. Their family consisted of five sons and two daughters: Sarah, wife of G. T. Millican; Horatio R., resides at Huntland, Tenn.; John J., resides at Iuka, Miss.; Capt. R. J.; Rebecca, wife of William Young, of Dallas, Texas; Hugh B., makes his home at Marietta, Miss.; and James K., resides at Huntland, Tenn. All the sons enlisted in the Confederate army in 1861, went direct to the front and were in all the engagements of their command. Capt. R. J. Moore was elected second lieutenant of his company at its organization, and in 1863 was promoted to the rank of captain, and filled that position ably and well until peace was declared. He was at the battle of Fort Donelson, Baker's creek, siege of Petersburg, and was wounded and captured at the last named engagement. He was taken to Johnson's island prison, retained there about three months, and was captured again at Fort Donelson. He was placed in the same prison and remained there six months, nine months in all at Johnson's island, being there at the final surrender. He was paroled in June, 1865, and then returned to his home in Tishomingo county, Miss., where he engaged in farming. He was married in 1864 to Miss Nancy S. Gaines, daughter of John S. and Eliza (Patton) Gaines, who came from Alabama to Mississippi in 1838, and were among the early settlers of the country. Mr. and Mrs. Gaines were the parents of thirteen children, five of whom are now living, Mrs. Moore being third in order of birth of the children. Mr. Gaines was a successful farmer and had accumulated considerable property before the war, being the owner of a large number of slaves. He died in Prentiss county, Miss., in 1879, at the age of sixty-five years. Captain Moore was elected county surveyor in 1888, and is the present incumbent of that position. He was a candidate for representative in 1878, but was defeated. He has made farming and milling his chief occupations during life, and has been quite successful in his chosen callings. Socially he is a member of the Masonic fraternity and the Knights of Honor organizations. He is public-spirited and enterprising, and extends a liberal hand to all laudable public enterprises. He and Mrs. Moore are members of the Christian church. To their marriage were born two children: Minnie, and Eddie (deceased).

Nelson Moore. The gentleman whose name heads this sketch is one of the oldest and most highly esteemed residents of Lauderdale county, Miss., for he was born in Darlington district of the Palmetto state in the month of January, 1808, the second in a family of nine children born to John and Betsey (King) Moore, both natives of North Carolina and of Revolutionary descent. They afterward became residents of South Carolina, where the father followed the calling of a farmer and for some time filled the position of justice of the peace. He and his wife were members of the Methodist Episcopal church at the time of their deaths. In 1838 Nelson Moore removed from South Carolina to Mississippi and located in Lauderdale county, where he is now living, before the Indians had gone from the country. Prior to leaving his native state he was married to Miss Icie Delt, by whom he became the father of four sons and three daughters: James, who died in Virginia in 1862 while in the Confederate service; Elias, who died in 1861; Mary, wife of John R. Cocke; Sarah, wife of William A. Rogers; John B., Thomas J., and Eliza, wife of William A. Rogers. Mr. Moore was among the very earliest settlers of this county and has been a resident of the county longer than any man now residing in it. His long residence here and his many noble qualities of mind and heart, have made him well and favorably known, and he is regarded by all as a high-minded old gentleman and as a useful, upright and worthy citizen. He has made farming his exclusive business through life, and is now the owner of one thousand five hundred acres of land, of which about four hundred acres are under cultivation and well improved. He is plain, practical and unassuming, and prior to the war was an extensive slaveowner. His wife, who died at her home in Lauderdale county in 1851, was a consistent member of the Methodist Episcopal church. Thomas J. Moore, their son, was educated in the common schools of the country and also attended Summerville college, of Noxubee county, Miss., for about three years. In 1863 he dropped his books and enlisted in company C, of the Second Mississippi cavalry, in Capt. William A. Roger's company, under General Forrest, and was with him throughout the various raids, and also with Hood in his Tennessee campaign, taking part in the battle of Franklin. He was wounded at Pulaski on the 25th of December, 1864, being shot through the left arm, after which he returned home and did not again enter the service. He was married in 1869 to Miss Sudie Twiley, a daughter of George Twiley, of Lauderdale county, and to their union three sons and two daughters have been born: Zadie (deceased), Jeffie B., George N., Heustis and an infant not named. Thomas J. Moore resides on his father's plantation, and looks after the interest of the place, as his father is quite feeble. He and his worthy wife are highly esteemed in the community in which they reside and she is a member of the Methodist Episcopal church.

William Walton Moore, M. D., one of Pike county's most eminent physicians, was born in Amite county, Miss., August 18, 1839, being the eldest of two sons and four daughters born to his parents, Thomas L. and Elizabeth (Swearingen) Moore, worthy and honored residents of Amite county. Thomas L. Moore was a prominent and extensive planter, and was born on the plantation on which he spent his life and died, his demise occurring in December, 1868. Although he was of a quiet, retiring and modest disposition, he was well known as one of the county's most benevolent and public-spirited citizens, and the good which he did in various unobtrusive ways will long be felt by those who survive him. His father, Samuel Moore, was the first of the family to settle in the county, having immigrated to this region from South Carolina about the year 1800. He, as well as his descendants, was prominently identified with the history and development of Amite county, and the prosperity which the rising generation are now enjoying was won by the unswerving energy and indomitable perseverance of such sturdy pioneers as Mr. Moore. William Walton Moore spent his boyhood days upon his father's plantation and in acquiring the foundation of his education in the neighboring schools and under his mother's care and guidance. By the time he attained his eighteenth year his knowledge of books well fitted him for entrance at a higher institution of learning, and he accordingly entered Mississippi college, at Clinton, where he pursued his studies with diligence for two years. Having acquired a taste for the study of medicine, he decided to make that his life calling, and in 1859 began the study of that science in the Eclectic Medical college at Cincinnati, Ohio, and was graduated as an M. D. in 1861. Immediately following this he attended one course of lectures, but before he could enter upon the practice of his profession to any great extent the coming clash of arms caused him to cast aside personal considerations to take up arms in defense of his home and section. In the summer of 1861 he enlisted as a member of company C, Seventh regiment of Mississippi volunteers, and was attached to the Army of Tennessee. He participated in all the engagements in which his command was engaged, including the battles of Shiloh, Chickamauga, Missionary Ridge, Fort Craige, Murfreesboro, Franklin and others, and at all times he bore himself in a manner becoming a soldier and gentleman. He officiated most of the time as surgeon and assistant surgeon, and at the battle of Murfreesboro he was left in charge of the wounded, and remained inside of the Federal lines for several months in the discharge of his duties. He afterward rejoined his regiment and surrendered with his command at Jonesboro, N. C., and after his return home the following fall entered the New Orleans school of medicine, and from this institution graduated in the spring of 1866. In April of that year he commenced practicing his profession at Summit, and here has since made his home, his services in a professional way being in great demand throughout the section in which he resides. In addition to this calling he is also interested in agriculture, and is the owner of plantations in Pike and Amite counties, particular attention being devoted to the raising of fine stock, in which he has wielded a wide influence through the county, the majority of plantations being well supplied with fine horses and cattle. He was the originator of the South Mississippi Fair association of Summit, of which he has been president since its organization. He also assisted is organizing, and is one of the stockholders as well as president of, the Summit cottonmills, which position was tendered him in recognition of his indefatigable efforts in securing the establishment of the industry at the town of Summit. He is a stockholder in the bank of Summit, and has always taken special interest in the upbuilding of the school system of the town, and for a number of years was a member of the board of education. To his efforts the splendid schools of Summit are largely due, and he always indorses every word and act that leads to progression and civilization, and is a man of very superior mental endowments, which have been strengthened and enriched by the highest culture. He is gentlemanly and courteous, and is very popular with all, not only professionally but socially, and may be said to be in a large measure a self-made man. He is a member of lodge No. 93 of the A. F. & A. M., in which order he has attained the chapter; and he also belongs to Summit lodge of the I. O. O. F., Summit lodge of the Knights of Pythias, and is a member of the Knights of Honor. In September, 1865, he was married to Miss Ary A. Felder, a native of Amite county, Miss., and daughter of James W. Felder, and granddaughter of Rev. Charles Felder, one of the pioneer Baptist ministers of this section, and a prominent man in his day. Mrs. Moore is an honored member of the Baptist church of Summit, and is active in woman's work. The Doctor is a leading democrat of his section, and has been a delegate to both state and county conventions, and chairman of the democratic executive committee of Pike county.

Capt. William Walker Moore, planter and merchant, was born in Madison, Miss., January 12, 1841. His parents were James J. and Elizabeth (Fleming) Moore. His father was born in Haywood county, N. C., in 1808. His mother was a native of York district, S. C. His paternal grandfather, Dr. William Moore, was of Scotch descent. The Flemings came from the north of Ireland, and on the maternal side of the latter family he traces his descent to Pennsylvania stock and to the Carolinas. His granduncles participated in the Revolutionary war, one of them, William, dying after the war from wounds received in battle. Gen. Francis Marion, being a cousin of the Moores of that generation, it is not improbable that some of them were of his cavalry force. Walker Fleming, uncle of our subject, served in the War of 1812, and family history places him at Fort Moultrie at the time of the attack on Charleston. James J. Moore, Capt. Walker Moore's father, was left an orphan by the early death of his father, and at an early age went forth to battle with the world, almost entirely untrained except to physical toil. Going to South Carolina he married there in 1830. In 1835 he removed to Madison county, where he remained until his death, in 1844, at the age of thirty-six. During his residence there, by industry and economical management, he obtained a sufficiency for the support and education of the large family. Not long after his removal to Mississippi he and his wife, although they had long been connected with the Presbyterian church of the old school, became members of the Cumberland Presbyterian organization then springing up in that part of the country, and in the faith of this church they lived and died. The mother survived to see the youngest of the children grown and married and passed away in 1878. The children in order of their birth are: Jane, Eliza, Mary Fleming, John Leander, Gustavus Adolphus, Roxana, William Walker, Catherine F. and Josie M. Of these all the males served in the late war until their military service was terminated by death or discharge. John Leander was in Texas when the war began and served with the Texan troops during its entire period. Gustavus Adolphus enlisted in company M, of Wirt Adams' regiment of cavalry, in 1862, and was one of the sergeants of that company. He contracted measles in the camp in northern Mississippi and partially recovered, but died of a relapse brought on by exposure. Capt. William Walker Moore attended the country schools near his home in his boyhood and then spent one and one-half years at Bethel college, Tennessee, and entered the sophomore class of the University of Mississippi in 1859. In 1861, while a member of the junior class, he joined a company of cavalry which had been organized by Captain, afterward General, John Davis, nephew of President Davis, which was nominally in the Tenth Mississippi regiment, although it was really the second regiment in order of organization. He also soon fell a victim to measles, became unfit for duty and was finally discharged in 1861. A part of the time he spent in the marine hospital near Pensacola. Returning home, his health was so far recruited as to enable him to assist in raising a company in answer to a call from the governor for sixty-day troops, and he was in the field again within three months from the time of his discharge. Of this company he was chosen orderly sergeant. Its captain was R. B. Campbell, a brother of Judge Campbell, of the supreme court and a veteran in the Mexican war. The company was of Bartlett's regiment and Alcorn's brigade. Notwithstanding the shortness of the campaign upon which it entered scarcely a man in the company escaped sickness. Returning home after being mustered out of service, Captain Moore assisted in enlisting men for a cavalry company which was organized by the election of W. R. Luckett as its captain, Addison Harvey as first lieutenant, William Walker Moore as second lieutenant, and John Smith, Jr., as third lieutenant. They received marching orders about June, 1862, to join Wirt Adams' regiment in northern Mississippi. Mr. Moore served in this company and this regiment until the close of the war. He became first lieutenant of the company, when Lieutenant, afterward Captain, Harvey was detached, and became its captain when Captain Luckett was killed. He served through the various skirmishes and battles in which the company participated from the battle of Boonville, July, 1862, to the battle of Sipsey, April

3, 1865, under command at different times of Generals Chalmers, Crosby, Bill Jackson, Armstrong, Adams and Forrest. There were many instances in Captain Moore's military career which would make interesting reading, did space permit their narration in these pages. They show that he was an intrepid soldier and that he possessed many of the qualities of a military leader. He was in command of the outposts under General Gregg at the battle of Raymond, May, 1863, when the Confederates surrendered to superior numbers only after a severe fight. July 4, 1864, he was placed for a time in command of Captain Yerger's company, which was in front of the charge which routed Elliott's brigade. After the surrender of Vicksburg, the Captain placed himself in command of a party of retreating scouts, who were being hard pressed by the Union cavalry, and saved the day for the Confederate cause. During the following November, while on a furlough, he hastily got together a small body of volunteers and did gallant service, though some may think it reckless, in defense of the Mississippi Central railroad bridge, near Canton, which was finally saved by Captain Yerger's arrival with two companies after Captain Moore and his devoted followers had been worsted by overwhelming numbers. The Captain was paroled at Gainesville, Ala., May 10, 1865. He married Miss Ernestine Watson, of Jefferson county, Miss., September 7, 1865. His wife's parents were Louis C. Watson and Martha Blanton, both natives of Jefferson county, Miss. The children by this marriage were: Anna, Gustavas Adolphus, Lewis C. Watson, Blanton Fleming, and James, Jr. He lived in Jefferson county until 1875, engaged in agriculture, has since lived in Issaquena and Sharkey counties, where he has planting interests, and in Vicksburg, but his home at present is in Port Gibson, Miss. He married his second wife, Miss Julia Rowan, whose parents were Thomas Rowan and Miss Clara Green, of Jefferson county, Miss. The children of the last marriage are: Clara C., Eliza, William Walker (deceased), Lilly, Kate and Helen Ross. In religion Mr. Moore is an Episcopalian, and he has a license from the bishop as lay reader, in which capacity he has acted since 1880. His wife is a Presbyterian. He served part of a term as magistrate for the people of Jefferson county, Miss., an office which he resigned on his removal to another locality. He ran for the legislature in Sharkey county, and was defeated. He was elected and served a term as a member of the board of levee commissioners from Sharkey, and was elected a member of the town council at Port Gibson and resigned on account of conflict of official duties with private affairs. He has had invitations at every election since becoming a citizen of Claiborne county to become a candidate for a member either of the house of representatives or the senate of the state legislature, but has declined. He is a member of no secret society.

Prof. Waldo W. Moore, president and principal of the Fairview college, located at Binnsville, Miss., is one of the most prominent educators of the state. The school which he now controls was opened in 1887, and has continued with an increased attendance each year. The faculty is composed of able and experienced teachers, each of whom is fully equal to the demands of his position. Binnsville is to be congratulated upon having a school so well equipped, as all well-ordered educational institutions must elevate the tone of the community. Professor Moore was born in Sumter county, Ala., February 26, 1860, and is a son of Capt. A. M. and Martha (Elliott) Moore. His father was born in Marengo county, Ala., August 6, 1830, and is a son of Robert and Ladocia (Hamilton) Moore, natives of Tennessee and North Carolina respectively. The paternal grandparents removed from Tennessee to Mississippi in 1816. Captain Moore was married in Sumter county, Ala., May 9, 1851, and four children were born of the union: Margaret E., now Mrs. McCaskill; Ladocia, who died in August, 1863; Rev. Marcus H., a minister of the Methodist Episcopal Church South; and Waldo W. The mother of these children was born in Greene county, Ala., in January,

1831, and was a daughter of Andrew and Anna (Knox) Elliott, natives of Tennessee. She died January 8, 1862. Captain Moore was married again in September, 1865, to Mary McCaskill, a daughter of Allen McCaskill, of South Carolina. She was born in South Carolina, in March, 1837. The result of this marriage was six children: Fannie C., Kate, Etta, Hans H., Andrew M. (who died in May, 1875) and Carrie. Mrs. Moore died January 25, 1891. In 1861 Captain Moore enlisted in company I, Fortieth Alabama volunteer infantry, of which he was elected captain. In 1864 he was taken prisoner in Georgia, and was sent to Johnson's island, Ohio. The most noted engagements in which he took part are Vicksburg, Atlanta and Lookout Mountain. He resigned in 1865. In January, 1867, he came to Kemper county, and located three miles south of Binnsville, where he followed farming for thirteen years. In 1881 he embarked in the mercantile trade, opening a store in Scooba. The same year he was elected a member of the house of representatives of Mississippi and filled the office very acceptably one term. He and his wife are members of the Methodist Episcopal Church South, as was also the mother of Professor Moore. The Captain was at one time a member of the Masonic order. Professor Moore was educated at the Southern university at Greensboro, Ala., and was graduated June 24, 1885. His first engagement was with the Methodist Episcopal Church South, in Lawrence county, Ala., where he remained until the opening of the school which he so ably conducts. He was married January 21, 1886, to Miss Hattie C. Jagers, a daughter of A. and Cornelia (Le Gette) Jagers. Her mother was a native of South Carolina, and removed to Kemper county about 1851. Her father was born in Mississippi. Professor Moore and his wife are members of the Methodist Episcopal Church South. He is democratic in his political opinions, and stanchly supports all issues of the party.

Benjamin H. Morehead is a successful merchant and planter at Ingleside, and is one of the best known, most popular and successful citizens of which Claiborne county, Miss., can boast. His birth occurred here in the month of July, 1841, to Bushrod W. Morehead, a native of Kentucky, in which state he resided until grown, receiving there his literary education. He then entered the Philadelphia (Pennsylvania) Medical college, and after graduating came to Mississippi to practice his profession, settling at Grand Gulf. After remaining there but a short time he came to Port Gibson, and followed his profession until his death in 1843, having obtained an eminent position as a practitioner and a very large practice among the leading citizens of this section. He was married to Miss Mary Ann Hughes, who was born and reared in Claiborne county, Miss., her father being Benjamin Hughes, a native of Kentucky, who came to Mississippi in his early manhood. One of his sons, Col. Henry Hughes, wrote a very creditable book on sociology, and during the war was first a private in the Claiborne guards, was afterward made captain of the same and was promoted to the rank of colonel of the Twelfth Mississippi regiment, serving until the reorganization of the regiment, and dying in 1862 of inflammatory rheumatism, which was the result of exposure. Mary Ann (Hughes) Morehead was the eldest of four children, all of whom lived to be grown and were educated in Claiborne county, with the exception of Mrs. Morehead, who was an attendant of the female seminary kept by Mrs. Tevis, at Shelbyville, Ky. After graduating and returning to her home in Mississippi she was married to Mr. Morehead, by whom she became the mother of three children: Julia Tevis (McAlpine), who resides on a plantation near Ingleside; Benjamin H. and a child that died in infancy. After the death of Mr. Morehead his widow married R. W. Harper, M. D., a native of Maryland, but at the time of his marriage a practicing physician of Port Gibson, which place continued to be his home until his death in April, 1867. This union resulted in the birth of one son,

Henry H., who is now an eminent lawyer of Barnum, Tex. He graduated from the law department of the University of Texas, since which time he has been in the active practice of his profession. The mother of these children remained a widow until her death, which occurred in the fall of 1876, she being an earnest member of the Presbyterian church and also of the benevolent aid society at the time of her death, which occurred at the home of her daughter, Mrs. McAlpine, near Ingleside. Benjamin H. Morehead attained his majority in the county of his birth, and with the exception of the time spent in the service of the Confederacy and when at school, has always resided here. He had just entered the senior class of the Oakland college when the war broke out and he immediately dropped his books, and in May, 1861, enlisted in the Claiborne guards, with which he served until after the seven days' fight around Richmond. He was wounded at Frazier's farm on Monday evening, June 30, 1862, his right arm being broken by a minie-ball. He then remained at home on furlough until he could again use his arm, when he became a member of the Fourth Mississippi regiment, of which he was made adjutant, serving in this capacity until the close of the war. He was in the skirmishes around Port Gibson and the engagement at Harrisburg, this being the principal battle in which he participated. He was active and faithful and did honorable service for the Confederacy, and won an excellent reputation for courage and fortitude. He was paroled at Jackson, Miss., in 1865, and returned home to take up the duties of planting and merchandising, and although he commenced at the bottom of the ladder, he has made steady progress toward the top and is now in easy circumstances financially. After following merchandising in Grand Gulf for three years he for one year worked with Mr. McAlpine. The following year he was married to Miss Mary T. Session, a native of Claiborne county, born and reared where she now lives, and after their marriage they settled on a plantation belonging to the latter, and about the time of the construction of the Louisville, New Orleans & Texas railroad Mr. Morehead opened a store at what is now called Ingelside, where he has since been doing a good business, the place receiving its name from the plantation of which he is the owner. Mrs. Morehead was educated at home by a private tutor, but finished her education in New Orleans. She is a daughter of Richard W. Sessions, a native of Adams county, Miss., and an early planter of that county. To Mr. and Mrs. Morehead seven children have been born, whose names are as follows: Robert H., who was educated at Chamberlain & Hunt's academy, at Port Gibson, is the depot agent at Ingleside; Richard S., who assists his father in the store, received his education in the same institution as his brother; Benjamin H., Howard S., Maria, William H. and Julia, all of whom are attendants at the above named academy. Mr. Morehead is a member of the Knights of Honor and Knights of Pythias at Port Gibson, is a democrat in politics and has been a member of the board of supervisors of the county, and in this capacity, as well as in every-day affairs of life, he is well liked and very popular. Mrs. Morehead is a member of the Presbyterian church and is a worthy and estimable lady.

John D. Morgan, of the well-known firm of Morgan, Robertson & Co., wholesale and retail grocers of Columbus, Miss., was born in the town in which he is now doing business in December, 1841, a son of John M. and C. L. (Prowell) Morgan, natives of South Carolina. The father came to Lowndes county, Miss., in 1835, his wife's arrival in this state preceding his by three years, and here they met and married. He was born in 1808, and consequently upon his arrival in this state he was about twenty-seven years of age. He first made his way hither on horseback in 1833, in order to view the country and buy land, and here purchased a tract in 1833, about seven miles west of Columbus, which was totally unimproved. He moved his effects hither in 1835, crossing the Tombigbee river on what

Eng'd by H.B. Hall's Sons, New York.

Very Truly Yours
J. M. C. Martin

The Goodspeed Pub. Co. Chicago.

was know as "Cold Friday," the coldest day that was ever known in the history of this country. He immediately located on and began improving his plantation, and in a little log cabin, which he erected, he lived in until 1846, when he moved to the house in which John D. Morgan is now residing, near Columbus, on the east side of the river. Here he died in 1877, his widow still surviving him, being now in her eighty-fourth year, and probably the oldest resident of the county. They were married in 1837, and their union resulted in the birth of three children, two of whom are living: Mrs. E. M. Moore and John D. The Morgan family originally came from Virginia, but in an early day became residents of South Carolina. The paternal grandfather and grandmother died in Mississippi and South Carolina respectively, the maternal grandmother, Mrs. Prowell, dying in the former state. The maternal grandfather was a soldier in the War of 1812. John D. Morgan was reared and educated in Columbus, but in 1861 left home and friends to take up arms in defense of the Confederate cause, becoming a member of the Tombigbee rangers. After serving until 1862 he received a discharge on account of disability, and went to his farm in Texas to recuperate. After some time he enlisted with General Maxy's command, with whom he served until the close of the war, surrendering in June, 1865, at Hempstead, Tex. He continued to make his home in Texas until 1869, after which he returned to Columbus, Miss., and in 1870 engaged in the mercantile business in the building now occupied by Walker & Donoghue, with whom he remained until 1884, when he built the large three-story brick building, 120x87½ feet, where he is now doing a wholesale and retail business. Mr. Morgan has large landed interests in Texas, besides some excellent property which he owns in Lowndes county, and in the city of Columbus. He is a practical and experienced man of business, is a shrewd financier, but his property has not been acquired at the expense of others, or by wronging a soul. He was married in 1866 to Miss Mary C. Couch, a native of Alabama, by whom he has three children: Judson A., John M. and Eugenia R. Mrs. Morgan and her children are members of the Baptist church.

John H. Morgan, clerk of Benton county, Miss., was born in Shelby county, Tenn., and there passed his boyhood and youth. On account of the breaking out of the war his early educational advantages were not of the best, but being a man of thought and observation he has made up for this to a great extent. He located in Tippah county, Miss., in 1868, and was residing where he now lives when the county of Benton was formed off Tippah and Marshall counties. He erected the first residence in Ashland, and was appointed a member of the board of aldermen of the town at the time of its organization. In 1871 he was appointed chancery clerk, a position held for one year, and then held the position of deputy chancery clerk under Allen Talbot and William Heedspeth. He then returned to Germantown, Shelby county, Tenn., in 1873, and was there married to Miss Mary Rogers, daughter of Jerry Rogers, of that place. The fruits of this union have been four interesting children. In 1877 Mr. Morgan was elected mayor of the town and was its first postmaster. He held the former position until 1883, when he was elected county clerk, and has held that office since. He discharges the duties of this office in a very efficient manner, and has fully testified to the wisdom of the people's choice. Mr. Morgan is a son of Dr. William N. and Mary (Welburn) Morgan, natives of Virginia and Alabama, respectively. Dr. Morgan graduated in medicine in Philadelphia, and was extensively known as a successful physician and surgeon. He died in 1867, at the age of fifty-three years. He had a brother, Rev. J. H. Morgan, who was a famous minister in the Cumberland Presbyterian church, and who ministered to the spiritual wants of his fellowman during almost his entire life.

J. H. Morris is the president and general manager of the Morris Ice company, of Jackson, Miss., and in discharging the duties of this position he has shown himself to be thoroughly competent and reliable. He was born in the city in which he now resides in 1846, the second of five children born to William and Martha (Jarvis) Morris, the former a native of New York and the latter of Maryland. William Morris came to Mississippi about 1837 and settled at Clinton, as a jeweler, but removed to Jackson in a short time and started a bank, which was the first and only one in the city until his death in 1854. Mrs. Morris survived him until 1866, when her death occurred. J. H. Morris was a resident of Jackson until the opening of the war, and there received a thorough and practical education. In 1861 he enlisted in the Burt rifles of the Eighteenth Mississippi regiment, army of northern Virginia, and was with this command until 1863, participating in all the engagements until the battle of Seven Pines. He was then discharged from the service on account of being under age and returned to Jackson, but was soon after appointed to the rank of lieutenant by General Johnston, later to first lieutenant, and finally brevet captain, and commanded his company for some time. He surrendered at Greenville, Ala., in 1865. His brother, William P., was born in 1844 and entered the Confederate army in 1862, and served until the close, mainly in the medical department. He was in the siege of Port Hudson when captured, was exchanged at the close of the war, and died in 1865, soon after his return home. Upon his return to Jackson, J. H. Morris became assistant agent of the Illinois Central railroad at that place, and retained this position until 1872, when he began dealing in ice and coal. In 1880 he built the first ice factory in Mississippi, but this was unfortunately burned in 1884. Mr. Morris at once erected his present factory, which is one of the very best in the country, and supplies, not only Jackson, but the surrounding country with ice. In 1884 the business was incorporated as the Morris Ice company and Judge J. A. T. Campbell was chosen president, and J. A. Morris, secretary, treasurer and general manager. The latter is now president and manager. Mr. Morris is an active and progressive man of business, and has made the business in which he is now engaged a decided success. He is the owner of much valuable property in West Jackson, and has erected and is the owner of several stores. He has been a hard worker for the democratic party, and although he has been a member of numerous conventions and on many important committees, he would never accept any office, much preferring to devote his attention to his business. He was married on the 12th of March, 1891, to Miss Lavinia Shelton, a daughter of Judge David Shelton (see sketch). Mr. Morris is a handsome gentleman of medium stature, has black hair and eyes, and is most courteous, genial and social. He has a very pleasant residence, and is devoted to his wife and home.

J. W. Morris, planter, Lexington, was born in South Carolina in 1842, and his parents, James and Mary Malvinia (Weems) Morris, were also natives of that state. The parents moved to Mississippi in 1845, and the father followed planting in Holmes county until his death in 1875. He was born in the year 1811. He was not a politician, but preferred the quiet, uneventful life of a farmer. J. W. Morris, the only child born to the above mentioned union, was but three years of age when he came with his parents to Mississippi. He was married in 1867 and subsequently resided in Durant for some time. From there he moved to Kentucky, made his home there for ten years, and then, returning to Holmes county, he located on his present place, where he has resided ever since. He has followed the occupation of a planter and is also the owner of a steam sawmill. His farm, which consists of sixteen hundred acres, has about six hundred acres under plow. His principal crops are cotton and corn. Mr. Morris enlisted in the Confederate army in 1861 as a private and served during the entire war in company G, Fourth Mississippi regiment. He participated in the following engagements: Fort Henry, Fort Donelson, was in all the battles of Hood's raid, and was at Port Gibson, Snyder's Bluff, Franklin and Blakely. Since that time Mr. Morris has followed planting and is one of the thoroughgoing, substantial men of the county. He is pleasant and social in his intercourse with all and has many warm friends. He is a member of the Methodist church and a liberal contributor to the same.

John T. Moseley (deceased) was a prominent merchant and banker of Kemper county, Miss., at Old Wahalak. He was born in Powhatan county, Va., in 1797, and was a son of William and Rebecca (Townes) Moseley. His father was a native of Virginia and became a prominent lawyer. Mr. Moseley was reared and married in Virginia. His wife was Mary W. Montague, daughter of M. Montague. She has borne him ten children: Nancy Rebecca, Sallie I., Wortley, Mariah, William X., George M., Mary W., Pattie, John T. and Anna B. Mr. Moseley moved to Mississippi in 1835 and located at Old Wahalak. He was for many years engaged in planting and selling general merchandise, and there in 1837 he opened the first bank, of which he was general manager and cashier. He was one of the most successful business men in this section, an Odd Fellow, and his wife a member of the Baptist church. He was a strong democrat, and while a resident of Virginia held several official positions in the state of Virginia. He was a prominent feature in the controversy which has become so well known in this county. He died in 1883 and was buried at Old Wahalak. His wife died in 1882 in the same county. He left a large estate, which included a considerable tract of land. John T. Moseley, Jr., was born in this county in 1845, at Old Wahalak. He received his early education here, and spent one year in school at Virginia. In 1863 he enlisted in company F, of the First Mississippi cavalry, though then but eighteen years of age. He took part in many hotly contested conflicts. He was in an engagement at Franklin and in many battles and skirmishes throughout Georgia. He was made a prisoner of war at Selma, Ala., but escaped and came home. After the war he engaged as a clerk for a grocery firm at Mobile. In 1872 he engaged in farming and has a tract of twelve hundred acres of land, which was a portion of his father's estate. For four years under the administration of President Cleveland he was in the railway mail service on the Mobile & Ohio railroad.

Robert J. Mosley, a well-known agriculturist of Kemper county, was born in Monroe county, Ala., in 1834, and is a son of Robert and Mary (Butler) Mosley. Robert Mosley was born in the year 1800, and is a son of Joel Mosley. He was a native of North Carolina, and was married in that state, immigrating to Kemper county, Miss., in 1838. He was first married to Rachel Riddle, but the children of this union are deceased. The second marriage, to Mary Butler, took place in Alabama, and eight children were born to them: William, Mary A., Conbacy, Sarah, Robert J., Amanda, Travers and Drucilla. The mother was born in South Carolina in 1812, and died in 1876; she was a member of the Baptist church. The father died in 1860; he was a prosperous planter, and a man of excellent business qualifications. He also belonged to the Baptist church. Robert J., the subject of this notice, was reared on a farm in Kemper county, and now resides on his father's old plantation, which consists of six hundred acres. He was married September 9, 1858, to Marian Gewin, a daughter of Thomas and Ruth (Newcomb) Gewin, natives of Alabama and Virginia respectively. Mrs. Mosley was born in Mississippi in 1843, her parents being early settlers of Kemper county. Her father was a man of wealth and influence, and an honored citizen. Mr. and Mrs. Mosley have had born to them thirteen children, three of whom are deceased: Mary E. is Mrs. Dr. Gewin, Anna is Mrs. Tartle, Robert lives in Meridian, Emma is Mrs. Davis, Gewin, Earl, Mattie, Howard, Walter and Ernest; those deceased are Richard,

Donnie B. and Marian. The parents are members of the Baptist church. Politically, Mr. Mosley is identified with the democratic party. He is a member of the Masonic order. In 1862, when there was a call for volunteers in the defense of the Southern cause, he enlisted, and served three years and four months. He was in the Thirty-fifth Mississippi volunteer infantry. He participated in the siege of Vicksburg; was at Corinth and Atlanta, Jonesboro and Chattanooga, and a number of skirmishes. He was taken prisoner at Vicksburg, and again at Blakely, from which point he was sent to Ship island, where he was held until the end of the war. He was a faithful and valiant soldier, and was loyal to his convictions to the end. Mrs. Mosley died October 30, 1887, and was buried at Blackwater church.

B. F. Moss, whose postoffice address is Mico, Jasper county, Miss., was born in Jones county, of this state, January 16, 1834. He is a son of Benjamin and Sarah E. (Hossey) Moss, both of whom were natives of South Carolina. Coming to Mississippi at an early day, they located in Wayne county, subsequently removing to Jones county, where he died in 1837. His widow removed to Jasper county, where she later married Rev. Isaac Anderson, and moved with him to Greene county, where she died in 1871. She was the mother of ten children, namely: Elizabeth, John, Ann, Samuel, Benjamin F., Andrew J., and three who died in infancy, by Mr. Moss, and one by Mr. Anderson, named Almeda. Benjamin F. Moss was educated in the home subscription schools of Jasper county, and since he was sixteen years old has fought the battle of life single-handed. He was married in Jasper county, Miss., September 22, 1853, to Miss Jane J., the daughter of William and Jennie (Collins) Hossey. After his marriage he located in the southwest part of Jasper county, and remained there until 1869, when he located upon the plantation upon which he now resides, and which has been his home ever since, except during two years, when he resided at Paulding, Miss. In 1874 he was elected to the office of assessor of Jasper county, in which he served with great fidelity for two years. In 1881 he was elected sheriff of Jasper county, and served one term to the entire satisfaction of his fellow-citizens. His wife died in March, 1882, and in 1883 he married Mrs. Mary E., the widow of John Wade, deceased, and a daughter of James and Pernelipa Ellis. Mr. Moss became the father of nineteen children, named as follows: Madison, Sarah J., William F., Saphronie A., deceased; Benjamin D., deceased; Beulah, Ada, Elizabeth E., Robert L., deceased; John W., deceased; Benjamin B., Samuel, Bert, B. L. These children were by his first wife, and Virgie V., Luther B., William F. and George H., who were twins, and an infant son, who died unnamed. Mr. Moss is the owner of one thousand nine hundred and fifty-five acres of land, of which there are about one hundred and sixty-five acres under cultivation. In 1861 he enlisted in company E, of the Eighth Mississippi regiment, and served until the close of the war. Upon the organization of the company he was elected a lieutenant of it, and in 1862 he was promoted to the rank of captain, and served in this rank. He participated in a number of battles, and was wounded in the left hand at the battle of Missionary Ridge. Besides this engagement, he was in engagements at Murfreesboro, Resaca, Selma, Ala., and a number of skirmishes. At Selma he was captured by the Federals, but made his escape by swimming the Alabama river, and came home to Jasper county. He is a member of the Masonic order and of the Baptist church. In all the relations of life he has the esteem of those with whom he comes in contact. His interest in the affairs of the town and county is great. He is always ready with his influence and money to aid any worthy movement, having in view the enhancement of the public weal.

Lewis A. Moss is a merchant of Edwards, Miss., who was born in New York city

March 8, 1840, the youngest of thirteen children born to Benjamin A. and Alice (Davis) Moss, both of whom were born in England, and came to the United States in 1832, settling in New York city where the father followed the calling of a merchant until 1849, when his death occurred. Lewis A. attended the public schools until about twelve years of age, when he ran away from home and went to California, where he remained until 1855, at which time he returned to his home in New York. While in the wild West he made plenty of money, receiving for his services as high as $150 per month and board. Upon his return to New York he began conducting an auction business, which he continued until he came South, in 1857. He first settled in Georgia where he remained until 1861, at which time he entered the Confederate service, joining company E, Fourth Georgia infantry, his entire service being confined to the state of Virginia, during which time he participated in the seven days fight at Richmond. He was ill in the hospital for some time, which prevented him taking part in the invasions of Maryland and Pennsylvania. He surrendered with Johnston, at Charleston, N. C., after which he came to Vicksburg, Miss., and engaged in general merchandising at which he was quite successful. Since 1875 he has conducted his present business in Edwards, and from a small beginning the business has increased to immense proportions, and now amounts to about $100,000 annually. He is the owner of about sixteen hundred acres of land, which he operates in connection with his store, of which twelve hundred and one acres are under cultivation, devoted to the raising of cotton and corn. He is said by many to be one of the greatest politicians of the state, but has interested himself in politics only at the earnest solicitation of his many friends. He has never held any political office himself, nor does he desire to, but has been instrumental in adding largely to the votes received by his political friends, and has always been a stanch democrat. He has been an alderman of Edwards for fourteen years, and is one of the school trustees, in both of which capacities he has done effective work, being especially interested in the cause of education. He has donated large sums of money to public enterprises and is very generous in aiding the needy and deserving poor, the generous and kind bestowal of his gifts, being warmly appreciated. Socially he is a member of the Masonic order and Royal Arch chapter, the K. of P., the K. of H., the American Legion of Honor, the Free Sons of Israel, and the I. O. of B. B. Mr. Moss was married April 14, 1871, to Miss Fannie Weil, a native of France, and by her became the father of nine children, three of whom are living, Carrie, Benjamin and Jacques, the other children dying in infancy. Although Mr. Moss began life for himself with no means he has been very successful, and now worth about $75,000, all the result of honest and persistent endeavor and good financial ability. His career, although somewhat checkered, has been an honorable one, and he has few, if any, enemies.

Dr. R. P. Moss, College Hill, Miss., has been prominently identified with the history of Lafayette county, for the past forty-seven years, and is well worthy of mention in this connection. He was born in Spartanburg district, S. C., in June, 1815, and is the seventh of a family of twelve children born to James and Emily (Harrison) Moss, natives of North and South Carolina respectively. The paternal grandfather was the son of one of six brothers who immigrated to America in the colonial days, and settled in Virginia; the mother was of Scotch descent. The parents reared their family in South Carolina, and there passed the remainder of their days. The father was a farmer, and a man of plain, practical habits; he died in 1859, and his wife died in 1829, in Spartanburg district, S. C. Dr. Moss, and one brother who lives in Texas, O. H. Moss, are the only surviving members of the once large family. The Doctor came from South Carolina to Abbeville, Miss., in 1844. He was then a single man, and a graduate of the medical department of the University of Pennsylvania,

He at once entered upon the practice of his chosen profession which he continued in Abbeville and vicinity for four years. In 1847 he was married to Miss Lucy A. E. Blakeley, a daughter of Samuel Blakeley. The following year he bought the farm on which he now lives; he continued his practice in connection with his agricultural pursuits until the outbreak of the Civil war. He was conscripted into the service in 1862, and served in the state militia under Colonel Brumley, doing guard duty. After the war he resumed his labors on the farm, and has continued to earn his living by tilling the soil. He and his wife have had born to them eleven children—six sons and five daughters: James A. (a practicing physician at College Hill), Samuel W., Oliver M., Robert L., Susan E. (wife of Dr. G. G. Buford), Sarah E. (wife of William P. Wadkins, of Memphis), Joseph E. W., Frances C. and Harriet Irene; the other two died in infancy. The Doctor is an unassuming man of practical habits, and takes no part in political affairs. He owns six hundred and forty acres of excellent land, three hundred of which are in a high state of cultivation. His son Robert attended the University at Oxford two years. Three daughters, Caroline, Elizabeth and Harriet, are students at the Female college of Oxford; Susan is a graduate of the Clarke Female institute. The family move in the best circles of society, and would be considered a desirable addition to any community. They have lent not only their influence to educational and religious enterprises, but have contributed liberally of their means. They are consistent members of the Presbyterian church.

Gen. Christopher H. Mott (deceased) was a prominent lawyer and politician of Marshall county for many years. He was born in Holly Springs, Miss., and was a student of Dr. Whitehorn. He served in the legislature several terms. He entered the Confederate army as a private, was elected colonel and subsequently brigadier-general and was killed at Williamsburg. He left a beautiful and accomplished wife, who afterward married Maj. John Phillips, of Columbus, Miss.

Like many of the representative citizens of Oktibbeha county, Miss., Capt. W. C. Muldrow was originally from the Palmetto state, his birth occurring in Darlington district in 1828, and his parents, Simon C. and Louise Adaline (Cannon) Muldrow, were natives also of that state. Simeon C. was born in Sumter district on the 18th of February, 1798, and was the son of John and Mary (Ellison) Muldrow. John Muldrow was reared in the Palmetto state and was married on the 7th of November, 1785, to Miss Ellison, who bore him six children, of whom Simeon C. was the youngest. The eldest son, Robert Muldrow, was at one time president of a railroad in South Carolina and a very wealthy man; a daughter, Agnes, married a Mr. Wilson; John Boyd Muldrow is a farmer in South Carolina; Matthew E. is also a farmer, and Mary married a Mr. Bingham. Simeon Connell was reared on a farm in Sumter county, educated at Princeton college and then studied law. He was married in Darlington district to Miss Louise A. Cannon, a native of Darlington district, born January 3, 1809, and the daughter of William H. and Sarah Ann (McTyre) Cannon. After his marriage Mr. Muldrow began practicing law in Darlington district, continued this three or four years and then removed to Claiborne county, Ala., where he followed tilling of the soil for two years. From there he went to Lowndes county, Miss. The six children born to his marriage are named in the order of their births as follows: William Cannon (subject), Robert (deceased, see sketch of Col. Muldrow), Sarah Ann Cordelia (deceased), Mary Louise (deceased), Eliza Jane (deceased) and Henry Lowndes (now in Starkville, see sketch of Colonel Muldrow). The father of these children continued farming in Lowndes county for five or six years and then removed to Oktibbeha county, where he was engaged in the same occupation up to the time of his death, which occurred on the 18th of December, 1853. He came to Mississippi with limited means and amassed considerable wealth. He was a man of fine intellect and was a great reader. Although he took no active part in political affairs he was well posted on all the popular topics of the day. He was a member of Oktibbeha (now Albert) lodge, A. F. & A. M., at Starkville, and he and wife hold membership in the Presbyterian church of old school. Four years after his death his widow married Isaac N. Davis, a native of Elbert county, Ga., and a gentleman who stood high in state affairs. He was a state elector on several occasions, served a number of years as state senator and was an orator of great eloquence at one time. He was educated for the legal profession, but followed agricultural pursuits the principal part of his days. He was a whig politically, but after his marriage with Mrs. Muldrow he changed to the democracy. Mr. Davis died on the 26th of June, 1860, and his widow survived him eight years, her death occurring on the 6th of June, 1868. William C. Muldrow received but a limited education in the public schools of his native district, but by his own exertions has become well posted on all subjects of interest and now has a good practical education. After the death of his father he took his place behind the plow, assumed charge of the plantation and, besides supporting the family, he paid off a debt on his father's estate amounting to $25,000. This property consisted of five hundred acres, to which William C. has added to, from time to time, until it increased to about twenty-five hundred acres. He sold that and now owns nearly seven hundred acres of land, five hundred acres of which are under cultivation. Like most of the farmers in the county, his principal crops are corn and cotton, and he is interested in stockraising. His farm is located on the Illinois Central railroad, five miles from West Point and one-half mile west of Muldrow. His brother, Colonel Muldrow, owns a large tract of land east of Muldrow Station. The land owned by our subject is in a high state of cultivation, and his system is productive of excellent results. He takes great pride in his farm, which, as before stated, is less than half a mile from the station which was erected by the Illinois Central railroad for the convenience of Captain Muldrow and his brother, Colonel Muldrow, of Starkville. Captain Muldrow's residence is beautifully situated and is surrounded by a fine park of about five acres, which is dotted here and there with great oak trees and many beds of choice flowers. The Captain exhibits great taste, not only in the selection of plants, but in the care and training of them. An archway covered with sweet-scented honeysuckle is over the front gate, the entrance to the house is up a broad flight of steps and from the front balcony a lovely view is obtained of the surrounding country. Everything is cozy and convenient about his place and his doors are ever open to his friends, of whom he has a host. In the latter part of 1860 Captain Muldrow enlisted as a private in company C, Fourteenth Mississippi infantry, serving about six months. At the battle of Fort Donelson he was captured and taken to Camp Douglas, where he was kept about nine months. He was exchanged at Vicksburg, Miss. By permission of President Davis the brother of our subject organized an independent company of cavalry, which Captain Muldrow joined as second lieutenant. He was promoted to first lieutenant in about a year and a half, and then became captain. He was in all the battles of General Sherman's raid and was in the engagements in Alabama, Mississippi, Georgia and South Carolina up to the line of North Carolina. He surrendered at Washington, Ga., and after returning home resumed his former occupation. The Captain has never married, his "home life," to quote his own words, "being so pleasant that I did not think of leaving it." He is a very genial, whole-souled gentleman and bears his years as lightly as many twenty years his junior. His farm is his pride and his most constant thought.

Col. Henry L. Muldrow, the most prominent lawyer of Starkville, and president of the

People's Savings bank at that place, was born in Lowndes county, Miss., in 1838. His parents, Simeon C. and Louise A. (Cannon) Muldrow, were natives respectively of Sumter and Darlington districts, S. C., the father born in 1798 and the mother in 1809. The elder Muldrow, passed his youth on a farm, received good educational advantages, and subsequently graduated from Princeton college, New Jersey. After this he studied law and practiced his profession for a few years in South Carolina and then removed to Claiborne county, Ala., where he led the life of an agriculturist. He was married in his native state about 1826, and in 1837 removed to Lowndes county, Miss., where he was among the first settlers. He located in the woods on Tibbee creek, improved a good farm, and there resided until about 1845, when he removed a few miles farther west into Oktibbeha county, again settling in the woods. He was a man of talent and excellent judgment, who by his honesty and industry amassed a good property. He never aspired to public positions, but was ever ready and willing to assist in all enterprises of a laudable nature. His death occurred in 1853. He was a member of the Presbyterian church. He was one of three sons and three daughters, born to the marriage of John Muldrow, who was of Irish descent and probably a native of the Palmetto state. The latter spent all his life, following the occupation of a planter in South Carolina, and served under General Marion in the Revolutionery war. The mother of Colonel Muldrow died in 1868. She was a member of the Presbyterian church, and a lady of rare accomplishments, having received her education at Barromville, N. C., a school of considerable note at that time. Her father, Hon. William H. Cannon, was of Scotch-Irish origin, was a wealthy planter, and one of the prominent men of South Carolina, representing the same in the state senate. He reared two sons and four daughters, the eldest son, Capt. William H., holding the rank of captain in the Florida war. Col. Henry L. Muldrow was one of three sons and three daughters, born to his parents, all the daughters dying when young. The eldest son, Capt. William C. Muldrow, is now one of the leading planters of Oktibbeha county. He was a captain in the Confederate army. Another son, Maj. Robert Muldrow, was a graduate of the State University of Mississippi, and when a young man represented Oktibbeha county in the legislature. His residence was in Kentucky, but died in Mississippi, in 1873, while visiting relatives. He served as major in Wirt Adams' cavalry during the war and was once wounded. Col. Henry L. Muldrow's early educational training was good, he having graduated from the literary department of the University of Mississippi in 1856, and from the law department in 1858. He then practiced at Starkville until April, 1861, when he joined the Oktibbeha rescue, afterward company C, Fourteenth Mississippi infantry as lieutenant, and was captured at Fort Donelson. He was imprisoned at Johnson's island for about seven months and was then exchanged. Upon the reorganization of the company he was made captain and operated in the Western campaign, in many of the most severe engagements until after the fall of Vicksburg. He then received orders from the war department at Richmond to raise a company of mounted scouts, which he did, and was then authorized, with Col. R. O. Perrin, to organize a regiment of which the latter was made colonel and Captain Muldrow, lieutenant-colonel. Upon the death of Colonel Perrin, which occurred soon after, our subject became colonel and commanded the regiment in General Johnston's army until the close of the war, surrendering with him after struggling gallantly with the enemy for four years. Prior to the war, in 1860, Colonel Muldrow was married to Miss Eliza D. Ervin, a native of Lowndes county, Miss., and the daughter of James W. and Ann J. (Jennings) Ervin, the father born in South Carolina and the mother in Georgia. Mr. and Mrs. Ervin were married in Mississippi, and after the death of the latter in 1860, Mr. Ervin removed to Alabama, where he followed planting until his death. To Colonel and Mrs. Muldrow was born a daughter,

Annie Louise, who is still living. Mrs. Muldrow is a member of the Presbyterian church. After the war Colonel Muldrow resumed the practice of law and his official career began in 1870 as district attorney of the sixth judicial district, serving about two years. He represented Oktibbeha county in the memorable legislature of 1876, and also served with credit and distinction in the XLVth, XLVIth, XLVIIth and XLVIIIth congress, declining re-election. In 1885 he was appointed first assistant secretary of the interior by President Cleveland, served until the close of the administration and then resigned. He then returned to his practice with his former partner, Hon. Wiley N. Nash, also one of the prominent lawyers of Mississippi. Colonel Muldrow was made president of the People's Savings bank, at Starkville, upon its organization in 1889 and he has since filled that position. He is also largely engaged in planting. The Colonel is a true type of the Southern gentleman, genial and hospitable, and he has secured a wide circle of friends, whom he holds tenaciously.

John J. Mulligan, of Vicksburg, Miss., is probably the most successful and extensive plumber in the entire South. He came to Vicksburg in youth as a mechanic, having previously learned the trade of a tinsmith. He soon engaged in business for himself, and is now doing a very large, reputable and lucrative business. He does an extensive wholesale business in tin, copper and sheet iron, tinners' supplies, fire and burglar-proof safes, engines, boilers, etc. He owns valuable property in Vicksburg, on Mulberry street, where he carries his stock, and from which he does his extensive business. He has recently completed the plumbing and cornice work on the new Vicksburg hotel and the Piazzo hotel. His fine work may be seen throughout Mississippi and adjoining states. Besides being a first-class plumber, he is filling the following responsible positions creditably to himself and satisfactorily to the citizens of Vicksburg: Treasurer of the Vicksburg Building association, treasurer of the Vicksburg fire department, president of the Washington fire department, and first lieutenant of the Catholic Knights of St. John.

Robert Mullin (deceased) was a resident of Grenada county, Miss., for over half a century, and during that period was one of the county's most active and prominent citizens. He was born in Belfast, Ireland, in 1818, and when a mere boy crossed the ocean to America, locating first in Dayton, Ohio, with a sister, Mrs. Margaret Thompson, who had immigrated to the United States a number of years before. In 1829 Mr. Mullin went to Kentucky and from there to Mississippi in 1838, locating at old Troy, Yalobusha county, a few miles below Grenada, on Yalobusha river, where he engaged in shipping cotton. Later he embarked in merchandising on a small scale, having but little to start with, but by his energy and close attention to business, soon became one of the leading merchants of the place. In all other enterprises undertaken by him he was very successful, and he purchased large tracts of land to which he added from time to time. About 1850 he purchased the place that he afterward named Evergreen plantation, consisting of twenty-two hundred acres of the choicest land in the county, and on this erected a large, two-story brick house, a very handsome and imposing structure. This building, standing on an elevation covered with magnolia and evergreen trees, commands a lovely view of the surrounding country and is picturesque in the extreme. On retiring from merchandising, Mr. Mullin made this place his home, where he wished to spend the rest of his days in quiet, but during the war he lost a great deal of his means, and after cessation of hostilities, he again engaged in merchandising in Grenada. There he worked with the vigor of former years and soon became one of the leading merchants of the county. He continued in business until 1884. He was a man of strong, vigorous mind, great originality, and was possessed of a high sense of honor and excellent judgment, which exerted a great influence over those with whom he came in contact, and he was often consulted for his opinion on different subjects. No one ever thought of doubting his word or impunging his motives. He was very conscientious, strictly honest in all his dealings and a thorough Christian man, although not a member of any church. In his early life he had joined the Methodist church, but thought he could not comply with all its rules and therefore withdrew. He led a good, moral life and those who knew him best loved and appreciated him most. He always contributed liberally to all worthy enterprises brought to his notice and with a willingness that made him popular with all. His death, which occurred on the 31st of May, 1885, was the occasion of universal sorrow, for all felt the loss that would be sustained by the departure of such a man. He was married in May, 1843, to Miss Mary Walton, a native of Tennessee, and daughter of Harris and Mary (Edwards) Walton, natives respectively of Tennessee and Georgia. Harris Walton and his family moved to Mississippi as early as 1838, settled in Marshall county, but the same year came to Yalobusha county, where he opened up a large plantation. He died at the age of fifty-eight years, and his wife when forty-six years of age. Both were members of the Methodist church. They were the parents of seven children, four of whom are yet living, and Mrs. Mullin being the eldest. She was nearly grown when she came with her parents to Mississippi. She is still living, is a member of the Methodist church and resides in Grenada with her daughter, Mrs. Laurance. She was a true companion to her husband and is one of the best of women, esteemed and respected by all. To Mr. and Mrs. Mullin were born nine children, six of whom survive at the present time: Appolis, wife of Capt. J. B. Wilson, resides in Bowling Green, Ky.; Annie, wife of Mr. Lake, of Memphis, Tenn.; Cora married John W. Griffis, of Grenada; Lillie, wife of F. G. Winn, of Clairmont, N. H.; Blanch married Samuel Laurance (deceased), who was a member of the firm of Doak & Laurance, merchants of Grenada, and to this union was born a bright little girl. The youngest of this family, Robert W. Mullin, was born on Evergreen plantation and supplemented the primary education received at Grenada by a thorough course in Roanoke college, Virginia, from which he graduated in 1882, taking a special course. From there he went to Bowling Green, Ky., engaged in stock trading for a few years and then returned to the old home place, where he has since resided engaged in stockraising. He is advanced and progressive in his ideas and is one of the prominent planters and stockfarmers of Grenada county. He selected for his companion in life Miss Effie Thomas, daughter of B. F. Thomas, and her death occurred on the 17th of April, 1890, at the age of twenty-one years. She left an infant daughter, Mary. Mrs. Mullin was educated at Blue Mount college, Ripley, Tenn., and was a lady of refinement and culture. Mr. Mullin adheres to the democratic party in his political views.

P. W. Mulvihill, dealer in general hardware, tinner and plumber, of Natchez, Miss., is the son of Michael and Mary (Creigan) Mulvihill, natives of Ireland; the father born in County Kerry and the mother in Limerick. The parents were married in their native country, and in 1848 sailed for Canada, where they remained but a short time and then moved to New York state. There they remained for about two years, and then moved to Illinois, and thence in 1858 to Natchez, Miss. Later yet they moved to Vicksburg, where the mother received her final summons, and where the father still resides. Although now retired from the active duties of life, he was formerly a railroad contractor and a merchant. He is a member of St. Mary's cathedral. He had two brothers and two sisters to cross the ocean to America. Mr. Mulvihill was the father of eleven children, only three sons now living, as follows: M. J., a prominent merchant at Vicksburg and one of the city's representative citizens, E. P., who is a hardware merchant at Colorado, Tex., and subject. Two daughters and four grandchildren died with yellow fever in Vicksburg in 1878. P. W. Mulvihill was born in New York city in 1850, secured a liberal education at the Brothers of the Sacred Heart, in Natchez, and in 1866 learned the tinner's trade, at which he worked for seventeen years. In the meantime he established himself in the hardware business, and now has an annual trade of probably $20,000. He is an energetic, thoroughgoing business man, and has the confidence and respect of all who know him. For four years he has been alderman of the Second ward; is a director in the Natchez Safe Deposit and Trust company; is president of the Phœnix Fire Company No. 7; was treasurer of the St. Joseph Total Abstinence and Benevolent society, and was once an officer of the state Knights of Workmen of Mississippi. He was married to Miss Bridget Gleeson, a native of Ireland, and daughter of John and Mary Gleeson, natives also of the Emerald isle. Her parents came to the United States and settled in Natchez in 1853. There they both died, the mother in about 1880 and he ten years later. To Mr. Mulvihill's marriage were born nine children, and he and family are members of St. Mary's cathedral.

There is no name more worthy of mention in the memorial department of these volumes than that of Jesse P. Myer, of Ellisville, Miss., who is the largest and most extensive retail merchant and cotton dealer in southern Mississippi, if not the largest in the state. This gentleman is a native-born Mississippian. His birthplace was in Jasper county, and he was born July 15, 1855. His father was Solomon Myer, who was born in Metz, Germany, about the year 1819, and came to the United States when quite young, settling about 1851 in Mississippi, where he married Miss Amanda Alexander, subsequently removing to Jasper county, where he became a merchant. Later he became a merchant of Clarke county and removed thence in 1883 to Jones county, where he died in February, 1891, his wife, who survived him, making her home with her son, Jesse P., at Ellisville. They were the parents of ten children: Joseph (deceased), Mary E., Amelia L., Jesse P., Josephine R., Sallie O. (deceased), Alexander S. (deceased), Nettie Forest, Charles S. and Ada C. Mr. Myer was educated at Shubuta, Miss., and at the age of seventeen years became a salesman in the employ of M. Greenhood, of Shubuta, a merchant of that place, in whose service he remained for several years. In 1879 he formed a co-partnership with N. B. Shelby to carry on a mercantile business at that place. This partnership was terminated by mutual consent in 1883, and Mr. Myer came to Ellisville, Miss., where he opened a store individually. Beginning with limited capital he gradually increased his stock as his trade warranted until now his business is very extensive. Some idea of its growth may be obtained when it is stated that in the first year he shipped three hundred bales of cotton and in 1890 he shipped more than four thousand bales. He carries the largest stock of general merchandise in southern Mississippi and ranks among the leading merchants in the state. He makes a specialty also of dealing in wool. He draws a very extensive and rapidly increasing trade from an area extending from sixty to seventy-five miles in all directions, and he has come to be known in the mercantile circles throughout the South. The town of Ellisville may be said to be coexistent with his enterprise there, and he has led in all improvements and done more perhaps than any other one man to secure its advancement and commercial prosperity. Mr. Myer was married in Heidelberg, Miss., May 14, 1884, to Miss Alice Lee Weens, a daughter of Lewis H. and Mary (Bachelor) Weens, who had four children: Alice Lee, Rutledge, Clara and another who died in infancy. Mr. and Mrs. Myer have had two children, Charles S., deceased, and Alma A. Mr. Myer is a member of the Knights of Pythias, and he and his wife are members of the Baptist church. The career of Mr. Myer illustrates what may be accomplished by characteristic American pluck and energy combined with unswerving honesty and faithfulness to community and to self; and such sketches as this point examples to the rising generation that may be followed with credit and success and result in still greater glory to Mississippi and the new South.

Prof. C. H. Myers was born in Union county, Miss., in February, 1861. He is a son of P. B. and Martha (Goodrich) Myers. His parents were natives of Alabama, and in that state they grew to maturity and were married. They removed to Union county in 1851, where Mr. Myers bought land and engaged in planting. About the beginning of the war he removed to Memphis Tenn., where he became a merchant. After the war he removed to a plantation near Memphis, which he managed in connection with his mercantile business until 1866, when he removed to Marshall county, Miss. His wife having died while he lived in Memphis, he married Miss Elizabeth Bridgewater. She soon died also, and he married for his third wife, Miss Jennie Wesson, of Marshall county. By his first wife, he had seven children, by his second wife, he had one child, and by his present wife, he has had three children. From Marshall county, he removed to Union county, where he engaged in planting. He was practically a successful business man, who never sought political preferment. Professor Myers began life for himself as a planter and schoolteacher. Having a great desire to so educate himself that he might become a successful teacher, he became a student at the State university at Oxford, in 1883. In 1884 he established a private school at Myrtle, Union county, where he has remained until the present time. His success here has been such that he has built up a small college, of which he is principal and owner. This institution has been of great usefulness to this part of the state, and its continued success seems assured. The number of pupils enrolled in 1891 was one hundred and fifty. In 1884, solely with his own capital, he built a good school building, which is adequate to the demands of the time. In 1887, the school having grown so rapidly that the accommodations were insufficient, he erected an additional building, and the college is now well equipped, both as regards buildings and apparatus. The institution is known as the Myrtle normal college, and is attended by students of both sexes. In 1890 Professor Myers obtained a charter of this college from the state legislature. Some idea of the growth of this institution may be had from a comparison of the roll of 1884 with that of 1891. The total number of students in the first mentioned year was sixteen. The college has good boarding facilities, and the college property embraces twenty acres of land on which are the college buildings and a fine residence, all of which Professor Myers is the sole owner. He deserves, and has been awarded great credit for his success in this useful enterprise, which is constantly growing in the confidence of the people in this and surrounding counties. The Professor is assisted in the management of the college by Mrs. Myers, who graduated at Oxford in the class of 1880. He married Mrs. Myers, who was Miss Jennie M. Ritz, in 1887. She is a daughter of Edmond and Jennie (Lark) Ritz. Her father was a native of Germany, and her mother was born in South Carolina. They were married in the state just mentioned in 1859, and removed from there to Washington, D. C., where they lived for ten years, when they located in Oxford, Miss. Mr. Ritz died in Memphis, Tenn., in 1883. Professor Myers is a member of the Methodist Episcopal church, and Mrs. Myers a member of the Baptist church. Professor Myers is almost wholly absorbed in the building up of the college, and it has been an honor to himself and a lasting benefit to the community, but he finds time and means to devote to laudable public enterprises of all kinds, which are of advantage and benefit to the community in which he lives.

On page three hundred and sixty-seven of this volume appears a biographical sketch of the late Hon. R. F. Beck (deceased). Mr. Beck died August 18, 1891, after the article mentioned had been printed, and it is deemed proper to supplement the above mentioned sketch with further details of the life of this remarkable man. In addition to the many public offices which he held, and the duties of which occupied so much of his valuable time, he still found leisure to devote himself to the demands of official positions such as the following: He was president of the following organizations: The Vicksburg Building association (for twelve years), the Yazoo and Tallahatchie Transportation company, the Vicksburg Builders and Traders' exchange, and the Gibraltar Publishing company, and he was an officer in the Vicksburg Wharf and Land company, the Delta Wharf and Land company, the Vicksburg Transfer company, the Vicksburg Wharf, Boat and Elevator company, the Delta Wharf, Boat and Elevator company, the Mississippi Home Insurance company, the First National bank of Vicksburg, the Vicksburg Fair association, the Vicksburg Driving club, the Benevolent Protective Order of Elks, and the Catholic Knights of America. All of these organizations held special meetings and passed suitable resolutions in respect to his death, and each sent to his late residence a beautiful floral offering. Almost every carriage, public and private, in the city was brought into requisition at his funeral and large numbers of people attended on horseback. The board of mayor and aldermen attended in a body and the city had a delegation of mounted police in uniform present. The carriages that bore the floral offerings were all beautifully draped in mourning, and the horses and drivers were decorated with crape. The procession to the cemetery was probably the largest ever seen in Vicksburg. The following account is taken from a local paper:

> Such an assemblage of the people as turned out yesterday to pay the last honors to the remains of Hon. R. F. Beck, has not been seen in many years. No less than seventy-six vehicles were in the procession, which extended several blocks, and spacious St. Paul's, where the funeral rites were celebrated, was so densely crowded that it seemed impossible for another person to gain admission. The ceremonies, which were grandly impressive, consisted of a requiem high mass, by Rev. Father Monti, and a chastely eloquent funeral oration, delivered by Rev. H. A. Picherit, whose polished and beautiful thoughts were never more appropriately expressed, even though he has delivered on frequent occasions productions which have moved the most stoical to tears, than on this occasion. His long friendship for the deceased gave him abundant qualifications as his eulogist, and this was most fittingly demonstrated in his touching tribute to his many virtues.
>
> The ceremonies at the church took place about 9 A. M. At their conclusion the mournful procession was reformed; the casket, buried beneath rare flowers, was reverently borne to the funeral car, and the march to the cemetery began. There were present in the funeral cortege Mayor R. V. Booth and the other members of the city council, preceded by Marshal Hammett and a detachment of police on horseback, the members of the Builders' exchange and representatives of all the city's institutions and organizations.
>
> Upon reaching the cemetery, the last rites of the church were pronounced by Rev. Father Picherit, the casket was deposited in its last resting-place, and the sorrowing throng turned sadly away.
>
> During the morning business was generally suspended by the members of the Builders and Traders' exchange, in honor of their deceased president.

Mr. Beck was a friendless young stranger when he located in Vicksburg at the close of the war, but he was possessed of brains, health, industry, good habits and indomitable energy. He soon became a builder and contractor, in which avocation he met with great success and which he followed until the day of his death. He was so constituted that he was a leader in whatever he devoted his energies to, whether it was business, political or social in its character. In the exciting events of the period following the war he took an active part, and was a prominent factor in the movement that overthrew radical rule in Vicksburg. He was first elected alderman and afterward mayor of Vicksburg. Soon after he was elected sheriff of his county, and re-elected two or three times. Later he was again elected mayor of Vicksburg for two successive terms. He took great interest in every movement that promised to aid the growth or welfare of the city, and no movement for the public good failed to receive help from him. His death while in the prime of life and at the zenith of his mental vigor, was a loss to Vicksburg and to the state. He was a devout member of St. Paul's congregation, and it was his regular custom to attend mass in the sacred edifice. In his death the church lost a true and stanch friend, and this may be said also of schools, which he assisted and encouraged in the most liberal and praiseworthy manner. His character may be summed up in the statement that he was a devoted husband, a loving father, a true friend and a thoroughly good man, and his place in the community will be hard to fill.

CHAPTER XIV.

CITIZENS' PRIVATE MEMOIRS, N.

Capt. George W. Naron, a member of the mercantile firm of Naron, Son & Mancill, at Maben, also the firm of G. W. Naron & Sons, Atlanta, Chickasaw county, was born in Coweta county, Ga., April 16, 1828, and was the third of nine children born to Thomas and Mary (Corker) Naron, natives respectively of South Carolina and Kentucky. The parents were married in Coweta county, Ga., and from there removed to Chambers county, Ala., thence to Randolph county, and in 1842 came to Chickasaw county, Miss., settling in a tent in the woods. Two years later they removed to near Little Rock, Ark., and there on the 22d of July of the same year (1844) Mr. Naron received his final summons. Mrs. Naron died two days later. The father was something of a speculator, and was of rather a roving disposition. He was a man of great endurance and was thoroughly acquainted with Indian life, having served in the Creek war as a sergeant, leaving a wife and several children at home, who were frequently obliged to protect themselves from the Indians by hiding in the woods. Mr. Naron was one of seven sons and one daughter born to the marriage of Eli Naron, who came to Chickasaw county in 1844, followed planting, and there passed his last days. He was in the War of 1812. His father was from the old country. Capt. George W. Naron became thoroughly familiar with the duties of the farm at an early age, but his educational advantages were not of the best, never having attended school more than six months altogether. He began for himself when sixteen years of age, and during the Mexican war he was in the quartermaster's department, serving about eight months in General Taylor's command. He then returned to Mississippi and in 1849 married Miss Mahala Few, a native of Morgan county, Ga., born in 1822, and the daughter of Clement and Sallie Few. Mr. Few was a successful planter, and died in Chickasaw county, Miss. His wife died in Georgia. Mrs. Naron, who died June 11, 1890, was the mother of seven children, four of whom are now living, viz.: Sara F., deceased wife of Rev. R. P. Gore; William W., a merchant of Eupora; J. Riley, died in 1891; Martha J. was the wife of F. P. Sinclair, of Eupora; Alonzo C., a merchant of Atlanta, Miss.; Rebecca O., wife of T. J. Mancill, of Maben; and Laura E., died in infancy. The mother of these children was a devout member of the Baptist church. Captain Naron was one of the early settlers of Chickasaw county, where he made his home until recently, when he moved to Maben, Oktibbeha county. He has followed the occupation of a farmer all his life, and is the owner of about thirteen hundred acres in Chickasaw, Calhoun and Webster counties, all the result of enterprise and industry on the part of the family. About 1875 Mr. Naron began merchandising at Atlanta, and since then has devoted his attention largely to that business, owning a large store at Maben and another at Atlanta. Early in the war Mr. Naron was made lieutenant of company H, Thirty-first Mississippi infantry, and later became captain of the company, operating in Mississippi the first year or two. He fought at Chickasaw Bayou, Baker's Creek, Jackson, and then on to Resaca, fighting all the way to Atlanta. From there he went to Franklin and Nashville, back to Mississippi, and rejoined General Johnston in North Carolina, surrendering with him after over four years of hardship and suffering. He was wounded three times. During that time his wife and children struggled hard to make a living and battled vigorously against all opposition. The Captain was for a number of years a prominent member of the Masonic fraternity, Atlanta lodge No. 362, having taken the past master degree, and he is now a member of New Hope lodge No. 224, at Maben. He is a member of the Baptist church. His wife was a noble companion, and much of his success in life the Captain attributes to her. She displayed wonderful fortitude during the war and supported the family instead of going to her people.

Wiley Norris Nash, of Starkville, Miss., is the son of Stephen Evans and Mariah Jane (Stanton) Nash. His father was born in South Carolina, October 27, 1807, and died on his plantation in the western part of Oktibbeha county, July 16, 1863. His mother, a native of North Carolina, was born October 12, 1822, and died in Starkville, Miss., October 26, 1859. His mother's family were among the pioneers of Alabama, and his father's family were pioneers, both of Alabama and Mississippi. The antecedents of this gentleman, when both lines are considered, have, first and last, occupied important places of trust and honor in positions religious, legal, political and military, extending back to and including the Revolutionary war. From this family have sprung worthy and honorable ministers, soldiers, judges and statesmen. The Nashes do not claim lineage from any great or titled family, yet the older members, or a number of them, claim a traditional motto, of which they are very proud, the English of which is "Faithful in everything."

Stephen E. Nash, the father of the immediate subject of this sketch, acquired a liberal education, and was a man of fine literary taste. He was a lawyer and practiced his profession for many years. At the date of his death he had retired from practice, and was farming somewhat extensively, and besides was a large owner of uncultivated woodlands mostly in the western portion of Oktibbeha county, Miss. In politics, before the war of 1861 broke out, he was a whig. He did not favor secession at the time and in the way it was brought about. When the troubles of 1861 confronted the people of the South he was a co-operationist, believing in the wisdom of all the slave-holding states co-operating together, and demanding in the Union, and as a whole their rights of property guaranteed to them by the constitution. He further believed that if war resulted it was best for the state to fight for its rights under the stars and stripes, and if a withdrawal was ultimately decided upon, as for the best for all the states to withdraw together. Although he was of this mind, when the war actually began, he went with, and heartily supported his section, and the action of his state taken in her sovereign capacity to the day of his death. To make the Southern cause a success, he gave up two of his sons, they being the only two near military age, and sent them to the front, before they were rarely able to bear arms, to do battle for their home and for their country, which was then invaded. Both of his boys were in the Confederate service at the surrender and on active duty at the front. As some evidence of the extent that this gentleman and this family were wrapped up in the fate of the young Confederacy, two incidents may be very properly mentioned in passing. The father (S. E. Nash) was almost heartbroken at the surrender of Vicksburg. It is said he hardly saw a well day after he heard positive news of the capitulation, its particulars and its extent. Vicksburg fell on the 4th day of July, A. D. 1863, and Stephen E. Nash died the 16th day of July, 1863, only twelve days later. The eldest daughter, Elvira Jane Nash, at the surrender was a schoolgirl at the Judson, in Marion, Ala. Owing it is said to some exposure, and the excitement and sorrow caused by the news of the surrender of the Southern armies, she sickened and died but a few days thereafter. Though in perfect health at that date, yet she lived but a short time after the fall of the Confederacy. The surrender took place in May, 1865, and her death occurred on the 4th of June following.

Wiley Norris Nash was born in Noxubee county, Miss., some fourteen miles south of Starkville, on the 6th day of April, 1846. His early childhood was passed less than thirty miles from where he now lives, in Noxubee and Winston counties, his father having moved to Starkville, Oktibbeha county, when this son was about six years old. Here most of his youth was spent, and here his mother, a lady of great worth and of a pure and lovely Christian character, died. The family moved when he was fifteen out in the western portion of Oktibbeha county, where they were living when the war broke out. Up to this time our subject's education had been well conducted, as it was for some twelve months thereafter. When the war began he was a mere boy, anxious even then to enter the service, his elder brother, James H. Nash, having joined the army soon after hostilities began. He was, however, kept at home and at school during the early part of that sanguinary conflict, but enlisted in the Confederate service at sixteen, being quite small for his age, weighing only ninety-six pounds. He served first, but not long, with state troops. He joined Adams' regiment of cavalry just before the fall of Vicksburg, with which he served a short time, being detached within a few months on extra hazardous duty with Harvey's scouts, with which command he served regularly until the day of the surrender, being at that date one of the sergeants of this company. When hostilities ceased he had seen hard service in Mississippi, Alabama, Georgia and Tennessee, mostly in Mississippi and Georgia. In each of these four states named members of this company lost their lives in the service of their country. In Mississippi, Mr. Nash saw most of his service in that portion of the state lying between Yazoo City and Natchez, and in that lying between Vicksburg and Meridian, and the larger part of this service was in Hinds, Warren and Claiborne counties. In Georgia he served in the campaigns of Generals Johnston and Hood. Harvey's scouts was organized under special military orders and was commanded by Capt. Addison Harvey, of Canton, Miss., one of the tried, one of the truest and one of the bravest sons of the South, a typical Southern soldier. This command served as a company during about one-half of the war, and carried on its roll first and last one hundred and twenty-eight men. Of this number during the time it was in service it lost in killed, wounded and captured, fifty-seven men. That is to say, there were twenty-nine captured, of which number sixteen made their escape and twelve were killed; there were sixteen wounded, of whom four were wounded twice. One of this four was wounded near Natchez, Miss., in a close fight with infantry, being shot and bayoneted in the same action. Of the wounded another was badly cut across the head in a fight with cavalry near Atlanta, Ga. Mr. Nash was severely wounded near Rome, Ga. In another fight during the time he

was in service he had his gun struck with a ball. He also had two of his horses slightly wounded, one while he was in a cavalry charge in Mississippi, and the other in Georgia in a fight with infantry. At the time Mr. Nash was wounded he was in charge of a squad of four men with orders to leave the company, then on the south bank of the Etawa river some ten miles above Rome, cross over and cut the telegraph wire just on the other side and return promptly. The party of five entered a rough boat or flat, and when within about twenty yards of the northern bank of the river some Federal infantry, before that time concealed, opened a deadly fire on the little squad. Mr. Nash, who was standing up in the boat, was shot through the outer muscle of the right thigh and fell overboard. He contrived to catch to the gunwale of the boat, however, as it was turning toward the southern shore, and was thus saved. The enemy continued to pour in their fire, splintering the boat at every volley, twice wounding Corporal Portwood, and killing outright J. Catlett, a brave and gallant soldier. Meanwhile Captain Harvey, with his company on the other side, opened fire on the Federal force, and under cover of this fire the party in the boat effected their escape. This company, though such was not its leading line of duty, did necessarily much special secret service, such as scouting for information, where generally one, two or three men were engaged, and squad scouting, where ten or fifteen men were, according to circumstances, sent out under a lieutenant or non-commissioned officer. The foregoing service was merely incidental, so to speak, or collateral to the main service in which Captain Harvey himself engaged personally and with the company proper. Mr. Nash, as a matter of preference as well as owing to his age, made a personal request of his captain to always keep him with the company, and never send him away from the command on special duty when this could possibly be avoided. This request Captain Harvey remembered and generally complied with. Captain Harvey always kept together as many of his command as possible, generally about thirty, and always in perfect fighting trim, ready to move together in a body on a moment's notice, as emergencies required. His program was to reconnoiter every position possible, and every force of the enemy moving or operating within range, never halting until he struck it, fighting whenever and wherever necessary. He moved very rapidly and would often strike a large command front, flank and rear in less than twenty-four hours, and be able to report to the nearest brigade or division commander the strength of the enemy's cavalry and infantry, supply wagons, ambulances, artillery and the name of the commanding officer, his objective point, etc. Mr. Nash was almost constantly with Captain Harvey during these expeditions and most of the time one of the non-commissioned officers, he not only saw but participated in much of this hazardous service. Though not the first sergeant, he often acted in that capacity, which position in any company, and especially in a company like this, is one of great trust and responsibility. In Georgia one of the special duties of Captain Harvey was to cut off Sherman's supply trains and impede in every way possible his transportation and means of communication. In this he was so successful that General Sherman found it necessary at one time to detail ten thousand men to look after his lines of communication, guard his supply trains, depots, railroad bridges, etc. Gen. Joseph E. Johnston, in his narrative, speaks very highly of the operations of Captain Harvey in the rear and on the flanks of Sherman's army in Georgia. General Sherman himself compares Harvey's scouts to "a nest of yellow jackets continually buzzing about my trains, and stinging severely when I attempted to drive them away." Gen. Stephen D. Lee, very high authority, says, speaking of this command: "They were everywhere conspicuous for activity, enterprise, persistence and intrepidity." In many instances no account was kept of the enemy killed and captured by Harvey's scouts, and those occasionally detailed to act under Captain Harvey's orders, and especially is this the case as to the time they were following Hood into Tennessee, or pursuing Wilson's command, which left Eastport on its famous raid just before the surrender. The following, however, is believed to be very near the mark: Harvey's charge into Jackson, Miss., killing Colonel Cromwell and capturing twenty-eight of his men, twenty-nine; killed in the fight with infantry at Natchez, Miss., forty; killed and captured in Sherman's campaign to Meridian, one hundred and thirty-eight; killed and captured in Sherman's Georgia compaign, one thousand three hundred; total, one thousand five hundred and seven.

Most of the foregoing pertaining to the army and the army life of Mr. Nash is taken from a sketch of Harvey's scouts by Col. J. F. H. Claiborne and designed by him as a part of his second volume of Claiborne's History of Mississippi. The second volume, unfortunately, was burnt, and Colonel Claiborne having departed this life, was never issued. The sketch alluded to, however, was published partly in the weekly *Clarion*, Jackson, Miss., and partly in the *East Mississippi Times*, Starkville, Miss., and the whole was afterward printed in pamplet form for private distribution. It would be proper, in this connection, to mention the following incidents which further illustrate the soldier life and soldier qualities of the subject of this sketch. In the Georgia campaign he saved in battle the life of John Lorance, who was badly cut with a sabre in a close fight with cavalry. To do this, after the fight was over, he went back to where it took place, passing beyond the Confederate lines. In front of the house where he found Lorance wounded, he captured two mounted Federal soldiers, one belonging to the quartermaster's department, the other a cavalryman. The wounded man had lost his horse in the fight that morning, had been captured by the enemy, and left at this farmhouse, being too badly injured to be moved at that time. Mr. Nash mounted his comrade on one of the captured horses and brought him back into the Confederate lines, had his wound dressed at his own expense, gave him one of the captured horses and sent him farther on to the rear, Mr. Nash returning to the front. This wound proved so severe that Lorance was never able again for military duty; he lived many years after this and died but recently in Jackson Miss., where his family are supposed to reside at this time. He was also largely instrumental in saving the life of another comrade, Alfred Land (now a practicing lawyer in Shreveport, La.), who was the party already mentioned as shot through and through and bayoneted in the breast, in a charge made by Captain Harvey, with his company of cavalry, on a much superior force of Federal infantry, near Natchez, Miss. These are the facts in connection with this incident: The infantry were routed and driven back inside their breastworks, leaving forty of their number dead on the field. The fight being over, Captain Harvey (who had himself been wounded in the action), supposing he would at once be pursued by an overwhelming force of fresh troops, gave orders to fall back by the road along which the fight had occurred. Land had been wounded in the hottest of the fray, and near the close of the fight and his wounds were supposed to be mortal. Two men were left with him, after the command had gone some little distance, a rear guard being established. They continued to move on in the direction of Washington, a small town a few miles almost east of Natchez, while P. L. Jordan and Mr. Williams (Jordan in a buggy that had been pressed into service, and Williams on horseback) were sent back after Land. Mr. Nash, being with rear guard, as they came along, volunteered to go back also. As they went on it was soon agreed that it would be unsafe and imprudent to go farther with a buggy, so it was decided that Jordan should stop where he was with the buggy, and that the other two should go on and see if the wounded man could be found. The two rode on for some distance, and over much of the battleground. It was soon evident that Land was not on that part of the field where he had been wounded. The thought here occurred to Mr. Nash that Land might be somewhere in the immediate vicinity, and that the place where he would be most likely found was off to the left of the Natchez road, in the woods a few hundred yards from where the fighting ceased. Supposing the two men with the wounded man would have tried to leave the field in that direction, Mr Nash proposed to Mr. Williams that if he would stay in the road and picket well toward Natchez, he would leave the road and go on to the left and in the woods and see if Land could be found. This being agreed, Mr. Nash went forward to attempt what he had volunteered to do. Going down some distance in the direction stated, he called for Land, but no voice replied that he could hear. He then rode still farther forward and still nearer Natchez toward a house in the woods. There he learned that three men had been seen going off in a certain direction; supposing these were the parties, he galloped down in the direction indicated and among some ravines, after calling Land and searching about a little, he found him at last and alone, down in a gully, his horse hitched near by. Mr. Land was deathly pale and to all appearance in a dying condition. Mr. Nash dismounted and tried to get him to mount; this he would make no effort to do, in his helpless condition. He could hardly speak above a whisper. He said he would certainly die, and desired to be left alone. Mr. Nash next brought Mr. Land's horse up and tried to lift Land so he could mount, but found this to be impossible. Mr. Nash's pony was small and much lower than the horse; Land was also lying or reclining upon the side of the gully. Taking in the situation he led his pony down on the lower side, or bottom of the gully, having thus the advantage of the ground, and with all the strength possible, and with some little effort on the part of the wounded man, he was thus enabled to lift him in the saddle. Land clasped the front of the saddle; he could not or did not take the reins so as to guide the horse. Mr. Nash, then mounting Land's horse and taking his pony's reins in hand, started back, riding Land's horse and leading his pony, which Land was now riding. He soon reached Mr. Williams, next the buggy, in which, by the side of Jordan, Land was placed, they driving off in the direction Captain Harvey had gone with his command. This done Mr. Nash again took his place with the rear guard. When Mr. Nash was wounded, as before stated, he received a sixty days fourlough; the day it expired he was back with the company, and though his wound troubled him at times, he served constantly, and on active duty until the close of the war. Mr. Nash was in Columbus, Ga., when it was heard that the army in Virginia had surrendered; Captain Harvey having followed to this point Wilson's raid from Eastport, Miss. The company after the death of Captain Harvey, who was killed in Columbus, Ga., turned and made its way with some difficulty back to Gainesville Ala., to Gen. W. H. Jackson's division of cavalry, to which Harvey's scouts belonged. The cavalry was then being paroled every day. Mr. Nash, with others of the company, concluded they would not surrender, but would make their way to the Mississippi river, cross over and join the army on the other side. Each of this party was to go home, spend a few days and all meet near Rodney, on the river, on June 4, then only a few days off. Mr. Nash having then no home, his father having died while he was in the army, and the family having broken up housekeeping, spent the few days allowed him with relatives, near Gainesville, Ala., but left in time to reach the Mississippi river on the evening of June 3, the day before the time agreed upon to meet. There he learned, for the first time, that the army on the other side had also surrendered. After resting himself and his horse a day or so, he went back some fifteen or twenty miles to Port Gibson, Miss., and surrendered, being paroled by the Federal officer in command of that post. He then started back again across the state of Mississippi, to Gainesville, Ala.

At the surrender Mr. Nash was but a few days past eighteen. Owing to the results of the war, Southern families, as a general rule, at that time had but little available means. Greatly desiring to complete his education, he started to school, for the first six or eight months attending the common schools of the country and then entering the University of Mississippi, first in the literary and then in the law department. He holds a certificate from the university, showing that at the time he entered the law class he was entitled to graduation in all the studies finished anterior to the senior year. Owing to limited means, and in order the sooner to be able to help his younger brothers and sisters he was compelled, in the fall of 1867, to leave the senior class in the literary department. This he regretted very much, being a regular member in good standing in the class of 1868, and all its members being among his nearest and dearest friends. Having studied law during two vacations under Hon. C. F. Miller, of Starkville, Miss., a first-class lawyer and a man of sterling worth and integrity, he was in the fall of 1867 enabled, on a strict examination, to enter (in everything except real estate) the senior law class of the University of Mississippi, under Hon. L. Q. C. Lamar. The junior class then being in real estate, he concluded to try and graduate the following commencement. For some four months he carried on both the junior and senior law studies, reciting with the juniors in the morning and the seniors in the evening. Later on he caught up with the regular senior class, leaving the juniors and becoming a regular senior about the first of January, 1868, graduating with his class the following June. This was at a time when the law course (as a general rule) required two years. While at the university, during the last six months of his second year, and during the whole of the last year, he labored under great financial embarrassment. Along with many other Mississippi boys, supposed to be in the same situation, in order to economize their means and be enabled to complete their education, they boarded themselves and thus reduced the cost of living to a minimum. They did their own marketing, made their own fires, cut their own wood, did their own cooking, washed their own dishes, etc. From such and similar action on the part of certain boys at the University of Mississippi, arose at that institution the system called "batching," Mr. Nash being among the first to "batch," by which many young men of limited means were enabled to gain a first-class education. He not only boarded himself in the manner stated, but sought, and during the greater part of the time he was in the law department, after he had become a regular senior, served in a position in the clerk's office of the United States district court at Oxford, Miss., where he worked until about two o'clock in the afternoon and then went and recited with the law class; thus most of the day was consumed; he did most of his studying at night.* It might be said at this point that Colonel Lamar trusted Mr. Nash for his tuition while a student in the law class, as well as loaned him, from his private library, the necessary law books; and thus he was enabled to pursue his studies to advantage. Again, when he left Oxford to purchase his first law books, he received a loan of $50 from Mrs. A. M. Quinche, the wife of one of the professors, and a noble Christian woman, and thus he was enabled to begin his law practice. Mr. Nash began the practice of law in Starkville, Miss., in the fall of 1868, still owing some $300 money borrowed to complete his education and to begin his law practice. As soon as possible, and out of the first money he made, he paid his indebtedness. After that he assisted largely in the education of his brothers and sisters, advancing freely of his own means as he accumulated, trusting them to refund the same when able. The children owned some wild lands, yet it was not available, there being no market for such lands at that time. He greatly assisted two of his brothers in securing their education, one graduating at the dental college in Baltimore, Md., the other at one of the

---

*The above position he secured through the influence of Hon. R. A. Hill, United States judge, and George R. Hill, one of his classmates.

medical schools in Louisville, Ky. Two sisters owe their education largely to his assistance, and both graduated at first-class female colleges. After practicing law for several years he took a regular commercial course, graduating on the 19th day of August, A. D. 1873, at Eastman's National Business college, Poughkeepsie, N. Y. Mr. Nash has been a practitioner before the supreme court of Mississippi for many years. In Washington, D. C., on January 19, 1881, on motion of Hon. Charles Devens, attorney general of the United States, he was duly admitted and qualified as an attorney and counsellor of the supreme court of the United States.

In 1874, Mr. Nash and Miss Alice Ervin were married. They have two children, Harry and Evie, Harry being the elder. The father of Mrs. Nash, Mr. James W. Ervin, was for a long time a large planter in the eastern portion of Oktibbeha county, Miss. Mr. Ervin belongs to a family from which has sprung some of the best citizens in Mississippi, many of whom have held important positions. Her father was among the first settlers of east Mississippi, was a leading citizen, a captain in the Confederate service, and for many years before his death a ruling elder in the Presbyterian church. After the war he moved to Pleasant Ridge, Ala., where he died a few years since at a ripe old age. Mrs. Ann C. Ervin (formerly Miss Ann Jennings) was the mother of Mrs. Nash; she died when Mrs. Nash was about three years old, regretted and beloved by all who knew her; she was a noble, kind-hearted Christian women. Shortly after Mr. Nash began the practice of law he received unsolicited the appointment of county attorney of Oktibbeha county, Miss. This position he resigned in a short time, preferring to follow his general practice. In 1875, "the year de white folks riz," he was elected district attorney. The district composed then the counties of Clay, Lowndes, Noxubee, Oktibbeha, and Winston. This office he held until 1880. In 1884, with Hon. J. S. Montgomery, he was elected to represent Oktibbeha county in the lower branch of the state legislature, in which capacity he served two years. In the legislature of 1884 he took an active part in all important legislation, and especially in the passage of the bill establishing the Industrial Institute and College for the White Girls of Mississippi. He labored faithfully for the passage of this bill from the time it came from the senate until it became a law a month or more thereafter. This bill passed the house of representatives at the night session, Wednesday, March 5, 1884, by a close vote of forty-five to forty-three. The speech made by Mr. Nash that night in support of the bill was printed and largely circulated over the state. Mr. Nash is a member of the Baptist church, and has always been liberal in his religious views. His father's family are generally Baptists; one of his father's brothers, Rev. O. L. Nash, was a Methodist minister, however, and as such, quite distinguished in the early days of Mississippi. His mother's family are generally Methodist; she however, after her marriage connected herself with the Baptist church, both father and mother being members of that church at their death. Mr. Nash's wife's family are Presbyterians, though his wife since their marriage has connected herself with the Baptist church. Two of his sisters are members of the Christian church. His stepmother, his father having married twice, and a half-sister are members of the Methodist church. Such facts tend to make most persons conservative and liberal in their religious views. Among several other fraternal, charitable and benevolent societies Mr. Nash belongs to the Independent Order of Odd Fellows in the grand lodge of Mississippi, and of this order he was in 1888 elected grand warden, in 1889, deputy grand master, and in 1890, he was elected grand master. At the expiration of his term as such, the grand lodge held in Meridian in May, 1891, unanimously passed a resolution most complimentary to Mr. Nash. Since Mr. Nash began the practice of law, not to mention many political speeches delivered in active and heated county, district and state campaigns, he has made a number of public literary addresses before different societies, schools and colleges in Mississippi. He joined while at college in 1868 the democratic party, and has voted with, and acted with that party ever since in both state and national matters. The first vote he ever polled was against the constitution of 1868, with its proscriptive clauses framed by aliens and by negroes who had been recently set free, and which was attempted to be forced upon the people of Mississippi at the point of the bayonet. In the many political, as well as social troubles through which the South has passed since the war Mr. Nash has always borne his part; some of them were fraught with great risk, peril and danger. When Mr. Nash started out in life, Starkville was quite a small inland town of some five hundred, or seven hundred inhabitants, with no lines of public transportation. It is now an important point in Mississippi with a population of two thousand, and has good railroad facilities with the Mississippi Agricultural and Mechanical college, a state institution located near the corporate limits. These improvements were secured mainly, some entirely, through the efforts of the public-spirited citizens of the town and county. This gentleman has been closely connected with, and has taken an active part in, every enterprise looking to the improvement of the town of Starkville, or of the county of Oktibbeha. He has given liberally of both his time and his means; he has labored hard whenever and wherever the interest and the prosperity of his town or county were concerned. Mr. Nash is now in the prime of life, is a lawyer in active practice and a close student, residing still in Starkville, Miss., where he was raised, where he first settled, and living among the same people to whom, he says, he owes most of his success in life. His present partner in the practice is Hon. H. L. Muldrow, a prominent lawyer, and one of the leading public men of Mississippi. Mr. Nash is regarded as a safe and successful practitioner, and an able advocate of any cause he espouses. As a speaker, he is convincing and forceful, at times brilliant. As a citizen, he has the good will of all who know him, and in politics, he is respected by his opponents.

Yalobusha county, Miss., is the home of many enterprising and prosperous agriculturists, and the history of the leading men of the state would not be complete without a sketch of some of the more prominent. James L. Nations was born in Yalobusha county, Miss., in 1856, and is the son of Calvin and Anna (Higgs) Nations, also natives of Mississippi. Joseph Nations, the father of Calvin, was a native of Tennessee, where he lived to man's estate; he then removed to Alabama and lived there until 1835, then coming to Yalobusha county, Miss., and engaging in farming. He continued this business until his death, which occurred when he was eighty-two years of age. He devoted the greater part of his time to the raising of livestock, and was very successful in this. He married Lucretia Brown, a native of Tennessee. She lived to be three-score and ten years old, the age allotted to man. She was a member of the Baptist church. Of this union there were born several children, three sons and three daughters of whom lived to maturity, and one of whom is living yet—James C. Nations, of Calhoun county, Miss. Calvin Nations was one of the younger members of the family. He died in Yalobusha county in the spring of 1858 at the age of twenty-six years, leaving a wife and one child. A second child was born after his death, Samuel C. Nations, who resides in this county and is a farmer by occupation. James L. Nations, our subject, is the other child. The mother died in 1865. She was married, a second time, to David Murphree, of this county, by whom she had two sons: David W. and Rolland, both residents of this county.

James L. Nations spent the greater part of his youth in his native county and received his education there. At the age of fourteen years he began to attend the free schools, and finished his schooling at the Banner academy. When he was twenty-two years of age he began teaching school in Calhoun county, and has followed the profession more or less ever since. Mr. Nations was united in marriage December 23, 1880, to Miss Josephine Gore, of Calhoun county, a daughter of Caleb Gore, a prominent pioneer of the county. Six children have been born to her parents, and she is the fifth and youngest daughter; born June 23, 1860. She was educated in the common schools of her native county. One child, Zelma, was born to Mr. and Mrs. Nations, October 5, 1882. They are among the most prominent families of the community, aiding in every movement that has for its object the advancement of the public, and thoroughly worthy of the respect in which they are held. In 1885 Mr. Nations settled on his present place, and has been actively engaged in tilling the soil and developing his farm. He has cleared considerable land until he has reached six hundred acres. Two hundred and sixty acres are under good cultivation. The plantation is one of the finest in the Pine Valley settlement, and few better are found in the county.

Starting in life with nothing, George Washington Neel, planter, Sardis, Miss., has made all his property by his own indomitable will and excellent management, and is not only one of the substantial men of the county, but is honored and respected as a representative citizen. He was born in Knoxville, Tenn., on the 2d of October, 1832, and was the fifth of seven children born to Joseph and Elizabeth (Mathes) Neel, natives of Kentucky and Tennessee respectively. The father was of Irish and the mother of Dutch-Welsh descent. Joseph Neel went to Tennessee when a young man and soon after his marriage removed to Alabama (Morgan county), where he remained only a few years and then came to Tishomingo county, locating in Panola county, where he made his home for twenty-four years. He moved to Arkansas in 1866, located on the Arkansas river about twelve miles above Arkansas Post, and there his life terminated in 1867. He had followed planting all his life in a modest way and to a limited extent. George W. Neel passed the principal part of his boyhood days in Panola county and his advantages for an education were quite limited. Being endowed with much natural ability, however, he has improved all his spare moments and is to-day a well informed man. He has also been quite successful in other respects and is considered one of the best business men in the county. During the struggle between the North and South (or in 1861) Mr. Neel enlisted in the Confederate army, company C, Twenty-ninth Mississippi regiment and participated in the battles of Chickamauga, Corinth and Missionary ridge, where he was captured and carried to Rock Island. There he remained for sixteen months and was then exchanged at the mouth of James river, reaching home just a few days before peace was declared. He immediately began to work on his badly wrecked farm, and to rebuild, for his house had been burned, and although the outlook was discouraging he never faltered but went resolutely to work and is to-day endowed with plenty. He is the owner of one thousand acres of land in Quitman and Panola counties and has one hundred and seventy-five acres under cultivation He has sold most of his real estate and invested the proceeds, with the exception of $40,000 stock in a mine in Park county, Colo., in good notes. His nuptials with Miss Fannie Rouzee, a native of Mississippi and the only child of James and Pauline E. (Neel) Rouzee, were celebrated in 1860. Mr. and Mrs. Rouzee were natives respectively of Georgia and Tennessee, and Mr. Rouzee's paternal grandfather was a Frenchman who came to America at an early period. Mrs. Neel is an Episcopalian, and Mr. Neel, though not a communicant, is a strong believer in and supporter of that church.

James E. Negus, president of the First National bank of Greenville, was originally from the Keystone state, his birth occurring in 1842. He was the third child of James E. and Isabella (Van Syckel) Negus, natives of Pennsylvania and New Jersey respectively. Both were representatives of old and prominent families. James E. Negus, Jr., remained in his native state until twelve years of age, after which he went to Europe and attended school in Germany for five years, and then spent two years more in France, Italy and other countries. Returning to his own country after the Civil war began, he entered the Federal army at the age of nineteen, in the Fifteenth Pennsylvania cavalry, and served until the close of the war, participating in many campaigns and in the battles of Murfreesboro, Chickamauga, Chattanooga and other engagements. After the war he went to New York city, in the employ of Hoyt, Spragues & Co. for about two years, but in 1867 he went to St. Louis and engaged in mercantile pursuits. From there he went south to Vicksburg, and thence in 1870 to Greenville, Miss., where he has since made his home. For about ten years he owned and managed most successfully the immense wharfboat business on the Mississippi river, which, prior to the railroads, was the most important interest to Greenville. After this he was one of the chief promoters in the building of the first railroad in the delta country, now the Georgia Pacific railroad. Still later he embarked in the banking business and was made president of the Merchants' bank. In 1887 this was organized into the First National bank, and Mr. Negus continued as president, and is the largest stockholder. This bank has a capital of $100,000 and a surplus of $30,000, and it is to-day one of the foremost banks in the state. In 1887 Mr. Negus was active in organizing the Planters' Compress and Warehouse company, with a capital of $100,000, and was elected president of this also. He is the owner of much valuable property in the city, including the substantial bank building, the large Temple building, his fine residence and others. In 1876 he married Miss Louisa Mosby McAllister, who was born here and was the daughter of Gen. A. W. McAllister, a native of Georgia, and one of the pioneers of this section of Mississippi. Four children were born to this marriage: Wade Hampton, Carrie Belle, William Engle and Susie Engle, all members of the Presbyterian church with their parents. Mr. Negus is to-day one of Greenville's most substantial and conservative citizens, and no one is held in higher esteem or has a more honored name in her commercial, social or religious circles.

Capt. Charles A. Neilson, a planter of Tallahatchie county, Miss., was born in Lowndes county, September 14, 1826. His parents are William W. and Sarah F. (Frazier) Neilson. His father was born in Ireland, and came with his parents to America at the age of six. He settled in Maryland and there his parents died. Mr. Neilson served as lieutenant in the United States army in the War of 1812; resigning, he was for a time in Philadelphia, where he married, soon after moving to Mississippi. At the time of his arrival there was but one log cabin where Columbus now is, and he may be recorded as having been one of the earliest pioneers in Lowndes county. He located nine miles northeast of the site of Columbus, where he cleared land, improved a good farm and passed the balance of his life as a successful farmer, dying about twelve years ago. He was the only member of his family who came to Mississippi. His wife was born in Philadelphia and died about 1836, a devout Episcopalian. Mr. Neilson was married a second time to Louisa P. Abert, a native of Culpeper county, Va., who came to Mississippi with her brother. Mr. Neilson and his family were members of the Methodist Episcopal church. Capt. C. A. Neilson was the third in order of birth of seven children, three sons and four daughters, born to his parents: Anna D., who became the wife of John M. Symons, of Columbus, and is now deceased; Capt. Edward Neilson was killed at Prairieville, Ky.; he was captain of a company known as the Reyburn Rifles, and previous to the war he had served several years as midshipman in the United States navy; Capt. Charles A.; Jane C., who became the wife of Capt. R. B. Covington and died in Texas; Captain Covington served through the entire period of the war, and was killed at Mobile almost immediately after Lee's surrender; William W. died in Lowndes county in 1863; Catharine C., the wife of Dr. James W. Hopkins, a physician and dentist at Columbus; Elizabeth B., died in infancy. By his second wife Mr. Neilson had four children: Of these the Hon. James A. Neilson, a well-known planter and lumberman, is the present state senator from Lowndes county; Sallie D. was the second born; Prof. John A. Neilson is the proctor of the Agricultural and Mechanical college in Columbus; Sophia married Sylvester Lewis, who is engaged in the banking business at St. Louis. Captain Neilson in his youth attended the public schools near his home, and was afterward for about eighteen months a student at La Grange college in Tennessee. During the Mexican war he enlisted in the Lowndes guards of the Second Mississippi infantry, commanded by Col. Reuben Davis, with which he did valiant service. During a portion of the time he was on garrison duty at Saltillo and Monterey. Returning to Mississippi after the war, he was married in 1852 to Julia A., a daughter of Benjamin P. and Catharine L. Clifford, both of whom were born near Charleston, S. C., where they were reared and married. At an early day Mrs. Neilson's parents came to Lowndes county, Miss., where Mr. Clifford was killed by a horse about thirty years ago. His wife survived until a few years since, dying in Tallahatchie county. Both were members of the Baptist church. Mrs. Neilson was born in Mississippi, and bore her husband no children. In 1861 Mr. Neilson joined the sixty-day troops, and served during the term of his enlistment, most of the time at Bowling Green, Ky. Later he enlisted in company H of the Thirty-fifth Mississippi infantry, and soon after was made commissary of that regiment, which position he filled till about the close of 1864, at which time, failing to secure a reappointment, he joined General Chalmer's cavalry, with which he served till the close of the war, surrendering at Gainesville, Ala. He was in the siege of Vicksburg and in various hard-fought engagements and skirmishes in Georgia and Mississippi. In 1867 he removed to Tallahatchie county, and lived in different places in that county until 1870, when he returned to Lowndes county; a year later, however, he went back to Tallahatchie county, locating on his present farm, ten miles west of Harrison Station. He is the owner of fourteen hundred acres of land, five hundred acres of which are under cultivation. The war left him comparatively bankrupt, but by industry and good management he has since retrieved his fortunes to a considerable extent, and is looked upon as a successful man. He has been for many years a member of the Columbus lodge No. 4, A. F. & A. M. Captain Neilson is a very pleasant gentleman to meet and a fine conversationalist, while he is respected by all who know him as an honest, straightforward man.

Hon. J. C. Neilson is a native of Lowndes county, Miss., where he was born on the 15th of April, 1838, to William W. and Louisa (Abert) Neilson, the former of whom was born in Ireland in 1792, and when about six years of age he was brought to the United States, and until he attained his eighteenth year was a resident of Baltimore. He then joined the United States army and became captain of a company in a regiment of United States regulars. After serving twelve years, during a part of which time he served in the Seminole war, he resigned at Pensacola, Fla., about 1821, and started North overland. As he passed through the country he saw its natural advantages so clearly and became so infatuated with it that here he concluded to make his future abiding place. He entered a large tract of land and afterward purchased other property during his lifetime, thus acquiring a large amount of real estate, a large part of which his son, J. C. Neilson, now owns. He found that the life suited him much better than soldiering and made this his calling until his death, which occurred in 1869. J. C. Neilson attended the common schools when young, after which he spent two years at an institution in Greene county, Ala. At the youthful age of seventeen years he began to engage earnestly in planting, which he followed with success until 1861, when he enlisted in a cavalry company. Possessing all the ardor of youth and of the native Southerner, he was very desirous of at once entering into active service and would not wait for his company to be ordered out but joined an infantry company as a private (the Columbus Rifles) of the Fourteenth Mississippi, and went to Corinth for organization. He was put into Buckner's division and at the battle of Fort Donelson was captured and was sent as a prisoner of war to Camp Douglas, Chicago, where he was kept in captivity for about four months. He then succeeded in making his escape by medium of a forged pass and made the best of his way home, where he remained until his regiment was reorganized at Clinton, Miss. He then rejoined his command and went to northern Mississippi. In the latter part of 1863 his command was joined to Johnston's army, after which he participated in the battles of Franklin; captured at Nashville, Tenn., sent again to Fort Douglas, but was released by exchange at the end of four months and sixteen days, he going to New Orleans, thence to the mouth of Red river for exchange. He was in the siege of Atlanta, and was promoted to second sergeant. His career as a soldier was marked by courage, faithfulness and endurance, and he was conspicuous for his strict adherence to duty. He returned to his home at the close of the war, where he at once set to work to rebuild his fallen fortunes. He was still the owner of a good sawmill, which had escaped the general destruction, and immediately succeeding the war this yielded him an enormous income and was the means of once more rendering him independent financially. Much of the lumber, which he sold during this period at good prices, was raised on his own land and sawed in his mill, and was thus clear gain. He is now the owner of ten hundred and forty acres of land, of which he has four hundred acres under cultivation, sixty of which are devoted to pasture and the rest to cotton principally. In addition to successfully conducting his sawmill and plantation he operates a gristmill for grinding corn and a fine steam cottongin, which does his own as well as some of his neighbors' ginning. He was first married in 1866 to Miss Mary B. Barry, a native of Lowndes county, whose parents were South Carolinians. To their union five children were born, three of whom are living: Louisa A., Anna Barry and Catherine Simms. The mother of these children died in 1878, and Mr. Neilson's second union was consummated December 3, 1879, to Miss Catherine Barry, by whom he has three children: J. Crawford, John Bruce and Sarah Danbridge. His children are all exceptionally refined and intelligent, and he takes much interest in their preparation for the active duties of life. Mr. Neilson has identified himself with the democratic party since the war, and in 1876 was elected by his numerous friends to the state legislature from Lowndes county, and while a member of that body he was the author of a bill for the protection of fish and for the manufacture of domestic wine. He was on the committee that framed an act for the protection of game, also the committee of registrations and elections and unfinished business, and in his encounters with members during their deliberations the admirable and lucid style in which he expressed himself, and his sound views on the subjects under discussion, placed him at once among the active and useful members of the legislature. In 1887 the distinction of state senator was conferred upon him, and owing to the faithful and able manner in which he has looked after the interests of his section he has since filled this position. He advocated bills for organizing the national guards, equalizing assessment of taxes, and supported the bill pensioning Confederate soldiers. He opposed the repeal of the law granting exemption to corporations, and was on the committee of agriculture and chairman of the committee on military affairs.

Hon. Benjamin F. Nelson, a retired planter of Copiah county, was born in Fauquier county, Va., in 1817, a son of George and Elizabeth (Porter) Nelson, who were born in Virginia. His father devoted his entire life to agricultural interests. He served his country in the War of 1812 and 1814. He and his wife reared eight children to manhood and womanhood, six of whom are now living: James M., of Booneville, Mo.; Louis P., of Virginia; Agnes, wife of B. B. Booth, of Virginia; Virginia, wife of Gus Ficklin of Virginia; Kate N., wife of T. Stark (deceased), of Virginia, and Benjamin F., of Copiah county, Miss. Our subject came to Copiah county in 1836, locating at Gallatin, where he served for about one year as assistant county surveyor. For three years thereafter he engaged in the mercantile business, but going out of trade he devoted his entire attention to planting. In 1841 he married Elma Graves, a daughter of James and Sarah (Holliday) Graves, of Copiah county. They had twelve children, the following of whom—five in number—are living: George B., of Hazlehurst; Dr. Thomas Y., of Copiah county; Anna, wife of Hiram B. Giant, of Hazlehurst; Agnes V., who lives at home; Sallie F., wife of Dr. Young, of Copiah county. Mr. Nelson has twenty-eight grandchildren, young and old, of whom he is justly proud. His wife died in 1889. For many years he has held the office of deputy sheriff in this county, and in 1840 he was elected a member of the legislature, in which capacity he served during one term. Mr. Nelson is one of the most respected residents as well as one of the oldest inhabitants of the county. His natural abilities are of a high order, and his business operations have been so successful that he has amassed considerable wealth. Although nearly seventy-five years of age, his health is yet good and he is active and mentally bright. His business and social standing are good, and his long experience has given him a fund of reminiscences which makes him an enjoyable and instructive companion to those who have any interest in listening to the tales of the past.

Frank C. Nelson, real estate agent of Jackson, Miss., was born in Carrollton, Carroll county, Miss., in 1858, the eldest of seven children born to James H. and Mary E. (Fendwick) Nelson, the former of whom was born in Tennessee. In 1846 the father came to Mississippi and until 1875 was engaged in merchandising in Carroll county. He was then elected to the position of deputy state treasurer, in which office he remained until his death in the fall of 1883. He was very successful as a man of business and filled the position of deputy state treasurer to the complete satisfaction of all concerned. His widow survives him and is a member of the Presbyterian church. The paternal grandfather, Richard R. Nelson, was a native of Tennessee, a lawyer by profession and came to Mississippi in 1846, locating at Carrollton, where he practiced his profession. He was a very able lawyer and was elected to the office of circuit judge, in which capacity he served for years. After retiring from the bench he for years enjoyed a large and profitable practice and was always spoken of in the highest terms. At the time of his death he was one of the most popular and prominent politicians of his county, and also held high rank as a citizen. Mary E. (Fendwick) Nelson was brought to Mississippi by her parents when an infant, but they died soon after, leaving her an orphan, consequently but little is known of them, but it is supposed that they originally came from Delaware. Frank C. Nelson was educated in Carrollton but at an early age began active labor for himself in a store, which calling he continued to follow in Greenwood for eight years. In 1876 he came to Jackson and in 1882 became interested in the Yazoo and Mississippi Delta Land business, which syndicate he represents in the controlling of two hundred and ninety-six thousand acres, all of which is in the delta, and placed on the market at liberal terms. He is the owner of five thousand six hundred acres of land in the delta, the most of which is exceptionally fertile and a considerable portion under cultivation, the rest being heavily covered with timber. Aside from this he owns some fine residence property in the city of Jackson and four hundred and eighty acres in Carroll county, which he is rapidly clearing and improving and will soon have a magnificent property. Mr. Nelson is an energetic young man of a high order of business attainments, and by giving earnest and careful attention to business he is enabled to transact any commission expeditiously, and to warrant satisfaction in every instance. He was one of the organizers of the Capital Cooperage and Manufacturing company, and is treasurer of the same. In 1881 he was united in marriage to Miss Ida Langley, a native of Jackson and a daughter of Willis Langley, a well known merchant of the city. To Mr. and Mrs. Nelson the following children having been born: Frank C., Jr., Fred., Bessie May, William Nugent, and Annie Marion. Mr. Nelson and his wife are members of the Episcopal church, in which he is a vestryman and secretary of the Sunday-school. Mr. Nelson's brothers and sisters are as follows: Willie F., who is engaged in planting in Carroll county; Mary, Samuel, Prentiss, Flora and Lillie, the two last named being still in school.

Dr. J. C. Nelson has been a resident of the town of Austin, Tunica county, Miss., since 1850, but has been a worthy citizen of the state since 1840. He was born in Tennessee October 5, 1818, to Robert and Mary (Combs) Nelson, both of whom were born in the Palmetto state, but were married in Tennessee, where they reared a family of six sons and two daughters, Stephen C., a resident of Humphreys county, Tenn., and Dr. J. C. being the only ones who are living. Those deceased are: George L., Joshua, William A., Robert L., Myra J., and Cora G., who became the wife of William B. Foster, of Tennessee. The parents of these children spent their declining years in Tennessee, and were there called from life in 1873 and 1878 respectively. Dr. J. C. Nelson is the only one of the family who came to Mississippi, and in Marshall county, of this state, he was married in 1845, Miss Mary C. Ferguson becoming his wife and in time the mother of his four children: Dr. William J., of Tunica; Mattie A., wife of W. G. Jaquess, clerk of the county court of Tunica county; Florence G., wife of W. A. Warfield, and Cora G., wife of Dr. M. J. Alexander. The mother of these children, who was a most estimable and intelligent lady, was called from life at Austin, Miss., in 1868, and the following year the Doctor's second marriage was consummated, his wife being Mrs. Virginia Perry, of Marshall county, Miss. Their union resulted in the birth of one child that is dead. The Doctor obtained his medical education in his native state, and his first practice was done in Pontotoc county, Miss., in 1845, since which time he has practiced continuously, now ranking among the oldest and most successful practitioners of the state. His success in life as a member of the medical fraternity, and his high position as a practitioner of the healing art have been obtained rather by the force of native talent and culture than by tact, and owing to his thorough knowledge of his profession and his long practice, it is conceded by all competent judges that he ranks among the eminent members of the medical brotherhood. His second wife was called from life in 1870, at her home in Austin, and the Doctor now makes his home with his daughter, Mrs. Cora Alexander, whose son, William J., is one of the leading physicians of the county. Although in his seventy-third year, Dr. Nelson shows but little the ravages of time, either mentally or physically, and yet has a good and paying practice. He has been a resident of the bottoms for over forty years, and as his health has always been very good, he has never been obliged to move to other climes to recuperate. He has always interested himself in the political affairs of his section, and his public services have been characterized by a noticeable devotion to the welfare of the county, and his fidelity and faithfulness in discharging the duties of the positions he has filled have been an excellent example to his successors, and has tended to make and keep the public service pure. His intelligent views on all subjects and the interest he took in public affairs soon placed him as a leader of his party, and in 1850 he was elected by his numerous friends to the position of clerk of the court of Tunica county, Miss., at which time there were but forty-eight voters in the county, he receiving forty-five of the votes polled. He filled this position with ability for twelve years, at the end of which time he was elected probate judge, in which capacity his sterling integrity, sound judgment, broad intelligence, and liberal and progressive ideas were exercised for the benefit of mankind. His decisions were not made without careful and painstaking study of the evidence adduced, and upon retiring from the bench at the end of three years he bore with him the confidence and respect of all. He was postmaster of Austin for a number of years, and is a worthy member of the Masonic fraternity.

Mrs. Luly L. Nelson, widow of Samuel Nelson, formerly a planter of Issaquena county, Miss., was born in this county on the farm where she now resides, and is the daughter of Zach and Martha (Bowie) Leatherman. Zach Leatherman was born in Mississippi in 1813, and like his father and grandfather before him was a wealthy planter and a slaveowner. He moved to Issaquena county in 1836, resided on Dunbarder plantation and managed the same for Mr. Dunbar for a number of years. He then bought the farm on which Mrs. Nelson now resides, which then consisted of five hundred and twenty-one acres, but which has since been added to until it now numbers fifteen hundred acres with seven hundred acres improved. It is now one of the handsomest plantations on the river. During the late war Mr. Leatherman practiced medicine and continued this for a few years afterward in Arkansas, where he made his home during those troublesome times. His death occurred in 1883, but his wife still survives. After his death she married Captain Burns, of Canada. By her first marriage she became the mother of three children, only Mrs. Nelson now living. One child died in infancy and the other, James B., received his final summons in January, 1891. Mrs. Nelson's paternal grandfather, Samuel Leatherman, was a native of Mississippi, and her great-grandfather was a native of the Keystone state, having emigrated to Mississippi when it was French territory. Her maternal grandparents, John J. and America (Watkins) Bowie, were natives of Louisiana and Mississippi respectively. The Bowie family was originally from Scotland, three brothers of that name having emigrated from that country to this at a very early period. One settled in Maryland, the other two in North Carolina, and the branch of the family of which Mrs. Nelson is a descendant came from the last named state. She is a relative of ex-Governor Bowie of Maryland, and is also a grand-niece of Col. James Bowie, after whom the world-famed bowie-knife was called, and who was one of the most wonderful men of his day. He was a brother of her grandfather Bowie. Mrs. Nelson was married to Samuel Nelson in 1873. He was a native of Tennessee, and was the son of Samuel Nelson, Sr., who was a soldier in the War of 1812. The elder Nelson moved to Mississippi at an early day and was quite prominent in the early settlement of Issaquena county. Samuel Nelson, Jr., served with distinction as a scout in the Confederate army during the Civil war and afterward became one of the prominent young planters of the county. He filled the office of levee commissioner and was holding that position at the time of his death, which occurred in 1883, at the age of forty-four years. By his marriage he became the father of one child, J. Howard Nelson, who is attending school at Memphis, Tennessee. Previous to this marriage Mr. Nelson had married a Miss Emma Holden of Thibodeaux, La., whose parents came from the Buckeye state. The fruits of this union were four children, three living: Emma H. N., wife of W. B. Wilmans, of Dallas, Texas; Samuel, of the Merchants' National bank, at Vicksburg, and William P., who resides in Greenville, Miss. Mr. Nelson was a member of the Knights of Pythias, Hay's Landing, lodge No. 16, was the first chancellor commander of the lodge, and the first member of the same to die. Mrs. Nelson is an intelligent and cultured lady and a very interesting conversationalist. She resides on her fine plantation near Arcadia, and uses excellent judgment in its management.

Shepherd S. Neville, a prominent planter and merchant of Giles, Kemper county, Miss., was born in Sumter county, Ala., in 1858, and is a son of William H. and Sharah H. (Spencer) Neville. William H. Neville, his father, was born in South Carolina in 1812, and was a son of William and Elizabeth (Lindsey) Neville. He merchandised for some years and afterward retired from business and engaged in planting, and removed to Sumter county, Ala., at an early day. He was married in Pickens county, Ala., in 1848, and reared a family of seven children: Robert S., William H., Jr., Belle, Helen, Shepherd S., Martha W., and Mary R. He was a man who was prosperous in business, and who took a deep interest in home enterprises. Politically he was a stanch democrat. He represented his county in the legislature in 1882, and was chairman of the democratic county committee of Sumter county. He was a member of the Masonic fraternity. His death occurred in 1887, in the month of July, in Sumter county, Ala. His wife was born in South Carolina in 1829, and she was a daughter of Shepard and Elizabeth (Harrison) Spencer. Her parents were both natives of South Carolina, and died in Noxubee county, Miss. She is living in Sumter county, Ala. Shepherd S. Neville was born in Sumter county, Ala., at Gainesville, in 1858, and received his education in the common schools of that day. At the age of seventeen years he engaged in the milling business and planting, which he continued until 1888. In that year he was united in marriage to Miss Maria C. Giles, only daughter of Simmons H. and Maria F. (Jones) Giles. He and his wife are zealous members of the Episcopal church. He is a democrat in his political views, and is a zealous supporter of the movements of that party. He owns about eight thousand acres of land in Sumter county, Ala., and Noxubee and Kemper counties, Miss.

Simmons H. Giles was a conspicuous character in the early settlement of Kemper county, where he located with his father in 1835. He was born in North Carolina in 1827, April 6th, and was a son of Jacob and Nancy L. (Harrison) Giles, natives of North Carolina. Jacob Giles was born July 27, 1799, and died April 22, 1860. He was a son of John Giles, a son of Nathaniel and Charity Giles, who was born August 29, 1750. Jacob Giles, as before stated, came to this county in 1835. He had poor educational advantages in his youth, but at the time of his death was one of the best informed and most public-spirited men of his day, whose sterling integrity and uprightness of life commanded the love and respect of all. Giles postoffice is named for him, he being the first settler in that community. He was married in North Carolina to Nancy L. Harrison, and they reared one of the four children born to them. He died in Kemper county, April 22, 1860, and his wife died January 3, 1885. Simmons H. was born in North Carolina April 6, 1827, and was educated at Jackson, Tenn. In 1854 he was married to Maria F. Jones, a daughter of Dr. B. A. and Maria (Cross) Jones. The father was a native of Virginia but removed to Tuscumbia, Ala., where he practiced medicine a number of years and finally settled in Sumter county, Ala., where he died in 1858, having given up medicine and successfully engaged in planting for twenty years in that county before his death. His wife died the same year. After his marriage Mr. Giles settled in Kemper county, and opened up a fine plantation, on which he built a beautiful residence. In 1860 he removed to the old plantation where his father had died. He and his wife reared one child, Maria C., who was born February 20, 1859. She is the wife of Shepherd S. Neville. In 1863 Mr. Giles enlisted in the Confederate service, and fought until the surrender. He was ever a friend of home enterprises, and contributed liberally of his means in the support of churches and educational institutions. He was a democrat, and a stanch adherent to the principles of his party. He was a very prosperous planter, owning about twelve thousand acres. He carried on a successful mercantile business in Scooba up to the time of his death, which occurred September 8, 1870. In his death the county lost a valued citizen, one whose sterling traits of character were an inspiration and in whom the poor and needy found ever a true friend and willing helper.

William Neville, a substantial merchant at Giles, Kemper county, Miss., was born in Sumter county, Ala., and is the eldest son of A. L. and Mary (McDow) Neville. The father was born in South Carolina in 1820, and removed thence to Greene county, Ala., in his boyhood; afterward he went to Sumter county. He was a son of William Neville, Sr., and Elizabeth (Lindsey) Neville. He was married in Greene county, Ala., in 1840, and seven children were born of the union: William, Samuel, Lucy, Mary, Andrew, Robert and James H. The mother died in 1852. She was born in 1820, in South Carolina, and was a daughter of William L. McDow. She was a worthy member of the Presbyterian church. After her death William Neville was married a second time, being united to Mrs. Nancy James. They had born to them three children: Pope, Fannie and George. The father died in Giles, Kemper county, in 1882. He was a member of the Presbyterian church, and in his political opinions adhered to the principles of the democratic party. At one time he was taxcollector of Sumter county. He was a merchant in Mobile, Ala., and was very prosperous. He was a man of deep integrity of character and a loyal citizen. Two of his sons were in the late war, William and Samuel; both were wounded, the latter at Seven Pines; he was an attorney by profession and died in Texas. William Neville spent his early days in Mobile, Ala., where he was a clerk in a store. In 1861 he enlisted in the Confederate army and was attached to the Third Alabama regiment. He saw some very hard service, participating in the battles of Seven Pines, Fredericksburg and Chancellorsville. At the last named place he received a gunshot wound which necessitated the amputation of his right foot. He was then discharged and sent to the hospital. After his recovery he went back to Sumter county, where he was engaged in merchandising. Later he became interested in farming. He was married in 1869 in Kemper county, Miss., to Miss Sallie P. Blocker, a daughter of George M. and Margaret (Perrin) Blocker. She was born in South Carolina in 1846 and was taken by her parents to Kemper county, Miss., in 1851. Mr. and Mrs. Neville are the parents of three children: Mary, George B. and Samuel A. The mother died in 1881. She was a member of the Episcopal church. Mr. Neville is identified with the democratic party and is well posted on all the leading issues of the day. He devotes his time and attention to his mercantile interests in Giles and is very successful. He is a member of the Episcopal church, and belongs to the Knights of Honor.

James H. Neville, district attorney of the second district of Mississippi, and practicing attorney at Scooba, Kemper county, Miss., was born in the state of Alabama, September 28th, 1852, and is the son of A. L. and Mary (McDow) Neville. His father was a native of South Carolina, born in 1820 and a son of William Neville. He was a wholesale merchant and cotton factor at Mobile, Ala., for ten years before his death, which occurred in 1882. He was actively interested in the political questions of the day, being allied with the democratic party. He was reared to the occupation of planting, but soon after he came of age he embarked in the mercantile trade, which he made his life's vocation. He was married in 1840 and seven children were born of the union: William, Lucy, Samuel, Mary, Andrew, Robert and James H. Mr. Neville was a man of rare business qualifications and held a position in the commercial circles of his county of which any man might have been proud. The mother of our subject was born in Greene county, Ala., and died in 1852, three days after the birth of James H. The father was married a second time to Mrs. James, of Mobile. Three children were born to them: Pope, Fannie and George. James H. Neville was reared in Sumter county, Ala., and was educated in the common schools. In 1871 he began the study of law and two years later he was admitted to the bar of Sumter county. In 1875 he removed to Kemper county, Miss., and located at Scooba, where he has since resided. In 1878 he was married at Scooba to Miss Susan Hart, a daughter of James E. and Susan (Harwood) Hart. They are the parents of three children: Florence, William and James. The parents are members of the Presbyterian church and take an active interest in all the movements of the community which tend to elevate the morals and improve the educational facilities. Mr. Neville is a democrat in his political views. He was elected district attorney in 1883 and was re-elected in 1887; was renominated for district attorney in July, 1891, for his third term without opposition. From 1878 to 1884 he was engaged in journalistic work, being during that time the editor of the Kemper *Herald*. He is a member of the Masonic order and of the Knights of Honor. In all his public career he has been a friend to the oppressed and a champion of the weak. He has displayed an unusual fitness for the work to which he has been called, and has reflected great credit upon his constituency.

Joseph and Edwin Newberger, who comprise the firm of Newberger Bros., are the sons of Leopold Newberger. The father began business in Coffeeville in 1842, and gained for himself the title of Old Reliable. No man in the state of Mississippi is more favorably and honorably known. He was born in Felheim, Bavaria, Germany, and emigrated to the United States at the age of sixteen years. He landed at Philadelphia in November, 1840, and journeyed thence by stage to Grenada, Miss., where his uncle, William Tandler, was a pioneer. The uncle gave him a stock of goods valued at about $20, with which he began to peddle in the country. He had but a limited education in his native language, and his knowledge of English was decidedly meager, so that his first business experience was anything but flattering; however, he was blessed with a great deal of determination, which is strongly characteristic of the German race, and he persevered until his efforts were crowned with success. He had been in this country but a year when Judge Carberry induced him to come to Coffeeville and go into business. Although he had but a few hundred dollars to invest, he rented a building and put in as large a stock as his means would permit; as his patronage grew he was enabled to increase his stock, and in an incredibly short time he took the lead among the merchants of Coffeeville He also dealt largely in slaves, being local agent for Forrest & Walton, of Memphis. In 1872 he went to New Orleans and engaged in the cotton commission business with the firm of R. Nugent & Co., remaining there for a period of three years, during which time he managed successfully both houses. He returned to Coffeeville, and in 1868 he established a branch store at Oakland, Miss., which is under the management of a son, Silvan Newberger. Mr. Newberger now resides in Louisville, Ky., where he has made his home since 1886, at which time he turned his business over to his sons. He was united in marriage in Louisville, Ky., in 1856, to Miss Esther Lichtenstader, whose father was a gentleman of great learning, a professor of one of the universities of Frankfort, Germany, and a member of a distinguished Jewish family; four of the brothers are connected with famous institutions of learning in Europe. Mrs. Newberger was a woman highly educated and of rare attainments; she took an especial delight in the rearing and training of his children, and was an ornament to the high social position which she occupied; she died in 1885, at the age of forty-eight years; she was born in Germany, and came to this country in 1856. To Mr. and Mrs. Newberger were born fourteen children, ten of whom are yet living: Joseph, Silvan, Charles, Dora, Hellen, Cornelia,

Edwin, Samuel, Isadore B. and Alma I.; those deceased are: Max, William, Josephine and Marcella. When a resident here Mr. Newberger took no especial part in politics further than to look after the interests of his people and the protection of his property. He is a man self-made, self-educated; he has been a constant reader and is thoroughly informed on all the leading topics of the day. In 1884 he became a Mason, joining Coffeeville lodge No. 83. For many years he was an alderman of the place and also served as town treasurer. He had a most beautiful home, which was known far and wide as the seat of the most elegant hospitality. Distinguished visitors to the place were often entertained there, and it was known as the home of prominent politicians when making a canvass. The children have been well educated, and in this a legacy has been bequeathed them of which no man can deprive them. Joseph Newberger, the eldest of the family, is a member of the Coffeeville lodge No. 83, A. F. & A. M., and he also belongs to Oakland lodge, I. O. O. F. In politics he takes an active interest and was tendered the nomination of state senator but declined; in a recent canvass he made more than twenty speeches in behalf of W. V. Moore, candidate for representative, and carried the election. Charles Newberger is also a member of the Masonic order. Joseph Newberger was the prime mover in the building of the new courthouse, and it was through his energy and untiring efforts that it was carried through. Newberger Bros. are the most extensive cotton dealers in northern Mississippi; they handle some twenty thousand bales yearly and do a business of $300,000 per annum. They buy cotton at all stations of the Illinois Central railroad of the Memphis branch, and have purchasing agents at Oxford, Coffeeville, Grenada, Vaiden, Eupora, Water Valley, Torrance, Winona, West Station, Tillatoba, Oakland and a number of smaller places. The property of the Newberger family is yet undivided, but it is all managed by the sons, each working for the interest of the whole. Charles Newberger is a traveling salesman for the firm of L. Moses & Co., Louisville, Ky.

John Newbery, Yazoo City, Miss. The gentleman whose name heads this brief biographical sketch dates his birth from the city of New Orleans, La., February 23, 1845. There were four children in the family, of whom he is the second. His parents were John P. and Caroline (Bower) Newbery, natives of North Carolina and Pennsylvania respectively. The father became a resident of Mississippi in 1855 and followed planting until his death, which occurred in 1867. His wife died the following year. The subject of this notice was reared in Mississippi and attended the private schools of the neighborhood until 1860, when he entered Dolbear's Commercial college at New Orleans. He was graduated from this institution in 1861, when he returned to his home to engage in husbandry. He now owns four hundred acres of land, cultivating two hundred and forty-five acres of the same. He was married in 1870 to Miss Lucy Ogden, of Mississippi, a daughter of Theophilus and Mary Ogden, who were also Mississippians by birth. Mr. and Mrs. Newbery are the parents of four children: Ella N., Kate H., Lucy and Estelle. When the late Civil war came and there was a call for volunteers Mr. Newbery enlisted, in 1861, in company F, Eighteenth Mississippi volunteer infantry, and was a member of this regiment until the battle of Gettysburg, when he was captured and carried to Fort Delaware; there he was held fifteen months, and after his release did not enter the service again. He participated in the engagements at Malvern hill, the seven days' fight around Richmond, the two battles of Fredericksburg, Gettysburg and Sharpsburg. Politically he affiliates with the democratic party. He is a member of the Masonic order. In all the walks of life he has exhibited that probity and honesty that have won for him hosts of friends and given him a place in the front ranks of the citizens of Yazoo county.

As a man of business Mr. David B. Newman's name and fame are coextensive with Jefferson and the surrounding counties. Every step of his financial and commercial career has been illustrated with acts of liberality, and with each vital interest of his section and his people he has been closely identified. If industry, hard work and ceaseless activity, united with a strong and determined perseverance, can accomplish anything in this world, Mr. Newman will undoubtedly become wealthy, for in him are to be found all the characteristics mentioned, and he deserves more than ordinary credit for his career thus far in life. He was born in Franklin county, Miss., October 15, 1860, his father, Maxwell Newman, being also born there. The grandfather, Solomon Newman, was a native of South Carolina, but when a young man came to Mississippi, and after some time being spent engaged in planting in Franklin county, of this state, he returned to the Palmetto state and married, returning hither with his bride. He became a wealthy planter, and on his large plantation he reared his family and resided until his death, having filled with success a number of local offices. Maxwell Newman was married in Franklin county to Miss Margaret Herring, a native of the county. Like his father before him he was an agriculturist, and on the plantation where he had labored faithfully to obtain a competency for himself and family he quietly breathed his last in 1864. His widow survives him at this writing, having borne her husband three sons and four daughters, all of whom grew to mature years. B. S. is a planter of Franklin county, and A. M. a merchant of Vicksburg, Miss. One sister is now deceased. The early boyhood of David B. Newman was spent in his native county, and in Hiwasse college he acquired a thorough practical education, completing an English course of study in 1879, soon after which he began teaching school, following this occupation in Jefferson county for one year, after which he clerked in a store at Union Church for a number of years. His next venture in earning his own living was to open a mercantile establishment near that place for one year, after which, in 1885, he formed a partnership with his brother, A. M. Newman, built a store and began business at McNair, their establishment being the second one opened at that point. The present firm of D. B. Newman & Co. was formed in 1890, and as their store room is large and roomy, their stock of general merchandise is well selected and large. Their trade, which amounts to about $40,000 annually, has been secured by honesty, fair dealing, and by studying and supplying the wants of the public. Mr. Newman has shown the best of judgment and tact, and as a natural result he is doing a thriving and constantly increasing business, and although he is yet a young man his outlook for the future is bright and promising. His marriage, which was celebrated in Franklin county, December 17, 1790, was to Miss Addie McNeil, a daughter of George McNeil (deceased). Mrs Newman was born and reared in Lincoln county, and being intelligent and well educated, she is proving a true helpmate to her husband.

Rev. James Milton Nicholson, one of the leading ministers of Kemper county, Miss., was born in Clarke county, Ala., February 12, 1830, and is a son of Theophilus and Rebecca S. (Goode) Nicholson. Theophilus Nicholson was a native of North Carolina and a son of Josiah Nicholson. He was married in Clarke county, Ala., having removed to that point from South Carolina in 1818. He was a farmer and was in good circumstances. In his politics he was a democrat. He died in 1844 and was buried on his plantation, which is now owned by the subject of this notice. He reared to mature years three of the seven children born to him and his estimable wife: Theodore L. (deceased), Josiah J. and James M. The mother of these children was born in Georgia in 1803, and was the daughter of William and Sarah (James) Goode. Her family were from Virginia, where they were well and favorably known. The maternal grandfather of our subject was a first cousin to Thomas Jefferson.

The mother died in Clarke county, Ala., in 1839. James M. spent his early life in this county, to which he removed with his father in 1839. His father purchased a large tract of land in Kemper county, and at the time of his death owned fourteen hundred acres. He received his education in his native state, principally at Howard college, Marion, Ala. In 1858 he entered the ministry and took charge of the old Wahalak Baptist church, of which he was pastor until 1866. The two years following he was at Meridian, Miss., and at the end of that time he came back to his plantation. He owns about fifteen hundred acres of land, which he has improved and brought to a high state of cultivation. Mr. Nicholson was married in 1856 to Miss Sallie E. Gordon, a daughter of James and Mary (Marsh) Gordon, natives of North Carolina. Mrs. Nicholson was born in Clarke county, Ala., in 1833. She died in 1880, and was buried in Sumter county, Ala. Two children were born to this union: James Milton, Jr., and Mary R., who died in childhood. James M., Jr., lived to be thirty-one years of age. He was born in Kemper county in 1857, and was educated at Meridian and at Howard college, Marion, Ala. He was married in 1884 to Miss Middleton E. Wiggins, a daughter of Thomas P. Wiggins. Four children were born to them, two of whom are living: Thomas Howard and James Milton, Jr., who reside with their grandfather. Mr. Nicholson, the son of our subject, was democratic in his political views. He belonged to the Grange in its palmy days. The Rev. Mr. Nicholson has for fifteen years been prominently connected with the ministerial work of this community. He has assisted in organizing a number of churches, and was the founder of the Baptist church at Binnsville, Kemper county. He has done a great amount of pioneer work in the church, and has been faithful and conscientious in the discharge of his duties.

Dr. J. E. Noble has devoted the greater part of his life to relieving the pains and ailments to which the human body is heir, and to his skill and talent the gratitude of hundreds is due. He is a native of Smith county, Miss., and was born in 1847 to Dr. Ezekiel and M. A. L. (Gammage) Noble, the former of whom was born in South Carolina and the latter in Alabama. The father was a graduate of the University of South Carolina and also of the Charleston Medical college, in which institution Prof. Samuel H. Dixon was a member of the faculty, occupying the same position thirty years later in Jefferson college, Philadelphia, of which noted institution of learning Dr. J. E. Noble was also a graduate. Dr. Ezekiel Noble removed to Smith county, Miss., in early manhood, where he became quite an extensive planter and popular and successful medical practitioner. His brother, Maj. Samuel Noble, represented Smith county, Miss., in the state legislature before the war. Dr. J. E. Noble received his initiatory training in the best schools in the section of the state in which he lived and later took a literary course in the State university at Oxford. Upon leaving college he taught school for a short time in Jasper county, and in the autumn of 1868 he entered the medical department of the University of Virginia, where he took one course of lectures. The following year he entered the Jefferson Medical college of Philadelphia, from which he graduated in 1870. He began the practice of his profession in Jasper county, Miss., and was there married in 1871 to Miss Florence R. Bender, a daughter of G. M. Bender, of that county. Succeeding this Dr. Noble practiced for a short time in Brandon, but in January, 1872, located at Fannin, near his mother, whose health was very bad, where he gave his exclusive attention to his profession for many years. He is a member of the Mississippi State Medical association. In the fall of 1880 he began merchandising, but the business grew so rapidly that it required the most of his attention, and he gradually retired from his professional duties, and for the past two years he has given his almost exclusive attention to his mercantile interests. He has a large interest in the Jackson Grocery company, of which he is vice president, and also owns a large amount of land and stock. He has always been interested in local and state politics, and although he has never sought office he has often represented his section in state and other conventions. He has been solicited through the local papers as well as by prominent citizens to become a candidate for the state senate, but has never yet accepted. He is an active member of the Baptist church, in which he is a deacon, and superintendent of the Sunday-school.

William S. Noble, planter, Canton, Miss. Not without justice Mr. Noble is conceded to hold a representative position among the prominent and successful planters of Madison county, and has continued steadily to pursue the even tenor of his way, which, no doubt, accounts for his prosperity. He was born in Madison county, Miss., May 24, 1833, and was the fourth in order of birth of five children born to William and Mary (Stowers) Noble, both natives of Mississippi. The father was a planter, and followed that occupation in his native state until his death in 1835. The mother followed him to the grave two years later. The paternal grandfather was a native of Maryland, and the maternal grandfather was born in Mississippi. William S. Noble became familiar with the duties of the farm at an early age, and secured a good practical education in the private schools of Mississippi. When it became necessary for him to choose some occupation, he very naturally selected that of planting, and this he has continued to pursue up to the present time. He was married in 1859 to Miss Fanny B. Helm, a native of Mississippi, and this union has resulted in the birth of six children: William H., Otway B., Battle, Minnie E., Birdie F. and Fanny. Mr. Noble is a member of the Farmers' Alliance, and in politics affiliates with the democratic party. He extends a liberal and willing hand to all laudable enterprises, and is prominent in all good work. He is a man of good business qualifications and excellent judgment.

Leland Noel, Lexington, Miss. The Noel family are of French descent. Their ancestors were among the Huguenots who were driven from France by religious persecutions in the latter part of the seventeenth century. They went to London, England. From there Edmond Noel came to Virginia about 1680, and located on the Rappahannock river. He engaged in mercantile and agricultural pursuits. His son James succeeded him, and was well circumstanced. James Noel had six sons: Edmond, Theodoric, James, William, Leonard and Callis, and two daughters. All of his sons served in the Revolutionary war, Callis being slain in battle. Theodoric was a Baptist minister, and served as chaplain. One of the daughters married Alfred Monroe, a brother of President James Monroe, and the other married Robert Garnett. Edmond Noel had seven daughters, three of whom were never married, and of the other four, Elizabeth was married to a Mr. Purdie, Nancy to George Turner, Niecie to a Mr. Richardson, and Sarah to a Mr. Motley, and after his death to a Mr. Sale. E. F. Noel, his youngest child and only son, was born in Essex county, Va., in 1793. He received a good education. He was married to Elizabeth F. Barton, daughter of Maj. Thomas Barton, and granddaughter of Ross Jones, a man of wealth and prominence. E. F. Noel engaged in farming and accumulated a large estate, including numerous slaves. He represented his native county with distinction in one or more terms of the Virginia legislature. He was a talented writer, and the author of several able essays against monopolies and the national banking system. He was one of the pioneers of Mississippi, having purchased a large tract of land near Franklin, in Holmes county, in 1835, which he placed in charge of his two oldest sons, Leland and Edmond B. He died in 1871, and his wife at about the same time. He had four sons: Leland, Edmond B., William L. and Henry R., the latter a physician of prominence in Baltimore, and who was one of the youngest surgeons in the Confederate army. E. F. Noel had seven daughters, two of whom, Emily and Julia, were never married, and of the other five Frances was married to the Rev. James Henshall, Eliza to Dr. John J. Wright, Rebecca to Dr. D. Sutton, and Louisa to Warring Lewis, who after her death married her sister Susan.

Leland, assisted by Edmond B., managed his father's plantation until 1848, when he purchased one of his own. At the beginning of the war he was in prosperous circumstances. In 1864 he lost his sight, but has continued to be interested and posted on all current matters. On April 2, 1851, he was married to Margaret, a daughter of Dr. B. W. Sanders. They were the parents of nine children, one of whom died in infancy, and the others are: Thomas D.; Elizabeth B., who is married to W. B. White; Edmond F., (see sketch); Benjamin S., Mary A., Henry L., Fannie J. and Annie S. Fannie J. was beautiful, amiable and one of the most dutiful and affectionate of daughters. She died October 21, 1890. Leland Noel has ever been an active supporter of the principles of the democratic party. Prior to the war he was a delegate to nearly all of the political conventions, and numbered among his friends many of the most prominent men of this state. With his wife and daughters he moved to Lexington, in 1886, leaving his old plantation in charge of his son Thomas D.

Edmond Favor Noel was born on his father's farm in Holmes county, Miss., on March 4, 1856. His father, Mr. Leland Noel, came from Virginia in 1835, being then about twenty years of age, and settled on a tract of land, a part of which he yet owns and has ever since cultivated. In 1835 his mother, Margaret Sanders, then but a few years old, was brought by her father, Dr. B. W. Sanders, from North Carolina to Franklin, in Holmes county, to which place his grandfather, Col. D. M. Dulaney, had by four or five years preceded him. The parents of E. F. Noel were married April 2, 1851. Nine children were born of that union, he being the second son and third child. Until his seventeenth year he had only such educational advantages as were afforded by irregular country schools, performing in the meanwhile such labor in the fields, and otherwise, as usually befalls a country boy of moderate circumstances. Prior to the war his father had been a well-to-do and successful farmer and a public-spirited citizen who actively participated in political affairs, though never aspiring to office, and who had the esteem and confidence of all who knew him. During the war, while sick, Mr. Noel was captured by Federal troops and subjected to such exposure in bad weather as caused the permanent loss of health and of his eyesight. Business reverses, immediately after the war, lost him all but land, and involved that. His uncle, Maj. D. W. Sanders, one of the leading lawyers in Louisville, Ky., took charge of E. F. Noel's education, in September, 1872, and sent him to the public high school of Louisville for three years, and afterward furnished him the opportunity of reading law at the high school in a class largely over a hundred students. He took third to the highest honor for general scholarship that year; the next to the highest the second year, and the third year, the very highest in the class. In March, 1877, he was admitted to the bar at Lexington, Miss., and commenced practicing law there, possessed of nothing but his professional services. At first he cleared expenses by abstracting land titles, and other services rendered older attorneys. He soon acquired a fair share of the law business of his county. His paternal and maternal ancestors had repeatedly represented the states of Virginia and North Carolina respectively in their legislatures. His grandfather, Dr. B. W. Sanders, was a member of the Mississippi legislature from Holmes county in 1838, at the time of his death. His granduncle, Thomas Dulaney, had formerly, and his uncle, D. W. Sanders, had subsequently held the same position. In 1881 E. F. Noel was, by a practically unanimous vote, elected to the legislature from that county. In the session that followed he served on the judiciary and other important committees. In company with a strong minority he supported bills for an equitable taxation and supervision of railroads, and earnestly opposed those provisions of the railroad charters passed at that session which exempted from taxation for twenty years their property of all kinds, and which virtually contracted away to those railroads the state's future right of supervision. He introduced and secured its passage through the house a constitutional amendment similar to the one just coming in force, fixing the terms of all state and county officers at four years, with quadrennial elections. This, however, failed in the senate.

In 1881 there were five candidates for the democratic nomination for district attorney before the convention for the Fifth judicial district, which embraces seven counties. After a spirited contest E. F. Noel received a considerable majority of the entire vote of the district, and his competitors, who ranked among the ablest and most popular lawyers of the district, withdrew, and he was nominated by acclamation, numbering among his most zealous supporters some of those who most earnestly opposed him in the election previous. At the election in 1887 he defeated, by over six thousand majority, the present United States district attorney, the most popular and influential republican in the district. He is now finishing his fourth year as district attorney. E. F. Noel was married to Miss Lula Hoskins, at Lexington, Miss., on June 4, 1890. All his life he has been a moral and temperate man, not using tobacco or intoxicating liquor. He has always been an unwavering and working democrat. He has served twice on the democratic state executive committee, twice on the congressional executive committee, and resigned the chairmanship of the democratic executive committee of his county in 1887 on entering the canvass.

No man in the state has ever served his country in an official capacity with more fidelity and sincerity than E. F. Noel. As a public prosecutor he is just and energetic, searching, sifting and thoroughly weighing every fact and circumstance material to the issue involved. He takes no unfair advantage, but presents his case strongly and irresistibly, and when he is once convinced that the defendant is innocent he seeks not his conviction, but immediately enters a nolle prosequi.

Henry Peyton Noland enjoys the reputation of being a substantial and progressive planter, and an intelligent and thoroughly posted man in all public affairs. He was born in Warren county, November 16, 1841, a son of Judge Pierce and Elizabeth L. (Galtmy) Noland, the former a native of Virginia and the latter of Adams county, Miss., where she was born in 1801, being descended from an old Dutch family of New York, the Killands, who were originally from Holland. Judge Pierce Noland was descended from a Revolutionary soldier, and at the age of thirteen years left home and came to Mississippi, and in time, by industry and frugality, he amassed quite a comfortable fortune. He also by self application fitted himself for the duties of a good citizen, and became an exceptionally well-informed man, although he never attended school but about three months during his life. He was judge of the county court of Jefferson county during the twenties, and in this capacity served with faithfulness and ability. He gave his eight children good advantages, and one of his sons, T. V. Noland, graduated from Princeton college and became a prominent attorney and citizen of Mississippi. Three of the other children graduated from Oakland college. Henry Peyton Noland attended a private school until he was twelve years of age, and at the age of fourteen entered Mississippi college, but a short time after returned home on account of ill-health and remained under the care of his parents for about six months. The following twelve months were then spent in Oakland college, and after remaining on the home place for about the same length of time, two months were spent in the Nashville military school.

Some fifteen months afterward he married Miss Annie Aldridge, a daughter of Dr. William O. Aldridge, of Kentucky, who acquired his medical education in New Orleans Medical college, and practiced his profession in Madison and Hinds counties. Mrs. Noland was born December 12, 1842, and received a high school education in the city of Jackson. Mr. Noland followed the calling of a planter until the opening of the war, then became a member of Capt. J. J. Cowan's company of artillery, First Mississippi regiment, stationed at Vicksburg, but was physically incapacitated for service and was discharged at the end of nine months. In 1863 he moved onto the plantation on which he is now residing, where he now owns about one thousand acres of land, of which three hundred are under cultivation. After the close of the war he began taking considerable interest in political matters, and has since been an active democrat. He filled the position of justice of the peace from 1876 to 1880, during which time he made an enviable record for himself. His sessions of court were models of order, and all concerned were given to understand that no favors would be shown, as had been the custom, but that even-handed justice would be meted out to all. He and his wife are Episcopalians in religious views. Their children are: Mary, Thomas Vaughn, Lily, Hugh Aldrich, Myra Ruth, Annie Aldrich and Edna Aubrey. Mary, Lily and Hugh are deceased.

In connection with his practice Dr. John R. Nolen, physician and surgeon, Tomnolen, Miss., is engaged in planting, and is also the present member of the state senate from Choctaw and Webster counties, Miss. He is a resident of old Greensboro, Webster county, Miss., where he was born in 1856, and is a son of Prof. John and Elizabeth (Dukins) Nolen, the former a native of Georgia, born in 1812, and the latter of Kentucky, born about 1827. Professor Nolen was of Irish descent, was a man of education and learning, and when still single, or in 1839, he came to what is now Webster county, where he taught school for a number of years. In 1843 he was elected circuit clerk of Choctaw county, and held that position for twelve consecutive years with credit to himself and his constituents. He was married in Greensboro, and there resided until his death, in 1868. Both he and wife were members in good standing in the Missionary Baptist church. He was a man of considerable influence and ability in his community, and was active in all public matters. He was the only member of his family who died in this county. During the latter part of the Civil war he served in the Confederate army. He showed his appreciation of secret organizations by becoming a member of Greensboro lodge No. 49, A. F. & A. M. His wife was a stepdaughter of Judge Thomas N. Davis, who came to Greensboro with his family in 1836. To Mr. and Mrs. Nolen were born nine children, who are named in the order of their births as follows: Alonzo, a soldier in the late war, was captured at Fort Donelson and was retained at Fort Delaware during nearly the entire war (he was killed in Arkansas in 1873); Susan is the widow of Frank Holloway; Edgar P., died in 1890 (he was a merchant and planter); Thomas; Dr. John R.; William C., a planter of Choctaw county; Eva, now Mrs. Stiff, of Texas; Lillian, died at the age of five years; and Lee, who is engaged in merchandising at Tomnolen station. Dr. John R. Nolen was reared to farm life, attended the Greensborough school until thirteen years of age, and then entered Hico academy, near Paducah, Ky. He subsequently studied medicine, first with Dr. D. M. Simmons, of Kentucky, and then with Dr. A. H. Bays, now of Eupora. During the winter of 1876-7 he attended the Louisville Medical college, and in 1878 graduated from Vanderbilt university, Nashville, Tenn. He at once began practicing at Greensboro, where he has since continued and is considered not only one of the leading physicians of the county, but is one of the most popular public men. In 1883 he celebrated his nuptials with Miss Zenie Holloway, a native of Choctaw county, Miss., and the daughter of William and Elizabeth Holloway. Mr. Holloway was a well-to-do planter of Choctaw county, where he died about 1874. His widow is now living at Greensboro. To Dr. and Mrs. Nolen were born four children. Dr. Nolen is the owner of nine hundred acres of land and has three hundred acres cleared, all the result of his own efforts. In 1887 he was elected to the lower house of the state legislature, and was chairman of the committee on public health and quarantines, also a member of the committee of ways and means and railroads. In 1889 he was elected to represent the thirteenth district, composed of the counties Choctaw, Webster, Clay and Oktibbeha, in the senate. He is a member of the Masonic fraternity, Greensboro lodge No. 49, and is past master. He is a member of the Farmers' Alliance, and he and Mrs. Nolen are members of the Missionary Baptist church.

Thomas N. Norrell, a well-to-do planter of Rankin county, Miss., whose parents came from South Carolina to Mississippi in the year 1800, was born on the 4th of July, 1815, in Claiborne county, Miss., being the youngest of five brothers and one sister, surviving members of a family of sixteen children born to Levi and Kate (Gwin) Norrell, both of whom were natives of South Carolina, but afterward became residents of Mississippi; he died in this state in 1823, his wife's death also occurring in that year. In the state of his birth Thomas N. Norrell was reared to the life of a planter, and in his youth acquired a practical education. He has been successful in the career he has marked out for himself, and his fine plantation comprises one thousand two hundred and sixty acres, located six miles south of Jackson, the principal part of the cultivated portion being devoted to the raising of cotton and corn. He also takes much interest in the raising of good stock, and, in fact, is a very practical and experienced planter and miller, the latter occupation having received his attention for many years. He justly merits the respect and esteem in which he is held by all classes, for his career has been honorable throughout, his kindly spirit has at all times manifested itself, and his intelligent and progressive views have placed him among the leading citizens of the county. He has been an active politician, and in 1880 his services to his party were recognized and he was elected by his many friends to represent Rankin county in the general assembly of the state, making a faithful legislator. He has also been a member of the board of supervisors of Rankin county two years. In 1854 he became a member of Evening Star lodge No. 70, of the A. F. & A. M., and has taken all the degrees in the Blue lodge. Since 1888 he has been a member of the Farmers' Alliance, which order he joined at Richland academy. He was married in 1845 to Miss Frances Parker, a native of Virginia, who was born in 1814, and by her has a family of seven children born, five of whom survive: Albert G. (who represented Yazoo county in the state legislature in 1882, 1884 and 1886, and for the past three years has held the position of United States commissioner in Utah territory), Mary E., William O., Laura F., Florence. The two sons are in Salt Lake City, Utah, practicing law, their education having been received in Oxford, Miss. The youngest son of this family represented Rankin county in the legislature in 1886. During the war Mr. Norrell enthusiastically espoused the Confederate cause and did all he could to bring matters to a successful issue for the South in the way of service, money and stock. He is an active member of the Methodist Episcopal church, but his estimable wife has long been a Baptist.

A. K. Northrop, D. D. S., Pass Christian, Miss., was born in St. Mary's parish, La., July 27, 1839, and is a son of Daniel and Christina (Knight) Northrop, natives of New Jersey and Louisiana, respectively. The father was a merchant, and removed to Louisiana in 1835, locating at Franklin, where he died of yellow fever in 1839. He had two sons, the

Doctor being the only surviving one. The mother was married, a second time, to John Hueston, editor of the Baton Rouge *Gazette*. Mr. Hueston was killed in a duel with L. C. Le Branch, a difference in political opinion being the cause of the encounter. By the second union two sons were born: J. C. Hueston, of the New York *Times*, and John Hueston, who was wounded and died in the Civil war. The widow now resides at Baton Rouge. The Doctor was educated at Baton Rouge, and was graduated from the Baltimore Dental college. He engaged in the practice of his profession, and for several years was one of the most prominent dentists along the coast. When there was a call for men to go out in behalf of the South, he enlisted in company E, Third Texas regiment, and served until hostilities ceased. He was third lieutenant, and was promoted to the position of captain. In 1867 he came to Mississippi, and as before stated, was successfully engaged in the practice of his profession, having his headquarters at Pass Christian. In 1873 he abandoned dentistry for mercantile pursuits, and has since carried on the business with great profit. He keeps the best stock of goods in Pass Christian, and has won a large patronage in that place and the surrounding country. He also deals in real estate, and has made some heavy transactions in that line. Dr. Northrop has also been identified with the politics of the county, having been county treasurer four years, and sheriff for the same length of time, and a member of the national democratic convention held in St. Louis in 1888. He was mayor of the town for two years, and has always taken an active interest in the growth and prosperity of the place. He is a member of the Masonic fraternity, and was largely instrumental in the erection of the Masonic hall at the pass. He is also a member of the American Legion of Honor. Dr. Northrop was married April 20, 1867, to Miss Helena Elmer, of Biloxi, Miss. They are now the parents of six sons and two daughters: A. E., J. D., Guy, George, James, Newton, Christina and Ruby. They are members of the Episcopal church. Dr. Northrop owns some good property in Pass Christian, and is in good circumstances.

Col. William Lewis Nugent, attorney at law, Jackson, Miss., is a native of Louisiana, and was born at East Baton Rouge parish, December 12, 1832, and is the son of John and Ann (Lewis) Nugent. The elder Nugent was born in the county of Westmeath, Ireland. He came to the United States when a lad of seventeen years, locating at Philadelphia, where he was employed as a clerk in the mercantile house of a Quaker. Two years later he was sent by his employer to Washington, Miss., to open up a branch house, where he continued in charge until he was twenty-one years of age, when the business was transferred entirely to him. Mr. Nugent successfully carried on this business until the year 1831, when he sold out and invested in a sugar plantation in Baton Rouge parish, which he operated two years, when he removed to Opelousas, La., where he reared his family. Mr. Nugent died in Jackson, Miss., in 1873, at the advanced age of eighty-five years. His wife was a native of Louisiana, and was the daughter of Judge Seth Lewis, a prominent lawyer of that state, and Nancy Hardeman, who was a native of Tennessee. The early life of William L. was common to that of most planters' sons. At the age of eight years he was placed in the state school at Opelousas, where he pursued his studies until he was fifteen years of age. At this period he was sent to Centenary college, Mississippi, where he was graduated in 1852. In August of that year Mr. Nugent removed to Greenville, Miss., where he continued to reside until 1872. For the first three years he was engaged as a private tutor. He then took up the study of law, reading in the office of A. F. Smith, and was admitted to the bar in the fall of 1856. He immediately opened an office and began the practice of law, which he continued with marked success until the breaking out of the war. He was then appointed inspector-general of the state. From this position he resigned in 1862, and entered the Confederate army as a private in company D, Eighteenth Mississippi, Col. P. B. Starke commanding. One of the principal engagements, while in this service, was at the battle of Franklin, Tenn., April 10, 1863, under Van Dorn. During the summer of this year he was promoted to the rank of captain, assigned to the adjutant-general's department, and ordered to report to Brig.-Gen. S. W. Ferguson. He served in this capacity until the early part of 1865, when, upon the petition of officers and men, he was promoted to the colonelcy of the Twelfth Mississippi cavalry. He was ordered west by General Beauregard to pick up the scattered men belonging to the command, and while out on this duty the surrender of the Confederacy was made. The war being over Colonel Nugent returned to his home in Greenville, and once more engaged in the peaceful occupation of the law. In 1872 he removed to Jackson, Miss. and became associated with W. and J. N. Yerger in the practice of his profession. His reputation as an able lawyer had preceded him, and he entered at once upon a lucrative practice. In 1875 he formed a copartnership with T. A. McWillie, under the firm name of Nugent & McWillie, which continues. Colonel Nugent was united in marriage November, 1860, to Eleanor, daughter of A. F. Smith. The issue of this marriage was one child, Eleanor, now the wife of Robert Somerville, of Greenville, Miss. Mrs. Nugent died December, 1865. Colonel Nugent was married the second time, February 25, 1870, to Aimée, daughter of John S. and Cecile Webb, of Alabama. To this union five children have been born: Cecile, Aimée, William L., Louis C., and Bessie W., all of whom are living at home. Colonel Nugent is a member of the Methodist Episcopal Church South. In politics he is a democrat.

This sketch would be incomplete without noting some of the personal characteristics of the subject. In form Colonel Nugent is tall, with a graceful, military bearing. His eyes are gray and beam with intellectual brightness, while his countenance, which is winning, is expressive of truth and goodness. He is a firm friend, a genial companion and a charitable neighbor. He was a firm believer in the right of secession and in the Confederacy, but since that question has been settled through the arbitrament of the sword he is a loyal and patriotic citizen of the Union. In one so gifted and versatile as Colonel Nugent it is difficult to draw a line, or to determine in which professional excellence he is most distinguished. He was endowed by nature with a mind of the finest quality, comprehensive, active, analytical and tenacious. The great powers of reason, imagination and memory are in perfect equipoise, and each the ready and faithful ally of the others. His collegiate education was more thorough than that of most students, for the reason that he studied for the acquisition of knowledge, and with little reference to the class distinctions that he won. His professional studies were pursued in the same spirit and were attended with the same results. His great purpose was the mastering of the science of law, and he has come about as near its attainment as any jurist ever did. It is difficult to imagine anything in the wide field of professional effort beyond the scope of his powers. This remarkable capacity is supplemented by an equally remarkable and untiring industry. Indeed, the form in which the admiration of his professional brethren is most frequently expressed presents the idea of rare efficiency and indefatigable labor. He works with the greatest celerity and works all the time. Even the manual portion of his labors partakes of these characteristics. He writes with unusual facility, and in the longest, most difficult and complex pleadings he rarely erases or interlines a word. He has practiced in all the courts known to our law system with great success, and the litigation in which he has taken part has been of an important nature. In the United States circuit and district courts, both at Jackson and at Oxford, and in the circuit, chancery and supreme courts of the state, he has long been a leading practitioner. He has also appeared from time to time with credit to the profession before the supreme court of the United States. Colonel Nugent is equally able both at law and in equity cases. One who heard him for the first time addressing the court would be apt to underrate his powers before a jury, for it is rarely the case that excellence in both branches are united in one person, yet his listener would be soon undeceived. No juryman ever listened to his advocacy of a cause who was not influenced by his legal arguments and logical reasoning. While making little pretension to oratory his language is a "well of pure English undefiled," and his expressions are so apt, his conceptions so clear, accompanied in the delivery by an electric-like energy, employing at the same instant both the flash and the stroke, that it becomes quite impossible to withstand their effect. He has the power of gathering all the facts of a cause in the grasp of his mind and retaining them for use at exactly the right point in his argument, and the manner of their employment is so just and their disclosed relation to each other so manifest, and yet so original and striking, that his arguments to the jury are often a revelation to those who have given the closest attention to the evidence. This is a much rarer faculty than is generally supposed. Indeed, it is really one of the attributes of genius. Colonel Nugent's briefs in the Mississippi reports disclose his fine style as a law-writer. They cover a period extending from the close of the late war to the present time, and these, with his pleadings, might be taken as models of composition by students of the profession. If it is true that a good bar makes a good bench, and that the labors of a lawyer largely contribute to the accuracy of the judge, then Colonel Nugent is in no small degree connected with the grand structure of Mississippi jurisprudence. He is yet in the meridian of his powers and is wholly engrossed by the calls of an extensive and lucrative practice, a great part of which relates to railway and other corporations. In association with his brethren of the bar he is ever courteous and considerate, and while faithful at all times to clients his high standard for the proprieties of the profession would prevent him from taking undue advantage of any laches that might be committed by opposing council. This is a quality that is not as common in the profession as it ought to be. Colonel Nugent is ever respectful and courteous to the court and enjoys the confidence and esteem of all the judges before whom he has practiced.

Maj. R. J. Nugent's parents, John and Ann (Lewis) Nugent, were natives respectively of Ireland and Louisiana. The father came to the United States about 1810, located first in Philadelphia, Penn., and later in Washington and Adams counties of that state, where he followed merchandising. In 1831 he moved to Louisiana, engaged in planting, and after the war passed the remainder of his days with his children. His death occurred in Jackson, Miss., in 1873. The maternal great-grandfather came to Mississippi in 1770, and settled on Black river. His son, Seth Lewis, became a prominent lawyer and was appointed supreme judge in 1800. He afterward went to Louisiana, was appointed probate judge, and died in that state about 1844. Maj. R. J. Nugent was born in Louisiana in 1834, and of the family of children born to his parents he was fourth in order of birth. He comes of old Welsh and Irish stock. He secured a liberal education in a college in Louisiana, and when a stripling of sixteen went to New Orleans, where he engaged in clerking. There he remained until 1862, and then entered the Confederate army in the Louisiana guards, as lieutenant of one of the companies. After the fall of New Orleans he went to Richmond, and was appointed to go to Louisiana and open the salt mines at New Iberia. He was subsequently attached to Morton's division, under General Taylor, and was in the battles of Banks' campaign as commissary. He was sent as a bearer of dispatches to Richmond by General Buckner, and was at Chester, S. C., at the evacuation of Richmond. He worked his way to Washington, S. C., and joined President Davis. After the war he engaged as bookkeeper in New Orleans, remained there for some time and then went to Washington county, Miss., and thence to Bolivar county, where he has since resided. He is the owner of fourteen hundred acres of land, Reville and Arcadia plantations, and is one of the foremost planters of the county. He was married in 1859 to Miss Coralie Smith, of Mississippi. She was a descendent of an old and honored family, and a relative of Jefferson Davis' family. Her death occurred in 1867, and she left three children: Ann, Mary Coralie and R. J., Jr. In 1884 Major Nugent was elected a member of the town board, was re-elected in 1890, and is the present incumbent of that position. He is an upright, conscientious and most highly respected citizen, not only in Bolivar county, but in the entire Yazoo delta. He is active in politics, but is no office seeker.

Maj. E. F. Nunn, farmer and stockman, Shuqualak, Miss. John Nunn was born in Georgia on Christmas day, 1796. He was married to Miss Jane Tubb, of Tennessee, and afterward followed planting for many years, although later in life he was engaged in merchandising. He emigrated to Noxubee county, Miss , in 1835, and purchased land from the government. He died in 1873. His son, E. F. Nunn, was born in Perry county, Ala., in 1826, and his early life was spent on a farm in that state. When but nine years of age he removed with his father to Noxubee county, Miss., where he attended the common schools at intervals. He engaged in farming on his own account at the age of nineteen years, and in 1849 he was married to Miss Mary Louise Anderson, of Winston county, Miss. He continued planting until the Civil war opened, when he went out as captain of a home company, which later formed a part of the Third Mississippi battalion, Hardcastle commanding. He saw his first fighting on Shiloh's bloody battlefield. Afterward his battalion was organized into the Thirty-third Mississippi regiment, with Hardcastle still commanding. After the battle of Perryville his regiment became the Forty-fifth Mississippi, commanded by Col. John D. Williams, of Tupelo, Miss., with Mr. Nunn as major. Major Nunn was in almost every engagement of Johnston's campaign before Atlanta, and later with Hood at Franklin. At that place he lost a hand almost on the spot where General Cleburne fell. At this time he was captured, taken to Nashville, and after a month's stay was taken to Fort Delaware, where he remained two months before he was exchanged. At the close of hostilities he engaged in planting and merchandising at Shuqualak, Noxubee county, Miss., and other points. Major Nunn is identified with all that goes to constitute the solid advancement of the state. He owns and operates ten thousand acres of land, principally in Noxubee county, and is engaged in milling, merchandising and stockraising. He is breeding Jersey cattle, fine horses and mules. He is a man of fine taste, as his registered cattle and other fine stock indicate. The Major is a Missionary Baptist. His marriage resulted in the birth of four children, two of whom died in infancy. A promising daughter, Miss Alice, died in 1889. Only one now survives, Miss M. Lillian. Major Nunn was a member of the legislature of 1877. As a business man he stands among the foremost, and indeed in every department of life he has built for himself a character which will reflect credit on his posterity. Those who know him best love to tell of his coolness and unquestioned bravery on the bloodiest fields. The Major's health has not been of the best for the past few years, and in obedience to medical advice he has, to a great extent, retired from active business.

The Nutt, or Knut, family. Arms: Party per fesse az. and erm. a pale counterchanged, three pheons ar. crest, on a chapeau gu. turned up erm. a pheon or between two wings expanded ar. The name of this family comes down from Scandinavian history and means a knot (Dutch, Knopp, a button or knot). The first king of Denmark of that name derived his name from the fact that he was found an infant in the woods of Holstein, with a silk scarf tied around him, and in the knot a gold ring. They were the Danes who overran southern and eastern England in the great Danish invasion. At the time of King Edward the Confessor, some forty odd lordships are recorded in Domesday as belonging to Knut, or Cnut. One is thus recorded: "Rainald Canut ten de rege 1. hid. in Chipeha Tochi tenuit T. R. E. Tra. e. i. Ibi. II. bord hnt dim Car. 7 VXX. 31. aoc pwti. 7 dimid molin redd. XV. fol. Tot ualuit 7 ual PXX. Solid." The parish of Knutstede (Knut's place) contains about one thousand acres. The church is an ancient Gothic building. The court is remarkable for two magnificent stone Gothic windows, and for the enormous oak pillars inside the hall, which are equally remarkable for their carving, as well as the dais in the baronial hall. It anciently belonged to a family of Knuts or Nutts. English heraldry first mentions them in County Kent; arms, a pheon ar. on a shield az. Thence in London, and next in County Essex. Knutstede in County Kent is now called Nursted. John Nutt, son of Thomas Nutt, of London, was clerk patron and parson of Berwick, and rector of Bexhill, County Essex. He was at that time worth half a million dollars. His son, William Nutt, was the emigrant to Virginia.

In 1666 William was high sheriff of Northumberland county, Va., and in the following year the colonel of the county. By his wife, Eliza, he had issue, Richard, who married Ann, daughter of William Downing, and had issue, Richard, who married Elizabeth Smith, and had issue, Richard, who married Alice Routh, and had issue, Richard, who married Elizabeth Rawlings, and had issue, Rush, the founder of the family in Mississippi. Having an independent turn of mind, Rush Nutt turned his back on the cock-fighting and fox-hunting pastimes of his people and fitted himself for the practice of medicine, in Philadelphia, under Dr. Rush, and became not only his friend, but also the friend of David Rittenhouse and Benjamin Franklin. After taking his degree he returned home and married, but was called upon to mourn the death of his wife six months later. Soon after this he started on horseback for the West, and in time reached Jefferson county, Miss., settling in the old town of Greenville, now wiped out, where he began practicing his profession. He soon purchased a large plantation near Rodney, called Laurel hill, and assisted in building the first brick church at that place, and afterward educated several young men for the ministry and medicine. His views were far ahead of the times in which he lived. He was industrious and enterprising, and, being a patron of education, was one of the three men who founded Oakland college, since changed to Alcorn university. Between 1833 and 1838 he made a tour of Greece, Turkey, Syria, the Holy Land and Egypt, being the first American to visit those regions, and was accompanied by his eldest son, Rittenhouse. After his return to his native land, he devoted his time to scientific studies and writing, and upon his death left valuable manuscripts.

His writings cover a number of scientific studies and show a mind of great thought and investigation. The manuscripts are still preserved by the family and will, when revised, be published. Learned men who have seen them compare them with the writings of Humboldt and Darwin. He turned his mind to agriculture and scientific study, and applied analytical chemistry to discover the plant foods, both those required by the plant and those found in the air and soil. He was so successful in this that after cotton had utterly failed, as a crop, as indigo had already done, he took the big Mexican plant and joining it with the Egyptian, produced a plant that became known as the Little Mexican cotton, the Petit Gulph, or Nutt, and from which all the cotton comes that is now raised in the United States to-day, except Sea Island cotton. He was married in Jefferson county, Miss., to Miss Eliza Ker, a daughter of

Judge David Ker, the founder and first presiding professor of Chapel Hill college, North Carolina, and judge of the supreme court of Mississippi territory, having been appointed by Mr. Jefferson. To their union several children were born: Rittenhouse married Miss Ellen Rowan, of Adams county, and left a family; Mary married Dr. Hugh Lyle, an Englishman by birth and an eminent physician; David died unmarried; Haller attended lectures at the University of Virginia and graduated in medicine in Louisville, and he was especially proficient in the dead languages, Hebrew, Greek and Latin. After the death of his father he was left guardian of his younger sisters, who were named Sarah, Eliza and Margaret, when he devoted his attention to agriculture, and became one of the most extensive planters of that section. He owned large estates in Louisiana and conducted his planting operations on scientific principles, thus securing large and fine crops, which commanded the best prices in the market. In connection with his father he had taken the crude Whitney gin and made it so perfect that from 1838 till the close of the war there was no improvement made. Following his father's steps in reasoning out natural causes and effects, he applied himself so assiduously to agriculture that he produced two or three times the amount of yield per acre more than his neighbors, and obtained eighteen to twenty per cent. per pound more for his cotton. He raised about thirty-five hundred bales of cotton a year. When a young man he acted as justice of the peace, as a favor to the neighbors, and for some years before his death served as president of the police jury of Tensas parish, La., and practically controlled and managed all the affairs of the parish. He was a student, and left behind him a large and choice library of standard works. During his lifetime he was a frequent contributor to the magazines of the day, both in Europe and the United States. His writings would fill volumes.

In numerous other instances he was ahead of the time in which he lived. In 1840 he was married to Miss Julia Augusta Williams (see sketch of Williams family) and in 1853 purchased the property near Natchez called Longwood. Here he began the erection of a magnificent residence which, although still uncompleted, is one of the loveliest of Southern homes. It is oriental in style. Mr. Sloan, of Philadelphia, was the architect. It is four stories and a basement in hight, surmounted by a domed cupola, that carries its apex to a hight that in 1860 exceeded the top of any church spire in Philadelphia, and in shape is octagonal, all the rooms being large, lofty and imposing. They center around a rotunda running up over one hundred feet and give a diameter to the building of one hundred feet. The finishing touches were being made in 1861 when the war broke out, and had this not put a stop to the work the building would have been completed in a few months. It occupies the site of the house in which Prentiss died. From the cupola can be seen a magnificent stretch of country in all directions, a fine view of the river being had for many miles. Mr. Nutt died in 1864, leaving his widow with a large family of children to care for during the turbulent and unsettled times of the war, and nobly did she perform the duties that were laid upon her shoulders. The family were Union during the war, and their losses amounted to several millions of dollars, their plantation being laid waste, and ruin left in the wake of tramping armies. Mrs. Nutt, knowing her husband's desire was to give to his children the advantages of a good education, set earnestly to work to fulfill his wishes and, although often at a great sacrifice to herself, she overcame all difficulties and they were given the advantages of the best schools of the South, and showed their appreciation of their worthy mother's efforts by applying themselves diligently to their books and becoming honorable men and women. They are all well established in life. Their names are as follows: Mary Ella resides with her mother; Haller is a planter; John Ker married Mary Worthington and is a prosperous planter of Washington county; Sargent Prentiss Knut, who has gone back to the old way of spelling the name, was educated near Philadelphia and finished a highly classical education at the University of Virginia, afterward studying law at Natchez, being now a successful practitioner of Washington, D. C.; Julia is single; Calvin R. married and resides in St. Louis, Mo., and Lily, who is the wife of James W. Ward of Washington county, are the members of the family now living. Those deceased are: Carrie, a renowned beauty and belle, and especially noted for her riding, who married Charles S. Forsyth, of Chicago, and died soon after her marriage; Fannie, who died in youth, and Austin, who was accidentally shot when a lad. The justness of a claim of this family against the government for property taken during the war has been well established in the courts of Washington and before congress.

The Ker family. The Kers of Scotland are a very ancient family, who inhabited the border. Sir Walter Scott tells a great deal of them in his "Tales of my Grandfather." The Dukes of Roxburgh and the Marquises of Lothian are younger branches of this family. David Ker, the founder of the family in Mississippi, was a native of Down Patrick, north Ireland, where so many Scotch people have settled. He was educated at Trinity college, Dublin, and emigrated with his wife, Mary, to North Carolina, before the Revolution. He founded Chapel Hill college, now the University of North Carolina, and was its first presiding professor. He migrated to Mississippi territory, and died there in 1805. He was appointed judge of the supreme court of the territory by Mr. Jefferson. He had issue: First, John (who married Mary K. Baker of Natchez, and had issue: Mary; Sarah, married to Butler; John Ker, who married Rosaltha Routh (see Routh); Lewis, Mary and William); second, David; third, Eliza (married to Dr. Rush Nutt, see Nutt); fourth, Martha (married to William Terry, and had issue: Sarah, married to —— Jeffries, and Eliza, married to Prince); fifth, Sarah (married to —— Cowden). Dr. John Ker, son of David, was an eminent physician. He was a surgeon in the state army in war with Indians, and also in the War of 1812. His son William is now engaged in the courts of Mississippi. He is a graduate of Harvard.

The Williams family. This family comes down from Sir Thomas De Bullen, one of the Knights of William the Conqueror. He overran a portion of Wales, and there took up his position. In course of time there came Sir William De Bullen, whose son, Sir Thomas, became designated as Sir Thomas Williams (on). He was the father of Ann Boulyne, or Ann De Bullen, the mother of Queen Elizabeth. Descendent from him was Barnett Williams, who came to Virginia with Lord Fairfax and married Mary Pierce, of Fredericksburg, and had issue Charles Pierce, who married Elizabeth Red, granddaughter of Col. John Minor, of Virginia. A few years later he migrated to Kentucky, where he became one of the pioneer settlers of Scott county. He became a wealthy planter, an influential citizen, and died on the magnificent plantation of which he had become the owner, at the age of eighty-three years. In his family were five sons and three daughters: Merritt, who lived all his life in Scott county; Archibald Pierce, who removed South and founded one of the wealthiest and best known families in Rapides parish, La., (one of his daughters married Judge Johnston, a son of Judge (Sibley) Johnston and a brother of Gen. Albert Sidney Johnston, and after his death she married the noted Philadelphia lawyer, Henry T. Gilpin, attorney-general of the United States); Maria Williams married William Payne and removed with him to Fayette, Mo., where their descendants are among the leading citizens of that state at the present time; Austin was educated in Kentucky, but about 1800 became a citizen of Natchez and a short time after turned his attention to planting in Louisiana, where he became well and prominently known. He was a member of the legislature of that state for some time, and died in 1847, his widow, who was formerly Miss Caroline M. Routh (see Routh), dying in 1863. To their union three sons and six daughters were born, who were as follows: Johnstone, who died in childhood; Annie E., married to Walton P. Smith (see sketch of Austin Smith); Julia Augusta, married to Haller Nutt (see sketch of the Nutt family); Catherine, married to Dr. John Brumley, of Virginia, who was taken prisoner during the war, and died of want; her death occurred before the war, in 1859; Caroline became the wife of Rev. Joseph R. Stratton, of Natchez (see sketch); Job Routh died single in Natchez, having been a noted society beau and a very popular gentleman of fashion of his day; Thomas served in the Confederate army on Gen. Dick Taylor's staff, and died in 1879, unmarried; Mary Louise resides with her sister in Washington county, and Irene is the wife of Merritt Williams, of Washington county (see sketch). All these children were given the advantages of the finest schools of the country. Their marriages resulted in the birth of large families, and they have ranked among the most popular and enterprising people of the sections in which they have resided. The other children born to Archibald Pierce Williams are as follows: Charles; Josiah; Frances, who married —— Chambers, now a wealthy planter of Rapides parish; John and Laura. Mr. Austin Williams was very wealthy and was very generous with his means, and made a point of giving each of his children a sum of money and ten negro slaves when they became of age. His house, Ashburn, near Natchez, was one of the most elegantly fitted up of any in the South. He was a man of unblemished reputation, and this worthy characteristic has been noticeable in all his descendants.

The Routh family. Arms or, three bars az. on a quarter ar., two lions passant gu. The Rouths are of the Danish invasion that accompanied William the Conqueror. The name means "the red." They are usually blondes, and a physical characteristic that has been present in the generations in England follows them to America, and we find here the same large physique of the Norseman. The founder of the family in Mississippi was Job Routh, who, when a mere lad, ran off from his family, then domineered by a disagreeable stepfather, and came out to the Southwest when the county was still under the Spanish flag. He was the first man of English blood to settle in Natchez. He married Ann Madeline, the daughter of —— Müller and his wife, nee Hawkins, both from Switzerland. Her brother was the venerable Christopher Miller, whom the old citizens of Natchez remember when, as a relic of the days gone by, with his brother-in-law he walked the streets of Natchez in his knee breeches and silk stockings and cutaway coat and three-cornered hat. Job Routh was industrious and hardworking, and it was not long before he accumulated a large fortune. He obtained a grant for land on Lake St. Joseph, in what is now Tensas parish, La., and there commenced planting cotton. As his children raised families, they, too, became planters in the same place, all retaining their fall and spring houses in the suburbs of Natchez till the breaking out of the late war, when they had under plow about twenty thousand acres of land and owned over five thousand slaves. The life these families lived on Lake St. Joseph has passed, never to return. Around the lake they possessed some fifteen homesteads, and during the winter each family had from one to three other families of relatives from Kentucky, Missouri, Arkansas and Virginia, visiting them, and their days and nights were one series of revelry and enjoyment, with dinners, balls, picnics, horse-racing, cock-fighting and boat races with crews composed of their slaves. Job Routh died ripe in years, and lies buried in the Routh graveyard that is to-day one of the landmarks of Natchez. Their children were: John, who married Nancy Smith and had issue; Matilda, who married Dr. Allen T. Bowie, from Maryland, and the brother of Mrs. Reverdy Johnson,

The Goodspeed Pub. Co. Chicago.

and whose children were John, Allen T., Thomas C., and Annie. Calvin, who married Ann Skillman and had issue; Andrew, who married Sue, daughter of Governor Dougherty of Georgia; Calvin, Annie, John and Matilda, and John Knox, who married Margaret Williams, sister of Mrs. S. S. Prentiss of Natchez, and had issue, Nannie, Jennie and Stella. John Routh was in his day called the Cotton King. His crop just before the war amounted to eight thousand eight hundred and forty-two bales in one year. He owned so many negroes that he did not know them all. His silver dinner service cost him $35,000. Elizabeth, who married Archibald Williams (see Williams family) Caroline, who married Austin Williams, brother of the above. Sarah, who married Colonel Walker, and had issue: Samuel, who married Eliza Baker of Virginia, Virginia, who married Samuel Hollingsworth of Maryland, and Martha, who married Zelliot, the brother of the latter. Ann, who married Isaac Ogden from New Jersey, and had issue. Eliza, who married William Cochran from New Jersey, and had issue: Wayne, Frank, who married Fredinka, daughter of the old Roman, General and Governor Quitman of Mississippi; John Routh, who married Josephine Marshall, and Mary, who married Clayton Pendleton of Virginia. Frank, who married Mary Lane, and had issue: Rosaltha, who married John Ker (see Ker), and Stebbins, who married Ann Stewart; (Mr. Frank Routh lived some years after the war, and was the last of his generation of old-timers. After his fortune had been swept away, and there seemed no hope of recovering it, he retired to the wilds of Catahoula parish, La., where his word became law among the small people around him. On one occasion when he visited Natchez, members of the family surrounded him and pleaded with him to come and make his home with them. His reply was: "No, by G—d, I would rather be a bull-dog in Catahoula than a d—d cur in Natchez.") Stephen, who married Eliza Sprague, and had issue: Alice, Horatio, Stephen, Pauline (a great beauty), who married Robert Percy (see Percy), Octo, Clarence, Job, who married Miss Jeffries of Mississippi, Charles, Earnest, and Amelia, who married N. Bayard Sadler of Georgia. Mary, who married first, Thomas Ellis, son of Colonel Ellis and Lady Percy, and had issue: Sarah, who married Samuel Dorsey from Maryland (it was she who left the beautiful place on the gulf, Beauvoir, and three plantations to Jefferson Davis), Thomas Percy, who married Appoline Ingraham, of New Orleans, and Inez, who married three times. She next married Charles Dahlgren, son of Barnard Dahlgren of Philadelphia, Swedish consul, and brother of Rear Admiral Dahlgren, United States navy, and by him had issue: Charles, Barnard, John Adolph (who married Miss DeMovel, of Tennessee), and Mortimer.

CHAPTER XV.

RECORDS OF A PRIVATE NATURE, O.

OAKLAND college is located in Claiborne county, thirty-five miles north of Natchez and five miles east of the Mississippi river. Rodney is the nearest landing place; Bruinsburg, three miles north, is the spot where Grant crossed the river and gained possession of the rear of the city of Vicksburg, and soon that city fell. Oakland college is situated in a region of country rendered interesting from many reminiscences of early times. Here was the scene of some characteristic incidents in the life of Gen. Andrew Jackson. A few miles from the college was the residence of Blennerhassett; here was the place of the capture of Aaron Burr; in this vicinity was the plantation of the amiable, patriotic and lamented Gen. Zachary Taylor. This region also possesses much interest, for it is the scene of the visits and labors of some of the earliest pioneers of Presbyterianism in the Southwest, Rickhow, Smylie and Montgomery, who came here when the dew of their youth was upon them, and laid the foundation of our churches. Here visited and preached Schermerhorn, S. J. Mills, Larned, Bullen and many others. The eccentric Lorenzo Dow here rode his mule and blew his horn and attracted crowds of the first settlers, preaching on housetops and haystacks, resembling Peter the Hermit, who once marshaled all Europe under the Crusaders' banner. The origin of Oakland college may be traced to a meeting of Presbyterian ministers held in the town of Baton Rouge, La., in April, 1829. * * * A committee was accordingly appointed, who, after an extensive correspondence, continued through several months, called a meeting of the friends of education at Bethel church, two miles from the present location of the college, on January 14, 1830. This meeting was composed of gentlemen from adjoining parishes in Louisiana, and from the counties of Claiborne, Amite, Wilkinson, Adams, Jefferson, Warren, Hinds and Madison, in Mississippi, and continued six days. The following resolution was presented:

Resolved, That it is expedient to establish and endow an institution of learning within our bounds, which, when complete, shall embrace the usual branches of science and literature taught in the colleges of our country, together with a preparatory English and German school, and theological professorship, or seminary.

This resolution was sustained by gentlemen from every part of the country represented in the meeting, and after considering it for three days it was unanimously adopted. A subscription was immediately opened to supply the requisite funds. Twelve thousand dollars were contributed for the purchase of a site and the erection of the building. Other committees were appointed to prepare constitution, etc., and make all necessary arrangements for opening the school.

On May 14 the school opened with three pupils, who had accompanied the president, Rev. Jeremiah Chamberlain, D. D., from Jackson, La., where he had been presiding over the College of Louisiana. On July 2, 1830, the first clearing was begun, on the magnificent oak ridge now occupied by the college buildings. At the end of the session, March 28, the school consisted of sixty-five pupils; the two more advanced formed a sophomore class, and there were five in the freshman class; the remainder in the English and classical. The president instructed the two college classes and the classical in the languages; his brother, Mr. John Chamberlain, afterward professor of chemistry and natural philosophy, instructed the classes in mathematics and in the English school. In 1831 it was chartered by the legislature of the state. In 1833 the first commencement was held, and Mr. James M. Smylie, ex-vice chancellor of this state, was the first graduate of Oakland college. This was the first commencement south of Tennessee, and Judge Smylie is the first native Mississippian who received the degree of A. B. in his own state. Such is the origin of Oakland college, which has aided in the education of nearly one thousand native youth, and which now has on its roll of graduates one hundred and twenty alumni, who are scattered throughout the Southwest, and occupied in the cultivation of the soil, or in the learned professions. There were about thirty cottages for the occupancy of pupils, residences for the president and professors, two handsome halls for literary societies, with libraries attached, a college library of upward of four thousand volumes, a philosophical, chemical and astronomical apparatus, which cost nearly $4,000, a main structure of brick, 112x60, containing a college chapel and prayerhall, lecture rooms, and other requisite accommodations. The institution has never received aid from the state or general government. Its funds have been secured by private liberality, etc. (See note of Chamberlain Hunt.) This college was purchased soon after the war by Governor Alcorn, and turned into a colored school, or agricultural college, and is in a very prosperous condition.

Chamberlain-Hunt academy is successor of Oakland college, and the following short sketch of its origin is taken from the correspondence of the *Times-Democrat:*

"In one of the most beautiful sections of the South, among the sweeping green hills and broad, umbrageous natural parks of Claiborne county, in the southwestern part of Mississippi, stood for years one of the most famous seats of learning in our Gulf states. This was Oakland college, the alma mater of many of the most prominent statesmen, jurists and divines now living in Louisiana and Mississippi. During a long era of sectional prosperity before the war, this college was celebrated throughout the entire South. When the irrepressible conflict commenced, its professors and students took four years' vacation, leaving their rules and books for a temporary diversion with rifles and bayonets. The former assiduous votaries of Minerva readily became ardent followers of Mars. Many of the alumni of old Oakland fell asleep in the broad bivouac of the dead which stretches under the sky from the banks of the Potomac to the distant borders of the Rio Grande. After the war no great effort was made to re-establish the institution in its old locality. Death had apparently disorganized the directory, and the general destruction of property involved in the conflict had sadly diminished the revenues of the college. Five years ago the grounds, buildings and properties of the college were purchased by the state from the synod of Mississippi. The proceeds of the sale were devoted to founding and endowing a new institution, which was to be made a worthy successor to Oakland. There was considerable competition among the cities and towns of this state in endeavoring to secure for themselves the site of the new school. Port Gibson manifestly offered the greatest inducements, and was accordingly chosen for its location. The school was chartered anew by the legislature under the name of the Chamberlain-Hunt academy, in honor to the memory of founders and presidents of Oakland college."

In the same vicinity, Bethel church (Presbyterian) was chartered in 1828, with William Young, L. Price, John Magruder and Smith C. Daniel, trustees. The church dates its organization from about 1826, with Rev. Samuel Hunter as pastor, who was a native of Ireland and a noble man. The present brick church of Bethel was built in about 1830, with Dr. Chamberlain as pastor. During that time, in addition to the support of their minister, the church contributed to the different boards of the church about $1,000 annually. In 1837, twenty-three were added to the church; in 1845 about fifty more. During thirty years of its prosperity the church contributed largely to the different boards of the church, to the tract cause, Bible society and Sunday-school union, the contributions oftentimes amounting to many thousands of dollars. A few noble planters supported a minister to labor among the slaves. At one time forty negroes, valued at $330,000, were liberated and sent to Liberia as missionaries. Thomas Freeland contributed $333 annually, between 1833 and 1843, to support a missionary in China. The college gave about the same amount, besides contributing to the various other church boards, theological seminary at Maryville, Tenn., Natchez Orphan asylum, etc. Those were palmy days—gone, never to return.

Dr. Charles E. Oatis is one of the most prominent physicians and surgeons of Hazlehurst. He was a native of Lawrence county, Miss., where he was born August 5, 1823. His father was John H. Oatis and his mother was Mary W. Buckley. The former was born near Milledgeville, Ga., in 1793, the latter in Barnwell district, S. C., May 13, 1795. They both located when comparatively young in Hancock county, Miss., where they were married, and from there they removed to Lawrence county, where Mr. Oatis died December 3, 1863, the mother surviving until May 12, 1886, only one day less than ninety-one years old. Both were for many years members of the Baptist church. Mr. Oatis was a very successful planter, a man of remarkable natural gifts and ability. His father died in Georgia when he was but a boy, leaving him without the advantages of an education, but being fond of reading and very industrious, he acquired a very large stock of useful knowledge, becoming well versed in law, history and medicine. His knowledge of the healing art was so well recognized that he was often called upon to practice among his neighbors, which he did with much success. A man of fine address and an exceedingly good conversationalist, he won and retained many friends and was universally esteemed for his good qualities. While not an officeseeker, he was active in all public affairs. Politically, he was an ardent democrat. Commissioned colonel by Governor Holmes, he served with distinction in one of the Indian wars; and he was a prominent member of the Masonic fraternity. He was one of four children, three sons and one daughter, born to Jeremiah Oatis, who died in Georgia; his mother, who before her marriage was Jane Sinkfield, married again and came at an early date to Hancock county, and afterward to Warren county, where she died. Dr. Oatis' grandfather, Edward Buckley, a native of South Carolina, removed from that state to Hancock county, Miss., and thence to Lawrence county before our subject was born, and became a prominent planter and reared a large family. The Doctor is the fifth of ten children born to his parents, five of whom are living: Adaline, the wife of Jesse Cannon, of Monticello, who is deceased; Col. Martin A., a graduate of the State university of Mississippi, who graduated in law from the Cumberland university, Lebanon, Tenn., and became a prominent lawyer of Cleburne, Tex., was Colonel of the Twenty-second Mississippi infantry, in which he served in the army of Tennessee, and was probate judge of Lawrence county after the war; Sarah, who is the widow of Thomas L. Watts, who died in the war; Adelaide, who is unmarried; C. C., the eldest, died in California; Dr. F. M., in Texas during the war; Amanda, the wife of S. A. Speights, in Lawrence county about the same time; Dr.

John J., died at Galveston, Tex., during the war while he was surgeon connected with a Confederate battery; W. A., who died in Warren county in 1878, and Dr. Charles E., who was reared on a farm and received a common school education, but later was a student for a short time at the Transylvania university at Lexington, Ky., from which institution he graduated in medicine in 1846. He practiced in Lawrence county until 1860, when he removed to Hazlehurst, where he has since lived, except the two years from 1874 to 1876, when he was a resident of Cleburne, Texas. During the war he was for a time assistant surgeon in the hospital at Hazlehurst. He is now the oldest medical practitioner in Copiah county, having practiced continuously for forty-five years, and is still in the enjoyment of good health and in great demand professionally throughout the surrounding country. He was married August 8, 1848, to Fannie T., daughter of Francis B. and Elizabeth (Tomlinson) Haynes. Mr. Haynes was born in North Carolina and came when a young man to Mississippi and became a prominent planter. He was married in Wilkinson county and afterward moved to Lawrence county, where he and his wife both died, she before and he during the war. Mr. and Mrs. Haynes had five children, three of whom served during the late war. Mrs. Oatis was born in Lawrence county and died September 29, 1886. She bore her husband four children, of whom Myra D. is the wife of John E. Mayes, a prominent merchant of Hazlehurst; and Dr. Charles E. Oatis, Jr., is a prominent practicing physician, who was educated at Cleburne, Tex., and studied medicine at Louisville, Ky., graduating from the college of physicians and surgeons of Baltimore in 1879, since when he has been a partner with his father and is now local surgeon of the Illinois Central railroad; Dr. Francis Bythel Oatis, eldest son of Dr. Charles E. and Frances T. Oatis, died at Benton, Bossier parish, La., December 2, 1876, aged twenty-four years, eight months and seventeen days; possessed of a mind of extraordinary power, every opportunity was given for its improvement, and with every pursuit open to him he chose that of doctor of medicine and graduated with honor at Louisville, Ky., in 1874; Mrs. Eulora H. Warrell, wife of Theodore M. Warrell and daughter of Dr. Oatis, died August 3, 1876. The Doctor is a dimitted Royal Arch Mason, and has been a member of the Baptist church for many years. He is five feet eleven inches high, is well proportioned and exceedingly well preserved. His integrity has always been unquestioned and he stands high as a citizen and in his profession.

Theodore T. Obryant, planter, Chapeltown, Miss. Mr. Obryant's parents, Levi R. and Amanda M. (Boyle) Obryant, were natives of Alabama and Mississippi respectively, and the father became an extensive planter of the last named state, whither he had moved in 1855. He died in 1883 and his wife followed him to the grave in 1890. The paternal grandparents were Owen and Vashti (Richardson) Obryant, and the maternal were Thomas F. and Cynthia (Whitten) Boyle, the last two natives of Alabama. Theodore T. Obryant was born in Panola county, Miss., on the 3d of December, 1861, attained his growth in Mississippi and secured his education in the public schools, which he attended until twenty-one years of age. He then went to Louisville, Ky., and took a course in the Southern Business college, graduating from the same in 1882, in bookkeeping. He immediately afterward was employed as bookkeeper for Storn & Brown, at Batesville, Miss., and was with this firm one year. After this he embarked in business for himself and formed a copartnership with R. S. Smyth under the firm title of Smyth & Obryant, this continuing one year. After the death of his father, he was obliged to go on the farm, where he has since remained. He is the owner of four hundred acres of land, three hundred acres under cultivation, and is a prominent young man of the county. He was elected a member of the board of supervisors in 1887, was re-elected in 1889 and holds that position at the present time. He is possessed of more than ordinary ability, comes of a good family, and is popular with all. Miss Cora Whitten, who became his wife in 1884, was born in Mississippi, and is a daughter of John A. and Martha E. Whitten, natives respectively of Alabama and Mississippi. Mr. Obryant's marriage has resulted in the birth of two children: Ruth and Olive. Mr. and Mrs. Obryant are members of the Methodist church, and he affiliates with the democratic party in his political views.

Denton O'Dell, planter, Chulahoma, Miss., is a native of the Empire state, his birth occurring in July, 1836, and is one of six children, two sons and four daughters, born to Isaac D. and Eliza Ann (Hauptman) O'Dell, both natives of New York state, the father born in Rockland county and the mother in New York city. The parents removed to Virginia in 1842, remained there ten years and then moved back to New York state. Their children were named in the order of their births as follows: Mary E. (deceased August 11th, 1847); Denton (subject), Hamilton (deceased November, 1856); Martha M. (deceased May 10th, 1858); Josephine, wife of J. B. Hastings, of Stony Point, N. Y.; Henrietta (deceased July 3, 1891), wife of Samuel King, of Monroe, N. Y., and Emma Z. O'Dell. The father was a farmer and followed that occupation all his life. His death occurred in 1858; his wife and two children also died that year. Mary E., the eldest daughter, died while in James City county, Va., 1847. Denton O'Dell came to Panola county, Miss., October 10th, 1859, alone, and in 1860 located in Chulahoma, Marshall county, of that state, where he followed the trade of carriage-maker. At the breaking out of the war he enlisted in company I, Nineteenth Mississippi infantry, under Col. Kit Mott, and was in the army of Virginia. He was in the battles of Evanston, Yorktown, Williamsburg, Fair Oaks, the seven days' fight before Richmond, and was wounded in the last named engagement, a minie-ball going through his left shoulder. This was a severe wound and he was taken to Chimborazo hospital at Richmond, Va., where he was attended by Dr. Shuford, of Holly Springs. He returned to his command just before the second battle of Manassas and was placed in charge of the litter bearers through that engagement. He was at Frederick city, Md., Harper's Ferry and in the Antietam fight his right arm was broken by a shell, and he was compelled to walk from there to Winchester, a distance of about thirty miles, before having his wound dressed, and from there to Staunton, a distance of over ninety miles, on one day's rations. From there he was taken back to Chimborazo hospital again and remained there about two months, after which he returned to his command at Fairfax Courthouse. He served after that on detailed duty until the final surrender at Appomattox in April, 1865. Returning to Chulahoma, Miss., he resumed his old occupation of wagon and carriage-making, and was married in October, 1865, to Frances Bloodworth (deceased 1884), daughter of Elisha W. and Elizabeth H. Bloodworth. The fruits of this union were twelve children—four sons and eight daughters: William Denton, in the employ of G. W. Fisher, of Memphis, Tenn.; Elisha Hamilton, Jesse D. and Charles; Elizabeth, wife of Robert Young; Martha M., wife of Robert L. Tucker, of Chulahoma; Stella, Henrietta, Josephine L., Ida (deceased), Kittie and an infant daughter (deceased). In 1876 he abandoned his trade of carriage-making and has since devoted his entire time to farming. He is now the owner of about seven hundred and forty acres of land, three hundred acres under cultivation, and also has a steam gin on his farm two miles south of Chulahoma. Mrs. O'Dell was a member of the Methodist Episcopal Church South. He is still a member of that church and also a member of the Masonic fraternity. He was a member of the board of supervisors of Marshall county for six years in succession, from 1884 to 1889, and is one of the most esteemed and respected citizens of the county.

James B. Oden, De Kalb, the present circuit clerk of Kemper county, Miss., was born in the county August 22, 1857, and is a son of John H. and Mary A. (Thomas) Oden. His father was born in Edgefield district, S. C., in 1815, and was a member of one of the old families of that state. There he spent his early life, and removed thence to Wayne county, Miss.; in 1840 he settled in Kemper county, where he engaged in a general milling business and in agriculture. He was married in his native state, and reared a family of twelve children, six of whom are living: Capt. George W.; Martha E., who is Mrs. Tinsley; Esther J., now Mrs. Saunders; Mary A., who is Mrs. Nall; Bell, who is Mrs. Ross; and James B., the subject of this biography. William E. was killed in battle; Thomas H. died at Savannah, Ga.; John died of yellow fever. The father died May 28, 1882. He was a Master Mason, a democrat in his politics, and a charter member of the Farmers' Grange. At an early day he was a member of the board of police. The mother of James B. was born in South Carolina, and was a daughter of Washington Thomas. She was an active member of the Methodist Episcopal church. Her death occurred in 1862. Mr. Oden was married a second time to Mrs. Susan Blakely, who lived one year. He was married again to Mrs. Ellen Drake, and two children were born of the union: Ella C. and Eliza L. James B. Oden was educated at Cooper institute, Miss., and was trained to the occupation of planting. In 1886 he was married to Miss Florence Roberts, a daughter of A. and Mary R. (Brittain) Roberts. Her parents were natives of Mississippi, and were married in Kemper county; the father was a farmer and miller by occupation. Mr. and Mrs. Oden are the parents of two children, John Albert, and James T. Mrs. Oden was born in 1868, and is one of a family of nine children. Mr. Oden affiliates with the democratic party, and takes an active part in all the deliberations of that body. He is a Master Mason, and is at the head of the Farmers' Alliance in this county. He is a man of untiring zeal in behalf of the county and all home interests, and is a citizen who has aided largely in the development of the county.

Among the representative establishments of Jackson, Miss., may be mentioned the house of E. T. Montgomery & Co., of which John H. Odeneal is the junior member. The business was established in 1887, and the stock of goods which they now carry is valued at about $20,000. Mr. Odeneal was born at Columbus, Miss., in 1842, the fourth in a family of seven children born to E. P. and Rosanna (Dearing) Odeneal, who were natives of the Old North state, but removed to Mississippi about 1833 and settled in Lowndes county, E. P. becoming one of its wealthiest planters. He died in 1877, and his wife in 1876, both being members of the Presbyterian church at the time of their deaths. The paternal grandfather was born in the Emerald isle, but at an early day came to America and took up his abode in North Carolina. John H. Odeneal was reared in the town of his birth, and in his youth was given advantages of a very superior nature, being educated in Nashville, Tenn., and Princeton, N. J. Before graduating, however, he left Princeton college to enter the Confederate army, enlisting in a company of the Tenth Mississippi infantry, with which he served one year, after which he went to Virginia and joined a company of Stuart's cavalry. In 1863 he entered the engineers' department, became a lieutenant, and served as such until the close of the war. After his return home he farmed for two years, but in 1868 again began following this occupation on the Yazoo river. In 1870 he came to Jackson, and, in partnership with Thomas E. Helm, he started the State Capital bank of Jackson, in which business he successfully remained until 1880, when he sold his interest and engaged in stockraising, with a small herd of blooded Jersey cattle. He now has a herd of one hundred thoroughbreds, and sells butter and milk in Jackson. He has one of the largest dairy farms in the South, comprising seven hundred and forty acres of land on the west side of Jackson, his milch cows amounting to over one hundred. He also has two other plantations in Hinds county, with six hundred and fifty acres under cultivation, and owns two thousand five hundred acres of timber land in Le Flore county, all of which will be extremely valuable in the future. In 1876 he erected a beautiful home in Jackson, and here he and his estimable wife have dispensed a generous hospitality. He was married in 1867 to Miss Annie Helm, a daughter of Thomas Helm, and to their union eight children have been born, all of whom are living. He and his wife are active members of the Presbyterian church, and are considered acquisitions to the social circles in which they move. Mr. Odeneal is a shrewd and far-seeing financier and a merchant of unblemished reputation, which has been built up by a steady adherence, throughout his long business history, to correct commercial principles.

John J. O'Ferrall (deceased) was one of the esteemed early settlers of Natchez, Miss., and while a resident of this section became prominently connected with the mercantile interests. He was born in Longford, Ireland, but in his youth came to the United States, and after a short residence in the city of New York he removed to St. Louis, in both of which places he devoted his time and attention to merchandising. About the year 1838 he took up his abode in the city of Natchez, and here, as time went on, became one of the wealthiest and most successful financiers of the place. He was a strictly honorable business man in every particular, devoted his time assiduously to his calling, was courteous and accommodating in his treatment of his patrons, which was no doubt the secret of his success. Soon after his arrival here he purchased sixteen acres of land near the city, which soon became known as O'Ferrall's, and on this place he erected a substantial business house, besides a number of other large buildings, and here his name and fame became co-extensive with Adams county and the surrounding country. His financial career was illustrated with many acts of liberality and kindness, and with every vital interest of this section he was closely identified. He was married in the city of New York to Miss Eliza O'Ferrall, a native of Ireland, and to them a family of twelve children were born: Eliza, a resident of Kansas; Mary, wife of Dr. John Murphy, of Natchez; John J.; William; Peter, a planter of Louisiana; Fannie, and several that died in early childhood. Mr. O'Ferrall was called from life in 1872 at the age of sixty-five years, having passed a well spent and useful life. In the space allotted in this volume it would be impossible to give a detailed account of his public and private career or to speak at length of his many sterling social and business qualities; suffice it to say that in every walk in life his career was above reproach. His wife died in 1882, having been a worthy Christian and a faithful wife and mother. John J. O'Ferrall, their son, was born in 1845, and in the city of Natchez, Miss., was reared and educated. During the late war, although he was not a Confederate soldier, he was taken a prisoner by the Federals during the early part of the war, and after some time spent in New Orleans he was sent to New York, and at the close of the war was exchanged from Elmira. After his return he clerked in Natchez for some time, and in the year 1870 first began taking charge of his present cottongin, which had been erected by his father in 1867. This gin is one of the best in this section of the country, and Mr. O'Ferrall gins more cotton than is turned out from any three gins in Adams county. The machinery is all of the latest improved, and is so thoroughly understood by Mr. O'Ferrall that two thousand bales are turned out annually. He is now in possession of his father's old place of sixteen acres, and on this property he has erected some twenty buildings, including his own handsome private residence. In Natchez (proper) he owns five dwellings at the corner of Pine and Jefferson streets, besides a magnificent plantation in the county, comprising one thousand one hundred acres, of which seven hundred acres are under cultivation. He also has two plantations in

Louisiana, one comprising one thousand acres and the other three hundred and sixty-five acres, and of this fine and valuable land seven hundred acres are under cultivation and are finely improved with excellent buildings, one of which is a stone one. Mr. O'Ferrall has led a very active life and has been very successful in his efforts to accumulate a competency, and by his own efforts has become one of the wealthiest residents of Adams county. He is president of the Natchez & Vidalia Steam Ferry company and in numerous other ways has shown himself to be an enterprising and pushing business man. He was married in Natchez in 1887, Miss Ella A. Tildsley becoming his wife, and to them two bright little children have been born: Lawrence Clapp and Thomas. Mrs. O'Ferrall is a daughter of Thomas Tildsley, who was one of the early settlers of Natchez and a contractor and builder by trade. The wedding of Mr. and Mrs. O'Ferrall was one of the largest ever celebrated in Natchez, and was held in the Catholic cathedral. The property of which Mr. O'Ferrall is the owner in Natchez has rapidly increased in value of late, for he has wisely improved it by erecting good buildings, and O'Ferrall's Corners is now a busy part of the town.

Gen. J. W. O'Ferrall, a prominent citizen of Enterprise, Clarke county, Miss., was born in Martinsburg, Berkeley county, Va., September 23, 1823. He was a son of John and Humric (House) O'Ferrall, the former a native of Virginia, who served in the War of 1812 and was for fifteen years a member of the legislature of that state. He was a prominent, public-spirited man, widely and favorably known. He was married in Maryland in 1821 and lived at Berkeley Springs, Morgan county, Va. He had a family of six children, namely: John, Ignatius, Peter, Lawrence, Richard and Eliza, all of whom grew to maturity. The mother died in 1830. The father remarried, and by his second wife had five children: Col. Charles T. O'Ferrall, who is prominent in Virginia politics; Virginia, Johnetta, Richard P., Laura. Mr. O'Ferrall died in 1856 in Virginia. In religion he was a Catholic. The early life of our subject was spent at Berkeley Springs. He received his education in his native state. He was married in 1851 to Miss Margaret Tolson of Newbern, Ala., a daughter of Fredric Tolson, a native of North Carolina, who has borne him four children, Merion, John, Thomas and Bessie, and who died in 1867, having lost her life on the coast while taking a voyage on board a vessel. Mr. O'Ferrall was married the second time to Miss Helen Gains Walton, daughter of Col. J. B. Walton, commander of the Washington artillery during the war. By this marriage he had two children, Edmond G. and Charles A. He and his wife are both members of the Episcopal church. Mr. O'Ferrall came to Enterprise in 1856 and established himself in the mercantile business in 1857, which he continued until the time of the war. During the war he was a brigadier-general. He has always been a prominent member of the democratic party and has served as a member of the city council. He is a member of the Masonic order. In connection with his other business he represents twelve insurance companies, some of which are among the most prominent in the country. He is an active, energetic business man, and takes a helpful interest in everything pertaining to the public benefit.

Richard O'Leary, M. D., was born in Georgia in 1828, the second in a family of eight children born to John Pearse and Catherine C. (Semmes) O'Leary, the father a native of Ireland and the mother of Georgia, the latter's ancestors being among the early settlers of Maryland and of French descent. Her father, Ignatius Semmes, was a successful practicing physician of Georgia. John Pearse O'Leary came from Ireland to the United States in his thirteenth year, and first made his home in Georgia. He had received a good education (for his years) in his native land, and after coming to this country he began the study of medicine in a school of Augusta, Ga., from which he graduated in his early manhood. In 1844 he came to Mississippi and settled in Madison county, where he became well known, and where he secured a large practice. He died in 1876, and his widow in 1888, both quite advanced in years, the former being an active practitioner until the day of his death. They were members of the Catholic church, and were worthy and useful members of society. Dr. Richard O'Leary, their son, was reared in Madison county, and was educated in Madison college and in Georgetown university. In 1858 he began the study of medicine, attending lectures at New York university, and graduated March 4, 1861. He then returned to his home in Mississippi and entered the Eighteenth Mississippi regiment as assistant surgeon, and was assigned to duty in the hospital at Richmond, where he remained during the war. In August, 1865, he settled at Vicksburg, where he has since been in the active practice of his profession, being accounted one of the highly successful medical practitioners of this section, and one of the leading ones of the state. He has been a leading man of Vicksburg for many years; has taken great interest in the improvement of the city, and is now erecting a handsome brick block, four stories in hight, one hundred feet front, on Crawford and Walnut streets, opposite the new Federal building. This is one of the most desirable localities in Vicksburg, and the fine block being erected by Dr. O'Leary will be a great improvement to the city. The building is designed for stores on the ground floor, and for offices above, the cost of the structure reaching the sum of $35,000. From 1874 to 1878 Dr. O'Leary was mayor of the city, and made a very faithful, zealous and competent official. During the yellow fever epidemic of 1878 he was one of its victims, but aside from this his health has always been remarkably good. He was married in 1867, but his wife died in 1883, leaving, besides her husband, a family of two sons and four daughters to mourn her loss. The Doctor's second union was to Mrs. N. A. Hartigan, and this union has resulted in the birth of a daughter.

Capt. William Oliver, Wesson, Miss. The South contains no treasure so rich as the fair fame of its children. Time evolves wondrous changes. "Empires crumble and fade away, governments perish and men decay," but the glory of our national existence must still remain so long as the names of those who aided in enlarging the boundaries of knowledge, who gave tone and high impress to its morals, who conserved its laws, or fought its battles, are remembered with gratitude. The men who stamp the impressions of their genius or their virtues on their own times, influence also the lives of those who follow, and they become the benefactors of after ages and of remote nations. Of such men the record should be carefully compiled, printed and preserved; and the South, above all other sections, owes it to its country and to the world to perpetuate such records, while it is yet possible to separate truth from fiction, in all that which pertains to the true character or relates to those who laid the foundation for a new and higher life—who have sustained it by their wisdom or adorned it by their talents. It should be constantly borne in mind that the South to day stands conspicuous among the countries of the world as a younger son grown to full and beautiful manhood from the ruins of a former bright and prosperous family; that it has passed successfully through an era of deep obscurity and wasted years of feeble infancy, and that it has stepped forth at maturity from the panoply of war like Minerva from the brain of Jove. Such is the character of the intrepid man whose memoir inspires these words.

Captain Oliver was endowed by nature with a powerful frame and vigorous intellect, undaunted courage, and a spirit of enterprise that peculiarly fitted him to encounter the perils and hardships of the time that tried men's souls. In a letter from Wesson to the *Southwestern Presbyterian* at the time of Captain Oliver's death, the Rev. T. S. West says:

"Some years ago I was on a rostrum before a large audience, witnessing some exercises of more or less interest. Turning my head a little to the right I noticed a man of singularly striking appearance, sitting near the platform; he was very handsome, had an open countenance with very forcible expression. I thought him one of the most imposing looking personages I had ever seen. He was about the age that men are the best looking, say fifty; his dark beard beginning to be threaded with gray. I said, mentally, 'I don't know who you are, nor what you are; but you stand above your fellows in whatever community you dwell, and you are a leader in your calling, whatever it may be.' He engaged my attention for some time; I turned and whispered to some one, 'Who is that?' The answer was, 'Captain Oliver, of Wesson.' I did not meet him again, until eighteen months ago, when I was appointed pastor in charge of the Methodist church of this place. We gradually grew intimate, and in his death I feel that I have lost a friend." William Oliver was born in Twiggs county, Ga., February 24, 1829. His father, Wiley Oliver, moved to Barbour county, Ala., in 1833. At the early age of eighteen we find William already occupying a position of trust, commanding the highest salary commanded in that day. On the 12th of October, 1847, he was married to Mary Milner Callaway, being at that time just eighteen years and eight months old; although so young, he made an admirable choice. When a little more than nineteen he began business for himself, in Eufaula, Ala. In 1853 he moved to Minden, La., and opened a business there with Mr. Drake. In 1855 the firm established a joint house in Trenton, La. Here he remained until the dark din of war rolled over our Southland. He had marked success in his ten or twelve years of mercantile life. He entered the Confederate service in the Thirty-first Louisiana regiment, with the rank of captain, and was assigned to duty in the quartermaster department. In 1866 he went to New Orleans, engaged in the cotton business with John T. Hardie, and was again successful. In 1870 the Mississippi Manufacturing company, at Wesson, Miss., passed into the hands of John T. Hardie and William Oliver. Captain Oliver, of the firm, came to Wesson and took charge of the mills, without any knowledge whatever of the manufacturing business. In the reorganization the name was changed to Mississippi Mills, with John T. Hardie, president, and William Oliver, secretary and treasurer. The plant at this time was worth about $100,000; after three years of successful management the mills were consumed by fire. This misfortune discouraged most of the stockholders; but Captain Oliver's three years' experience led him to believe that the thing could be made a grand success under proper management. About this time John T. Hardie, the leading stockholder, proposed to buy or sell. Captain Oliver saw his opportunity, and had the adroitness to interest in this enterprise Col. Ed. Richardson, the commercial king of Mississippi. So John T. Hardie and others were bought out; the company newly organized, the stock increased to $340,000, with Col. Ed. Richardson president, and Captain Oliver, the general manager, in the office of secretary and treasurer. In eighteen years, from 1873 to 1891, without any additional capital except profits reinvested, the factory grew to that magnificent plant at Wesson to-day, with $2,000,000, dispensing its blessings to thousands of the poor, and with comfortably increasing dividends to the stockholders, who are confined almost wholly to the Richardson and Oliver families. Since the death of Col. Ed. Richardson, his son, John P., has been president of the company; he married Mary Ella, second daughter of Captain Oliver. Rilla E., the eldest daughter, married Dr. R. W. Rea. His only son, John M. Oliver, is a successful young merchant at Wesson.

Colonel Richardson was asked one day why he did not put more money in factories, as his Wesson interests had proven so profitable. He said: "I would be glad to do so if I could get more William Olivers to manage them." Capt. William Oliver's wife, Mary Milner Callaway, died January 10, 1883: she that had been the comfort and joy of his young life, that had increased the strength of his mature manhood, proven herself to be the fitting companion of such a man, passed away, with the praise and blessing of all who knew and loved her. After a suitable season in silence and sad solitude, recognizing the truth of God's word that it is not good that man should be alone, he married again; this time, a niece of his first wife, Melissa D. Callaway. This also proved a wise choice, for she was a stay to him in trials, and a comfort to the last hour of his life; he said that parting from her and his children was the saddest thing connected with passing away from this life. The sting of death, itself, he did not fear. He said a short time before he died: "While I have been ready to defend what I regarded as my rights, I have acted with a good conscience toward my fellow-men, and I go out into eternity trusting only in my Lord." Men who had business dealings with him pronounced him honest and fair. The world called him charitable; he sympathized with the suffering, and his hand was open to the wants of the needy. During his residence in New Orleans he became the warm friend and admirer of Rev. Dr. B. M. Palmer, and united with his church in 1867. For a period of eighteen years he held the office of elder in the Presbyterian church at Wesson. One who knew him well said: "The Captain differs from most men; as he grows richer he grows better." It is exceedingly common for men to grow in worldliness as they grow in worldly goods, but it was not the case with the subject of this sketch. Some men are too busy to worship God; this man, although very busy, attended church regularly; if his own pastor was away he went to some other church to worship; he taught a class in Sabbath-school, was equally at home in managing a factory or conducting a prayer-meeting. He took interest in the affairs of the community, the public school, the municipal government, or whatever was of interest to the people. He was specially interested in the welfare of the operatives in the mill; he called them his people. The old women were heard often to say: "The Captain has been mighty good to us; when we came here and had nothing the children soon got work in the mill, and we got credit at the store until we could pay up." The Captain had an eye to the morals of his people, and refused to employ any disreputable person. His devotion to his home was very beautiful; its lovely surroundings attest to his exquisite taste and love for flowers. A profusion of greenhouse plants and rare flowers grace his extensive lawn, and gladden the eyes of all; it was his delight and recreation to wander among them, and in their beauty seek oblivion from the sordid cares of business. As a homemaker, one sees the loveliest traits of his character brought to light; his home was first with him always, nothing had precedence before it. It was his delight to make those about him, young and old, happy, and he was ever thinking of the wants and pleasures of others.

Never was more solicitude expressed in a community for a sick man than was expressed during his last illness. Never was there such a crowd at a funeral; the church was packed, all the standing room in the aisles was occupied, the yard was filled, the masses about the windows, with stretched umbrellas in the drizzling rain. Some one remarked that during a part of the funeral service there was scarcely a dry eye in the house. This remarkable man left to his family not only nearly $400,000, which he had accumulated, but also the rich heritage of a good name, an unsullied reputation. A man of wonderful magnetism, he drew about him a host of friends, who deeply mourn his loss. He went down to the grave much loved and greatly honored. The glorious Fourth of July, as we term it, was a sad day for Wesson when Captain Oliver lay in state. He died on the 3d of July, 1891, at 9 o'clock P. M. On the 3d of July, 1890, the people of the mills presented him with a gold-headed cane, in token of their devotion. He died upon the anniversary of this expression of their love.

B. F. Ormond, Meridian, Miss., was born in Greene county, N. C., in January, 1849, and is the sixth of a family of nine children. His parents, Fletcher and Fanny (Sugg) Ormond, were natives of North Carolina, and there grew to maturity, were married, and died. The father was a merchant in his early days, and was also a brick manufacturer and planter. He and his wife both died in 1861. They were consistent members of the Methodist Episcopal church. There are only five of the family now living: Thomas, John, William, Julia, wife of O. C. Thomas, and B. F., the subject of this notice. He was educated at the Cooper institute at Spring Hill, Miss., and at the University of Kentucky. After leaving school he devoted his time and attention to the mercantile business at Lauderdale, Miss., forming a copartnership with his brother and E. C. Eason in 1869. This relationship existed one year, when Mr. Ormond purchased Mr. Eason's interest, and finally bought the entire business. He conducted the business alone until December, 1881, and then sold out, going to Meridian. The following year he embarked in the wholesale provision business under the firm name of Branch, Ormond & McInnis. This partnership continued until 1886, when Mr. Ormond bought the interest of Mr. Branch, the firm name being changed to Ormond & McInnis. At the end of one year he purchased Mr. McInnis' interest, and conducted the business under the firm name of Ormond & Co. until July, 1890. His brother, W. H. Ormond, was then admitted as a partner to the business; they are now doing an extensive trade in groceries and cotton, and are one of the largest wholesale concerns in the place. Mr. Ormond is connected with some of the most important banking institutions of Meridian, and is also a stockholder of the Insurance, Building and Loan association. He has been very successful in all his business enterprises, and is considered one of the most progressive and energetic men of Meridian. In 1870 he was married to Miss Batty Watts, and they had born to them nine children, six of whom are living: Ella, J. B., Earl (deceased), Marion, Robert, Wayne (deceased), John W., Marie (deceased), Marguerite. The eldest daughter, Ella, is a graduate of the East Mississippi Female college and has taken a post-graduate course at Pulaski, Tenn. James B. has been a student at the Southern university at Greensboro, Ala., and the other children are yet attending the public schools. Mr. Ormond is a member of the Masonic fraternity, and he and his wife belong to the Methodist Episcopal church. Politically he affiliates with the democratic party, but takes no active part in the movements of that body. All educational enterprises are sure of a hearty support in Mr. Ormond, and he has contributed liberally to the churches.

Dr. T. T. Orendorff, a physician and surgeon of Rolling Fork, Miss., was born in Breckinridge county, Ky., on the 11th of April, 1847, and is a son of M. and Mary (Cain) Orendorff, natives of Virginia, born in 1822 and 1826, respectively. Both families removed to Kentucky in an early day, where the young couple was married in 1840, in Breckinridge county, and where Mr. Orendorff died in 1853; his wife still survives him. She is a daughter of Thomas and Ona (Meador) Cain, natives of Virginia, and long since dead; the former was a son of Micajah and Elizabeth (Wilkerson) Cain, and the latter a daughter of Benjamin and Mary H. (Morris) Meador. The Orendorffs were originally from the lower Palatinate, Germany, and were descended from noble ancestry. They were driven from their native country of the Rhine nearly two centuries ago by Louis XIV. on account of their religious opinions. They fled to England and eventually made their way to America, the future land of the free and home of the brave, prior to the Revolutionary war. Members of the family settled in Maryland, Virginia and Pennsylvania, and the tradition goes that many of the male members became active soldiers in the war for independence. From these pioneers, representatives have penetrated half the states of the Union, as a family reunion, held at Bloomington, Ill., in October, 1886, found representatives present from seventeen states and territories. This fraternal gathering developed many family traits, characteristics and peculiarities, one of which is worthy of note: in all this prolific family not a member of it has ever been known to have been tried in court for a criminal offense. Dr. Orendorff, the subject of this sketch, is the fourth in a family of seven children, five sons and two daughters, all of whom, except the youngest son, Thomas Jesse, are living. He was brought up on a farm and received the benefits of the common schools, finishing off a good English education at the Brandenburg (Kentucky) academy. After leaving school he was for some time employed in a country store, during which time his evenings and leisure hours were occupied in reading medicine. Thus, by energy and perseverance, he was qualified to enter the Kentucky school of medicine at Louisville, in the fall of 1868, attending his first course of lectures. He then spent eighteen months in one of the city hospitals, after which, in 1871, he graduated from the Kentucky school of medicine. Immediately after being graduated he went to Mississippi and located in the Deer Creek valley, Sharkey county, where he has practiced his profession ever since and where, by that courtesy and politeness which are his strongest characteristics, and a close attention to his patrons, he has won flattering success. In 1880 he made a trip to Europe and spent the year in visiting the hospitals of Edinburgh, London, Paris, Berlin, etc., and in making a tour of most of the countries of the old world. In 1882, in addition to his medical practice he engaged in cotton planting, and is now the owner of some two thousand acres of fine land in the Deer Creek valley, in Sharkey county, on the cultivated portion of which he raises about eight hundred bales of cotton annually. He is also the owner of some valuable property in Memphis, Florence, Ala., and in El Paso, Tex. All of his possessions have been won by his own individual efforts and persevering industry. Although he has often been urged to run for office, he has invariably refused, party politics having no charms for him. Dr. Orendorff's brothers and sisters are as follows: Prof. Henry, who is a practicing physician, holds a chair in the Kentucky school of medicine, from which he graduated in 1871, and in which he has been a professor for twelve years; Capt. C. C. is connected with the Southern Palace Car company at Memphis, Tenn.; Edmonia B. was educated at Bethlehem convent in Kentucky, and is a cultured and accomplished lady. She is the wife of Col. W. H. Perrin, connected with the Louisville *Courier-Journal* and one of its ablest writers; William A. is a cotton planter in Sharkey county, as was Thomas J. until his death, which occurred in March, 1891; Lena, who married the late Dr. Edward S. Crosier, of New Albany, Ind., an accomplished scholar, scientist and physician, and for seventeen years in charge of the surveyor's office in the United States customhouse at Louisville, Ky., and also for years a professor in the Louisville Medical college. Dr. Orendorff is one of the most progressive and public-spirited men in Sharkey county, and makes an intelligent and judicious use of his means and ability. His knowledge of matters in general is broad and comprehensive, and, being a close observer, his extensive travel in this country and Europe has been of material benefit to him. He is a member of the Mississippi State Medical association, and of the fraternity of A. F. & A. M., of the Knights of Honor and of the American Legion of Honor.

J. A. Orr, ex-judge and attorney at law of Columbus, Miss., was born in Anderson county, S. C., April 10, 1828, and inherits many of the sterling qualities of his Scotch ancestors. His paternal great-grandfather, Robert Orr, was of Scotch origin although born in the north of Ireland, and in the year 1720 became a resident of America, settling in Pennsylvania but afterward moving to the Palmetto state, where his last days were spent. He left two brothers in Pennsylvania, who became prominent planters and merchants. His son Jehu followed in his father's footsteps and became a planter, but when the Revolutionary war came up he dropped all personal considerations to espouse the cause of the colonists, as did five of his brothers. His son Christopher, father of J. A. Orr, was born in South Carolina, where he was reared, and wooed and won for his bride Miss Martha McCann, a noble and estimable young lady and a native of the same state as himself. About 1843 he became attracted to the eastern section of Mississippi by the famed fertility of its virgin soil, and at that date he cast his fortunes in that favored region, and although he was first a resident of Chickasaw county he subsequently removed to Pontotoc county, where he was called from life. His family consisted of five children: Jane S., who became the wife of W. H. Calhoun; James L., who was speaker of the XXXVIIIth Congress, Confederate state senator, governor of South Carolina and died while minister to Russia in 1873; Martha E., wife of Gen. J. W. Miller; H. C., an eminent physician of Lee county; and Judge J. A. The latter was brought to Mississippi at the age of fifteen years but was educated at Princeton, New Jersey, and at an early age he imbibed those principles of honor and probity which are so characteristic of those of his nativity. He inherited the gracious and kindly nature of both his parents and, being a lad of quick discernment and possessing a retentive memory, he imbibed the best literary thought in the English language and thus in part received ideas and impressions which have distinguished him at the bar and as a civilian. After deciding upon law as his life calling and giving it some study he began practicing in 1849, but in 1850 assumed the duties of secretary of the Mississippi senate, in which capacity his varied attainments soon made him conspicuous. In 1852-3 he represented his county in the state legislature and in 1854-5 filled the high position of United States district attorney, the following year being presidential elector for Buchanan. In 1857-9 he was school commissioner for Chickasaw county and an active member of the secession convention in 1860. He was a member of the provisional congress from February, 1861, to February, 1862, at which time he raised the Thirty-first Mississippi regiment of fourteen hundred men, of which he was the honored commander until March, 1864, during which time he was a participant in the battles of Coffeeville, Baton Rouge, siege of Vicksburg, Baker's creek, Jackson and others. He was the volunteer aid of General Forrest and General Lee at the battle of Harrisburg. During the last eighteen months of the existence of the Confederate government he was a member of the Confederate congress, and was appointed by the committee of foreign affairs to make its report to congress, which provided for the appointment of the Hampton Roads commission.

Mr. Orr furnishes us with a history of the celebrated Hampton Roads conference never before published. There was a large minority in the Confederate congress who, for more than a year preceding the surrender of General Lee, thought the war could and should be ended by negotiation. President Lincoln had, in his annual message to the congress of the United States, asserted that the Southern states—erring sisters, as he termed them—could at any time, of their own volition, resume their allegiance to, and occupy their position in the government of the United States, including their representation in congress. The same assurance was authoritatively given by Hon. F. P. Blair, Sr., in his missives to the Confederate officials. Every shade of resolution, from those proposing to die in the last ditch to those of unconditional surrender, was referred to the committee on foreign affairs. The resolutions here given were finally adopted by the committee and reported to the house. This report and the action of the house thereon led to the appointment of the Hampton Roads commission. On the next day, Friday, February 13, 1865, Mr. Dupre announced in secret session that the president would appoint three gentlemen to confer with the president of the United States, or such as he might designate. He did appoint Vice President Stevens, Senator Hunter and Judge Campbell of Alabama, and on Saturday evening, January 14th, those gentlemen left Richmond with their commission, which closed with the historic words, "peace to the two countries." When the commission was read by President Lincoln, he construed it to mean that the basis of the conference involved the recognition of the Confederacy as a separate government, and terminated the official interview. The following is an extract from the proceedings of the secret session of the Confederate congress:

The house being in secret session, Mr. Foster moved that the house resolve itself into open session, which motion did not prevail. Mr. Orr, from the committe on foreign affairs, reported the following resolutions:

Resolved, That the independence of the Confederate states of America, based upon the constitutional compact between the sovereign states composing the Confederacy, and maintained through nearly four years of gigantic war, justly claims from their former associates, and from the world, its recognition as a rightful fact.

Resolved, That we hail with gratification the just and sound sentiment manifested by a large portion of the people of the United States, since the last session of our congress, that all associations of these American states ought to be voluntary and not forcible, and we give a hearty response to their views and wishes for a suspension of the present conflict of arms, and an appeal to the forum of reason, to see if the matters in controversy cannot be properly and justly adjusted by negotiation, without the further effusion of blood.

Resolved, That, being wedded to no particular or exclusive mode of initiating or inaugurating negotiations looking to a peaceful settlement and adjustment of the questions now in issue between the United States and the Confederate States, it is the judgment of this house, that if it should be more agreeable to the government and people of the United States, or even a large and respectable portion of them, that the question should be submitted to the consideration of commissioners from each state, one or more, in the character of a convention, of all the states, than to plenipotentiaries appointed in the usual way, then such a plan of initiating negotiations should be acceded to or proposed on our side; such a convention being acceded to or proposed as an advisory body only, the commissioners or delegates to it being authorized by the treaty-making power of each government respectively, not to form any agreement or compact between states, but simply to confer, consult, and after freely entertaining and hearing all propositions and suggestions, to agree, if possible, upon some plan of peace, to be proposed by them to their respective governments. The mode of inaugurating negotiations, in the opinion of the house, would be relieved of all possible constitutional objections by the consent of the proper constitutional authorities of the two governments. With such consent the proposed delegates would but act, in any view of the subject, as commissioners appointed in any other way, to negotiate for peace, and whatever they might agree upon or propose, would be subject to the approval or disapproval of the two governments respectively.

Resolved, Inasmuch as the authorities at Washington have heretofore rejected all formal offers for a free interchange of views looking to negotiations made by our authorities, and as we deem it a high duty, not only to our gallant citizen soldiers in the field, but to the whole body of our people, as well as our duty to the cause of humanity, civilization and Christianity, that the chosen representatives of the people of the several states of the Confederacy upon this floor should omit or neglect no effort in our power to bring about negotiations, if possible; therefore, be it further

Resolved, That the president of the Confederate States be informed of these resolves, and that he be requested to grant permission to three persons to be selected by this house—the members from each state voting in such selection by states, and a majority of all the votes being necessary to a choice in each case—to cross our lines, who shall immediately proceed to ask and obtain, if possible, an informal interview or conference with the authorities at Washington, or any person or persons who may be appointed by them, to meet the persons so sent on our side, to see if any such plan of inaugurating negotiations for peace, upon the basis above set forth, can be agreed upon, and if not, to ascertain any other, or what terms, if any, of a peaceful settlement, may be proposed by the authorities at Washington; and the said commissioners shall be authorized to bring into view the possibility of coöperation between the Confederate and United States, in maintaining the principles and policy of the Monroe doctrine, in the event of a prompt recognition of the independence of the former by the government of the latter, and to report the result

of their effort and action to the president and to this house; and should this effort fail, we shall have the consolation of knowing that we, in our high and responsible trust, have done our duty. We shall have given assurance to our people, that we have done all that we, in our position and capacity, can do, to end the strife upon just and honorable principles, and the rejection of the overtures by the president of the United States will afford additional evidence to the people of these states that he is waging this unnatural war, not for peace or for the good of his country, but for the purpose of the most unholy ambition, while it will demonstrate to our people that his object as to them is nothing short of an unconditional subjugation or extinction.

Mr. Perkins from the same committee, in behalf of himself and his colleague, Mr. Snead, submitted a minority report, which was laid upon the table. Mr. Orr moved that the resolutions be postponed until Saturday next, made the special order for that day at twelve o'clock, and printed. Mr. Staples moved to amend the motion of Mr. Orr, by striking out the same and inserting in lieu thereof the following, viz.: "That the resolutions be postponed until the bill to amend the act to organize forces to serve during the war is disposed of." Mr. Dupre called the question, which was ordered. Mr. Orr demanded the yeas and nays, which were ordered and recorded as follows, viz.: Yeas forty-two, nays thirty-eight; yeas— Messrs. Barksdale, Batson, Baylor, Branch, Burnett, Carroll, Chilton, Chrisman, Clark, Clusky, Conrad, Conrow, Darden, Dickinson, Dupre, Ewing, Farrow, Foster, Funsten, Gholsen, Goode, Gray, Hanly, Hatcher, Hilton, Holliday, Johnstone, Lyon, Miles, Miller, Norton, Perkins, Pugh, Read, Rives, Russell, Sexton, Simpson, Staples, Welsh, Wilkes, and Mr. Speaker; nays—Messrs. Anderson, Baldwin, Bell, Blandford, Boyce, Bradley, E. M. Bruce, H. W. Bruce, Clopton, Coylar, Cruikshank, De Jarnette, Echols, Elliot, Fuller, Garland, Gilmer, Holder, Lamkin, J. M. Leach, Lester, Logan, Machen, Manhall, McCallum, McMullin, Menees, Moore, Orr, Shewmanke, J. M. Smith, W. E. Smith, Smith of Alabama, Tripplett, Turner, Villere, Wickham and Witherspoon. So the amendment of Mr. Staples was agreed to. Mr. Lyon submitted the following amendment to the motion of Mr. Orr as amended: Add to the end thereof the following, "and until the tax and other bills for the relief of the treasury shall be disposed of." Pending which Mr. Read moved to reconsider the vote by which the amendment of Mr. Staples was agreed to; pending which, on motion of Mr. McMullin, the house resolved itself into open session.

Although, as shown, the negotiations of this commission were declined, several hours were spent by Mr. Lincoln, Mr. Seward, Mr. Stevens, Mr. Campbell and Mr. Hunter in agreeable and amicable social intercourse. Mr. Orr was judge of the Sixth judicial district for six years from the 10th of May, 1870, and, upon taking his seat, found that district, which was largely composed of blacks, in a chaotic condition, the preceding judge having been George F. Brown, of Ohio, who sought to instill into the minds of the negro the ideas of equality. During the years that Judge Orr filled this trying position he administered justice with an even hand, and his work was eminently satisfactory. The frequent affirmance of his decisions by the supreme court attested his profound knowledge and astute judgment of the noble science of law. He has been ardently devoted to the cause of education all his life, and has served his state as a trustee of the Mississippi university for twenty years, and has never missed a meeting of the board. While a resident of Houston, Miss., he was a partner of Gen. W. S. Featherston for eight years, and for the past fifteen years has been associated in his practice with ex-Governor Simms. In his career at the bar he has ever been laborious in research, and his brilliant mental endowments, his rare power of oratory, his logical and ornate style of speaking and writing, his sagacity, his skill in planning, and his sound and sober judgment admirably fit him for the arena of law. He is still an active practitioner, although he has considerably passed the three-score year milestone of his life, and gives promise of spending many more years in battling for right and for the interests of the section in which he resides, for he retains to the fullest extent his vigor of mind and intellect. He is a prominent member of the First Presbyterian church and is a member of the board of elders. He was first married to Miss Lizzie, daughter of William Gates, of Chickasaw county, in 1852, and by her is the father of three children: William G., an eminent attorney of Okolona, Miss.; Christopher and Lizzie. Mr. Orr's second union was to Miss Cornelia Vandegraff, by whom he has two children: Mrs. Franklin Harris, of Chattanooga, Tenn., a very fine musician, and Miss Pauline V., who is professor of English literature in the State Female college of Mississippi, filling a like position at Mount Eagle, Tenn.

Eugene C. Orrick, the senior member of the firm of Orrick & Baker, a very prominent law firm of Indianola, the county seat of Sunflower county, is a young man, having been born on January 3, 1864, in Canton, Miss., where he was reared and received his elementary education. He took a full collegiate course at that most admirable institution of learning, Notre Dame university, Notre Dame, Ind., graduating with high honors in 1882. He was admitted to the bar in Canton in 1884, and after practicing there for about a year he removed to Indianola, where together with his partner, Mr. J. H. Baker, he has built up a most excellent practice. Mr. Orrick interests himself to some extent in politics and is a stanch democrat. He is chairman of the county executive committee and is now serving his second term as superintendent of public education. The ancestors of Mr. Orrick are of English descent, having settled in this country long prior to the Revolutionary war. His father, N. C. Orrick, was born in Virginia, in October, 1836, and was reared and educated in that state. He moved to Mississippi in 1859, and after being in the state for a short while located in Canton, where he now resides. Mrs. Orrick, a daughter of John R. Semmes, is a native of Georgia, but was reared in Mississippi.

Nicholas Cromwell Orrick, merchant, Canton, Miss., was born in Morgan county, Va., near Martinsburg, October 27, 1837, and of the eight children born to Cromwell and Mary (Johnson) Orrick he was seventh in order of birth. The parents were natives of Virginia and Maryland, respectively. The father was a planter on the Potomac river. He held important offices in his state and county, serving with credit as probate judge for some time, as a member of the Virginia legislature for a number of years and in the senate of Virginia. He was a gentleman of wealth and culture. He died in his native state in 1857, when but sixty-four years of age. He was the son of Nicholas and Mary (Pendleton) Orrick, natives of Maryland and Virginia, respectively. Nicholas Orrick, for whom the subject of this sketch is named, was one of the most prominent men in his state. In the year 1784, he was one of a committee to witness a test of steam navigation invented by one James Rumsey, who according to the reports of congress (Vol. 70, XXIVth congress) was the original inventor of steam navigation. The committee consisted of Charles Morrow, Nicholas Orrick, Gen. George Washington, Gen. Horatio Gates and Henry Bedinger; General Washington signing an affidavit to the effect that the invention was a success. The boat was launched on the Potomac river in Berkeley county, Va., within a few miles of where the subject of this sketch was born. Mr. Rumsey went to England and soon after related to Fulton what he had done. He died in England before he had fully developed his wonderful discovery. Fulton then came to America and fully demonstrated to the world what Mr. Rumsey had discovered, to all of which the records of the XXIVth congress testify.

William Orrick, the great-grandfather of our subject, was a native of Baltimore county, Md. The Orrick family originated in England in the days of the Saxons. The maternal grandparents of Nicholas Cromwell Orrick, William and Betty Pendleton, were natives of

Virginia and of English ancestry. For more than two hundred years this family had been Episcopalians.

Nicholas Cromwell Orrick was reared in his native state, attended school at Hancock, Md., at Berryville, Va., then Winchester academy, and finished at the University of Virginia in 1855. Soon after he began the study of medicine, attending lectures at the Universities of Virginia and Philadelphia, but on account of failing health he abandoned the profession, although he still continued to study. Pending the settlement of his father's estate he left home before he was twenty years old, came West, and after drifting about through the West and South for some time, finally settled in Jackson, Miss., where he was engaged as a bookkeeper for some time by John W. Robinson. He was then sent by his employer to Canton, Madison county, and there he has since made his home. He has been a hard student all his life and has a finished scientific education. He has a fertile brain and has invented some of the most useful implements known to the public. In 1890 he lost by accident while working with some machinery the first and second fingers of his right hand, and to replace them he applied to the best known artists in the United States; but failing to find any one who could supply his want he went to work, and with astonishing results, for he made two fingers with which he can write and can use nearly as well as the natural members, and which are so perfect in shape and color that the imitation can not be detected except by critical examination, a thing never before accomplished. He is an inveterate reader and reads only the best literature. If he wishes to invent anything Mr. Orrick at once consults the best scientific authorities and studies and experiments until he obtains the desired results. Thus he has made his knowledge useful to himself and the world. His life is one of purpose.

In 1861 he enlisted in the Confederate army, company I, Tenth Mississippi regiment, Madison rifles, under Capt. Joseph Davis, and was sent to Fort McRea, Fla., where he remained until transferred to the army of Virginia. He participated in the Valley campaign under Stonewall Jackson, and was wounded in the left elbow and disabled from further service. While at Winchester he was appointed by General Jackson to drill the recruits for heavy artillery service, and was complimented by that general for his excellency and proficiency in performing his duty. He had been a military student and made that branch of knowledge useful. He came to Canton, Miss., in 1859, and was engaged as bookkeeper for Robinson, Mayson & Co., a large firm whose annual business equals $250,000 in Canton, besides a larger business in Jackson. Mr. Orrick was married in 1864, to Miss Mary Semmes, a native of Georgia, and daughter of John R. Semmes. The fruits of this union have been eleven children: Eugene C., a very successful lawyer, now practicing in Indianola, Miss., but who has just formed a copartnership with Mr. Hogsett, of Fort Worth, Tex., at which place he will make his future home; Lucy Semmes, has had special advantages in the study of drawing and painting, and whose productions have received much praise from art critics; she is a writer of much fluency and vigor; her literary efforts have been published in some of the leading journals North and South; Alphonse Paul is in business with his father, a youth of fine character and a superb pianist; Mary Bena, whose specialty is being a violinist of very high order; Pauline, Louise, Edna, Madeleine and Gertrude at school; John and Zita, deceased. Mr. Orrick and family are members of the Catholic church, although his ancestors for over two centuries back have been Episcopalians. He investigated the subject of religion wholly by himself and for himself, and educated himself into the Catholic church. After the war he found the two administrators of his father's estate had been killed in the army. The estate being located between the hostile lines a new administrator was appointed by the court. The courthouse and public records were burned. The property was sold by the new administrator. When the war closed it was found his bond was worthless; this entire splendid estate was consequently lost to the heirs. Mr. Orrick, finding himself without means, applied to his former employer, John W. Robinson, for a loan of $5,000. Mr. Robinson gave him the money without a line of security or anything but a verbal promise. This sum was immediately invested and in three months returned, leaving Mr. Orrick with $4,000 of his own profits. With this beginning he started in the mercantile business in 1869. He has raised and educated a large family, has a beautiful and attractive home, and with a business which, with the revenues derived from his patents, places him in easy circumstances. Mr. Orrick takes great pride in his family, and well he may, for all his children are bright and quick at whatever they undertake. All are good musicians, and his eldest daughters are specially talented in music and art.

Rev. Charles H. Otken, LL. D., was born in 1839, in the parish of Orleans, La. His parents were respectable. His father was a skillful mechanic. His mother possessed more than ordinary intellectual qualities and great force of character. She died when the subject of this sketch was about six years old. After the mother's death his father placed his three sons in different families. Charles lived with his uncle Coleman, whose first wife was his father's sister. He had married again, and this second wife, whom Charles called aunt, was not related to him. His uncle placed Charles in the public school of Carrollton, La.; here he learned his letters; he attended this school for about two years. After this his father sent him to a school about a half-mile north of Carrollton. This coast school, as it was called, was regarded as more select than the former, consisting largely of the children of wealthy planters. He also attended a private school, where he studied French and German. He had learned the rudiments of the two languages when a Mr. George, a merchant of the town, desired Charles to take a position as clerk in his store. The offer was accepted. From this time on Charles earned his own living. He was now about eleven years old; he remained here some four or five years. It was a store of general merchandise; he soon familiarized himself with the business. He was attentive to business, industrious and honest, frank and cheerful by nature; he was not too proud to do any honorable work, but too proud to do a mean thing.

He used no profane language, nor did he use tobacco in any form, neither did he touch liquor of any kind. He never was away from his place of business for a single day, nor from his employer's home after eight o'clock at night. His excellent habits gave him the name of the model boy. During his clerkship he occupied a room in the store; slept there at night. There was no iron safe in the house and no bank in the town. The gold and silver were kept in sacks and banknotes in a book, all of which were in charge of Charles. Up to his seventeenth year he knew nothing of practical religion. Ceremonial observances were not unknown to him—the dead forms of worship that touch no heart. The Bible was to him a sealed book. Belief in Christ as a personal Savior was an inexplicable mystery; he saw no necessity for such belief. At this time he became acquainted with a Baptist minister and through him with Christian people who believed in the great doctrines of conversion and justification by faith in Christ. He attended their meetings, heard the gospel in its charming simplicity as he had never heard it before. He now for the first time in his life made the gracious discovery that he was a sinful being and a sinner. Thus convicted, he saw the need of a Savior. He joyfully accepted Christ as his Savior. He felt that a wonderful change had taken place in his spiritual being. He soon after united with the Coliseum Place Baptist church of New Orleans, joyfully following his Lord and Master in the ordinance of baptism by immersion.

In 1856 he matriculated as a student of Mississippi college, located at Clinton, Miss., and remained there three and a half years. After the college suspended work at the outbreak of the Civil war he taught a school for a few months at Edwards depot, and from there, in 1861, joined the Charlton rifles at Grenada. This company formed a part of the Third Mississippi battalion, afterward changed to the Forty-fifth Mississippi regiment. In 1862 he was appointed chaplain of this regiment; resigned the chaplaincy in 1864, and in the same year he was ordained a Baptist minister in the St. Francis Street Baptist church, of Mobile, Ala. During most of the period that he served as chaplain he was a licentiate minister. After the war closed he went to Amite county, Miss., at the suggestion of Rev. J. B. Hamberlin. Here he taught school and served as pastor of Liberty Baptist church and Mount Vernon church. In 1866 he married Emily Jane, daughter of James E. and Frances Lee, of Amite county. Rev. Dr. B. Sears, agent of the Peabody fund, having visited the town of Summit, in Pike county, Miss., offered that community a thousand dollars annually if they would establish a public school. The proposition was accepted by the people. At the suggestion of a friend, Mr. Otken applied for the principalship of this school, in 1867, and, after a rigid examination, was elected principal of the Peabody public school. The school opened with twenty-seven pupils. The school prospered from the beginning. The third session a pay high school was added to the free school, Mr. Otken serving as principal of both. The highest enrollment during any one year was three hundred and forty-seven pupils. He served nine years as principal of the two schools, when he declined a re-election. During seven years of this period he was also the pastor of the Summit Baptist church. During his pastorate it became one of the best organized and strongest churches on the Illinois Central railroad in south Mississippi.

An effort having been made by Mr. Otken and Rev. S. S. Relyea to establish a female school of high order at Summit, Mr. Otken, after the death of his friend, Rev. Relyea, decided to commence such a school upon a modest basis. This was done in the year 1877. He bought two squares of ground containing a two-story building, originally intended for a school. To accomplish his object, he sought the assistance of personal friends upon the condition that he would open such a school and continue it at least five years. Upon this condition, Mrs. Elceba Bates, an aunt of Mrs. Otken, donated to the enterprise $1,000; Mrs. Mary Lee donated $750. This lady was a cousin of Mrs. Otken. The surname of both was Lee. Mrs. Margaret Silliman, a friend, of East Feliciana parish, La., donated $1,000. This lady promised to donate $6,000 in addition to her first gift. She failed in carrying out her benevolent design on account of her sudden death. The school was named Lee Female college, in honor of the two lady relatives, and chartered in 1877. It has had fourteen continuous sessions and has sent out fifty-seven graduates. Many of its pupils have been fitted as teachers of the public schools.

When the war closed Dr. Otken, in addition to his labors as a teacher and pastor, completed by hard work the studies usually pursued in the classical course at college. Mississippi college twice honored him, without solicitation on his part, first with the degree of A. M. and later with the degree of LL. D. When Prof. Thomas S. Gathright resigned the office of state superintendent of public education in Mississippi this gentleman and Prof. Charles L. Patton called upon Gov. J. M. Stone and urged him to appoint Dr. Otken to fill the vacancy. The result of the interview led to a dispatch to come to Jackson. Dr. Otken wired his friends declining the office. In 1877 he was appointed by Governor Stone a trustee of the University of Mississippi. He served four years. For nine years he has served Mississippi college as a trustee, having been three times appointed by the Baptist state convention. He is now serving his fourth term as a trustee of this college. He declined invitations to accept the pastorate from the First Baptist church of New Orleans, and various churches in Mississippi and Texas. He also declined the presidency of a school in Texas, and the superintendency of public education in one of the most flourishing cities in Alabama. Believing that his life work was in south Mississippi, he has devoted his energies to its educational and religious upbuilding. In denominational matters Dr. Otken advocated with great earnestness the work of Sunday-schools, especially their efficiency; benevolence for ministerial education, missions, systematic pastoral support and thorough organization in all the work of Christian churches. For years he stood almost alone in the advocacy of these subjects, combating prejudices and deeply rooted customs. Rev. Dr. J. R. Graves asked him in 1865, in the town of Magnolia, "Brother Otken, do you wish to be a popular preacher?" Often, after closing the discussion on one of these subjects, he felt that his popularity had received a deadly wound. But these discussions have borne rich fruitage in the churches of the Mississippi Baptist association—the oldest Baptist association in the state. Invitations to deliver addresses before schools and on general education have been frequent. He has spoken much on education in south Mississippi. He delivered also, by invitation on the occasion of death, eulogies on the characters of Gen. Robert E. Lee, President James A. Garfield and Hon. Jefferson Davis. Dr. Otken is recognized at his home and where he is best known as a Christian gentleman. He is genial and unobtrusive in his manners, firm and conscientious in his convictions, clear in his opinions, and formulates his own judgment of men and measures.

Capt. Robert A. Owen. A glance at the genealogy of Mr. Owen's family shows that his people were worthy and honored residents of the famous Blue Grass region of Kentucky. He was born in the month of April, 1834, and was the eldest of a family of three children born to his parents, Richard T., his brother, being still a resident of Kentucky and deeply interested in the municipal affairs of the county in which he lives. He was first lieutenant of a company in the Confederate States army, and during his entire service, which lasted throughout the entire war, he bore himself with intrepid valor and displayed the sagacity, coolness and discipline of the trained soldier. He was terribly wounded at the battle of Antietam, it was supposed fatally so, but the fates were on his side and he still lives, being a useful citizen of Kentucky. Catherine, the sister of Capt. Robert A. Owen, also resides in Kentucky and is a finely educated lady. Their father, Taylor G. Owen, was born on Blue Grass soil in the month of October, 1806, but his ancestors were of old Virginia stock, so well known in history. He was a real Southern gentleman, of the old school, and in his veins flowed some of the best and bravest blood of which America can boast, and of which he was deservedly proud. He was given a practical education in boyhood and, possessing a mind naturally brilliant, his career was a successful one and he became wealthy. He dispensed his means with an unstinted hand when necessity called and supported worthy enterprises of a public nature both by purse and influence. He departed this life in 1845, and his wife, whose maiden name was Mary A. McGrath, passed from life on the 26th of January, 1889, having attained the advanced age of eighty-one years. She, like her husband, was a Kentuckian by birth and was finely educated, being a graduate of Science Hill Female college of Shelbyville. Capt. Robert A. Owen, who has early become distinguished in Mississippi history, was in his youth given the advantages of Shelby college, and being a youth of practical views he made good use of his opportunities, and upon leaving that institution was better fitted than the average to make his own way in the world. Upon his return home he turned his attention to the pursuit of agriculture, but was engaged in steamboating at the coming of the clash of arms, which caused him to drop his private pursuit to enlist in the famous Claiborne guards, of Claiborne county, Miss. He entered as a private, but for his pronounced bravery, skill and strict adherence to his duties he was promoted to the position of first sergeant of his company (company K Twelfth Mississippi volunteers), being transferred from this regiment to Morgan's command March 12, 1863. He bore with him valuable papers and credentials from his captain and adjutant and a warm letter from his commanding colonel, M. B. Harris. He took an active part in about thirty-seven battles and skirmishes, the following of which are among the most important: Yorktown, Williamsburg, Seven Pines, seven days' fight around Richmond, second battle of Manassas, the Maryland campaign, Harper's Ferry, Antietam, the battles in the Shenandoah valley, Fredericksburg, and Shelbyville. Captain Owen was one of only three men of his company who was not wounded nor captured. He was never absent on account of sickness during his service, was at all times ready for duty, and in an engagement set an excellent example to his men, for he displayed indomitable courage, coolness and a determination to do or die. He was promoted to a lieutenancy in General Morgan's command, and by order of Jefferson Davis, of whom he was a personal acquaintance and friend, he was sent to the Mississippi valley, of which region he had a thorough knowledge, having been engaged in steamboating on the Mississippi river; being promoted to the rank of captain in a battalion which was detailed to convey Mr. Davis across that river after he had evacuated Virginia and North Carolina. Captain Owen relates many interesting war experiences and tells of a skirmish at Osceola, Miss., which is well worthy of mention. He, with only fourteen brave followers, made a running skirmish against eight hundred Union troops under a Yankee captain by the name of Owen, from Indiana, but were driven back to Port Gibson. The Captain and his command surrendered at Jackson, Miss., May 13, 1865, after which he returned to his home, once more to take up his river life, which he continued until his marriage and then entered upon the occupation of planting. He and wife are the owners of a magnificent plantation of one thousand five hundred acres, known as the Scrogy plantation, an English title. They are devout members of the St. James Episcopal church of Port Gibson, and for their many admirable qualities hold a high social position in the history of Claiborne county. They possess that true hospitality and generosity for which the Southern people are so famous, and are kind, genial, gracious and deferential, and both have the happy faculty of making the poorest and humblest feel the dignity of being men. They are warm advocates of education and their two children are to be given every advantage. Mrs. Owen was formerly Miss Eleanor Jefferies, a member of the noted Jefferies family, further mention of which is made in the Memoirs of Mississippi. Her union with Mr. Owen was celebrated at Port Gibson by Rev. John G. Jones, on the 16th of August, 1876. Nathaniel Jefferies, their eldest child, is now ten years of age and is attending the Port Gibson Female college, their little daughter, Mary, being also an attendant of that institution. Captain Owen is a Knight Templar in the Masonic fraternity and is now past commander in that order.

Samuel D. Owen, of New Albany, Union county, Miss., was born and reared in Tippah county, Miss., and grew to manhood on his father's plantation there. William E. Owen, his father, was born in Tennessee, and when he was two years of age his parents removed to a point near Decatur, Ala., where he grew to maturity. He came to Tippah county, Miss., in 1836 and secured a plantation, but soon returned to Alabama, where he remained until 1841, when he came again to Tippah county, where he made his home until 1871. During that year he located in Lincoln county, Ark., where he lived but two years, dying in 1873 at the age of sixty. He was a planter during all of his active life. At the age of eighteen Samuel

D. Owen entered school at Ripley, and after a due course of study he acquired a practical education which enabled him to engage in the profession of teaching, which he continued for two years. He then read medicine and clerked in the drugstore of Drs. Murray & Alexander. After a year spent thus he went to Orizaba, Tippah county, Miss., and from there came a year later to New Albany, where he has since lived. He was engaged in merchandising until 1877, when he was appointed deputy sheriff and in this capacity he served during two years. In the fall of 1879 he was elected chancery clerk and served his fellow-citizens in that capacity for four years with great credit. After two years' retirement he was again elected to the same office, which he has filled to the present time, and is now the nominee of the democratic party for another term of four years. He has given such care and attention to the duties devolving upon him that he has gained the good opinion of the leading citizens of all classes, without respect to party. He was married in 1873 to Miss Hettie Williamson, a daughter of that old pioneer, J. H. Williamson of New Albany. Mr. Owen is a member of the Masonic fraternity, of the Independent Order of Odd Fellows, of the Knights of Honor, and has been secretary of the Masonic order of New Albany since 1873. He and his good wife are members of the Missionary Baptist church. He is a liberal patron of all worthy enterprises of public character, and a generous contributor to every good cause that is brought to his attention.

George W. Owens, planter, was born in Russellville, Ky., on the 3d of September, 1837, to James M. and George Ann E. (Dismukes) Owens, the former a Kentuckian, born December 25, 1812, and the latter a native of Tennessee, born in 1816, their marriage taking place in the latter state in 1836, George W. being their first child. Their union resulted in the birth of seven sons and four daughters, five of whom are still living. The parents removed from Kentucky to Tunica county, Miss., in January, 1851, where they had purchased land in 1846, consisting of two tracts of one thousand two hundred and eighty acres each, all wild land, and here they set energetically to work to clear their property and to erect good and substantial buildings thereon. Mrs. Owens died in 1872, on the plantation near Tunica, and Mr. Owens passed from life four years later, in Austin. George W. Owens was reared to a knowledge of agricultural life in this county, and since starting out in life for himself he has shown that he possesses practical, progressive and intelligent ideas and is singularly self-reliant and independent. He is the owner of about six hundred acres of valuable and fertile farming land, of which about one hundred acres are under cultivation, but has not followed the life of a planter since 1868, and has been a resident of Austin since 1871. He has held the office of county surveyor for the past eighteen years, was mayor of the town of Austin for four years and is one of the leading citizens of the county, for he has done much to place her among the leading counties of the state, and is most highly respected and esteemed by her citizens. The family of which he is a member were among the first settlers of this region and were well known for their liberality in aiding worthy causes and for advancing every interest tending to develop and improve the region. Mrs. Owens is a worthy and active member of the Methodist Episcopal church, but Mr. Owens is a Baptist. In the early part of the Civil war he enlisted in the Confederate service and remained true to the cause for which the South was fighting until hostilities were closed by the surrender of General Lee. He was in the battles around Vicksburg, at Iuka, Corinth, Jackson, besides various other engagements, but was never captured, and wounded only once during his entire service. He returned to Tunica county at the close of the war, and once more turned his attention to planting, but, as above stated, abandoned it in 1868 and turned his attention to diversified farming and stockraising. Mr. Owens is a finely educated gentleman, having graduated from Bethel college, of Russellville, in Kentucky, in 1858, since which time he has kept thoroughly posted on the current topics of the day, and has taken a prominent part in the various affairs of the county. He is dignified, yet cordial in his manners, is of fair complexion, and his eyes are a bright blue.

www.ingramcontent.com/pod-product-compliance
Lightning Source LLC
Chambersburg PA
CBHW080719300426
44114CB00019B/2422